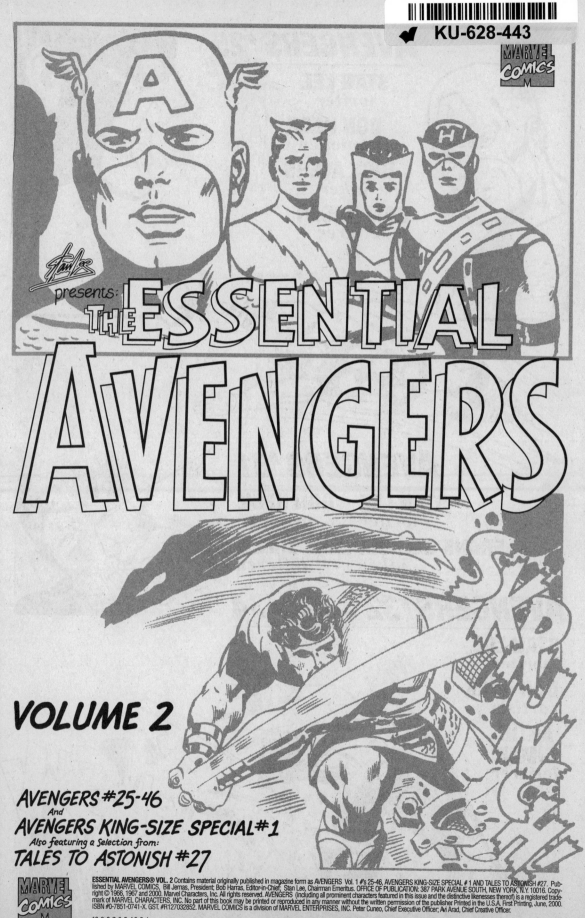

Stan Lee presents: THE ESSENTIAL AVENGERS

VOLUME 2

AVENGERS #25-46
And
AVENGERS KING-SIZE SPECIAL #1
Also featuring a Selection from:
TALES TO ASTONISH #27

ESSENTIAL AVENGERS® VOL. 2 Contains material originally published in magazine form as AVENGERS Vol. 1 #'s 25-46, AVENGERS KING-SIZE SPECIAL # 1 AND TALES TO ASTONISH #27. Published by MARVEL COMICS, Bill Jemas, President; Bob Harras, Editor-in-Chief; Stan Lee, Chairman Emeritus. OFFICE OF PUBLICATION: 387 PARK AVENUE SOUTH, NEW YORK, N.Y. 10016. Copyright © 1966, 1967 and 2000. Marvel Characters, Inc. All rights reserved. AVENGERS (including all prominent characters featured in this issue and the distinctive likenesses thereof) is a registered trademark of MARVEL CHARACTERS, INC. No part of this book may be printed or reproduced in any manner without the written permission of the publisher Printed in the U.S.A. First Printing, June, 2000. ISBN #0-7851-0741-X. GST. #R127032852. MARVEL COMICS is a division of MARVEL ENTERPRISES, INC. Peter Cuneo, Chief Executive Officer; Avi Arad, Chief Creative Officer.

10 9 8 7 6 5 4 3 2 1

AVENGERS #25

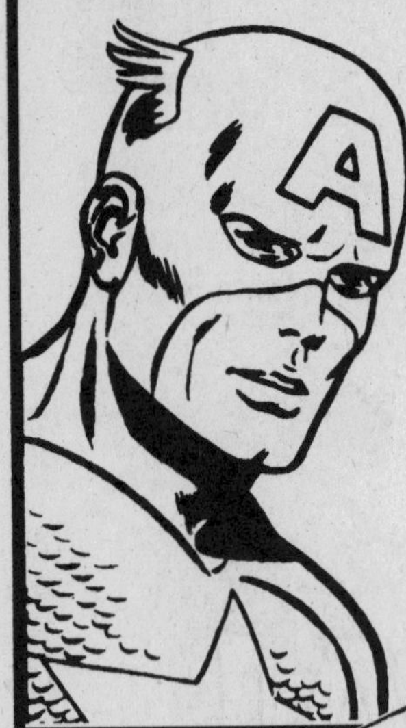

STAN LEE
writer

DON HECK
penciler

DICK AYERS
inker

SAM ROSEN
letterer

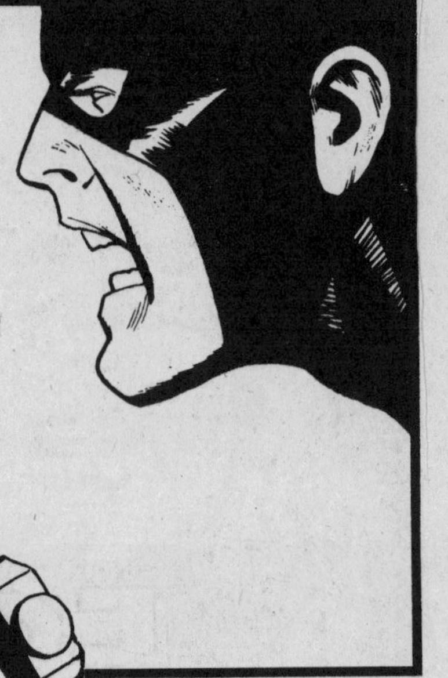

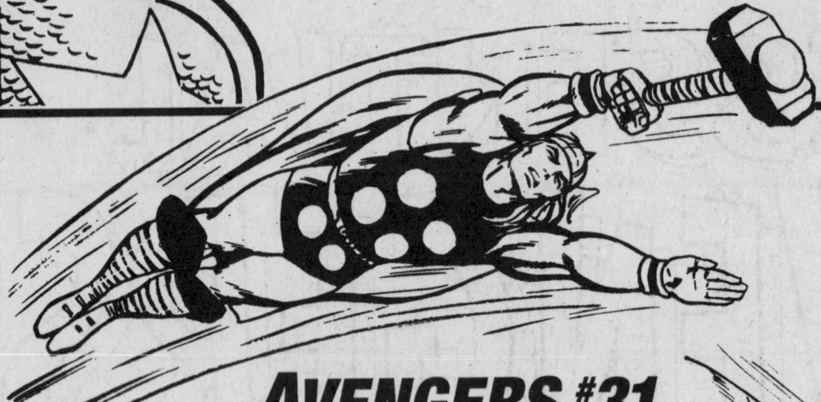

AVENGERS #31

STAN LEE
writer

DON HECK
penciler

FRANK GIACOIA
inker

ART SIMEK
letterer

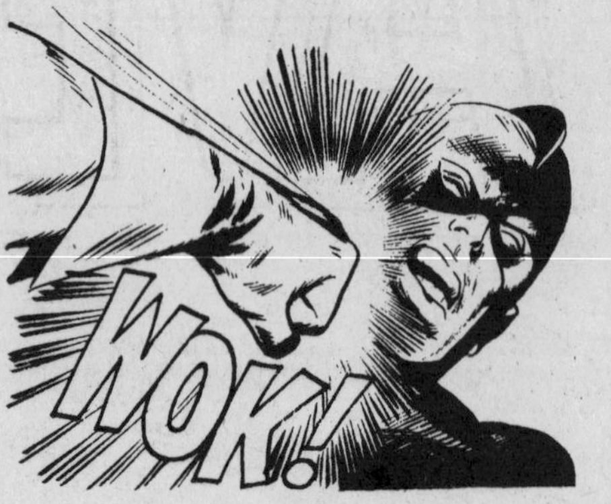
WOK!

AVENGERS #32 *through* #34

STAN LEE
writer

DON HECK
artist

ARTIE SIMEK
letterer

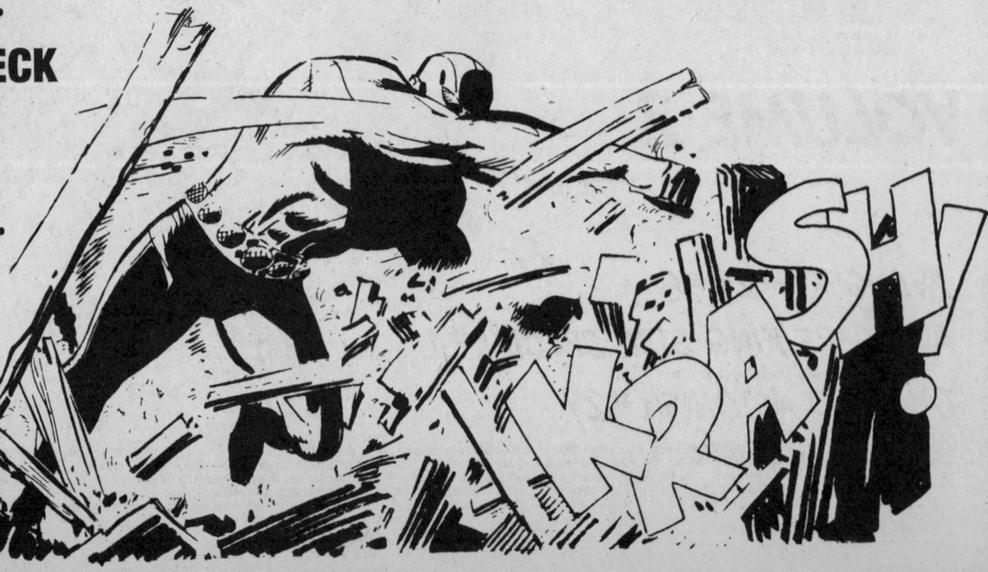
KRASH!

AVENGERS #26

STAN LEE
writer

DON HECK
penciler

FRANK GIACOIA
inker

ARTIE SIMEK
letterer

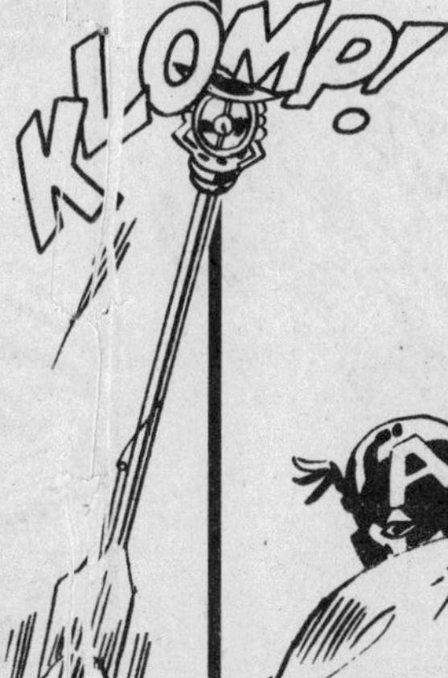
K-LOMP!

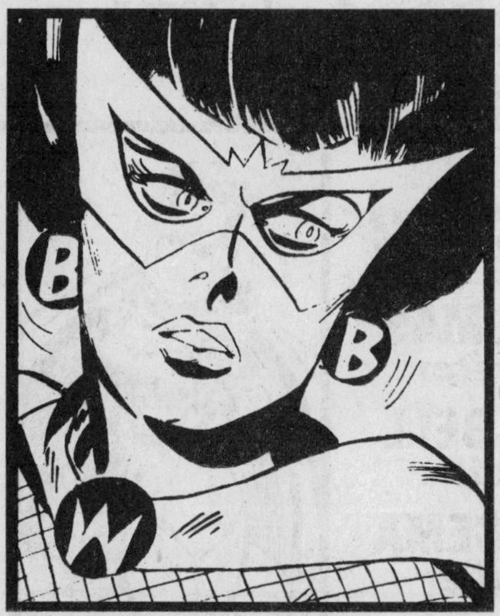

AVENGERS #27-30

STAN LEE
writer

DON HECK
penciler

FRANK GIACOIA
inker

SAM ROSEN
letterer

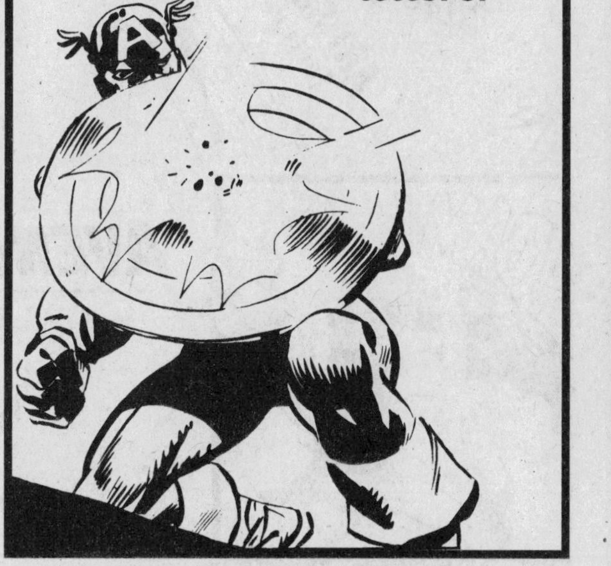

AVENGERS #35-36

ROY THOMAS
writer

DON HECK
artist

SAM ROSEN
letterer

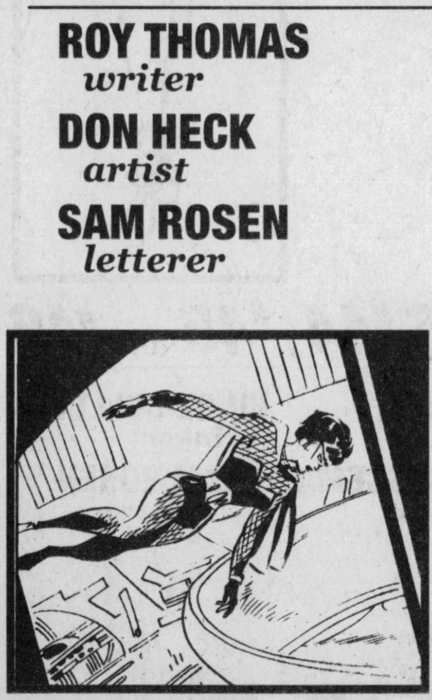

AVENGERS #37

ROY THOMAS
writer

DON HECK
artist

ARTIE SIMEK
letterer

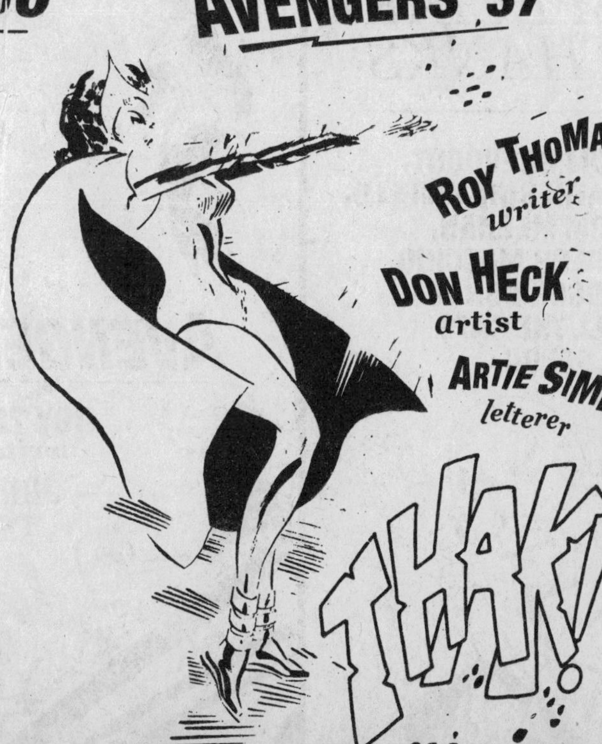
THAK!

AVENGERS #38 and #39

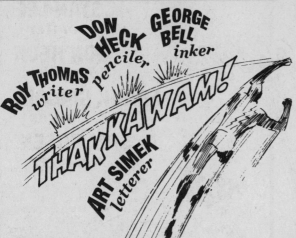

ROY THOMAS
writer

DON HECK
penciler

GEORGE BELL
inker

THAKKAWAM!

ART SIMEK
letterer

AVENGERS #40

ROY THOMAS
writer

DON HECK
penciler

GEORGE BELL
inker

SAM ROSEN
letterer

KBAM!

SPECIAL THANKS:

TOM BREVOORT,
CATHERINE CIVELLO,
TOM MEEHAN,
RALPH MACCHIO,
ROGER BONAS and
ALL THE CATS
at REPRO.

AVENGERS #43

ROY THOMAS
writer

GEORGE BELL
penciler

JOHN BUSCEMA
inker

JERRY MANN
letterer

AVENGERS #44, #45 and #46

ROY THOMAS
writer

JOHN BUSCEMA
penciler

VINCE COLLETTA
inker

SAM ROSEN
letterer

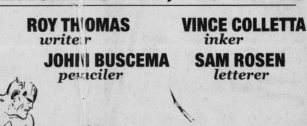

AVENGERS #41 and #42

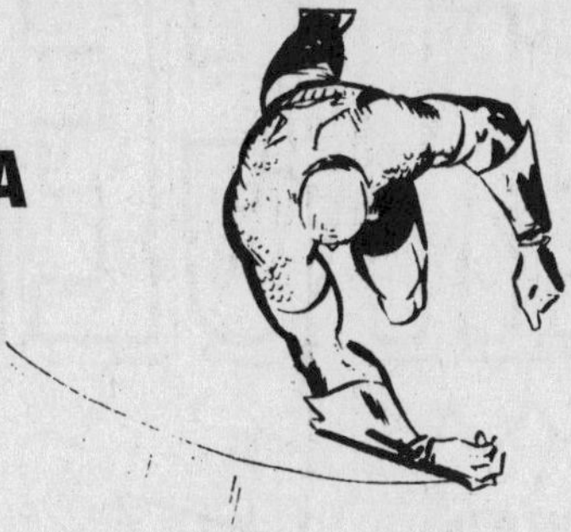

ROY THOMAS
writer

JOHN BUSCEMA
penciler

GEORGE BELL
inker

ARTIE SIMEK
letterer

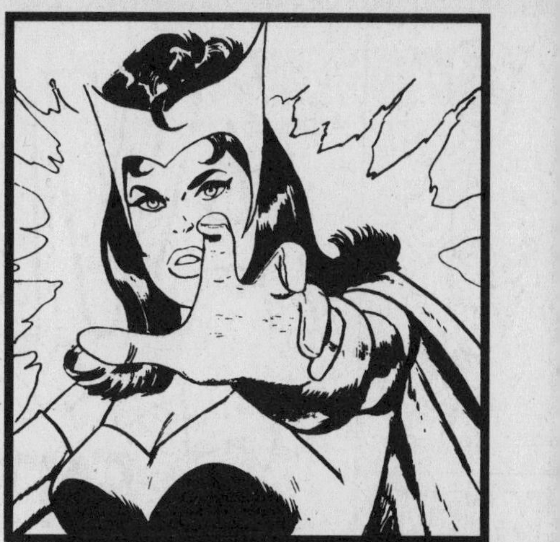

AVENGERS ANNUAL #1

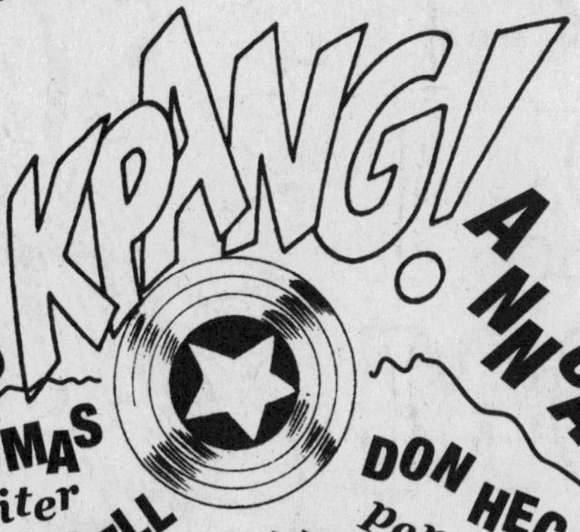
KPANG!

ROY THOMAS
writer

DON HECK
penciler

GEORGE BELL
inker

ARTIE SIMEK
letterer

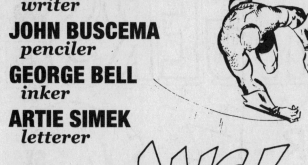

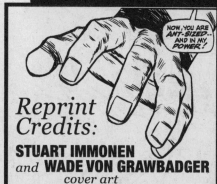

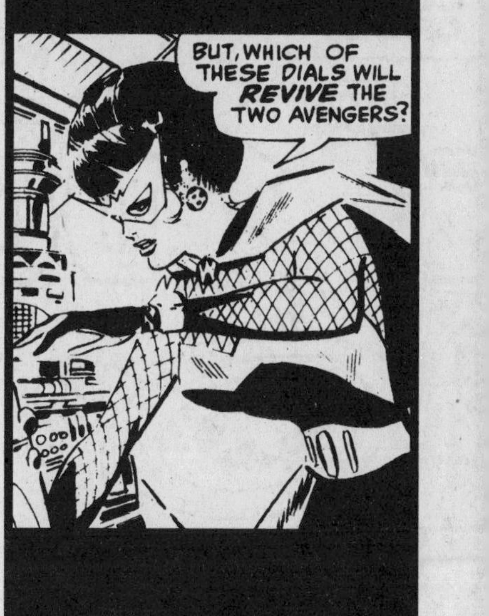
BUT, WHICH OF THESE DIALS WILL REVIVE THE TWO AVENGERS?

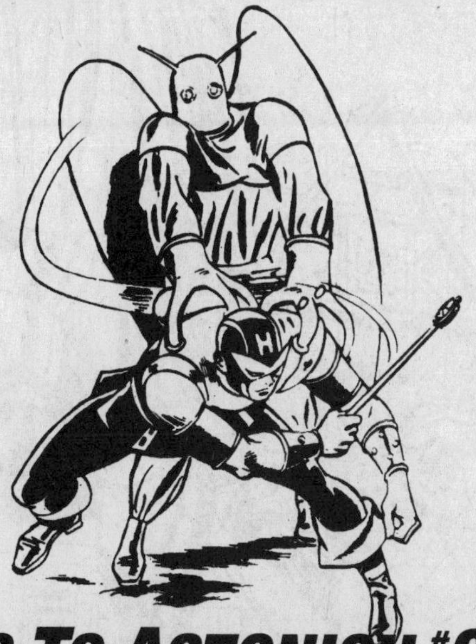

TALES TO ASTONISH #27

STAN LEE and **LARRY LIEBER**
writers

JACK KIRBY
penciler

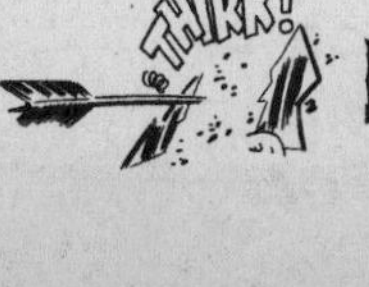
THKK!

DICK AYERS
inker

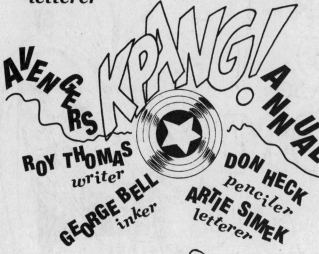

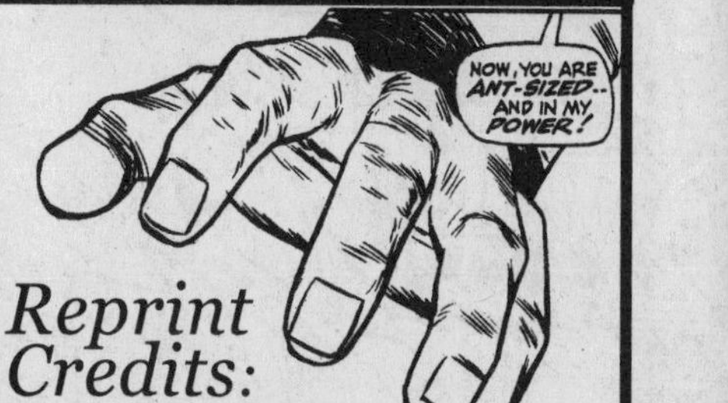
NOW, YOU ARE ANT-SIZED-- AND IN MY POWER!

Reprint Credits:

STUART IMMONEN
and **WADE VON GRAWBADGER**
cover art

STEVE BUCCELLATO
cover color

JONATHAN BABCOCK
interior design & touch-ups

SUZANNE GAFFNEY and
THOMAS VELAZQUEZ
cover design

POLLY WATSON
and **MARIE JAVINS**
reprint editors

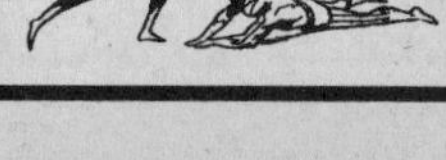

BOB HARRAS
editor in chief

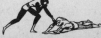

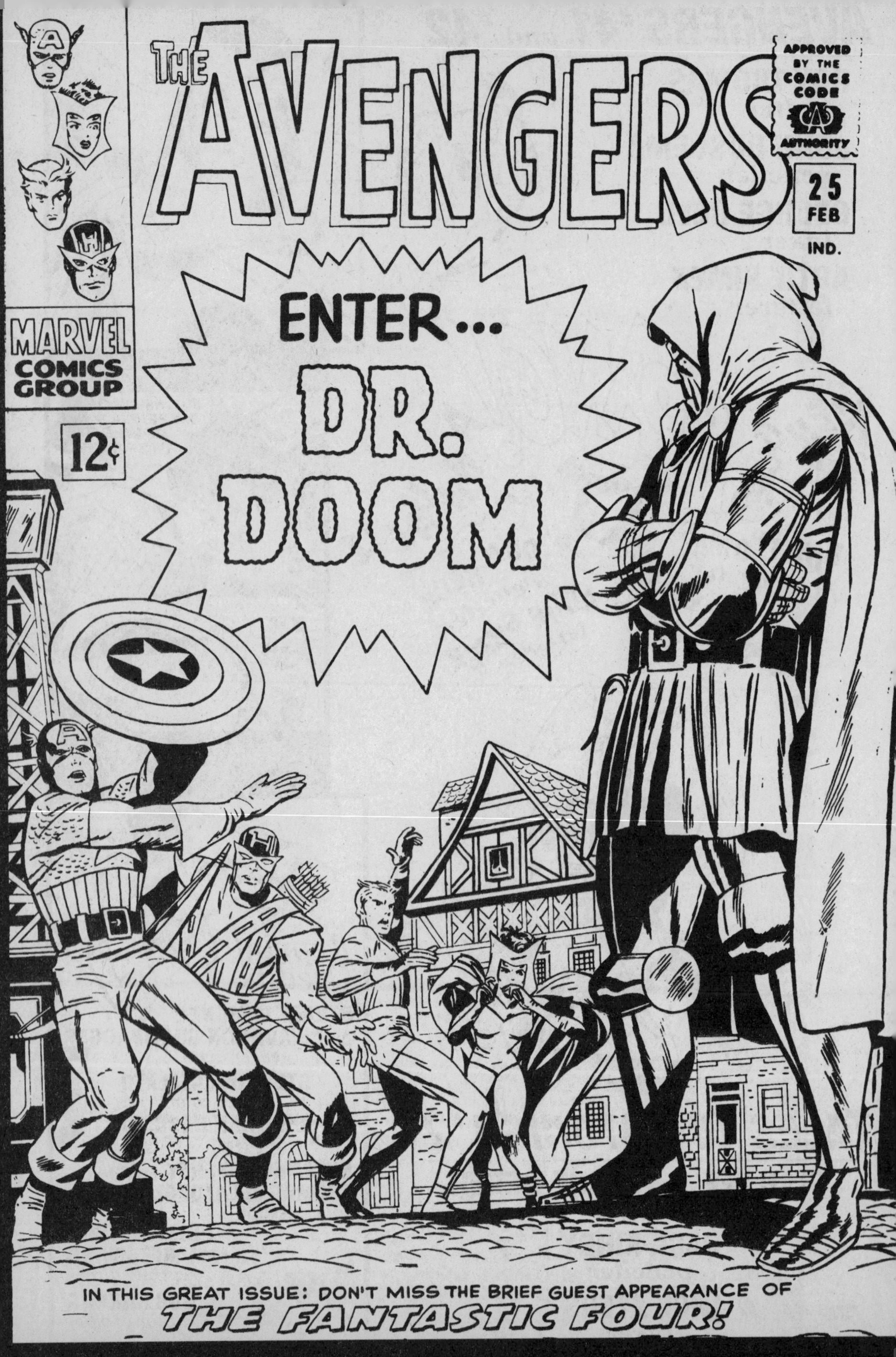
THE AVENGERS
APPROVED BY THE COMICS CODE AUTHORITY
25
FEB
IND.
MARVEL COMICS GROUP
12¢
ENTER... DR. DOOM
IN THIS GREAT ISSUE: DON'T MISS THE BRIEF GUEST APPEARANCE OF
THE FANTASTIC FOUR!

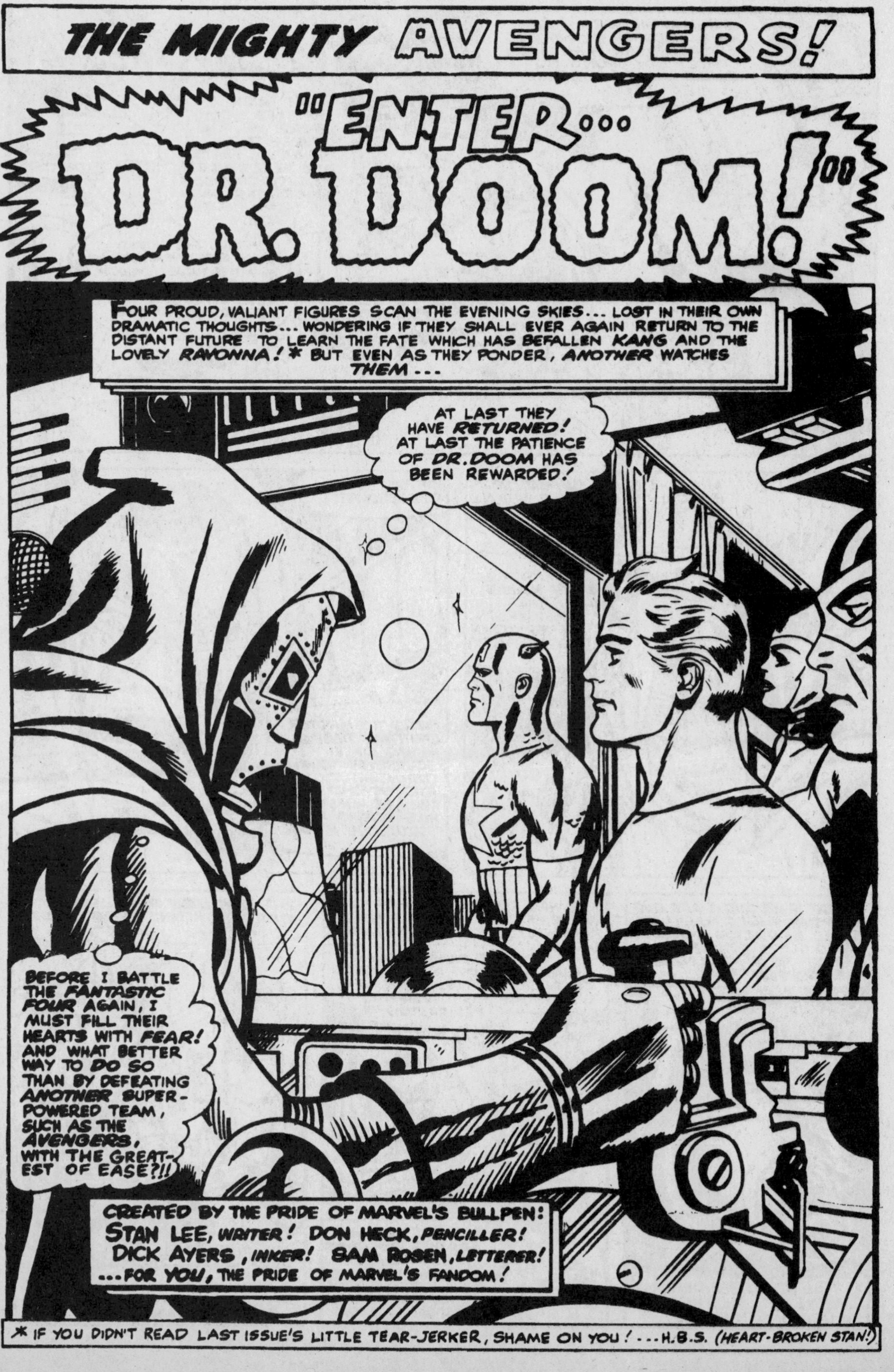
THE MIGHTY AVENGERS!
"ENTER... DR. DOOM!"
FOUR PROUD, VALIANT FIGURES SCAN THE EVENING SKIES... LOST IN THEIR OWN DRAMATIC THOUGHTS... WONDERING IF THEY SHALL EVER AGAIN RETURN TO THE DISTANT FUTURE TO LEARN THE FATE WHICH HAS BEFALLEN KANG AND THE LOVELY RAVONNA! * BUT EVEN AS THEY PONDER, ANOTHER WATCHES THEM...
AT LAST THEY HAVE RETURNED! AT LAST THE PATIENCE OF DR. DOOM HAS BEEN REWARDED!
BEFORE I BATTLE THE FANTASTIC FOUR AGAIN, I MUST FILL THEIR HEARTS WITH FEAR! AND WHAT BETTER WAY TO DO SO THAN BY DEFEATING ANOTHER SUPER-POWERED TEAM, SUCH AS THE AVENGERS, WITH THE GREATEST OF EASE?!!
CREATED BY THE PRIDE OF MARVEL'S BULLPEN: STAN LEE, WRITER! DON HECK, PENCILLER! DICK AYERS, INKER! SAM ROSEN, LETTERER! ...FOR YOU, THE PRIDE OF MARVEL'S FANDOM!
* IF YOU DIDN'T READ LAST ISSUE'S LITTLE TEAR-JERKER, SHAME ON YOU! ...H.B.S. (HEART-BROKEN STAN!)

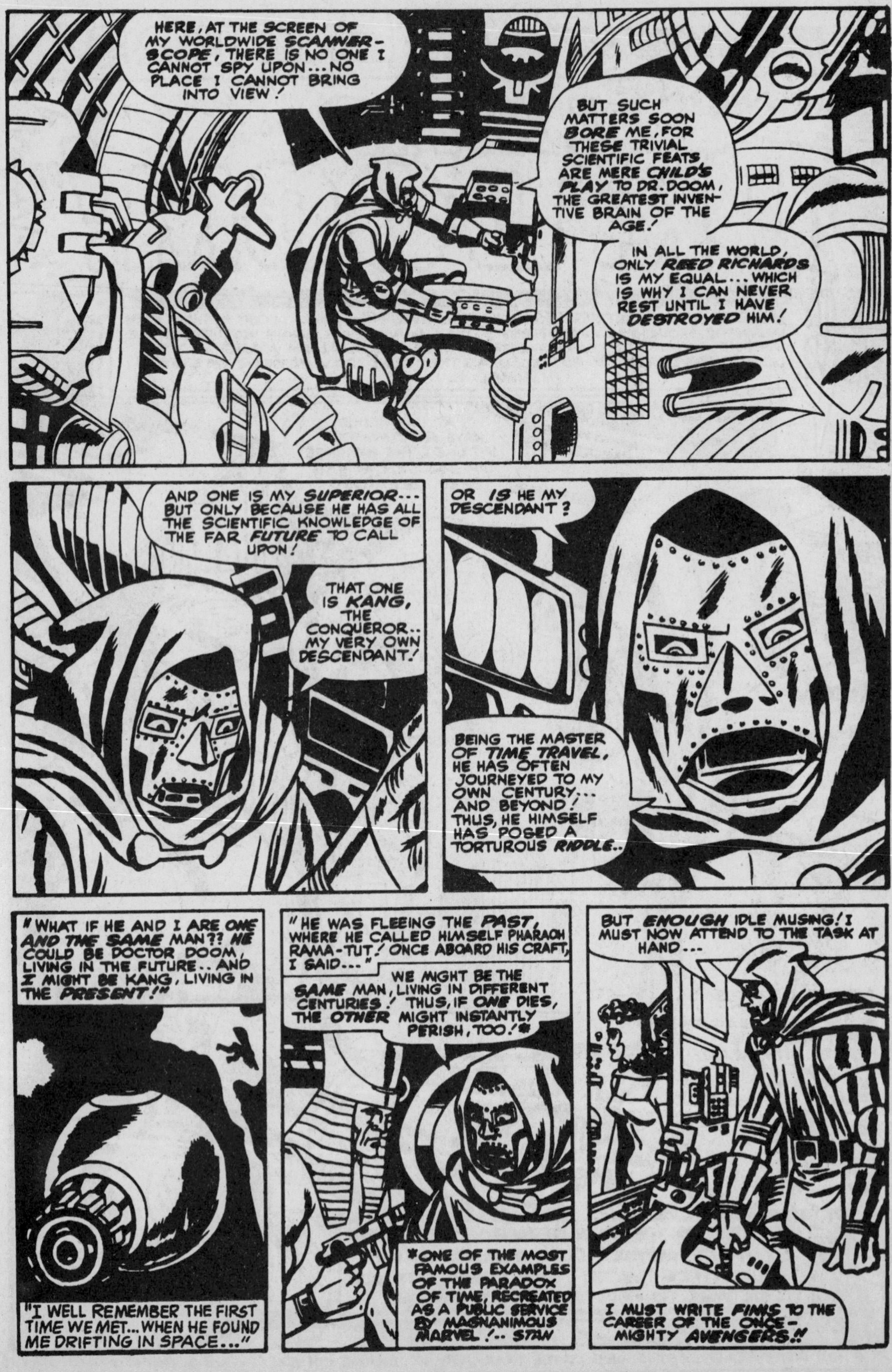
HERE, AT THE SCREEN OF MY WORLDWIDE SCANNER-SCOPE, THERE IS NO ONE I CANNOT SPY UPON... NO PLACE I CANNOT BRING INTO VIEW!
BUT SUCH MATTERS SOON BORE ME, FOR THESE TRIVIAL SCIENTIFIC FEATS ARE MERE CHILD'S PLAY TO DR. DOOM, THE GREATEST INVENTIVE BRAIN OF THE AGE!
IN ALL THE WORLD, ONLY REED RICHARDS IS MY EQUAL... WHICH IS WHY I CAN NEVER REST UNTIL I HAVE DESTROYED HIM!
AND ONE IS MY SUPERIOR... BUT ONLY BECAUSE HE HAS ALL THE SCIENTIFIC KNOWLEDGE OF THE FAR FUTURE TO CALL UPON!
THAT ONE IS KANG, THE CONQUEROR.. MY VERY OWN DESCENDANT!
OR IS HE MY DESCENDANT?
BEING THE MASTER OF TIME TRAVEL, HE HAS OFTEN JOURNEYED TO MY OWN CENTURY... AND BEYOND! THUS, HE HIMSELF HAS POSED A TORTUROUS RIDDLE..
"WHAT IF HE AND I ARE ONE AND THE SAME MAN?? HE COULD BE DOCTOR DOOM, LIVING IN THE FUTURE.. AND I MIGHT BE KANG, LIVING IN THE PRESENT!"
"I WELL REMEMBER THE FIRST TIME WE MET... WHEN HE FOUND ME DRIFTING IN SPACE..."
"HE WAS FLEEING THE PAST, WHERE HE CALLED HIMSELF PHARAOH RAMA-TUT! ONCE ABOARD HIS CRAFT, I SAID..."
WE MIGHT BE THE SAME MAN, LIVING IN DIFFERENT CENTURIES! THUS, IF ONE DIES, THE OTHER MIGHT INSTANTLY PERISH, TOO!*
*ONE OF THE MOST FAMOUS EXAMPLES OF THE PARADOX OF TIME, RECREATED AS A PUBLIC SERVICE BY MAGNANIMOUS MARVEL!-- STAN
BUT ENOUGH IDLE MUSING! I MUST NOW ATTEND TO THE TASK AT HAND...
I MUST WRITE FINIS TO THE CAREER OF THE ONCE-MIGHTY AVENGERS!!

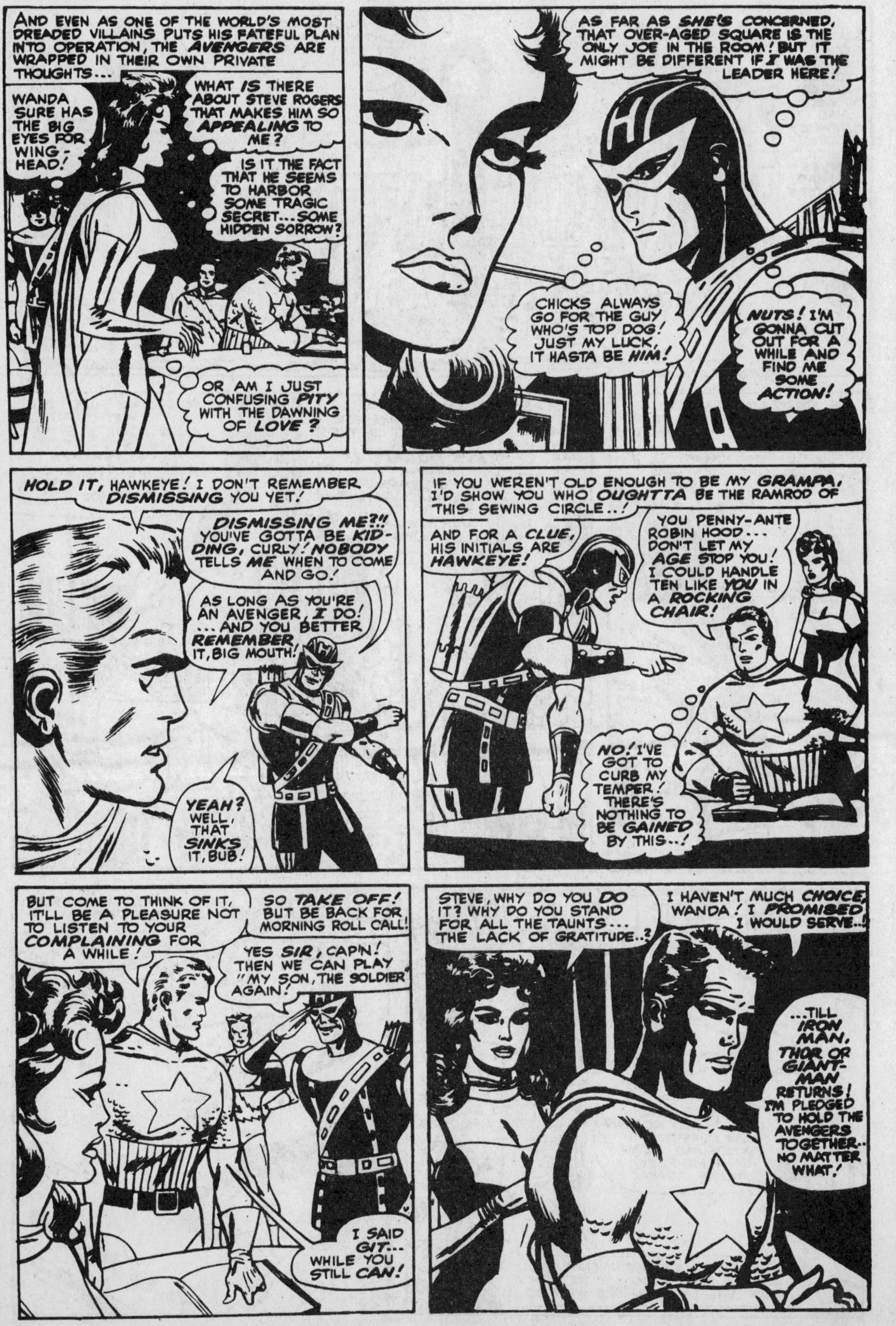

AND EVEN AS ONE OF THE WORLD'S MOST DREADED VILLAINS PUTS HIS FATEFUL PLAN INTO OPERATION, THE AVENGERS ARE WRAPPED IN THEIR OWN PRIVATE THOUGHTS...
WANDA SURE HAS THE BIG EYES FOR WING-HEAD!
WHAT IS THERE ABOUT STEVE ROGERS THAT MAKES HIM SO APPEALING TO ME?
IS IT THE FACT THAT HE SEEMS TO HARBOR SOME TRAGIC SECRET... SOME HIDDEN SORROW?
OR AM I JUST CONFUSING PITY WITH THE DAWNING OF LOVE?
AS FAR AS SHE'S CONCERNED, THAT OVER-AGED SQUARE IS THE ONLY JOE IN THE ROOM! BUT IT MIGHT BE DIFFERENT IF I WAS THE LEADER HERE!
CHICKS ALWAYS GO FOR THE GUY WHO'S TOP DOG! JUST MY LUCK, IT HASTA BE HIM!
NUTS! I'M GONNA CUT OUT FOR A WHILE AND FIND ME SOME ACTION!
HOLD IT, HAWKEYE! I DON'T REMEMBER DISMISSING YOU YET!
DISMISSING ME?!! YOU'VE GOTTA BE KID-DING, CURLY! NOBODY TELLS ME WHEN TO COME AND GO!
AS LONG AS YOU'RE AN AVENGER, I DO! ...AND YOU BETTER REMEMBER IT, BIG MOUTH!
YEAH? WELL, THAT SINKS IT, BUB!
IF YOU WEREN'T OLD ENOUGH TO BE MY GRAMPA, I'D SHOW YOU WHO OUGHTTA BE THE RAMROD OF THIS SEWING CIRCLE..!
AND FOR A CLUE, HIS INITIALS ARE HAWKEYE!
YOU PENNY-ANTE ROBIN HOOD... DON'T LET MY AGE STOP YOU! I COULD HANDLE TEN LIKE YOU IN A ROCKING CHAIR!
NO! I'VE GOT TO CURB MY TEMPER! THERE'S NOTHING TO BE GAINED BY THIS..!
BUT COME TO THINK OF IT, IT'LL BE A PLEASURE NOT TO LISTEN TO YOUR COMPLAINING FOR A WHILE!
SO TAKE OFF! BUT BE BACK FOR MORNING ROLL CALL!
YES SIR, CAP'N! THEN WE CAN PLAY "MY SON, THE SOLDIER" AGAIN!
I SAID GIT... WHILE YOU STILL CAN!
STEVE, WHY DO YOU DO IT? WHY DO YOU STAND FOR ALL THE TAUNTS... THE LACK OF GRATITUDE..?
I HAVEN'T MUCH CHOICE, WANDA! I PROMISED I WOULD SERVE...!
...TILL IRON MAN, THOR OR GIANT-MAN RETURNS! I'M PLEDGED TO HOLD THE AVENGERS TOGETHER.. NO MATTER WHAT!

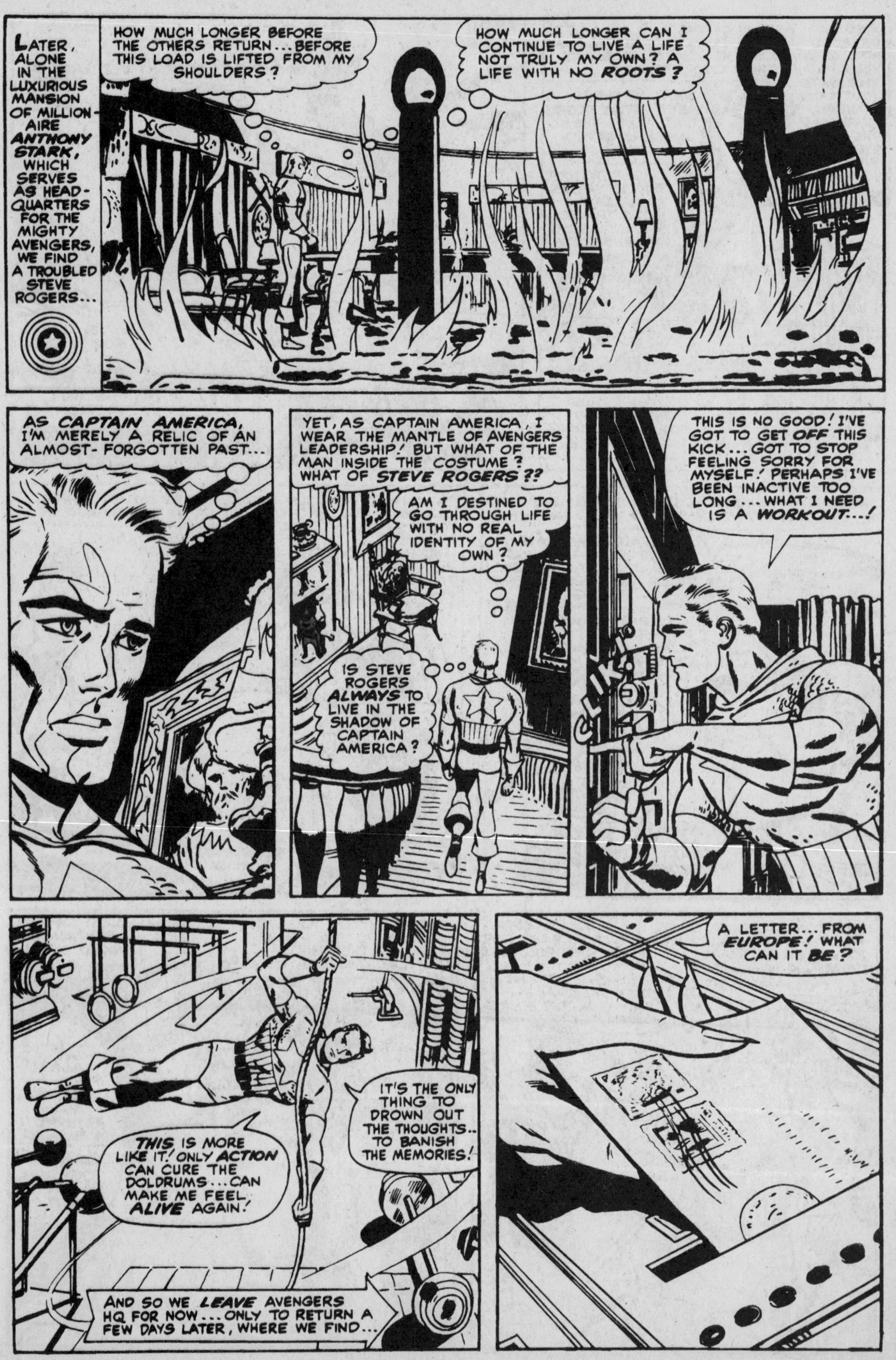
LATER, ALONE IN THE LUXURIOUS MANSION OF MILLIONAIRE ANTHONY STARK, WHICH SERVES AS HEADQUARTERS FOR THE MIGHTY AVENGERS, WE FIND A TROUBLED STEVE ROGERS...
HOW MUCH LONGER BEFORE THE OTHERS RETURN... BEFORE THIS LOAD IS LIFTED FROM MY SHOULDERS?
HOW MUCH LONGER CAN I CONTINUE TO LIVE A LIFE NOT TRULY MY OWN? A LIFE WITH NO ROOTS?
AS CAPTAIN AMERICA, I'M MERELY A RELIC OF AN ALMOST-FORGOTTEN PAST...
YET, AS CAPTAIN AMERICA, I WEAR THE MANTLE OF AVENGERS LEADERSHIP! BUT WHAT OF THE MAN INSIDE THE COSTUME? WHAT OF STEVE ROGERS??
AM I DESTINED TO GO THROUGH LIFE WITH NO REAL IDENTITY OF MY OWN?
IS STEVE ROGERS ALWAYS TO LIVE IN THE SHADOW OF CAPTAIN AMERICA?
THIS IS NO GOOD! I'VE GOT TO GET OFF THIS KICK... GOT TO STOP FEELING SORRY FOR MYSELF! PERHAPS I'VE BEEN INACTIVE TOO LONG... WHAT I NEED IS A WORKOUT...!
THIS IS MORE LIKE IT! ONLY ACTION CAN CURE THE DOLDRUMS... CAN MAKE ME FEEL ALIVE AGAIN!
IT'S THE ONLY THING TO DROWN OUT THE THOUGHTS.. TO BANISH THE MEMORIES!
AND SO WE LEAVE AVENGERS HQ FOR NOW... ONLY TO RETURN A FEW DAYS LATER, WHERE WE FIND...
A LETTER... FROM EUROPE! WHAT CAN IT BE?

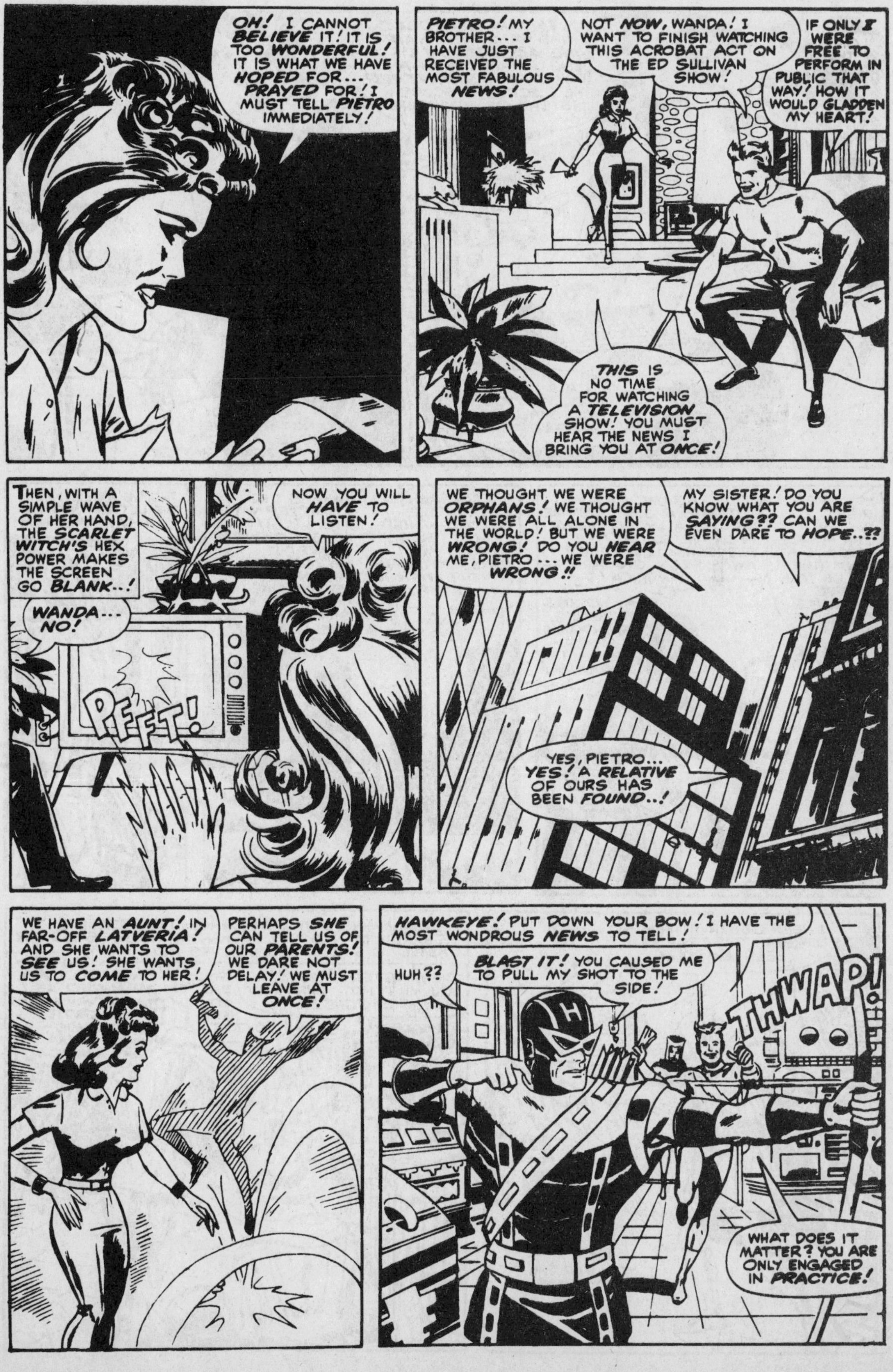

OH! I CANNOT BELIEVE IT! IT IS TOO WONDERFUL! IT IS WHAT WE HAVE HOPED FOR... PRAYED FOR! I MUST TELL PIETRO IMMEDIATELY!
PIETRO! MY BROTHER... I HAVE JUST RECEIVED THE MOST FABULOUS NEWS!
NOT NOW, WANDA! I WANT TO FINISH WATCHING THIS ACROBAT ACT ON THE ED SULLIVAN SHOW!
IF ONLY I WERE FREE TO PERFORM IN PUBLIC THAT WAY! HOW IT WOULD GLADDEN MY HEART!
THIS IS NO TIME FOR WATCHING A TELEVISION SHOW! YOU MUST HEAR THE NEWS I BRING YOU AT ONCE!
THEN, WITH A SIMPLE WAVE OF HER HAND, THE SCARLET WITCH'S HEX POWER MAKES THE SCREEN GO BLANK..!
NOW YOU WILL HAVE TO LISTEN!
WANDA... NO!
PFFFT!
WE THOUGHT WE WERE ORPHANS! WE THOUGHT WE WERE ALL ALONE IN THE WORLD! BUT WE WERE WRONG! DO YOU HEAR ME, PIETRO... WE WERE WRONG!!
MY SISTER! DO YOU KNOW WHAT YOU ARE SAYING?? CAN WE EVEN DARE TO HOPE..??
YES, PIETRO... YES! A RELATIVE OF OURS HAS BEEN FOUND..!
WE HAVE AN AUNT! IN FAR-OFF LATVERIA! AND SHE WANTS TO SEE US! SHE WANTS US TO COME TO HER!
PERHAPS SHE CAN TELL US OF OUR PARENTS! WE DARE NOT DELAY! WE MUST LEAVE AT ONCE!
HAWKEYE! PUT DOWN YOUR BOW! I HAVE THE MOST WONDROUS NEWS TO TELL!
HUH??
BLAST IT! YOU CAUSED ME TO PULL MY SHOT TO THE SIDE!
THWAP!
WHAT DOES IT MATTER? YOU ARE ONLY ENGAGED IN PRACTICE!

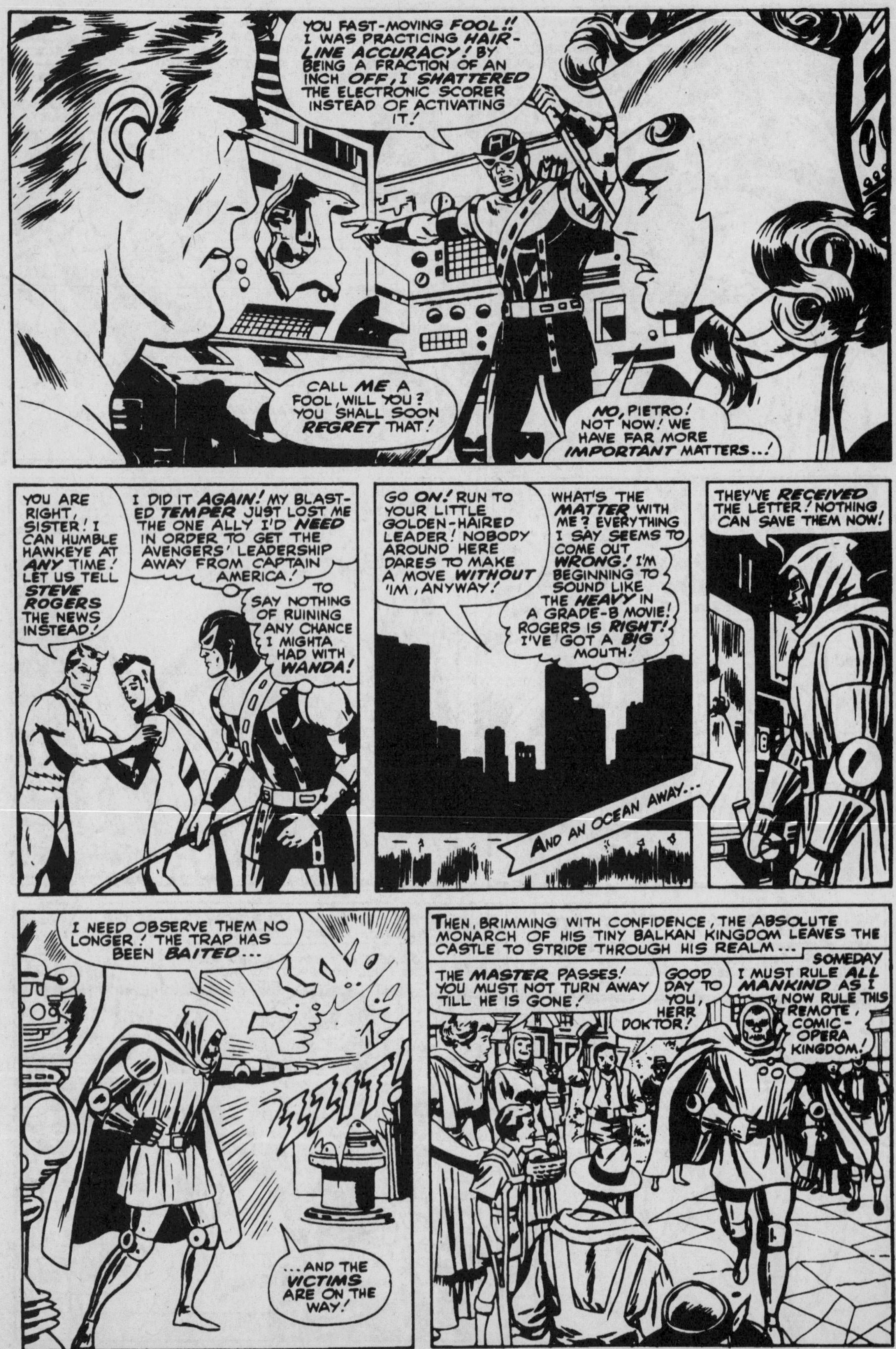
YOU FAST-MOVING FOOL!! I WAS PRACTICING HAIR-LINE ACCURACY! BY BEING A FRACTION OF AN INCH OFF, I SHATTERED THE ELECTRONIC SCORER INSTEAD OF ACTIVATING IT!
CALL ME A FOOL, WILL YOU? YOU SHALL SOON REGRET THAT!
NO, PIETRO! NOT NOW! WE HAVE FAR MORE IMPORTANT MATTERS...!
YOU ARE RIGHT, SISTER! I CAN HUMBLE HAWKEYE AT ANY TIME! LET US TELL STEVE ROGERS THE NEWS INSTEAD!
I DID IT AGAIN! MY BLASTED TEMPER JUST LOST ME THE ONE ALLY I'D NEED IN ORDER TO GET THE AVENGERS' LEADERSHIP AWAY FROM CAPTAIN AMERICA!
TO SAY NOTHING OF RUINING ANY CHANCE I MIGHTA HAD WITH WANDA!
GO ON! RUN TO YOUR LITTLE GOLDEN-HAIRED LEADER! NOBODY AROUND HERE DARES TO MAKE A MOVE WITHOUT 'IM, ANYWAY!
WHAT'S THE MATTER WITH ME? EVERYTHING I SAY SEEMS TO COME OUT WRONG! I'M BEGINNING TO SOUND LIKE THE HEAVY IN A GRADE-B MOVIE! ROGERS IS RIGHT! I'VE GOT A BIG MOUTH!
AND AN OCEAN AWAY...
THEY'VE RECEIVED THE LETTER! NOTHING CAN SAVE THEM NOW!
I NEED OBSERVE THEM NO LONGER! THE TRAP HAS BEEN BAITED...
FZZZT!
...AND THE VICTIMS ARE ON THE WAY!
THEN, BRIMMING WITH CONFIDENCE, THE ABSOLUTE MONARCH OF HIS TINY BALKAN KINGDOM LEAVES THE CASTLE TO STRIDE THROUGH HIS REALM...
THE MASTER PASSES! YOU MUST NOT TURN AWAY TILL HE IS GONE!
GOOD DAY TO YOU, HERR DOKTOR!
SOMEDAY I MUST RULE ALL MANKIND AS I NOW RULE THIS REMOTE, COMIC-OPERA KINGDOM!

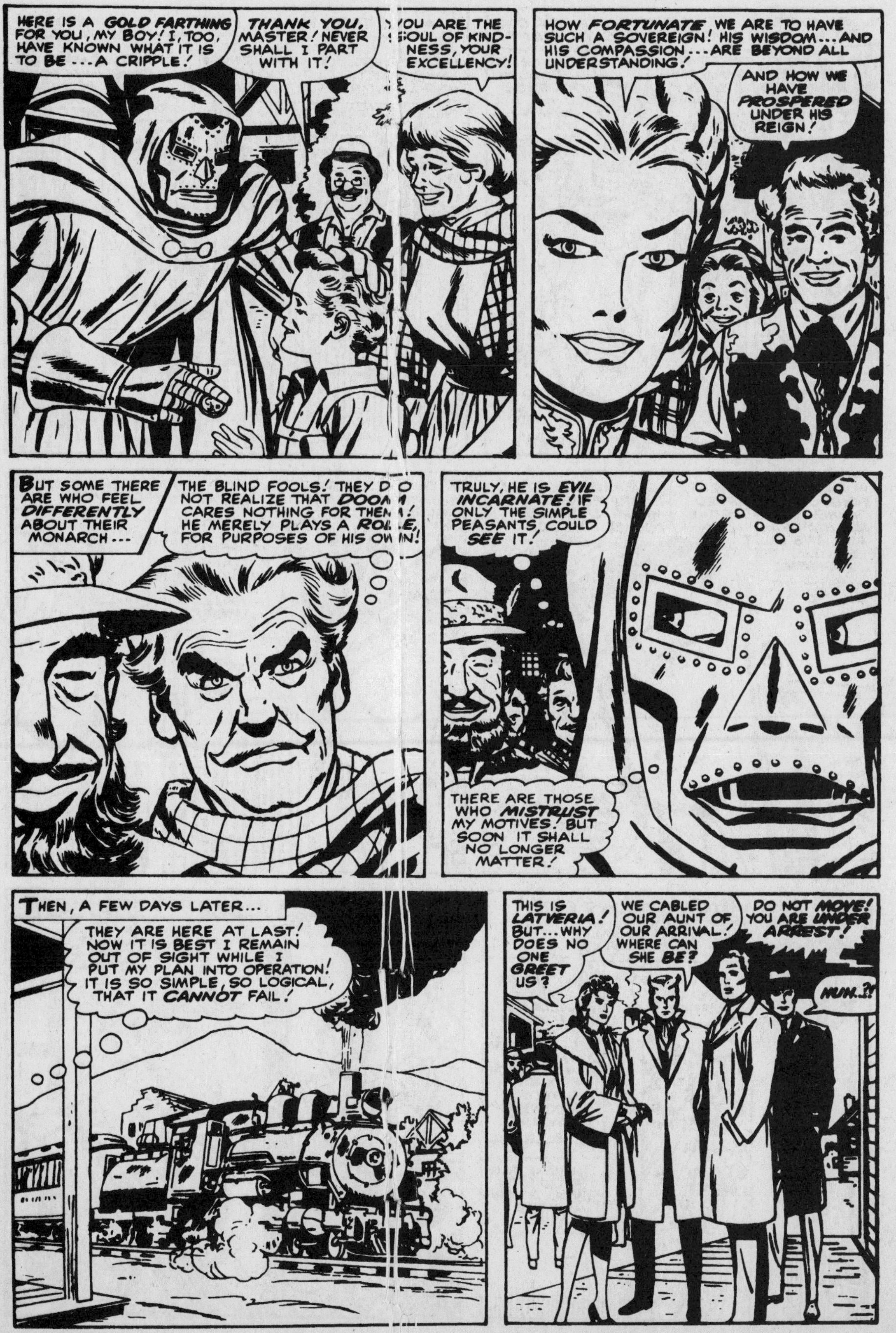
HERE IS A GOLD FARTHING FOR YOU, MY BOY! I, TOO, HAVE KNOWN WHAT IT IS TO BE... A CRIPPLE!
THANK YOU, MASTER! NEVER SHALL I PART WITH IT!
YOU ARE THE SOUL OF KINDNESS, YOUR EXCELLENCY!
HOW FORTUNATE WE ARE TO HAVE SUCH A SOVEREIGN! HIS WISDOM... AND HIS COMPASSION... ARE BEYOND ALL UNDERSTANDING!
AND HOW WE HAVE PROSPERED UNDER HIS REIGN!
BUT SOME THERE ARE WHO FEEL DIFFERENTLY ABOUT THEIR MONARCH...
THE BLIND FOOLS! THEY DO NOT REALIZE THAT DOOM CARES NOTHING FOR THEM! HE MERELY PLAYS A ROLE, FOR PURPOSES OF HIS OWN!
TRULY, HE IS EVIL INCARNATE! IF ONLY THE SIMPLE PEASANTS COULD SEE IT!
THERE ARE THOSE WHO MISTRUST MY MOTIVES! BUT SOON IT SHALL NO LONGER MATTER!
THEN, A FEW DAYS LATER...
THEY ARE HERE AT LAST! NOW IT IS BEST I REMAIN OUT OF SIGHT WHILE I PUT MY PLAN INTO OPERATION! IT IS SO SIMPLE, SO LOGICAL, THAT IT CANNOT FAIL!
THIS IS LATVERIA! BUT... WHY DOES NO ONE GREET US?
WE CABLED OUR AUNT OF OUR ARRIVAL! WHERE CAN SHE BE?
DO NOT MOVE! YOU ARE UNDER ARREST!
HUH..?!

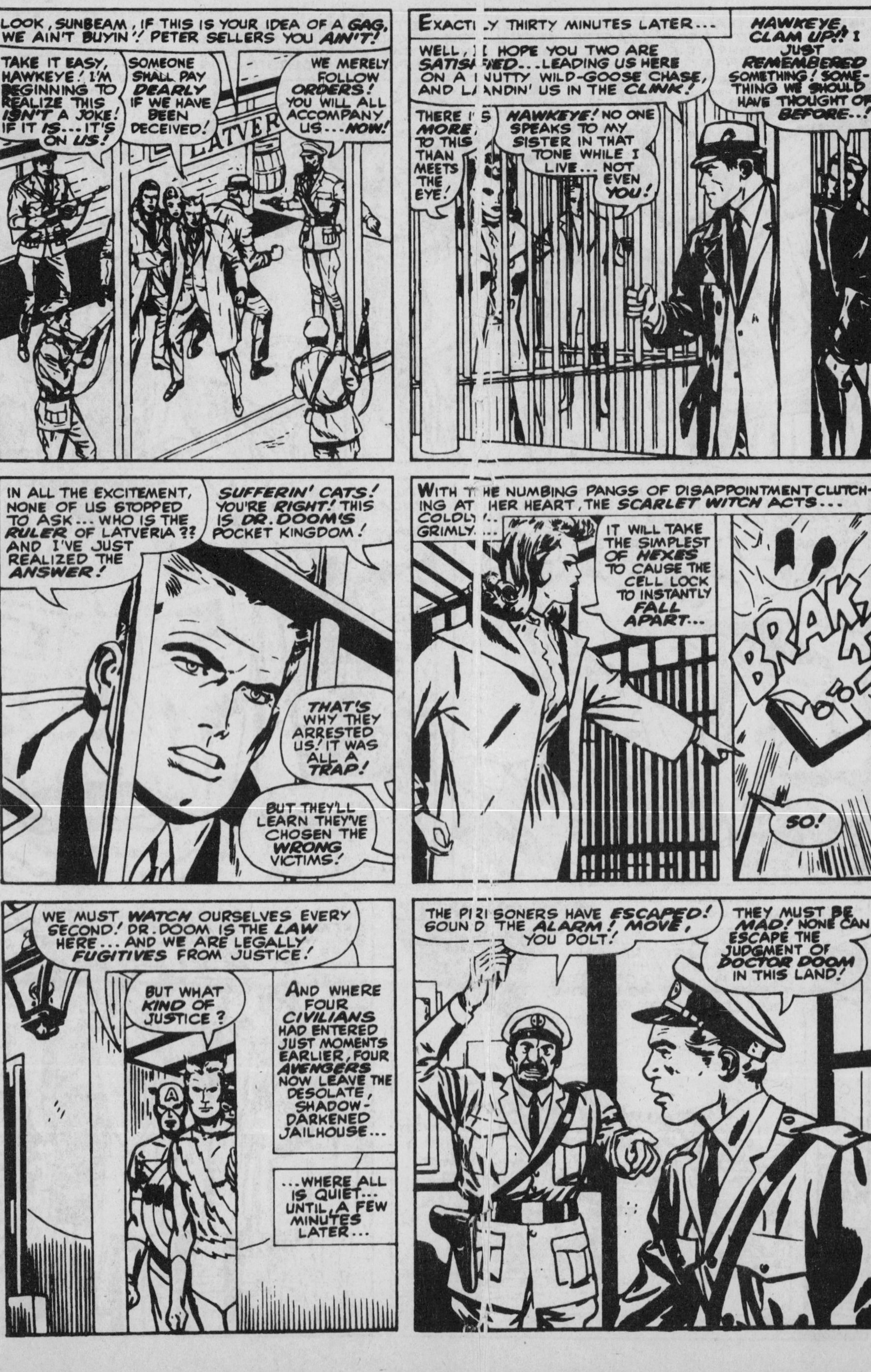
LOOK, SUNBEAM, IF THIS IS YOUR IDEA OF A GAG, WE AIN'T BUYIN'! PETER SELLERS YOU AIN'T!
TAKE IT EASY, HAWKEYE! I'M BEGINNING TO REALIZE THIS ISN'T A JOKE! IF IT IS... IT'S ON US!
SOMEONE SHALL PAY DEARLY IF WE HAVE BEEN DECEIVED!
WE MERELY FOLLOW ORDERS! YOU WILL ALL ACCOMPANY US... NOW!
LATVER
EXACTLY THIRTY MINUTES LATER...
WELL, I HOPE YOU TWO ARE SATISFIED... LEADING US HERE ON A NUTTY WILD-GOOSE CHASE, AND LANDIN' US IN THE CLINK!
THERE IS MORE TO THIS THAN MEETS THE EYE!
HAWKEYE! NO ONE SPEAKS TO MY SISTER IN THAT TONE WHILE I LIVE... NOT EVEN YOU!
HAWKEYE, CLAM UP!! I JUST REMEMBERED SOMETHING! SOMETHING WE SHOULD HAVE THOUGHT OF BEFORE..!
IN ALL THE EXCITEMENT, NONE OF US STOPPED TO ASK... WHO IS THE RULER OF LATVERIA?? AND I'VE JUST REALIZED THE ANSWER!
SUFFERIN' CATS! YOU'RE RIGHT! THIS IS DR. DOOM'S POCKET KINGDOM!
THAT'S WHY THEY ARRESTED US! IT WAS ALL A TRAP!
BUT THEY'LL LEARN THEY'VE CHOSEN THE WRONG VICTIMS!
WITH THE NUMBING PANGS OF DISAPPOINTMENT CLUTCHING AT HER HEART, THE SCARLET WITCH ACTS... COLDLY... GRIMLY...
IT WILL TAKE THE SIMPLEST OF HEXES TO CAUSE THE CELL LOCK TO INSTANTLY FALL APART...
BRAKK!
SO!
WE MUST WATCH OURSELVES EVERY SECOND! DR. DOOM IS THE LAW HERE... AND WE ARE LEGALLY FUGITIVES FROM JUSTICE!
BUT WHAT KIND OF JUSTICE?
AND WHERE FOUR CIVILIANS HAD ENTERED JUST MOMENTS EARLIER, FOUR AVENGERS NOW LEAVE THE DESOLATE, SHADOW-DARKENED JAILHOUSE...
...WHERE ALL IS QUIET... UNTIL A FEW MINUTES LATER...
THE PRISONERS HAVE ESCAPED! SOUND THE ALARM! MOVE, YOU DOLT!
THEY MUST BE MAD! NONE CAN ESCAPE THE JUDGMENT OF DOCTOR DOOM IN THIS LAND!

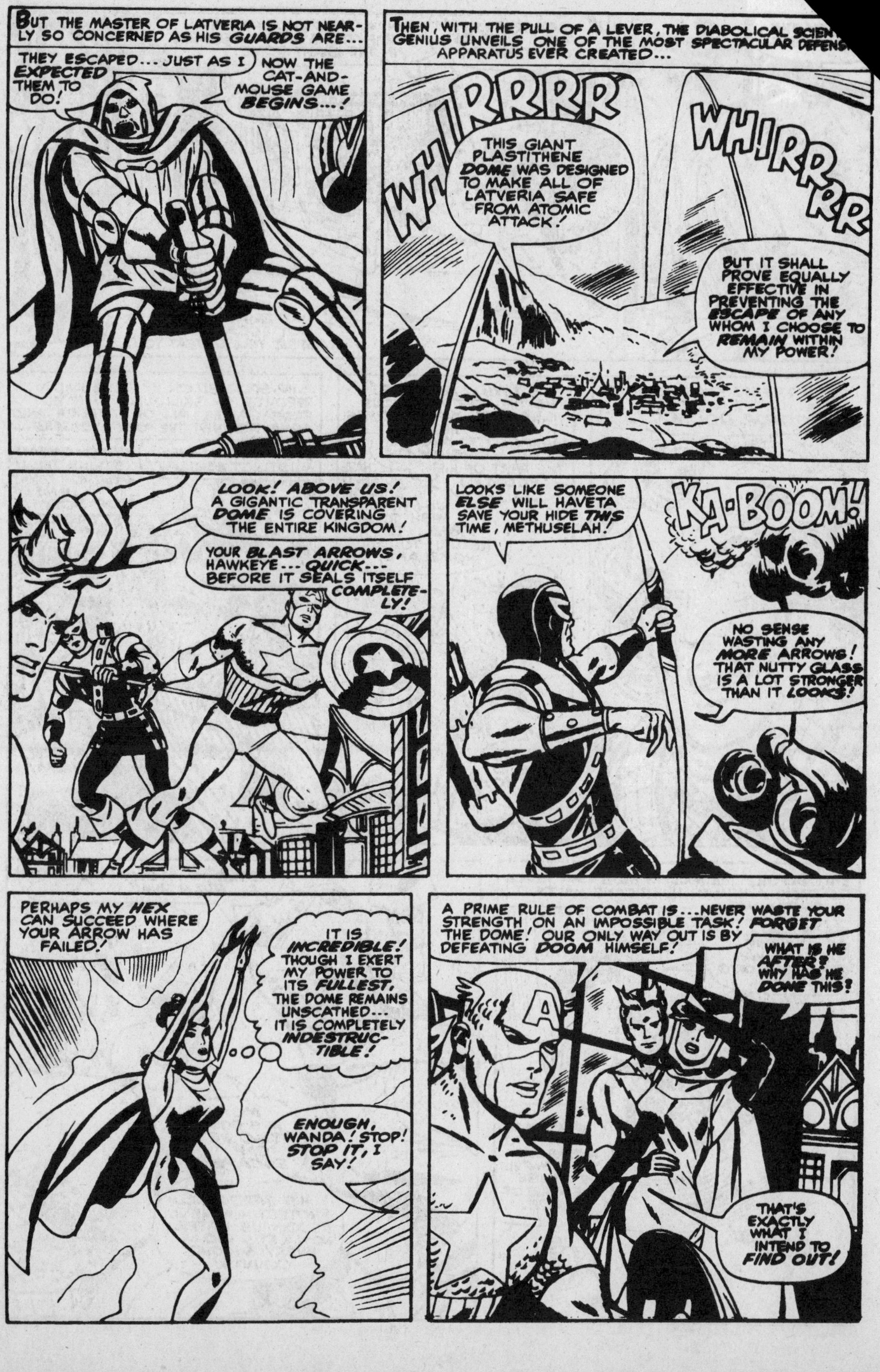

BUT THE MASTER OF LATVERIA IS NOT NEARLY SO CONCERNED AS HIS GUARDS ARE...
THEY ESCAPED... JUST AS I EXPECTED THEM TO DO!
NOW THE CAT-AND-MOUSE GAME BEGINS...!
THEN, WITH THE PULL OF A LEVER, THE DIABOLICAL SCIENT GENIUS UNVEILS ONE OF THE MOST SPECTACULAR DEFENS APPARATUS EVER CREATED...
WHIRRRR
THIS GIANT PLASTITHENE DOME WAS DESIGNED TO MAKE ALL OF LATVERIA SAFE FROM ATOMIC ATTACK!
WHIRRRRR
BUT IT SHALL PROVE EQUALLY EFFECTIVE IN PREVENTING THE ESCAPE OF ANY WHOM I CHOOSE TO REMAIN WITHIN MY POWER!
LOOK! ABOVE US! A GIGANTIC TRANSPARENT DOME IS COVERING THE ENTIRE KINGDOM!
YOUR BLAST ARROWS, HAWKEYE... QUICK... BEFORE IT SEALS ITSELF COMPLETELY!
LOOKS LIKE SOMEONE ELSE WILL HAVETA SAVE YOUR HIDE THIS TIME, METHUSELAH!
KA-BOOM!
NO SENSE WASTING ANY MORE ARROWS! THAT NUTTY GLASS IS A LOT STRONGER THAN IT LOOKS!
PERHAPS MY HEX CAN SUCCEED WHERE YOUR ARROW HAS FAILED!
IT IS INCREDIBLE! THOUGH I EXERT MY POWER TO ITS FULLEST, THE DOME REMAINS UNSCATHED... IT IS COMPLETELY INDESTRUCTIBLE!
ENOUGH, WANDA! STOP! STOP IT, I SAY!
A PRIME RULE OF COMBAT IS...NEVER WASTE YOUR STRENGTH ON AN IMPOSSIBLE TASK! FORGET THE DOME! OUR ONLY WAY OUT IS BY DEFEATING DOOM HIMSELF!
WHAT IS HE AFTER? WHY HAS HE DONE THIS?
THAT'S EXACTLY WHAT I INTEND TO FIND OUT!

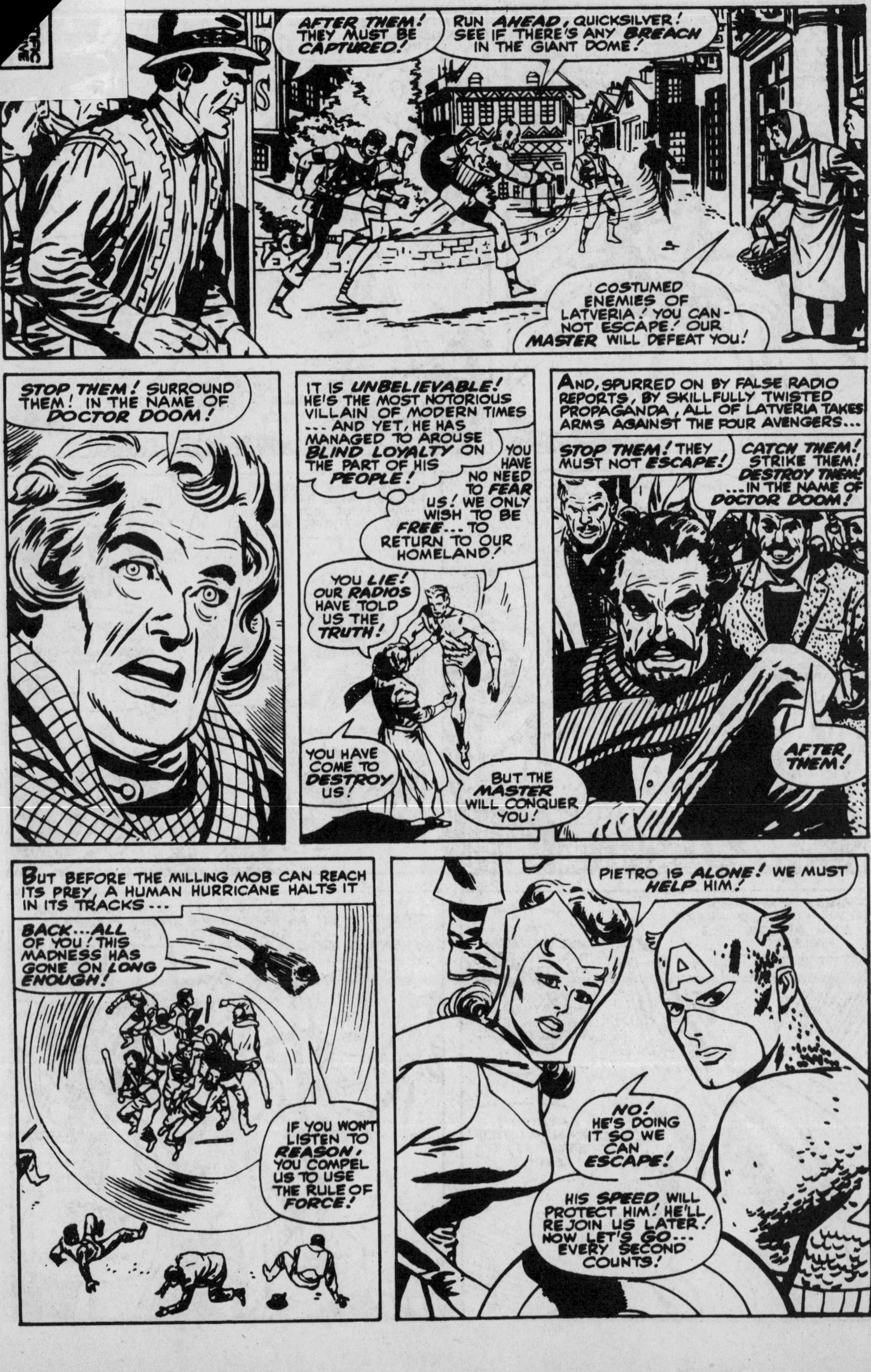

AFTER THEM! THEY MUST BE CAPTURED!
RUN AHEAD, QUICKSILVER! SEE IF THERE'S ANY BREACH IN THE GIANT DOME!
COSTUMED ENEMIES OF LATVERIA! YOU CAN-NOT ESCAPE! OUR MASTER WILL DEFEAT YOU!
STOP THEM! SURROUND THEM! IN THE NAME OF DOCTOR DOOM!
IT IS UNBELIEVABLE! HE'S THE MOST NOTORIOUS VILLAIN OF MODERN TIMES ... AND YET, HE HAS MANAGED TO AROUSE BLIND LOYALTY ON THE PART OF HIS PEOPLE!
YOU HAVE NO NEED TO FEAR US! WE ONLY WISH TO BE FREE... TO RETURN TO OUR HOMELAND!
YOU LIE! OUR RADIOS HAVE TOLD US THE TRUTH!
YOU HAVE COME TO DESTROY US!
BUT THE MASTER WILL CONQUER YOU!
AND, SPURRED ON BY FALSE RADIO REPORTS, BY SKILLFULLY TWISTED PROPAGANDA, ALL OF LATVERIA TAKES ARMS AGAINST THE FOUR AVENGERS...
STOP THEM! THEY MUST NOT ESCAPE!
CATCH THEM! STRIKE THEM! DESTROY THEM! ...IN THE NAME OF DOCTOR DOOM!
AFTER THEM!
BUT BEFORE THE MILLING MOB CAN REACH ITS PREY, A HUMAN HURRICANE HALTS IT IN ITS TRACKS...
BACK...ALL OF YOU! THIS MADNESS HAS GONE ON LONG ENOUGH!
IF YOU WON'T LISTEN TO REASON, YOU COMPEL US TO USE THE RULE OF FORCE!
PIETRO IS ALONE! WE MUST HELP HIM!
NO! HE'S DOING IT SO WE CAN ESCAPE!
HIS SPEED WILL PROTECT HIM! HE'LL REJOIN US LATER! NOW LET'S GO... EVERY SECOND COUNTS!

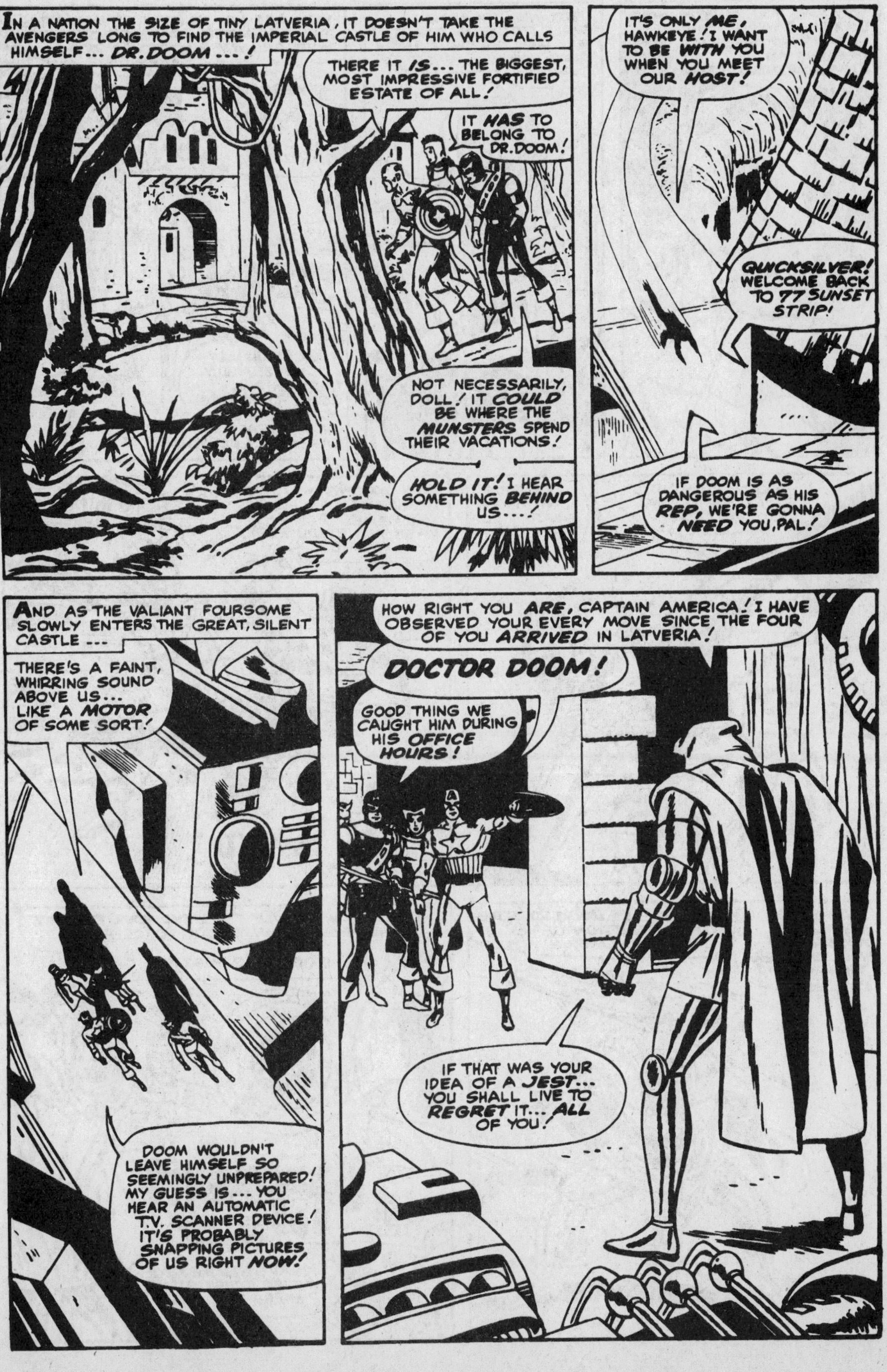
IN A NATION THE SIZE OF TINY LATVERIA, IT DOESN'T TAKE THE AVENGERS LONG TO FIND THE IMPERIAL CASTLE OF HIM WHO CALLS HIMSELF... DR. DOOM ...!
THERE IT IS... THE BIGGEST, MOST IMPRESSIVE FORTIFIED ESTATE OF ALL!
IT HAS TO BELONG TO DR. DOOM!
NOT NECESSARILY, DOLL! IT COULD BE WHERE THE MUNSTERS SPEND THEIR VACATIONS!
HOLD IT! I HEAR SOMETHING BEHIND US...!
IT'S ONLY ME, HAWKEYE! I WANT TO BE WITH YOU WHEN YOU MEET OUR HOST!
QUICKSILVER! WELCOME BACK TO 77 SUNSET STRIP!
IF DOOM IS AS DANGEROUS AS HIS REP, WE'RE GONNA NEED YOU, PAL!
AND AS THE VALIANT FOURSOME SLOWLY ENTERS THE GREAT, SILENT CASTLE ---
THERE'S A FAINT, WHIRRING SOUND ABOVE US... LIKE A MOTOR OF SOME SORT!
DOOM WOULDN'T LEAVE HIMSELF SO SEEMINGLY UNPREPARED! MY GUESS IS... YOU HEAR AN AUTOMATIC T.V. SCANNER DEVICE! IT'S PROBABLY SNAPPING PICTURES OF US RIGHT NOW!
HOW RIGHT YOU ARE, CAPTAIN AMERICA! I HAVE OBSERVED YOUR EVERY MOVE SINCE THE FOUR OF YOU ARRIVED IN LATVERIA!
DOCTOR DOOM!
GOOD THING WE CAUGHT HIM DURING HIS OFFICE HOURS!
IF THAT WAS YOUR IDEA OF A JEST... YOU SHALL LIVE TO REGRET IT... ALL OF YOU!

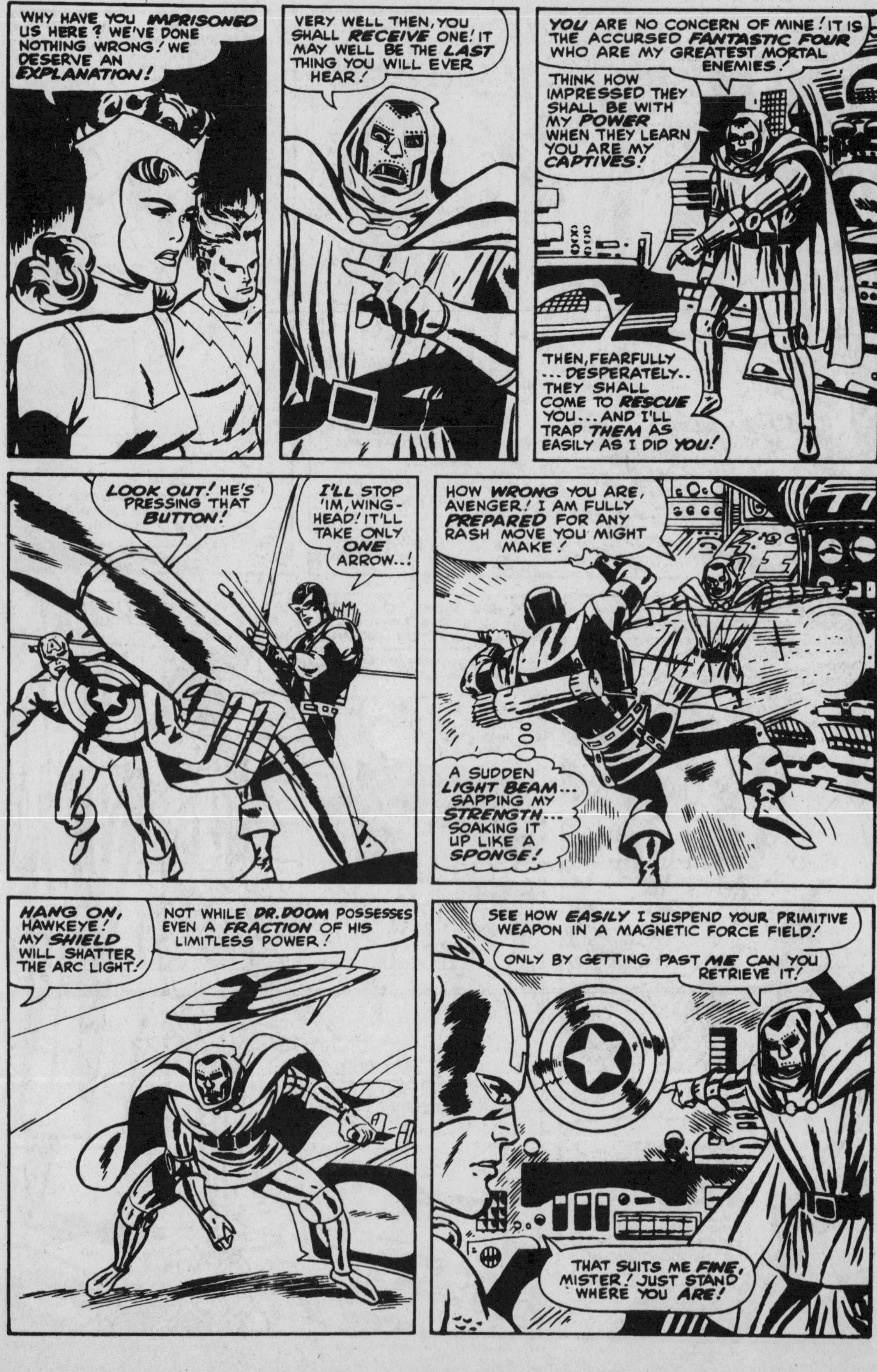
WHY HAVE YOU IMPRISONED US HERE? WE'VE DONE NOTHING WRONG! WE DESERVE AN EXPLANATION!
VERY WELL THEN, YOU SHALL RECEIVE ONE! IT MAY WELL BE THE LAST THING YOU WILL EVER HEAR!
YOU ARE NO CONCERN OF MINE! IT IS THE ACCURSED FANTASTIC FOUR WHO ARE MY GREATEST MORTAL ENEMIES!
THINK HOW IMPRESSED THEY SHALL BE WITH MY POWER WHEN THEY LEARN YOU ARE MY CAPTIVES!
THEN, FEARFULLY ... DESPERATELY.. THEY SHALL COME TO RESCUE YOU... AND I'LL TRAP THEM AS EASILY AS I DID YOU!
LOOK OUT! HE'S PRESSING THAT BUTTON!
I'LL STOP 'IM, WING-HEAD! IT'LL TAKE ONLY ONE ARROW..!
HOW WRONG YOU ARE, AVENGER! I AM FULLY PREPARED FOR ANY RASH MOVE YOU MIGHT MAKE!
A SUDDEN LIGHT BEAM... SAPPING MY STRENGTH... SOAKING IT UP LIKE A SPONGE!
HANG ON, HAWKEYE! MY SHIELD WILL SHATTER THE ARC LIGHT!
NOT WHILE DR. DOOM POSSESSES EVEN A FRACTION OF HIS LIMITLESS POWER!
SEE HOW EASILY I SUSPEND YOUR PRIMITIVE WEAPON IN A MAGNETIC FORCE FIELD!
ONLY BY GETTING PAST ME CAN YOU RETRIEVE IT!
THAT SUITS ME FINE, MISTER! JUST STAND WHERE YOU ARE!

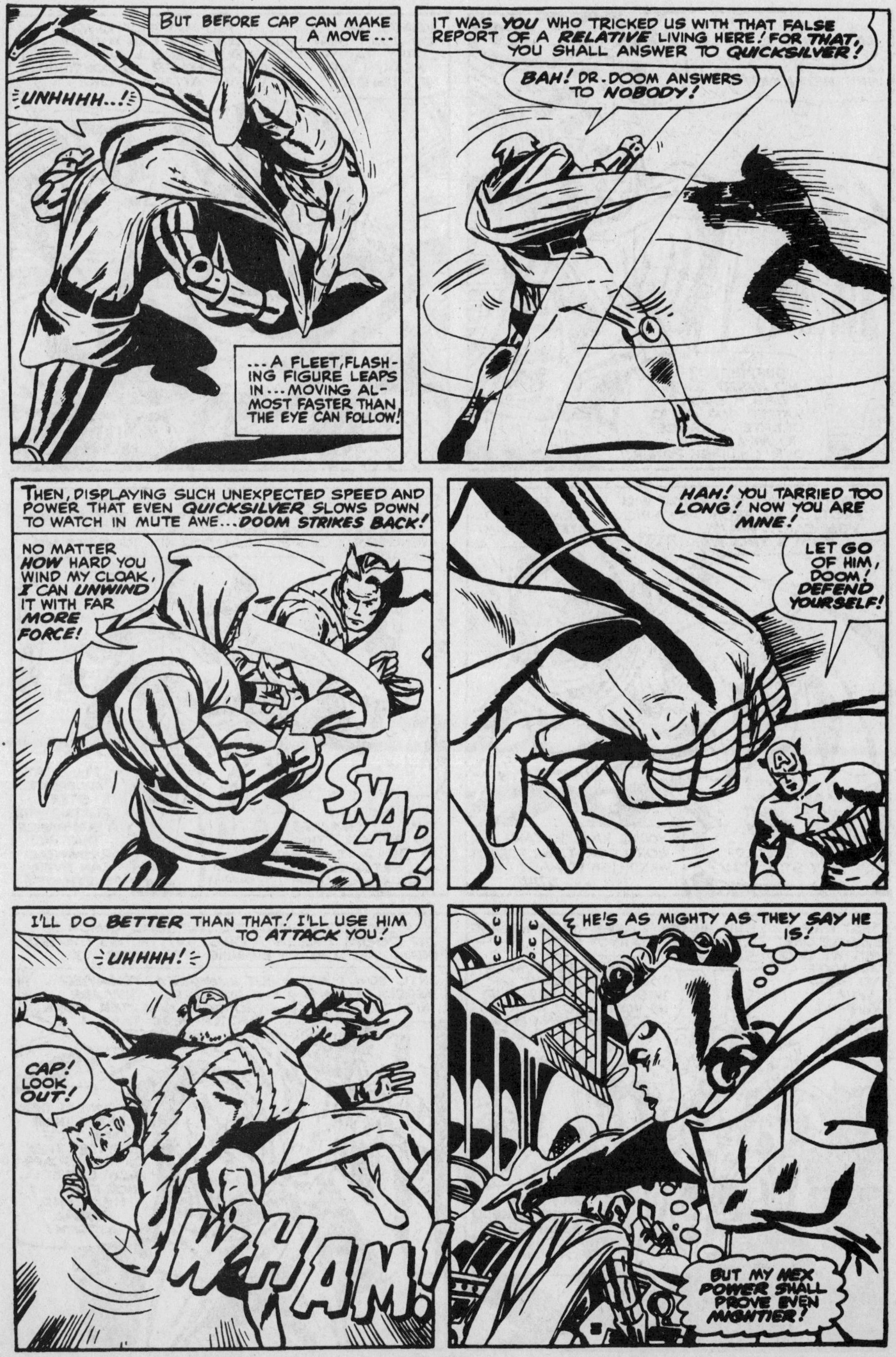

BUT BEFORE CAP CAN MAKE A MOVE...
UNHHHH..!
...A FLEET, FLASHING FIGURE LEAPS IN...MOVING ALMOST FASTER THAN THE EYE CAN FOLLOW!
IT WAS YOU WHO TRICKED US WITH THAT FALSE REPORT OF A RELATIVE LIVING HERE! FOR THAT, YOU SHALL ANSWER TO QUICKSILVER!
BAH! DR. DOOM ANSWERS TO NOBODY!
THEN, DISPLAYING SUCH UNEXPECTED SPEED AND POWER THAT EVEN QUICKSILVER SLOWS DOWN TO WATCH IN MUTE AWE...DOOM STRIKES BACK!
NO MATTER HOW HARD YOU WIND MY CLOAK, I CAN UNWIND IT WITH FAR MORE FORCE!
SNAP!
HAH! YOU TARRIED TOO LONG! NOW YOU ARE MINE!
LET GO OF HIM, DOOM! DEFEND YOURSELF!
I'LL DO BETTER THAN THAT! I'LL USE HIM TO ATTACK YOU!
UNHHH!
CAP! LOOK OUT!
WHAM!
HE'S AS MIGHTY AS THEY SAY HE IS!
BUT MY HEX POWER SHALL PROVE EVEN MIGHTIER!

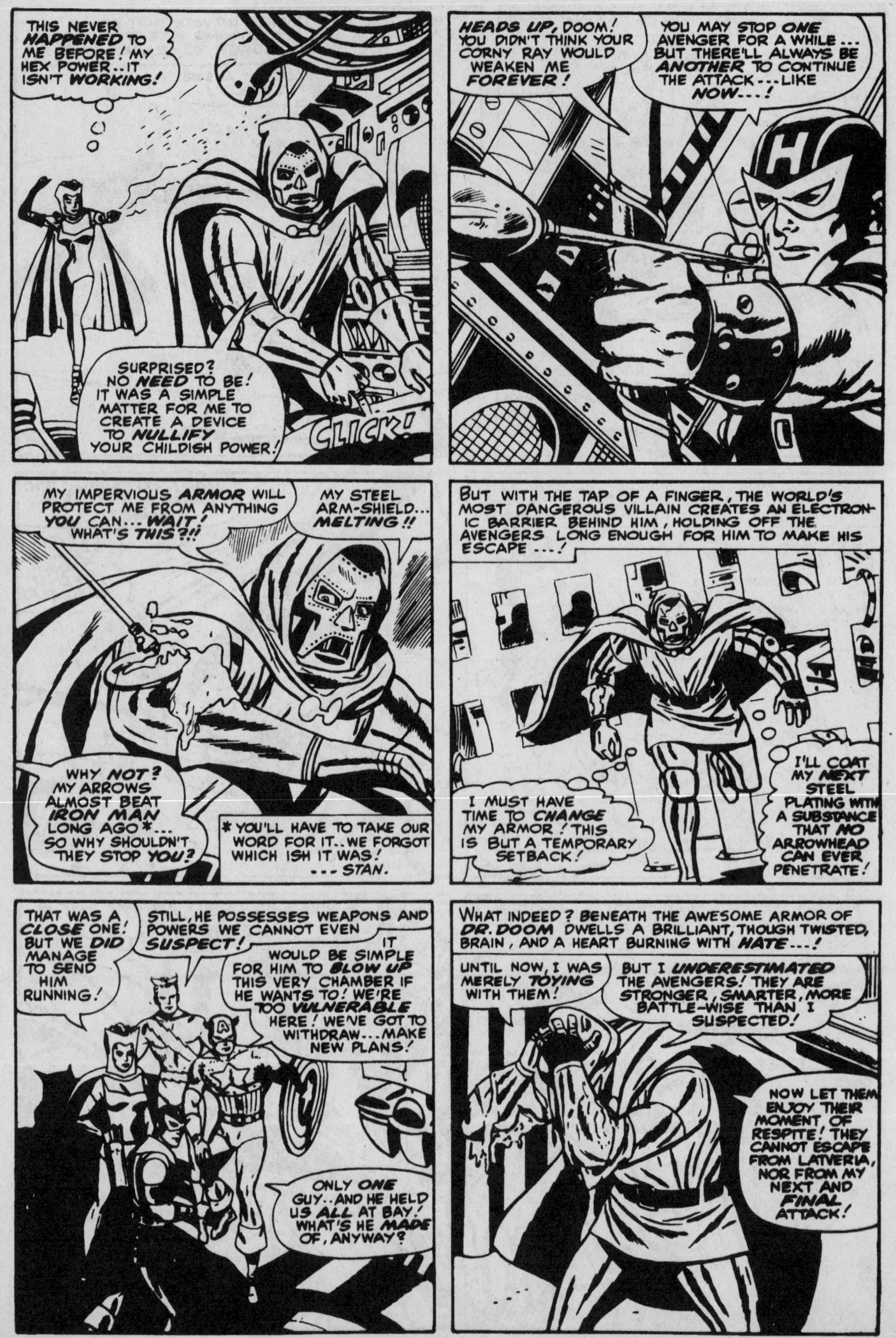

THIS NEVER HAPPENED TO ME BEFORE! MY HEX POWER..IT ISN'T WORKING!
SURPRISED? NO NEED TO BE! IT WAS A SIMPLE MATTER FOR ME TO CREATE A DEVICE TO NULLIFY YOUR CHILDISH POWER!
CLICK!
HEADS UP, DOOM! YOU DIDN'T THINK YOUR CORNY RAY WOULD WEAKEN ME FOREVER!
YOU MAY STOP ONE AVENGER FOR A WHILE ... BUT THERE'LL ALWAYS BE ANOTHER TO CONTINUE THE ATTACK---LIKE NOW---!
MY IMPERVIOUS ARMOR WILL PROTECT ME FROM ANYTHING YOU CAN... WAIT! WHAT'S THIS?!!
MY STEEL ARM-SHIELD... MELTING!!
WHY NOT? MY ARROWS ALMOST BEAT IRON MAN LONG AGO*... SO WHY SHOULDN'T THEY STOP YOU?
* YOU'LL HAVE TO TAKE OUR WORD FOR IT.. WE FORGOT WHICH ISH IT WAS! --- STAN.
BUT WITH THE TAP OF A FINGER, THE WORLD'S MOST DANGEROUS VILLAIN CREATES AN ELECTRONIC BARRIER BEHIND HIM, HOLDING OFF THE AVENGERS LONG ENOUGH FOR HIM TO MAKE HIS ESCAPE ---!
I MUST HAVE TIME TO CHANGE MY ARMOR! THIS IS BUT A TEMPORARY SETBACK!
I'LL COAT MY NEXT STEEL PLATING WITH A SUBSTANCE THAT NO ARROWHEAD CAN EVER PENETRATE!
THAT WAS A CLOSE ONE! BUT WE DID MANAGE TO SEND HIM RUNNING!
STILL, HE POSSESSES WEAPONS AND POWERS WE CANNOT EVEN SUSPECT!
IT WOULD BE SIMPLE FOR HIM TO BLOW UP THIS VERY CHAMBER IF HE WANTS TO! WE'RE TOO VULNERABLE HERE! WE'VE GOT TO WITHDRAW... MAKE NEW PLANS!
ONLY ONE GUY.. AND HE HELD US ALL AT BAY! WHAT'S HE MADE OF, ANYWAY?
WHAT INDEED? BENEATH THE AWESOME ARMOR OF DR. DOOM DWELLS A BRILLIANT, THOUGH TWISTED, BRAIN, AND A HEART BURNING WITH HATE---!
UNTIL NOW, I WAS MERELY TOYING WITH THEM!
BUT I UNDERESTIMATED THE AVENGERS! THEY ARE STRONGER, SMARTER, MORE BATTLE-WISE THAN I SUSPECTED!
NOW LET THEM ENJOY THEIR MOMENT OF RESPITE! THEY CANNOT ESCAPE FROM LATVERIA, NOR FROM MY NEXT AND FINAL ATTACK!

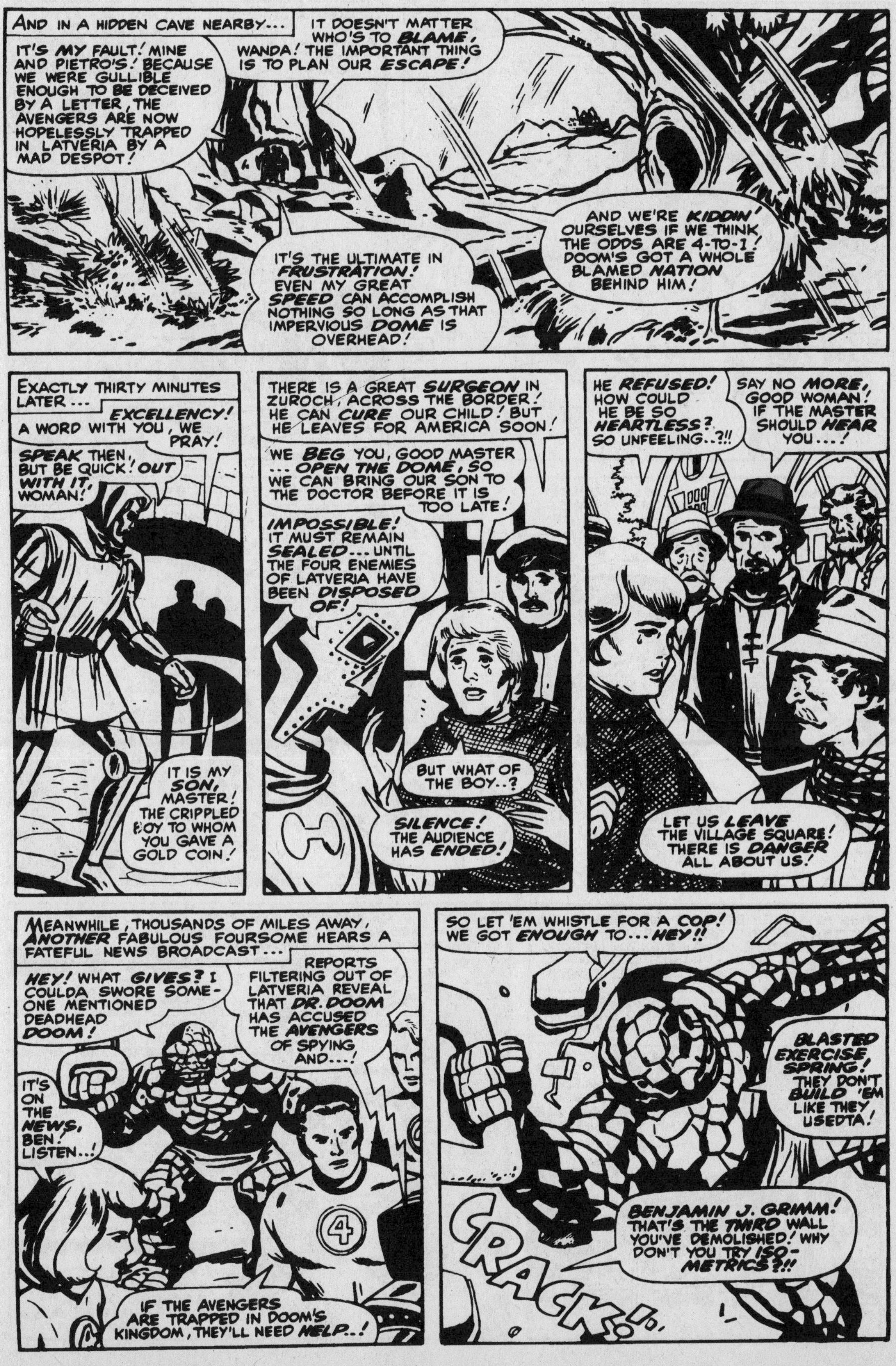

AND IN A HIDDEN CAVE NEARBY...
IT'S MY FAULT! MINE AND PIETRO'S! BECAUSE WE WERE GULLIBLE ENOUGH TO BE DECEIVED BY A LETTER, THE AVENGERS ARE NOW HOPELESSLY TRAPPED IN LATVERIA BY A MAD DESPOT!
IT DOESN'T MATTER WHO'S TO BLAME, WANDA! THE IMPORTANT THING IS TO PLAN OUR ESCAPE!
IT'S THE ULTIMATE IN FRUSTRATION! EVEN MY GREAT SPEED CAN ACCOMPLISH NOTHING SO LONG AS THAT IMPERVIOUS DOME IS OVERHEAD!
AND WE'RE KIDDIN' OURSELVES IF WE THINK THE ODDS ARE 4-TO-1! DOOM'S GOT A WHOLE BLAMED NATION BEHIND HIM!
EXACTLY THIRTY MINUTES LATER...
EXCELLENCY! A WORD WITH YOU, WE PRAY!
SPEAK THEN, BUT BE QUICK! OUT WITH IT, WOMAN!
IT IS MY SON, MASTER! THE CRIPPLED BOY TO WHOM YOU GAVE A GOLD COIN!
THERE IS A GREAT SURGEON IN ZUROCH, ACROSS THE BORDER! HE CAN CURE OUR CHILD! BUT HE LEAVES FOR AMERICA SOON!
WE BEG YOU, GOOD MASTER ... OPEN THE DOME, SO WE CAN BRING OUR SON TO THE DOCTOR BEFORE IT IS TOO LATE!
IMPOSSIBLE! IT MUST REMAIN SEALED... UNTIL THE FOUR ENEMIES OF LATVERIA HAVE BEEN DISPOSED OF!
BUT WHAT OF THE BOY..?
SILENCE! THE AUDIENCE HAS ENDED!
HE REFUSED! HOW COULD HE BE SO HEARTLESS? SO UNFEELING..?!!
SAY NO MORE, GOOD WOMAN! IF THE MASTER SHOULD HEAR YOU....!
LET US LEAVE THE VILLAGE SQUARE! THERE IS DANGER ALL ABOUT US!
MEANWHILE, THOUSANDS OF MILES AWAY, ANOTHER FABULOUS FOURSOME HEARS A FATEFUL NEWS BROADCAST...
HEY! WHAT GIVES? I COULDA SWORE SOME-ONE MENTIONED DEADHEAD DOOM!
REPORTS FILTERING OUT OF LATVERIA REVEAL THAT DR. DOOM HAS ACCUSED THE AVENGERS OF SPYING AND...!
IT'S ON THE NEWS, BEN. LISTEN..!
IF THE AVENGERS ARE TRAPPED IN DOOM'S KINGDOM, THEY'LL NEED HELP..!
SO LET 'EM WHISTLE FOR A COP! WE GOT ENOUGH TO... HEY!!
BLASTED EXERCISE SPRING! THEY DON'T BUILD 'EM LIKE THEY USEDTA!
CRACK!
BENJAMIN J. GRIMM! THAT'S THE THIRD WALL YOU'VE DEMOLISHED! WHY DON'T YOU TRY ISO-METRICS?!!

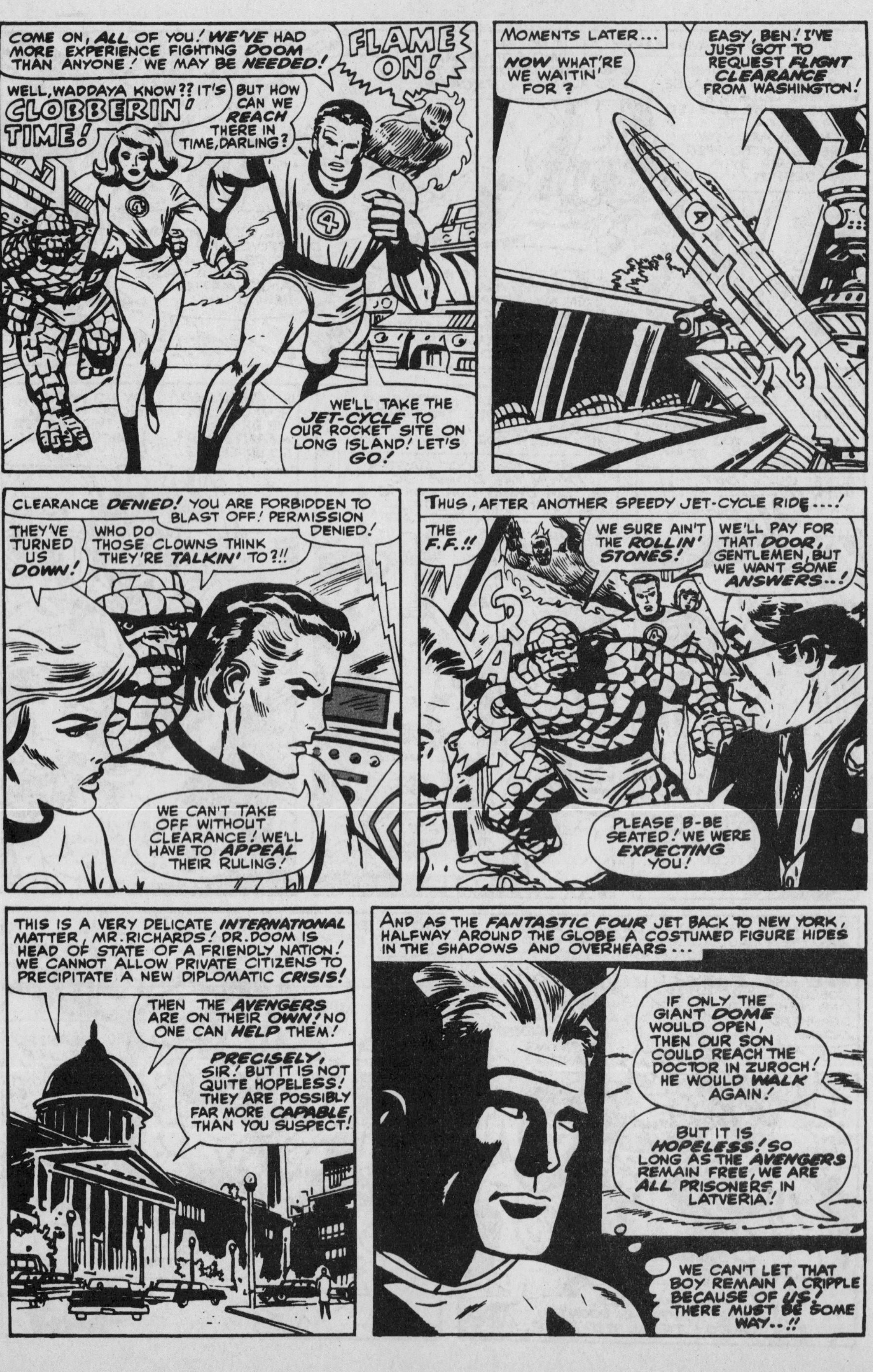

COME ON, ALL OF YOU! WE'VE HAD MORE EXPERIENCE FIGHTING DOOM THAN ANYONE! WE MAY BE NEEDED!
FLAME ON!
WELL, WADDAYA KNOW?? IT'S CLOBBERIN' TIME!
BUT HOW CAN WE REACH THERE IN TIME, DARLING?
WE'LL TAKE THE JET-CYCLE TO OUR ROCKET SITE ON LONG ISLAND! LET'S GO!
MOMENTS LATER...
NOW WHAT'RE WE WAITIN' FOR?
EASY, BEN! I'VE JUST GOT TO REQUEST FLIGHT CLEARANCE FROM WASHINGTON!
CLEARANCE DENIED! YOU ARE FORBIDDEN TO BLAST OFF! PERMISSION DENIED!
THEY'VE TURNED US DOWN!
WHO DO THOSE CLOWNS THINK THEY'RE TALKIN' TO?!!
WE CAN'T TAKE OFF WITHOUT CLEARANCE! WE'LL HAVE TO APPEAL THEIR RULING!
THUS, AFTER ANOTHER SPEEDY JET-CYCLE RIDE....!
THE F.F.!!
WE SURE AIN'T THE ROLLIN' STONES!
WE'LL PAY FOR THAT DOOR, GENTLEMEN, BUT WE WANT SOME ANSWERS..!
CRACK
PLEASE B-BE SEATED! WE WERE EXPECTING YOU!
THIS IS A VERY DELICATE INTERNATIONAL MATTER, MR. RICHARDS! DR. DOOM IS HEAD OF STATE OF A FRIENDLY NATION! WE CANNOT ALLOW PRIVATE CITIZENS TO PRECIPITATE A NEW DIPLOMATIC CRISIS!
THEN THE AVENGERS ARE ON THEIR OWN! NO ONE CAN HELP THEM!
PRECISELY, SIR! BUT IT IS NOT QUITE HOPELESS! THEY ARE POSSIBLY FAR MORE CAPABLE THAN YOU SUSPECT!
AND AS THE FANTASTIC FOUR JET BACK TO NEW YORK, HALFWAY AROUND THE GLOBE A COSTUMED FIGURE HIDES IN THE SHADOWS AND OVERHEARS...
IF ONLY THE GIANT DOME WOULD OPEN, THEN OUR SON COULD REACH THE DOCTOR IN ZUROCH! HE WOULD WALK AGAIN!
BUT IT IS HOPELESS! SO LONG AS THE AVENGERS REMAIN FREE, WE ARE ALL PRISONERS IN LATVERIA!
WE CAN'T LET THAT BOY REMAIN A CRIPPLE BECAUSE OF US! THERE MUST BE SOME WAY..!!

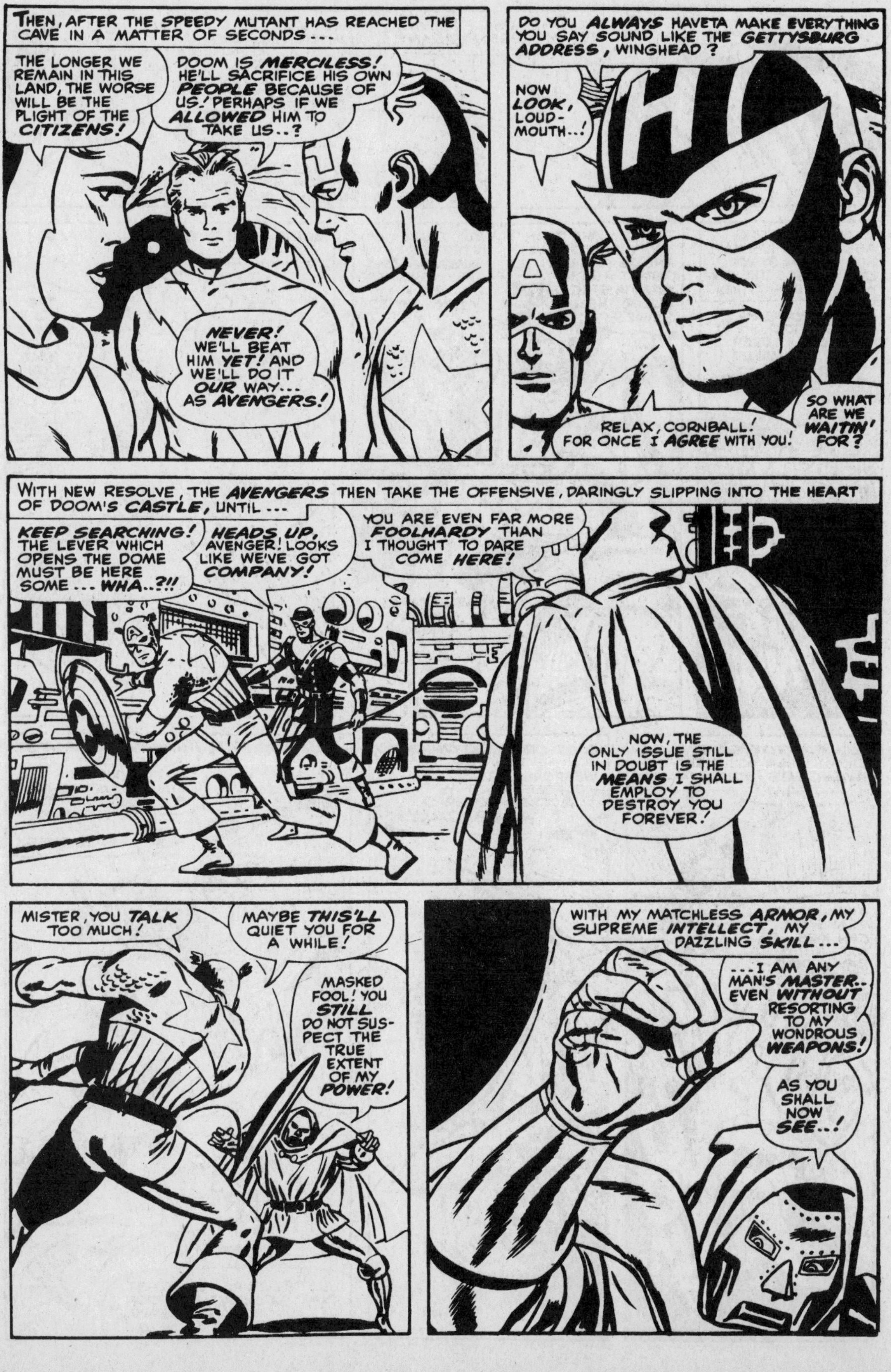
THEN, AFTER THE SPEEDY MUTANT HAS REACHED THE CAVE IN A MATTER OF SECONDS ...
THE LONGER WE REMAIN IN THIS LAND, THE WORSE WILL BE THE PLIGHT OF THE CITIZENS!
DOOM IS MERCILESS! HE'LL SACRIFICE HIS OWN PEOPLE BECAUSE OF US! PERHAPS IF WE ALLOWED HIM TO TAKE US..?
NEVER! WE'LL BEAT HIM YET! AND WE'LL DO IT OUR WAY... AS AVENGERS!
DO YOU ALWAYS HAVETA MAKE EVERYTHING YOU SAY SOUND LIKE THE GETTYSBURG ADDRESS, WINGHEAD?
NOW LOOK, LOUD-MOUTH...!
RELAX, CORNBALL! FOR ONCE I AGREE WITH YOU!
SO WHAT ARE WE WAITIN' FOR?
WITH NEW RESOLVE, THE AVENGERS THEN TAKE THE OFFENSIVE, DARINGLY SLIPPING INTO THE HEART OF DOOM'S CASTLE, UNTIL ...
KEEP SEARCHING! THE LEVER WHICH OPENS THE DOME MUST BE HERE SOME ... WHA..?!!
HEADS UP, AVENGER! LOOKS LIKE WE'VE GOT COMPANY!
YOU ARE EVEN FAR MORE FOOLHARDY THAN I THOUGHT TO DARE COME HERE!
NOW, THE ONLY ISSUE STILL IN DOUBT IS THE MEANS I SHALL EMPLOY TO DESTROY YOU FOREVER!
MISTER, YOU TALK TOO MUCH!
MAYBE THIS'LL QUIET YOU FOR A WHILE!
MASKED FOOL! YOU STILL DO NOT SUSPECT THE TRUE EXTENT OF MY POWER!
WITH MY MATCHLESS ARMOR, MY SUPREME INTELLECT, MY DAZZLING SKILL ...
... I AM ANY MAN'S MASTER.. EVEN WITHOUT RESORTING TO MY WONDROUS WEAPONS!
AS YOU SHALL NOW SEE..!

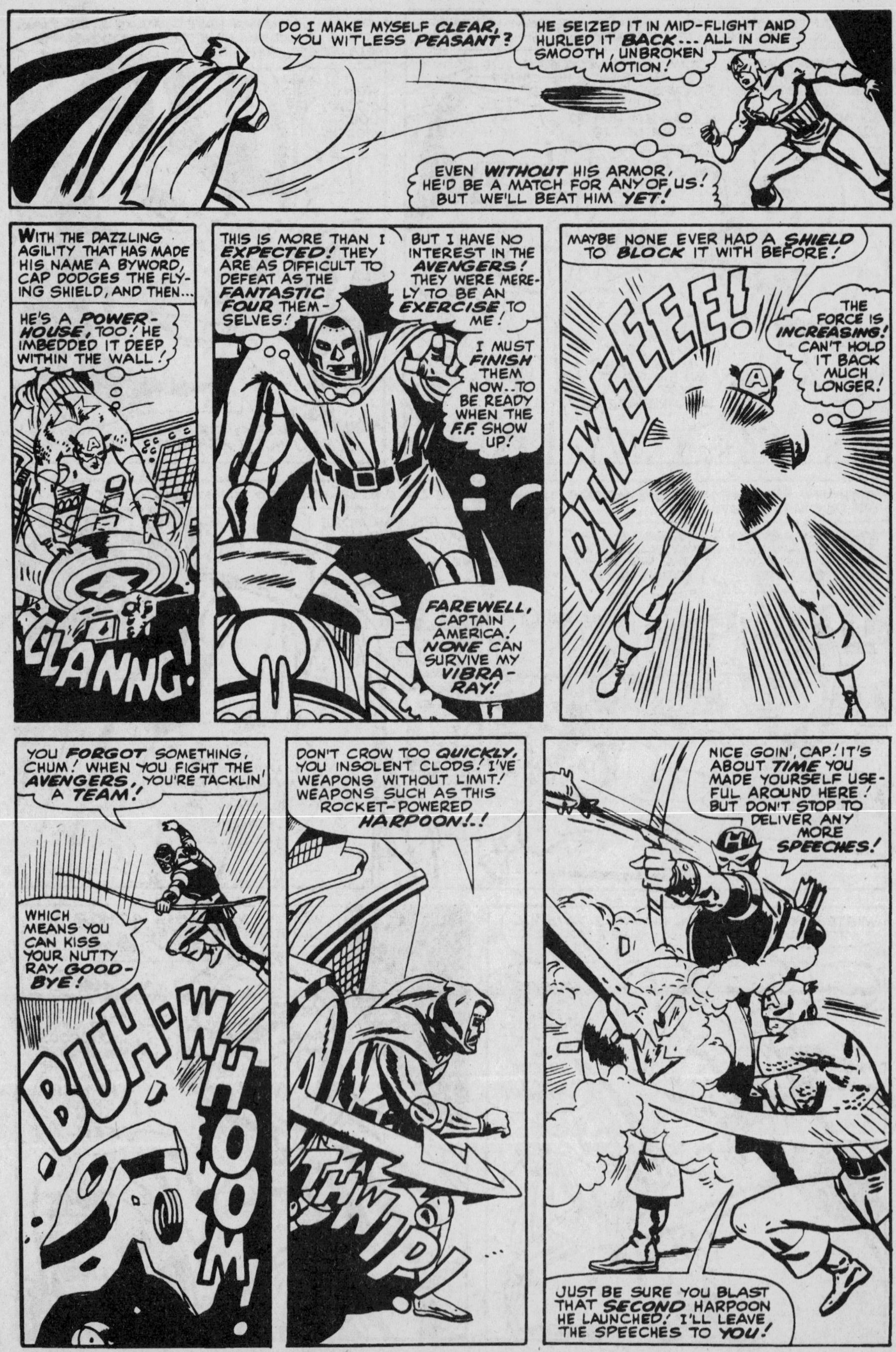
DO I MAKE MYSELF CLEAR, YOU WITLESS PEASANT?
HE SEIZED IT IN MID-FLIGHT AND HURLED IT BACK... ALL IN ONE SMOOTH, UNBROKEN MOTION!
EVEN WITHOUT HIS ARMOR, HE'D BE A MATCH FOR ANY OF US! BUT WE'LL BEAT HIM YET!
WITH THE DAZZLING AGILITY THAT HAS MADE HIS NAME A BYWORD, CAP DODGES THE FLYING SHIELD, AND THEN...
HE'S A POWER-HOUSE, TOO! HE IMBEDDED IT DEEP WITHIN THE WALL!
CLANNG!
THIS IS MORE THAN I EXPECTED! THEY ARE AS DIFFICULT TO DEFEAT AS THE FANTASTIC FOUR THEMSELVES!
BUT I HAVE NO INTEREST IN THE AVENGERS! THEY WERE MERELY TO BE AN EXERCISE TO ME!
I MUST FINISH THEM NOW..TO BE READY WHEN THE F.F. SHOW UP!
FAREWELL, CAPTAIN AMERICA! NONE CAN SURVIVE MY VIBRA-RAY!
MAYBE NONE EVER HAD A SHIELD TO BLOCK IT WITH BEFORE!
PITWEEEE!
THE FORCE IS INCREASING! CAN'T HOLD IT BACK MUCH LONGER!
YOU FORGOT SOMETHING, CHUM! WHEN YOU FIGHT THE AVENGERS, YOU'RE TACKLIN' A TEAM!
WHICH MEANS YOU CAN KISS YOUR NUTTY RAY GOOD-BYE!
BUH-WHOOM!
DON'T CROW TOO QUICKLY, YOU INSOLENT CLODS! I'VE WEAPONS WITHOUT LIMIT! WEAPONS SUCH AS THIS ROCKET-POWERED HARPOON!.!
THWIP!
NICE GOIN', CAP! IT'S ABOUT TIME YOU MADE YOURSELF USEFUL AROUND HERE! BUT DON'T STOP TO DELIVER ANY MORE SPEECHES!
JUST BE SURE YOU BLAST THAT SECOND HARPOON HE LAUNCHED! I'LL LEAVE THE SPEECHES TO YOU!

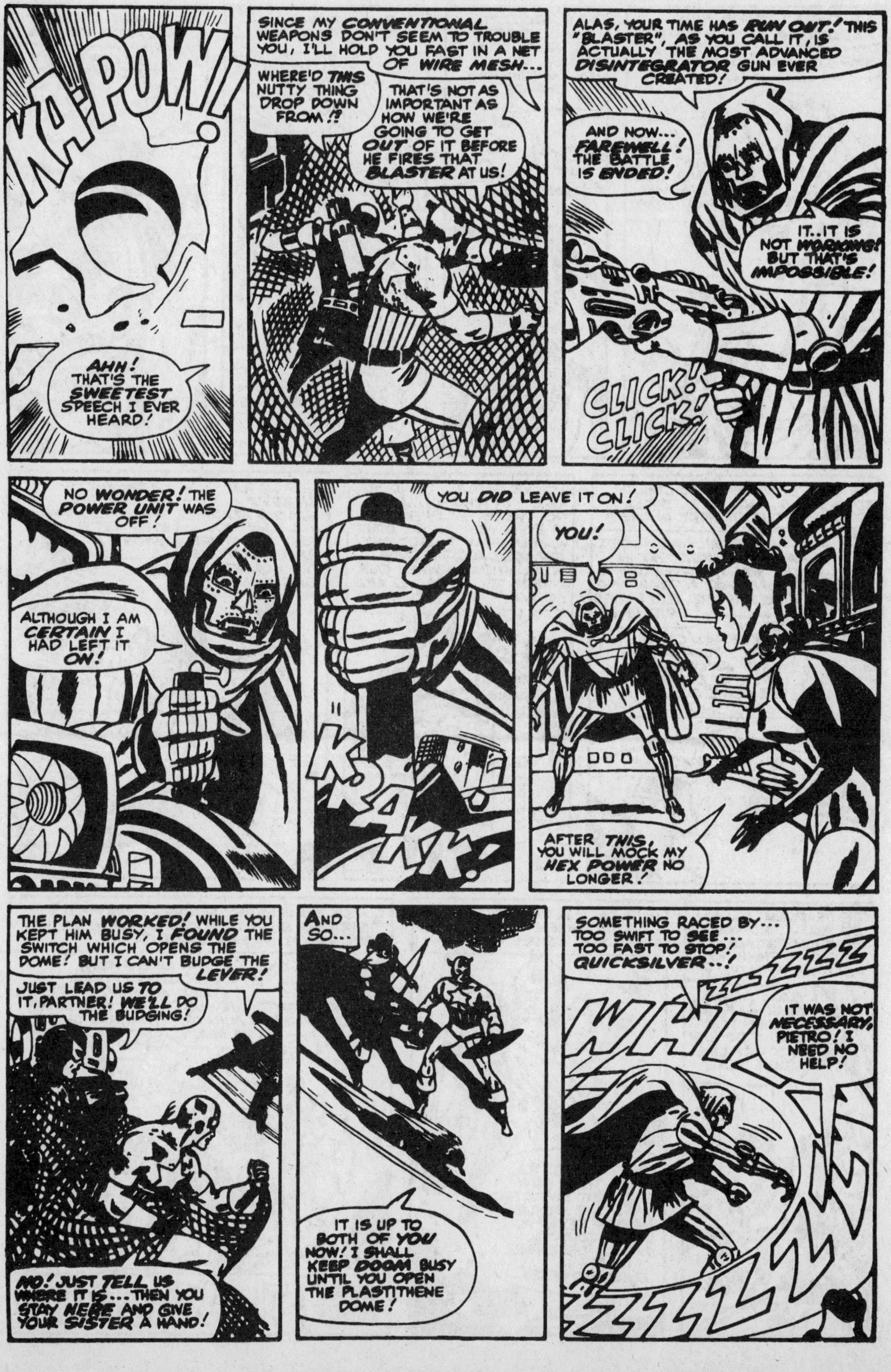
KA-POW!!
AHH! THAT'S THE SWEETEST SPEECH I EVER HEARD!
SINCE MY CONVENTIONAL WEAPONS DON'T SEEM TO TROUBLE YOU, I'LL HOLD YOU FAST IN A NET OF WIRE MESH...
WHERE'D THIS NUTTY THING DROP DOWN FROM!?
THAT'S NOT AS IMPORTANT AS HOW WE'RE GOING TO GET OUT OF IT BEFORE HE FIRES THAT BLASTER AT US!
ALAS, YOUR TIME HAS RUN OUT! THIS "BLASTER", AS YOU CALL IT, IS ACTUALLY THE MOST ADVANCED DISINTEGRATOR GUN EVER CREATED!
AND NOW... FAREWELL! THE BATTLE IS ENDED!
IT..IT IS NOT WORKING! BUT THAT'S IMPOSSIBLE!
CLICK! CLICK!
NO WONDER! THE POWER UNIT WAS OFF!
ALTHOUGH I AM CERTAIN I HAD LEFT IT ON!
YOU DID LEAVE IT ON!
KRAKK!
YOU!
AFTER THIS, YOU WILL MOCK MY HEX POWER NO LONGER!
THE PLAN WORKED! WHILE YOU KEPT HIM BUSY, I FOUND THE SWITCH WHICH OPENS THE DOME! BUT I CAN'T BUDGE THE LEVER!
JUST LEAD US TO IT, PARTNER! WE'LL DO THE BUDGING!
NO! JUST TELL US WHERE IT IS...THEN YOU STAY HERE AND GIVE YOUR SISTER A HAND!
AND SO...
IT IS UP TO BOTH OF YOU NOW! I SHALL KEEP DOOM BUSY UNTIL YOU OPEN THE PLASTITHENE DOME!
SOMETHING RACED BY... TOO SWIFT TO SEE... TOO FAST TO STOP! QUICKSILVER...!
ZZZZZZ
WHII
IT WAS NOT NECESSARY, PIETRO! I NEED NO HELP!
ZZZZZZ

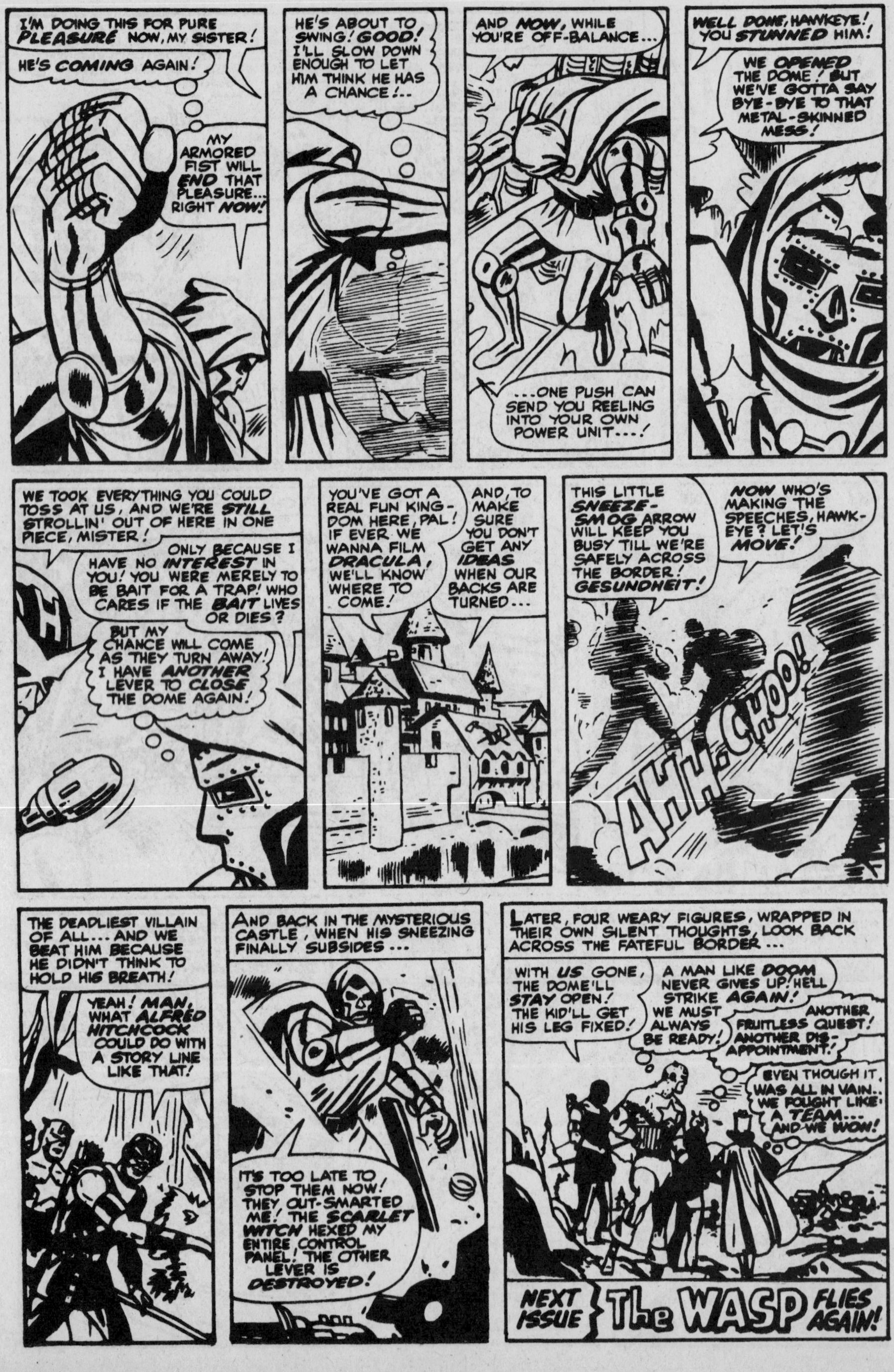
I'M DOING THIS FOR PURE PLEASURE NOW, MY SISTER!
HE'S COMING AGAIN!
MY ARMORED FIST WILL END THAT PLEASURE... RIGHT NOW!
HE'S ABOUT TO SWING! GOOD! I'LL SLOW DOWN ENOUGH TO LET HIM THINK HE HAS A CHANCE!..
AND NOW, WHILE YOU'RE OFF-BALANCE...
...ONE PUSH CAN SEND YOU REELING INTO YOUR OWN POWER UNIT...!
WELL DONE, HAWKEYE! YOU STUNNED HIM!
WE OPENED THE DOME! BUT WE'VE GOTTA SAY BYE-BYE TO THAT METAL-SKINNED MESS!
WE TOOK EVERYTHING YOU COULD TOSS AT US, AND WE'RE STILL STROLLIN' OUT OF HERE IN ONE PIECE, MISTER!
ONLY BECAUSE I HAVE NO INTEREST IN YOU! YOU WERE MERELY TO BE BAIT FOR A TRAP! WHO CARES IF THE BAIT LIVES OR DIES?
BUT MY CHANCE WILL COME AS THEY TURN AWAY! I HAVE ANOTHER LEVER TO CLOSE THE DOME AGAIN!
YOU'VE GOT A REAL FUN KING-DOM HERE, PAL! IF EVER WE WANNA FILM DRACULA, WE'LL KNOW WHERE TO COME!
AND, TO MAKE SURE YOU DON'T GET ANY IDEAS WHEN OUR BACKS ARE TURNED...
THIS LITTLE SNEEZE-SMOG ARROW WILL KEEP YOU BUSY TILL WE'RE SAFELY ACROSS THE BORDER! GESUNDHEIT!
NOW WHO'S MAKING THE SPEECHES, HAWK-EYE? LET'S MOVE!
AHH-CHOO!
THE DEADLIEST VILLAIN OF ALL... AND WE BEAT HIM BECAUSE HE DIDN'T THINK TO HOLD HIS BREATH!
YEAH! MAN, WHAT ALFRED HITCHCOCK COULD DO WITH A STORY LINE LIKE THAT!
AND BACK IN THE MYSTERIOUS CASTLE, WHEN HIS SNEEZING FINALLY SUBSIDES...
IT'S TOO LATE TO STOP THEM NOW! THEY OUT-SMARTED ME! THE SCARLET WITCH HEXED MY ENTIRE CONTROL PANEL! THE OTHER LEVER IS DESTROYED!
LATER, FOUR WEARY FIGURES, WRAPPED IN THEIR OWN SILENT THOUGHTS, LOOK BACK ACROSS THE FATEFUL BORDER...
WITH US GONE, THE DOME'LL STAY OPEN! THE KID'LL GET HIS LEG FIXED!
A MAN LIKE DOOM NEVER GIVES UP! HE'LL STRIKE AGAIN! WE MUST ALWAYS BE READY!
ANOTHER FRUITLESS QUEST! ANOTHER DIS-APPOINTMENT!
EVEN THOUGH IT WAS ALL IN VAIN.. WE FOUGHT LIKE A TEAM... AND WE WON!
NEXT ISSUE The WASP FLIES AGAIN!

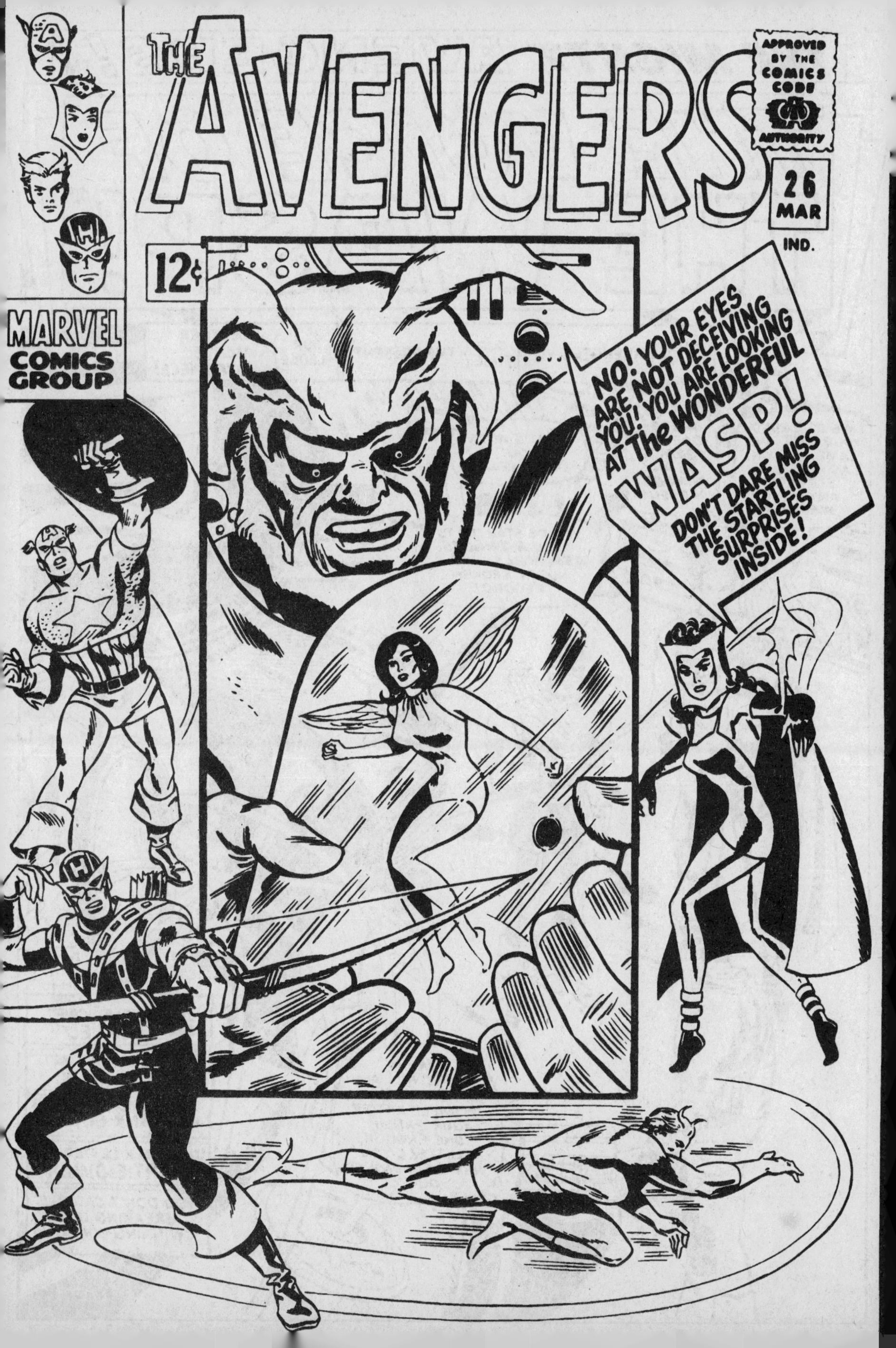

THE AVENGERS
APPROVED BY THE COMICS CODE AUTHORITY
26 MAR
IND.
12¢
MARVEL COMICS GROUP
NO! YOUR EYES ARE NOT DECEIVING YOU! YOU ARE LOOKING AT The WONDERFUL WASP!
DON'T DARE MISS THE STARTLING SURPRISES INSIDE!

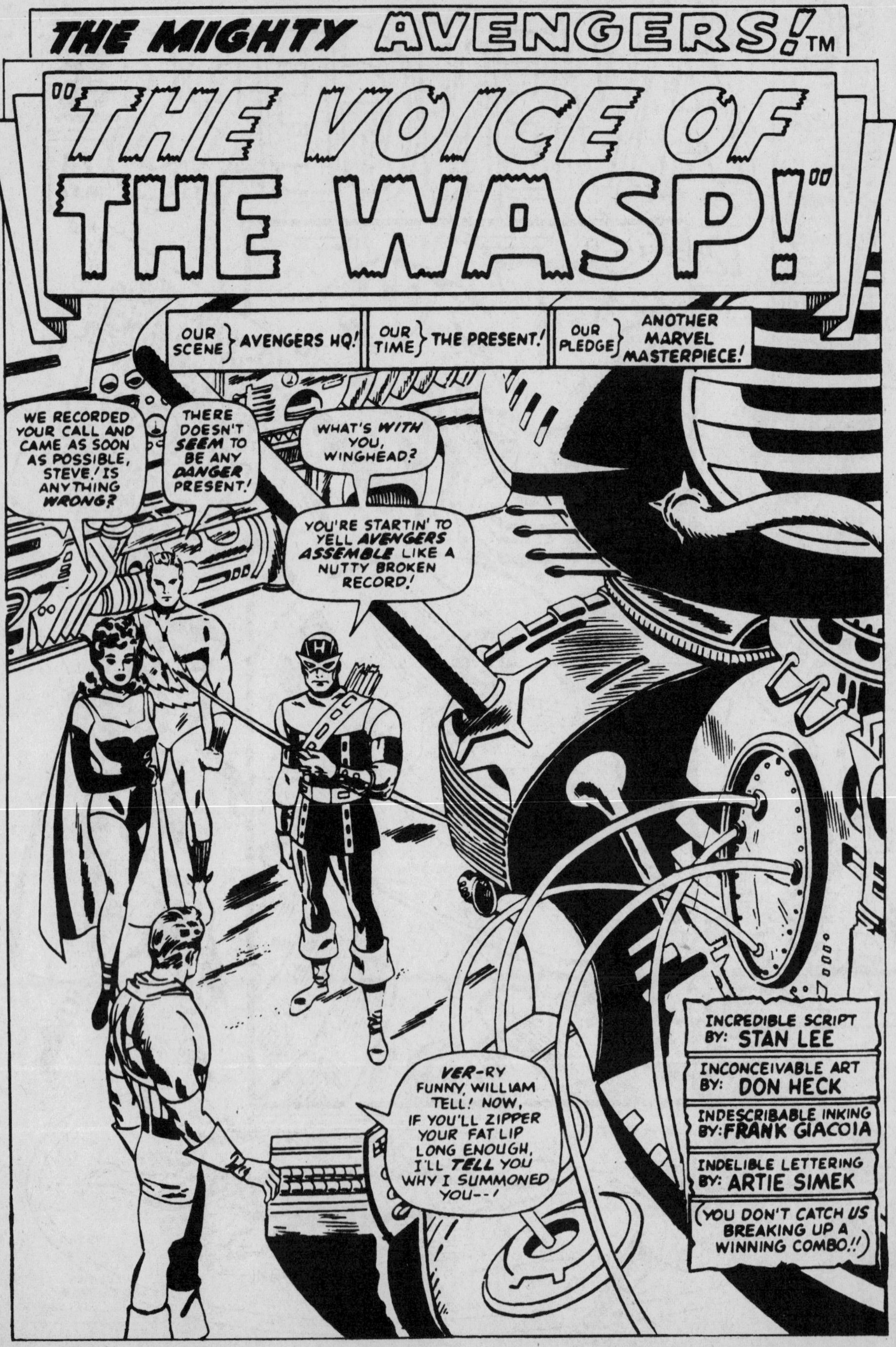
THE MIGHTY AVENGERS!™
"THE VOICE OF THE WASP!"
OUR SCENE } AVENGERS HQ!
OUR TIME } THE PRESENT!
OUR PLEDGE } ANOTHER MARVEL MASTERPIECE!
WE RECORDED YOUR CALL AND CAME AS SOON AS POSSIBLE, STEVE! IS ANYTHING WRONG?
THERE DOESN'T SEEM TO BE ANY DANGER PRESENT!
WHAT'S WITH YOU, WINGHEAD?
YOU'RE STARTIN' TO YELL AVENGERS ASSEMBLE LIKE A NUTTY BROKEN RECORD!
VER-RY FUNNY, WILLIAM TELL! NOW, IF YOU'LL ZIPPER YOUR FAT LIP LONG ENOUGH, I'LL TELL YOU WHY I SUMMONED YOU--!
INCREDIBLE SCRIPT BY: STAN LEE
INCONCEIVABLE ART BY: DON HECK
INDESCRIBABLE INKING BY: FRANK GIACOIA
INDELIBLE LETTERING BY: ARTIE SIMEK
(YOU DON'T CATCH US BREAKING UP A WINNING COMBO!!)

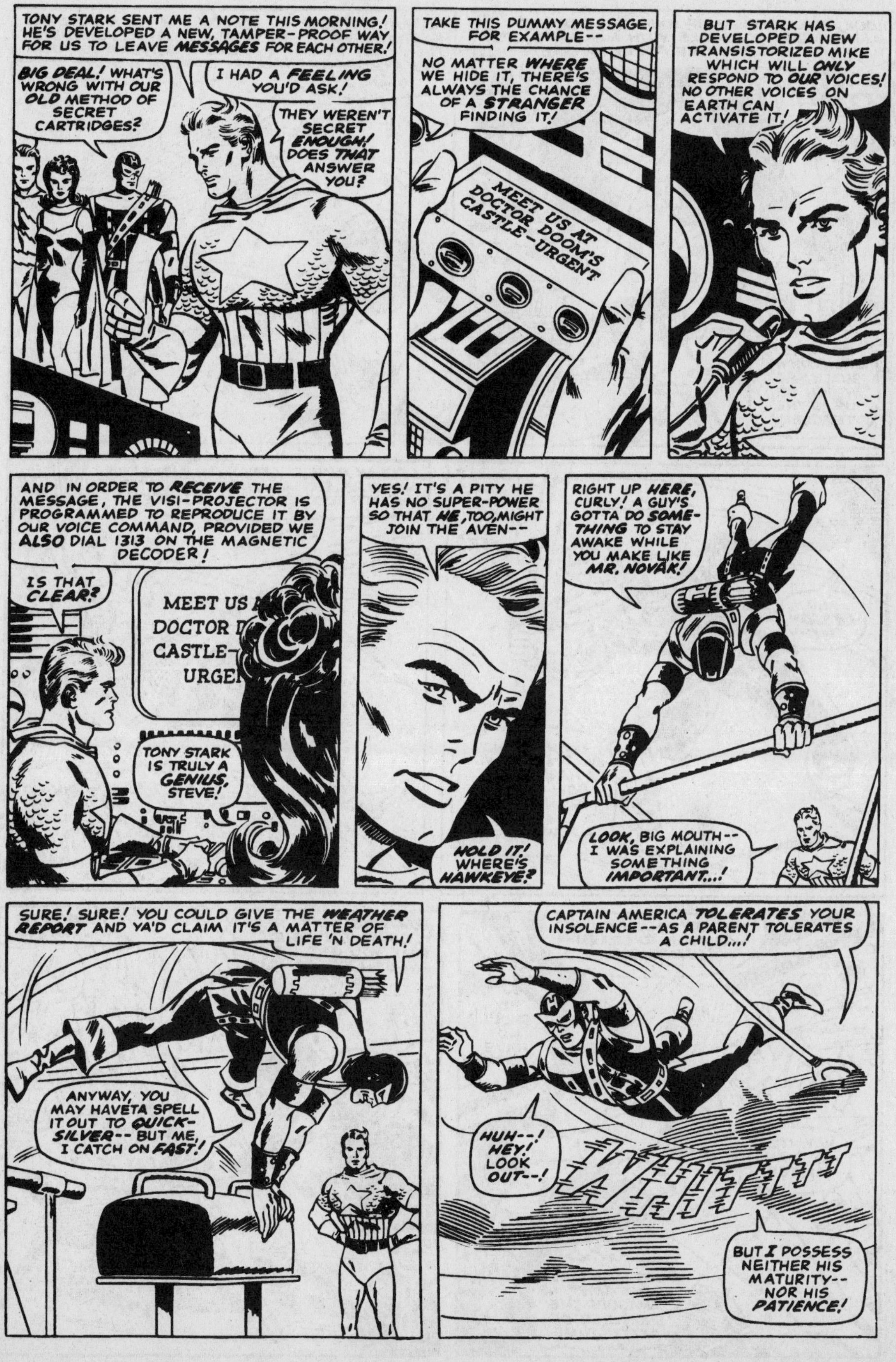
TONY STARK SENT ME A NOTE THIS MORNING! HE'S DEVELOPED A NEW, TAMPER-PROOF WAY FOR US TO LEAVE MESSAGES FOR EACH OTHER!
BIG DEAL! WHAT'S WRONG WITH OUR OLD METHOD OF SECRET CARTRIDGES?
I HAD A FEELING YOU'D ASK!
THEY WEREN'T SECRET ENOUGH! DOES THAT ANSWER YOU?
TAKE THIS DUMMY MESSAGE, FOR EXAMPLE--
NO MATTER WHERE WE HIDE IT, THERE'S ALWAYS THE CHANCE OF A STRANGER FINDING IT!
MEET US AT DOCTOR DOOM'S CASTLE-URGENT
BUT STARK HAS DEVELOPED A NEW TRANSISTORIZED MIKE WHICH WILL ONLY RESPOND TO OUR VOICES! NO OTHER VOICES ON EARTH CAN ACTIVATE IT!
AND IN ORDER TO RECEIVE THE MESSAGE, THE VISI-PROJECTOR IS PROGRAMMED TO REPRODUCE IT BY OUR VOICE COMMAND, PROVIDED WE ALSO DIAL 1313 ON THE MAGNETIC DECODER!
IS THAT CLEAR?
TONY STARK IS TRULY A GENIUS, STEVE!
YES! IT'S A PITY HE HAS NO SUPER-POWER SO THAT ME, TOO, MIGHT JOIN THE AVEN--
HOLD IT! WHERE'S HAWKEYE?
RIGHT UP HERE, CURLY! A GUY'S GOTTA DO SOMETHING TO STAY AWAKE WHILE YOU MAKE LIKE MR. NOVAK!
LOOK, BIG MOUTH-- I WAS EXPLAINING SOMETHING IMPORTANT...!
SURE! SURE! YOU COULD GIVE THE WEATHER REPORT AND YA'D CLAIM IT'S A MATTER OF LIFE 'N DEATH!
ANYWAY, YOU MAY HAVETA SPELL IT OUT TO QUICK-SILVER-- BUT ME, I CATCH ON FAST!
CAPTAIN AMERICA TOLERATES YOUR INSOLENCE--AS A PARENT TOLERATES A CHILD...!
HUH--! HEY! LOOK OUT--!
WHITTT
BUT I POSSESS NEITHER HIS MATURITY-- NOR HIS PATIENCE!

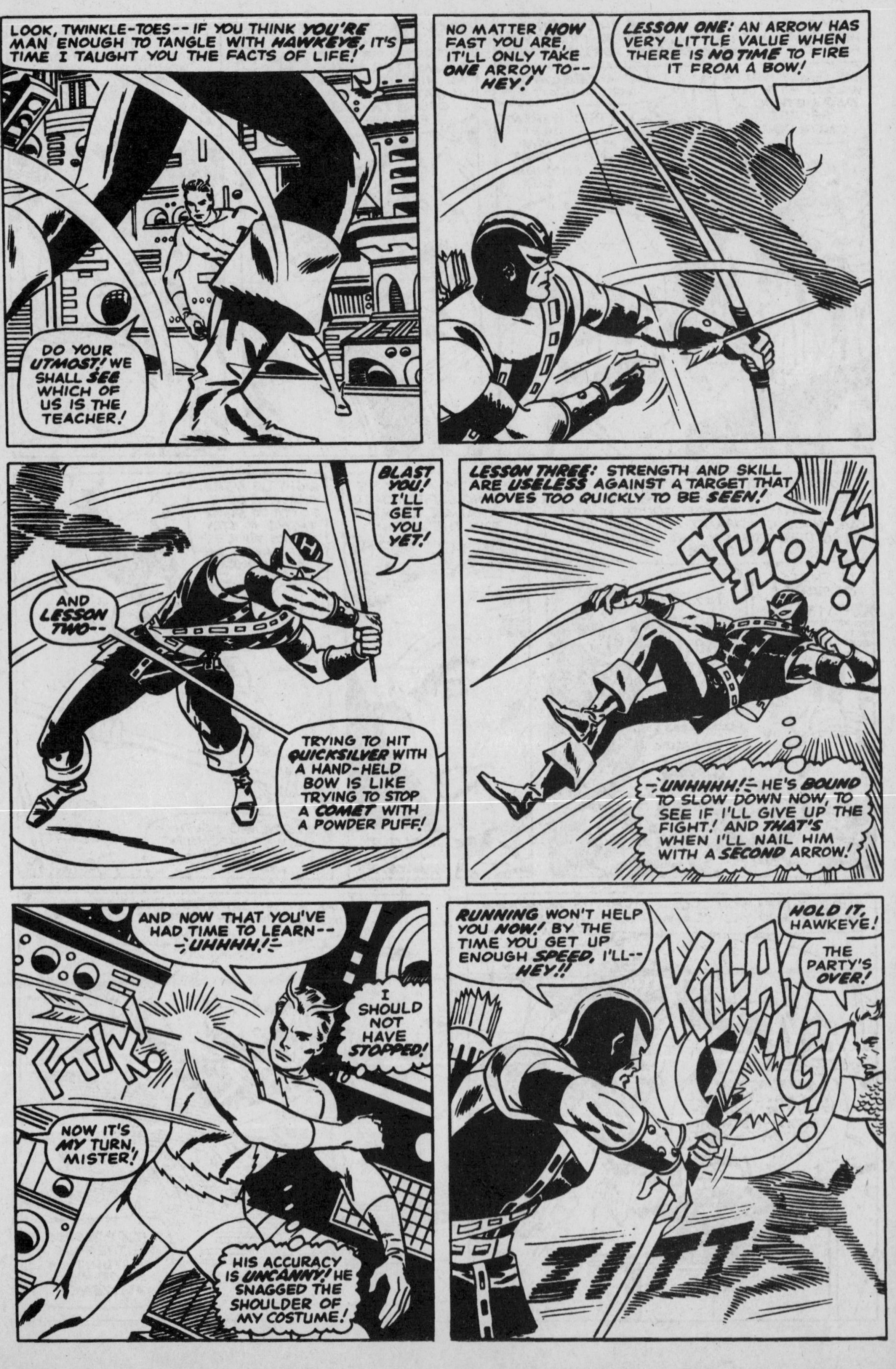

LOOK, TWINKLE-TOES-- IF YOU THINK YOU'RE MAN ENOUGH TO TANGLE WITH HAWKEYE, IT'S TIME I TAUGHT YOU THE FACTS OF LIFE!
DO YOUR UTMOST! WE SHALL SEE WHICH OF US IS THE TEACHER!
NO MATTER HOW FAST YOU ARE, IT'LL ONLY TAKE ONE ARROW TO-- HEY!
LESSON ONE: AN ARROW HAS VERY LITTLE VALUE WHEN THERE IS NO TIME TO FIRE IT FROM A BOW!
AND LESSON TWO--
BLAST YOU! I'LL GET YOU YET!
TRYING TO HIT QUICKSILVER WITH A HAND-HELD BOW IS LIKE TRYING TO STOP A COMET WITH A POWDER PUFF!
LESSON THREE: STRENGTH AND SKILL ARE USELESS AGAINST A TARGET THAT MOVES TOO QUICKLY TO BE SEEN!
THOK!
-UNHHHH!- HE'S BOUND TO SLOW DOWN NOW, TO SEE IF I'LL GIVE UP THE FIGHT! AND THAT'S WHEN I'LL NAIL HIM WITH A SECOND ARROW!
AND NOW THAT YOU'VE HAD TIME TO LEARN-- -UHHHH!-
FTK
I SHOULD NOT HAVE STOPPED!
NOW IT'S MY TURN, MISTER!
HIS ACCURACY IS UNCANNY! HE SNAGGED THE SHOULDER OF MY COSTUME!
RUNNING WON'T HELP YOU NOW! BY THE TIME YOU GET UP ENOUGH SPEED, I'LL-- HEY!!
KLANG!
HOLD IT, HAWKEYE!
THE PARTY'S OVER!
ZIT

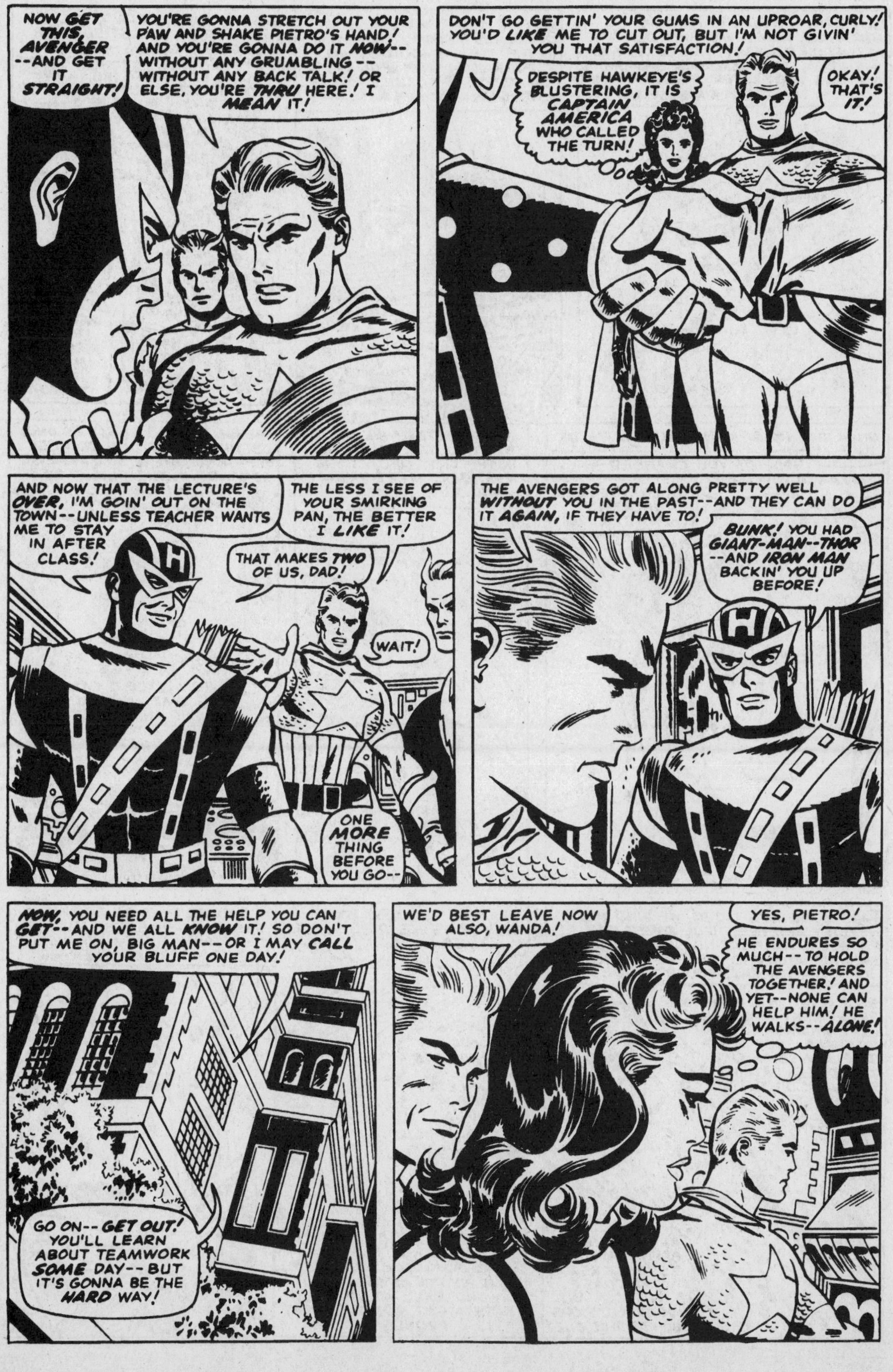
NOW GET THIS, AVENGER --AND GET IT STRAIGHT!
YOU'RE GONNA STRETCH OUT YOUR PAW AND SHAKE PIETRO'S HAND! AND YOU'RE GONNA DO IT NOW-- WITHOUT ANY GRUMBLING-- WITHOUT ANY BACK TALK! OR ELSE, YOU'RE THRU HERE! I MEAN IT!
DON'T GO GETTIN' YOUR GUMS IN AN UPROAR, CURLY! YOU'D LIKE ME TO CUT OUT, BUT I'M NOT GIVIN' YOU THAT SATISFACTION!
DESPITE HAWKEYE'S BLUSTERING, IT IS CAPTAIN AMERICA WHO CALLED THE TURN!
OKAY! THAT'S IT!
AND NOW THAT THE LECTURE'S OVER, I'M GOIN' OUT ON THE TOWN--UNLESS TEACHER WANTS ME TO STAY IN AFTER CLASS!
THE LESS I SEE OF YOUR SMIRKING PAN, THE BETTER I LIKE IT!
THAT MAKES TWO OF US, DAD!
WAIT!
ONE MORE THING BEFORE YOU GO--
THE AVENGERS GOT ALONG PRETTY WELL WITHOUT YOU IN THE PAST--AND THEY CAN DO IT AGAIN, IF THEY HAVE TO!
BUNK! YOU HAD GIANT-MAN--THOR --AND IRON MAN BACKIN' YOU UP BEFORE!
NOW, YOU NEED ALL THE HELP YOU CAN GET--AND WE ALL KNOW IT! SO DON'T PUT ME ON, BIG MAN--OR I MAY CALL YOUR BLUFF ONE DAY!
GO ON--GET OUT! YOU'LL LEARN ABOUT TEAMWORK SOME DAY--BUT IT'S GONNA BE THE HARD WAY!
WE'D BEST LEAVE NOW ALSO, WANDA!
YES, PIETRO!
HE ENDURES SO MUCH--TO HOLD THE AVENGERS TOGETHER! AND YET--NONE CAN HELP HIM! HE WALKS--ALONE!

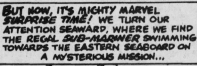
BUT NOW, IT'S MIGHTY MARVEL *SURPRISE TIME!* WE TURN OUR ATTENTION SEAWARD, WHERE WE FIND THE REGAL *SUB-MARINER* SWIMMING TOWARDS THE EASTERN SEABOARD ON A MYSTERIOUS MISSION...

BUT IT IS NOT *NAMOR* WHO CONCERNS US NOW! RATHER, IT IS THE STILL-SMOULDERING EXPLORATION *SHIP* WHICH HE HAS JUST LEFT... *(AS SEEN IN ASTONISH #78--ON SALE NOW!!)*

AND ESPECIALLY THE TWO STARTLINGLY FAMILIAR CHARACTERS WHOM WE SEE ABOARD THE DAMAGED VESSEL...

HENRY! SUB-MARINER IS HEADING FOR NEW YORK! YOU'VE GOT TO CHANGE INTO *GIANT-MAN* AND *STOP* HIM!

I CAN'T, JAN! I MUST REMAIN HERE--AND FINISH THE JOB I'VE STARTED!

BUT THE CITY MUST BE *WARNED!* WHAT'LL WE DO?

OUR RADIO'S *DEAD*--DUE TO THE FIRE! THAT MEANS IT'S UP TO *YOU*--!

ONLY THE *WASP* CAN REACH SHORE IN TIME--!

WHA-?!! YOU CHANGED--- INSTANTANEOUSLY!

'NATCH! I'VE BEEN SECRETLY *PRACTICING* FOR MONTHS!

JAN--*LISTEN!* WE DON'T WANT TO START A *PANIC* IN THE CITY! CONTACT THE *AVENGERS*--LET *THEM* HANDLE IT!

WILL DO, HANDSOME! DON'T WORRY ABOUT A THING! I'M ON MY WAY!

BE *CAREFUL,* HONEY!

THE BIG, LOVABLE LUG! HE'S ONLY LETTING ME *DO* THIS BECAUSE HE KNOWS THERE'S NO *DANGER* INVOLVED IN THE FLIGHT TO SHORE.

ALTHOUGH IT'S TOO FAR TO MAKE IT *NON-STOP,* I CAN BECOME NORMAL-SIZED AND *FLOAT* FOR A WHILE WHEN I GET TIRED!

THUS, SOME TIME LATER, WE FIND THE WEALTHY AND BEAUTIFUL *JANET VAN DYNE,* CALMLY FLOATING SOMEWHERE IN THE VAST ATLANTIC, WRAPPED IN HER OWN SILENT THOUGHTS...

SINCE GOING INTO TEMPORARY RETIREMENT WITH HANK, I LEFT MY WASP COSTUME ON SHORE--BUT FOR A SIMPLE MISSION LIKE THIS ONE, A BATHING SUIT WILL DO JUST AS WELL!

AT THE RATE I'VE BEEN TRAVELING, I SHOULD REACH THE COAST WITHOUT ANY ADDITIONAL STOPS SUCH AS THIS ONE!

IF ONLY WE KNEW *WHY* NAMOR IS HEADING FOR AMERICA AGAIN!

I HOPE THE *AVENGERS* WILL BE ABLE TO *COPE* WITH HIM!

BUT WITHIN *SECONDS,* THE WONDERFUL *WASP* WILL FACE A FAR MORE *URGENT* PROBLEM...

A PROBLEM THAT *BEGINS* WHEN A POWERFUL HAND SUDDENLY PULLS A STRANGELY DANGEROUS *LEVER*--!

NOW--!

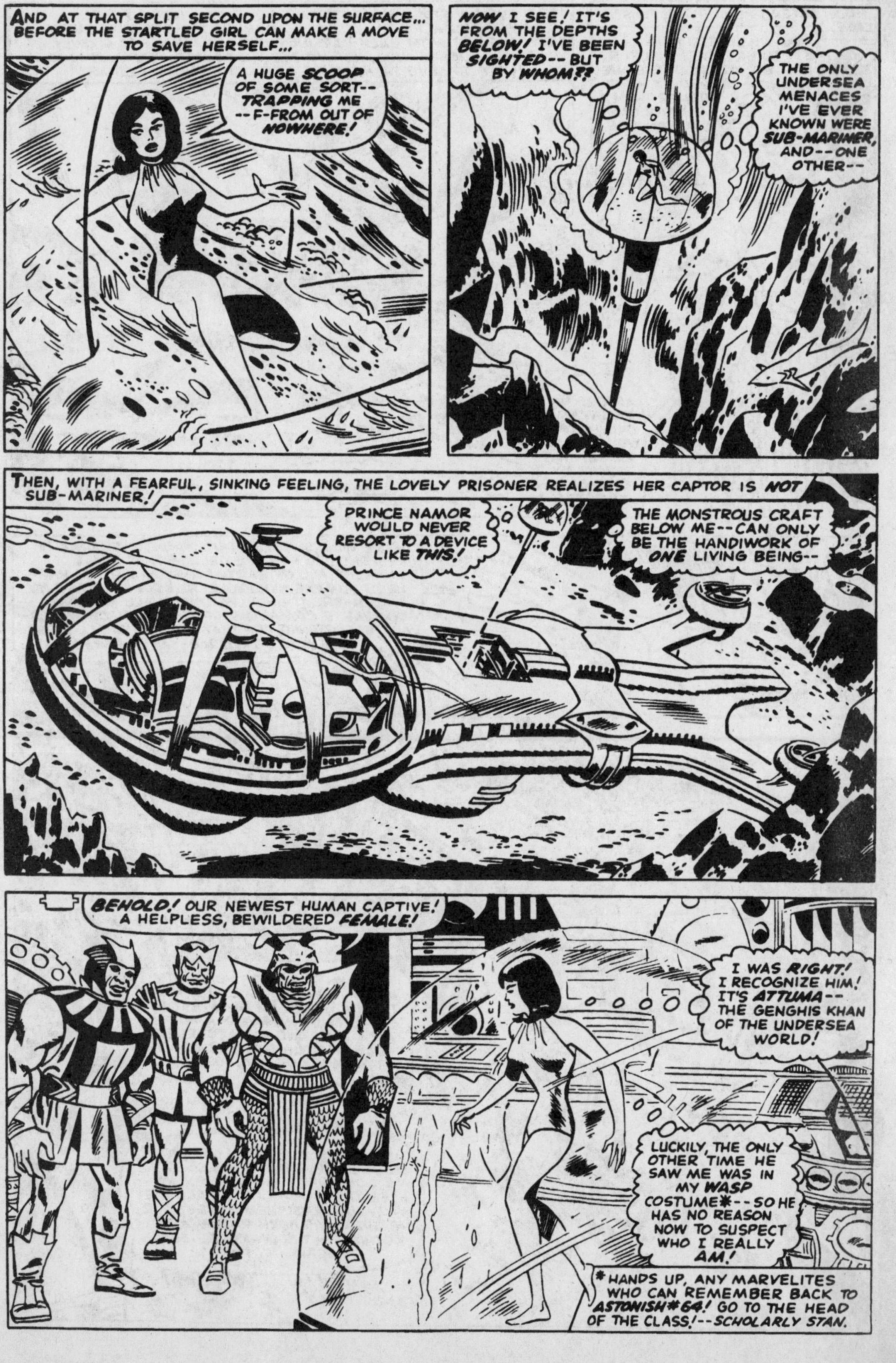
AND AT THAT SPLIT SECOND UPON THE SURFACE... BEFORE THE STARTLED GIRL CAN MAKE A MOVE TO SAVE HERSELF...
A HUGE SCOOP OF SOME SORT--TRAPPING ME --F-FROM OUT OF NOWHERE!
NOW I SEE! IT'S FROM THE DEPTHS BELOW! I'VE BEEN SIGHTED--BUT BY WHOM??
THE ONLY UNDERSEA MENACES I'VE EVER KNOWN WERE SUB-MARINER, AND--ONE OTHER--
THEN, WITH A FEARFUL, SINKING FEELING, THE LOVELY PRISONER REALIZES HER CAPTOR IS NOT SUB-MARINER!
PRINCE NAMOR WOULD NEVER RESORT TO A DEVICE LIKE THIS!
THE MONSTROUS CRAFT BELOW ME--CAN ONLY BE THE HANDIWORK OF ONE LIVING BEING--
BEHOLD! OUR NEWEST HUMAN CAPTIVE! A HELPLESS, BEWILDERED FEMALE!
I WAS RIGHT! I RECOGNIZE HIM! IT'S ATTUMA--THE GENGHIS KHAN OF THE UNDERSEA WORLD!
LUCKILY, THE ONLY OTHER TIME HE SAW ME WAS IN MY WASP COSTUME*--SO HE HAS NO REASON NOW TO SUSPECT WHO I REALLY AM!
*HANDS UP, ANY MARVELITES WHO CAN REMEMBER BACK TO ASTONISH #64! GO TO THE HEAD OF THE CLASS!--SCHOLARLY STAN.

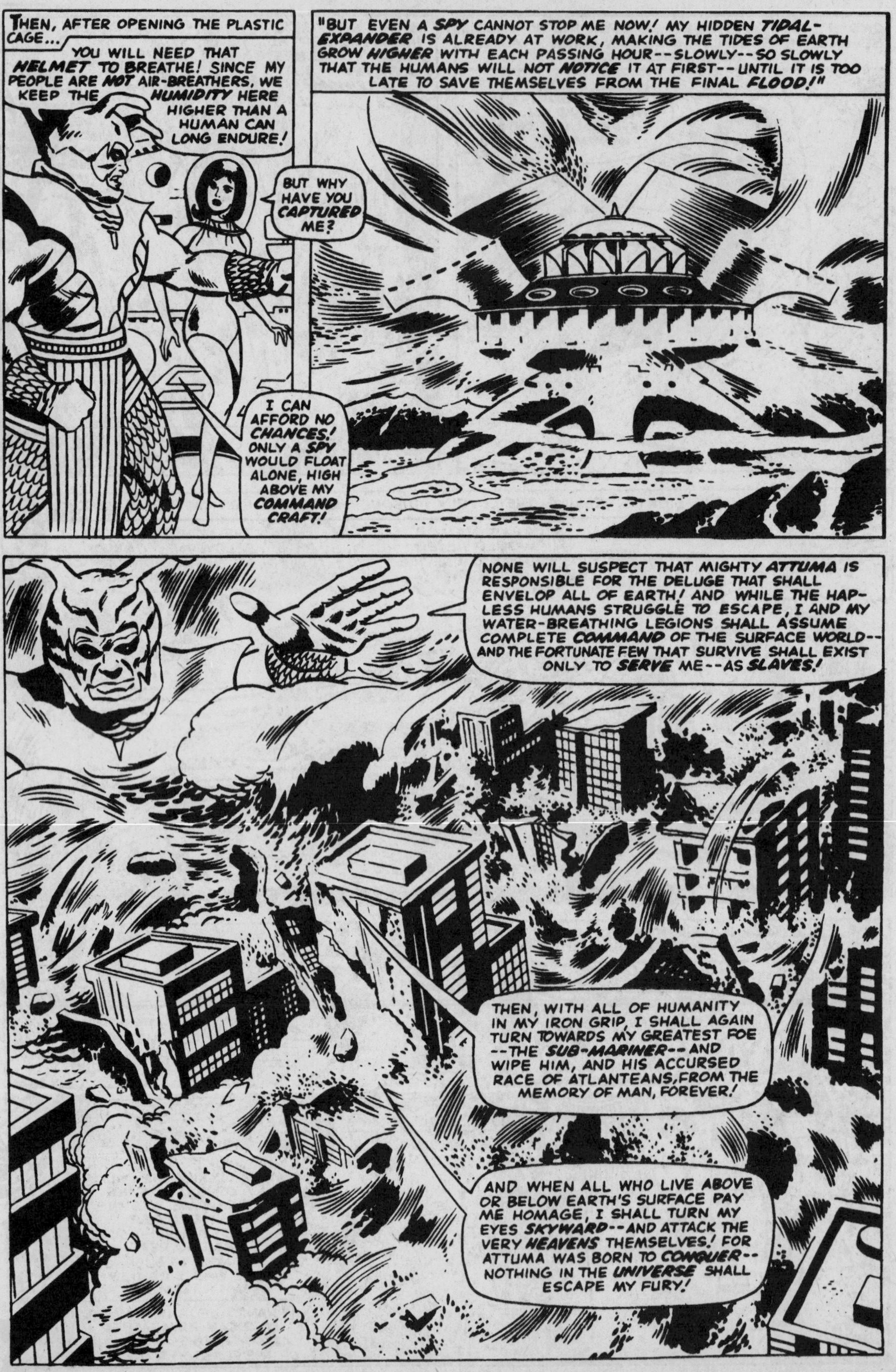
THEN, AFTER OPENING THE PLASTIC CAGE...
YOU WILL NEED THAT HELMET TO BREATHE! SINCE MY PEOPLE ARE NOT AIR-BREATHERS, WE KEEP THE HUMIDITY HERE HIGHER THAN A HUMAN CAN LONG ENDURE!
BUT WHY HAVE YOU CAPTURED ME?
I CAN AFFORD NO CHANCES! ONLY A SPY WOULD FLOAT ALONE, HIGH ABOVE MY COMMAND CRAFT!
"BUT EVEN A SPY CANNOT STOP ME NOW! MY HIDDEN TIDAL-EXPANDER IS ALREADY AT WORK, MAKING THE TIDES OF EARTH GROW HIGHER WITH EACH PASSING HOUR--SLOWLY--SO SLOWLY THAT THE HUMANS WILL NOT NOTICE IT AT FIRST--UNTIL IT IS TOO LATE TO SAVE THEMSELVES FROM THE FINAL FLOOD!"
NONE WILL SUSPECT THAT MIGHTY ATTUMA IS RESPONSIBLE FOR THE DELUGE THAT SHALL ENVELOP ALL OF EARTH! AND WHILE THE HAPLESS HUMANS STRUGGLE TO ESCAPE, I AND MY WATER-BREATHING LEGIONS SHALL ASSUME COMPLETE COMMAND OF THE SURFACE WORLD--AND THE FORTUNATE FEW THAT SURVIVE SHALL EXIST ONLY TO SERVE ME--AS SLAVES!
THEN, WITH ALL OF HUMANITY IN MY IRON GRIP, I SHALL AGAIN TURN TOWARDS MY GREATEST FOE --THE SUB-MARINER-- AND WIPE HIM, AND HIS ACCURSED RACE OF ATLANTEANS, FROM THE MEMORY OF MAN, FOREVER!
AND WHEN ALL WHO LIVE ABOVE OR BELOW EARTH'S SURFACE PAY ME HOMAGE, I SHALL TURN MY EYES SKYWARD--AND ATTACK THE VERY HEAVENS THEMSELVES! FOR ATTUMA WAS BORN TO CONQUER--NOTHING IN THE UNIVERSE SHALL ESCAPE MY FURY!

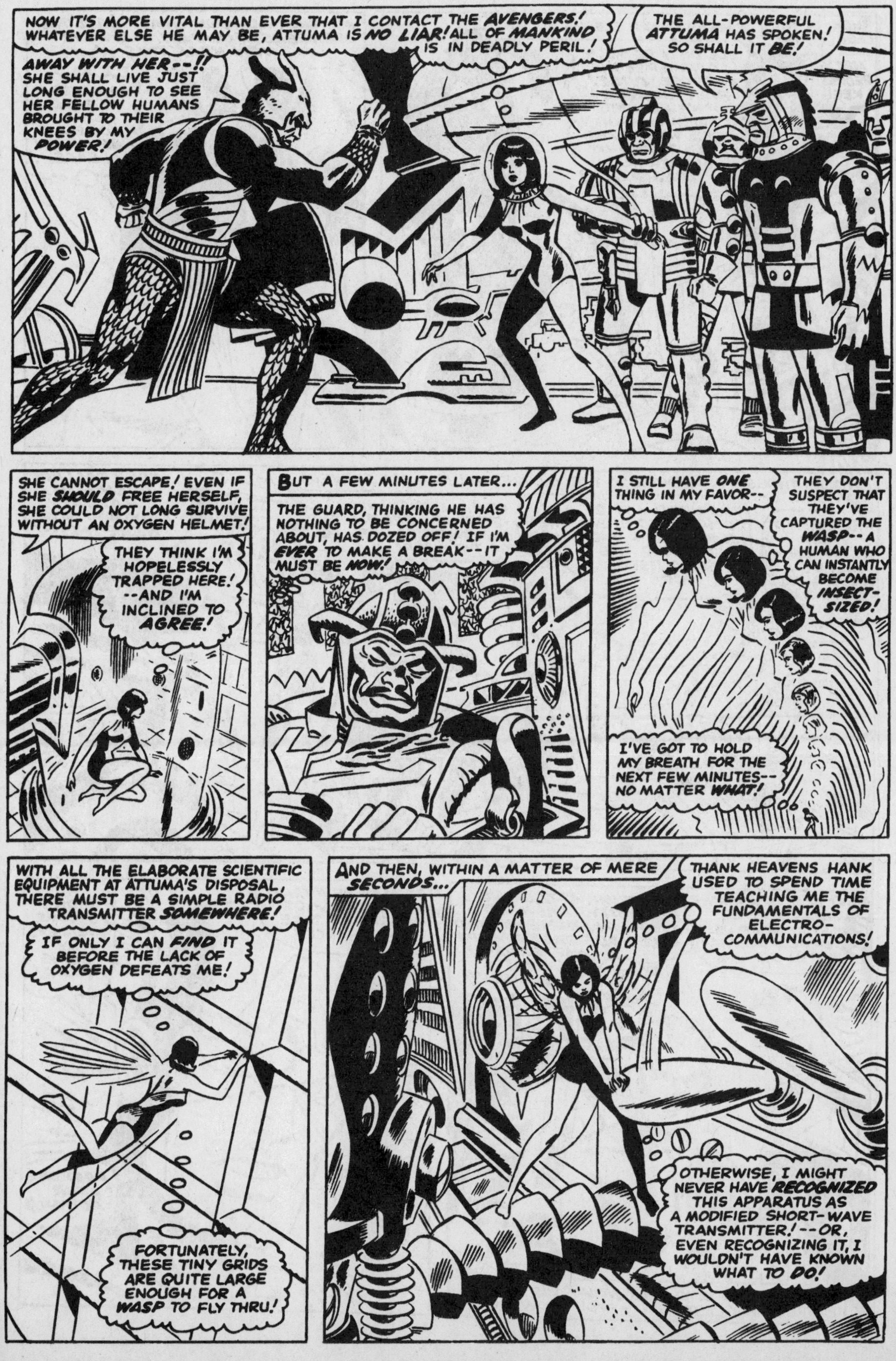

NOW IT'S MORE VITAL THAN EVER THAT I CONTACT THE AVENGERS! WHATEVER ELSE HE MAY BE, ATTUMA IS NO LIAR! ALL OF MANKIND IS IN DEADLY PERIL!
THE ALL-POWERFUL ATTUMA HAS SPOKEN! SO SHALL IT BE!
AWAY WITH HER--!! SHE SHALL LIVE JUST LONG ENOUGH TO SEE HER FELLOW HUMANS BROUGHT TO THEIR KNEES BY MY POWER!
SHE CANNOT ESCAPE! EVEN IF SHE SHOULD FREE HERSELF, SHE COULD NOT LONG SURVIVE WITHOUT AN OXYGEN HELMET!
THEY THINK I'M HOPELESSLY TRAPPED HERE! --AND I'M INCLINED TO AGREE!
BUT A FEW MINUTES LATER...
THE GUARD, THINKING HE HAS NOTHING TO BE CONCERNED ABOUT, HAS DOZED OFF! IF I'M EVER TO MAKE A BREAK--IT MUST BE NOW!
I STILL HAVE ONE THING IN MY FAVOR--
THEY DON'T SUSPECT THAT THEY'VE CAPTURED THE WASP--A HUMAN WHO CAN INSTANTLY BECOME INSECT-SIZED!
I'VE GOT TO HOLD MY BREATH FOR THE NEXT FEW MINUTES--NO MATTER WHAT!
WITH ALL THE ELABORATE SCIENTIFIC EQUIPMENT AT ATTUMA'S DISPOSAL, THERE MUST BE A SIMPLE RADIO TRANSMITTER SOMEWHERE!
IF ONLY I CAN FIND IT BEFORE THE LACK OF OXYGEN DEFEATS ME!
FORTUNATELY, THESE TINY GRIDS ARE QUITE LARGE ENOUGH FOR A WASP TO FLY THRU!
AND THEN, WITHIN A MATTER OF MERE SECONDS...
THANK HEAVENS HANK USED TO SPEND TIME TEACHING ME THE FUNDAMENTALS OF ELECTRO-COMMUNICATIONS!
OTHERWISE, I MIGHT NEVER HAVE RECOGNIZED THIS APPARATUS AS A MODIFIED SHORT-WAVE TRANSMITTER! --OR, EVEN RECOGNIZING IT, I WOULDN'T HAVE KNOWN WHAT TO DO!

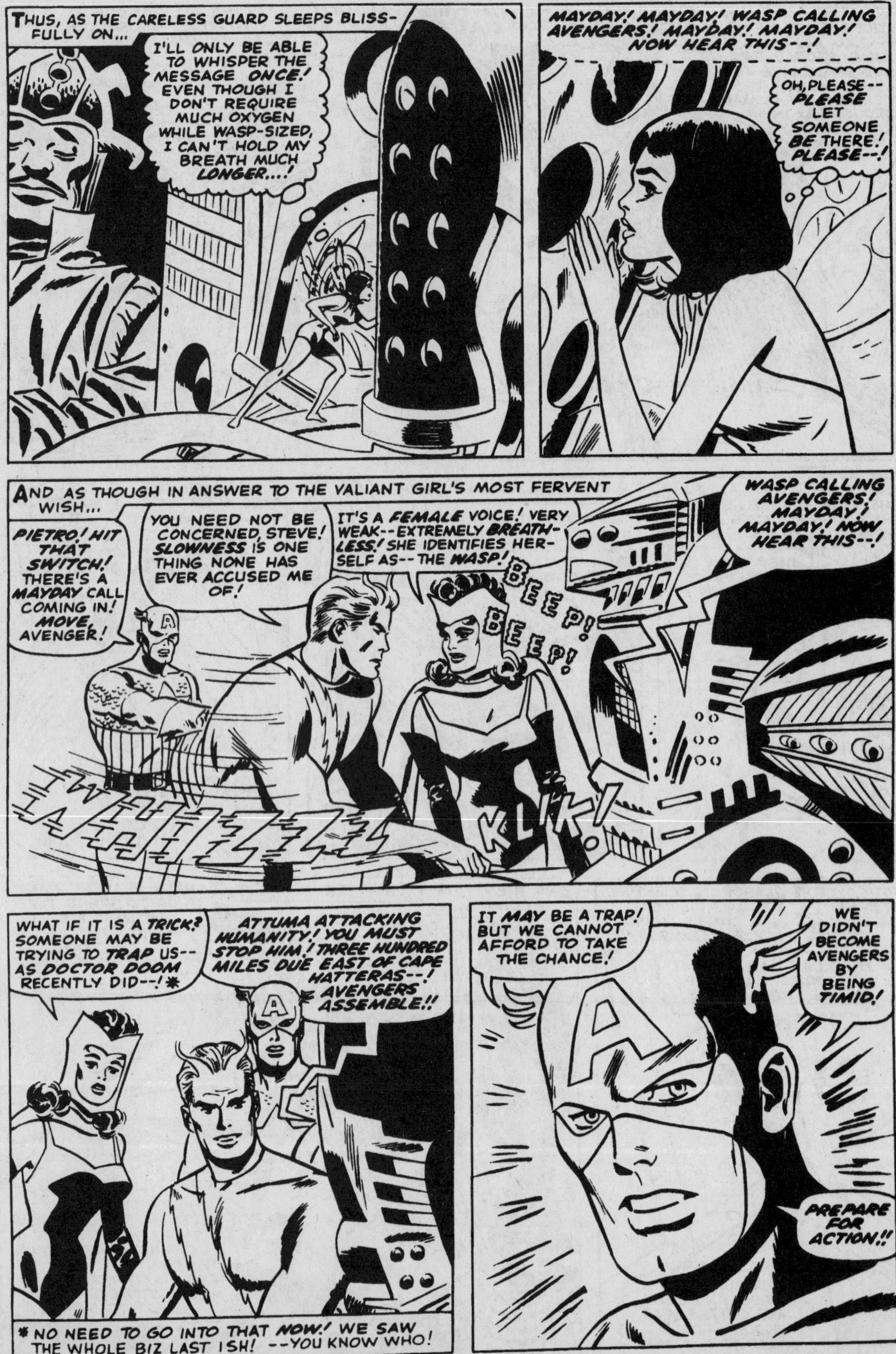
THUS, AS THE CARELESS GUARD SLEEPS BLISS-FULLY ON...
I'LL ONLY BE ABLE TO WHISPER THE MESSAGE ONCE! EVEN THOUGH I DON'T REQUIRE MUCH OXYGEN WHILE WASP-SIZED, I CAN'T HOLD MY BREATH MUCH LONGER....!
MAYDAY! MAYDAY! WASP CALLING AVENGERS! MAYDAY! MAYDAY! NOW HEAR THIS--!
OH, PLEASE-- PLEASE LET SOMEONE BE THERE! PLEASE--!
AND AS THOUGH IN ANSWER TO THE VALIANT GIRL'S MOST FERVENT WISH...
PIETRO! HIT THAT SWITCH! THERE'S A MAYDAY CALL COMING IN! MOVE, AVENGER!
YOU NEED NOT BE CONCERNED, STEVE! SLOWNESS IS ONE THING NONE HAS EVER ACCUSED ME OF!
IT'S A FEMALE VOICE! VERY WEAK--EXTREMELY BREATH-LESS! SHE IDENTIFIES HER-SELF AS-- THE WASP!
WASP CALLING AVENGERS! MAYDAY! MAYDAY! NOW HEAR THIS--!
BEEP! BEEP!
TWHIZZZ
KLIK!
WHAT IF IT IS A TRICK? SOMEONE MAY BE TRYING TO TRAP US-- AS DOCTOR DOOM RECENTLY DID--! *
ATTUMA ATTACKING HUMANITY! YOU MUST STOP HIM! THREE HUNDRED MILES DUE EAST OF CAPE HATTERAS--! AVENGERS ASSEMBLE!!
* NO NEED TO GO INTO THAT NOW! WE SAW THE WHOLE BIZ LAST ISH! --YOU KNOW WHO!
IT MAY BE A TRAP! BUT WE CANNOT AFFORD TO TAKE THE CHANCE!
WE DIDN'T BECOME AVENGERS BY BEING TIMID!
PREPARE FOR ACTION!!

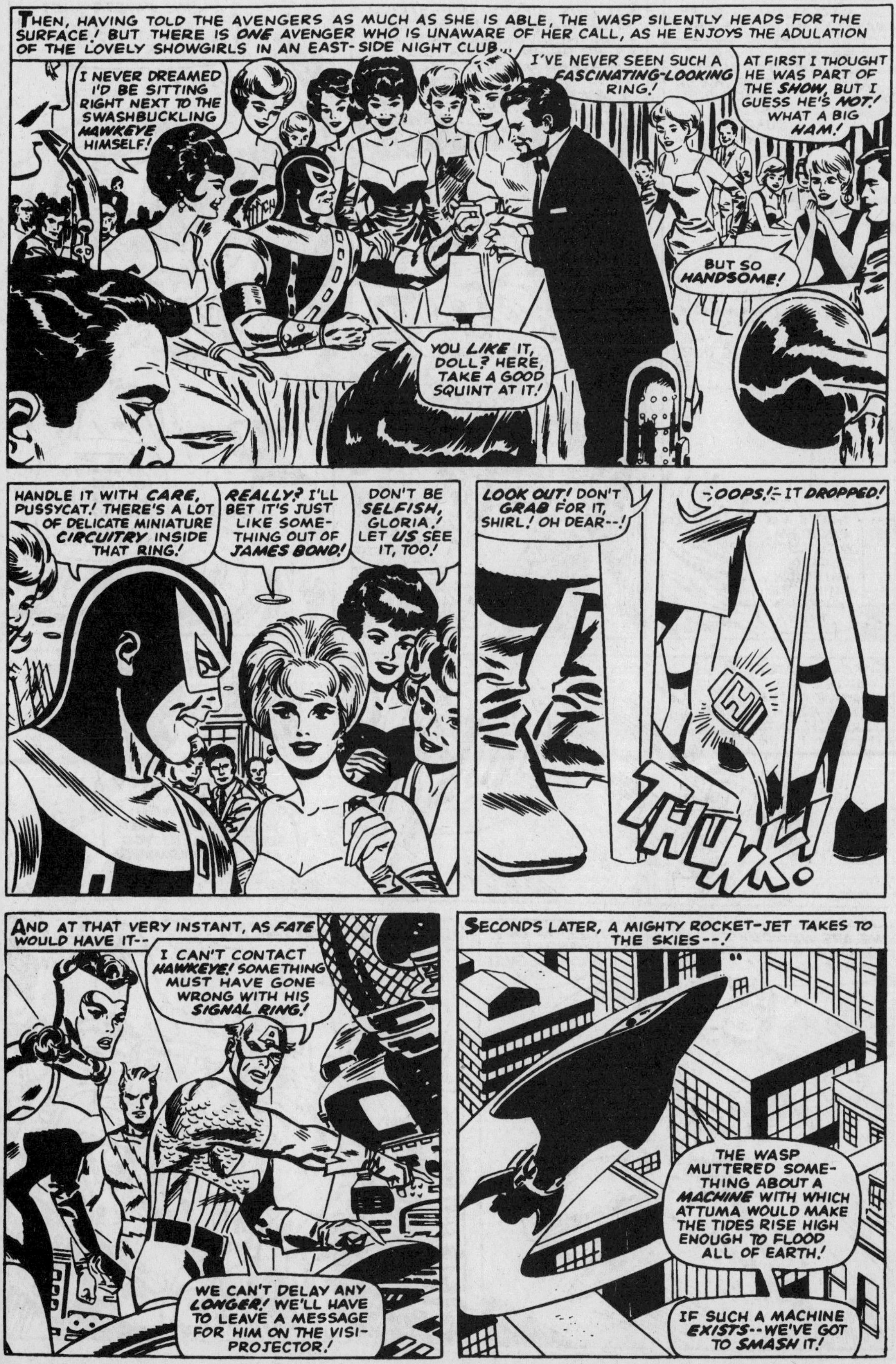
THEN, HAVING TOLD THE AVENGERS AS MUCH AS SHE IS ABLE, THE WASP SILENTLY HEADS FOR THE SURFACE! BUT THERE IS ONE AVENGER WHO IS UNAWARE OF HER CALL, AS HE ENJOYS THE ADULATION OF THE LOVELY SHOWGIRLS IN AN EAST-SIDE NIGHT CLUB...
I NEVER DREAMED I'D BE SITTING RIGHT NEXT TO THE SWASHBUCKLING HAWKEYE HIMSELF!
I'VE NEVER SEEN SUCH A FASCINATING-LOOKING RING!
AT FIRST I THOUGHT HE WAS PART OF THE SHOW, BUT I GUESS HE'S NOT! WHAT A BIG HAM!
BUT SO HANDSOME!
YOU LIKE IT, DOLL? HERE, TAKE A GOOD SQUINT AT IT!
HANDLE IT WITH CARE, PUSSYCAT! THERE'S A LOT OF DELICATE MINIATURE CIRCUITRY INSIDE THAT RING!
REALLY? I'LL BET IT'S JUST LIKE SOMETHING OUT OF JAMES BOND!
DON'T BE SELFISH, GLORIA! LET US SEE IT, TOO!
LOOK OUT! DON'T GRAB FOR IT, SHIRL! OH DEAR--!
OOPS! IT DROPPED!
THUNK!
AND AT THAT VERY INSTANT, AS FATE WOULD HAVE IT--
I CAN'T CONTACT HAWKEYE! SOMETHING MUST HAVE GONE WRONG WITH HIS SIGNAL RING!
WE CAN'T DELAY ANY LONGER! WE'LL HAVE TO LEAVE A MESSAGE FOR HIM ON THE VISI-PROJECTOR!
SECONDS LATER, A MIGHTY ROCKET-JET TAKES TO THE SKIES--!
THE WASP MUTTERED SOMETHING ABOUT A MACHINE WITH WHICH ATTUMA WOULD MAKE THE TIDES RISE HIGH ENOUGH TO FLOOD ALL OF EARTH!
IF SUCH A MACHINE EXISTS--WE'VE GOT TO SMASH IT!

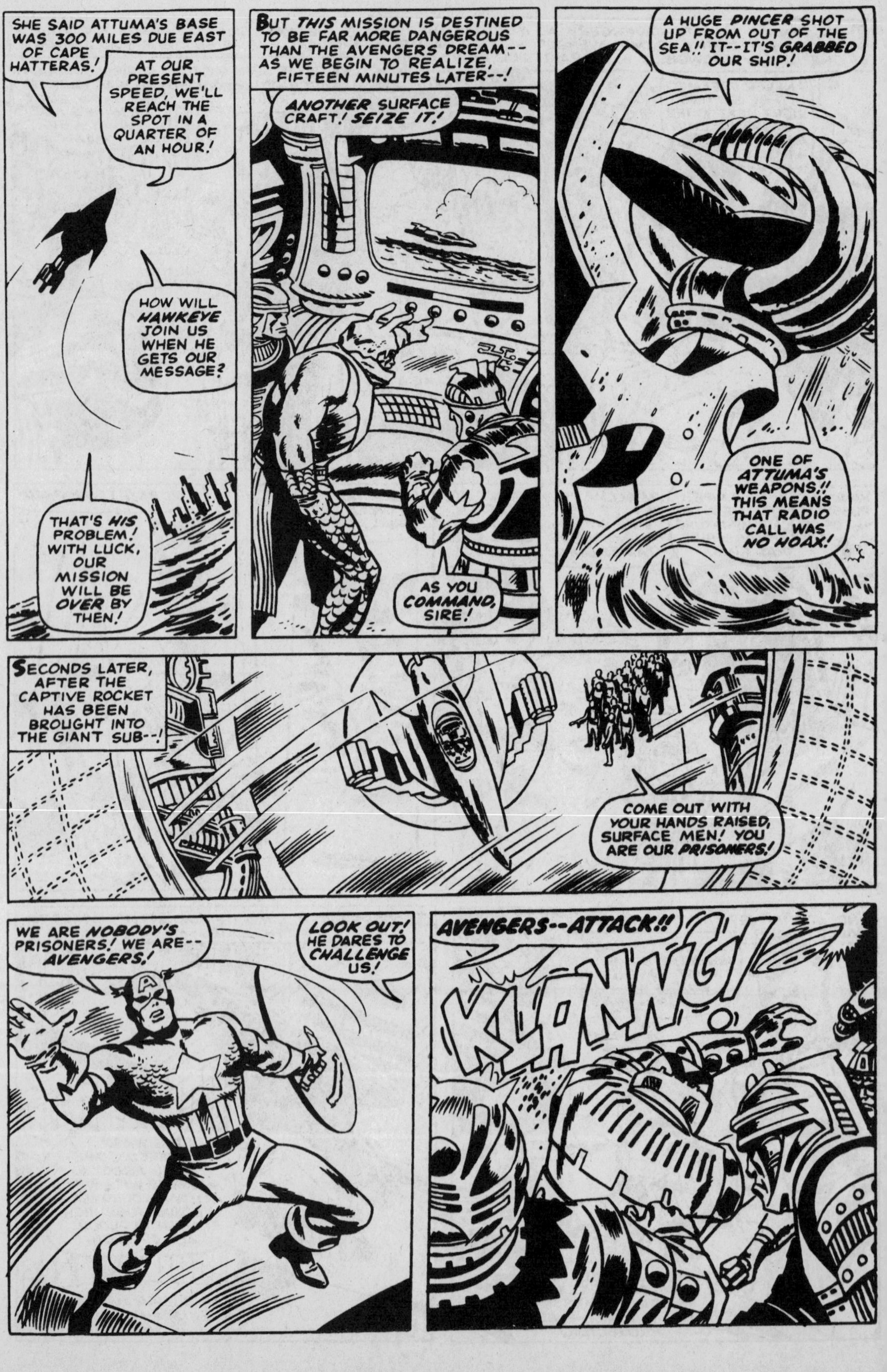
SHE SAID ATTUMA'S BASE WAS 300 MILES DUE EAST OF CAPE HATTERAS!
AT OUR PRESENT SPEED, WE'LL REACH THE SPOT IN A QUARTER OF AN HOUR!
HOW WILL HAWKEYE JOIN US WHEN HE GETS OUR MESSAGE?
THAT'S HIS PROBLEM! WITH LUCK, OUR MISSION WILL BE OVER BY THEN!
BUT THIS MISSION IS DESTINED TO BE FAR MORE DANGEROUS THAN THE AVENGERS DREAM-- AS WE BEGIN TO REALIZE, FIFTEEN MINUTES LATER--!
ANOTHER SURFACE CRAFT! SEIZE IT!
AS YOU COMMAND, SIRE!
A HUGE PINCER SHOT UP FROM OUT OF THE SEA!! IT--IT'S GRABBED OUR SHIP!
ONE OF ATTUMA'S WEAPONS!! THIS MEANS THAT RADIO CALL WAS NO HOAX!
SECONDS LATER, AFTER THE CAPTIVE ROCKET HAS BEEN BROUGHT INTO THE GIANT SUB--!
COME OUT WITH YOUR HANDS RAISED, SURFACE MEN! YOU ARE OUR PRISONERS!
WE ARE NOBODY'S PRISONERS! WE ARE-- AVENGERS!
LOOK OUT! HE DARES TO CHALLENGE US!
AVENGERS--ATTACK!!
KLANNG!

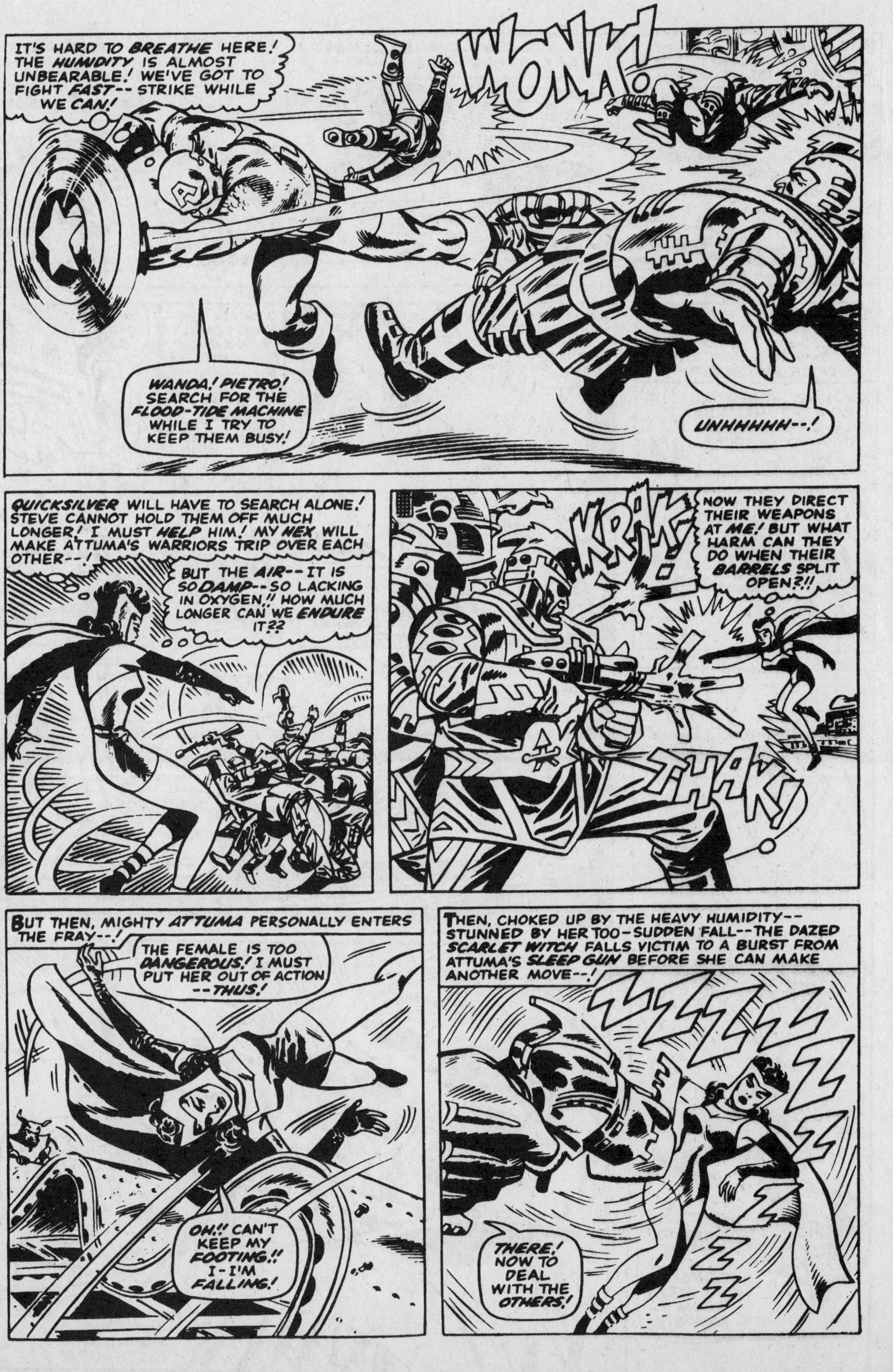

IT'S HARD TO BREATHE HERE! THE HUMIDITY IS ALMOST UNBEARABLE! WE'VE GOT TO FIGHT FAST-- STRIKE WHILE WE CAN!
WONK!
WANDA! PIETRO! SEARCH FOR THE FLOOD-TIDE MACHINE WHILE I TRY TO KEEP THEM BUSY!
UNHHHHH--!
QUICKSILVER WILL HAVE TO SEARCH ALONE! STEVE CANNOT HOLD THEM OFF MUCH LONGER! I MUST HELP HIM! MY HEX WILL MAKE ATTUMA'S WARRIORS TRIP OVER EACH OTHER--!
BUT THE AIR-- IT IS SO DAMP-- SO LACKING IN OXYGEN!! HOW MUCH LONGER CAN WE ENDURE IT??
KRAK!
NOW THEY DIRECT THEIR WEAPONS AT ME! BUT WHAT HARM CAN THEY DO WHEN THEIR BARRELS SPLIT OPEN?!!
THAK!
BUT THEN, MIGHTY ATTUMA PERSONALLY ENTERS THE FRAY--!
THE FEMALE IS TOO DANGEROUS! I MUST PUT HER OUT OF ACTION --THUS!
OH!! CAN'T KEEP MY FOOTING!! I-I'M FALLING!
THEN, CHOKED UP BY THE HEAVY HUMIDITY-- STUNNED BY HER TOO-SUDDEN FALL--THE DAZED SCARLET WITCH FALLS VICTIM TO A BURST FROM ATTUMA'S SLEEP GUN BEFORE SHE CAN MAKE ANOTHER MOVE--!
THERE! NOW TO DEAL WITH THE OTHERS!

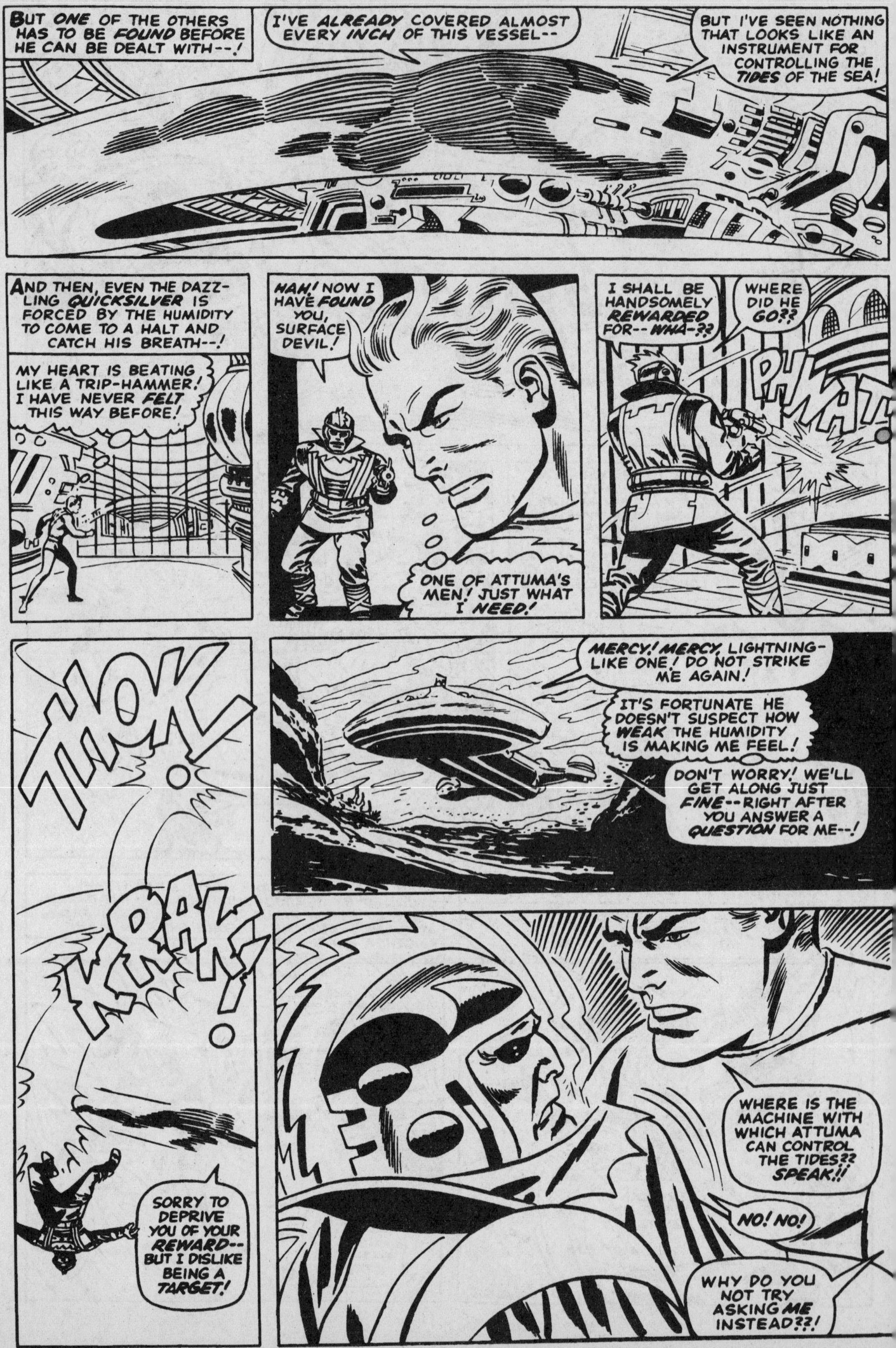
BUT ONE OF THE OTHERS HAS TO BE FOUND BEFORE HE CAN BE DEALT WITH--!
I'VE ALREADY COVERED ALMOST EVERY INCH OF THIS VESSEL--
BUT I'VE SEEN NOTHING THAT LOOKS LIKE AN INSTRUMENT FOR CONTROLLING THE TIDES OF THE SEA!
AND THEN, EVEN THE DAZZLING QUICKSILVER IS FORCED BY THE HUMIDITY TO COME TO A HALT AND CATCH HIS BREATH--!
MY HEART IS BEATING LIKE A TRIP-HAMMER! I HAVE NEVER FELT THIS WAY BEFORE!
HAH! NOW I HAVE FOUND YOU, SURFACE DEVIL!
ONE OF ATTUMA'S MEN! JUST WHAT I NEED!
I SHALL BE HANDSOMELY REWARDED FOR-- WHA-??
WHERE DID HE GO??
PHWAT
THOK
KRAK!
SORRY TO DEPRIVE YOU OF YOUR REWARD-- BUT I DISLIKE BEING A TARGET!
MERCY! MERCY, LIGHTNING-LIKE ONE! DO NOT STRIKE ME AGAIN!
IT'S FORTUNATE HE DOESN'T SUSPECT HOW WEAK THE HUMIDITY IS MAKING ME FEEL!
DON'T WORRY! WE'LL GET ALONG JUST FINE--RIGHT AFTER YOU ANSWER A QUESTION FOR ME--!
WHERE IS THE MACHINE WITH WHICH ATTUMA CAN CONTROL THE TIDES?? SPEAK!!
NO! NO!
WHY DO YOU NOT TRY ASKING ME INSTEAD??!

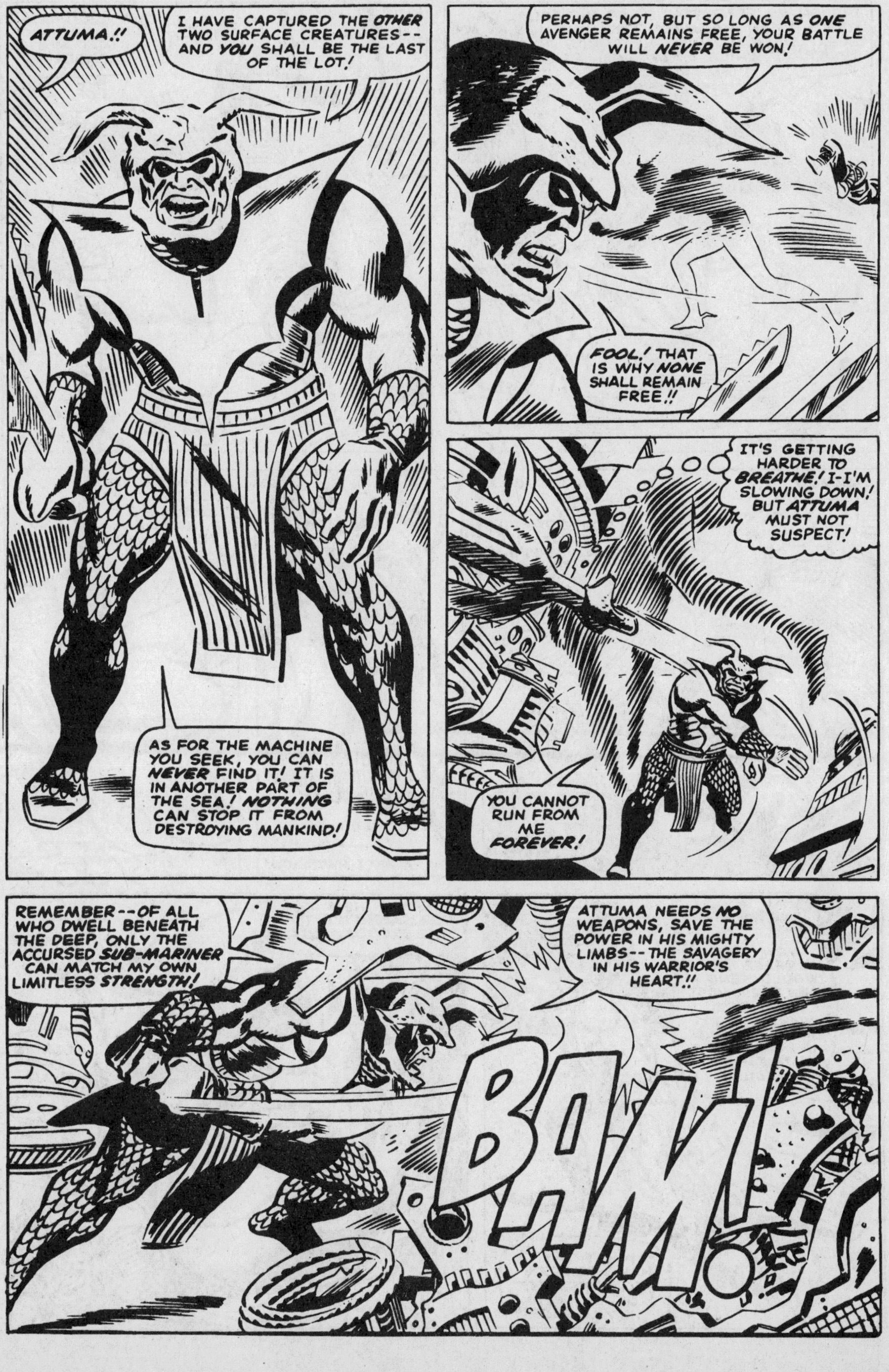
ATTUMA.!!
I HAVE CAPTURED THE OTHER TWO SURFACE CREATURES-- AND YOU SHALL BE THE LAST OF THE LOT!
AS FOR THE MACHINE YOU SEEK, YOU CAN NEVER FIND IT! IT IS IN ANOTHER PART OF THE SEA! NOTHING CAN STOP IT FROM DESTROYING MANKIND!
PERHAPS NOT, BUT SO LONG AS ONE AVENGER REMAINS FREE, YOUR BATTLE WILL NEVER BE WON!
FOOL! THAT IS WHY NONE SHALL REMAIN FREE.!!
IT'S GETTING HARDER TO BREATHE! I-I'M SLOWING DOWN! BUT ATTUMA MUST NOT SUSPECT!
YOU CANNOT RUN FROM ME FOREVER!
REMEMBER--OF ALL WHO DWELL BENEATH THE DEEP, ONLY THE ACCURSED SUB-MARINER CAN MATCH MY OWN LIMITLESS STRENGTH!
ATTUMA NEEDS NO WEAPONS, SAVE THE POWER IN HIS MIGHTY LIMBS--THE SAVAGERY IN HIS WARRIOR'S HEART.!!
BAM!

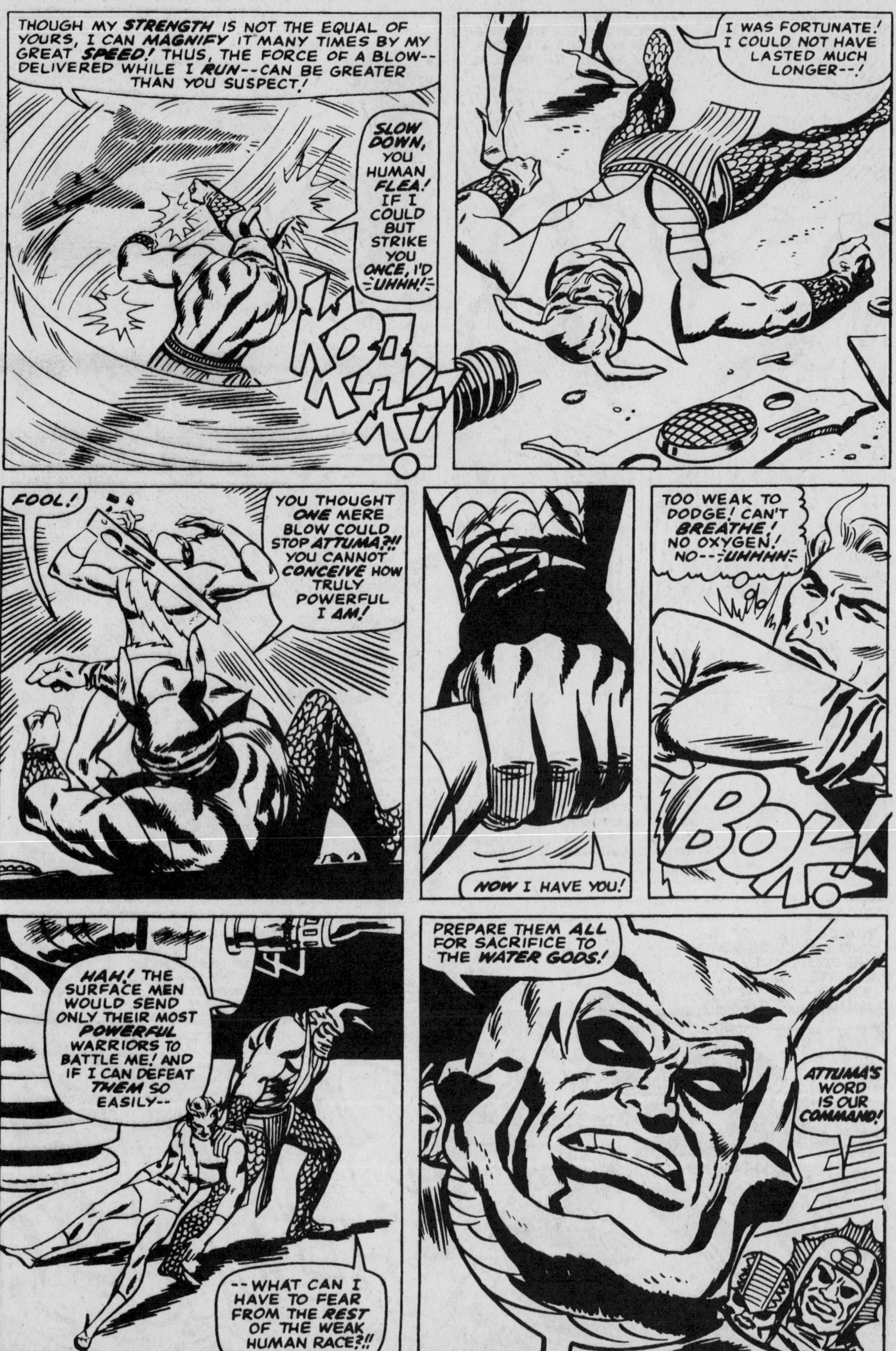
THOUGH MY STRENGTH IS NOT THE EQUAL OF YOURS, I CAN MAGNIFY IT MANY TIMES BY MY GREAT SPEED! THUS, THE FORCE OF A BLOW-- DELIVERED WHILE I RUN--CAN BE GREATER THAN YOU SUSPECT!
SLOW DOWN, YOU HUMAN FLEA! IF I COULD BUT STRIKE YOU ONCE, I'D UHHH!
KRAKK!
I WAS FORTUNATE! I COULD NOT HAVE LASTED MUCH LONGER--!
FOOL!
YOU THOUGHT ONE MERE BLOW COULD STOP ATTUMA?!! YOU CANNOT CONCEIVE HOW TRULY POWERFUL I AM!
NOW I HAVE YOU!
TOO WEAK TO DODGE! CAN'T BREATHE! NO OXYGEN! NO--UHHHH!
BOK!
HAH! THE SURFACE MEN WOULD SEND ONLY THEIR MOST POWERFUL WARRIORS TO BATTLE ME! AND IF I CAN DEFEAT THEM SO EASILY--
--WHAT CAN I HAVE TO FEAR FROM THE REST OF THE WEAK HUMAN RACE?!!
PREPARE THEM ALL FOR SACRIFICE TO THE WATER GODS!
ATTUMA'S WORD IS OUR COMMAND!

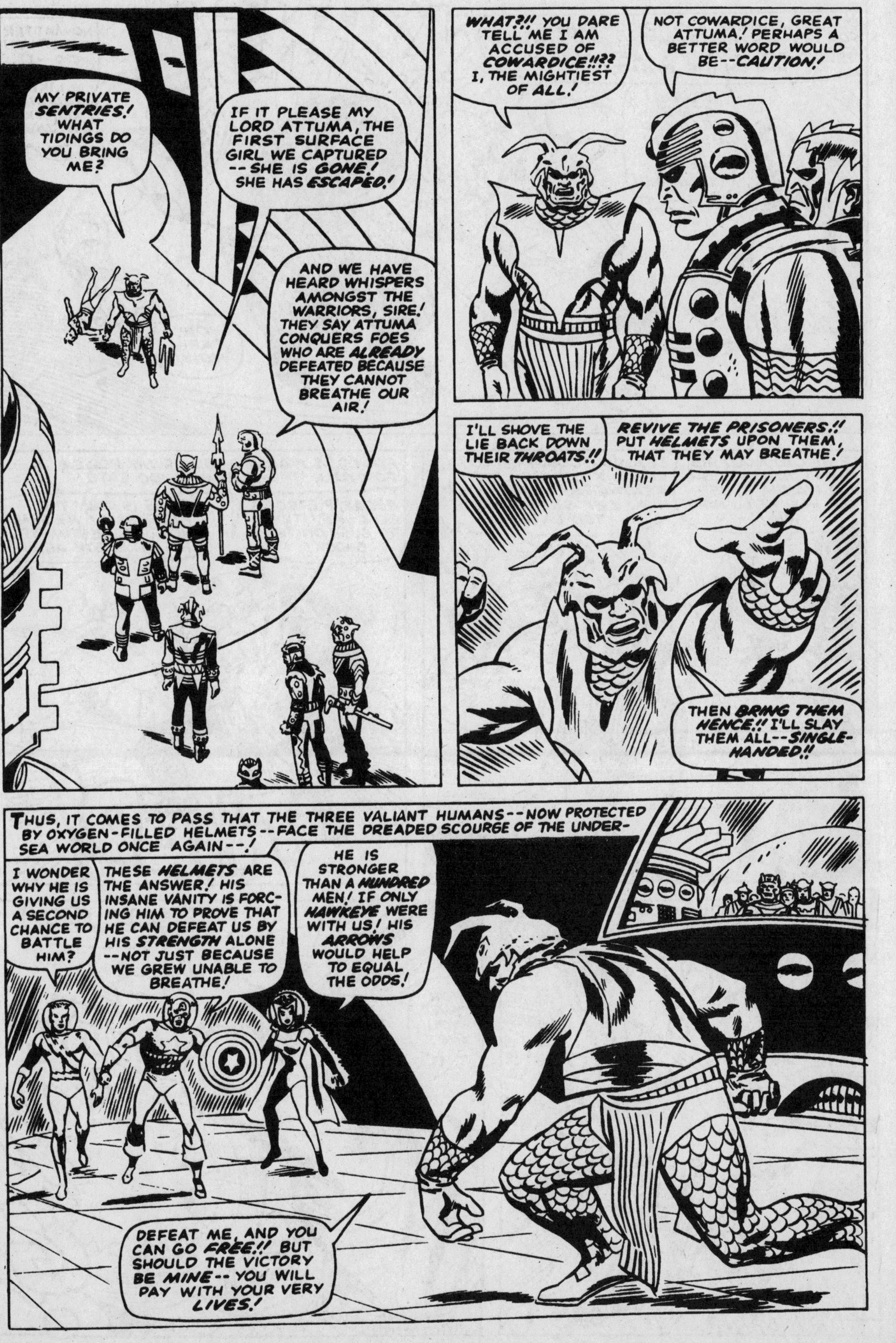
MY PRIVATE SENTRIES! WHAT TIDINGS DO YOU BRING ME?
IF IT PLEASE MY LORD ATTUMA, THE FIRST SURFACE GIRL WE CAPTURED -- SHE IS GONE! SHE HAS ESCAPED!
AND WE HAVE HEARD WHISPERS AMONGST THE WARRIORS, SIRE! THEY SAY ATTUMA CONQUERS FOES WHO ARE ALREADY DEFEATED BECAUSE THEY CANNOT BREATHE OUR AIR!
WHAT?!! YOU DARE TELL ME I AM ACCUSED OF COWARDICE!!?? I, THE MIGHTIEST OF ALL!
NOT COWARDICE, GREAT ATTUMA! PERHAPS A BETTER WORD WOULD BE--CAUTION!
I'LL SHOVE THE LIE BACK DOWN THEIR THROATS!!
REVIVE THE PRISONERS!! PUT HELMETS UPON THEM, THAT THEY MAY BREATHE!
THEN BRING THEM HENCE!! I'LL SLAY THEM ALL--SINGLE-HANDED!!
THUS, IT COMES TO PASS THAT THE THREE VALIANT HUMANS--NOW PROTECTED BY OXYGEN-FILLED HELMETS--FACE THE DREADED SCOURGE OF THE UNDER-SEA WORLD ONCE AGAIN--!
I WONDER WHY HE IS GIVING US A SECOND CHANCE TO BATTLE HIM?
THESE HELMETS ARE THE ANSWER! HIS INSANE VANITY IS FORCING HIM TO PROVE THAT HE CAN DEFEAT US BY HIS STRENGTH ALONE --NOT JUST BECAUSE WE GREW UNABLE TO BREATHE!
HE IS STRONGER THAN A HUNDRED MEN! IF ONLY HAWKEYE WERE WITH US! HIS ARROWS WOULD HELP TO EQUAL THE ODDS!
DEFEAT ME, AND YOU CAN GO FREE!! BUT SHOULD THE VICTORY BE MINE-- YOU WILL PAY WITH YOUR VERY LIVES!

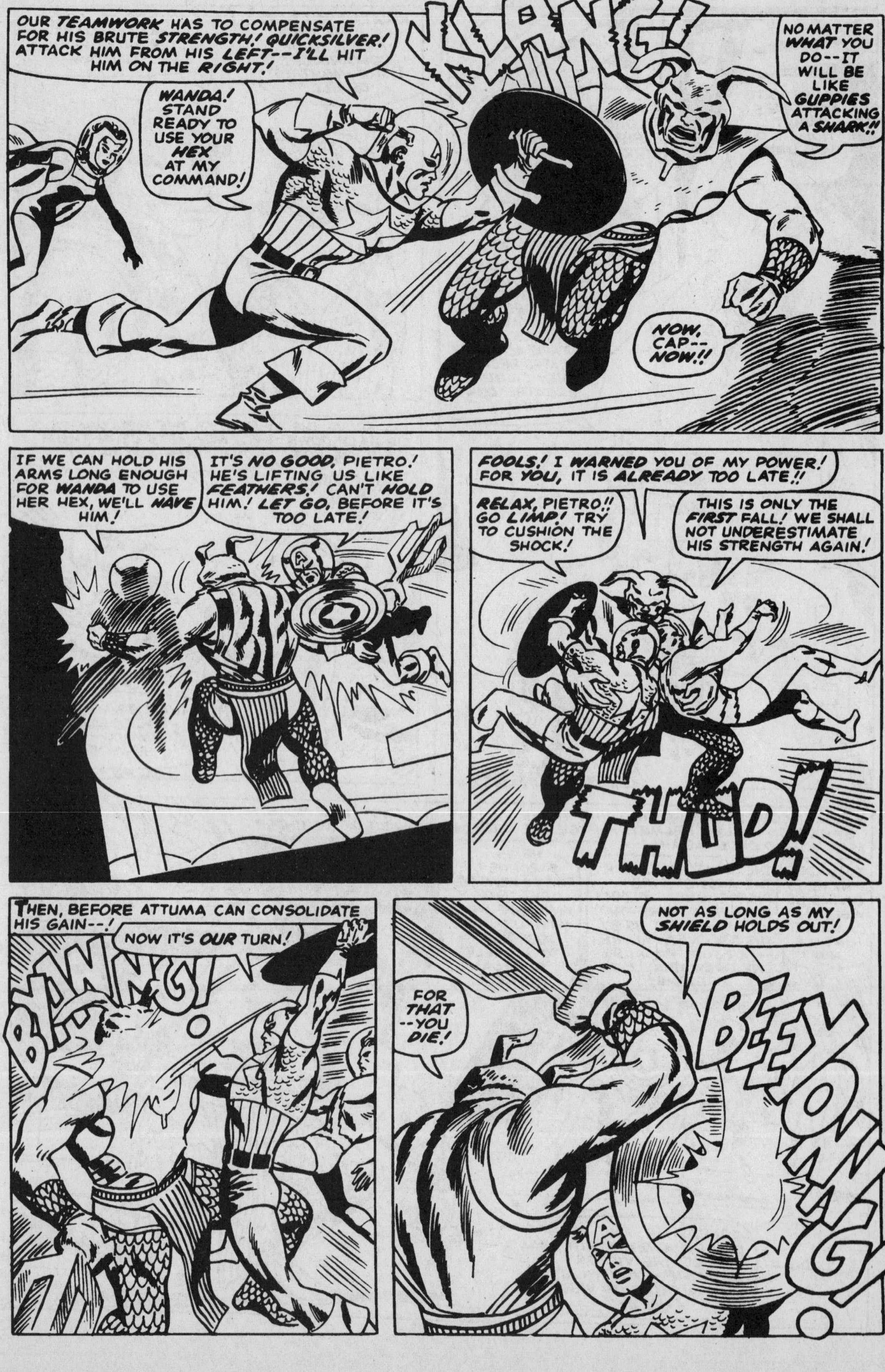

OUR TEAMWORK HAS TO COMPENSATE FOR HIS BRUTE STRENGTH! QUICKSILVER! ATTACK HIM FROM HIS LEFT--I'LL HIT HIM ON THE RIGHT!
KLANG!
NO MATTER WHAT YOU DO--IT WILL BE LIKE GUPPIES ATTACKING A SHARK!!
WANDA! STAND READY TO USE YOUR HEX AT MY COMMAND!
NOW, CAP-- NOW!!
IF WE CAN HOLD HIS ARMS LONG ENOUGH FOR WANDA TO USE HER HEX, WE'LL HAVE HIM!
IT'S NO GOOD, PIETRO! HE'S LIFTING US LIKE FEATHERS! CAN'T HOLD HIM! LET GO, BEFORE IT'S TOO LATE!
FOOLS! I WARNED YOU OF MY POWER! FOR YOU, IT IS ALREADY TOO LATE!!
RELAX, PIETRO!! GO LIMP! TRY TO CUSHION THE SHOCK!
THIS IS ONLY THE FIRST FALL! WE SHALL NOT UNDERESTIMATE HIS STRENGTH AGAIN!
THUD!
THEN, BEFORE ATTUMA CAN CONSOLIDATE HIS GAIN--!
NOW IT'S OUR TURN!
BWANNG!
NOT AS LONG AS MY SHIELD HOLDS OUT!
FOR THAT --YOU DIE!
BEEYONNNG!

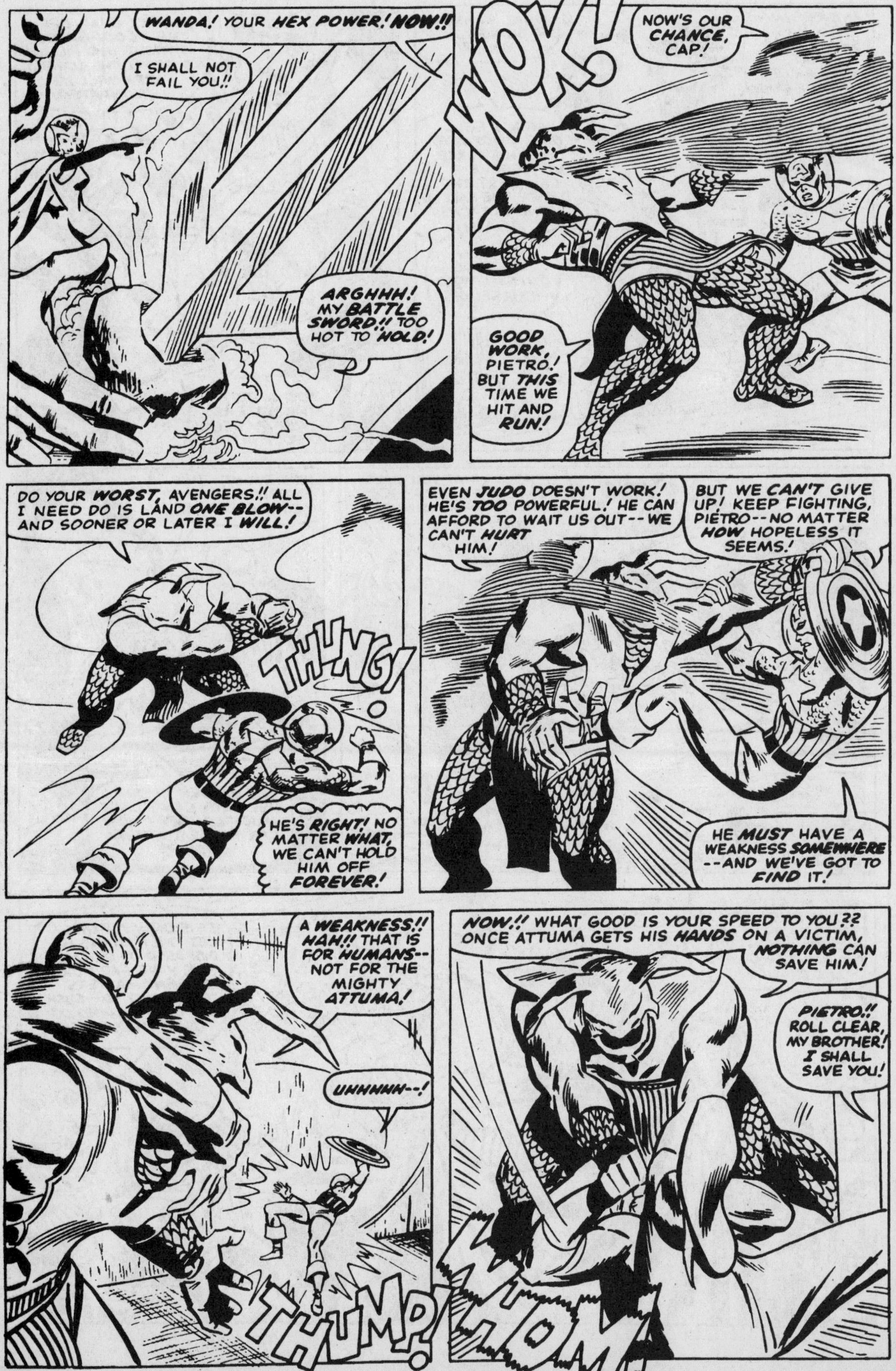
WANDA! YOUR HEX POWER! NOW!!
I SHALL NOT FAIL YOU!!
ARGHHH! MY BATTLE SWORD!! TOO HOT TO HOLD!
WOK!
NOW'S OUR CHANCE, CAP!
GOOD WORK, PIETRO! BUT THIS TIME WE HIT AND RUN!
DO YOUR WORST, AVENGERS!! ALL I NEED DO IS LAND ONE BLOW-- AND SOONER OR LATER I WILL!
THUNG!
HE'S RIGHT! NO MATTER WHAT, WE CAN'T HOLD HIM OFF FOREVER!
EVEN JUDO DOESN'T WORK! HE'S TOO POWERFUL! HE CAN AFFORD TO WAIT US OUT--WE CAN'T HURT HIM!
BUT WE CAN'T GIVE UP! KEEP FIGHTING, PIETRO--NO MATTER HOW HOPELESS IT SEEMS!
HE MUST HAVE A WEAKNESS SOMEWHERE --AND WE'VE GOT TO FIND IT!
A WEAKNESS!! NAH!! THAT IS FOR HUMANS-- NOT FOR THE MIGHTY ATTUMA!
UHHHHH--!
THUMP!
NOW!! WHAT GOOD IS YOUR SPEED TO YOU?? ONCE ATTUMA GETS HIS HANDS ON A VICTIM, NOTHING CAN SAVE HIM!
PIETRO!! ROLL CLEAR, MY BROTHER! I SHALL SAVE YOU!
WHOM!

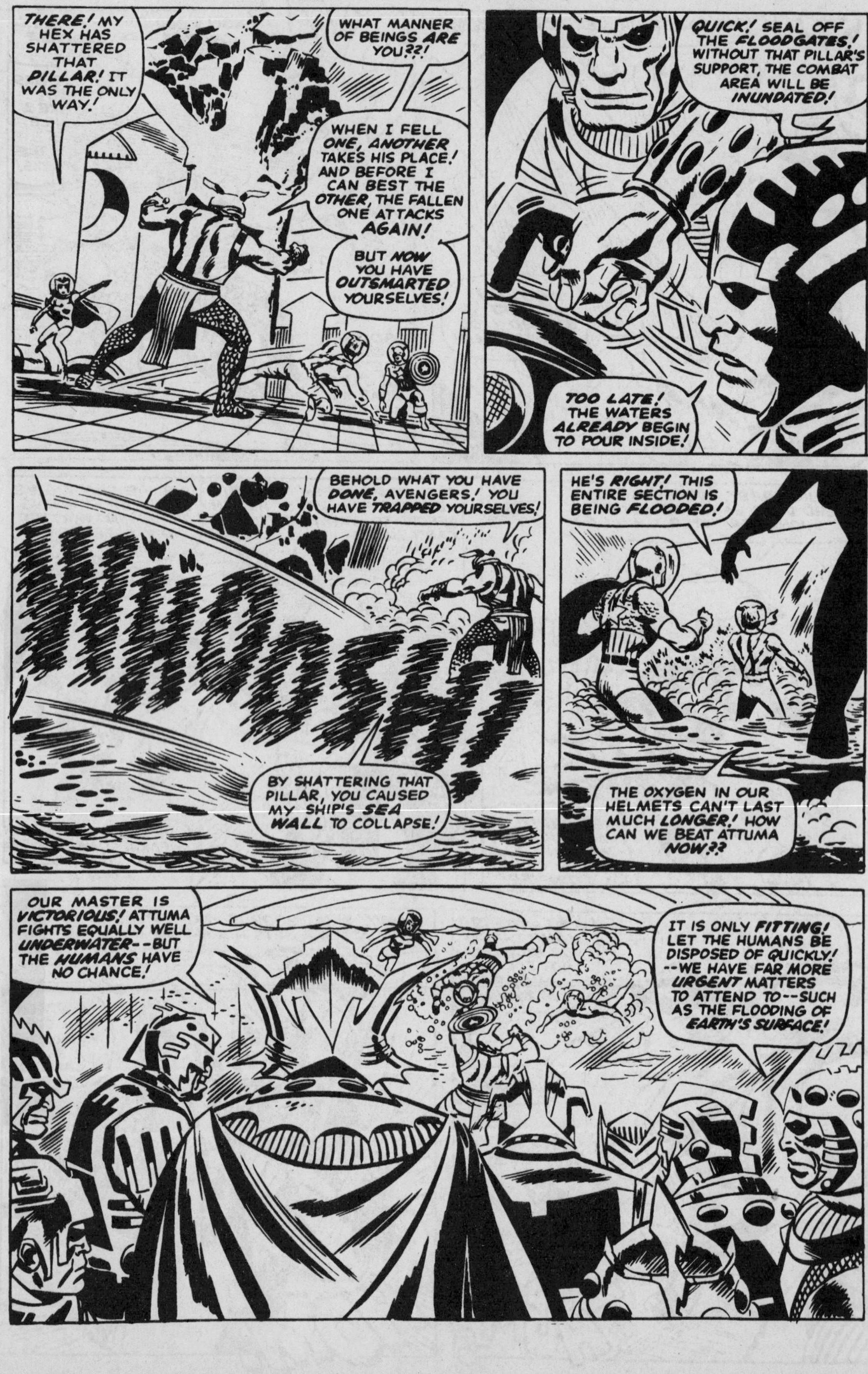
THERE! MY HEX HAS SHATTERED THAT PILLAR! IT WAS THE ONLY WAY!
WHAT MANNER OF BEINGS ARE YOU??!
WHEN I FELL ONE, ANOTHER TAKES HIS PLACE! AND BEFORE I CAN BEST THE OTHER, THE FALLEN ONE ATTACKS AGAIN!
BUT NOW YOU HAVE OUTSMARTED YOURSELVES!
QUICK! SEAL OFF THE FLOODGATES! WITHOUT THAT PILLAR'S SUPPORT, THE COMBAT AREA WILL BE INUNDATED!
TOO LATE! THE WATERS ALREADY BEGIN TO POUR INSIDE!
BEHOLD WHAT YOU HAVE DONE, AVENGERS! YOU HAVE TRAPPED YOURSELVES!
WHOOSH!
BY SHATTERING THAT PILLAR, YOU CAUSED MY SHIP'S SEA WALL TO COLLAPSE!
HE'S RIGHT! THIS ENTIRE SECTION IS BEING FLOODED!
THE OXYGEN IN OUR HELMETS CAN'T LAST MUCH LONGER! HOW CAN WE BEAT ATTUMA NOW??
OUR MASTER IS VICTORIOUS! ATTUMA FIGHTS EQUALLY WELL UNDERWATER--BUT THE HUMANS HAVE NO CHANCE!
IT IS ONLY FITTING! LET THE HUMANS BE DISPOSED OF QUICKLY! --WE HAVE FAR MORE URGENT MATTERS TO ATTEND TO--SUCH AS THE FLOODING OF EARTH'S SURFACE!

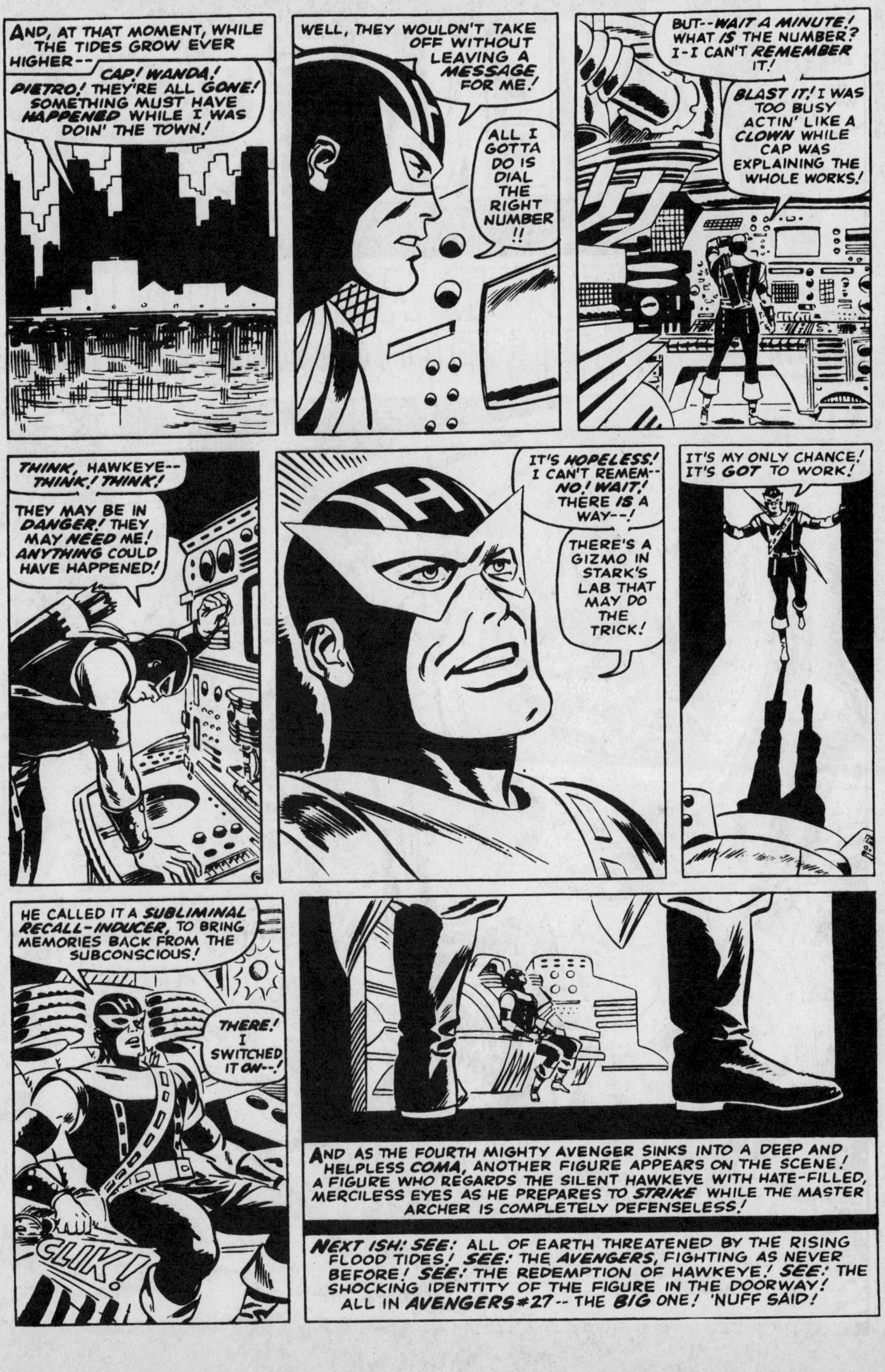

AND, AT THAT MOMENT, WHILE THE TIDES GROW EVER HIGHER--
CAP! WANDA! PIETRO! THEY'RE ALL GONE! SOMETHING MUST HAVE HAPPENED WHILE I WAS DOIN' THE TOWN!
WELL, THEY WOULDN'T TAKE OFF WITHOUT LEAVING A MESSAGE FOR ME!
ALL I GOTTA DO IS DIAL THE RIGHT NUMBER!!
BUT--WAIT A MINUTE! WHAT IS THE NUMBER? I-I CAN'T REMEMBER IT!
BLAST IT! I WAS TOO BUSY ACTIN' LIKE A CLOWN WHILE CAP WAS EXPLAINING THE WHOLE WORKS!
THINK, HAWKEYE-- THINK! THINK!
THEY MAY BE IN DANGER! THEY MAY NEED ME! ANYTHING COULD HAVE HAPPENED!
IT'S HOPELESS! I CAN'T REMEM-- NO! WAIT! THERE IS A WAY--!
THERE'S A GIZMO IN STARK'S LAB THAT MAY DO THE TRICK!
IT'S MY ONLY CHANCE! IT'S GOT TO WORK!
HE CALLED IT A SUBLIMINAL RECALL-INDUCER, TO BRING MEMORIES BACK FROM THE SUBCONSCIOUS!
THERE! I SWITCHED IT ON--!
CLIK!
AND AS THE FOURTH MIGHTY AVENGER SINKS INTO A DEEP AND HELPLESS COMA, ANOTHER FIGURE APPEARS ON THE SCENE! A FIGURE WHO REGARDS THE SILENT HAWKEYE WITH HATE-FILLED, MERCILESS EYES AS HE PREPARES TO STRIKE WHILE THE MASTER ARCHER IS COMPLETELY DEFENSELESS!
NEXT ISH: SEE: ALL OF EARTH THREATENED BY THE RISING FLOOD TIDES! SEE: THE AVENGERS, FIGHTING AS NEVER BEFORE! SEE: THE REDEMPTION OF HAWKEYE! SEE: THE SHOCKING IDENTITY OF THE FIGURE IN THE DOORWAY! ALL IN AVENGERS #27 -- THE BIG ONE! 'NUFF SAID!

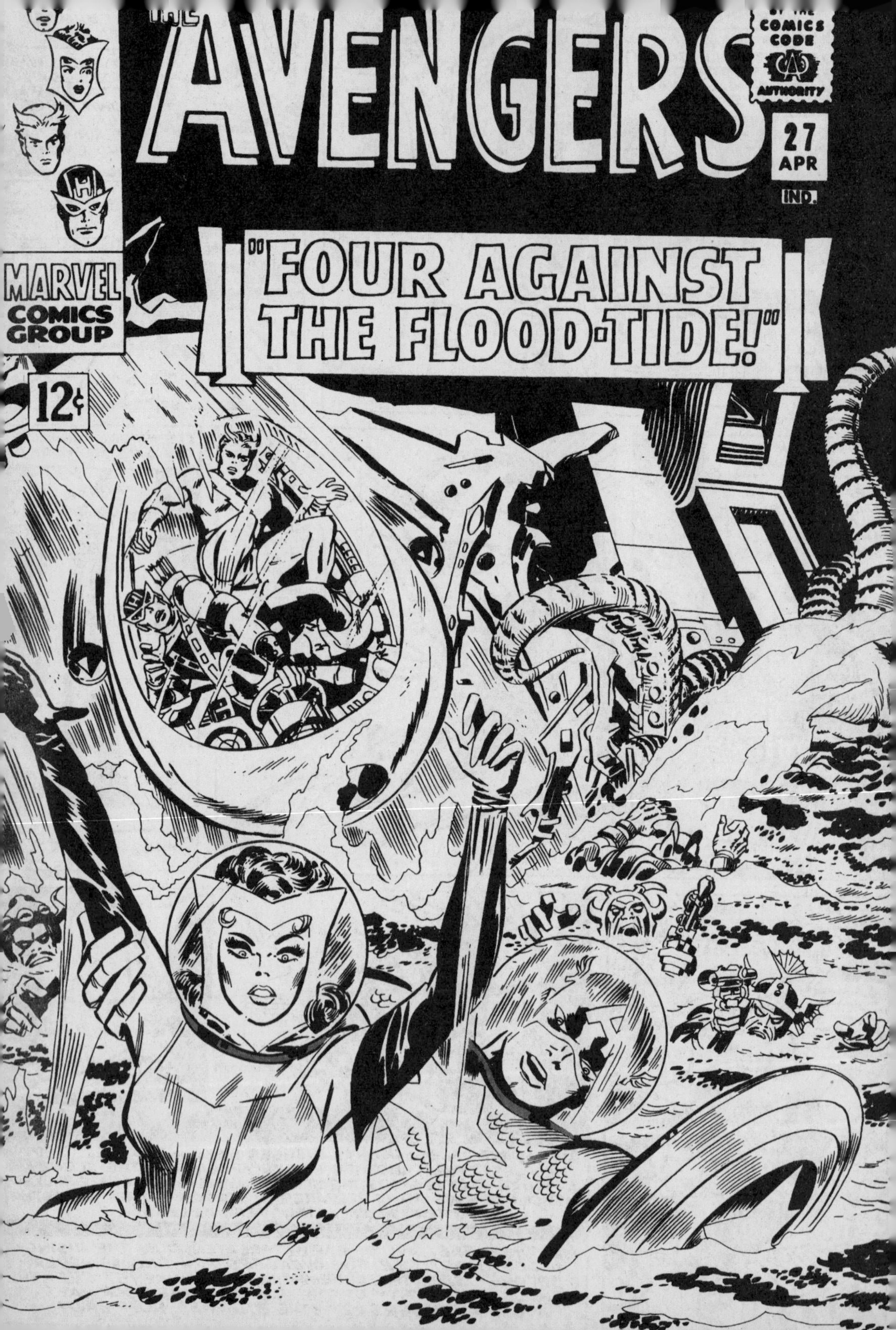
THE AVENGERS
APPROVED BY THE COMICS CODE AUTHORITY
27
APR
IND.
MARVEL COMICS GROUP
12¢
"FOUR AGAINST THE FLOOD-TIDE!"

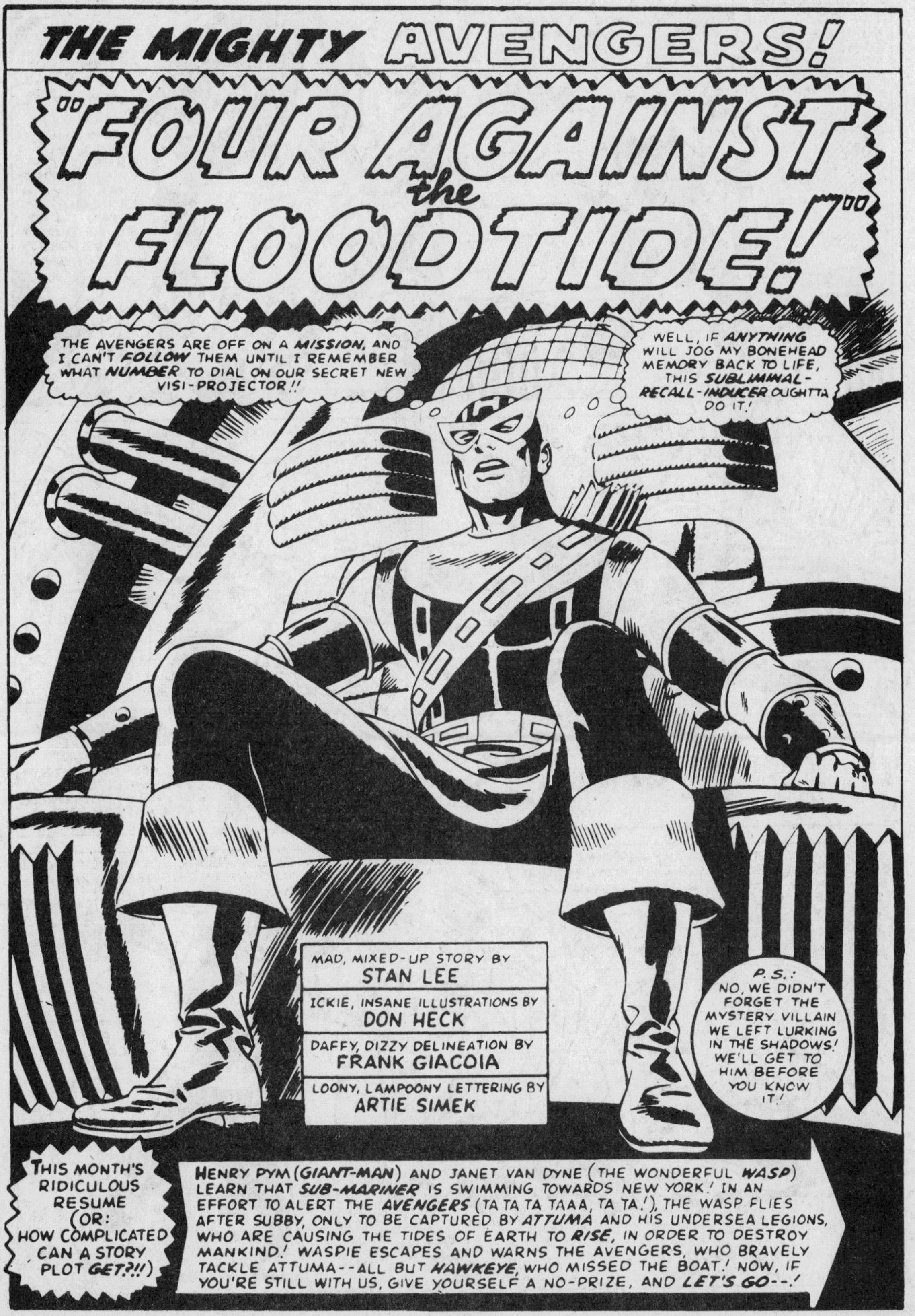
THE MIGHTY AVENGERS!
"FOUR AGAINST the FLOODTIDE!"
THE AVENGERS ARE OFF ON A MISSION, AND I CAN'T FOLLOW THEM UNTIL I REMEMBER WHAT NUMBER TO DIAL ON OUR SECRET NEW VISI-PROJECTOR!!
WELL, IF ANYTHING WILL JOG MY BONEHEAD MEMORY BACK TO LIFE, THIS SUBLIMINAL-RECALL-INDUCER OUGHTTA DO IT!
MAD, MIXED-UP STORY BY STAN LEE
ICKIE, INSANE ILLUSTRATIONS BY DON HECK
DAFFY, DIZZY DELINEATION BY FRANK GIACOIA
LOONY, LAMPOONY LETTERING BY ARTIE SIMEK
P.S.: NO, WE DIDN'T FORGET THE MYSTERY VILLAIN WE LEFT LURKING IN THE SHADOWS! WE'LL GET TO HIM BEFORE YOU KNOW IT!
THIS MONTH'S RIDICULOUS RESUME (OR: HOW COMPLICATED CAN A STORY PLOT GET?!!)
HENRY PYM (GIANT-MAN) AND JANET VAN DYNE (THE WONDERFUL WASP) LEARN THAT SUB-MARINER IS SWIMMING TOWARDS NEW YORK! IN AN EFFORT TO ALERT THE AVENGERS (TA TA TA TAAA, TA TA!), THE WASP FLIES AFTER SUBBY, ONLY TO BE CAPTURED BY ATTUMA AND HIS UNDERSEA LEGIONS, WHO ARE CAUSING THE TIDES OF EARTH TO RISE, IN ORDER TO DESTROY MANKIND! WASPIE ESCAPES AND WARNS THE AVENGERS, WHO BRAVELY TACKLE ATTUMA--ALL BUT HAWKEYE, WHO MISSED THE BOAT! NOW, IF YOU'RE STILL WITH US, GIVE YOURSELF A NO-PRIZE, AND LET'S GO--!

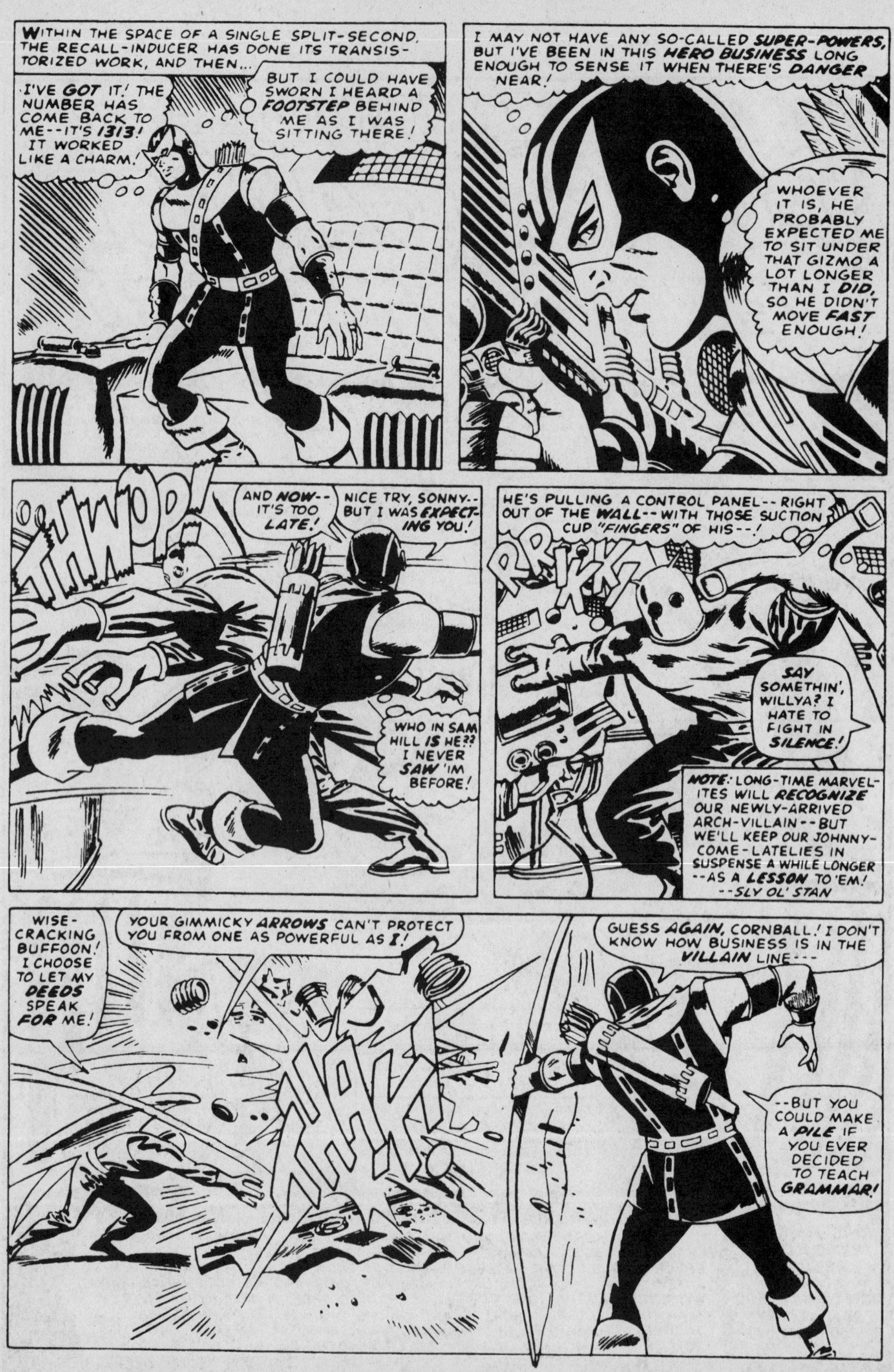
WITHIN THE SPACE OF A SINGLE SPLIT-SECOND, THE RECALL-INDUCER HAS DONE ITS TRANSISTORIZED WORK, AND THEN...
I'VE GOT IT! THE NUMBER HAS COME BACK TO ME--IT'S 1313! IT WORKED LIKE A CHARM!
BUT I COULD HAVE SWORN I HEARD A FOOTSTEP BEHIND ME AS I WAS SITTING THERE!
I MAY NOT HAVE ANY SO-CALLED SUPER-POWERS, BUT I'VE BEEN IN THIS HERO BUSINESS LONG ENOUGH TO SENSE IT WHEN THERE'S DANGER NEAR!
WHOEVER IT IS, HE PROBABLY EXPECTED ME TO SIT UNDER THAT GIZMO A LOT LONGER THAN I DID, SO HE DIDN'T MOVE FAST ENOUGH!
THWOP!
AND NOW--IT'S TOO LATE!
NICE TRY, SONNY--BUT I WAS EXPECTING YOU!
WHO IN SAM HILL IS HE?? I NEVER SAW 'IM BEFORE!
HE'S PULLING A CONTROL PANEL--RIGHT OUT OF THE WALL--WITH THOSE SUCTION CUP "FINGERS" OF HIS--!
RRIKK!
SAY SOMETHIN', WILLYA? I HATE TO FIGHT IN SILENCE!
NOTE: LONG-TIME MARVELITES WILL RECOGNIZE OUR NEWLY-ARRIVED ARCH-VILLAIN--BUT WE'LL KEEP OUR JOHNNY-COME-LATELIES IN SUSPENSE A WHILE LONGER--AS A LESSON TO 'EM! --SLY OL' STAN
WISE-CRACKING BUFFOON! I CHOOSE TO LET MY DEEDS SPEAK FOR ME!
YOUR GIMMICKY ARROWS CAN'T PROTECT YOU FROM ONE AS POWERFUL AS I!
THAK!
GUESS AGAIN, CORNBALL! I DON'T KNOW HOW BUSINESS IS IN THE VILLAIN LINE---
--BUT YOU COULD MAKE A PILE IF YOU EVER DECIDED TO TEACH GRAMMAR!

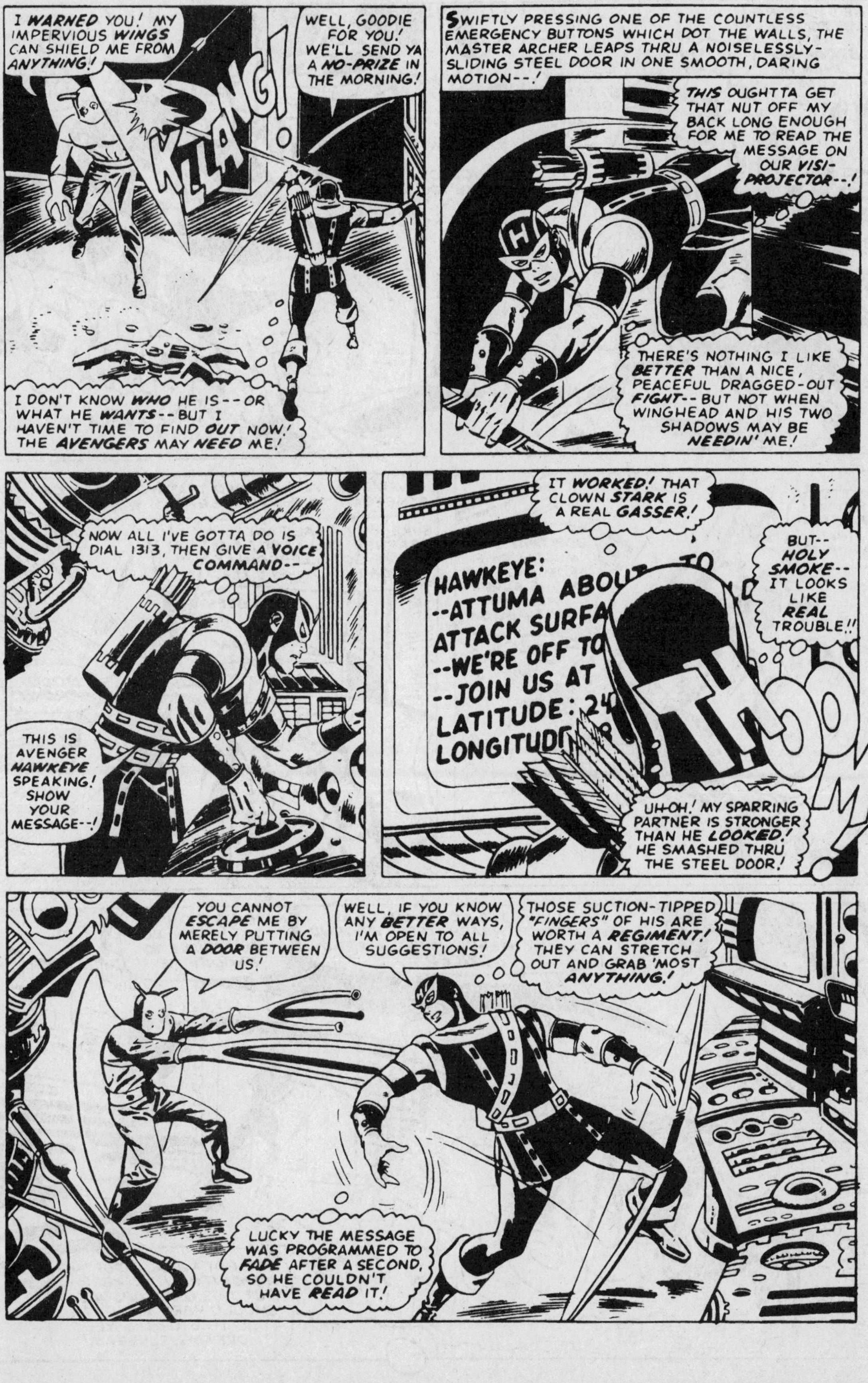
I WARNED YOU! MY IMPERVIOUS WINGS CAN SHIELD ME FROM ANYTHING!
WELL, GOODIE FOR YOU! WE'LL SEND YA A NO-PRIZE IN THE MORNING!
KLLANG!
I DON'T KNOW WHO HE IS--OR WHAT HE WANTS--BUT I HAVEN'T TIME TO FIND OUT NOW! THE AVENGERS MAY NEED ME!
SWIFTLY PRESSING ONE OF THE COUNTLESS EMERGENCY BUTTONS WHICH DOT THE WALLS, THE MASTER ARCHER LEAPS THRU A NOISELESSLY-SLIDING STEEL DOOR IN ONE SMOOTH, DARING MOTION--!
THIS OUGHTTA GET THAT NUT OFF MY BACK LONG ENOUGH FOR ME TO READ THE MESSAGE ON OUR VISI-PROJECTOR--!
THERE'S NOTHING I LIKE BETTER THAN A NICE, PEACEFUL DRAGGED-OUT FIGHT--BUT NOT WHEN WINGHEAD AND HIS TWO SHADOWS MAY BE NEEDIN' ME!
NOW ALL I'VE GOTTA DO IS DIAL 1313, THEN GIVE A VOICE COMMAND--
THIS IS AVENGER HAWKEYE SPEAKING! SHOW YOUR MESSAGE--!
IT WORKED! THAT CLOWN STARK IS A REAL GASSER!
HAWKEYE:
--ATTUMA ABOU
ATTACK SURFA
--WE'RE OFF TO
--JOIN US AT
LATITUDE: 2
LONGITUD
BUT--HOLY SMOKE--IT LOOKS LIKE REAL TROUBLE!!
THOOM!
UH-OH! MY SPARRING PARTNER IS STRONGER THAN HE LOOKED! HE SMASHED THRU THE STEEL DOOR!
YOU CANNOT ESCAPE ME BY MERELY PUTTING A DOOR BETWEEN US!
WELL, IF YOU KNOW ANY BETTER WAYS, I'M OPEN TO ALL SUGGESTIONS!
THOSE SUCTION-TIPPED "FINGERS" OF HIS ARE WORTH A REGIMENT! THEY CAN STRETCH OUT AND GRAB 'MOST ANYTHING!
LUCKY THE MESSAGE WAS PROGRAMMED TO FADE AFTER A SECOND, SO HE COULDN'T HAVE READ IT!

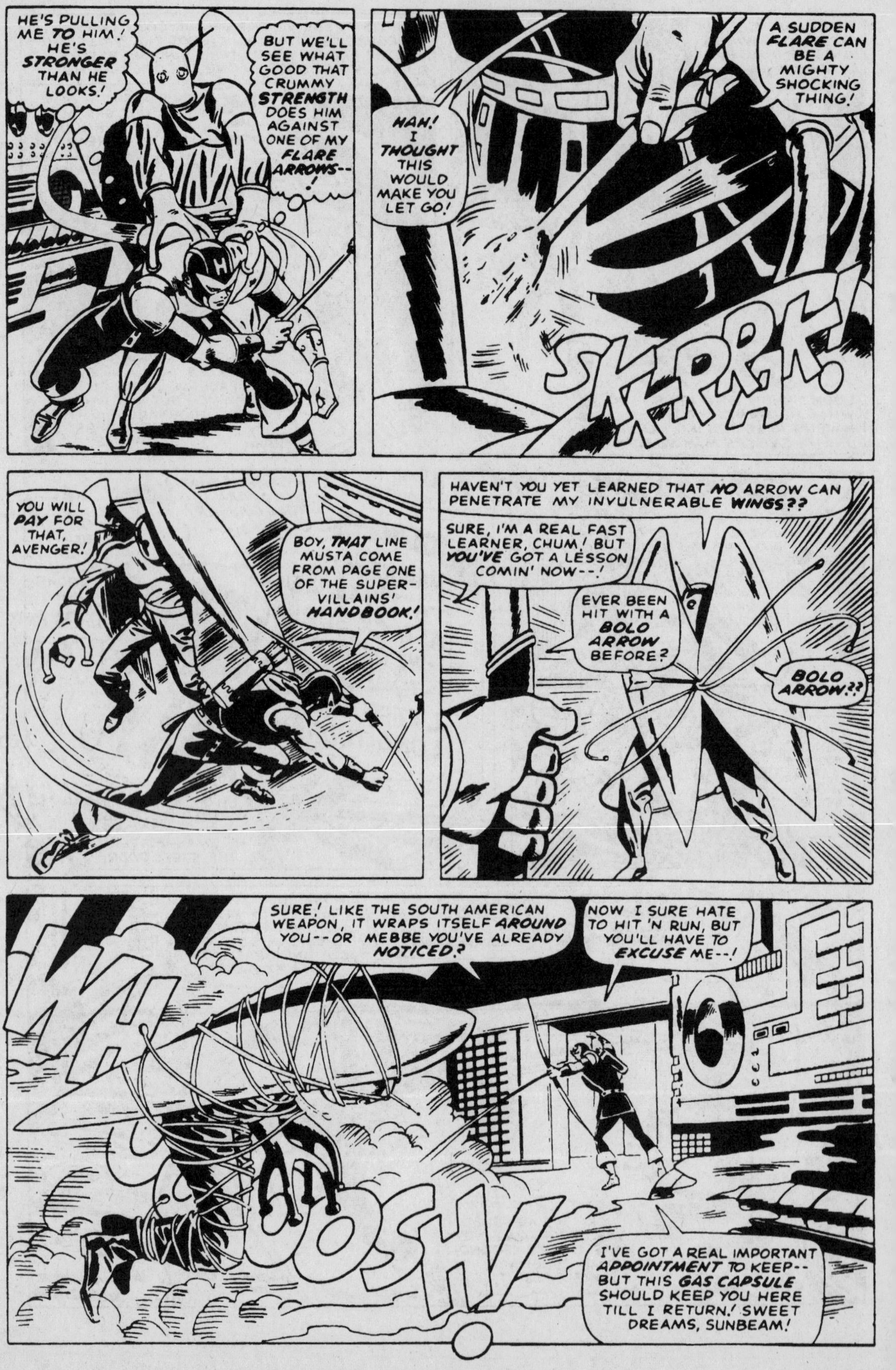
HE'S PULLING ME TO HIM! HE'S STRONGER THAN HE LOOKS!
BUT WE'LL SEE WHAT GOOD THAT CRUMMY STRENGTH DOES HIM AGAINST ONE OF MY FLARE ARROWS--!
A SUDDEN FLARE CAN BE A MIGHTY SHOCKING THING!
HAH! I THOUGHT THIS WOULD MAKE YOU LET GO!
SKRPPAK!
YOU WILL PAY FOR THAT, AVENGER!
BOY, THAT LINE MUSTA COME FROM PAGE ONE OF THE SUPER-VILLAINS' HANDBOOK!
HAVEN'T YOU YET LEARNED THAT NO ARROW CAN PENETRATE MY INVULNERABLE WINGS??
SURE, I'M A REAL FAST LEARNER, CHUM! BUT YOU'VE GOT A LESSON COMIN' NOW--!
EVER BEEN HIT WITH A BOLO ARROW BEFORE?
BOLO ARROW??
SURE! LIKE THE SOUTH AMERICAN WEAPON, IT WRAPS ITSELF AROUND YOU--OR MEBBE YOU'VE ALREADY NOTICED?
NOW I SURE HATE TO HIT 'N RUN, BUT YOU'LL HAVE TO EXCUSE ME--!
WHOOSH!
I'VE GOT A REAL IMPORTANT APPOINTMENT TO KEEP--BUT THIS GAS CAPSULE SHOULD KEEP YOU HERE TILL I RETURN! SWEET DREAMS, SUNBEAM!

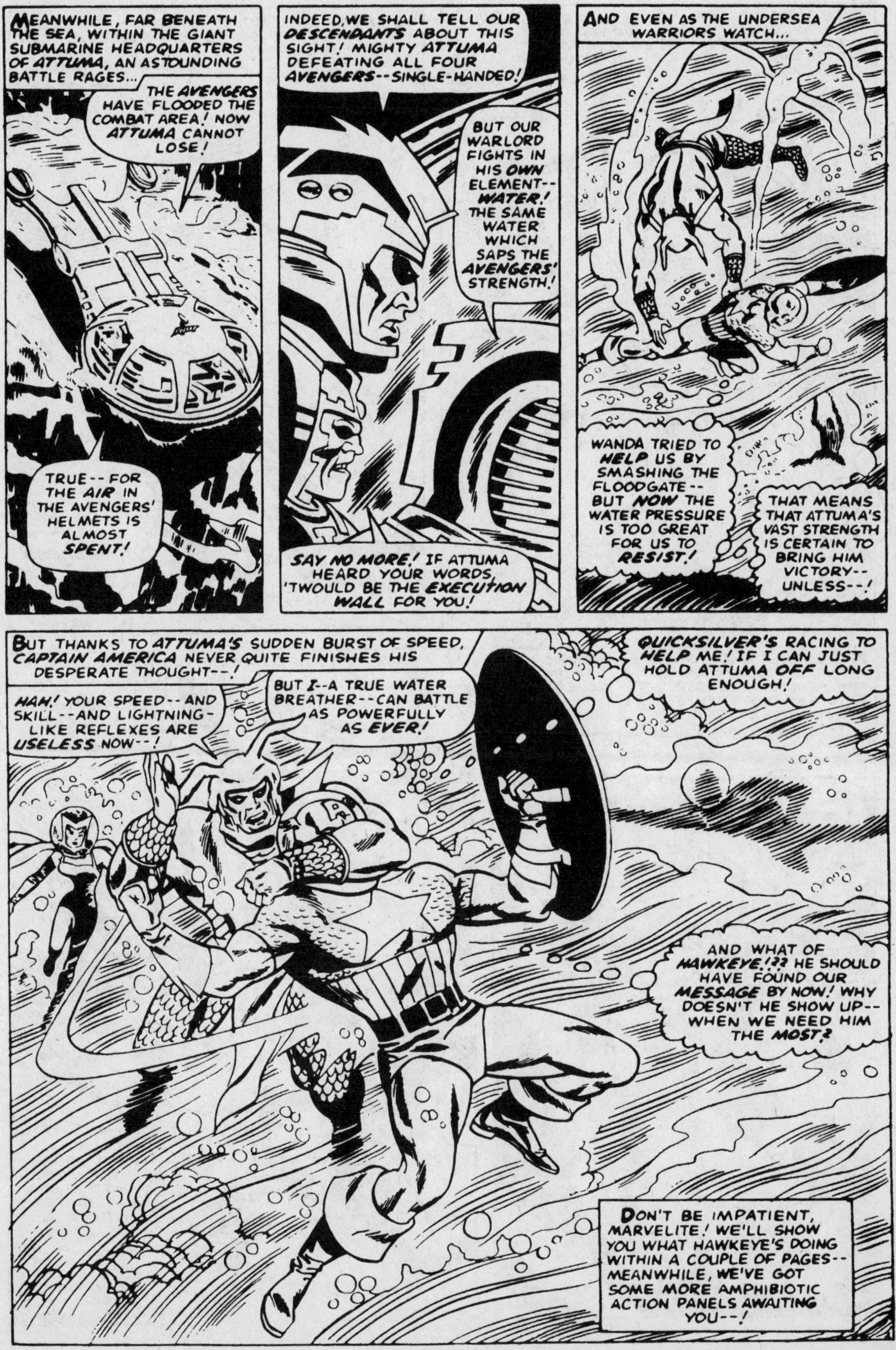
MEANWHILE, FAR BENEATH THE SEA, WITHIN THE GIANT SUBMARINE HEADQUARTERS OF ATTUMA, AN ASTOUNDING BATTLE RAGES...
THE AVENGERS HAVE FLOODED THE COMBAT AREA! NOW ATTUMA CANNOT LOSE!
TRUE--FOR THE AIR IN THE AVENGERS' HELMETS IS ALMOST SPENT!
INDEED, WE SHALL TELL OUR DESCENDANTS ABOUT THIS SIGHT! MIGHTY ATTUMA DEFEATING ALL FOUR AVENGERS--SINGLE-HANDED!
BUT OUR WARLORD FIGHTS IN HIS OWN ELEMENT--WATER! THE SAME WATER WHICH SAPS THE AVENGERS' STRENGTH!
SAY NO MORE! IF ATTUMA HEARD YOUR WORDS, 'TWOULD BE THE EXECUTION WALL FOR YOU!
AND EVEN AS THE UNDERSEA WARRIORS WATCH...
WANDA TRIED TO HELP US BY SMASHING THE FLOODGATE--BUT NOW THE WATER PRESSURE IS TOO GREAT FOR US TO RESIST!
THAT MEANS THAT ATTUMA'S VAST STRENGTH IS CERTAIN TO BRING HIM VICTORY--UNLESS--!
BUT THANKS TO ATTUMA'S SUDDEN BURST OF SPEED, CAPTAIN AMERICA NEVER QUITE FINISHES HIS DESPERATE THOUGHT--!
HAH! YOUR SPEED--AND SKILL--AND LIGHTNING-LIKE REFLEXES ARE USELESS NOW--!
BUT I--A TRUE WATER BREATHER--CAN BATTLE AS POWERFULLY AS EVER!
QUICKSILVER'S RACING TO HELP ME! IF I CAN JUST HOLD ATTUMA OFF LONG ENOUGH!
AND WHAT OF HAWKEYE!?? HE SHOULD HAVE FOUND OUR MESSAGE BY NOW! WHY DOESN'T HE SHOW UP--WHEN WE NEED HIM THE MOST?
DON'T BE IMPATIENT, MARVELITE! WE'LL SHOW YOU WHAT HAWKEYE'S DOING WITHIN A COUPLE OF PAGES--MEANWHILE, WE'VE GOT SOME MORE AMPHIBIOTIC ACTION PANELS AWAITING YOU--!

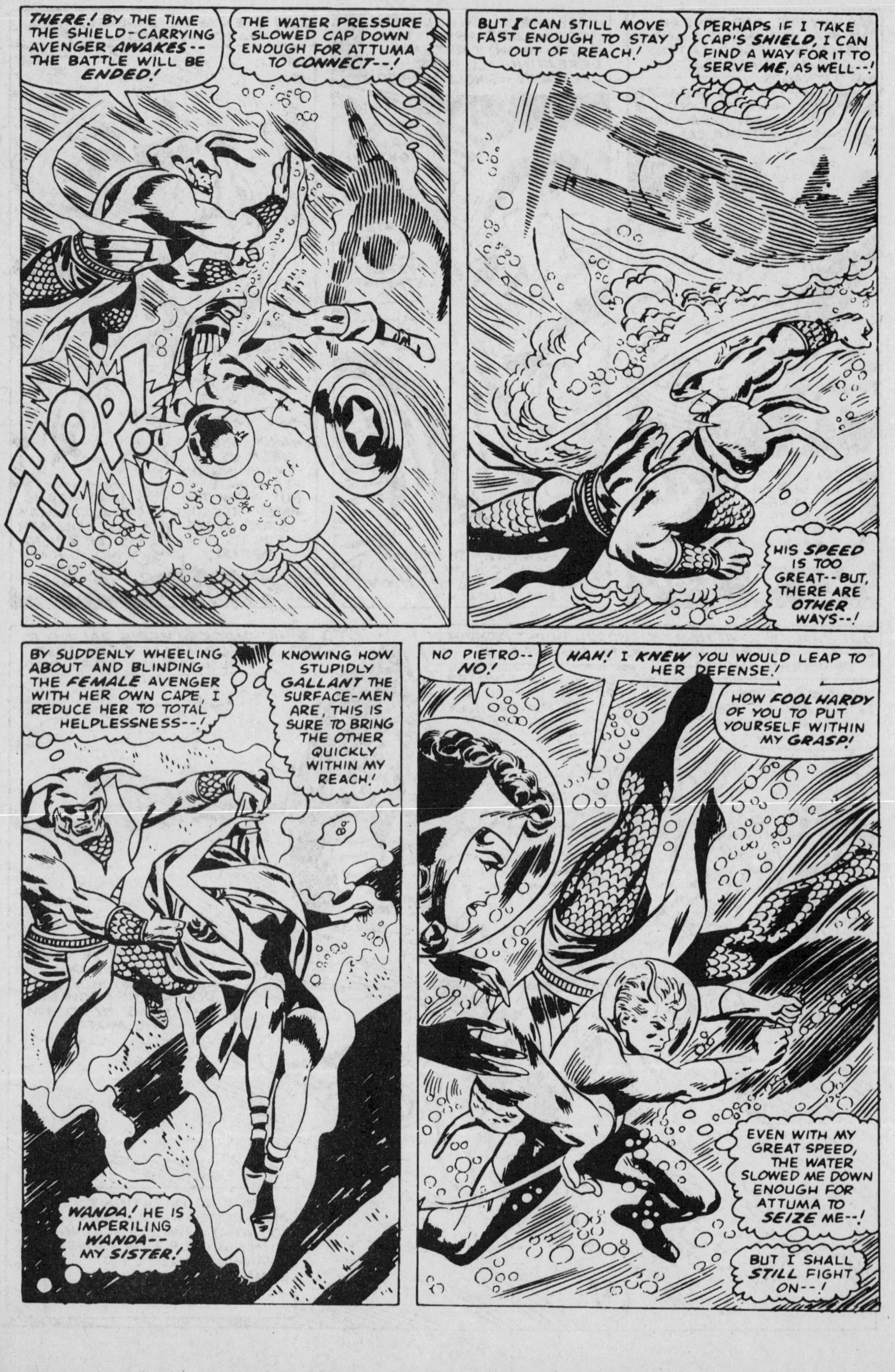
THERE! BY THE TIME THE SHIELD-CARRYING AVENGER AWAKES-- THE BATTLE WILL BE ENDED!
THE WATER PRESSURE SLOWED CAP DOWN ENOUGH FOR ATTUMA TO CONNECT--!
THOP!
BUT I CAN STILL MOVE FAST ENOUGH TO STAY OUT OF REACH!
PERHAPS IF I TAKE CAP'S SHIELD, I CAN FIND A WAY FOR IT TO SERVE ME, AS WELL--!
HIS SPEED IS TOO GREAT--BUT, THERE ARE OTHER WAYS--!
BY SUDDENLY WHEELING ABOUT AND BLINDING THE FEMALE AVENGER WITH HER OWN CAPE, I REDUCE HER TO TOTAL HELPLESSNESS--!
KNOWING HOW STUPIDLY GALLANT THE SURFACE-MEN ARE, THIS IS SURE TO BRING THE OTHER QUICKLY WITHIN MY REACH!
WANDA! HE IS IMPERILING WANDA-- MY SISTER!
NO PIETRO-- NO!
HAH! I KNEW YOU WOULD LEAP TO HER DEFENSE!
HOW FOOLHARDY OF YOU TO PUT YOURSELF WITHIN MY GRASP!
EVEN WITH MY GREAT SPEED, THE WATER SLOWED ME DOWN ENOUGH FOR ATTUMA TO SEIZE ME--!
BUT I SHALL STILL FIGHT ON--!

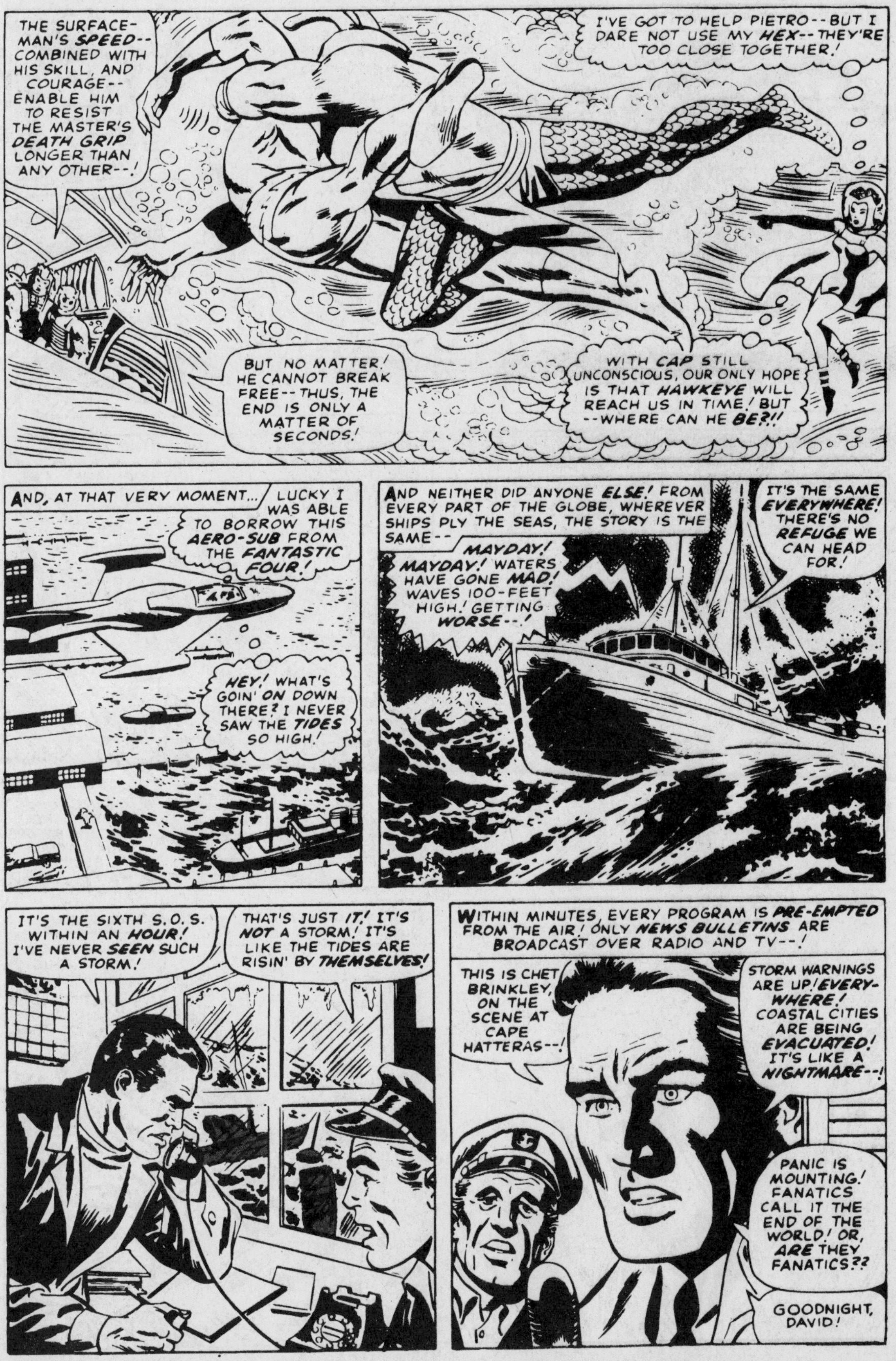
THE SURFACE-MAN'S SPEED--COMBINED WITH HIS SKILL, AND COURAGE--ENABLE HIM TO RESIST THE MASTER'S DEATH GRIP LONGER THAN ANY OTHER--!
I'VE GOT TO HELP PIETRO--BUT I DARE NOT USE MY HEX--THEY'RE TOO CLOSE TOGETHER!
BUT NO MATTER! HE CANNOT BREAK FREE--THUS, THE END IS ONLY A MATTER OF SECONDS!
WITH CAP STILL UNCONSCIOUS, OUR ONLY HOPE IS THAT HAWKEYE WILL REACH US IN TIME! BUT --WHERE CAN HE BE?!!
AND, AT THAT VERY MOMENT...
LUCKY I WAS ABLE TO BORROW THIS AERO-SUB FROM THE FANTASTIC FOUR!
HEY! WHAT'S GOIN' ON DOWN THERE? I NEVER SAW THE TIDES SO HIGH!
AND NEITHER DID ANYONE ELSE! FROM EVERY PART OF THE GLOBE, WHEREVER SHIPS PLY THE SEAS, THE STORY IS THE SAME--
IT'S THE SAME EVERYWHERE! THERE'S NO REFUGE WE CAN HEAD FOR!
MAYDAY! MAYDAY! WATERS HAVE GONE MAD! WAVES 100-FEET HIGH! GETTING WORSE--!
IT'S THE SIXTH S.O.S. WITHIN AN HOUR! I'VE NEVER SEEN SUCH A STORM!
THAT'S JUST IT! IT'S NOT A STORM! IT'S LIKE THE TIDES ARE RISIN' BY THEMSELVES!
WITHIN MINUTES, EVERY PROGRAM IS PRE-EMPTED FROM THE AIR! ONLY NEWS BULLETINS ARE BROADCAST OVER RADIO AND TV--!
THIS IS CHET BRINKLEY, ON THE SCENE AT CAPE HATTERAS--!
STORM WARNINGS ARE UP! EVERY-WHERE! COASTAL CITIES ARE BEING EVACUATED! IT'S LIKE A NIGHTMARE--!
PANIC IS MOUNTING! FANATICS CALL IT THE END OF THE WORLD! OR, ARE THEY FANATICS??
GOODNIGHT, DAVID!

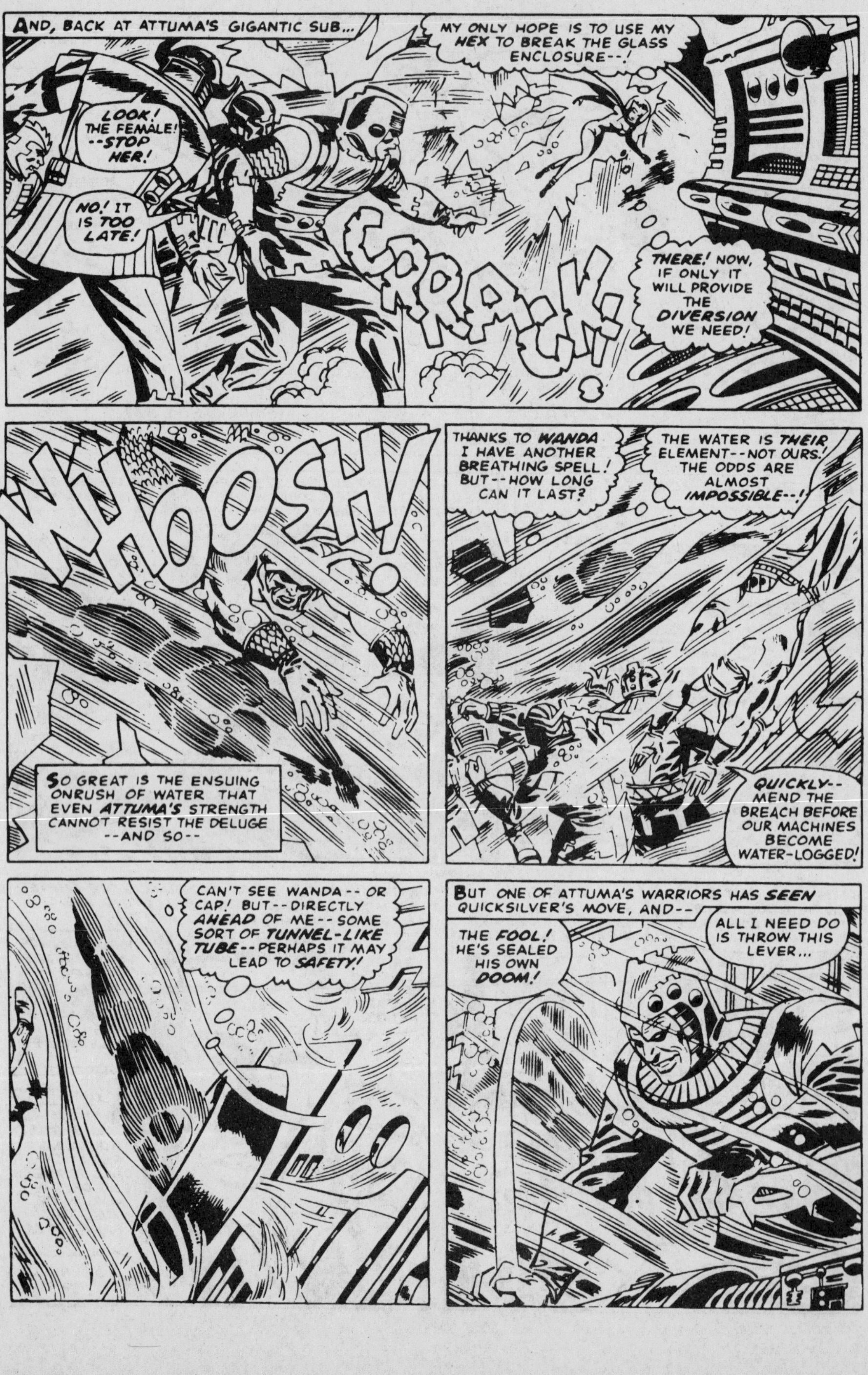

AND, BACK AT ATTUMA'S GIGANTIC SUB...
MY ONLY HOPE IS TO USE MY HEX TO BREAK THE GLASS ENCLOSURE--!
LOOK! THE FEMALE! --STOP HER!
NO! IT IS TOO LATE!
CRRACK!
THERE! NOW, IF ONLY IT WILL PROVIDE THE DIVERSION WE NEED!
WHOOSH!
SO GREAT IS THE ENSUING ONRUSH OF WATER THAT EVEN ATTUMA'S STRENGTH CANNOT RESIST THE DELUGE --AND SO--
THANKS TO WANDA I HAVE ANOTHER BREATHING SPELL! BUT--HOW LONG CAN IT LAST?
THE WATER IS THEIR ELEMENT--NOT OURS! THE ODDS ARE ALMOST IMPOSSIBLE--!
QUICKLY-- MEND THE BREACH BEFORE OUR MACHINES BECOME WATER-LOGGED!
CAN'T SEE WANDA-- OR CAP! BUT--DIRECTLY AHEAD OF ME--SOME SORT OF TUNNEL-LIKE TUBE--PERHAPS IT MAY LEAD TO SAFETY!
BUT ONE OF ATTUMA'S WARRIORS HAS SEEN QUICKSILVER'S MOVE, AND--
THE FOOL! HE'S SEALED HIS OWN DOOM!
ALL I NEED DO IS THROW THIS LEVER...

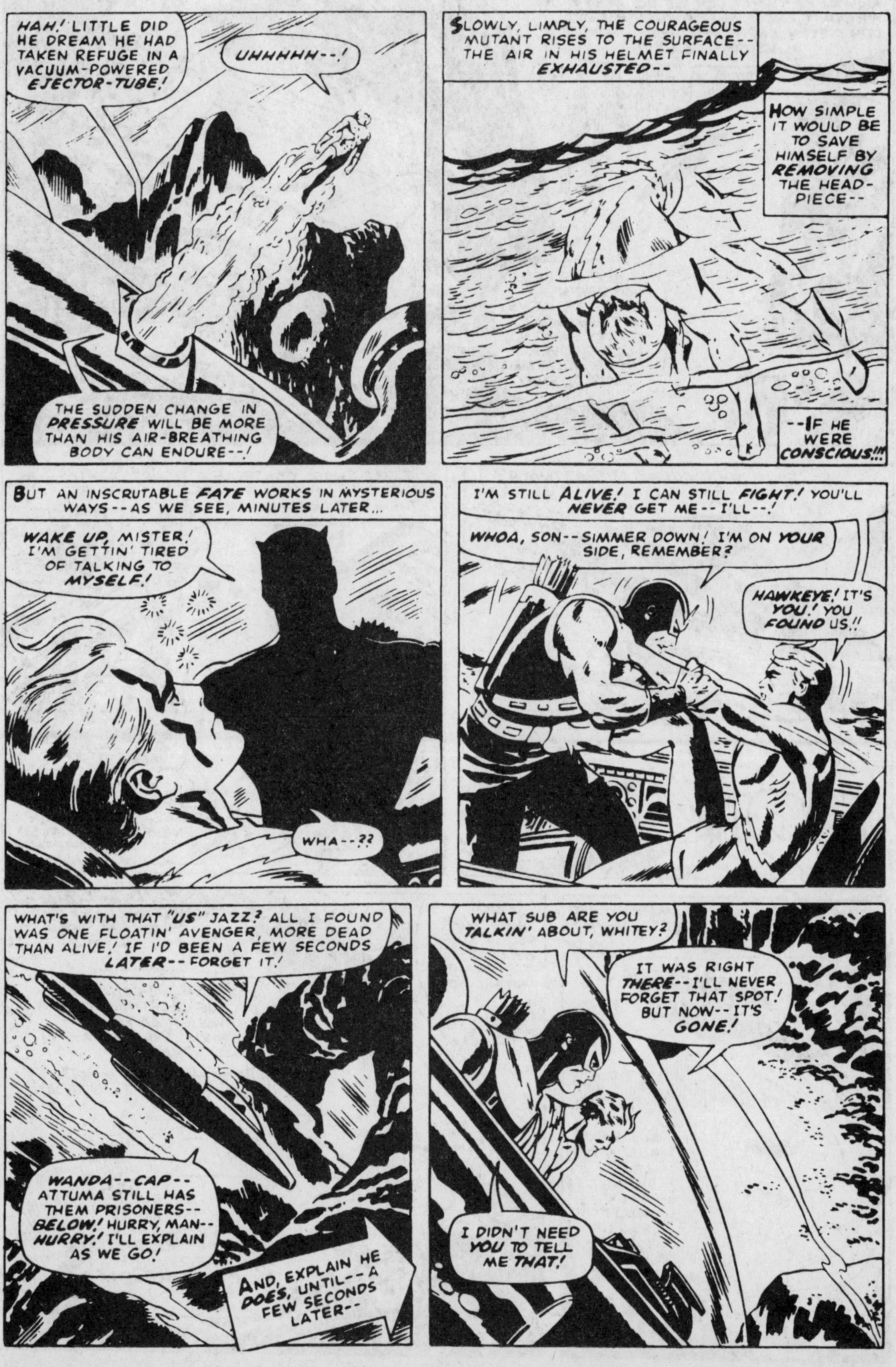
HAH! LITTLE DID HE DREAM HE HAD TAKEN REFUGE IN A VACUUM-POWERED EJECTOR-TUBE!
UHHHHH--!
THE SUDDEN CHANGE IN PRESSURE WILL BE MORE THAN HIS AIR-BREATHING BODY CAN ENDURE--!
SLOWLY, LIMPLY, THE COURAGEOUS MUTANT RISES TO THE SURFACE--THE AIR IN HIS HELMET FINALLY EXHAUSTED--
HOW SIMPLE IT WOULD BE TO SAVE HIMSELF BY REMOVING THE HEAD-PIECE--
--IF HE WERE CONSCIOUS!!!
BUT AN INSCRUTABLE FATE WORKS IN MYSTERIOUS WAYS--AS WE SEE, MINUTES LATER...
WAKE UP, MISTER! I'M GETTIN' TIRED OF TALKING TO MYSELF!
WHA--??
I'M STILL ALIVE! I CAN STILL FIGHT! YOU'LL NEVER GET ME--I'LL--!
WHOA, SON--SIMMER DOWN! I'M ON YOUR SIDE, REMEMBER?
HAWKEYE! IT'S YOU! YOU FOUND US!!
WHAT'S WITH THAT "US" JAZZ? ALL I FOUND WAS ONE FLOATIN' AVENGER, MORE DEAD THAN ALIVE! IF I'D BEEN A FEW SECONDS LATER--FORGET IT!
WANDA--CAP--ATTUMA STILL HAS THEM PRISONERS--BELOW! HURRY, MAN--HURRY! I'LL EXPLAIN AS WE GO!
AND, EXPLAIN HE DOES, UNTIL--A FEW SECONDS LATER--
WHAT SUB ARE YOU TALKIN' ABOUT, WHITEY?
IT WAS RIGHT THERE--I'LL NEVER FORGET THAT SPOT! BUT NOW--IT'S GONE!
I DIDN'T NEED YOU TO TELL ME THAT!

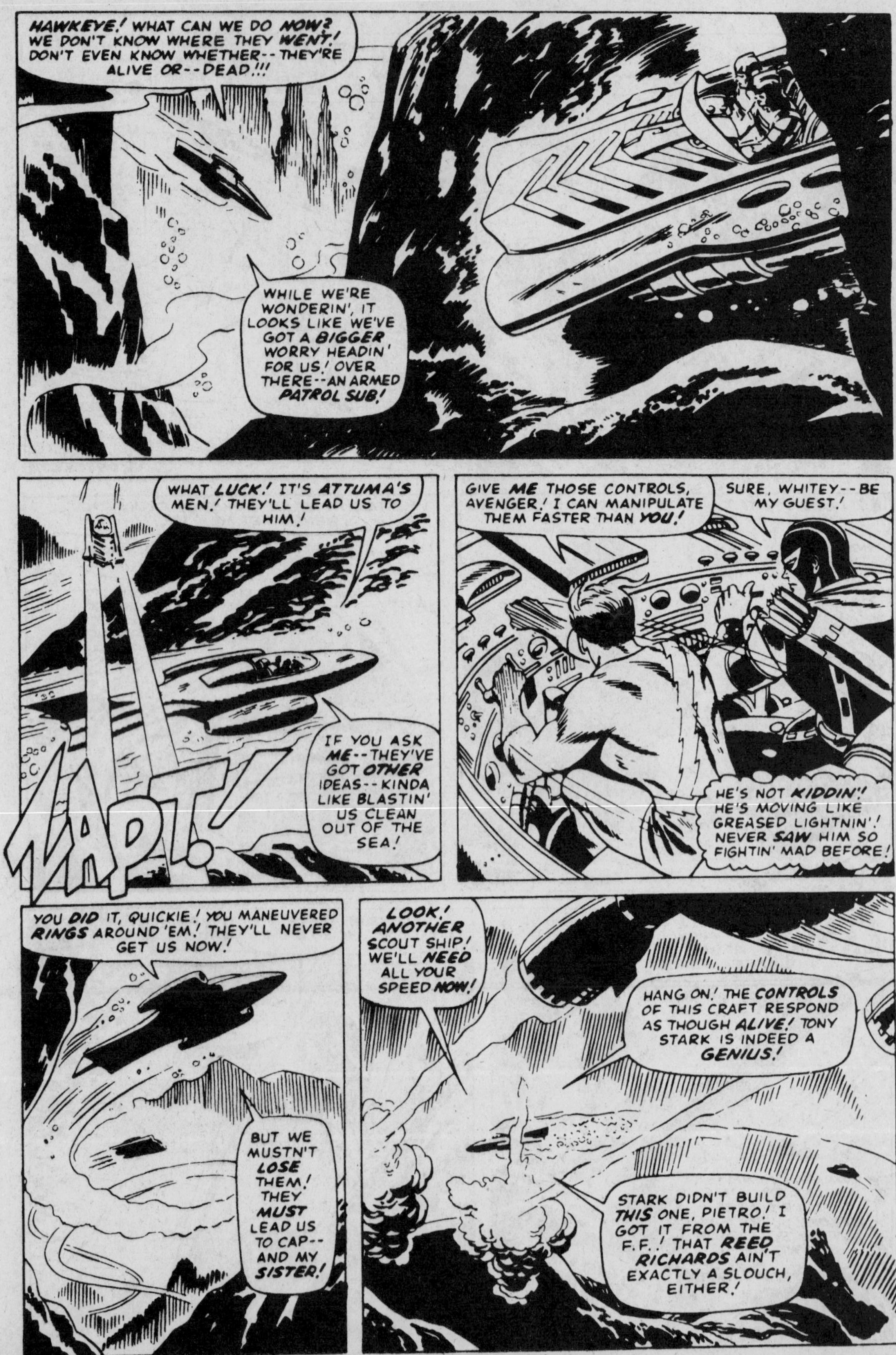
HAWKEYE! WHAT CAN WE DO NOW? WE DON'T KNOW WHERE THEY WENT! DON'T EVEN KNOW WHETHER-- THEY'RE ALIVE OR--DEAD!!!
WHILE WE'RE WONDERIN', IT LOOKS LIKE WE'VE GOT A BIGGER WORRY HEADIN' FOR US! OVER THERE--AN ARMED PATROL SUB!
WHAT LUCK! IT'S ATTUMA'S MEN! THEY'LL LEAD US TO HIM!
IF YOU ASK ME--THEY'VE GOT OTHER IDEAS--KINDA LIKE BLASTIN' US CLEAN OUT OF THE SEA!
ZAP!!
GIVE ME THOSE CONTROLS, AVENGER! I CAN MANIPULATE THEM FASTER THAN YOU!
SURE, WHITEY--BE MY GUEST!
HE'S NOT KIDDIN'! HE'S MOVING LIKE GREASED LIGHTNIN'! NEVER SAW HIM SO FIGHTIN' MAD BEFORE!
YOU DID IT, QUICKIE! YOU MANEUVERED RINGS AROUND 'EM! THEY'LL NEVER GET US NOW!
BUT WE MUSTN'T LOSE THEM! THEY MUST LEAD US TO CAP--AND MY SISTER!
LOOK! ANOTHER SCOUT SHIP! WE'LL NEED ALL YOUR SPEED NOW!
HANG ON! THE CONTROLS OF THIS CRAFT RESPOND AS THOUGH ALIVE! TONY STARK IS INDEED A GENIUS!
STARK DIDN'T BUILD THIS ONE, PIETRO! I GOT IT FROM THE F.F.! THAT REED RICHARDS AIN'T EXACTLY A SLOUCH, EITHER!

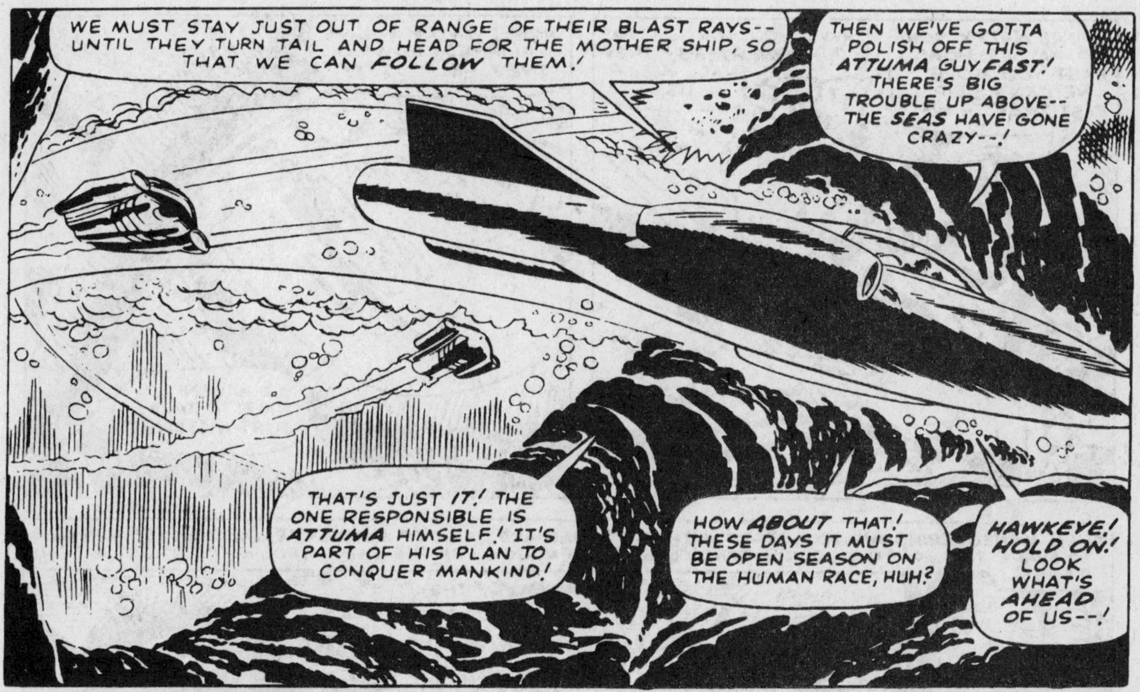
WE MUST STAY JUST OUT OF RANGE OF THEIR BLAST RAYS-- UNTIL THEY TURN TAIL AND HEAD FOR THE MOTHER SHIP, SO THAT WE CAN FOLLOW THEM!
THEN WE'VE GOTTA POLISH OFF THIS ATTUMA GUY FAST! THERE'S BIG TROUBLE UP ABOVE-- THE SEAS HAVE GONE CRAZY--!
THAT'S JUST IT! THE ONE RESPONSIBLE IS ATTUMA HIMSELF! IT'S PART OF HIS PLAN TO CONQUER MANKIND!
HOW ABOUT THAT! THESE DAYS IT MUST BE OPEN SEASON ON THE HUMAN RACE, HUH?
HAWKEYE! HOLD ON! LOOK WHAT'S AHEAD OF US--!

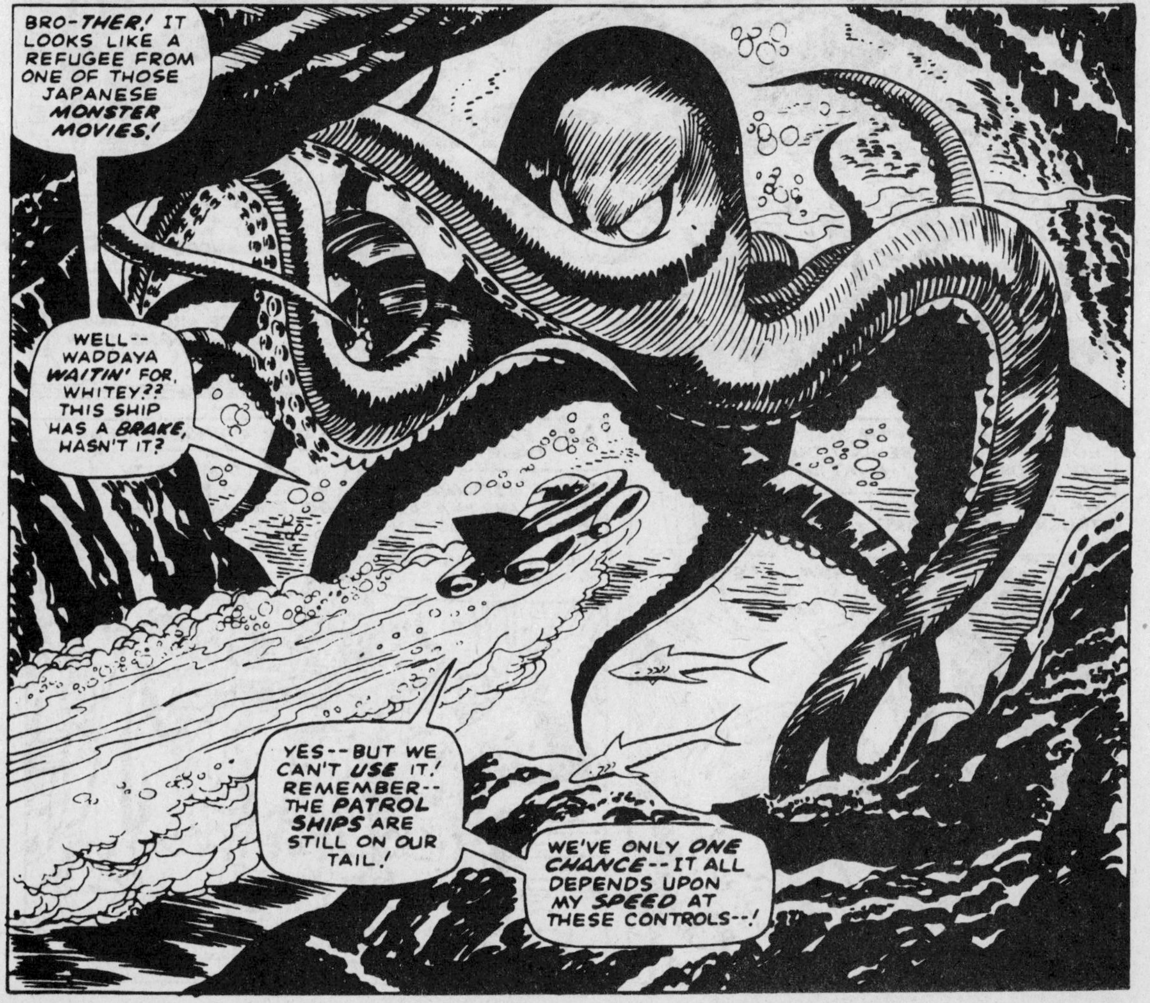
BRO-THER! IT LOOKS LIKE A REFUGEE FROM ONE OF THOSE JAPANESE MONSTER MOVIES!
WELL-- WADDAYA WAITIN' FOR, WHITEY?? THIS SHIP HAS A BRAKE, HASN'T IT?
YES--BUT WE CAN'T USE IT! REMEMBER-- THE PATROL SHIPS ARE STILL ON OUR TAIL!
WE'VE ONLY ONE CHANCE--IT ALL DEPENDS UPON MY SPEED AT THESE CONTROLS--!

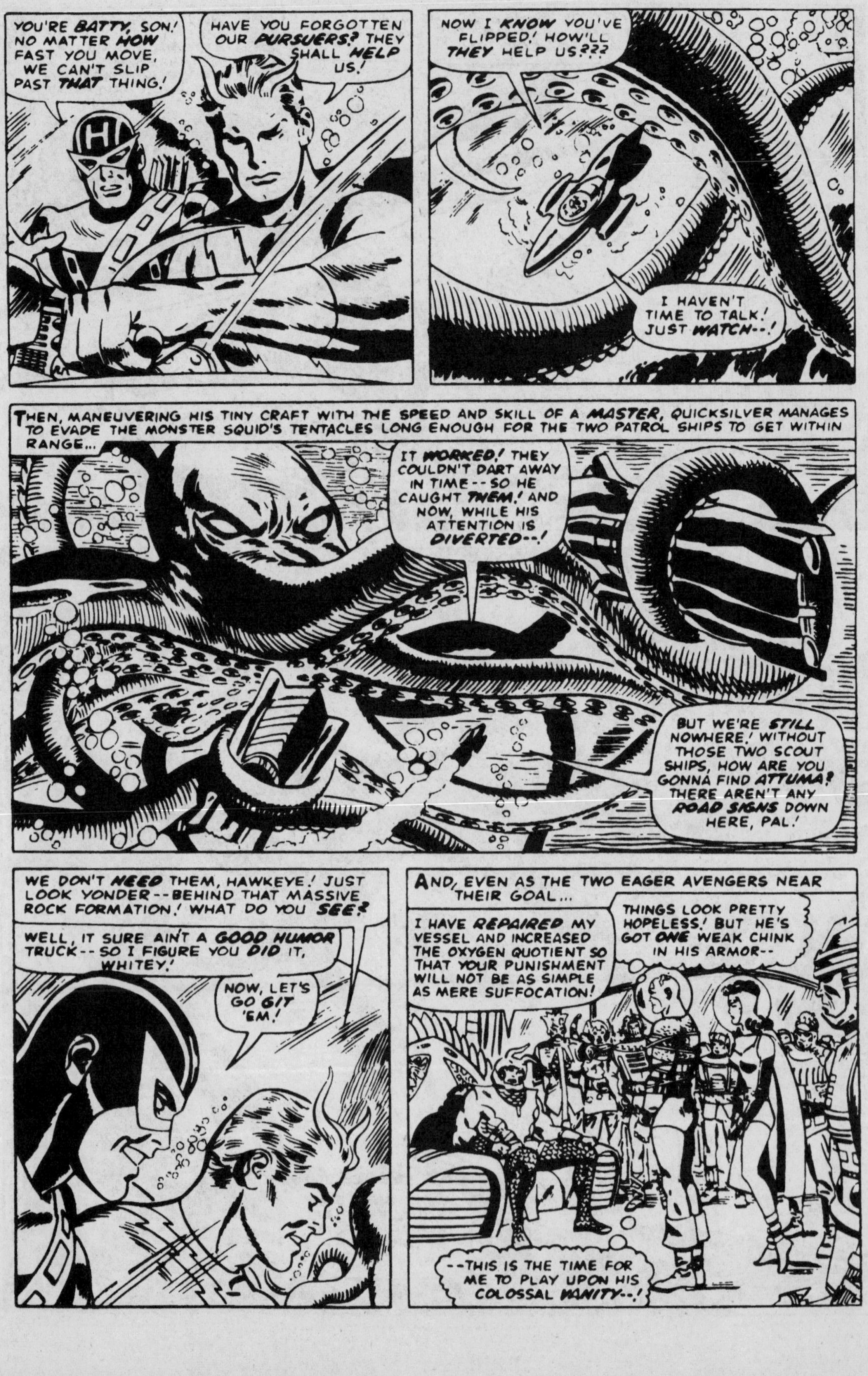

YOU'RE BATTY, SON! NO MATTER HOW FAST YOU MOVE, WE CAN'T SLIP PAST THAT THING!
HAVE YOU FORGOTTEN OUR PURSUERS? THEY SHALL HELP US!
NOW I KNOW YOU'VE FLIPPED! HOW'LL THEY HELP US???
I HAVEN'T TIME TO TALK! JUST WATCH--!
THEN, MANEUVERING HIS TINY CRAFT WITH THE SPEED AND SKILL OF A MASTER, QUICKSILVER MANAGES TO EVADE THE MONSTER SQUID'S TENTACLES LONG ENOUGH FOR THE TWO PATROL SHIPS TO GET WITHIN RANGE...
IT WORKED! THEY COULDN'T DART AWAY IN TIME--SO HE CAUGHT THEM! AND NOW, WHILE HIS ATTENTION IS DIVERTED--!
BUT WE'RE STILL NOWHERE! WITHOUT THOSE TWO SCOUT SHIPS, HOW ARE YOU GONNA FIND ATTUMA? THERE AREN'T ANY ROAD SIGNS DOWN HERE, PAL!
WE DON'T NEED THEM, HAWKEYE! JUST LOOK YONDER--BEHIND THAT MASSIVE ROCK FORMATION! WHAT DO YOU SEE?
WELL, IT SURE AIN'T A GOOD HUMOR TRUCK--SO I FIGURE YOU DID IT, WHITEY!
NOW, LET'S GO GIT 'EM!
AND, EVEN AS THE TWO EAGER AVENGERS NEAR THEIR GOAL...
I HAVE REPAIRED MY VESSEL AND INCREASED THE OXYGEN QUOTIENT SO THAT YOUR PUNISHMENT WILL NOT BE AS SIMPLE AS MERE SUFFOCATION!
THINGS LOOK PRETTY HOPELESS! BUT HE'S GOT ONE WEAK CHINK IN HIS ARMOR--
--THIS IS THE TIME FOR ME TO PLAY UPON HIS COLOSSAL VANITY--!

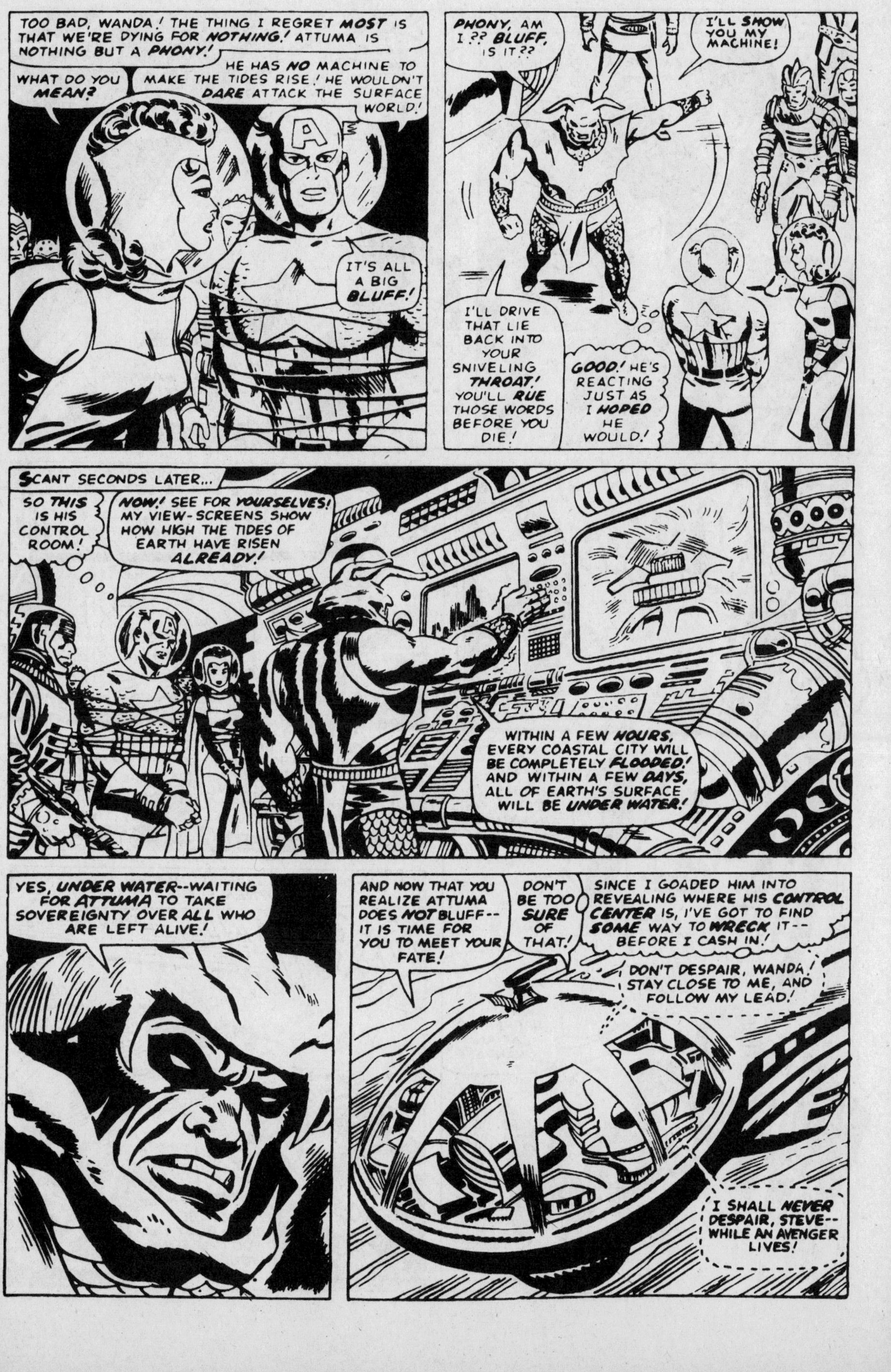
TOO BAD, WANDA! THE THING I REGRET MOST IS THAT WE'RE DYING FOR NOTHING! ATTUMA IS NOTHING BUT A PHONY!
WHAT DO YOU MEAN?
HE HAS NO MACHINE TO MAKE THE TIDES RISE! HE WOULDN'T DARE ATTACK THE SURFACE WORLD!
IT'S ALL A BIG BLUFF!
PHONY, AM I?? BLUFF, IS IT??
I'LL SHOW YOU MY MACHINE!
I'LL DRIVE THAT LIE BACK INTO YOUR SNIVELING THROAT! YOU'LL RUE THOSE WORDS BEFORE YOU DIE!
GOOD! HE'S REACTING JUST AS I HOPED HE WOULD!
SCANT SECONDS LATER...
SO THIS IS HIS CONTROL ROOM!
NOW! SEE FOR YOURSELVES! MY VIEW-SCREENS SHOW HOW HIGH THE TIDES OF EARTH HAVE RISEN ALREADY!
WITHIN A FEW HOURS, EVERY COASTAL CITY WILL BE COMPLETELY FLOODED! AND WITHIN A FEW DAYS, ALL OF EARTH'S SURFACE WILL BE UNDER WATER!
YES, UNDER WATER--WAITING FOR ATTUMA TO TAKE SOVEREIGNTY OVER ALL WHO ARE LEFT ALIVE!
AND NOW THAT YOU REALIZE ATTUMA DOES NOT BLUFF--IT IS TIME FOR YOU TO MEET YOUR FATE!
DON'T BE TOO SURE OF THAT!
SINCE I GOADED HIM INTO REVEALING WHERE HIS CONTROL CENTER IS, I'VE GOT TO FIND SOME WAY TO WRECK IT--BEFORE I CASH IN!
DON'T DESPAIR, WANDA! STAY CLOSE TO ME, AND FOLLOW MY LEAD!
I SHALL NEVER DESPAIR, STEVE--WHILE AN AVENGER LIVES!

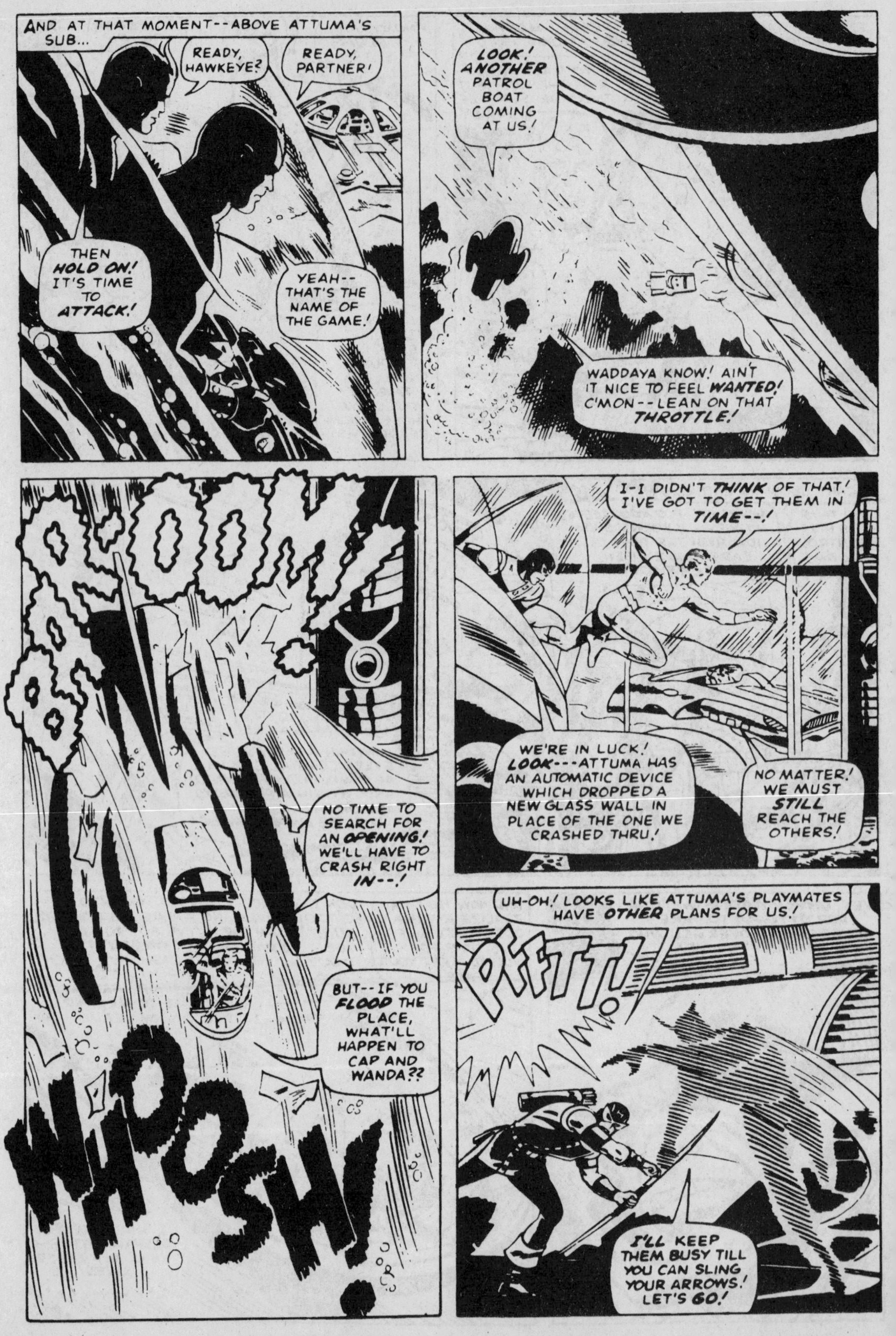

AND AT THAT MOMENT--ABOVE ATTUMA'S SUB...
READY, HAWKEYE?
READY, PARTNER!
THEN HOLD ON! IT'S TIME TO ATTACK!
YEAH--THAT'S THE NAME OF THE GAME!
LOOK! ANOTHER PATROL BOAT COMING AT US!
WADDAYA KNOW! AIN'T IT NICE TO FEEL WANTED! C'MON--LEAN ON THAT THROTTLE!
B-BOOM!
NO TIME TO SEARCH FOR AN OPENING! WE'LL HAVE TO CRASH RIGHT IN--!
BUT--IF YOU FLOOD THE PLACE, WHAT'LL HAPPEN TO CAP AND WANDA??
WHOOSH!
I-I DIDN'T THINK OF THAT! I'VE GOT TO GET THEM IN TIME--!
WE'RE IN LUCK! LOOK---ATTUMA HAS AN AUTOMATIC DEVICE WHICH DROPPED A NEW GLASS WALL IN PLACE OF THE ONE WE CRASHED THRU!
NO MATTER! WE MUST STILL REACH THE OTHERS!
UH-OH! LOOKS LIKE ATTUMA'S PLAYMATES HAVE OTHER PLANS FOR US!
PFFTT!
I'LL KEEP THEM BUSY TILL YOU CAN SLING YOUR ARROWS! LET'S GO!

BOK! **THAK!** **WHAK!**

MAN! I NEVER THOUGHT EVEN *QUICKSILVER* COULD MOVE SO FAST! WHEN HIS *SISTER'S* IN DANGER, HE DOESN'T KID AROUND!

NOTHIN' HE NEEDS FROM *ME*--EXCEPT MAYBE *APPLAUSE!*

BIK! **ZAP!** **WHP!** **THIP!**

THAT TAKES CARE OF *ALL* OF THEM!

LET *THIS* BE AN ANSWER TO THOSE WHO CLAIM THE *NEW* AVENGERS ARE LACKING IN *POWER!*

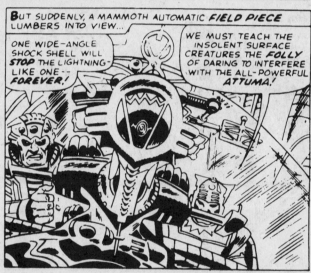

BUT SUDDENLY, A MAMMOTH AUTOMATIC *FIELD PIECE* LUMBERS INTO VIEW...

ONE WIDE-ANGLE SHOCK SHELL WILL *STOP* THE LIGHTNING-LIKE ONE--*FOREVER!*

WE MUST TEACH THE INSOLENT SURFACE CREATURES THE *FOLLY* OF DARING TO INTERFERE WITH THE ALL-POWERFUL *ATTUMA!*

BUT BEFORE THE FATEFUL BUTTON CAN BE PRESSED...

BEHOLD--!

THE *OTHER ONE*-- HE HAS FIRED AN *ARROW!*

AND TRUER WORDS WERE NEVER MUMBLED!

BJOINNNG!

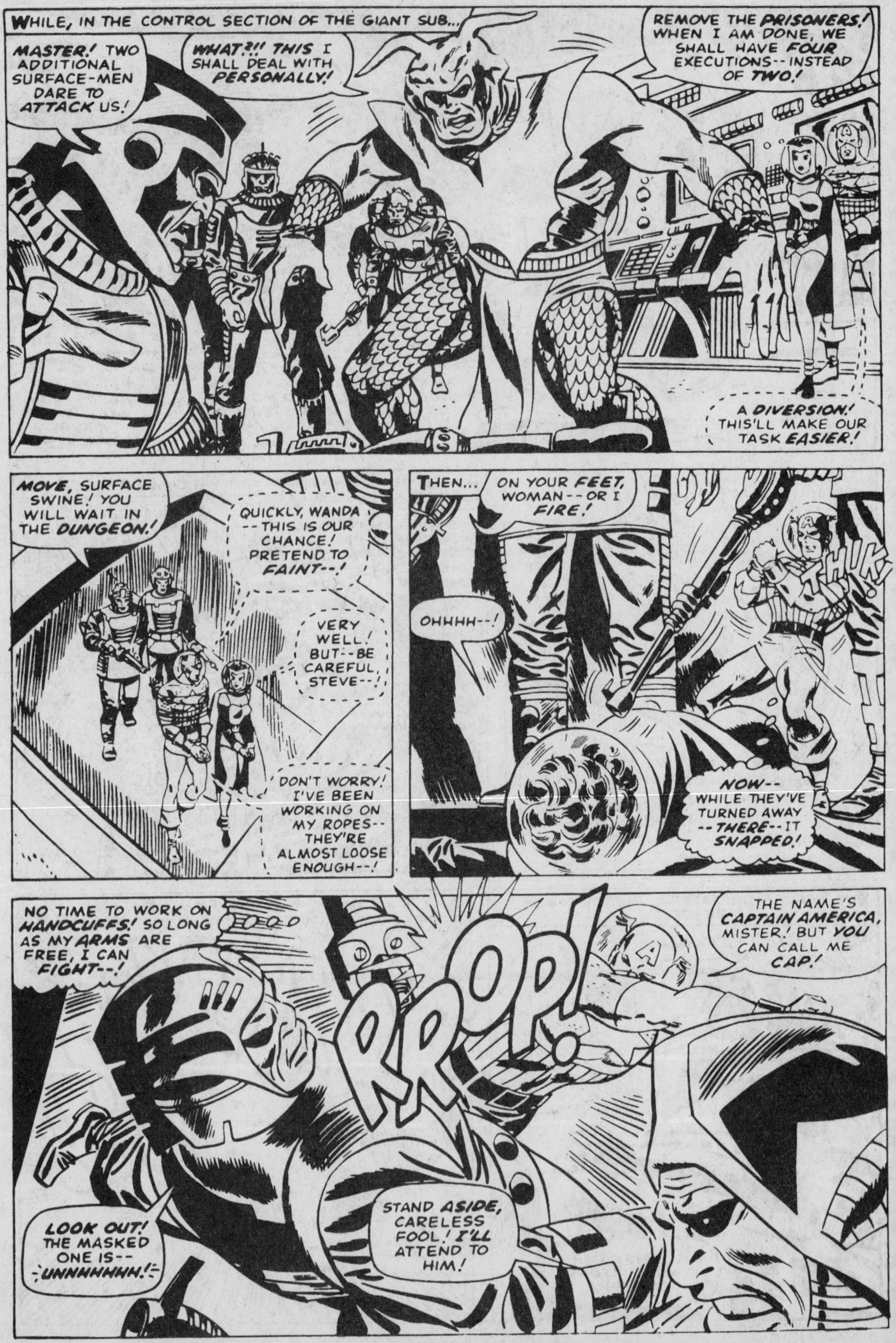
WHILE, IN THE CONTROL SECTION OF THE GIANT SUB...
MASTER! TWO ADDITIONAL SURFACE-MEN DARE TO ATTACK US!
WHAT?!! THIS I SHALL DEAL WITH PERSONALLY!
REMOVE THE PRISONERS! WHEN I AM DONE, WE SHALL HAVE FOUR EXECUTIONS--INSTEAD OF TWO!
A DIVERSION! THIS'LL MAKE OUR TASK EASIER!
MOVE, SURFACE SWINE! YOU WILL WAIT IN THE DUNGEON!
QUICKLY, WANDA--THIS IS OUR CHANCE! PRETEND TO FAINT--!
VERY WELL! BUT--BE CAREFUL, STEVE--!
DON'T WORRY! I'VE BEEN WORKING ON MY ROPES--THEY'RE ALMOST LOOSE ENOUGH--!
THEN...
ON YOUR FEET, WOMAN--OR I FIRE!
OHHHH--!
THIK!
NOW--WHILE THEY'VE TURNED AWAY--THERE--IT SNAPPED!
NO TIME TO WORK ON HANDCUFFS! SO LONG AS MY ARMS ARE FREE, I CAN FIGHT--!
RROOP!
THE NAME'S CAPTAIN AMERICA, MISTER! BUT YOU CAN CALL ME CAP!
LOOK OUT! THE MASKED ONE IS----UNNHHHHH!
STAND ASIDE, CARELESS FOOL! I'LL ATTEND TO HIM!

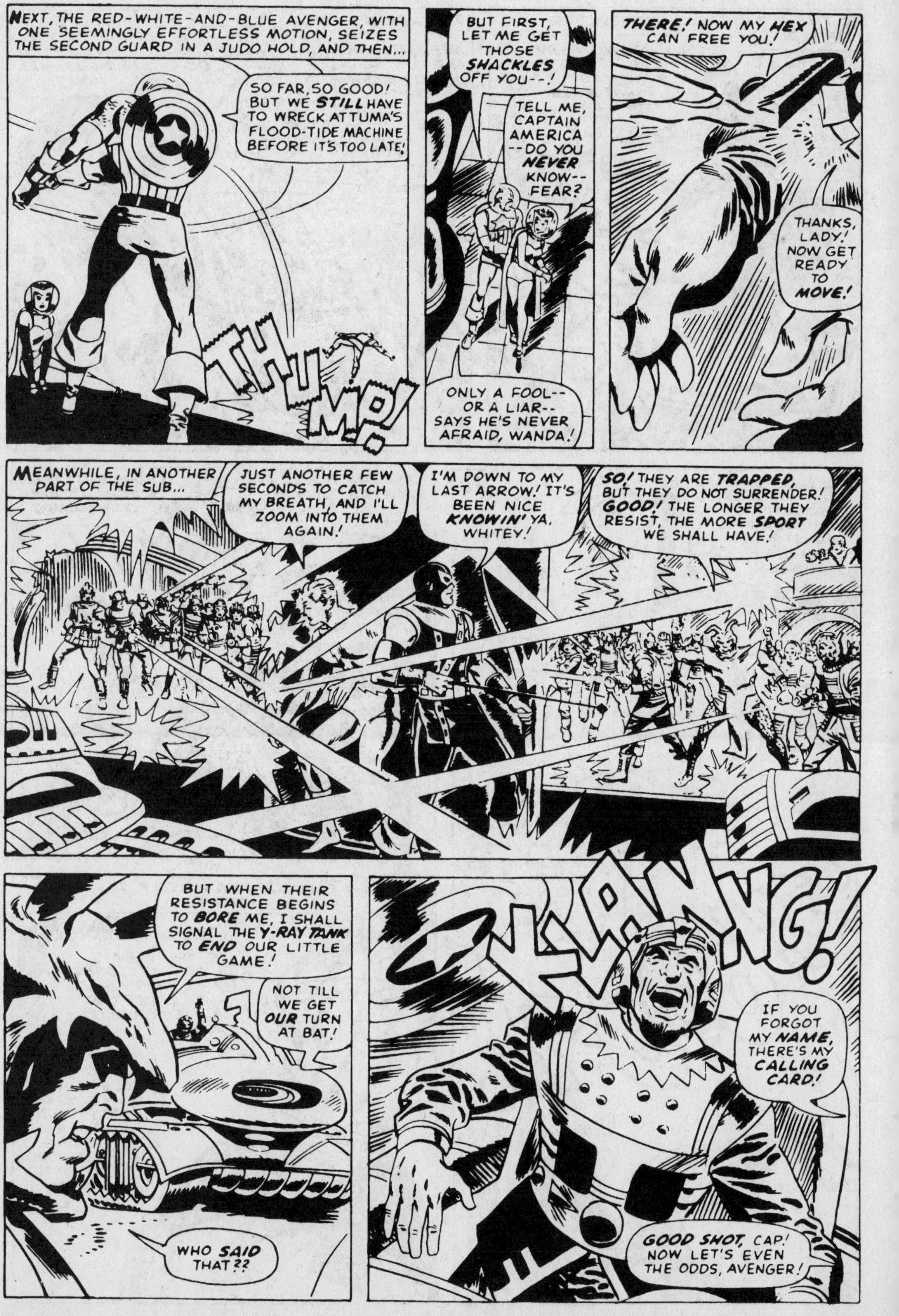
NEXT, THE RED-WHITE-AND-BLUE AVENGER, WITH ONE SEEMINGLY EFFORTLESS MOTION, SEIZES THE SECOND GUARD IN A JUDO HOLD, AND THEN...
SO FAR, SO GOOD! BUT WE STILL HAVE TO WRECK ATTUMA'S FLOOD-TIDE MACHINE BEFORE IT'S TOO LATE!
THUMP!
BUT FIRST, LET ME GET THOSE SHACKLES OFF YOU--!
TELL ME, CAPTAIN AMERICA --DO YOU NEVER KNOW-- FEAR?
ONLY A FOOL-- OR A LIAR-- SAYS HE'S NEVER AFRAID, WANDA!
THERE! NOW MY HEX CAN FREE YOU!
THANKS, LADY! NOW GET READY TO MOVE!
MEANWHILE, IN ANOTHER PART OF THE SUB...
JUST ANOTHER FEW SECONDS TO CATCH MY BREATH, AND I'LL ZOOM INTO THEM AGAIN!
I'M DOWN TO MY LAST ARROW! IT'S BEEN NICE KNOWIN' YA, WHITEY!
SO! THEY ARE TRAPPED, BUT THEY DO NOT SURRENDER! GOOD! THE LONGER THEY RESIST, THE MORE SPORT WE SHALL HAVE!
BUT WHEN THEIR RESISTANCE BEGINS TO BORE ME, I SHALL SIGNAL THE Y-RAY TANK TO END OUR LITTLE GAME!
NOT TILL WE GET OUR TURN AT BAT!
WHO SAID THAT??
KLANNG!
IF YOU FORGOT MY NAME, THERE'S MY CALLING CARD!
GOOD SHOT, CAP! NOW LET'S EVEN THE ODDS, AVENGER!

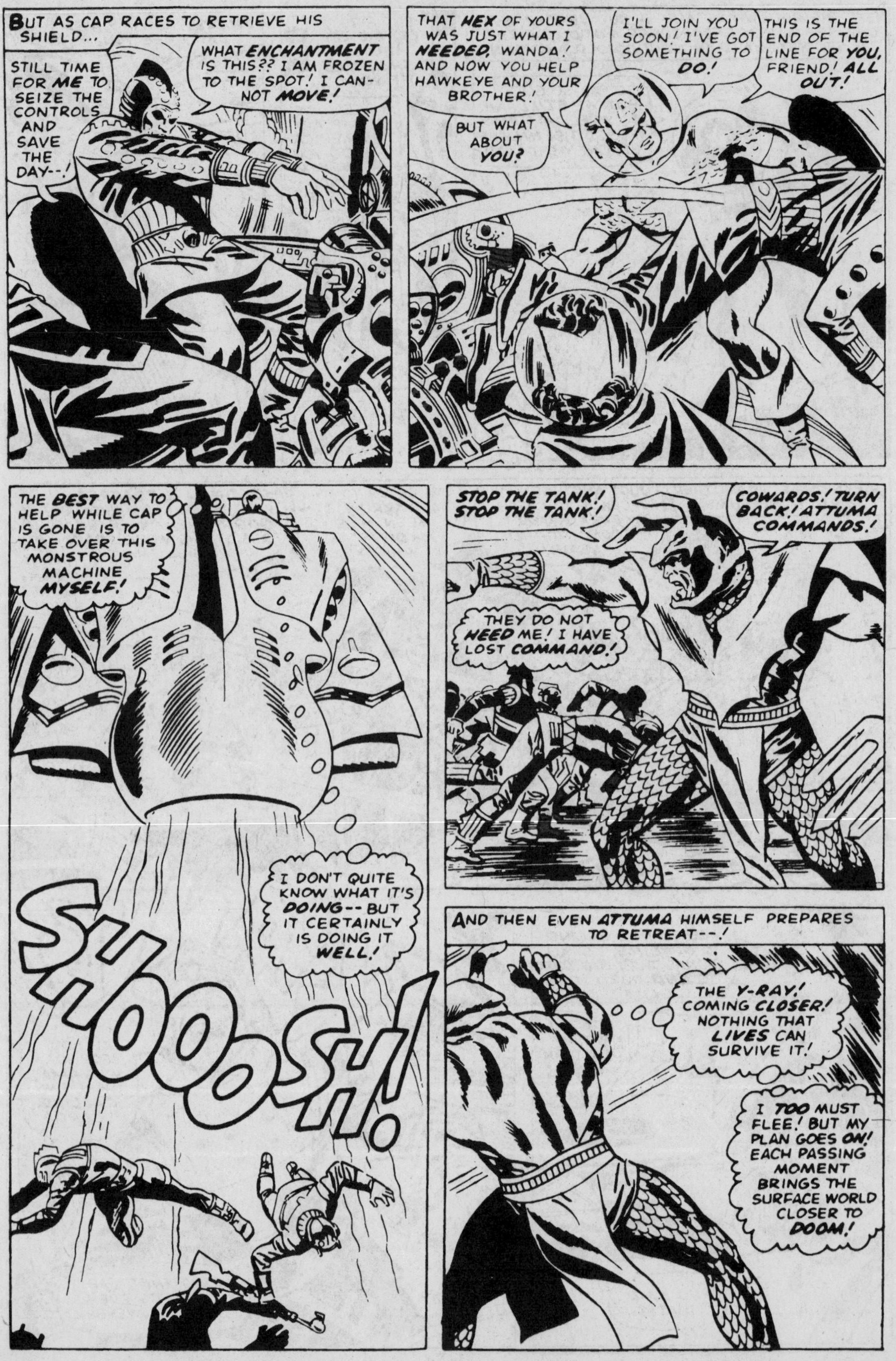
BUT AS CAP RACES TO RETRIEVE HIS SHIELD...
STILL TIME FOR ME TO SEIZE THE CONTROLS AND SAVE THE DAY--!
WHAT ENCHANTMENT IS THIS?? I AM FROZEN TO THE SPOT! I CAN-NOT MOVE!
THAT HEX OF YOURS WAS JUST WHAT I NEEDED, WANDA! AND NOW YOU HELP HAWKEYE AND YOUR BROTHER!
BUT WHAT ABOUT YOU?
I'LL JOIN YOU SOON! I'VE GOT SOMETHING TO DO!
THIS IS THE END OF THE LINE FOR YOU, FRIEND! ALL OUT!
THE BEST WAY TO HELP WHILE CAP IS GONE IS TO TAKE OVER THIS MONSTROUS MACHINE MYSELF!
I DON'T QUITE KNOW WHAT IT'S DOING-- BUT IT CERTAINLY IS DOING IT WELL!
SHOOOSH!
STOP THE TANK! STOP THE TANK!
COWARDS! TURN BACK! ATTUMA COMMANDS!
THEY DO NOT NEED ME! I HAVE LOST COMMAND!
AND THEN EVEN ATTUMA HIMSELF PREPARES TO RETREAT--!
THE Y-RAY! COMING CLOSER! NOTHING THAT LIVES CAN SURVIVE IT!
I TOO MUST FLEE! BUT MY PLAN GOES ON! EACH PASSING MOMENT BRINGS THE SURFACE WORLD CLOSER TO DOOM!

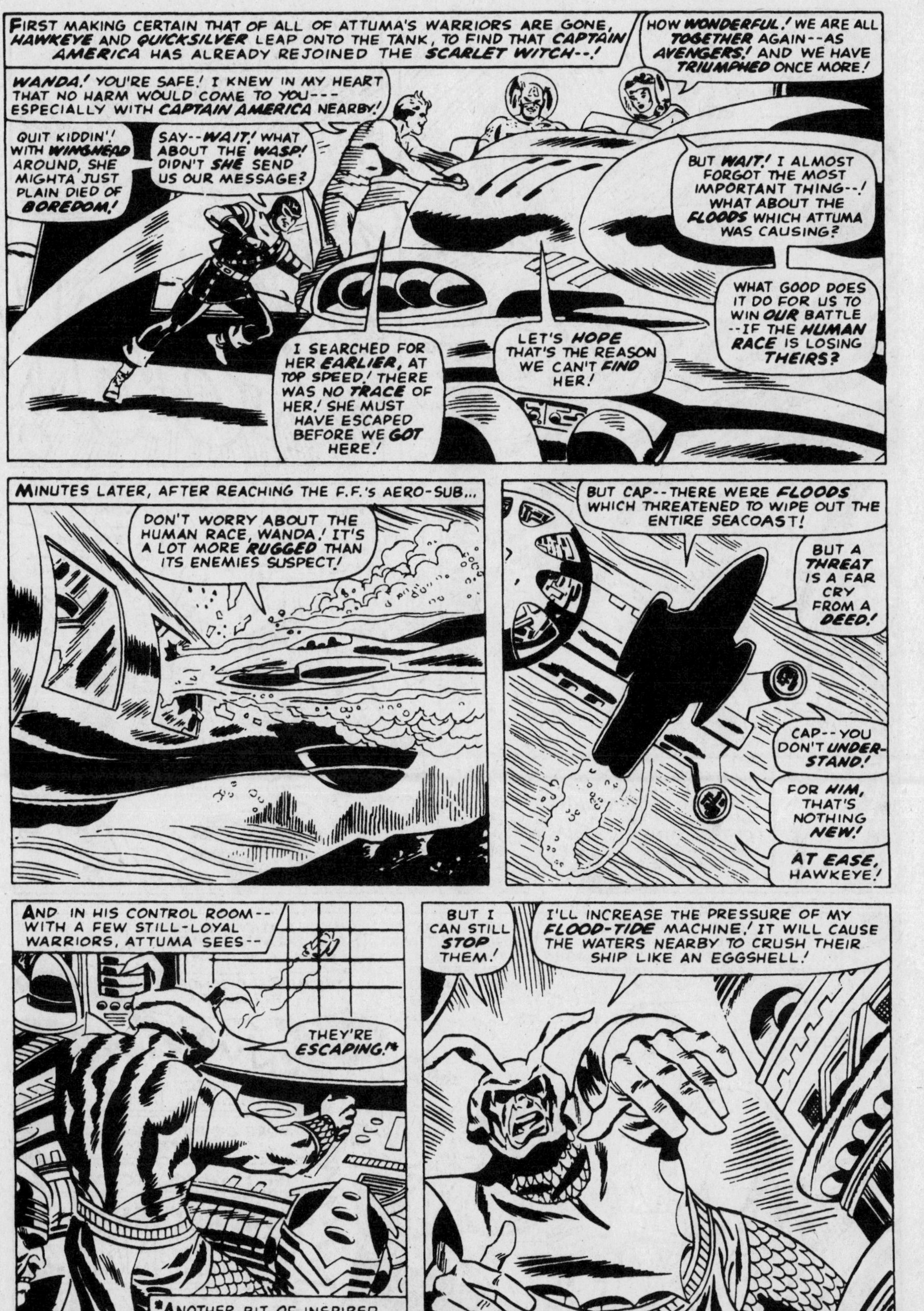
FIRST MAKING CERTAIN THAT OF ALL OF ATTUMA'S WARRIORS ARE GONE, HAWKEYE AND QUICKSILVER LEAP ONTO THE TANK, TO FIND THAT CAPTAIN AMERICA HAS ALREADY REJOINED THE SCARLET WITCH--!
HOW WONDERFUL! WE ARE ALL TOGETHER AGAIN--AS AVENGERS! AND WE HAVE TRIUMPHED ONCE MORE!
WANDA! YOU'RE SAFE! I KNEW IN MY HEART THAT NO HARM WOULD COME TO YOU--- ESPECIALLY WITH CAPTAIN AMERICA NEARBY!
QUIT KIDDIN'! WITH WINGHEAD AROUND, SHE MIGHTA JUST PLAIN DIED OF BOREDOM!
SAY--WAIT! WHAT ABOUT THE WASP! DIDN'T SHE SEND US OUR MESSAGE?
I SEARCHED FOR HER EARLIER, AT TOP SPEED! THERE WAS NO TRACE OF HER! SHE MUST HAVE ESCAPED BEFORE WE GOT HERE!
LET'S HOPE THAT'S THE REASON WE CAN'T FIND HER!
BUT WAIT! I ALMOST FORGOT THE MOST IMPORTANT THING--! WHAT ABOUT THE FLOODS WHICH ATTUMA WAS CAUSING?
WHAT GOOD DOES IT DO FOR US TO WIN OUR BATTLE --IF THE HUMAN RACE IS LOSING THEIRS?
MINUTES LATER, AFTER REACHING THE F.F.'S AERO-SUB...
DON'T WORRY ABOUT THE HUMAN RACE, WANDA! IT'S A LOT MORE RUGGED THAN ITS ENEMIES SUSPECT!
BUT CAP--THERE WERE FLOODS WHICH THREATENED TO WIPE OUT THE ENTIRE SEACOAST!
BUT A THREAT IS A FAR CRY FROM A DEED!
CAP--YOU DON'T UNDER-STAND!
FOR HIM, THAT'S NOTHING NEW!
AT EASE, HAWKEYE!
AND IN HIS CONTROL ROOM-- WITH A FEW STILL-LOYAL WARRIORS, ATTUMA SEES--
THEY'RE ESCAPING!*
*ANOTHER BIT OF INSPIRED DIALOGUE BY SLEEPY STAN!
BUT I CAN STILL STOP THEM!
I'LL INCREASE THE PRESSURE OF MY FLOOD-TIDE MACHINE! IT WILL CAUSE THE WATERS NEARBY TO CRUSH THEIR SHIP LIKE AN EGGSHELL!

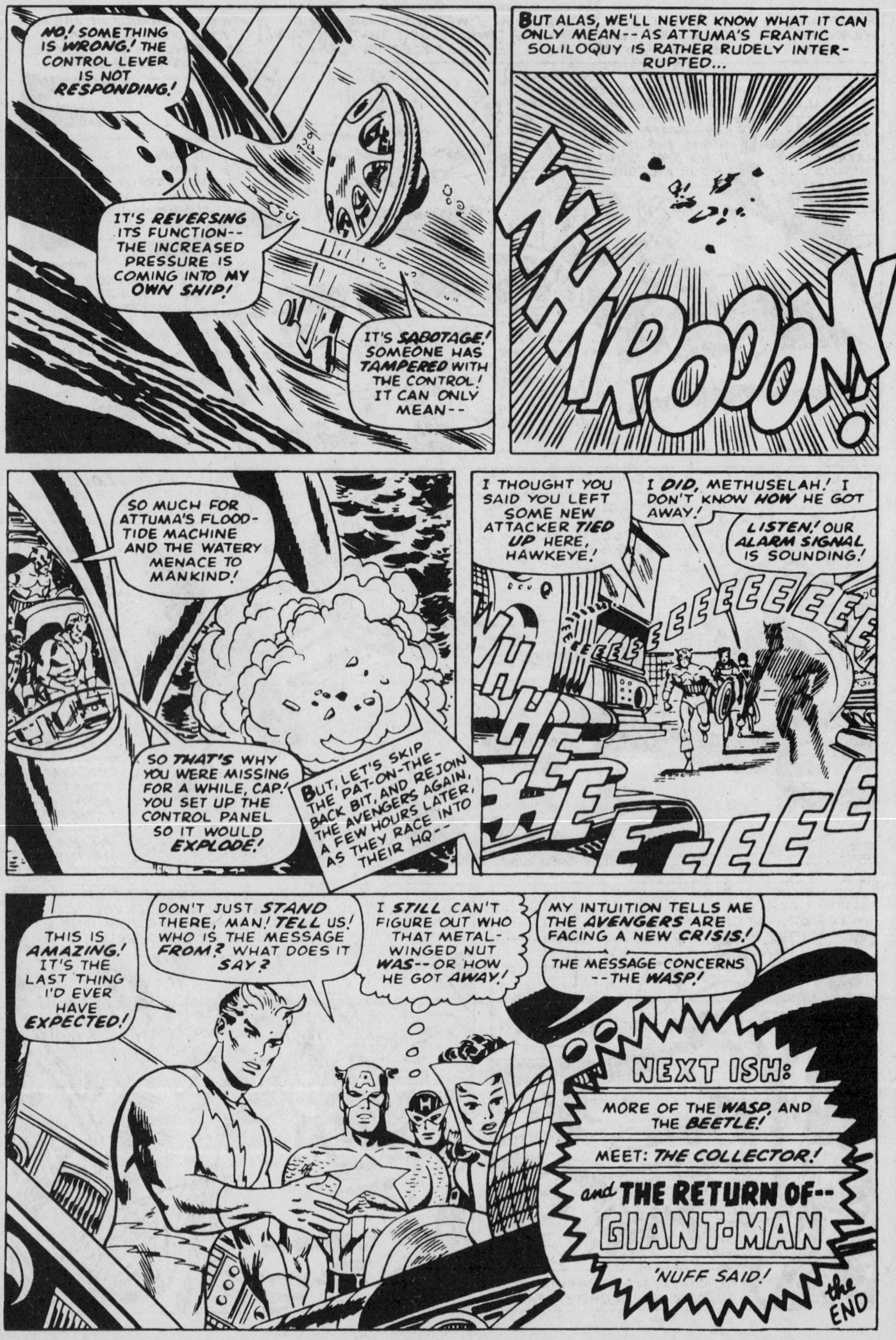
NO! SOMETHING IS WRONG! THE CONTROL LEVER IS NOT RESPONDING!
IT'S REVERSING ITS FUNCTION-- THE INCREASED PRESSURE IS COMING INTO MY OWN SHIP!
IT'S SABOTAGE! SOMEONE HAS TAMPERED WITH THE CONTROL! IT CAN ONLY MEAN--
BUT ALAS, WE'LL NEVER KNOW WHAT IT CAN ONLY MEAN--AS ATTUMA'S FRANTIC SOLILOQUY IS RATHER RUDELY INTERRUPTED...
WHROOOOM!
SO MUCH FOR ATTUMA'S FLOOD-TIDE MACHINE AND THE WATERY MENACE TO MANKIND!
SO THAT'S WHY YOU WERE MISSING FOR A WHILE, CAP! YOU SET UP THE CONTROL PANEL SO IT WOULD EXPLODE!
BUT, LET'S SKIP THE PAT-ON-THE-BACK BIT, AND REJOIN THE AVENGERS AGAIN, A FEW HOURS LATER, AS THEY RACE INTO THEIR HQ--
I THOUGHT YOU SAID YOU LEFT SOME NEW ATTACKER TIED UP HERE, HAWKEYE!
I DID, METHUSELAH! I DON'T KNOW HOW HE GOT AWAY!
LISTEN! OUR ALARM SIGNAL IS SOUNDING!
EEEEEEEEEEE
WHHEEEEEEE
THIS IS AMAZING! IT'S THE LAST THING I'D EVER HAVE EXPECTED!
DON'T JUST STAND THERE, MAN! TELL US! WHO IS THE MESSAGE FROM? WHAT DOES IT SAY?
I STILL CAN'T FIGURE OUT WHO THAT METAL-WINGED NUT WAS--OR HOW HE GOT AWAY!
MY INTUITION TELLS ME THE AVENGERS ARE FACING A NEW CRISIS!
THE MESSAGE CONCERNS --THE WASP!
NEXT ISH:
MORE OF THE WASP, AND THE BEETLE!
MEET: THE COLLECTOR!
and THE RETURN OF-- GIANT-MAN
'NUFF SAID!
the END

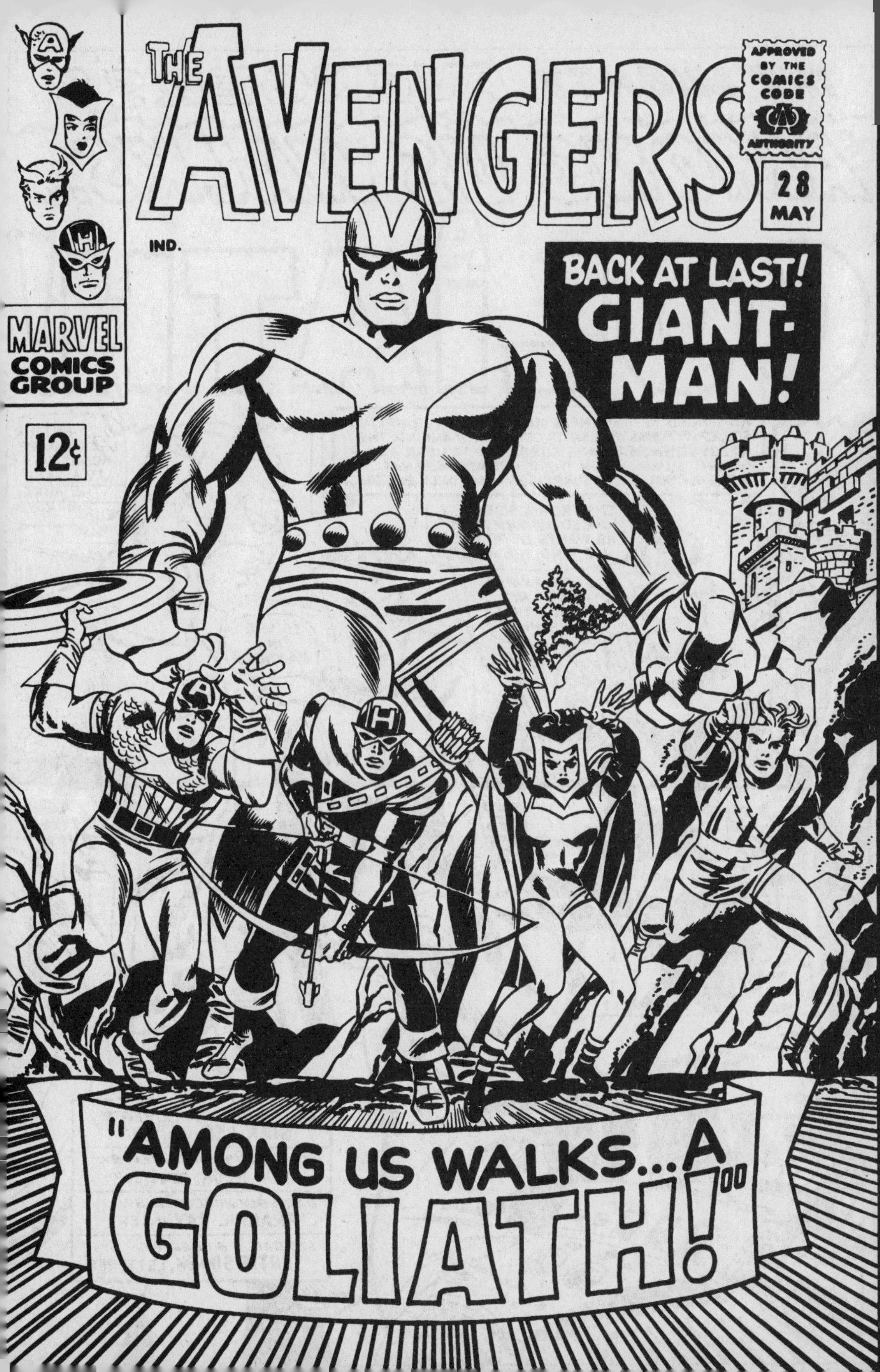
THE AVENGERS
APPROVED BY THE COMICS CODE AUTHORITY
28
MAY
IND.
MARVEL COMICS GROUP
12¢
BACK AT LAST! GIANT-MAN!
"AMONG US WALKS... A GOLIATH!"

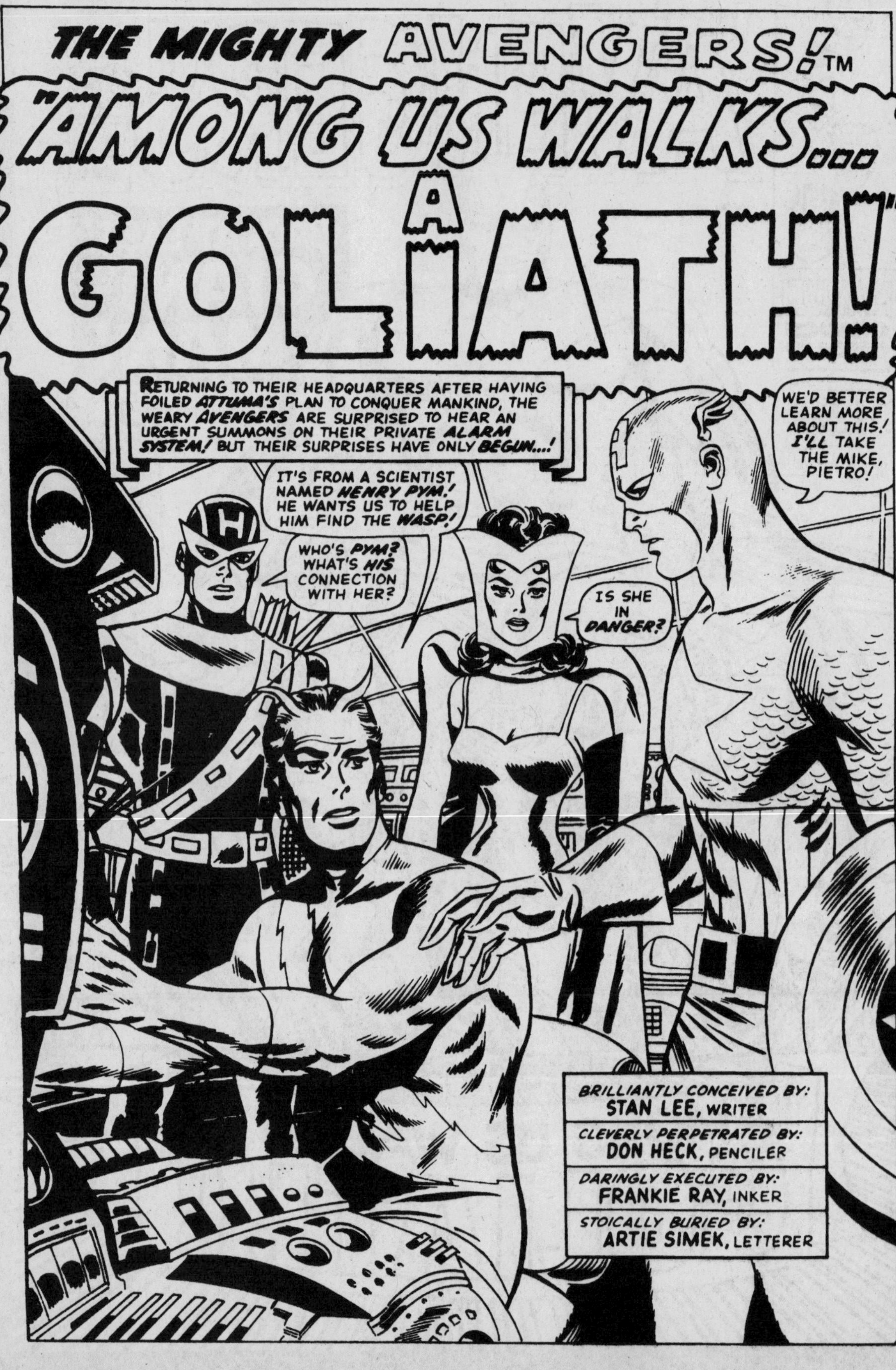
THE MIGHTY AVENGERS!™
"AMONG US WALKS... A GOLIATH!"
RETURNING TO THEIR HEADQUARTERS AFTER HAVING FOILED ATTUMA'S PLAN TO CONQUER MANKIND, THE WEARY AVENGERS ARE SURPRISED TO HEAR AN URGENT SUMMONS ON THEIR PRIVATE ALARM SYSTEM! BUT THEIR SURPRISES HAVE ONLY BEGUN...!
IT'S FROM A SCIENTIST NAMED HENRY PYM! HE WANTS US TO HELP HIM FIND THE WASP!
WHO'S PYM? WHAT'S HIS CONNECTION WITH HER?
IS SHE IN DANGER?
WE'D BETTER LEARN MORE ABOUT THIS! I'LL TAKE THE MIKE, PIETRO!
BRILLIANTLY CONCEIVED BY: STAN LEE, WRITER
CLEVERLY PERPETRATED BY: DON HECK, PENCILER
DARINGLY EXECUTED BY: FRANKIE RAY, INKER
STOICALLY BURIED BY: ARTIE SIMEK, LETTERER

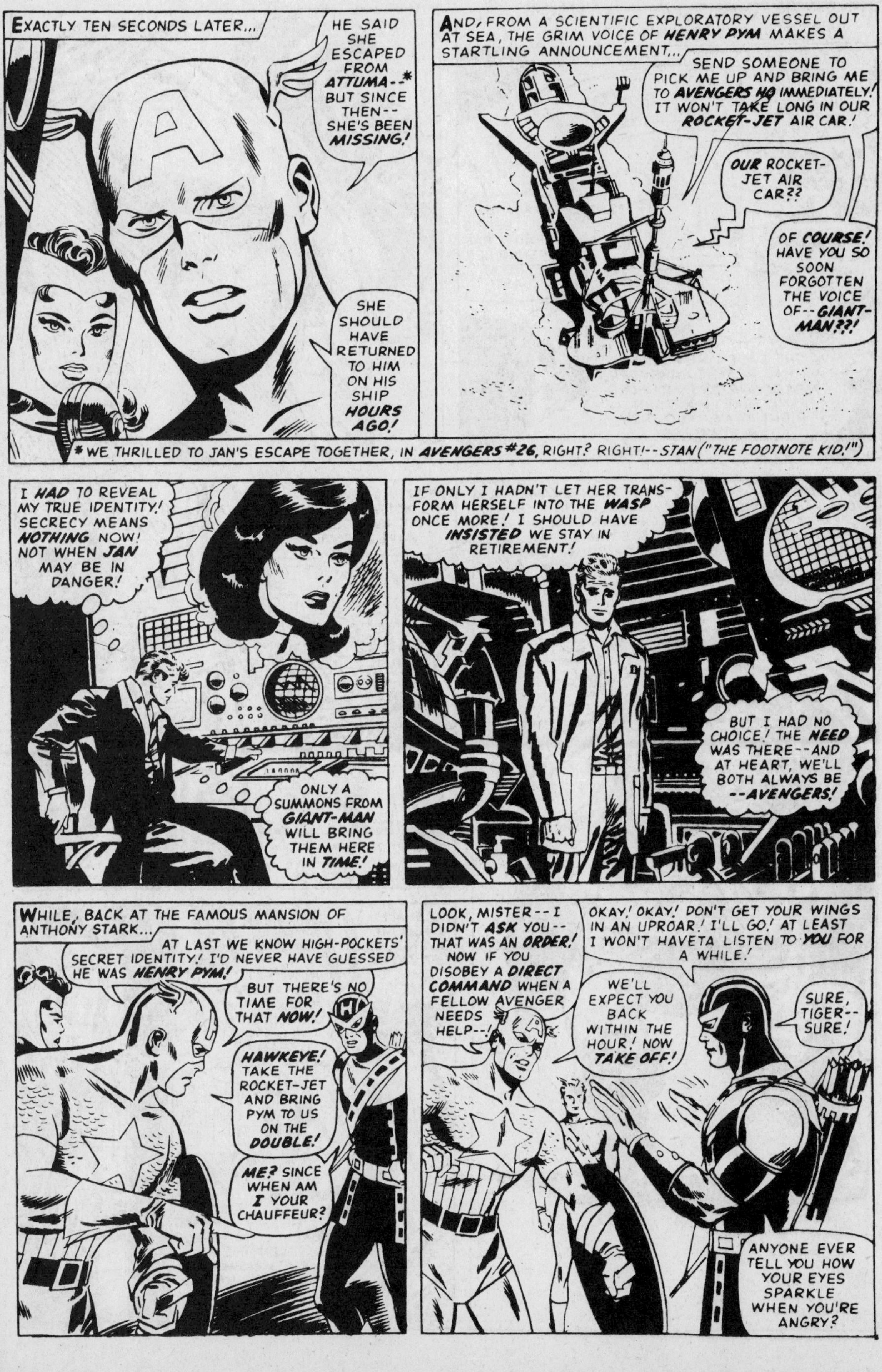
EXACTLY TEN SECONDS LATER...
HE SAID SHE ESCAPED FROM ATTUMA--* BUT SINCE THEN--SHE'S BEEN MISSING!
SHE SHOULD HAVE RETURNED TO HIM ON HIS SHIP HOURS AGO!
AND, FROM A SCIENTIFIC EXPLORATORY VESSEL OUT AT SEA, THE GRIM VOICE OF HENRY PYM MAKES A STARTLING ANNOUNCEMENT...
SEND SOMEONE TO PICK ME UP AND BRING ME TO AVENGERS HQ IMMEDIATELY! IT WON'T TAKE LONG IN OUR ROCKET-JET AIR CAR!
OUR ROCKET-JET AIR CAR??
OF COURSE! HAVE YOU SO SOON FORGOTTEN THE VOICE OF--GIANT-MAN??!
* WE THRILLED TO JAN'S ESCAPE TOGETHER, IN AVENGERS #26, RIGHT? RIGHT!--STAN ("THE FOOTNOTE KID!")
I HAD TO REVEAL MY TRUE IDENTITY! SECRECY MEANS NOTHING NOW! NOT WHEN JAN MAY BE IN DANGER!
ONLY A SUMMONS FROM GIANT-MAN WILL BRING THEM HERE IN TIME!
IF ONLY I HADN'T LET HER TRANSFORM HERSELF INTO THE WASP ONCE MORE! I SHOULD HAVE INSISTED WE STAY IN RETIREMENT!
BUT I HAD NO CHOICE! THE NEED WAS THERE--AND AT HEART, WE'LL BOTH ALWAYS BE --AVENGERS!
WHILE, BACK AT THE FAMOUS MANSION OF ANTHONY STARK...
AT LAST WE KNOW HIGH-POCKETS' SECRET IDENTITY! I'D NEVER HAVE GUESSED HE WAS HENRY PYM!
BUT THERE'S NO TIME FOR THAT NOW!
HAWKEYE! TAKE THE ROCKET-JET AND BRING PYM TO US ON THE DOUBLE!
ME? SINCE WHEN AM I YOUR CHAUFFEUR?
LOOK, MISTER--I DIDN'T ASK YOU--THAT WAS AN ORDER! NOW IF YOU DISOBEY A DIRECT COMMAND WHEN A FELLOW AVENGER NEEDS HELP--!
OKAY! OKAY! DON'T GET YOUR WINGS IN AN UPROAR! I'LL GO! AT LEAST I WON'T HAVETA LISTEN TO YOU FOR A WHILE!
WE'LL EXPECT YOU BACK WITHIN THE HOUR! NOW TAKE OFF!
SURE, TIGER--SURE!
ANYONE EVER TELL YOU HOW YOUR EYES SPARKLE WHEN YOU'RE ANGRY?

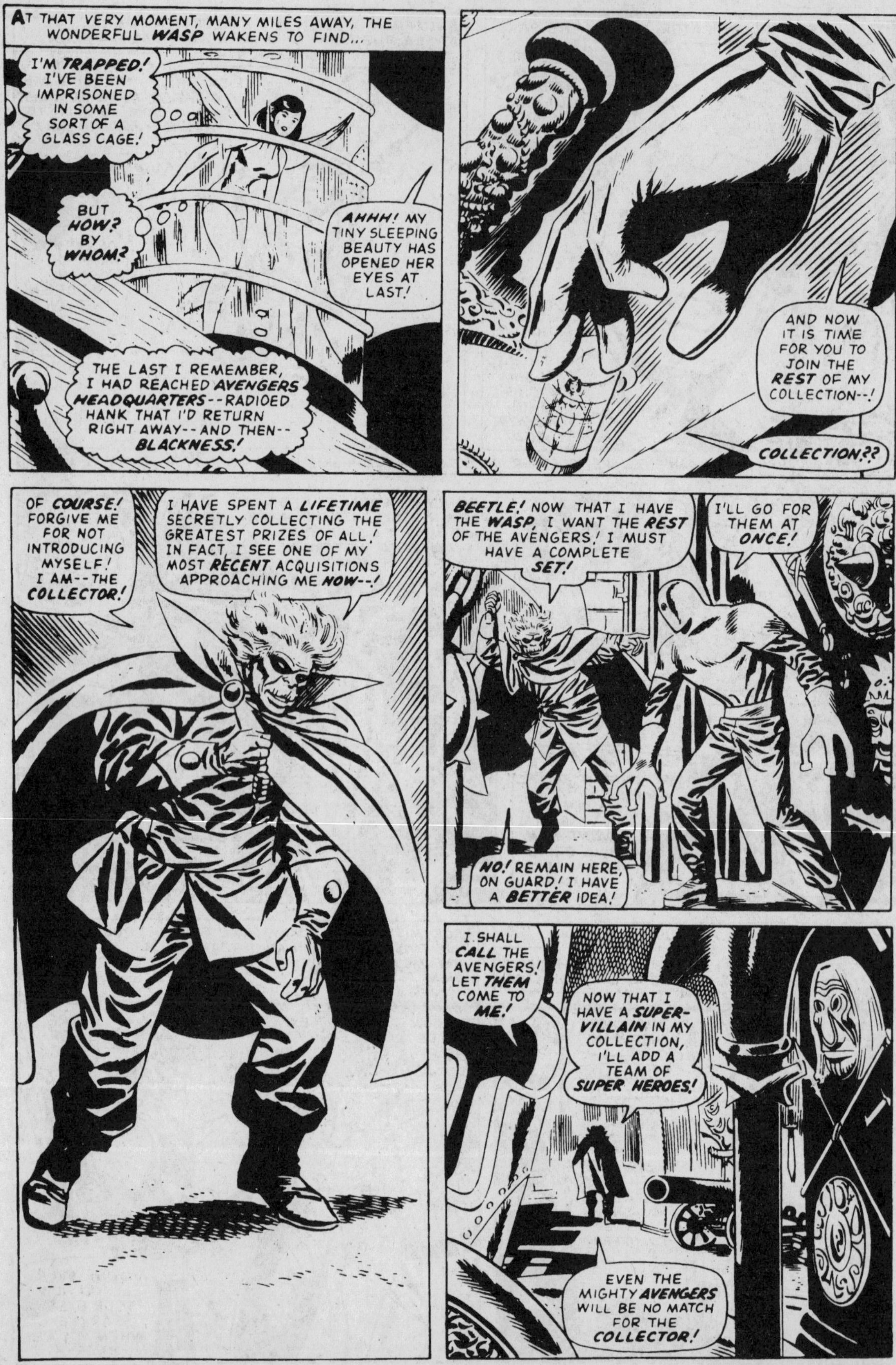

AT THAT VERY MOMENT, MANY MILES AWAY, THE WONDERFUL WASP WAKENS TO FIND...
I'M TRAPPED! I'VE BEEN IMPRISONED IN SOME SORT OF A GLASS CAGE!
BUT HOW? BY WHOM?
AHHH! MY TINY SLEEPING BEAUTY HAS OPENED HER EYES AT LAST!
THE LAST I REMEMBER, I HAD REACHED AVENGERS HEADQUARTERS--RADIOED HANK THAT I'D RETURN RIGHT AWAY--AND THEN--BLACKNESS!
AND NOW IT IS TIME FOR YOU TO JOIN THE REST OF MY COLLECTION--!
COLLECTION??
OF COURSE! FORGIVE ME FOR NOT INTRODUCING MYSELF! I AM--THE COLLECTOR!
I HAVE SPENT A LIFETIME SECRETLY COLLECTING THE GREATEST PRIZES OF ALL! IN FACT, I SEE ONE OF MY MOST RECENT ACQUISITIONS APPROACHING ME NOW--!
BEETLE! NOW THAT I HAVE THE WASP, I WANT THE REST OF THE AVENGERS! I MUST HAVE A COMPLETE SET!
I'LL GO FOR THEM AT ONCE!
NO! REMAIN HERE, ON GUARD! I HAVE A BETTER IDEA!
I SHALL CALL THE AVENGERS! LET THEM COME TO ME!
NOW THAT I HAVE A SUPER-VILLAIN IN MY COLLECTION, I'LL ADD A TEAM OF SUPER HEROES!
EVEN THE MIGHTY AVENGERS WILL BE NO MATCH FOR THE COLLECTOR!

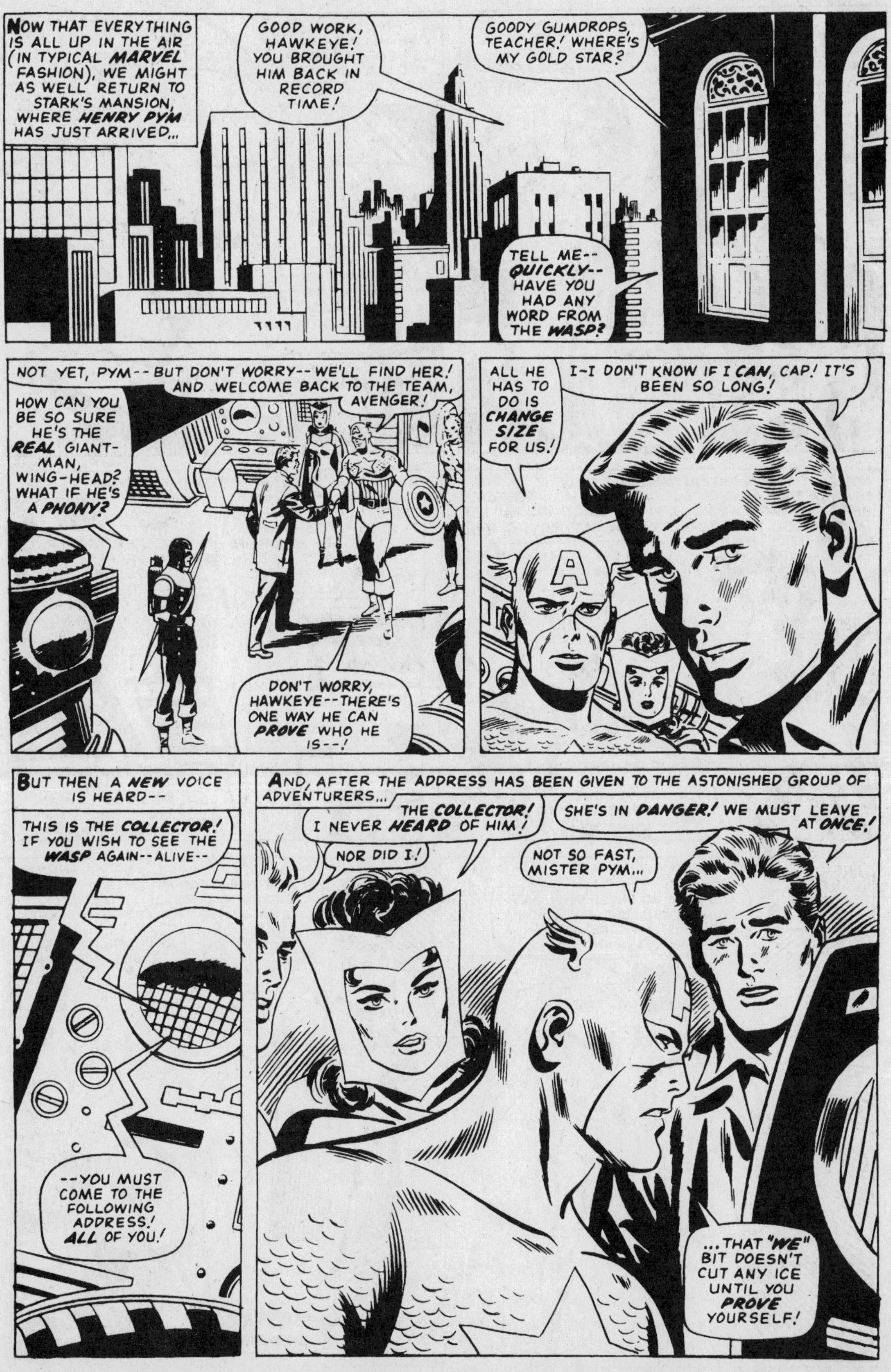
NOW THAT EVERYTHING IS ALL UP IN THE AIR (IN TYPICAL MARVEL FASHION), WE MIGHT AS WELL RETURN TO STARK'S MANSION, WHERE HENRY PYM HAS JUST ARRIVED...
GOOD WORK, HAWKEYE! YOU BROUGHT HIM BACK IN RECORD TIME!
GOODY GUMDROPS, TEACHER! WHERE'S MY GOLD STAR?
TELL ME--QUICKLY--HAVE YOU HAD ANY WORD FROM THE WASP?
NOT YET, PYM--BUT DON'T WORRY--WE'LL FIND HER! AND WELCOME BACK TO THE TEAM, AVENGER!
HOW CAN YOU BE SO SURE HE'S THE REAL GIANT-MAN, WING-HEAD? WHAT IF HE'S A PHONY?
DON'T WORRY, HAWKEYE--THERE'S ONE WAY HE CAN PROVE WHO HE IS--!
ALL HE HAS TO DO IS CHANGE SIZE FOR US!
I-I DON'T KNOW IF I CAN, CAP! IT'S BEEN SO LONG!
BUT THEN A NEW VOICE IS HEARD--
THIS IS THE COLLECTOR! IF YOU WISH TO SEE THE WASP AGAIN--ALIVE--
--YOU MUST COME TO THE FOLLOWING ADDRESS! ALL OF YOU!
AND, AFTER THE ADDRESS HAS BEEN GIVEN TO THE ASTONISHED GROUP OF ADVENTURERS...
THE COLLECTOR! I NEVER HEARD OF HIM!
NOR DID I!
SHE'S IN DANGER! WE MUST LEAVE AT ONCE!
NOT SO FAST, MISTER PYM...
...THAT "WE" BIT DOESN'T CUT ANY ICE UNTIL YOU PROVE YOURSELF!

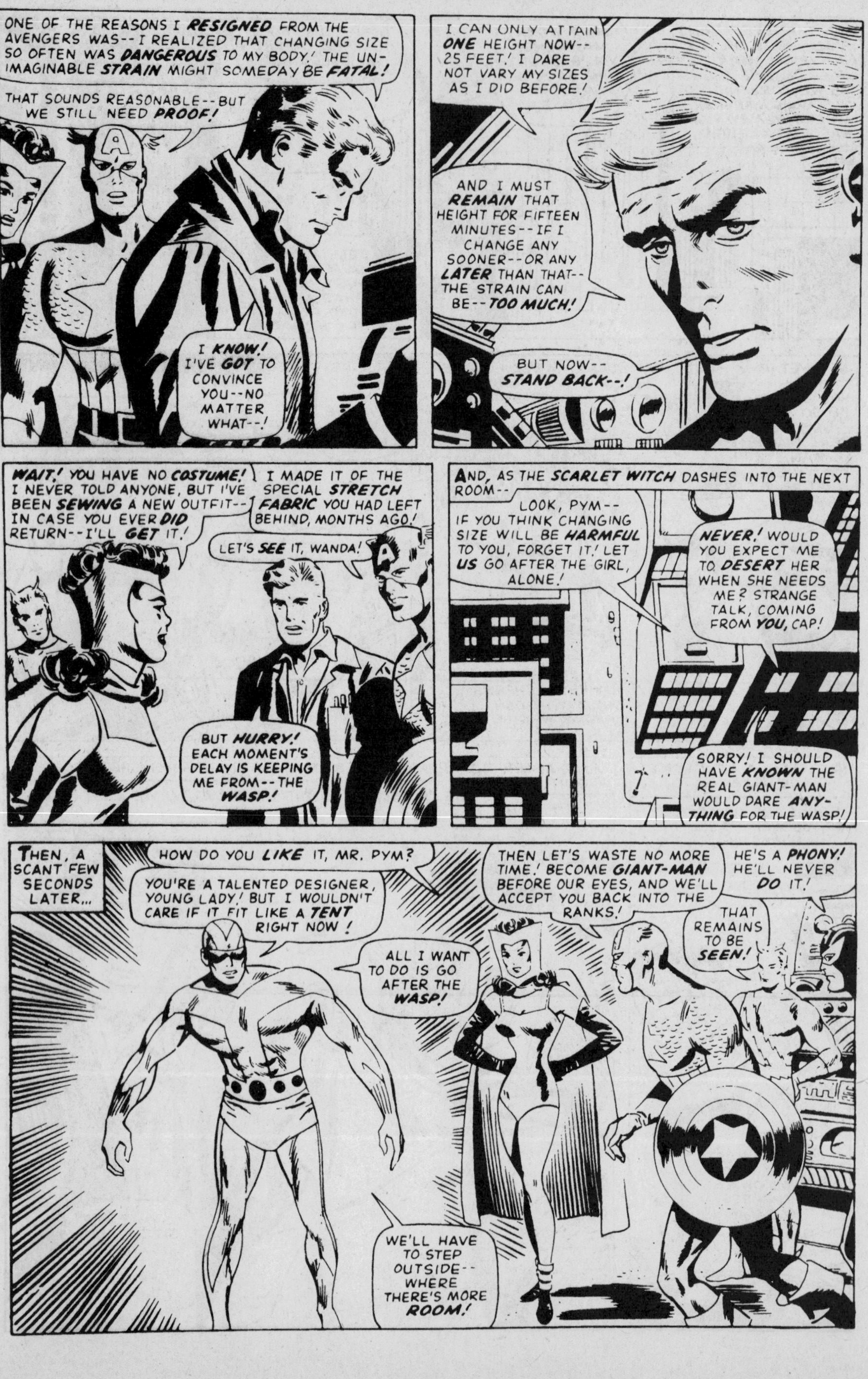

ONE OF THE REASONS I RESIGNED FROM THE AVENGERS WAS--I REALIZED THAT CHANGING SIZE SO OFTEN WAS DANGEROUS TO MY BODY! THE UNIMAGINABLE STRAIN MIGHT SOMEDAY BE FATAL!
THAT SOUNDS REASONABLE--BUT WE STILL NEED PROOF!
I KNOW! I'VE GOT TO CONVINCE YOU--NO MATTER WHAT--!
I CAN ONLY ATTAIN ONE HEIGHT NOW--25 FEET! I DARE NOT VARY MY SIZES AS I DID BEFORE!
AND I MUST REMAIN THAT HEIGHT FOR FIFTEEN MINUTES--IF I CHANGE ANY SOONER--OR ANY LATER THAN THAT--THE STRAIN CAN BE--TOO MUCH!
BUT NOW--STAND BACK--!
WAIT! YOU HAVE NO COSTUME! I NEVER TOLD ANYONE, BUT I'VE BEEN SEWING A NEW OUTFIT--IN CASE YOU EVER DID RETURN--I'LL GET IT!
I MADE IT OF THE SPECIAL STRETCH FABRIC YOU HAD LEFT BEHIND, MONTHS AGO!
LET'S SEE IT, WANDA!
BUT HURRY! EACH MOMENT'S DELAY IS KEEPING ME FROM--THE WASP!
AND, AS THE SCARLET WITCH DASHES INTO THE NEXT ROOM--
LOOK, PYM--IF YOU THINK CHANGING SIZE WILL BE HARMFUL TO YOU, FORGET IT! LET US GO AFTER THE GIRL, ALONE!
NEVER! WOULD YOU EXPECT ME TO DESERT HER WHEN SHE NEEDS ME? STRANGE TALK, COMING FROM YOU, CAP!
SORRY! I SHOULD HAVE KNOWN THE REAL GIANT-MAN WOULD DARE ANYTHING FOR THE WASP!
THEN, A SCANT FEW SECONDS LATER...
HOW DO YOU LIKE IT, MR. PYM?
YOU'RE A TALENTED DESIGNER, YOUNG LADY! BUT I WOULDN'T CARE IF IT FIT LIKE A TENT RIGHT NOW!
ALL I WANT TO DO IS GO AFTER THE WASP!
WE'LL HAVE TO STEP OUTSIDE--WHERE THERE'S MORE ROOM!
THEN LET'S WASTE NO MORE TIME! BECOME GIANT-MAN BEFORE OUR EYES, AND WE'LL ACCEPT YOU BACK INTO THE RANKS!
HE'S A PHONY! HE'LL NEVER DO IT!
THAT REMAINS TO BE SEEN!

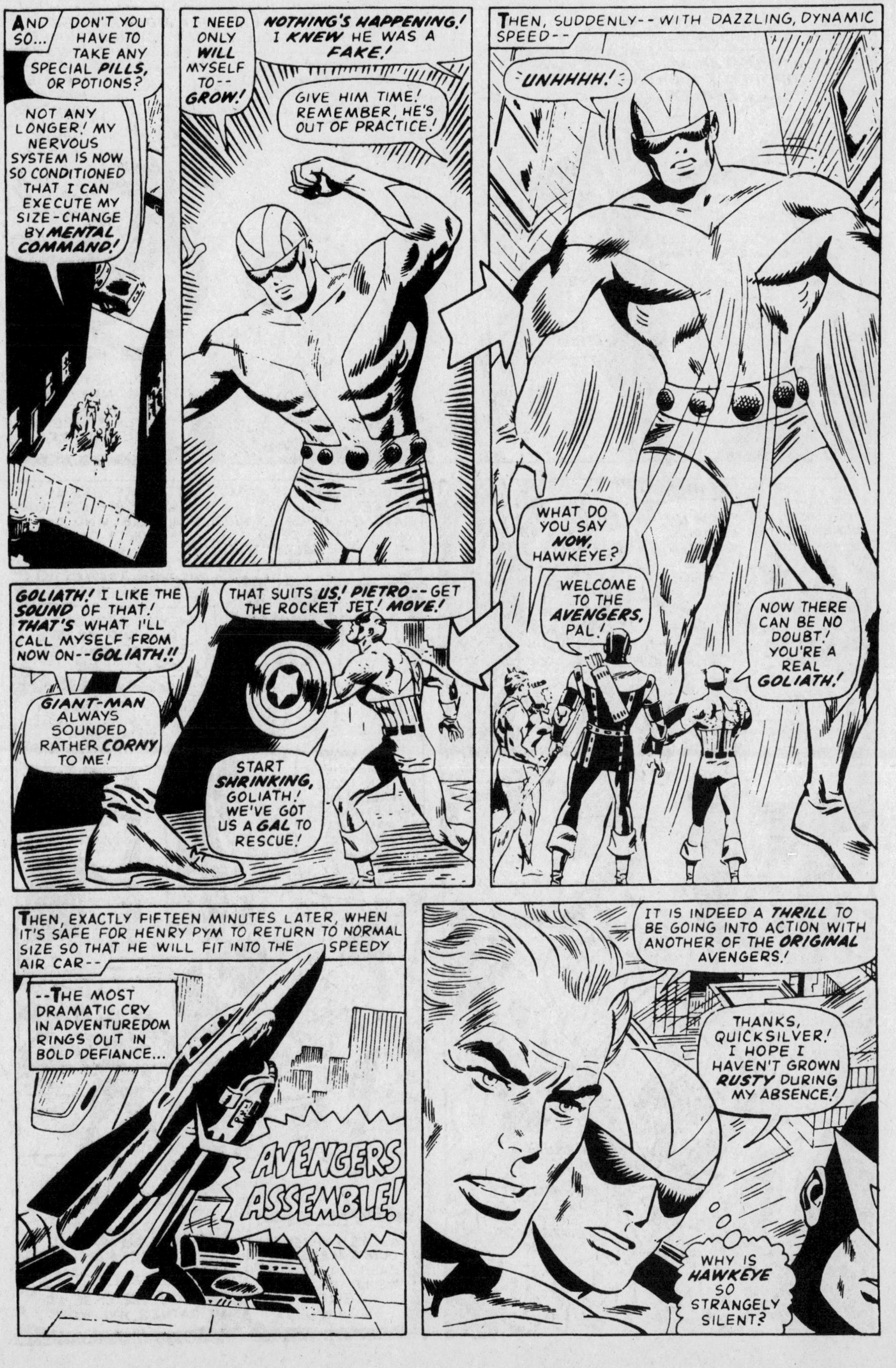
AND SO...
DON'T YOU HAVE TO TAKE ANY SPECIAL PILLS, OR POTIONS?
NOT ANY LONGER! MY NERVOUS SYSTEM IS NOW SO CONDITIONED THAT I CAN EXECUTE MY SIZE-CHANGE BY MENTAL COMMAND!
I NEED ONLY WILL MYSELF TO--GROW!
NOTHING'S HAPPENING! I KNEW HE WAS A FAKE!
GIVE HIM TIME! REMEMBER, HE'S OUT OF PRACTICE!
THEN, SUDDENLY--WITH DAZZLING, DYNAMIC SPEED--
UNHHHH!
WHAT DO YOU SAY NOW, HAWKEYE?
WELCOME TO THE AVENGERS, PAL!
NOW THERE CAN BE NO DOUBT! YOU'RE A REAL GOLIATH!
GOLIATH! I LIKE THE SOUND OF THAT! THAT'S WHAT I'LL CALL MYSELF FROM NOW ON--GOLIATH!!
GIANT-MAN ALWAYS SOUNDED RATHER CORNY TO ME!
THAT SUITS US! PIETRO--GET THE ROCKET JET! MOVE!
START SHRINKING, GOLIATH! WE'VE GOT US A GAL TO RESCUE!
THEN, EXACTLY FIFTEEN MINUTES LATER, WHEN IT'S SAFE FOR HENRY PYM TO RETURN TO NORMAL SIZE SO THAT HE WILL FIT INTO THE SPEEDY AIR CAR--
--THE MOST DRAMATIC CRY IN ADVENTUREDOM RINGS OUT IN BOLD DEFIANCE...
AVENGERS ASSEMBLE!
IT IS INDEED A THRILL TO BE GOING INTO ACTION WITH ANOTHER OF THE ORIGINAL AVENGERS!
THANKS, QUICKSILVER! I HOPE I HAVEN'T GROWN RUSTY DURING MY ABSENCE!
WHY IS HAWKEYE SO STRANGELY SILENT?

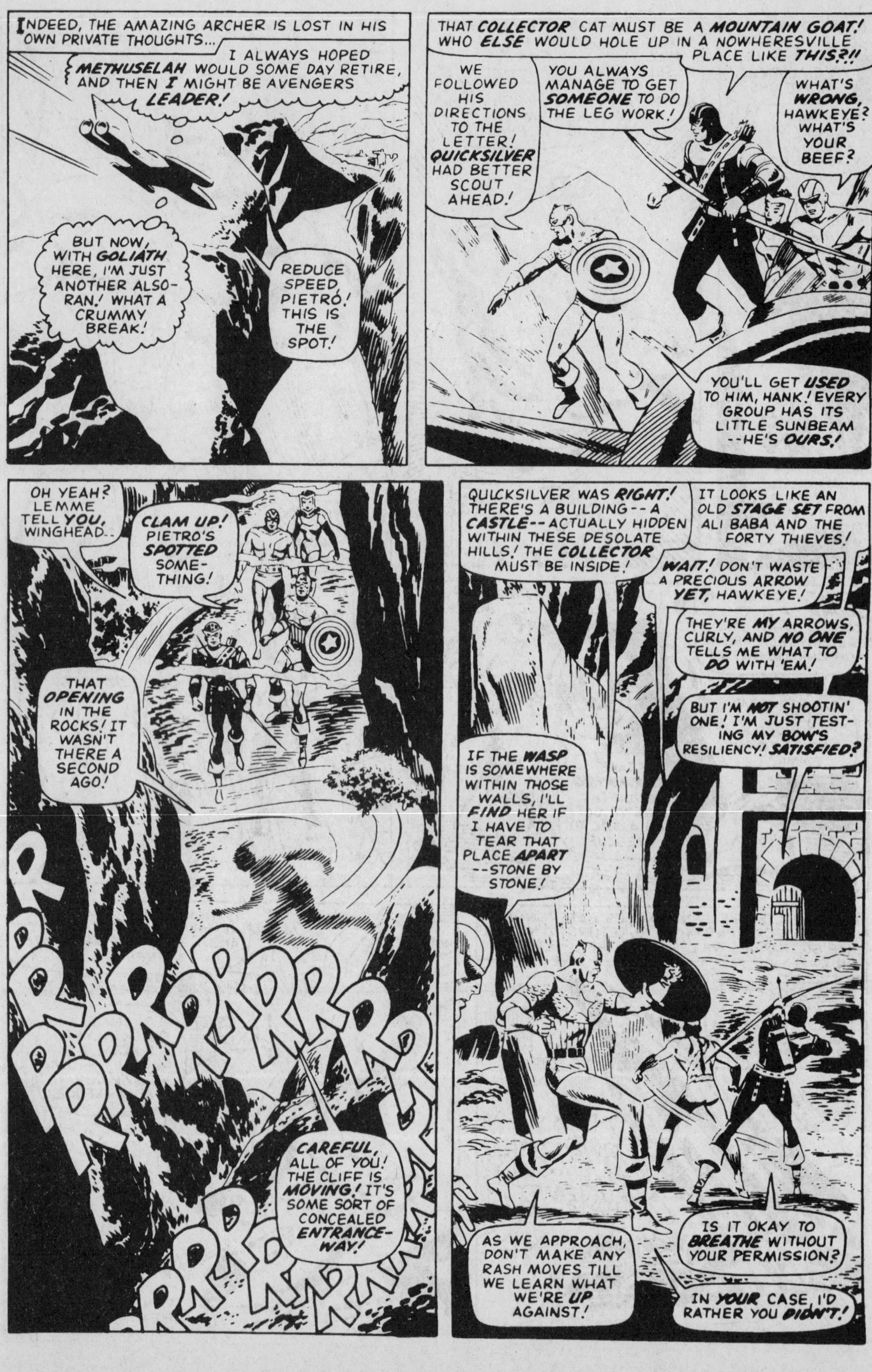
INDEED, THE AMAZING ARCHER IS LOST IN HIS OWN PRIVATE THOUGHTS...
I ALWAYS HOPED METHUSELAH WOULD SOME DAY RETIRE, AND THEN I MIGHT BE AVENGERS LEADER!
BUT NOW, WITH GOLIATH HERE, I'M JUST ANOTHER ALSO-RAN! WHAT A CRUMMY BREAK!
REDUCE SPEED PIETRO! THIS IS THE SPOT!
THAT COLLECTOR CAT MUST BE A MOUNTAIN GOAT! WHO ELSE WOULD HOLE UP IN A NOWHERESVILLE PLACE LIKE THIS?!!
WE FOLLOWED HIS DIRECTIONS TO THE LETTER! QUICKSILVER HAD BETTER SCOUT AHEAD!
YOU ALWAYS MANAGE TO GET SOMEONE TO DO THE LEG WORK!
WHAT'S WRONG, HAWKEYE? WHAT'S YOUR BEEF?
YOU'LL GET USED TO HIM, HANK! EVERY GROUP HAS ITS LITTLE SUNBEAM --HE'S OURS!
OH YEAH? LEMME TELL YOU, WINGHEAD...
CLAM UP! PIETRO'S SPOTTED SOMETHING!
THAT OPENING IN THE ROCKS! IT WASN'T THERE A SECOND AGO!
CAREFUL, ALL OF YOU! THE CLIFF IS MOVING! IT'S SOME SORT OF CONCEALED ENTRANCE-WAY!
QUICKSILVER WAS RIGHT! THERE'S A BUILDING-- A CASTLE-- ACTUALLY HIDDEN WITHIN THESE DESOLATE HILLS! THE COLLECTOR MUST BE INSIDE!
IT LOOKS LIKE AN OLD STAGE SET FROM ALI BABA AND THE FORTY THIEVES!
WAIT! DON'T WASTE A PRECIOUS ARROW YET, HAWKEYE!
THEY'RE MY ARROWS, CURLY, AND NO ONE TELLS ME WHAT TO DO WITH 'EM!
BUT I'M NOT SHOOTIN' ONE! I'M JUST TESTING MY BOW'S RESILIENCY! SATISFIED?
IF THE WASP IS SOMEWHERE WITHIN THOSE WALLS, I'LL FIND HER IF I HAVE TO TEAR THAT PLACE APART --STONE BY STONE!
AS WE APPROACH, DON'T MAKE ANY RASH MOVES TILL WE LEARN WHAT WE'RE UP AGAINST!
IS IT OKAY TO BREATHE WITHOUT YOUR PERMISSION?
IN YOUR CASE, I'D RATHER YOU DIDN'T!

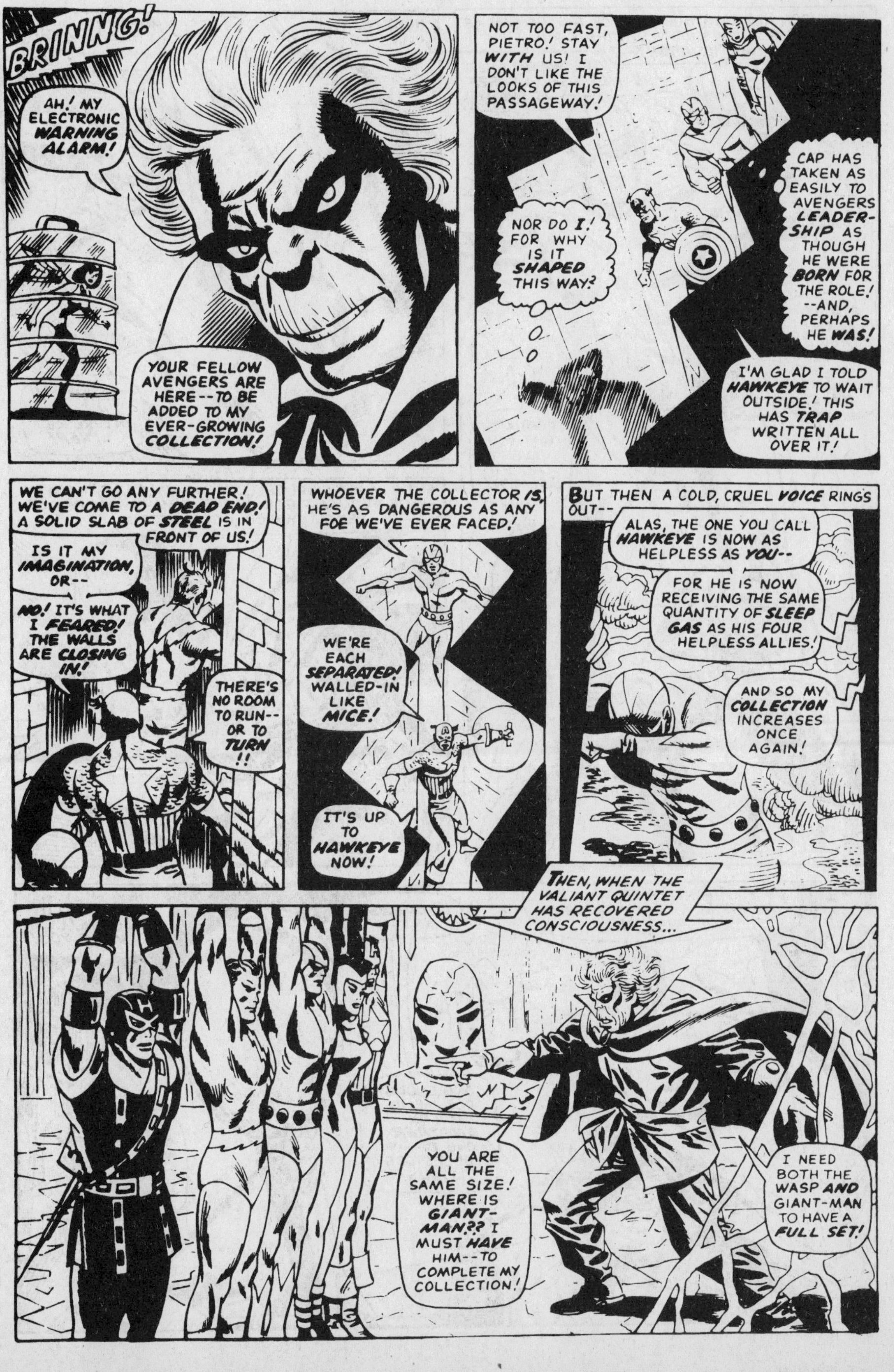
BRINNG!
AH! MY ELECTRONIC WARNING ALARM!
YOUR FELLOW AVENGERS ARE HERE--TO BE ADDED TO MY EVER-GROWING COLLECTION!
NOT TOO FAST, PIETRO! STAY WITH US! I DON'T LIKE THE LOOKS OF THIS PASSAGEWAY!
NOR DO I! FOR WHY IS IT SHAPED THIS WAY?
CAP HAS TAKEN AS EASILY TO AVENGERS LEADER-SHIP AS THOUGH HE WERE BORN FOR THE ROLE! --AND, PERHAPS HE WAS!
I'M GLAD I TOLD HAWKEYE TO WAIT OUTSIDE! THIS HAS TRAP WRITTEN ALL OVER IT!
WE CAN'T GO ANY FURTHER! WE'VE COME TO A DEAD END! A SOLID SLAB OF STEEL IS IN FRONT OF US!
IS IT MY IMAGINATION, OR--
NO! IT'S WHAT I FEARED! THE WALLS ARE CLOSING IN!
THERE'S NO ROOM TO RUN--OR TO TURN!!
WHOEVER THE COLLECTOR IS, HE'S AS DANGEROUS AS ANY FOE WE'VE EVER FACED!
WE'RE EACH SEPARATED! WALLED-IN LIKE MICE!
IT'S UP TO HAWKEYE NOW!
BUT THEN A COLD, CRUEL VOICE RINGS OUT--
ALAS, THE ONE YOU CALL HAWKEYE IS NOW AS HELPLESS AS YOU--
FOR HE IS NOW RECEIVING THE SAME QUANTITY OF SLEEP GAS AS HIS FOUR HELPLESS ALLIES!
AND SO MY COLLECTION INCREASES ONCE AGAIN!
THEN, WHEN THE VALIANT QUINTET HAS RECOVERED CONSCIOUSNESS...
YOU ARE ALL THE SAME SIZE! WHERE IS GIANT-MAN?? I MUST HAVE HIM--TO COMPLETE MY COLLECTION!
I NEED BOTH THE WASP AND GIANT-MAN TO HAVE A FULL SET!

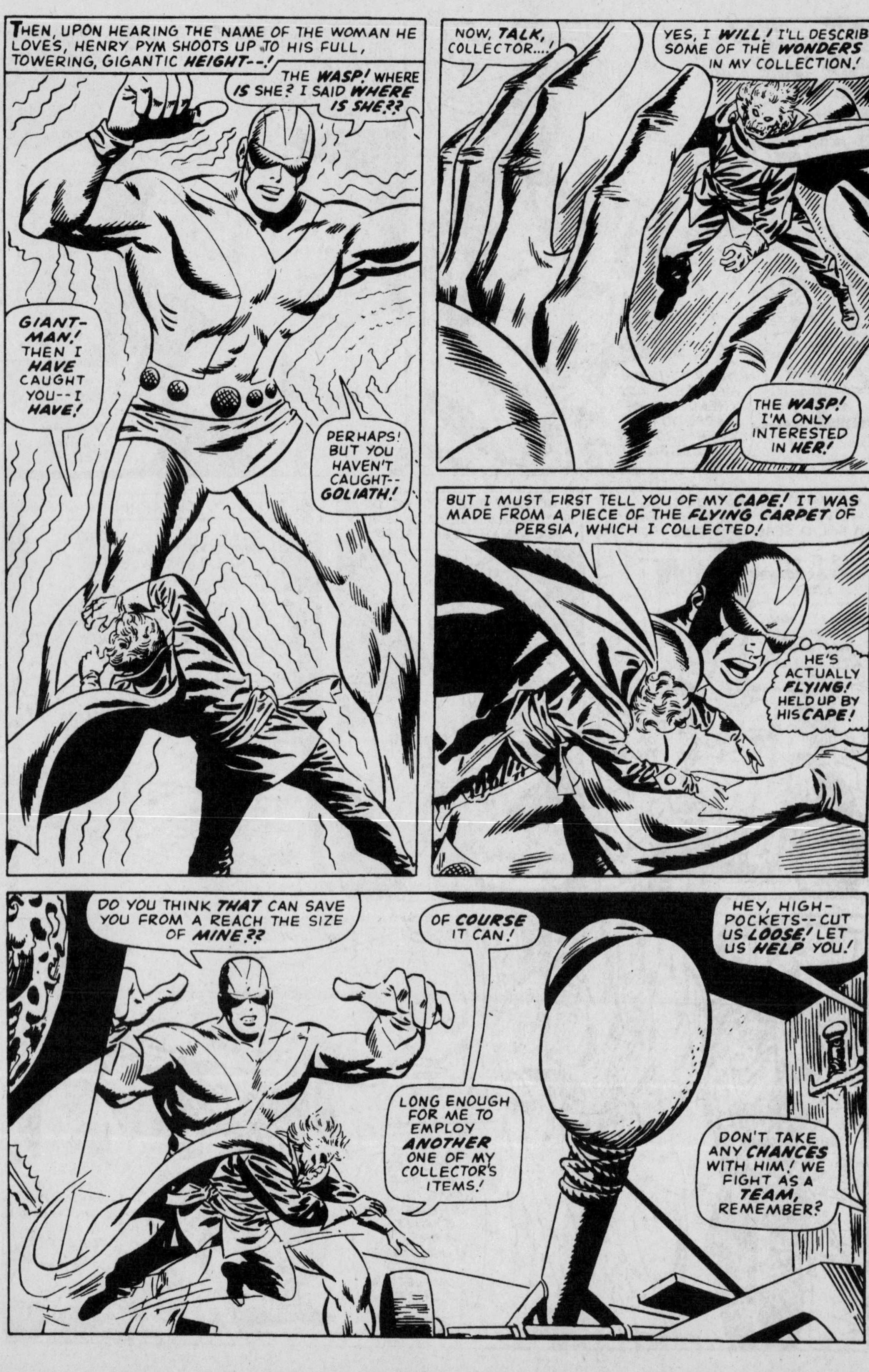
THEN, UPON HEARING THE NAME OF THE WOMAN HE LOVES, HENRY PYM SHOOTS UP TO HIS FULL, TOWERING, GIGANTIC HEIGHT--!
THE WASP! WHERE IS SHE? I SAID WHERE IS SHE??
GIANT-MAN! THEN I HAVE CAUGHT YOU--I HAVE!
PERHAPS! BUT YOU HAVEN'T CAUGHT--GOLIATH!
NOW, TALK, COLLECTOR...!
YES, I WILL! I'LL DESCRIBE SOME OF THE WONDERS IN MY COLLECTION!
THE WASP! I'M ONLY INTERESTED IN HER!
BUT I MUST FIRST TELL YOU OF MY CAPE! IT WAS MADE FROM A PIECE OF THE FLYING CARPET OF PERSIA, WHICH I COLLECTED!
HE'S ACTUALLY FLYING! HELD UP BY HIS CAPE!
DO YOU THINK THAT CAN SAVE YOU FROM A REACH THE SIZE OF MINE??
OF COURSE IT CAN!
LONG ENOUGH FOR ME TO EMPLOY ANOTHER ONE OF MY COLLECTOR'S ITEMS!
HEY, HIGH-POCKETS--CUT US LOOSE! LET US HELP YOU!
DON'T TAKE ANY CHANCES WITH HIM! WE FIGHT AS A TEAM, REMEMBER?

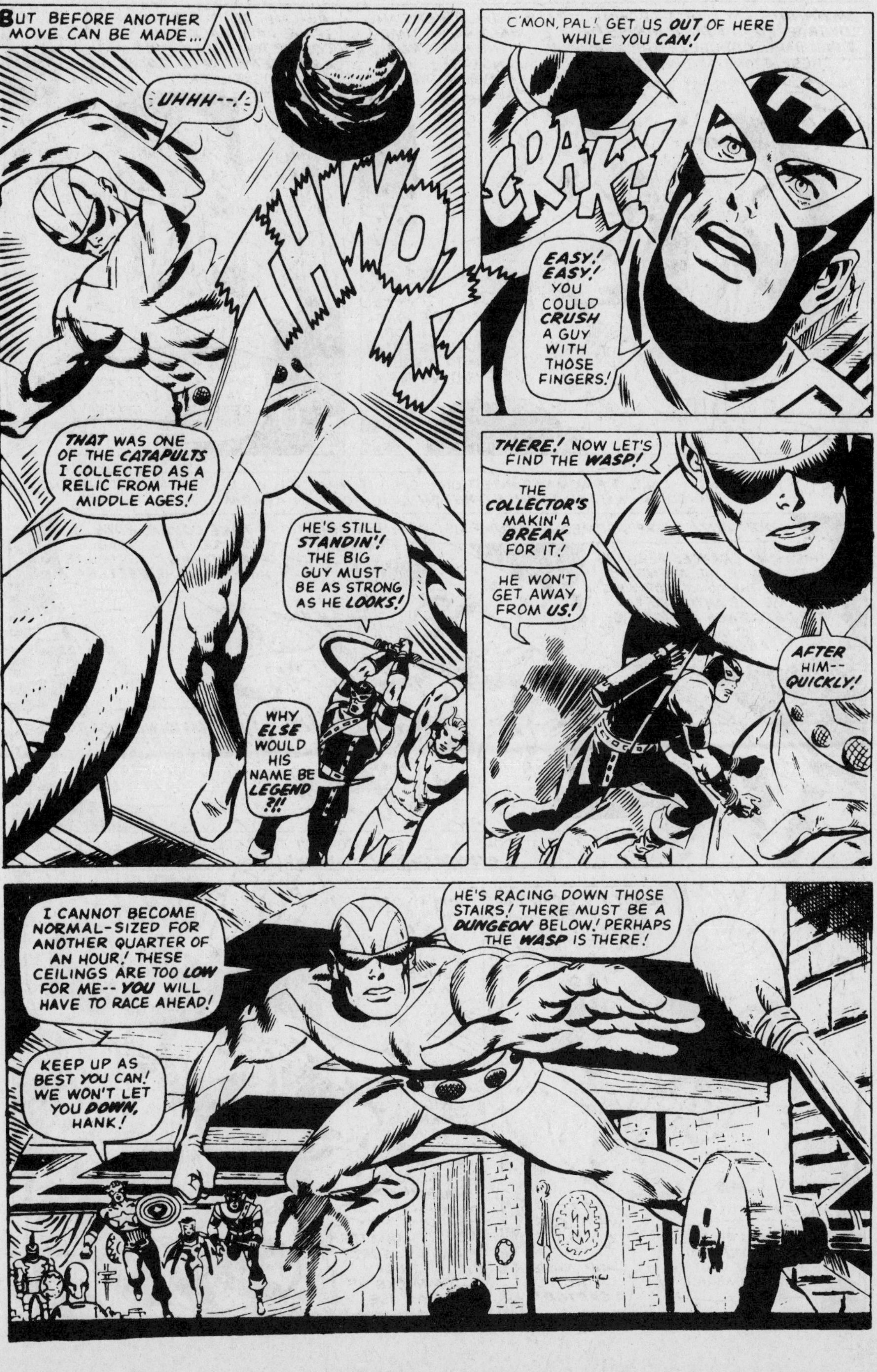
BUT BEFORE ANOTHER MOVE CAN BE MADE...
UHHH--!
THWOK
THAT WAS ONE OF THE CATAPULTS I COLLECTED AS A RELIC FROM THE MIDDLE AGES!
HE'S STILL STANDIN'! THE BIG GUY MUST BE AS STRONG AS HE LOOKS!
WHY ELSE WOULD HIS NAME BE LEGEND ?!!
C'MON, PAL! GET US OUT OF HERE WHILE YOU CAN!
CRAK!
EASY! EASY! YOU COULD CRUSH A GUY WITH THOSE FINGERS!
THERE! NOW LET'S FIND THE WASP!
THE COLLECTOR'S MAKIN' A BREAK FOR IT!
HE WON'T GET AWAY FROM US!
AFTER HIM-- QUICKLY!
I CANNOT BECOME NORMAL-SIZED FOR ANOTHER QUARTER OF AN HOUR! THESE CEILINGS ARE TOO LOW FOR ME-- YOU WILL HAVE TO RACE AHEAD!
HE'S RACING DOWN THOSE STAIRS! THERE MUST BE A DUNGEON BELOW! PERHAPS THE WASP IS THERE!
KEEP UP AS BEST YOU CAN! WE WON'T LET YOU DOWN, HANK!

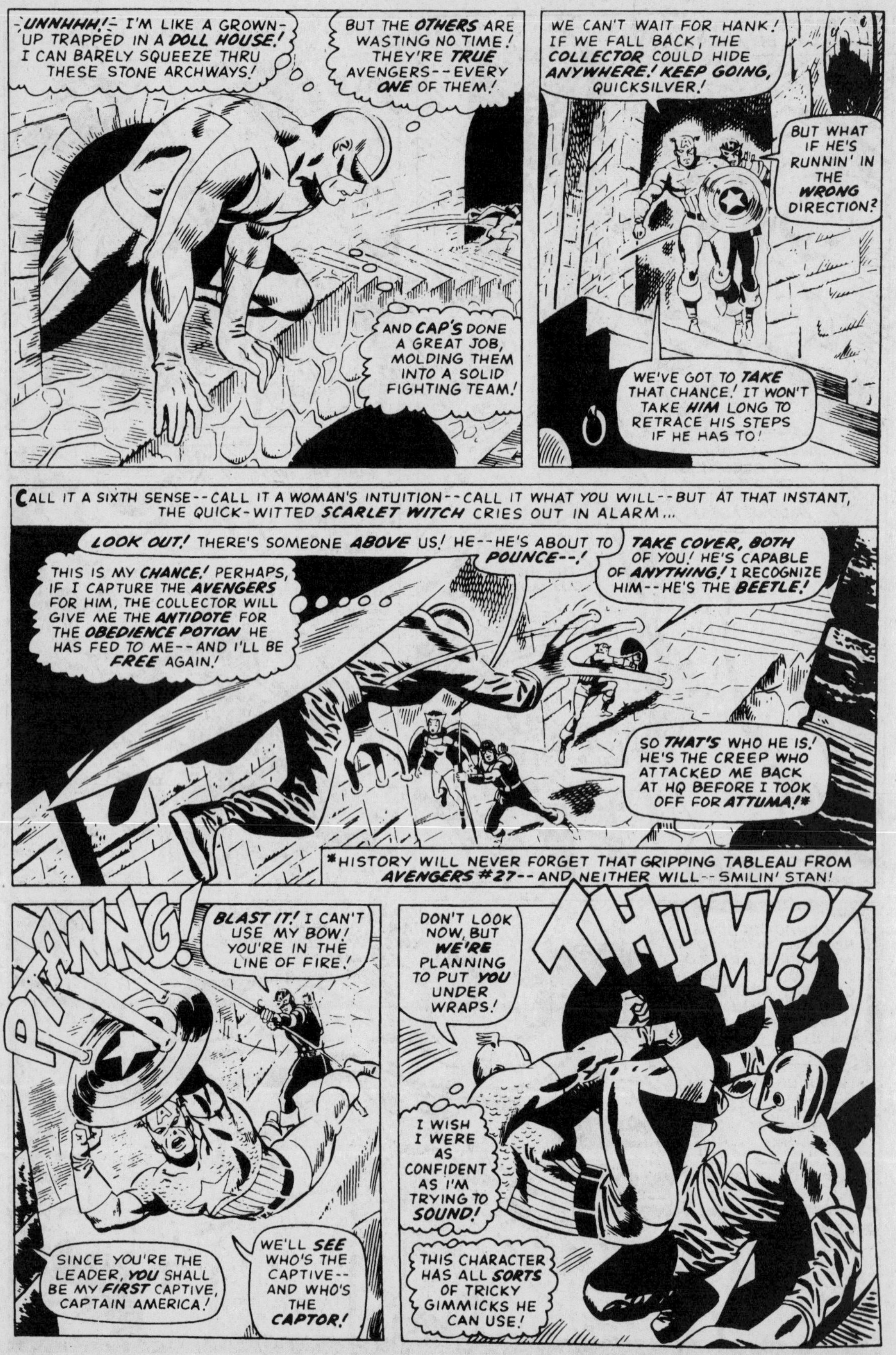
-UNNHHH!- I'M LIKE A GROWN-UP TRAPPED IN A DOLL HOUSE! I CAN BARELY SQUEEZE THRU THESE STONE ARCHWAYS!
BUT THE OTHERS ARE WASTING NO TIME! THEY'RE TRUE AVENGERS--EVERY ONE OF THEM!
AND CAP'S DONE A GREAT JOB, MOLDING THEM INTO A SOLID FIGHTING TEAM!
WE CAN'T WAIT FOR HANK! IF WE FALL BACK, THE COLLECTOR COULD HIDE ANYWHERE! KEEP GOING, QUICKSILVER!
BUT WHAT IF HE'S RUNNIN' IN THE WRONG DIRECTION?
WE'VE GOT TO TAKE THAT CHANCE! IT WON'T TAKE HIM LONG TO RETRACE HIS STEPS IF HE HAS TO!
CALL IT A SIXTH SENSE--CALL IT A WOMAN'S INTUITION--CALL IT WHAT YOU WILL--BUT AT THAT INSTANT, THE QUICK-WITTED SCARLET WITCH CRIES OUT IN ALARM...
LOOK OUT! THERE'S SOMEONE ABOVE US! HE--HE'S ABOUT TO POUNCE--!
THIS IS MY CHANCE! PERHAPS, IF I CAPTURE THE AVENGERS FOR HIM, THE COLLECTOR WILL GIVE ME THE ANTIDOTE FOR THE OBEDIENCE POTION HE HAS FED TO ME--AND I'LL BE FREE AGAIN!
TAKE COVER, BOTH OF YOU! HE'S CAPABLE OF ANYTHING! I RECOGNIZE HIM--HE'S THE BEETLE!
SO THAT'S WHO HE IS! HE'S THE CREEP WHO ATTACKED ME BACK AT HQ BEFORE I TOOK OFF FOR ATTUMA!*
*HISTORY WILL NEVER FORGET THAT GRIPPING TABLEAU FROM AVENGERS #27--AND NEITHER WILL--SMILIN' STAN!
PTANNG!
BLAST IT! I CAN'T USE MY BOW! YOU'RE IN THE LINE OF FIRE!
SINCE YOU'RE THE LEADER, YOU SHALL BE MY FIRST CAPTIVE, CAPTAIN AMERICA!
WE'LL SEE WHO'S THE CAPTIVE--AND WHO'S THE CAPTOR!
THUMP!
DON'T LOOK NOW, BUT WE'RE PLANNING TO PUT YOU UNDER WRAPS!
I WISH I WERE AS CONFIDENT AS I'M TRYING TO SOUND!
THIS CHARACTER HAS ALL SORTS OF TRICKY GIMMICKS HE CAN USE!

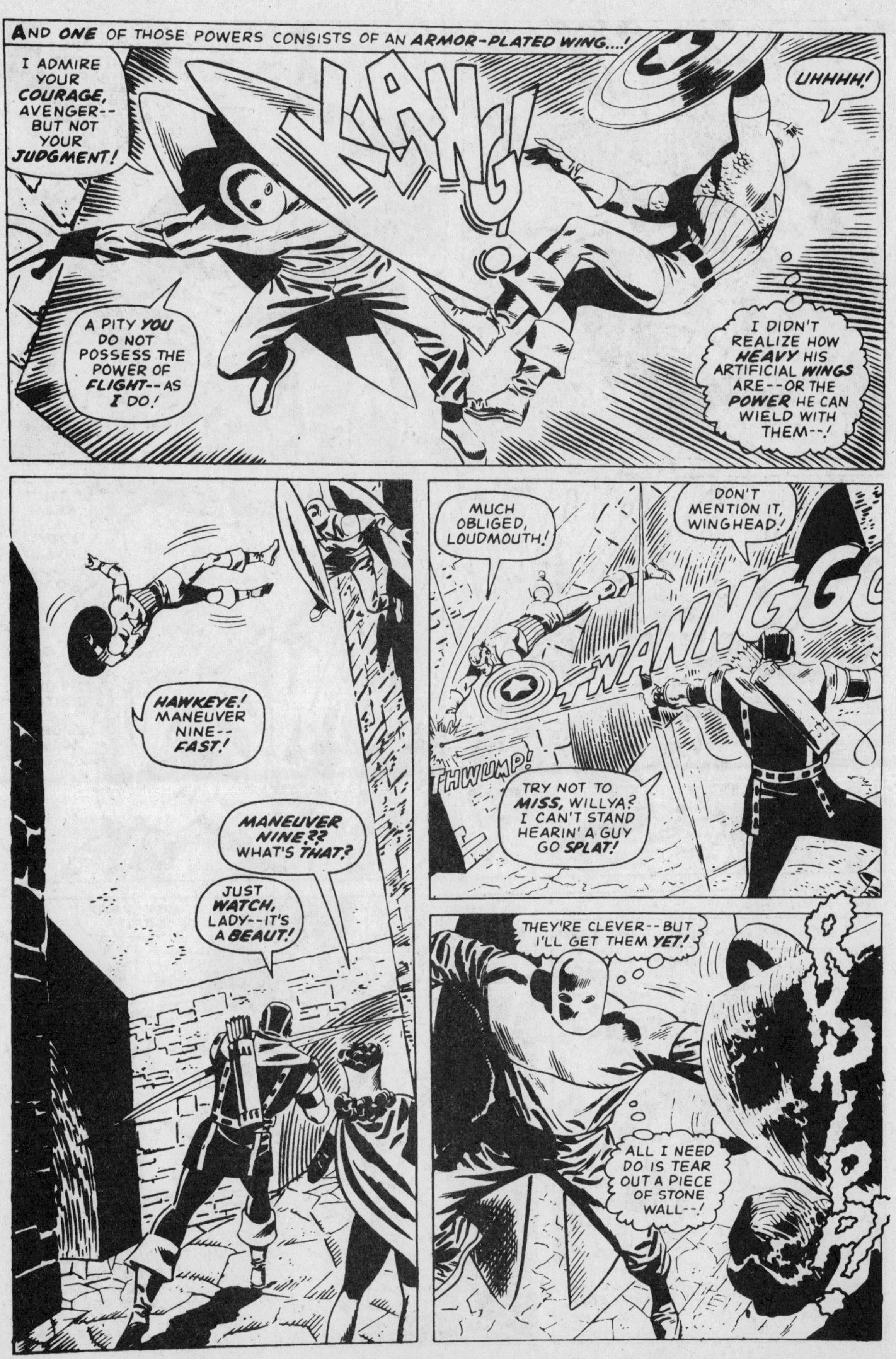
AND ONE OF THOSE POWERS CONSISTS OF AN ARMOR-PLATED WING...!
I ADMIRE YOUR COURAGE, AVENGER-- BUT NOT YOUR JUDGMENT!
KLANG!
UHHHH!
A PITY YOU DO NOT POSSESS THE POWER OF FLIGHT--AS I DO!
I DIDN'T REALIZE HOW HEAVY HIS ARTIFICIAL WINGS ARE--OR THE POWER HE CAN WIELD WITH THEM--!
HAWKEYE! MANEUVER NINE--FAST!
MANEUVER NINE?? WHAT'S THAT?
JUST WATCH, LADY--IT'S A BEAUT!
MUCH OBLIGED, LOUDMOUTH!
DON'T MENTION IT, WINGHEAD!
TWANNGG
THWUMP!
TRY NOT TO MISS, WILLYA? I CAN'T STAND HEARIN' A GUY GO SPLAT!
THEY'RE CLEVER--BUT I'LL GET THEM YET!
ALL I NEED DO IS TEAR OUT A PIECE OF STONE WALL--!

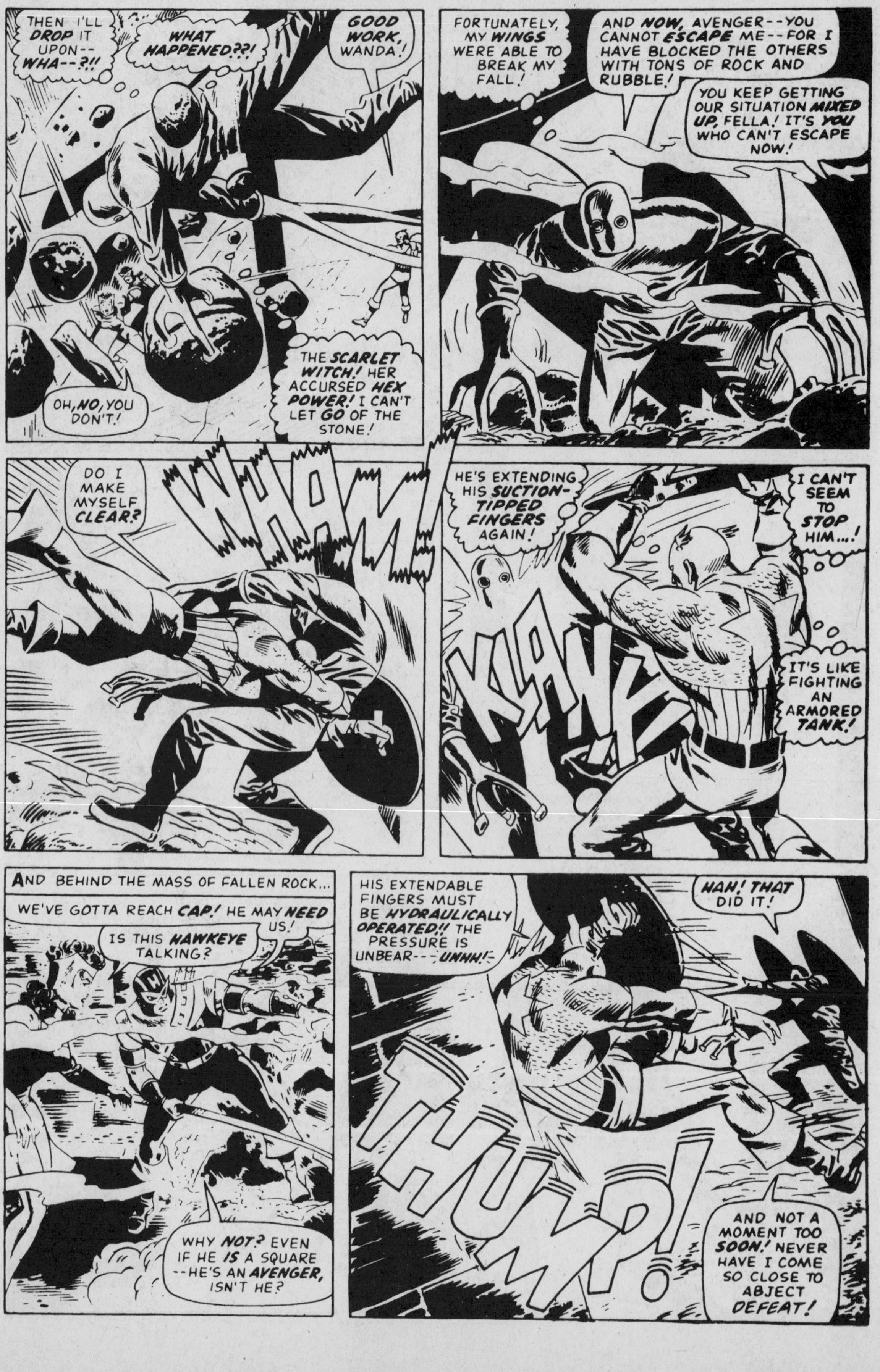

THEN I'LL DROP IT UPON-- WHA--?!!
WHAT HAPPENED??!
GOOD WORK, WANDA!
THE SCARLET WITCH! HER ACCURSED HEX POWER! I CAN'T LET GO OF THE STONE!
OH, NO, YOU DON'T!
FORTUNATELY, MY WINGS WERE ABLE TO BREAK MY FALL!
AND NOW, AVENGER--YOU CANNOT ESCAPE ME--FOR I HAVE BLOCKED THE OTHERS WITH TONS OF ROCK AND RUBBLE!
YOU KEEP GETTING OUR SITUATION MIXED UP, FELLA! IT'S YOU WHO CAN'T ESCAPE NOW!
DO I MAKE MYSELF CLEAR?
WHAM!
HE'S EXTENDING HIS SUCTION-TIPPED FINGERS AGAIN!
I CAN'T SEEM TO STOP HIM....!
KLANK
IT'S LIKE FIGHTING AN ARMORED TANK!
AND BEHIND THE MASS OF FALLEN ROCK...
WE'VE GOTTA REACH CAP! HE MAY NEED US!
IS THIS HAWKEYE TALKING?
WHY NOT? EVEN IF HE IS A SQUARE --HE'S AN AVENGER, ISN'T HE?
HIS EXTENDABLE FINGERS MUST BE HYDRAULICALLY OPERATED!! THE PRESSURE IS UNBEAR---UNHH!
HAH! THAT DID IT!
THUMP!
AND NOT A MOMENT TOO SOON! NEVER HAVE I COME SO CLOSE TO ABJECT DEFEAT!

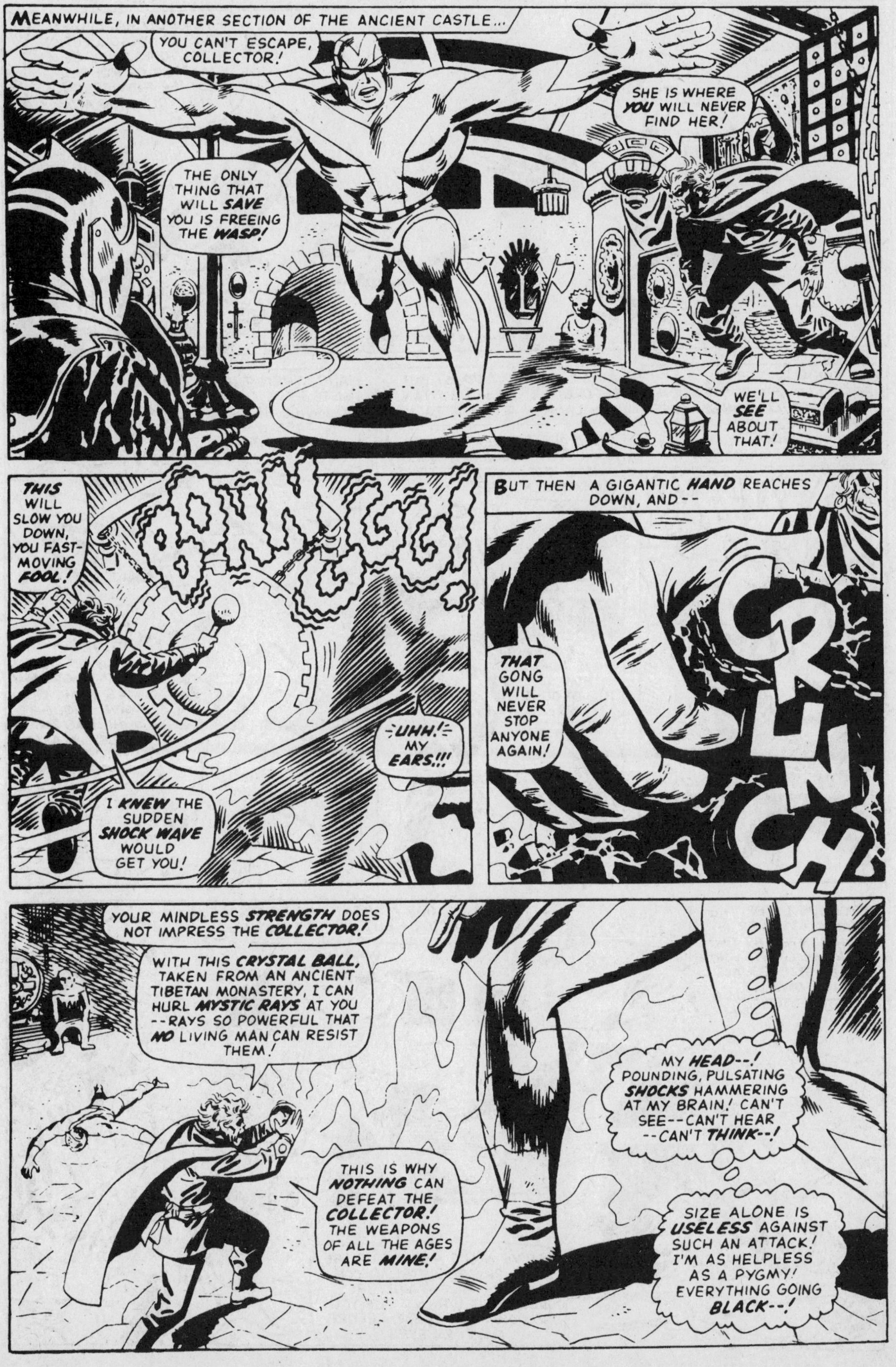
MEANWHILE, IN ANOTHER SECTION OF THE ANCIENT CASTLE...
YOU CAN'T ESCAPE, COLLECTOR!
SHE IS WHERE YOU WILL NEVER FIND HER!
THE ONLY THING THAT WILL SAVE YOU IS FREEING THE WASP!
WE'LL SEE ABOUT THAT!
THIS WILL SLOW YOU DOWN, YOU FAST-MOVING FOOL!
BONNGG!
UHH! MY EARS!!!
I KNEW THE SUDDEN SHOCK WAVE WOULD GET YOU!
BUT THEN A GIGANTIC HAND REACHES DOWN, AND--
THAT GONG WILL NEVER STOP ANYONE AGAIN!
CRUNCH
YOUR MINDLESS STRENGTH DOES NOT IMPRESS THE COLLECTOR!
WITH THIS CRYSTAL BALL, TAKEN FROM AN ANCIENT TIBETAN MONASTERY, I CAN HURL MYSTIC RAYS AT YOU --RAYS SO POWERFUL THAT NO LIVING MAN CAN RESIST THEM!
MY HEAD--! POUNDING, PULSATING SHOCKS HAMMERING AT MY BRAIN! CAN'T SEE--CAN'T HEAR --CAN'T THINK--!
THIS IS WHY NOTHING CAN DEFEAT THE COLLECTOR! THE WEAPONS OF ALL THE AGES ARE MINE!
SIZE ALONE IS USELESS AGAINST SUCH AN ATTACK! I'M AS HELPLESS AS A PYGMY! EVERYTHING GOING BLACK--!

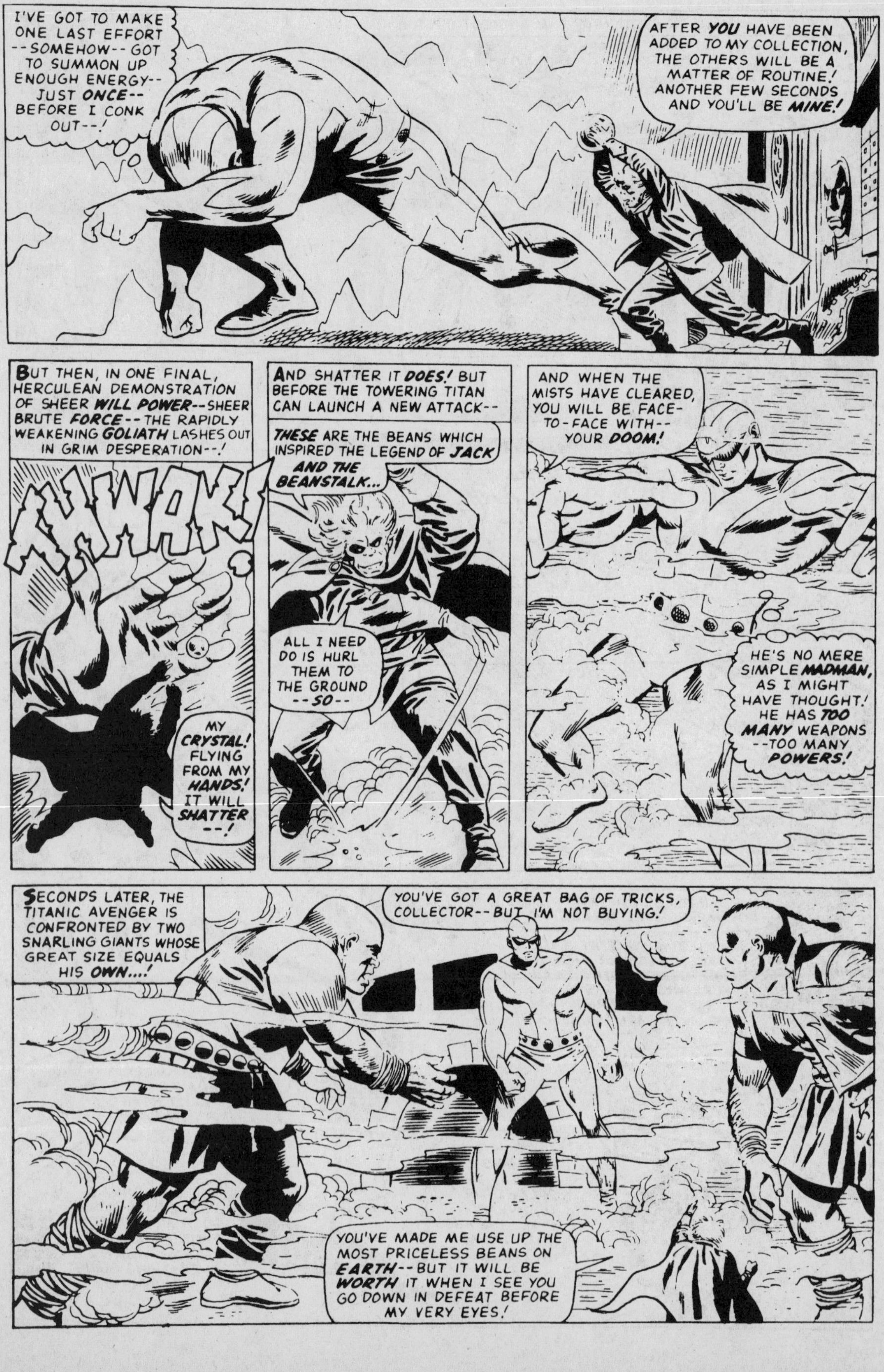
I'VE GOT TO MAKE ONE LAST EFFORT --SOMEHOW-- GOT TO SUMMON UP ENOUGH ENERGY-- JUST ONCE-- BEFORE I CONK OUT--!
AFTER YOU HAVE BEEN ADDED TO MY COLLECTION, THE OTHERS WILL BE A MATTER OF ROUTINE! ANOTHER FEW SECONDS AND YOU'LL BE MINE!
BUT THEN, IN ONE FINAL, HERCULEAN DEMONSTRATION OF SHEER WILL POWER--SHEER BRUTE FORCE--THE RAPIDLY WEAKENING GOLIATH LASHES OUT IN GRIM DESPERATION--!
THWAK!
MY CRYSTAL! FLYING FROM MY HANDS! IT WILL SHATTER--!
AND SHATTER IT DOES! BUT BEFORE THE TOWERING TITAN CAN LAUNCH A NEW ATTACK--
THESE ARE THE BEANS WHICH INSPIRED THE LEGEND OF JACK AND THE BEANSTALK...
ALL I NEED DO IS HURL THEM TO THE GROUND --SO--
AND WHEN THE MISTS HAVE CLEARED, YOU WILL BE FACE-TO-FACE WITH-- YOUR DOOM!
HE'S NO MERE SIMPLE MADMAN, AS I MIGHT HAVE THOUGHT! HE HAS TOO MANY WEAPONS --TOO MANY POWERS!
SECONDS LATER, THE TITANIC AVENGER IS CONFRONTED BY TWO SNARLING GIANTS WHOSE GREAT SIZE EQUALS HIS OWN...!
YOU'VE GOT A GREAT BAG OF TRICKS, COLLECTOR--BUT I'M NOT BUYING!
YOU'VE MADE ME USE UP THE MOST PRICELESS BEANS ON EARTH--BUT IT WILL BE WORTH IT WHEN I SEE YOU GO DOWN IN DEFEAT BEFORE MY VERY EYES!

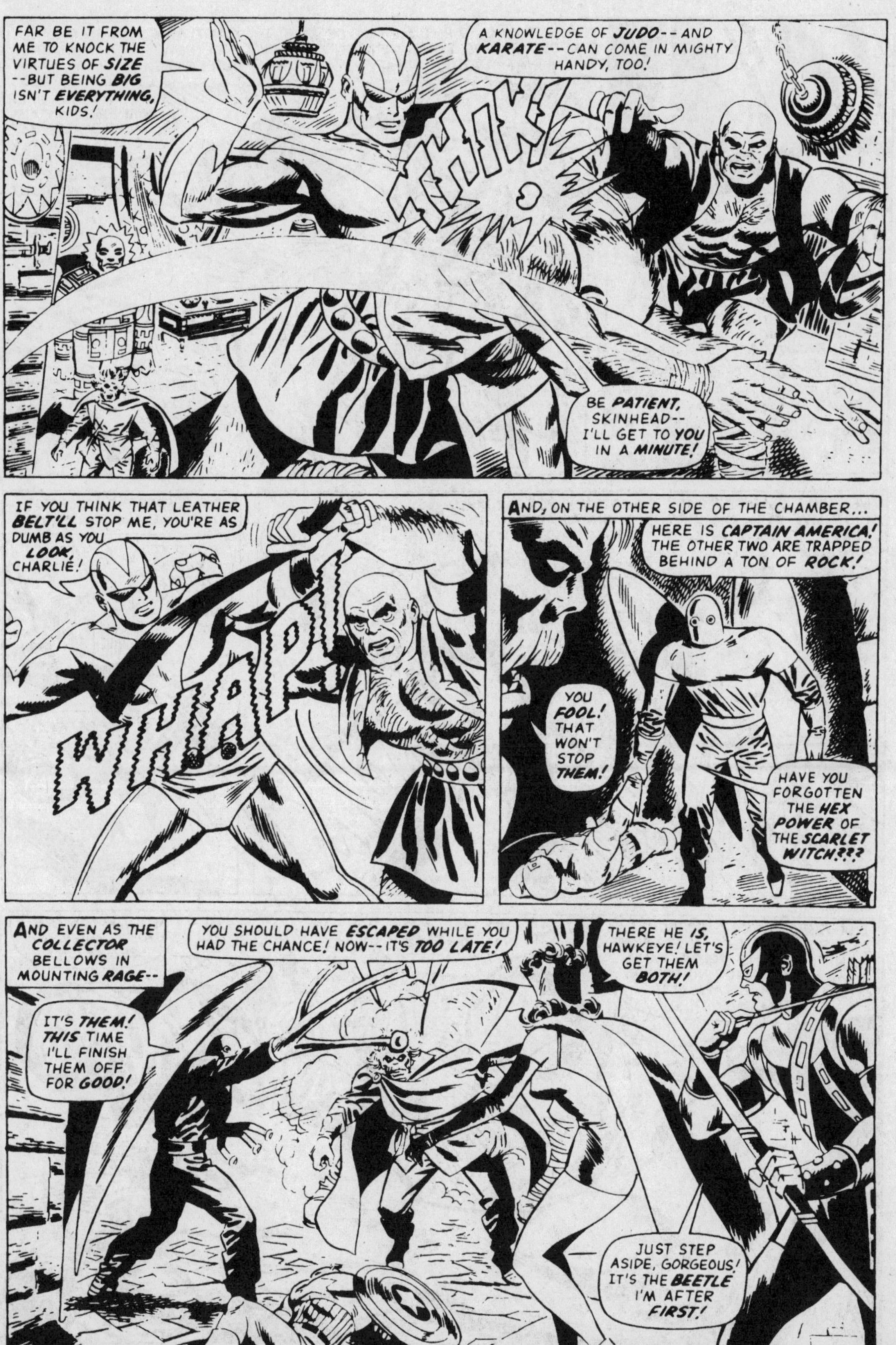
FAR BE IT FROM ME TO KNOCK THE VIRTUES OF SIZE --BUT BEING BIG ISN'T EVERYTHING, KIDS!
A KNOWLEDGE OF JUDO-- AND KARATE--CAN COME IN MIGHTY HANDY, TOO!
THOK!
BE PATIENT, SKINHEAD-- I'LL GET TO YOU IN A MINUTE!
IF YOU THINK THAT LEATHER BELT'LL STOP ME, YOU'RE AS DUMB AS YOU LOOK, CHARLIE!
WHAP!
AND, ON THE OTHER SIDE OF THE CHAMBER...
HERE IS CAPTAIN AMERICA! THE OTHER TWO ARE TRAPPED BEHIND A TON OF ROCK!
YOU FOOL! THAT WON'T STOP THEM!
HAVE YOU FORGOTTEN THE HEX POWER OF THE SCARLET WITCH???
AND EVEN AS THE COLLECTOR BELLOWS IN MOUNTING RAGE--
YOU SHOULD HAVE ESCAPED WHILE YOU HAD THE CHANCE! NOW--IT'S TOO LATE!
THERE HE IS, HAWKEYE! LET'S GET THEM BOTH!
IT'S THEM! THIS TIME I'LL FINISH THEM OFF FOR GOOD!
JUST STEP ASIDE, GORGEOUS! IT'S THE BEETLE I'M AFTER FIRST!

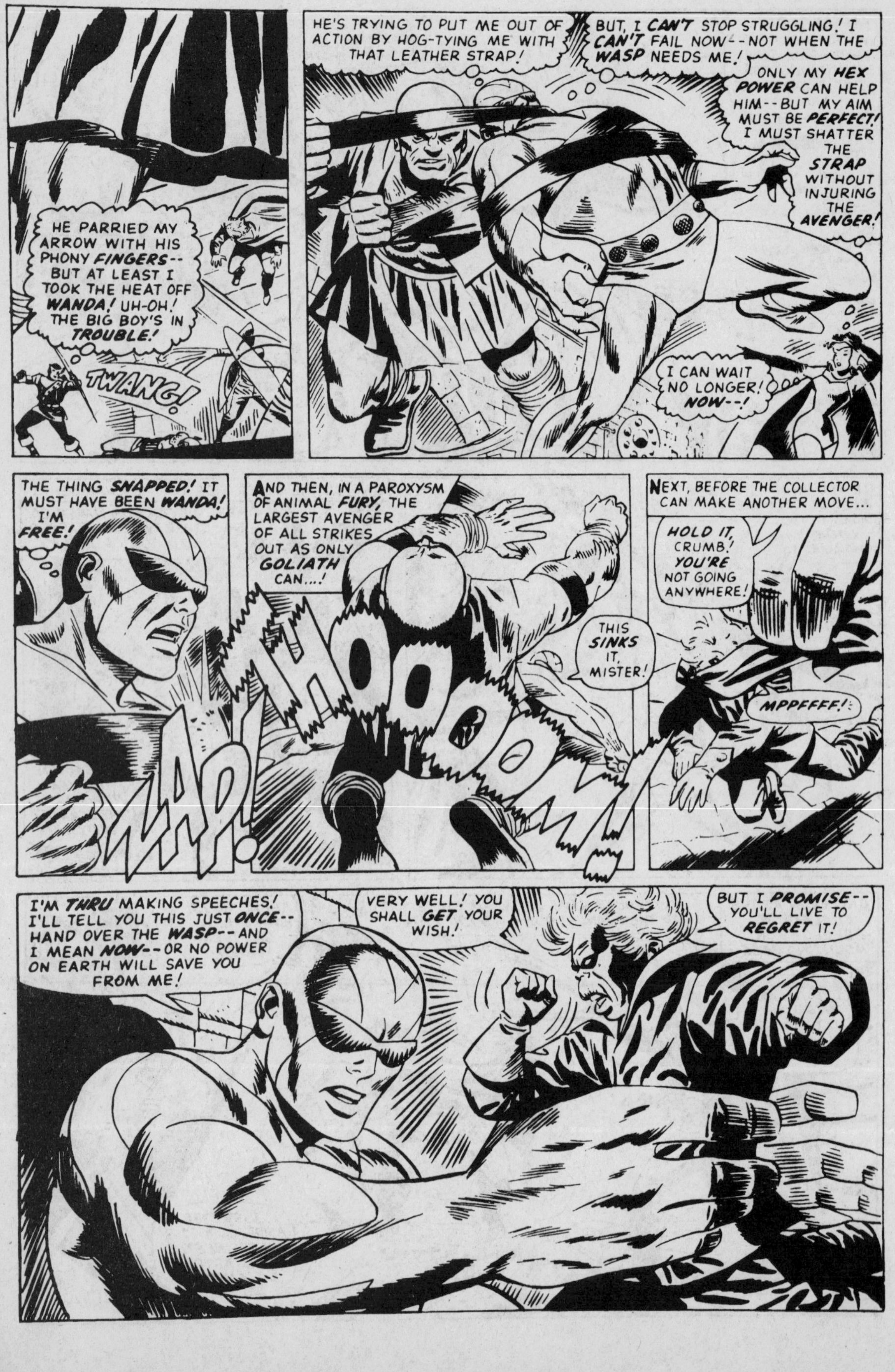
HE PARRIED MY ARROW WITH HIS PHONY FINGERS-- BUT AT LEAST I TOOK THE HEAT OFF WANDA! UH-OH! THE BIG BOY'S IN TROUBLE!
TWANG!
HE'S TRYING TO PUT ME OUT OF ACTION BY HOG-TYING ME WITH THAT LEATHER STRAP!
BUT, I CAN'T STOP STRUGGLING! I CAN'T FAIL NOW--NOT WHEN THE WASP NEEDS ME!
ONLY MY HEX POWER CAN HELP HIM--BUT MY AIM MUST BE PERFECT! I MUST SHATTER THE STRAP WITHOUT INJURING THE AVENGER!
I CAN WAIT NO LONGER! NOW--!
THE THING SNAPPED! IT MUST HAVE BEEN WANDA! I'M FREE!
AND THEN, IN A PAROXYSM OF ANIMAL FURY, THE LARGEST AVENGER OF ALL STRIKES OUT AS ONLY GOLIATH CAN...!
THOOOOM!
ZAP!
NEXT, BEFORE THE COLLECTOR CAN MAKE ANOTHER MOVE...
HOLD IT, CRUMB! YOU'RE NOT GOING ANYWHERE!
THIS SINKS IT, MISTER!
MPPFFFF!
I'M THRU MAKING SPEECHES! I'LL TELL YOU THIS JUST ONCE-- HAND OVER THE WASP--AND I MEAN NOW--OR NO POWER ON EARTH WILL SAVE YOU FROM ME!
VERY WELL! YOU SHALL GET YOUR WISH!
BUT I PROMISE-- YOU'LL LIVE TO REGRET IT!

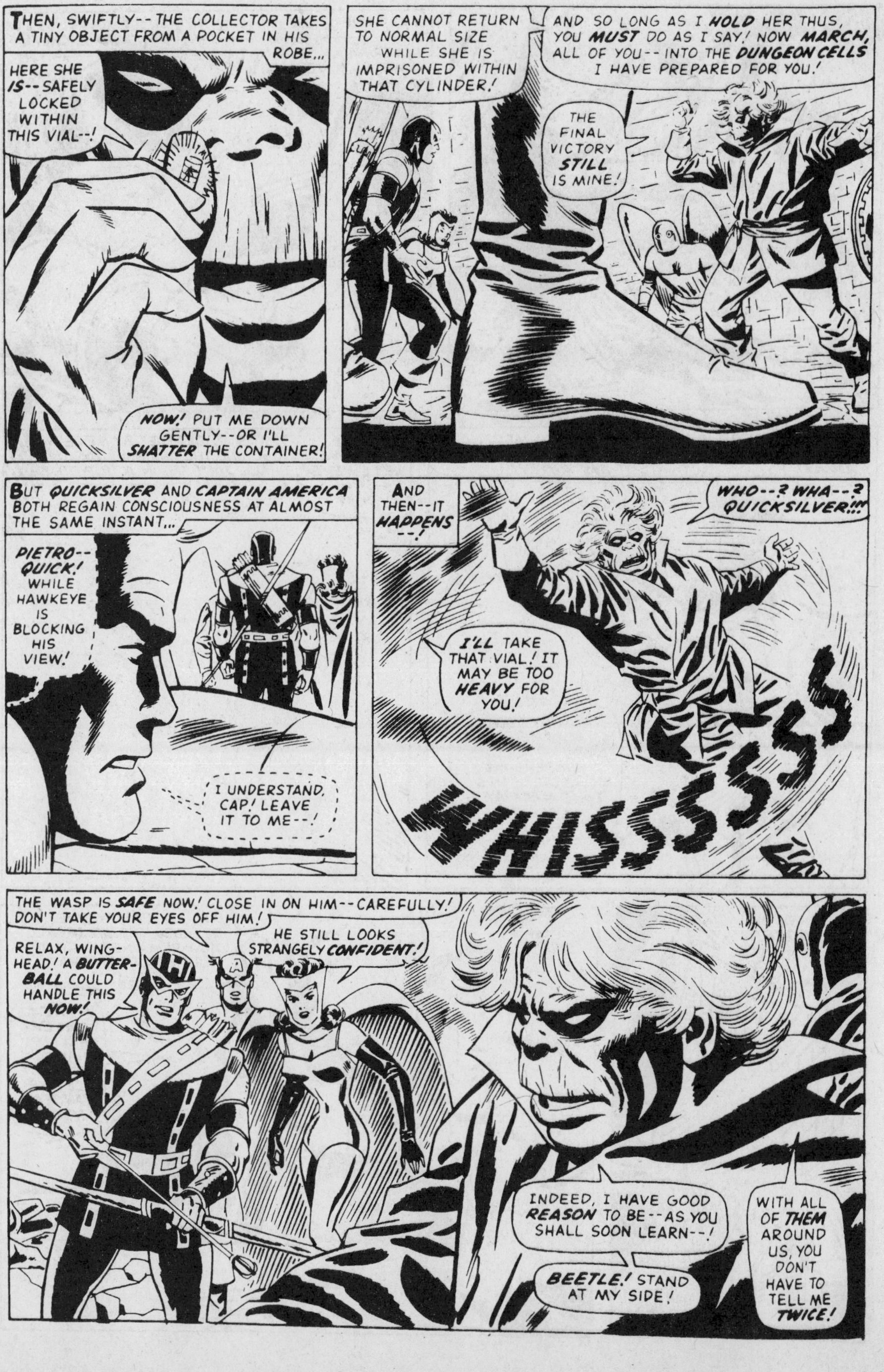
THEN, SWIFTLY--THE COLLECTOR TAKES A TINY OBJECT FROM A POCKET IN HIS ROBE...
HERE SHE IS--SAFELY LOCKED WITHIN THIS VIAL--!
NOW! PUT ME DOWN GENTLY--OR I'LL SHATTER THE CONTAINER!
SHE CANNOT RETURN TO NORMAL SIZE WHILE SHE IS IMPRISONED WITHIN THAT CYLINDER!
AND SO LONG AS I HOLD HER THUS, YOU MUST DO AS I SAY! NOW MARCH, ALL OF YOU--INTO THE DUNGEON CELLS I HAVE PREPARED FOR YOU!
THE FINAL VICTORY STILL IS MINE!
BUT QUICKSILVER AND CAPTAIN AMERICA BOTH REGAIN CONSCIOUSNESS AT ALMOST THE SAME INSTANT...
PIETRO--QUICK! WHILE HAWKEYE IS BLOCKING HIS VIEW!
I UNDERSTAND, CAP! LEAVE IT TO ME--!
AND THEN--IT HAPPENS--!
WHO--? WHA--? QUICKSILVER!!!
I'LL TAKE THAT VIAL! IT MAY BE TOO HEAVY FOR YOU!
WHISSSSSS
THE WASP IS SAFE NOW! CLOSE IN ON HIM--CAREFULLY! DON'T TAKE YOUR EYES OFF HIM!
RELAX, WING-HEAD! A BUTTER-BALL COULD HANDLE THIS NOW!
HE STILL LOOKS STRANGELY CONFIDENT!
INDEED, I HAVE GOOD REASON TO BE--AS YOU SHALL SOON LEARN--!
BEETLE! STAND AT MY SIDE!
WITH ALL OF THEM AROUND US, YOU DON'T HAVE TO TELL ME TWICE!

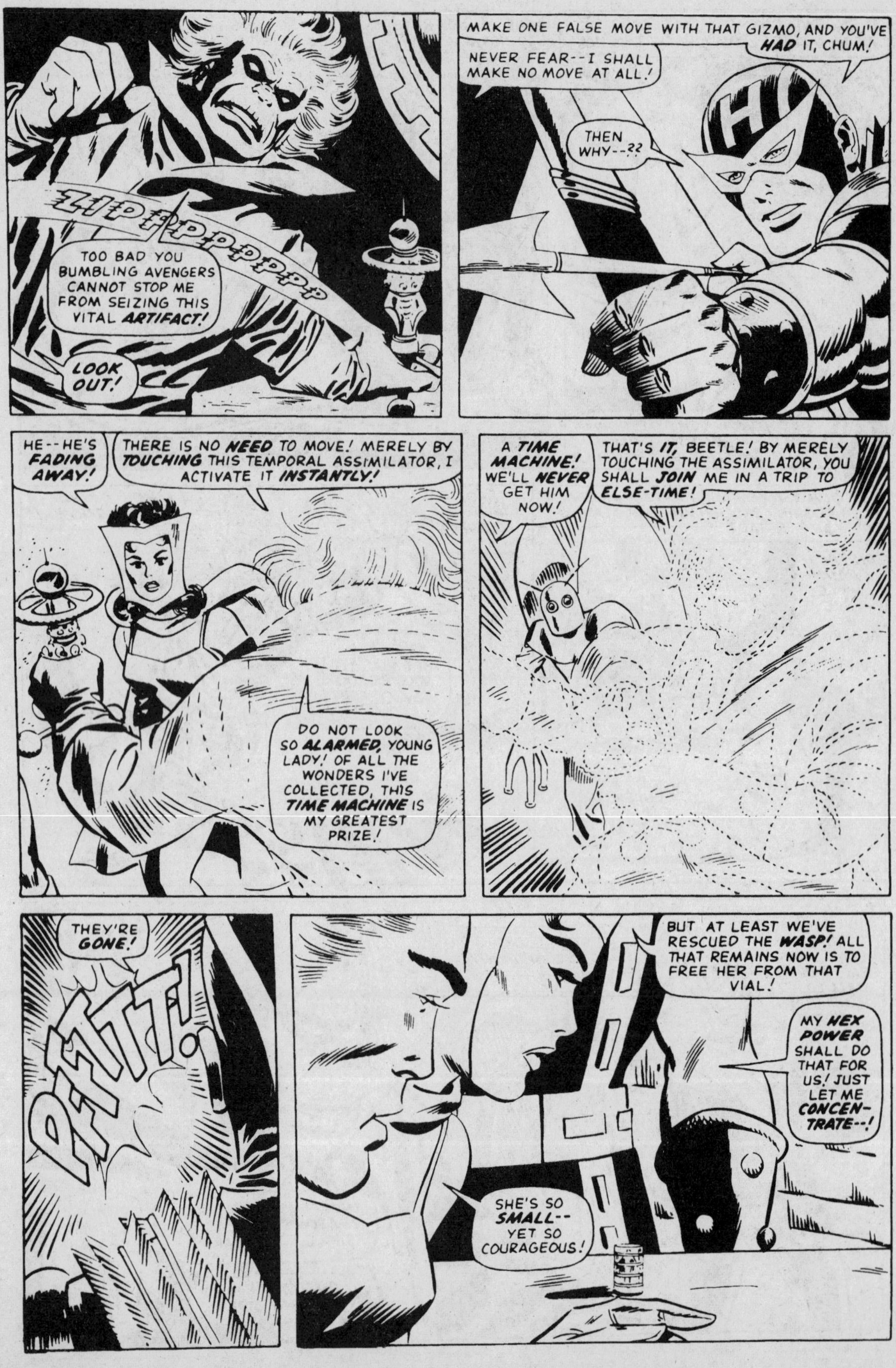

ZIPPPPPPPPPP
TOO BAD YOU BUMBLING AVENGERS CANNOT STOP ME FROM SEIZING THIS VITAL ARTIFACT!
LOOK OUT!
MAKE ONE FALSE MOVE WITH THAT GIZMO, AND YOU'VE HAD IT, CHUM!
NEVER FEAR--I SHALL MAKE NO MOVE AT ALL!
THEN WHY--??
HE--HE'S FADING AWAY!
THERE IS NO NEED TO MOVE! MERELY BY TOUCHING THIS TEMPORAL ASSIMILATOR, I ACTIVATE IT INSTANTLY!
DO NOT LOOK SO ALARMED, YOUNG LADY! OF ALL THE WONDERS I'VE COLLECTED, THIS TIME MACHINE IS MY GREATEST PRIZE!
A TIME MACHINE! WE'LL NEVER GET HIM NOW!
THAT'S IT, BEETLE! BY MERELY TOUCHING THE ASSIMILATOR, YOU SHALL JOIN ME IN A TRIP TO ELSE-TIME!
THEY'RE GONE!
PFFTT!
BUT AT LEAST WE'VE RESCUED THE WASP! ALL THAT REMAINS NOW IS TO FREE HER FROM THAT VIAL!
MY HEX POWER SHALL DO THAT FOR US! JUST LET ME CONCEN-TRATE--!
SHE'S SO SMALL--YET SO COURAGEOUS!

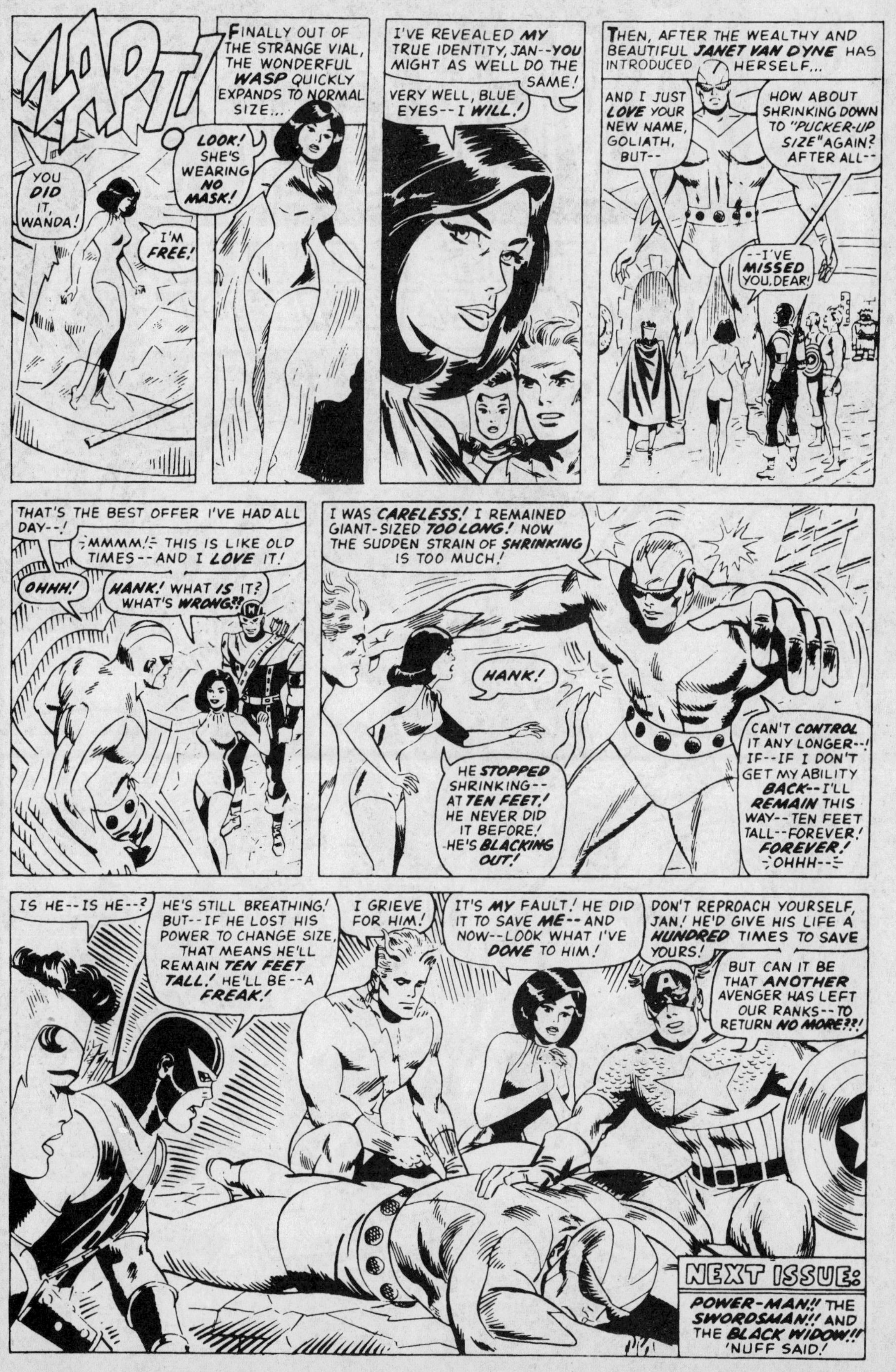
ZAPT!
YOU DID IT, WANDA!
I'M FREE!
FINALLY OUT OF THE STRANGE VIAL, THE WONDERFUL WASP QUICKLY EXPANDS TO NORMAL SIZE...
LOOK! SHE'S WEARING NO MASK!
I'VE REVEALED MY TRUE IDENTITY, JAN--YOU MIGHT AS WELL DO THE SAME!
VERY WELL, BLUE EYES--I WILL.!
THEN, AFTER THE WEALTHY AND BEAUTIFUL JANET VAN DYNE HAS INTRODUCED HERSELF...
AND I JUST LOVE YOUR NEW NAME, GOLIATH, BUT--
HOW ABOUT SHRINKING DOWN TO "PUCKER-UP SIZE" AGAIN? AFTER ALL--
--I'VE MISSED YOU, DEAR!
THAT'S THE BEST OFFER I'VE HAD ALL DAY--!
MMMM! THIS IS LIKE OLD TIMES--AND I LOVE IT!
OHHH!
HANK! WHAT IS IT? WHAT'S WRONG?!
I WAS CARELESS! I REMAINED GIANT-SIZED TOO LONG! NOW THE SUDDEN STRAIN OF SHRINKING IS TOO MUCH!
HANK!
HE STOPPED SHRINKING--AT TEN FEET! HE NEVER DID IT BEFORE! HE'S BLACKING OUT!
CAN'T CONTROL IT ANY LONGER--! IF--IF I DON'T GET MY ABILITY BACK--I'LL REMAIN THIS WAY--TEN FEET TALL--FOREVER! FOREVER! OHHH--
IS HE--IS HE--?
HE'S STILL BREATHING! BUT--IF HE LOST HIS POWER TO CHANGE SIZE, THAT MEANS HE'LL REMAIN TEN FEET TALL! HE'LL BE--A FREAK!
I GRIEVE FOR HIM!
IT'S MY FAULT! HE DID IT TO SAVE ME--AND NOW--LOOK WHAT I'VE DONE TO HIM!
DON'T REPROACH YOURSELF, JAN! HE'D GIVE HIS LIFE A HUNDRED TIMES TO SAVE YOURS!
BUT CAN IT BE THAT ANOTHER AVENGER HAS LEFT OUR RANKS--TO RETURN NO MORE?!
NEXT ISSUE:
POWER-MAN!! THE SWORDSMAN!! AND THE BLACK WIDOW!! 'NUFF SAID!

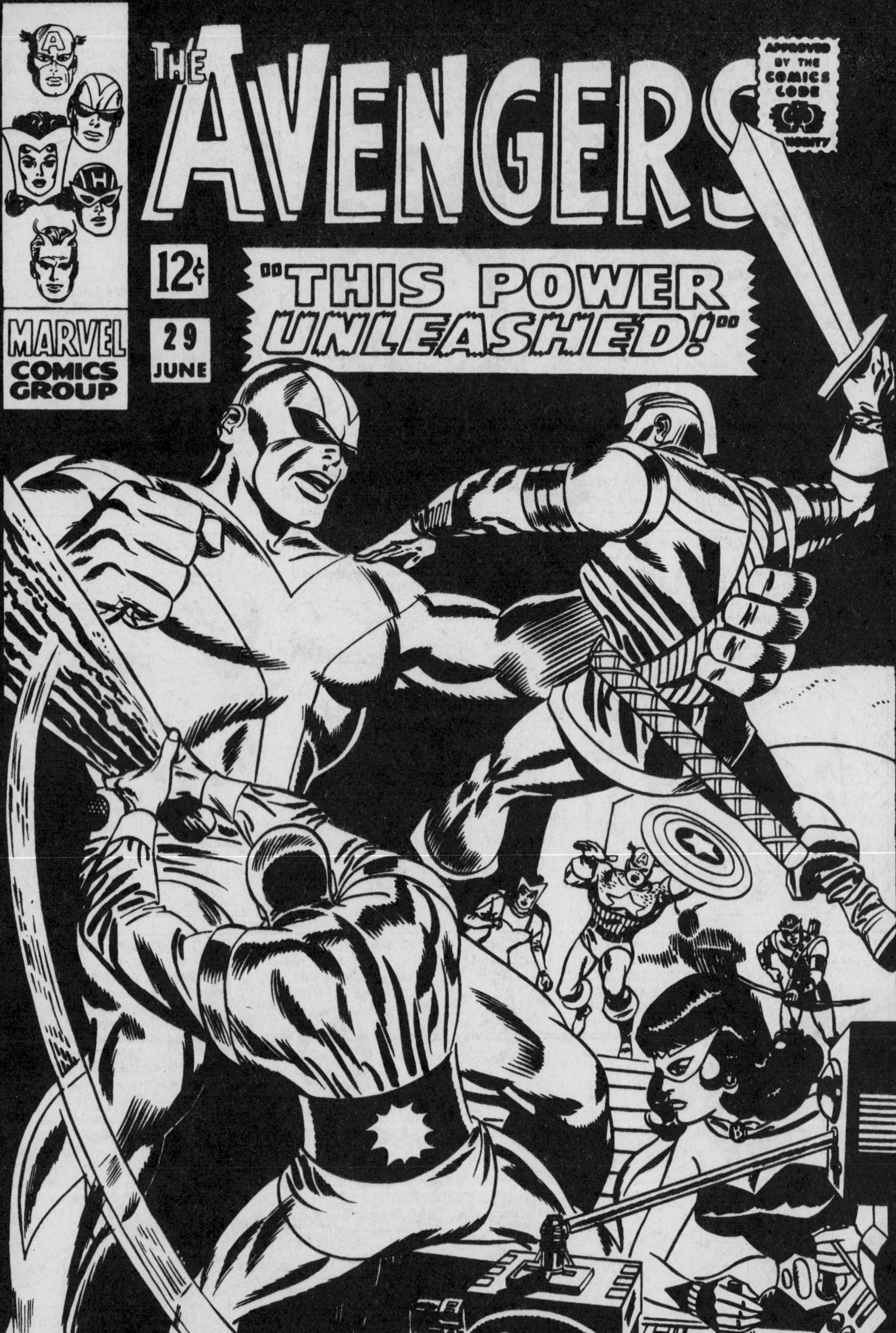
THE AVENGERS
APPROVED BY THE COMICS CODE AUTHORITY
12¢
"THIS POWER UNLEASHED!"
MARVEL COMICS GROUP
29
JUNE

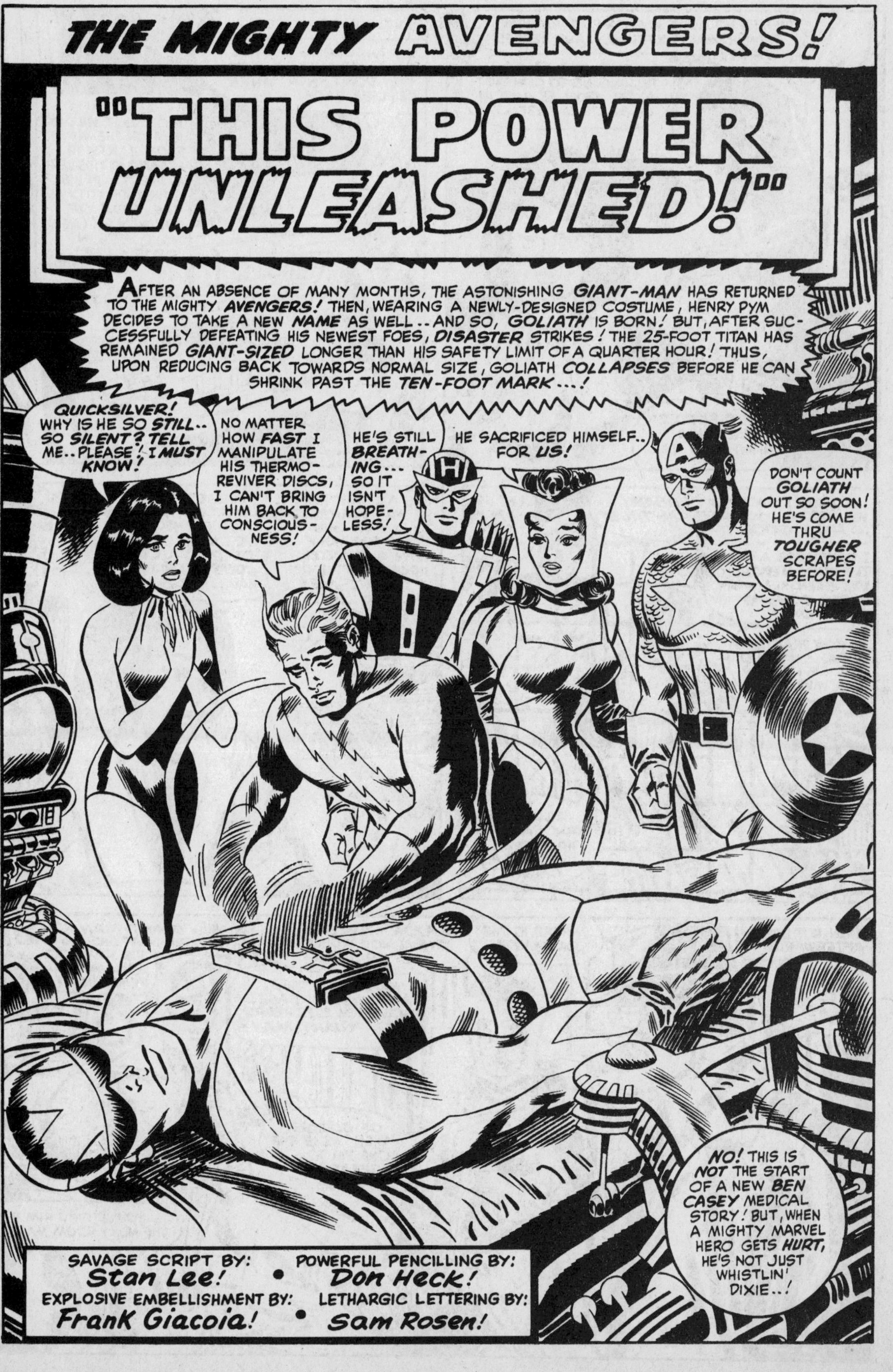
THE MIGHTY AVENGERS!
"THIS POWER UNLEASHED!"
AFTER AN ABSENCE OF MANY MONTHS, THE ASTONISHING GIANT-MAN HAS RETURNED TO THE MIGHTY AVENGERS! THEN, WEARING A NEWLY-DESIGNED COSTUME, HENRY PYM DECIDES TO TAKE A NEW NAME AS WELL.. AND SO, GOLIATH IS BORN! BUT, AFTER SUCCESSFULLY DEFEATING HIS NEWEST FOES, DISASTER STRIKES! THE 25-FOOT TITAN HAS REMAINED GIANT-SIZED LONGER THAN HIS SAFETY LIMIT OF A QUARTER HOUR! THUS, UPON REDUCING BACK TOWARDS NORMAL SIZE, GOLIATH COLLAPSES BEFORE HE CAN SHRINK PAST THE TEN-FOOT MARK...!
QUICKSILVER! WHY IS HE SO STILL.. SO SILENT? TELL ME.. PLEASE! I MUST KNOW!
NO MATTER HOW FAST I MANIPULATE HIS THERMO-REVIVER DISCS, I CAN'T BRING HIM BACK TO CONSCIOUSNESS!
HE'S STILL BREATHING... SO IT ISN'T HOPELESS!
HE SACRIFICED HIMSELF.. FOR US!
DON'T COUNT GOLIATH OUT SO SOON! HE'S COME THRU TOUGHER SCRAPES BEFORE!
NO! THIS IS NOT THE START OF A NEW BEN CASEY MEDICAL STORY! BUT, WHEN A MIGHTY MARVEL HERO GETS HURT, HE'S NOT JUST WHISTLIN' DIXIE..!
SAVAGE SCRIPT BY: Stan Lee! • POWERFUL PENCILLING BY: Don Heck!
EXPLOSIVE EMBELLISHMENT BY: Frank Giacoia! • LETHARGIC LETTERING BY: Sam Rosen!

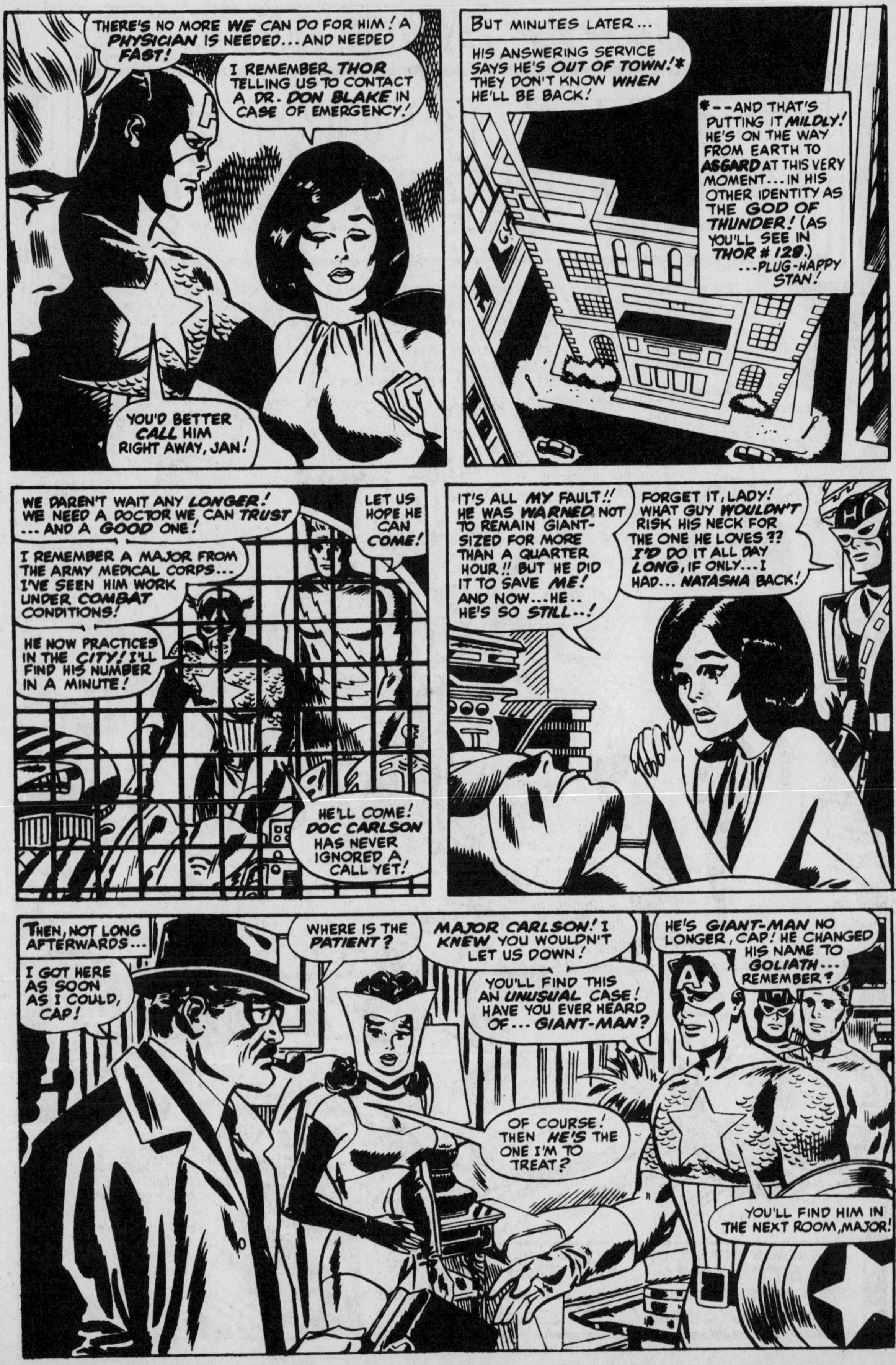
THERE'S NO MORE WE CAN DO FOR HIM! A PHYSICIAN IS NEEDED... AND NEEDED FAST!
I REMEMBER THOR TELLING US TO CONTACT A DR. DON BLAKE IN CASE OF EMERGENCY!
YOU'D BETTER CALL HIM RIGHT AWAY, JAN!
BUT MINUTES LATER...
HIS ANSWERING SERVICE SAYS HE'S OUT OF TOWN!* THEY DON'T KNOW WHEN HE'LL BE BACK!
*--AND THAT'S PUTTING IT MILDLY! HE'S ON THE WAY FROM EARTH TO ASGARD AT THIS VERY MOMENT... IN HIS OTHER IDENTITY AS THE GOD OF THUNDER! (AS YOU'LL SEE IN THOR # 128.) ---PLUG-HAPPY STAN!
WE DAREN'T WAIT ANY LONGER! WE NEED A DOCTOR WE CAN TRUST ... AND A GOOD ONE!
LET US HOPE HE CAN COME!
I REMEMBER A MAJOR FROM THE ARMY MEDICAL CORPS... I'VE SEEN HIM WORK UNDER COMBAT CONDITIONS!
HE NOW PRACTICES IN THE CITY! I'LL FIND HIS NUMBER IN A MINUTE!
HE'LL COME! DOC CARLSON HAS NEVER IGNORED A CALL YET!
IT'S ALL MY FAULT!! HE WAS WARNED NOT TO REMAIN GIANT-SIZED FOR MORE THAN A QUARTER HOUR!! BUT HE DID IT TO SAVE ME! AND NOW... HE.. HE'S SO STILL...!
FORGET IT, LADY! WHAT GUY WOULDN'T RISK HIS NECK FOR THE ONE HE LOVES?? I'D DO IT ALL DAY LONG, IF ONLY... I HAD... NATASHA BACK!
THEN, NOT LONG AFTERWARDS...
I GOT HERE AS SOON AS I COULD, CAP!
WHERE IS THE PATIENT?
MAJOR CARLSON! I KNEW YOU WOULDN'T LET US DOWN!
YOU'LL FIND THIS AN UNUSUAL CASE! HAVE YOU EVER HEARD OF... GIANT-MAN?
HE'S GIANT-MAN NO LONGER, CAP! HE CHANGED HIS NAME TO GOLIATH--- REMEMBER?
OF COURSE! THEN HE'S THE ONE I'M TO TREAT?
YOU'LL FIND HIM IN THE NEXT ROOM, MAJOR!

GOOD HEAVENS! THIS MAN IS ACTUALLY *TEN FEET TALL!*

HE *HAD* BEEN 25 FEET... BUT *COLLAPSED* WHILE SHRINKING!

CHANGING HIS SIZE SO RAPIDLY ALL THESE YEARS HAS UNDOUBTEDLY PUT TOO GREAT A *STRAIN* UPON HIS BODY...!

WE'VE BEEN APPLYING *THERMO-REVIVER* DISCS... BUT THEY HAVEN'T HELPED!

REMOVE THEM NOW, SON! I WANT TO BE LEFT *ALONE* WITH THE PATIENT FOR A WHILE!

EXACTLY A HALF HOUR LATER, DR. CARLSON SUMMONS THE AVENGERS INTO THE SILENT CHAMBER ONCE AGAIN...

I'VE COMPLETED MY EXAMINATION OF HIM! I HAVE *TWO* REPORTS FOR YOU... ONE GOOD... THE OTHER *BAD!*

FIRST OF ALL, HIS TREMENDOUS *STRENGTH* WILL ENABLE GOLIATH TO *RECOVER!*

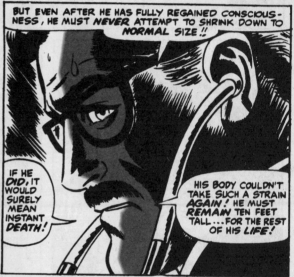

BUT EVEN AFTER HE HAS FULLY REGAINED CONSCIOUS-NESS, HE MUST *NEVER* ATTEMPT TO SHRINK DOWN TO *NORMAL* SIZE!!

IF HE *DID,* IT WOULD SURELY MEAN INSTANT *DEATH!*

HIS BODY COULDN'T TAKE SUCH A STRAIN *AGAIN!* HE MUST *REMAIN* TEN FEET TALL... FOR THE REST OF HIS *LIFE!*

THEN, FINALLY...

WHEW! I FEEL AS THOUGH I'VE BEEN THROUGH A *WRINGER!* HOW..HOW LONG HAVE I BEEN *OUT?*

ONLY A FEW HOURS... BUT YOU MUST TAKE IT *EASY!* NO VIOLENT EXERCISE FOR A WHILE!

HANK... DARLING! YOU'RE *ALIVE!* THAT'S ALL THAT *MATTERS!*

THEN, BEFORE THE PHYSICIAN TURNS TO LEAVE, CAPTAIN AMERICA SPEAKS TO HIM IN A SECLUDED CORNER OF THE DOWNSTAIRS WING...

MAJOR...ARE YOU *SURE* THAT GOLIATH WILL NEVER AGAIN BE ABLE TO REVERT TO HIS NORMAL SIZE?

NOTHING IS 100% CERTAIN IN MEDICINE, CAP... BUT, JUDGING BY HIS PRESENT CONDITION, I'M AFRAID HE'S DESTINED TO REMAIN A TEN-FOOTER FOR AS LONG AS HE *LIVES!*

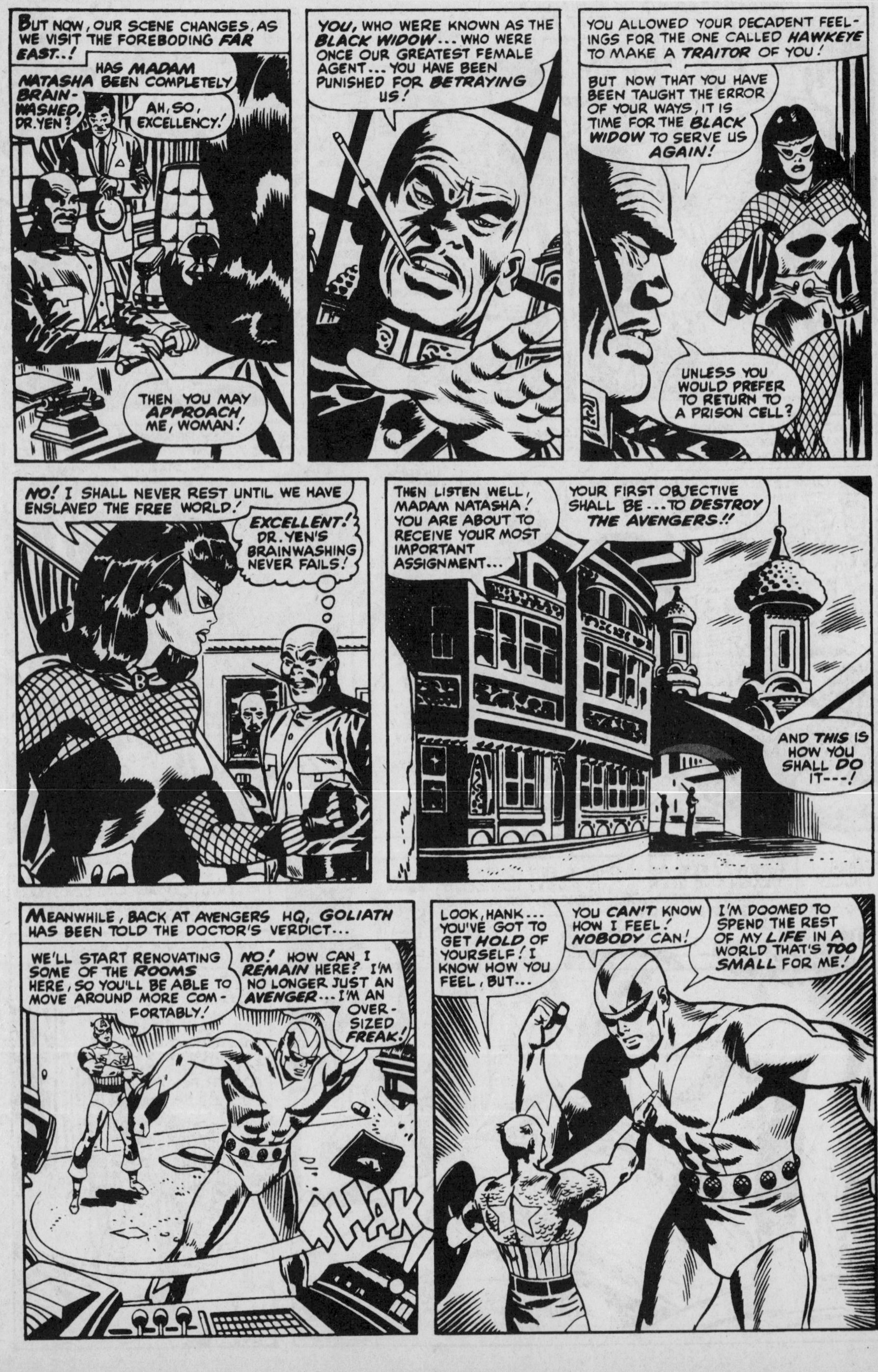
BUT NOW, OUR SCENE CHANGES, AS WE VISIT THE FOREBODING FAR EAST..!
HAS MADAM NATASHA BEEN COMPLETELY BRAIN-WASHED, DR. YEN?
AH, SO, EXCELLENCY!
THEN YOU MAY APPROACH, ME, WOMAN!
YOU, WHO WERE KNOWN AS THE BLACK WIDOW... WHO WERE ONCE OUR GREATEST FEMALE AGENT... YOU HAVE BEEN PUNISHED FOR BETRAYING US!
YOU ALLOWED YOUR DECADENT FEEL-INGS FOR THE ONE CALLED HAWKEYE TO MAKE A TRAITOR OF YOU!
BUT NOW THAT YOU HAVE BEEN TAUGHT THE ERROR OF YOUR WAYS, IT IS TIME FOR THE BLACK WIDOW TO SERVE US AGAIN!
UNLESS YOU WOULD PREFER TO RETURN TO A PRISON CELL?
NO! I SHALL NEVER REST UNTIL WE HAVE ENSLAVED THE FREE WORLD!
EXCELLENT! DR. YEN'S BRAINWASHING NEVER FAILS!
THEN LISTEN WELL, MADAM NATASHA! YOU ARE ABOUT TO RECEIVE YOUR MOST IMPORTANT ASSIGNMENT...
YOUR FIRST OBJECTIVE SHALL BE... TO DESTROY THE AVENGERS!!
AND THIS IS HOW YOU SHALL DO IT---!
MEANWHILE, BACK AT AVENGERS HQ, GOLIATH HAS BEEN TOLD THE DOCTOR'S VERDICT...
WE'LL START RENOVATING SOME OF THE ROOMS HERE, SO YOU'LL BE ABLE TO MOVE AROUND MORE COM-FORTABLY!
NO! HOW CAN I REMAIN HERE? I'M NO LONGER JUST AN AVENGER... I'M AN OVER-SIZED FREAK!
THAK
LOOK, HANK... YOU'VE GOT TO GET HOLD OF YOURSELF! I KNOW HOW YOU FEEL, BUT...
YOU CAN'T KNOW HOW I FEEL! NOBODY CAN!
I'M DOOMED TO SPEND THE REST OF MY LIFE IN A WORLD THAT'S TOO SMALL FOR ME!

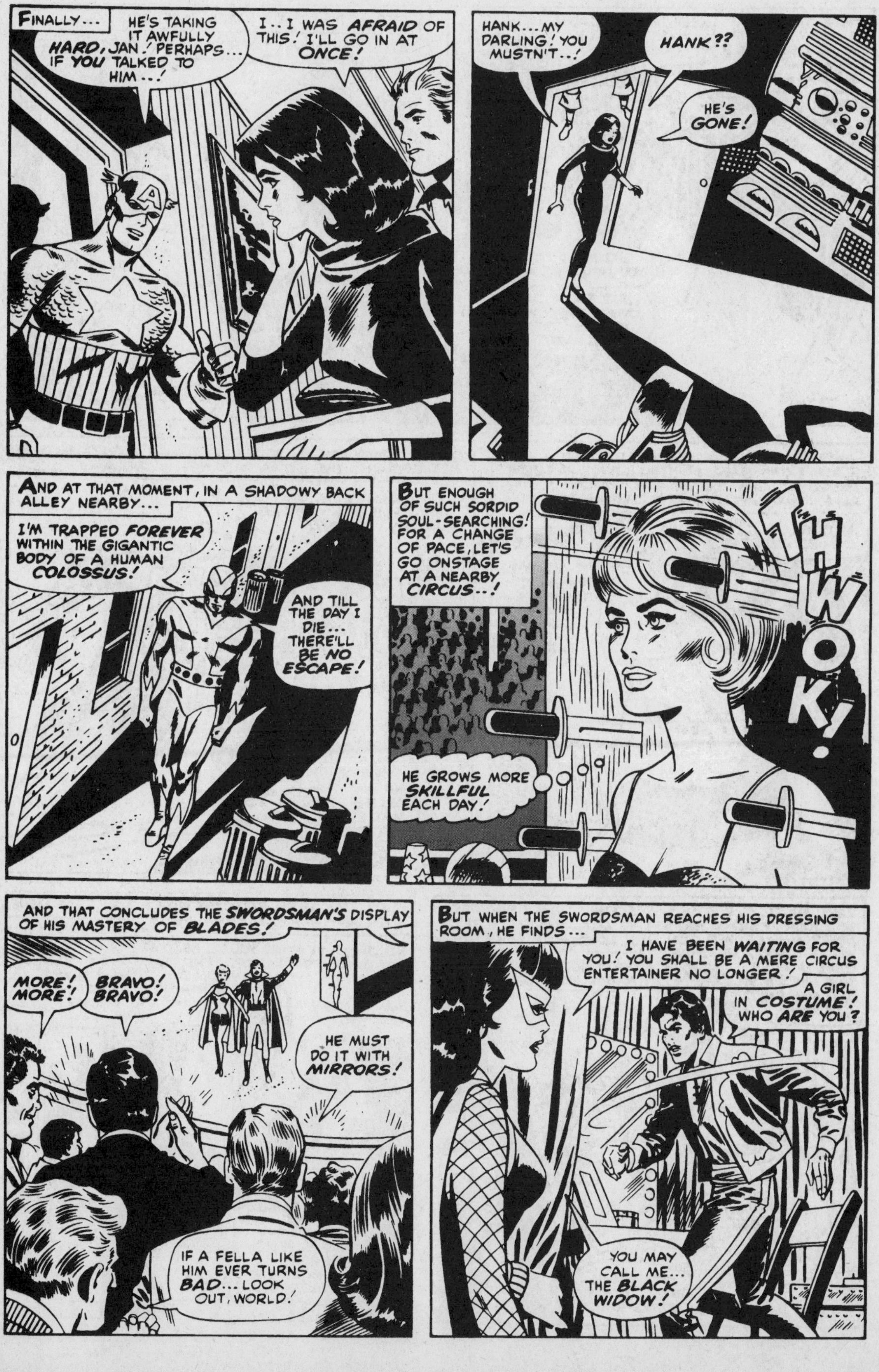
FINALLY...
HE'S TAKING IT AWFULLY HARD, JAN! PERHAPS... IF YOU TALKED TO HIM...!
I.. I WAS AFRAID OF THIS! I'LL GO IN AT ONCE!
HANK... MY DARLING! YOU MUSTN'T...!
HANK??
HE'S GONE!
AND AT THAT MOMENT, IN A SHADOWY BACK ALLEY NEARBY...
I'M TRAPPED FOREVER WITHIN THE GIGANTIC BODY OF A HUMAN COLOSSUS!
AND TILL THE DAY I DIE... THERE'LL BE NO ESCAPE!
BUT ENOUGH OF SUCH SORDID SOUL-SEARCHING! FOR A CHANGE OF PACE, LET'S GO ONSTAGE AT A NEARBY CIRCUS...!
THWOK!
HE GROWS MORE SKILLFUL EACH DAY!
AND THAT CONCLUDES THE SWORDSMAN'S DISPLAY OF HIS MASTERY OF BLADES!
MORE! MORE!
BRAVO! BRAVO!
HE MUST DO IT WITH MIRRORS!
IF A FELLA LIKE HIM EVER TURNS BAD... LOOK OUT, WORLD!
BUT WHEN THE SWORDSMAN REACHES HIS DRESSING ROOM, HE FINDS...
I HAVE BEEN WAITING FOR YOU! YOU SHALL BE A MERE CIRCUS ENTERTAINER NO LONGER!
A GIRL IN COSTUME! WHO ARE YOU?
YOU MAY CALL ME... THE BLACK WIDOW!

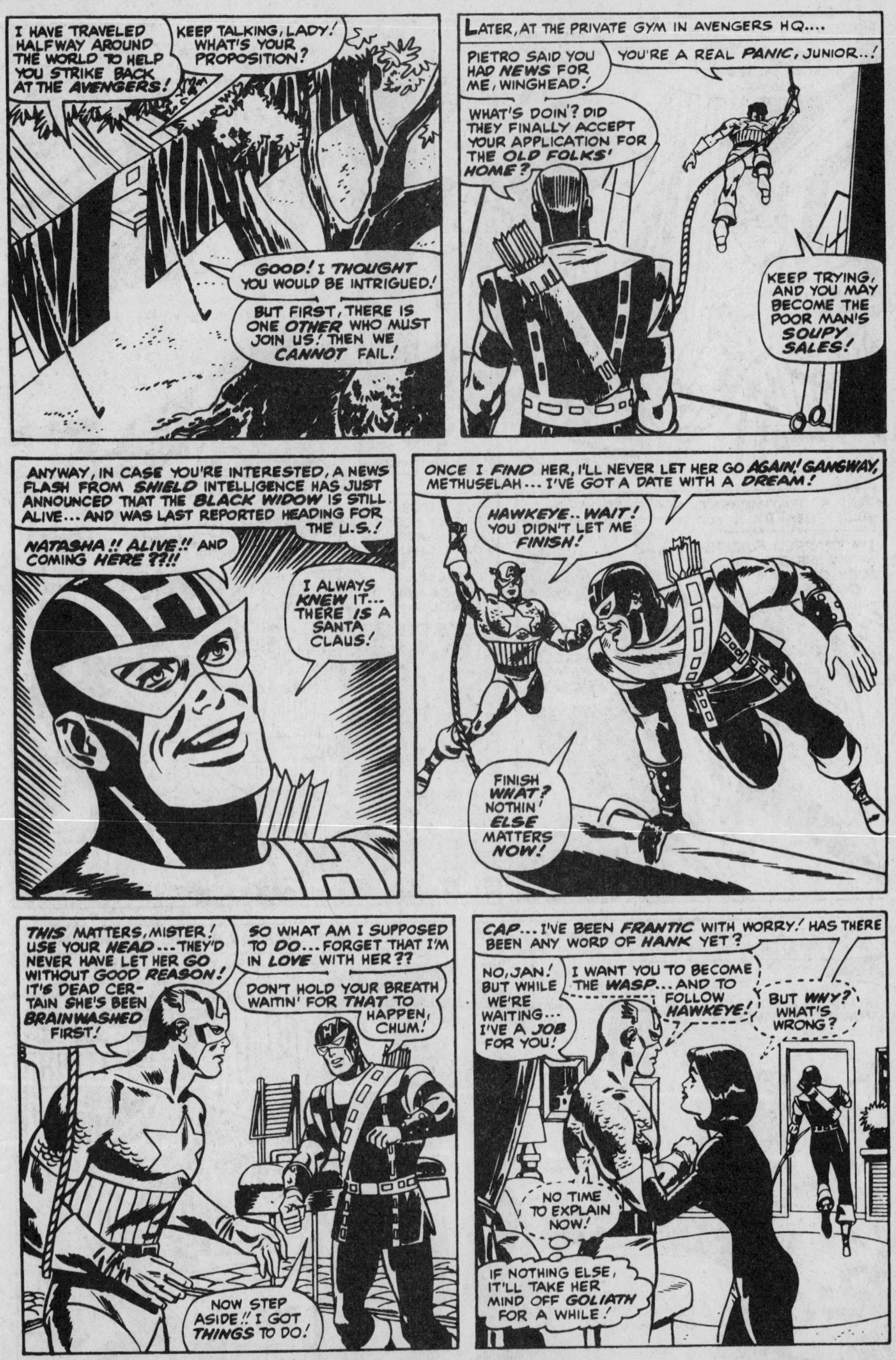

I HAVE TRAVELED HALFWAY AROUND THE WORLD TO HELP YOU STRIKE BACK AT THE AVENGERS!
KEEP TALKING, LADY! WHAT'S YOUR PROPOSITION?
GOOD! I THOUGHT YOU WOULD BE INTRIGUED!
BUT FIRST, THERE IS ONE OTHER WHO MUST JOIN US! THEN WE CANNOT FAIL!
LATER, AT THE PRIVATE GYM IN AVENGERS HQ....
PIETRO SAID YOU HAD NEWS FOR ME, WINGHEAD!
YOU'RE A REAL PANIC, JUNIOR..!
WHAT'S DOIN'? DID THEY FINALLY ACCEPT YOUR APPLICATION FOR THE OLD FOLKS' HOME?
KEEP TRYING, AND YOU MAY BECOME THE POOR MAN'S SOUPY SALES!
ANYWAY, IN CASE YOU'RE INTERESTED, A NEWS FLASH FROM SHIELD INTELLIGENCE HAS JUST ANNOUNCED THAT THE BLACK WIDOW IS STILL ALIVE... AND WAS LAST REPORTED HEADING FOR THE U.S.!
NATASHA!! ALIVE!! AND COMING HERE??!!
I ALWAYS KNEW IT... THERE IS A SANTA CLAUS!
ONCE I FIND HER, I'LL NEVER LET HER GO AGAIN! GANGWAY, METHUSELAH... I'VE GOT A DATE WITH A DREAM!
HAWKEYE.. WAIT! YOU DIDN'T LET ME FINISH!
FINISH WHAT? NOTHIN' ELSE MATTERS NOW!
THIS MATTERS, MISTER! USE YOUR HEAD... THEY'D NEVER HAVE LET HER GO WITHOUT GOOD REASON! IT'S DEAD CERTAIN SHE'S BEEN BRAINWASHED FIRST!
SO WHAT AM I SUPPOSED TO DO... FORGET THAT I'M IN LOVE WITH HER??
DON'T HOLD YOUR BREATH WAITIN' FOR THAT TO HAPPEN, CHUM!
NOW STEP ASIDE!! I GOT THINGS TO DO!
CAP... I'VE BEEN FRANTIC WITH WORRY! HAS THERE BEEN ANY WORD OF HANK YET?
NO, JAN! BUT WHILE WE'RE WAITING... I'VE A JOB FOR YOU!
I WANT YOU TO BECOME THE WASP... AND TO FOLLOW HAWKEYE!
BUT WHY? WHAT'S WRONG?
NO TIME TO EXPLAIN NOW!
IF NOTHING ELSE, IT'LL TAKE HER MIND OFF GOLIATH FOR A WHILE!

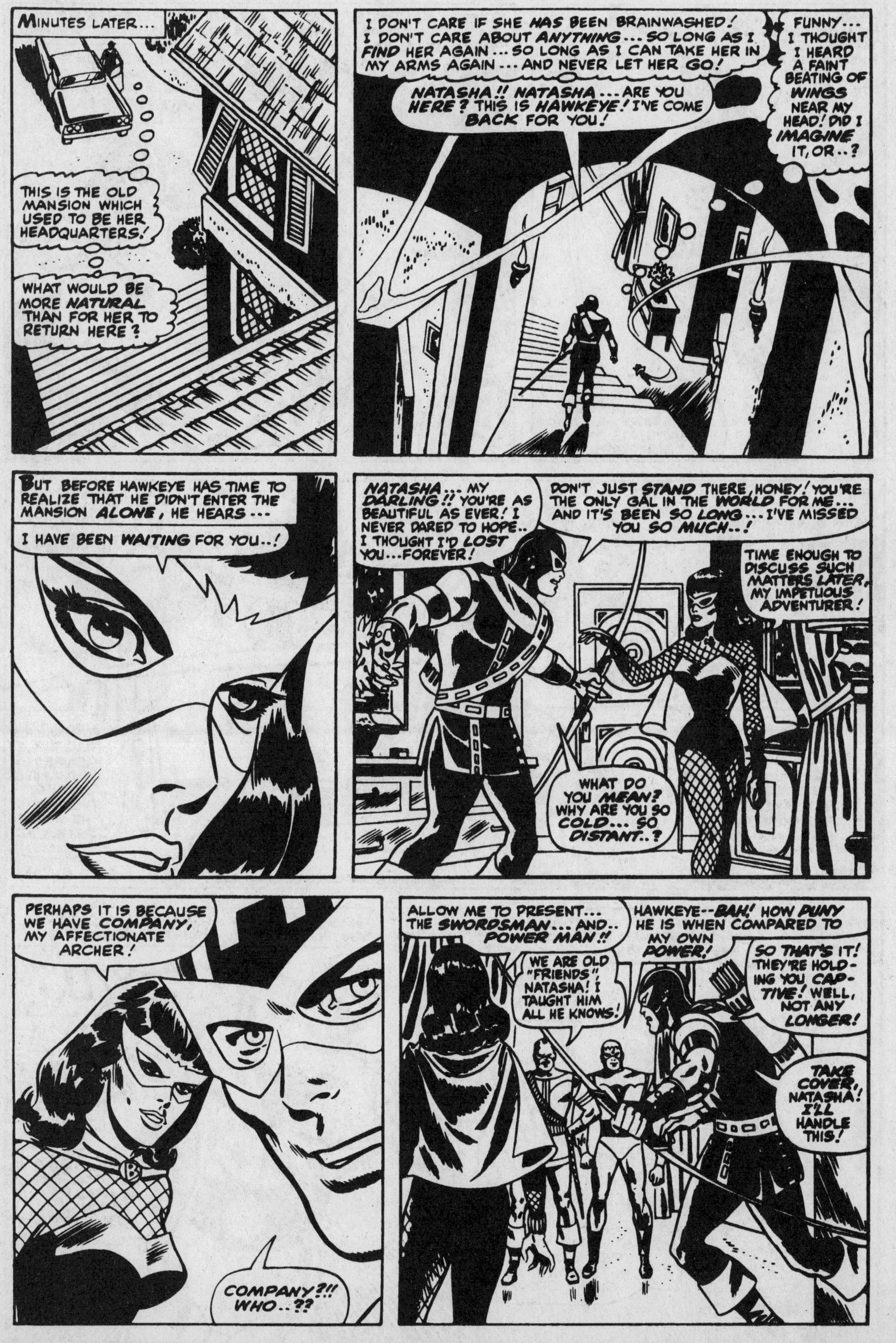

MINUTES LATER...
THIS IS THE OLD MANSION WHICH USED TO BE HER HEADQUARTERS!
WHAT WOULD BE MORE NATURAL THAN FOR HER TO RETURN HERE?
I DON'T CARE IF SHE HAS BEEN BRAINWASHED! I DON'T CARE ABOUT ANYTHING... SO LONG AS I FIND HER AGAIN... SO LONG AS I CAN TAKE HER IN MY ARMS AGAIN... AND NEVER LET HER GO!
NATASHA!! NATASHA... ARE YOU HERE? THIS IS HAWKEYE! I'VE COME BACK FOR YOU!
FUNNY... I THOUGHT I HEARD A FAINT BEATING OF WINGS NEAR MY HEAD! DID I IMAGINE IT, OR..?
BUT BEFORE HAWKEYE HAS TIME TO REALIZE THAT HE DIDN'T ENTER THE MANSION ALONE, HE HEARS...
I HAVE BEEN WAITING FOR YOU..!
NATASHA... MY DARLING!! YOU'RE AS BEAUTIFUL AS EVER! I NEVER DARED TO HOPE.. I THOUGHT I'D LOST YOU...FOREVER!
DON'T JUST STAND THERE, HONEY! YOU'RE THE ONLY GAL IN THE WORLD FOR ME... AND IT'S BEEN SO LONG... I'VE MISSED YOU SO MUCH..!
TIME ENOUGH TO DISCUSS SUCH MATTERS LATER, MY IMPETUOUS ADVENTURER!
WHAT DO YOU MEAN? WHY ARE YOU SO COLD... SO DISTANT..?
PERHAPS IT IS BECAUSE WE HAVE COMPANY, MY AFFECTIONATE ARCHER!
COMPANY?!! WHO..??
ALLOW ME TO PRESENT... THE SWORDSMAN... AND.. POWER MAN!!
HAWKEYE--BAH! HOW PUNY HE IS WHEN COMPARED TO MY OWN POWER!
WE ARE OLD "FRIENDS", NATASHA! I TAUGHT HIM ALL HE KNOWS!
SO THAT'S IT! THEY'RE HOLDING YOU CAPTIVE! WELL, NOT ANY LONGER!
TAKE COVER, NATASHA! I'LL HANDLE THIS!

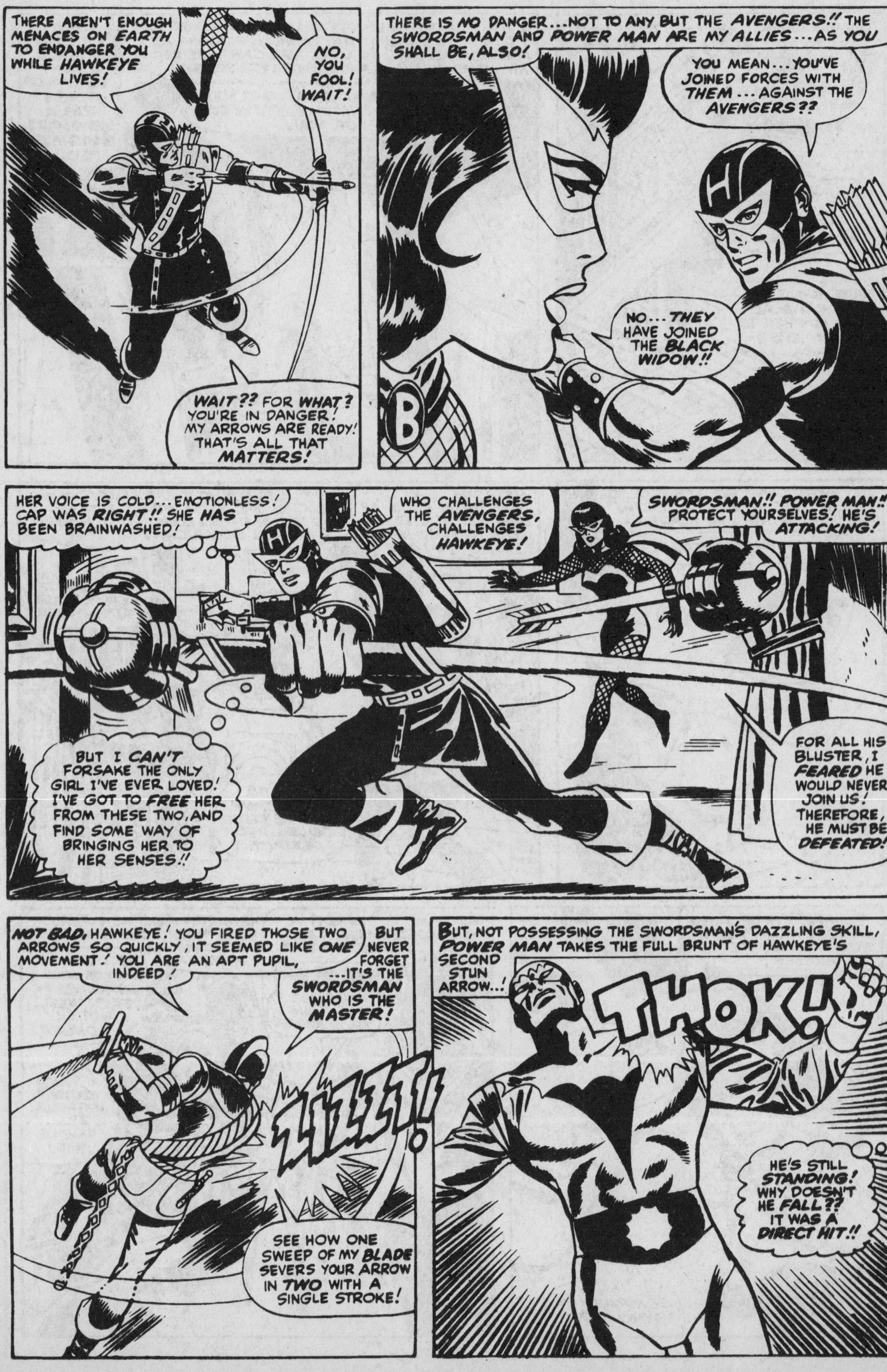
THERE AREN'T ENOUGH MENACES ON EARTH TO ENDANGER YOU WHILE HAWKEYE LIVES!
NO, YOU FOOL! WAIT!
WAIT?? FOR WHAT? YOU'RE IN DANGER! MY ARROWS ARE READY! THAT'S ALL THAT MATTERS!
THERE IS NO DANGER...NOT TO ANY BUT THE AVENGERS!! THE SWORDSMAN AND POWER MAN ARE MY ALLIES...AS YOU SHALL BE, ALSO!
YOU MEAN...YOU'VE JOINED FORCES WITH THEM...AGAINST THE AVENGERS??
NO...THEY HAVE JOINED THE BLACK WIDOW!!
HER VOICE IS COLD...EMOTIONLESS! CAP WAS RIGHT!! SHE HAS BEEN BRAINWASHED!
WHO CHALLENGES THE AVENGERS, CHALLENGES HAWKEYE!
SWORDSMAN!! POWER MAN!! PROTECT YOURSELVES! HE'S ATTACKING!
BUT I CAN'T FORSAKE THE ONLY GIRL I'VE EVER LOVED! I'VE GOT TO FREE HER FROM THESE TWO, AND FIND SOME WAY OF BRINGING HER TO HER SENSES!!
FOR ALL HIS BLUSTER, I FEARED HE WOULD NEVER JOIN US! THEREFORE, HE MUST BE DEFEATED!
NOT BAD, HAWKEYE! YOU FIRED THOSE TWO ARROWS SO QUICKLY, IT SEEMED LIKE ONE MOVEMENT! YOU ARE AN APT PUPIL, INDEED!
BUT NEVER FORGET ...IT'S THE SWORDSMAN WHO IS THE MASTER!
ZIZZZT!
SEE HOW ONE SWEEP OF MY BLADE SEVERS YOUR ARROW IN TWO WITH A SINGLE STROKE!
BUT, NOT POSSESSING THE SWORDSMAN'S DAZZLING SKILL, POWER MAN TAKES THE FULL BRUNT OF HAWKEYE'S SECOND STUN ARROW...!
THOK!
HE'S STILL STANDING! WHY DOESN'T HE FALL?? IT WAS A DIRECT HIT!!

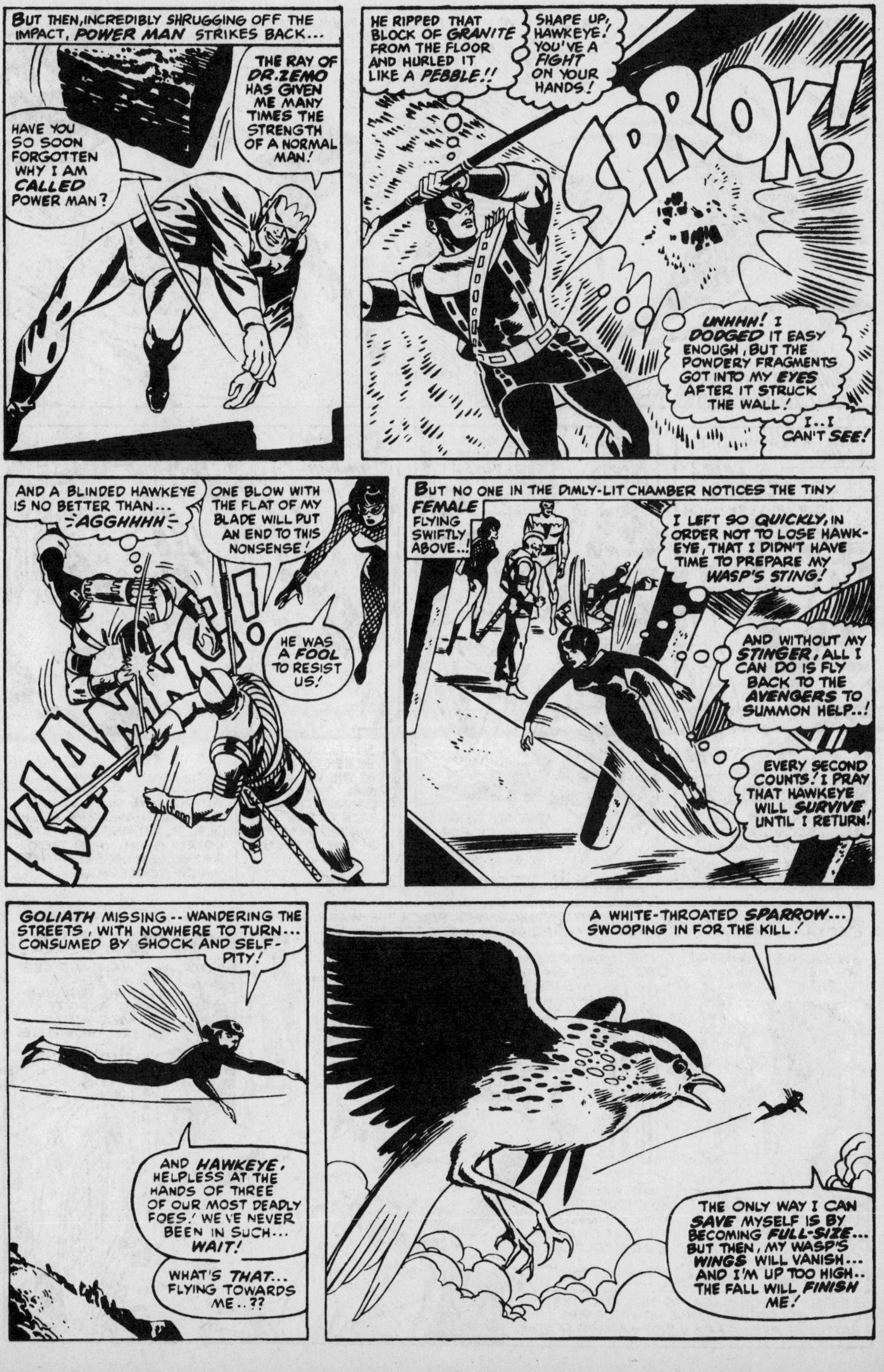

BUT THEN, INCREDIBLY SHRUGGING OFF THE IMPACT, POWER MAN STRIKES BACK...
HAVE YOU SO SOON FORGOTTEN WHY I AM CALLED POWER MAN?
THE RAY OF DR. ZEMO HAS GIVEN ME MANY TIMES THE STRENGTH OF A NORMAL MAN!
HE RIPPED THAT BLOCK OF GRANITE FROM THE FLOOR AND HURLED IT LIKE A PEBBLE!!
SHAPE UP, HAWKEYE! YOU'VE A FIGHT ON YOUR HANDS!
SPROK!
UNHHH! I DODGED IT EASY ENOUGH, BUT THE POWDERY FRAGMENTS GOT INTO MY EYES AFTER IT STRUCK THE WALL!
I..I CAN'T SEE!
AND A BLINDED HAWKEYE IS NO BETTER THAN... AGGHHHH
ONE BLOW WITH THE FLAT OF MY BLADE WILL PUT AN END TO THIS NONSENSE!
HE WAS A FOOL TO RESIST US!
BUT NO ONE IN THE DIMLY-LIT CHAMBER NOTICES THE TINY FEMALE FLYING SWIFTLY ABOVE...
I LEFT SO QUICKLY, IN ORDER NOT TO LOSE HAWKEYE, THAT I DIDN'T HAVE TIME TO PREPARE MY WASP'S STING!
AND WITHOUT MY STINGER, ALL I CAN DO IS FLY BACK TO THE AVENGERS TO SUMMON HELP..!
EVERY SECOND COUNTS! I PRAY THAT HAWKEYE WILL SURVIVE UNTIL I RETURN!
GOLIATH MISSING -- WANDERING THE STREETS, WITH NOWHERE TO TURN... CONSUMED BY SHOCK AND SELF-PITY!
AND HAWKEYE, HELPLESS AT THE HANDS OF THREE OF OUR MOST DEADLY FOES! WE'VE NEVER BEEN IN SUCH... WAIT!
WHAT'S THAT... FLYING TOWARDS ME..??
A WHITE-THROATED SPARROW... SWOOPING IN FOR THE KILL!
THE ONLY WAY I CAN SAVE MYSELF IS BY BECOMING FULL-SIZE... BUT THEN, MY WASP'S WINGS WILL VANISH... AND I'M UP TOO HIGH.. THE FALL WILL FINISH ME!

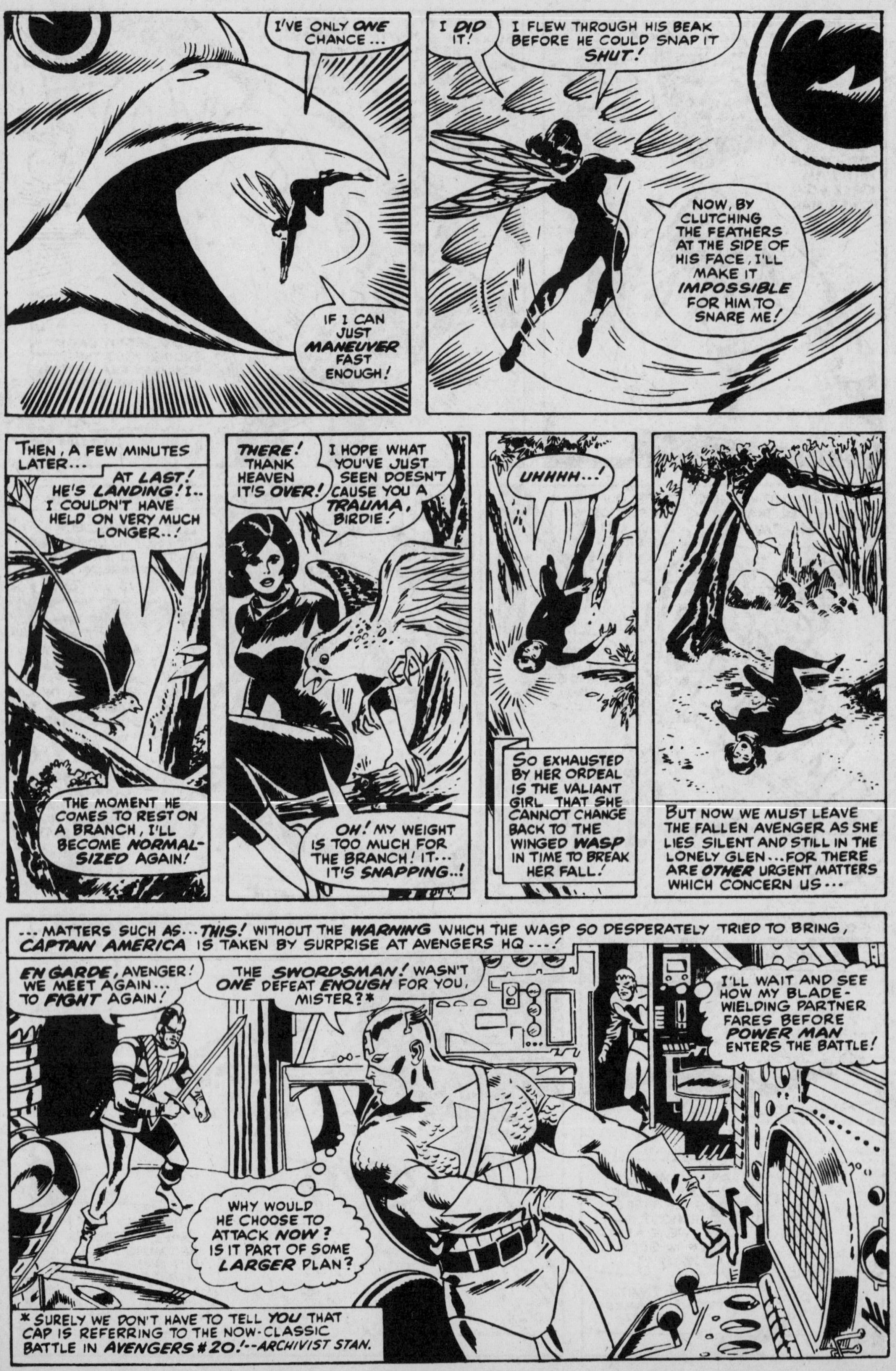

I'VE ONLY ONE CHANCE...
IF I CAN JUST MANEUVER FAST ENOUGH!
I DID IT!
I FLEW THROUGH HIS BEAK BEFORE HE COULD SNAP IT SHUT!
NOW, BY CLUTCHING THE FEATHERS AT THE SIDE OF HIS FACE, I'LL MAKE IT IMPOSSIBLE FOR HIM TO SNARE ME!
THEN, A FEW MINUTES LATER...
AT LAST! HE'S LANDING! I.. I COULDN'T HAVE HELD ON VERY MUCH LONGER...!
THE MOMENT HE COMES TO REST ON A BRANCH, I'LL BECOME NORMAL-SIZED AGAIN!
THERE! THANK HEAVEN IT'S OVER!
I HOPE WHAT YOU'VE JUST SEEN DOESN'T CAUSE YOU A TRAUMA, BIRDIE!
OH! MY WEIGHT IS TOO MUCH FOR THE BRANCH! IT... IT'S SNAPPING..!
UHHHH...!
SO EXHAUSTED BY HER ORDEAL IS THE VALIANT GIRL THAT SHE CANNOT CHANGE BACK TO THE WINGED WASP IN TIME TO BREAK HER FALL!
BUT NOW WE MUST LEAVE THE FALLEN AVENGER AS SHE LIES SILENT AND STILL IN THE LONELY GLEN...FOR THERE ARE OTHER URGENT MATTERS WHICH CONCERN US...
...MATTERS SUCH AS...THIS! WITHOUT THE WARNING WHICH THE WASP SO DESPERATELY TRIED TO BRING, CAPTAIN AMERICA IS TAKEN BY SURPRISE AT AVENGERS HQ---!
EN GARDE, AVENGER! WE MEET AGAIN... TO FIGHT AGAIN!
THE SWORDSMAN! WASN'T ONE DEFEAT ENOUGH FOR YOU, MISTER?*
I'LL WAIT AND SEE HOW MY BLADE-WIELDING PARTNER FARES BEFORE POWER MAN ENTERS THE BATTLE!
WHY WOULD HE CHOOSE TO ATTACK NOW? IS IT PART OF SOME LARGER PLAN?
* SURELY WE DON'T HAVE TO TELL YOU THAT CAP IS REFERRING TO THE NOW-CLASSIC BATTLE IN AVENGERS #20!--ARCHIVIST STAN.

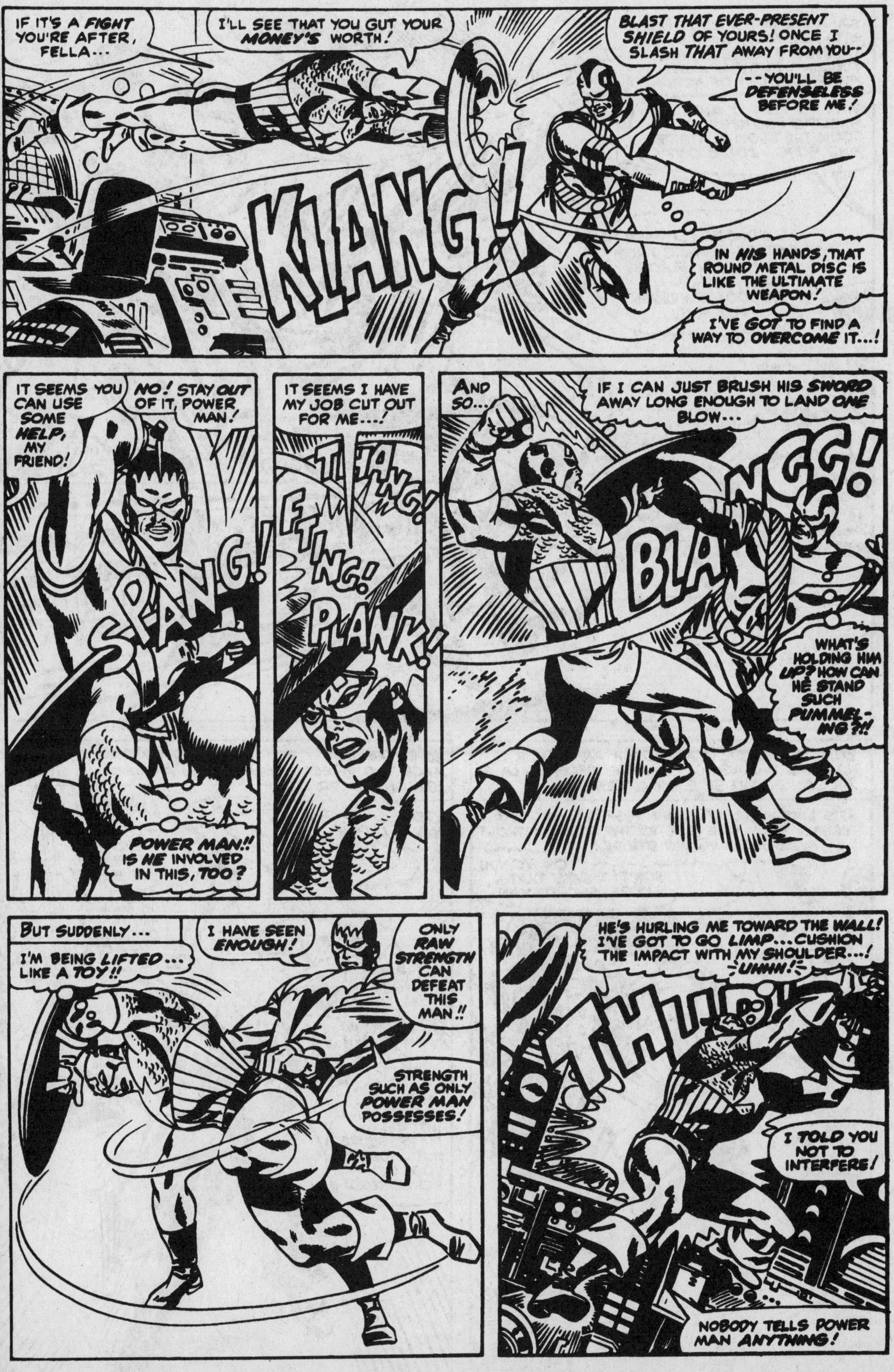
IF IT'S A FIGHT YOU'RE AFTER, FELLA...
I'LL SEE THAT YOU GUT YOUR MONEY'S WORTH!
BLAST THAT EVER-PRESENT SHIELD OF YOURS! ONCE I SLASH THAT AWAY FROM YOU--
--YOU'LL BE DEFENSELESS BEFORE ME!
KLANG!
IN HIS HANDS, THAT ROUND METAL DISC IS LIKE THE ULTIMATE WEAPON!
I'VE GOT TO FIND A WAY TO OVERCOME IT...!
IT SEEMS YOU CAN USE SOME HELP, MY FRIEND!
NO! STAY OUT OF IT, POWER MAN!
SPANG!
POWER MAN!! IS HE INVOLVED IN THIS, TOO?
IT SEEMS I HAVE MY JOB CUT OUT FOR ME...!
THANG!
FTING!
PLANK!
AND SO...
IF I CAN JUST BRUSH HIS SWORD AWAY LONG ENOUGH TO LAND ONE BLOW...
BLANGG!
WHAT'S HOLDING HIM UP? HOW CAN HE STAND SUCH PUMMEL-ING?!!
BUT SUDDENLY...
I'M BEING LIFTED... LIKE A TOY!!
I HAVE SEEN ENOUGH!
ONLY RAW STRENGTH CAN DEFEAT THIS MAN!!
STRENGTH SUCH AS ONLY POWER MAN POSSESSES!
HE'S HURLING ME TOWARD THE WALL! I'VE GOT TO GO LIMP... CUSHION THE IMPACT WITH MY SHOULDER...!
UHHN!
I TOLD YOU NOT TO INTERFERE!
NOBODY TELLS POWER MAN ANYTHING!

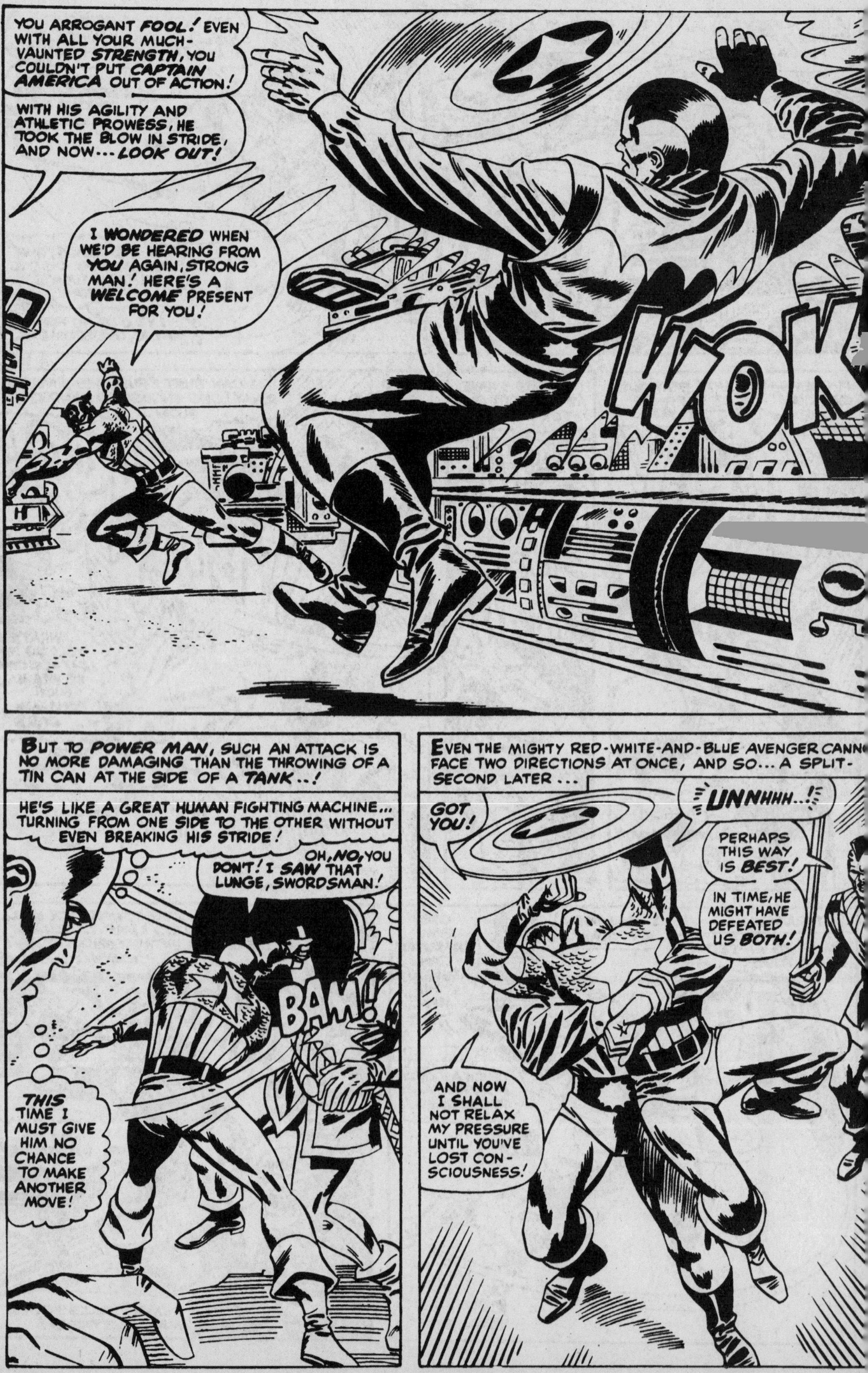
YOU ARROGANT FOOL! EVEN WITH ALL YOUR MUCH-VAUNTED STRENGTH, YOU COULDN'T PUT CAPTAIN AMERICA OUT OF ACTION!
WITH HIS AGILITY AND ATHLETIC PROWESS, HE TOOK THE BLOW IN STRIDE, AND NOW... LOOK OUT!
I WONDERED WHEN WE'D BE HEARING FROM YOU AGAIN, STRONG MAN! HERE'S A WELCOME PRESENT FOR YOU!
WOK
BUT TO POWER MAN, SUCH AN ATTACK IS NO MORE DAMAGING THAN THE THROWING OF A TIN CAN AT THE SIDE OF A TANK..!
HE'S LIKE A GREAT HUMAN FIGHTING MACHINE... TURNING FROM ONE SIDE TO THE OTHER WITHOUT EVEN BREAKING HIS STRIDE!
OH, NO, YOU DON'T! I SAW THAT LUNGE, SWORDSMAN!
BAM!
THIS TIME I MUST GIVE HIM NO CHANCE TO MAKE ANOTHER MOVE!
EVEN THE MIGHTY RED-WHITE-AND-BLUE AVENGER CANN FACE TWO DIRECTIONS AT ONCE, AND SO... A SPLIT-SECOND LATER...
GOT YOU!
UNNHHH..!
PERHAPS THIS WAY IS BEST!
IN TIME, HE MIGHT HAVE DEFEATED US BOTH!
AND NOW I SHALL NOT RELAX MY PRESSURE UNTIL YOU'VE LOST CON-SCIOUSNESS!

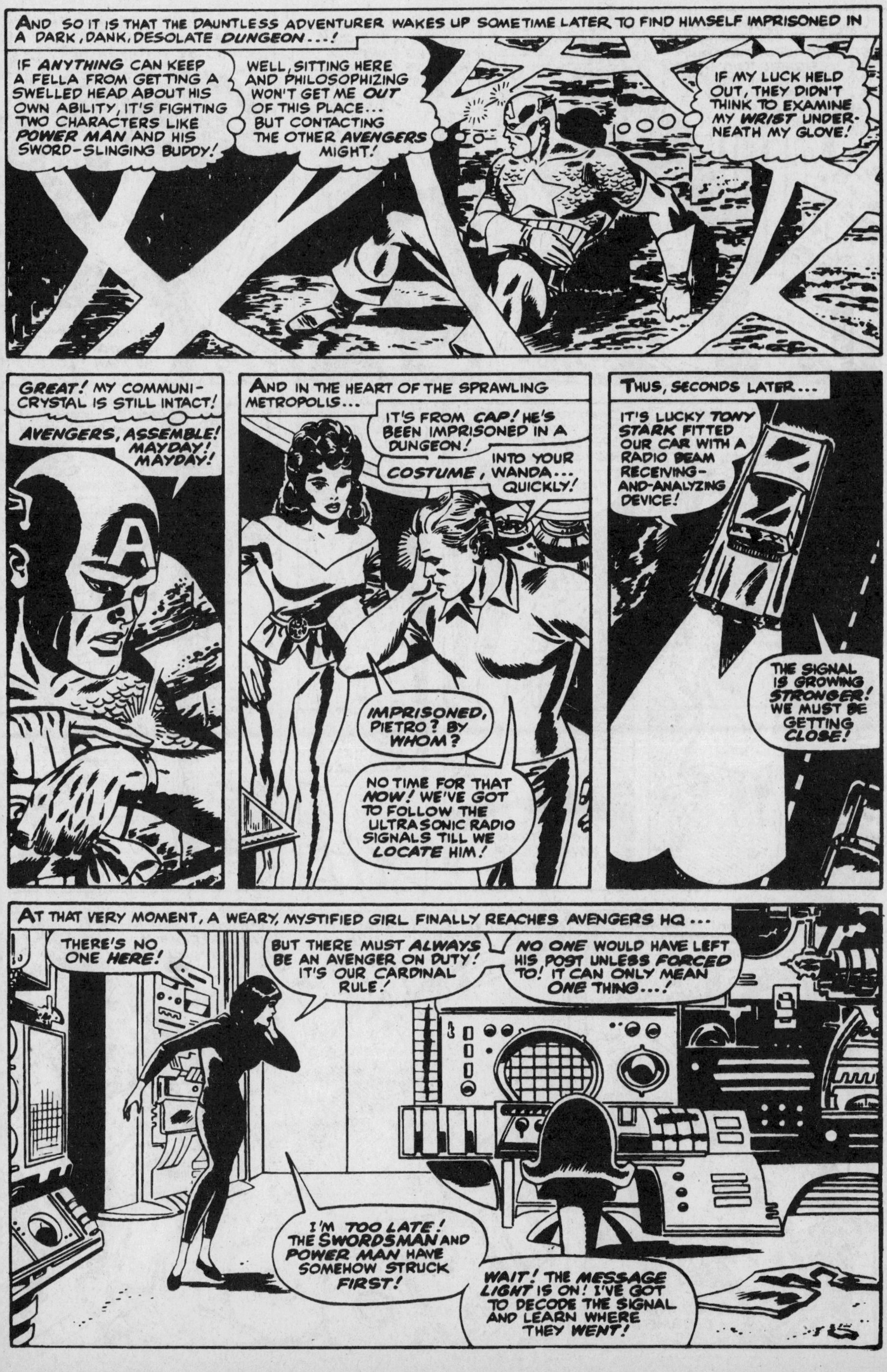
AND SO IT IS THAT THE DAUNTLESS ADVENTURER WAKES UP SOMETIME LATER TO FIND HIMSELF IMPRISONED IN A DARK, DANK, DESOLATE DUNGEON...!
IF ANYTHING CAN KEEP A FELLA FROM GETTING A SWELLED HEAD ABOUT HIS OWN ABILITY, IT'S FIGHTING TWO CHARACTERS LIKE POWER MAN AND HIS SWORD-SLINGING BUDDY!
WELL, SITTING HERE AND PHILOSOPHIZING WON'T GET ME OUT OF THIS PLACE... BUT CONTACTING THE OTHER AVENGERS MIGHT!
IF MY LUCK HELD OUT, THEY DIDN'T THINK TO EXAMINE MY WRIST UNDERNEATH MY GLOVE!
GREAT! MY COMMUNI-CRYSTAL IS STILL INTACT!
AVENGERS, ASSEMBLE! MAYDAY! MAYDAY!
AND IN THE HEART OF THE SPRAWLING METROPOLIS...
IT'S FROM CAP! HE'S BEEN IMPRISONED IN A DUNGEON!
COSTUME, INTO YOUR WANDA... QUICKLY!
IMPRISONED, PIETRO? BY WHOM?
NO TIME FOR THAT NOW! WE'VE GOT TO FOLLOW THE ULTRASONIC RADIO SIGNALS TILL WE LOCATE HIM!
THUS, SECONDS LATER...
IT'S LUCKY TONY STARK FITTED OUR CAR WITH A RADIO BEAM RECEIVING-AND-ANALYZING DEVICE!
THE SIGNAL IS GROWING STRONGER! WE MUST BE GETTING CLOSE!
AT THAT VERY MOMENT, A WEARY, MYSTIFIED GIRL FINALLY REACHES AVENGERS HQ...
THERE'S NO ONE HERE!
BUT THERE MUST ALWAYS BE AN AVENGER ON DUTY! IT'S OUR CARDINAL RULE!
NO ONE WOULD HAVE LEFT HIS POST UNLESS FORCED TO! IT CAN ONLY MEAN ONE THING...!
I'M TOO LATE! THE SWORDSMAN AND POWER MAN HAVE SOMEHOW STRUCK FIRST!
WAIT! THE MESSAGE LIGHT IS ON! I'VE GOT TO DECODE THE SIGNAL AND LEARN WHERE THEY WENT!

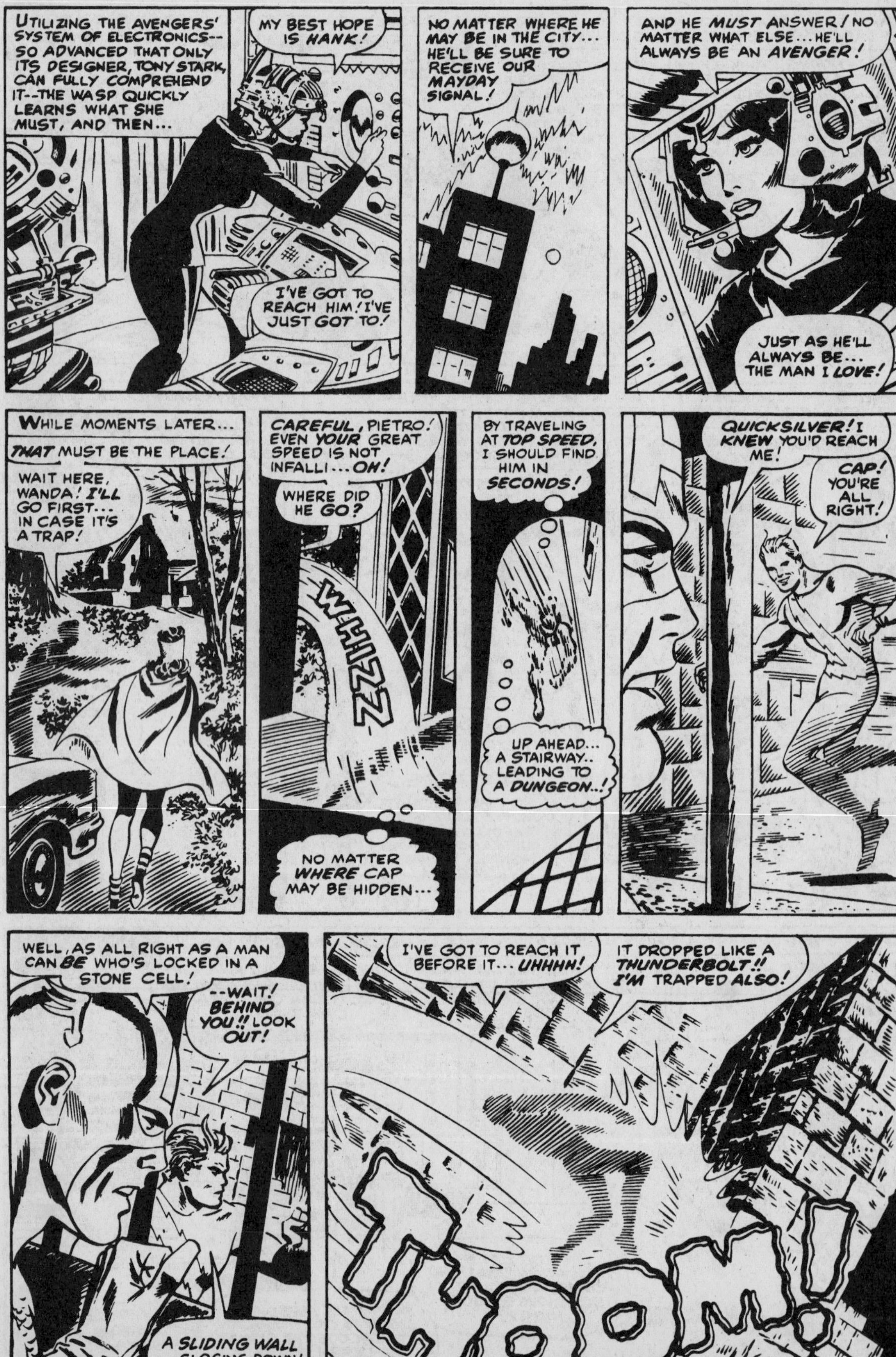

UTILIZING THE AVENGERS' SYSTEM OF ELECTRONICS-- SO ADVANCED THAT ONLY ITS DESIGNER, TONY STARK, CAN FULLY COMPREHEND IT--THE WASP QUICKLY LEARNS WHAT SHE MUST, AND THEN...
MY BEST HOPE IS HANK!
I'VE GOT TO REACH HIM! I'VE JUST GOT TO!
NO MATTER WHERE HE MAY BE IN THE CITY... HE'LL BE SURE TO RECEIVE OUR MAYDAY SIGNAL!
AND HE MUST ANSWER! NO MATTER WHAT ELSE... HE'LL ALWAYS BE AN AVENGER!
JUST AS HE'LL ALWAYS BE... THE MAN I LOVE!
WHILE MOMENTS LATER...
THAT MUST BE THE PLACE!
WAIT HERE, WANDA! I'LL GO FIRST... IN CASE IT'S A TRAP!
CAREFUL, PIETRO! EVEN YOUR GREAT SPEED IS NOT INFALLI... OH!
WHERE DID HE GO?
WHIZZZ
NO MATTER WHERE CAP MAY BE HIDDEN...
BY TRAVELING AT TOP SPEED, I SHOULD FIND HIM IN SECONDS!
UP AHEAD... A STAIRWAY.. LEADING TO A DUNGEON...!
QUICKSILVER! I KNEW YOU'D REACH ME!
CAP! YOU'RE ALL RIGHT!
WELL, AS ALL RIGHT AS A MAN CAN BE WHO'S LOCKED IN A STONE CELL!
--WAIT! BEHIND YOU!! LOOK OUT!
A SLIDING WALL .. CLOSING DOWN!
I'VE GOT TO REACH IT BEFORE IT... UHHHH!
IT DROPPED LIKE A THUNDERBOLT!! I'M TRAPPED ALSO!
THOOM!

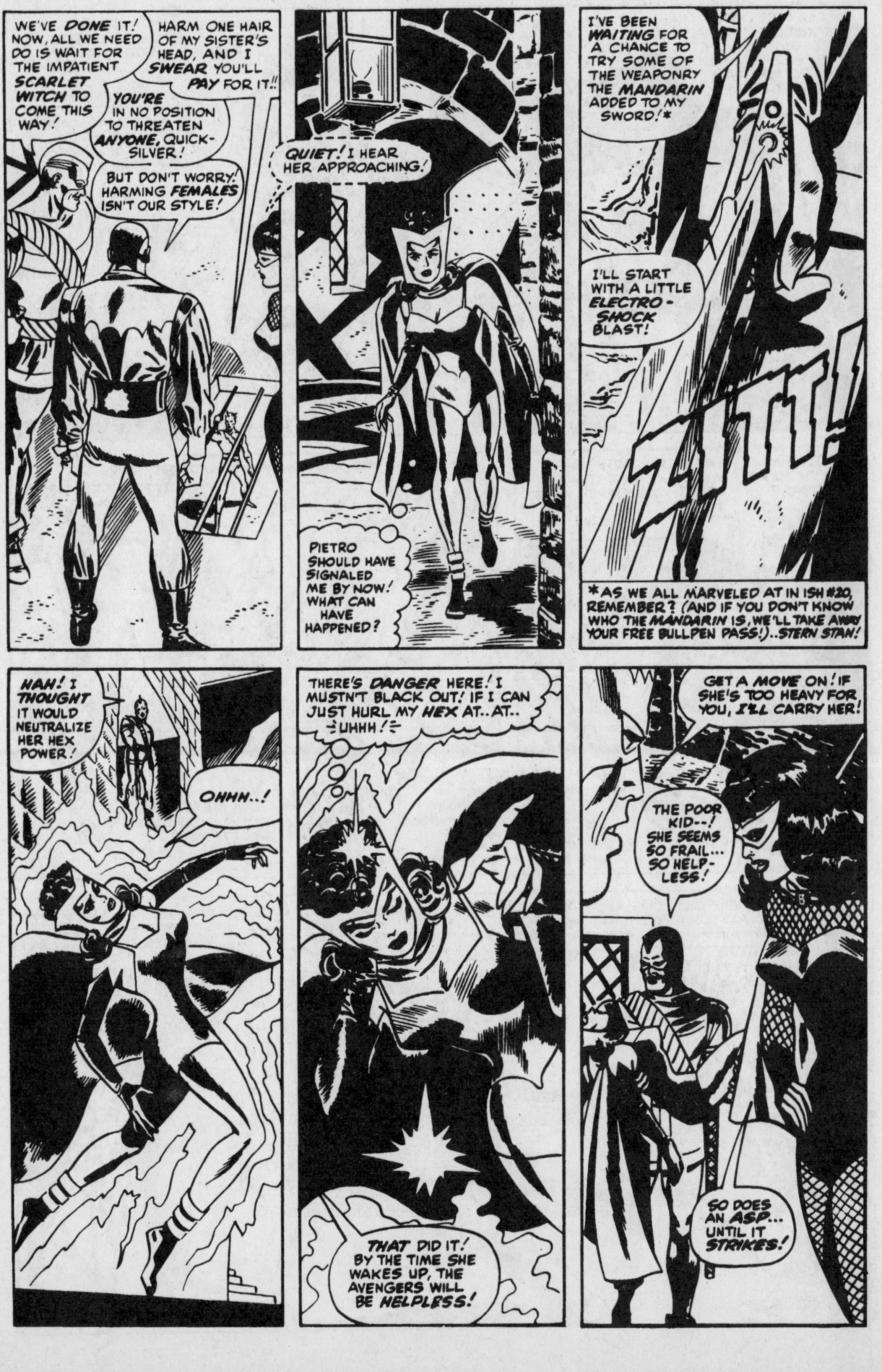
WE'VE DONE IT! NOW, ALL WE NEED DO IS WAIT FOR THE IMPATIENT SCARLET WITCH TO COME THIS WAY!
HARM ONE HAIR OF MY SISTER'S HEAD, AND I SWEAR YOU'LL PAY FOR IT!!
YOU'RE IN NO POSITION TO THREATEN ANYONE, QUICK-SILVER!
BUT DON'T WORRY! HARMING FEMALES ISN'T OUR STYLE!
QUIET! I HEAR HER APPROACHING!
PIETRO SHOULD HAVE SIGNALED ME BY NOW! WHAT CAN HAVE HAPPENED?
I'VE BEEN WAITING FOR A CHANCE TO TRY SOME OF THE WEAPONRY THE MANDARIN ADDED TO MY SWORD!*
I'LL START WITH A LITTLE ELECTRO-SHOCK BLAST!
ZITT!
*AS WE ALL MARVELED AT IN ISH #20, REMEMBER? (AND IF YOU DON'T KNOW WHO THE MANDARIN IS, WE'LL TAKE AWAY YOUR FREE BULLPEN PASS!)..STERN STAN!
HAH! I THOUGHT IT WOULD NEUTRALIZE HER HEX POWER!
OHHH..!
THERE'S DANGER HERE! I MUSTN'T BLACK OUT! IF I CAN JUST HURL MY HEX AT..AT.. UHHH!
THAT DID IT! BY THE TIME SHE WAKES UP, THE AVENGERS WILL BE HELPLESS!
GET A MOVE ON! IF SHE'S TOO HEAVY FOR YOU, I'LL CARRY HER!
THE POOR KID--! SHE SEEMS SO FRAIL... SO HELP-LESS!
SO DOES AN ASP... UNTIL IT STRIKES!

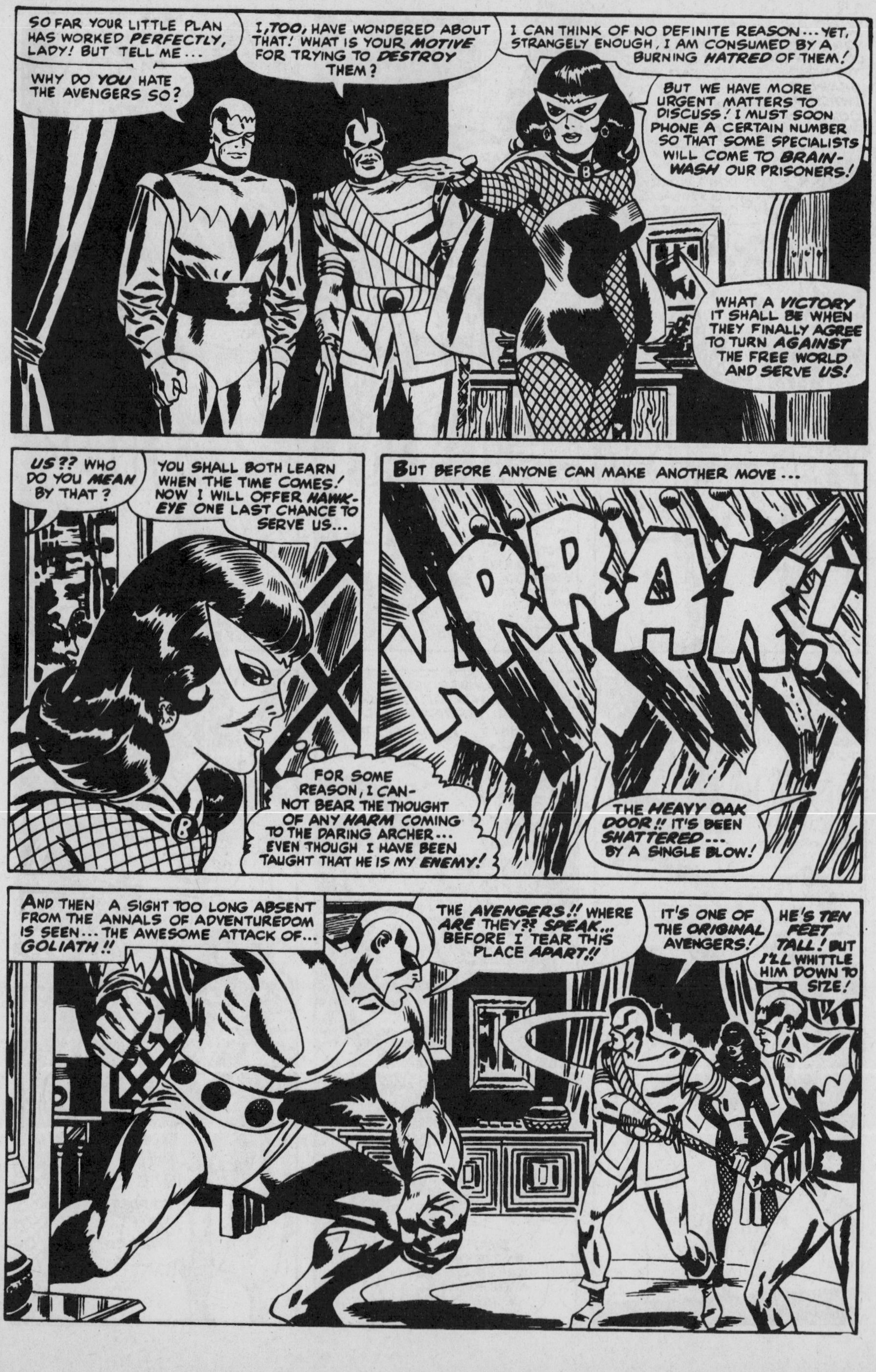
SO FAR YOUR LITTLE PLAN HAS WORKED PERFECTLY, LADY! BUT TELL ME...
WHY DO YOU HATE THE AVENGERS SO?
I, TOO, HAVE WONDERED ABOUT THAT! WHAT IS YOUR MOTIVE FOR TRYING TO DESTROY THEM?
I CAN THINK OF NO DEFINITE REASON... YET, STRANGELY ENOUGH, I AM CONSUMED BY A BURNING HATRED OF THEM!
BUT WE HAVE MORE URGENT MATTERS TO DISCUSS! I MUST SOON PHONE A CERTAIN NUMBER SO THAT SOME SPECIALISTS WILL COME TO BRAIN-WASH OUR PRISONERS!
WHAT A VICTORY IT SHALL BE WHEN THEY FINALLY AGREE TO TURN AGAINST THE FREE WORLD AND SERVE US!
US?? WHO DO YOU MEAN BY THAT?
YOU SHALL BOTH LEARN WHEN THE TIME COMES! NOW I WILL OFFER HAWK-EYE ONE LAST CHANCE TO SERVE US...
FOR SOME REASON, I CAN-NOT BEAR THE THOUGHT OF ANY HARM COMING TO THE DARING ARCHER... EVEN THOUGH I HAVE BEEN TAUGHT THAT HE IS MY ENEMY!
BUT BEFORE ANYONE CAN MAKE ANOTHER MOVE...
KRRAK!
THE HEAVY OAK DOOR!! IT'S BEEN SHATTERED... BY A SINGLE BLOW!
AND THEN A SIGHT TOO LONG ABSENT FROM THE ANNALS OF ADVENTUREDOM IS SEEN... THE AWESOME ATTACK OF... GOLIATH!!
THE AVENGERS!! WHERE ARE THEY?? SPEAK... BEFORE I TEAR THIS PLACE APART!!
IT'S ONE OF THE ORIGINAL AVENGERS!
HE'S TEN FEET TALL! BUT I'LL WHITTLE HIM DOWN TO SIZE!

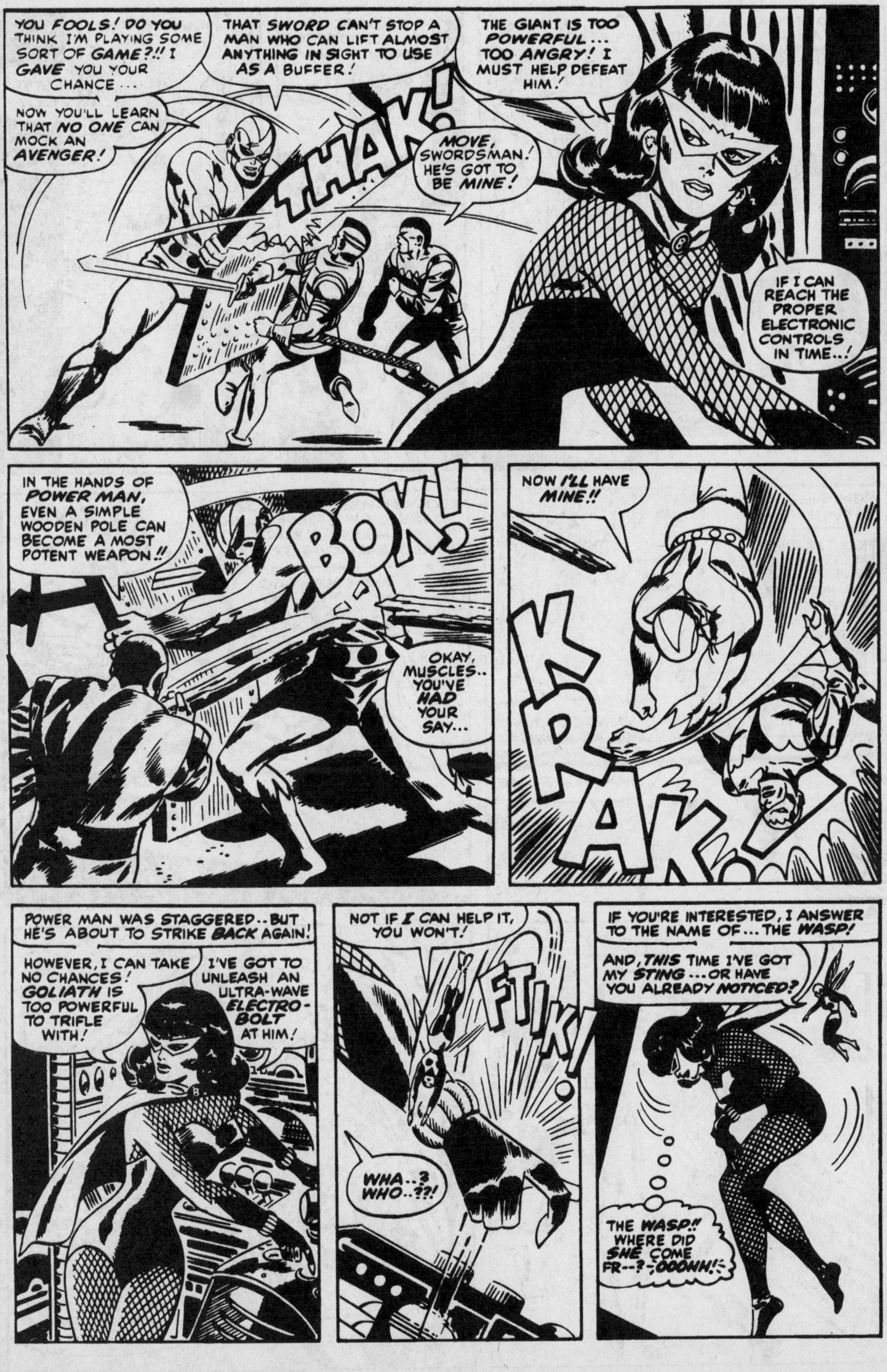
YOU FOOLS! DO YOU THINK I'M PLAYING SOME SORT OF GAME?!! I GAVE YOU YOUR CHANCE...
NOW YOU'LL LEARN THAT NO ONE CAN MOCK AN AVENGER!
THAT SWORD CAN'T STOP A MAN WHO CAN LIFT ALMOST ANYTHING IN SIGHT TO USE AS A BUFFER!
THAK!
MOVE, SWORDSMAN! HE'S GOT TO BE MINE!
THE GIANT IS TOO POWERFUL... TOO ANGRY! I MUST HELP DEFEAT HIM!
IF I CAN REACH THE PROPER ELECTRONIC CONTROLS IN TIME...!
IN THE HANDS OF POWER MAN, EVEN A SIMPLE WOODEN POLE CAN BECOME A MOST POTENT WEAPON!!
BOK!
OKAY, MUSCLES.. YOU'VE HAD YOUR SAY...
NOW I'LL HAVE MINE!!
KRAK!
POWER MAN WAS STAGGERED..BUT HE'S ABOUT TO STRIKE BACK AGAIN!
HOWEVER, I CAN TAKE NO CHANCES! GOLIATH IS TOO POWERFUL TO TRIFLE WITH!
I'VE GOT TO UNLEASH AN ULTRA-WAVE ELECTRO-BOLT AT HIM!
NOT IF I CAN HELP IT, YOU WON'T!
FTIK!
WHA..? WHO..??!
IF YOU'RE INTERESTED, I ANSWER TO THE NAME OF... THE WASP!
AND, THIS TIME I'VE GOT MY STING...OR HAVE YOU ALREADY NOTICED?
THE WASP!! WHERE DID SHE COME FR--?-OOOHH!

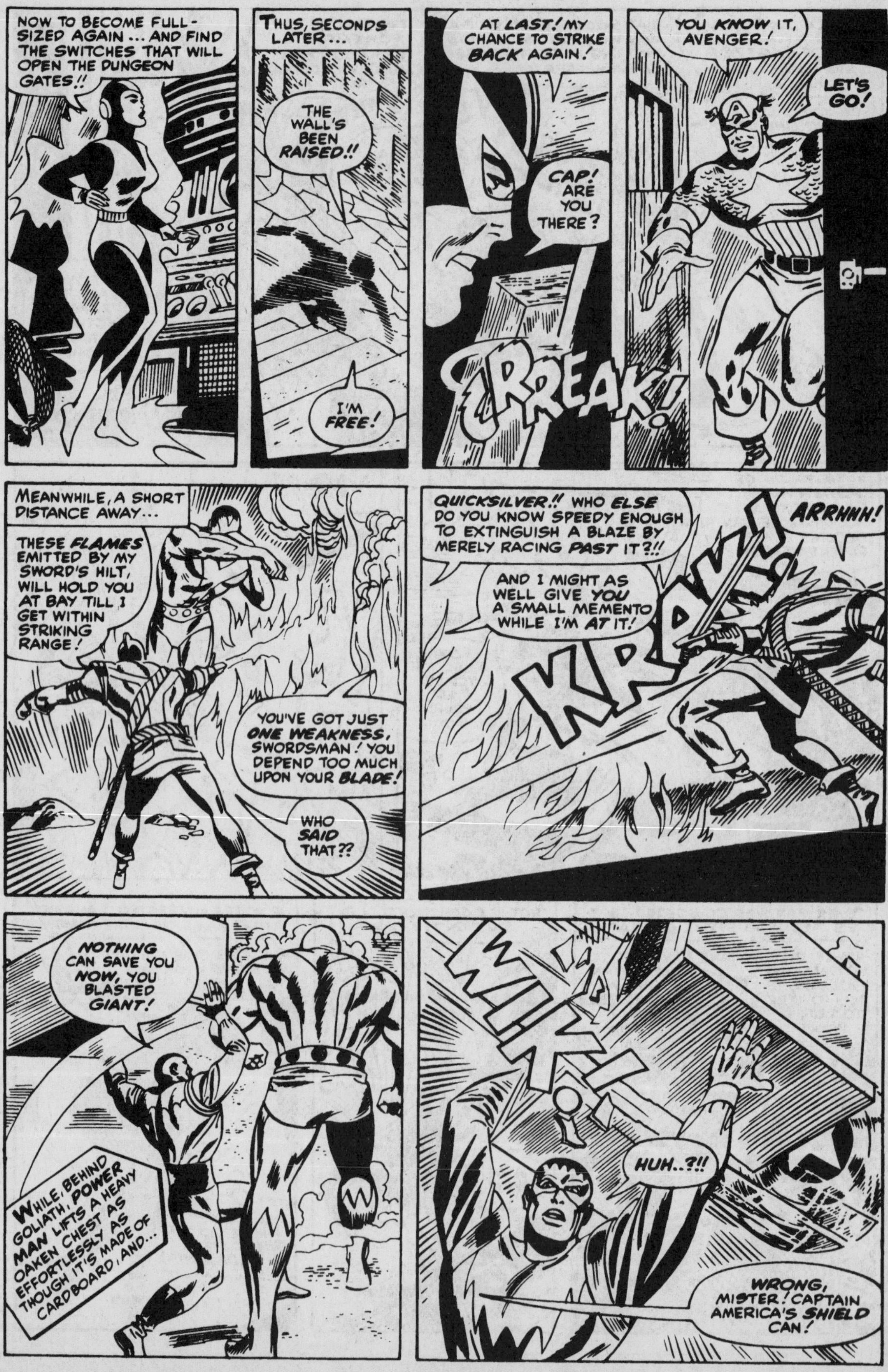
NOW TO BECOME FULL-SIZED AGAIN ... AND FIND THE SWITCHES THAT WILL OPEN THE DUNGEON GATES!!
THUS, SECONDS LATER...
THE WALL'S BEEN RAISED!!
I'M FREE!
AT LAST! MY CHANCE TO STRIKE BACK AGAIN!
CAP! ARE YOU THERE?
CRREAK!
YOU KNOW IT, AVENGER!
LET'S GO!
MEANWHILE, A SHORT DISTANCE AWAY...
THESE FLAMES EMITTED BY MY SWORD'S HILT, WILL HOLD YOU AT BAY TILL I GET WITHIN STRIKING RANGE!
YOU'VE GOT JUST ONE WEAKNESS, SWORDSMAN! YOU DEPEND TOO MUCH UPON YOUR BLADE!
WHO SAID THAT??
QUICKSILVER!! WHO ELSE DO YOU KNOW SPEEDY ENOUGH TO EXTINGUISH A BLAZE BY MERELY RACING PAST IT?!!
AND I MIGHT AS WELL GIVE YOU A SMALL MEMENTO WHILE I'M AT IT!
ARRHHH!
KRAK!
NOTHING CAN SAVE YOU NOW, YOU BLASTED GIANT!
WHILE, BEHIND GOLIATH, POWER MAN LIFTS A HEAVY OAKEN CHEST AS EFFORTLESSLY AS THOUGH IT'S MADE OF CARDBOARD, AND...
WHAT?!
HUH..?!!
WRONG, MISTER! CAPTAIN AMERICA'S SHIELD CAN!

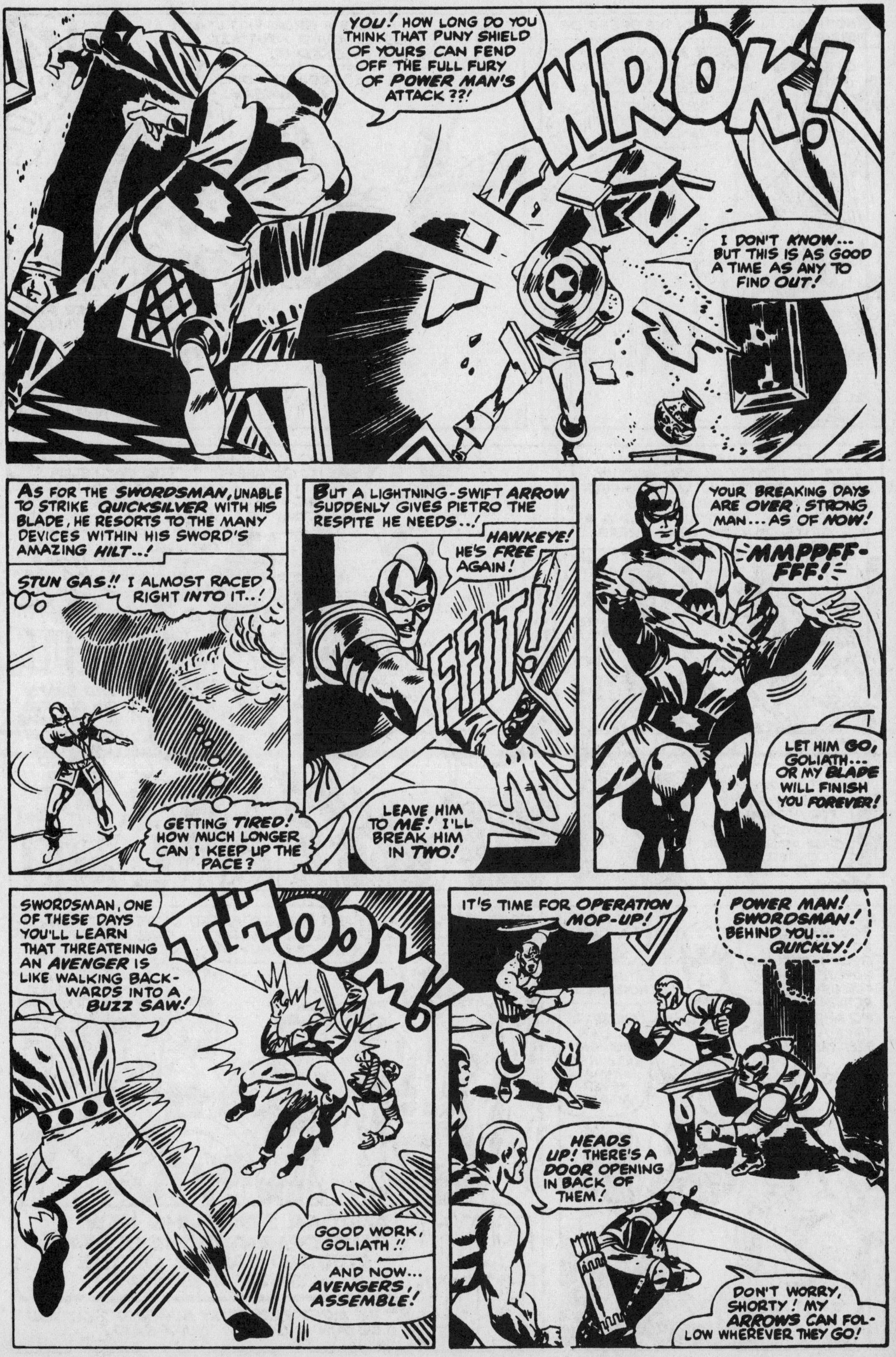
YOU! HOW LONG DO YOU THINK THAT PUNY SHIELD OF YOURS CAN FEND OFF THE FULL FURY OF POWER MAN'S ATTACK ??!
WROK!
I DON'T KNOW... BUT THIS IS AS GOOD A TIME AS ANY TO FIND OUT!
AS FOR THE SWORDSMAN, UNABLE TO STRIKE QUICKSILVER WITH HIS BLADE, HE RESORTS TO THE MANY DEVICES WITHIN HIS SWORD'S AMAZING HILT..!
STUN GAS!! I ALMOST RACED RIGHT INTO IT..!
GETTING TIRED! HOW MUCH LONGER CAN I KEEP UP THE PACE?
BUT A LIGHTNING-SWIFT ARROW SUDDENLY GIVES PIETRO THE RESPITE HE NEEDS..!
HAWKEYE! HE'S FREE AGAIN!
FFIT!
LEAVE HIM TO ME! I'LL BREAK HIM IN TWO!
YOUR BREAKING DAYS ARE OVER, STRONG MAN... AS OF NOW!
MMPPFF-FFF!
LET HIM GO, GOLIATH... OR MY BLADE WILL FINISH YOU FOREVER!
SWORDSMAN, ONE OF THESE DAYS YOU'LL LEARN THAT THREATENING AN AVENGER IS LIKE WALKING BACK-WARDS INTO A BUZZ SAW!
THOOM!
GOOD WORK, GOLIATH!!
AND NOW... AVENGERS, ASSEMBLE!
IT'S TIME FOR OPERATION MOP-UP!
POWER MAN! SWORDSMAN! BEHIND YOU... QUICKLY!
HEADS UP! THERE'S A DOOR OPENING IN BACK OF THEM!
DON'T WORRY, SHORTY! MY ARROWS CAN FOL-LOW WHEREVER THEY GO!

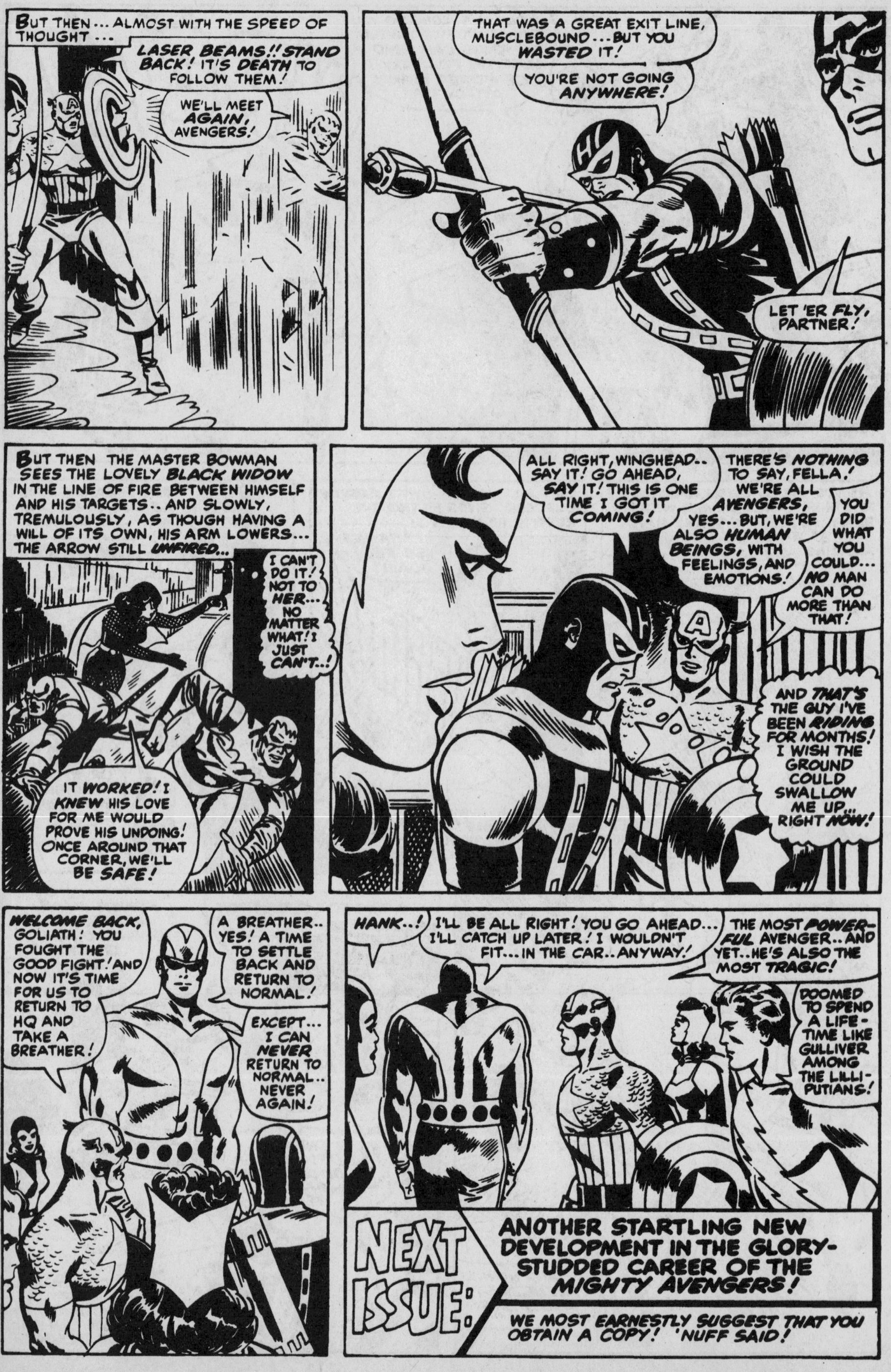
BUT THEN ... ALMOST WITH THE SPEED OF THOUGHT ...
LASER BEAMS!! STAND BACK! IT'S DEATH TO FOLLOW THEM!
WE'LL MEET AGAIN, AVENGERS!
THAT WAS A GREAT EXIT LINE, MUSCLEBOUND ... BUT YOU WASTED IT!
YOU'RE NOT GOING ANYWHERE!
LET 'ER FLY, PARTNER!
BUT THEN THE MASTER BOWMAN SEES THE LOVELY BLACK WIDOW IN THE LINE OF FIRE BETWEEN HIMSELF AND HIS TARGETS .. AND SLOWLY, TREMULOUSLY, AS THOUGH HAVING A WILL OF ITS OWN, HIS ARM LOWERS ... THE ARROW STILL UNFIRED...
I CAN'T DO IT! NOT TO HER... NO MATTER WHAT! I JUST CAN'T..!
IT WORKED! I KNEW HIS LOVE FOR ME WOULD PROVE HIS UNDOING! ONCE AROUND THAT CORNER, WE'LL BE SAFE!
ALL RIGHT, WINGHEAD.. SAY IT! GO AHEAD, SAY IT! THIS IS ONE TIME I GOT IT COMING!
THERE'S NOTHING TO SAY, FELLA! WE'RE ALL AVENGERS, YES ... BUT, WE'RE ALSO HUMAN BEINGS, WITH FEELINGS, AND EMOTIONS!
YOU DID WHAT YOU COULD... NO MAN CAN DO MORE THAN THAT!
AND THAT'S THE GUY I'VE BEEN RIDING FOR MONTHS! I WISH THE GROUND COULD SWALLOW ME UP... RIGHT NOW!
WELCOME BACK, GOLIATH! YOU FOUGHT THE GOOD FIGHT! AND NOW IT'S TIME FOR US TO RETURN TO HQ AND TAKE A BREATHER!
A BREATHER.. YES! A TIME TO SETTLE BACK AND RETURN TO NORMAL!
EXCEPT... I CAN NEVER RETURN TO NORMAL... NEVER AGAIN!
HANK..!
I'LL BE ALL RIGHT! YOU GO AHEAD... I'LL CATCH UP LATER! I WOULDN'T FIT... IN THE CAR.. ANYWAY!
THE MOST POWER-FUL AVENGER .. AND YET.. HE'S ALSO THE MOST TRAGIC!
DOOMED TO SPEND A LIFE-TIME LIKE GULLIVER AMONG THE LILLI-PUTIANS!
NEXT ISSUE:
ANOTHER STARTLING NEW DEVELOPMENT IN THE GLORY-STUDDED CAREER OF THE MIGHTY AVENGERS!
WE MOST EARNESTLY SUGGEST THAT YOU OBTAIN A COPY! 'NUFF SAID!

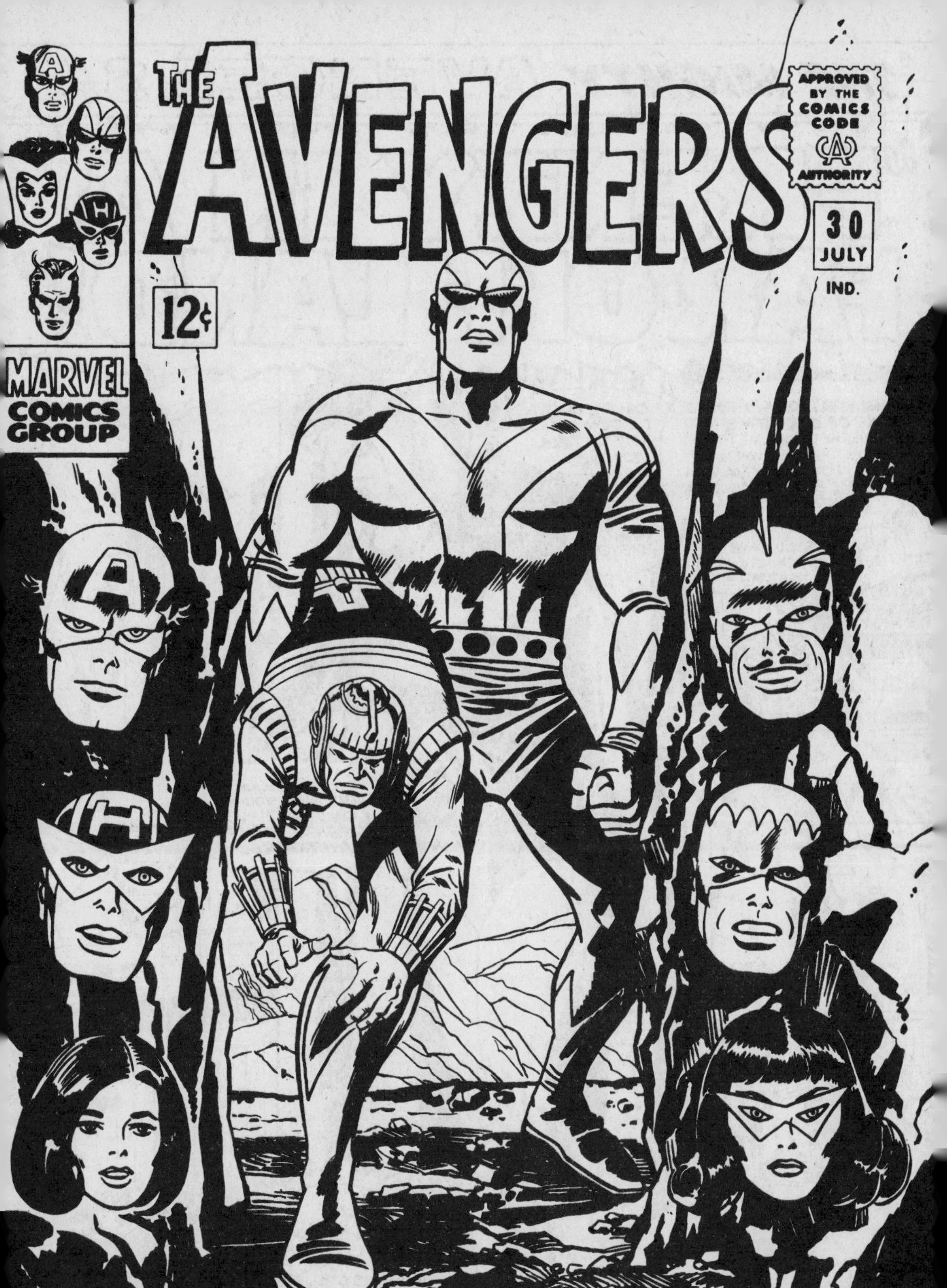
THE AVENGERS
APPROVED BY THE COMICS CODE AUTHORITY
30
JULY
IND.
12¢
MARVEL COMICS GROUP
"FRENZY IN A FAR-OFF LAND!"

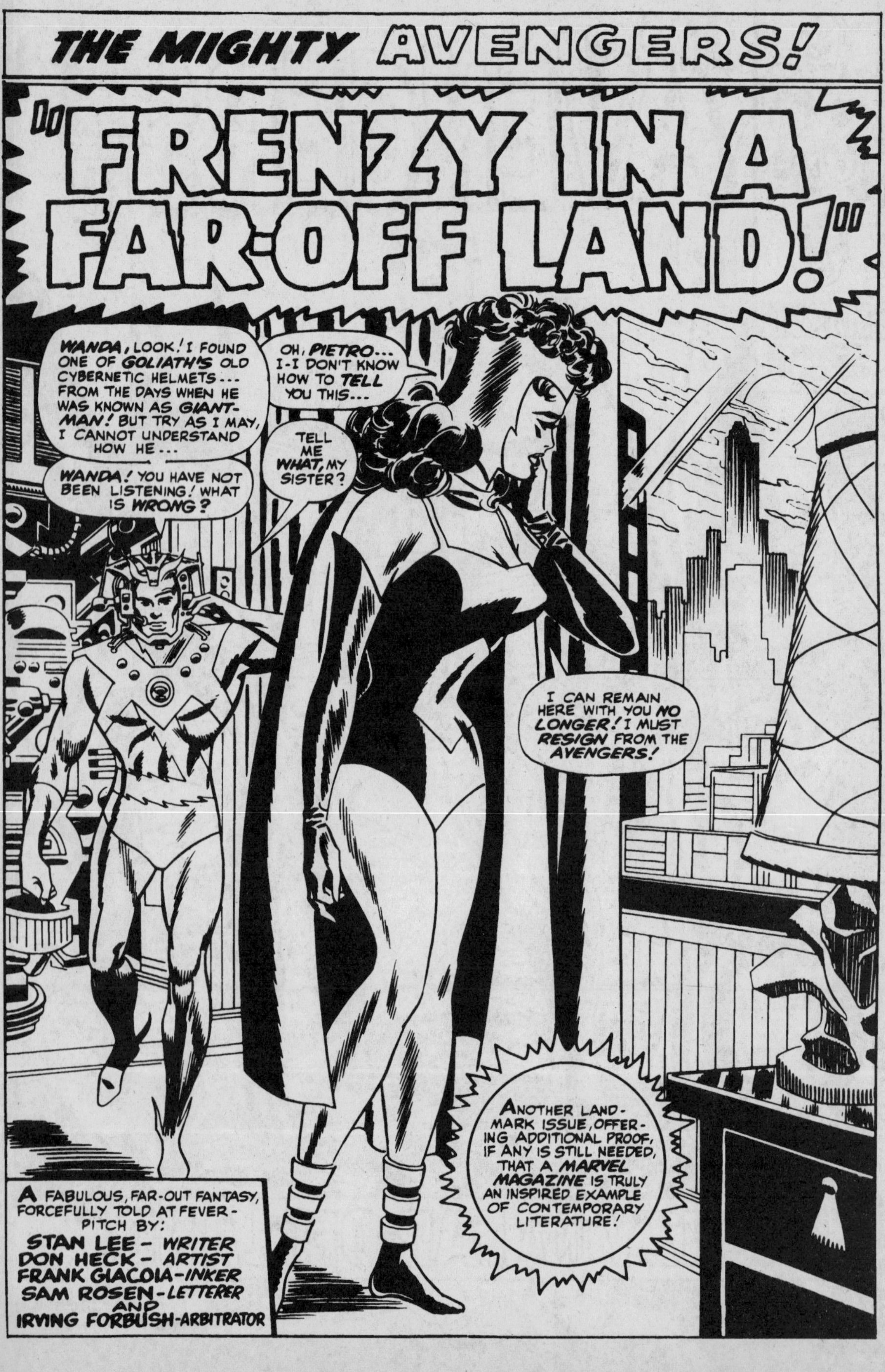

THE MIGHTY AVENGERS!
"FRENZY IN A FAR-OFF LAND!"
WANDA, LOOK! I FOUND ONE OF GOLIATH'S OLD CYBERNETIC HELMETS... FROM THE DAYS WHEN HE WAS KNOWN AS GIANT-MAN! BUT TRY AS I MAY, I CANNOT UNDERSTAND HOW HE...
OH, PIETRO... I-I DON'T KNOW HOW TO TELL YOU THIS...
WANDA! YOU HAVE NOT BEEN LISTENING! WHAT IS WRONG?
TELL ME WHAT, MY SISTER?
I CAN REMAIN HERE WITH YOU NO LONGER! I MUST RESIGN FROM THE AVENGERS!
ANOTHER LANDMARK ISSUE, OFFERING ADDITIONAL PROOF, IF ANY IS STILL NEEDED, THAT A MARVEL MAGAZINE IS TRULY AN INSPIRED EXAMPLE OF CONTEMPORARY LITERATURE!
A FABULOUS, FAR-OUT FANTASY, FORCEFULLY TOLD AT FEVER-PITCH BY:
STAN LEE - WRITER
DON HECK - ARTIST
FRANK GIACOIA - INKER
SAM ROSEN - LETTERER
AND
IRVING FORBUSH - ARBITRATOR

LEAVE THE *AVENGERS* ?!! BUT... *WHY* ??

I'D JUST BE A *HANDICAP* TO ALL OF YOU! DIDN'T YOU NOTICE HOW *LITTLE* I HELPED RECENTLY WHEN WE FOUGHT *POWER MAN*, THE *SWORDS-MAN*, AND THE *BLACK-WIDOW* ?*

*AVENGERS #29... WHAT ELSE ?.. LOGICAL STAN.

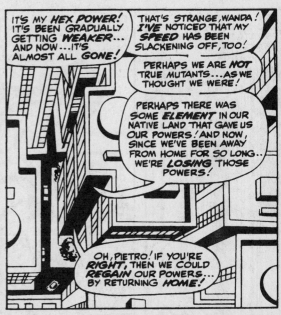

IT'S MY *HEX POWER!* IT'S BEEN GRADUALLY GETTING *WEAKER*... AND NOW...IT'S ALMOST ALL *GONE!*

THAT'S STRANGE, WANDA! *I'VE* NOTICED THAT MY *SPEED* HAS BEEN SLACKENING OFF, TOO!

PERHAPS WE ARE *NOT* TRUE MUTANTS...AS WE THOUGHT WE WERE!

PERHAPS THERE WAS SOME *ELEMENT* IN OUR NATIVE LAND THAT GAVE US OUR POWERS! AND NOW, SINCE WE'VE BEEN AWAY FROM HOME FOR SO LONG.. WE'RE *LOSING* THOSE POWERS!

OH, PIETRO! IF YOU'RE *RIGHT*, THEN WE COULD *REGAIN* OUR POWERS... BY RETURNING *HOME!*

AT ANY RATE, WE MUST *TRY* IT! WE SHALL RETURN TO EUROPE *IMMEDIATELY!* I'LL TELL THE *OTHER* MEMBERS OF..OH, HERE'S CAP!

NO NEED TO EXPLAIN, PIETRO! I COULDN'T HELP OVERHEARING!

THEN...YOU *UNDERSTAND*, STEVE ?

OF *COURSE* I DO, WANDA!

AND SO WILL THE *OTHERS* WHEN I TELL THEM ABOUT IT! YOU HAVE BOTH SERVED LONG AND WELL! LET'S CONSIDER THIS A *VACATION*, WHICH YOU RICHLY DESERVE!

LUCKILY, *GOLIATH* HAS RETURNED TO US AGAIN... SO WE'LL HAVE HIS *POWER* DURING YOUR ABSENCE!

BUT PERHAPS *CAPTAIN AMERICA'S* CONFIDENCE IN GOLIATH IS NOT FULLY WARRANTED! FOR THE NEXT DAY... AFTER *QUICKSILVER* AND THE *SCARLET WITCH* HAVE DEPARTED FOR EUROPE ---

HANK, DARLING! YOU'VE BEEN CLOSETED IN THERE ALL DAY! YOU HAVEN'T EVEN *EATEN!*

GO AWAY, JAN! I'M NOT HUNGRY!

BUT YOU *MUST* EAT--ESPECIALLY SINCE YOU'RE NOW *TEN FEET TALL!* YOU NEED MORE FOOD THAN *EVER!*

TEN FEET TALL! A LIVING *FREAK*... A VIRTUAL *MONSTROSITY*... UNABLE TO EVER REDUCE TO MY NORMAL SIZE!

ONCE I WAS AMONG THE MOST *ENVIED* OF MEN... ADMIRED... RESPECTED.. AND.. *LOVED*... BY JAN!

BUT *NOW*... I'M NOTHING MORE THAN A *GROTESQUE OBJECT OF PITY!* WHEREAS I USED TO CHERISH THE *LOVE* OF JANET VAN DYNE...I CANNOT BEAR HER *SYMPATHY!*

HANK.. MY DEAREST.. WHY WON'T YOU OPEN THE DOOR ? WHY WON'T YOU *ANSWER* ME ? I...I *LOVE* YOU, HANK! I WANT TO *SHARE* YOUR TROUBLES...!

OH, JAN.. JAN! I LOVE YOU *TOO MUCH* TO LET YOU BURDEN YOUR-SELF WITH ME NOW! I CAN'T STAND SEEING THE *SADNESS* IN YOUR EYES...!

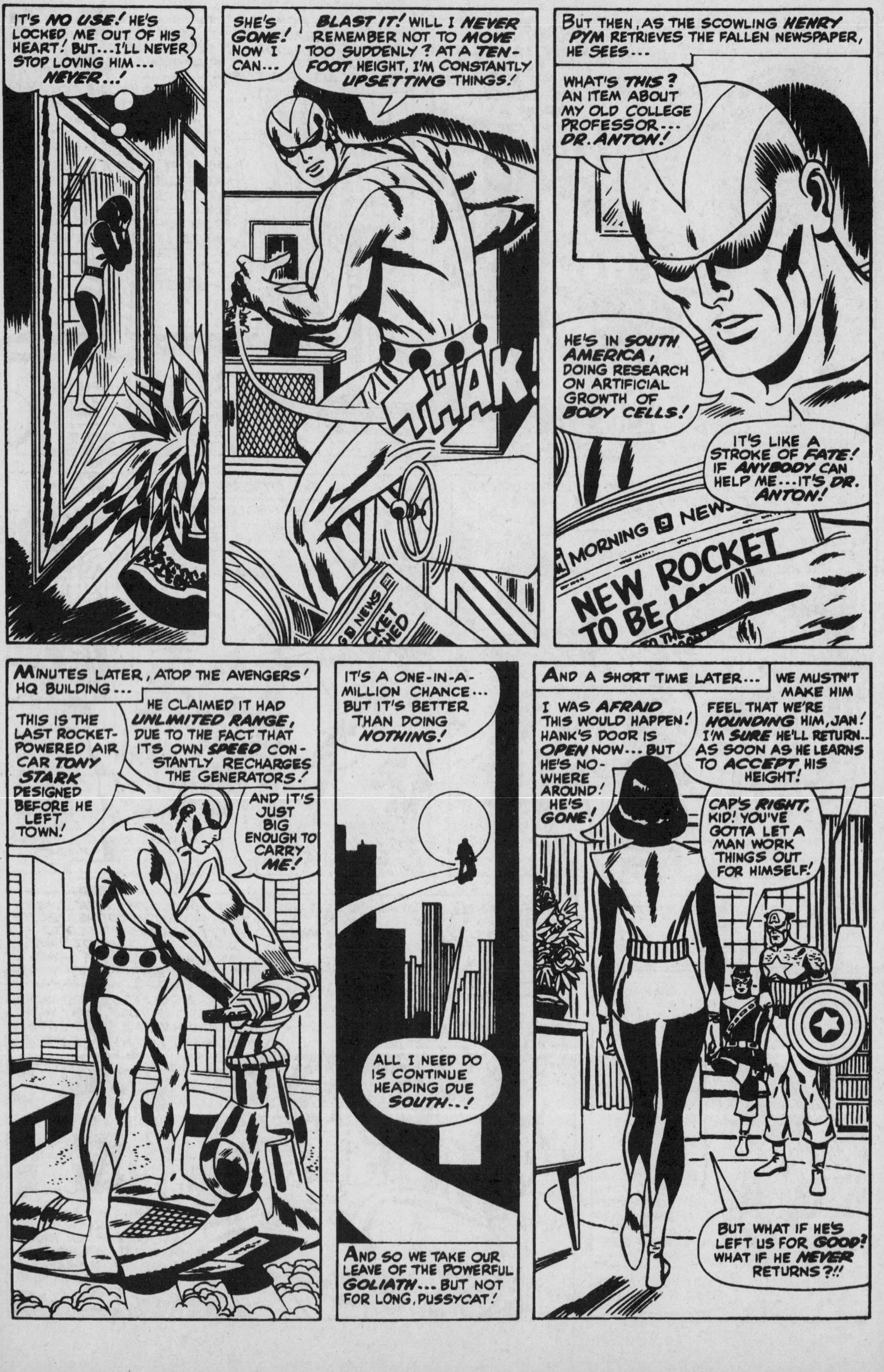

IT'S NO USE! HE'S LOCKED ME OUT OF HIS HEART! BUT... I'LL NEVER STOP LOVING HIM... NEVER...!
SHE'S GONE! NOW I CAN...
BLAST IT! WILL I NEVER REMEMBER NOT TO MOVE TOO SUDDENLY? AT A TEN-FOOT HEIGHT, I'M CONSTANTLY UPSETTING THINGS!
THAK!
BUT THEN, AS THE SCOWLING HENRY PYM RETRIEVES THE FALLEN NEWSPAPER, HE SEES...
WHAT'S THIS? AN ITEM ABOUT MY OLD COLLEGE PROFESSOR... DR. ANTON!
HE'S IN SOUTH AMERICA, DOING RESEARCH ON ARTIFICIAL GROWTH OF BODY CELLS!
IT'S LIKE A STROKE OF FATE! IF ANYBODY CAN HELP ME... IT'S DR. ANTON!
MORNING NEWS
NEW ROCKET TO BE
MINUTES LATER, ATOP THE AVENGERS' HQ BUILDING...
THIS IS THE LAST ROCKET-POWERED AIR CAR TONY STARK DESIGNED BEFORE HE LEFT TOWN!
HE CLAIMED IT HAD UNLIMITED RANGE, DUE TO THE FACT THAT ITS OWN SPEED CONSTANTLY RECHARGES THE GENERATORS!
AND IT'S JUST BIG ENOUGH TO CARRY ME!
IT'S A ONE-IN-A-MILLION CHANCE... BUT IT'S BETTER THAN DOING NOTHING!
ALL I NEED DO IS CONTINUE HEADING DUE SOUTH...!
AND SO WE TAKE OUR LEAVE OF THE POWERFUL GOLIATH... BUT NOT FOR LONG, PUSSYCAT!
AND A SHORT TIME LATER...
I WAS AFRAID THIS WOULD HAPPEN! HANK'S DOOR IS OPEN NOW... BUT HE'S NOWHERE AROUND! HE'S GONE!
WE MUSTN'T MAKE HIM FEEL THAT WE'RE HOUNDING HIM, JAN! I'M SURE HE'LL RETURN... AS SOON AS HE LEARNS TO ACCEPT HIS HEIGHT!
CAP'S RIGHT, KID! YOU'VE GOTTA LET A MAN WORK THINGS OUT FOR HIMSELF!
BUT WHAT IF HE'S LEFT US FOR GOOD? WHAT IF HE NEVER RETURNS?!!

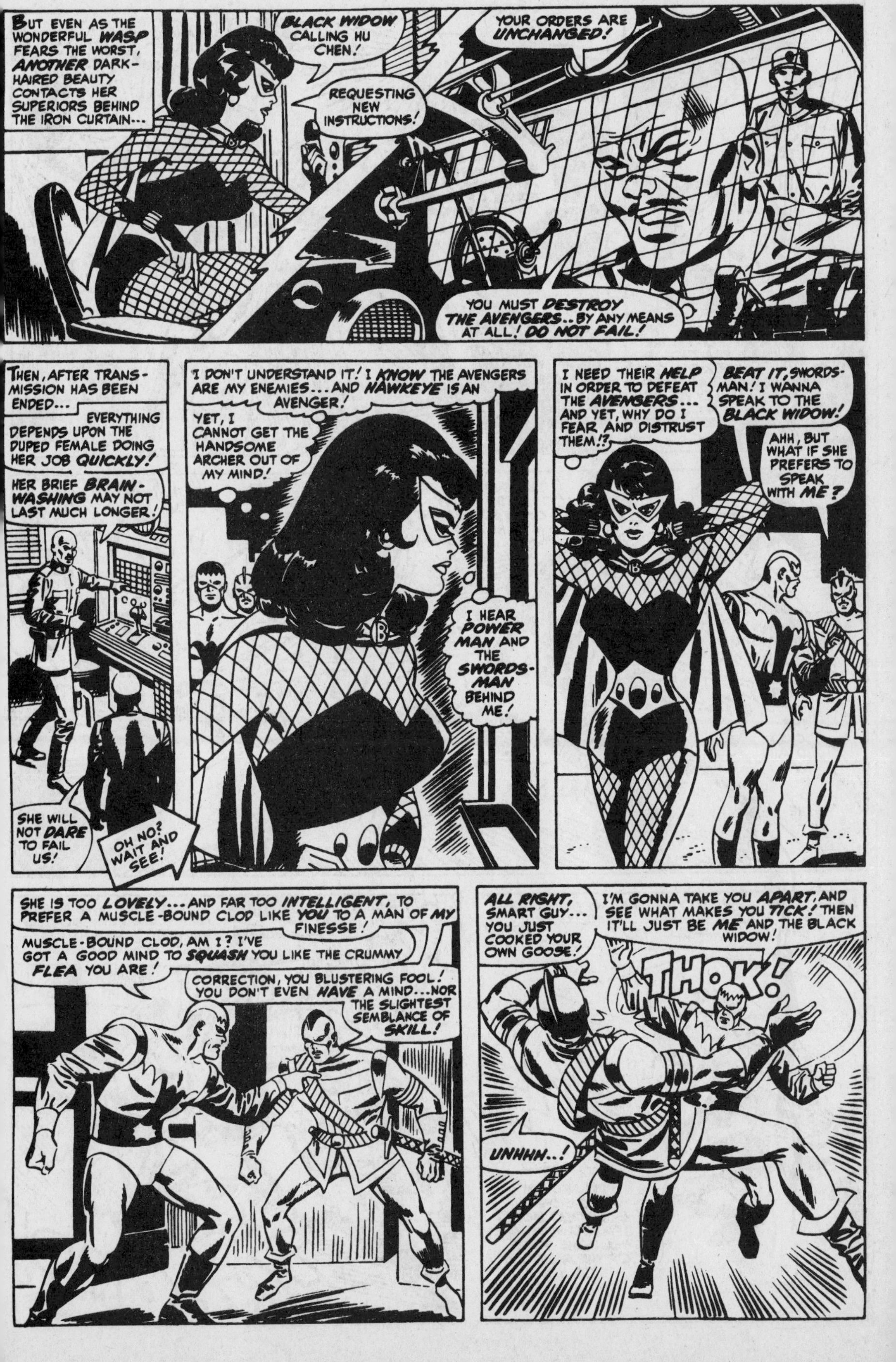

BUT EVEN AS THE WONDERFUL WASP FEARS THE WORST, ANOTHER DARK-HAIRED BEAUTY CONTACTS HER SUPERIORS BEHIND THE IRON CURTAIN...
BLACK WIDOW CALLING HU CHEN!
REQUESTING NEW INSTRUCTIONS!
YOUR ORDERS ARE UNCHANGED!
YOU MUST DESTROY THE AVENGERS.. BY ANY MEANS AT ALL! DO NOT FAIL!
THEN, AFTER TRANSMISSION HAS BEEN ENDED...
EVERYTHING DEPENDS UPON THE DUPED FEMALE DOING HER JOB QUICKLY!
HER BRIEF BRAIN-WASHING MAY NOT LAST MUCH LONGER!
SHE WILL NOT DARE TO FAIL US!
OH NO? WAIT AND SEE!
I DON'T UNDERSTAND IT! I KNOW THE AVENGERS ARE MY ENEMIES... AND HAWKEYE IS AN AVENGER!
YET, I CANNOT GET THE HANDSOME ARCHER OUT OF MY MIND!
I HEAR POWER MAN AND THE SWORDSMAN BEHIND ME!
I NEED THEIR HELP IN ORDER TO DEFEAT THE AVENGERS... AND YET, WHY DO I FEAR AND DISTRUST THEM!?
BEAT IT, SWORDSMAN! I WANNA SPEAK TO THE BLACK WIDOW!
AHH, BUT WHAT IF SHE PREFERS TO SPEAK WITH ME?
SHE IS TOO LOVELY... AND FAR TOO INTELLIGENT, TO PREFER A MUSCLE-BOUND CLOD LIKE YOU TO A MAN OF MY FINESSE!
MUSCLE-BOUND CLOD, AM I? I'VE GOT A GOOD MIND TO SQUASH YOU LIKE THE CRUMMY FLEA YOU ARE!
CORRECTION, YOU BLUSTERING FOOL! YOU DON'T EVEN HAVE A MIND... NOR THE SLIGHTEST SEMBLANCE OF SKILL!
ALL RIGHT, SMART GUY... YOU JUST COOKED YOUR OWN GOOSE!
I'M GONNA TAKE YOU APART, AND SEE WHAT MAKES YOU TICK! THEN IT'LL JUST BE ME AND THE BLACK WIDOW!
THOK!
UNHHH...!

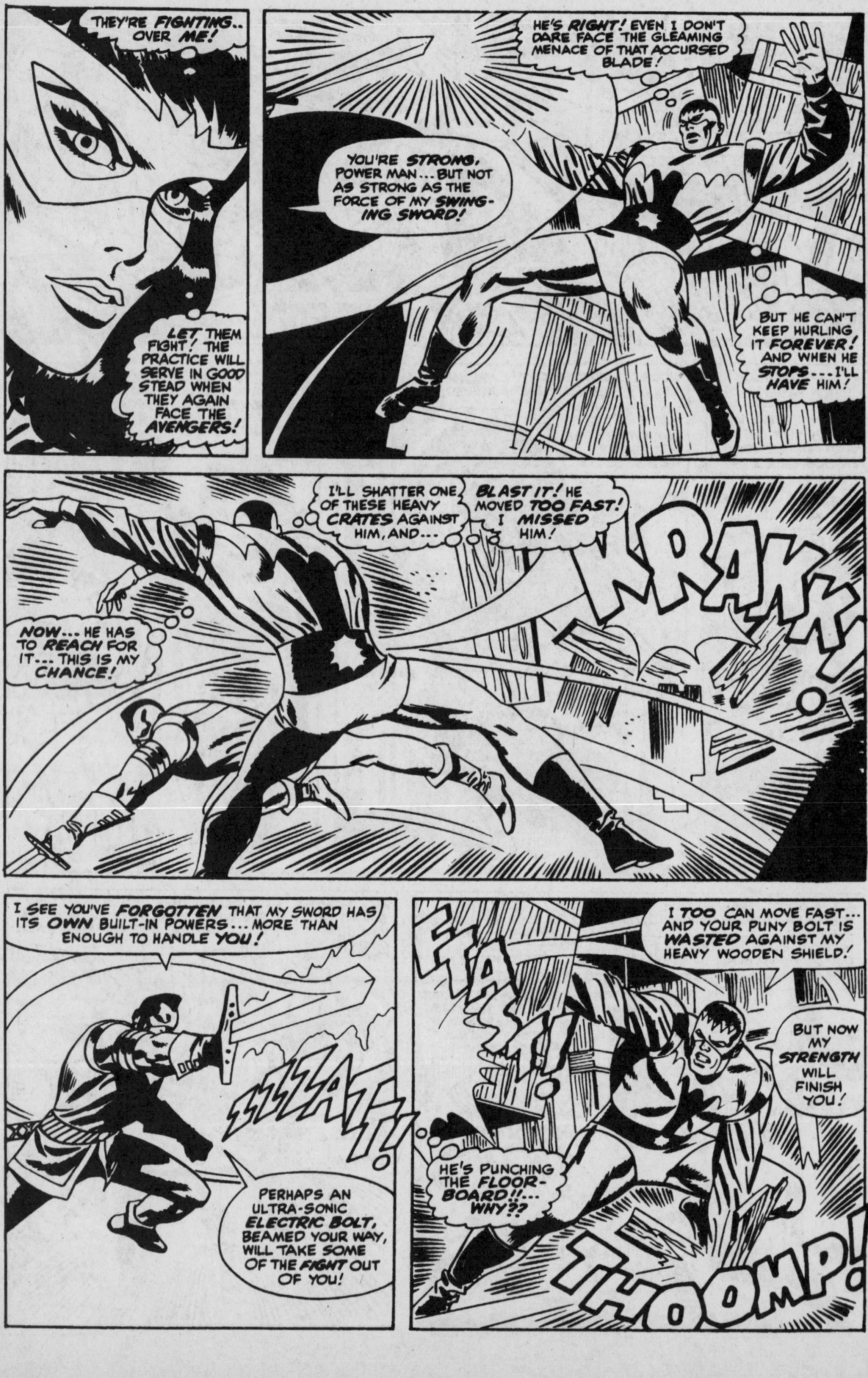
THEY'RE FIGHTING.. OVER ME!
LET THEM FIGHT! THE PRACTICE WILL SERVE IN GOOD STEAD WHEN THEY AGAIN FACE THE AVENGERS!
HE'S RIGHT! EVEN I DON'T DARE FACE THE GLEAMING MENACE OF THAT ACCURSED BLADE!
YOU'RE STRONG, POWER MAN... BUT NOT AS STRONG AS THE FORCE OF MY SWINGING SWORD!
BUT HE CAN'T KEEP HURLING IT FOREVER! AND WHEN HE STOPS...I'LL HAVE HIM!
I'LL SHATTER ONE OF THESE HEAVY CRATES AGAINST HIM, AND...
BLAST IT! HE MOVED TOO FAST! I MISSED HIM!
KRAKK!
NOW... HE HAS TO REACH FOR IT... THIS IS MY CHANCE!
I SEE YOU'VE FORGOTTEN THAT MY SWORD HAS ITS OWN BUILT-IN POWERS... MORE THAN ENOUGH TO HANDLE YOU!
ZZZAT!!
PERHAPS AN ULTRA-SONIC ELECTRIC BOLT, BEAMED YOUR WAY, WILL TAKE SOME OF THE FIGHT OUT OF YOU!
I TOO CAN MOVE FAST... AND YOUR PUNY BOLT IS WASTED AGAINST MY HEAVY WOODEN SHIELD!
FTASSH!
BUT NOW MY STRENGTH WILL FINISH YOU!
HE'S PUNCHING THE FLOOR-BOARD!!... WHY??
THOOMP!

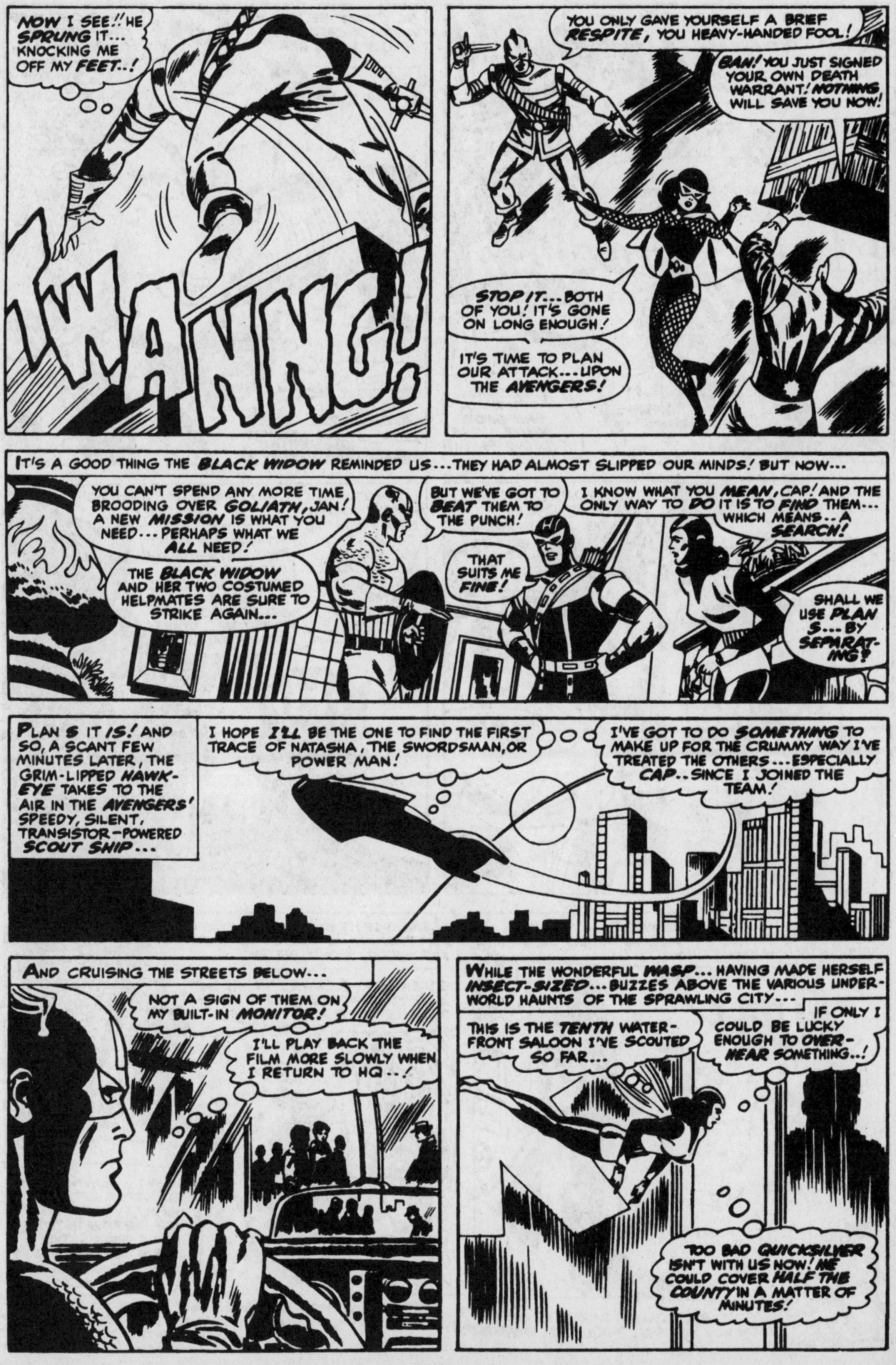

NOW I SEE!! HE SPRUNG IT... KNOCKING ME OFF MY FEET..!
WANNG!
YOU ONLY GAVE YOURSELF A BRIEF RESPITE, YOU HEAVY-HANDED FOOL!
BAH! YOU JUST SIGNED YOUR OWN DEATH WARRANT! NOTHING WILL SAVE YOU NOW!
STOP IT... BOTH OF YOU! IT'S GONE ON LONG ENOUGH!
IT'S TIME TO PLAN OUR ATTACK... UPON THE AVENGERS!
IT'S A GOOD THING THE BLACK WIDOW REMINDED US... THEY HAD ALMOST SLIPPED OUR MINDS! BUT NOW...
YOU CAN'T SPEND ANY MORE TIME BROODING OVER GOLIATH, JAN! A NEW MISSION IS WHAT YOU NEED... PERHAPS WHAT WE ALL NEED!
THE BLACK WIDOW AND HER TWO COSTUMED HELPMATES ARE SURE TO STRIKE AGAIN...
BUT WE'VE GOT TO BEAT THEM TO THE PUNCH!
THAT SUITS ME FINE!
I KNOW WHAT YOU MEAN, CAP! AND THE ONLY WAY TO DO IT IS TO FIND THEM... WHICH MEANS.. A SEARCH!
SHALL WE USE PLAN S... BY SEPARATING?
PLAN S IT IS! AND SO, A SCANT FEW MINUTES LATER, THE GRIM-LIPPED HAWK-EYE TAKES TO THE AIR IN THE AVENGERS' SPEEDY, SILENT, TRANSISTOR-POWERED SCOUT SHIP...
I HOPE I'LL BE THE ONE TO FIND THE FIRST TRACE OF NATASHA, THE SWORDSMAN, OR POWER MAN!
I'VE GOT TO DO SOMETHING TO MAKE UP FOR THE CRUMMY WAY I'VE TREATED THE OTHERS... ESPECIALLY CAP.. SINCE I JOINED THE TEAM!
AND CRUISING THE STREETS BELOW...
NOT A SIGN OF THEM ON MY BUILT-IN MONITOR!
I'LL PLAY BACK THE FILM MORE SLOWLY WHEN I RETURN TO HQ..!
WHILE THE WONDERFUL WASP... HAVING MADE HERSELF INSECT-SIZED... BUZZES ABOVE THE VARIOUS UNDER-WORLD HAUNTS OF THE SPRAWLING CITY...
THIS IS THE TENTH WATER-FRONT SALOON I'VE SCOUTED SO FAR...
IF ONLY I COULD BE LUCKY ENOUGH TO OVER-HEAR SOMETHING..!
TOO BAD QUICKSILVER ISN'T WITH US NOW! HE COULD COVER HALF THE COUNTY IN A MATTER OF MINUTES!

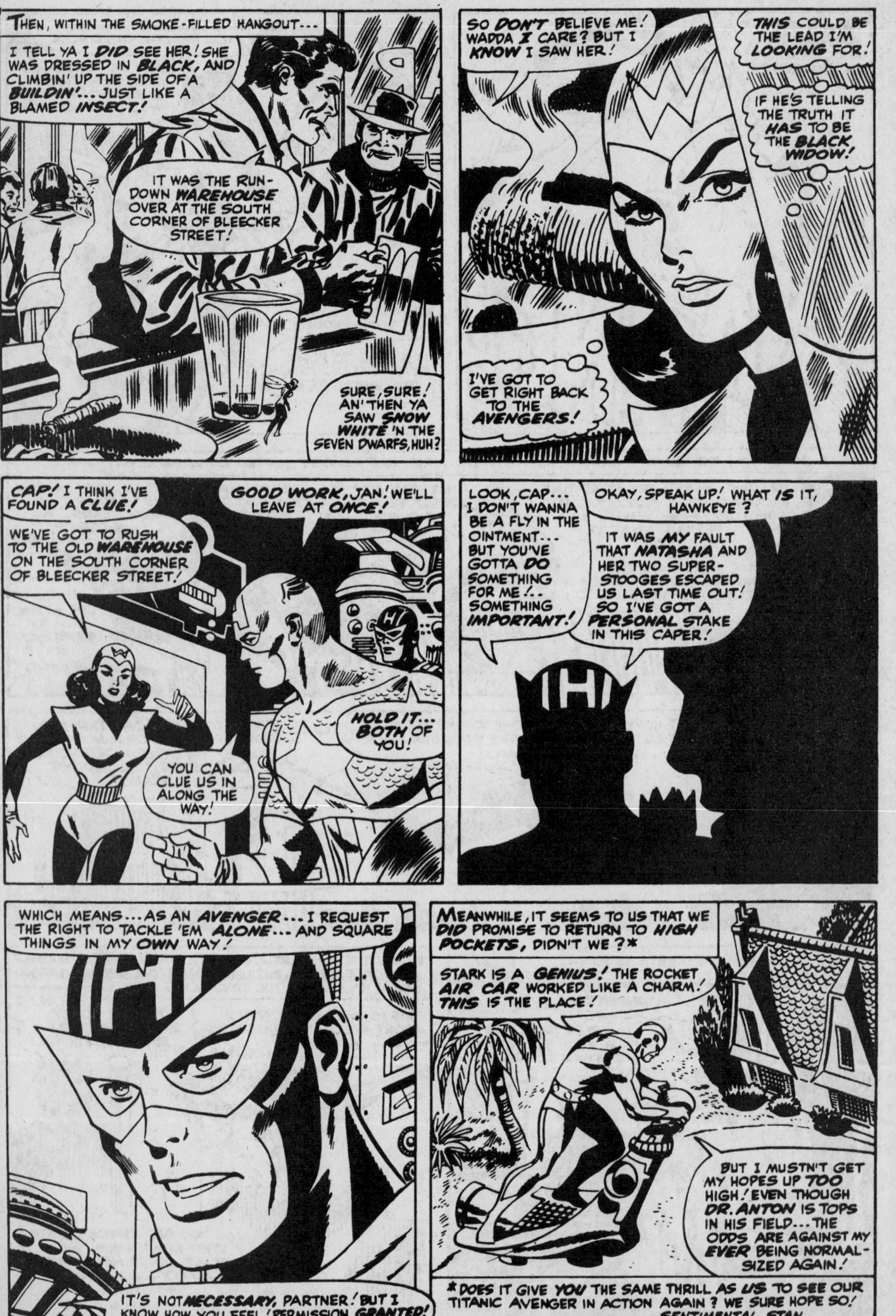
THEN, WITHIN THE SMOKE-FILLED HANGOUT...
I TELL YA I DID SEE HER! SHE WAS DRESSED IN BLACK, AND CLIMBIN' UP THE SIDE OF A BUILDIN'... JUST LIKE A BLAMED INSECT!
IT WAS THE RUN-DOWN WAREHOUSE OVER AT THE SOUTH CORNER OF BLEECKER STREET!
SURE, SURE! AN' THEN YA SAW SNOW WHITE 'N THE SEVEN DWARFS, HUH?
SO DON'T BELIEVE ME! WADDA I CARE? BUT I KNOW I SAW HER!
THIS COULD BE THE LEAD I'M LOOKING FOR!
IF HE'S TELLING THE TRUTH IT HAS TO BE THE BLACK WIDOW!
I'VE GOT TO GET RIGHT BACK TO THE AVENGERS!
CAP! I THINK I'VE FOUND A CLUE!
WE'VE GOT TO RUSH TO THE OLD WAREHOUSE ON THE SOUTH CORNER OF BLEECKER STREET!
GOOD WORK, JAN! WE'LL LEAVE AT ONCE!
HOLD IT... BOTH OF YOU!
YOU CAN CLUE US IN ALONG THE WAY!
LOOK, CAP... I DON'T WANNA BE A FLY IN THE OINTMENT... BUT YOU'VE GOTTA DO SOMETHING FOR ME!.. SOMETHING IMPORTANT!
OKAY, SPEAK UP! WHAT IS IT, HAWKEYE?
IT WAS MY FAULT THAT NATASHA AND HER TWO SUPER-STOOGES ESCAPED US LAST TIME OUT! SO I'VE GOT A PERSONAL STAKE IN THIS CAPER!
WHICH MEANS... AS AN AVENGER... I REQUEST THE RIGHT TO TACKLE 'EM ALONE... AND SQUARE THINGS IN MY OWN WAY!
IT'S NOT NECESSARY, PARTNER! BUT I KNOW HOW YOU FEEL! PERMISSION GRANTED!
MEANWHILE, IT SEEMS TO US THAT WE DID PROMISE TO RETURN TO HIGH POCKETS, DIDN'T WE?*
STARK IS A GENIUS! THE ROCKET AIR CAR WORKED LIKE A CHARM! THIS IS THE PLACE!
BUT I MUSTN'T GET MY HOPES UP TOO HIGH! EVEN THOUGH DR. ANTON IS TOPS IN HIS FIELD... THE ODDS ARE AGAINST MY EVER BEING NORMAL-SIZED AGAIN!
*DOES IT GIVE YOU THE SAME THRILL AS US TO SEE OUR TITANIC AVENGER IN ACTION AGAIN? WE SURE HOPE SO! ...SENTIMENTAL STAN.

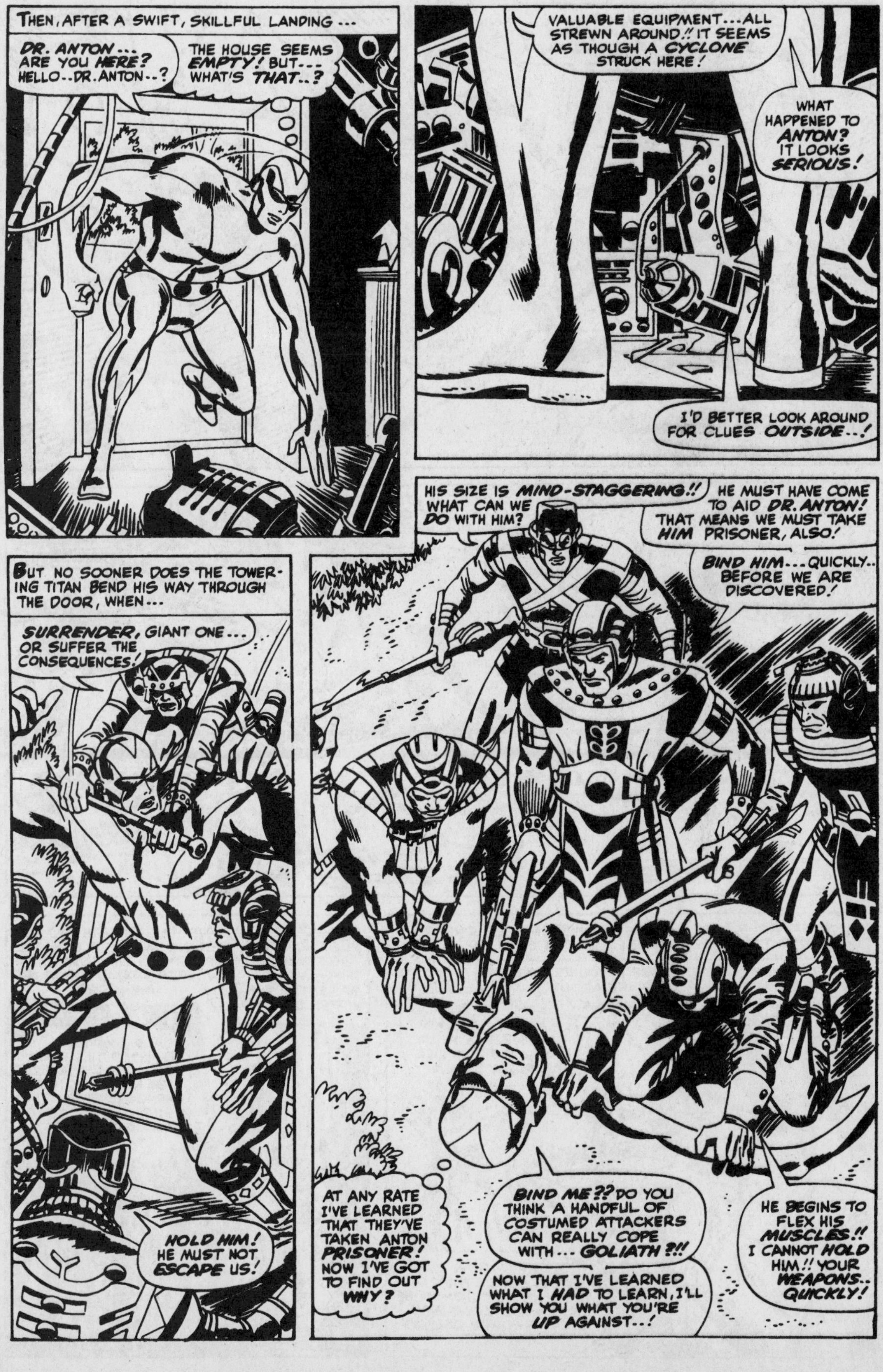

THEN, AFTER A SWIFT, SKILLFUL LANDING ...
DR. ANTON ... ARE YOU HERE? HELLO..DR. ANTON..?
THE HOUSE SEEMS EMPTY! BUT--- WHAT'S THAT..?
VALUABLE EQUIPMENT...ALL STREWN AROUND!! IT SEEMS AS THOUGH A CYCLONE STRUCK HERE!
WHAT HAPPENED TO ANTON? IT LOOKS SERIOUS!
I'D BETTER LOOK AROUND FOR CLUES OUTSIDE..!
BUT NO SOONER DOES THE TOWERING TITAN BEND HIS WAY THROUGH THE DOOR, WHEN...
SURRENDER, GIANT ONE... OR SUFFER THE CONSEQUENCES!
HOLD HIM! HE MUST NOT ESCAPE US!
HIS SIZE IS MIND-STAGGERING!! WHAT CAN WE DO WITH HIM?
HE MUST HAVE COME TO AID DR. ANTON! THAT MEANS WE MUST TAKE HIM PRISONER, ALSO!
BIND HIM...QUICKLY.. BEFORE WE ARE DISCOVERED!
AT ANY RATE I'VE LEARNED THAT THEY'VE TAKEN ANTON PRISONER! NOW I'VE GOT TO FIND OUT WHY?
BIND ME?? DO YOU THINK A HANDFUL OF COSTUMED ATTACKERS CAN REALLY COPE WITH... GOLIATH?!!
NOW THAT I'VE LEARNED WHAT I HAD TO LEARN, I'LL SHOW YOU WHAT YOU'RE UP AGAINST..!
HE BEGINS TO FLEX HIS MUSCLES!! I CANNOT HOLD HIM!! YOUR WEAPONS.. QUICKLY!

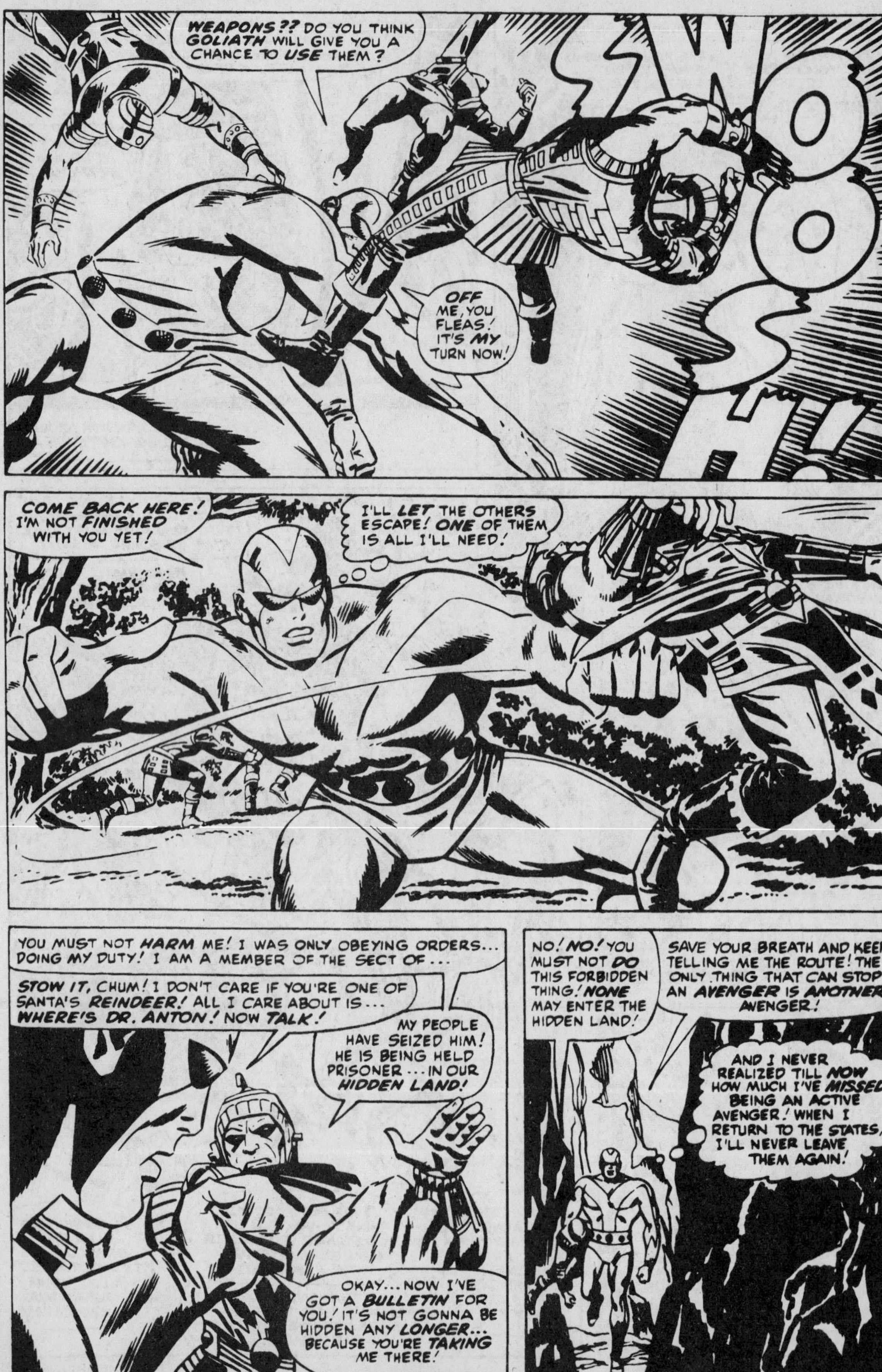
WEAPONS?? DO YOU THINK GOLIATH WILL GIVE YOU A CHANCE TO USE THEM?
SWOOSH!
OFF ME, YOU FLEAS! IT'S MY TURN NOW!
COME BACK HERE! I'M NOT FINISHED WITH YOU YET!
I'LL LET THE OTHERS ESCAPE! ONE OF THEM IS ALL I'LL NEED!
YOU MUST NOT HARM ME! I WAS ONLY OBEYING ORDERS... DOING MY DUTY! I AM A MEMBER OF THE SECT OF...
STOW IT, CHUM! I DON'T CARE IF YOU'RE ONE OF SANTA'S REINDEER! ALL I CARE ABOUT IS... WHERE'S DR. ANTON! NOW TALK!
MY PEOPLE HAVE SEIZED HIM! HE IS BEING HELD PRISONER... IN OUR HIDDEN LAND!
OKAY... NOW I'VE GOT A BULLETIN FOR YOU! IT'S NOT GONNA BE HIDDEN ANY LONGER... BECAUSE YOU'RE TAKING ME THERE!
NO! NO! YOU MUST NOT DO THIS FORBIDDEN THING! NONE MAY ENTER THE HIDDEN LAND!
SAVE YOUR BREATH AND KEEP TELLING ME THE ROUTE! THE ONLY THING THAT CAN STOP AN AVENGER IS ANOTHER AVENGER!
AND I NEVER REALIZED TILL NOW HOW MUCH I'VE MISSED BEING AN ACTIVE AVENGER! WHEN I RETURN TO THE STATES, I'LL NEVER LEAVE THEM AGAIN!

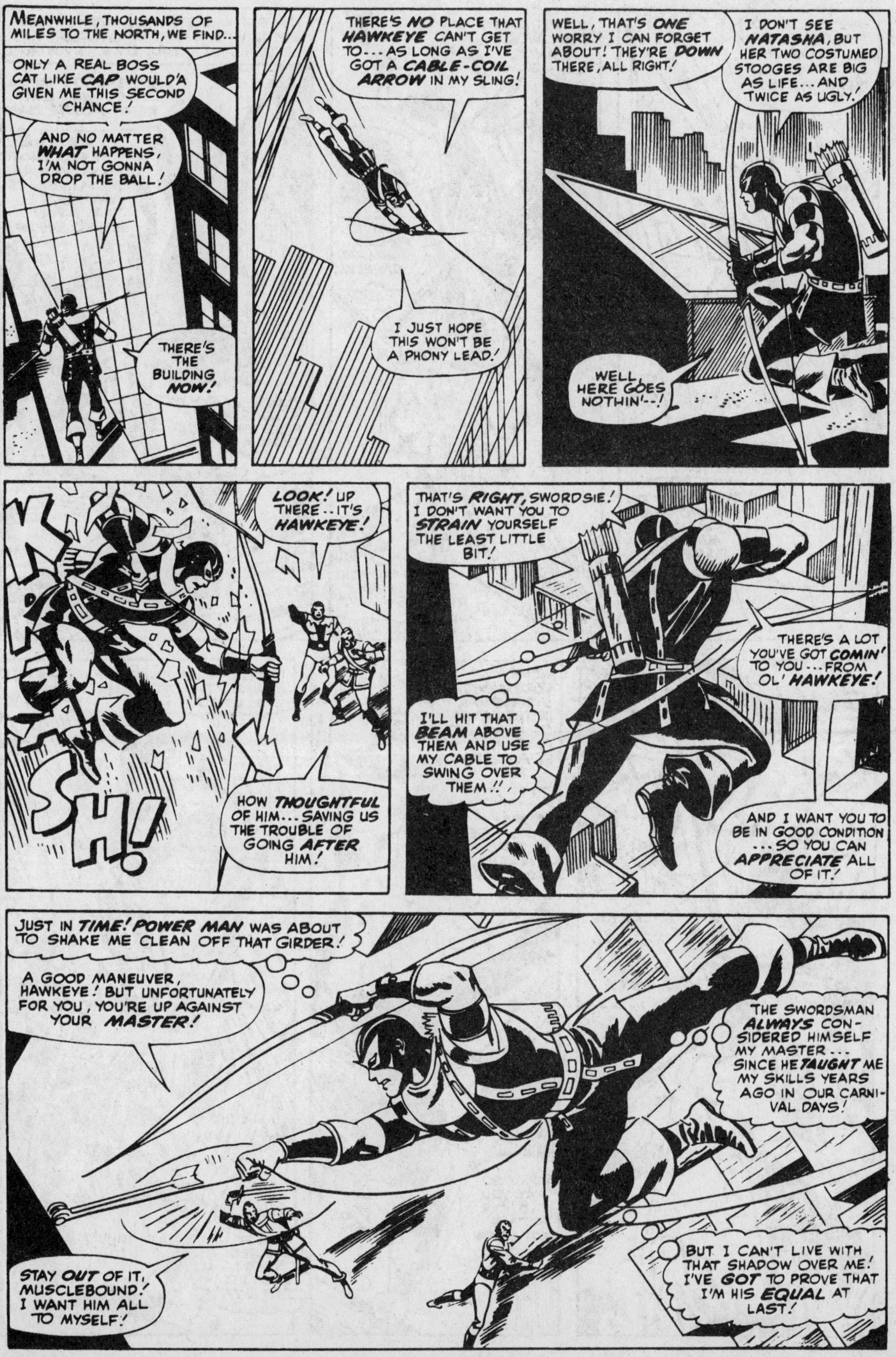
MEANWHILE, THOUSANDS OF MILES TO THE NORTH, WE FIND...
ONLY A REAL BOSS CAT LIKE CAP WOULD'A GIVEN ME THIS SECOND CHANCE!
AND NO MATTER WHAT HAPPENS, I'M NOT GONNA DROP THE BALL!
THERE'S THE BUILDING NOW!
THERE'S NO PLACE THAT HAWKEYE CAN'T GET TO... AS LONG AS I'VE GOT A CABLE-COIL ARROW IN MY SLING!
I JUST HOPE THIS WON'T BE A PHONY LEAD!
WELL, THAT'S ONE WORRY I CAN FORGET ABOUT! THEY'RE DOWN THERE, ALL RIGHT!
I DON'T SEE NATASHA, BUT HER TWO COSTUMED STOOGES ARE BIG AS LIFE... AND TWICE AS UGLY!
WELL, HERE GOES NOTHIN'--!
K-RASH!
LOOK! UP THERE.. IT'S HAWKEYE!
HOW THOUGHTFUL OF HIM... SAVING US THE TROUBLE OF GOING AFTER HIM!
THAT'S RIGHT, SWORDSIE! I DON'T WANT YOU TO STRAIN YOURSELF THE LEAST LITTLE BIT!
THERE'S A LOT YOU'VE GOT COMIN' TO YOU... FROM OL' HAWKEYE!
I'LL HIT THAT BEAM ABOVE THEM AND USE MY CABLE TO SWING OVER THEM!!
AND I WANT YOU TO BE IN GOOD CONDITION ... SO YOU CAN APPRECIATE ALL OF IT!
JUST IN TIME! POWER MAN WAS ABOUT TO SHAKE ME CLEAN OFF THAT GIRDER!
A GOOD MANEUVER, HAWKEYE! BUT UNFORTUNATELY FOR YOU, YOU'RE UP AGAINST YOUR MASTER!
THE SWORDSMAN ALWAYS CONSIDERED HIMSELF MY MASTER ... SINCE HE TAUGHT ME MY SKILLS YEARS AGO IN OUR CARNIVAL DAYS!
BUT I CAN'T LIVE WITH THAT SHADOW OVER ME! I'VE GOT TO PROVE THAT I'M HIS EQUAL AT LAST!
STAY OUT OF IT, MUSCLEBOUND! I WANT HIM ALL TO MYSELF!

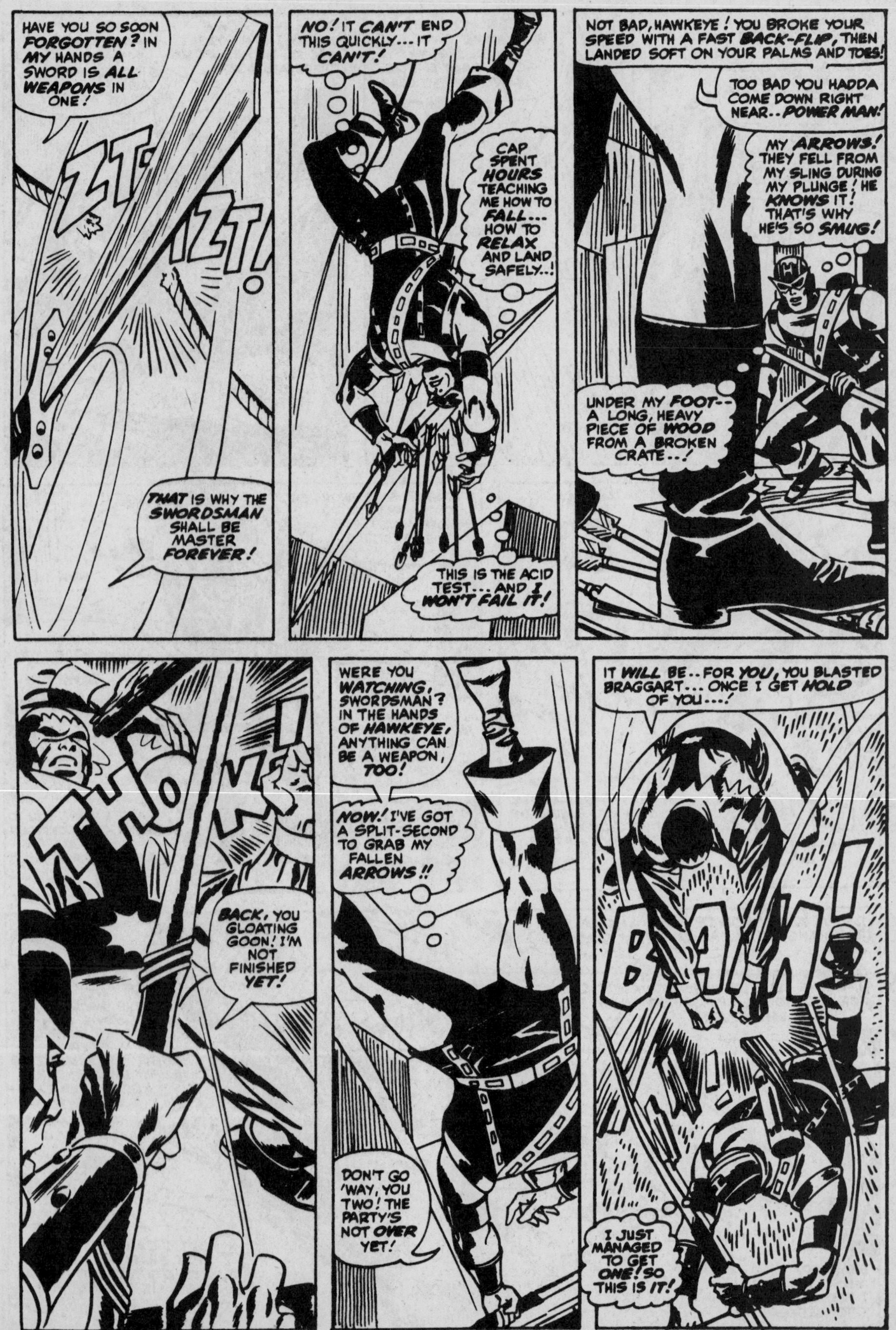
HAVE YOU SO SOON FORGOTTEN? IN MY HANDS A SWORD IS ALL WEAPONS IN ONE!
ZT-ZZT!
THAT IS WHY THE SWORDSMAN SHALL BE MASTER FOREVER!
NO! IT CAN'T END THIS QUICKLY--- IT CAN'T!
CAP SPENT HOURS TEACHING ME HOW TO FALL... HOW TO RELAX AND LAND SAFELY..!
THIS IS THE ACID TEST... AND I WON'T FAIL IT!
NOT BAD, HAWKEYE! YOU BROKE YOUR SPEED WITH A FAST BACK-FLIP, THEN LANDED SOFT ON YOUR PALMS AND TOES!
TOO BAD YOU HADDA COME DOWN RIGHT NEAR.. POWER MAN!
MY ARROWS! THEY FELL FROM MY SLING DURING MY PLUNGE! HE KNOWS IT! THAT'S WHY HE'S SO SMUG!
UNDER MY FOOT-- A LONG, HEAVY PIECE OF WOOD FROM A BROKEN CRATE..!
THOK!
BACK, YOU GLOATING GOON! I'M NOT FINISHED YET!
WERE YOU WATCHING, SWORDSMAN? IN THE HANDS OF HAWKEYE, ANYTHING CAN BE A WEAPON, TOO!
NOW! I'VE GOT A SPLIT-SECOND TO GRAB MY FALLEN ARROWS!!
DON'T GO 'WAY, YOU TWO! THE PARTY'S NOT OVER YET!
IT WILL BE.. FOR YOU, YOU BLASTED BRAGGART... ONCE I GET HOLD OF YOU---!
BAM!
I JUST MANAGED TO GET ONE! SO THIS IS IT!

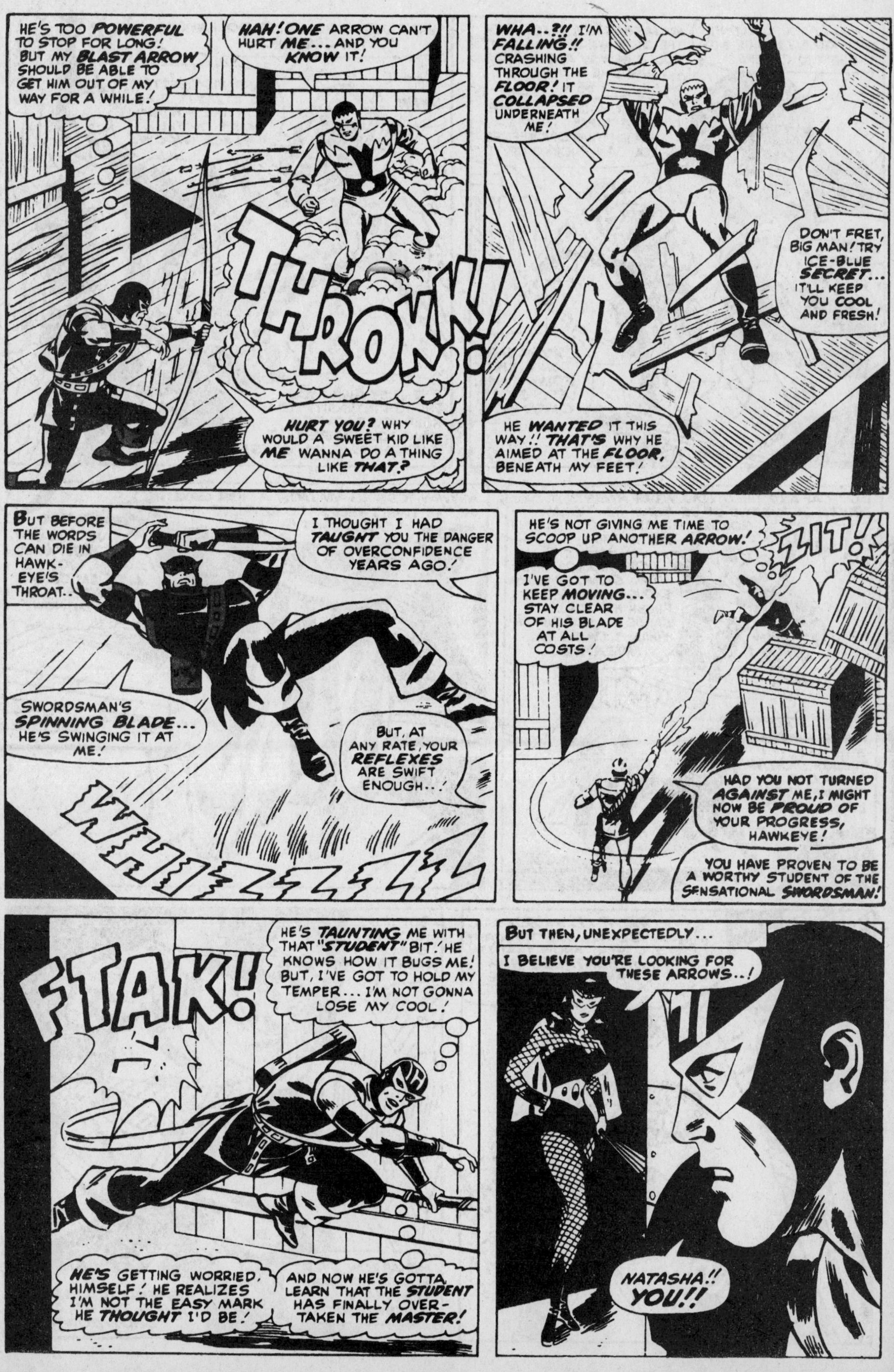

HE'S TOO POWERFUL TO STOP FOR LONG! BUT MY BLAST ARROW SHOULD BE ABLE TO GET HIM OUT OF MY WAY FOR A WHILE!
HAH! ONE ARROW CAN'T HURT ME... AND YOU KNOW IT!
THROKK!
HURT YOU? WHY WOULD A SWEET KID LIKE ME WANNA DO A THING LIKE THAT?
WHA..?!! I'M FALLING!! CRASHING THROUGH THE FLOOR! IT COLLAPSED UNDERNEATH ME!
DON'T FRET, BIG MAN! TRY ICE-BLUE SECRET... IT'LL KEEP YOU COOL AND FRESH!
HE WANTED IT THIS WAY!! THAT'S WHY HE AIMED AT THE FLOOR, BENEATH MY FEET!
BUT BEFORE THE WORDS CAN DIE IN HAWK-EYE'S THROAT..
I THOUGHT I HAD TAUGHT YOU THE DANGER OF OVERCONFIDENCE YEARS AGO!
SWORDSMAN'S SPINNING BLADE... HE'S SWINGING IT AT ME!
BUT, AT ANY RATE, YOUR REFLEXES ARE SWIFT ENOUGH...!
WHIZZZZZ
HE'S NOT GIVING ME TIME TO SCOOP UP ANOTHER ARROW!
ZIT!
I'VE GOT TO KEEP MOVING... STAY CLEAR OF HIS BLADE AT ALL COSTS!
HAD YOU NOT TURNED AGAINST ME, I MIGHT NOW BE PROUD OF YOUR PROGRESS, HAWKEYE!
YOU HAVE PROVEN TO BE A WORTHY STUDENT OF THE SENSATIONAL SWORDSMAN!
FTAK!
HE'S TAUNTING ME WITH THAT "STUDENT" BIT! HE KNOWS HOW IT BUGS ME! BUT, I'VE GOT TO HOLD MY TEMPER... I'M NOT GONNA LOSE MY COOL!
HE'S GETTING WORRIED, HIMSELF! HE REALIZES I'M NOT THE EASY MARK HE THOUGHT I'D BE!
AND NOW HE'S GOTTA LEARN THAT THE STUDENT HAS FINALLY OVER-TAKEN THE MASTER!
BUT THEN, UNEXPECTEDLY...
I BELIEVE YOU'RE LOOKING FOR THESE ARROWS..!
NATASHA!! YOU!!

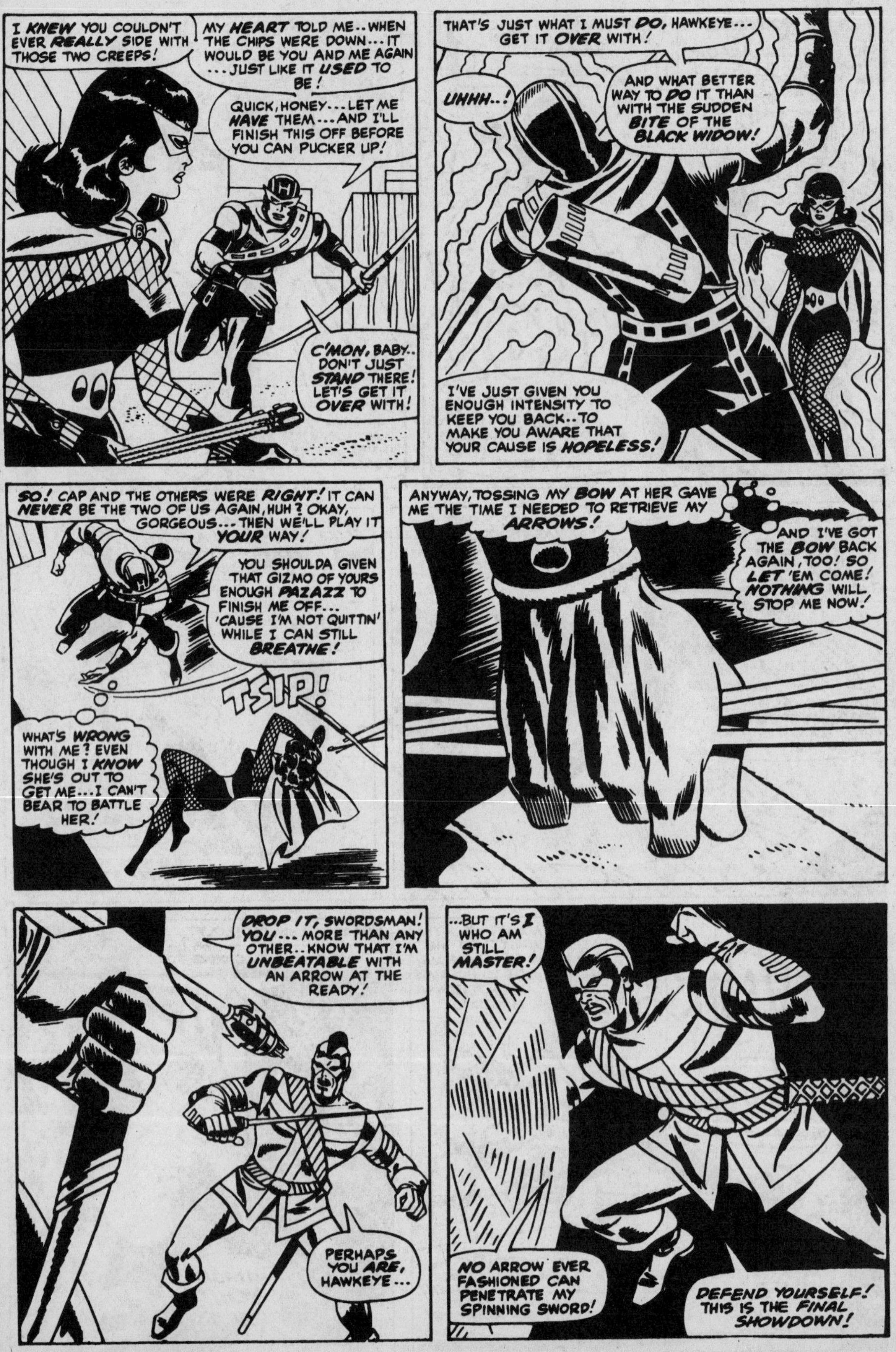
I KNEW YOU COULDN'T EVER REALLY SIDE WITH THOSE TWO CREEPS!
MY HEART TOLD ME.. WHEN THE CHIPS WERE DOWN... IT WOULD BE YOU AND ME AGAIN ... JUST LIKE IT USED TO BE!
QUICK, HONEY... LET ME HAVE THEM... AND I'LL FINISH THIS OFF BEFORE YOU CAN PUCKER UP!
C'MON, BABY.. DON'T JUST STAND THERE! LET'S GET IT OVER WITH!
THAT'S JUST WHAT I MUST DO, HAWKEYE... GET IT OVER WITH!
UHHH..!
AND WHAT BETTER WAY TO DO IT THAN WITH THE SUDDEN BITE OF THE BLACK WIDOW!
I'VE JUST GIVEN YOU ENOUGH INTENSITY TO KEEP YOU BACK.. TO MAKE YOU AWARE THAT YOUR CAUSE IS HOPELESS!
SO! CAP AND THE OTHERS WERE RIGHT! IT CAN NEVER BE THE TWO OF US AGAIN, HUH? OKAY, GORGEOUS... THEN WE'LL PLAY IT YOUR WAY!
YOU SHOULDA GIVEN THAT GIZMO OF YOURS ENOUGH PAZAZZ TO FINISH ME OFF... 'CAUSE I'M NOT QUITTIN' WHILE I CAN STILL BREATHE!
TSIP!
WHAT'S WRONG WITH ME? EVEN THOUGH I KNOW SHE'S OUT TO GET ME... I CAN'T BEAR TO BATTLE HER!
ANYWAY, TOSSING MY BOW AT HER GAVE ME THE TIME I NEEDED TO RETRIEVE MY ARROWS!
AND I'VE GOT THE BOW BACK AGAIN, TOO! SO LET 'EM COME! NOTHING WILL STOP ME NOW!
DROP IT, SWORDSMAN! YOU... MORE THAN ANY OTHER.. KNOW THAT I'M UNBEATABLE WITH AN ARROW AT THE READY!
PERHAPS YOU ARE, HAWKEYE...
...BUT IT'S I WHO AM STILL MASTER!
NO ARROW EVER FASHIONED CAN PENETRATE MY SPINNING SWORD!
DEFEND YOURSELF! THIS IS THE FINAL SHOWDOWN!

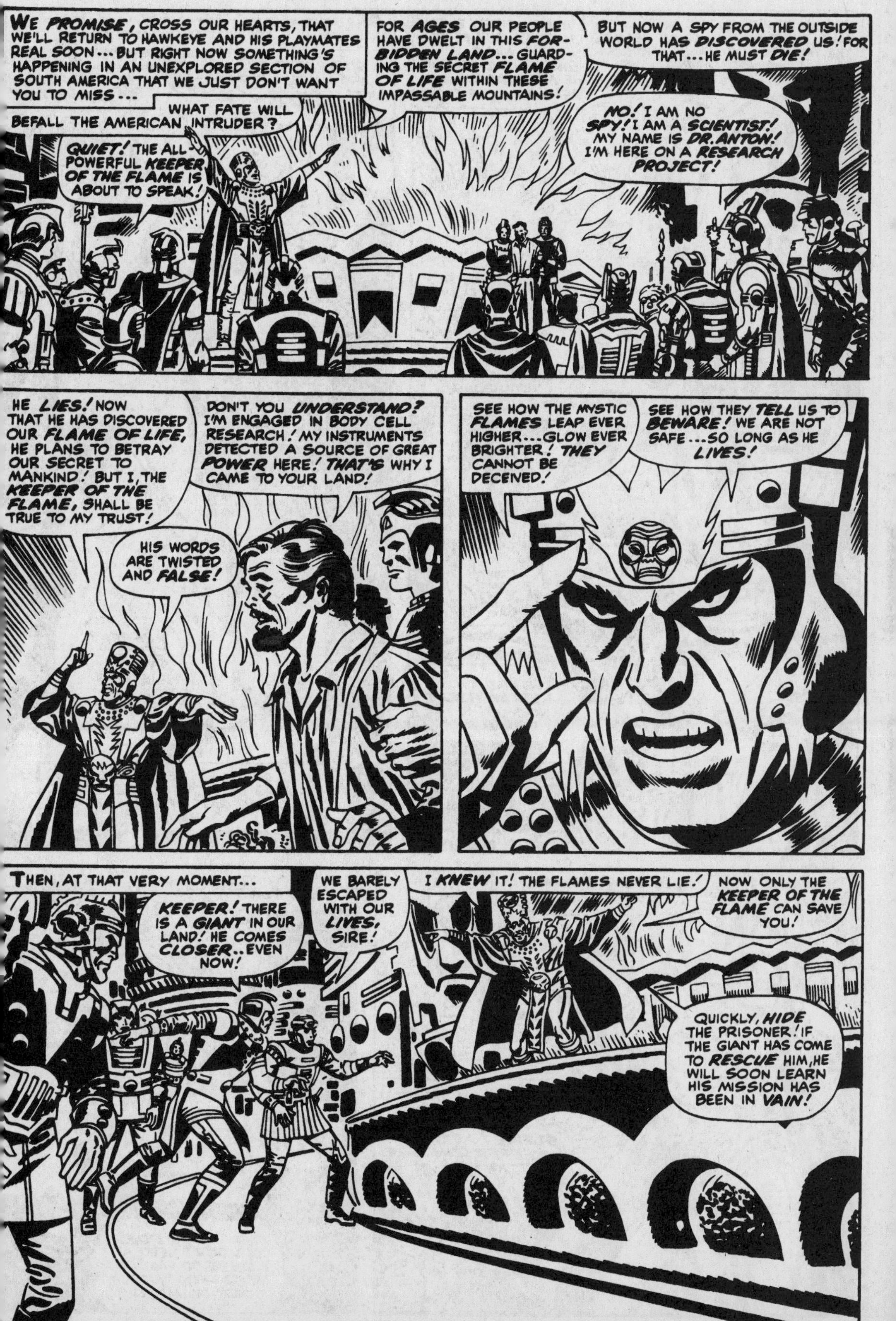
WE PROMISE, CROSS OUR HEARTS, THAT WE'LL RETURN TO HAWKEYE AND HIS PLAYMATES REAL SOON... BUT RIGHT NOW SOMETHING'S HAPPENING IN AN UNEXPLORED SECTION OF SOUTH AMERICA THAT WE JUST DON'T WANT YOU TO MISS...
WHAT FATE WILL BEFALL THE AMERICAN INTRUDER?
FOR AGES OUR PEOPLE HAVE DWELT IN THIS FORBIDDEN LAND... GUARDING THE SECRET FLAME OF LIFE WITHIN THESE IMPASSABLE MOUNTAINS!
BUT NOW A SPY FROM THE OUTSIDE WORLD HAS DISCOVERED US! FOR THAT... HE MUST DIE!
QUIET! THE ALL-POWERFUL KEEPER OF THE FLAME IS ABOUT TO SPEAK!
NO! I AM NO SPY! I AM A SCIENTIST! MY NAME IS DR. ANTON! I'M HERE ON A RESEARCH PROJECT!
HE LIES! NOW THAT HE HAS DISCOVERED OUR FLAME OF LIFE, HE PLANS TO BETRAY OUR SECRET TO MANKIND! BUT I, THE KEEPER OF THE FLAME, SHALL BE TRUE TO MY TRUST!
DON'T YOU UNDERSTAND? I'M ENGAGED IN BODY CELL RESEARCH! MY INSTRUMENTS DETECTED A SOURCE OF GREAT POWER HERE! THAT'S WHY I CAME TO YOUR LAND!
HIS WORDS ARE TWISTED AND FALSE!
SEE HOW THE MYSTIC FLAMES LEAP EVER HIGHER... GLOW EVER BRIGHTER! THEY CANNOT BE DECEIVED!
SEE HOW THEY TELL US TO BEWARE! WE ARE NOT SAFE... SO LONG AS HE LIVES!
THEN, AT THAT VERY MOMENT...
KEEPER! THERE IS A GIANT IN OUR LAND! HE COMES CLOSER.. EVEN NOW!
WE BARELY ESCAPED WITH OUR LIVES, SIRE!
I KNEW IT! THE FLAMES NEVER LIE!
NOW ONLY THE KEEPER OF THE FLAME CAN SAVE YOU!
QUICKLY, HIDE THE PRISONER! IF THE GIANT HAS COME TO RESCUE HIM, HE WILL SOON LEARN HIS MISSION HAS BEEN IN VAIN!

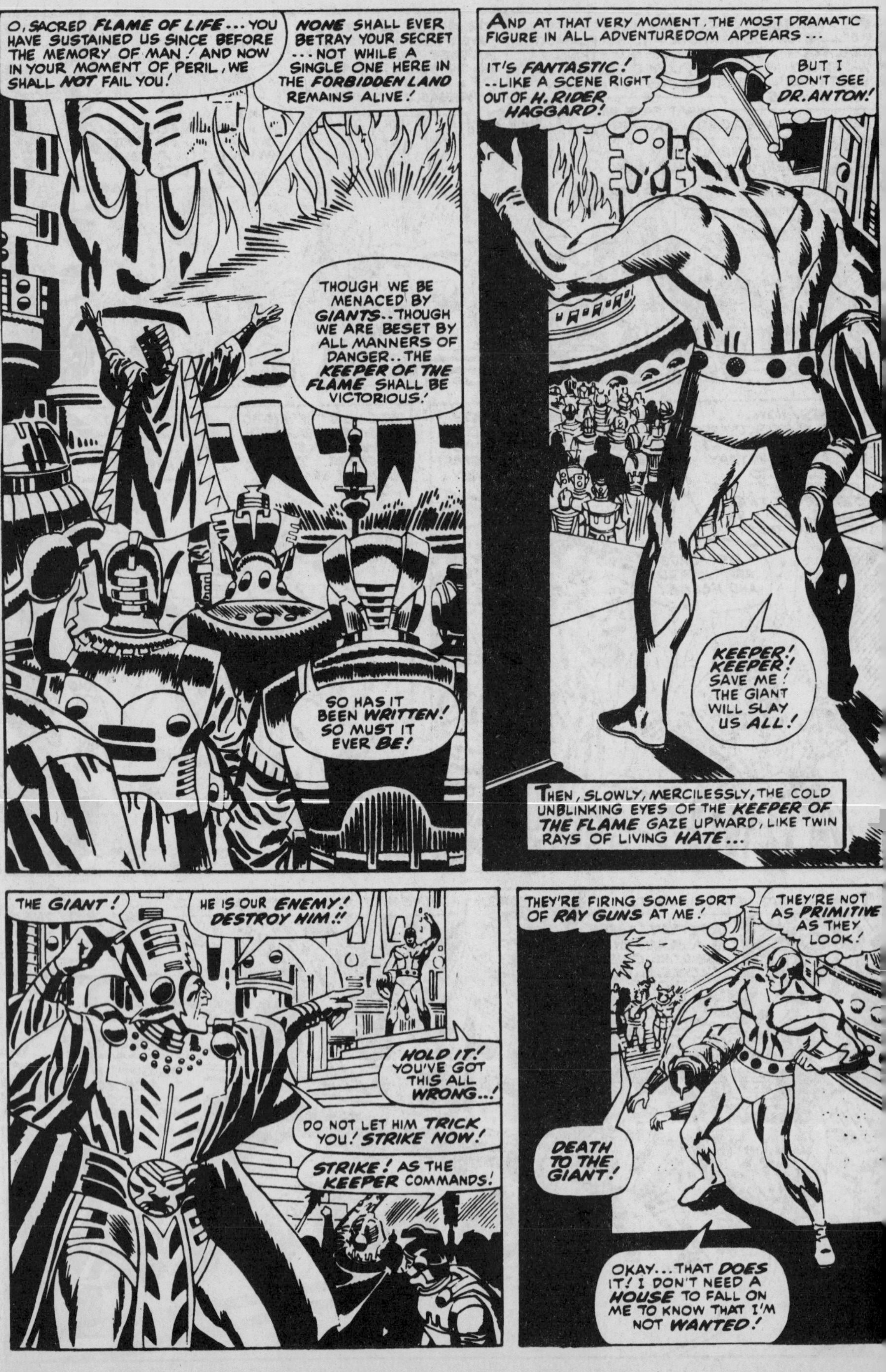
O, SACRED FLAME OF LIFE... YOU HAVE SUSTAINED US SINCE BEFORE THE MEMORY OF MAN! AND NOW IN YOUR MOMENT OF PERIL, WE SHALL NOT FAIL YOU!
NONE SHALL EVER BETRAY YOUR SECRET ...NOT WHILE A SINGLE ONE HERE IN THE FORBIDDEN LAND REMAINS ALIVE!
THOUGH WE BE MENACED BY GIANTS.. THOUGH WE ARE BESET BY ALL MANNERS OF DANGER.. THE KEEPER OF THE FLAME SHALL BE VICTORIOUS!
SO HAS IT BEEN WRITTEN! SO MUST IT EVER BE!
AND AT THAT VERY MOMENT, THE MOST DRAMATIC FIGURE IN ALL ADVENTUREDOM APPEARS...
IT'S FANTASTIC! ..LIKE A SCENE RIGHT OUT OF H. RIDER HAGGARD!
BUT I DON'T SEE DR. ANTON!
KEEPER! KEEPER! SAVE ME! THE GIANT WILL SLAY US ALL!
THEN, SLOWLY, MERCILESSLY, THE COLD UNBLINKING EYES OF THE KEEPER OF THE FLAME GAZE UPWARD, LIKE TWIN RAYS OF LIVING HATE...
THE GIANT!
HE IS OUR ENEMY! DESTROY HIM!!
HOLD IT! YOU'VE GOT THIS ALL WRONG...!
DO NOT LET HIM TRICK YOU! STRIKE NOW!
STRIKE! AS THE KEEPER COMMANDS!
THEY'RE FIRING SOME SORT OF RAY GUNS AT ME!
THEY'RE NOT AS PRIMITIVE AS THEY LOOK!
DEATH TO THE GIANT!
OKAY... THAT DOES IT! I DON'T NEED A HOUSE TO FALL ON ME TO KNOW THAT I'M NOT WANTED!

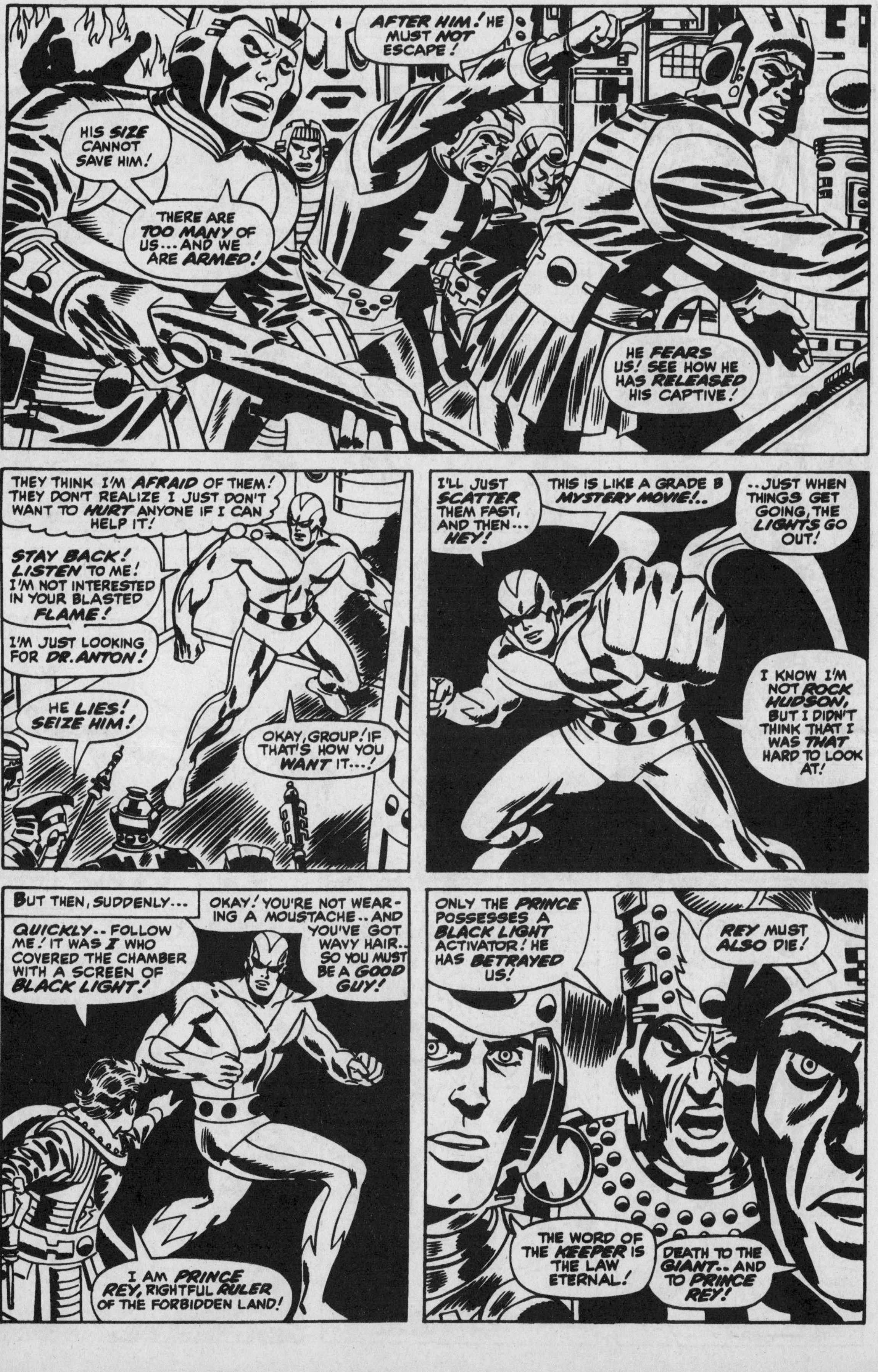
AFTER HIM! HE MUST NOT ESCAPE!
HIS SIZE CANNOT SAVE HIM!
THERE ARE TOO MANY OF US... AND WE ARE ARMED!
HE FEARS US! SEE HOW HE HAS RELEASED HIS CAPTIVE!
THEY THINK I'M AFRAID OF THEM! THEY DON'T REALIZE I JUST DON'T WANT TO HURT ANYONE IF I CAN HELP IT!
STAY BACK! LISTEN TO ME! I'M NOT INTERESTED IN YOUR BLASTED FLAME!
I'M JUST LOOKING FOR DR. ANTON!
HE LIES! SEIZE HIM!
OKAY, GROUP! IF THAT'S HOW YOU WANT IT...!
I'LL JUST SCATTER THEM FAST, AND THEN... HEY!
THIS IS LIKE A GRADE B MYSTERY MOVIE!..
..JUST WHEN THINGS GET GOING, THE LIGHTS GO OUT!
I KNOW I'M NOT ROCK HUDSON, BUT I DIDN'T THINK THAT I WAS THAT HARD TO LOOK AT!
BUT THEN, SUDDENLY...
QUICKLY.. FOLLOW ME! IT WAS I WHO COVERED THE CHAMBER WITH A SCREEN OF BLACK LIGHT!
OKAY! YOU'RE NOT WEARING A MOUSTACHE.. AND YOU'VE GOT WAVY HAIR.. SO YOU MUST BE A GOOD GUY!
I AM PRINCE REY, RIGHTFUL RULER OF THE FORBIDDEN LAND!
ONLY THE PRINCE POSSESSES A BLACK LIGHT ACTIVATOR! HE HAS BETRAYED US!
REY MUST ALSO DIE!
THE WORD OF THE KEEPER IS THE LAW ETERNAL!
DEATH TO THE GIANT.. AND TO PRINCE REY!

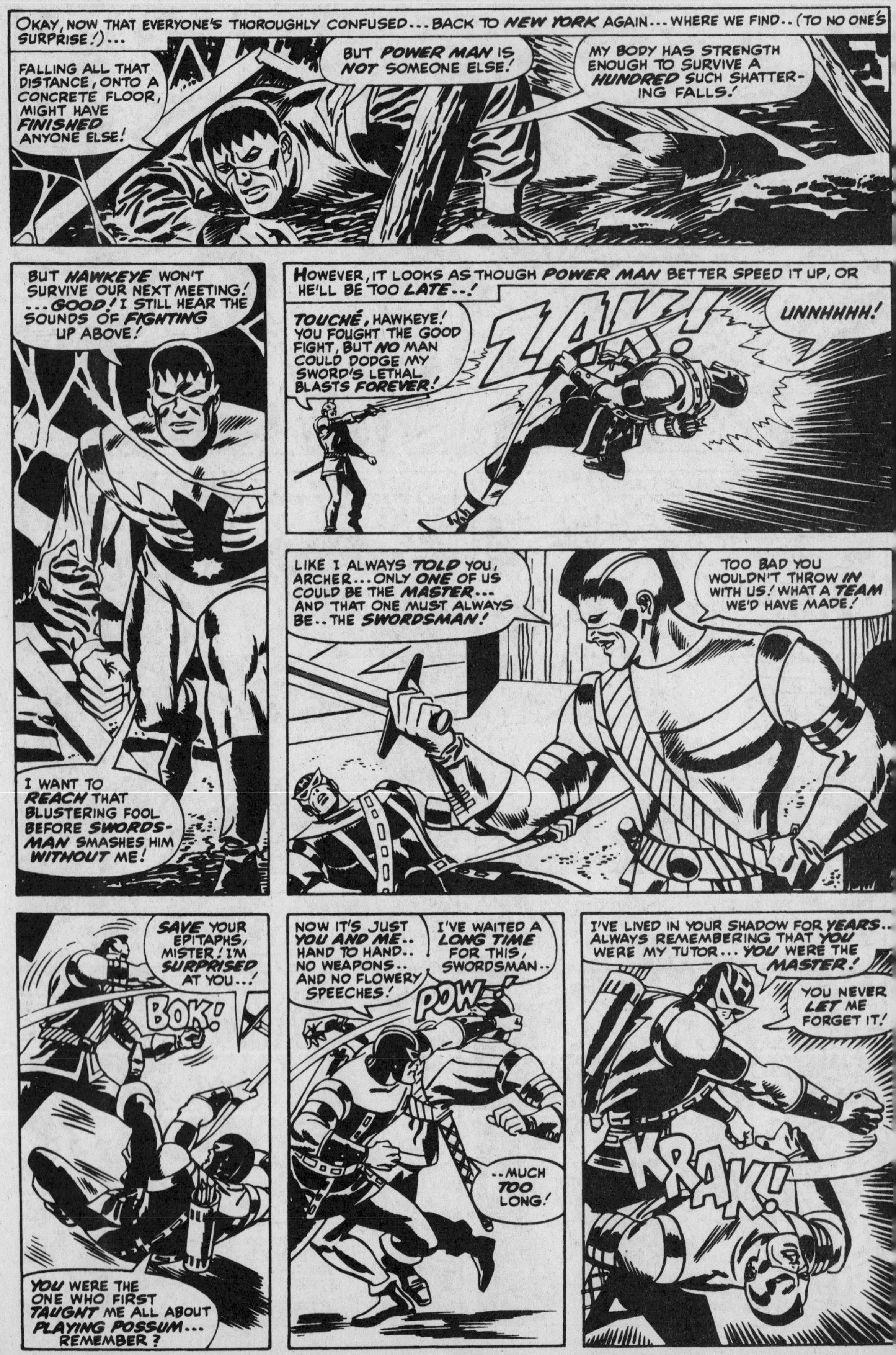
OKAY, NOW THAT EVERYONE'S THOROUGHLY CONFUSED... BACK TO NEW YORK AGAIN... WHERE WE FIND.. (TO NO ONE'S SURPRISE!)...
FALLING ALL THAT DISTANCE, ONTO A CONCRETE FLOOR, MIGHT HAVE FINISHED ANYONE ELSE!
BUT POWER MAN IS NOT SOMEONE ELSE!
MY BODY HAS STRENGTH ENOUGH TO SURVIVE A HUNDRED SUCH SHATTERING FALLS!
BUT HAWKEYE WON'T SURVIVE OUR NEXT MEETING! ...GOOD! I STILL HEAR THE SOUNDS OF FIGHTING UP ABOVE!
I WANT TO REACH THAT BLUSTERING FOOL BEFORE SWORDSMAN SMASHES HIM WITHOUT ME!
HOWEVER, IT LOOKS AS THOUGH POWER MAN BETTER SPEED IT UP, OR HE'LL BE TOO LATE..!
TOUCHÉ, HAWKEYE! YOU FOUGHT THE GOOD FIGHT, BUT NO MAN COULD DODGE MY SWORD'S LETHAL BLASTS FOREVER!
ZAK!
UNNHHHH!
LIKE I ALWAYS TOLD YOU, ARCHER... ONLY ONE OF US COULD BE THE MASTER... AND THAT ONE MUST ALWAYS BE.. THE SWORDSMAN!
TOO BAD YOU WOULDN'T THROW IN WITH US! WHAT A TEAM WE'D HAVE MADE!
SAVE YOUR EPITAPHS, MISTER! I'M SURPRISED AT YOU...!
BOK!
YOU WERE THE ONE WHO FIRST TAUGHT ME ALL ABOUT PLAYING POSSUM... REMEMBER?
NOW IT'S JUST YOU AND ME.. HAND TO HAND.. NO WEAPONS.. AND NO FLOWERY SPEECHES!
I'VE WAITED A LONG TIME FOR THIS, SWORDSMAN..
POW
..MUCH TOO LONG!
I'VE LIVED IN YOUR SHADOW FOR YEARS.. ALWAYS REMEMBERING THAT YOU WERE MY TUTOR... YOU WERE THE MASTER!
YOU NEVER LET ME FORGET IT!
KRAK!

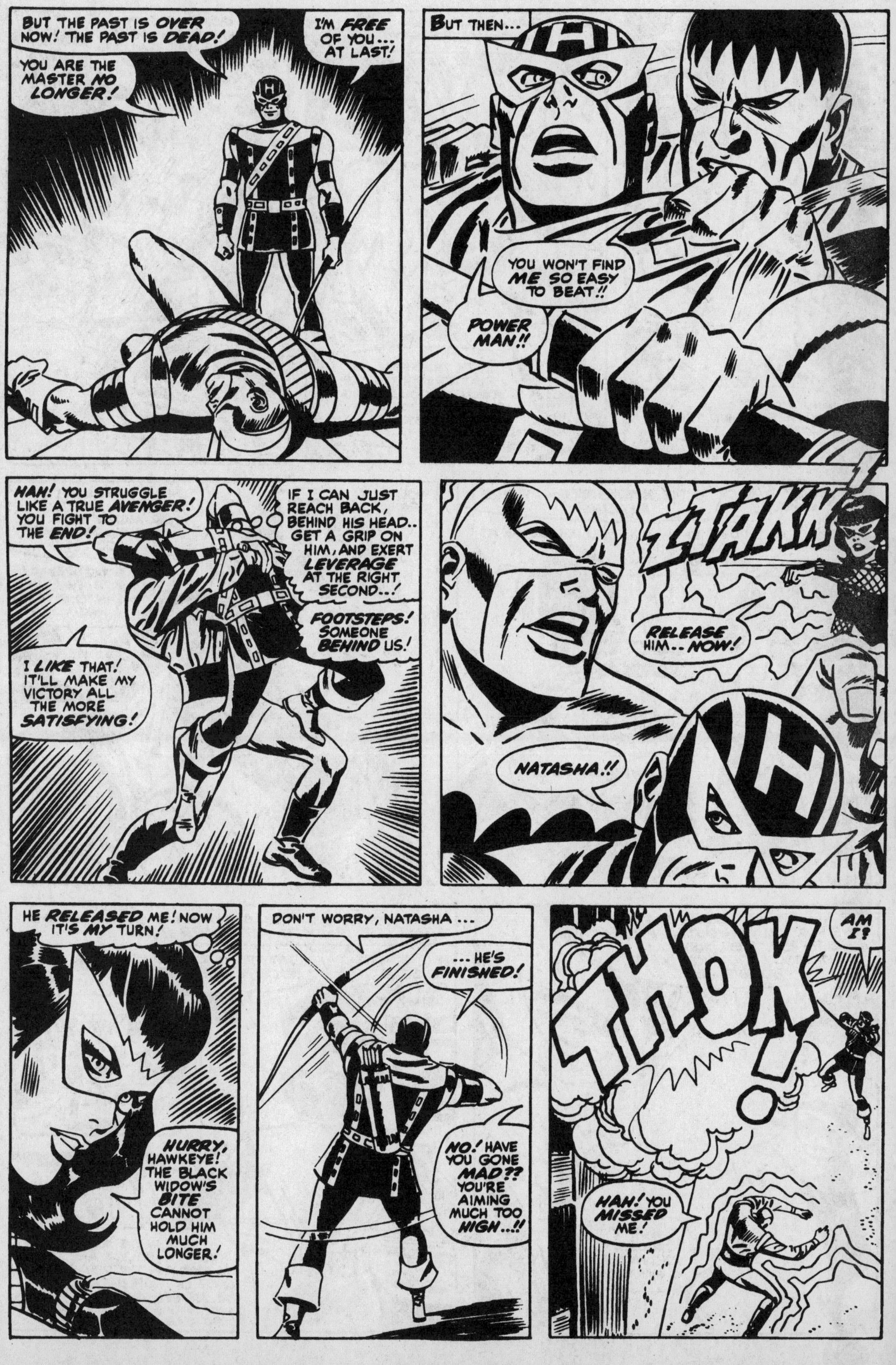
BUT THE PAST IS OVER NOW! THE PAST IS DEAD!
YOU ARE THE MASTER NO LONGER!
I'M FREE OF YOU... AT LAST!
BUT THEN...
YOU WON'T FIND ME SO EASY TO BEAT!!
POWER MAN!!
HAH! YOU STRUGGLE LIKE A TRUE AVENGER! YOU FIGHT TO THE END!
IF I CAN JUST REACH BACK, BEHIND HIS HEAD.. GET A GRIP ON HIM, AND EXERT LEVERAGE AT THE RIGHT SECOND...!
FOOTSTEPS! SOMEONE BEHIND US!
I LIKE THAT! IT'LL MAKE MY VICTORY ALL THE MORE SATISFYING!
ZTAKK!
RELEASE HIM.. NOW!
NATASHA!!
HE RELEASED ME! NOW IT'S MY TURN!
HURRY, HAWKEYE! THE BLACK WIDOW'S BITE CANNOT HOLD HIM MUCH LONGER!
DON'T WORRY, NATASHA ...
... HE'S FINISHED!
NO! HAVE YOU GONE MAD?? YOU'RE AIMING MUCH TOO HIGH...!!
AM I?
THOK!
HAH! YOU MISSED ME!

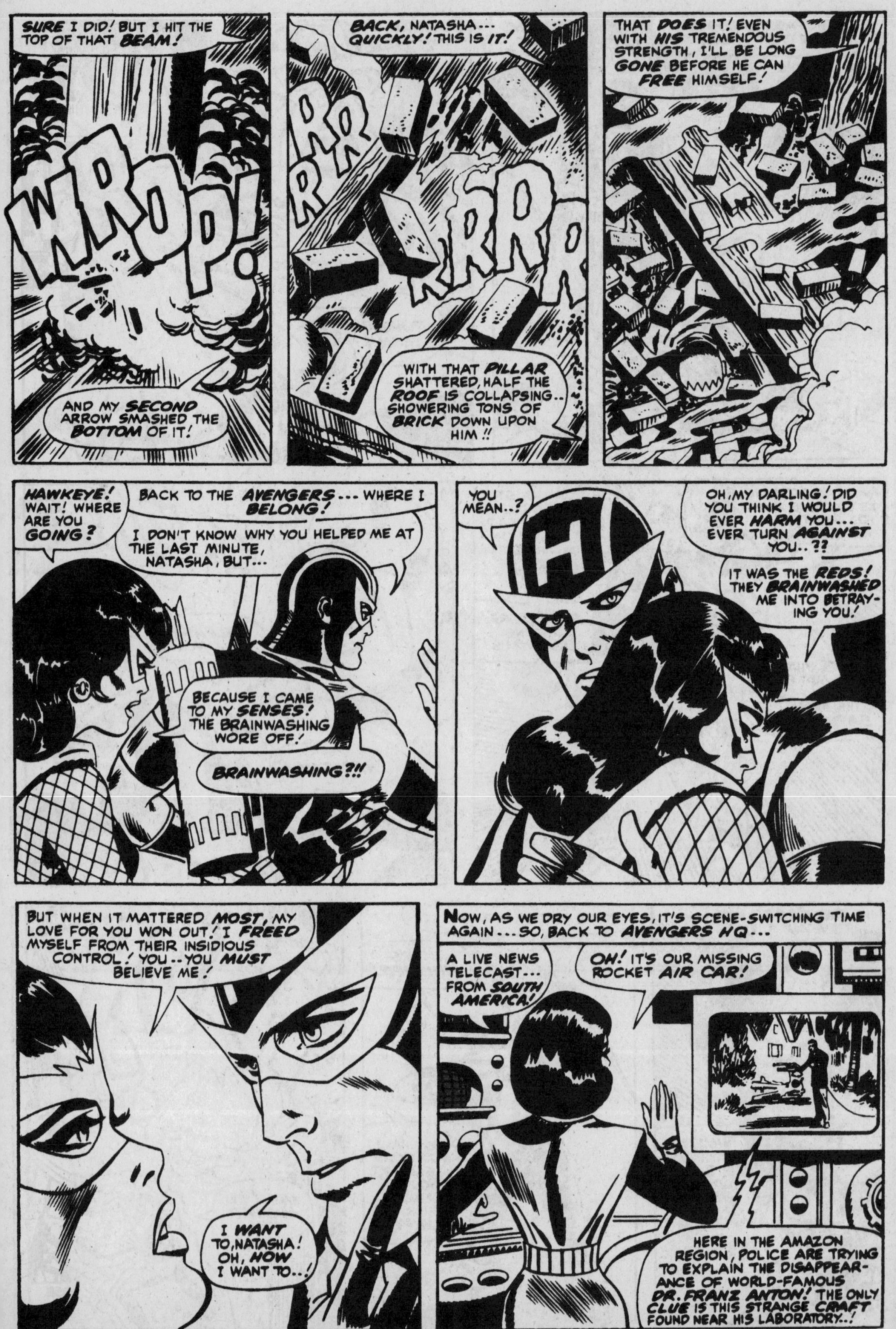
SURE I DID! BUT I HIT THE TOP OF THAT BEAM!
WROP!
AND MY SECOND ARROW SMASHED THE BOTTOM OF IT!
BACK, NATASHA... QUICKLY! THIS IS IT!
RRR
RRRR
WITH THAT PILLAR SHATTERED, HALF THE ROOF IS COLLAPSING.. SHOWERING TONS OF BRICK DOWN UPON HIM!!
THAT DOES IT! EVEN WITH HIS TREMENDOUS STRENGTH, I'LL BE LONG GONE BEFORE HE CAN FREE HIMSELF!
HAWKEYE! WAIT! WHERE ARE YOU GOING?
BACK TO THE AVENGERS --- WHERE I BELONG!
I DON'T KNOW WHY YOU HELPED ME AT THE LAST MINUTE, NATASHA, BUT...
BECAUSE I CAME TO MY SENSES! THE BRAINWASHING WORE OFF!
BRAINWASHING?!!
YOU MEAN..?
OH, MY DARLING! DID YOU THINK I WOULD EVER HARM YOU... EVER TURN AGAINST YOU..??
IT WAS THE REDS! THEY BRAINWASHED ME INTO BETRAYING YOU!
BUT WHEN IT MATTERED MOST, MY LOVE FOR YOU WON OUT! I FREED MYSELF FROM THEIR INSIDIOUS CONTROL! YOU--YOU MUST BELIEVE ME!
I WANT TO, NATASHA! OH, HOW I WANT TO..!
NOW, AS WE DRY OUR EYES, IT'S SCENE-SWITCHING TIME AGAIN... SO, BACK TO AVENGERS HQ...
A LIVE NEWS TELECAST... FROM SOUTH AMERICA!
OH! IT'S OUR MISSING ROCKET AIR CAR!
HERE IN THE AMAZON REGION, POLICE ARE TRYING TO EXPLAIN THE DISAPPEARANCE OF WORLD-FAMOUS DR. FRANZ ANTON! THE ONLY CLUE IS THIS STRANGE CRAFT FOUND NEAR HIS LABORATORY..!

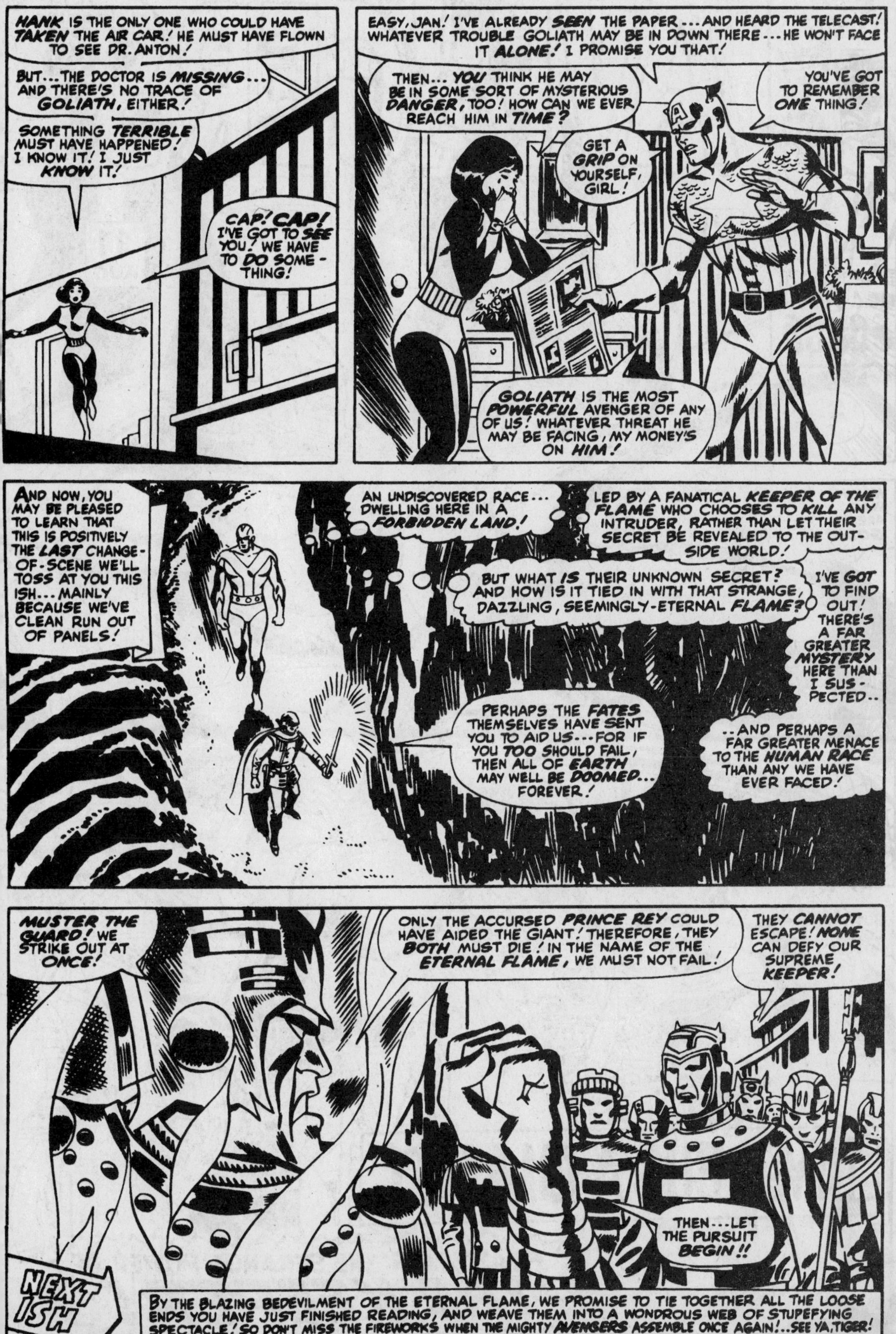

HANK IS THE ONLY ONE WHO COULD HAVE TAKEN THE AIR CAR! HE MUST HAVE FLOWN TO SEE DR. ANTON!
BUT... THE DOCTOR IS MISSING... AND THERE'S NO TRACE OF GOLIATH, EITHER!
SOMETHING TERRIBLE MUST HAVE HAPPENED! I KNOW IT! I JUST KNOW IT!
CAP! CAP! I'VE GOT TO SEE YOU! WE HAVE TO DO SOME-THING!
EASY, JAN! I'VE ALREADY SEEN THE PAPER... AND HEARD THE TELECAST! WHATEVER TROUBLE GOLIATH MAY BE IN DOWN THERE... HE WON'T FACE IT ALONE! I PROMISE YOU THAT!
THEN... YOU THINK HE MAY BE IN SOME SORT OF MYSTERIOUS DANGER, TOO! HOW CAN WE EVER REACH HIM IN TIME?
GET A GRIP ON YOURSELF, GIRL!
YOU'VE GOT TO REMEMBER ONE THING!
GOLIATH IS THE MOST POWERFUL AVENGER OF ANY OF US! WHATEVER THREAT HE MAY BE FACING, MY MONEY'S ON HIM!
AND NOW, YOU MAY BE PLEASED TO LEARN THAT THIS IS POSITIVELY THE LAST CHANGE-OF-SCENE WE'LL TOSS AT YOU THIS ISH... MAINLY BECAUSE WE'VE CLEAN RUN OUT OF PANELS!
AN UNDISCOVERED RACE... DWELLING HERE IN A FORBIDDEN LAND!
LED BY A FANATICAL KEEPER OF THE FLAME WHO CHOOSES TO KILL ANY INTRUDER, RATHER THAN LET THEIR SECRET BE REVEALED TO THE OUT-SIDE WORLD!
BUT WHAT IS THEIR UNKNOWN SECRET? AND HOW IS IT TIED IN WITH THAT STRANGE, DAZZLING, SEEMINGLY-ETERNAL FLAME?
I'VE GOT TO FIND OUT! THERE'S A FAR GREATER MYSTERY HERE THAN I SUS-PECTED..
PERHAPS THE FATES THEMSELVES HAVE SENT YOU TO AID US... FOR IF YOU TOO SHOULD FAIL, THEN ALL OF EARTH MAY WELL BE DOOMED... FOREVER!
..AND PERHAPS A FAR GREATER MENACE TO THE HUMAN RACE THAN ANY WE HAVE EVER FACED!
MUSTER THE GUARD! WE STRIKE OUT AT ONCE!
ONLY THE ACCURSED PRINCE REY COULD HAVE AIDED THE GIANT! THEREFORE, THEY BOTH MUST DIE! IN THE NAME OF THE ETERNAL FLAME, WE MUST NOT FAIL!
THEY CANNOT ESCAPE! NONE CAN DEFY OUR SUPREME KEEPER!
THEN... LET THE PURSUIT BEGIN!!
NEXT ISH
BY THE BLAZING BEDEVILMENT OF THE ETERNAL FLAME, WE PROMISE TO TIE TOGETHER ALL THE LOOSE ENDS YOU HAVE JUST FINISHED READING, AND WEAVE THEM INTO A WONDROUS WEB OF STUPEFYING SPECTACLE! SO DON'T MISS THE FIREWORKS WHEN THE MIGHTY AVENGERS ASSEMBLE ONCE AGAIN!...SEE YA, TIGER!

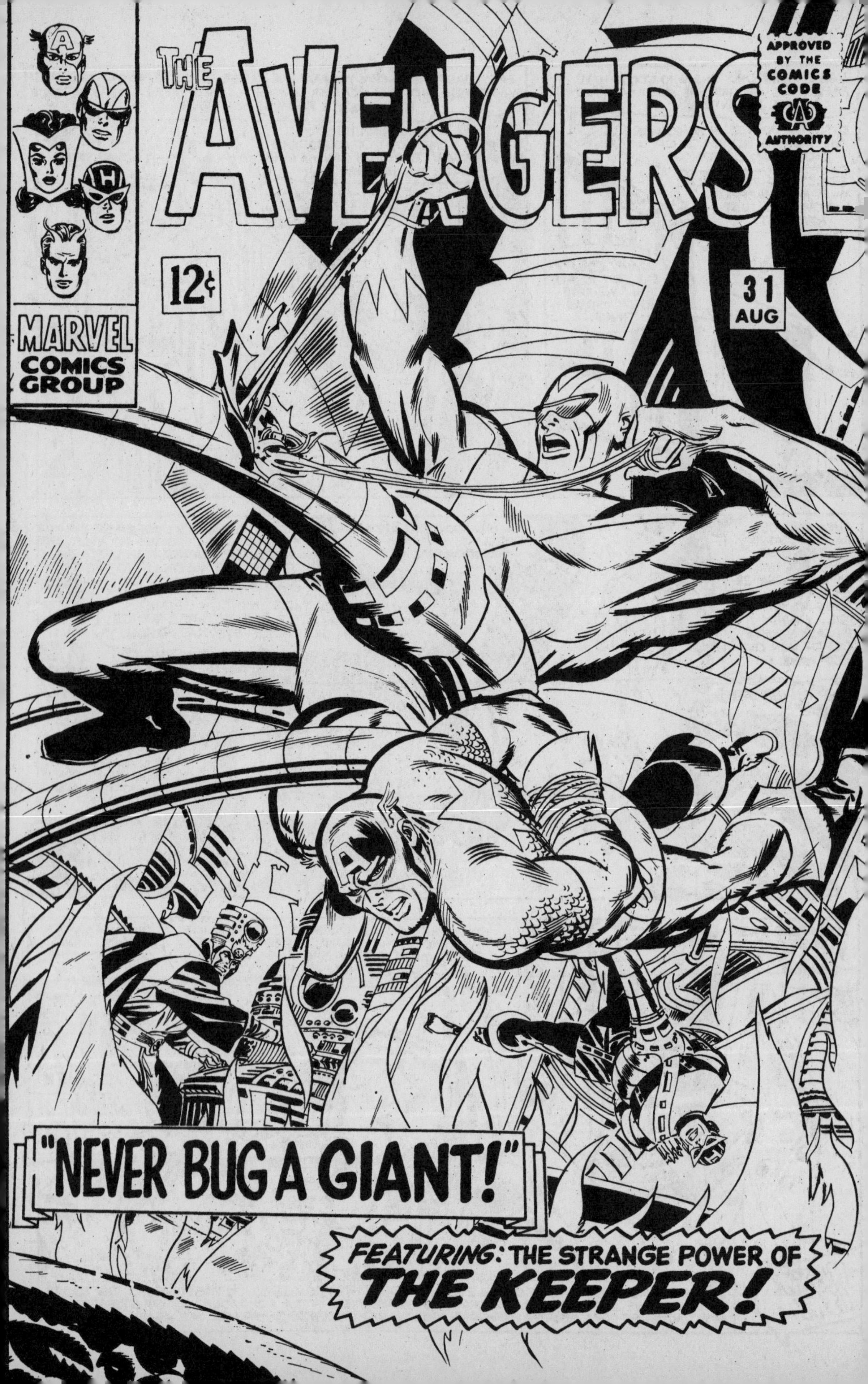
THE AVENGERS
APPROVED BY THE COMICS CODE AUTHORITY
12¢
31 AUG
MARVEL COMICS GROUP
"NEVER BUG A GIANT!"
FEATURING: THE STRANGE POWER OF THE KEEPER!

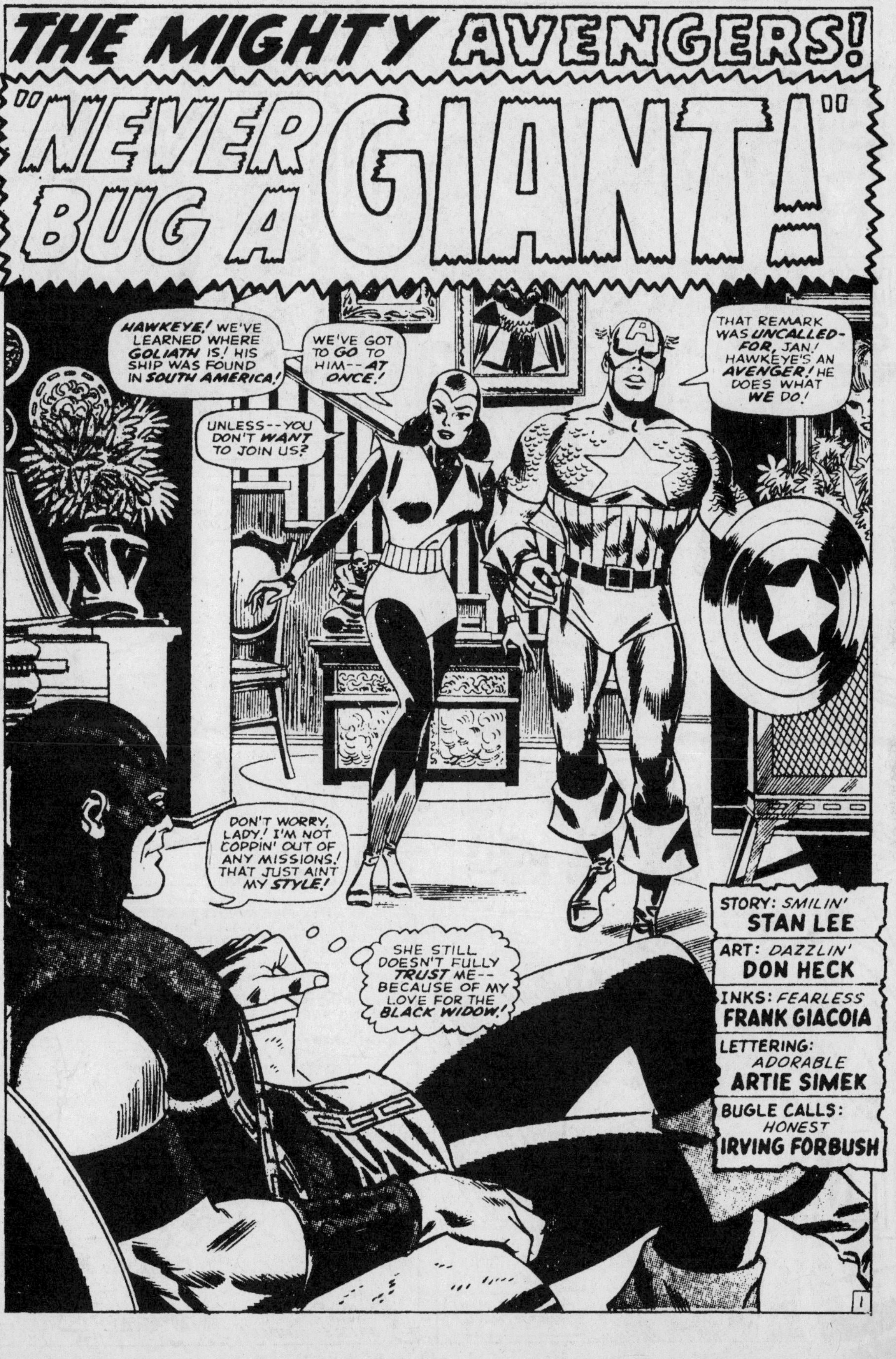
THE MIGHTY AVENGERS!
"NEVER BUG A GIANT!"
HAWKEYE! WE'VE LEARNED WHERE GOLIATH IS! HIS SHIP WAS FOUND IN SOUTH AMERICA!
WE'VE GOT TO GO TO HIM--AT ONCE!
UNLESS--YOU DON'T WANT TO JOIN US?
THAT REMARK WAS UNCALLED-FOR, JAN! HAWKEYE'S AN AVENGER! HE DOES WHAT WE DO!
DON'T WORRY, LADY! I'M NOT COPPIN' OUT OF ANY MISSIONS! THAT JUST AINT MY STYLE!
SHE STILL DOESN'T FULLY TRUST ME--BECAUSE OF MY LOVE FOR THE BLACK WIDOW!
STORY: SMILIN' STAN LEE
ART: DAZZLIN' DON HECK
INKS: FEARLESS FRANK GIACOIA
LETTERING: ADORABLE ARTIE SIMEK
BUGLE CALLS: HONEST IRVING FORBUSH
1

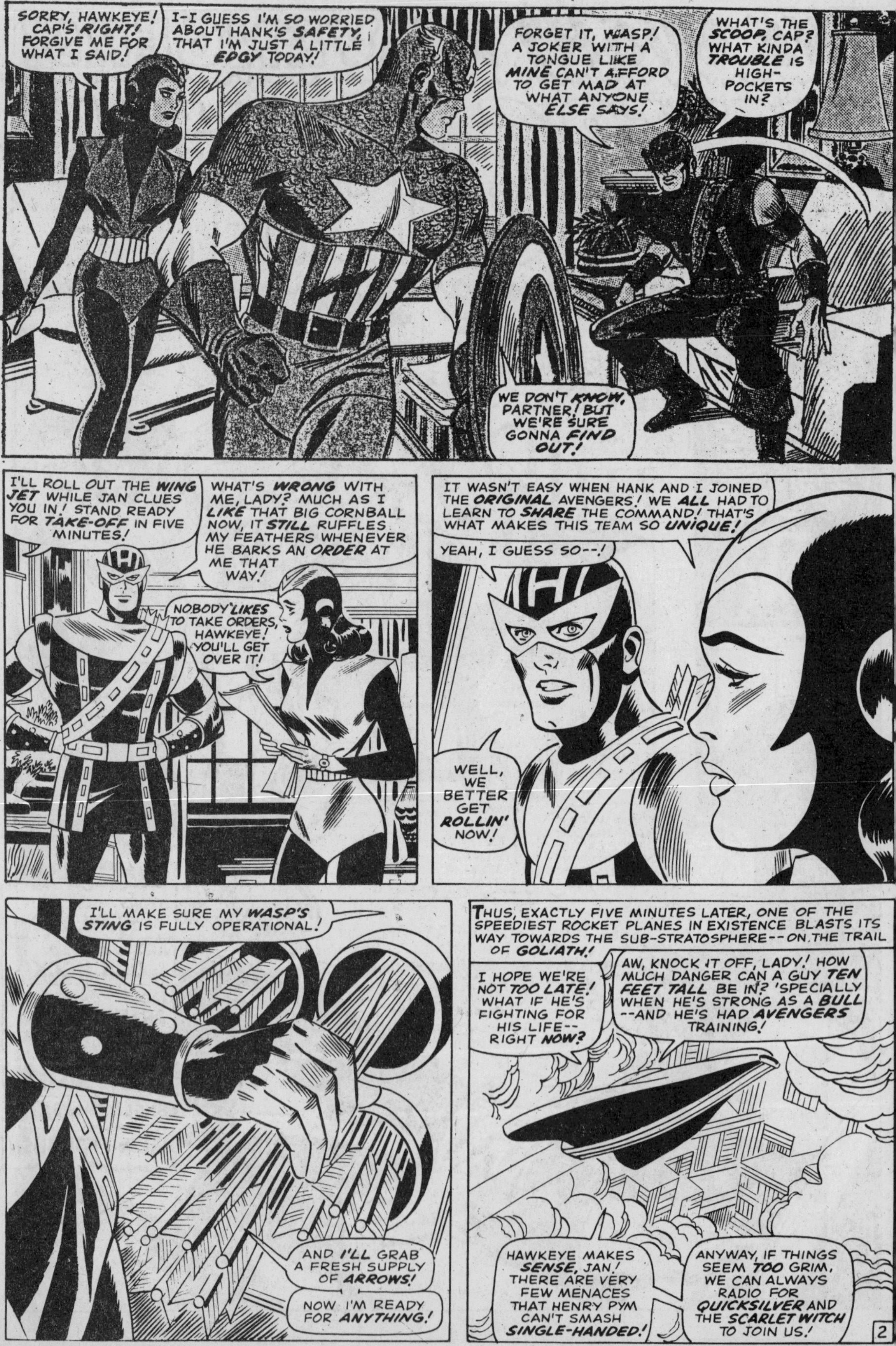
SORRY, HAWKEYE! CAP'S RIGHT! FORGIVE ME FOR WHAT I SAID!
I-I GUESS I'M SO WORRIED ABOUT HANK'S SAFETY, THAT I'M JUST A LITTLE EDGY TODAY!
FORGET IT, WASP! A JOKER WITH A TONGUE LIKE MINE CAN'T AFFORD TO GET MAD AT WHAT ANYONE ELSE SAYS!
WHAT'S THE SCOOP, CAP? WHAT KINDA TROUBLE IS HIGH-POCKETS IN?
WE DON'T KNOW, PARTNER! BUT WE'RE SURE GONNA FIND OUT!
I'LL ROLL OUT THE WING JET WHILE JAN CLUES YOU IN! STAND READY FOR TAKE-OFF IN FIVE MINUTES!
WHAT'S WRONG WITH ME, LADY? MUCH AS I LIKE THAT BIG CORNBALL NOW, IT STILL RUFFLES MY FEATHERS WHENEVER HE BARKS AN ORDER AT ME THAT WAY!
NOBODY LIKES TO TAKE ORDERS, HAWKEYE! YOU'LL GET OVER IT!
IT WASN'T EASY WHEN HANK AND I JOINED THE ORIGINAL AVENGERS! WE ALL HAD TO LEARN TO SHARE THE COMMAND! THAT'S WHAT MAKES THIS TEAM SO UNIQUE!
YEAH, I GUESS SO--!
WELL, WE BETTER GET ROLLIN' NOW!
I'LL MAKE SURE MY WASP'S STING IS FULLY OPERATIONAL!
AND I'LL GRAB A FRESH SUPPLY OF ARROWS!
NOW I'M READY FOR ANYTHING!
THUS, EXACTLY FIVE MINUTES LATER, ONE OF THE SPEEDIEST ROCKET PLANES IN EXISTENCE BLASTS ITS WAY TOWARDS THE SUB-STRATOSPHERE--ON THE TRAIL OF GOLIATH!
I HOPE WE'RE NOT TOO LATE! WHAT IF HE'S FIGHTING FOR HIS LIFE--RIGHT NOW?
AW, KNOCK IT OFF, LADY! HOW MUCH DANGER CAN A GUY TEN FEET TALL BE IN? 'SPECIALLY WHEN HE'S STRONG AS A BULL--AND HE'S HAD AVENGERS TRAINING!
HAWKEYE MAKES SENSE, JAN! THERE ARE VERY FEW MENACES THAT HENRY PYM CAN'T SMASH SINGLE-HANDED!
ANYWAY, IF THINGS SEEM TOO GRIM, WE CAN ALWAYS RADIO FOR QUICKSILVER AND THE SCARLET WITCH TO JOIN US!
2

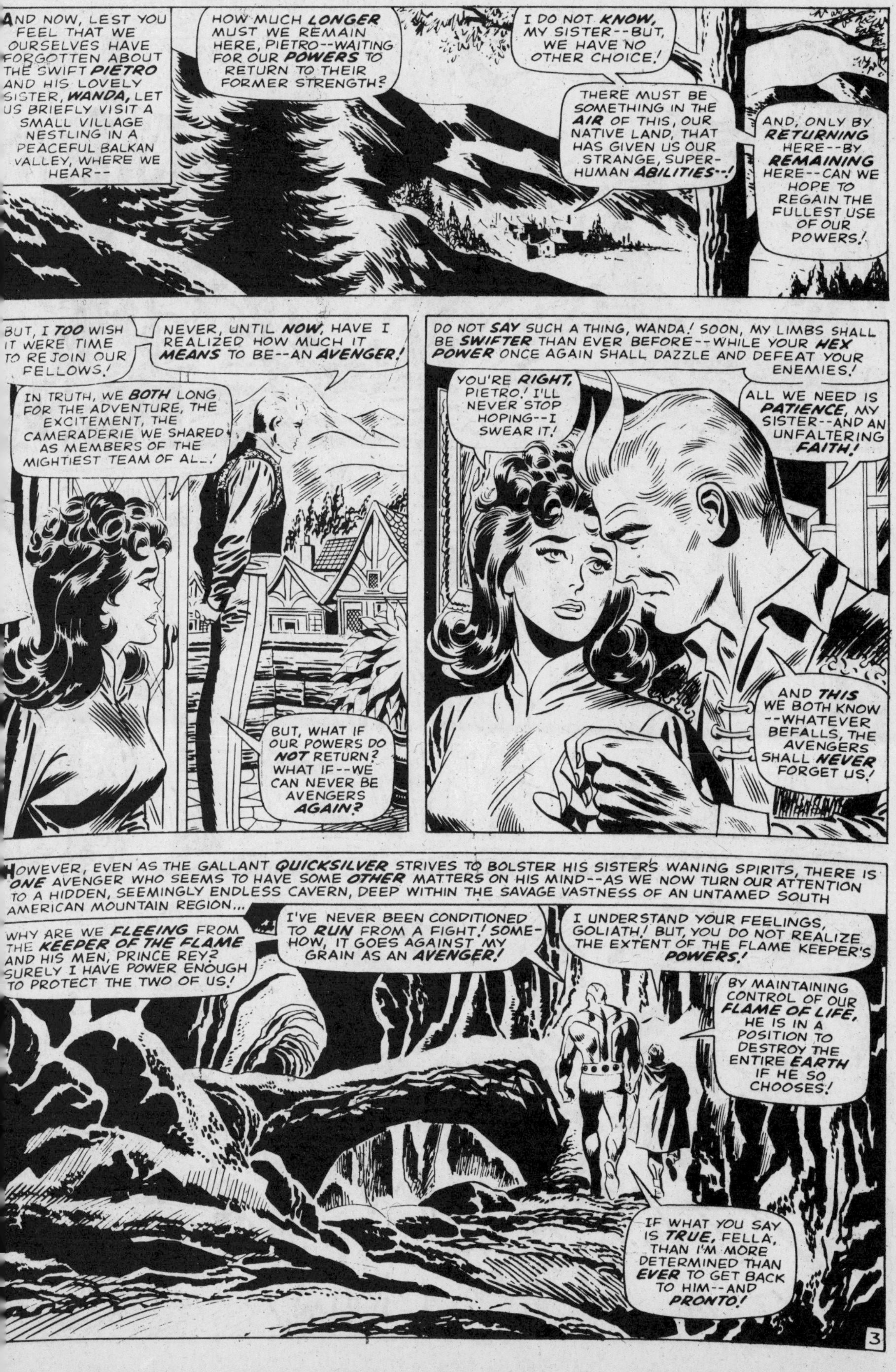
AND NOW, LEST YOU FEEL THAT WE OURSELVES HAVE FORGOTTEN ABOUT THE SWIFT PIETRO AND HIS LOVELY SISTER, WANDA, LET US BRIEFLY VISIT A SMALL VILLAGE NESTLING IN A PEACEFUL BALKAN VALLEY, WHERE WE HEAR--
HOW MUCH LONGER MUST WE REMAIN HERE, PIETRO--WAITING FOR OUR POWERS TO RETURN TO THEIR FORMER STRENGTH?
I DO NOT KNOW, MY SISTER--BUT, WE HAVE NO OTHER CHOICE!
THERE MUST BE SOMETHING IN THE AIR OF THIS, OUR NATIVE LAND, THAT HAS GIVEN US OUR STRANGE, SUPER-HUMAN ABILITIES--!
AND, ONLY BY RETURNING HERE--BY REMAINING HERE--CAN WE HOPE TO REGAIN THE FULLEST USE OF OUR POWERS!
BUT, I TOO WISH IT WERE TIME TO REJOIN OUR FELLOWS!
NEVER, UNTIL NOW, HAVE I REALIZED HOW MUCH IT MEANS TO BE--AN AVENGER!
IN TRUTH, WE BOTH LONG FOR THE ADVENTURE, THE EXCITEMENT, THE CAMERADERIE WE SHARED AS MEMBERS OF THE MIGHTIEST TEAM OF ALL!
BUT, WHAT IF OUR POWERS DO NOT RETURN? WHAT IF--WE CAN NEVER BE AVENGERS AGAIN?
DO NOT SAY SUCH A THING, WANDA! SOON, MY LIMBS SHALL BE SWIFTER THAN EVER BEFORE--WHILE YOUR HEX POWER ONCE AGAIN SHALL DAZZLE AND DEFEAT YOUR ENEMIES!
YOU'RE RIGHT, PIETRO! I'LL NEVER STOP HOPING--I SWEAR IT!
ALL WE NEED IS PATIENCE, MY SISTER--AND AN UNFALTERING FAITH!
AND THIS WE BOTH KNOW--WHATEVER BEFALLS, THE AVENGERS SHALL NEVER FORGET US!
HOWEVER, EVEN AS THE GALLANT QUICKSILVER STRIVES TO BOLSTER HIS SISTER'S WANING SPIRITS, THERE IS ONE AVENGER WHO SEEMS TO HAVE SOME OTHER MATTERS ON HIS MIND--AS WE NOW TURN OUR ATTENTION TO A HIDDEN, SEEMINGLY ENDLESS CAVERN, DEEP WITHIN THE SAVAGE VASTNESS OF AN UNTAMED SOUTH AMERICAN MOUNTAIN REGION...
WHY ARE WE FLEEING FROM THE KEEPER OF THE FLAME AND HIS MEN, PRINCE REY? SURELY I HAVE POWER ENOUGH TO PROTECT THE TWO OF US!
I'VE NEVER BEEN CONDITIONED TO RUN FROM A FIGHT! SOMEHOW, IT GOES AGAINST MY GRAIN AS AN AVENGER!
I UNDERSTAND YOUR FEELINGS, GOLIATH! BUT, YOU DO NOT REALIZE THE EXTENT OF THE FLAME KEEPER'S POWERS!
BY MAINTAINING CONTROL OF OUR FLAME OF LIFE, HE IS IN A POSITION TO DESTROY THE ENTIRE EARTH IF HE SO CHOOSES!
IF WHAT YOU SAY IS TRUE, FELLA, THAN I'M MORE DETERMINED THAN EVER TO GET BACK TO HIM--AND PRONTO!

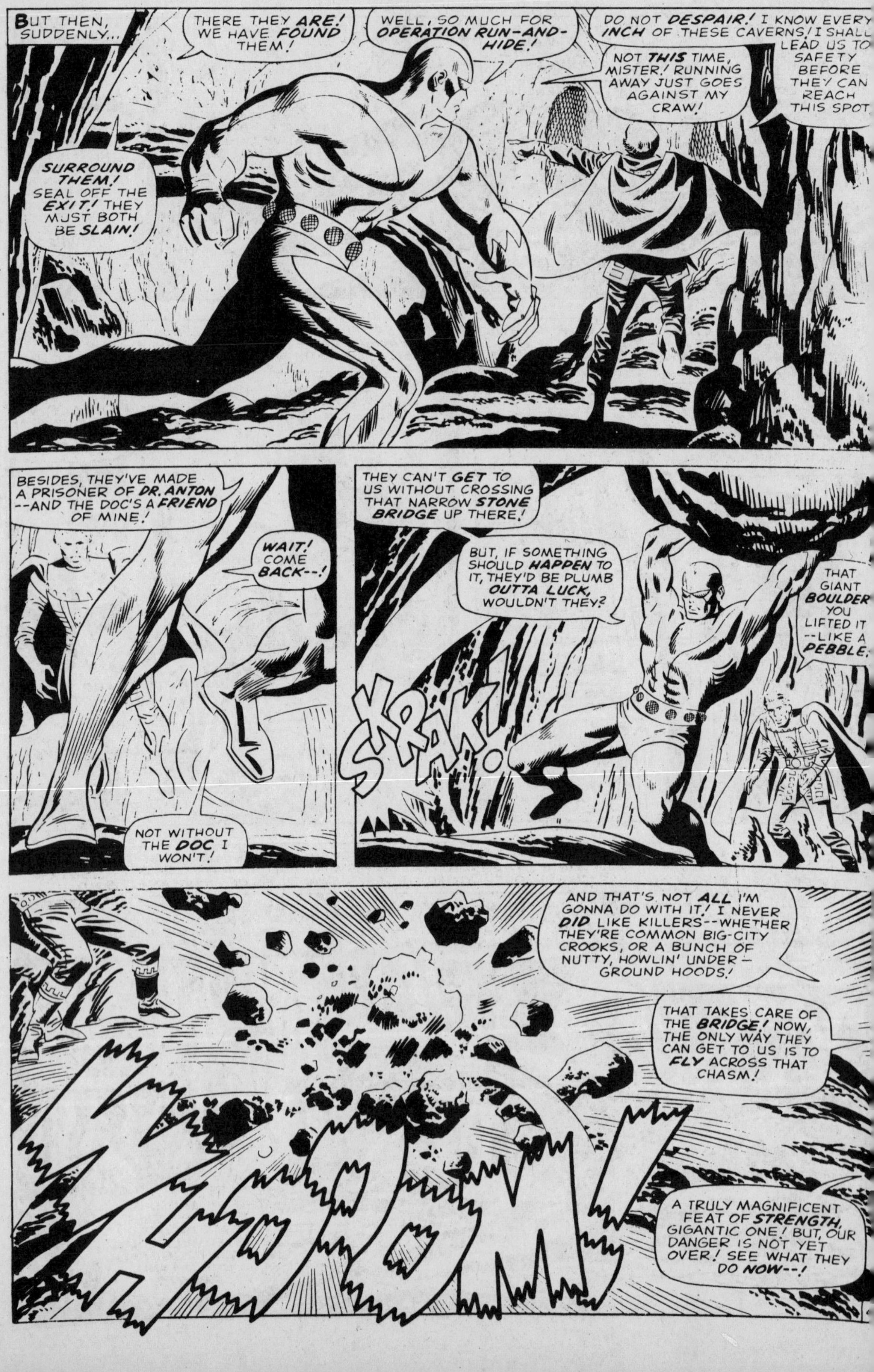

BUT THEN, SUDDENLY...
THERE THEY ARE! WE HAVE FOUND THEM!
WELL, SO MUCH FOR OPERATION RUN-AND-HIDE!
DO NOT DESPAIR! I KNOW EVERY INCH OF THESE CAVERNS! I SHALL LEAD US TO SAFETY BEFORE THEY CAN REACH THIS SPOT
NOT THIS TIME, MISTER! RUNNING AWAY JUST GOES AGAINST MY CRAW!
SURROUND THEM! SEAL OFF THE EXIT! THEY MUST BOTH BE SLAIN!
BESIDES, THEY'VE MADE A PRISONER OF DR. ANTON --AND THE DOC'S A FRIEND OF MINE!
WAIT! COME BACK--!
NOT WITHOUT THE DOC I WON'T!
THEY CAN'T GET TO US WITHOUT CROSSING THAT NARROW STONE BRIDGE UP THERE!
BUT, IF SOMETHING SHOULD HAPPEN TO IT, THEY'D BE PLUMB OUTTA LUCK, WOULDN'T THEY?
THAT GIANT BOULDER YOU LIFTED IT --LIKE A PEBBLE!
SKRAK!
AND THAT'S NOT ALL I'M GONNA DO WITH IT! I NEVER DID LIKE KILLERS--WHETHER THEY'RE COMMON BIG-CITY CROOKS, OR A BUNCH OF NUTTY, HOWLIN' UNDER-GROUND HOODS!
THAT TAKES CARE OF THE BRIDGE! NOW, THE ONLY WAY THEY CAN GET TO US IS TO FLY ACROSS THAT CHASM!
A TRULY MAGNIFICENT FEAT OF STRENGTH, GIGANTIC ONE! BUT, OUR DANGER IS NOT YET OVER! SEE WHAT THEY DO NOW--!

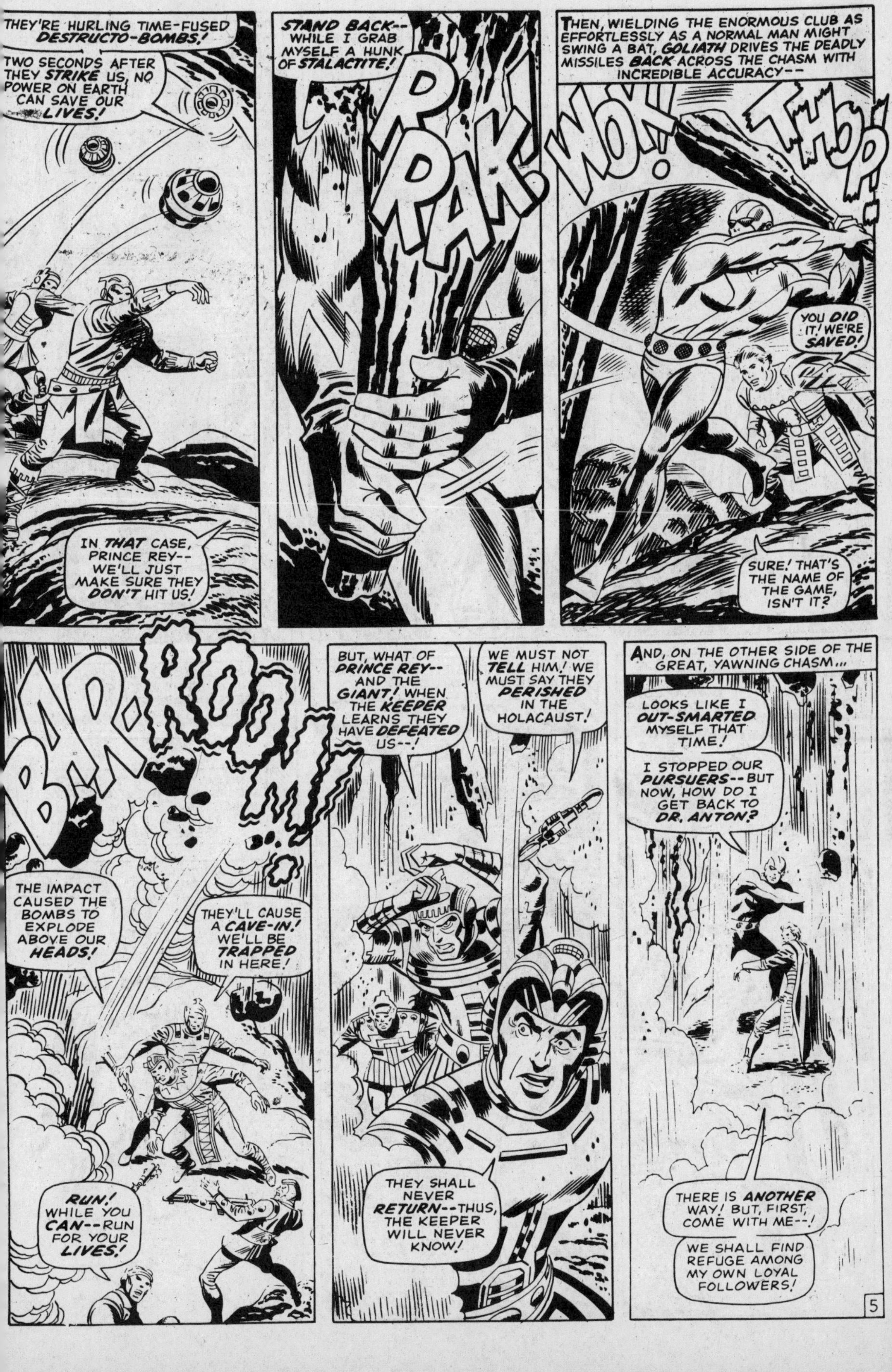
THEY'RE HURLING TIME-FUSED DESTRUCTO-BOMBS!
TWO SECONDS AFTER THEY STRIKE US, NO POWER ON EARTH CAN SAVE OUR LIVES!
IN THAT CASE, PRINCE REY-- WE'LL JUST MAKE SURE THEY DON'T HIT US!
STAND BACK-- WHILE I GRAB MYSELF A HUNK OF STALACTITE!
R-RAK.
THEN, WIELDING THE ENORMOUS CLUB AS EFFORTLESSLY AS A NORMAL MAN MIGHT SWING A BAT, GOLIATH DRIVES THE DEADLY MISSILES BACK ACROSS THE CHASM WITH INCREDIBLE ACCURACY--
WOK!
THOP!
YOU DID IT! WE'RE SAVED!
SURE! THAT'S THE NAME OF THE GAME, ISN'T IT?
BA-R-ROOM!
THE IMPACT CAUSED THE BOMBS TO EXPLODE ABOVE OUR HEADS!
THEY'LL CAUSE A CAVE-IN! WE'LL BE TRAPPED IN HERE!
RUN! WHILE YOU CAN--RUN FOR YOUR LIVES!
BUT, WHAT OF PRINCE REY-- AND THE GIANT! WHEN THE KEEPER LEARNS THEY HAVE DEFEATED US--!
WE MUST NOT TELL HIM! WE MUST SAY THEY PERISHED IN THE HOLACAUST!
THEY SHALL NEVER RETURN--THUS, THE KEEPER WILL NEVER KNOW!
AND, ON THE OTHER SIDE OF THE GREAT, YAWNING CHASM...
LOOKS LIKE I OUT-SMARTED MYSELF THAT TIME!
I STOPPED OUR PURSUERS--BUT NOW, HOW DO I GET BACK TO DR. ANTON?
THERE IS ANOTHER WAY! BUT, FIRST, COME WITH ME--!
WE SHALL FIND REFUGE AMONG MY OWN LOYAL FOLLOWERS!

THEN, A FEW MINUTES LATER...

CRREEKK!

SINCE THE KEEPER SEIZED TOTAL POWER, MY OWN FOLLOWERS HAVE HIDDEN HERE, WAITING FOR THE DAY OF REBELLION!

THAT DAY'LL COME --SOON AS YOU SHOW ME THE WAY TO RETURN TO THE OTHER SIDE OF THE CAVERN!

IT IS OUR PRINCE! BUT-- THERE IS A GIANT BESIDE HIM!

THERE IS NO NEED FOR ALARM! THIS IS GOLIATH! HE SHALL BE OUR MOST POWERFUL ALLY!

WHO WOULD DARE PLACE HIS TRUST IN ONE SO HUGE?

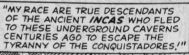

THIS IS A MIGHTY GROOVY PLACE YOU'VE GOT DOWN HERE, PRINCE REY!

WITH ALL THIS GOING FOR YOU, WHY WOULD YOU WANT TO BOTHER WITH THE KEEPER AND HIS BATTY LITTLE BONFIRE?

IT IS PRECISELY BECAUSE OF THAT FIRE THAT THE KEEPER MUST BE DEFEATED!

WHAT MAKES IT SO IMPORTANT? WHY DO THEY TRY TO KEEP IT HIDDEN FROM THE OUTSIDE WORLD?

BECAUSE IT IS THE GREATEST SOURCE OF POWER MANKIND HAS EVER KNOWN!

THOSE EVER-BURNING FLAMES ARE FED BY ENDLESS QUANTITIES OF SPECIALLY-TREATED COBALT!

COBALT! THE ELEMENT WE'RE WORKING WITH TODAY-- TO PRODUCE AN ALL-POWERFUL COBALT BOMB!!

EXACTLY! THAT IS NO SIMPLE FIRE THE KEEPER GUARDS! WITHIN ITS FLAMING FURY IS POWER ENOUGH TO DESTROY THE EARTH!

"MY RACE ARE TRUE DESCENDANTS OF THE ANCIENT INCAS WHO FLED TO THESE UNDERGROUND CAVERNS CENTURIES AGO TO ESCAPE THE TYRANNY OF THE CONQUISTADORES!"

"AND, WITHIN THESE CAVES, WE FOUND--THE FIRE! FIRE, WHICH GAVE US WARMTH, AND LIGHT, AND ENERGY FOR GENERATIONS!"

"FIRE--WHICH WAS ALWAYS GUARDED BY--A KEEPER OF THE FLAME!"

6

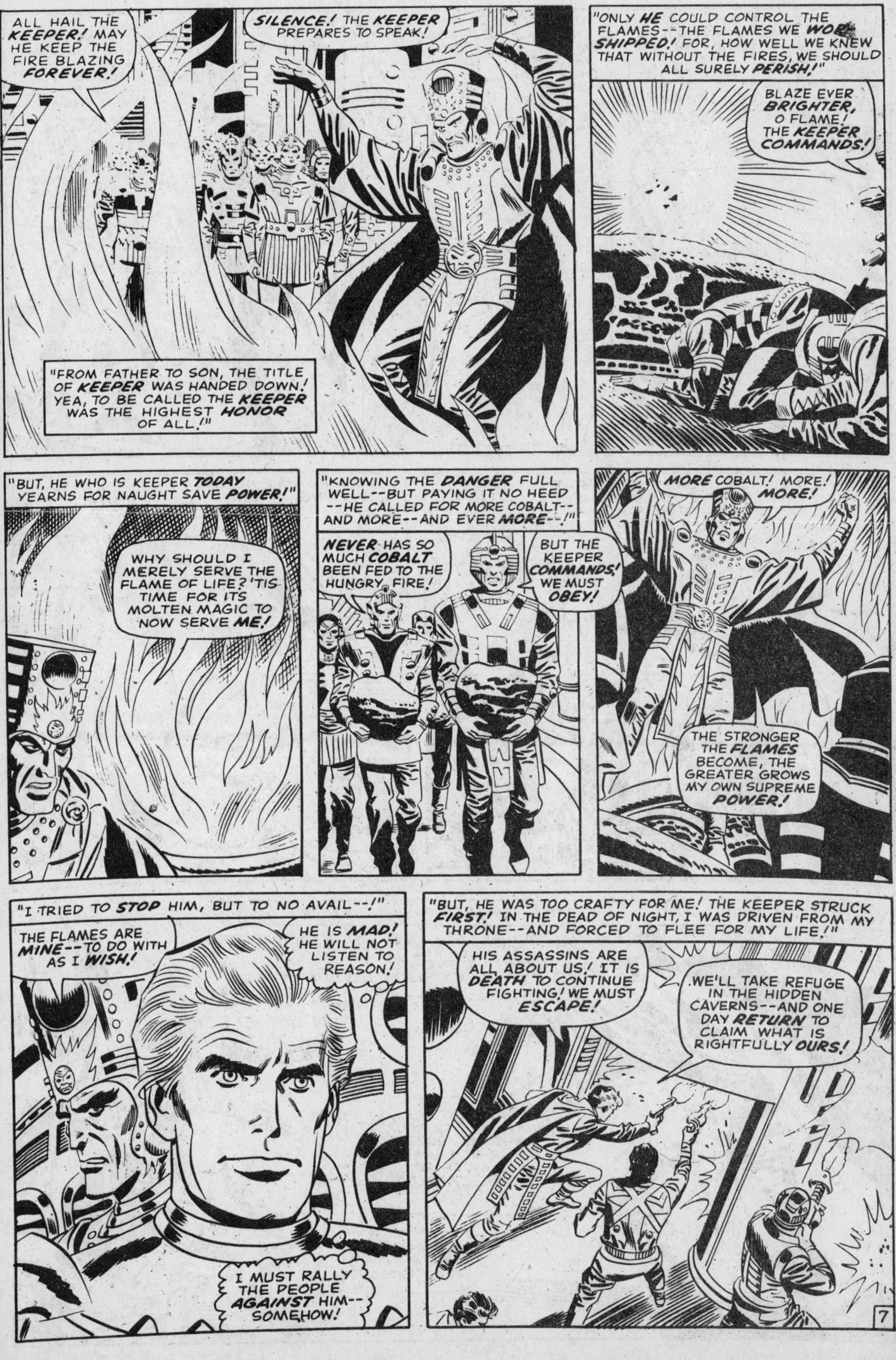
ALL HAIL THE KEEPER! MAY HE KEEP THE FIRE BLAZING FOREVER!
SILENCE! THE KEEPER PREPARES TO SPEAK!
"FROM FATHER TO SON, THE TITLE OF KEEPER WAS HANDED DOWN! YEA, TO BE CALLED THE KEEPER WAS THE HIGHEST HONOR OF ALL!"
"ONLY HE COULD CONTROL THE FLAMES--THE FLAMES WE WORSHIPPED! FOR, HOW WELL WE KNEW THAT WITHOUT THE FIRES, WE SHOULD ALL SURELY PERISH!"
BLAZE EVER BRIGHTER, O FLAME! THE KEEPER COMMANDS!
"BUT, HE WHO IS KEEPER TODAY YEARNS FOR NAUGHT SAVE POWER!"
WHY SHOULD I MERELY SERVE THE FLAME OF LIFE? 'TIS TIME FOR ITS MOLTEN MAGIC TO NOW SERVE ME!
"KNOWING THE DANGER FULL WELL--BUT PAYING IT NO HEED--HE CALLED FOR MORE COBALT--AND MORE--AND EVER MORE--!"
NEVER HAS SO MUCH COBALT BEEN FED TO THE HUNGRY FIRE!
BUT THE KEEPER COMMANDS! WE MUST OBEY!
MORE COBALT! MORE! MORE!
THE STRONGER THE FLAMES BECOME, THE GREATER GROWS MY OWN SUPREME POWER!
"I TRIED TO STOP HIM, BUT TO NO AVAIL--!"
THE FLAMES ARE MINE--TO DO WITH AS I WISH!
HE IS MAD! HE WILL NOT LISTEN TO REASON!
I MUST RALLY THE PEOPLE AGAINST HIM--SOMEHOW!
"BUT, HE WAS TOO CRAFTY FOR ME! THE KEEPER STRUCK FIRST! IN THE DEAD OF NIGHT, I WAS DRIVEN FROM MY THRONE--AND FORCED TO FLEE FOR MY LIFE!"
HIS ASSASSINS ARE ALL ABOUT US! IT IS DEATH TO CONTINUE FIGHTING! WE MUST ESCAPE!
WE'LL TAKE REFUGE IN THE HIDDEN CAVERNS--AND ONE DAY RETURN TO CLAIM WHAT IS RIGHTFULLY OURS!
7

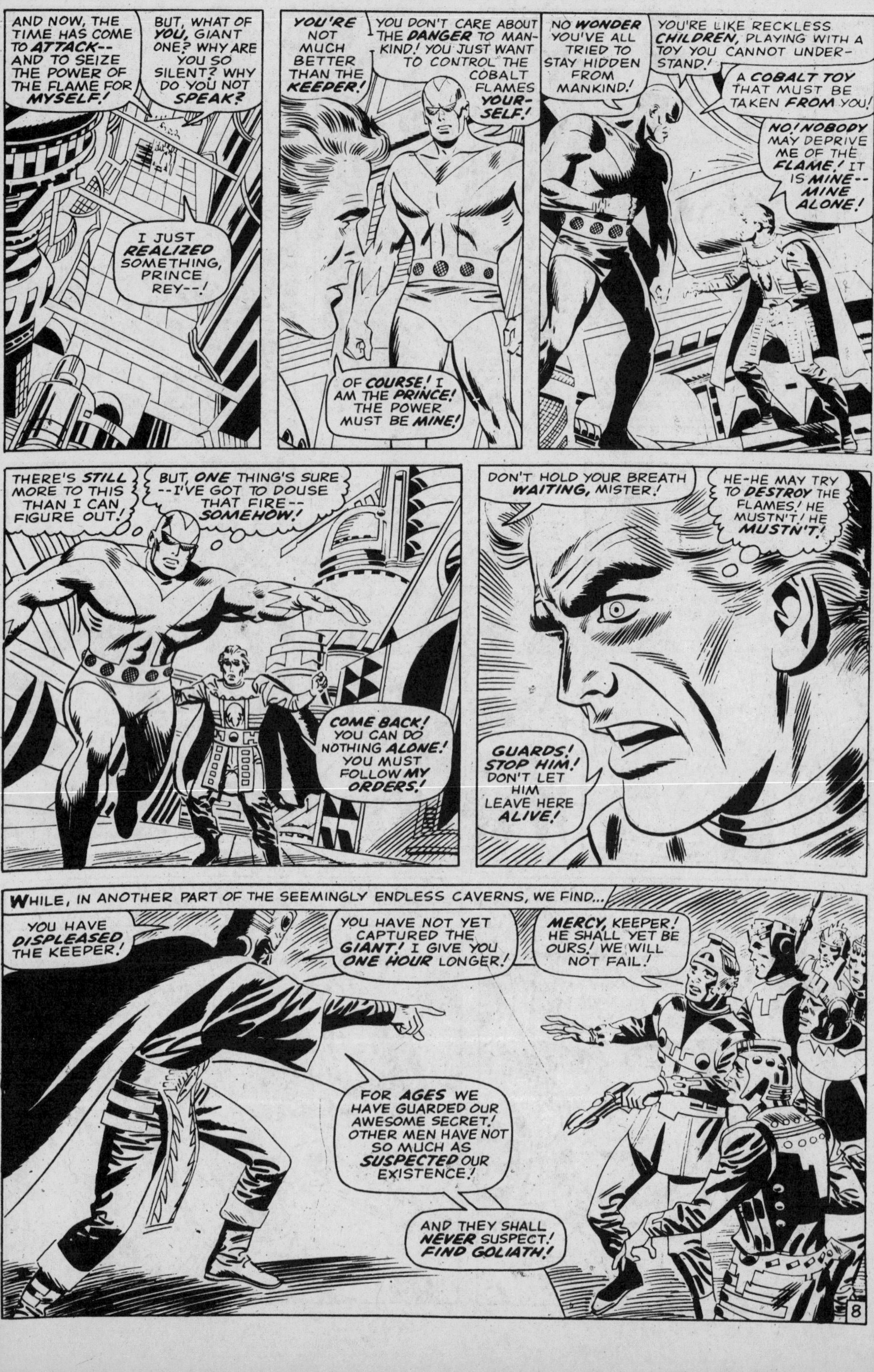
AND NOW, THE TIME HAS COME TO ATTACK-- AND TO SEIZE THE POWER OF THE FLAME FOR MYSELF!
BUT, WHAT OF YOU, GIANT ONE? WHY ARE YOU SO SILENT? WHY DO YOU NOT SPEAK?
I JUST REALIZED SOMETHING, PRINCE REY--!
YOU'RE NOT MUCH BETTER THAN THE KEEPER!
YOU DON'T CARE ABOUT THE DANGER TO MANKIND! YOU JUST WANT TO CONTROL THE COBALT FLAMES YOURSELF!
OF COURSE! I AM THE PRINCE! THE POWER MUST BE MINE!
NO WONDER YOU'VE ALL TRIED TO STAY HIDDEN FROM MANKIND!
YOU'RE LIKE RECKLESS CHILDREN, PLAYING WITH A TOY YOU CANNOT UNDERSTAND!
A COBALT TOY THAT MUST BE TAKEN FROM YOU!
NO! NOBODY MAY DEPRIVE ME OF THE FLAME! IT IS MINE-- MINE ALONE!
THERE'S STILL MORE TO THIS THAN I CAN FIGURE OUT!
BUT, ONE THING'S SURE --I'VE GOT TO DOUSE THAT FIRE-- SOMEHOW!
COME BACK! YOU CAN DO NOTHING ALONE! YOU MUST FOLLOW MY ORDERS!
DON'T HOLD YOUR BREATH WAITING, MISTER!
HE-HE MAY TRY TO DESTROY THE FLAMES! HE MUSTN'T! HE MUSTN'T!
GUARDS! STOP HIM! DON'T LET HIM LEAVE HERE ALIVE!
WHILE, IN ANOTHER PART OF THE SEEMINGLY ENDLESS CAVERNS, WE FIND...
YOU HAVE DISPLEASED THE KEEPER!
YOU HAVE NOT YET CAPTURED THE GIANT! I GIVE YOU ONE HOUR LONGER!
MERCY, KEEPER! HE SHALL YET BE OURS! WE WILL NOT FAIL!
FOR AGES WE HAVE GUARDED OUR AWESOME SECRET! OTHER MEN HAVE NOT SO MUCH AS SUSPECTED OUR EXISTENCE!
AND THEY SHALL NEVER SUSPECT! FIND GOLIATH!
8

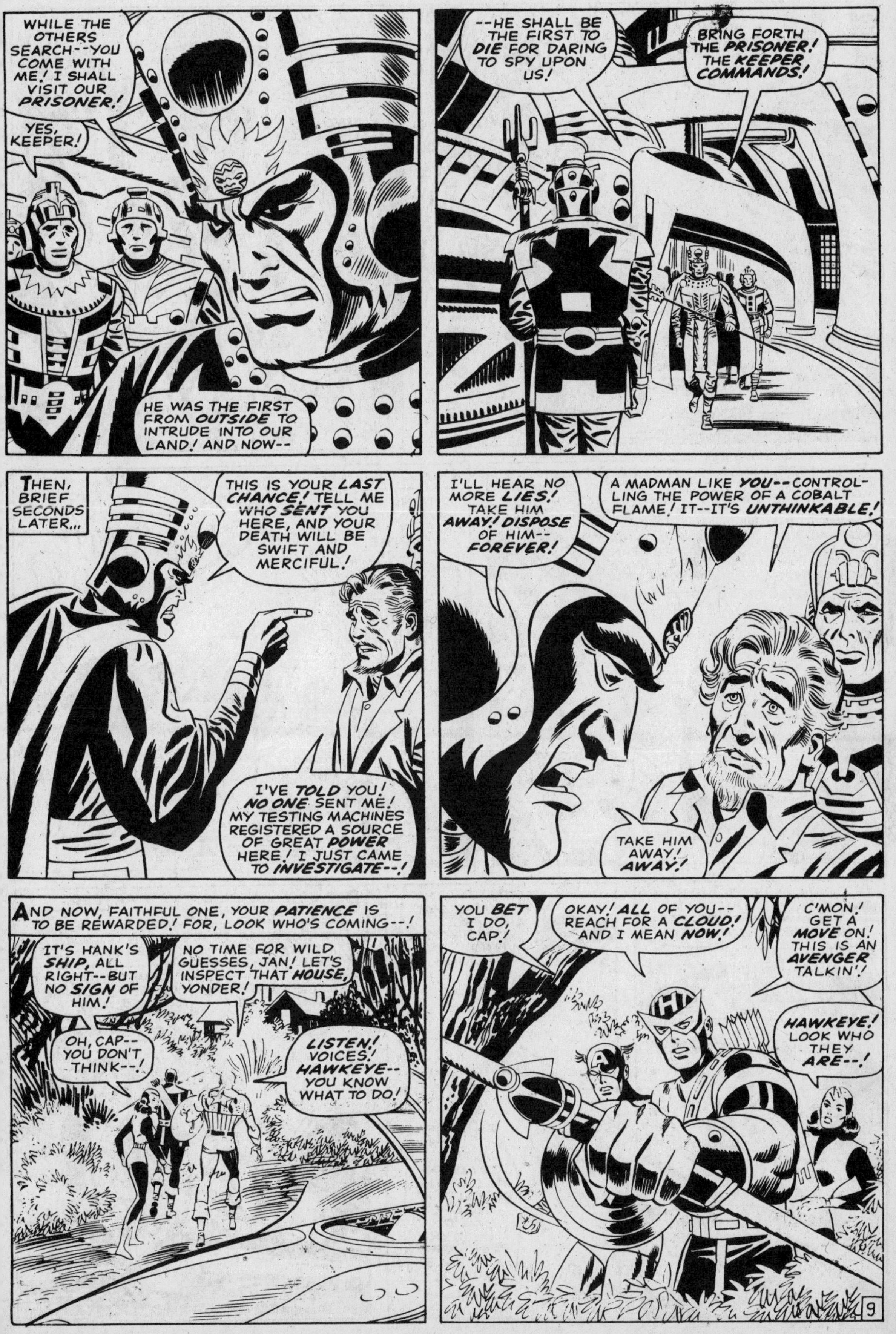
WHILE THE OTHERS SEARCH--YOU COME WITH ME! I SHALL VISIT OUR PRISONER!
YES, KEEPER!
HE WAS THE FIRST FROM OUTSIDE TO INTRUDE INTO OUR LAND! AND NOW--
--HE SHALL BE THE FIRST TO DIE FOR DARING TO SPY UPON US!
BRING FORTH THE PRISONER! THE KEEPER COMMANDS!
THEN, BRIEF SECONDS LATER...
THIS IS YOUR LAST CHANCE! TELL ME WHO SENT YOU HERE, AND YOUR DEATH WILL BE SWIFT AND MERCIFUL!
I'VE TOLD YOU! NO ONE SENT ME! MY TESTING MACHINES REGISTERED A SOURCE OF GREAT POWER HERE! I JUST CAME TO INVESTIGATE--!
I'LL HEAR NO MORE LIES! TAKE HIM AWAY! DISPOSE OF HIM--FOREVER!
A MADMAN LIKE YOU--CONTROLLING THE POWER OF A COBALT FLAME! IT--IT'S UNTHINKABLE!
TAKE HIM AWAY! AWAY!
AND NOW, FAITHFUL ONE, YOUR PATIENCE IS TO BE REWARDED! FOR, LOOK WHO'S COMING--!
IT'S HANK'S SHIP, ALL RIGHT--BUT NO SIGN OF HIM!
NO TIME FOR WILD GUESSES, JAN! LET'S INSPECT THAT HOUSE, YONDER!
OH, CAP--YOU DON'T THINK--!
LISTEN! VOICES! HAWKEYE--YOU KNOW WHAT TO DO!
YOU BET I DO, CAP!
OKAY! ALL OF YOU--REACH FOR A CLOUD! AND I MEAN NOW!
C'MON! GET A MOVE ON! THIS IS AN AVENGER TALKIN'!
HAWKEYE! LOOK WHO THEY ARE--!
9

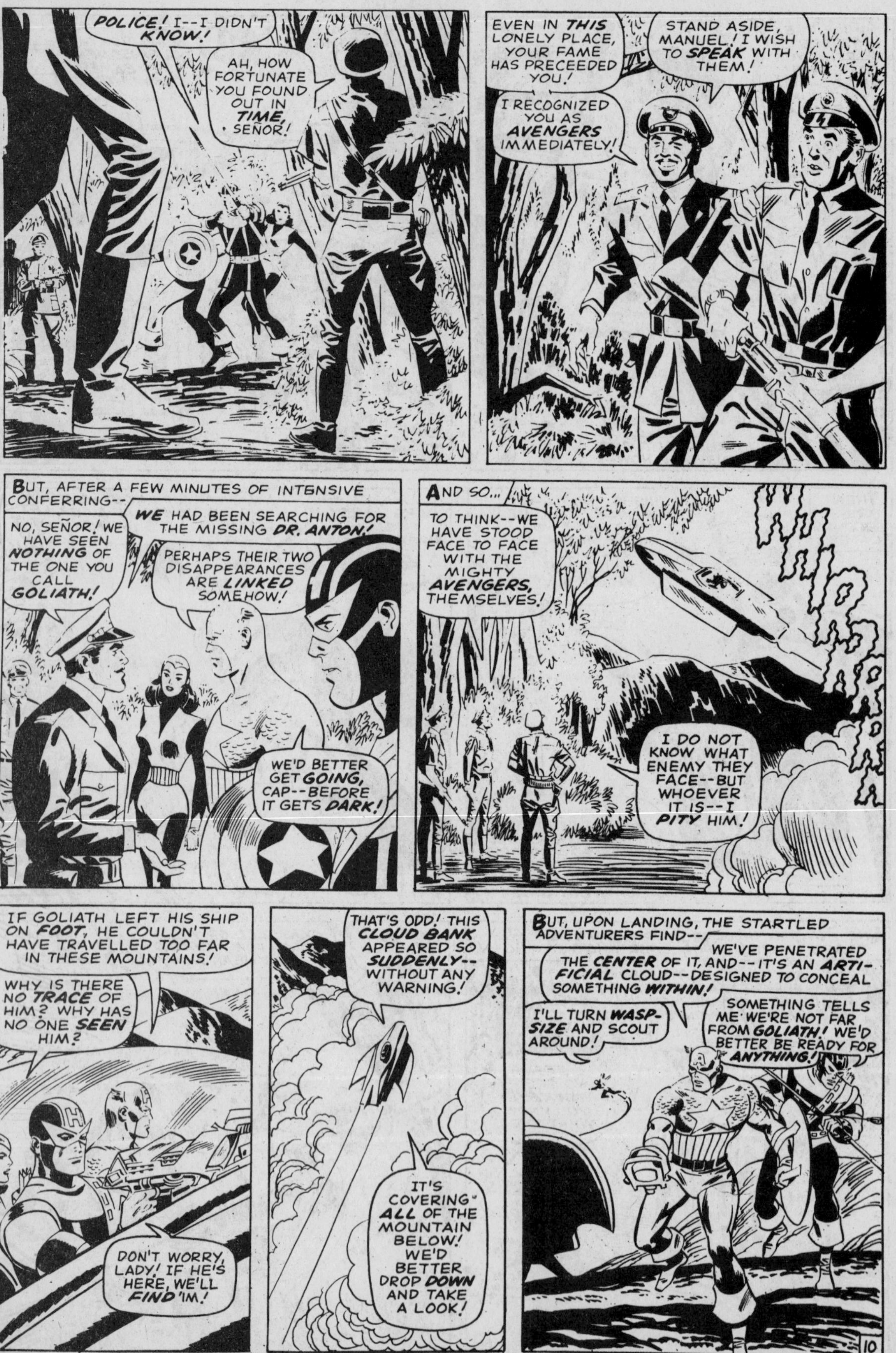
POLICE! I--I DIDN'T KNOW!
AH, HOW FORTUNATE YOU FOUND OUT IN TIME, SEÑOR!
EVEN IN THIS LONELY PLACE, YOUR FAME HAS PRECEEDED YOU!
I RECOGNIZED YOU AS AVENGERS IMMEDIATELY!
STAND ASIDE, MANUEL! I WISH TO SPEAK WITH THEM!
BUT, AFTER A FEW MINUTES OF INTENSIVE CONFERRING--
NO, SEÑOR! WE HAVE SEEN NOTHING OF THE ONE YOU CALL GOLIATH!
WE HAD BEEN SEARCHING FOR THE MISSING DR. ANTON!
PERHAPS THEIR TWO DISAPPEARANCES ARE LINKED SOMEHOW!
WE'D BETTER GET GOING, CAP--BEFORE IT GETS DARK!
AND SO...
TO THINK--WE HAVE STOOD FACE TO FACE WITH THE MIGHTY AVENGERS, THEMSELVES!
WHRRRR
I DO NOT KNOW WHAT ENEMY THEY FACE--BUT WHOEVER IT IS--I PITY HIM!
IF GOLIATH LEFT HIS SHIP ON FOOT, HE COULDN'T HAVE TRAVELLED TOO FAR IN THESE MOUNTAINS!
WHY IS THERE NO TRACE OF HIM? WHY HAS NO ONE SEEN HIM?
DON'T WORRY, LADY! IF HE'S HERE, WE'LL FIND 'IM!
THAT'S ODD! THIS CLOUD BANK APPEARED SO SUDDENLY--WITHOUT ANY WARNING!
IT'S COVERING ALL OF THE MOUNTAIN BELOW! WE'D BETTER DROP DOWN AND TAKE A LOOK!
BUT, UPON LANDING, THE STARTLED ADVENTURERS FIND--
WE'VE PENETRATED THE CENTER OF IT, AND--IT'S AN ARTI-FICIAL CLOUD--DESIGNED TO CONCEAL SOMETHING WITHIN!
I'LL TURN WASP-SIZE AND SCOUT AROUND!
SOMETHING TELLS ME WE'RE NOT FAR FROM GOLIATH! WE'D BETTER BE READY FOR ANYTHING!
10

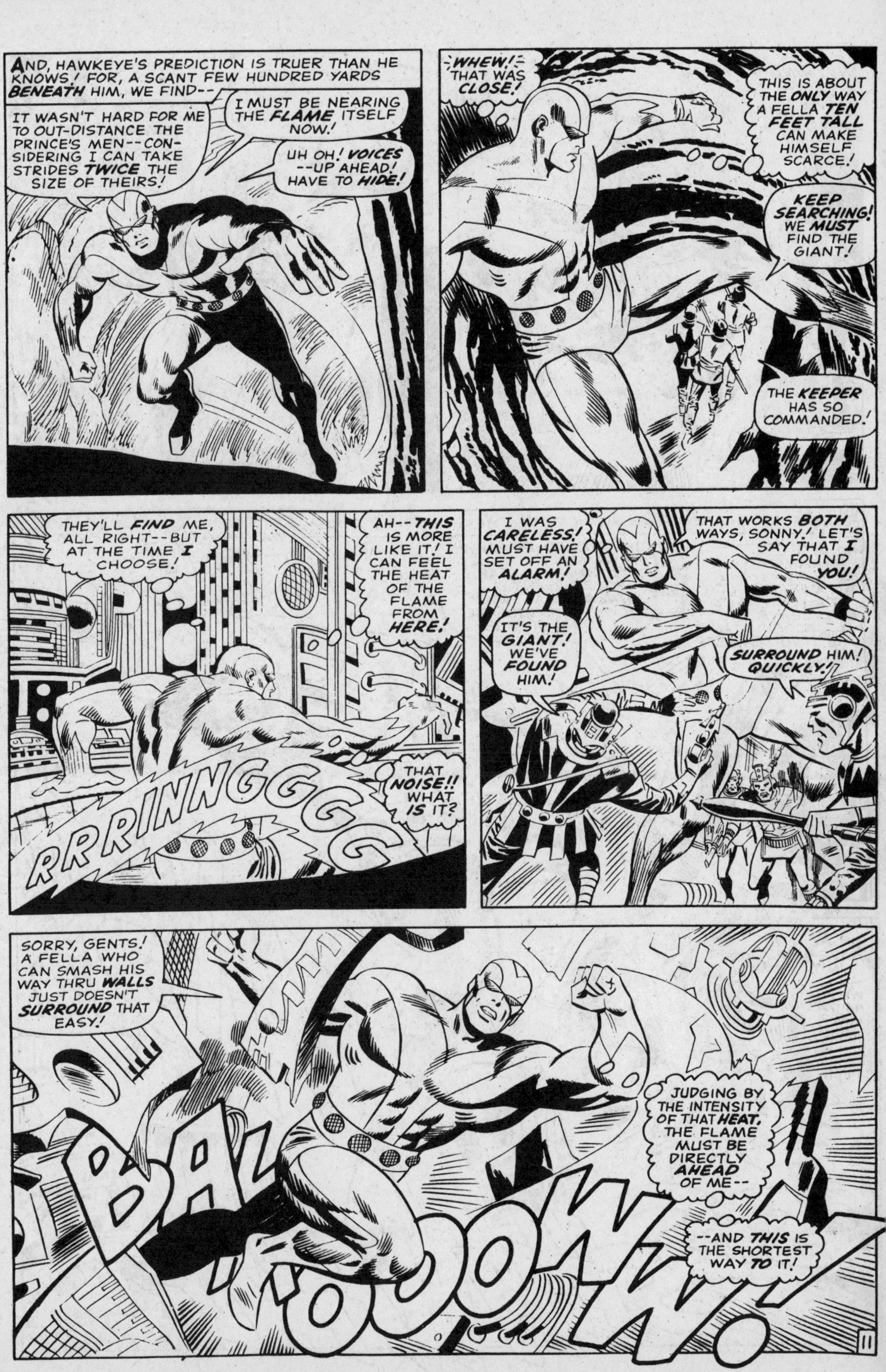

AND, HAWKEYE'S PREDICTION IS TRUER THAN HE KNOWS! FOR, A SCANT FEW HUNDRED YARDS BENEATH HIM, WE FIND--
IT WASN'T HARD FOR ME TO OUT-DISTANCE THE PRINCE'S MEN--CONSIDERING I CAN TAKE STRIDES TWICE THE SIZE OF THEIRS!
I MUST BE NEARING THE FLAME ITSELF NOW!
UH OH! VOICES --UP AHEAD! HAVE TO HIDE!
WHEW! THAT WAS CLOSE!
THIS IS ABOUT THE ONLY WAY A FELLA TEN FEET TALL CAN MAKE HIMSELF SCARCE!
KEEP SEARCHING! WE MUST FIND THE GIANT!
THE KEEPER HAS SO COMMANDED!
THEY'LL FIND ME, ALL RIGHT--BUT AT THE TIME I CHOOSE!
AH--THIS IS MORE LIKE IT! I CAN FEEL THE HEAT OF THE FLAME FROM HERE!
THAT NOISE!! WHAT IS IT?
RRRINNGGGG
I WAS CARELESS! MUST HAVE SET OFF AN ALARM!
THAT WORKS BOTH WAYS, SONNY! LET'S SAY THAT I FOUND YOU!
IT'S THE GIANT! WE'VE FOUND HIM!
SURROUND HIM! QUICKLY!
SORRY, GENTS! A FELLA WHO CAN SMASH HIS WAY THRU WALLS JUST DOESN'T SURROUND THAT EASY!
JUDGING BY THE INTENSITY OF THAT HEAT, THE FLAME MUST BE DIRECTLY AHEAD OF ME--
--AND THIS IS THE SHORTEST WAY TO IT!
BADOOOOM!

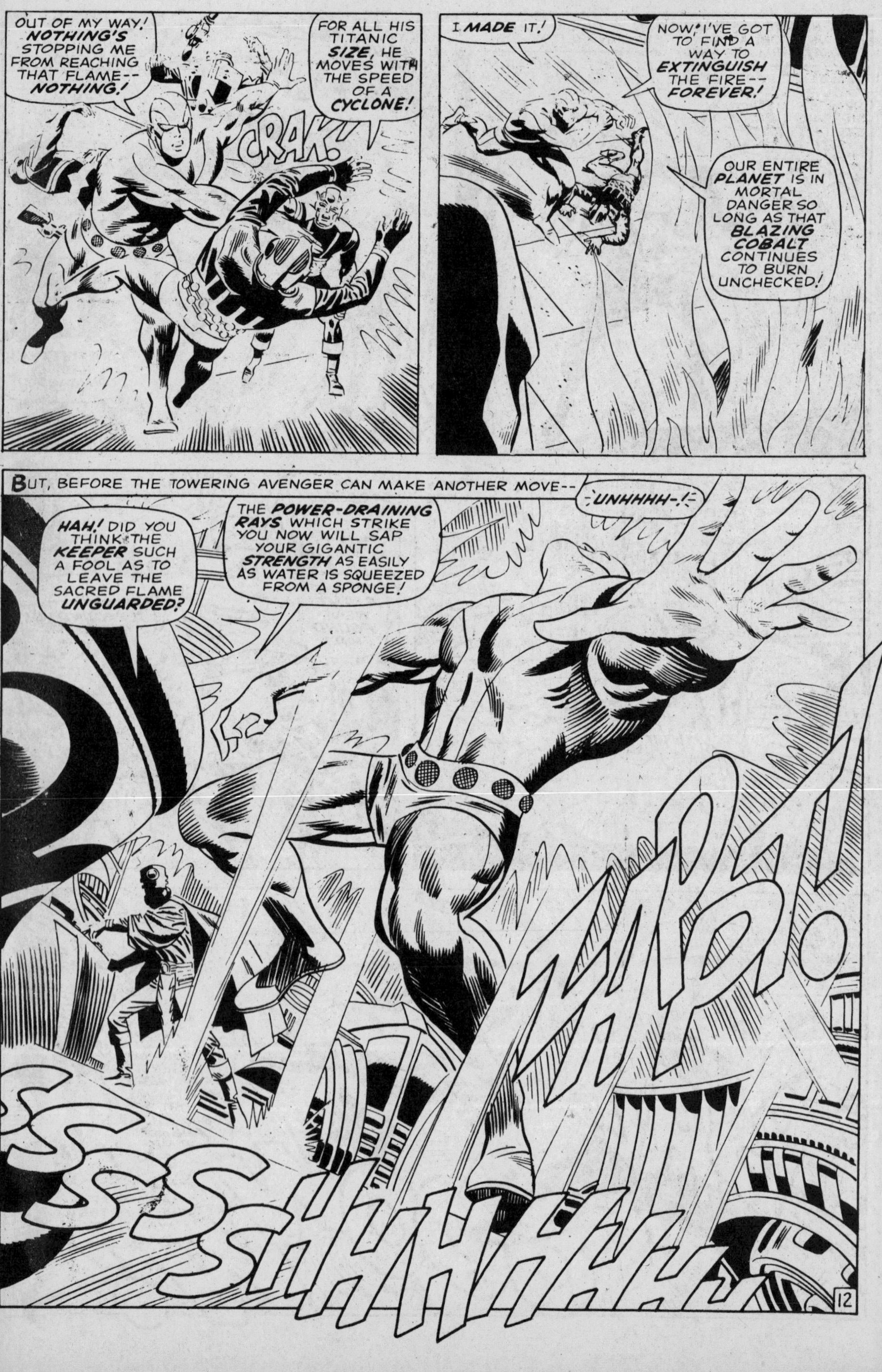
OUT OF MY WAY! NOTHING'S STOPPING ME FROM REACHING THAT FLAME-- NOTHING!
FOR ALL HIS TITANIC SIZE, HE MOVES WITH THE SPEED OF A CYCLONE!
CRAK!
I MADE IT!
NOW, I'VE GOT TO FIND A WAY TO EXTINGUISH THE FIRE-- FOREVER!
OUR ENTIRE PLANET IS IN MORTAL DANGER SO LONG AS THAT BLAZING COBALT CONTINUES TO BURN UNCHECKED!
BUT, BEFORE THE TOWERING AVENGER CAN MAKE ANOTHER MOVE--
HAH! DID YOU THINK THE KEEPER SUCH A FOOL AS TO LEAVE THE SACRED FLAME UNGUARDED?
THE POWER-DRAINING RAYS WHICH STRIKE YOU NOW WILL SAP YOUR GIGANTIC STRENGTH AS EASILY AS WATER IS SQUEEZED FROM A SPONGE!
UNHHHH-!
ZAPP!
SSSHHHHHH
12

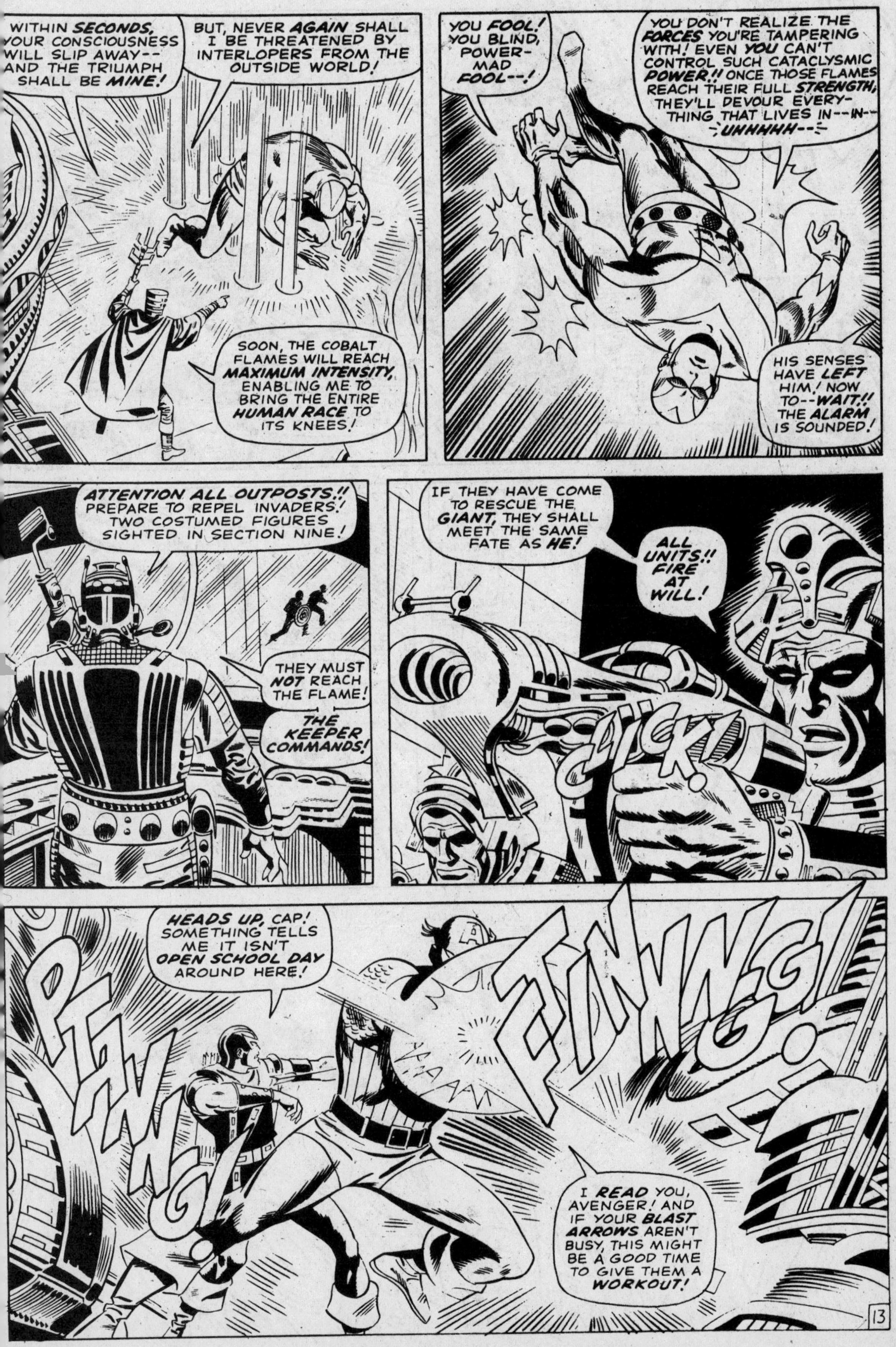
WITHIN SECONDS, YOUR CONSCIOUSNESS WILL SLIP AWAY-- AND THE TRIUMPH SHALL BE MINE!
BUT, NEVER AGAIN SHALL I BE THREATENED BY INTERLOPERS FROM THE OUTSIDE WORLD!
SOON, THE COBALT FLAMES WILL REACH MAXIMUM INTENSITY, ENABLING ME TO BRING THE ENTIRE HUMAN RACE TO ITS KNEES!
YOU FOOL! YOU BLIND, POWER-MAD FOOL--!
YOU DON'T REALIZE THE FORCES YOU'RE TAMPERING WITH! EVEN YOU CAN'T CONTROL SUCH CATACLYSMIC POWER!! ONCE THOSE FLAMES REACH THEIR FULL STRENGTH, THEY'LL DEVOUR EVERY-THING THAT LIVES IN--IN-- UNHHHH--
HIS SENSES HAVE LEFT HIM! NOW TO--WAIT!! THE ALARM IS SOUNDED!
ATTENTION ALL OUTPOSTS!! PREPARE TO REPEL INVADERS! TWO COSTUMED FIGURES SIGHTED IN SECTION NINE!
THEY MUST NOT REACH THE FLAME!
THE KEEPER COMMANDS!
IF THEY HAVE COME TO RESCUE THE GIANT, THEY SHALL MEET THE SAME FATE AS HE!
ALL UNITS!! FIRE AT WILL!
CLICK!
HEADS UP, CAP! SOMETHING TELLS ME IT ISN'T OPEN SCHOOL DAY AROUND HERE!
PTWNG!
PTWNNG!
I READ YOU, AVENGER! AND IF YOUR BLAST ARROWS AREN'T BUSY, THIS MIGHT BE A GOOD TIME TO GIVE THEM A WORKOUT!

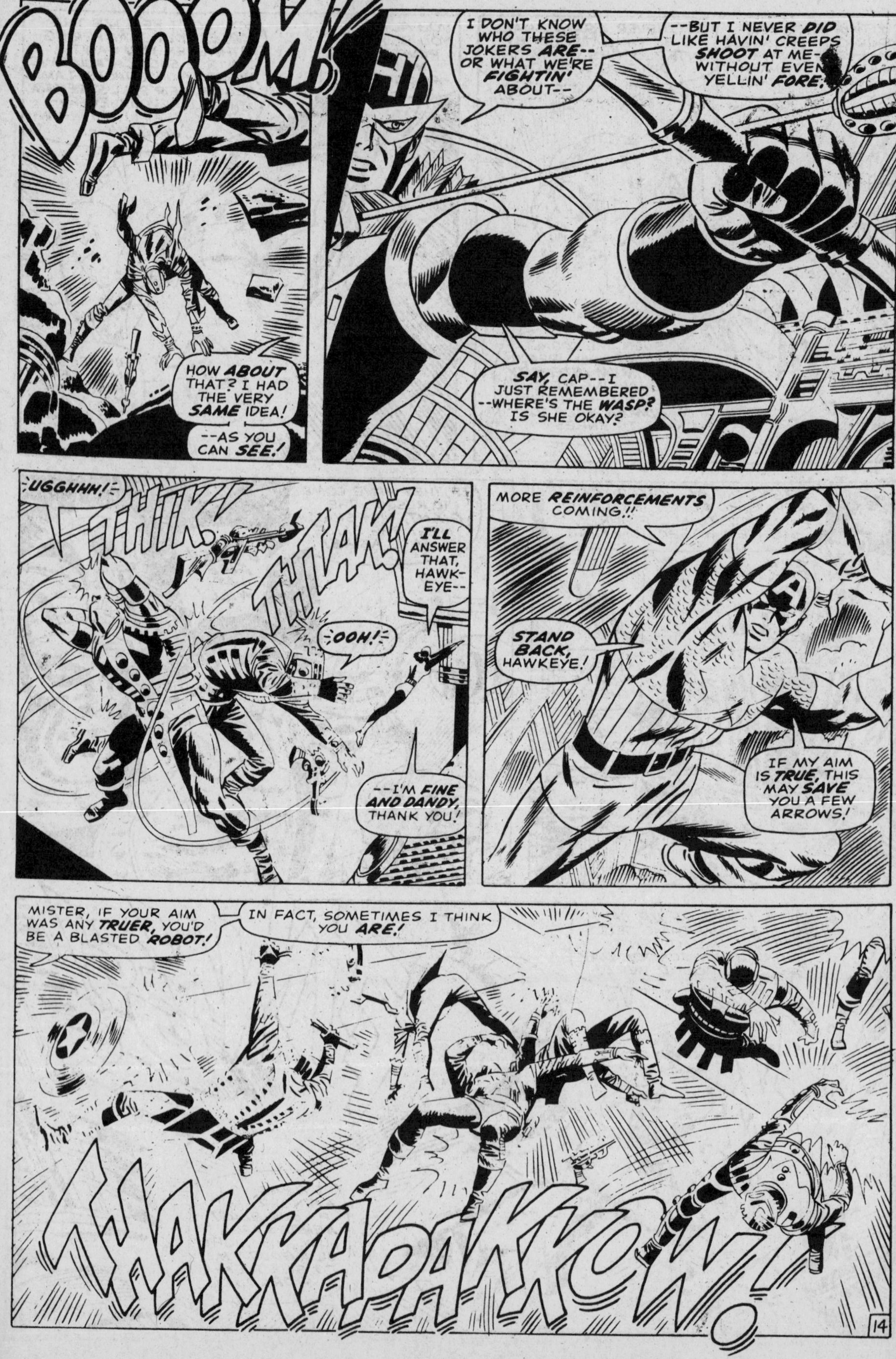
BOOOM!
HOW ABOUT THAT? I HAD THE VERY SAME IDEA!
--AS YOU CAN SEE!
I DON'T KNOW WHO THESE JOKERS ARE--OR WHAT WE'RE FIGHTIN' ABOUT--
--BUT I NEVER DID LIKE HAVIN' CREEPS SHOOT AT ME--WITHOUT EVEN YELLIN' FORE!
SAY, CAP--I JUST REMEMBERED--WHERE'S THE WASP? IS SHE OKAY?
UGGHHH!
THIK!
THAK!
I'LL ANSWER THAT, HAWKEYE--
OOH!
--I'M FINE AND DANDY, THANK YOU!
MORE REINFORCEMENTS COMING!!
STAND BACK, HAWKEYE!
IF MY AIM IS TRUE, THIS MAY SAVE YOU A FEW ARROWS!
MISTER, IF YOUR AIM WAS ANY TRUER, YOU'D BE A BLASTED ROBOT!
IN FACT, SOMETIMES I THINK YOU ARE!
WHAKKADAKKOW!

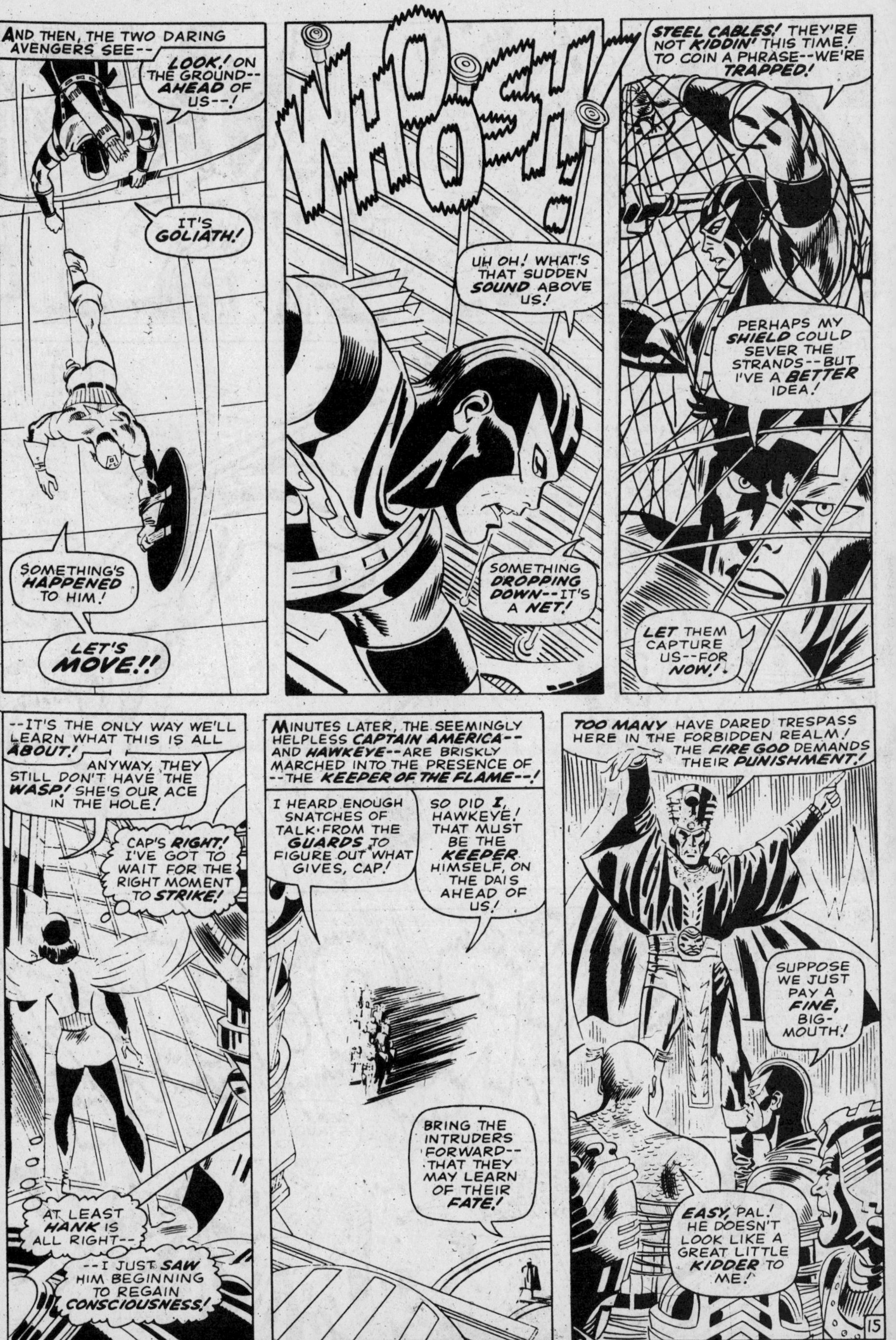
AND THEN, THE TWO DARING AVENGERS SEE--
LOOK! ON THE GROUND--AHEAD OF US--!
IT'S GOLIATH!
SOMETHING'S HAPPENED TO HIM!
LET'S MOVE!!
WHOOSH!
UH OH! WHAT'S THAT SUDDEN SOUND ABOVE US!
SOMETHING DROPPING DOWN--IT'S A NET!
STEEL CABLES! THEY'RE NOT KIDDIN' THIS TIME! TO COIN A PHRASE--WE'RE TRAPPED!
PERHAPS MY SHIELD COULD SEVER THE STRANDS--BUT I'VE A BETTER IDEA!
LET THEM CAPTURE US--FOR NOW!
--IT'S THE ONLY WAY WE'LL LEARN WHAT THIS IS ALL ABOUT!
ANYWAY, THEY STILL DON'T HAVE THE WASP! SHE'S OUR ACE IN THE HOLE!
CAP'S RIGHT! I'VE GOT TO WAIT FOR THE RIGHT MOMENT TO STRIKE!
AT LEAST HANK IS ALL RIGHT--
--I JUST SAW HIM BEGINNING TO REGAIN CONSCIOUSNESS!
MINUTES LATER, THE SEEMINGLY HELPLESS CAPTAIN AMERICA--AND HAWKEYE--ARE BRISKLY MARCHED INTO THE PRESENCE OF --THE KEEPER OF THE FLAME--!
I HEARD ENOUGH SNATCHES OF TALK FROM THE GUARDS TO FIGURE OUT WHAT GIVES, CAP!
SO DID I, HAWKEYE! THAT MUST BE THE KEEPER HIMSELF, ON THE DAIS AHEAD OF US!
BRING THE INTRUDERS FORWARD--THAT THEY MAY LEARN OF THEIR FATE!
TOO MANY HAVE DARED TRESPASS HERE IN THE FORBIDDEN REALM! THE FIRE GOD DEMANDS THEIR PUNISHMENT!
SUPPOSE WE JUST PAY A FINE, BIG-MOUTH!
EASY, PAL! HE DOESN'T LOOK LIKE A GREAT LITTLE KIDDER TO ME!
15

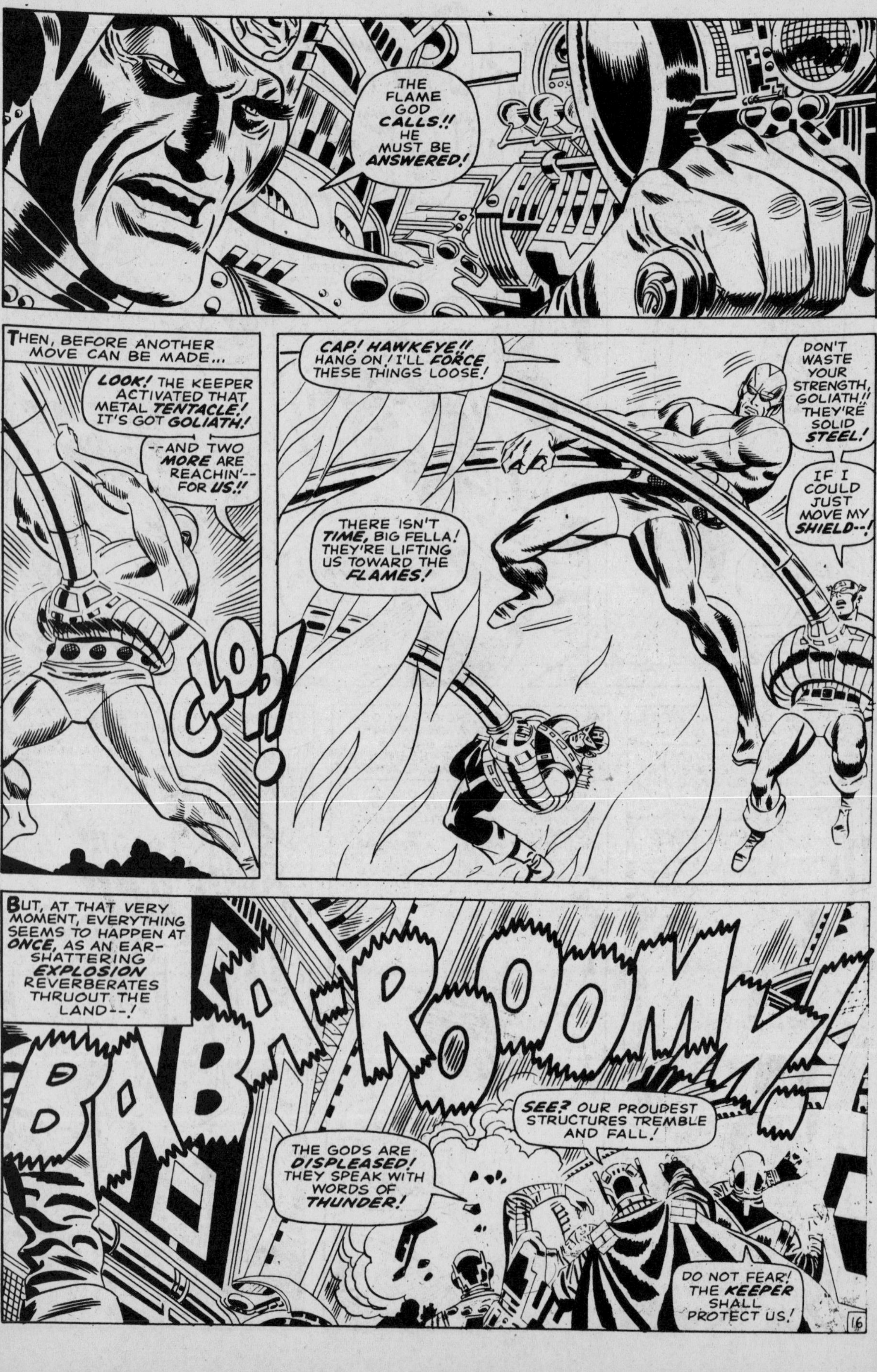
THE FLAME GOD CALLS!! HE MUST BE ANSWERED!
THEN, BEFORE ANOTHER MOVE CAN BE MADE...
LOOK! THE KEEPER ACTIVATED THAT METAL TENTACLE! IT'S GOT GOLIATH!
--AND TWO MORE ARE REACHIN'-- FOR US!!
CLOP!
CAP! HAWKEYE!! HANG ON! I'LL FORCE THESE THINGS LOOSE!
DON'T WASTE YOUR STRENGTH, GOLIATH!! THEY'RE SOLID STEEL!
IF I COULD JUST MOVE MY SHIELD--!
THERE ISN'T TIME, BIG FELLA! THEY'RE LIFTING US TOWARD THE FLAMES!
BUT, AT THAT VERY MOMENT, EVERYTHING SEEMS TO HAPPEN AT ONCE, AS AN EAR-SHATTERING EXPLOSION REVERBERATES THRUOUT THE LAND--!
BA-BA-ROOM!
SEE? OUR PROUDEST STRUCTURES TREMBLE AND FALL!
THE GODS ARE DISPLEASED! THEY SPEAK WITH WORDS OF THUNDER!
DO NOT FEAR! THE KEEPER SHALL PROTECT US!

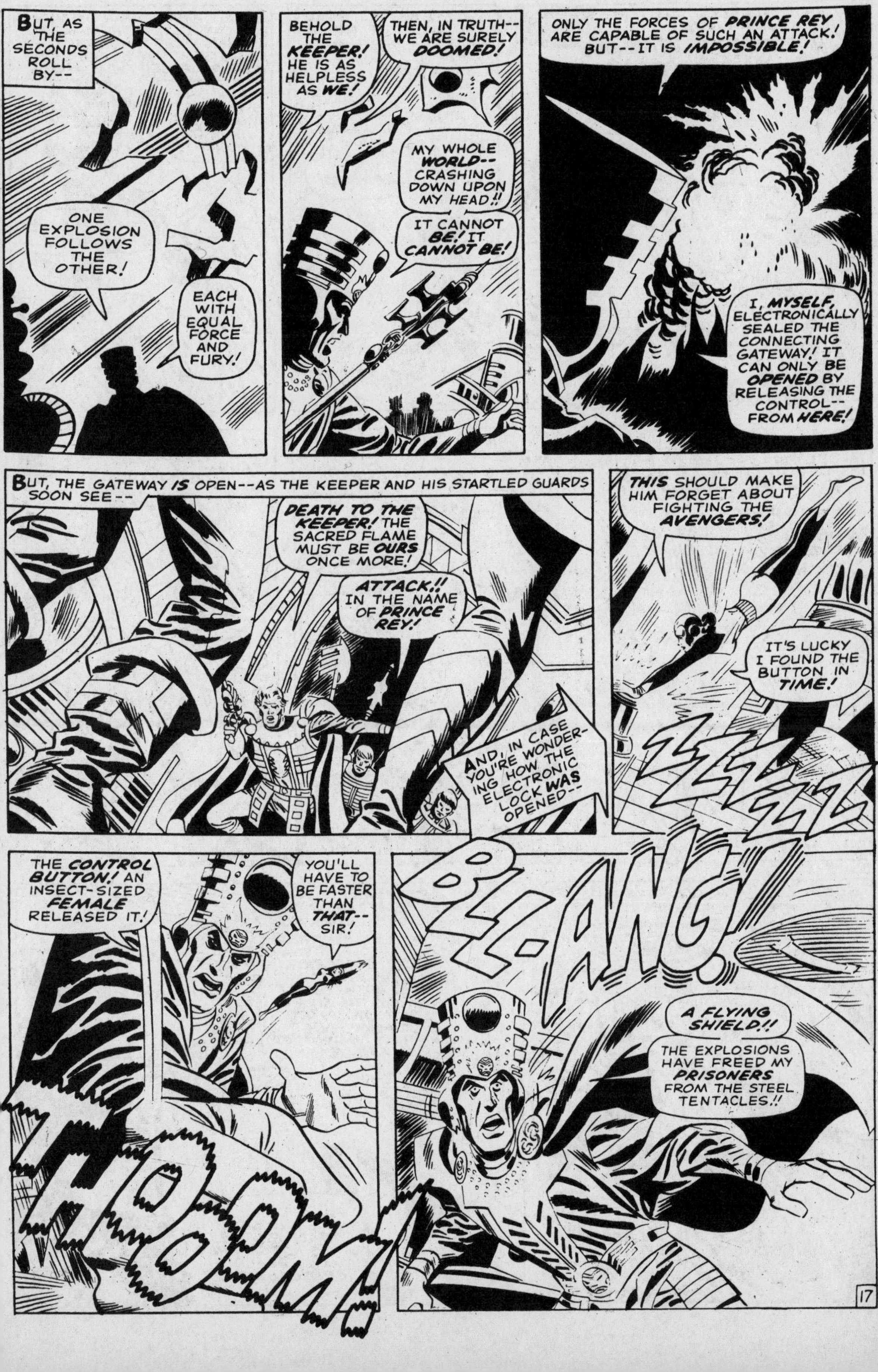

BUT, AS THE SECONDS ROLL BY--
ONE EXPLOSION FOLLOWS THE OTHER!
EACH WITH EQUAL FORCE AND FURY!
BEHOLD THE KEEPER! HE IS AS HELPLESS AS WE!
THEN, IN TRUTH-- WE ARE SURELY DOOMED!
MY WHOLE WORLD-- CRASHING DOWN UPON MY HEAD!!
IT CANNOT BE! IT CANNOT BE!
ONLY THE FORCES OF PRINCE REY ARE CAPABLE OF SUCH AN ATTACK! BUT-- IT IS IMPOSSIBLE!
I, MYSELF, ELECTRONICALLY SEALED THE CONNECTING GATEWAY! IT CAN ONLY BE OPENED BY RELEASING THE CONTROL-- FROM HERE!
BUT, THE GATEWAY IS OPEN--AS THE KEEPER AND HIS STARTLED GUARDS SOON SEE--
DEATH TO THE KEEPER! THE SACRED FLAME MUST BE OURS ONCE MORE!
ATTACK!! IN THE NAME OF PRINCE REY!
AND, IN CASE YOU'RE WONDERING HOW THE ELECTRONIC LOCK WAS OPENED--
THIS SHOULD MAKE HIM FORGET ABOUT FIGHTING THE AVENGERS!
IT'S LUCKY I FOUND THE BUTTON IN TIME!
ZZZZZZ
THE CONTROL BUTTON! AN INSECT-SIZED FEMALE RELEASED IT!
YOU'LL HAVE TO BE FASTER THAN THAT-- SIR!
THOOM!
BL-ANG!
A FLYING SHIELD!!
THE EXPLOSIONS HAVE FREED MY PRISONERS FROM THE STEEL TENTACLES!!

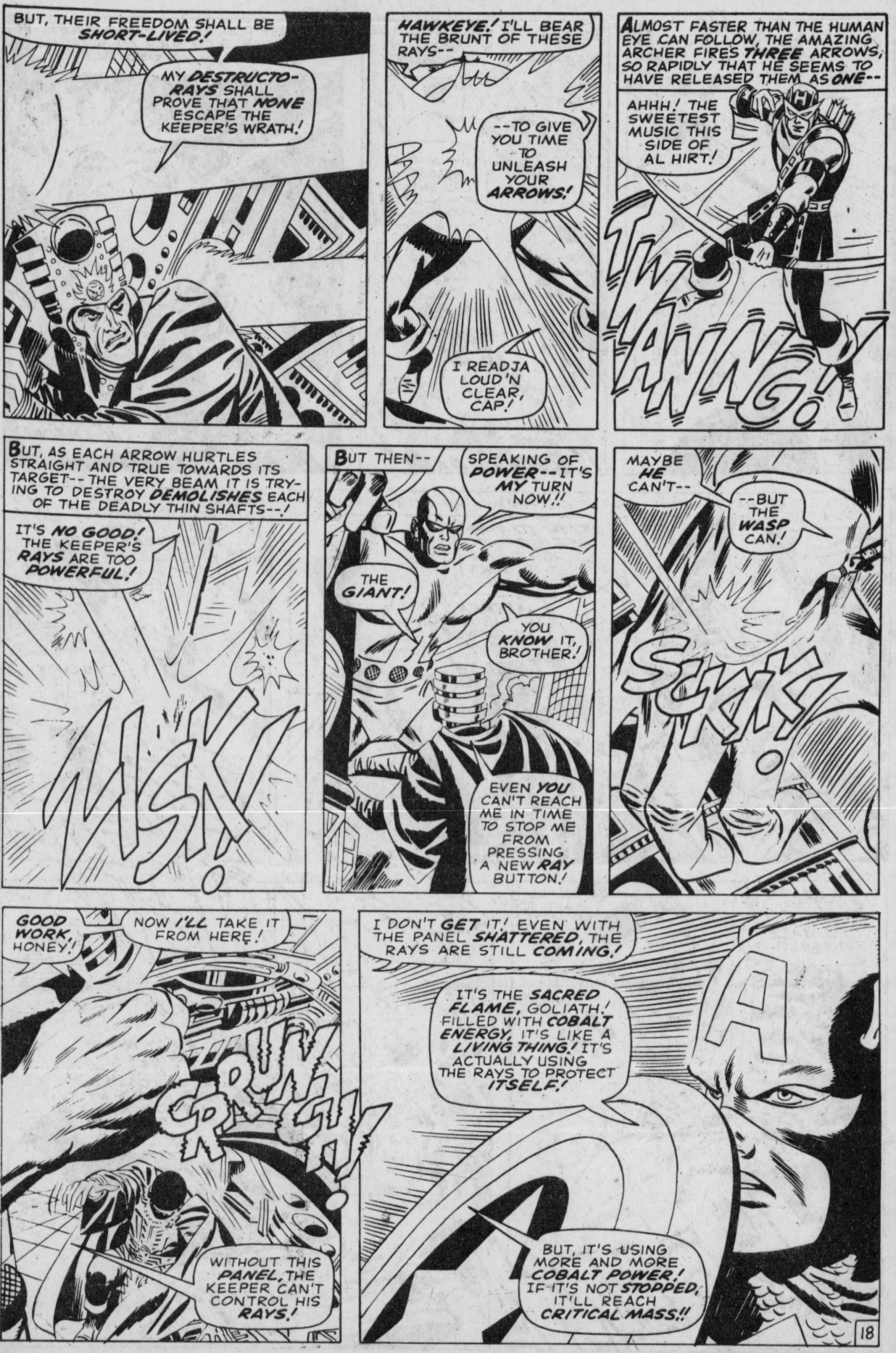
BUT, THEIR FREEDOM SHALL BE SHORT-LIVED!
MY DESTRUCTO-RAYS SHALL PROVE THAT NONE ESCAPE THE KEEPER'S WRATH!
HAWKEYE! I'LL BEAR THE BRUNT OF THESE RAYS--
--TO GIVE YOU TIME TO UNLEASH YOUR ARROWS!
I READJA LOUD'N CLEAR, CAP!
ALMOST FASTER THAN THE HUMAN EYE CAN FOLLOW, THE AMAZING ARCHER FIRES THREE ARROWS, SO RAPIDLY THAT HE SEEMS TO HAVE RELEASED THEM AS ONE--
AHHH! THE SWEETEST MUSIC THIS SIDE OF AL HIRT!
TWANNNG!
BUT, AS EACH ARROW HURTLES STRAIGHT AND TRUE TOWARDS ITS TARGET-- THE VERY BEAM IT IS TRYING TO DESTROY DEMOLISHES EACH OF THE DEADLY THIN SHAFTS--!
IT'S NO GOOD! THE KEEPER'S RAYS ARE TOO POWERFUL!
WSSK!
BUT THEN--
SPEAKING OF POWER--IT'S MY TURN NOW!!
THE GIANT!
YOU KNOW IT, BROTHER!
EVEN YOU CAN'T REACH ME IN TIME TO STOP ME FROM PRESSING A NEW RAY BUTTON!
MAYBE HE CAN'T--
--BUT THE WASP CAN!
SCHKK!
GOOD WORK, HONEY!
NOW I'LL TAKE IT FROM HERE!
CRRUNNCH!
WITHOUT THIS PANEL, THE KEEPER CAN'T CONTROL HIS RAYS!
I DON'T GET IT! EVEN WITH THE PANEL SHATTERED, THE RAYS ARE STILL COMING!
IT'S THE SACRED FLAME, GOLIATH! FILLED WITH COBALT ENERGY, IT'S LIKE A LIVING THING! IT'S ACTUALLY USING THE RAYS TO PROTECT ITSELF!
BUT, IT'S USING MORE AND MORE COBALT POWER! IF IT'S NOT STOPPED, IT'LL REACH CRITICAL MASS!!
18

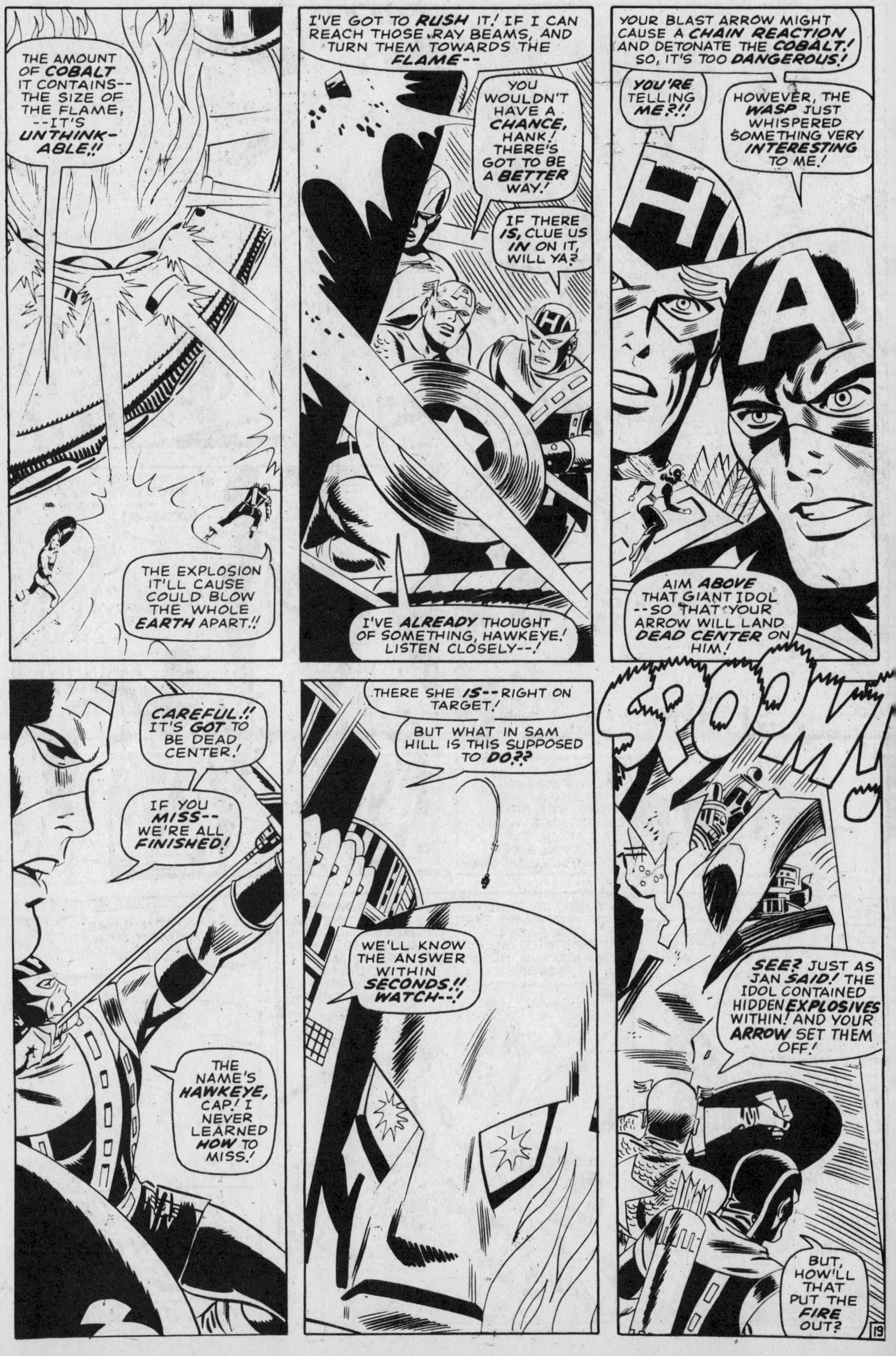
THE AMOUNT OF COBALT IT CONTAINS-- THE SIZE OF THE FLAME, --IT'S UNTHINK-ABLE!!
THE EXPLOSION IT'LL CAUSE COULD BLOW THE WHOLE EARTH APART!!
I'VE GOT TO RUSH IT! IF I CAN REACH THOSE RAY BEAMS, AND TURN THEM TOWARDS THE FLAME--
YOU WOULDN'T HAVE A CHANCE, HANK! THERE'S GOT TO BE A BETTER WAY!
IF THERE IS, CLUE US IN ON IT, WILL YA?
I'VE ALREADY THOUGHT OF SOMETHING, HAWKEYE! LISTEN CLOSELY--!
YOUR BLAST ARROW MIGHT CAUSE A CHAIN REACTION AND DETONATE THE COBALT! SO, IT'S TOO DANGEROUS!
YOU'RE TELLING ME?!!
HOWEVER, THE WASP JUST WHISPERED SOMETHING VERY INTERESTING TO ME!
AIM ABOVE THAT GIANT IDOL --SO THAT YOUR ARROW WILL LAND DEAD CENTER ON HIM!
CAREFUL!! IT'S GOT TO BE DEAD CENTER!
IF YOU MISS-- WE'RE ALL FINISHED!
THE NAME'S HAWKEYE, CAP! I NEVER LEARNED HOW TO MISS!
THERE SHE IS-- RIGHT ON TARGET!
BUT WHAT IN SAM HILL IS THIS SUPPOSED TO DO??
WE'LL KNOW THE ANSWER WITHIN SECONDS!! WATCH--!
SPOOM!
SEE? JUST AS JAN SAID! THE IDOL CONTAINED HIDDEN EXPLOSIVES WITHIN! AND YOUR ARROW SET THEM OFF!
BUT, HOW'LL THAT PUT THE FIRE OUT?
19

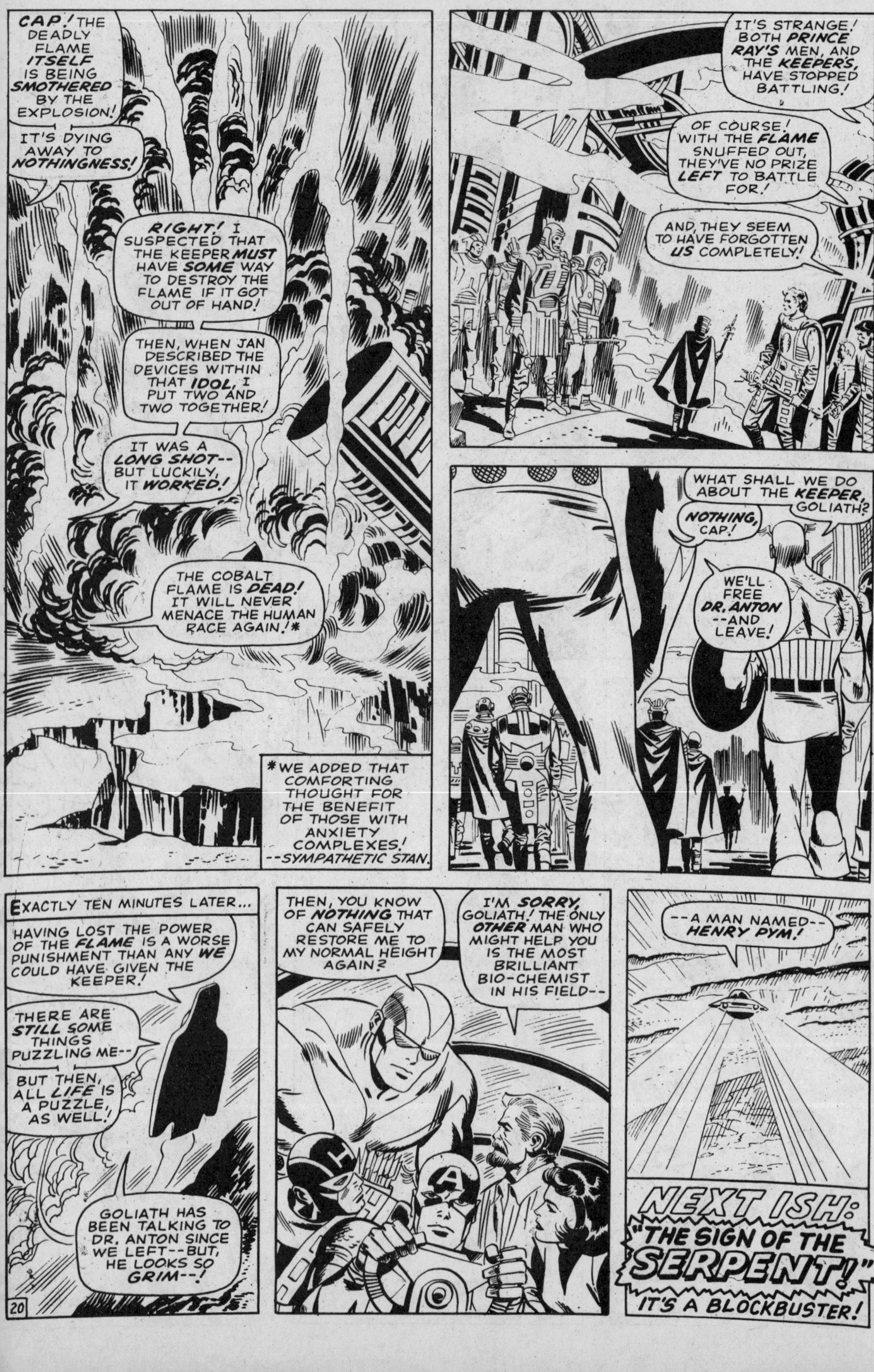
CAP! THE DEADLY FLAME ITSELF IS BEING SMOTHERED BY THE EXPLOSION!
IT'S DYING AWAY TO NOTHINGNESS!
RIGHT! I SUSPECTED THAT THE KEEPER MUST HAVE SOME WAY TO DESTROY THE FLAME IF IT GOT OUT OF HAND!
THEN, WHEN JAN DESCRIBED THE DEVICES WITHIN THAT IDOL, I PUT TWO AND TWO TOGETHER!
IT WAS A LONG SHOT-- BUT LUCKILY, IT WORKED!
THE COBALT FLAME IS DEAD! IT WILL NEVER MENACE THE HUMAN RACE AGAIN!*
*WE ADDED THAT COMFORTING THOUGHT FOR THE BENEFIT OF THOSE WITH ANXIETY COMPLEXES! --SYMPATHETIC STAN.
IT'S STRANGE! BOTH PRINCE RAY'S MEN, AND THE KEEPER'S, HAVE STOPPED BATTLING!
OF COURSE! WITH THE FLAME SNUFFED OUT, THEY'VE NO PRIZE LEFT TO BATTLE FOR!
AND, THEY SEEM TO HAVE FORGOTTEN US COMPLETELY!
WHAT SHALL WE DO ABOUT THE KEEPER, GOLIATH?
NOTHING, CAP!
WE'LL FREE DR. ANTON --AND LEAVE!
EXACTLY TEN MINUTES LATER...
HAVING LOST THE POWER OF THE FLAME IS A WORSE PUNISHMENT THAN ANY WE COULD HAVE GIVEN THE KEEPER!
THERE ARE STILL SOME THINGS PUZZLING ME--
BUT THEN, ALL LIFE IS A PUZZLE, AS WELL!
GOLIATH HAS BEEN TALKING TO DR. ANTON SINCE WE LEFT--BUT, HE LOOKS SO GRIM--!
20
THEN, YOU KNOW OF NOTHING THAT CAN SAFELY RESTORE ME TO MY NORMAL HEIGHT AGAIN?
I'M SORRY, GOLIATH! THE ONLY OTHER MAN WHO MIGHT HELP YOU IS THE MOST BRILLIANT BIO-CHEMIST IN HIS FIELD--
--A MAN NAMED-- HENRY PYM!
NEXT ISH: "THE SIGN OF THE SERPENT!"
IT'S A BLOCKBUSTER!

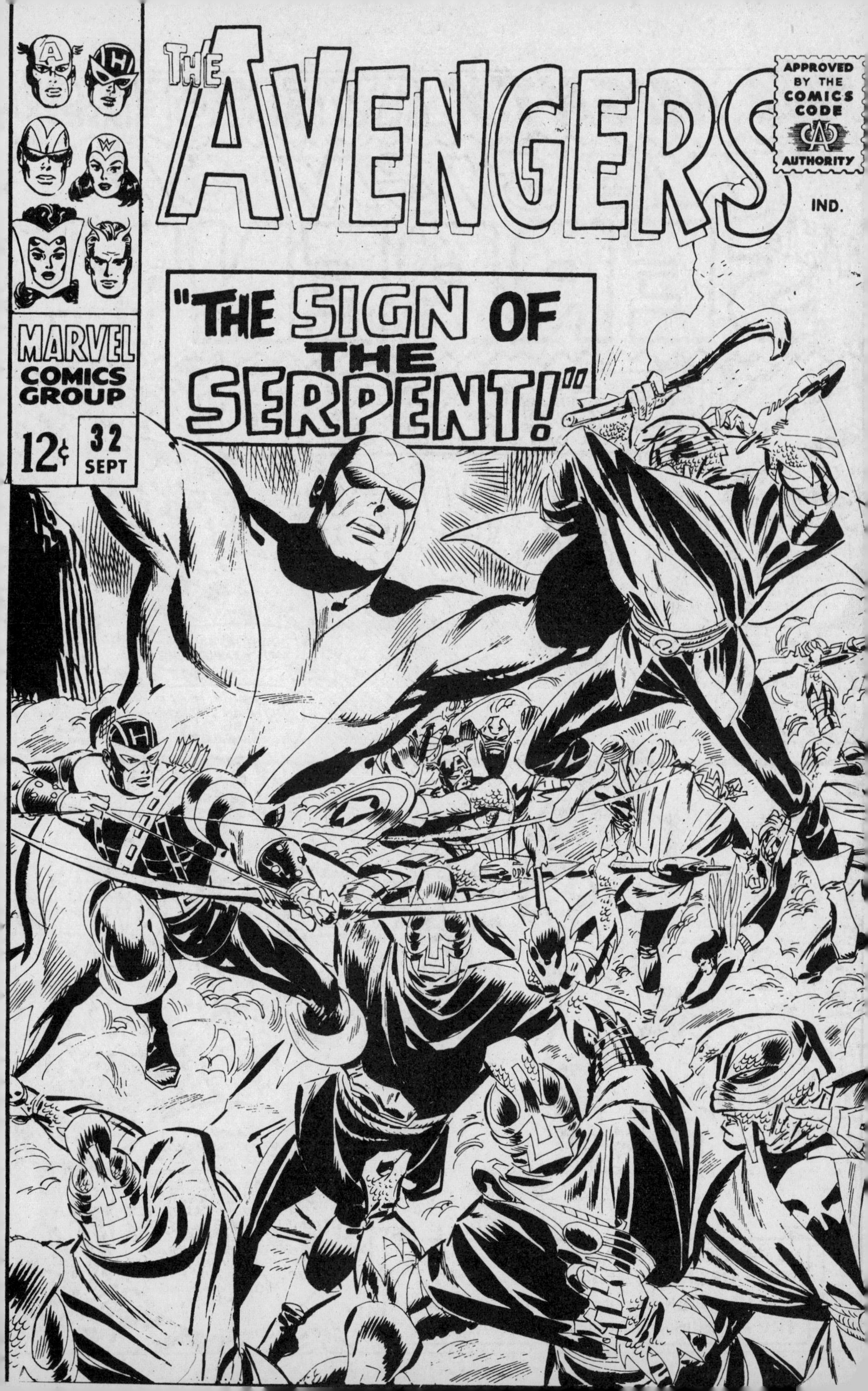

THE AVENGERS
APPROVED BY THE COMICS CODE AUTHORITY
IND.
MARVEL COMICS GROUP
12¢
32 SEPT
"THE SIGN OF THE SERPENT!"

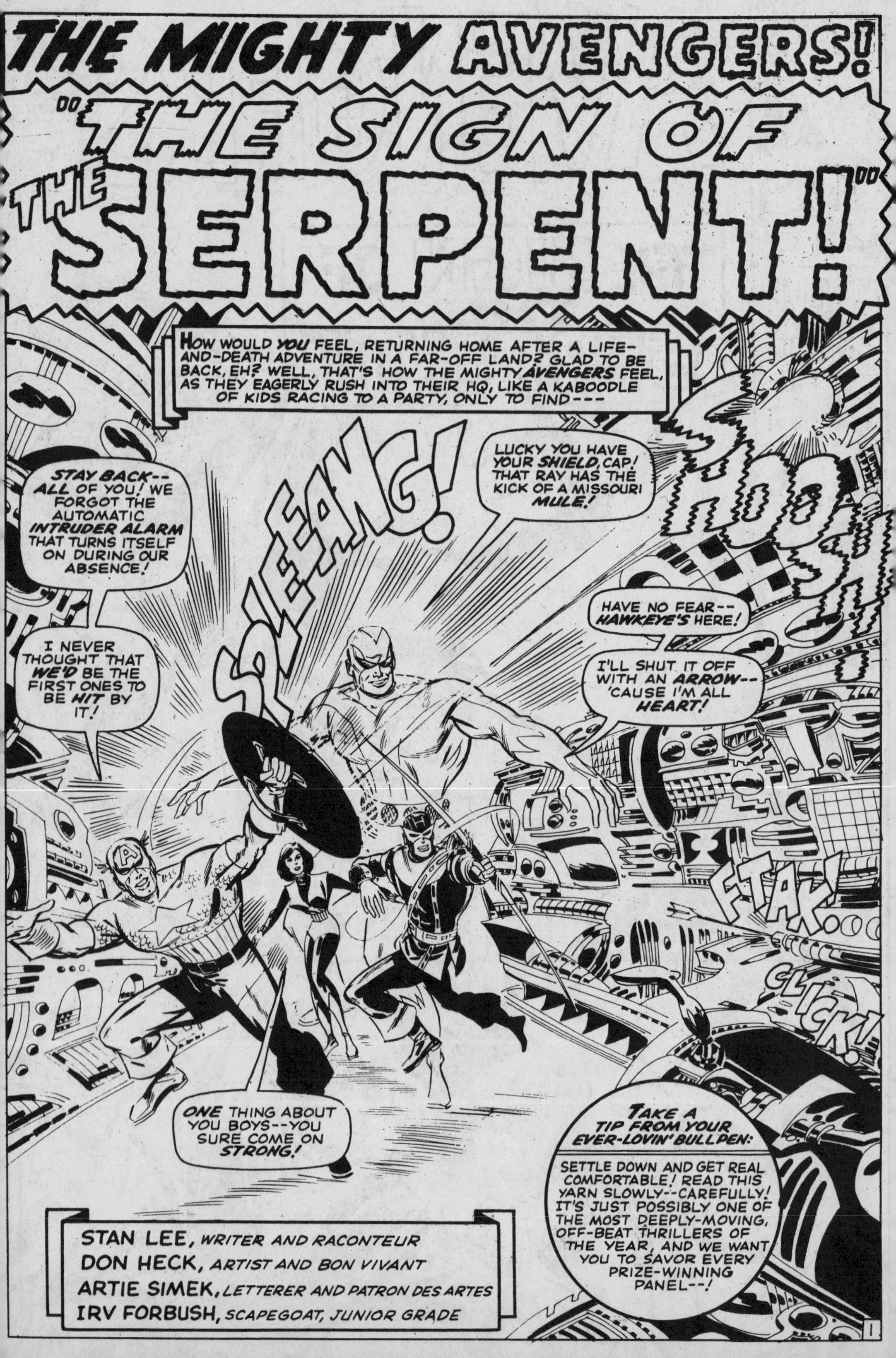
THE MIGHTY AVENGERS!
"THE SIGN OF THE SERPENT!"
HOW WOULD YOU FEEL, RETURNING HOME AFTER A LIFE-AND-DEATH ADVENTURE IN A FAR-OFF LAND? GLAD TO BE BACK, EH? WELL, THAT'S HOW THE MIGHTY AVENGERS FEEL, AS THEY EAGERLY RUSH INTO THEIR HQ, LIKE A KABOODLE OF KIDS RACING TO A PARTY, ONLY TO FIND---
STAY BACK-- ALL OF YOU! WE FORGOT THE AUTOMATIC INTRUDER ALARM THAT TURNS ITSELF ON DURING OUR ABSENCE!
I NEVER THOUGHT THAT WE'D BE THE FIRST ONES TO BE HIT BY IT!
SPIEEANG!
LUCKY YOU HAVE YOUR SHIELD, CAP! THAT RAY HAS THE KICK OF A MISSOURI MULE!
SHOOOSH
HAVE NO FEAR-- HAWKEYE'S HERE!
I'LL SHUT IT OFF WITH AN ARROW-- 'CAUSE I'M ALL HEART!
FTAK!
CLICK!
ONE THING ABOUT YOU BOYS--YOU SURE COME ON STRONG!
TAKE A TIP FROM YOUR EVER-LOVIN' BULLPEN:
SETTLE DOWN AND GET REAL COMFORTABLE! READ THIS YARN SLOWLY--CAREFULLY! IT'S JUST POSSIBLY ONE OF THE MOST DEEPLY-MOVING, OFF-BEAT THRILLERS OF THE YEAR, AND WE WANT YOU TO SAVOR EVERY PRIZE-WINNING PANEL--!
STAN LEE, WRITER AND RACONTEUR
DON HECK, ARTIST AND BON VIVANT
ARTIE SIMEK, LETTERER AND PATRON DES ARTES
IRV FORBUSH, SCAPEGOAT, JUNIOR GRADE
1

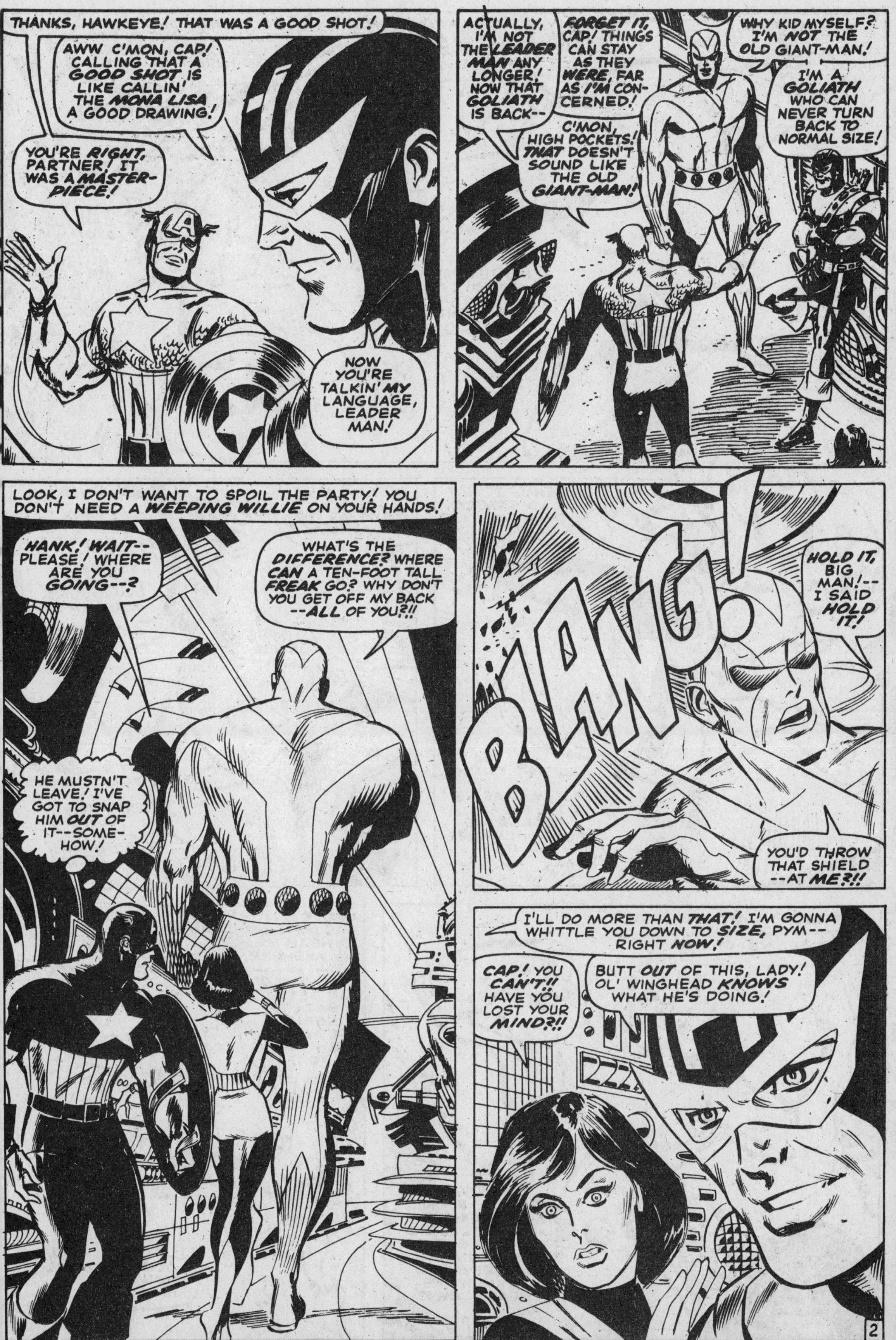
THANKS, HAWKEYE! THAT WAS A GOOD SHOT!
AWW C'MON, CAP! CALLING THAT A GOOD SHOT IS LIKE CALLIN' THE MONA LISA A GOOD DRAWING!
YOU'RE RIGHT, PARTNER! IT WAS A MASTER-PIECE!
NOW YOU'RE TALKIN' MY LANGUAGE, LEADER MAN!
ACTUALLY, I'M NOT THE LEADER MAN ANY LONGER! NOW THAT GOLIATH IS BACK--
FORGET IT, CAP! THINGS CAN STAY AS THEY WERE, FAR AS I'M CON-CERNED!
C'MON, HIGH POCKETS! THAT DOESN'T SOUND LIKE THE OLD GIANT-MAN!
WHY KID MYSELF? I'M NOT THE OLD GIANT-MAN!
I'M A GOLIATH WHO CAN NEVER TURN BACK TO NORMAL SIZE!
LOOK, I DON'T WANT TO SPOIL THE PARTY! YOU DON'T NEED A WEEPING WILLIE ON YOUR HANDS!
HANK! WAIT-- PLEASE! WHERE ARE YOU GOING--?
WHAT'S THE DIFFERENCE? WHERE CAN A TEN-FOOT TALL FREAK GO? WHY DON'T YOU GET OFF MY BACK --ALL OF YOU?!!
HE MUSTN'T LEAVE! I'VE GOT TO SNAP HIM OUT OF IT--SOME-HOW!
BLANG!
HOLD IT, BIG MAN!-- I SAID HOLD IT!
YOU'D THROW THAT SHIELD --AT ME?!!
I'LL DO MORE THAN THAT! I'M GONNA WHITTLE YOU DOWN TO SIZE, PYM-- RIGHT NOW!
CAP! YOU CAN'T!! HAVE YOU LOST YOUR MIND?!!
BUTT OUT OF THIS, LADY! OL' WINGHEAD KNOWS WHAT HE'S DOING!
2

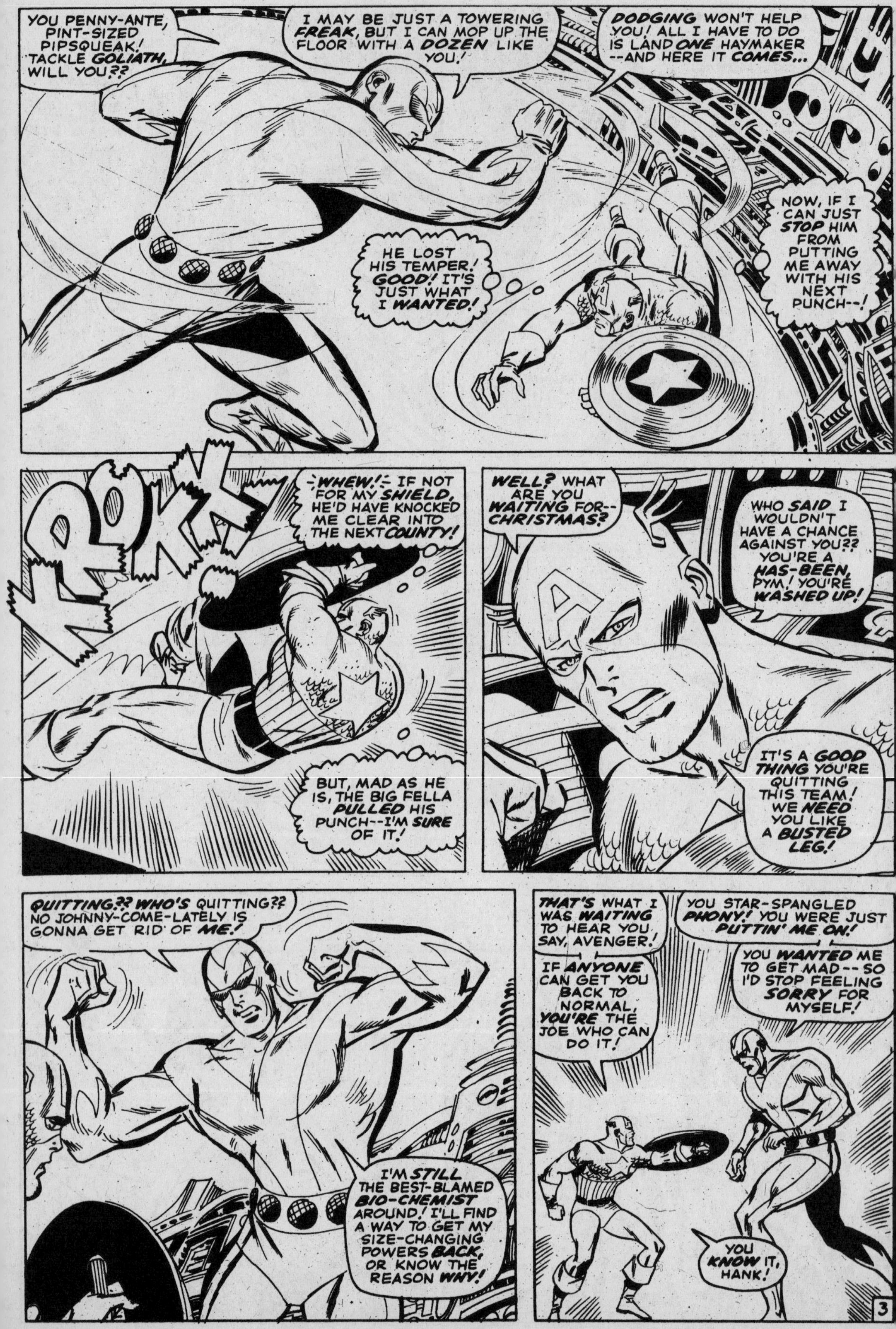
YOU PENNY-ANTE, PINT-SIZED PIPSQUEAK! TACKLE GOLIATH, WILL YOU??
I MAY BE JUST A TOWERING FREAK, BUT I CAN MOP UP THE FLOOR WITH A DOZEN LIKE YOU!
DODGING WON'T HELP YOU! ALL I HAVE TO DO IS LAND ONE HAYMAKER --AND HERE IT COMES...
HE LOST HIS TEMPER! GOOD! IT'S JUST WHAT I WANTED!
NOW, IF I CAN JUST STOP HIM FROM PUTTING ME AWAY WITH HIS NEXT PUNCH--!
KROK!
-WHEW!- IF NOT FOR MY SHIELD, HE'D HAVE KNOCKED ME CLEAR INTO THE NEXT COUNTY!
BUT, MAD AS HE IS, THE BIG FELLA PULLED HIS PUNCH--I'M SURE OF IT!
WELL? WHAT ARE YOU WAITING FOR--CHRISTMAS?
WHO SAID I WOULDN'T HAVE A CHANCE AGAINST YOU?? YOU'RE A HAS-BEEN, PYM! YOU'RE WASHED UP!
IT'S A GOOD THING YOU'RE QUITTING THIS TEAM! WE NEED YOU LIKE A BUSTED LEG!
QUITTING?? WHO'S QUITTING?? NO JOHNNY-COME-LATELY IS GONNA GET RID OF ME!
I'M STILL THE BEST-BLAMED BIO-CHEMIST AROUND! I'LL FIND A WAY TO GET MY SIZE-CHANGING POWERS BACK, OR KNOW THE REASON WHY!
THAT'S WHAT I WAS WAITING TO HEAR YOU SAY, AVENGER!
IF ANYONE CAN GET YOU BACK TO NORMAL, YOU'RE THE JOE WHO CAN DO IT!
YOU STAR-SPANGLED PHONY! YOU WERE JUST PUTTIN' ME ON!
YOU WANTED ME TO GET MAD -- SO I'D STOP FEELING SORRY FOR MYSELF!
YOU KNOW IT, HANK!
3

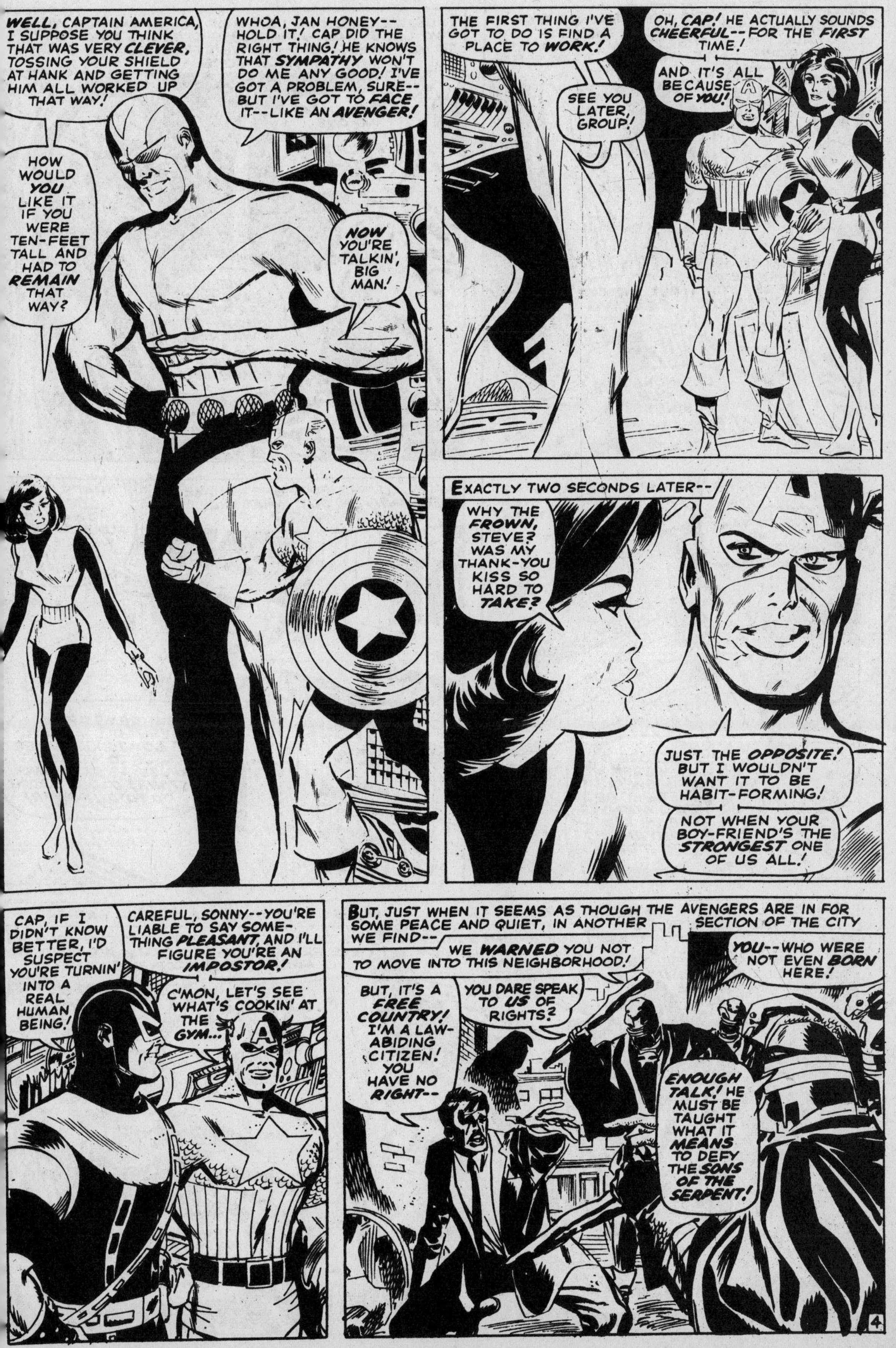
WELL, CAPTAIN AMERICA, I SUPPOSE YOU THINK THAT WAS VERY CLEVER, TOSSING YOUR SHIELD AT HANK AND GETTING HIM ALL WORKED UP THAT WAY!
HOW WOULD YOU LIKE IT IF YOU WERE TEN-FEET TALL AND HAD TO REMAIN THAT WAY?
WHOA, JAN HONEY-- HOLD IT! CAP DID THE RIGHT THING! HE KNOWS THAT SYMPATHY WON'T DO ME ANY GOOD! I'VE GOT A PROBLEM, SURE-- BUT I'VE GOT TO FACE IT--LIKE AN AVENGER!
NOW YOU'RE TALKIN', BIG MAN!
THE FIRST THING I'VE GOT TO DO IS FIND A PLACE TO WORK!
SEE YOU LATER, GROUP!
OH, CAP! HE ACTUALLY SOUNDS CHEERFUL--FOR THE FIRST TIME!
AND IT'S ALL BECAUSE OF YOU!
EXACTLY TWO SECONDS LATER--
WHY THE FROWN, STEVE? WAS MY THANK-YOU KISS SO HARD TO TAKE?
JUST THE OPPOSITE! BUT I WOULDN'T WANT IT TO BE HABIT-FORMING!
NOT WHEN YOUR BOY-FRIEND'S THE STRONGEST ONE OF US ALL!
CAP, IF I DIDN'T KNOW BETTER, I'D SUSPECT YOU'RE TURNIN' INTO A REAL HUMAN BEING!
CAREFUL, SONNY--YOU'RE LIABLE TO SAY SOMETHING PLEASANT, AND I'LL FIGURE YOU'RE AN IMPOSTOR!
C'MON, LET'S SEE WHAT'S COOKIN' AT THE GYM...
BUT, JUST WHEN IT SEEMS AS THOUGH THE AVENGERS ARE IN FOR SOME PEACE AND QUIET, IN ANOTHER SECTION OF THE CITY WE FIND--
WE WARNED YOU NOT TO MOVE INTO THIS NEIGHBORHOOD!
YOU--WHO WERE NOT EVEN BORN HERE!
BUT, IT'S A FREE COUNTRY! I'M A LAW-ABIDING CITIZEN! YOU HAVE NO RIGHT--
YOU DARE SPEAK TO US OF RIGHTS?
ENOUGH TALK! HE MUST BE TAUGHT WHAT IT MEANS TO DEFY THE SONS OF THE SERPENT!
4

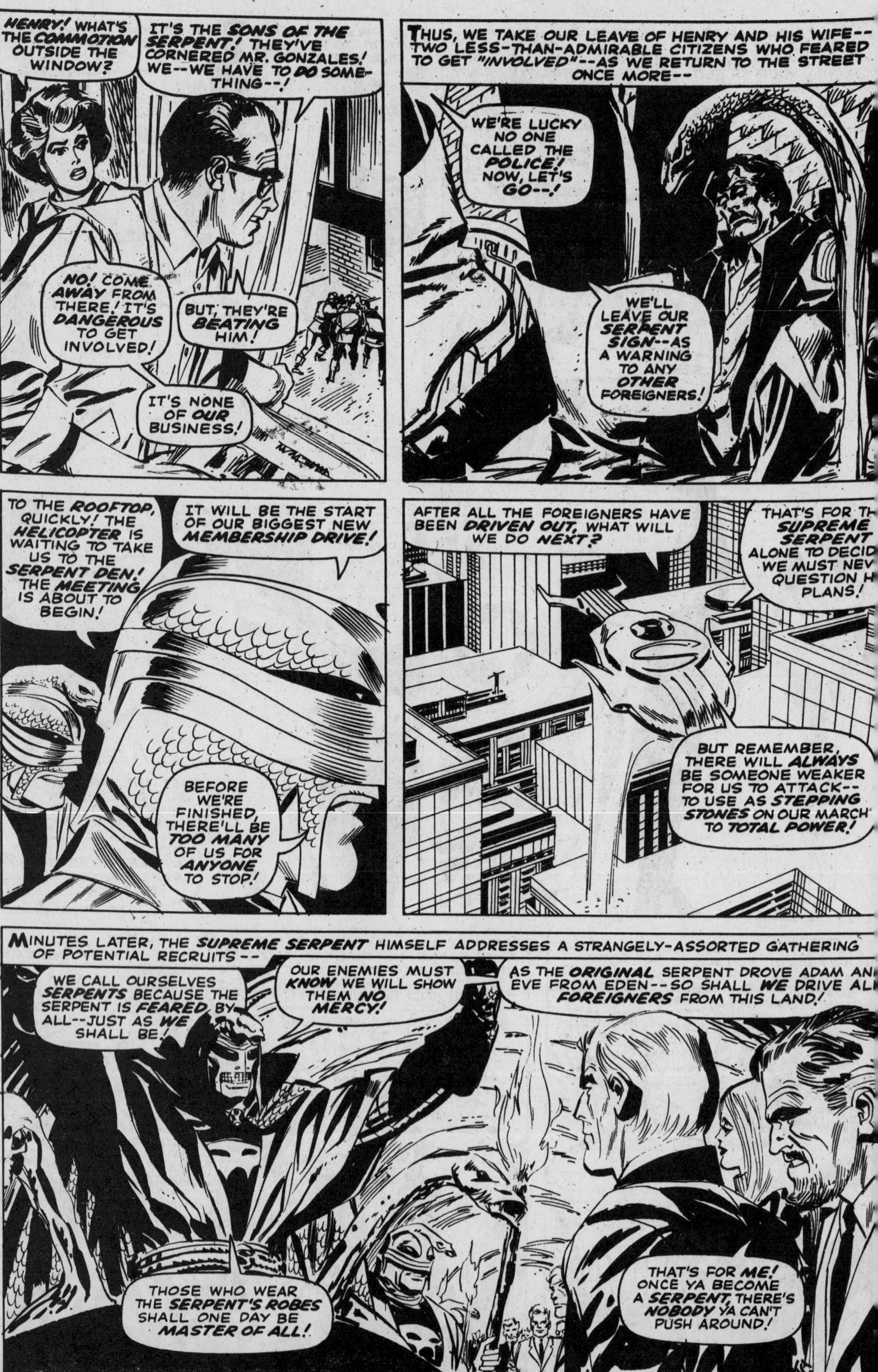
HENRY! WHAT'S THE COMMOTION OUTSIDE THE WINDOW?
IT'S THE SONS OF THE SERPENT! THEY'VE CORNERED MR. GONZALES! WE--WE HAVE TO DO SOMETHING--!
NO! COME AWAY FROM THERE! IT'S DANGEROUS TO GET INVOLVED!
BUT, THEY'RE BEATING HIM!
IT'S NONE OF OUR BUSINESS!
THUS, WE TAKE OUR LEAVE OF HENRY AND HIS WIFE--TWO LESS-THAN-ADMIRABLE CITIZENS WHO FEARED TO GET "INVOLVED"--AS WE RETURN TO THE STREET ONCE MORE--
WE'RE LUCKY NO ONE CALLED THE POLICE! NOW, LET'S GO--!
WE'LL LEAVE OUR SERPENT SIGN--AS A WARNING TO ANY OTHER FOREIGNERS!
TO THE ROOFTOP, QUICKLY! THE HELICOPTER IS WAITING TO TAKE US TO THE SERPENT DEN! THE MEETING IS ABOUT TO BEGIN!
IT WILL BE THE START OF OUR BIGGEST NEW MEMBERSHIP DRIVE!
BEFORE WE'RE FINISHED, THERE'LL BE TOO MANY OF US FOR ANYONE TO STOP!
AFTER ALL THE FOREIGNERS HAVE BEEN DRIVEN OUT, WHAT WILL WE DO NEXT?
THAT'S FOR TH SUPREME SERPENT ALONE TO DECID WE MUST NEV QUESTION H PLANS!
BUT REMEMBER, THERE WILL ALWAYS BE SOMEONE WEAKER FOR US TO ATTACK--TO USE AS STEPPING STONES ON OUR MARCH TO TOTAL POWER!
MINUTES LATER, THE SUPREME SERPENT HIMSELF ADDRESSES A STRANGELY-ASSORTED GATHERING OF POTENTIAL RECRUITS--
WE CALL OURSELVES SERPENTS BECAUSE THE SERPENT IS FEARED BY ALL--JUST AS WE SHALL BE!
OUR ENEMIES MUST KNOW WE WILL SHOW THEM NO MERCY!
AS THE ORIGINAL SERPENT DROVE ADAM AN EVE FROM EDEN--SO SHALL WE DRIVE AL FOREIGNERS FROM THIS LAND!
THOSE WHO WEAR THE SERPENT'S ROBES SHALL ONE DAY BE MASTER OF ALL!
THAT'S FOR ME! ONCE YA BECOME A SERPENT, THERE'S NOBODY YA CAN'T PUSH AROUND!

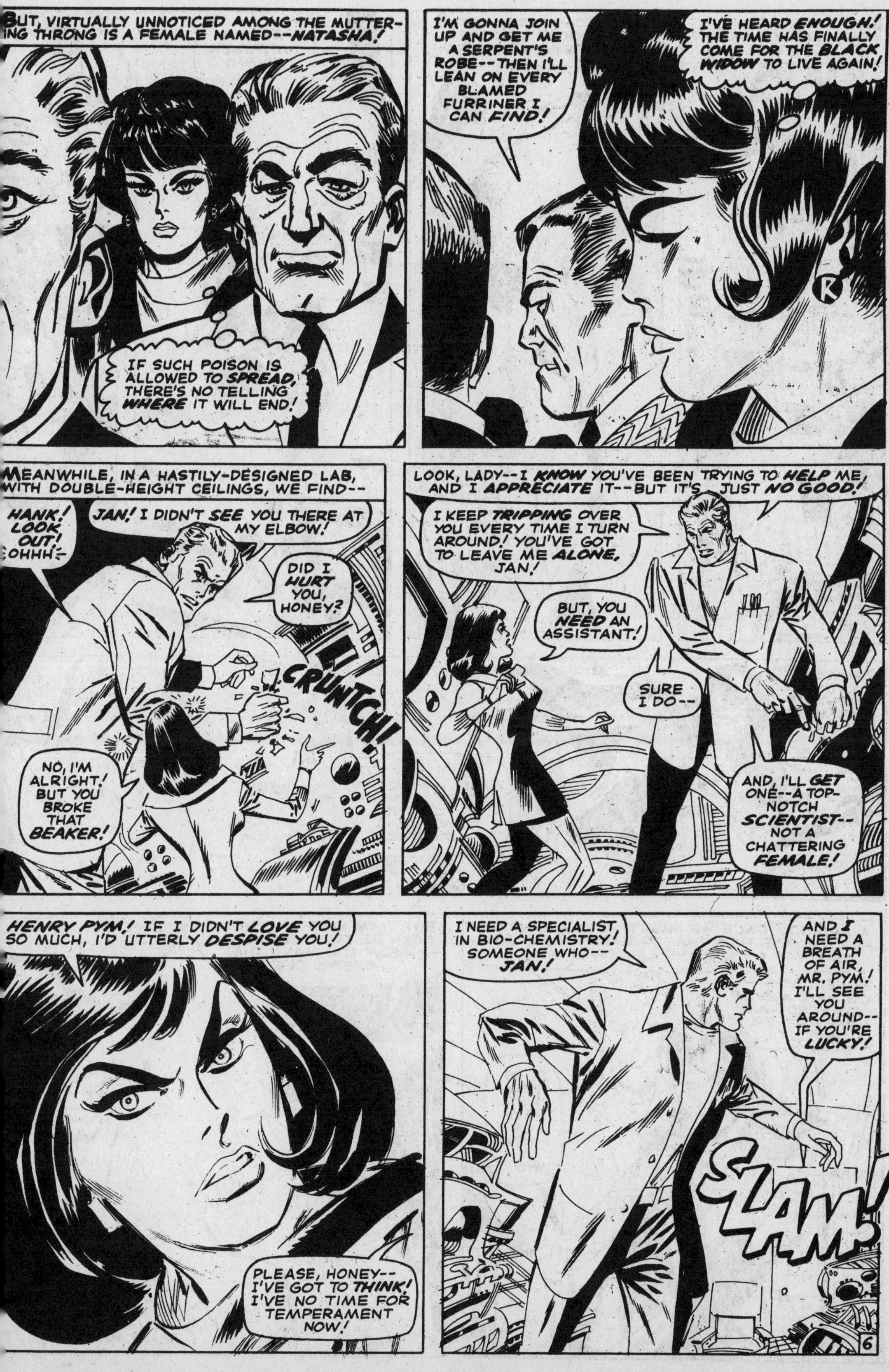
BUT, VIRTUALLY UNNOTICED AMONG THE MUTTERING THRONG IS A FEMALE NAMED--NATASHA!
IF SUCH POISON IS ALLOWED TO SPREAD, THERE'S NO TELLING WHERE IT WILL END!
I'M GONNA JOIN UP AND GET ME A SERPENT'S ROBE--THEN I'LL LEAN ON EVERY BLAMED FURRINER I CAN FIND!
I'VE HEARD ENOUGH! THE TIME HAS FINALLY COME FOR THE BLACK WIDOW TO LIVE AGAIN!
MEANWHILE, IN A HASTILY-DESIGNED LAB, WITH DOUBLE-HEIGHT CEILINGS, WE FIND--
HANK! LOOK OUT! OHHH!
JAN! I DIDN'T SEE YOU THERE AT MY ELBOW!
DID I HURT YOU, HONEY?
CRUNTCH!
NO, I'M ALRIGHT! BUT YOU BROKE THAT BEAKER!
LOOK, LADY--I KNOW YOU'VE BEEN TRYING TO HELP ME, AND I APPRECIATE IT--BUT IT'S JUST NO GOOD!
I KEEP TRIPPING OVER YOU EVERY TIME I TURN AROUND! YOU'VE GOT TO LEAVE ME ALONE, JAN!
BUT, YOU NEED AN ASSISTANT!
SURE I DO--
AND, I'LL GET ONE--A TOP-NOTCH SCIENTIST--NOT A CHATTERING FEMALE!
HENRY PYM! IF I DIDN'T LOVE YOU SO MUCH, I'D UTTERLY DESPISE YOU!
PLEASE, HONEY--I'VE GOT TO THINK! I'VE NO TIME FOR TEMPERAMENT NOW!
I NEED A SPECIALIST IN BIO-CHEMISTRY! SOMEONE WHO--JAN!
AND I NEED A BREATH OF AIR, MR. PYM! I'LL SEE YOU AROUND--IF YOU'RE LUCKY!
SLAM!
6

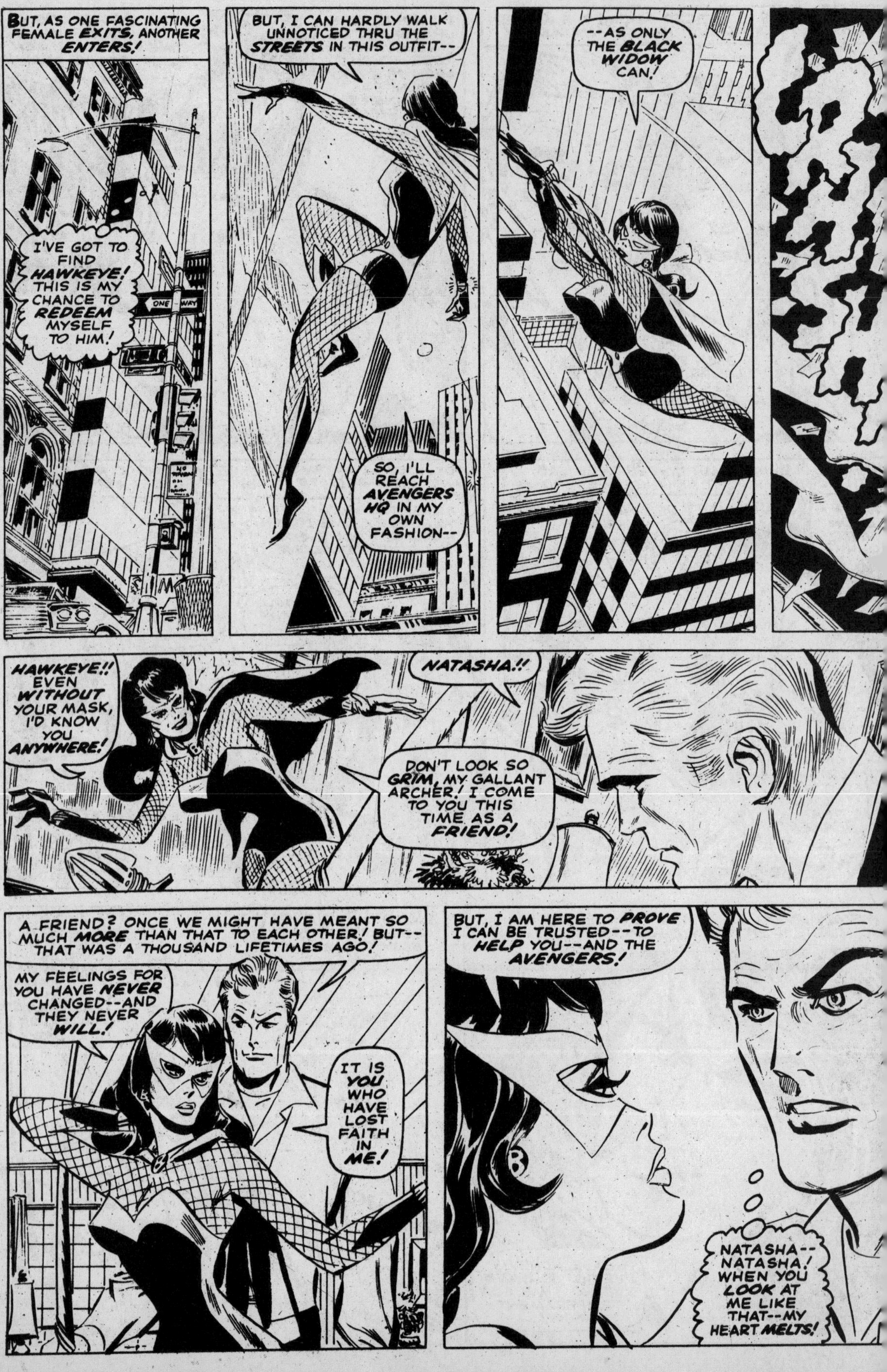
BUT, AS ONE FASCINATING FEMALE EXITS, ANOTHER ENTERS!
I'VE GOT TO FIND HAWKEYE! THIS IS MY CHANCE TO REDEEM MYSELF TO HIM!
ONE WAY
BUT, I CAN HARDLY WALK UNNOTICED THRU THE STREETS IN THIS OUTFIT--
SO, I'LL REACH AVENGERS HQ IN MY OWN FASHION--
--AS ONLY THE BLACK WIDOW CAN!
HAWKEYE!! EVEN WITHOUT YOUR MASK, I'D KNOW YOU ANYWHERE!
NATASHA!!
DON'T LOOK SO GRIM, MY GALLANT ARCHER! I COME TO YOU THIS TIME AS A FRIEND!
A FRIEND? ONCE WE MIGHT HAVE MEANT SO MUCH MORE THAN THAT TO EACH OTHER! BUT--THAT WAS A THOUSAND LIFETIMES AGO!
MY FEELINGS FOR YOU HAVE NEVER CHANGED--AND THEY NEVER WILL!
IT IS YOU WHO HAVE LOST FAITH IN ME!
BUT, I AM HERE TO PROVE I CAN BE TRUSTED--TO HELP YOU--AND THE AVENGERS!
NATASHA--NATASHA! WHEN YOU LOOK AT ME LIKE THAT--MY HEART MELTS!

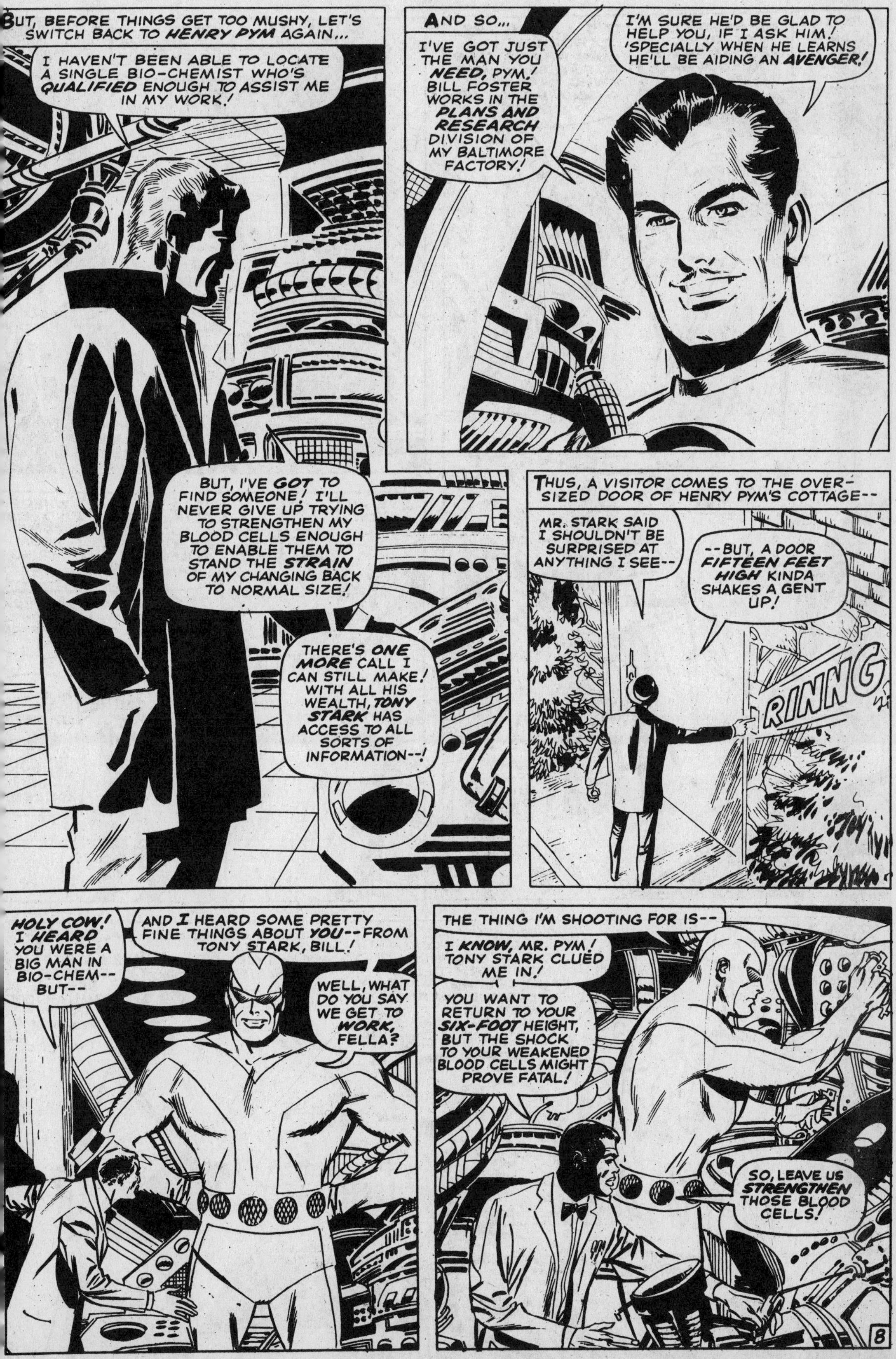
BUT, BEFORE THINGS GET TOO MUSHY, LET'S SWITCH BACK TO HENRY PYM AGAIN...
I HAVEN'T BEEN ABLE TO LOCATE A SINGLE BIO-CHEMIST WHO'S QUALIFIED ENOUGH TO ASSIST ME IN MY WORK!
BUT, I'VE GOT TO FIND SOMEONE! I'LL NEVER GIVE UP TRYING TO STRENGTHEN MY BLOOD CELLS ENOUGH TO ENABLE THEM TO STAND THE STRAIN OF MY CHANGING BACK TO NORMAL SIZE!
THERE'S ONE MORE CALL I CAN STILL MAKE! WITH ALL HIS WEALTH, TONY STARK HAS ACCESS TO ALL SORTS OF INFORMATION--!
AND SO...
I'VE GOT JUST THE MAN YOU NEED, PYM! BILL FOSTER WORKS IN THE PLANS AND RESEARCH DIVISION OF MY BALTIMORE FACTORY!
I'M SURE HE'D BE GLAD TO HELP YOU, IF I ASK HIM! 'SPECIALLY WHEN HE LEARNS HE'LL BE AIDING AN AVENGER!
THUS, A VISITOR COMES TO THE OVER-SIZED DOOR OF HENRY PYM'S COTTAGE--
MR. STARK SAID I SHOULDN'T BE SURPRISED AT ANYTHING I SEE--
--BUT, A DOOR FIFTEEN FEET HIGH KINDA SHAKES A GENT UP!
RINNG
HOLY COW! I HEARD YOU WERE A BIG MAN IN BIO-CHEM-- BUT--
AND I HEARD SOME PRETTY FINE THINGS ABOUT YOU--FROM TONY STARK, BILL!
WELL, WHAT DO YOU SAY WE GET TO WORK, FELLA?
THE THING I'M SHOOTING FOR IS--
I KNOW, MR. PYM! TONY STARK CLUED ME IN!
YOU WANT TO RETURN TO YOUR SIX-FOOT HEIGHT, BUT THE SHOCK TO YOUR WEAKENED BLOOD CELLS MIGHT PROVE FATAL!
SO, LEAVE US STRENGTHEN THOSE BLOOD CELLS!
8

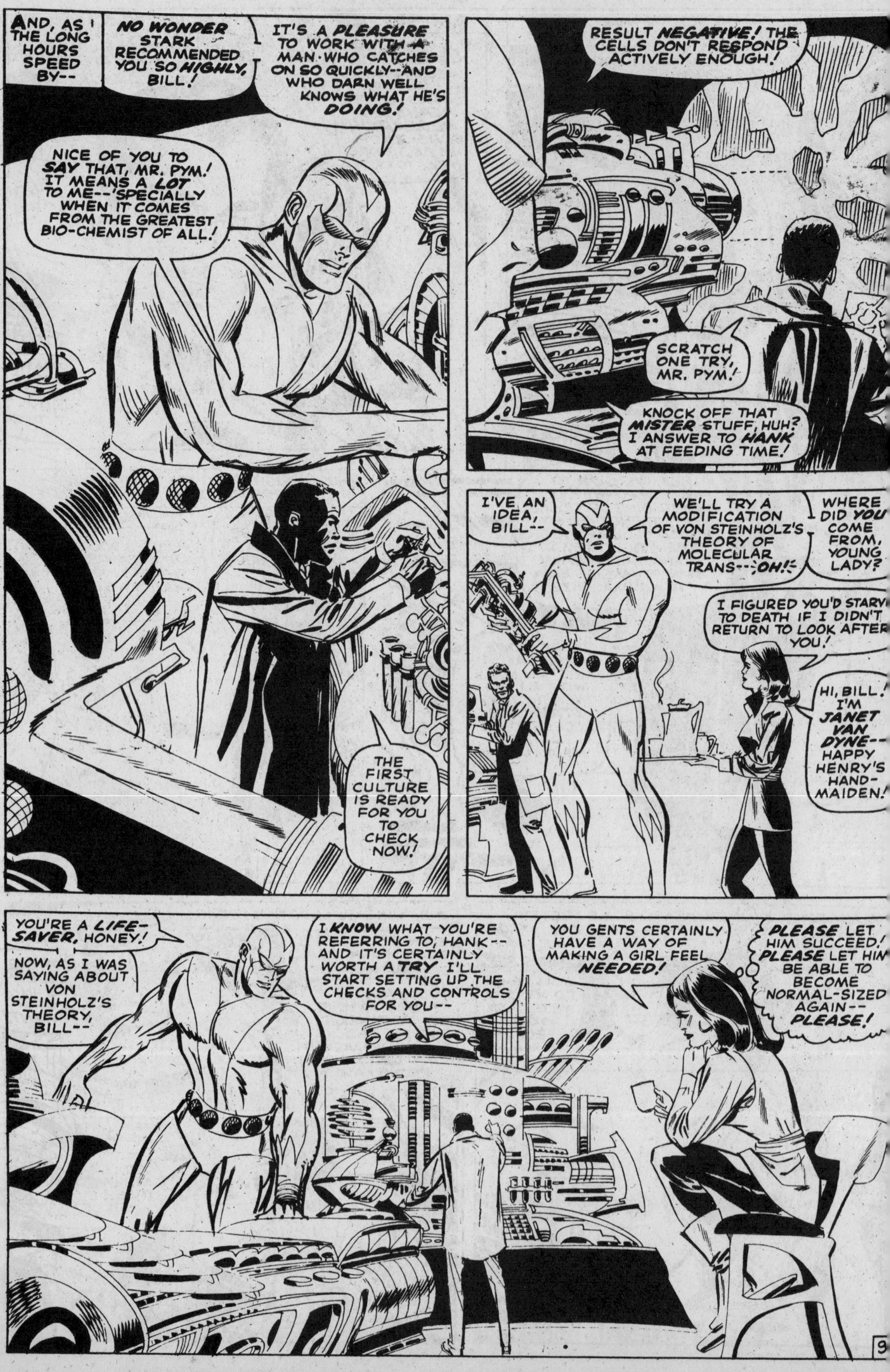
AND, AS THE LONG HOURS SPEED BY--
NO WONDER STARK RECOMMENDED YOU SO HIGHLY, BILL!
IT'S A PLEASURE TO WORK WITH A MAN WHO CATCHES ON SO QUICKLY--AND WHO DARN WELL KNOWS WHAT HE'S DOING!
NICE OF YOU TO SAY THAT, MR. PYM! IT MEANS A LOT TO ME--'SPECIALLY WHEN IT COMES FROM THE GREATEST BIO-CHEMIST OF ALL!
THE FIRST CULTURE IS READY FOR YOU TO CHECK NOW!
RESULT NEGATIVE! THE CELLS DON'T RESPOND ACTIVELY ENOUGH!
SCRATCH ONE TRY, MR. PYM!
KNOCK OFF THAT MISTER STUFF, HUH? I ANSWER TO HANK AT FEEDING TIME!
I'VE AN IDEA, BILL--
WE'LL TRY A MODIFICATION OF VON STEINHOLZ'S THEORY OF MOLECULAR TRANS--;OH!-
WHERE DID YOU COME FROM, YOUNG LADY?
I FIGURED YOU'D STARVE TO DEATH IF I DIDN'T RETURN TO LOOK AFTER YOU!
HI, BILL! I'M JANET VAN DYNE-- HAPPY HENRY'S HAND-MAIDEN!
YOU'RE A LIFE-SAVER, HONEY!
NOW, AS I WAS SAYING ABOUT VON STEINHOLZ'S THEORY, BILL--
I KNOW WHAT YOU'RE REFERRING TO, HANK--AND IT'S CERTAINLY WORTH A TRY I'LL START SETTING UP THE CHECKS AND CONTROLS FOR YOU--
YOU GENTS CERTAINLY HAVE A WAY OF MAKING A GIRL FEEL NEEDED!
PLEASE LET HIM SUCCEED! PLEASE LET HIM BE ABLE TO BECOME NORMAL-SIZED AGAIN-- PLEASE!

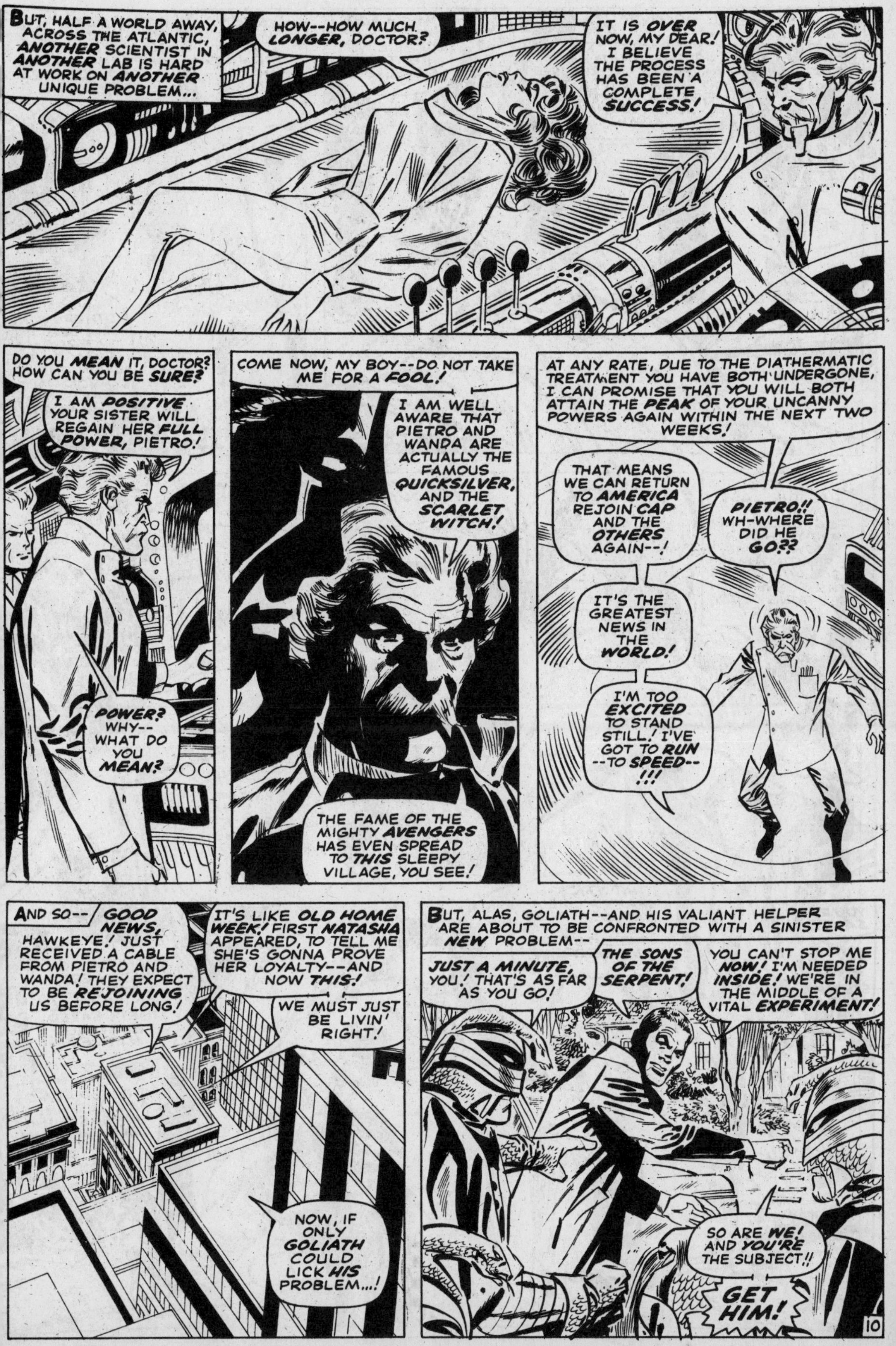
BUT, HALF A WORLD AWAY, ACROSS THE ATLANTIC, ANOTHER SCIENTIST IN ANOTHER LAB IS HARD AT WORK ON ANOTHER UNIQUE PROBLEM...
HOW--HOW MUCH LONGER, DOCTOR?
IT IS OVER NOW, MY DEAR! I BELIEVE THE PROCESS HAS BEEN A COMPLETE SUCCESS!
DO YOU MEAN IT, DOCTOR? HOW CAN YOU BE SURE?
I AM POSITIVE YOUR SISTER WILL REGAIN HER FULL POWER, PIETRO!
POWER? WHY-- WHAT DO YOU MEAN?
COME NOW, MY BOY--DO NOT TAKE ME FOR A FOOL!
I AM WELL AWARE THAT PIETRO AND WANDA ARE ACTUALLY THE FAMOUS QUICKSILVER, AND THE SCARLET WITCH!
THE FAME OF THE MIGHTY AVENGERS HAS EVEN SPREAD TO THIS SLEEPY VILLAGE, YOU SEE!
AT ANY RATE, DUE TO THE DIATHERMATIC TREATMENT YOU HAVE BOTH UNDERGONE, I CAN PROMISE THAT YOU WILL BOTH ATTAIN THE PEAK OF YOUR UNCANNY POWERS AGAIN WITHIN THE NEXT TWO WEEKS!
THAT MEANS WE CAN RETURN TO AMERICA REJOIN CAP AND THE OTHERS AGAIN--!
IT'S THE GREATEST NEWS IN THE WORLD!
I'M TOO EXCITED TO STAND STILL! I'VE GOT TO RUN --TO SPEED-- !!!
PIETRO!! WH-WHERE DID HE GO??
AND SO--
GOOD NEWS, HAWKEYE! JUST RECEIVED A CABLE FROM PIETRO AND WANDA! THEY EXPECT TO BE REJOINING US BEFORE LONG!
IT'S LIKE OLD HOME WEEK! FIRST NATASHA APPEARED, TO TELL ME SHE'S GONNA PROVE HER LOYALTY--AND NOW THIS!
WE MUST JUST BE LIVIN' RIGHT!
NOW, IF ONLY GOLIATH COULD LICK HIS PROBLEM...!
BUT, ALAS, GOLIATH--AND HIS VALIANT HELPER ARE ABOUT TO BE CONFRONTED WITH A SINISTER NEW PROBLEM--
JUST A MINUTE, YOU! THAT'S AS FAR AS YOU GO!
THE SONS OF THE SERPENT!
YOU CAN'T STOP ME NOW! I'M NEEDED INSIDE! WE'RE IN THE MIDDLE OF A VITAL EXPERIMENT!
SO ARE WE! AND YOU'RE THE SUBJECT!!
GET HIM!
10

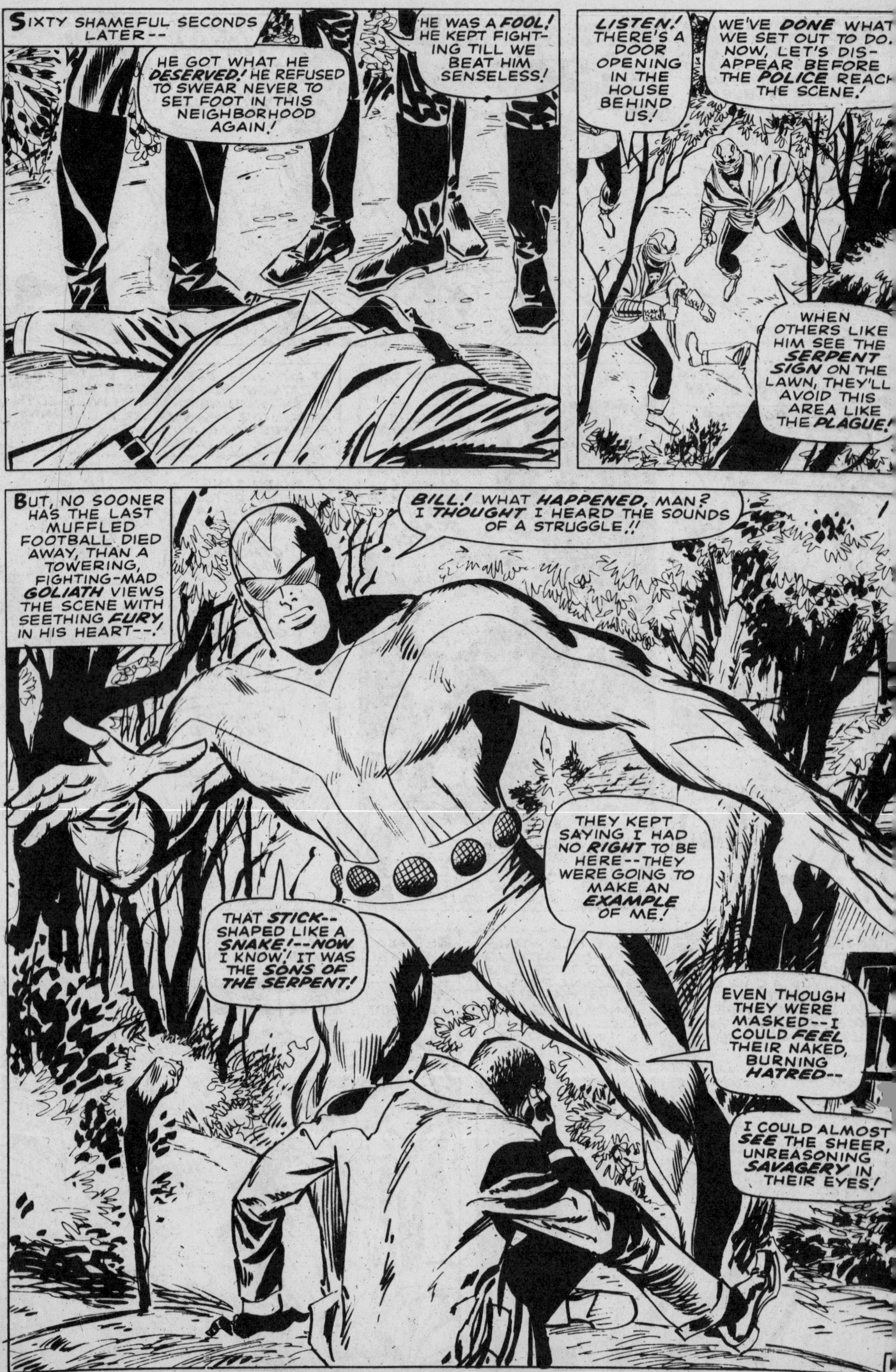
SIXTY SHAMEFUL SECONDS LATER--
HE GOT WHAT HE DESERVED! HE REFUSED TO SWEAR NEVER TO SET FOOT IN THIS NEIGHBORHOOD AGAIN!
HE WAS A FOOL! HE KEPT FIGHTING TILL WE BEAT HIM SENSELESS!
LISTEN! THERE'S A DOOR OPENING IN THE HOUSE BEHIND US!
WE'VE DONE WHAT WE SET OUT TO DO. NOW, LET'S DISAPPEAR BEFORE THE POLICE REACH THE SCENE!
WHEN OTHERS LIKE HIM SEE THE SERPENT SIGN ON THE LAWN, THEY'LL AVOID THIS AREA LIKE THE PLAGUE!
BUT, NO SOONER HAS THE LAST MUFFLED FOOTBALL DIED AWAY, THAN A TOWERING, FIGHTING-MAD GOLIATH VIEWS THE SCENE WITH SEETHING FURY IN HIS HEART--!
BILL! WHAT HAPPENED, MAN? I THOUGHT I HEARD THE SOUNDS OF A STRUGGLE!!
THEY KEPT SAYING I HAD NO RIGHT TO BE HERE--THEY WERE GOING TO MAKE AN EXAMPLE OF ME!
THAT STICK--SHAPED LIKE A SNAKE!--NOW I KNOW! IT WAS THE SONS OF THE SERPENT!
EVEN THOUGH THEY WERE MASKED--I COULD FEEL THEIR NAKED, BURNING HATRED--
I COULD ALMOST SEE THE SHEER, UNREASONING SAVAGERY IN THEIR EYES!

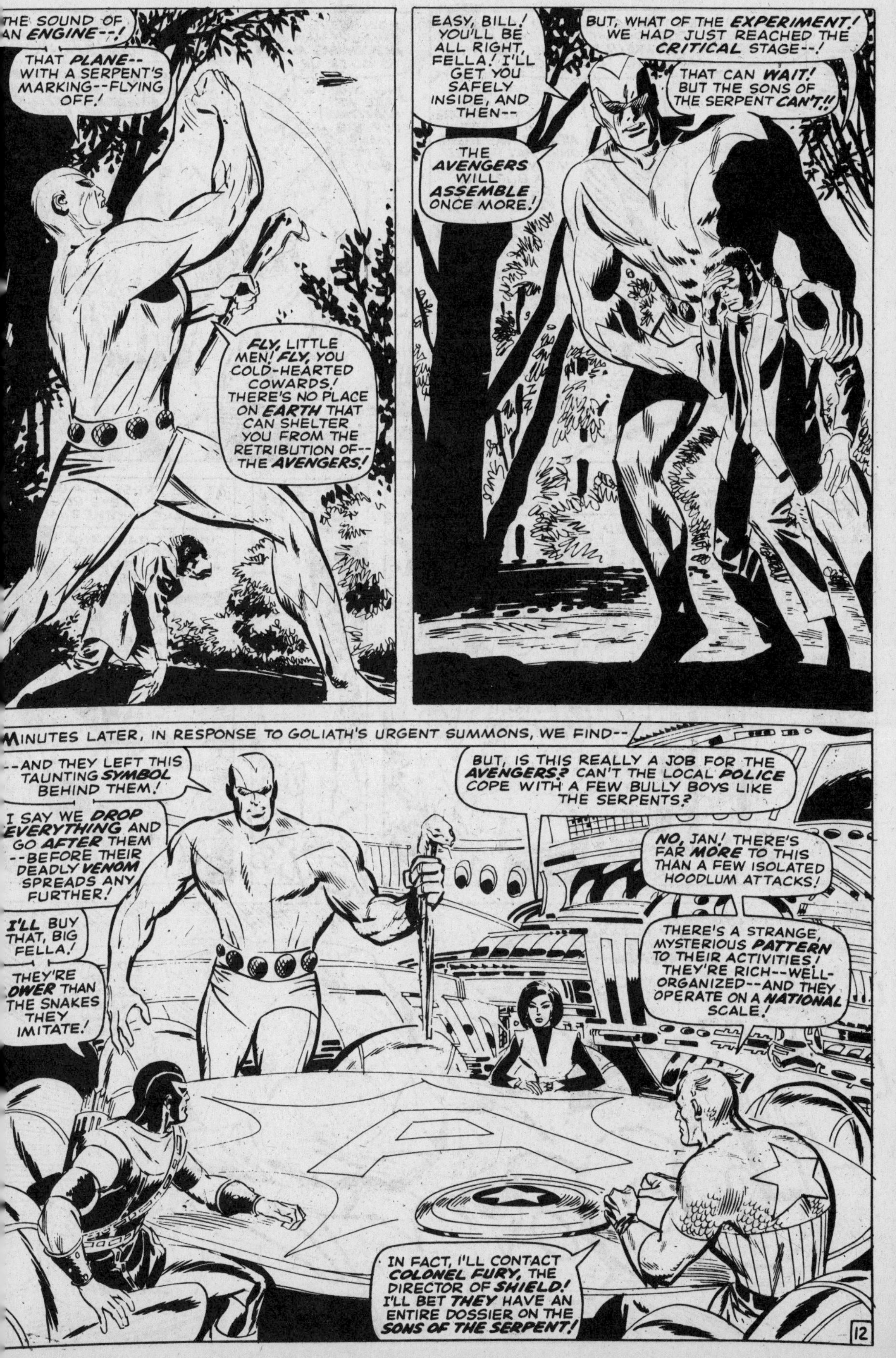
THE SOUND OF AN ENGINE--!
THAT PLANE--WITH A SERPENT'S MARKING--FLYING OFF!
FLY, LITTLE MEN! FLY, YOU COLD-HEARTED COWARDS! THERE'S NO PLACE ON EARTH THAT CAN SHELTER YOU FROM THE RETRIBUTION OF--THE AVENGERS!
EASY, BILL! YOU'LL BE ALL RIGHT, FELLA! I'LL GET YOU SAFELY INSIDE, AND THEN--
THE AVENGERS WILL ASSEMBLE ONCE MORE!
BUT, WHAT OF THE EXPERIMENT! WE HAD JUST REACHED THE CRITICAL STAGE--!
THAT CAN WAIT! BUT THE SONS OF THE SERPENT CAN'T!!
MINUTES LATER, IN RESPONSE TO GOLIATH'S URGENT SUMMONS, WE FIND--
--AND THEY LEFT THIS TAUNTING SYMBOL BEHIND THEM!
I SAY WE DROP EVERYTHING AND GO AFTER THEM --BEFORE THEIR DEADLY VENOM SPREADS ANY FURTHER!
I'LL BUY THAT, BIG FELLA!
THEY'RE OWER THAN THE SNAKES THEY IMITATE!
BUT, IS THIS REALLY A JOB FOR THE AVENGERS? CAN'T THE LOCAL POLICE COPE WITH A FEW BULLY BOYS LIKE THE SERPENTS?
NO, JAN! THERE'S FAR MORE TO THIS THAN A FEW ISOLATED HOODLUM ATTACKS!
THERE'S A STRANGE, MYSTERIOUS PATTERN TO THEIR ACTIVITIES! THEY'RE RICH--WELL-ORGANIZED--AND THEY OPERATE ON A NATIONAL SCALE!
IN FACT, I'LL CONTACT COLONEL FURY, THE DIRECTOR OF SHIELD! I'LL BET THEY HAVE AN ENTIRE DOSSIER ON THE SONS OF THE SERPENT!
12

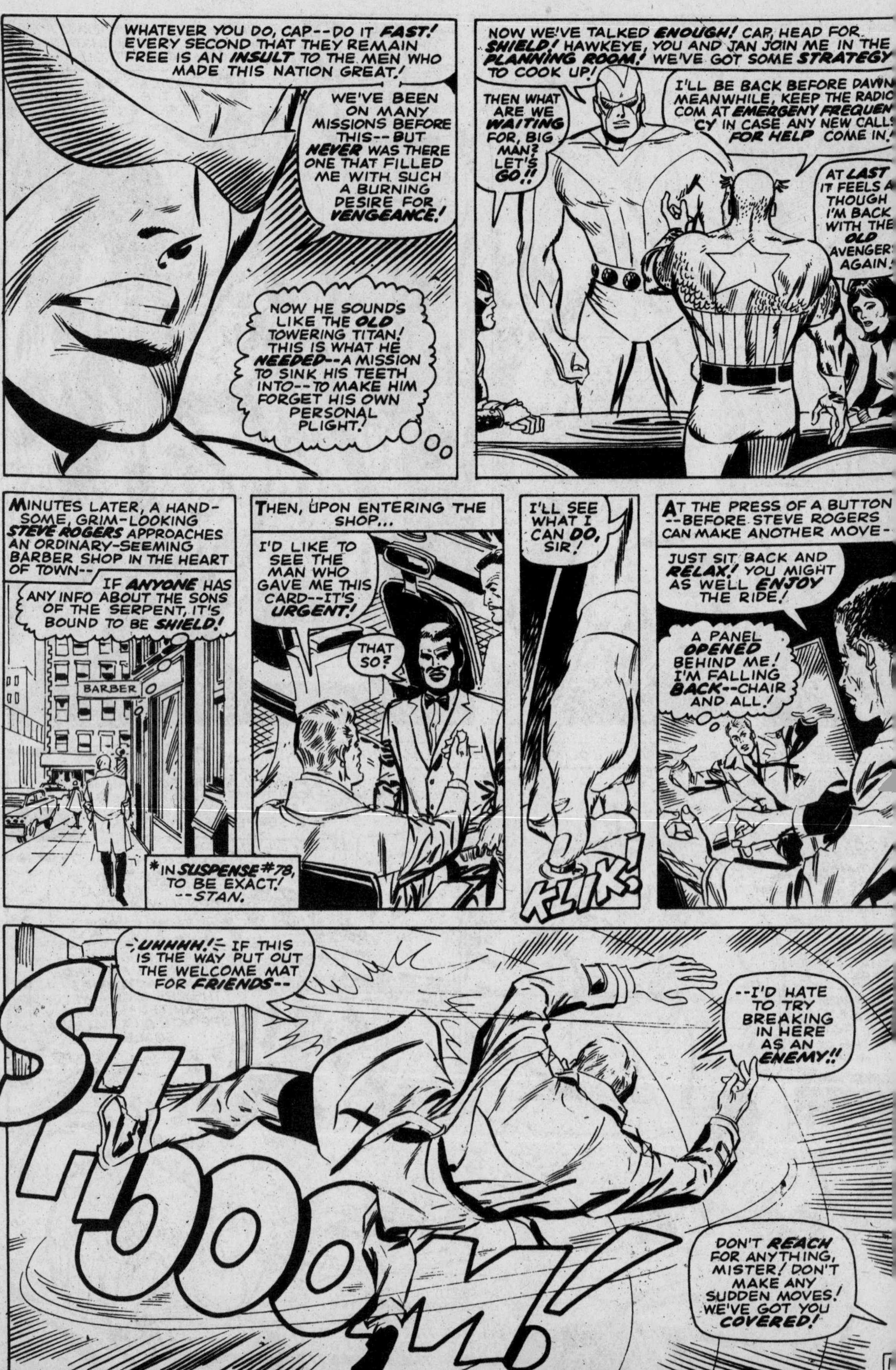

WHATEVER YOU DO, CAP--DO IT FAST! EVERY SECOND THAT THEY REMAIN FREE IS AN INSULT TO THE MEN WHO MADE THIS NATION GREAT!
WE'VE BEEN ON MANY MISSIONS BEFORE THIS--BUT NEVER WAS THERE ONE THAT FILLED ME WITH SUCH A BURNING DESIRE FOR VENGEANCE!
NOW HE SOUNDS LIKE THE OLD TOWERING TITAN! THIS IS WHAT HE NEEDED--A MISSION TO SINK HIS TEETH INTO--TO MAKE HIM FORGET HIS OWN PERSONAL PLIGHT!
NOW WE'VE TALKED ENOUGH! CAP, HEAD FOR SHIELD! HAWKEYE, YOU AND JAN JOIN ME IN THE PLANNING ROOM! WE'VE GOT SOME STRATEGY TO COOK UP!
THEN WHAT ARE WE WAITING FOR, BIG MAN? LET'S GO!!
I'LL BE BACK BEFORE DAWN! MEANWHILE, KEEP THE RADIO COM AT EMERGENCY FREQUENCY IN CASE ANY NEW CALLS FOR HELP COME IN!
AT LAST IT FEELS AS THOUGH I'M BACK WITH THE OLD AVENGERS AGAIN!
MINUTES LATER, A HANDSOME, GRIM-LOOKING STEVE ROGERS APPROACHES AN ORDINARY-SEEMING BARBER SHOP IN THE HEART OF TOWN--
IF ANYONE HAS ANY INFO ABOUT THE SONS OF THE SERPENT, IT'S BOUND TO BE SHIELD!
BARBER
*IN SUSPENSE #78, TO BE EXACT! --STAN.
THEN, UPON ENTERING THE SHOP...
I'D LIKE TO SEE THE MAN WHO GAVE ME THIS CARD--IT'S URGENT!
THAT SO?
I'LL SEE WHAT I CAN DO, SIR!
KLIK!
AT THE PRESS OF A BUTTON --BEFORE STEVE ROGERS CAN MAKE ANOTHER MOVE--
JUST SIT BACK AND RELAX! YOU MIGHT AS WELL ENJOY THE RIDE!
A PANEL OPENED BEHIND ME! I'M FALLING BACK--CHAIR AND ALL!
UHNHH!- IF THIS IS THE WAY PUT OUT THE WELCOME MAT FOR FRIENDS--
--I'D HATE TO TRY BREAKING IN HERE AS AN ENEMY!!
SHOOOM!
DON'T REACH FOR ANYTHING, MISTER! DON'T MAKE ANY SUDDEN MOVES! WE'VE GOT YOU COVERED!

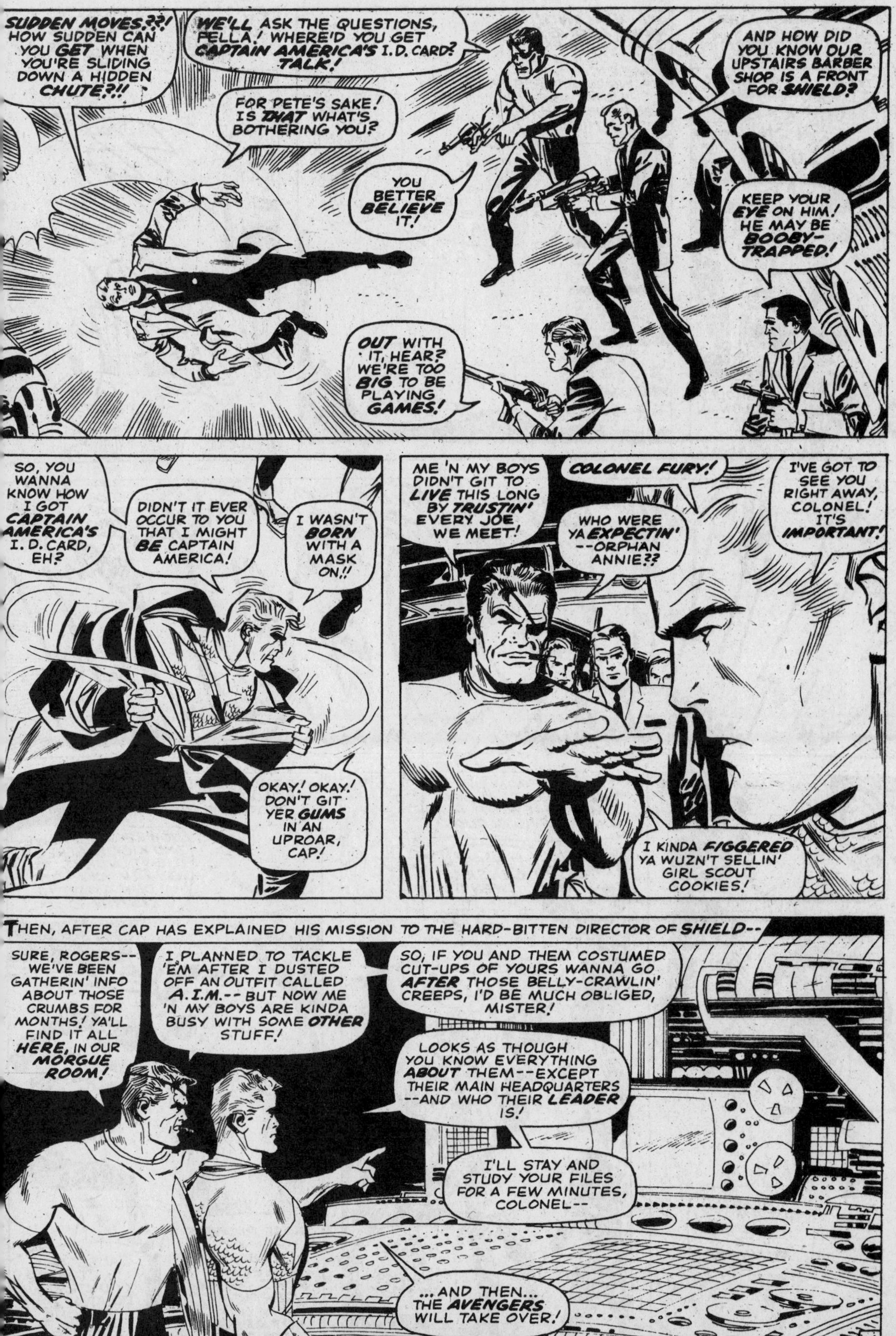
SUDDEN MOVES??! HOW SUDDEN CAN YOU GET WHEN YOU'RE SLIDING DOWN A HIDDEN CHUTE?!!
WE'LL ASK THE QUESTIONS, FELLA! WHERE'D YOU GET CAPTAIN AMERICA'S I.D. CARD? TALK!
FOR PETE'S SAKE! IS THAT WHAT'S BOTHERING YOU?
YOU BETTER BELIEVE IT!
AND HOW DID YOU KNOW OUR UPSTAIRS BARBER SHOP IS A FRONT FOR SHIELD?
KEEP YOUR EYE ON HIM! HE MAY BE BOOBY-TRAPPED!
OUT WITH IT, HEAR? WE'RE TOO BIG TO BE PLAYING GAMES!
SO, YOU WANNA KNOW HOW I GOT CAPTAIN AMERICA'S I. D. CARD, EH?
DIDN'T IT EVER OCCUR TO YOU THAT I MIGHT BE CAPTAIN AMERICA!
I WASN'T BORN WITH A MASK ON!!
OKAY! OKAY! DON'T GIT YER GUMS IN AN UPROAR, CAP!
ME 'N MY BOYS DIDN'T GIT TO LIVE THIS LONG BY TRUSTIN' EVERY JOE WE MEET!
COLONEL FURY!
WHO WERE YA EXPECTIN' --ORPHAN ANNIE??
I'VE GOT TO SEE YOU RIGHT AWAY, COLONEL! IT'S IMPORTANT!
I KINDA FIGGERED YA WUZN'T SELLIN' GIRL SCOUT COOKIES!
THEN, AFTER CAP HAS EXPLAINED HIS MISSION TO THE HARD-BITTEN DIRECTOR OF SHIELD--
SURE, ROGERS-- WE'VE BEEN GATHERIN' INFO ABOUT THOSE CRUMBS FOR MONTHS! YA'LL FIND IT ALL HERE, IN OUR MORGUE ROOM!
I PLANNED TO TACKLE 'EM AFTER I DUSTED OFF AN OUTFIT CALLED A.I.M.-- BUT NOW ME 'N MY BOYS ARE KINDA BUSY WITH SOME OTHER STUFF!
SO, IF YOU AND THEM COSTUMED CUT-UPS OF YOURS WANNA GO AFTER THOSE BELLY-CRAWLIN' CREEPS, I'D BE MUCH OBLIGED, MISTER!
LOOKS AS THOUGH YOU KNOW EVERYTHING ABOUT THEM--EXCEPT THEIR MAIN HEADQUARTERS --AND WHO THEIR LEADER IS!
I'LL STAY AND STUDY YOUR FILES FOR A FEW MINUTES, COLONEL--
...AND THEN... THE AVENGERS WILL TAKE OVER!
14

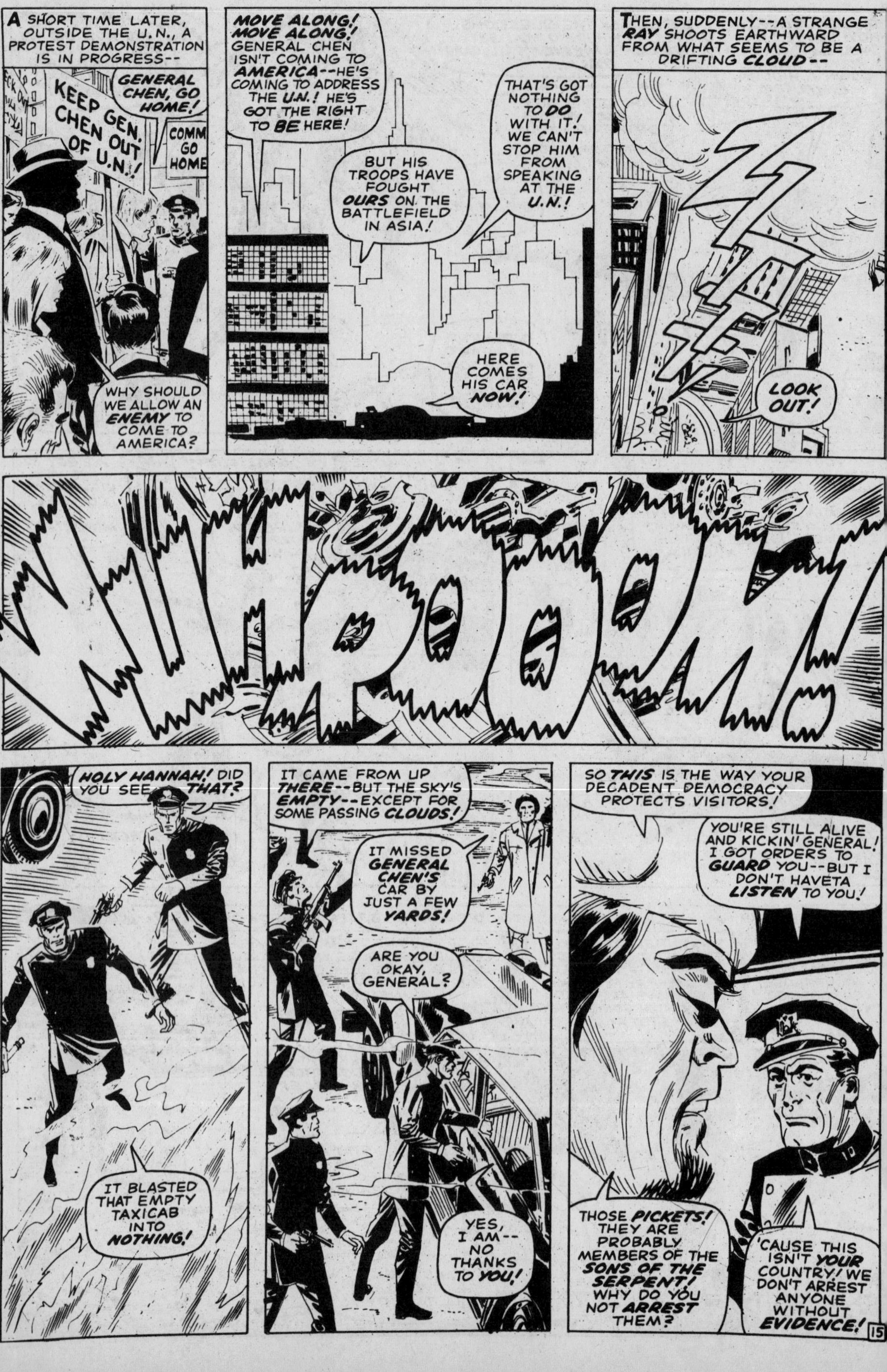

A SHORT TIME LATER, OUTSIDE THE U.N., A PROTEST DEMONSTRATION IS IN PROGRESS--
KEEP GEN. CHEN OUT OF U.N.!
GENERAL CHEN, GO HOME!
COMM GO HOME
WHY SHOULD WE ALLOW AN ENEMY TO COME TO AMERICA?
MOVE ALONG! MOVE ALONG! GENERAL CHEN ISN'T COMING TO AMERICA--HE'S COMING TO ADDRESS THE U.N.! HE'S GOT THE RIGHT TO BE HERE!
BUT HIS TROOPS HAVE FOUGHT OURS ON THE BATTLEFIELD IN ASIA!
THAT'S GOT NOTHING TO DO WITH IT! WE CAN'T STOP HIM FROM SPEAKING AT THE U.N.!
HERE COMES HIS CAR NOW!
THEN, SUDDENLY--A STRANGE RAY SHOOTS EARTHWARD FROM WHAT SEEMS TO BE A DRIFTING CLOUD--
ZZZT
LOOK OUT!
WHROOM!
HOLY HANNAH! DID YOU SEE THAT?
IT BLASTED THAT EMPTY TAXICAB INTO NOTHING!
IT CAME FROM UP THERE--BUT THE SKY'S EMPTY--EXCEPT FOR SOME PASSING CLOUDS!
IT MISSED GENERAL CHEN'S CAR BY JUST A FEW YARDS!
ARE YOU OKAY, GENERAL?
YES, I AM--NO THANKS TO YOU!
SO THIS IS THE WAY YOUR DECADENT DEMOCRACY PROTECTS VISITORS!
YOU'RE STILL ALIVE AND KICKIN' GENERAL! I GOT ORDERS TO GUARD YOU--BUT I DON'T HAVETA LISTEN TO YOU!
THOSE PICKETS! THEY ARE PROBABLY MEMBERS OF THE SONS OF THE SERPENT! WHY DO YOU NOT ARREST THEM?
'CAUSE THIS ISN'T YOUR COUNTRY! WE DON'T ARREST ANYONE WITHOUT EVIDENCE!

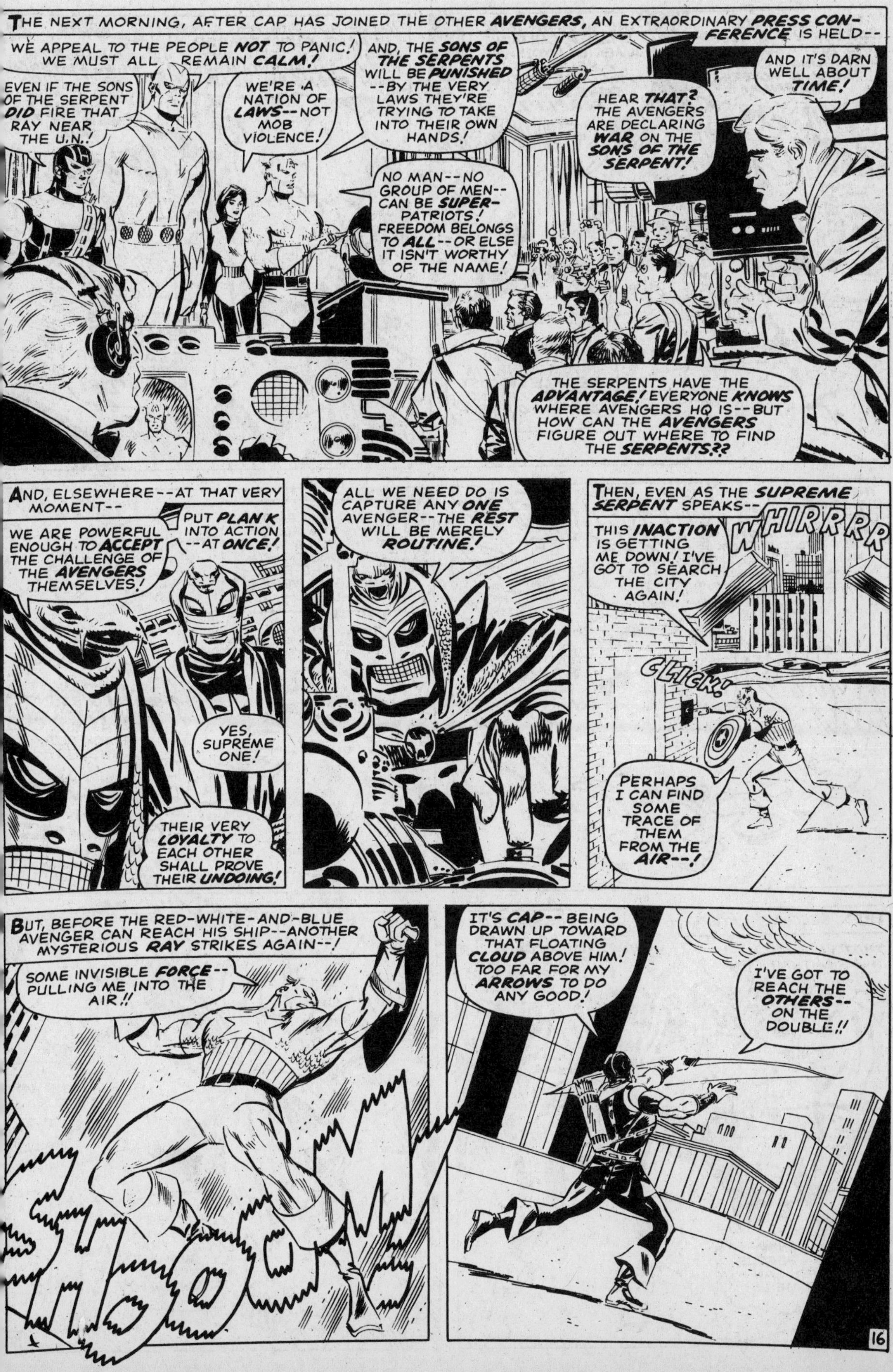
THE NEXT MORNING, AFTER CAP HAS JOINED THE OTHER AVENGERS, AN EXTRAORDINARY PRESS CONFERENCE IS HELD--
WE APPEAL TO THE PEOPLE NOT TO PANIC! WE MUST ALL REMAIN CALM!
EVEN IF THE SONS OF THE SERPENT DID FIRE THAT RAY NEAR THE U.N.!
WE'RE A NATION OF LAWS--NOT MOB VIOLENCE!
AND, THE SONS OF THE SERPENTS WILL BE PUNISHED --BY THE VERY LAWS THEY'RE TRYING TO TAKE INTO THEIR OWN HANDS!
NO MAN--NO GROUP OF MEN--CAN BE SUPER-PATRIOTS! FREEDOM BELONGS TO ALL--OR ELSE IT ISN'T WORTHY OF THE NAME!
HEAR THAT? THE AVENGERS ARE DECLARING WAR ON THE SONS OF THE SERPENT!
AND IT'S DARN WELL ABOUT TIME!
THE SERPENTS HAVE THE ADVANTAGE! EVERYONE KNOWS WHERE AVENGERS HQ IS--BUT HOW CAN THE AVENGERS FIGURE OUT WHERE TO FIND THE SERPENTS??
AND, ELSEWHERE--AT THAT VERY MOMENT--
WE ARE POWERFUL ENOUGH TO ACCEPT THE CHALLENGE OF THE AVENGERS THEMSELVES!
PUT PLAN K INTO ACTION --AT ONCE!
YES, SUPREME ONE!
THEIR VERY LOYALTY TO EACH OTHER SHALL PROVE THEIR UNDOING!
ALL WE NEED DO IS CAPTURE ANY ONE AVENGER--THE REST WILL BE MERELY ROUTINE!
THEN, EVEN AS THE SUPREME SERPENT SPEAKS--
THIS INACTION IS GETTING ME DOWN! I'VE GOT TO SEARCH THE CITY AGAIN!
WHIRRRR
CLICK!
PERHAPS I CAN FIND SOME TRACE OF THEM FROM THE AIR--!
BUT, BEFORE THE RED-WHITE-AND-BLUE AVENGER CAN REACH HIS SHIP--ANOTHER MYSTERIOUS RAY STRIKES AGAIN--!
SOME INVISIBLE FORCE--PULLING ME INTO THE AIR!!
SHOOM
IT'S CAP--BEING DRAWN UP TOWARD THAT FLOATING CLOUD ABOVE HIM! TOO FAR FOR MY ARROWS TO DO ANY GOOD!
I'VE GOT TO REACH THE OTHERS--ON THE DOUBLE!!
16

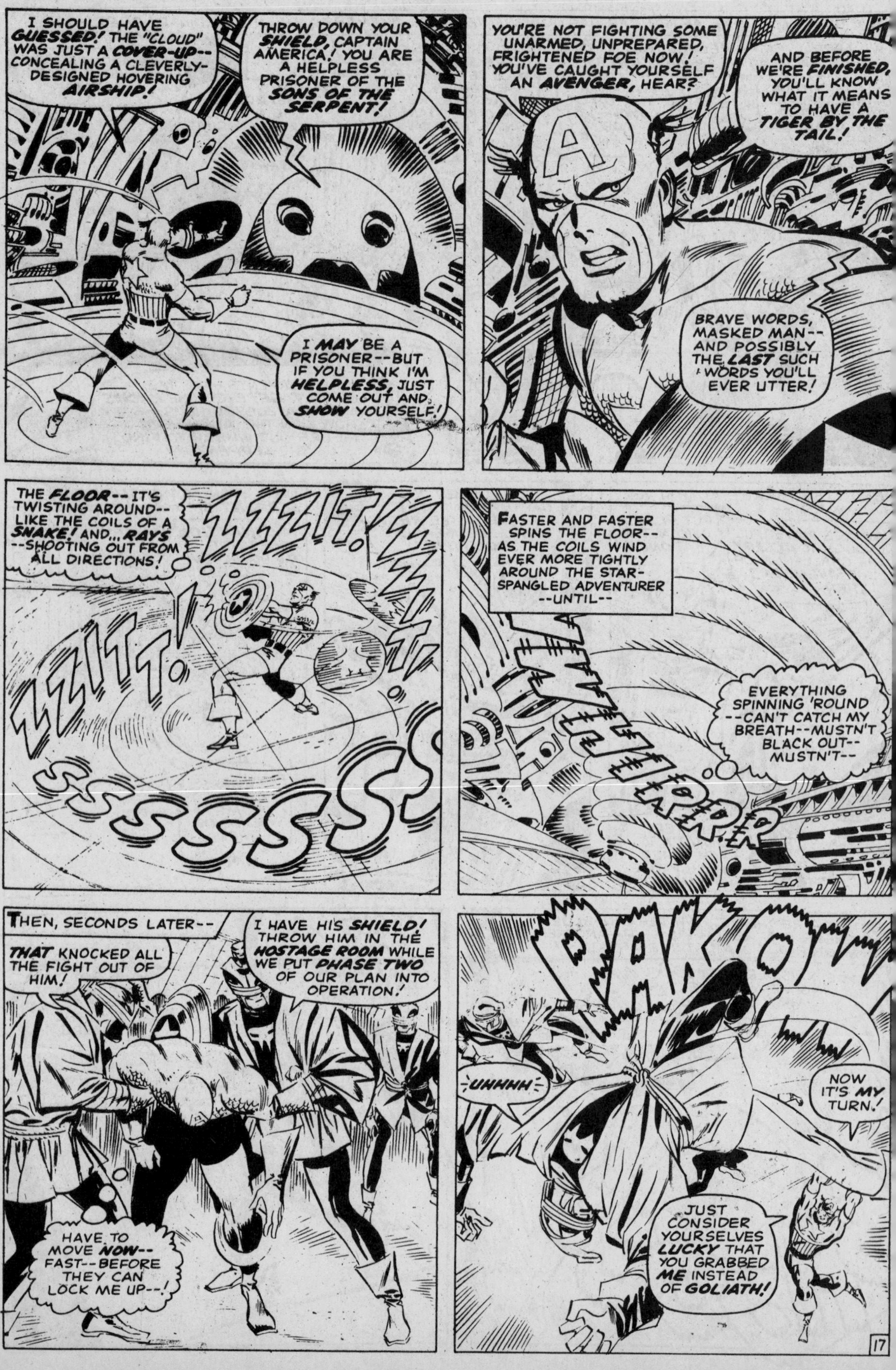

I SHOULD HAVE GUESSED! THE "CLOUD" WAS JUST A COVER-UP-- CONCEALING A CLEVERLY-DESIGNED HOVERING AIRSHIP!
THROW DOWN YOUR SHIELD, CAPTAIN AMERICA! YOU ARE A HELPLESS PRISONER OF THE SONS OF THE SERPENT!
I MAY BE A PRISONER--BUT IF YOU THINK I'M HELPLESS, JUST COME OUT AND SHOW YOURSELF!
YOU'RE NOT FIGHTING SOME UNARMED, UNPREPARED, FRIGHTENED FOE NOW! YOU'VE CAUGHT YOURSELF AN AVENGER, HEAR?
AND BEFORE WE'RE FINISHED, YOU'LL KNOW WHAT IT MEANS TO HAVE A TIGER BY THE TAIL!
BRAVE WORDS, MASKED MAN-- AND POSSIBLY THE LAST SUCH WORDS YOU'LL EVER UTTER!
THE FLOOR--IT'S TWISTING AROUND-- LIKE THE COILS OF A SNAKE! AND... RAYS --SHOOTING OUT FROM ALL DIRECTIONS!
ZZZIT!
ZZIT!
ZZIT!
ZZIT!
SSSSSS
FASTER AND FASTER SPINS THE FLOOR-- AS THE COILS WIND EVER MORE TIGHTLY AROUND THE STAR-SPANGLED ADVENTURER --UNTIL--
WHIRRRR
EVERYTHING SPINNING 'ROUND --CAN'T CATCH MY BREATH--MUSTN'T BLACK OUT-- MUSTN'T--
THEN, SECONDS LATER--
THAT KNOCKED ALL THE FIGHT OUT OF HIM!
I HAVE HIS SHIELD! THROW HIM IN THE HOSTAGE ROOM WHILE WE PUT PHASE TWO OF OUR PLAN INTO OPERATION!
HAVE TO MOVE NOW-- FAST--BEFORE THEY CAN LOCK ME UP--!
PAKOW
UNHHH
NOW IT'S MY TURN!
JUST CONSIDER YOURSELVES LUCKY THAT YOU GRABBED ME INSTEAD OF GOLIATH!

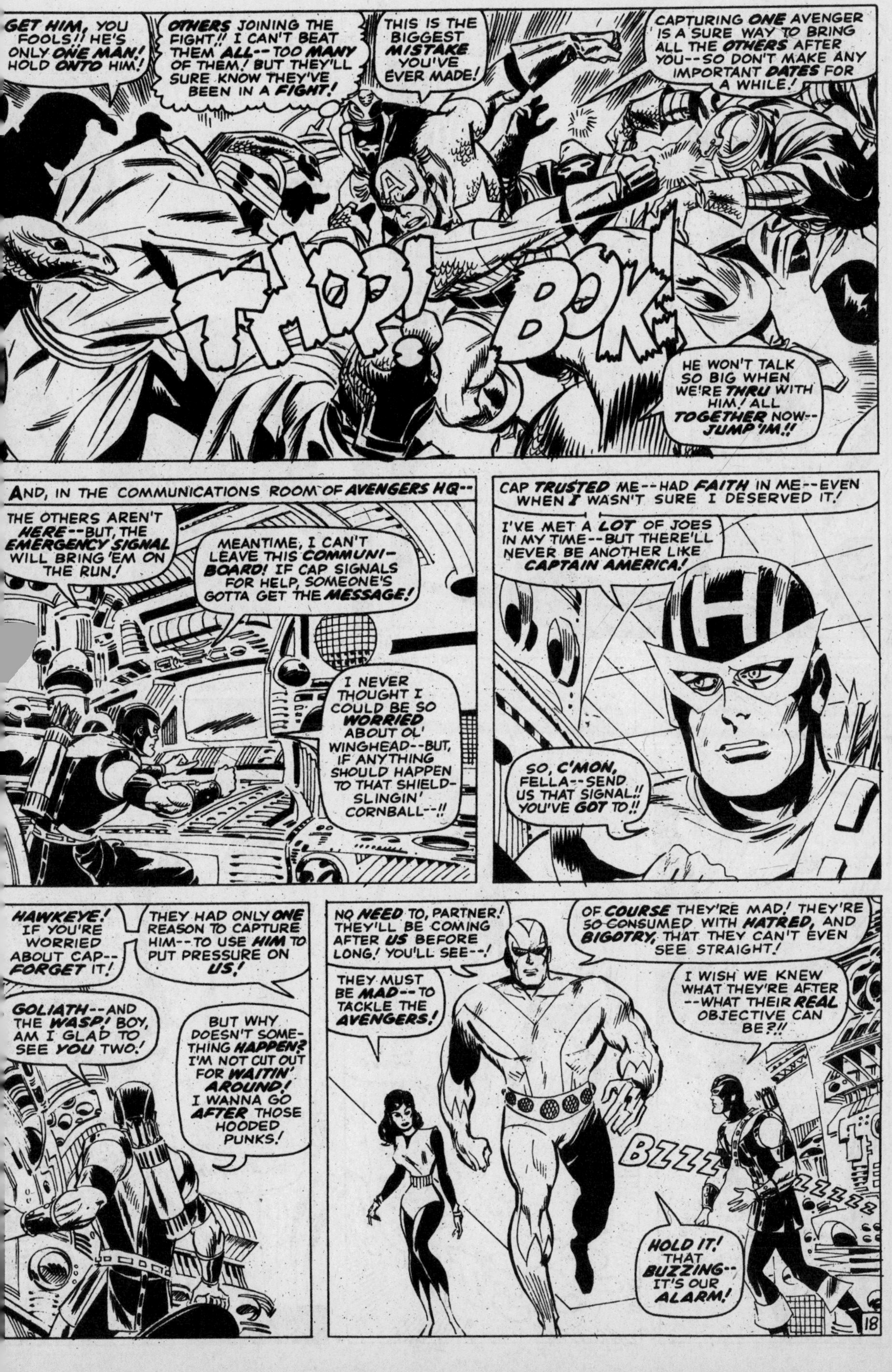
GET HIM, YOU FOOLS!! HE'S ONLY ONE MAN! HOLD ONTO HIM!
OTHERS JOINING THE FIGHT!! I CAN'T BEAT THEM ALL--TOO MANY OF THEM! BUT THEY'LL SURE KNOW THEY'VE BEEN IN A FIGHT!
THIS IS THE BIGGEST MISTAKE YOU'VE EVER MADE!
CAPTURING ONE AVENGER IS A SURE WAY TO BRING ALL THE OTHERS AFTER YOU--SO DON'T MAKE ANY IMPORTANT DATES FOR A WHILE!
THOP!
BOK!
HE WON'T TALK SO BIG WHEN WE'RE THRU WITH HIM! ALL TOGETHER NOW--JUMP 'IM!!
AND, IN THE COMMUNICATIONS ROOM OF AVENGERS HQ--
THE OTHERS AREN'T HERE--BUT, THE EMERGENCY SIGNAL WILL BRING 'EM ON THE RUN!
MEANTIME, I CAN'T LEAVE THIS COMMUNI-BOARD! IF CAP SIGNALS FOR HELP, SOMEONE'S GOTTA GET THE MESSAGE!
I NEVER THOUGHT I COULD BE SO WORRIED ABOUT OL' WINGHEAD--BUT, IF ANYTHING SHOULD HAPPEN TO THAT SHIELD-SLINGIN' CORNBALL--!!
CAP TRUSTED ME--HAD FAITH IN ME--EVEN WHEN I WASN'T SURE I DESERVED IT!
I'VE MET A LOT OF JOES IN MY TIME--BUT THERE'LL NEVER BE ANOTHER LIKE CAPTAIN AMERICA!
SO, C'MON, FELLA--SEND US THAT SIGNAL!! YOU'VE GOT TO!!
HAWKEYE! IF YOU'RE WORRIED ABOUT CAP--FORGET IT!
THEY HAD ONLY ONE REASON TO CAPTURE HIM--TO USE HIM TO PUT PRESSURE ON US!
GOLIATH--AND THE WASP! BOY, AM I GLAD TO SEE YOU TWO!
BUT WHY DOESN'T SOMETHING HAPPEN? I'M NOT CUT OUT FOR WAITIN' AROUND! I WANNA GO AFTER THOSE HOODED PUNKS!
NO NEED TO, PARTNER! THEY'LL BE COMING AFTER US BEFORE LONG! YOU'LL SEE--!
THEY MUST BE MAD--TO TACKLE THE AVENGERS!
OF COURSE THEY'RE MAD! THEY'RE SO CONSUMED WITH HATRED, AND BIGOTRY, THAT THEY CAN'T EVEN SEE STRAIGHT!
I WISH WE KNEW WHAT THEY'RE AFTER--WHAT THEIR REAL OBJECTIVE CAN BE?!!
BZZZZ
ZZZZZZ
HOLD IT! THAT BUZZING--IT'S OUR ALARM!
18

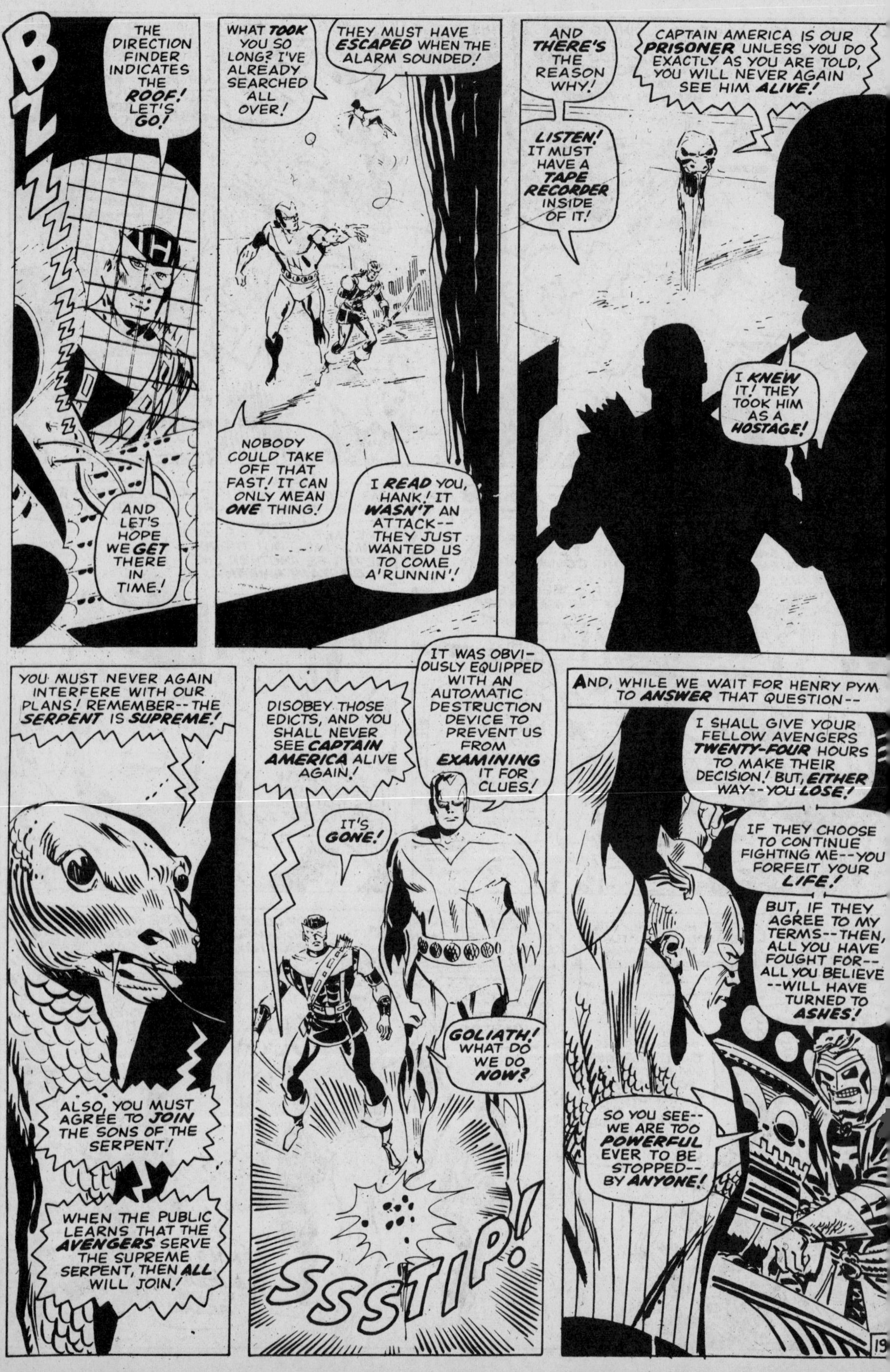
B Z Z Z Z Z Z Z Z Z Z
THE DIRECTION FINDER INDICATES THE ROOF! LET'S GO!
AND LET'S HOPE WE GET THERE IN TIME!
WHAT TOOK YOU SO LONG? I'VE ALREADY SEARCHED ALL OVER!
THEY MUST HAVE ESCAPED WHEN THE ALARM SOUNDED!
NOBODY COULD TAKE OFF THAT FAST! IT CAN ONLY MEAN ONE THING!
I READ YOU, HANK! IT WASN'T AN ATTACK-- THEY JUST WANTED US TO COME A'RUNNIN'!
AND THERE'S THE REASON WHY!
CAPTAIN AMERICA IS OUR PRISONER UNLESS YOU DO EXACTLY AS YOU ARE TOLD, YOU WILL NEVER AGAIN SEE HIM ALIVE!
LISTEN! IT MUST HAVE A TAPE RECORDER INSIDE OF IT!
I KNEW IT! THEY TOOK HIM AS A HOSTAGE!
YOU MUST NEVER AGAIN INTERFERE WITH OUR PLANS! REMEMBER-- THE SERPENT IS SUPREME!
ALSO, YOU MUST AGREE TO JOIN THE SONS OF THE SERPENT!
WHEN THE PUBLIC LEARNS THAT THE AVENGERS SERVE THE SUPREME SERPENT, THEN ALL WILL JOIN!
DISOBEY THOSE EDICTS, AND YOU SHALL NEVER SEE CAPTAIN AMERICA ALIVE AGAIN!
IT WAS OBVIOUSLY EQUIPPED WITH AN AUTOMATIC DESTRUCTION DEVICE TO PREVENT US FROM EXAMINING IT FOR CLUES!
IT'S GONE!
GOLIATH! WHAT DO WE DO NOW?
SSSTIP!
AND, WHILE WE WAIT FOR HENRY PYM TO ANSWER THAT QUESTION--
I SHALL GIVE YOUR FELLOW AVENGERS TWENTY-FOUR HOURS TO MAKE THEIR DECISION! BUT, EITHER WAY--YOU LOSE!
IF THEY CHOOSE TO CONTINUE FIGHTING ME--YOU FORFEIT YOUR LIFE!
BUT, IF THEY AGREE TO MY TERMS--THEN, ALL YOU HAVE FOUGHT FOR--ALL YOU BELIEVE--WILL HAVE TURNED TO ASHES!
SO YOU SEE--WE ARE TOO POWERFUL EVER TO BE STOPPED--BY ANYONE!
19

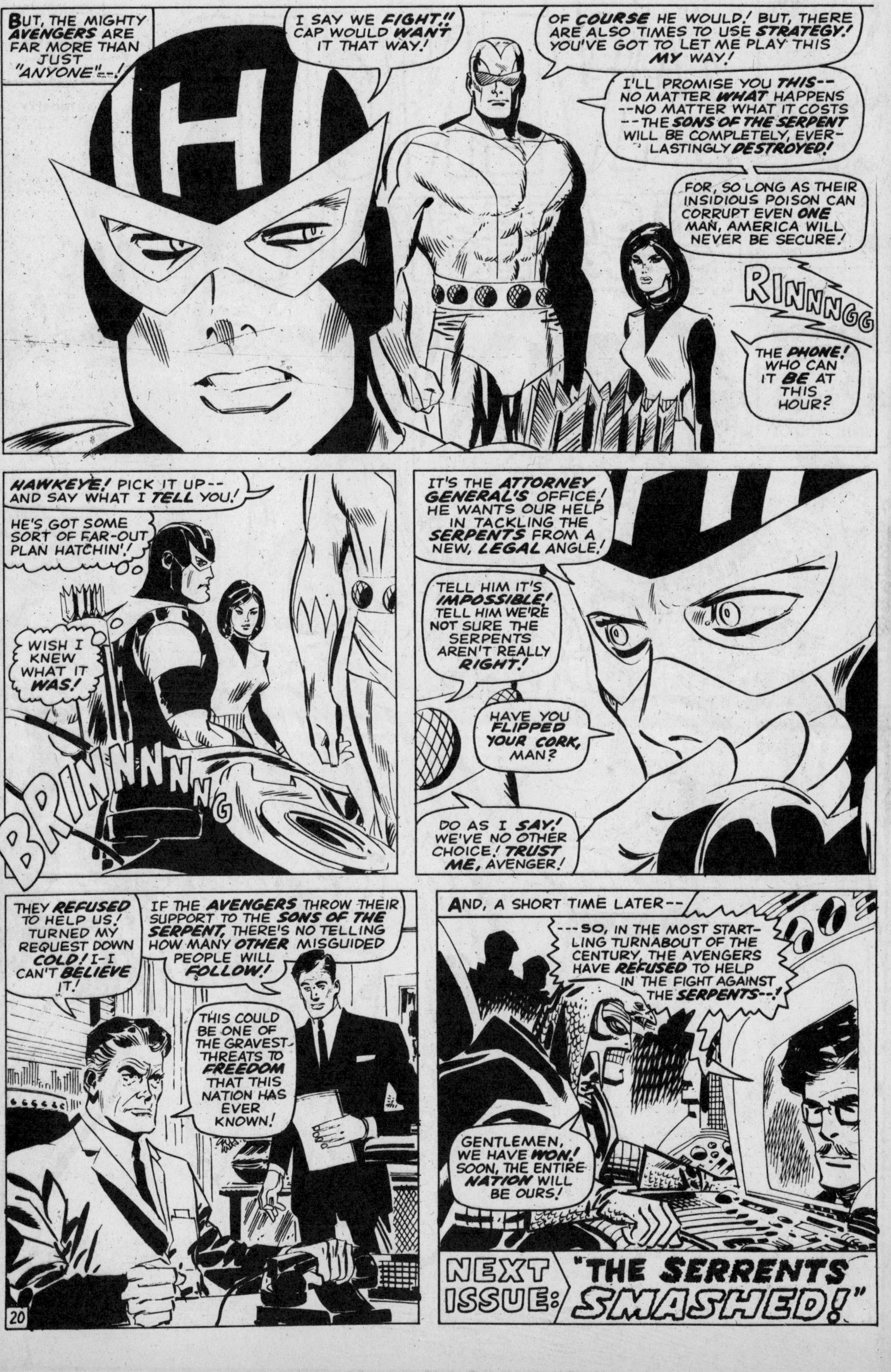

BUT, THE MIGHTY AVENGERS ARE FAR MORE THAN JUST "ANYONE"--!
I SAY WE FIGHT!! CAP WOULD WANT IT THAT WAY!
OF COURSE HE WOULD! BUT, THERE ARE ALSO TIMES TO USE STRATEGY! YOU'VE GOT TO LET ME PLAY THIS MY WAY!
I'LL PROMISE YOU THIS-- NO MATTER WHAT HAPPENS --NO MATTER WHAT IT COSTS --THE SONS OF THE SERPENT WILL BE COMPLETELY, EVER-LASTINGLY DESTROYED!
FOR, SO LONG AS THEIR INSIDIOUS POISON CAN CORRUPT EVEN ONE MAN, AMERICA WILL NEVER BE SECURE!
RINNNGG
THE PHONE! WHO CAN IT BE AT THIS HOUR?
HAWKEYE! PICK IT UP-- AND SAY WHAT I TELL YOU!
HE'S GOT SOME SORT OF FAR-OUT PLAN HATCHIN'!
WISH I KNEW WHAT IT WAS!
BRINNNNNNG
IT'S THE ATTORNEY GENERAL'S OFFICE! HE WANTS OUR HELP IN TACKLING THE SERPENTS FROM A NEW, LEGAL ANGLE!
TELL HIM IT'S IMPOSSIBLE! TELL HIM WE'RE NOT SURE THE SERPENTS AREN'T REALLY RIGHT!
HAVE YOU FLIPPED YOUR CORK, MAN?
DO AS I SAY! WE'VE NO OTHER CHOICE! TRUST ME, AVENGER!
THEY REFUSED TO HELP US! TURNED MY REQUEST DOWN COLD! I-I CAN'T BELIEVE IT!
IF THE AVENGERS THROW THEIR SUPPORT TO THE SONS OF THE SERPENT, THERE'S NO TELLING HOW MANY OTHER MISGUIDED PEOPLE WILL FOLLOW!
THIS COULD BE ONE OF THE GRAVEST THREATS TO FREEDOM THAT THIS NATION HAS EVER KNOWN!
AND, A SHORT TIME LATER--
---SO, IN THE MOST STARTLING TURNABOUT OF THE CENTURY, THE AVENGERS HAVE REFUSED TO HELP IN THE FIGHT AGAINST THE SERPENTS--!
GENTLEMEN, WE HAVE WON! SOON, THE ENTIRE NATION WILL BE OURS!
NEXT ISSUE: "THE SERRENTS SMASHED!"
20

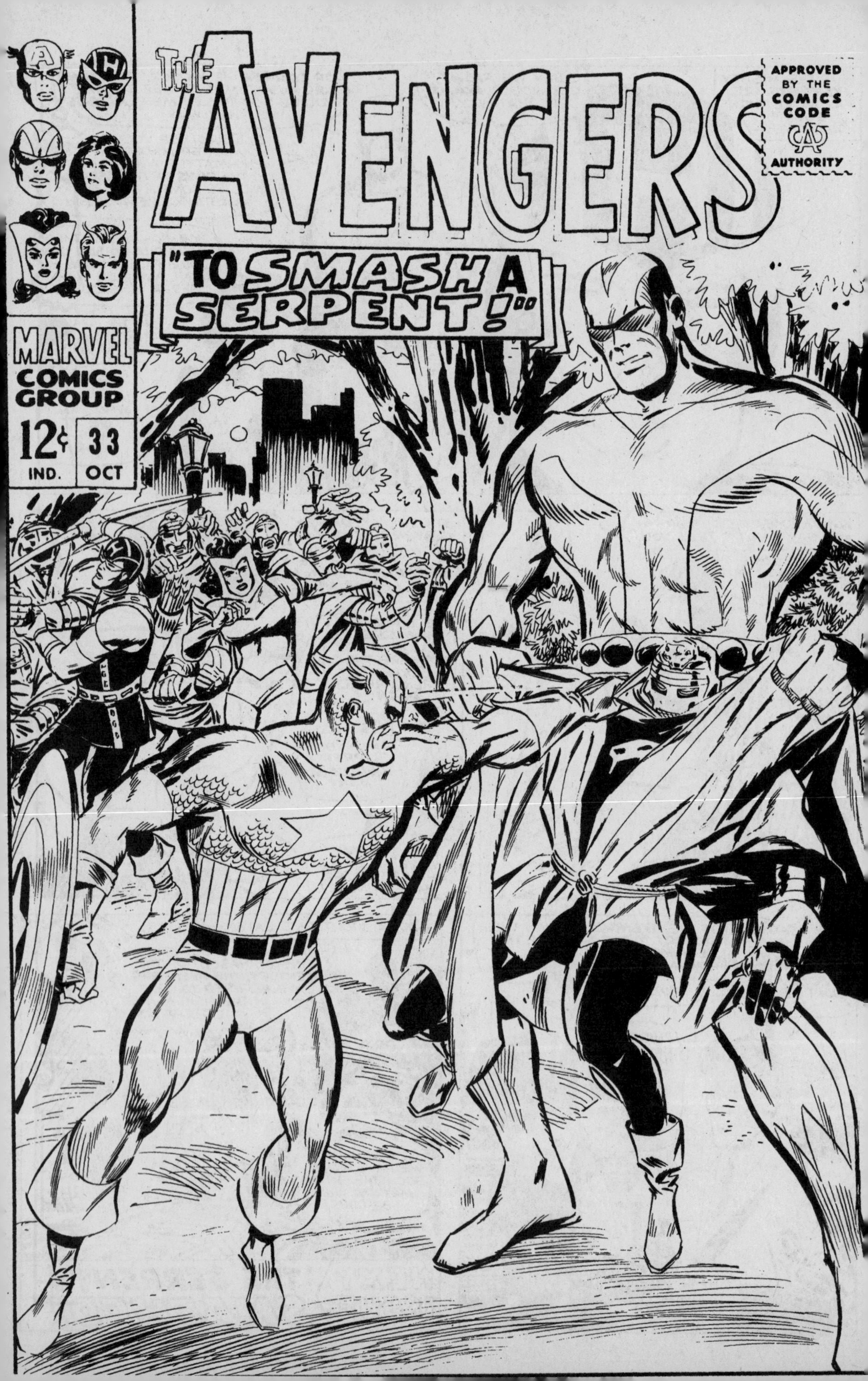
THE AVENGERS
"TO SMASH A SERPENT!"
MARVEL COMICS GROUP
12¢ IND.
33 OCT
APPROVED BY THE COMICS CODE AUTHORITY

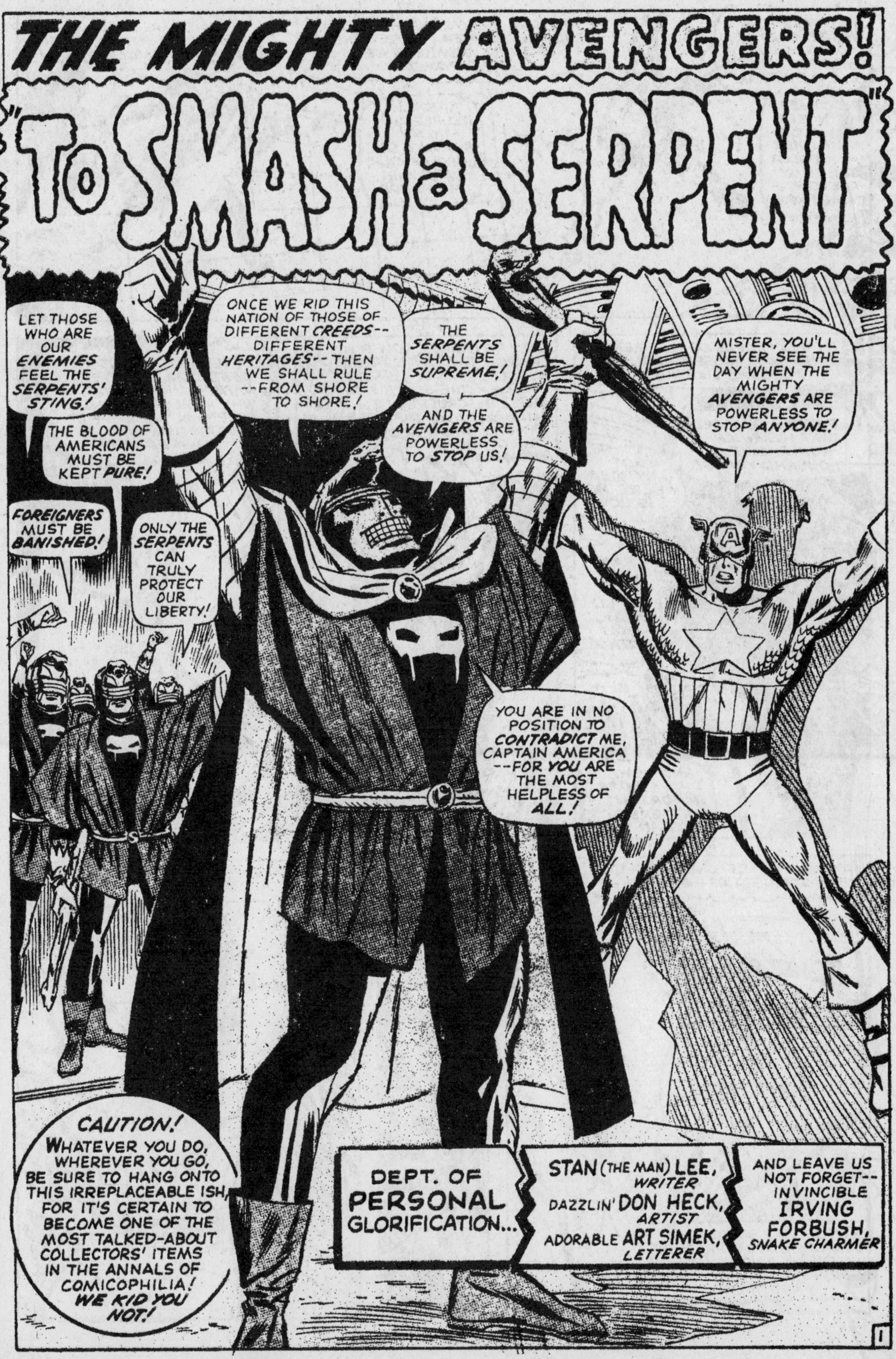
THE MIGHTY AVENGERS!
"To SMASH a SERPENT"
LET THOSE WHO ARE OUR ENEMIES FEEL THE SERPENTS' STING!
THE BLOOD OF AMERICANS MUST BE KEPT PURE!
FOREIGNERS MUST BE BANISHED!
ONLY THE SERPENTS CAN TRULY PROTECT OUR LIBERTY!
ONCE WE RID THIS NATION OF THOSE OF DIFFERENT CREEDS-- DIFFERENT HERITAGES-- THEN WE SHALL RULE --FROM SHORE TO SHORE!
THE SERPENTS SHALL BE SUPREME!
AND THE AVENGERS ARE POWERLESS TO STOP US!
MISTER, YOU'LL NEVER SEE THE DAY WHEN THE MIGHTY AVENGERS ARE POWERLESS TO STOP ANYONE!
YOU ARE IN NO POSITION TO CONTRADICT ME, CAPTAIN AMERICA --FOR YOU ARE THE MOST HELPLESS OF ALL!
CAUTION! WHATEVER YOU DO, WHEREVER YOU GO, BE SURE TO HANG ONTO THIS IRREPLACEABLE ISH, FOR IT'S CERTAIN TO BECOME ONE OF THE MOST TALKED-ABOUT COLLECTORS' ITEMS IN THE ANNALS OF COMICOPHILIA! WE KID YOU NOT!
DEPT. OF PERSONAL GLORIFICATION...
STAN (THE MAN) LEE, WRITER
DAZZLIN' DON HECK, ARTIST
ADORABLE ART SIMEK, LETTERER
AND LEAVE US NOT FORGET-- INVINCIBLE IRVING FORBUSH, SNAKE CHARMER
1

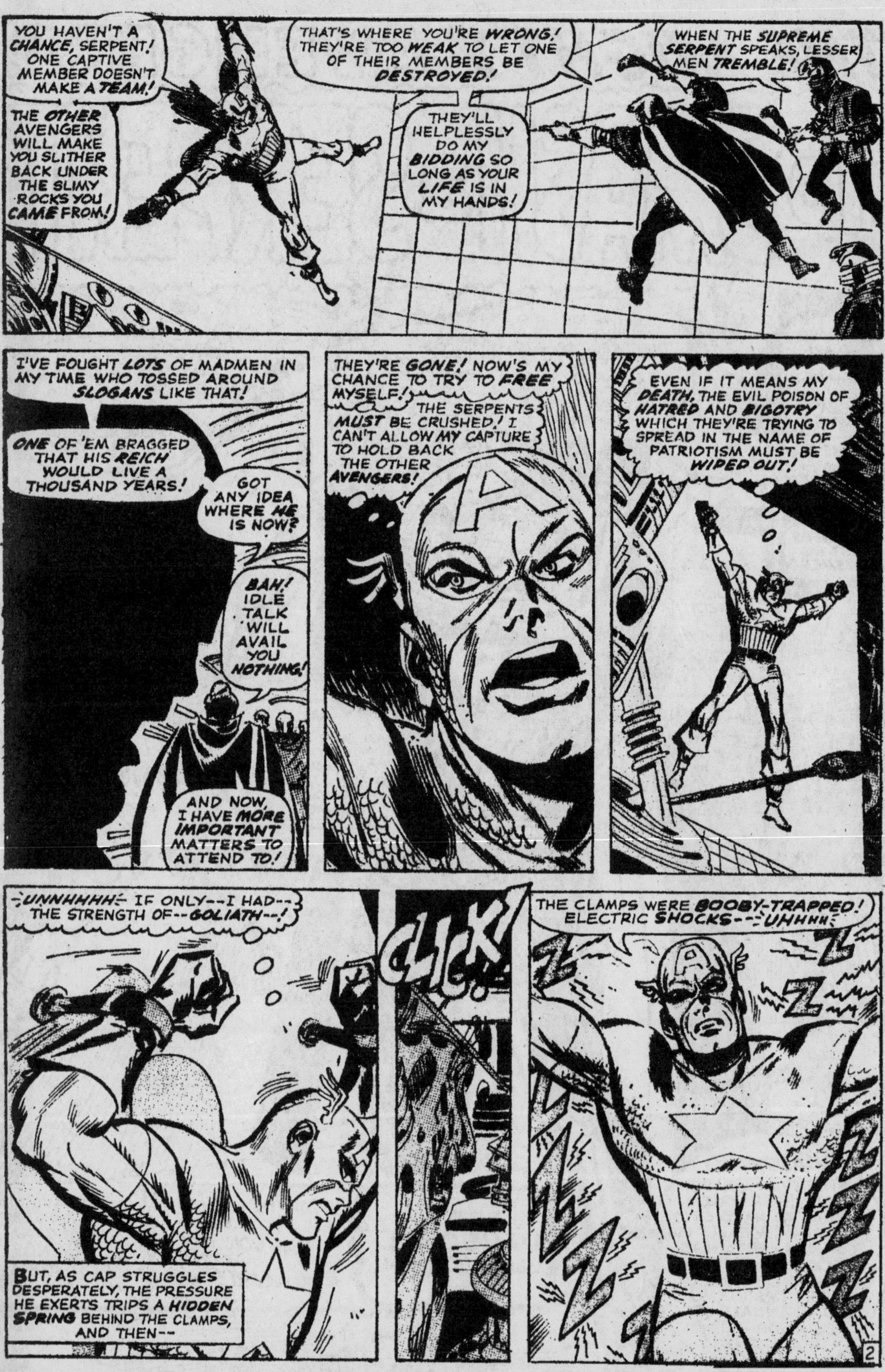

YOU HAVEN'T A CHANCE, SERPENT! ONE CAPTIVE MEMBER DOESN'T MAKE A TEAM!
THE OTHER AVENGERS WILL MAKE YOU SLITHER BACK UNDER THE SLIMY ROCKS YOU CAME FROM!
THAT'S WHERE YOU'RE WRONG! THEY'RE TOO WEAK TO LET ONE OF THEIR MEMBERS BE DESTROYED!
THEY'LL HELPLESSLY DO MY BIDDING SO LONG AS YOUR LIFE IS IN MY HANDS!
WHEN THE SUPREME SERPENT SPEAKS, LESSER MEN TREMBLE!
I'VE FOUGHT LOTS OF MADMEN IN MY TIME WHO TOSSED AROUND SLOGANS LIKE THAT!
ONE OF 'EM BRAGGED THAT HIS REICH WOULD LIVE A THOUSAND YEARS!
GOT ANY IDEA WHERE HE IS NOW?
BAH! IDLE TALK WILL AVAIL YOU NOTHING!
AND NOW, I HAVE MORE IMPORTANT MATTERS TO ATTEND TO!
THEY'RE GONE! NOW'S MY CHANCE TO TRY TO FREE MYSELF!
THE SERPENTS MUST BE CRUSHED! I CAN'T ALLOW MY CAPTURE TO HOLD BACK THE OTHER AVENGERS!
EVEN IF IT MEANS MY DEATH, THE EVIL POISON OF HATRED AND BIGOTRY WHICH THEY'RE TRYING TO SPREAD IN THE NAME OF PATRIOTISM MUST BE WIPED OUT!
UNNHHHH-- IF ONLY--I HAD-- THE STRENGTH OF--GOLIATH--!
BUT, AS CAP STRUGGLES DESPERATELY, THE PRESSURE HE EXERTS TRIPS A HIDDEN SPRING BEHIND THE CLAMPS, AND THEN--
CLICK!
THE CLAMPS WERE BOOBY-TRAPPED! ELECTRIC SHOCKS-- --UHHHH!
2

FOOL! YOU MIGHT HAVE JOINED US, AND BEEN ONE OF THE SUPREME ONES!

INSTEAD, YOU CHOSE TO CAST YOUR LOT WITH THE RABBLE! THOSE WHO DEFY US ARE TRAITORS--AND YOU, LIKE THEY, DESERVE NO MERCY!

SO SPEAKS THE SERPENT!

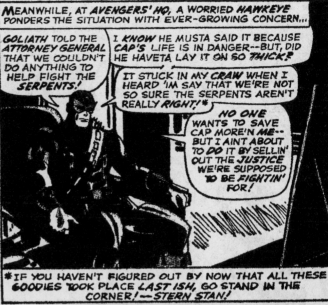

MEANWHILE, AT AVENGERS' HQ, A WORRIED HAWKEYE PONDERS THE SITUATION WITH EVER-GROWING CONCERN...

GOLIATH TOLD THE ATTORNEY GENERAL THAT WE COULDN'T DO ANYTHING TO HELP FIGHT THE SERPENTS!

I KNOW HE MUSTA SAID IT BECAUSE CAP'S LIFE IS IN DANGER--BUT, DID HE HAVETA LAY IT ON SO THICK?

IT STUCK IN MY CRAW WHEN I HEARD 'IM SAY THAT WE'RE NOT SO SURE THE SERPENTS AREN'T REALLY RIGHT!*

NO ONE WANTS TO SAVE CAP MORE'N ME--BUT I AIN'T ABOUT TO DO IT BY SELLIN' OUT THE JUSTICE WE'RE SUPPOSED TO BE FIGHTIN' FOR!

*IF YOU HAVEN'T FIGURED OUT BY NOW THAT ALL THESE GOODIES TOOK PLACE LAST ISH, GO STAND IN THE CORNER!--STERN STAN!

OUR ALARM BUZZER!

IT'S ABOUT TIME--NOW--MEBBE THERE'LL BE A CHANCE FOR A FELLA TO GET INTO ACTION!

I DUNNO WHERE HIGH-POCKETS AND THE WASP ARE--BUT IT DOESN'T MATTER--

NO MATTER WHO'S OUT THERE, OL' HAWKEYE'LL BE ABLE TO HANDLE 'EM!

I'M IN LUCK! IT'S A COUPLE'A THOSE LOW-DOWN, SCURVY, MURDEROUS COWARDS!

I CAN ALMOST SMELL 'EM FROM HERE!

HOLD IT, CREEPS! ONE FALSE MOVE--EVEN ONE MISERABLE MISS--AND YOU'RE DONE FOR!

HAWKEYE!

WHO WERE YA EXPECTIN'--YOGI BEAR??

BUT, SUDDENLY--

NOW, NOW, PARTNER--THAT'S NO WAY TO TREAT GUESTS! WHERE ARE YOUR MANNERS?

GOLIATH! HAVE YA POPPED YOUR CORK? WHAT IN BLAZES DO YA THINK YOU'RE DOIN'?!

SAVING YOU FROM MAKING A HASTY MISTAKE, CHUM! THEY WERE HERE TO SEE ME!

WE CAME TO PRESENT THE DEMANDS OF THE SUPREME SERPENT!

YOU WILL DO WELL TO REMEMBER--IF WE ARE INTERFERED WITH CAPTAIN AMERICA WILL DIE! YOU DARE NOT FIGHT US!

3

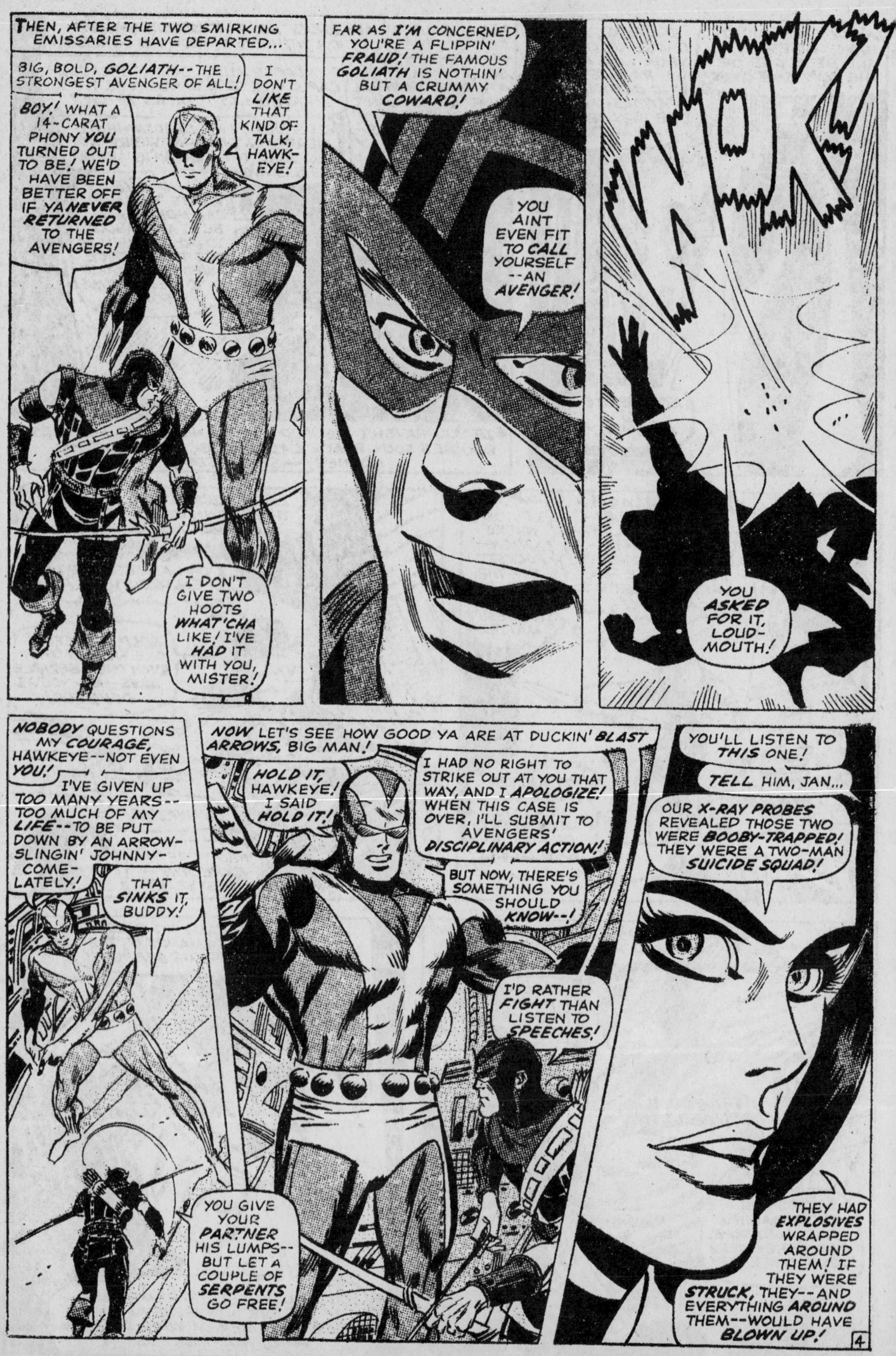
THEN, AFTER THE TWO SMIRKING EMISSARIES HAVE DEPARTED...
BIG, BOLD, GOLIATH--THE STRONGEST AVENGER OF ALL!
BOY! WHAT A 14-CARAT PHONY YOU TURNED OUT TO BE! WE'D HAVE BEEN BETTER OFF IF YA NEVER RETURNED TO THE AVENGERS!
I DON'T LIKE THAT KIND OF TALK, HAWKEYE!
I DON'T GIVE TWO HOOTS WHAT'CHA LIKE! I'VE HAD IT WITH YOU, MISTER!
FAR AS I'M CONCERNED, YOU'RE A FLIPPIN' FRAUD! THE FAMOUS GOLIATH IS NOTHIN' BUT A CRUMMY COWARD!
YOU AINT EVEN FIT TO CALL YOURSELF --AN AVENGER!
WOK!
YOU ASKED FOR IT, LOUD-MOUTH!
NOBODY QUESTIONS MY COURAGE, HAWKEYE--NOT EVEN YOU!
I'VE GIVEN UP TOO MANY YEARS--TOO MUCH OF MY LIFE--TO BE PUT DOWN BY AN ARROW-SLINGIN' JOHNNY-COME-LATELY!
THAT SINKS IT, BUDDY!
NOW LET'S SEE HOW GOOD YA ARE AT DUCKIN' BLAST ARROWS, BIG MAN!
HOLD IT, HAWKEYE! I SAID HOLD IT!
I HAD NO RIGHT TO STRIKE OUT AT YOU THAT WAY, AND I APOLOGIZE! WHEN THIS CASE IS OVER, I'LL SUBMIT TO AVENGERS' DISCIPLINARY ACTION!
BUT NOW, THERE'S SOMETHING YOU SHOULD KNOW--!
I'D RATHER FIGHT THAN LISTEN TO SPEECHES!
YOU GIVE YOUR PARTNER HIS LUMPS--BUT LET A COUPLE OF SERPENTS GO FREE!
YOU'LL LISTEN TO THIS ONE!
TELL HIM, JAN...
OUR X-RAY PROBES REVEALED THOSE TWO WERE BOOBY-TRAPPED! THEY WERE A TWO-MAN SUICIDE SQUAD!
THEY HAD EXPLOSIVES WRAPPED AROUND THEM! IF THEY WERE STRUCK, THEY--AND EVERYTHING AROUND THEM--WOULD HAVE BLOWN UP!
4

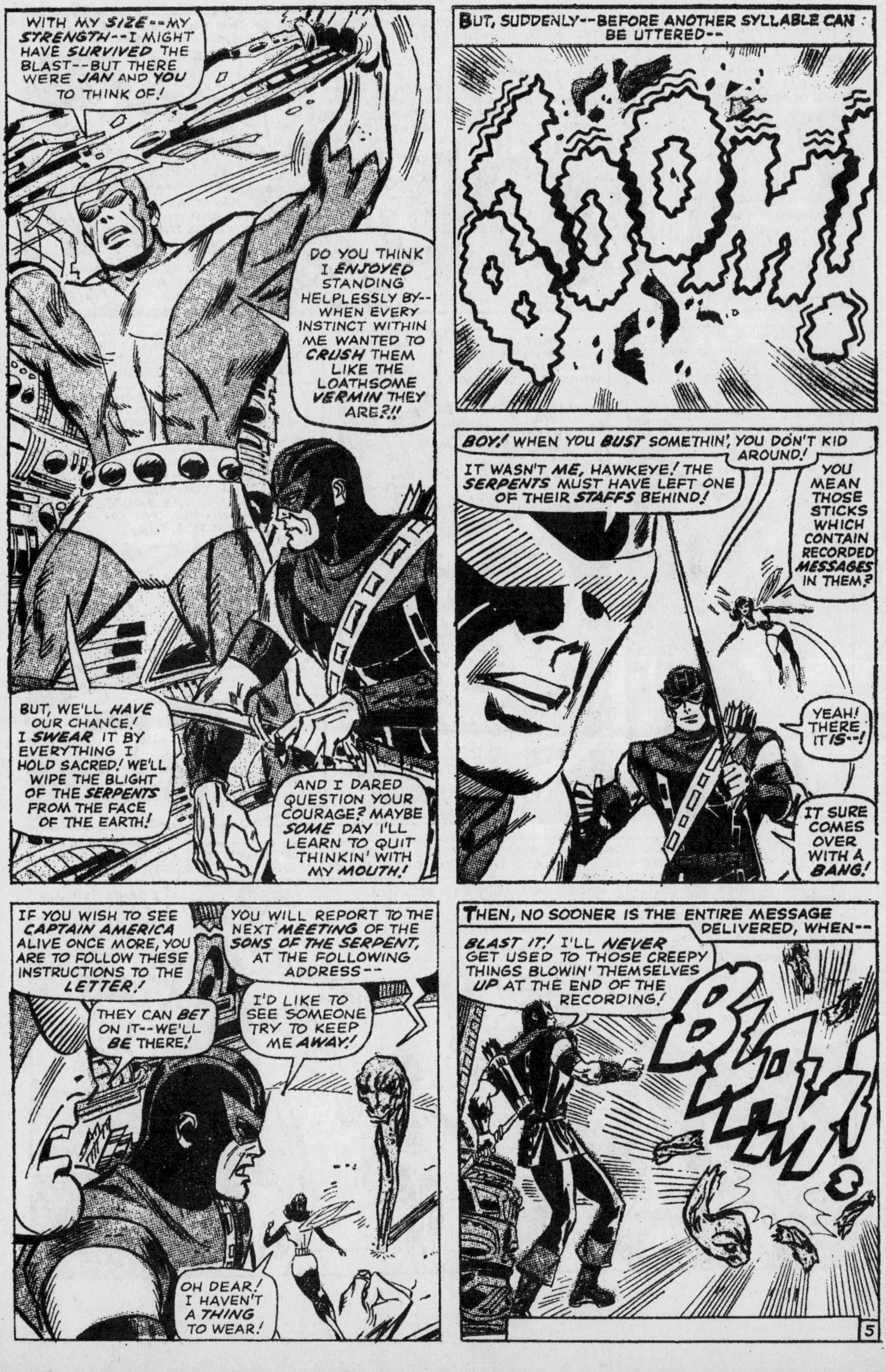
WITH MY SIZE--MY STRENGTH--I MIGHT HAVE SURVIVED THE BLAST--BUT THERE WERE JAN AND YOU TO THINK OF!
DO YOU THINK I ENJOYED STANDING HELPLESSLY BY--WHEN EVERY INSTINCT WITHIN ME WANTED TO CRUSH THEM LIKE THE LOATHSOME VERMIN THEY ARE?!!
BUT, WE'LL HAVE OUR CHANCE! I SWEAR IT BY EVERYTHING I HOLD SACRED! WE'LL WIPE THE BLIGHT OF THE SERPENTS FROM THE FACE OF THE EARTH!
AND I DARED QUESTION YOUR COURAGE? MAYBE SOME DAY I'LL LEARN TO QUIT THINKIN' WITH MY MOUTH!
BUT, SUDDENLY--BEFORE ANOTHER SYLLABLE CAN BE UTTERED--
BOOM!
BOY! WHEN YOU BUST SOMETHIN', YOU DON'T KID AROUND!
IT WASN'T ME, HAWKEYE! THE SERPENTS MUST HAVE LEFT ONE OF THEIR STAFFS BEHIND!
YOU MEAN THOSE STICKS WHICH CONTAIN RECORDED MESSAGES IN THEM?
YEAH! THERE IT IS--!
IT SURE COMES OVER WITH A BANG!
IF YOU WISH TO SEE CAPTAIN AMERICA ALIVE ONCE MORE, YOU ARE TO FOLLOW THESE INSTRUCTIONS TO THE LETTER!
YOU WILL REPORT TO THE NEXT MEETING OF THE SONS OF THE SERPENT, AT THE FOLLOWING ADDRESS--
THEY CAN BET ON IT--WE'LL BE THERE!
I'D LIKE TO SEE SOMEONE TRY TO KEEP ME AWAY!
OH DEAR! I HAVEN'T A THING TO WEAR!
THEN, NO SOONER IS THE ENTIRE MESSAGE DELIVERED, WHEN--
BLAST IT! I'LL NEVER GET USED TO THOSE CREEPY THINGS BLOWIN' THEMSELVES UP AT THE END OF THE RECORDING!
BLAM!

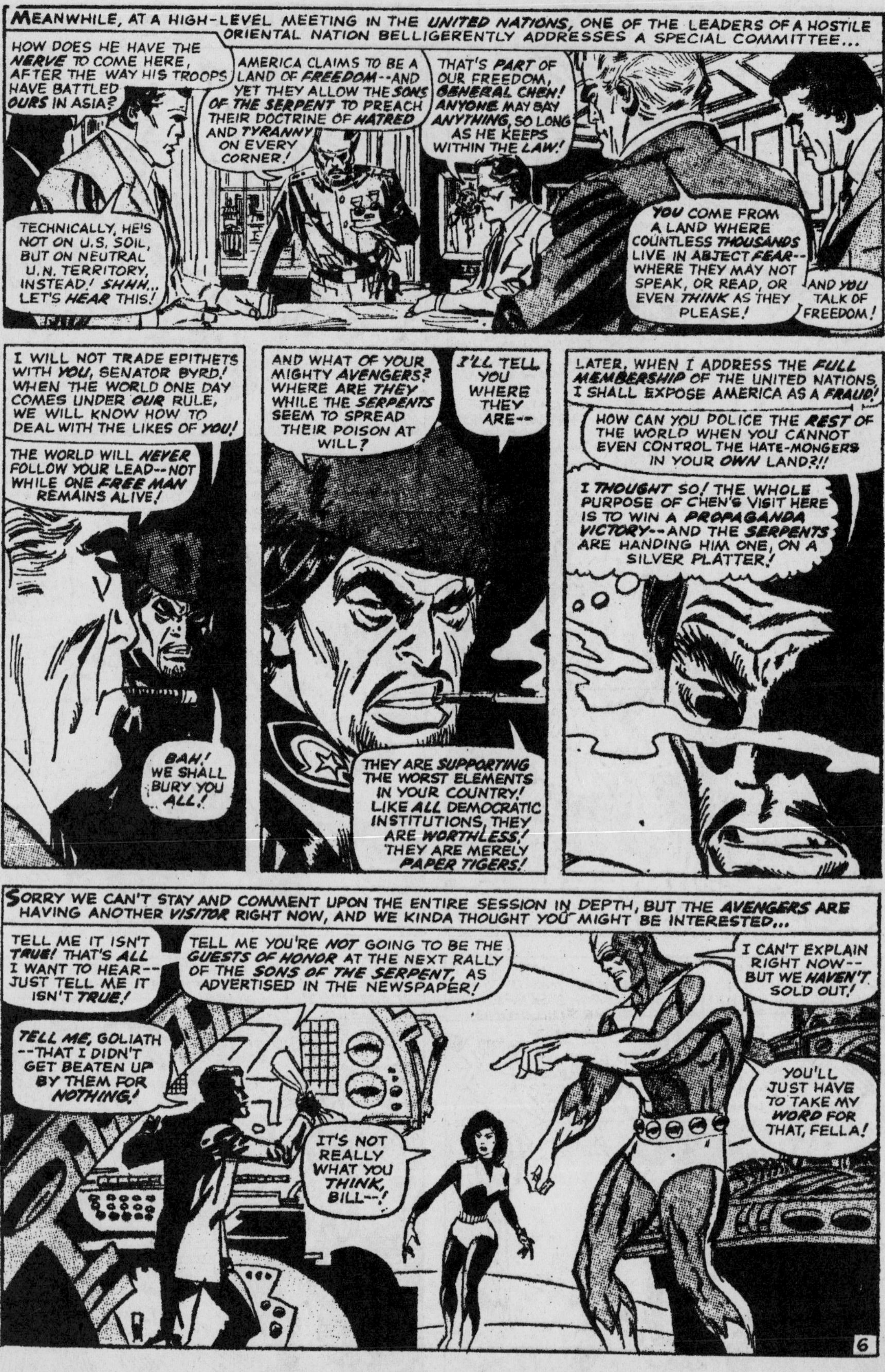
MEANWHILE, AT A HIGH-LEVEL MEETING IN THE UNITED NATIONS, ONE OF THE LEADERS OF A HOSTILE ORIENTAL NATION BELLIGERENTLY ADDRESSES A SPECIAL COMMITTEE...
HOW DOES HE HAVE THE NERVE TO COME HERE, AFTER THE WAY HIS TROOPS HAVE BATTLED OURS IN ASIA?
AMERICA CLAIMS TO BE A LAND OF FREEDOM--AND YET THEY ALLOW THE SONS OF THE SERPENT TO PREACH THEIR DOCTRINE OF HATRED AND TYRANNY ON EVERY CORNER!
THAT'S PART OF OUR FREEDOM, GENERAL CHEN! ANYONE MAY SAY ANYTHING, SO LONG AS HE KEEPS WITHIN THE LAW!
TECHNICALLY, HE'S NOT ON U.S. SOIL, BUT ON NEUTRAL U.N. TERRITORY, INSTEAD! SHHH... LET'S HEAR THIS!
YOU COME FROM A LAND WHERE COUNTLESS THOUSANDS LIVE IN ABJECT FEAR--WHERE THEY MAY NOT SPEAK, OR READ, OR EVEN THINK AS THEY PLEASE!
AND YOU TALK OF FREEDOM!
I WILL NOT TRADE EPITHETS WITH YOU, SENATOR BYRD! WHEN THE WORLD ONE DAY COMES UNDER OUR RULE, WE WILL KNOW HOW TO DEAL WITH THE LIKES OF YOU!
THE WORLD WILL NEVER FOLLOW YOUR LEAD--NOT WHILE ONE FREE MAN REMAINS ALIVE!
BAH! WE SHALL BURY YOU ALL!
AND WHAT OF YOUR MIGHTY AVENGERS? WHERE ARE THEY WHILE THE SERPENTS SEEM TO SPREAD THEIR POISON AT WILL?
I'LL TELL YOU WHERE THEY ARE--
THEY ARE SUPPORTING THE WORST ELEMENTS IN YOUR COUNTRY! LIKE ALL DEMOCRATIC INSTITUTIONS, THEY ARE WORTHLESS! THEY ARE MERELY PAPER TIGERS!
LATER, WHEN I ADDRESS THE FULL MEMBERSHIP OF THE UNITED NATIONS I SHALL EXPOSE AMERICA AS A FRAUD!
HOW CAN YOU POLICE THE REST OF THE WORLD WHEN YOU CANNOT EVEN CONTROL THE HATE-MONGERS IN YOUR OWN LAND?!!
I THOUGHT SO! THE WHOLE PURPOSE OF CHEN'S VISIT HERE IS TO WIN A PROPAGANDA VICTORY--AND THE SERPENTS ARE HANDING HIM ONE, ON A SILVER PLATTER!
SORRY WE CAN'T STAY AND COMMENT UPON THE ENTIRE SESSION IN DEPTH, BUT THE AVENGERS ARE HAVING ANOTHER VISITOR RIGHT NOW, AND WE KINDA THOUGHT YOU MIGHT BE INTERESTED...
TELL ME IT ISN'T TRUE! THAT'S ALL I WANT TO HEAR--JUST TELL ME IT ISN'T TRUE!
TELL ME YOU'RE NOT GOING TO BE THE GUESTS OF HONOR AT THE NEXT RALLY OF THE SONS OF THE SERPENT, AS ADVERTISED IN THE NEWSPAPER!
I CAN'T EXPLAIN RIGHT NOW--BUT WE HAVEN'T SOLD OUT!
TELL ME, GOLIATH--THAT I DIDN'T GET BEATEN UP BY THEM FOR NOTHING!
IT'S NOT REALLY WHAT YOU THINK, BILL--!
YOU'LL JUST HAVE TO TAKE MY WORD FOR THAT, FELLA!
6

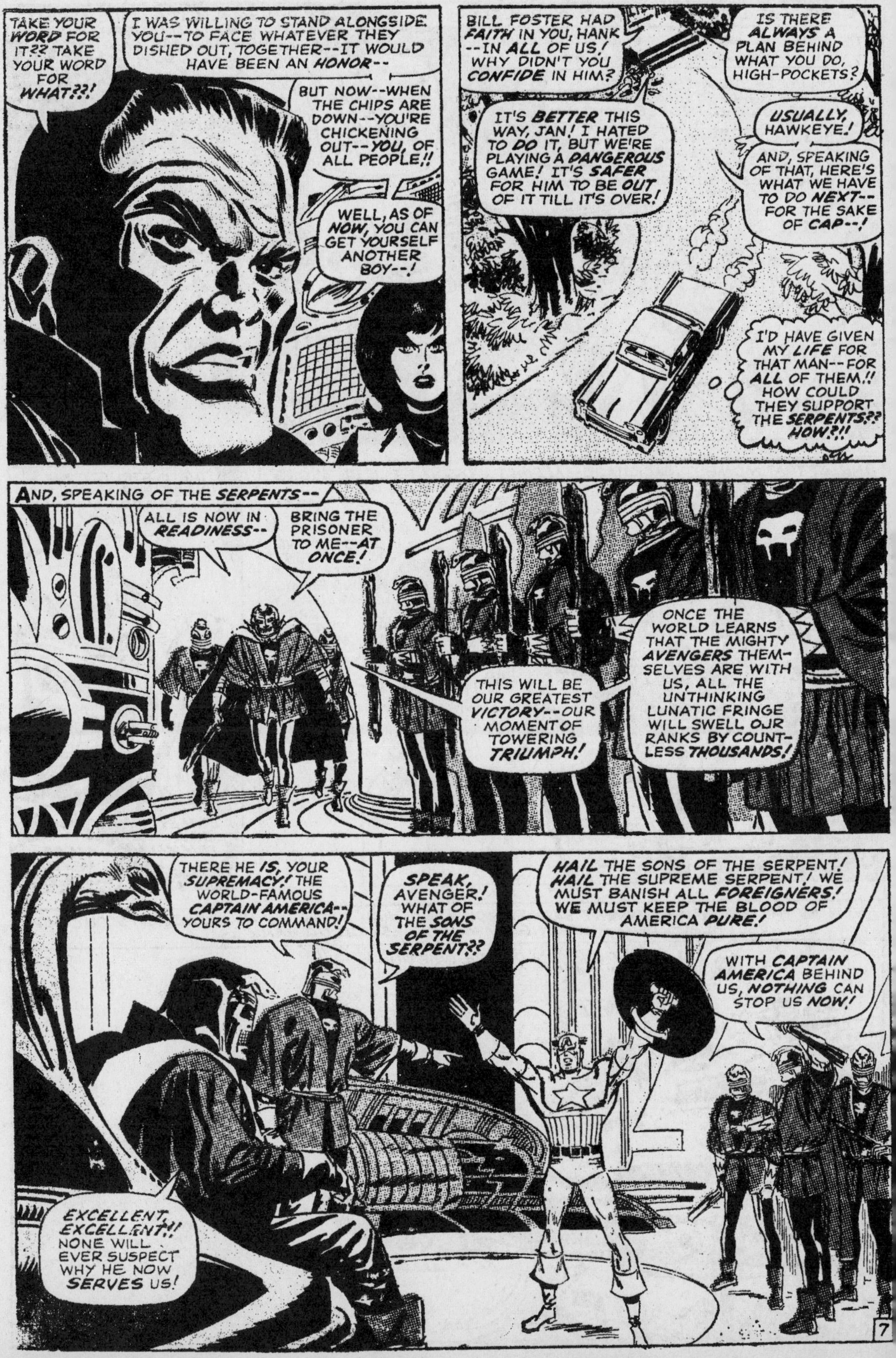
TAKE YOUR WORD FOR IT?? TAKE YOUR WORD FOR WHAT??!
I WAS WILLING TO STAND ALONGSIDE YOU--TO FACE WHATEVER THEY DISHED OUT, TOGETHER--IT WOULD HAVE BEEN AN HONOR--
BUT NOW--WHEN THE CHIPS ARE DOWN--YOU'RE CHICKENING OUT--YOU, OF ALL PEOPLE!!
WELL, AS OF NOW, YOU CAN GET YOURSELF ANOTHER BOY--!
BILL FOSTER HAD FAITH IN YOU, HANK --IN ALL OF US! WHY DIDN'T YOU CONFIDE IN HIM?
IT'S BETTER THIS WAY, JAN! I HATED TO DO IT, BUT WE'RE PLAYING A DANGEROUS GAME! IT'S SAFER FOR HIM TO BE OUT OF IT TILL IT'S OVER!
IS THERE ALWAYS A PLAN BEHIND WHAT YOU DO, HIGH-POCKETS?
USUALLY, HAWKEYE!
AND, SPEAKING OF THAT, HERE'S WHAT WE HAVE TO DO NEXT--FOR THE SAKE OF CAP--!
I'D HAVE GIVEN MY LIFE FOR THAT MAN--FOR ALL OF THEM!! HOW COULD THEY SUPPORT THE SERPENTS?? HOW?!!
AND, SPEAKING OF THE SERPENTS--
ALL IS NOW IN READINESS--
BRING THE PRISONER TO ME--AT ONCE!
THIS WILL BE OUR GREATEST VICTORY--OUR MOMENT OF TOWERING TRIUMPH!
ONCE THE WORLD LEARNS THAT THE MIGHTY AVENGERS THEMSELVES ARE WITH US, ALL THE UNTHINKING LUNATIC FRINGE WILL SWELL OUR RANKS BY COUNTLESS THOUSANDS!
THERE HE IS, YOUR SUPREMACY! THE WORLD-FAMOUS CAPTAIN AMERICA--YOURS TO COMMAND!
SPEAK, AVENGER! WHAT OF THE SONS OF THE SERPENT??
HAIL THE SONS OF THE SERPENT! HAIL THE SUPREME SERPENT! WE MUST BANISH ALL FOREIGNERS! WE MUST KEEP THE BLOOD OF AMERICA PURE!
WITH CAPTAIN AMERICA BEHIND US, NOTHING CAN STOP US NOW!
EXCELLENT, EXCELLENT!! NONE WILL EVER SUSPECT WHY HE NOW SERVES US!
7

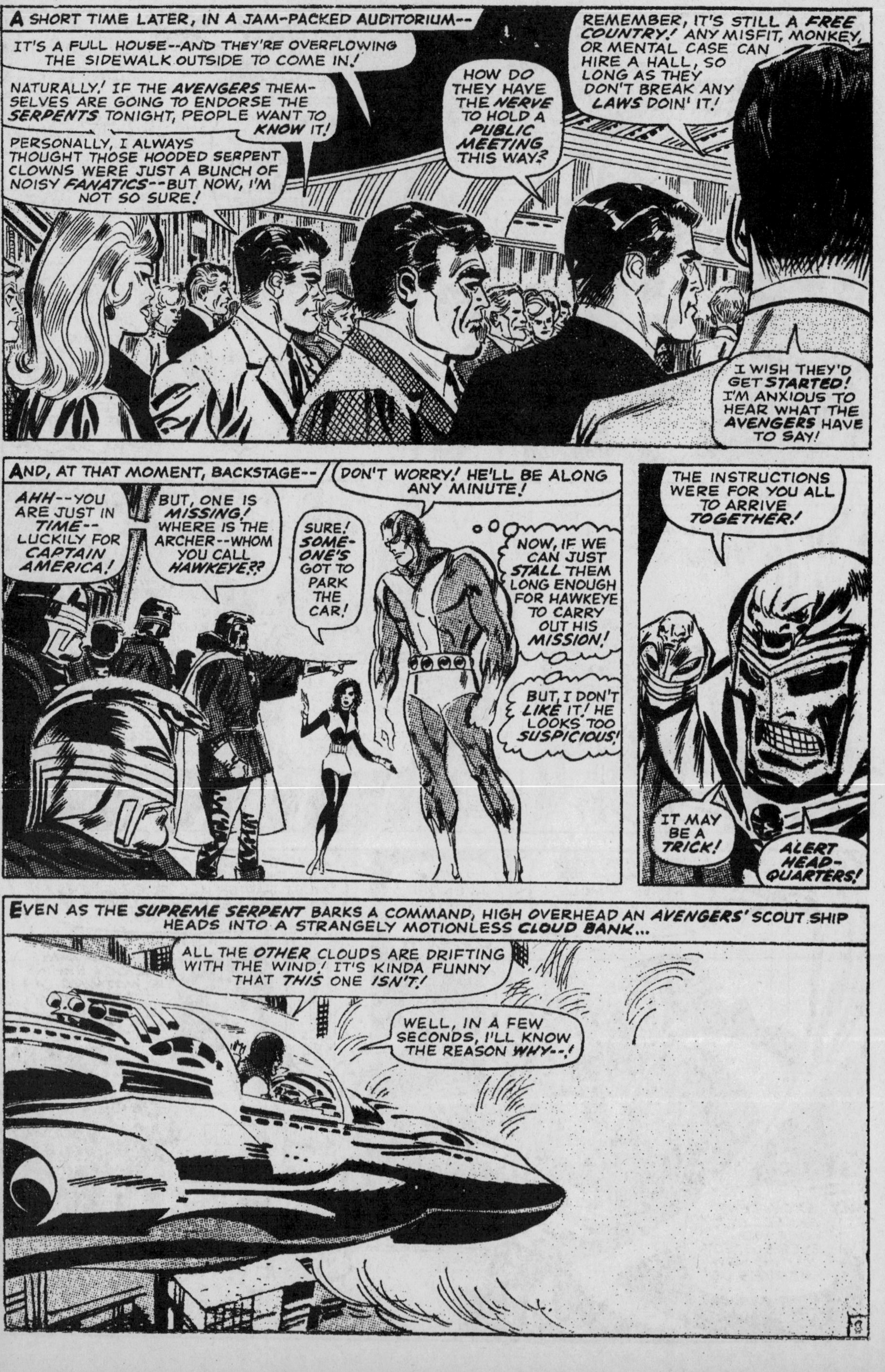
A SHORT TIME LATER, IN A JAM-PACKED AUDITORIUM--
IT'S A FULL HOUSE--AND THEY'RE OVERFLOWING THE SIDEWALK OUTSIDE TO COME IN!
NATURALLY! IF THE AVENGERS THEMSELVES ARE GOING TO ENDORSE THE SERPENTS TONIGHT, PEOPLE WANT TO KNOW IT!
PERSONALLY, I ALWAYS THOUGHT THOSE HOODED SERPENT CLOWNS WERE JUST A BUNCH OF NOISY FANATICS--BUT NOW, I'M NOT SO SURE!
HOW DO THEY HAVE THE NERVE TO HOLD A PUBLIC MEETING THIS WAY?
REMEMBER, IT'S STILL A FREE COUNTRY! ANY MISFIT, MONKEY, OR MENTAL CASE CAN HIRE A HALL, SO LONG AS THEY DON'T BREAK ANY LAWS DOIN' IT!
I WISH THEY'D GET STARTED! I'M ANXIOUS TO HEAR WHAT THE AVENGERS HAVE TO SAY!
AND, AT THAT MOMENT, BACKSTAGE--
AHH--YOU ARE JUST IN TIME--LUCKILY FOR CAPTAIN AMERICA!
BUT, ONE IS MISSING! WHERE IS THE ARCHER--WHOM YOU CALL HAWKEYE??
DON'T WORRY! HE'LL BE ALONG ANY MINUTE!
SURE! SOMEONE'S GOT TO PARK THE CAR!
NOW, IF WE CAN JUST STALL THEM LONG ENOUGH FOR HAWKEYE TO CARRY OUT HIS MISSION!
BUT, I DON'T LIKE IT! HE LOOKS TOO SUSPICIOUS!
THE INSTRUCTIONS WERE FOR YOU ALL TO ARRIVE TOGETHER!
IT MAY BE A TRICK!
ALERT HEADQUARTERS!
EVEN AS THE SUPREME SERPENT BARKS A COMMAND, HIGH OVERHEAD AN AVENGERS' SCOUT SHIP HEADS INTO A STRANGELY MOTIONLESS CLOUD BANK...
ALL THE OTHER CLOUDS ARE DRIFTING WITH THE WIND! IT'S KINDA FUNNY THAT THIS ONE ISN'T!
WELL, IN A FEW SECONDS, I'LL KNOW THE REASON WHY--!
8

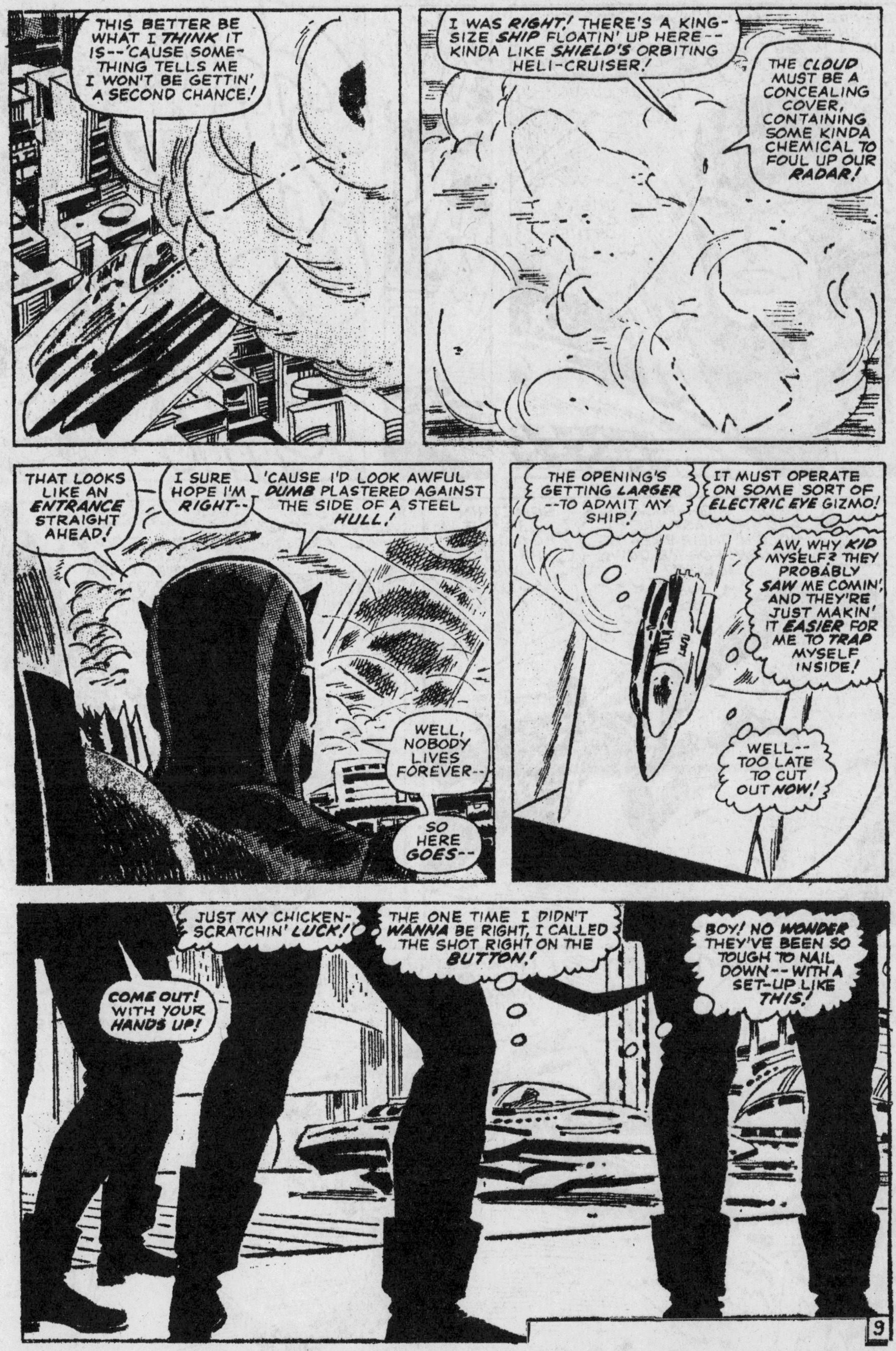
THIS BETTER BE WHAT I THINK IT IS--'CAUSE SOMETHING TELLS ME I WON'T BE GETTIN' A SECOND CHANCE!
I WAS RIGHT! THERE'S A KING-SIZE SHIP FLOATIN' UP HERE--KINDA LIKE SHIELD'S ORBITING HELI-CRUISER!
THE CLOUD MUST BE A CONCEALING COVER, CONTAINING SOME KINDA CHEMICAL TO FOUL UP OUR RADAR!
THAT LOOKS LIKE AN ENTRANCE STRAIGHT AHEAD!
I SURE HOPE I'M RIGHT--
'CAUSE I'D LOOK AWFUL DUMB PLASTERED AGAINST THE SIDE OF A STEEL HULL!
WELL, NOBODY LIVES FOREVER--
SO HERE GOES--
THE OPENING'S GETTING LARGER --TO ADMIT MY SHIP!
IT MUST OPERATE ON SOME SORT OF ELECTRIC EYE GIZMO!
AW, WHY KID MYSELF? THEY PROBABLY SAW ME COMIN', AND THEY'RE JUST MAKIN' IT EASIER FOR ME TO TRAP MYSELF INSIDE!
WELL-- TOO LATE TO CUT OUT NOW!
COME OUT! WITH YOUR HANDS UP!
JUST MY CHICKEN-SCRATCHIN' LUCK!
THE ONE TIME I DIDN'T WANNA BE RIGHT, I CALLED THE SHOT RIGHT ON THE BUTTON!
BOY! NO WONDER THEY'VE BEEN SO TOUGH TO NAIL DOWN-- WITH A SET-UP LIKE THIS!
9

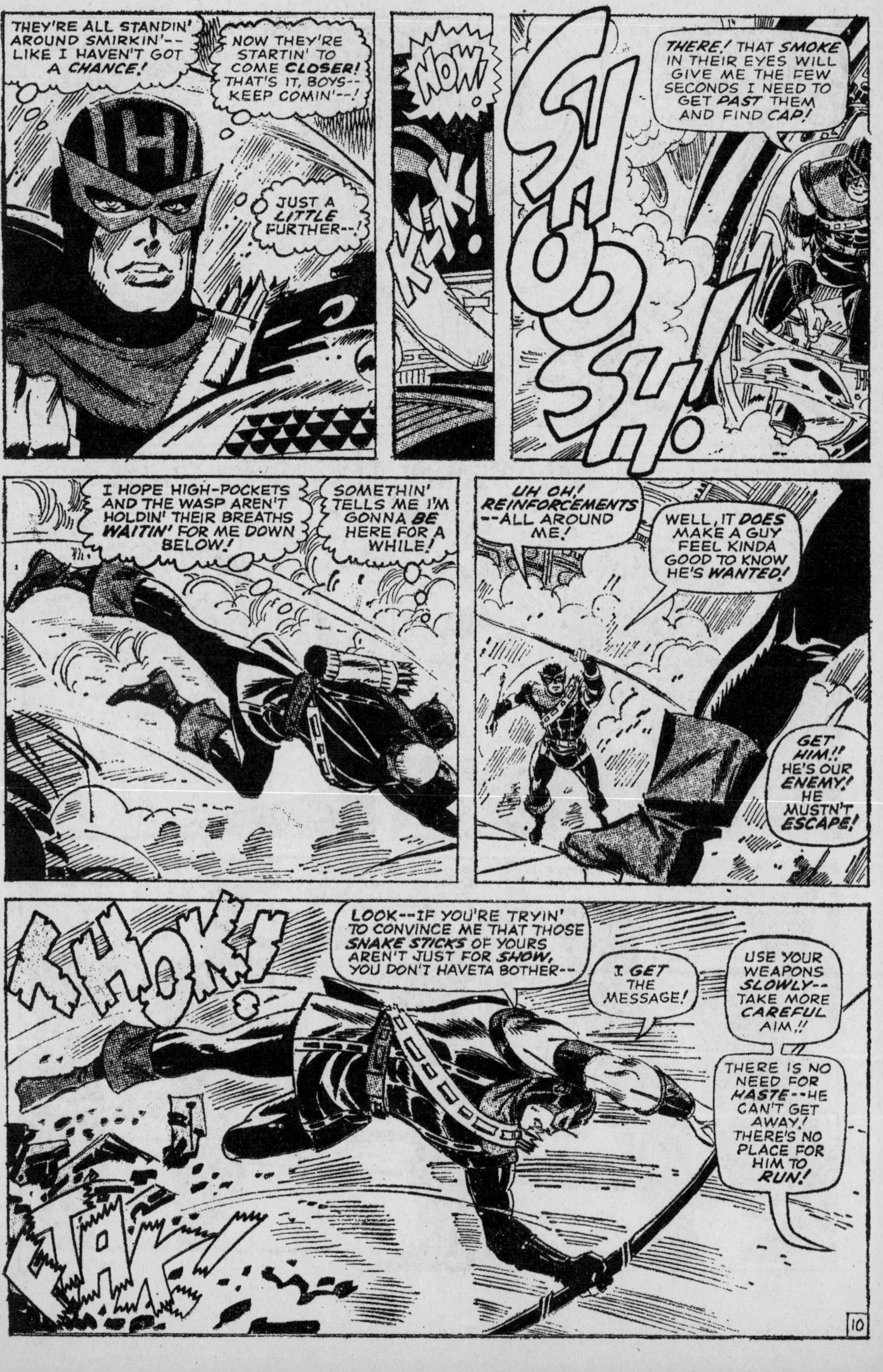
THEY'RE ALL STANDIN' AROUND SMIRKIN'-- LIKE I HAVEN'T GOT A CHANCE!
NOW THEY'RE STARTIN' TO COME CLOSER! THAT'S IT, BOYS-- KEEP COMIN'--!
JUST A LITTLE FURTHER--!
NOW!
THERE! THAT SMOKE IN THEIR EYES WILL GIVE ME THE FEW SECONDS I NEED TO GET PAST THEM AND FIND CAP!
SHOOOSH!
I HOPE HIGH-POCKETS AND THE WASP AREN'T HOLDIN' THEIR BREATHS WAITIN' FOR ME DOWN BELOW!
SOMETHIN' TELLS ME I'M GONNA BE HERE FOR A WHILE!
UH OH! REINFORCEMENTS --ALL AROUND ME!
WELL, IT DOES MAKE A GUY FEEL KINDA GOOD TO KNOW HE'S WANTED!
GET HIM!! HE'S OUR ENEMY! HE MUSTN'T ESCAPE!
THOK!
LOOK--IF YOU'RE TRYIN' TO CONVINCE ME THAT THOSE SNAKE STICKS OF YOURS AREN'T JUST FOR SHOW, YOU DON'T HAVETA BOTHER--
I GET THE MESSAGE!
USE YOUR WEAPONS SLOWLY-- TAKE MORE CAREFUL AIM!!
THERE IS NO NEED FOR HASTE--HE CAN'T GET AWAY! THERE'S NO PLACE FOR HIM TO RUN!
TAK!
10

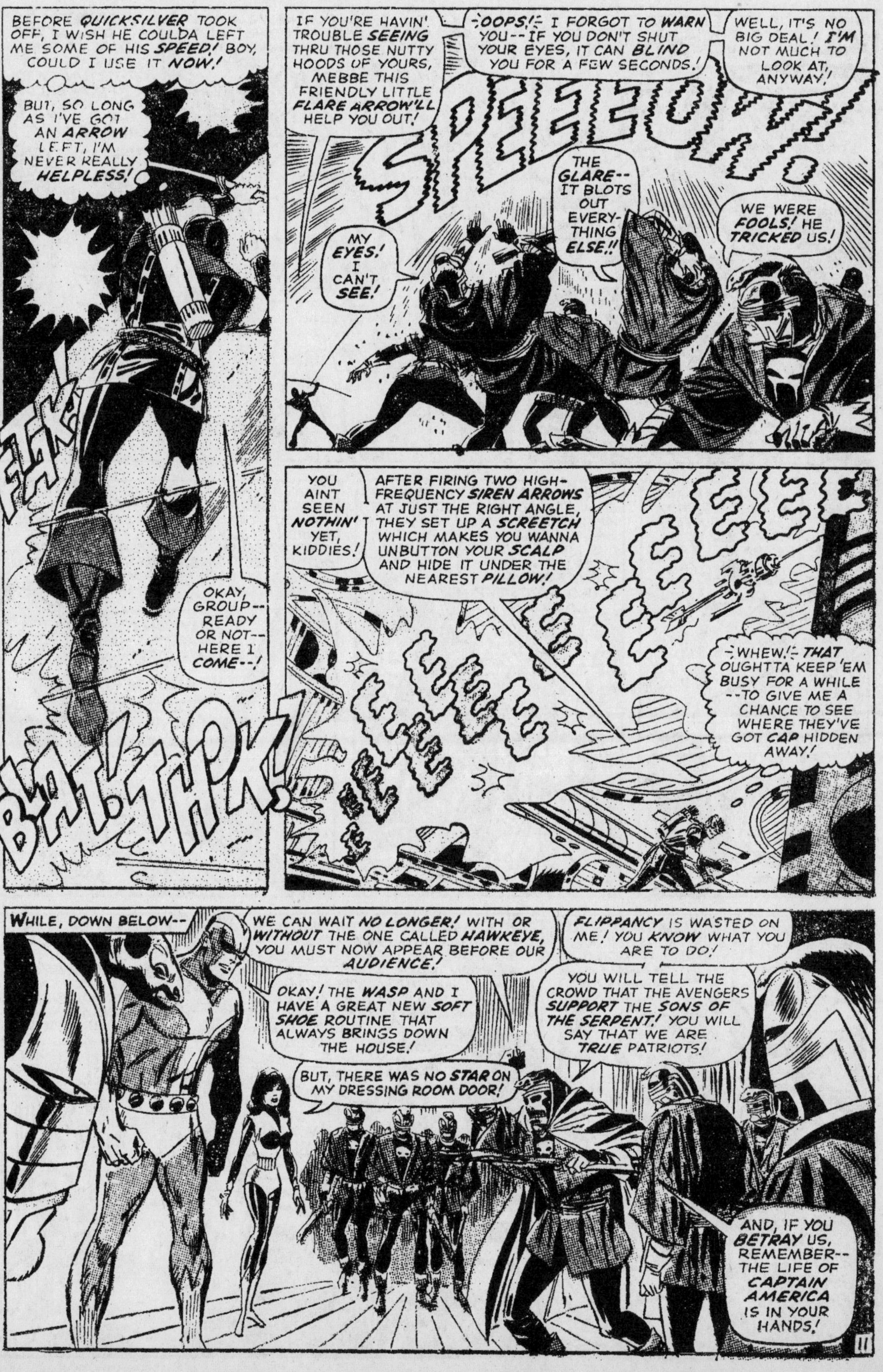

BEFORE QUICKSILVER TOOK OFF, I WISH HE COULDA LEFT ME SOME OF HIS SPEED! BOY, COULD I USE IT NOW!
BUT, SO LONG AS I'VE GOT AN ARROW LEFT, I'M NEVER REALLY HELPLESS!
FTTK!
OKAY, GROUP-- READY OR NOT-- HERE I COME--!
BLAT! THPK!
IF YOU'RE HAVIN' TROUBLE SEEING THRU THOSE NUTTY HOODS OF YOURS, MEBBE THIS FRIENDLY LITTLE FLARE ARROW'LL HELP YOU OUT!
OOPS! I FORGOT TO WARN YOU--IF YOU DON'T SHUT YOUR EYES, IT CAN BLIND YOU FOR A FEW SECONDS!
WELL, IT'S NO BIG DEAL! I'M NOT MUCH TO LOOK AT, ANYWAY!
SPEEEOWW!
THE GLARE-- IT BLOTS OUT EVERY-THING ELSE!!
MY EYES! I CAN'T SEE!
WE WERE FOOLS! HE TRICKED US!
YOU AINT SEEN NOTHIN' YET, KIDDIES!
AFTER FIRING TWO HIGH-FREQUENCY SIREN ARROWS AT JUST THE RIGHT ANGLE, THEY SET UP A SCREETCH WHICH MAKES YOU WANNA UNBUTTON YOUR SCALP AND HIDE IT UNDER THE NEAREST PILLOW!
EEEEE
WHEW! THAT OUGHTTA KEEP 'EM BUSY FOR A WHILE --TO GIVE ME A CHANCE TO SEE WHERE THEY'VE GOT CAP HIDDEN AWAY!
WHILE, DOWN BELOW--
WE CAN WAIT NO LONGER! WITH OR WITHOUT THE ONE CALLED HAWKEYE, YOU MUST NOW APPEAR BEFORE OUR AUDIENCE!
OKAY! THE WASP AND I HAVE A GREAT NEW SOFT SHOE ROUTINE THAT ALWAYS BRINGS DOWN THE HOUSE!
BUT, THERE WAS NO STAR ON MY DRESSING ROOM DOOR!
FLIPPANCY IS WASTED ON ME! YOU KNOW WHAT YOU ARE TO DO!
YOU WILL TELL THE CROWD THAT THE AVENGERS SUPPORT THE SONS OF THE SERPENT! YOU WILL SAY THAT WE ARE TRUE PATRIOTS!
AND, IF YOU BETRAY US, REMEMBER-- THE LIFE OF CAPTAIN AMERICA IS IN YOUR HANDS!
11

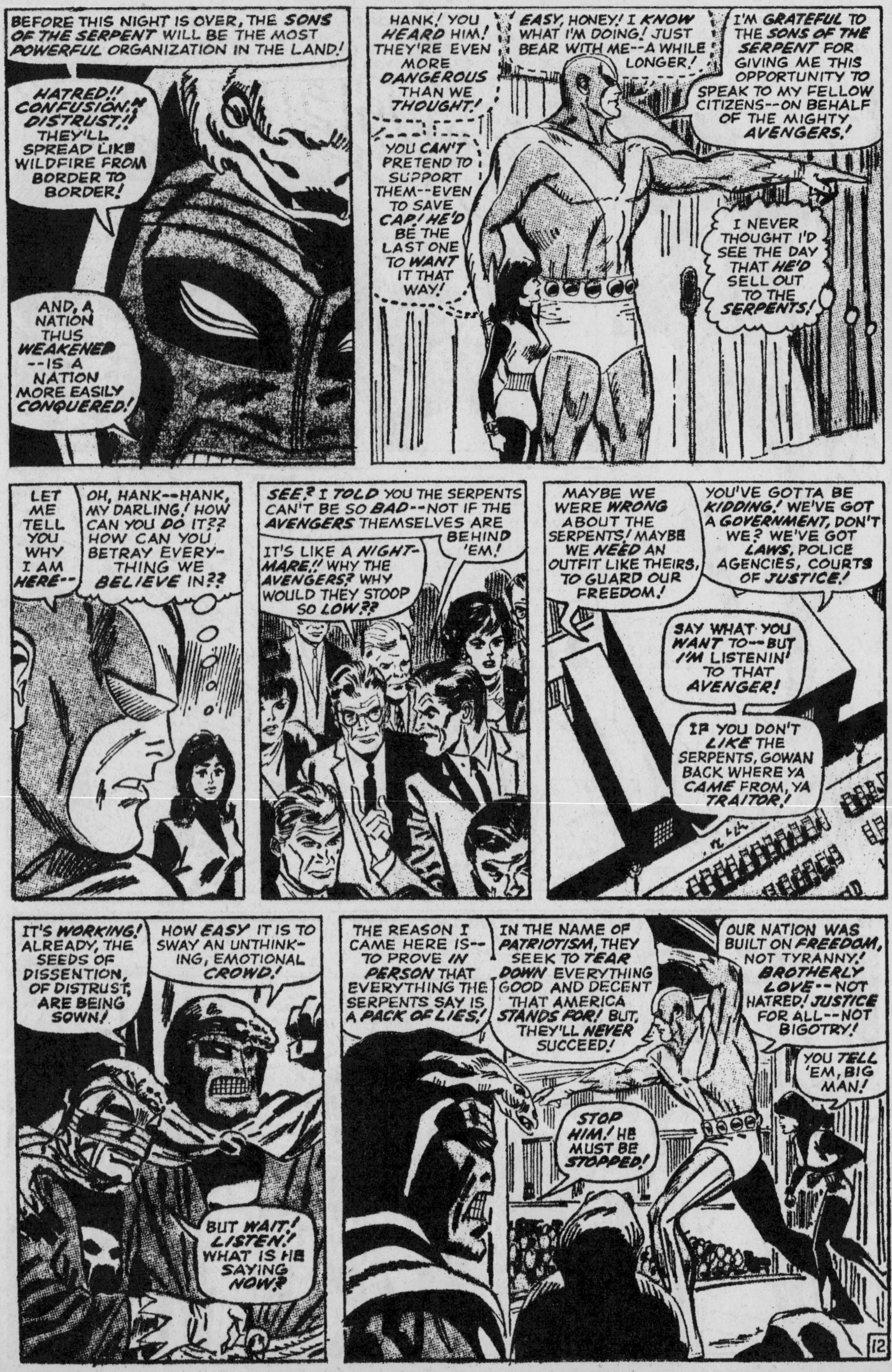
BEFORE THIS NIGHT IS OVER, THE SONS OF THE SERPENT WILL BE THE MOST POWERFUL ORGANIZATION IN THE LAND!
HATRED!! CONFUSION!! DISTRUST!! THEY'LL SPREAD LIKE WILDFIRE FROM BORDER TO BORDER!
AND, A NATION THUS WEAKENED --IS A NATION MORE EASILY CONQUERED!
HANK! YOU HEARD HIM! THEY'RE EVEN MORE DANGEROUS THAN WE THOUGHT!
YOU CAN'T PRETEND TO SUPPORT THEM--EVEN TO SAVE CAP! HE'D BE THE LAST ONE TO WANT IT THAT WAY!
EASY, HONEY! I KNOW WHAT I'M DOING! JUST BEAR WITH ME--A WHILE LONGER!
I'M GRATEFUL TO THE SONS OF THE SERPENT FOR GIVING ME THIS OPPORTUNITY TO SPEAK TO MY FELLOW CITIZENS--ON BEHALF OF THE MIGHTY AVENGERS!
I NEVER THOUGHT I'D SEE THE DAY THAT HE'D SELL OUT TO THE SERPENTS!
LET ME TELL YOU WHY I AM HERE--
OH, HANK--HANK, MY DARLING! HOW CAN YOU DO IT?? HOW CAN YOU BETRAY EVERYTHING WE BELIEVE IN??
SEE? I TOLD YOU THE SERPENTS CAN'T BE SO BAD--NOT IF THE AVENGERS THEMSELVES ARE BEHIND 'EM!
IT'S LIKE A NIGHTMARE!! WHY THE AVENGERS? WHY WOULD THEY STOOP SO LOW??
MAYBE WE WERE WRONG ABOUT THE SERPENTS! MAYBE WE NEED AN OUTFIT LIKE THEIRS, TO GUARD OUR FREEDOM!
YOU'VE GOTTA BE KIDDING! WE'VE GOT A GOVERNMENT, DON'T WE? WE'VE GOT LAWS, POLICE AGENCIES, COURTS OF JUSTICE!
SAY WHAT YOU WANT TO--BUT I'M LISTENIN' TO THAT AVENGER!
IF YOU DON'T LIKE THE SERPENTS, GOWAN BACK WHERE YA CAME FROM, YA TRAITOR!
IT'S WORKING! ALREADY, THE SEEDS OF DISSENTION, OF DISTRUST, ARE BEING SOWN!
HOW EASY IT IS TO SWAY AN UNTHINKING, EMOTIONAL CROWD!
BUT WAIT! LISTEN! WHAT IS HE SAYING NOW?
THE REASON I CAME HERE IS--TO PROVE IN PERSON THAT EVERYTHING THE SERPENTS SAY IS A PACK OF LIES!
IN THE NAME OF PATRIOTISM, THEY SEEK TO TEAR DOWN EVERYTHING GOOD AND DECENT THAT AMERICA STANDS FOR! BUT, THEY'LL NEVER SUCCEED!
OUR NATION WAS BUILT ON FREEDOM, NOT TYRANNY! BROTHERLY LOVE--NOT HATRED! JUSTICE FOR ALL--NOT BIGOTRY!
YOU TELL 'EM, BIG MAN!
STOP HIM! HE MUST BE STOPPED!
12

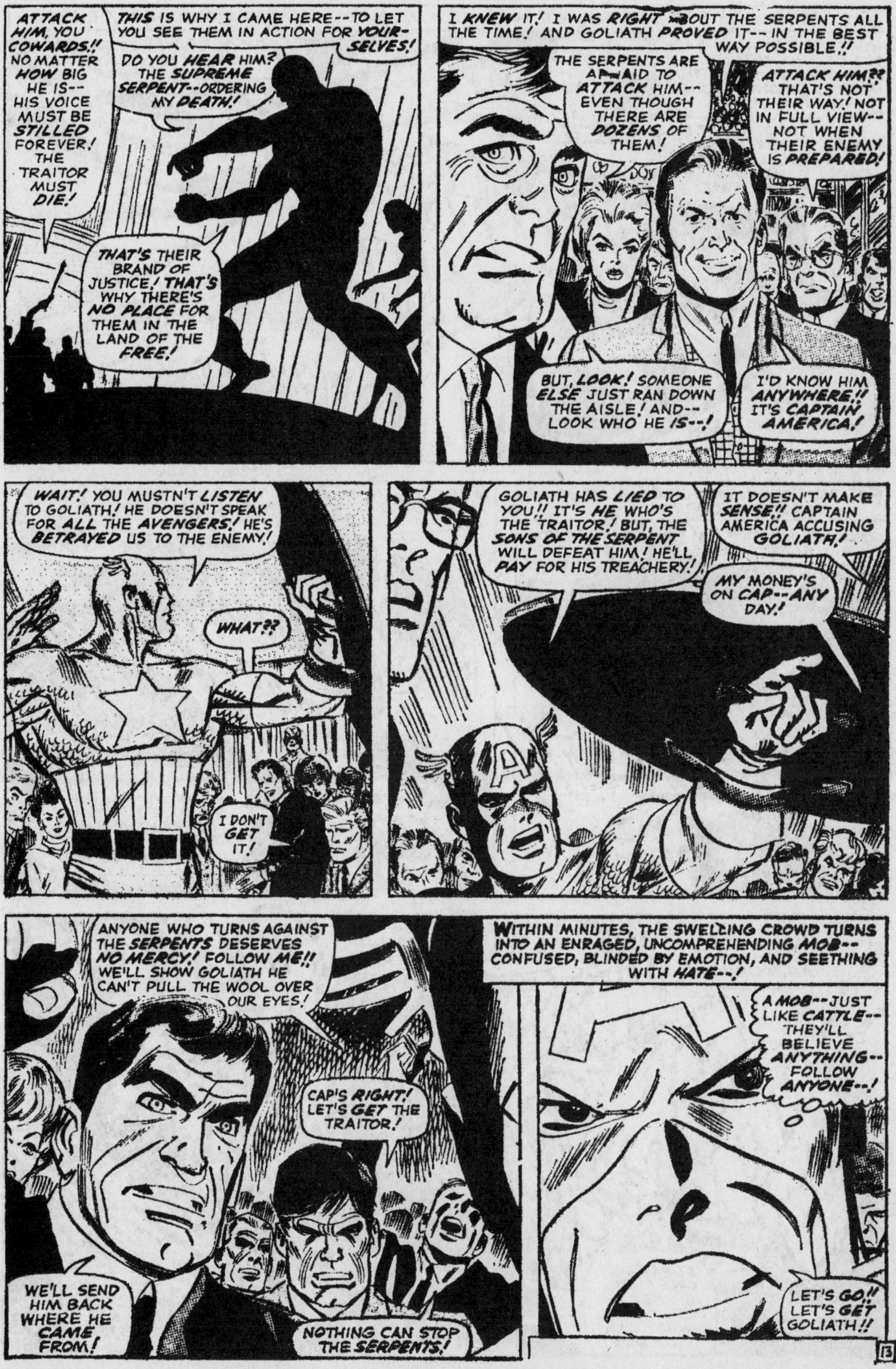
ATTACK HIM, YOU COWARDS!! NO MATTER HOW BIG HE IS-- HIS VOICE MUST BE STILLED FOREVER! THE TRAITOR MUST DIE!
THIS IS WHY I CAME HERE--TO LET YOU SEE THEM IN ACTION FOR YOURSELVES!
DO YOU HEAR HIM? THE SUPREME SERPENT--ORDERING MY DEATH!
THAT'S THEIR BRAND OF JUSTICE! THAT'S WHY THERE'S NO PLACE FOR THEM IN THE LAND OF THE FREE!
I KNEW IT! I WAS RIGHT ABOUT THE SERPENTS ALL THE TIME! AND GOLIATH PROVED IT-- IN THE BEST WAY POSSIBLE!!
THE SERPENTS ARE AFRAID TO ATTACK HIM-- EVEN THOUGH THERE ARE DOZENS OF THEM!
ATTACK HIM?? THAT'S NOT THEIR WAY! NOT IN FULL VIEW-- NOT WHEN THEIR ENEMY IS PREPARED!
BUT, LOOK! SOMEONE ELSE JUST RAN DOWN THE AISLE! AND-- LOOK WHO HE IS--!
I'D KNOW HIM ANYWHERE!! IT'S CAPTAIN AMERICA!
WAIT! YOU MUSTN'T LISTEN TO GOLIATH! HE DOESN'T SPEAK FOR ALL THE AVENGERS! HE'S BETRAYED US TO THE ENEMY!
WHAT??
I DON'T GET IT!
GOLIATH HAS LIED TO YOU!! IT'S HE WHO'S THE TRAITOR! BUT, THE SONS OF THE SERPENT WILL DEFEAT HIM! HE'LL PAY FOR HIS TREACHERY!
IT DOESN'T MAKE SENSE!! CAPTAIN AMERICA ACCUSING GOLIATH!
MY MONEY'S ON CAP--ANY DAY!
ANYONE WHO TURNS AGAINST THE SERPENTS DESERVES NO MERCY! FOLLOW ME!! WE'LL SHOW GOLIATH HE CAN'T PULL THE WOOL OVER OUR EYES!
CAP'S RIGHT! LET'S GET THE TRAITOR!
WE'LL SEND HIM BACK WHERE HE CAME FROM!
NOTHING CAN STOP THE SERPENTS!
WITHIN MINUTES, THE SWELLING CROWD TURNS INTO AN ENRAGED, UNCOMPREHENDING MOB-- CONFUSED, BLINDED BY EMOTION, AND SEETHING WITH HATE--!
A MOB--JUST LIKE CATTLE-- THEY'LL BELIEVE ANYTHING-- FOLLOW ANYONE--!
LET'S GO!! LET'S GET GOLIATH!!
13

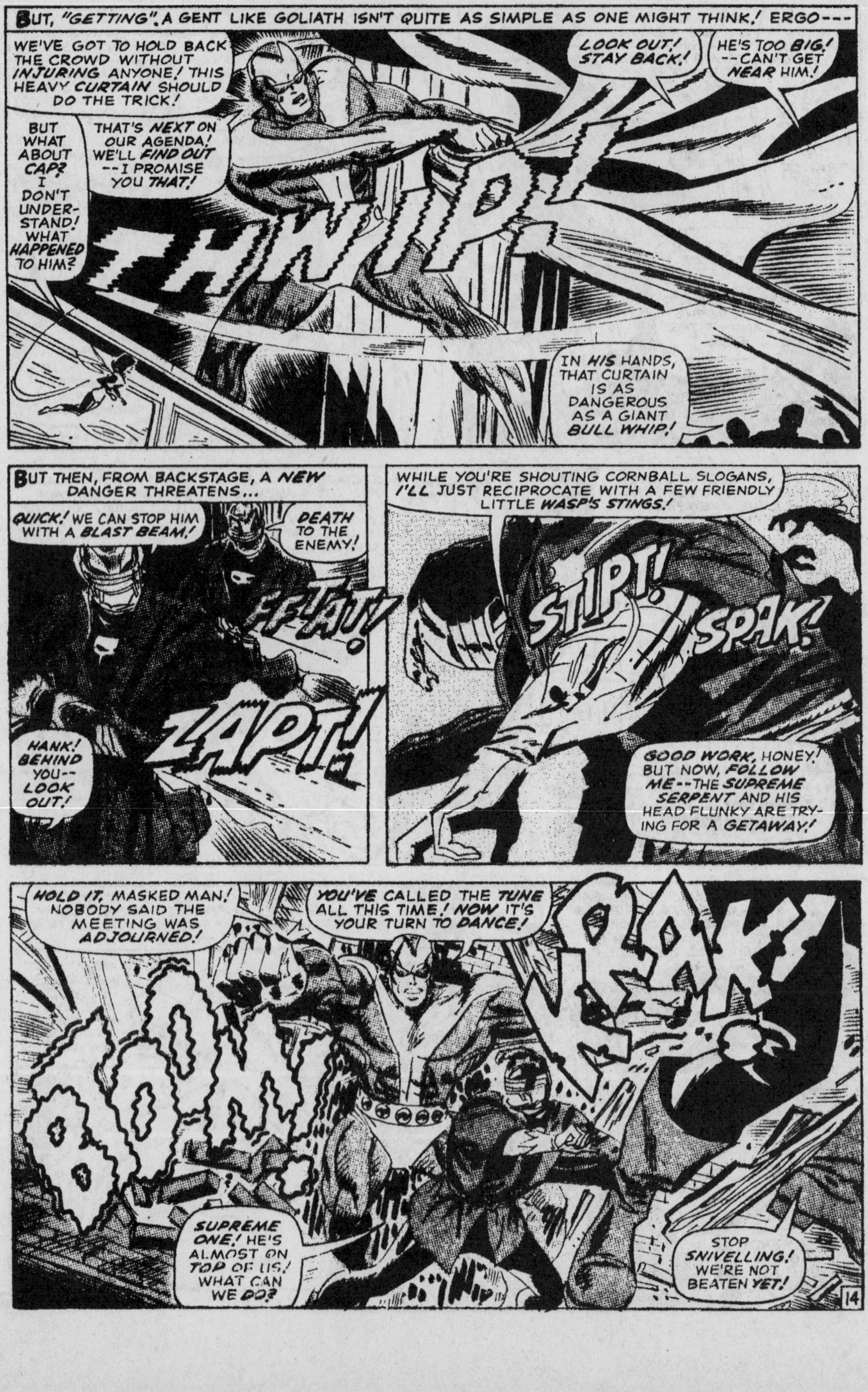

BUT, "GETTING", A GENT LIKE GOLIATH ISN'T QUITE AS SIMPLE AS ONE MIGHT THINK! ERGO---
WE'VE GOT TO HOLD BACK THE CROWD WITHOUT INJURING ANYONE! THIS HEAVY CURTAIN SHOULD DO THE TRICK!
LOOK OUT! STAY BACK!
HE'S TOO BIG! --CAN'T GET NEAR HIM!
BUT WHAT ABOUT CAP? I DON'T UNDERSTAND! WHAT HAPPENED TO HIM?
THAT'S NEXT ON OUR AGENDA! WE'LL FIND OUT --I PROMISE YOU THAT!
THWIPP!
IN HIS HANDS, THAT CURTAIN IS AS DANGEROUS AS A GIANT BULL WHIP!
BUT THEN, FROM BACKSTAGE, A NEW DANGER THREATENS...
QUICK! WE CAN STOP HIM WITH A BLAST BEAM!
DEATH TO THE ENEMY!
FFLAT!
ZAPT!
HANK! BEHIND YOU-- LOOK OUT!
WHILE YOU'RE SHOUTING CORNBALL SLOGANS, I'LL JUST RECIPROCATE WITH A FEW FRIENDLY LITTLE WASP'S STINGS!
STIPT!
SPAK!
GOOD WORK, HONEY! BUT NOW, FOLLOW ME--THE SUPREME SERPENT AND HIS HEAD FLUNKY ARE TRYING FOR A GETAWAY!
HOLD IT, MASKED MAN! NOBODY SAID THE MEETING WAS ADJOURNED!
YOU'VE CALLED THE TUNE ALL THIS TIME! NOW IT'S YOUR TURN TO DANCE!
POK!
BOOM!
SUPREME ONE! HE'S ALMOST ON TOP OF US! WHAT CAN WE DO?
STOP SNIVELLING! WE'RE NOT BEATEN YET!

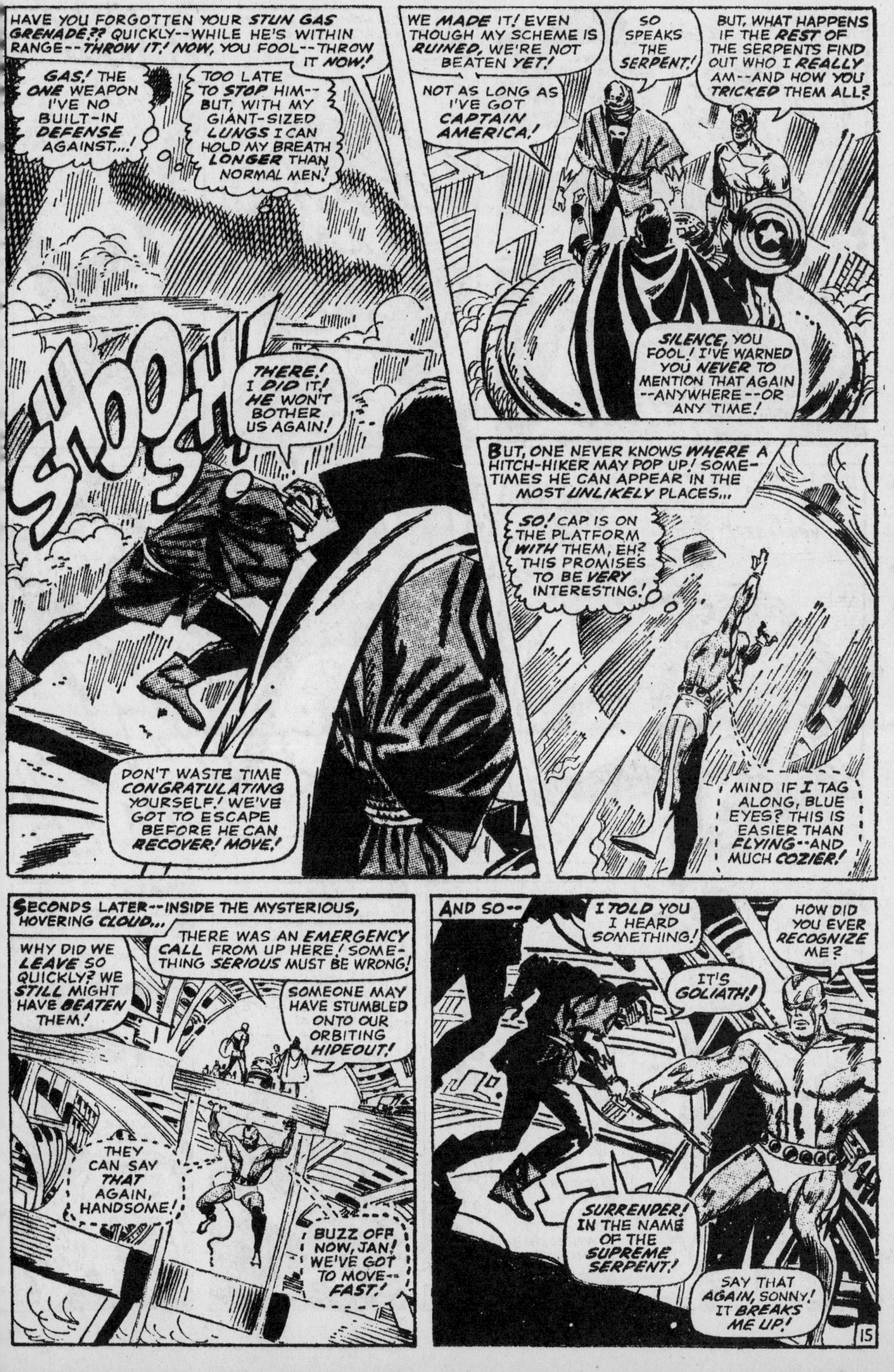

HAVE YOU FORGOTTEN YOUR STUN GAS GRENADE?? QUICKLY--WHILE HE'S WITHIN RANGE--THROW IT! NOW, YOU FOOL--THROW IT NOW!
GAS! THE ONE WEAPON I'VE NO BUILT-IN DEFENSE AGAINST...!
TOO LATE TO STOP HIM--BUT, WITH MY GIANT-SIZED LUNGS I CAN HOLD MY BREATH LONGER THAN NORMAL MEN!
SHOOSH!
THERE! I DID IT! HE WON'T BOTHER US AGAIN!
DON'T WASTE TIME CONGRATULATING YOURSELF! WE'VE GOT TO ESCAPE BEFORE HE CAN RECOVER! MOVE!
WE MADE IT! EVEN THOUGH MY SCHEME IS RUINED, WE'RE NOT BEATEN YET!
NOT AS LONG AS I'VE GOT CAPTAIN AMERICA!
SO SPEAKS THE SERPENT!
BUT, WHAT HAPPENS IF THE REST OF THE SERPENTS FIND OUT WHO I REALLY AM--AND HOW YOU TRICKED THEM ALL?
SILENCE, YOU FOOL! I'VE WARNED YOU NEVER TO MENTION THAT AGAIN--ANYWHERE--OR ANY TIME!
BUT, ONE NEVER KNOWS WHERE A HITCH-HIKER MAY POP UP! SOMETIMES HE CAN APPEAR IN THE MOST UNLIKELY PLACES...
SO! CAP IS ON THE PLATFORM WITH THEM, EH? THIS PROMISES TO BE VERY INTERESTING!
MIND IF I TAG ALONG, BLUE EYES? THIS IS EASIER THAN FLYING--AND MUCH COZIER!
SECONDS LATER--INSIDE THE MYSTERIOUS, HOVERING CLOUD...
WHY DID WE LEAVE SO QUICKLY? WE STILL MIGHT HAVE BEATEN THEM!
THERE WAS AN EMERGENCY CALL FROM UP HERE! SOMETHING SERIOUS MUST BE WRONG!
SOMEONE MAY HAVE STUMBLED ONTO OUR ORBITING HIDEOUT!
THEY CAN SAY THAT AGAIN, HANDSOME!
BUZZ OFF NOW, JAN! WE'VE GOT TO MOVE--FAST!
AND SO--
I TOLD YOU I HEARD SOMETHING!
HOW DID YOU EVER RECOGNIZE ME?
IT'S GOLIATH!
SURRENDER! IN THE NAME OF THE SUPREME SERPENT!
SAY THAT AGAIN, SONNY! IT BREAKS ME UP!
15

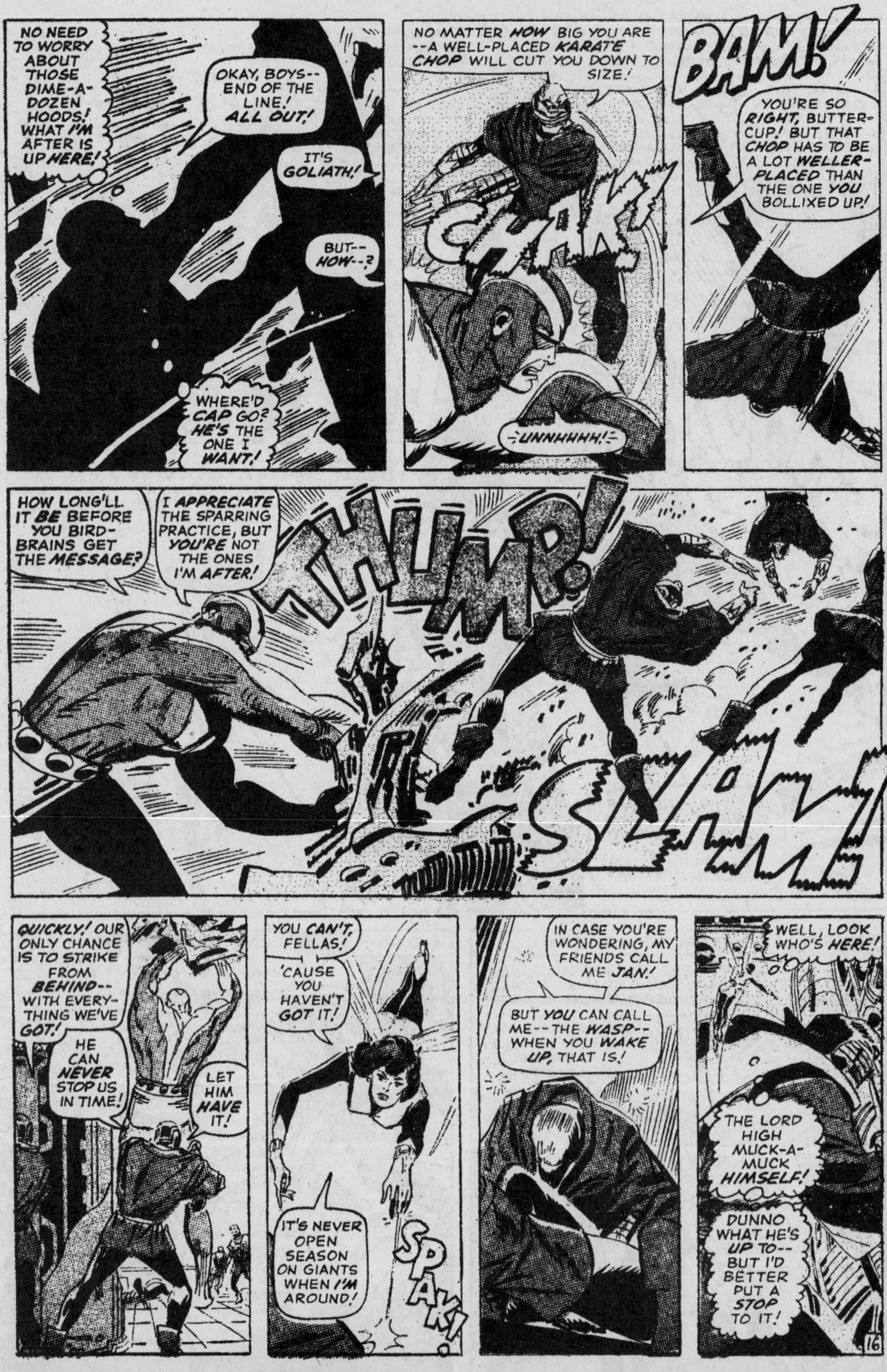
NO NEED TO WORRY ABOUT THOSE DIME-A-DOZEN HOODS! WHAT I'M AFTER IS UP HERE!
OKAY, BOYS-- END OF THE LINE! ALL OUT!
IT'S GOLIATH!
BUT-- HOW--?
WHERE'D CAP GO? HE'S THE ONE I WANT!
NO MATTER HOW BIG YOU ARE --A WELL-PLACED KARATE CHOP WILL CUT YOU DOWN TO SIZE!
CHAK!
UNNHHHH!
BAM!
YOU'RE SO RIGHT, BUTTER-CUP! BUT THAT CHOP HAS TO BE A LOT WELLER-PLACED THAN THE ONE YOU BOLLIXED UP!
HOW LONG'LL IT BE BEFORE YOU BIRD-BRAINS GET THE MESSAGE?
I APPRECIATE THE SPARRING PRACTICE, BUT YOU'RE NOT THE ONES I'M AFTER!
THUMP!
SLAM!
QUICKLY! OUR ONLY CHANCE IS TO STRIKE FROM BEHIND-- WITH EVERY-THING WE'VE GOT!
HE CAN NEVER STOP US IN TIME!
LET HIM HAVE IT!
YOU CAN'T, FELLAS!
'CAUSE YOU HAVEN'T GOT IT!
IT'S NEVER OPEN SEASON ON GIANTS WHEN I'M AROUND!
SPAK!
IN CASE YOU'RE WONDERING, MY FRIENDS CALL ME JAN!
BUT YOU CAN CALL ME-- THE WASP-- WHEN YOU WAKE UP, THAT IS!
WELL, LOOK WHO'S HERE!
THE LORD HIGH MUCK-A-MUCK HIMSELF!
DUNNO WHAT HE'S UP TO-- BUT I'D BETTER PUT A STOP TO IT!
16

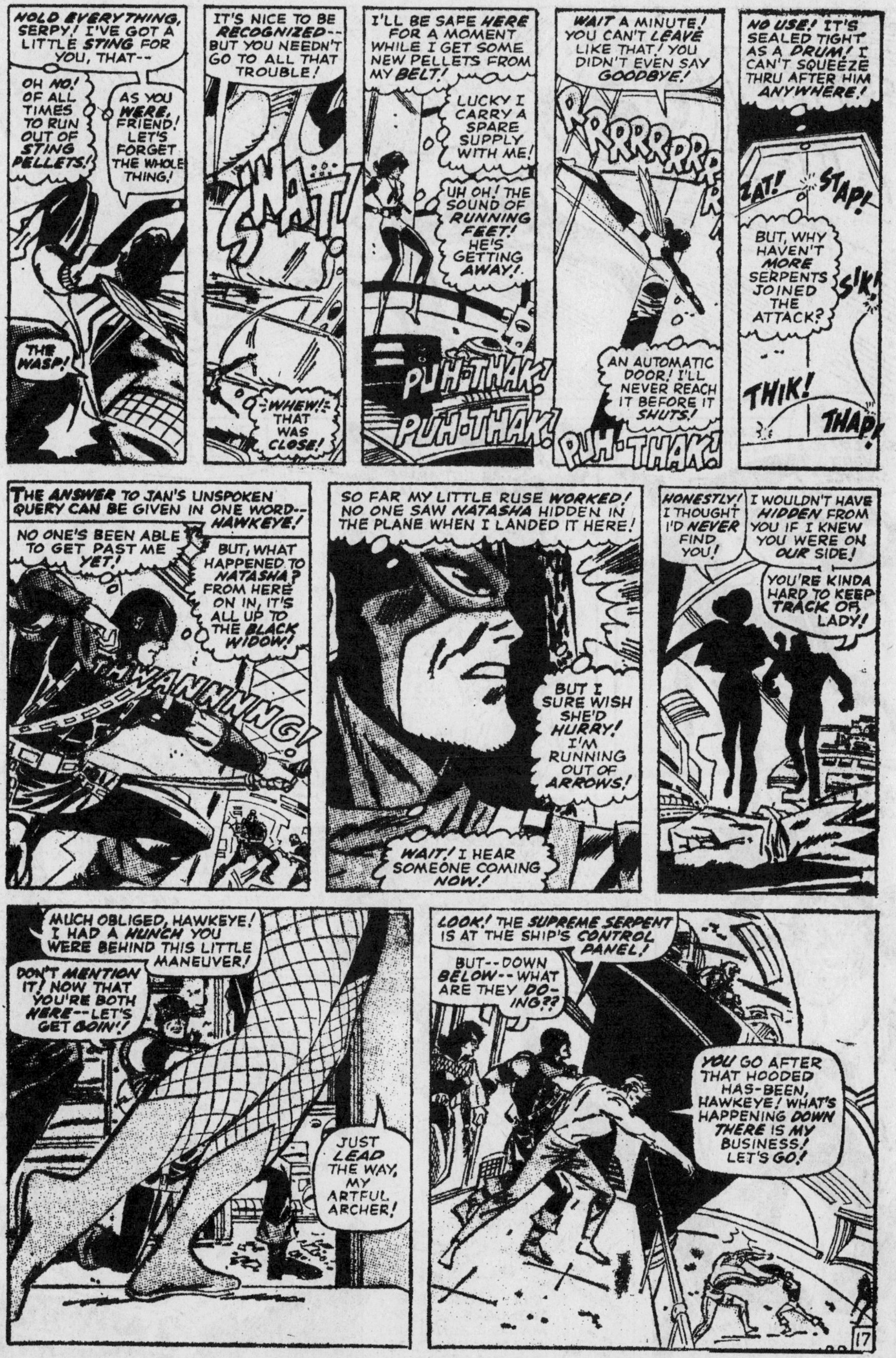
HOLD EVERYTHING, SERPY! I'VE GOT A LITTLE STING FOR YOU, THAT--
OH NO! OF ALL TIMES TO RUN OUT OF STING PELLETS!
AS YOU WERE, FRIEND! LET'S FORGET THE WHOLE THING!
THE WASP!
IT'S NICE TO BE RECOGNIZED-- BUT YOU NEEDN'T GO TO ALL THAT TROUBLE!
SNAT!
WHEW! THAT WAS CLOSE!
I'LL BE SAFE HERE FOR A MOMENT WHILE I GET SOME NEW PELLETS FROM MY BELT!
LUCKY I CARRY A SPARE SUPPLY WITH ME!
UH OH! THE SOUND OF RUNNING FEET! HE'S GETTING AWAY!
PUH-THAK! PUH-THAK!
WAIT A MINUTE! YOU CAN'T LEAVE LIKE THAT! YOU DIDN'T EVEN SAY GOODBYE!
RRRRRRRRR
AN AUTOMATIC DOOR! I'LL NEVER REACH IT BEFORE IT SHUTS!
PUH-THAK!
NO USE! IT'S SEALED TIGHT AS A DRUM! I CAN'T SQUEEZE THRU AFTER HIM ANYWHERE!
ZAT! STAP!
BUT, WHY HAVEN'T MORE SERPENTS JOINED THE ATTACK?
SIK!
THIK! THAP!
THE ANSWER TO JAN'S UNSPOKEN QUERY CAN BE GIVEN IN ONE WORD-- HAWKEYE!
NO ONE'S BEEN ABLE TO GET PAST ME YET!
BUT, WHAT HAPPENED TO NATASHA? FROM HERE ON IN, IT'S ALL UP TO THE BLACK WIDOW!
THWANNNNG!
SO FAR MY LITTLE RUSE WORKED! NO ONE SAW NATASHA HIDDEN IN THE PLANE WHEN I LANDED IT HERE!
BUT I SURE WISH SHE'D HURRY! I'M RUNNING OUT OF ARROWS!
WAIT! I HEAR SOMEONE COMING NOW!
HONESTLY! I THOUGHT I'D NEVER FIND YOU!
I WOULDN'T HAVE HIDDEN FROM YOU IF I KNEW YOU WERE ON OUR SIDE!
YOU'RE KINDA HARD TO KEEP TRACK OF, LADY!
MUCH OBLIGED, HAWKEYE! I HAD A HUNCH YOU WERE BEHIND THIS LITTLE MANEUVER!
DON'T MENTION IT! NOW THAT YOU'RE BOTH HERE--LET'S GET GOIN'!
JUST LEAD THE WAY, MY ARTFUL ARCHER!
LOOK! THE SUPREME SERPENT IS AT THE SHIP'S CONTROL PANEL!
BUT--DOWN BELOW--WHAT ARE THEY DOING??
YOU GO AFTER THAT HOODED HAS-BEEN, HAWKEYE! WHAT'S HAPPENING DOWN THERE IS MY BUSINESS! LET'S GO!
17

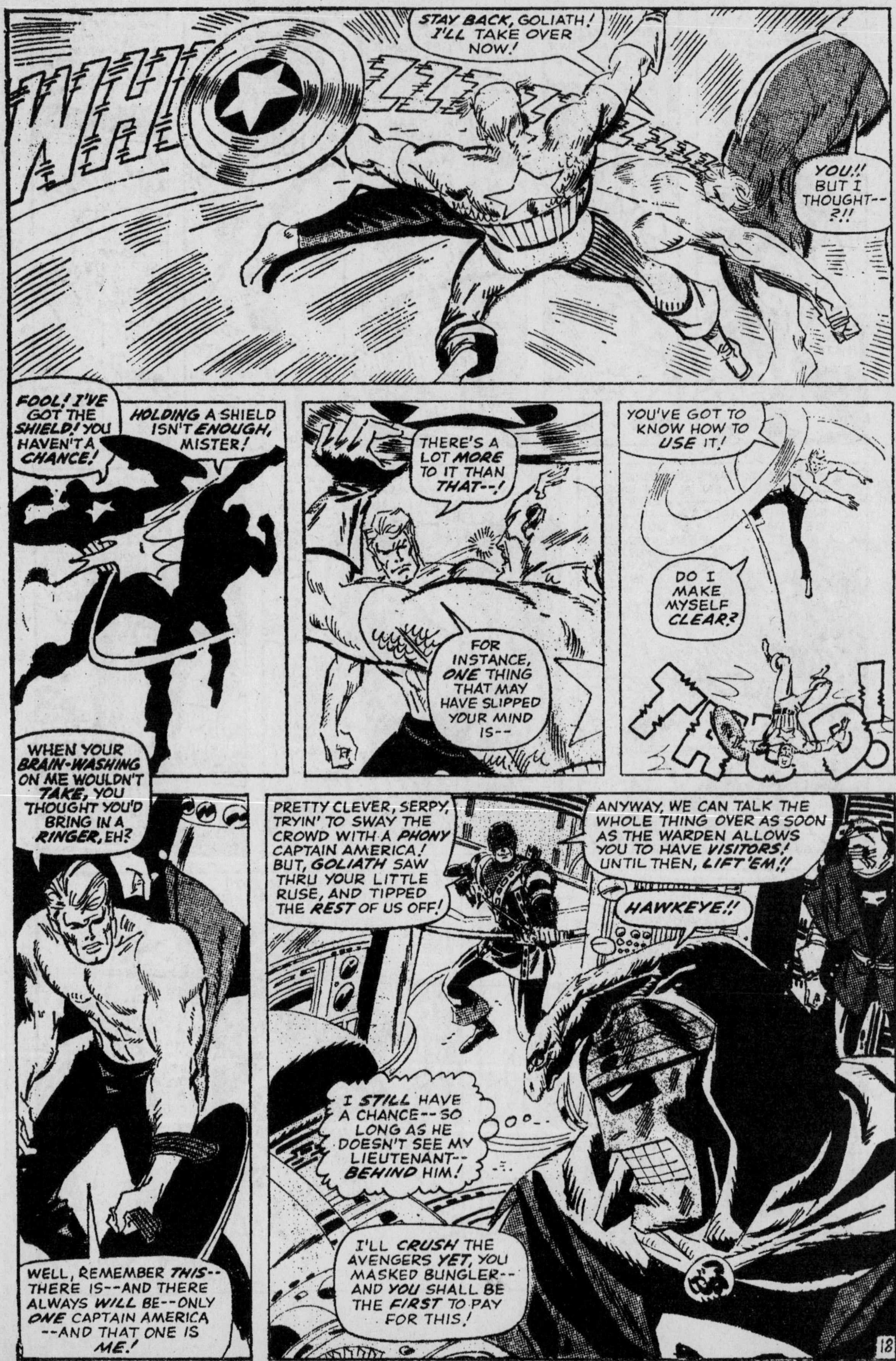
STAY BACK, GOLIATH! I'LL TAKE OVER NOW!
WHHZZZZ
YOU!! BUT I THOUGHT--?!!
FOOL! I'VE GOT THE SHIELD! YOU HAVEN'T A CHANCE!
HOLDING A SHIELD ISN'T ENOUGH, MISTER!
THERE'S A LOT MORE TO IT THAN THAT--!
FOR INSTANCE, ONE THING THAT MAY HAVE SLIPPED YOUR MIND IS--
YOU'VE GOT TO KNOW HOW TO USE IT!
DO I MAKE MYSELF CLEAR?
THUD!
WHEN YOUR BRAIN-WASHING ON ME WOULDN'T TAKE, YOU THOUGHT YOU'D BRING IN A RINGER, EH?
WELL, REMEMBER THIS--THERE IS--AND THERE ALWAYS WILL BE--ONLY ONE CAPTAIN AMERICA--AND THAT ONE IS ME!
PRETTY CLEVER, SERPY, TRYIN' TO SWAY THE CROWD WITH A PHONY CAPTAIN AMERICA! BUT, GOLIATH SAW THRU YOUR LITTLE RUSE, AND TIPPED THE REST OF US OFF!
ANYWAY, WE CAN TALK THE WHOLE THING OVER AS SOON AS THE WARDEN ALLOWS YOU TO HAVE VISITORS! UNTIL THEN, LIFT 'EM!!
HAWKEYE!!
I STILL HAVE A CHANCE--SO LONG AS HE DOESN'T SEE MY LIEUTENANT--BEHIND HIM!
I'LL CRUSH THE AVENGERS YET, YOU MASKED BUNGLER--AND YOU SHALL BE THE FIRST TO PAY FOR THIS!

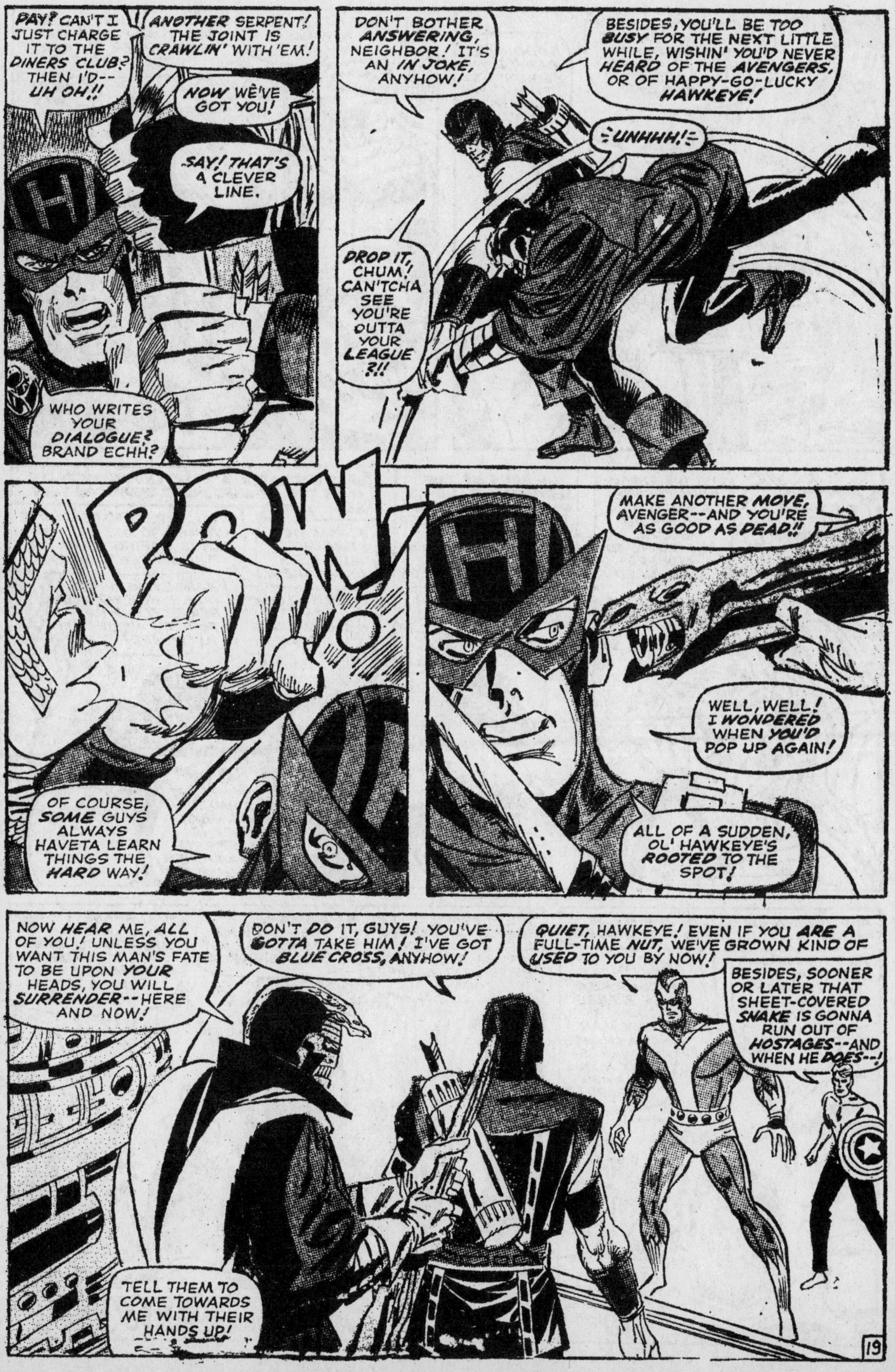
PAY? CAN'T I JUST CHARGE IT TO THE DINERS CLUB? THEN I'D-- UH OH!!
ANOTHER SERPENT! THE JOINT IS CRAWLIN' WITH 'EM!
NOW WE'VE GOT YOU!
SAY! THAT'S A CLEVER LINE.
WHO WRITES YOUR DIALOGUE? BRAND ECHH?
DON'T BOTHER ANSWERING, NEIGHBOR! IT'S AN IN JOKE, ANYHOW!
BESIDES, YOU'LL BE TOO BUSY FOR THE NEXT LITTLE WHILE, WISHIN' YOU'D NEVER HEARD OF THE AVENGERS, OR OF HAPPY-GO-LUCKY HAWKEYE!
UNHHH!
DROP IT, CHUM! CAN'TCHA SEE YOU'RE OUTTA YOUR LEAGUE ?!!
POW!
OF COURSE, SOME GUYS ALWAYS HAVETA LEARN THINGS THE HARD WAY!
MAKE ANOTHER MOVE, AVENGER--AND YOU'RE AS GOOD AS DEAD!!
WELL, WELL! I WONDERED WHEN YOU'D POP UP AGAIN!
ALL OF A SUDDEN, OL' HAWKEYE'S ROOTED TO THE SPOT!
NOW HEAR ME, ALL OF YOU! UNLESS YOU WANT THIS MAN'S FATE TO BE UPON YOUR HEADS, YOU WILL SURRENDER--HERE AND NOW!
DON'T DO IT, GUYS! YOU'VE GOTTA TAKE HIM! I'VE GOT BLUE CROSS, ANYHOW!
QUIET, HAWKEYE! EVEN IF YOU ARE A FULL-TIME NUT, WE'VE GROWN KIND OF USED TO YOU BY NOW!
BESIDES, SOONER OR LATER THAT SHEET-COVERED SNAKE IS GONNA RUN OUT OF HOSTAGES--AND WHEN HE DOES--!
TELL THEM TO COME TOWARDS ME WITH THEIR HANDS UP!
19

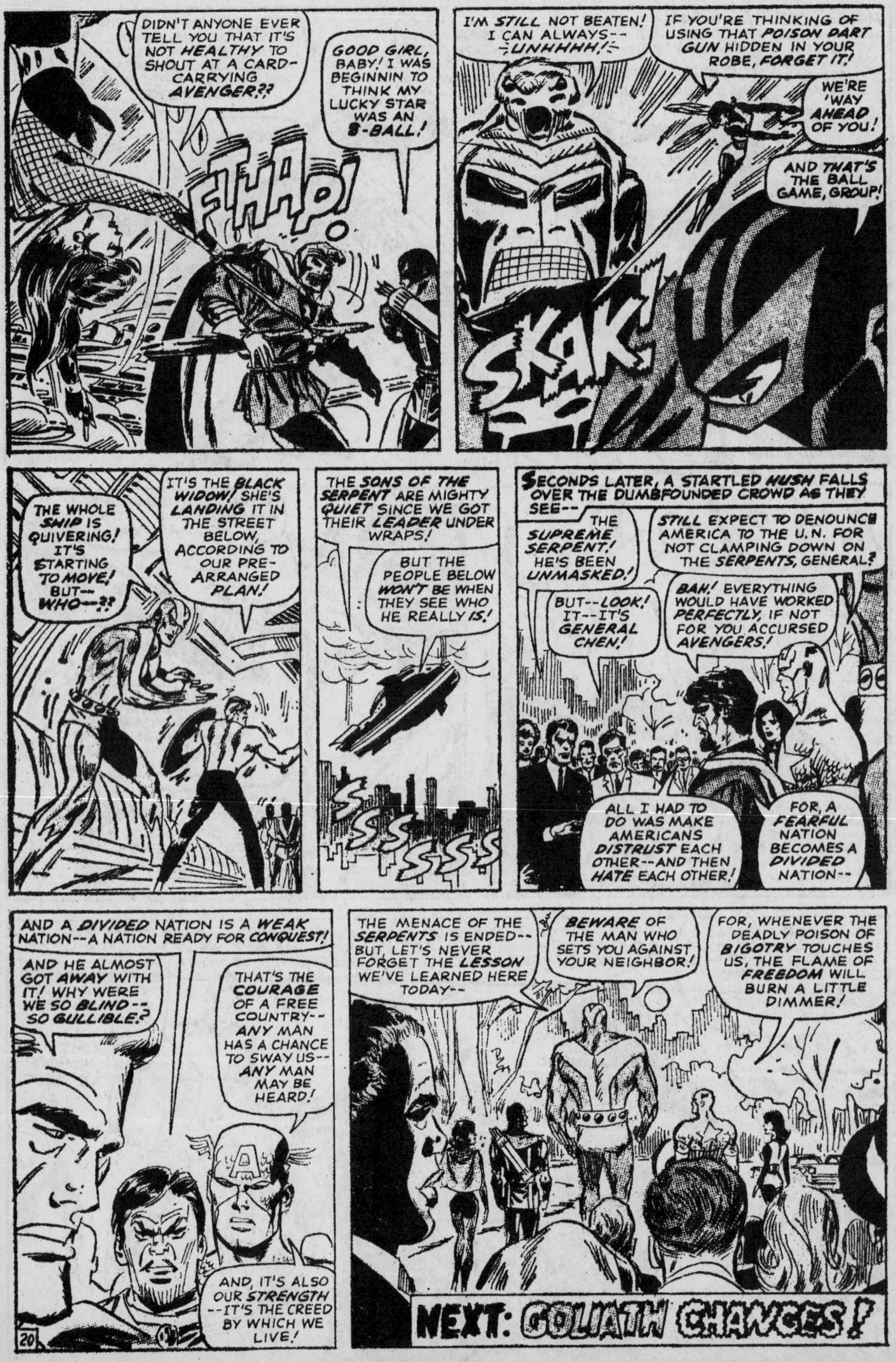
DIDN'T ANYONE EVER TELL YOU THAT IT'S NOT HEALTHY TO SHOUT AT A CARD-CARRYING AVENGER?!?
GOOD GIRL, BABY! I WAS BEGINNIN TO THINK MY LUCKY STAR WAS AN 8-BALL!
FTHAP!
I'M STILL NOT BEATEN! I CAN ALWAYS-- UNHHHH!
IF YOU'RE THINKING OF USING THAT POISON DART GUN HIDDEN IN YOUR ROBE, FORGET IT!
WE'RE 'WAY AHEAD OF YOU!
AND THAT'S THE BALL GAME, GROUP!
SKAK!
THE WHOLE SHIP IS QUIVERING! IT'S STARTING TO MOVE! BUT-- WHO--?!?
IT'S THE BLACK WIDOW! SHE'S LANDING IT IN THE STREET BELOW, ACCORDING TO OUR PRE-ARRANGED PLAN!
THE SONS OF THE SERPENT ARE MIGHTY QUIET SINCE WE GOT THEIR LEADER UNDER WRAPS!
BUT THE PEOPLE BELOW WON'T BE WHEN THEY SEE WHO HE REALLY IS!
SSSSSS
SECONDS LATER, A STARTLED HUSH FALLS OVER THE DUMBFOUNDED CROWD AS THEY SEE--
THE SUPREME SERPENT! HE'S BEEN UNMASKED!
BUT--LOOK! IT--IT'S GENERAL CHEN!
STILL EXPECT TO DENOUNCE AMERICA TO THE U.N. FOR NOT CLAMPING DOWN ON THE SERPENTS, GENERAL?
BAH! EVERYTHING WOULD HAVE WORKED PERFECTLY, IF NOT FOR YOU ACCURSED AVENGERS!
ALL I HAD TO DO WAS MAKE AMERICANS DISTRUST EACH OTHER--AND THEN HATE EACH OTHER!
FOR, A FEARFUL NATION BECOMES A DIVIDED NATION--
AND A DIVIDED NATION IS A WEAK NATION--A NATION READY FOR CONQUEST!
AND HE ALMOST GOT AWAY WITH IT! WHY WERE WE SO BLIND--SO GULLIBLE?
THAT'S THE COURAGE OF A FREE COUNTRY--ANY MAN HAS A CHANCE TO SWAY US--ANY MAN MAY BE HEARD!
AND, IT'S ALSO OUR STRENGTH--IT'S THE CREED BY WHICH WE LIVE!
THE MENACE OF THE SERPENTS IS ENDED--BUT, LET'S NEVER FORGET THE LESSON WE'VE LEARNED HERE TODAY--
BEWARE OF THE MAN WHO SETS YOU AGAINST YOUR NEIGHBOR!
FOR, WHENEVER THE DEADLY POISON OF BIGOTRY TOUCHES US, THE FLAME OF FREEDOM WILL BURN A LITTLE DIMMER!
NEXT: GOLIATH CHANGES!

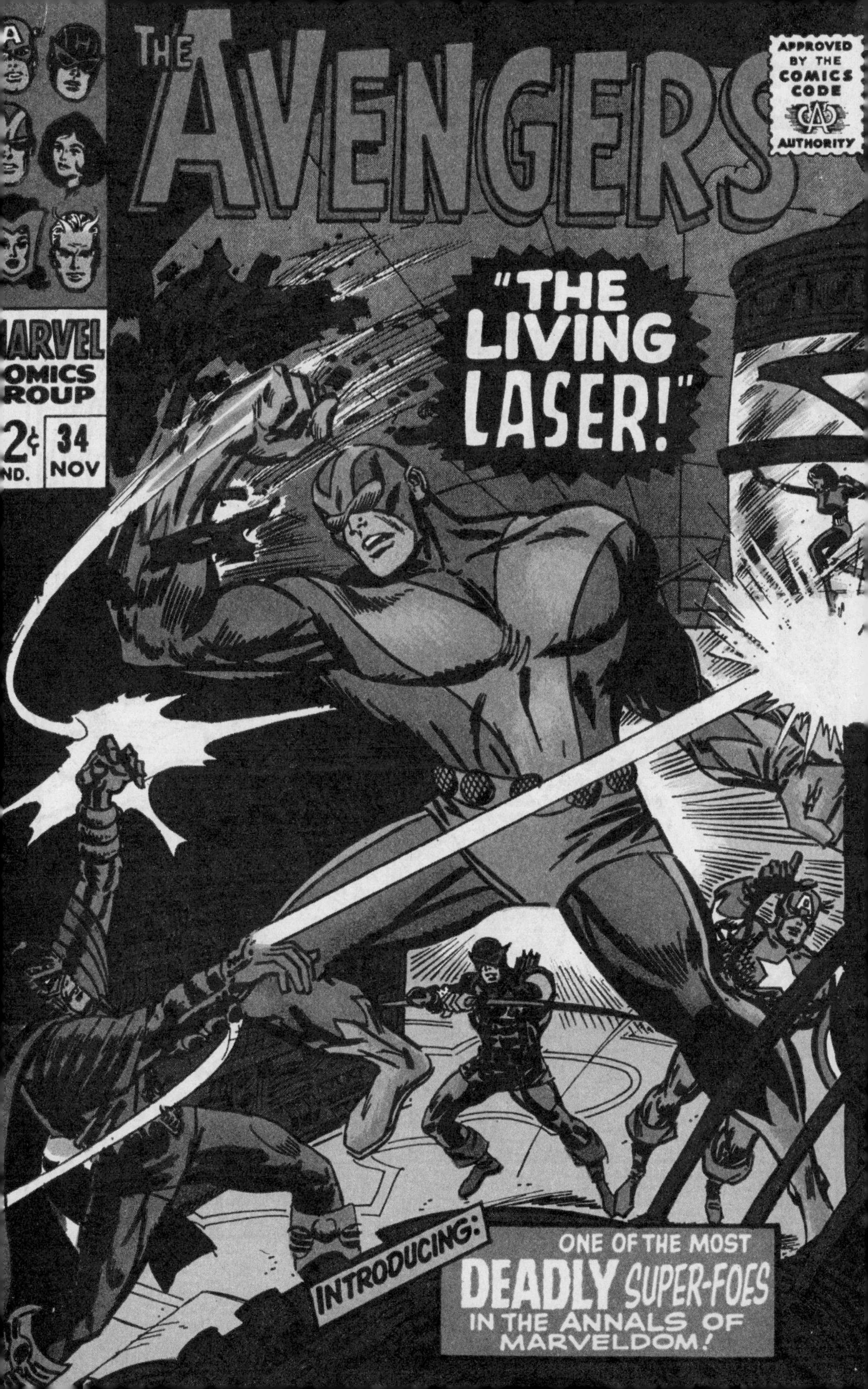
THE AVENGERS
APPROVED BY THE COMICS CODE AUTHORITY
MARVEL COMICS GROUP
34 NOV
"THE LIVING LASER!"
INTRODUCING:
ONE OF THE MOST DEADLY SUPER-FOES IN THE ANNALS OF MARVELDOM!

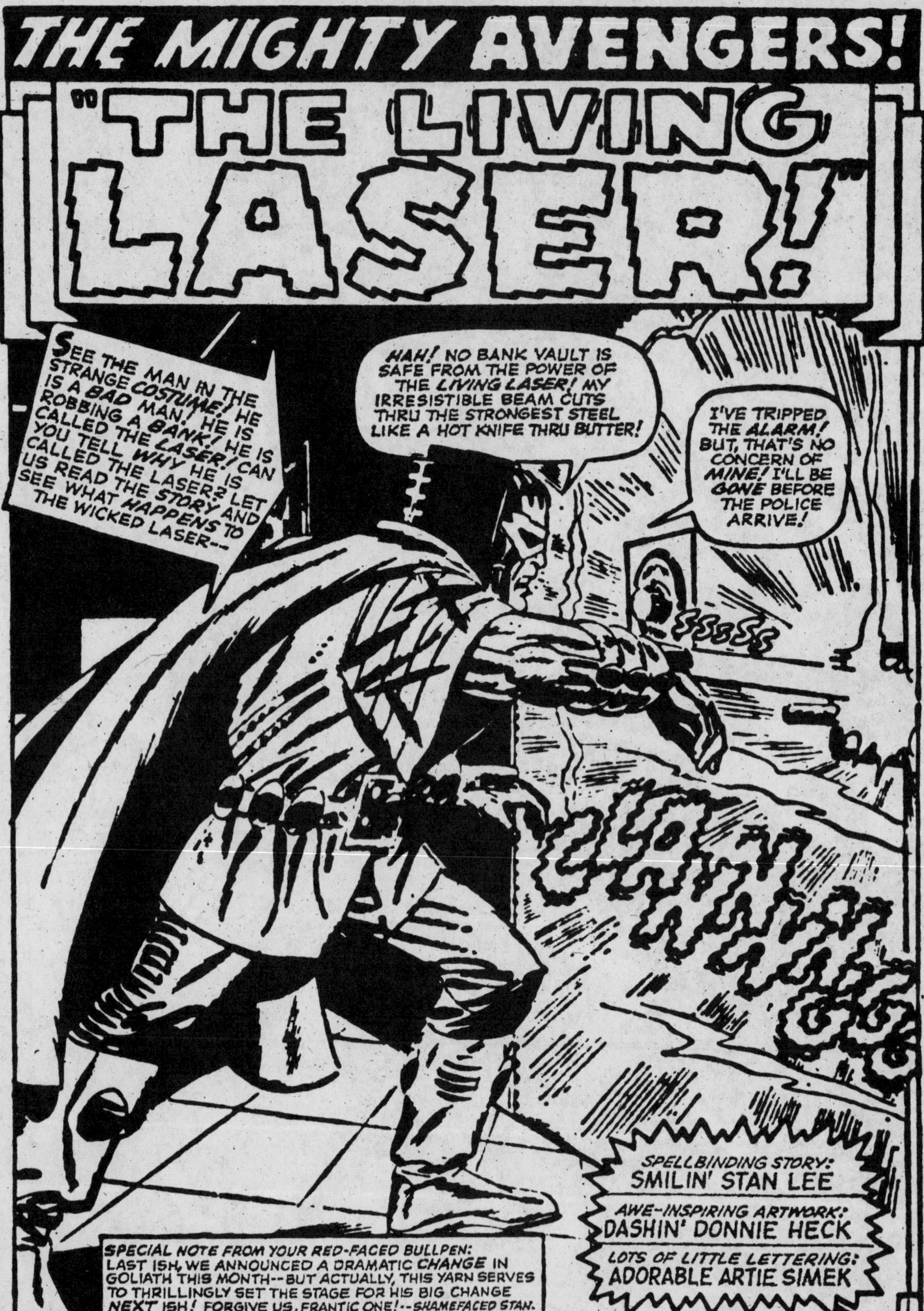
THE MIGHTY AVENGERS!
"THE LIVING LASER!"
SEE THE MAN IN THE STRANGE COSTUME! HE IS A BAD MAN! HE IS ROBBING A BANK! HE IS CALLED THE LASER! CAN YOU TELL WHY HE IS CALLED THE LASER? LET US READ THE STORY AND SEE WHAT HAPPENS TO THE WICKED LASER--
HAH! NO BANK VAULT IS SAFE FROM THE POWER OF THE LIVING LASER! MY IRRESISTIBLE BEAM CUTS THRU THE STRONGEST STEEL LIKE A HOT KNIFE THRU BUTTER!
I'VE TRIPPED THE ALARM! BUT, THAT'S NO CONCERN OF MINE! I'LL BE GONE BEFORE THE POLICE ARRIVE!
SPELLBINDING STORY: SMILIN' STAN LEE
AWE-INSPIRING ARTWORK: DASHIN' DONNIE HECK
LOTS OF LITTLE LETTERING: ADORABLE ARTIE SIMEK
SPECIAL NOTE FROM YOUR RED-FACED BULLPEN: LAST ISH, WE ANNOUNCED A DRAMATIC CHANGE IN GOLIATH THIS MONTH--BUT ACTUALLY, THIS YARN SERVES TO THRILLINGLY SET THE STAGE FOR HIS BIG CHANGE NEXT ISH! FORGIVE US, FRANTIC ONE!--SHAMEFACED STAN.

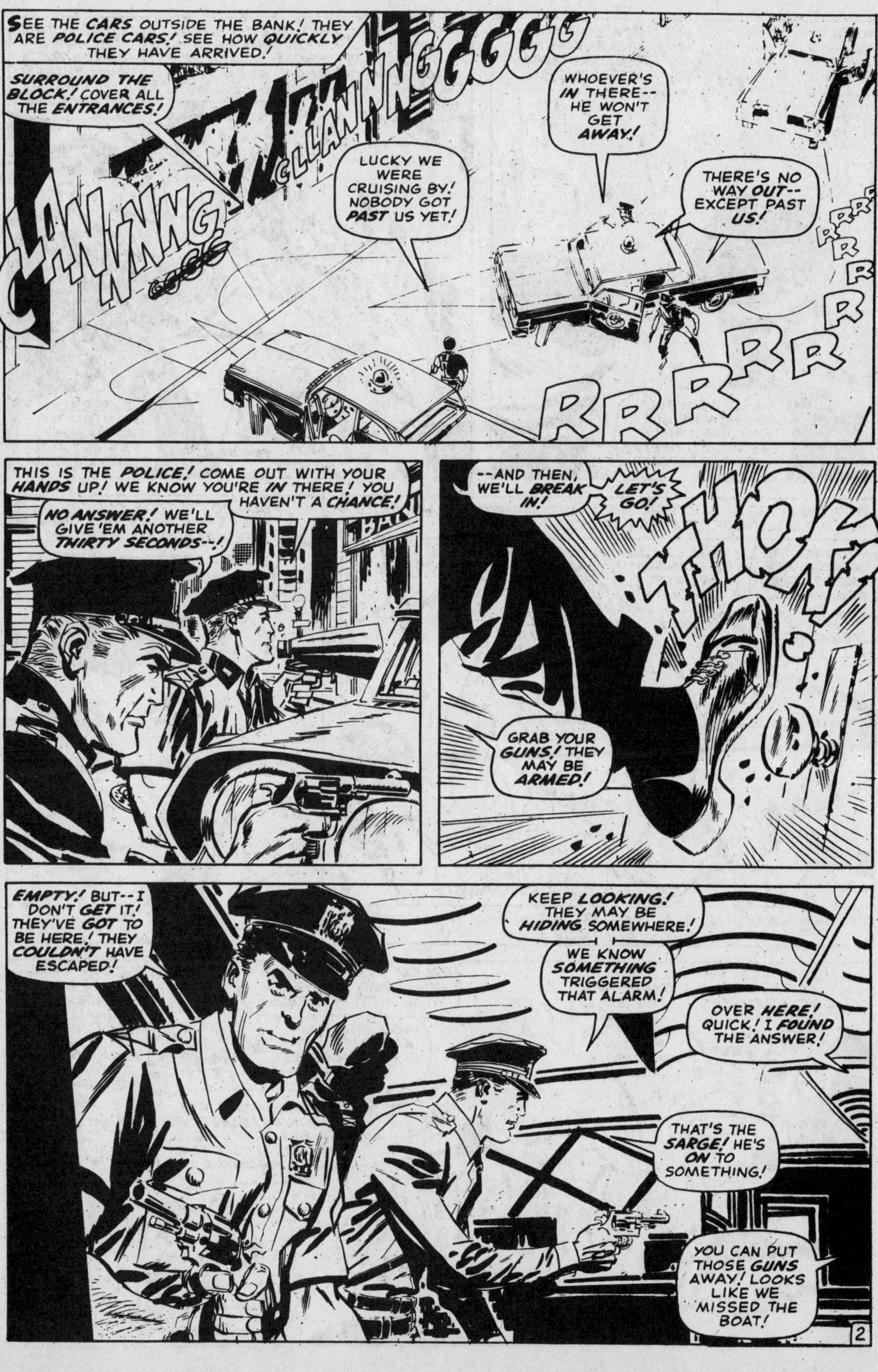
SEE THE CARS OUTSIDE THE BANK! THEY ARE POLICE CARS! SEE HOW QUICKLY THEY HAVE ARRIVED!
SURROUND THE BLOCK! COVER ALL THE ENTRANCES!
CLANNNNG
CLLANNNGGGGG
LUCKY WE WERE CRUISING BY! NOBODY GOT PAST US YET!
WHOEVER'S IN THERE-- HE WON'T GET AWAY!
THERE'S NO WAY OUT-- EXCEPT PAST US!
RRRRRRRRRRR
THIS IS THE POLICE! COME OUT WITH YOUR HANDS UP! WE KNOW YOU'RE IN THERE! YOU HAVEN'T A CHANCE!
NO ANSWER! WE'LL GIVE 'EM ANOTHER THIRTY SECONDS--!
--AND THEN, WE'LL BREAK IN!
LET'S GO!
THOK!
GRAB YOUR GUNS! THEY MAY BE ARMED!
EMPTY! BUT--I DON'T GET IT! THEY'VE GOT TO BE HERE! THEY COULDN'T HAVE ESCAPED!
KEEP LOOKING! THEY MAY BE HIDING SOMEWHERE!
WE KNOW SOMETHING TRIGGERED THAT ALARM!
OVER HERE! QUICK! I FOUND THE ANSWER!
THAT'S THE SARGE! HE'S ON TO SOMETHING!
YOU CAN PUT THOSE GUNS AWAY! LOOKS LIKE WE MISSED THE BOAT!
2

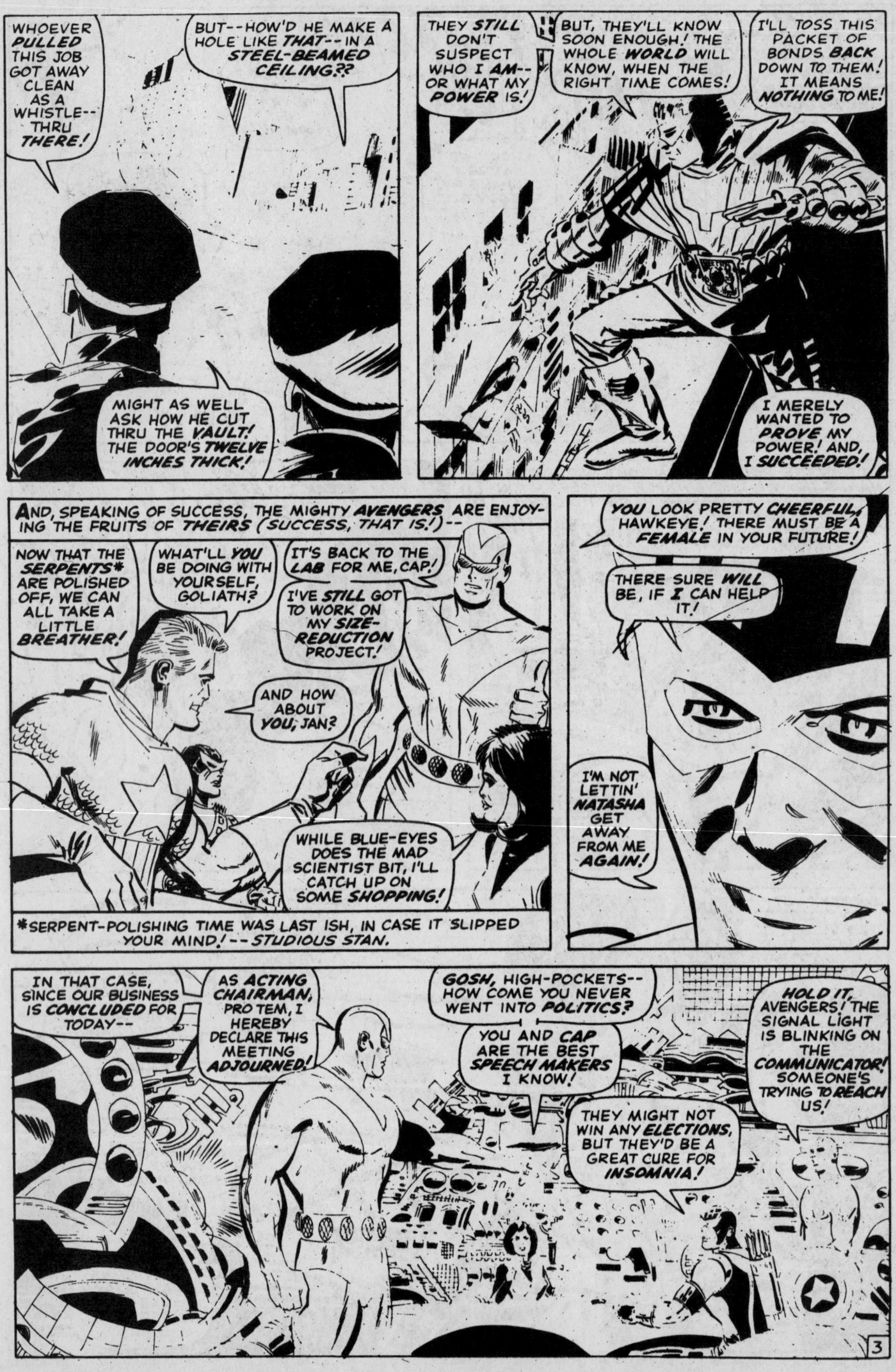
WHOEVER PULLED THIS JOB GOT AWAY CLEAN AS A WHISTLE--THRU THERE!
BUT--HOW'D HE MAKE A HOLE LIKE THAT--IN A STEEL-BEAMED CEILING??
MIGHT AS WELL ASK HOW HE CUT THRU THE VAULT! THE DOOR'S TWELVE INCHES THICK!
THEY STILL DON'T SUSPECT WHO I AM--OR WHAT MY POWER IS!
BUT, THEY'LL KNOW SOON ENOUGH! THE WHOLE WORLD WILL KNOW, WHEN THE RIGHT TIME COMES!
I'LL TOSS THIS PACKET OF BONDS BACK DOWN TO THEM! IT MEANS NOTHING TO ME!
I MERELY WANTED TO PROVE MY POWER! AND, I SUCCEEDED!
AND, SPEAKING OF SUCCESS, THE MIGHTY AVENGERS ARE ENJOYING THE FRUITS OF THEIRS (SUCCESS, THAT IS!)--
NOW THAT THE SERPENTS* ARE POLISHED OFF, WE CAN ALL TAKE A LITTLE BREATHER!
WHAT'LL YOU BE DOING WITH YOURSELF, GOLIATH?
IT'S BACK TO THE LAB FOR ME, CAP!
I'VE STILL GOT TO WORK ON MY SIZE-REDUCTION PROJECT!
AND HOW ABOUT YOU, JAN?
WHILE BLUE-EYES DOES THE MAD SCIENTIST BIT, I'LL CATCH UP ON SOME SHOPPING!
*SERPENT-POLISHING TIME WAS LAST ISH, IN CASE IT SLIPPED YOUR MIND!--STUDIOUS STAN.
YOU LOOK PRETTY CHEERFUL, HAWKEYE! THERE MUST BE A FEMALE IN YOUR FUTURE!
THERE SURE WILL BE, IF I CAN HELP IT!
I'M NOT LETTIN' NATASHA GET AWAY FROM ME AGAIN!
IN THAT CASE, SINCE OUR BUSINESS IS CONCLUDED FOR TODAY--
AS ACTING CHAIRMAN, PRO TEM, I HEREBY DECLARE THIS MEETING ADJOURNED!
GOSH, HIGH-POCKETS--HOW COME YOU NEVER WENT INTO POLITICS?
YOU AND CAP ARE THE BEST SPEECH MAKERS I KNOW!
THEY MIGHT NOT WIN ANY ELECTIONS, BUT THEY'D BE A GREAT CURE FOR INSOMNIA!
HOLD IT, AVENGERS! THE SIGNAL LIGHT IS BLINKING ON THE COMMUNICATOR! SOMEONE'S TRYING TO REACH US!
3

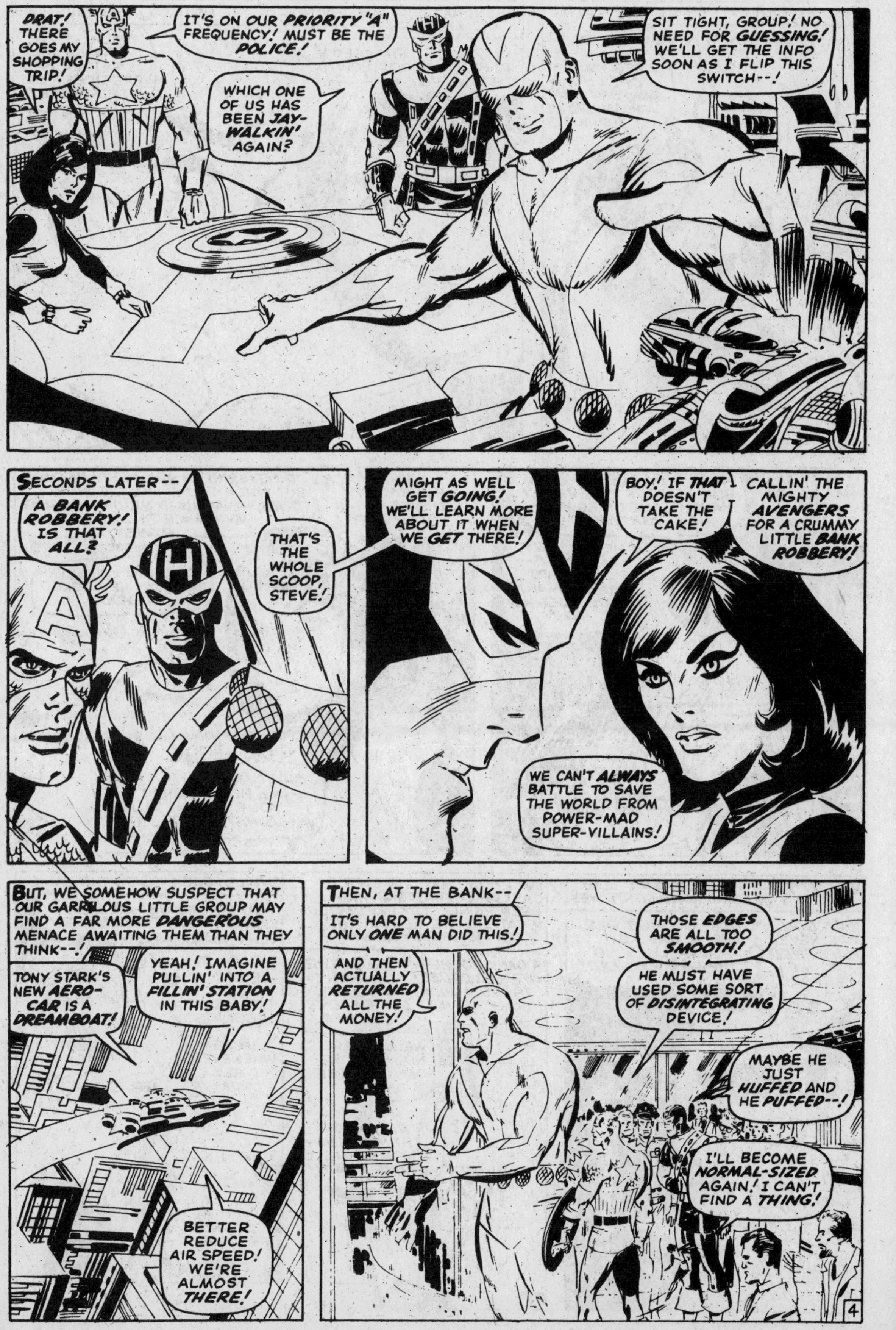
DRAT! THERE GOES MY SHOPPING TRIP!
IT'S ON OUR PRIORITY "A" FREQUENCY! MUST BE THE POLICE!
WHICH ONE OF US HAS BEEN JAY-WALKIN' AGAIN?
SIT TIGHT, GROUP! NO NEED FOR GUESSING! WE'LL GET THE INFO SOON AS I FLIP THIS SWITCH--!
SECONDS LATER--
A BANK ROBBERY! IS THAT ALL?
THAT'S THE WHOLE SCOOP, STEVE!
MIGHT AS WELL GET GOING! WE'LL LEARN MORE ABOUT IT WHEN WE GET THERE!
BOY! IF THAT DOESN'T TAKE THE CAKE!
CALLIN' THE MIGHTY AVENGERS FOR A CRUMMY LITTLE BANK ROBBERY!
WE CAN'T ALWAYS BATTLE TO SAVE THE WORLD FROM POWER-MAD SUPER-VILLAINS!
BUT, WE SOMEHOW SUSPECT THAT OUR GARRULOUS LITTLE GROUP MAY FIND A FAR MORE DANGEROUS MENACE AWAITING THEM THAN THEY THINK--!
TONY STARK'S NEW AERO-CAR IS A DREAMBOAT!
YEAH! IMAGINE PULLIN' INTO A FILLIN' STATION IN THIS BABY!
BETTER REDUCE AIR SPEED! WE'RE ALMOST THERE!
THEN, AT THE BANK--
IT'S HARD TO BELIEVE ONLY ONE MAN DID THIS!
AND THEN ACTUALLY RETURNED ALL THE MONEY!
THOSE EDGES ARE ALL TOO SMOOTH!
HE MUST HAVE USED SOME SORT OF DISINTEGRATING DEVICE!
MAYBE HE JUST HUFFED AND HE PUFFED--!
I'LL BECOME NORMAL-SIZED AGAIN! I CAN'T FIND A THING!
4

MINUTES LATER--

WHY, JANET VAN DYNE!!

I BEG YOUR-- OH! LUCY BARTON! WHAT A WONDERFUL SURPRISE!

I HAVEN'T SEEN YOU SINCE YOUR COMING OUT PARTY!

THEN, AFTER A FEW ROUNDS OF THE USUAL FEMALE QUESTIONS AND ANSWERS--

--AND YOU'RE ENGAGED TO BE MARRIED? HOW THRILLING!

ACTUALLY, MY FIANCE'S FATHER IS PRESIDENT OF THIS BANK!

WHAT IS IT, LUCY? WHAT'S WRONG?

I JUST SAW MY EX-BOY FRIEND, ARTHUR PARKS!

WHEN I BROKE UP WITH HIM, HE TOOK IT TERRIBLY HARD! SOMETIMES HE-- HE FRIGHTENS ME!

HE'S A VERY INTENSE-LOOKING YOUNG MAN! WHAT DOES HE DO?

HE'S A RESEARCH PHYSICIST! SCIENCE IS HIS WHOLE LIFE!

I'D NEVER SEEN HIM ANGRY BEFORE, BUT WHEN I TOLD HIM WE WERE THRU, HE ACCUSED ME OF CHOOSING MY FIANCE BECAUSE OF HIS MONEY!

JAN! DID YOU SEE-- THE WAY HE LOOKED AT YOU?

OH, IT MUST HAVE BEEN YOUR IMAGINATION!

BUT WE KNOW THAT IT WASN'T LUCY BARTON'S IMAGINATION--DON'T WE?

THAT GIRL! THIS NEVER HAPPENED TO ME BEFORE!

ONE LOOK AT HER, AND IT WAS AS THOUGH LUCY NO LONGER EXISTED!

SHE'S THE WASP! I RECOGNIZED HER ON SIGHT!

I'VE GOT TO MEET HER-- SOMEHOW!

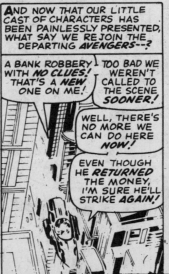

AND NOW THAT OUR LITTLE CAST OF CHARACTERS HAS BEEN PAINLESSLY PRESENTED, WHAT SAY WE REJOIN THE DEPARTING AVENGERS--?

A BANK ROBBERY WITH NO CLUES! THAT'S A NEW ONE ON ME!

TOO BAD WE WEREN'T CALLED TO THE SCENE SOONER!

WELL, THERE'S NO MORE WE CAN DO HERE NOW!

EVEN THOUGH HE RETURNED THE MONEY, I'M SURE HE'LL STRIKE AGAIN!

WHILE, BACK INSIDE THE BANK--

THAT'S STRANGE! ARTHUR SEEMS TO HAVE VANISHED!

IF ONLY I COULD LOSE THAT FEELING OF DANGER WHENEVER I SEE HIM!

AND--THE WAY HE LOOKED AT JAN--!

5

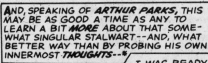

AND, SPEAKING OF *ARTHUR PARKS*, THIS MAY BE AS GOOD A TIME AS ANY TO LEARN A BIT *MORE* ABOUT THAT SOMEWHAT SINGULAR STALWART--AND, WHAT BETTER WAY THAN BY PROBING HIS OWN INNERMOST *THOUGHTS*--*

IT DOESN'T SEEM *POSSIBLE!*

WHEN *LUCY* BROKE OFF WITH ME, I THOUGHT MY *LIFE* HAD ENDED!

I WAS READY TO DO *ANYTHING* TO PROVE I WAS *BETTER* THAN THAT *BANKER'S SON* SHE DECIDED TO MARRY!

*ALTHOUGH *WIRE-TAPPING* IS ILLEGAL IN CERTAIN AREAS, FORTUNATELY FOR COMICDOM, *MIND-TAPPING* IS STILL PERMISSIBLE WHEN NECESSARY! --*SOCIOLOGICAL STAN.*

AND NOW--AFTER JUST ONE FLEEPING GLIMPSE OF THE *WASP*--LUCY MEANS *NOTHING* TO ME!

I NEVER BELIEVED IN LOVE AT FIRST SIGHT BEFORE --UNTIL *TODAY!*

BUT--WHAT DO I DO *NOW?* SHE'S THE PARTNER OF THE MOST *POWERFUL* AVENGER OF ALL!

BUT, THAT DOESN'T HAVE TO STOP *ME!*

MY *OWN* NEW-FOUND POWER HAS BEEN ABLE TO GET ME ALL THE MONEY I CAN EVER NEED! AND, IT'S GIVEN ME SOMETHING FAR *GREATER* THAN MERE WEALTH--

IT'S GIVEN ME A *WEAPON*--ONE STRONG ENOUGH TO DEFEAT THE AVENGERS *THEMSELVES,* IF THEY SHOULD EVER DARE *OPPOSE* ME!

I HAD ORIGINALLY STUMBLED UPON MY DISCOVERY WHILE DOING PURE *RESEARCH*--A DISCOVERY ALLOWING ME TO *HARNESS* ONE OF THE MOST AWESOME SOURCES OF ENERGY ON EARTH!

BUT NOW, I'M *THRU* WITH RESERCH! MY DISCOVERY WILL BE USED TO SERVE NO ONE BUT *MYSELF!*

AND, THERE'S NO TIME LIKE THE *PRESENT!*

IF *ANYONE* CAN WIN THE WONDERFUL *WASP* AWAY FROM *GOLIATH,* ONLY *ONE MAN* CAN DO IT! AND *I'M* THAT MAN!

FOR, *NO ONE* CAN MATCH THE POWER OF--

THE *LIVING LASER!*

6

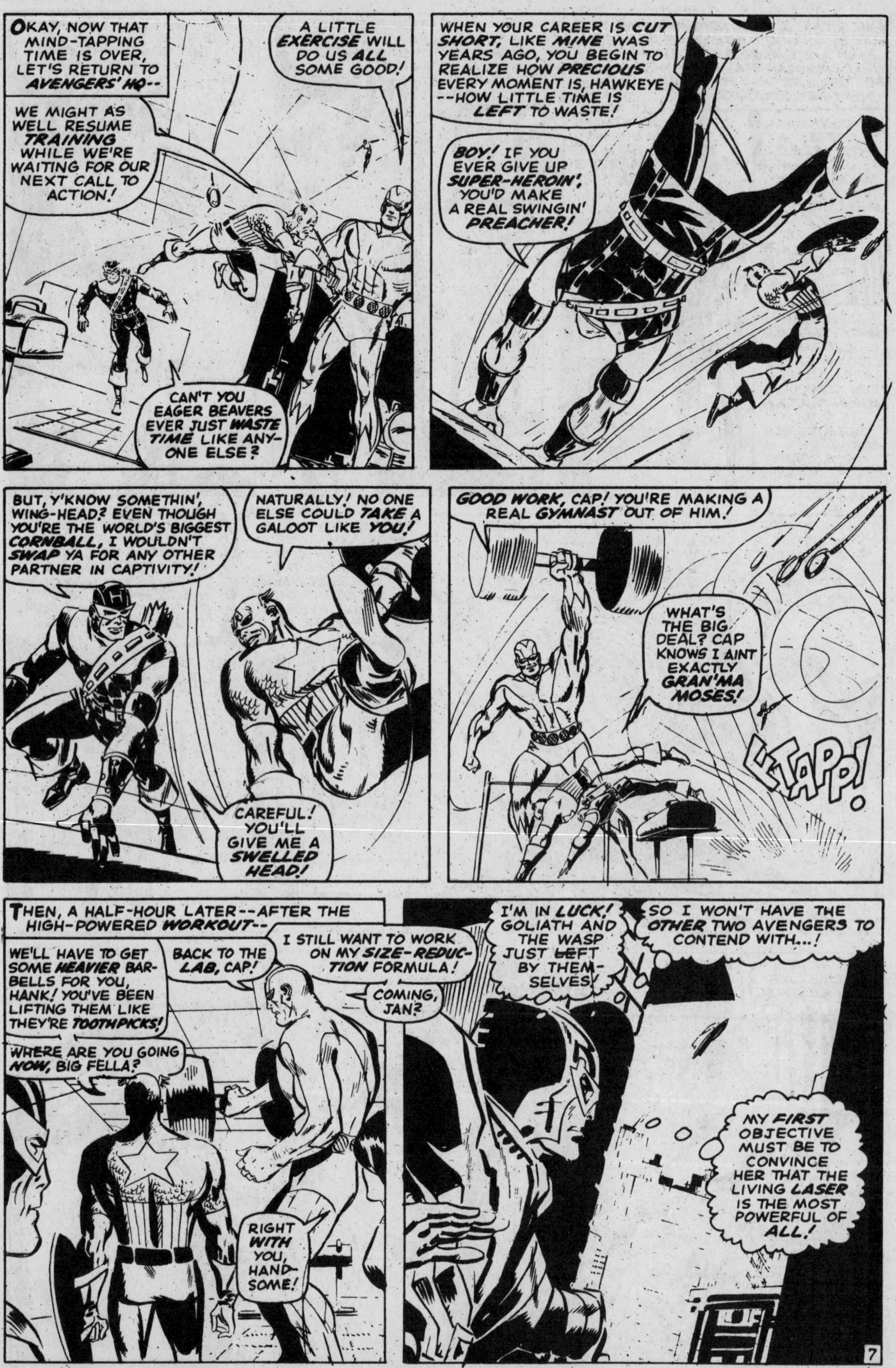
OKAY, NOW THAT MIND-TAPPING TIME IS OVER, LET'S RETURN TO AVENGERS' HQ--
WE MIGHT AS WELL RESUME TRAINING WHILE WE'RE WAITING FOR OUR NEXT CALL TO ACTION!
A LITTLE EXERCISE WILL DO US ALL SOME GOOD!
CAN'T YOU EAGER BEAVERS EVER JUST WASTE TIME LIKE ANY-ONE ELSE?
WHEN YOUR CAREER IS CUT SHORT, LIKE MINE WAS YEARS AGO, YOU BEGIN TO REALIZE HOW PRECIOUS EVERY MOMENT IS, HAWKEYE --HOW LITTLE TIME IS LEFT TO WASTE!
BOY! IF YOU EVER GIVE UP SUPER-HEROIN', YOU'D MAKE A REAL SWINGIN' PREACHER!
BUT, Y'KNOW SOMETHIN', WING-HEAD? EVEN THOUGH YOU'RE THE WORLD'S BIGGEST CORNBALL, I WOULDN'T SWAP YA FOR ANY OTHER PARTNER IN CAPTIVITY!
NATURALLY! NO ONE ELSE COULD TAKE A GALOOT LIKE YOU!
CAREFUL! YOU'LL GIVE ME A SWELLED HEAD!
GOOD WORK, CAP! YOU'RE MAKING A REAL GYMNAST OUT OF HIM!
WHAT'S THE BIG DEAL? CAP KNOWS I AINT EXACTLY GRAN'MA MOSES!
THTAPP!
THEN, A HALF-HOUR LATER--AFTER THE HIGH-POWERED WORKOUT--
WE'LL HAVE TO GET SOME HEAVIER BAR-BELLS FOR YOU, HANK! YOU'VE BEEN LIFTING THEM LIKE THEY'RE TOOTHPICKS!
BACK TO THE LAB, CAP!
I STILL WANT TO WORK ON MY SIZE-REDUCTION FORMULA!
COMING, JAN?
WHERE ARE YOU GOING NOW, BIG FELLA?
RIGHT WITH YOU, HAND-SOME!
I'M IN LUCK! GOLIATH AND THE WASP JUST LEFT BY THEM-SELVES!
SO I WON'T HAVE THE OTHER TWO AVENGERS TO CONTEND WITH...!
MY FIRST OBJECTIVE MUST BE TO CONVINCE HER THAT THE LIVING LASER IS THE MOST POWERFUL OF ALL!

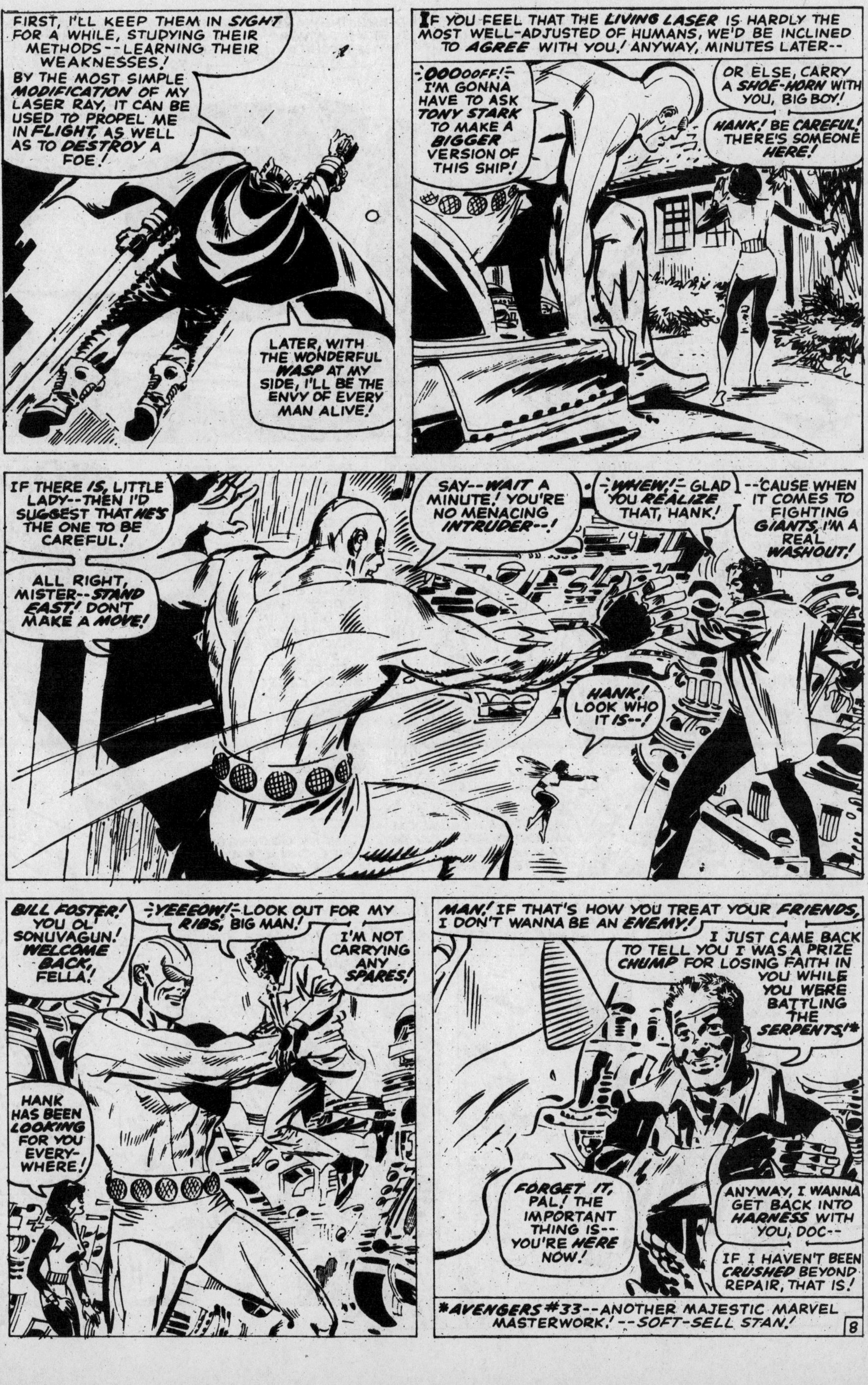
FIRST, I'LL KEEP THEM IN SIGHT FOR A WHILE, STUDYING THEIR METHODS--LEARNING THEIR WEAKNESSES!
BY THE MOST SIMPLE MODIFICATION OF MY LASER RAY, IT CAN BE USED TO PROPEL ME IN FLIGHT, AS WELL AS TO DESTROY A FOE!
LATER, WITH THE WONDERFUL WASP AT MY SIDE, I'LL BE THE ENVY OF EVERY MAN ALIVE!
IF YOU FEEL THAT THE LIVING LASER IS HARDLY THE MOST WELL-ADJUSTED OF HUMANS, WE'D BE INCLINED TO AGREE WITH YOU! ANYWAY, MINUTES LATER--
OOOOOFF! I'M GONNA HAVE TO ASK TONY STARK TO MAKE A BIGGER VERSION OF THIS SHIP!
OR ELSE, CARRY A SHOE-HORN WITH YOU, BIG BOY!
HANK! BE CAREFUL! THERE'S SOMEONE HERE!
IF THERE IS, LITTLE LADY--THEN I'D SUGGEST THAT HE'S THE ONE TO BE CAREFUL!
ALL RIGHT, MISTER--STAND EAST! DON'T MAKE A MOVE!
SAY--WAIT A MINUTE! YOU'RE NO MENACING INTRUDER--!
WHEW! GLAD YOU REALIZE THAT, HANK!
--CAUSE WHEN IT COMES TO FIGHTING GIANTS, I'M A REAL WASHOUT!
HANK! LOOK WHO IT IS--!
BILL FOSTER! YOU OL' SONUVAGUN! WELCOME BACK, FELLA!
YEEEOW! LOOK OUT FOR MY RIBS, BIG MAN!
I'M NOT CARRYING ANY SPARES!
HANK HAS BEEN LOOKING FOR YOU EVERYWHERE!
MAN! IF THAT'S HOW YOU TREAT YOUR FRIENDS, I DON'T WANNA BE AN ENEMY!
I JUST CAME BACK TO TELL YOU I WAS A PRIZE CHUMP FOR LOSING FAITH IN YOU WHILE YOU WERE BATTLING THE SERPENTS!*
FORGET IT, PAL! THE IMPORTANT THING IS--YOU'RE HERE NOW!
ANYWAY, I WANNA GET BACK INTO HARNESS WITH YOU, DOC--
IF I HAVEN'T BEEN CRUSHED BEYOND REPAIR, THAT IS!
*AVENGERS #33--ANOTHER MAJESTIC MARVEL MASTERWORK! --SOFT-SELL STAN!
8

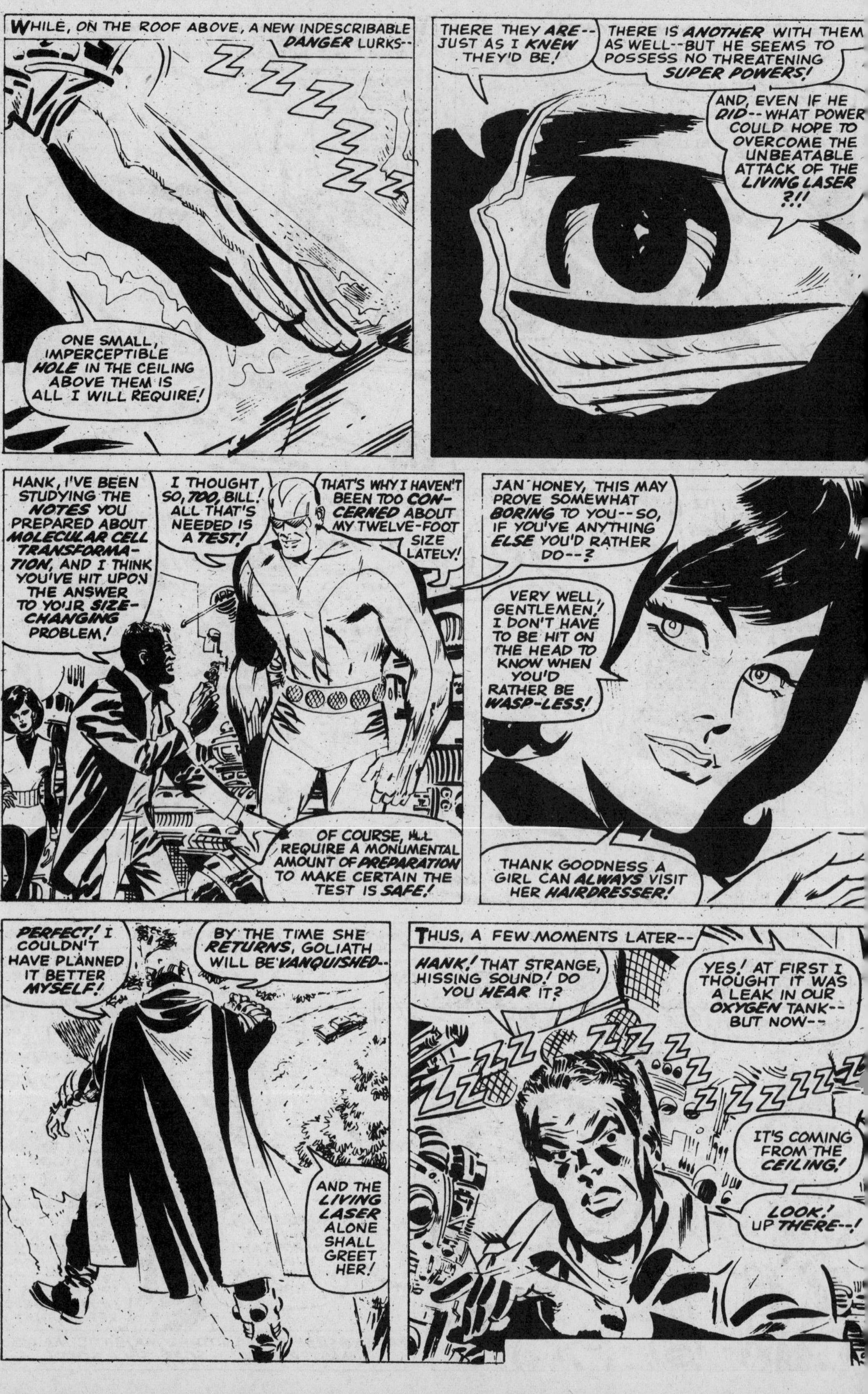

WHILE, ON THE ROOF ABOVE, A NEW INDESCRIBABLE DANGER LURKS--
ZZZZZZ
ONE SMALL, IMPERCEPTIBLE HOLE IN THE CEILING ABOVE THEM IS ALL I WILL REQUIRE!
THERE THEY ARE-- JUST AS I KNEW THEY'D BE!
THERE IS ANOTHER WITH THEM AS WELL--BUT HE SEEMS TO POSSESS NO THREATENING SUPER POWERS!
AND, EVEN IF HE DID--WHAT POWER COULD HOPE TO OVERCOME THE UNBEATABLE ATTACK OF THE LIVING LASER ?!!
HANK, I'VE BEEN STUDYING THE NOTES YOU PREPARED ABOUT MOLECULAR CELL TRANSFORMATION, AND I THINK YOU'VE HIT UPON THE ANSWER TO YOUR SIZE-CHANGING PROBLEM!
I THOUGHT SO, TOO, BILL! ALL THAT'S NEEDED IS A TEST!
THAT'S WHY I HAVEN'T BEEN TOO CONCERNED ABOUT MY TWELVE-FOOT SIZE LATELY!
OF COURSE, REQUIRE A MONUMENTAL AMOUNT OF PREPARATION TO MAKE CERTAIN THE TEST IS SAFE!
JAN HONEY, THIS MAY PROVE SOMEWHAT BORING TO YOU--SO, IF YOU'VE ANYTHING ELSE YOU'D RATHER DO--?
VERY WELL, GENTLEMEN! I DON'T HAVE TO BE HIT ON THE HEAD TO KNOW WHEN YOU'D RATHER BE WASP-LESS!
THANK GOODNESS A GIRL CAN ALWAYS VISIT HER HAIRDRESSER!
PERFECT! I COULDN'T HAVE PLANNED IT BETTER MYSELF!
BY THE TIME SHE RETURNS, GOLIATH WILL BE VANQUISHED--
AND THE LIVING LASER ALONE SHALL GREET HER!
THUS, A FEW MOMENTS LATER--
HANK! THAT STRANGE, HISSING SOUND! DO YOU HEAR IT?
YES! AT FIRST I THOUGHT IT WAS A LEAK IN OUR OXYGEN TANK--BUT NOW--
ZZZZZZZZZZZZZZZZ
IT'S COMING FROM THE CEILING!
LOOK! UP THERE--!

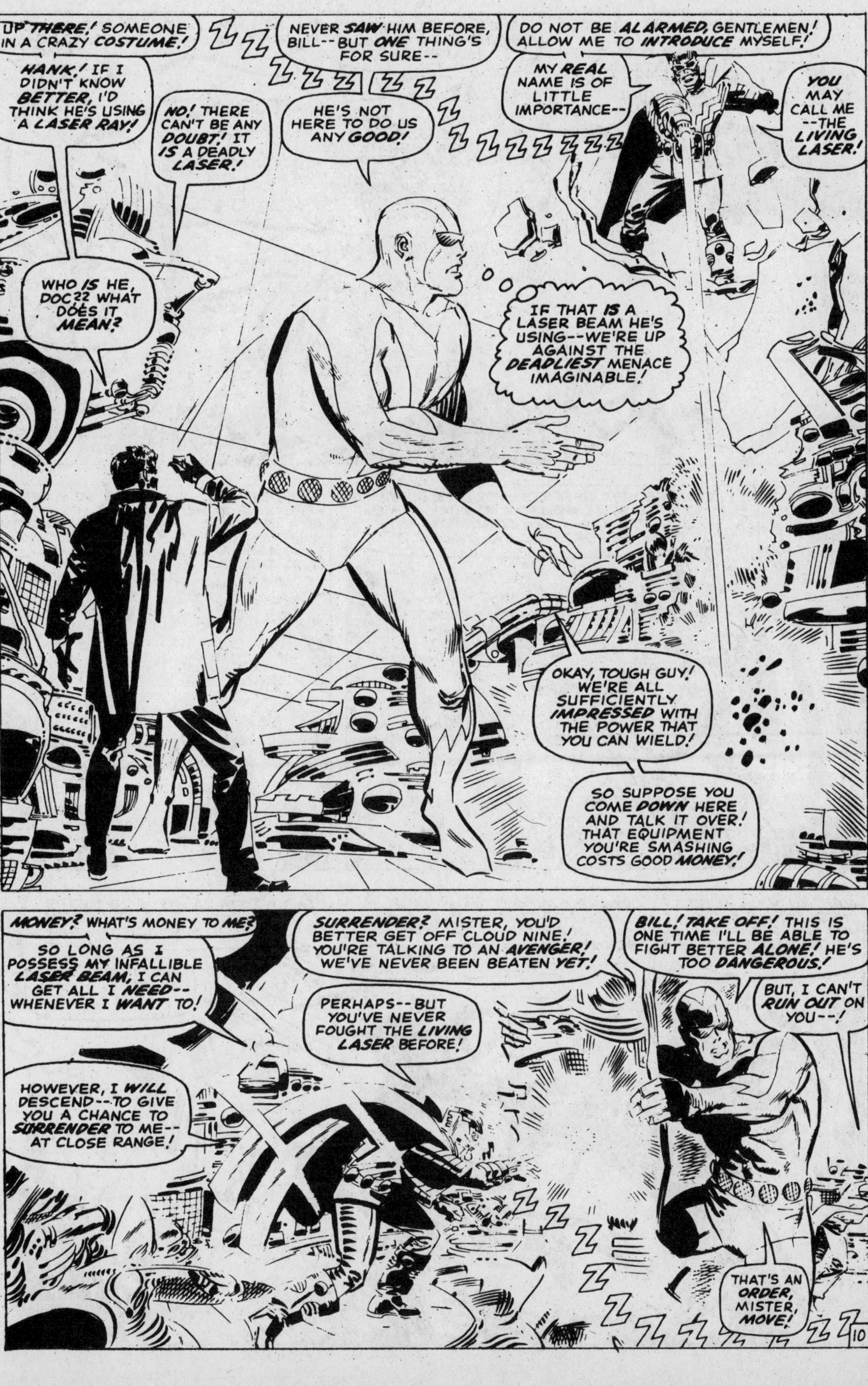
UP THERE! SOMEONE IN A CRAZY COSTUME!
HANK! IF I DIDN'T KNOW BETTER, I'D THINK HE'S USING A LASER RAY!
NO! THERE CAN'T BE ANY DOUBT! IT IS A DEADLY LASER!
NEVER SAW HIM BEFORE, BILL--BUT ONE THING'S FOR SURE--
HE'S NOT HERE TO DO US ANY GOOD!
DO NOT BE ALARMED, GENTLEMEN! ALLOW ME TO INTRODUCE MYSELF!
MY REAL NAME IS OF LITTLE IMPORTANCE--
YOU MAY CALL ME --THE LIVING LASER!
WHO IS HE, DOC?? WHAT DOES IT MEAN?
IF THAT IS A LASER BEAM HE'S USING--WE'RE UP AGAINST THE DEADLIEST MENACE IMAGINABLE!
OKAY, TOUGH GUY! WE'RE ALL SUFFICIENTLY IMPRESSED WITH THE POWER THAT YOU CAN WIELD!
SO SUPPOSE YOU COME DOWN HERE AND TALK IT OVER! THAT EQUIPMENT YOU'RE SMASHING COSTS GOOD MONEY!
MONEY? WHAT'S MONEY TO ME?
SO LONG AS I POSSESS MY INFALLIBLE LASER BEAM, I CAN GET ALL I NEED--WHENEVER I WANT TO!
HOWEVER, I WILL DESCEND--TO GIVE YOU A CHANCE TO SURRENDER TO ME--AT CLOSE RANGE!
SURRENDER? MISTER, YOU'D BETTER GET OFF CLOUD NINE! YOU'RE TALKING TO AN AVENGER! WE'VE NEVER BEEN BEATEN YET!
PERHAPS--BUT YOU'VE NEVER FOUGHT THE LIVING LASER BEFORE!
BILL! TAKE OFF! THIS IS ONE TIME I'LL BE ABLE TO FIGHT BETTER ALONE! HE'S TOO DANGEROUS!
BUT, I CAN'T RUN OUT ON YOU--!
THAT'S AN ORDER, MISTER, MOVE!

THAT WAS *CONSIDERATE* OF YOU, GOLIATH!

OR, COULD IT BE THAT YOU WANTED NO *WITNESS* TO YOUR IMPENDING *DEFEAT??*

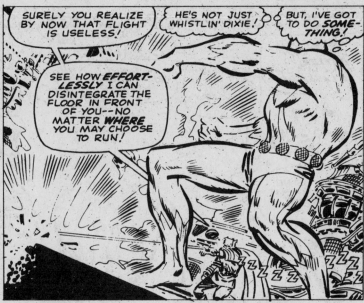

SURELY YOU REALIZE BY NOW THAT FLIGHT IS USELESS!

HE'S NOT JUST WHISTLIN' DIXIE!

BUT, I'VE GOT TO DO *SOME-THING!*

SEE HOW *EFFORT-LESSLY* I CAN DISINTEGRATE THE FLOOR IN FRONT OF YOU--NO MATTER *WHERE* YOU MAY CHOOSE TO RUN!

THE MIGHTY *GOLIATH!* HAH! HOW *EASILY* I THWART YOU AT EVERY TURN!

I ADMIRE YOUR EFFORTS--HOWEVER BUMBLING --TO SEIZE SOME *WEAPON* TO HURL AT ME... BUT NOTICE HOW I CAN *ELIMINATE* ANY-THING BEFORE YOU CAN *TOUCH* IT!

WEAPON MY *FOOT!* I'VE SOMETHING *ELSE* IN MIND!

GOOD! BY APPEARING TO BE AT A LOSS FOR WHAT TO DO NEXT, I MANAGED TO MAKE IT TO THE SPOT I WANT.

LIKE SO MANY *OTHERS,* HIS *OVER-CONFIDENCE* COULD BE HIS UNDOING--

IF I'M *LUCKY!*

RUN, GOLIATH! *RUN*--LIKE THE HIGHLY-TOUTED *FAILURE* YOU REALLY ARE!

HAH! IN YOUR BLIND, UNREASONING *PANIC,* YOU CRASHED RIGHT INTO THAT SOLID *WALL!*

I CRASHED *INTO* IT, ALL RIGHT--BUT IT WASN'T IN *PANIC,* SONNY BOY!

A FELLA *MY* SIZE NEEDS PLENTY OF *ELBOW* ROOM TO DO HIS FIGHTING IN--

AND, THAT'S JUST WHAT I'M GONNA *GET!*

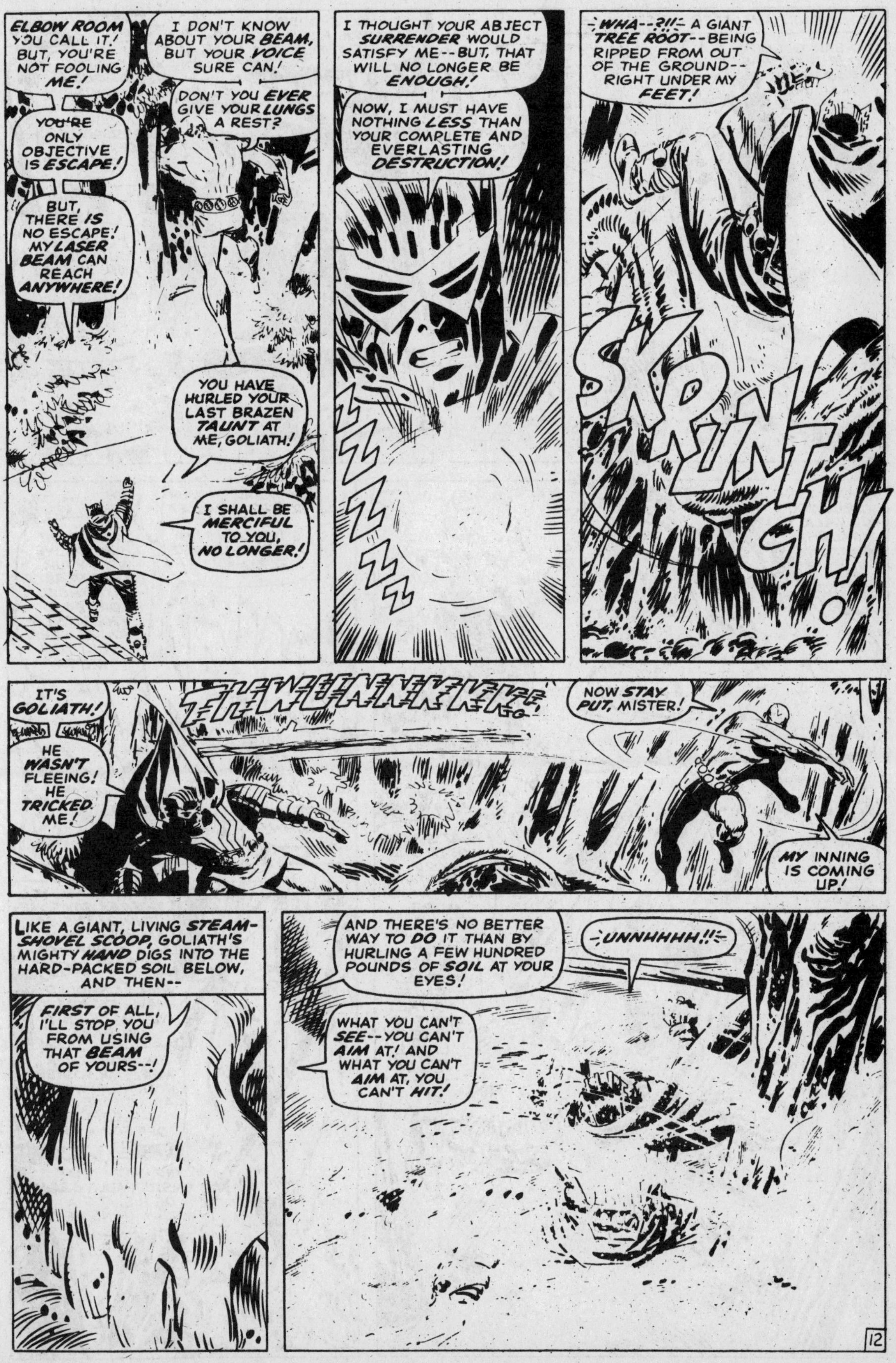
ELBOW ROOM YOU CALL IT! BUT, YOU'RE NOT FOOLING ME!
YOU'RE ONLY OBJECTIVE IS ESCAPE!
BUT, THERE IS NO ESCAPE! MY LASER BEAM CAN REACH ANYWHERE!
I DON'T KNOW ABOUT YOUR BEAM, BUT YOUR VOICE SURE CAN!
DON'T YOU EVER GIVE YOUR LUNGS A REST?
YOU HAVE HURLED YOUR LAST BRAZEN TAUNT AT ME, GOLIATH!
I SHALL BE MERCIFUL TO YOU, NO LONGER!
I THOUGHT YOUR ABJECT SURRENDER WOULD SATISFY ME--BUT, THAT WILL NO LONGER BE ENOUGH!
NOW, I MUST HAVE NOTHING LESS THAN YOUR COMPLETE AND EVERLASTING DESTRUCTION!
WHA--?!!- A GIANT TREE ROOT--BEING RIPPED FROM OUT OF THE GROUND--RIGHT UNDER MY FEET!
SKRUNTCH!
THWUNNKKK
IT'S GOLIATH!
HE WASN'T FLEEING! HE TRICKED ME!
NOW STAY PUT, MISTER!
MY INNING IS COMING UP!
LIKE A GIANT, LIVING STEAM-SHOVEL SCOOP, GOLIATH'S MIGHTY HAND DIGS INTO THE HARD-PACKED SOIL BELOW, AND THEN--
FIRST OF ALL, I'LL STOP YOU FROM USING THAT BEAM OF YOURS--!
AND THERE'S NO BETTER WAY TO DO IT THAN BY HURLING A FEW HUNDRED POUNDS OF SOIL AT YOUR EYES!
WHAT YOU CAN'T SEE--YOU CAN'T AIM AT! AND WHAT YOU CAN'T AIM AT, YOU CAN'T HIT!
UNNHHHH!!
12

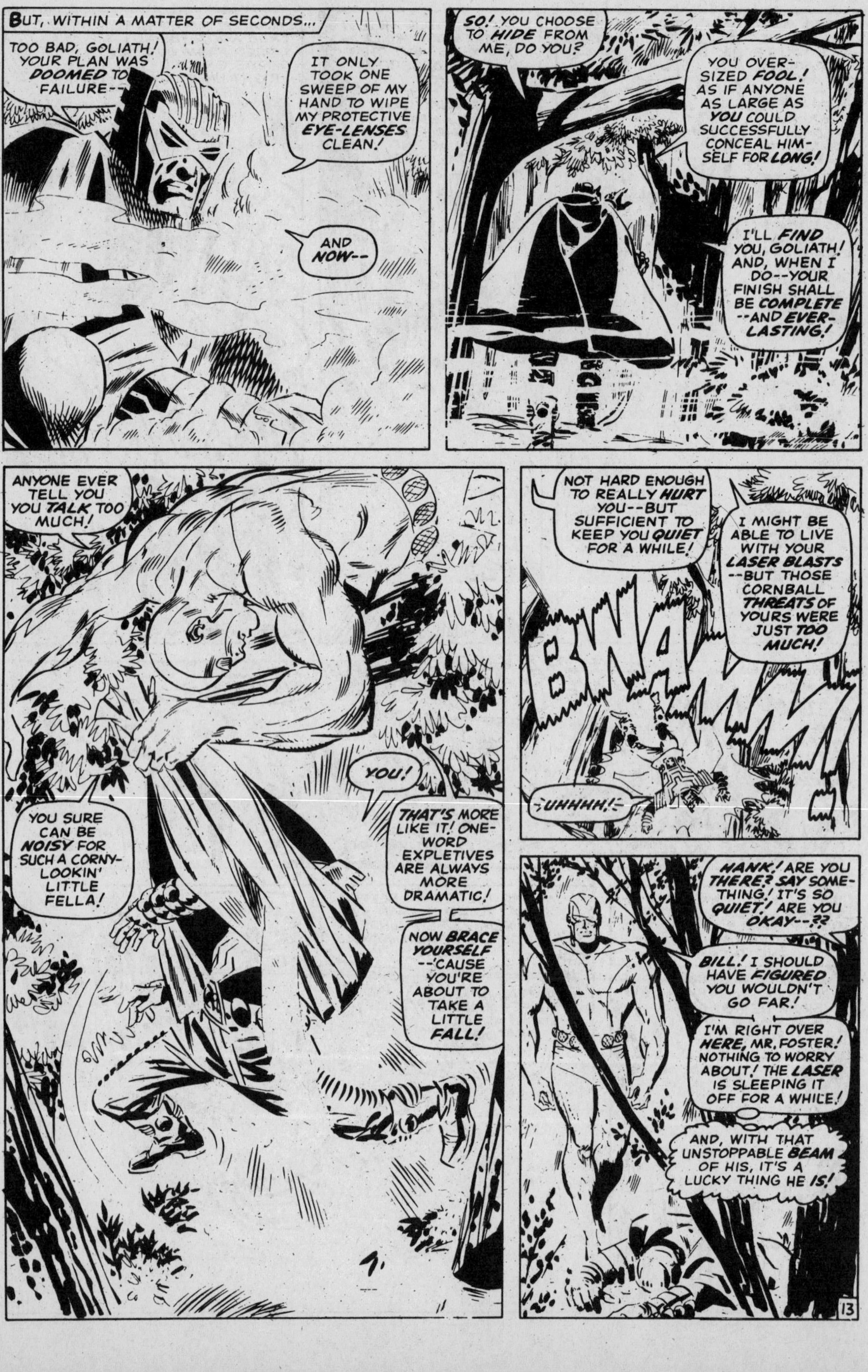
BUT, WITHIN A MATTER OF SECONDS...
TOO BAD, GOLIATH! YOUR PLAN WAS DOOMED TO FAILURE--
IT ONLY TOOK ONE SWEEP OF MY HAND TO WIPE MY PROTECTIVE EYE-LENSES CLEAN!
AND NOW--
SO! YOU CHOOSE TO HIDE FROM ME, DO YOU?
YOU OVER-SIZED FOOL! AS IF ANYONE AS LARGE AS YOU COULD SUCCESSFULLY CONCEAL HIM-SELF FOR LONG!
I'LL FIND YOU, GOLIATH! AND, WHEN I DO--YOUR FINISH SHALL BE COMPLETE --AND EVER-LASTING!
ANYONE EVER TELL YOU YOU TALK TOO MUCH!
YOU!
YOU SURE CAN BE NOISY FOR SUCH A CORNY-LOOKIN' LITTLE FELLA!
THAT'S MORE LIKE IT! ONE-WORD EXPLETIVES ARE ALWAYS MORE DRAMATIC!
NOW BRACE YOURSELF --'CAUSE YOU'RE ABOUT TO TAKE A LITTLE FALL!
NOT HARD ENOUGH TO REALLY HURT YOU--BUT SUFFICIENT TO KEEP YOU QUIET FOR A WHILE!
I MIGHT BE ABLE TO LIVE WITH YOUR LASER BLASTS --BUT THOSE CORNBALL THREATS OF YOURS WERE JUST TOO MUCH!
BWAMM
UHHHH!
HANK! ARE YOU THERE? SAY SOME-THING! IT'S SO QUIET! ARE YOU OKAY--??
BILL! I SHOULD HAVE FIGURED YOU WOULDN'T GO FAR!
I'M RIGHT OVER HERE, MR. FOSTER! NOTHING TO WORRY ABOUT! THE LASER IS SLEEPING IT OFF FOR A WHILE!
AND, WITH THAT UNSTOPPABLE BEAM OF HIS, IT'S A LUCKY THING HE IS!
13

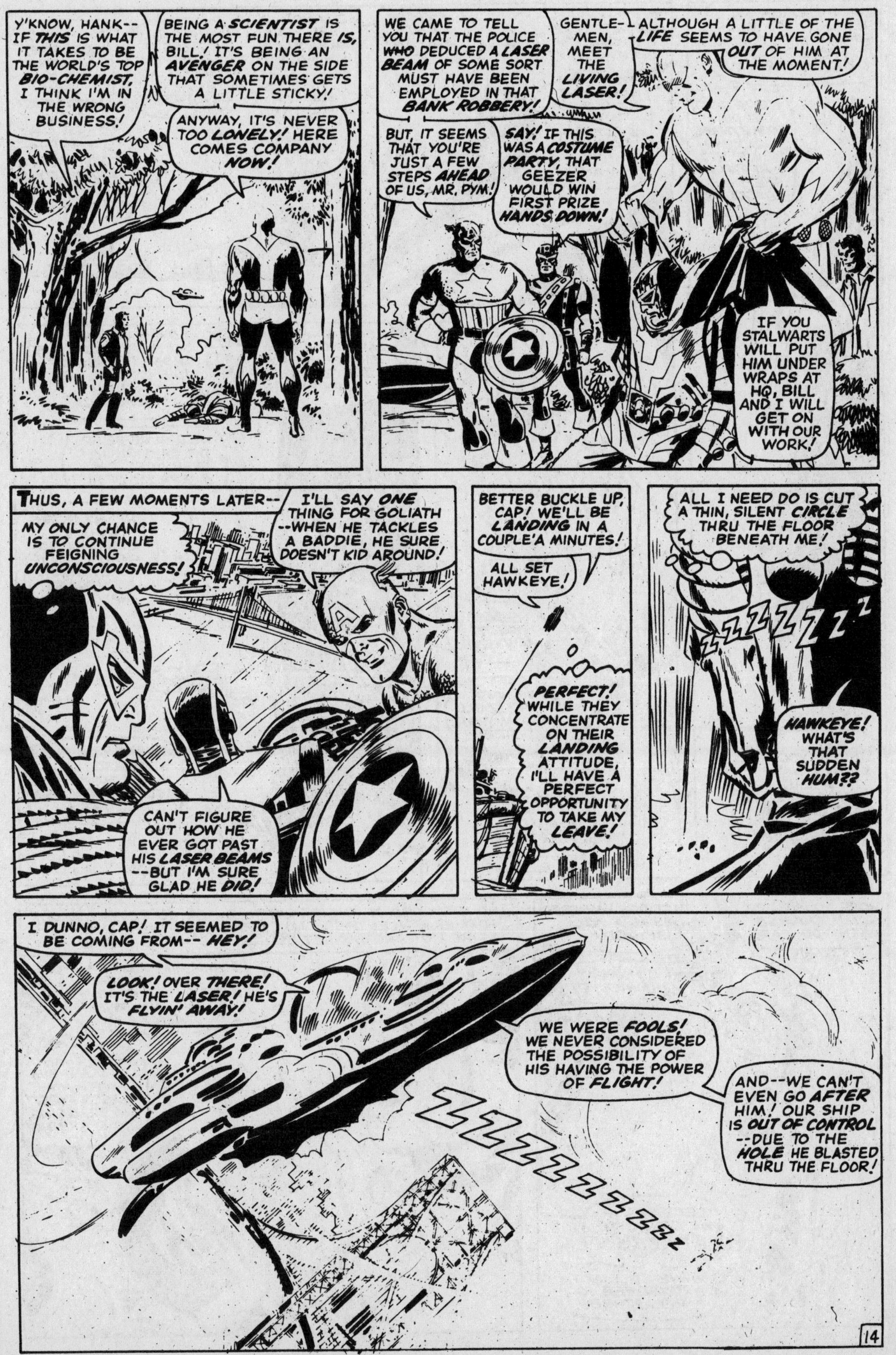

Y'KNOW, HANK-- IF THIS IS WHAT IT TAKES TO BE THE WORLD'S TOP BIO-CHEMIST, I THINK I'M IN THE WRONG BUSINESS!
BEING A SCIENTIST IS THE MOST FUN THERE IS, BILL! IT'S BEING AN AVENGER ON THE SIDE THAT SOMETIMES GETS A LITTLE STICKY!
ANYWAY, IT'S NEVER TOO LONELY! HERE COMES COMPANY NOW!
WE CAME TO TELL YOU THAT THE POLICE WHO DEDUCED A LASER BEAM OF SOME SORT MUST HAVE BEEN EMPLOYED IN THAT BANK ROBBERY!
GENTLE-MEN, MEET THE LIVING LASER!
ALTHOUGH A LITTLE OF THE LIFE SEEMS TO HAVE GONE OUT OF HIM AT THE MOMENT!
BUT, IT SEEMS THAT YOU'RE JUST A FEW STEPS AHEAD OF US, MR. PYM!
SAY! IF THIS WAS A COSTUME PARTY, THAT GEEZER WOULD WIN FIRST PRIZE HANDS DOWN!
IF YOU STALWARTS WILL PUT HIM UNDER WRAPS AT HQ, BILL AND I WILL GET ON WITH OUR WORK!
THUS, A FEW MOMENTS LATER--
MY ONLY CHANCE IS TO CONTINUE FEIGNING UNCONSCIOUSNESS!
I'LL SAY ONE THING FOR GOLIATH --WHEN HE TACKLES A BADDIE, HE SURE DOESN'T KID AROUND!
CAN'T FIGURE OUT HOW HE EVER GOT PAST HIS LASER BEAMS --BUT I'M SURE GLAD HE DID!
BETTER BUCKLE UP, CAP! WE'LL BE LANDING IN A COUPLE'A MINUTES!
ALL SET HAWKEYE!
PERFECT! WHILE THEY CONCENTRATE ON THEIR LANDING ATTITUDE, I'LL HAVE A PERFECT OPPORTUNITY TO TAKE MY LEAVE!
ALL I NEED DO IS CUT A THIN, SILENT CIRCLE THRU THE FLOOR BENEATH ME!
ZZZZZZZZ
HAWKEYE! WHAT'S THAT SUDDEN HUM??
I DUNNO, CAP! IT SEEMED TO BE COMING FROM-- HEY!
LOOK! OVER THERE! IT'S THE LASER! HE'S FLYIN' AWAY!
WE WERE FOOLS! WE NEVER CONSIDERED THE POSSIBILITY OF HIS HAVING THE POWER OF FLIGHT!
AND--WE CAN'T EVEN GO AFTER HIM! OUR SHIP IS OUT OF CONTROL --DUE TO THE HOLE HE BLASTED THRU THE FLOOR!
ZZZZZZZZZZZZZ

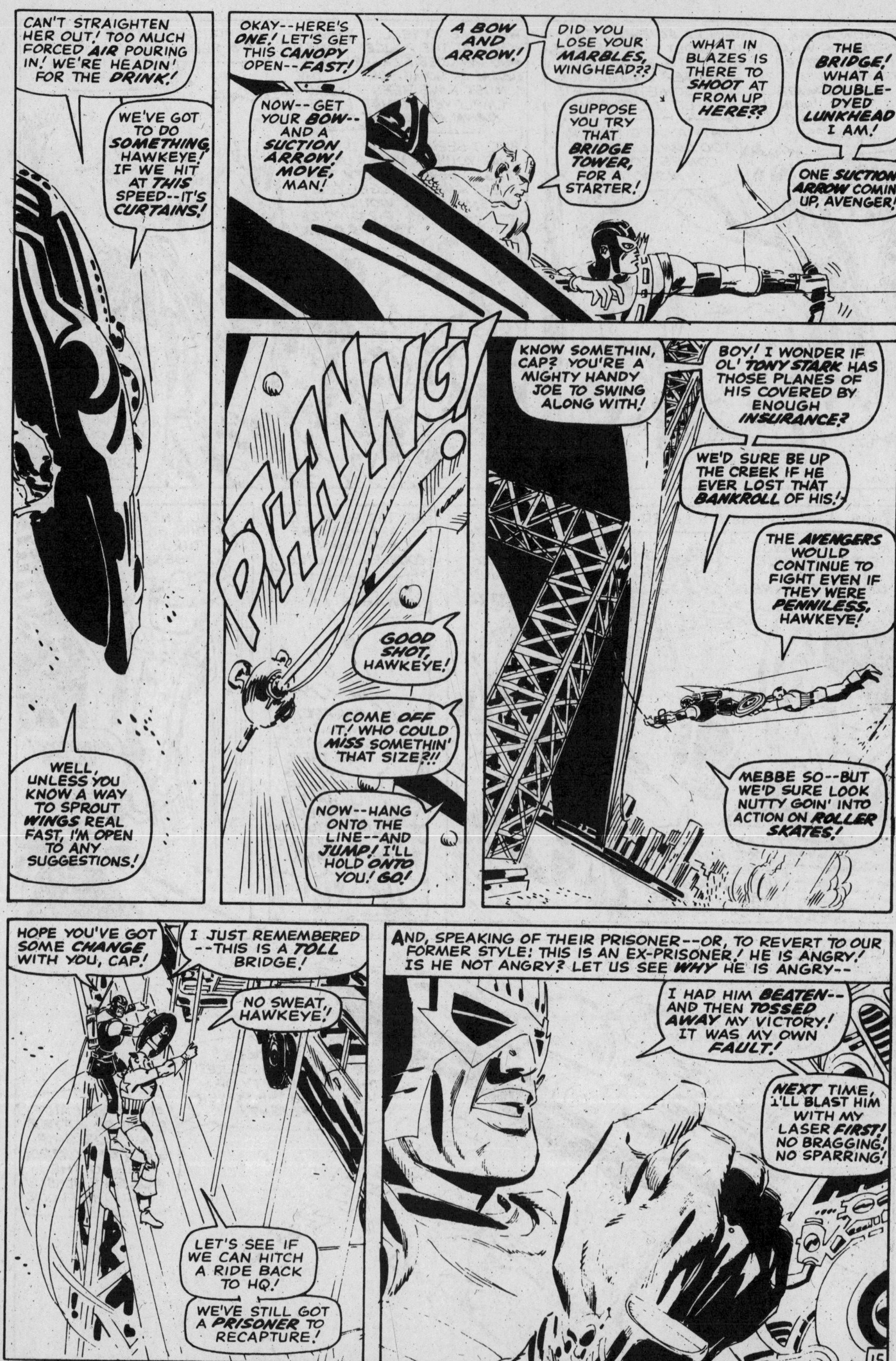
CAN'T STRAIGHTEN HER OUT! TOO MUCH FORCED AIR POURING IN! WE'RE HEADIN' FOR THE DRINK!
WE'VE GOT TO DO SOMETHING, HAWKEYE! IF WE HIT AT THIS SPEED--IT'S CURTAINS!
WELL, UNLESS YOU KNOW A WAY TO SPROUT WINGS REAL FAST, I'M OPEN TO ANY SUGGESTIONS!
OKAY--HERE'S ONE! LET'S GET THIS CANOPY OPEN--FAST!
NOW--GET YOUR BOW--AND A SUCTION ARROW! MOVE, MAN!
A BOW AND ARROW!
DID YOU LOSE YOUR MARBLES, WINGHEAD??
WHAT IN BLAZES IS THERE TO SHOOT AT FROM UP HERE??
SUPPOSE YOU TRY THAT BRIDGE TOWER, FOR A STARTER!
THE BRIDGE! WHAT A DOUBLE-DYED LUNKHEAD I AM!
ONE SUCTION ARROW COMIN' UP, AVENGER!
PTHANNG!
GOOD SHOT, HAWKEYE!
COME OFF IT! WHO COULD MISS SOMETHIN' THAT SIZE?!!
NOW--HANG ONTO THE LINE--AND JUMP! I'LL HOLD ONTO YOU! GO!
KNOW SOMETHIN, CAP? YOU'RE A MIGHTY HANDY JOE TO SWING ALONG WITH!
BOY! I WONDER IF OL' TONY STARK HAS THOSE PLANES OF HIS COVERED BY ENOUGH INSURANCE?
WE'D SURE BE UP THE CREEK IF HE EVER LOST THAT BANKROLL OF HIS!
THE AVENGERS WOULD CONTINUE TO FIGHT EVEN IF THEY WERE PENNILESS, HAWKEYE!
MEBBE SO--BUT WE'D SURE LOOK NUTTY GOIN' INTO ACTION ON ROLLER SKATES!
HOPE YOU'VE GOT SOME CHANGE WITH YOU, CAP!
I JUST REMEMBERED--THIS IS A TOLL BRIDGE!
NO SWEAT, HAWKEYE!
LET'S SEE IF WE CAN HITCH A RIDE BACK TO HQ!
WE'VE STILL GOT A PRISONER TO RECAPTURE!
AND, SPEAKING OF THEIR PRISONER--OR, TO REVERT TO OUR FORMER STYLE: THIS IS AN EX-PRISONER! HE IS ANGRY! IS HE NOT ANGRY? LET US SEE WHY HE IS ANGRY--
I HAD HIM BEATEN--AND THEN TOSSED AWAY MY VICTORY! IT WAS MY OWN FAULT!
NEXT TIME, I'LL BLAST HIM WITH MY LASER FIRST! NO BRAGGING! NO SPARRING!
15

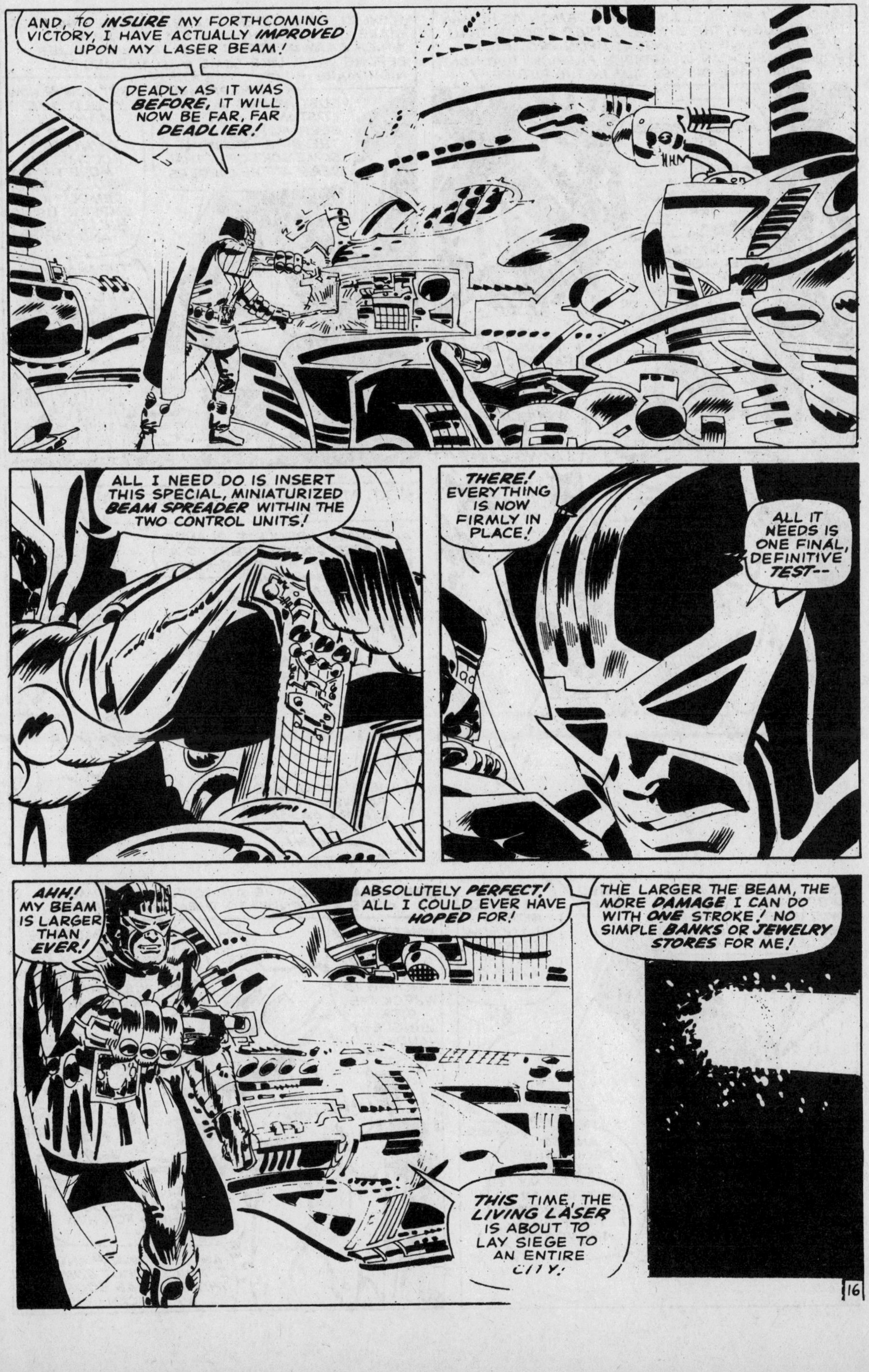
AND, TO INSURE MY FORTHCOMING VICTORY, I HAVE ACTUALLY IMPROVED UPON MY LASER BEAM!
DEADLY AS IT WAS BEFORE, IT WILL NOW BE FAR, FAR DEADLIER!
ALL I NEED DO IS INSERT THIS SPECIAL, MINIATURIZED BEAM SPREADER WITHIN THE TWO CONTROL UNITS!
THERE! EVERYTHING IS NOW FIRMLY IN PLACE!
ALL IT NEEDS IS ONE FINAL, DEFINITIVE TEST--
AHH! MY BEAM IS LARGER THAN EVER!
ABSOLUTELY PERFECT! ALL I COULD EVER HAVE HOPED FOR!
THE LARGER THE BEAM, THE MORE DAMAGE I CAN DO WITH ONE STROKE! NO SIMPLE BANKS OR JEWELRY STORES FOR ME!
THIS TIME, THE LIVING LASER IS ABOUT TO LAY SIEGE TO AN ENTIRE CITY!
16

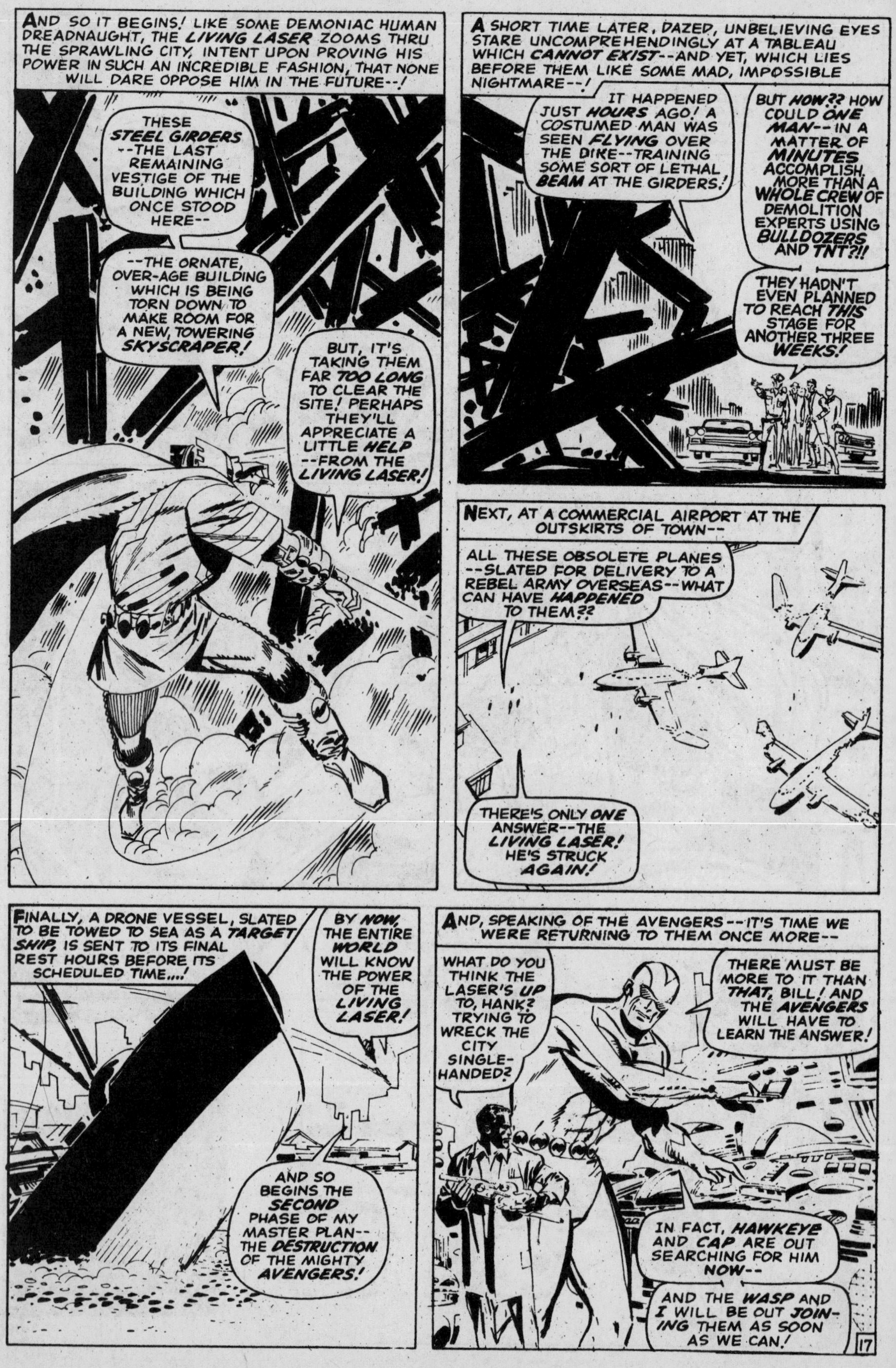

AND SO IT BEGINS! LIKE SOME DEMONIAC HUMAN DREADNAUGHT, THE LIVING LASER ZOOMS THRU THE SPRAWLING CITY, INTENT UPON PROVING HIS POWER IN SUCH AN INCREDIBLE FASHION, THAT NONE WILL DARE OPPOSE HIM IN THE FUTURE--!
THESE STEEL GIRDERS --THE LAST REMAINING VESTIGE OF THE BUILDING WHICH ONCE STOOD HERE--
--THE ORNATE, OVER-AGE BUILDING WHICH IS BEING TORN DOWN TO MAKE ROOM FOR A NEW, TOWERING SKYSCRAPER!
BUT, IT'S TAKING THEM FAR TOO LONG TO CLEAR THE SITE! PERHAPS THEY'LL APPRECIATE A LITTLE HELP --FROM THE LIVING LASER!
A SHORT TIME LATER, DAZED, UNBELIEVING EYES STARE UNCOMPREHENDINGLY AT A TABLEAU WHICH CANNOT EXIST--AND YET, WHICH LIES BEFORE THEM LIKE SOME MAD, IMPOSSIBLE NIGHTMARE--!
IT HAPPENED JUST HOURS AGO! A COSTUMED MAN WAS SEEN FLYING OVER THE DIKE--TRAINING SOME SORT OF LETHAL BEAM AT THE GIRDERS!
BUT HOW?? HOW COULD ONE MAN--IN A MATTER OF MINUTES ACCOMPLISH MORE THAN A WHOLE CREW OF DEMOLITION EXPERTS USING BULLDOZERS AND TNT?!!
THEY HADN'T EVEN PLANNED TO REACH THIS STAGE FOR ANOTHER THREE WEEKS!
NEXT, AT A COMMERCIAL AIRPORT AT THE OUTSKIRTS OF TOWN--
ALL THESE OBSOLETE PLANES --SLATED FOR DELIVERY TO A REBEL ARMY OVERSEAS--WHAT CAN HAVE HAPPENED TO THEM??
THERE'S ONLY ONE ANSWER--THE LIVING LASER! HE'S STRUCK AGAIN!
FINALLY, A DRONE VESSEL, SLATED TO BE TOWED TO SEA AS A TARGET SHIP, IS SENT TO ITS FINAL REST HOURS BEFORE ITS SCHEDULED TIME...!
BY NOW, THE ENTIRE WORLD WILL KNOW THE POWER OF THE LIVING LASER!
AND SO BEGINS THE SECOND PHASE OF MY MASTER PLAN--THE DESTRUCTION OF THE MIGHTY AVENGERS!
AND, SPEAKING OF THE AVENGERS--IT'S TIME WE WERE RETURNING TO THEM ONCE MORE--
WHAT DO YOU THINK THE LASER'S UP TO, HANK? TRYING TO WRECK THE CITY SINGLE-HANDED?
THERE MUST BE MORE TO IT THAN THAT, BILL! AND THE AVENGERS WILL HAVE TO LEARN THE ANSWER!
IN FACT, HAWKEYE AND CAP ARE OUT SEARCHING FOR HIM NOW--
AND THE WASP AND I WILL BE OUT JOINING THEM AS SOON AS WE CAN!

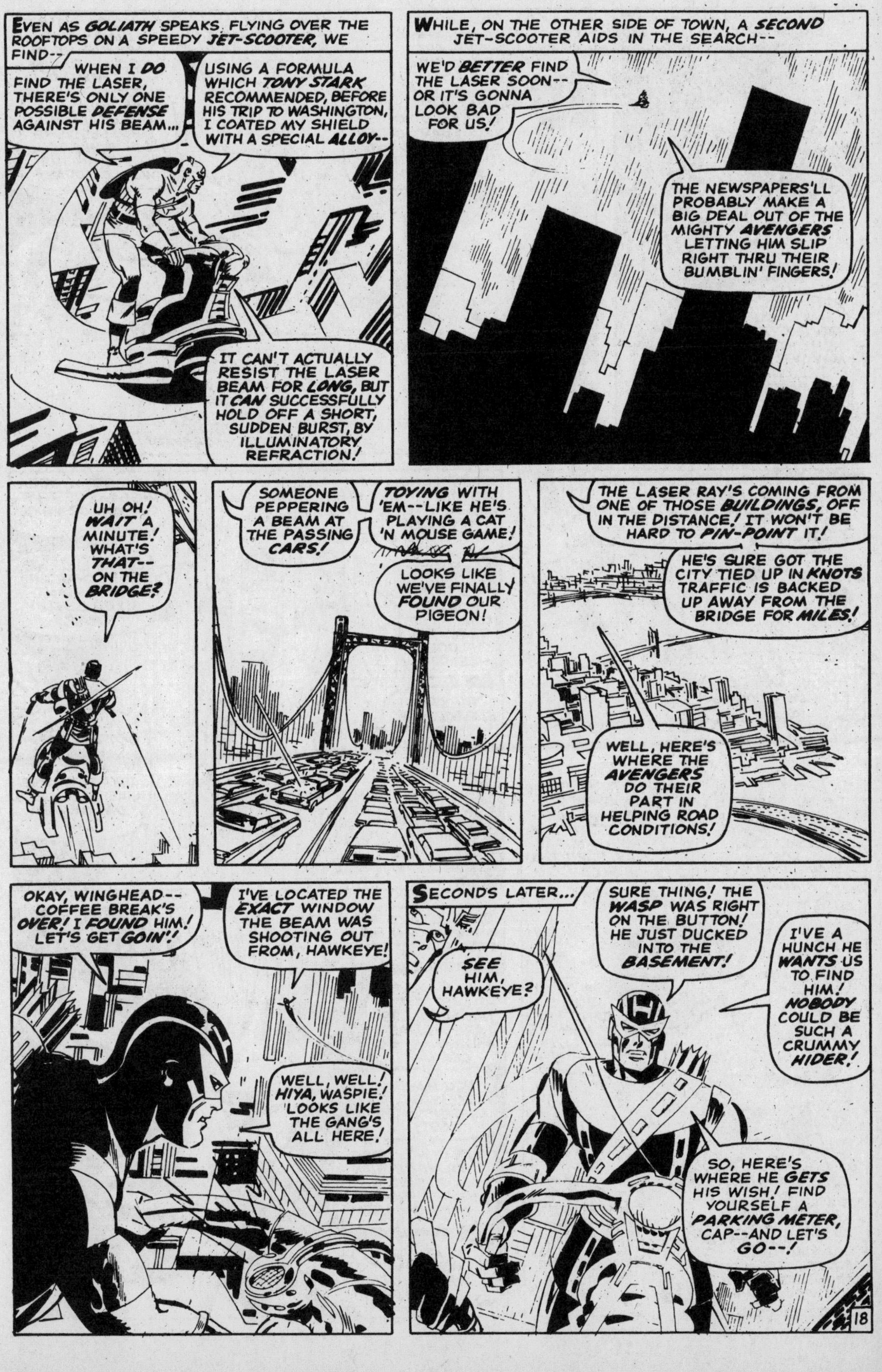
EVEN AS GOLIATH SPEAKS, FLYING OVER THE ROOFTOPS ON A SPEEDY JET-SCOOTER, WE FIND--
WHEN I DO FIND THE LASER, THERE'S ONLY ONE POSSIBLE DEFENSE AGAINST HIS BEAM...
USING A FORMULA WHICH TONY STARK RECOMMENDED, BEFORE HIS TRIP TO WASHINGTON, I COATED MY SHIELD WITH A SPECIAL ALLOY--
IT CAN'T ACTUALLY RESIST THE LASER BEAM FOR LONG, BUT IT CAN SUCCESSFULLY HOLD OFF A SHORT, SUDDEN BURST, BY ILLUMINATORY REFRACTION!
WHILE, ON THE OTHER SIDE OF TOWN, A SECOND JET-SCOOTER AIDS IN THE SEARCH--
WE'D BETTER FIND THE LASER SOON--OR IT'S GONNA LOOK BAD FOR US!
THE NEWSPAPERS'LL PROBABLY MAKE A BIG DEAL OUT OF THE MIGHTY AVENGERS LETTING HIM SLIP RIGHT THRU THEIR BUMBLIN' FINGERS!
UH OH! WAIT A MINUTE! WHAT'S THAT--ON THE BRIDGE?
SOMEONE PEPPERING A BEAM AT THE PASSING CARS!
TOYING WITH 'EM--LIKE HE'S PLAYING A CAT 'N MOUSE GAME!
LOOKS LIKE WE'VE FINALLY FOUND OUR PIGEON!
THE LASER RAY'S COMING FROM ONE OF THOSE BUILDINGS, OFF IN THE DISTANCE! IT WON'T BE HARD TO PIN-POINT IT!
HE'S SURE GOT THE CITY TIED UP IN KNOTS TRAFFIC IS BACKED UP AWAY FROM THE BRIDGE FOR MILES!
WELL, HERE'S WHERE THE AVENGERS DO THEIR PART IN HELPING ROAD CONDITIONS!
OKAY, WINGHEAD--COFFEE BREAK'S OVER! I FOUND HIM! LET'S GET GOIN'!
I'VE LOCATED THE EXACT WINDOW THE BEAM WAS SHOOTING OUT FROM, HAWKEYE!
WELL, WELL! HIYA, WASPIE! LOOKS LIKE THE GANG'S ALL HERE!
SECONDS LATER...
SEE HIM, HAWKEYE?
SURE THING! THE WASP WAS RIGHT ON THE BUTTON! HE JUST DUCKED INTO THE BASEMENT!
I'VE A HUNCH HE WANTS US TO FIND HIM! NOBODY COULD BE SUCH A CRUMMY HIDER!
SO, HERE'S WHERE HE GETS HIS WISH! FIND YOURSELF A PARKING METER, CAP--AND LET'S GO--!

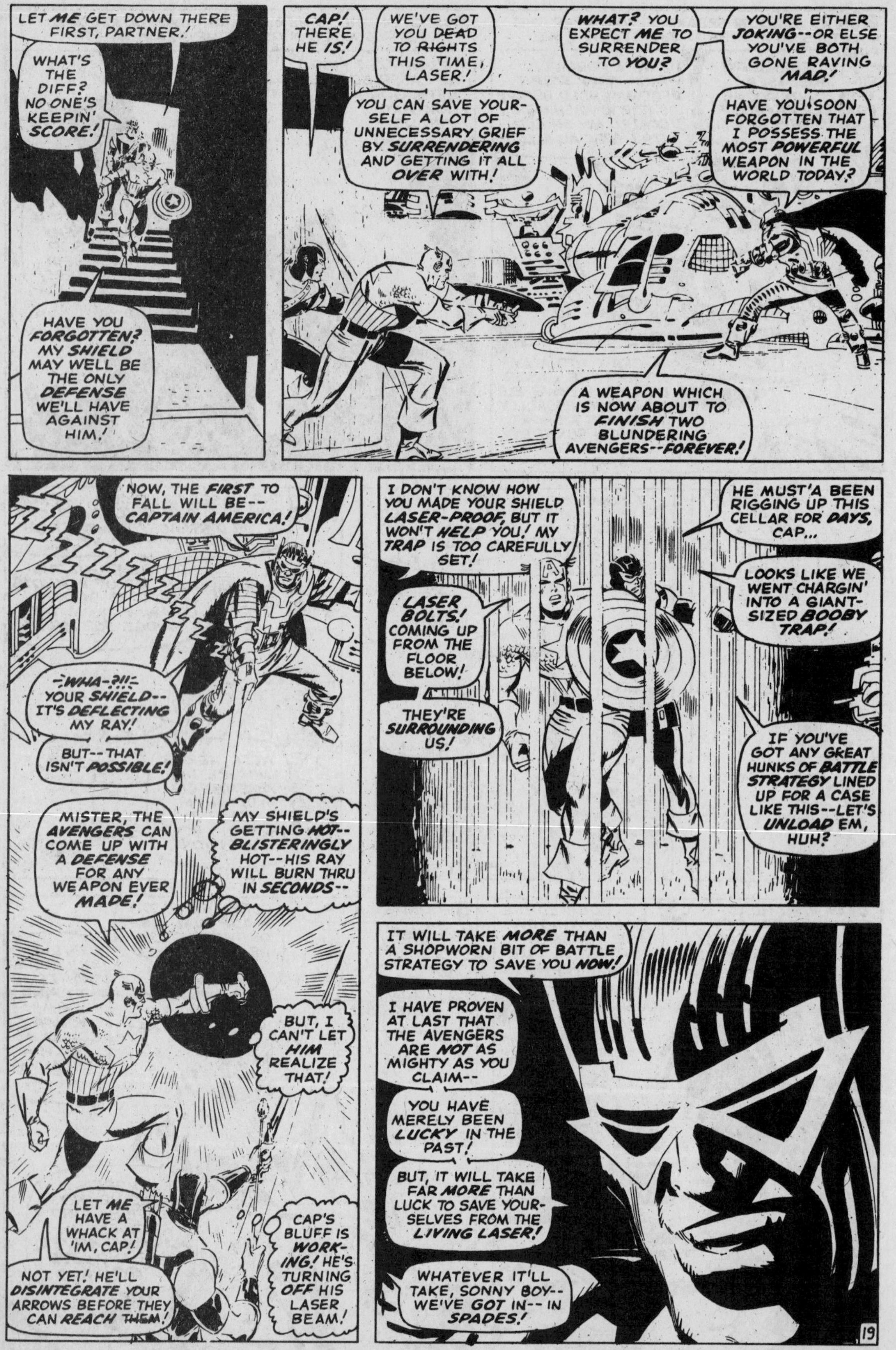
LET ME GET DOWN THERE FIRST, PARTNER!
WHAT'S THE DIFF? NO ONE'S KEEPIN' SCORE!
HAVE YOU FORGOTTEN? MY SHIELD MAY WELL BE THE ONLY DEFENSE WE'LL HAVE AGAINST HIM!
CAP! THERE HE IS!
WE'VE GOT YOU DEAD TO RIGHTS THIS TIME, LASER!
YOU CAN SAVE YOURSELF A LOT OF UNNECESSARY GRIEF BY SURRENDERING AND GETTING IT ALL OVER WITH!
WHAT? YOU EXPECT ME TO SURRENDER TO YOU?
YOU'RE EITHER JOKING--OR ELSE YOU'VE BOTH GONE RAVING MAD!
HAVE YOU SOON FORGOTTEN THAT I POSSESS THE MOST POWERFUL WEAPON IN THE WORLD TODAY?
A WEAPON WHICH IS NOW ABOUT TO FINISH TWO BLUNDERING AVENGERS--FOREVER!
NOW, THE FIRST TO FALL WILL BE-- CAPTAIN AMERICA!
-WHA-?!!- YOUR SHIELD-- IT'S DEFLECTING MY RAY!
BUT--THAT ISN'T POSSIBLE!
MISTER, THE AVENGERS CAN COME UP WITH A DEFENSE FOR ANY WEAPON EVER MADE!
MY SHIELD'S GETTING HOT-- BLISTERINGLY HOT--HIS RAY WILL BURN THRU IN SECONDS--
BUT, I CAN'T LET HIM REALIZE THAT!
LET ME HAVE A WHACK AT 'IM, CAP!
NOT YET! HE'LL DISINTEGRATE YOUR ARROWS BEFORE THEY CAN REACH THEM!
CAP'S BLUFF IS WORKING! HE'S TURNING OFF HIS LASER BEAM!
I DON'T KNOW HOW YOU MADE YOUR SHIELD LASER-PROOF, BUT IT WON'T HELP YOU! MY TRAP IS TOO CAREFULLY SET!
LASER BOLTS! COMING UP FROM THE FLOOR BELOW!
THEY'RE SURROUNDING US!
HE MUST'A BEEN RIGGING UP THIS CELLAR FOR DAYS, CAP...
LOOKS LIKE WE WENT CHARGIN' INTO A GIANT-SIZED BOOBY TRAP!
IF YOU'VE GOT ANY GREAT HUNKS OF BATTLE STRATEGY LINED UP FOR A CASE LIKE THIS--LET'S UNLOAD EM, HUH?
IT WILL TAKE MORE THAN A SHOPWORN BIT OF BATTLE STRATEGY TO SAVE YOU NOW!
I HAVE PROVEN AT LAST THAT THE AVENGERS ARE NOT AS MIGHTY AS YOU CLAIM--
YOU HAVE MERELY BEEN LUCKY IN THE PAST!
BUT, IT WILL TAKE FAR MORE THAN LUCK TO SAVE YOURSELVES FROM THE LIVING LASER!
WHATEVER IT'LL TAKE, SONNY BOY-- WE'VE GOT IN-- IN SPADES!
19

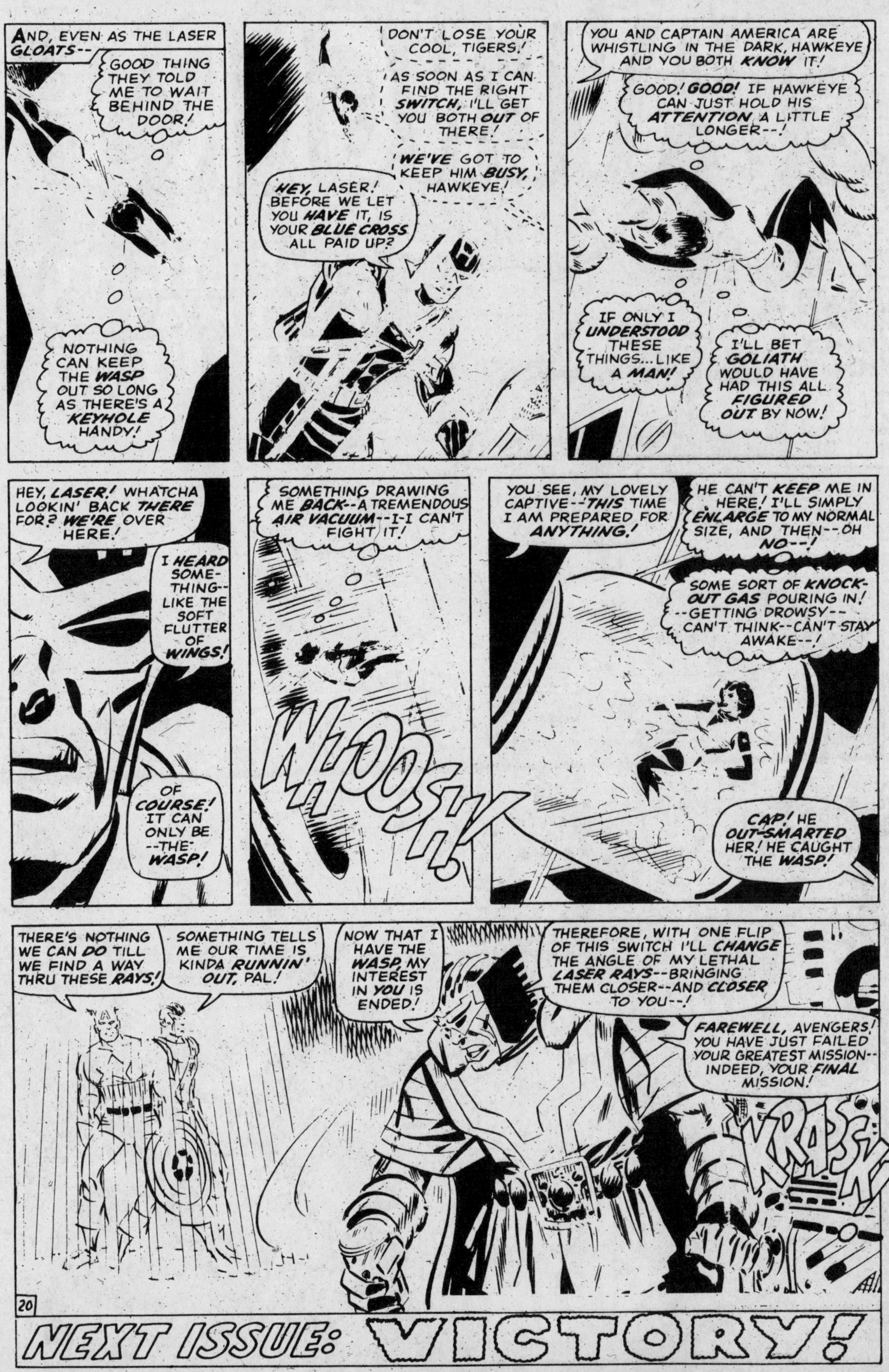
AND, EVEN AS THE LASER GLOATS--
GOOD THING THEY TOLD ME TO WAIT BEHIND THE DOOR!
NOTHING CAN KEEP THE WASP OUT SO LONG AS THERE'S A KEYHOLE HANDY!
DON'T LOSE YOUR COOL, TIGERS!
AS SOON AS I CAN FIND THE RIGHT SWITCH, I'LL GET YOU BOTH OUT OF THERE!
WE'VE GOT TO KEEP HIM BUSY, HAWKEYE!
HEY, LASER! BEFORE WE LET YOU HAVE IT, IS YOUR BLUE CROSS ALL PAID UP?
YOU AND CAPTAIN AMERICA ARE WHISTLING IN THE DARK, HAWKEYE AND YOU BOTH KNOW IT!
GOOD! GOOD! IF HAWKEYE CAN JUST HOLD HIS ATTENTION A LITTLE LONGER--!
IF ONLY I UNDERSTOOD THESE THINGS...LIKE A MAN!
I'LL BET GOLIATH WOULD HAVE HAD THIS ALL FIGURED OUT BY NOW!
HEY, LASER! WHATCHA LOOKIN' BACK THERE FOR? WE'RE OVER HERE!
I HEARD SOMETHING--LIKE THE SOFT FLUTTER OF WINGS!
OF COURSE! IT CAN ONLY BE --THE WASP!
SOMETHING DRAWING ME BACK--A TREMENDOUS AIR VACUUM--I-I CAN'T FIGHT IT!
WHOOSH!
YOU SEE, MY LOVELY CAPTIVE--THIS TIME I AM PREPARED FOR ANYTHING!
HE CAN'T KEEP ME IN HERE! I'LL SIMPLY ENLARGE TO MY NORMAL SIZE, AND THEN--OH NO--!
SOME SORT OF KNOCK-OUT GAS POURING IN! --GETTING DROWSY-- CAN'T THINK--CAN'T STAY AWAKE--!
CAP! HE OUT-SMARTED HER! HE CAUGHT THE WASP!
THERE'S NOTHING WE CAN DO TILL WE FIND A WAY THRU THESE RAYS!
SOMETHING TELLS ME OUR TIME IS KINDA RUNNIN' OUT, PAL!
NOW THAT I HAVE THE WASP, MY INTEREST IN YOU IS ENDED!
THEREFORE, WITH ONE FLIP OF THIS SWITCH I'LL CHANGE THE ANGLE OF MY LETHAL LASER RAYS--BRINGING THEM CLOSER--AND CLOSER TO YOU--!
FAREWELL, AVENGERS! YOU HAVE JUST FAILED YOUR GREATEST MISSION--INDEED, YOUR FINAL MISSION!
KRASH!
20
NEXT ISSUE: VICTORY!

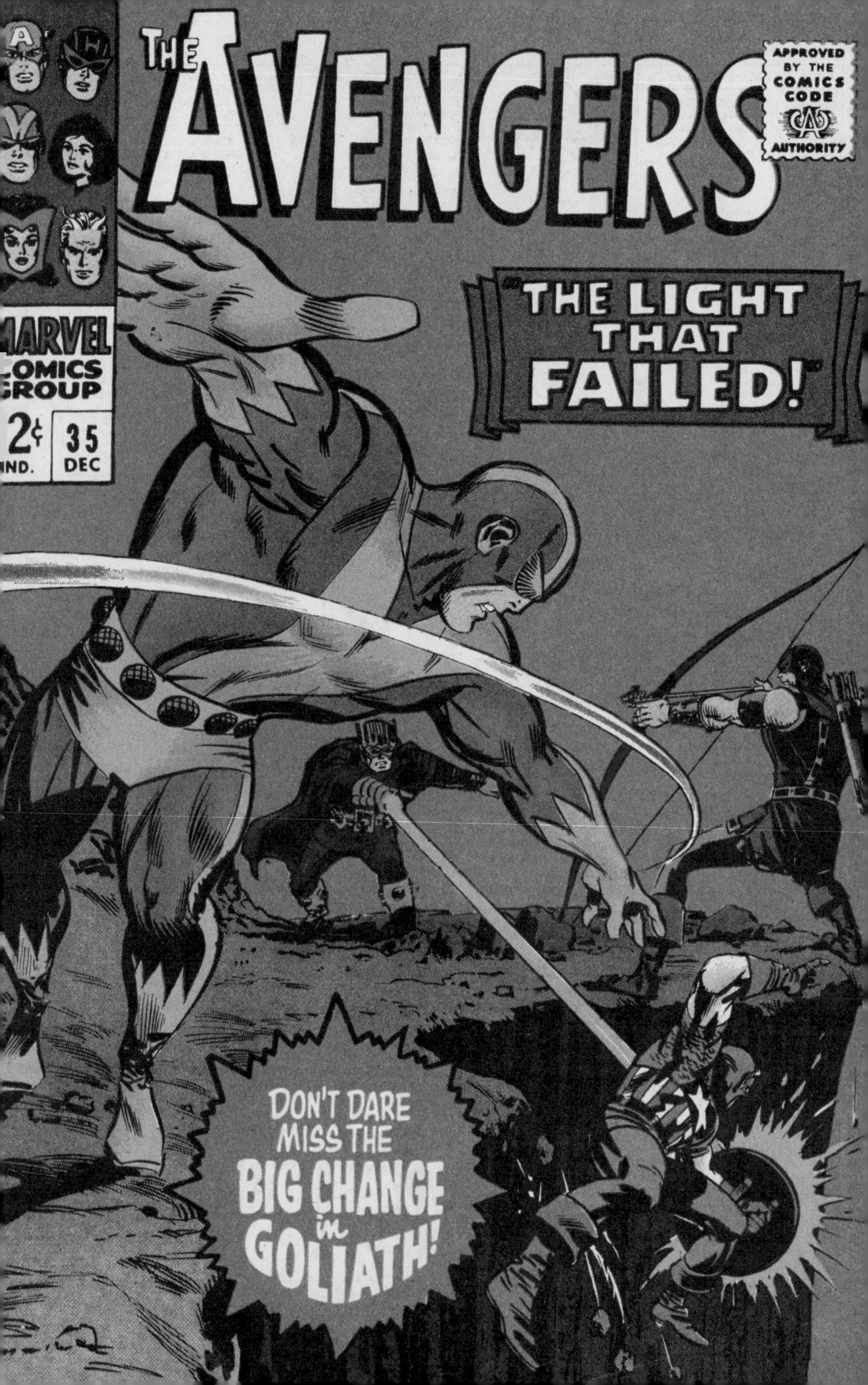
THE AVENGERS
APPROVED BY THE COMICS CODE AUTHORITY
MARVEL COMICS GROUP
12¢
IND.
35
DEC
"THE LIGHT THAT FAILED!"
DON'T DARE MISS THE BIG CHANGE in GOLIATH!

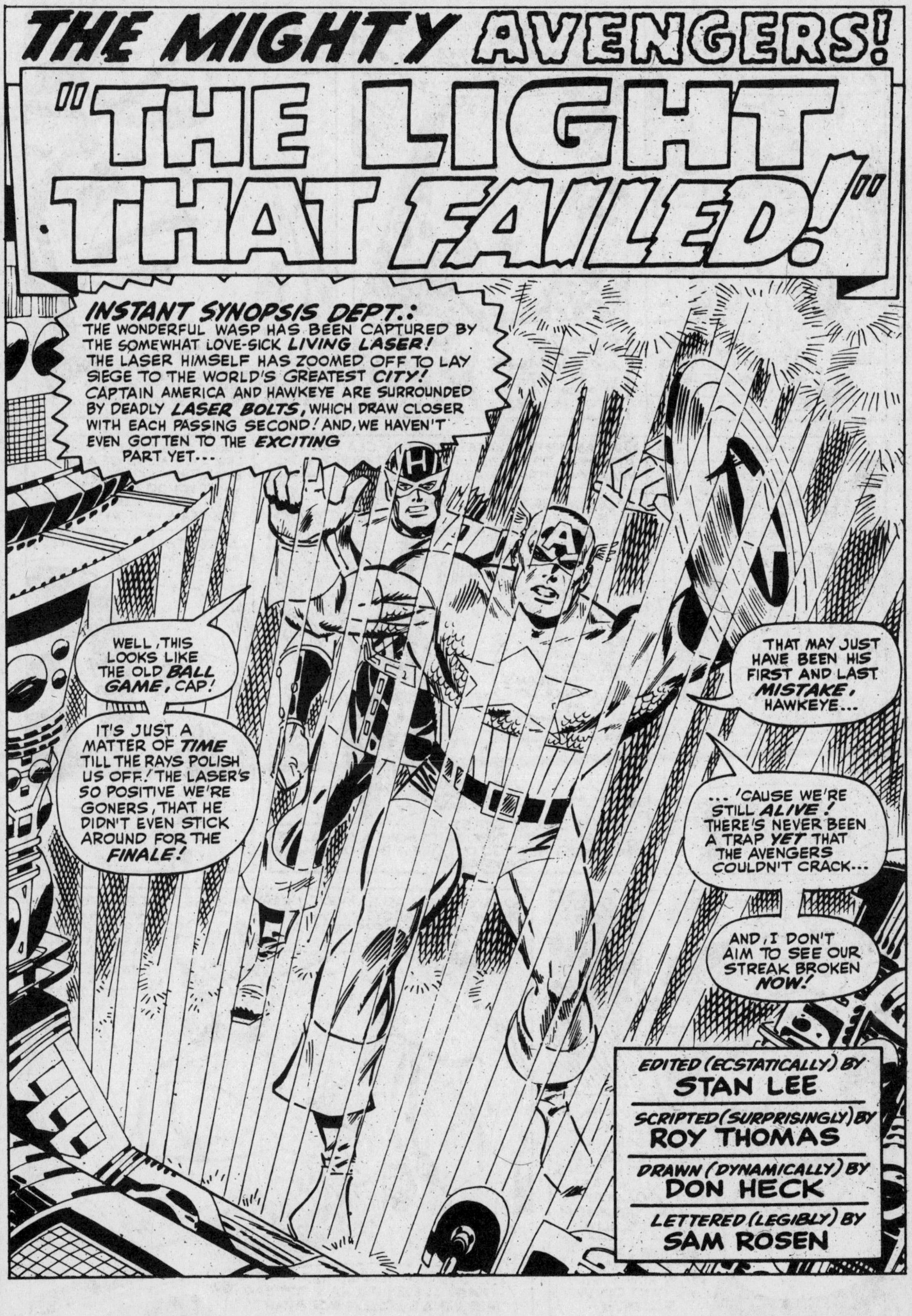
THE MIGHTY AVENGERS!
"THE LIGHT THAT FAILED!"
INSTANT SYNOPSIS DEPT.: THE WONDERFUL WASP HAS BEEN CAPTURED BY THE SOMEWHAT LOVE-SICK LIVING LASER! THE LASER HIMSELF HAS ZOOMED OFF TO LAY SIEGE TO THE WORLD'S GREATEST CITY! CAPTAIN AMERICA AND HAWKEYE ARE SURROUNDED BY DEADLY LASER BOLTS, WHICH DRAW CLOSER WITH EACH PASSING SECOND! AND, WE HAVEN'T EVEN GOTTEN TO THE EXCITING PART YET...
WELL, THIS LOOKS LIKE THE OLD BALL GAME, CAP!
IT'S JUST A MATTER OF TIME TILL THE RAYS POLISH US OFF! THE LASER'S SO POSITIVE WE'RE GONERS, THAT HE DIDN'T EVEN STICK AROUND FOR THE FINALE!
THAT MAY JUST HAVE BEEN HIS FIRST AND LAST MISTAKE, HAWKEYE...
...'CAUSE WE'RE STILL ALIVE! THERE'S NEVER BEEN A TRAP YET THAT THE AVENGERS COULDN'T CRACK...
AND, I DON'T AIM TO SEE OUR STREAK BROKEN NOW!
EDITED (ECSTATICALLY) BY STAN LEE
SCRIPTED (SURPRISINGLY) BY ROY THOMAS
DRAWN (DYNAMICALLY) BY DON HECK
LETTERED (LEGIBLY) BY SAM ROSEN

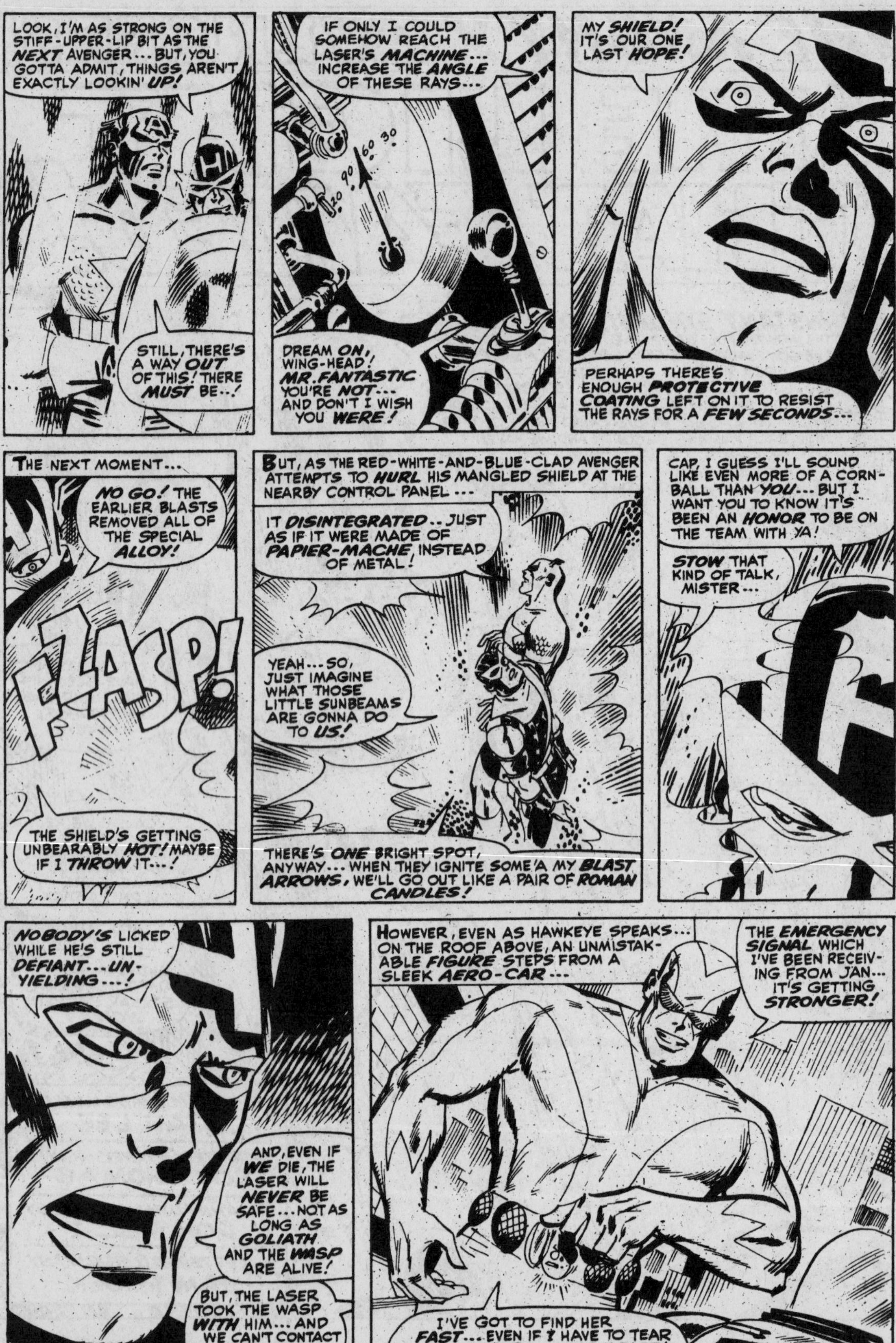
LOOK, I'M AS STRONG ON THE STIFF-UPPER-LIP BIT AS THE NEXT AVENGER... BUT, YOU GOTTA ADMIT, THINGS AREN'T EXACTLY LOOKIN' UP!
STILL, THERE'S A WAY OUT OF THIS! THERE MUST BE..!
IF ONLY I COULD SOMEHOW REACH THE LASER'S MACHINE... INCREASE THE ANGLE OF THESE RAYS...
20 90 60 30
DREAM ON, WING-HEAD! MR. FANTASTIC YOU'RE NOT... AND DON'T I WISH YOU WERE!
MY SHIELD! IT'S OUR ONE LAST HOPE!
PERHAPS THERE'S ENOUGH PROTECTIVE COATING LEFT ON IT TO RESIST THE RAYS FOR A FEW SECONDS...
THE NEXT MOMENT...
NO GO! THE EARLIER BLASTS REMOVED ALL OF THE SPECIAL ALLOY!
FZASP!
THE SHIELD'S GETTING UNBEARABLY HOT! MAYBE IF I THROW IT...!
BUT, AS THE RED-WHITE-AND-BLUE-CLAD AVENGER ATTEMPTS TO HURL HIS MANGLED SHIELD AT THE NEARBY CONTROL PANEL...
IT DISINTEGRATED.. JUST AS IF IT WERE MADE OF PAPIER-MACHE, INSTEAD OF METAL!
YEAH... SO, JUST IMAGINE WHAT THOSE LITTLE SUNBEAMS ARE GONNA DO TO US!
THERE'S ONE BRIGHT SPOT, ANYWAY... WHEN THEY IGNITE SOME'A MY BLAST ARROWS, WE'LL GO OUT LIKE A PAIR OF ROMAN CANDLES!
CAP, I GUESS I'LL SOUND LIKE EVEN MORE OF A CORN-BALL THAN YOU... BUT I WANT YOU TO KNOW IT'S BEEN AN HONOR TO BE ON THE TEAM WITH YA!
STOW THAT KIND OF TALK, MISTER...
NOBODY'S LICKED WHILE HE'S STILL DEFIANT... UN-YIELDING...!
AND, EVEN IF WE DIE, THE LASER WILL NEVER BE SAFE... NOT AS LONG AS GOLIATH AND THE WASP ARE ALIVE!
BUT, THE LASER TOOK THE WASP WITH HIM... AND WE CAN'T CONTACT GOLIATH!
HOWEVER, EVEN AS HAWKEYE SPEAKS... ON THE ROOF ABOVE, AN UNMISTAKABLE FIGURE STEPS FROM A SLEEK AERO-CAR...
THE EMERGENCY SIGNAL WHICH I'VE BEEN RECEIVING FROM JAN... IT'S GETTING STRONGER!
I'VE GOT TO FIND HER FAST... EVEN IF I HAVE TO TEAR THIS WHOLE BUILDING APART!
2

IN AN INCREDIBLY SHORT SPAN OF TIME, THE MOST POWERFUL OF THE AVENGERS HAS ZEROED IN ON THE *BASEMENT LAIR* OF THE LIVING LASER, AS...

THE SIGNALS' VIBRATIONS HAVE REACHED THEIR *HIGHEST PEAK!* THE WASP MUST BE IN THAT CLOSED ROOM DOWN THE *CORRIDOR!*

IF ANY *HARM* HAS COME TO HER, NOTHING ON *EARTH* WILL STOP THE VENGEANCE OF.. *GOLIATH!*

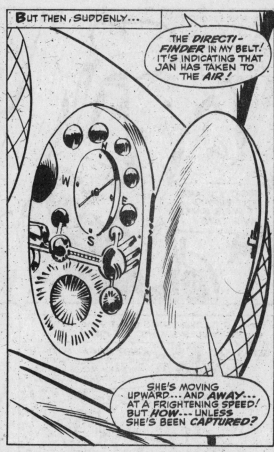

BUT THEN, SUDDENLY...

THE *DIRECTI-FINDER* IN MY BELT! IT'S INDICATING THAT JAN HAS TAKEN TO THE *AIR!*

SHE'S MOVING UPWARD....AND *AWAY*...AT A FRIGHTENING SPEED! BUT *HOW*---UNLESS SHE'S BEEN *CAPTURED?*

AND *THAT*, AS HENRY PYM WILL SOON LEARN, IS EXACTLY WHAT *HAS* HAPPENED TO THE MINIATURIZED WASP... FOR, AT THAT PRECISE INSTANT, ON THE OTHER SIDE OF THE BUILDING...

WITH THE *WASP* AS MY PRISONER INSIDE THIS *PLEXIGLASS JAR*, I HAVE NO MORE INTEREST IN THE OTHER AVENGERS!

I'LL MOVE ON TO MY *SECOND* HEADQUARTERS, AFTER CAUSING A BIT MORE *RANDOM DESTRUCTION*--TO DEMONSTRATE MY POWER BEYOND THE SHADOW OF A DOUBT!

FOR THEN, HOW CAN JANET VAN DYNE FAIL TO *FALL IN LOVE* WITH THE MAN WHO IS NOW *MIGHTIER* THAN GOLIATH HIMSELF?

MEANWHILE, LET US NOT FORGET OUR TWO IMPERILED STALWARTS IN THE LASER'S LAB...FOR, THEY HAVE SOMETHING LESS APPEALING THAN *ROMANCE* ON THEIR MINDS...

WE CAN'T HAVE OVER THIRTY *SECONDS* LEFT BEFORE THESE CRUMMY RAYS FINISH US OFF! I *ALREADY* FEEL LIKE I'M STANDIN' ON A *POSTAGE STAMP!*

FUNNY..I ALWAYS THOUGHT THAT, WHEN I WENT UNDER, IT'D BE IN *COMBAT*---NOT IN SOME MUSTY, ABANDONED *BASEMENT!*

HOLD IT, AVENGER..DON'T YOU *HEAR SOMETHING..?* *FOOTSTEPS*...FOOTSTEPS HEAVY ENOUGH TO MAKE THE *FLOOR* TREMBLE! IT CAN ONLY BE...

3.

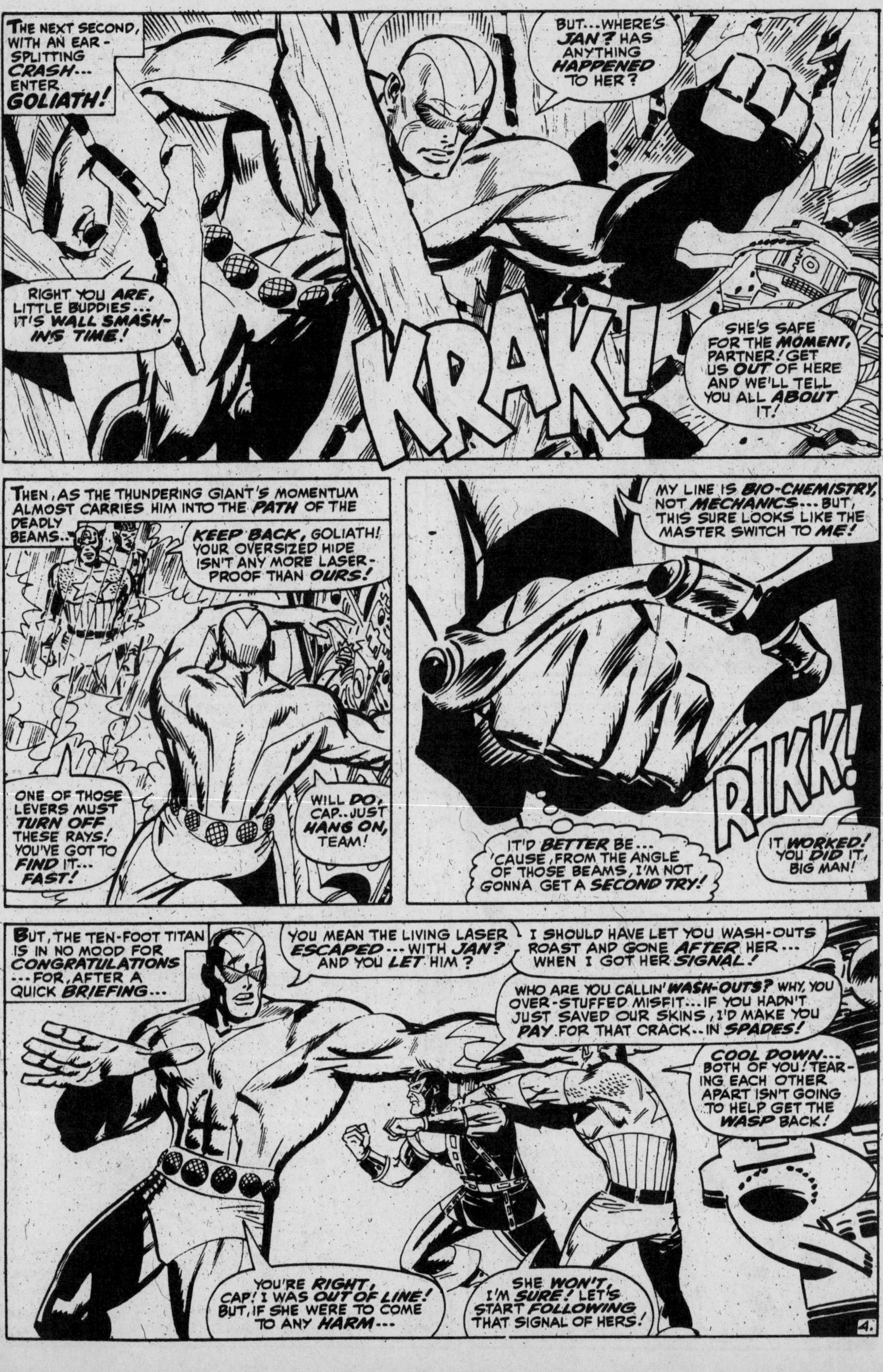
THE NEXT SECOND, WITH AN EAR-SPLITTING CRASH... ENTER GOLIATH!
BUT...WHERE'S JAN? HAS ANYTHING HAPPENED TO HER?
RIGHT YOU ARE, LITTLE BUDDIES... IT'S WALL SMASHIN' TIME!
KRAK!
SHE'S SAFE FOR THE MOMENT, PARTNER! GET US OUT OF HERE AND WE'LL TELL YOU ALL ABOUT IT!
THEN, AS THE THUNDERING GIANT'S MOMENTUM ALMOST CARRIES HIM INTO THE PATH OF THE DEADLY BEAMS...
KEEP BACK, GOLIATH! YOUR OVERSIZED HIDE ISN'T ANY MORE LASER-PROOF THAN OURS!
ONE OF THOSE LEVERS MUST TURN OFF THESE RAYS! YOU'VE GOT TO FIND IT... FAST!
WILL DO, CAP.. JUST HANG ON, TEAM!
MY LINE IS BIO-CHEMISTRY, NOT MECHANICS... BUT, THIS SURE LOOKS LIKE THE MASTER SWITCH TO ME!
RIKK!
IT'D BETTER BE... 'CAUSE, FROM THE ANGLE OF THOSE BEAMS, I'M NOT GONNA GET A SECOND TRY!
IT WORKED! YOU DID IT, BIG MAN!
BUT, THE TEN-FOOT TITAN IS IN NO MOOD FOR CONGRATULATIONS ...FOR, AFTER A QUICK BRIEFING...
YOU MEAN THE LIVING LASER ESCAPED... WITH JAN? AND YOU LET HIM?
I SHOULD HAVE LET YOU WASH-OUTS ROAST AND GONE AFTER HER... WHEN I GOT HER SIGNAL!
WHO ARE YOU CALLIN' WASH-OUTS? WHY, YOU OVER-STUFFED MISFIT... IF YOU HADN'T JUST SAVED OUR SKINS, I'D MAKE YOU PAY FOR THAT CRACK.. IN SPADES!
COOL DOWN... BOTH OF YOU! TEARING EACH OTHER APART ISN'T GOING TO HELP GET THE WASP BACK!
YOU'RE RIGHT, CAP! I WAS OUT OF LINE! BUT, IF SHE WERE TO COME TO ANY HARM---
SHE WON'T, I'M SURE! LET'S START FOLLOWING THAT SIGNAL OF HERS!
4.

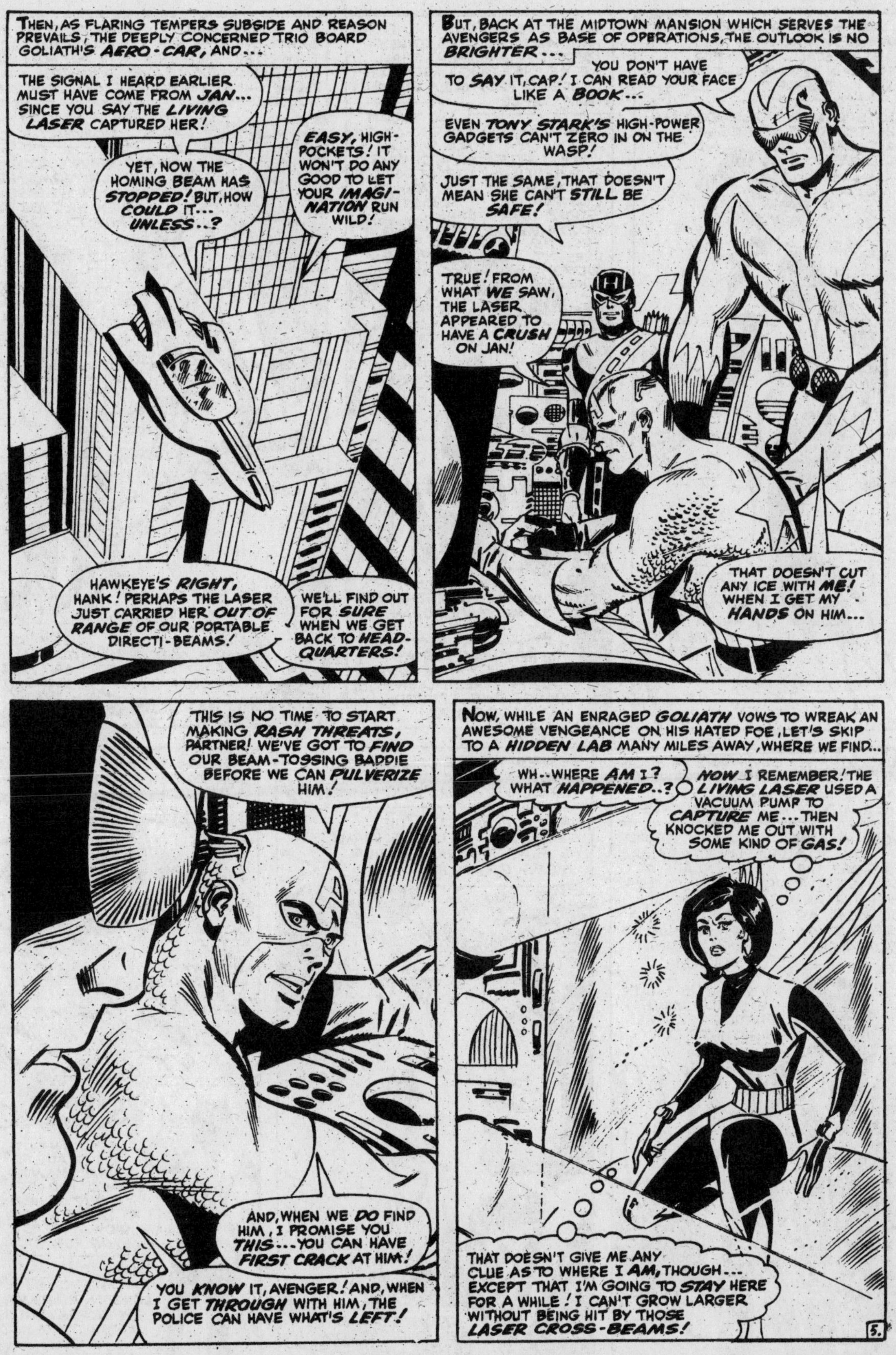

THEN, AS FLARING TEMPERS SUBSIDE AND REASON PREVAILS, THE DEEPLY CONCERNED TRIO BOARD GOLIATH'S AERO-CAR, AND...
THE SIGNAL I HEARD EARLIER MUST HAVE COME FROM JAN... SINCE YOU SAY THE LIVING LASER CAPTURED HER!
YET, NOW THE HOMING BEAM HAS STOPPED! BUT, HOW COULD IT... UNLESS..?
EASY, HIGH-POCKETS! IT WON'T DO ANY GOOD TO LET YOUR IMAGINATION RUN WILD!
HAWKEYE'S RIGHT, HANK! PERHAPS THE LASER JUST CARRIED HER OUT OF RANGE OF OUR PORTABLE DIRECTI-BEAMS!
WE'LL FIND OUT FOR SURE WHEN WE GET BACK TO HEADQUARTERS!
BUT, BACK AT THE MIDTOWN MANSION WHICH SERVES THE AVENGERS AS BASE OF OPERATIONS, THE OUTLOOK IS NO BRIGHTER...
YOU DON'T HAVE TO SAY IT, CAP! I CAN READ YOUR FACE LIKE A BOOK...
EVEN TONY STARK'S HIGH-POWER GADGETS CAN'T ZERO IN ON THE WASP!
JUST THE SAME, THAT DOESN'T MEAN SHE CAN'T STILL BE SAFE!
TRUE! FROM WHAT WE SAW, THE LASER APPEARED TO HAVE A CRUSH ON JAN!
THAT DOESN'T CUT ANY ICE WITH ME! WHEN I GET MY HANDS ON HIM...
THIS IS NO TIME TO START MAKING RASH THREATS, PARTNER! WE'VE GOT TO FIND OUR BEAM-TOSSING BADDIE BEFORE WE CAN PULVERIZE HIM!
AND, WHEN WE DO FIND HIM, I PROMISE YOU THIS... YOU CAN HAVE FIRST CRACK AT HIM!
YOU KNOW IT, AVENGER! AND, WHEN I GET THROUGH WITH HIM, THE POLICE CAN HAVE WHAT'S LEFT!
NOW, WHILE AN ENRAGED GOLIATH VOWS TO WREAK AN AWESOME VENGEANCE ON HIS HATED FOE, LET'S SKIP TO A HIDDEN LAB MANY MILES AWAY, WHERE WE FIND...
WH-- WHERE AM I? WHAT HAPPENED..?
NOW I REMEMBER! THE LIVING LASER USED A VACUUM PUMP TO CAPTURE ME... THEN KNOCKED ME OUT WITH SOME KIND OF GAS!
THAT DOESN'T GIVE ME ANY CLUE AS TO WHERE I AM, THOUGH... EXCEPT THAT I'M GOING TO STAY HERE FOR A WHILE! I CAN'T GROW LARGER WITHOUT BEING HIT BY THOSE LASER CROSS-BEAMS!
5.

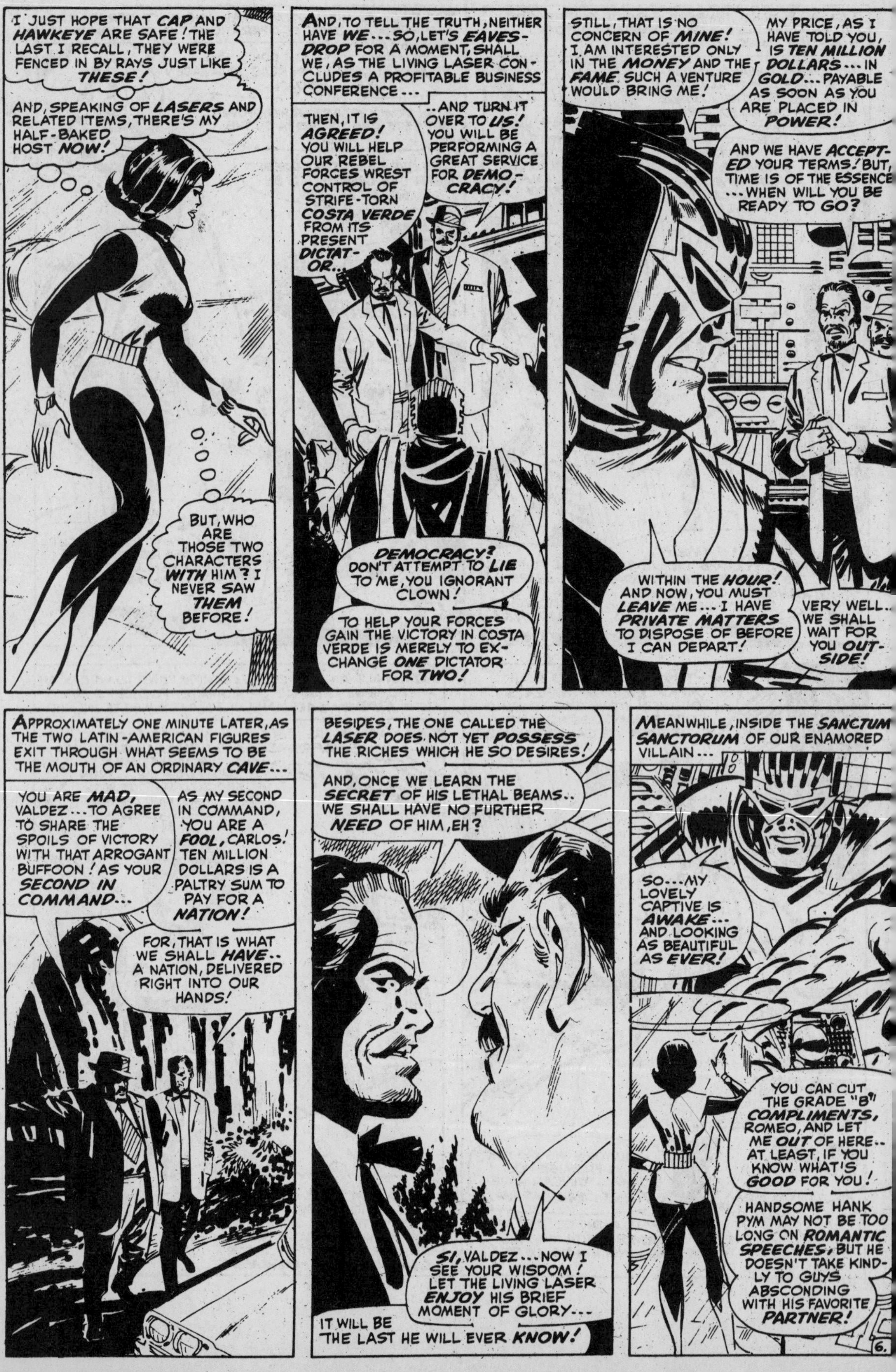
I JUST HOPE THAT CAP AND HAWKEYE ARE SAFE! THE LAST I RECALL, THEY WERE FENCED IN BY RAYS JUST LIKE THESE!
AND, SPEAKING OF LASERS AND RELATED ITEMS, THERE'S MY HALF-BAKED HOST NOW!
BUT, WHO ARE THOSE TWO CHARACTERS WITH HIM? I NEVER SAW THEM BEFORE!
AND, TO TELL THE TRUTH, NEITHER HAVE WE... SO, LET'S EAVES-DROP FOR A MOMENT, SHALL WE, AS THE LIVING LASER CONCLUDES A PROFITABLE BUSINESS CONFERENCE...
THEN, IT IS AGREED! YOU WILL HELP OUR REBEL FORCES WREST CONTROL OF STRIFE-TORN COSTA VERDE FROM ITS PRESENT DICTATOR...
..AND TURN IT OVER TO US! YOU WILL BE PERFORMING A GREAT SERVICE FOR DEMOCRACY!
DEMOCRACY? DON'T ATTEMPT TO LIE TO ME, YOU IGNORANT CLOWN!
TO HELP YOUR FORCES GAIN THE VICTORY IN COSTA VERDE IS MERELY TO EXCHANGE ONE DICTATOR FOR TWO!
STILL, THAT IS NO CONCERN OF MINE! I AM INTERESTED ONLY IN THE MONEY AND THE FAME SUCH A VENTURE WOULD BRING ME!
MY PRICE, AS I HAVE TOLD YOU, IS TEN MILLION DOLLARS... IN GOLD... PAYABLE AS SOON AS YOU ARE PLACED IN POWER!
AND WE HAVE ACCEPTED YOUR TERMS! BUT, TIME IS OF THE ESSENCE ...WHEN WILL YOU BE READY TO GO?
WITHIN THE HOUR! AND NOW, YOU MUST LEAVE ME... I HAVE PRIVATE MATTERS TO DISPOSE OF BEFORE I CAN DEPART!
VERY WELL.. WE SHALL WAIT FOR YOU OUTSIDE!
APPROXIMATELY ONE MINUTE LATER, AS THE TWO LATIN-AMERICAN FIGURES EXIT THROUGH WHAT SEEMS TO BE THE MOUTH OF AN ORDINARY CAVE...
YOU ARE MAD, VALDEZ... TO AGREE TO SHARE THE SPOILS OF VICTORY WITH THAT ARROGANT BUFFOON! AS YOUR SECOND IN COMMAND...
AS MY SECOND IN COMMAND, YOU ARE A FOOL, CARLOS! TEN MILLION DOLLARS IS A PALTRY SUM TO PAY FOR A NATION!
FOR, THAT IS WHAT WE SHALL HAVE.. A NATION, DELIVERED RIGHT INTO OUR HANDS!
BESIDES, THE ONE CALLED THE LASER DOES NOT YET POSSESS THE RICHES WHICH HE SO DESIRES!
AND, ONCE WE LEARN THE SECRET OF HIS LETHAL BEAMS.. WE SHALL HAVE NO FURTHER NEED OF HIM, EH?
SI, VALDEZ... NOW I SEE YOUR WISDOM! LET THE LIVING LASER ENJOY HIS BRIEF MOMENT OF GLORY...
IT WILL BE THE LAST HE WILL EVER KNOW!
MEANWHILE, INSIDE THE SANCTUM SANCTORUM OF OUR ENAMORED VILLAIN...
SO... MY LOVELY CAPTIVE IS AWAKE... AND LOOKING AS BEAUTIFUL AS EVER!
YOU CAN CUT THE GRADE "B" COMPLIMENTS, ROMEO, AND LET ME OUT OF HERE.. AT LEAST, IF YOU KNOW WHAT'S GOOD FOR YOU!
HANDSOME HANK PYM MAY NOT BE TOO LONG ON ROMANTIC SPEECHES, BUT HE DOESN'T TAKE KINDLY TO GUYS ABSCONDING WITH HIS FAVORITE PARTNER!
6.

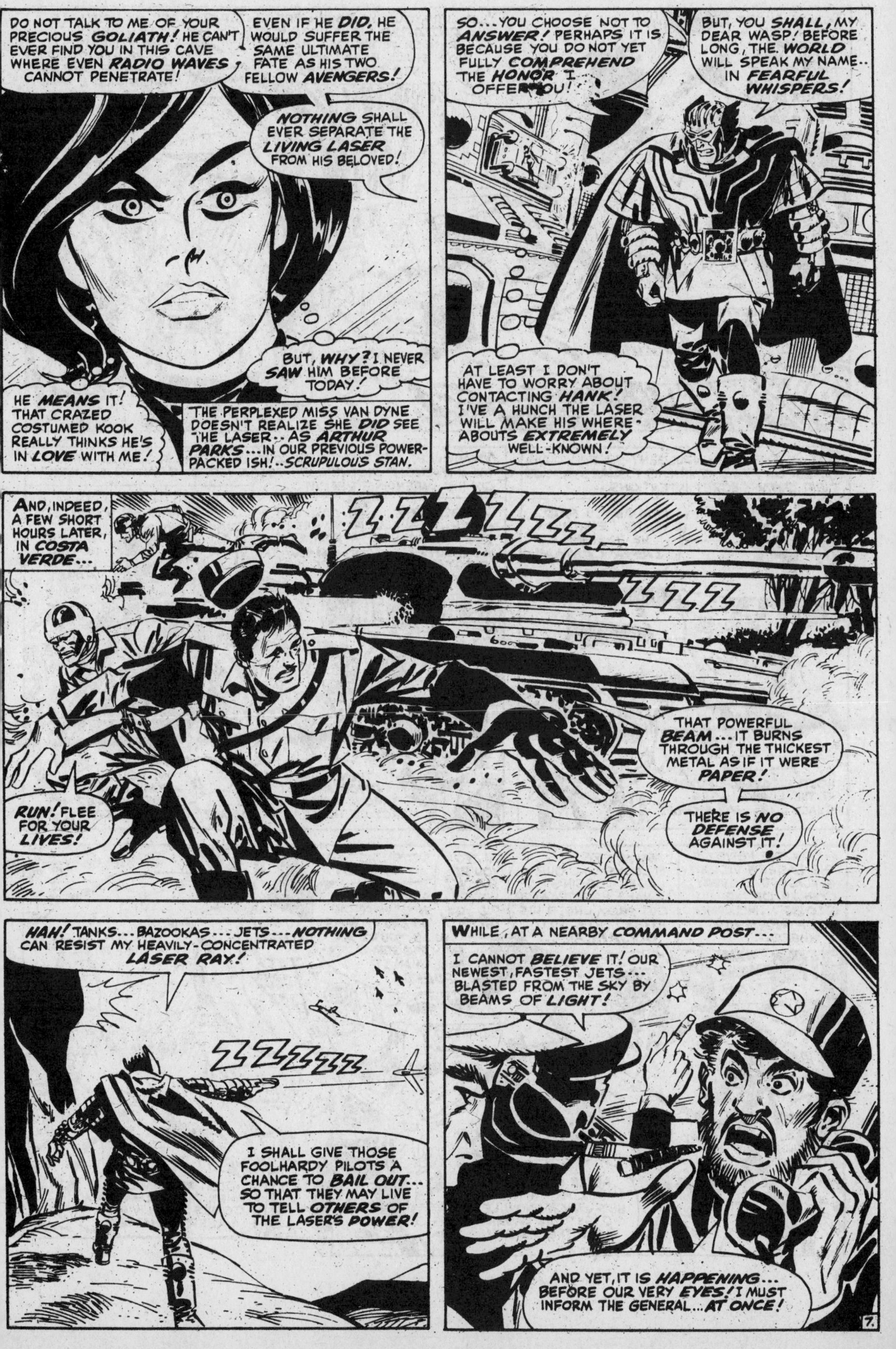
DO NOT TALK TO ME OF YOUR PRECIOUS GOLIATH! HE CAN'T EVER FIND YOU IN THIS CAVE WHERE EVEN RADIO WAVES CANNOT PENETRATE!
EVEN IF HE DID, HE WOULD SUFFER THE SAME ULTIMATE FATE AS HIS TWO FELLOW AVENGERS!
NOTHING SHALL EVER SEPARATE THE LIVING LASER FROM HIS BELOVED!
BUT, WHY? I NEVER SAW HIM BEFORE TODAY!
HE MEANS IT! THAT CRAZED COSTUMED KOOK REALLY THINKS HE'S IN LOVE WITH ME!
THE PERPLEXED MISS VAN DYNE DOESN'T REALIZE SHE DID SEE THE LASER.. AS ARTHUR PARKS... IN OUR PREVIOUS POWER-PACKED ISH!..SCRUPULOUS STAN.
SO... YOU CHOOSE NOT TO ANSWER! PERHAPS IT IS BECAUSE YOU DO NOT YET FULLY COMPREHEND THE HONOR I OFFER YOU!
BUT, YOU SHALL, MY DEAR WASP! BEFORE LONG, THE WORLD WILL SPEAK MY NAME.. IN FEARFUL WHISPERS!
AT LEAST I DON'T HAVE TO WORRY ABOUT CONTACTING HANK! I'VE A HUNCH THE LASER WILL MAKE HIS WHEREABOUTS EXTREMELY WELL-KNOWN!
AND, INDEED, A FEW SHORT HOURS LATER, IN COSTA VERDE...
ZZZZZZZ
ZZZZ
RUN! FLEE FOR YOUR LIVES!
THAT POWERFUL BEAM... IT BURNS THROUGH THE THICKEST METAL AS IF IT WERE PAPER!
THERE IS NO DEFENSE AGAINST IT!
HAH! TANKS... BAZOOKAS... JETS... NOTHING CAN RESIST MY HEAVILY-CONCENTRATED LASER RAY!
ZZZZZZZ
I SHALL GIVE THOSE FOOLHARDY PILOTS A CHANCE TO BAIL OUT... SO THAT THEY MAY LIVE TO TELL OTHERS OF THE LASER'S POWER!
WHILE, AT A NEARBY COMMAND POST...
I CANNOT BELIEVE IT! OUR NEWEST, FASTEST JETS... BLASTED FROM THE SKY BY BEAMS OF LIGHT!
AND YET, IT IS HAPPENING... BEFORE OUR VERY EYES! I MUST INFORM THE GENERAL... AT ONCE!
7.

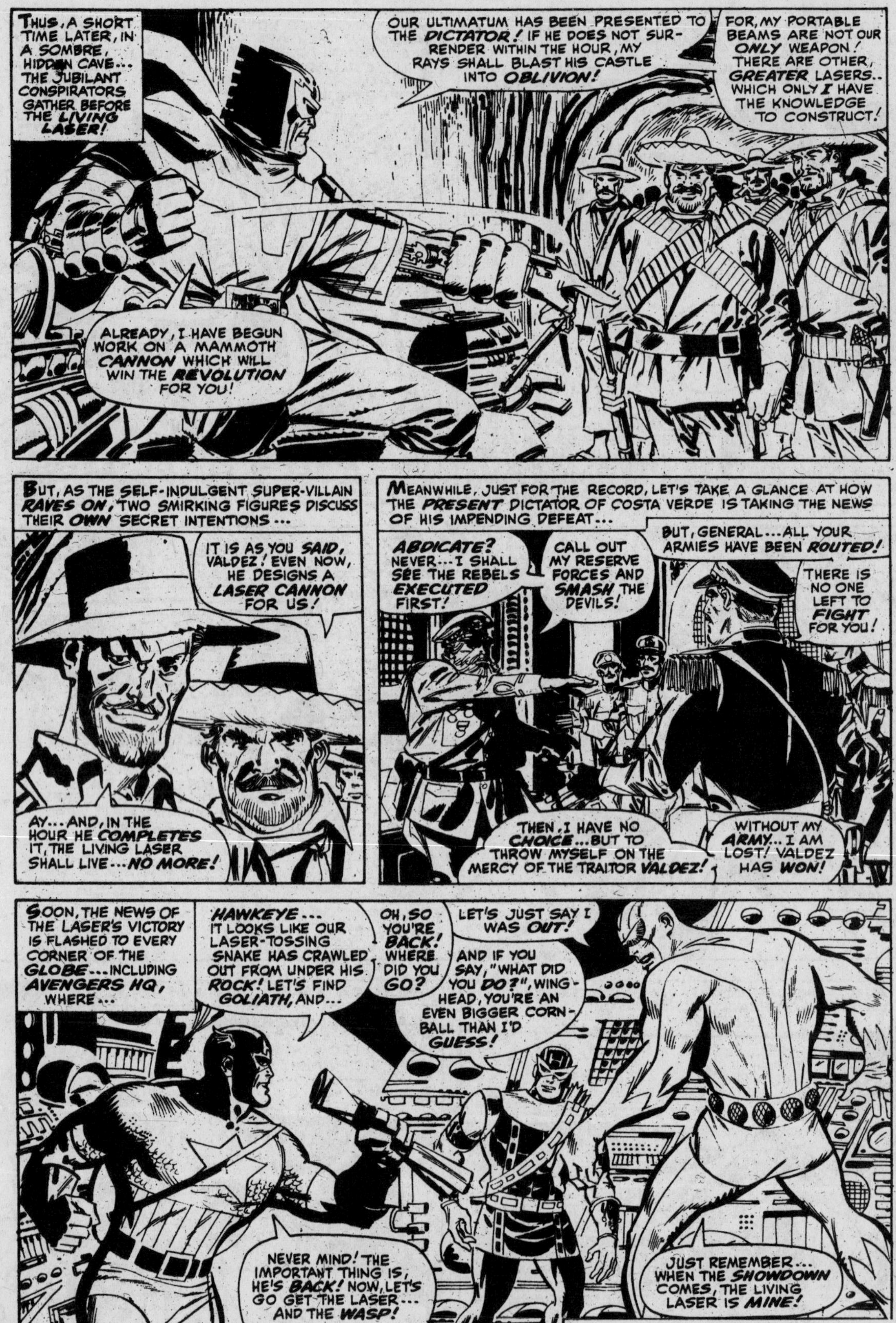
THUS, A SHORT TIME LATER, IN A SOMBRE, HIDDEN CAVE... THE JUBILANT CONSPIRATORS GATHER BEFORE THE LIVING LASER!
OUR ULTIMATUM HAS BEEN PRESENTED TO THE DICTATOR! IF HE DOES NOT SURRENDER WITHIN THE HOUR, MY RAYS SHALL BLAST HIS CASTLE INTO OBLIVION!
FOR, MY PORTABLE BEAMS ARE NOT OUR ONLY WEAPON! THERE ARE OTHER, GREATER LASERS.. WHICH ONLY I HAVE THE KNOWLEDGE TO CONSTRUCT!
ALREADY, I HAVE BEGUN WORK ON A MAMMOTH CANNON WHICH WILL WIN THE REVOLUTION FOR YOU!
BUT, AS THE SELF-INDULGENT SUPER-VILLAIN RAVES ON, TWO SMIRKING FIGURES DISCUSS THEIR OWN SECRET INTENTIONS...
IT IS AS YOU SAID, VALDEZ! EVEN NOW, HE DESIGNS A LASER CANNON FOR US!
AY... AND, IN THE HOUR HE COMPLETES IT, THE LIVING LASER SHALL LIVE... NO MORE!
MEANWHILE, JUST FOR THE RECORD, LET'S TAKE A GLANCE AT HOW THE PRESENT DICTATOR OF COSTA VERDE IS TAKING THE NEWS OF HIS IMPENDING DEFEAT...
ABDICATE? NEVER... I SHALL SEE THE REBELS EXECUTED FIRST!
CALL OUT MY RESERVE FORCES AND SMASH THE DEVILS!
BUT, GENERAL... ALL YOUR ARMIES HAVE BEEN ROUTED!
THERE IS NO ONE LEFT TO FIGHT FOR YOU!
THEN, I HAVE NO CHOICE... BUT TO THROW MYSELF ON THE MERCY OF THE TRAITOR VALDEZ!
WITHOUT MY ARMY... I AM LOST! VALDEZ HAS WON!
SOON, THE NEWS OF THE LASER'S VICTORY IS FLASHED TO EVERY CORNER OF THE GLOBE... INCLUDING AVENGERS HQ, WHERE...
HAWKEYE... IT LOOKS LIKE OUR LASER-TOSSING SNAKE HAS CRAWLED OUT FROM UNDER HIS ROCK! LET'S FIND GOLIATH, AND...
OH, SO YOU'RE BACK! WHERE DID YOU GO?
LET'S JUST SAY I WAS OUT!
AND IF YOU SAY, "WHAT DID YOU DO?", WING-HEAD, YOU'RE AN EVEN BIGGER CORN-BALL THAN I'D GUESS!
NEVER MIND! THE IMPORTANT THING IS, HE'S BACK! NOW, LET'S GO GET THE LASER... AND THE WASP!
JUST REMEMBER... WHEN THE SHOWDOWN COMES, THE LIVING LASER IS MINE!

SCANT MOMENTS LATER, IN ONE OF THEIR MANY SLEEK CRAFT, THREE AVENGERS ZOOM THROUGH THE AIR ABOVE THE WORLD'S MOST FAMOUS SKYLINE...

YOU'VE BEEN QUIET A FULL *TEN SECONDS*, HAWKEYE! WHAT'S THE SPECIAL *OCCASION*?

I WAS JUST THINKIN' ABOUT ALL THESE CLASSY *GO-BUGGIES* THAT TONY STARK KEEPS TURNIN' OUT FOR US!

NO *WONDER* YA DON'T READ MUCH ABOUT HIM GOIN' TO THE *PLAYBOY CLUB* ANY MORE!

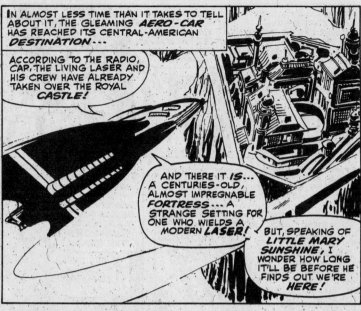

IN ALMOST LESS TIME THAN IT TAKES TO TELL ABOUT IT, THE GLEAMING *AERO-CAR* HAS REACHED ITS CENTRAL-AMERICAN *DESTINATION*...

ACCORDING TO THE RADIO, CAP, THE LIVING LASER AND HIS CREW HAVE ALREADY TAKEN OVER THE ROYAL *CASTLE*!

AND THERE IT *IS*... A CENTURIES-OLD, ALMOST IMPREGNABLE *FORTRESS*... A STRANGE SETTING FOR ONE WHO WIELDS A MODERN *LASER*!

BUT, SPEAKING OF *LITTLE MARY SUNSHINE*, I WONDER HOW LONG IT'LL BE BEFORE HE FINDS OUT WE'RE *HERE*!

THE NEXT SECOND, THE-RED-WHITE-AND-BLUE SENTINEL RECEIVES HIS ANSWER FROM AN *UNEXPECTED QUARTER*, AS...

THE *FOOLS*! WHEN I LEARNED OF THEIR ESCAPE FROM MY TRAP, DID THEY NOT THINK I WOULD BE *READY* FOR THEM?

I'LL *END* THEIR PUNY ATTACK... WITH A TEST-BLAST FROM MY PERFECTED *LASER CANNON*!

AND, HIGH ABOVE...

UH-OH! YOU GOT ANY *MORE* BRIGHT QUESTIONS, WINGHEAD?

WE'RE *SPINNING OUT*! HAWKEYE... GOLIATH... GET READY TO *HIT*!

SPLUNCH!

LET'S *HOPE* NOT, HAWKEYE! WE'RE GOING TO BE UP AGAINST AN ENTIRE REBEL *ARMY*... AND WE NEED ALL THE BREAKS WE CAN *GET*!

PERFECT *SPLASHDOWN*, CAP! I WONDER IF THE LIVING LASER KNOWS THAT THIS BABY DOUBLES AS A *SUBMARINE*?

I'M WORRIED ABOUT *GOLIATH*! FIRST HE *DISAPPEARED* FOR AN HOUR AFTER JAN WAS CAPTURED... AND NOW HE'S SO GRIMLY *SILENT*!

I HOPE HE DOESN'T TRY ANYTHING *RASH* WHEN WE RUN INTO THE *LIVING LASER*!

9.

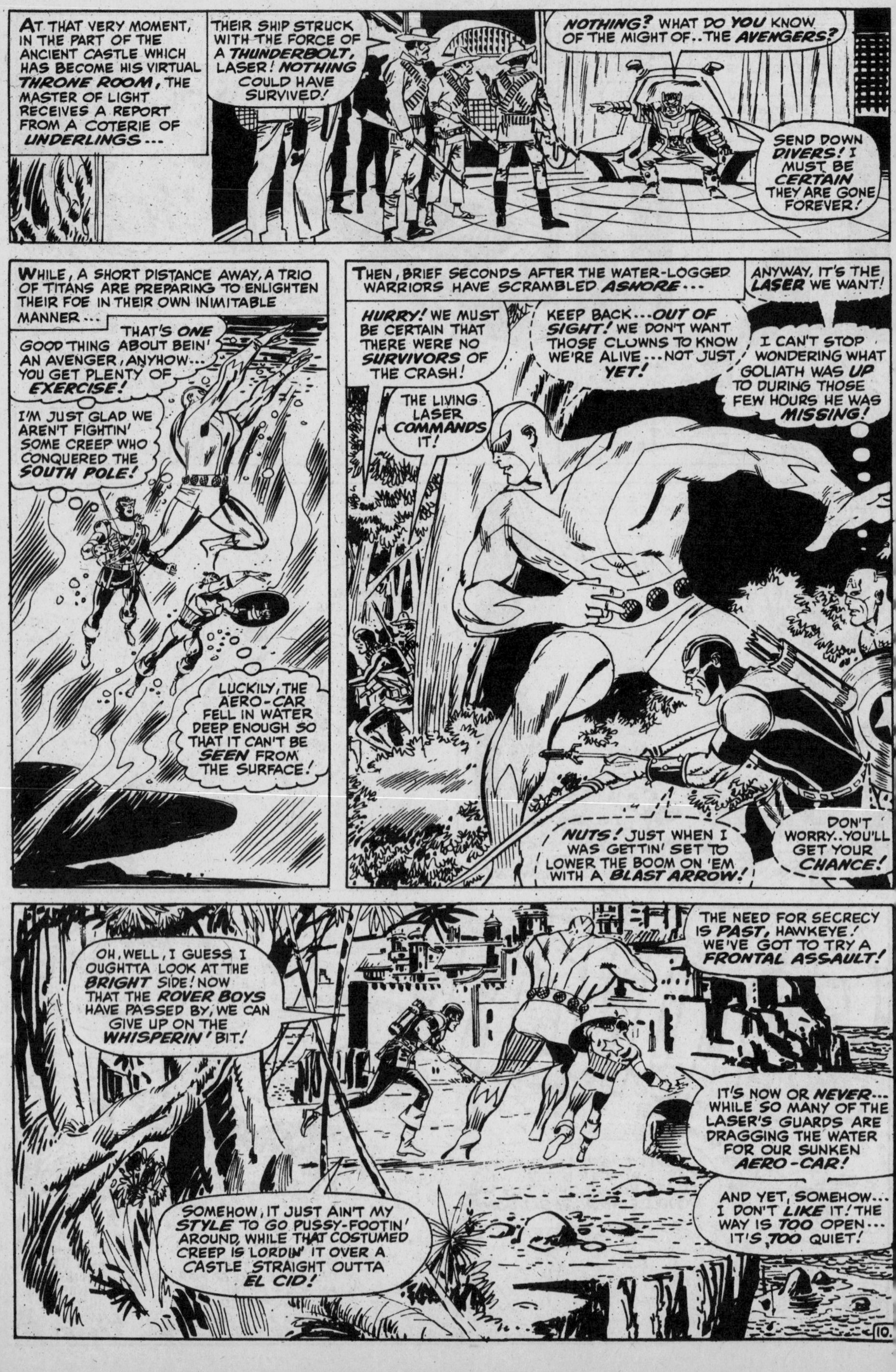
AT THAT VERY MOMENT, IN THE PART OF THE ANCIENT CASTLE WHICH HAS BECOME HIS VIRTUAL THRONE ROOM, THE MASTER OF LIGHT RECEIVES A REPORT FROM A COTERIE OF UNDERLINGS...
THEIR SHIP STRUCK WITH THE FORCE OF A THUNDERBOLT, LASER! NOTHING COULD HAVE SURVIVED!
NOTHING? WHAT DO YOU KNOW OF THE MIGHT OF..THE AVENGERS?
SEND DOWN DIVERS! I MUST BE CERTAIN THEY ARE GONE FOREVER!
WHILE, A SHORT DISTANCE AWAY, A TRIO OF TITANS ARE PREPARING TO ENLIGHTEN THEIR FOE IN THEIR OWN INIMITABLE MANNER...
THAT'S ONE GOOD THING ABOUT BEIN' AN AVENGER, ANYHOW... YOU GET PLENTY OF EXERCISE!
I'M JUST GLAD WE AREN'T FIGHTIN' SOME CREEP WHO CONQUERED THE SOUTH POLE!
LUCKILY, THE AERO-CAR FELL IN WATER DEEP ENOUGH SO THAT IT CAN'T BE SEEN FROM THE SURFACE!
THEN, BRIEF SECONDS AFTER THE WATER-LOGGED WARRIORS HAVE SCRAMBLED ASHORE...
HURRY! WE MUST BE CERTAIN THAT THERE WERE NO SURVIVORS OF THE CRASH!
THE LIVING LASER COMMANDS IT!
KEEP BACK...OUT OF SIGHT! WE DON'T WANT THOSE CLOWNS TO KNOW WE'RE ALIVE...NOT JUST YET!
ANYWAY, IT'S THE LASER WE WANT!
I CAN'T STOP WONDERING WHAT GOLIATH WAS UP TO DURING THOSE FEW HOURS HE WAS MISSING!
NUTS! JUST WHEN I WAS GETTIN' SET TO LOWER THE BOOM ON 'EM WITH A BLAST ARROW!
DON'T WORRY..YOU'LL GET YOUR CHANCE!
OH, WELL, I GUESS I OUGHTTA LOOK AT THE BRIGHT SIDE! NOW THAT THE ROVER BOYS HAVE PASSED BY, WE CAN GIVE UP ON THE WHISPERIN' BIT!
THE NEED FOR SECRECY IS PAST, HAWKEYE! WE'VE GOT TO TRY A FRONTAL ASSAULT!
IT'S NOW OR NEVER... WHILE SO MANY OF THE LASER'S GUARDS ARE DRAGGING THE WATER FOR OUR SUNKEN AERO-CAR!
SOMEHOW, IT JUST AIN'T MY STYLE TO GO PUSSY-FOOTIN' AROUND, WHILE THAT COSTUMED CREEP IS LORDIN' IT OVER A CASTLE STRAIGHT OUTTA EL CID!
AND YET, SOMEHOW... I DON'T LIKE IT! THE WAY IS TOO OPEN... IT'S TOO QUIET!
10.

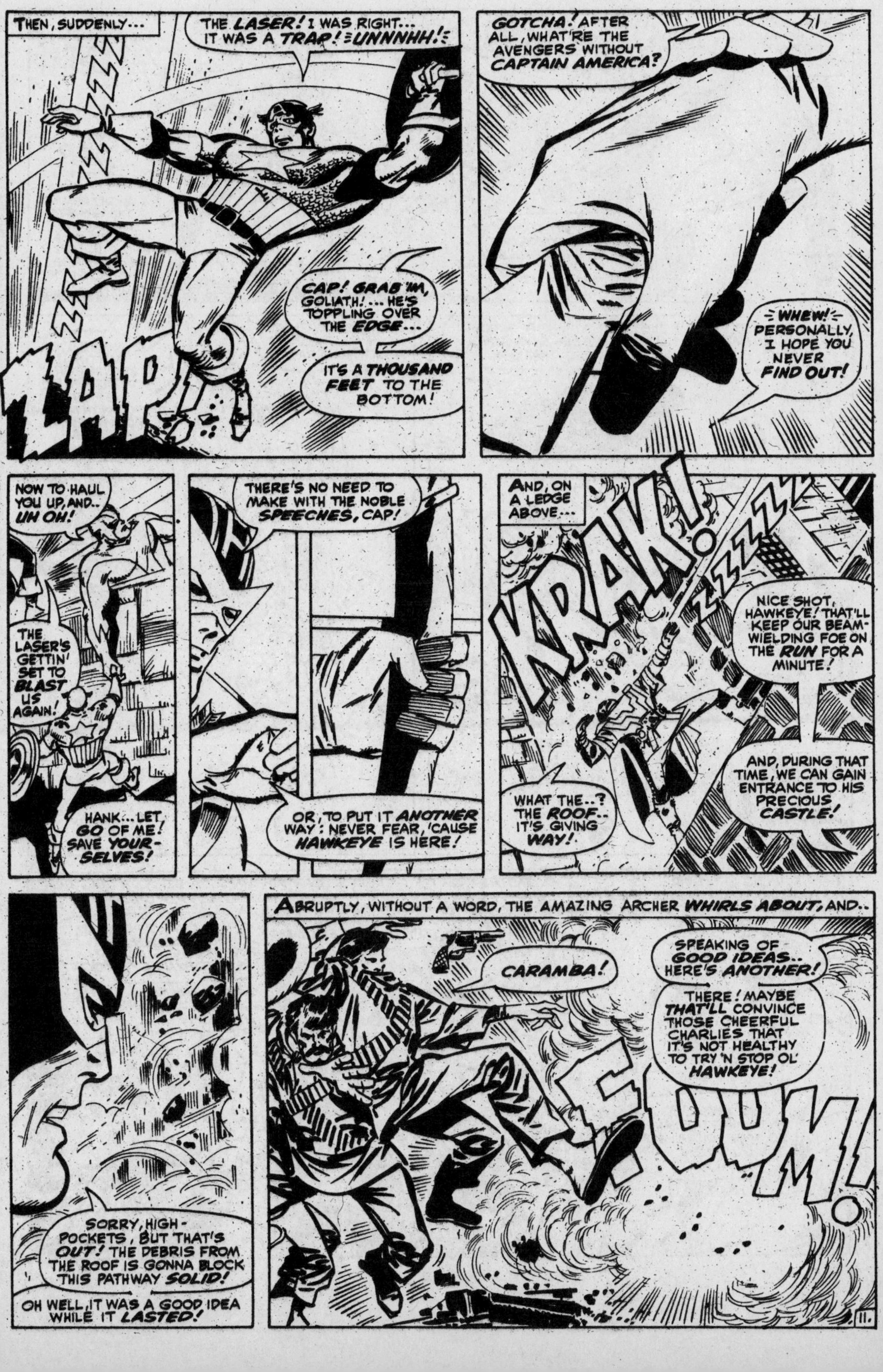
THEN, SUDDENLY...
THE LASER! I WAS RIGHT... IT WAS A TRAP! UNNNHH!
ZAP
CAP! GRAB 'IM, GOLIATH!... HE'S TOPPLING OVER THE EDGE...
IT'S A THOUSAND FEET TO THE BOTTOM!
GOTCHA! AFTER ALL, WHAT'RE THE AVENGERS WITHOUT CAPTAIN AMERICA?
WHEW! PERSONALLY, I HOPE YOU NEVER FIND OUT!
NOW TO HAUL YOU UP, AND.. UH OH!
THE LASER'S GETTIN' SET TO BLAST US AGAIN!
HANK... LET GO OF ME! SAVE YOURSELVES!
THERE'S NO NEED TO MAKE WITH THE NOBLE SPEECHES, CAP!
OR, TO PUT IT ANOTHER WAY: NEVER FEAR, 'CAUSE HAWKEYE IS HERE!
AND, ON A LEDGE ABOVE...
KRAK!
NICE SHOT, HAWKEYE! THAT'LL KEEP OUR BEAM-WIELDING FOE ON THE RUN FOR A MINUTE!
AND, DURING THAT TIME, WE CAN GAIN ENTRANCE TO HIS PRECIOUS CASTLE!
WHAT THE..? THE ROOF.. IT'S GIVING WAY!
SORRY, HIGH-POCKETS, BUT THAT'S OUT! THE DEBRIS FROM THE ROOF IS GONNA BLOCK THIS PATHWAY SOLID!
OH WELL, IT WAS A GOOD IDEA WHILE IT LASTED!
ABRUPTLY, WITHOUT A WORD, THE AMAZING ARCHER WHIRLS ABOUT, AND..
CARAMBA!
SPEAKING OF GOOD IDEAS.. HERE'S ANOTHER!
THERE! MAYBE THAT'LL CONVINCE THOSE CHEERFUL CHARLIES THAT IT'S NOT HEALTHY TO TRY 'N STOP OL' HAWKEYE!
FOOM!
11.

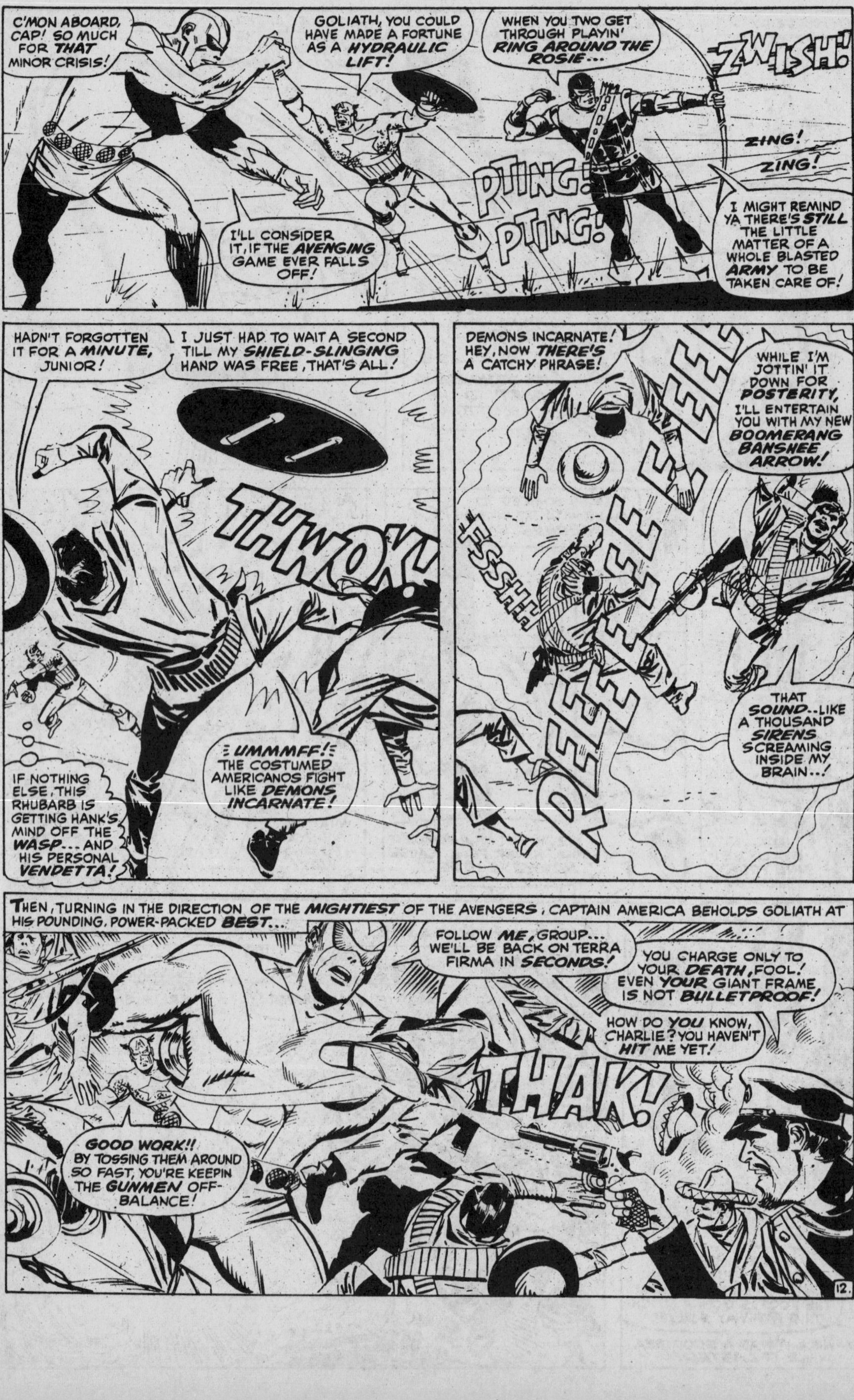

C'MON ABOARD, CAP! SO MUCH FOR THAT MINOR CRISIS!
GOLIATH, YOU COULD HAVE MADE A FORTUNE AS A HYDRAULIC LIFT!
I'LL CONSIDER IT, IF THE AVENGING GAME EVER FALLS OFF!
WHEN YOU TWO GET THROUGH PLAYIN' RING AROUND THE ROSIE...
ZWISH!
ZING!
ZING!
PTING!
PTING!
I MIGHT REMIND YA THERE'S STILL THE LITTLE MATTER OF A WHOLE BLASTED ARMY TO BE TAKEN CARE OF!
HADN'T FORGOTTEN IT FOR A MINUTE, JUNIOR!
I JUST HAD TO WAIT A SECOND TILL MY SHIELD-SLINGING HAND WAS FREE, THAT'S ALL!
THWOK!
IF NOTHING ELSE, THIS RHUBARB IS GETTING HANK'S MIND OFF THE WASP... AND HIS PERSONAL VENDETTA!
UMMMFF! THE COSTUMED AMERICANOS FIGHT LIKE DEMONS INCARNATE!
DEMONS INCARNATE! HEY, NOW THERE'S A CATCHY PHRASE!
WHILE I'M JOTTIN' IT DOWN FOR POSTERITY, I'LL ENTERTAIN YOU WITH MY NEW BOOMERANG BANSHEE ARROW!
FSSHH
REEEEEEEEEE
THAT SOUND..LIKE A THOUSAND SIRENS SCREAMING INSIDE MY BRAIN..!
THEN, TURNING IN THE DIRECTION OF THE MIGHTIEST OF THE AVENGERS, CAPTAIN AMERICA BEHOLDS GOLIATH AT HIS POUNDING, POWER-PACKED BEST...
FOLLOW ME, GROUP... WE'LL BE BACK ON TERRA FIRMA IN SECONDS!
YOU CHARGE ONLY TO YOUR DEATH, FOOL! EVEN YOUR GIANT FRAME IS NOT BULLETPROOF!
HOW DO YOU KNOW, CHARLIE? YOU HAVEN'T HIT ME YET!
THAK!
GOOD WORK!! BY TOSSING THEM AROUND SO FAST, YOU'RE KEEPIN THE GUNMEN OFF-BALANCE!
12.

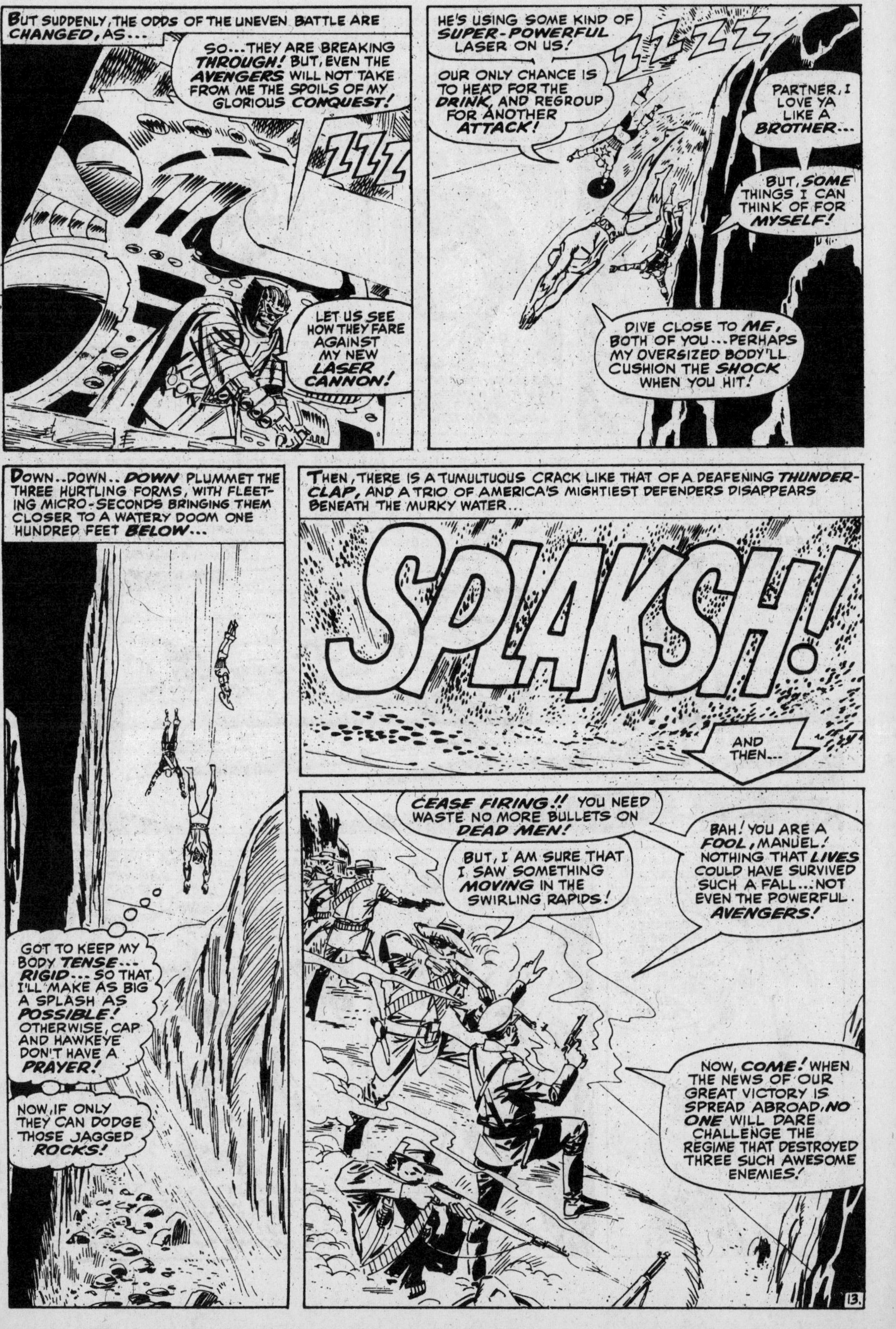

BUT SUDDENLY, THE ODDS OF THE UNEVEN BATTLE ARE CHANGED, AS...
SO...THEY ARE BREAKING THROUGH! BUT, EVEN THE AVENGERS WILL NOT TAKE FROM ME THE SPOILS OF MY GLORIOUS CONQUEST!
ZZZ
LET US SEE HOW THEY FARE AGAINST MY NEW LASER CANNON!
HE'S USING SOME KIND OF SUPER-POWERFUL LASER ON US!
OUR ONLY CHANCE IS TO HEAD FOR THE DRINK, AND REGROUP FOR ANOTHER ATTACK!
ZZZZZ
PARTNER, I LOVE YA LIKE A BROTHER...
BUT, SOME THINGS I CAN THINK OF FOR MYSELF!
DIVE CLOSE TO ME, BOTH OF YOU...PERHAPS MY OVERSIZED BODY'LL CUSHION THE SHOCK WHEN YOU HIT!
DOWN..DOWN..DOWN PLUMMET THE THREE HURTLING FORMS, WITH FLEETING MICRO-SECONDS BRINGING THEM CLOSER TO A WATERY DOOM ONE HUNDRED FEET BELOW...
GOT TO KEEP MY BODY TENSE... RIGID... SO THAT I'LL MAKE AS BIG A SPLASH AS POSSIBLE! OTHERWISE, CAP AND HAWKEYE DON'T HAVE A PRAYER!
NOW, IF ONLY THEY CAN DODGE THOSE JAGGED ROCKS!
THEN, THERE IS A TUMULTUOUS CRACK LIKE THAT OF A DEAFENING THUNDER-CLAP, AND A TRIO OF AMERICA'S MIGHTIEST DEFENDERS DISAPPEARS BENEATH THE MURKY WATER...
SPLAKSH!
AND THEN...
CEASE FIRING!! YOU NEED WASTE NO MORE BULLETS ON DEAD MEN!
BUT, I AM SURE THAT I SAW SOMETHING MOVING IN THE SWIRLING RAPIDS!
BAH! YOU ARE A FOOL, MANUEL! NOTHING THAT LIVES COULD HAVE SURVIVED SUCH A FALL...NOT EVEN THE POWERFUL AVENGERS!
NOW, COME! WHEN THE NEWS OF OUR GREAT VICTORY IS SPREAD ABROAD, NO ONE WILL DARE CHALLENGE THE REGIME THAT DESTROYED THREE SUCH AWESOME ENEMIES!
13.

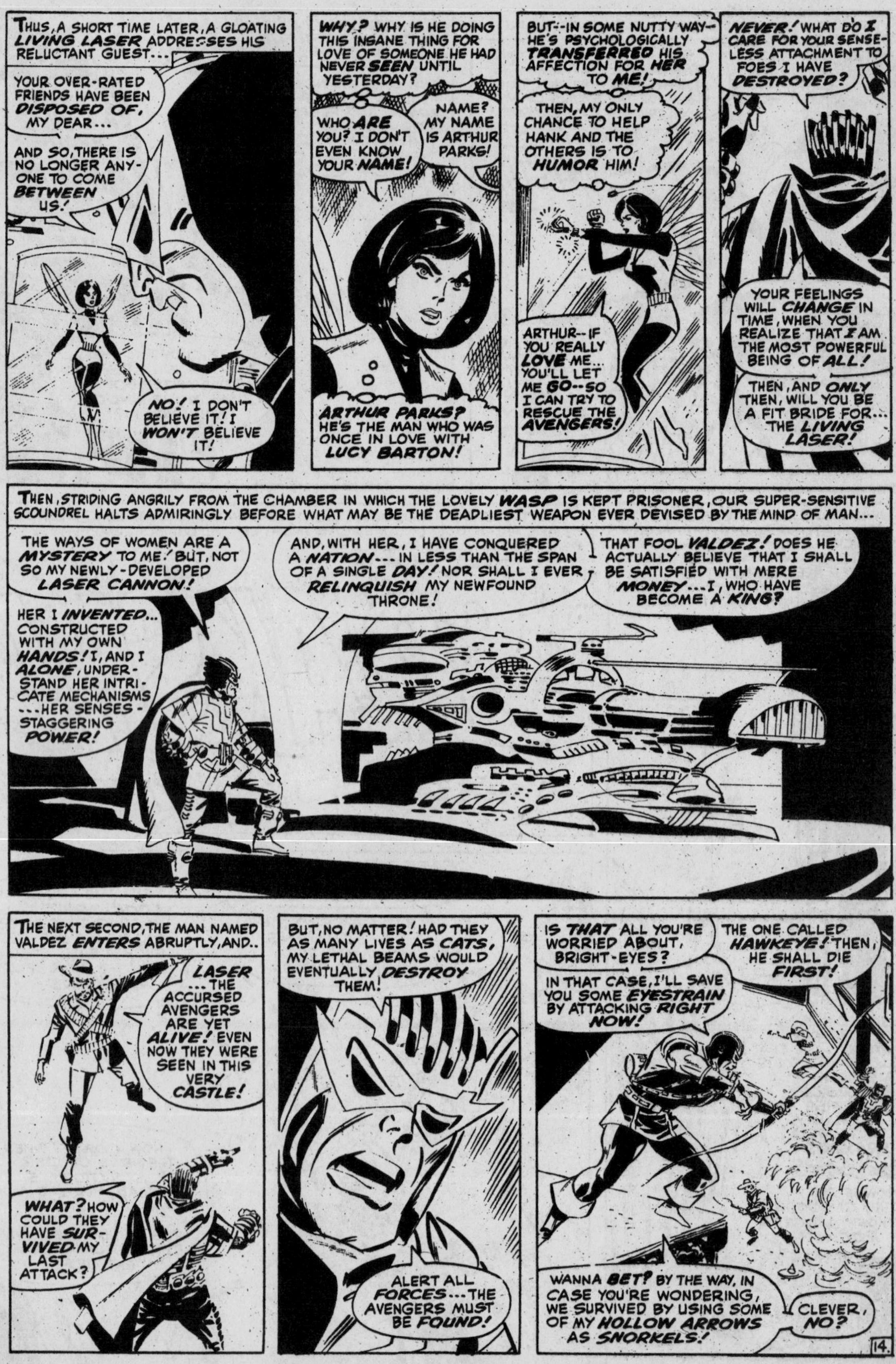
THUS, A SHORT TIME LATER, A GLOATING LIVING LASER ADDRESSES HIS RELUCTANT GUEST...
YOUR OVER-RATED FRIENDS HAVE BEEN DISPOSED OF, MY DEAR...
AND SO, THERE IS NO LONGER ANYONE TO COME BETWEEN US!
NO! I DON'T BELIEVE IT! I WON'T BELIEVE IT!
WHY? WHY IS HE DOING THIS INSANE THING FOR LOVE OF SOMEONE HE HAD NEVER SEEN UNTIL YESTERDAY?
WHO ARE YOU? I DON'T EVEN KNOW YOUR NAME!
NAME? MY NAME IS ARTHUR PARKS!
ARTHUR PARKS? HE'S THE MAN WHO WAS ONCE IN LOVE WITH LUCY BARTON!
BUT--IN SOME NUTTY WAY--HE'S PSYCHOLOGICALLY TRANSFERRED HIS AFFECTION FOR HER TO ME!
THEN, MY ONLY CHANCE TO HELP HANK AND THE OTHERS IS TO HUMOR HIM!
ARTHUR--IF YOU REALLY LOVE ME... YOU'LL LET ME GO--SO I CAN TRY TO RESCUE THE AVENGERS!
NEVER! WHAT DO I CARE FOR YOUR SENSELESS ATTACHMENT TO FOES I HAVE DESTROYED?
YOUR FEELINGS WILL CHANGE IN TIME, WHEN YOU REALIZE THAT I AM THE MOST POWERFUL BEING OF ALL!
THEN, AND ONLY THEN, WILL YOU BE A FIT BRIDE FOR... THE LIVING LASER!
THEN, STRIDING ANGRILY FROM THE CHAMBER IN WHICH THE LOVELY WASP IS KEPT PRISONER, OUR SUPER-SENSITIVE SCOUNDREL HALTS ADMIRINGLY BEFORE WHAT MAY BE THE DEADLIEST WEAPON EVER DEVISED BY THE MIND OF MAN...
THE WAYS OF WOMEN ARE A MYSTERY TO ME! BUT, NOT SO MY NEWLY-DEVELOPED LASER CANNON!
HER I INVENTED... CONSTRUCTED WITH MY OWN HANDS! I, AND I ALONE, UNDERSTAND HER INTRICATE MECHANISMS ---HER SENSES-STAGGERING POWER!
AND, WITH HER, I HAVE CONQUERED A NATION--- IN LESS THAN THE SPAN OF A SINGLE DAY! NOR SHALL I EVER RELINQUISH MY NEWFOUND THRONE!
THAT FOOL VALDEZ! DOES HE ACTUALLY BELIEVE THAT I SHALL BE SATISFIED WITH MERE MONEY...I, WHO HAVE BECOME A KING?
THE NEXT SECOND, THE MAN NAMED VALDEZ ENTERS ABRUPTLY, AND..
LASER ...THE ACCURSED AVENGERS ARE YET ALIVE! EVEN NOW THEY WERE SEEN IN THIS VERY CASTLE!
WHAT? HOW COULD THEY HAVE SURVIVED MY LAST ATTACK?
BUT, NO MATTER! HAD THEY AS MANY LIVES AS CATS, MY LETHAL BEAMS WOULD EVENTUALLY DESTROY THEM!
ALERT ALL FORCES... THE AVENGERS MUST BE FOUND!
IS THAT ALL YOU'RE WORRIED ABOUT, BRIGHT-EYES?
IN THAT CASE, I'LL SAVE YOU SOME EYESTRAIN BY ATTACKING RIGHT NOW!
THE ONE CALLED HAWKEYE! THEN, HE SHALL DIE FIRST!
WANNA BET? BY THE WAY, IN CASE YOU'RE WONDERING, WE SURVIVED BY USING SOME OF MY HOLLOW ARROWS AS SNORKELS!
CLEVER, NO?

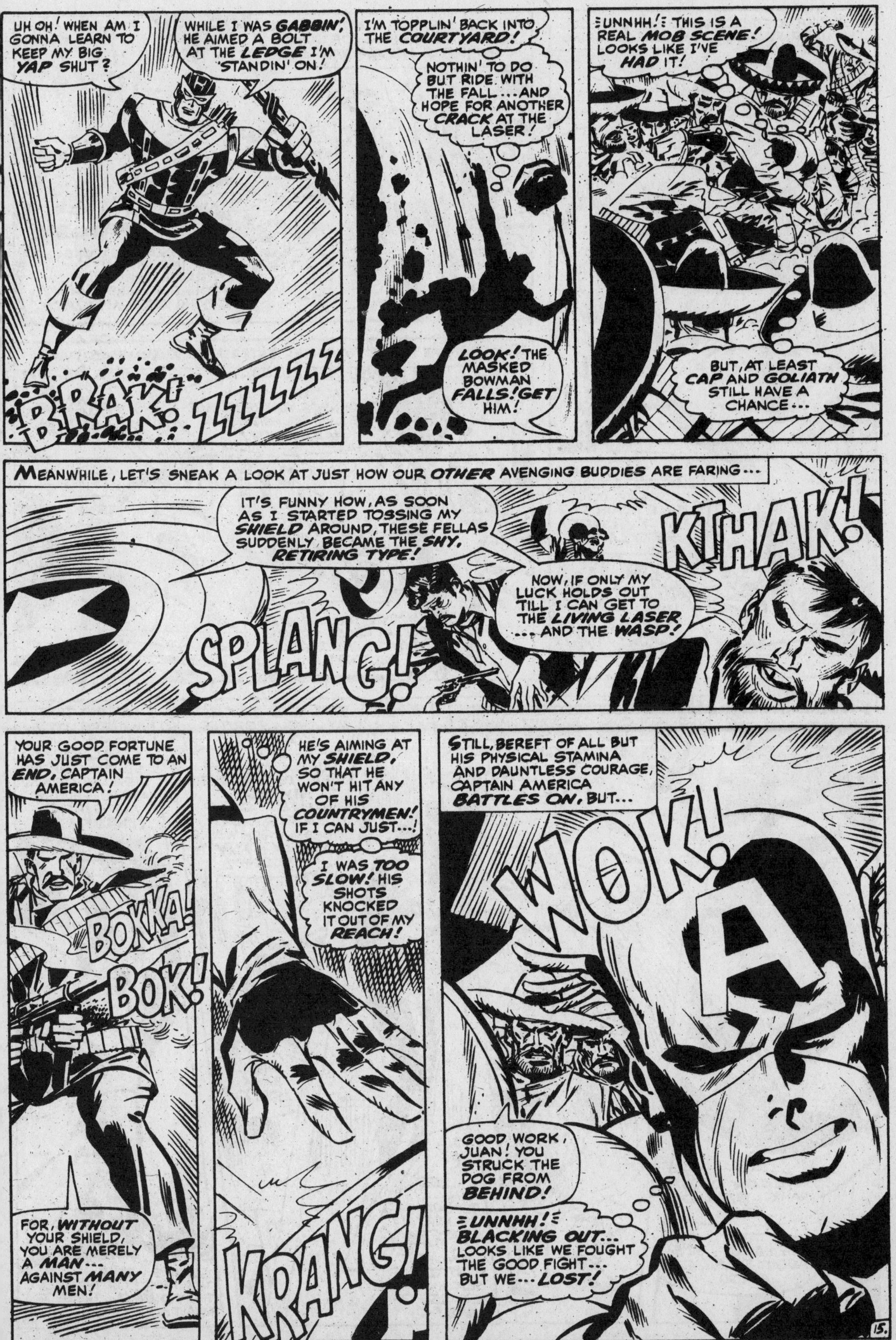
UH OH! WHEN AM I GONNA LEARN TO KEEP MY BIG YAP SHUT?
WHILE I WAS GABBIN', HE AIMED A BOLT AT THE LEDGE I'M 'STANDIN' ON!
BRAK!
ZZZZZ
I'M TOPPLIN' BACK INTO THE COURTYARD!
NOTHIN' TO DO BUT RIDE WITH THE FALL...AND HOPE FOR ANOTHER CRACK AT THE LASER!
LOOK! THE MASKED BOWMAN FALLS! GET HIM!
UNNHH! THIS IS A REAL MOB SCENE! LOOKS LIKE I'VE HAD IT!
BUT, AT LEAST CAP AND GOLIATH STILL HAVE A CHANCE...
MEANWHILE, LET'S SNEAK A LOOK AT JUST HOW OUR OTHER AVENGING BUDDIES ARE FARING...
IT'S FUNNY HOW, AS SOON AS I STARTED TOSSING MY SHIELD AROUND, THESE FELLAS SUDDENLY BECAME THE SHY, RETIRING TYPE!
KTHAK!
NOW, IF ONLY MY LUCK HOLDS OUT TILL I CAN GET TO THE LIVING LASER ...AND THE WASP!
SPLANG!
YOUR GOOD FORTUNE HAS JUST COME TO AN END, CAPTAIN AMERICA!
BOKKA!
BOK!
FOR, WITHOUT YOUR SHIELD, YOU ARE MERELY A MAN... AGAINST MANY MEN!
HE'S AIMING AT MY SHIELD, SO THAT HE WON'T HIT ANY OF HIS COUNTRYMEN! IF I CAN JUST...!
I WAS TOO SLOW! HIS SHOTS KNOCKED IT OUT OF MY REACH!
KRANG!
STILL, BEREFT OF ALL BUT HIS PHYSICAL STAMINA AND DAUNTLESS COURAGE, CAPTAIN AMERICA BATTLES ON, BUT...
WOK!
GOOD WORK, JUAN! YOU STRUCK THE DOG FROM BEHIND!
UNNHH! BLACKING OUT... LOOKS LIKE WE FOUGHT THE GOOD FIGHT... BUT WE... LOST!
15.

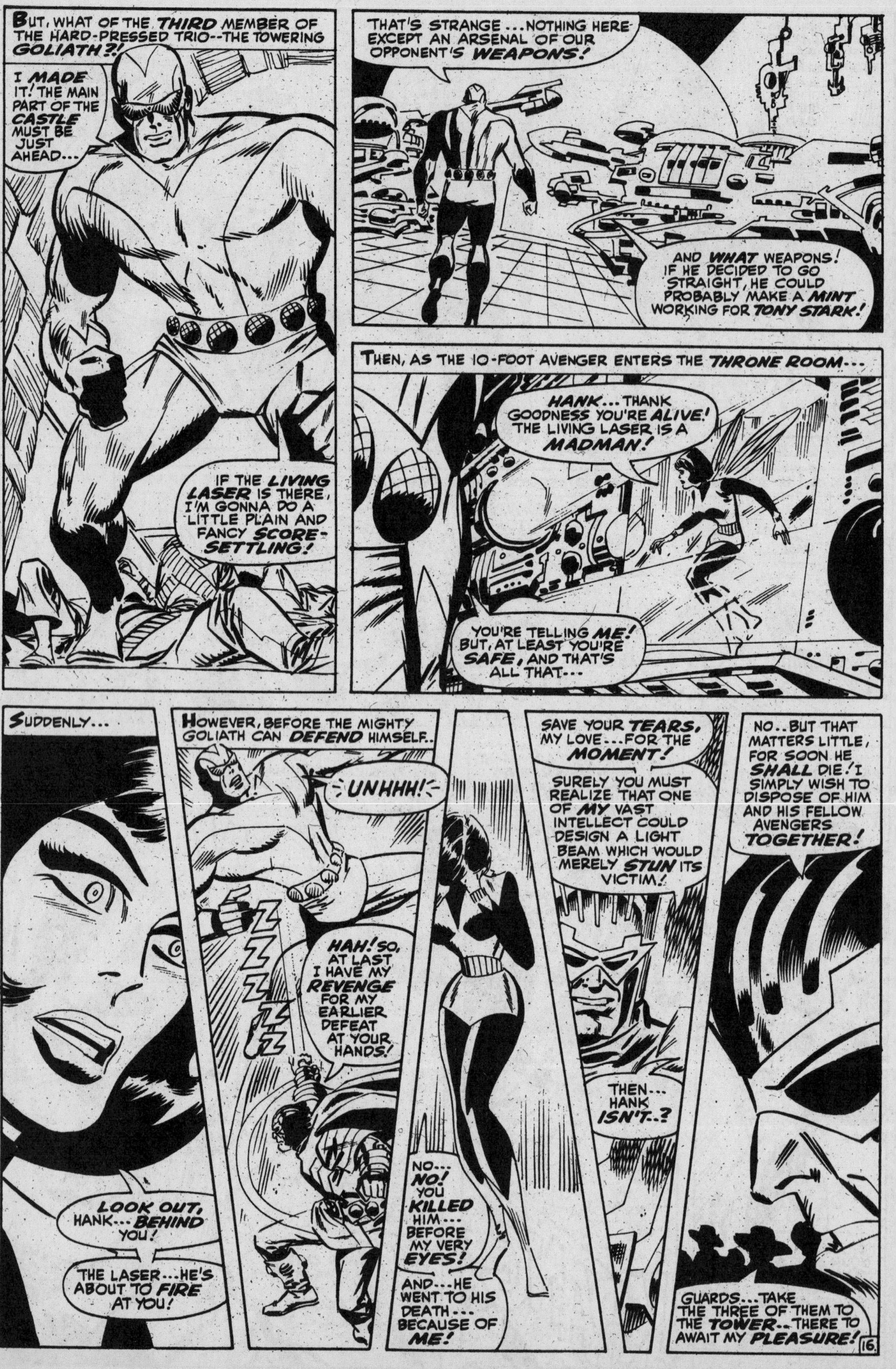
BUT, WHAT OF THE THIRD MEMBER OF THE HARD-PRESSED TRIO--THE TOWERING GOLIATH?!
I MADE IT! THE MAIN PART OF THE CASTLE MUST BE JUST AHEAD...
IF THE LIVING LASER IS THERE, I'M GONNA DO A LITTLE PLAIN AND FANCY SCORE-SETTLING!
THAT'S STRANGE...NOTHING HERE EXCEPT AN ARSENAL OF OUR OPPONENT'S WEAPONS!
AND WHAT WEAPONS! IF HE DECIDED TO GO STRAIGHT, HE COULD PROBABLY MAKE A MINT WORKING FOR TONY STARK!
THEN, AS THE 10-FOOT AVENGER ENTERS THE THRONE ROOM...
HANK...THANK GOODNESS YOU'RE ALIVE! THE LIVING LASER IS A MADMAN!
YOU'RE TELLING ME! BUT, AT LEAST YOU'RE SAFE, AND THAT'S ALL THAT...
SUDDENLY...
LOOK OUT, HANK...BEHIND YOU!
THE LASER...HE'S ABOUT TO FIRE AT YOU!
HOWEVER, BEFORE THE MIGHTY GOLIATH CAN DEFEND HIMSELF..
UNHHH!
HAH! SO, AT LAST I HAVE MY REVENGE FOR MY EARLIER DEFEAT AT YOUR HANDS!
NO... NO! YOU KILLED HIM... BEFORE MY VERY EYES!
AND...HE WENT TO HIS DEATH... BECAUSE OF ME!
SAVE YOUR TEARS, MY LOVE...FOR THE MOMENT!
SURELY YOU MUST REALIZE THAT ONE OF MY VAST INTELLECT COULD DESIGN A LIGHT BEAM WHICH WOULD MERELY STUN ITS VICTIM!
THEN... HANK ISN'T..?
NO..BUT THAT MATTERS LITTLE, FOR SOON HE SHALL DIE! I SIMPLY WISH TO DISPOSE OF HIM AND HIS FELLOW AVENGERS TOGETHER!
GUARDS...TAKE THE THREE OF THEM TO THE TOWER..THERE TO AWAIT MY PLEASURE!

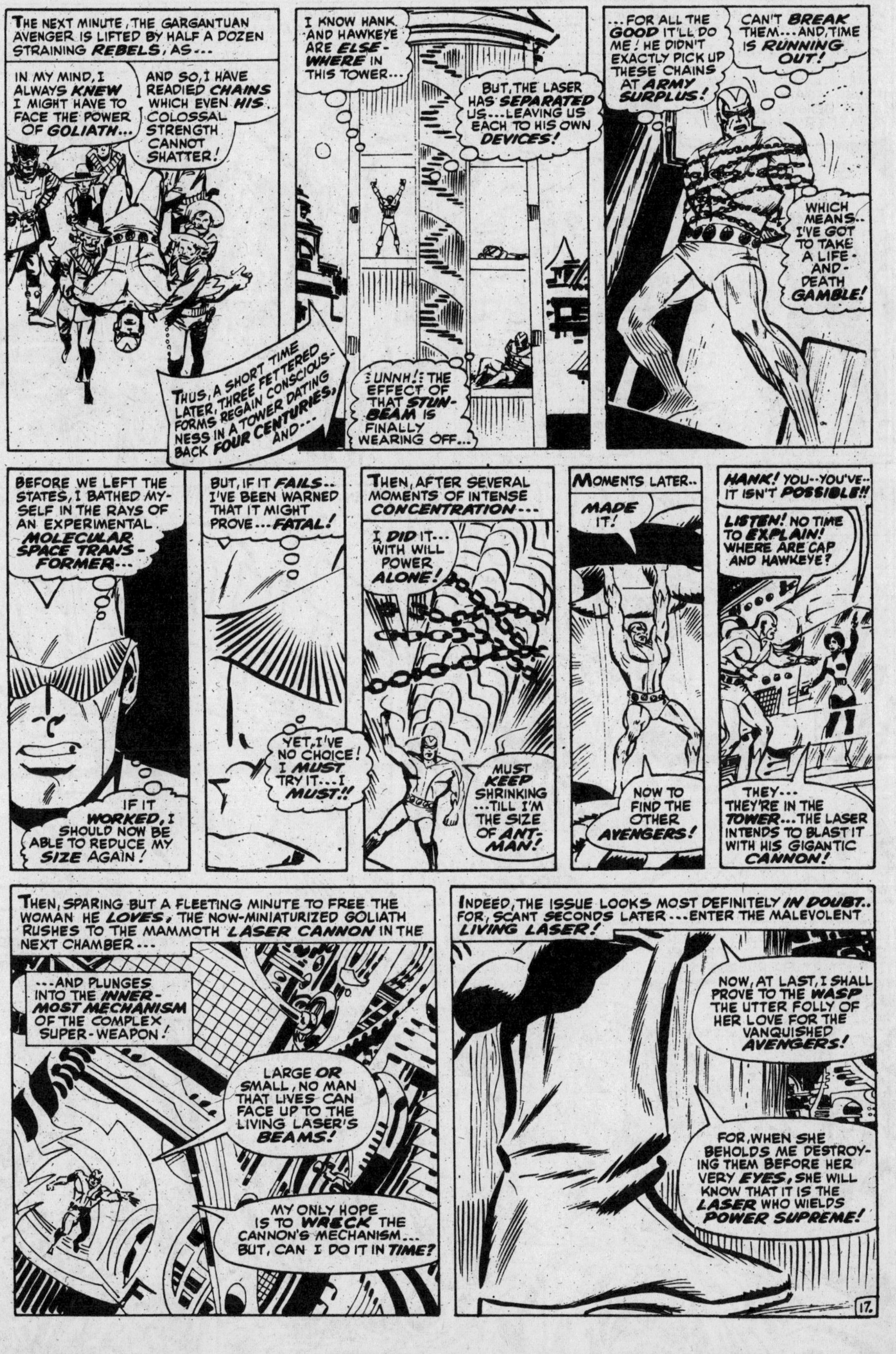
THE NEXT MINUTE, THE GARGANTUAN AVENGER IS LIFTED BY HALF A DOZEN STRAINING REBELS, AS...
IN MY MIND, I ALWAYS KNEW I MIGHT HAVE TO FACE THE POWER OF GOLIATH...
AND SO, I HAVE READIED CHAINS WHICH EVEN HIS COLOSSAL STRENGTH CANNOT SHATTER!
THUS, A SHORT TIME LATER, THREE FETTERED FORMS REGAIN CONSCIOUSNESS IN A TOWER DATING BACK FOUR CENTURIES, AND...
I KNOW HANK AND HAWKEYE ARE ELSEWHERE IN THIS TOWER...
BUT, THE LASER HAS SEPARATED US...LEAVING US EACH TO HIS OWN DEVICES!
UNNH! THE EFFECT OF THAT STUN-BEAM IS FINALLY WEARING OFF...
...FOR ALL THE GOOD IT'LL DO ME! HE DIDN'T EXACTLY PICK UP THESE CHAINS AT ARMY SURPLUS!
CAN'T BREAK THEM...AND, TIME IS RUNNING OUT!
WHICH MEANS.. I'VE GOT TO TAKE A LIFE-AND-DEATH GAMBLE!
BEFORE WE LEFT THE STATES, I BATHED MYSELF IN THE RAYS OF AN EXPERIMENTAL MOLECULAR SPACE TRANSFORMER...
IF IT WORKED, I SHOULD NOW BE ABLE TO REDUCE MY SIZE AGAIN!
BUT, IF IT FAILS.. I'VE BEEN WARNED THAT IT MIGHT PROVE...FATAL!
YET, I'VE NO CHOICE! I MUST TRY IT...I MUST!!
THEN, AFTER SEVERAL MOMENTS OF INTENSE CONCENTRATION...
I DID IT... WITH WILL POWER ALONE!
MUST KEEP SHRINKING ...TILL I'M THE SIZE OF ANT-MAN!
MOMENTS LATER..
MADE IT!
NOW TO FIND THE OTHER AVENGERS!
HANK! YOU--YOU'VE.. IT ISN'T POSSIBLE!!
LISTEN! NO TIME TO EXPLAIN! WHERE ARE CAP AND HAWKEYE?
THEY... THEY'RE IN THE TOWER...THE LASER INTENDS TO BLAST IT WITH HIS GIGANTIC CANNON!
THEN, SPARING BUT A FLEETING MINUTE TO FREE THE WOMAN HE LOVES, THE NOW-MINIATURIZED GOLIATH RUSHES TO THE MAMMOTH LASER CANNON IN THE NEXT CHAMBER...
...AND PLUNGES INTO THE INNER-MOST MECHANISM OF THE COMPLEX SUPER-WEAPON!
LARGE OR SMALL, NO MAN THAT LIVES CAN FACE UP TO THE LIVING LASER'S BEAMS!
MY ONLY HOPE IS TO WRECK THE CANNON'S MECHANISM... BUT, CAN I DO IT IN TIME?
INDEED, THE ISSUE LOOKS MOST DEFINITELY IN DOUBT.. FOR, SCANT SECONDS LATER...ENTER THE MALEVOLENT LIVING LASER!
NOW, AT LAST, I SHALL PROVE TO THE WASP THE UTTER FOLLY OF HER LOVE FOR THE VANQUISHED AVENGERS!
FOR, WHEN SHE BEHOLDS ME DESTROYING THEM BEFORE HER VERY EYES, SHE WILL KNOW THAT IT IS THE LASER WHO WIELDS POWER SUPREME!
17.

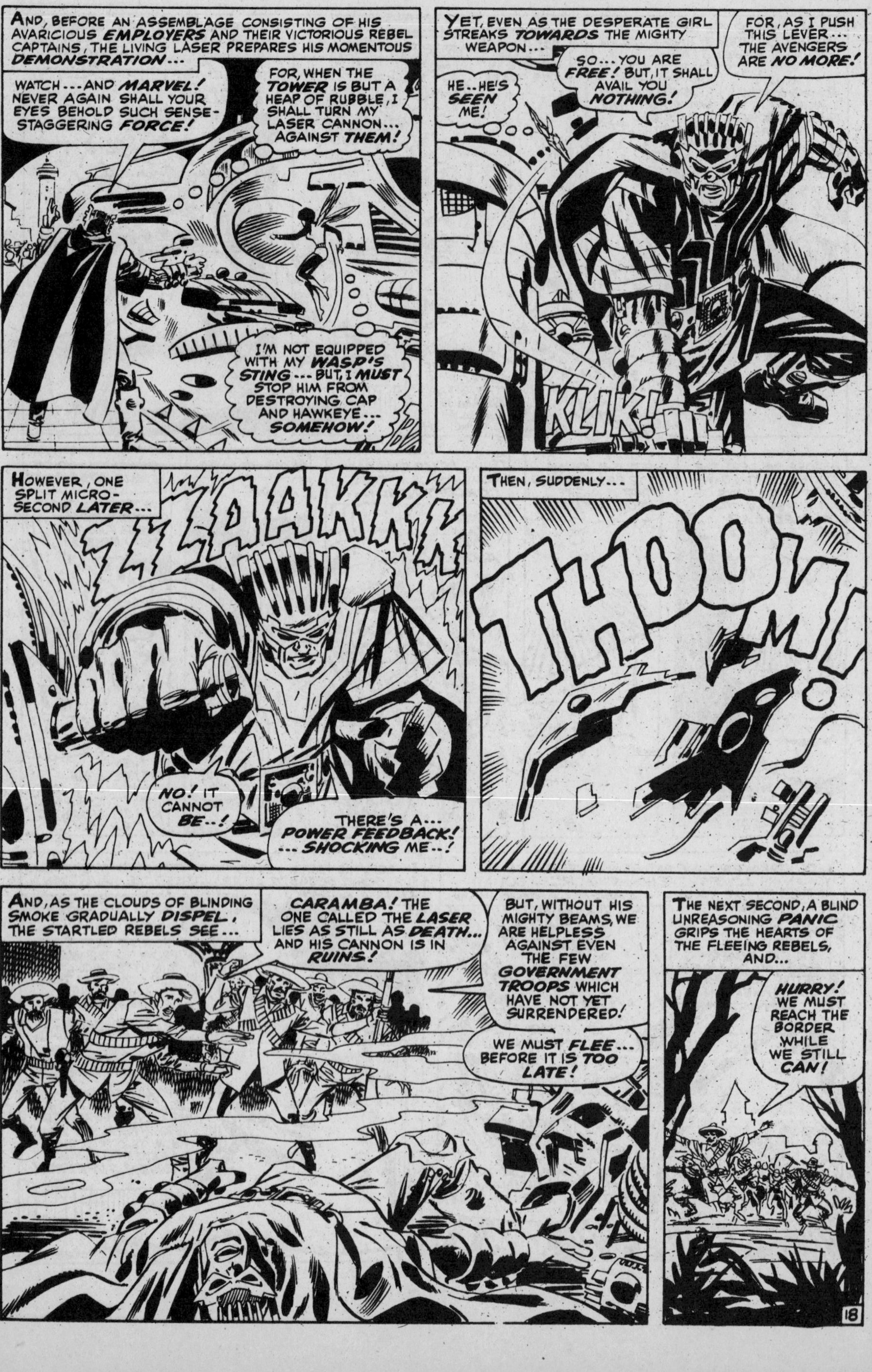
AND, BEFORE AN ASSEMBLAGE CONSISTING OF HIS AVARICIOUS EMPLOYERS AND THEIR VICTORIOUS REBEL CAPTAINS, THE LIVING LASER PREPARES HIS MOMENTOUS DEMONSTRATION...
WATCH...AND MARVEL! NEVER AGAIN SHALL YOUR EYES BEHOLD SUCH SENSE-STAGGERING FORCE!
FOR, WHEN THE TOWER IS BUT A HEAP OF RUBBLE, I SHALL TURN MY LASER CANNON... AGAINST THEM!
I'M NOT EQUIPPED WITH MY WASP'S STING... BUT, I MUST STOP HIM FROM DESTROYING CAP AND HAWKEYE... SOMEHOW!
YET, EVEN AS THE DESPERATE GIRL STREAKS TOWARDS THE MIGHTY WEAPON...
HE..HE'S SEEN ME!
SO...YOU ARE FREE! BUT, IT SHALL AVAIL YOU NOTHING!
FOR, AS I PUSH THIS LEVER... THE AVENGERS ARE NO MORE!
KLIK!
HOWEVER, ONE SPLIT MICRO-SECOND LATER...
ZZAAKKK
NO! IT CANNOT BE..!
THERE'S A... POWER FEEDBACK! ...SHOCKING ME..!
THEN, SUDDENLY...
THOOM
AND, AS THE CLOUDS OF BLINDING SMOKE GRADUALLY DISPEL, THE STARTLED REBELS SEE...
CARAMBA! THE ONE CALLED THE LASER LIES AS STILL AS DEATH... AND HIS CANNON IS IN RUINS!
BUT, WITHOUT HIS MIGHTY BEAMS, WE ARE HELPLESS AGAINST EVEN THE FEW GOVERNMENT TROOPS WHICH HAVE NOT YET SURRENDERED!
WE MUST FLEE... BEFORE IT IS TOO LATE!
THE NEXT SECOND, A BLIND UNREASONING PANIC GRIPS THE HEARTS OF THE FLEEING REBELS, AND...
HURRY! WE MUST REACH THE BORDER WHILE WE STILL CAN!
18

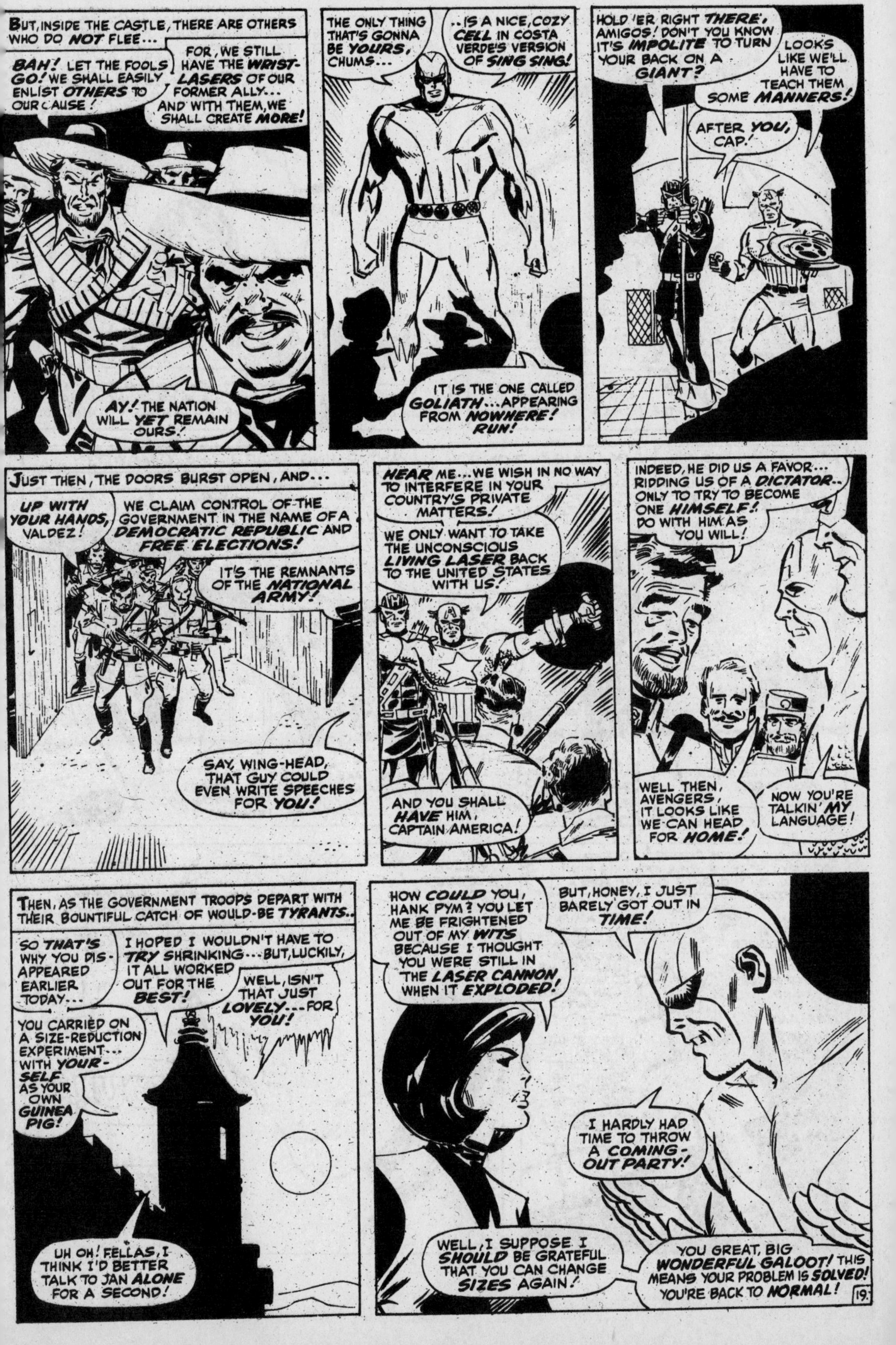

BUT, INSIDE THE CASTLE, THERE ARE OTHERS WHO DO NOT FLEE...
BAH! LET THE FOOLS GO! WE SHALL EASILY ENLIST OTHERS TO OUR CAUSE!
FOR, WE STILL HAVE THE WRIST-LASERS OF OUR FORMER ALLY... AND WITH THEM, WE SHALL CREATE MORE!
AY! THE NATION WILL YET REMAIN OURS!
THE ONLY THING THAT'S GONNA BE YOURS, CHUMS...
..IS A NICE, COZY CELL IN COSTA VERDE'S VERSION OF SING SING!
IT IS THE ONE CALLED GOLIATH...APPEARING FROM NOWHERE! RUN!
HOLD 'ER RIGHT THERE, AMIGOS! DON'T YOU KNOW IT'S IMPOLITE TO TURN YOUR BACK ON A GIANT?
LOOKS LIKE WE'LL HAVE TO TEACH THEM SOME MANNERS!
AFTER YOU, CAP!
JUST THEN, THE DOORS BURST OPEN, AND...
UP WITH YOUR HANDS, VALDEZ!
WE CLAIM CONTROL OF THE GOVERNMENT IN THE NAME OF A DEMOCRATIC REPUBLIC AND FREE ELECTIONS!
IT'S THE REMNANTS OF THE NATIONAL ARMY!
SAY, WING-HEAD, THAT GUY COULD EVEN WRITE SPEECHES FOR YOU!
HEAR ME...WE WISH IN NO WAY TO INTERFERE IN YOUR COUNTRY'S PRIVATE MATTERS!
WE ONLY WANT TO TAKE THE UNCONSCIOUS LIVING LASER BACK TO THE UNITED STATES WITH US!
AND YOU SHALL HAVE HIM, CAPTAIN AMERICA!
INDEED, HE DID US A FAVOR... RIDDING US OF A DICTATOR.. ONLY TO TRY TO BECOME ONE HIMSELF! DO WITH HIM AS YOU WILL!
WELL THEN, AVENGERS, IT LOOKS LIKE WE CAN HEAD FOR HOME!
NOW YOU'RE TALKIN' MY LANGUAGE!
THEN, AS THE GOVERNMENT TROOPS DEPART WITH THEIR BOUNTIFUL CATCH OF WOULD-BE TYRANTS..
SO THAT'S WHY YOU DIS-APPEARED EARLIER TODAY...
I HOPED I WOULDN'T HAVE TO TRY SHRINKING...BUT, LUCKILY, IT ALL WORKED OUT FOR THE BEST!
WELL, ISN'T THAT JUST LOVELY...FOR YOU!
YOU CARRIED ON A SIZE-REDUCTION EXPERIMENT... WITH YOUR-SELF AS YOUR OWN GUINEA PIG!
UH OH! FELLAS, I THINK I'D BETTER TALK TO JAN ALONE FOR A SECOND!
HOW COULD YOU, HANK PYM? YOU LET ME BE FRIGHTENED OUT OF MY WITS BECAUSE I THOUGHT YOU WERE STILL IN THE LASER CANNON, WHEN IT EXPLODED!
BUT, HONEY, I JUST BARELY GOT OUT IN TIME!
I HARDLY HAD TIME TO THROW A COMING-OUT PARTY!
WELL, I SUPPOSE I SHOULD BE GRATEFUL THAT YOU CAN CHANGE SIZES AGAIN!
YOU GREAT, BIG WONDERFUL GALOOT! THIS MEANS YOUR PROBLEM IS SOLVED! YOU'RE BACK TO NORMAL!
19

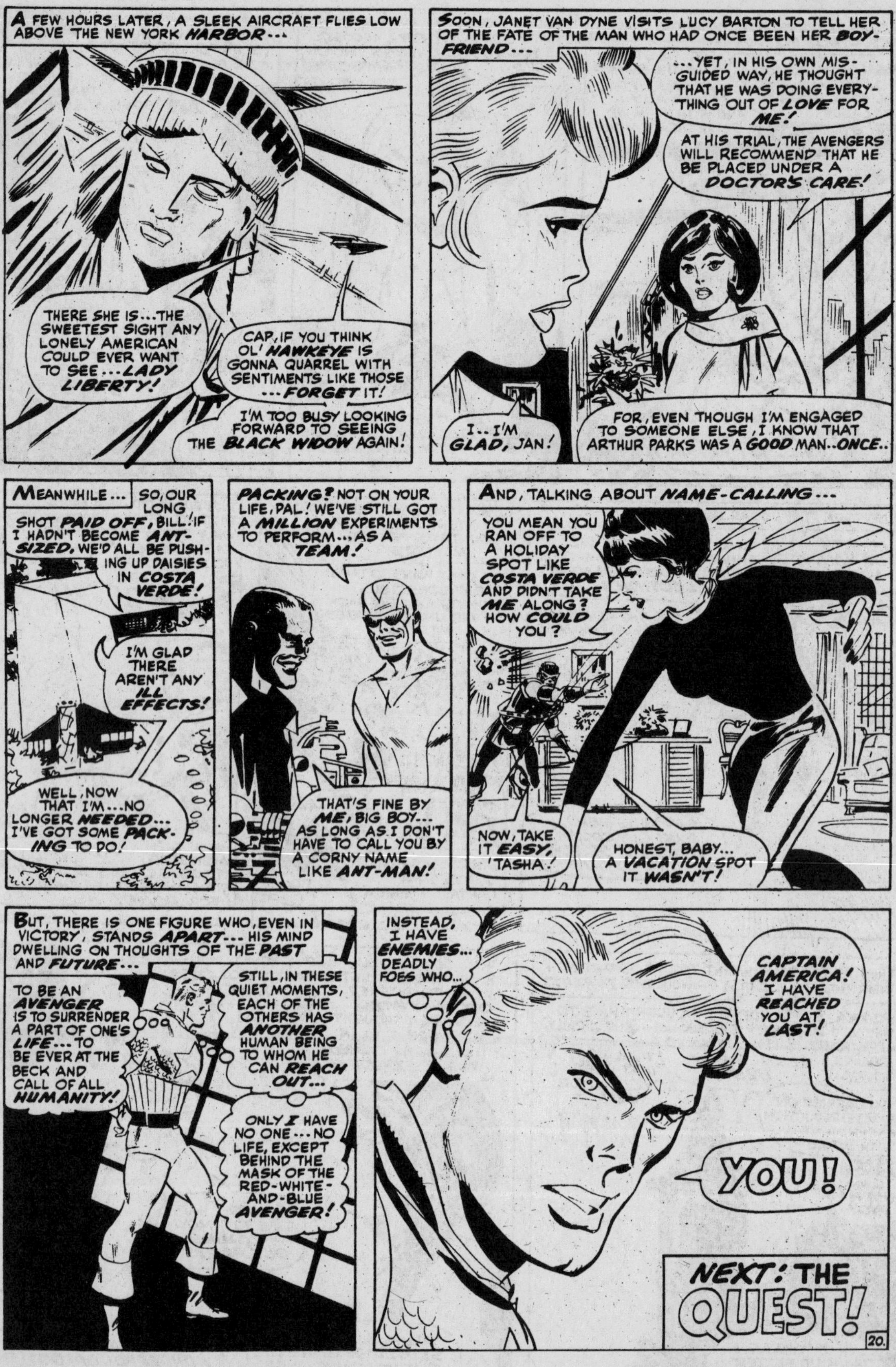
A FEW HOURS LATER, A SLEEK AIRCRAFT FLIES LOW ABOVE THE NEW YORK HARBOR...
THERE SHE IS...THE SWEETEST SIGHT ANY LONELY AMERICAN COULD EVER WANT TO SEE...LADY LIBERTY!
CAP, IF YOU THINK OL' HAWKEYE IS GONNA QUARREL WITH SENTIMENTS LIKE THOSE ...FORGET IT!
I'M TOO BUSY LOOKING FORWARD TO SEEING THE BLACK WIDOW AGAIN!
SOON, JANET VAN DYNE VISITS LUCY BARTON TO TELL HER OF THE FATE OF THE MAN WHO HAD ONCE BEEN HER BOY-FRIEND...
...YET, IN HIS OWN MIS-GUIDED WAY, HE THOUGHT THAT HE WAS DOING EVERY-THING OUT OF LOVE FOR ME!
AT HIS TRIAL, THE AVENGERS WILL RECOMMEND THAT HE BE PLACED UNDER A DOCTOR'S CARE!
I.. I'M GLAD, JAN!
FOR, EVEN THOUGH I'M ENGAGED TO SOMEONE ELSE, I KNOW THAT ARTHUR PARKS WAS A GOOD MAN..ONCE..
MEANWHILE...
SO, OUR LONG SHOT PAID OFF, BILL! IF I HADN'T BECOME ANT-SIZED, WE'D ALL BE PUSHING UP DAISIES IN COSTA VERDE!
I'M GLAD THERE AREN'T ANY ILL EFFECTS!
WELL, NOW THAT I'M...NO LONGER NEEDED... I'VE GOT SOME PACKING TO DO!
PACKING? NOT ON YOUR LIFE, PAL! WE'VE STILL GOT A MILLION EXPERIMENTS TO PERFORM...AS A TEAM!
THAT'S FINE BY ME, BIG BOY... AS LONG AS I DON'T HAVE TO CALL YOU BY A CORNY NAME LIKE ANT-MAN!
AND, TALKING ABOUT NAME-CALLING...
YOU MEAN YOU RAN OFF TO A HOLIDAY SPOT LIKE COSTA VERDE AND DIDN'T TAKE ME ALONG? HOW COULD YOU?
NOW, TAKE IT EASY, 'TASHA!
HONEST, BABY... A VACATION SPOT IT WASN'T!
BUT, THERE IS ONE FIGURE WHO, EVEN IN VICTORY, STANDS APART... HIS MIND DWELLING ON THOUGHTS OF THE PAST AND FUTURE...
TO BE AN AVENGER IS TO SURRENDER A PART OF ONE'S LIFE...TO BE EVER AT THE BECK AND CALL OF ALL HUMANITY!
STILL, IN THESE QUIET MOMENTS, EACH OF THE OTHERS HAS ANOTHER HUMAN BEING TO WHOM HE CAN REACH OUT...
ONLY I HAVE NO ONE...NO LIFE, EXCEPT BEHIND THE MASK OF THE RED-WHITE-AND-BLUE AVENGER!
INSTEAD, I HAVE ENEMIES... DEADLY FOES WHO...
CAPTAIN AMERICA! I HAVE REACHED YOU AT LAST!
YOU!
NEXT: THE QUEST!
20.

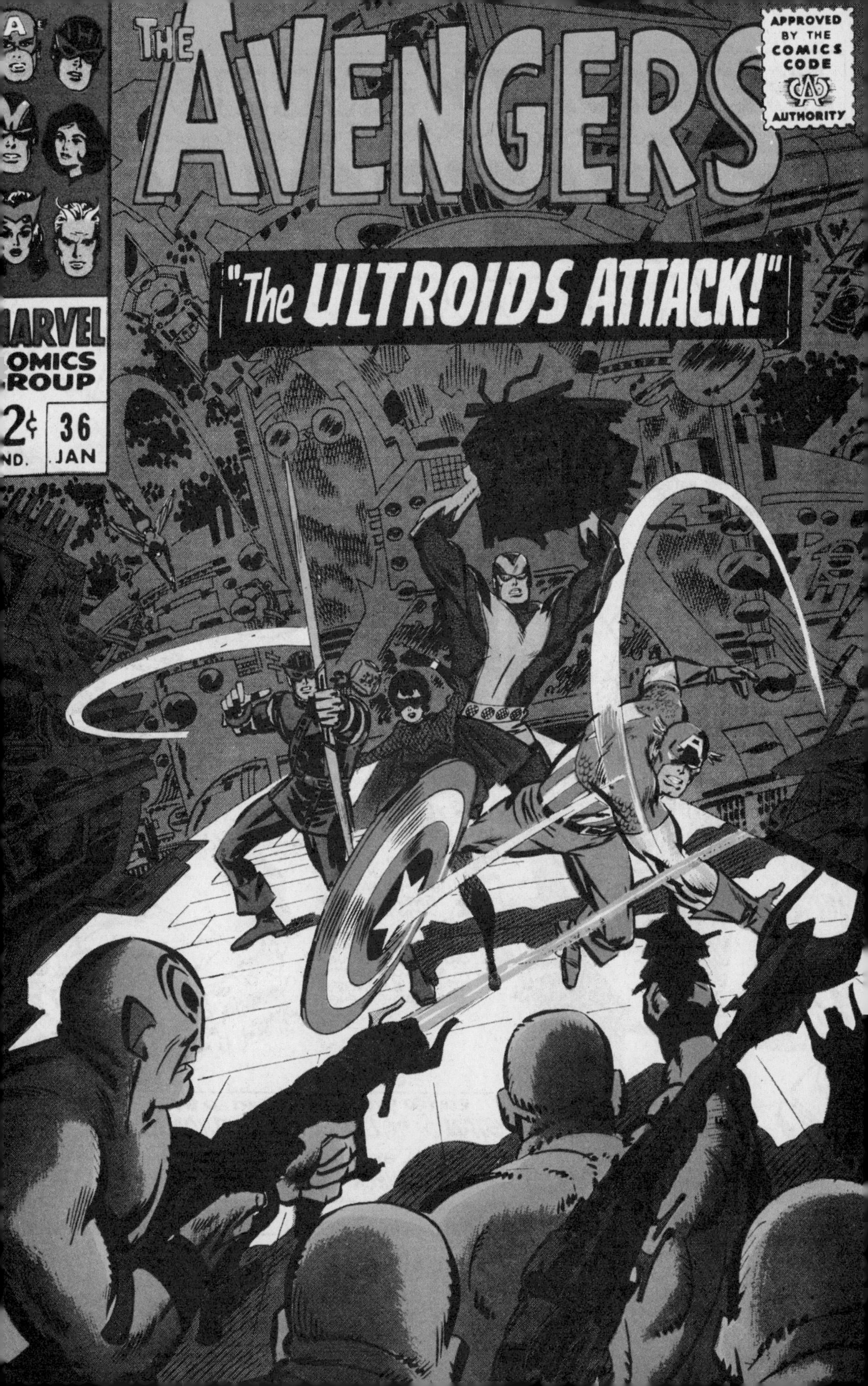

THE AVENGERS
APPROVED BY THE COMICS CODE CA AUTHORITY
"The ULTROIDS ATTACK!"
MARVEL COMICS GROUP
12¢
36 JAN
IND.

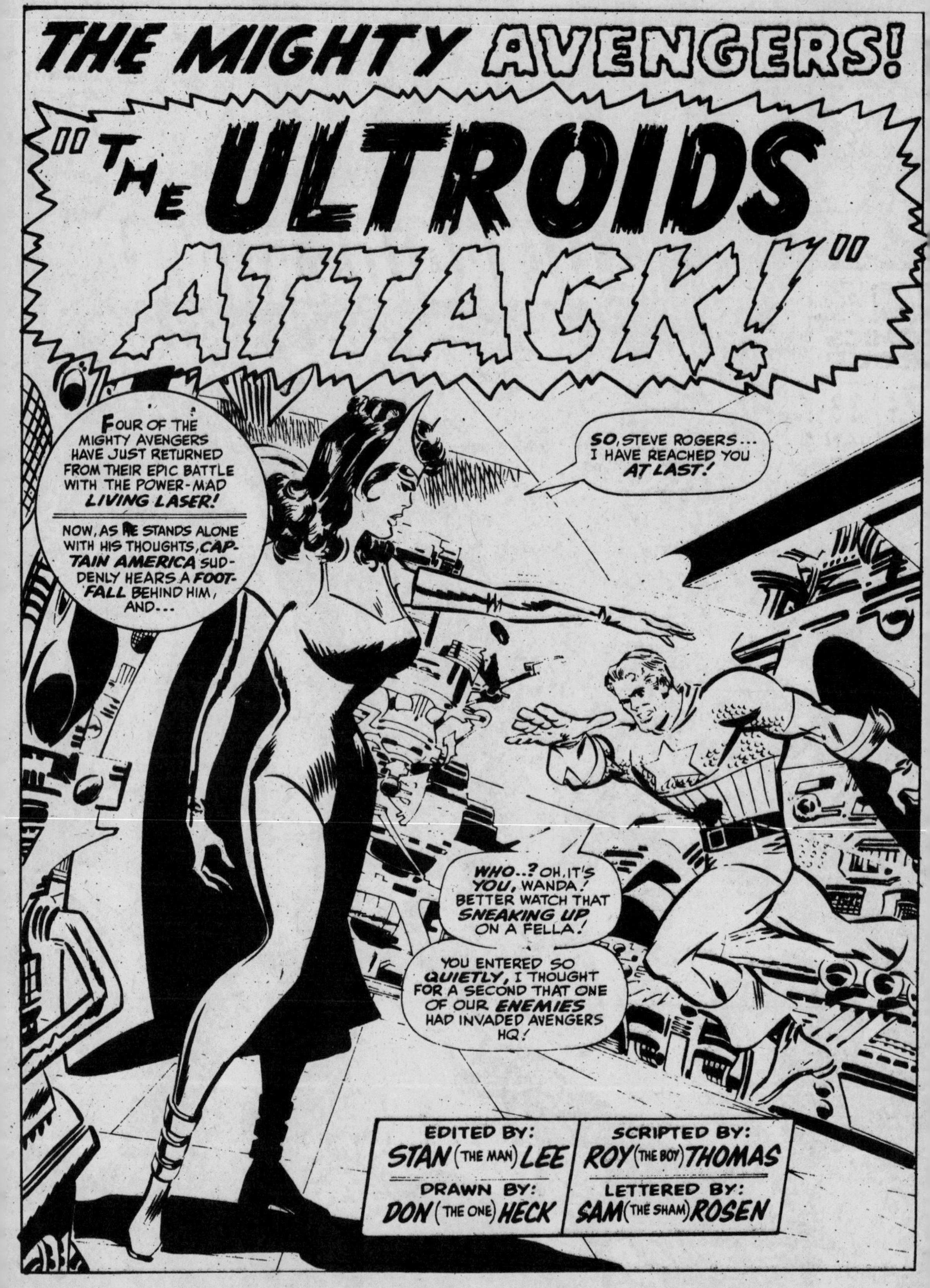
THE MIGHTY AVENGERS!
"THE ULTROIDS ATTACK!"
FOUR OF THE MIGHTY AVENGERS HAVE JUST RETURNED FROM THEIR EPIC BATTLE WITH THE POWER-MAD LIVING LASER!
NOW, AS HE STANDS ALONE WITH HIS THOUGHTS, CAPTAIN AMERICA SUDDENLY HEARS A FOOTFALL BEHIND HIM, AND...
SO, STEVE ROGERS... I HAVE REACHED YOU AT LAST!
WHO..? OH, IT'S YOU, WANDA! BETTER WATCH THAT SNEAKING UP ON A FELLA!
YOU ENTERED SO QUIETLY, I THOUGHT FOR A SECOND THAT ONE OF OUR ENEMIES HAD INVADED AVENGERS HQ!
EDITED BY: STAN (THE MAN) LEE
SCRIPTED BY: ROY (THE BOY) THOMAS
DRAWN BY: DON (THE ONE) HECK
LETTERED BY: SAM (THE SHAM) ROSEN

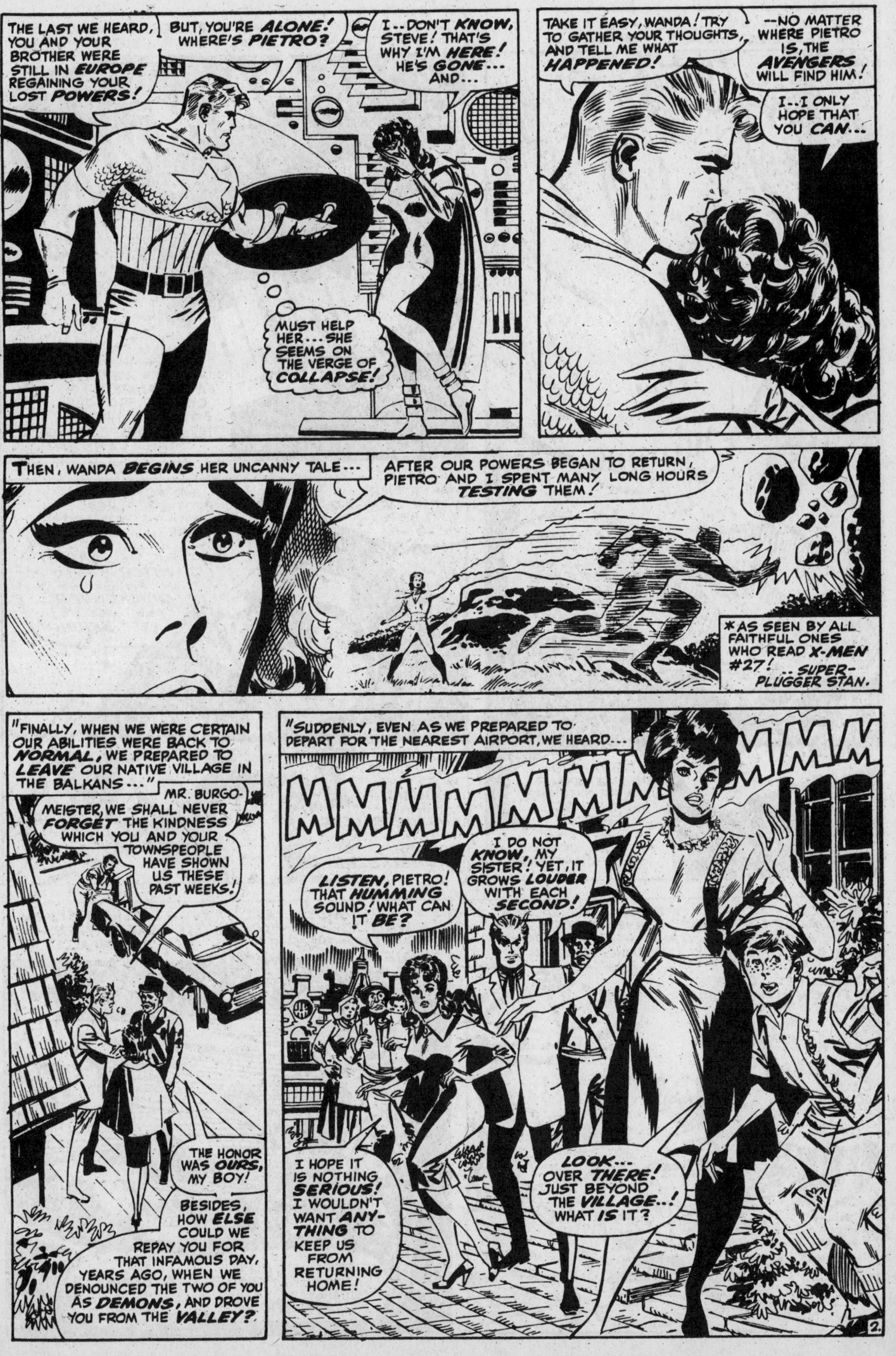
THE LAST WE HEARD, YOU AND YOUR BROTHER WERE STILL IN EUROPE REGAINING YOUR LOST POWERS!
BUT, YOU'RE ALONE! WHERE'S PIETRO?
I..DON'T KNOW, STEVE! THAT'S WHY I'M HERE! HE'S GONE... AND...
MUST HELP HER... SHE SEEMS ON THE VERGE OF COLLAPSE!
TAKE IT EASY, WANDA! TRY TO GATHER YOUR THOUGHTS, AND TELL ME WHAT HAPPENED!
--NO MATTER WHERE PIETRO IS, THE AVENGERS WILL FIND HIM!
I..I ONLY HOPE THAT YOU CAN...
THEN, WANDA BEGINS HER UNCANNY TALE...
AFTER OUR POWERS BEGAN TO RETURN, PIETRO AND I SPENT MANY LONG HOURS TESTING THEM!
*AS SEEN BY ALL FAITHFUL ONES WHO READ X-MEN #27! ...SUPER-PLUGGER STAN.
"FINALLY, WHEN WE WERE CERTAIN OUR ABILITIES WERE BACK TO NORMAL, WE PREPARED TO LEAVE OUR NATIVE VILLAGE IN THE BALKANS..."
MR. BURGOMEISTER, WE SHALL NEVER FORGET THE KINDNESS WHICH YOU AND YOUR TOWNSPEOPLE HAVE SHOWN US THESE PAST WEEKS!
THE HONOR WAS OURS, MY BOY!
BESIDES, HOW ELSE COULD WE REPAY YOU FOR THAT INFAMOUS DAY, YEARS AGO, WHEN WE DENOUNCED THE TWO OF YOU AS DEMONS, AND DROVE YOU FROM THE VALLEY?
"SUDDENLY, EVEN AS WE PREPARED TO DEPART FOR THE NEAREST AIRPORT, WE HEARD...
MMMMMMMMMMMMMM
LISTEN, PIETRO! THAT HUMMING SOUND! WHAT CAN IT BE?
I DO NOT KNOW, MY SISTER! YET, IT GROWS LOUDER WITH EACH SECOND!
I HOPE IT IS NOTHING SERIOUS! I WOULDN'T WANT ANYTHING TO KEEP US FROM RETURNING HOME!
LOOK... OVER THERE! JUST BEYOND THE VILLAGE..! WHAT IS IT?
2.

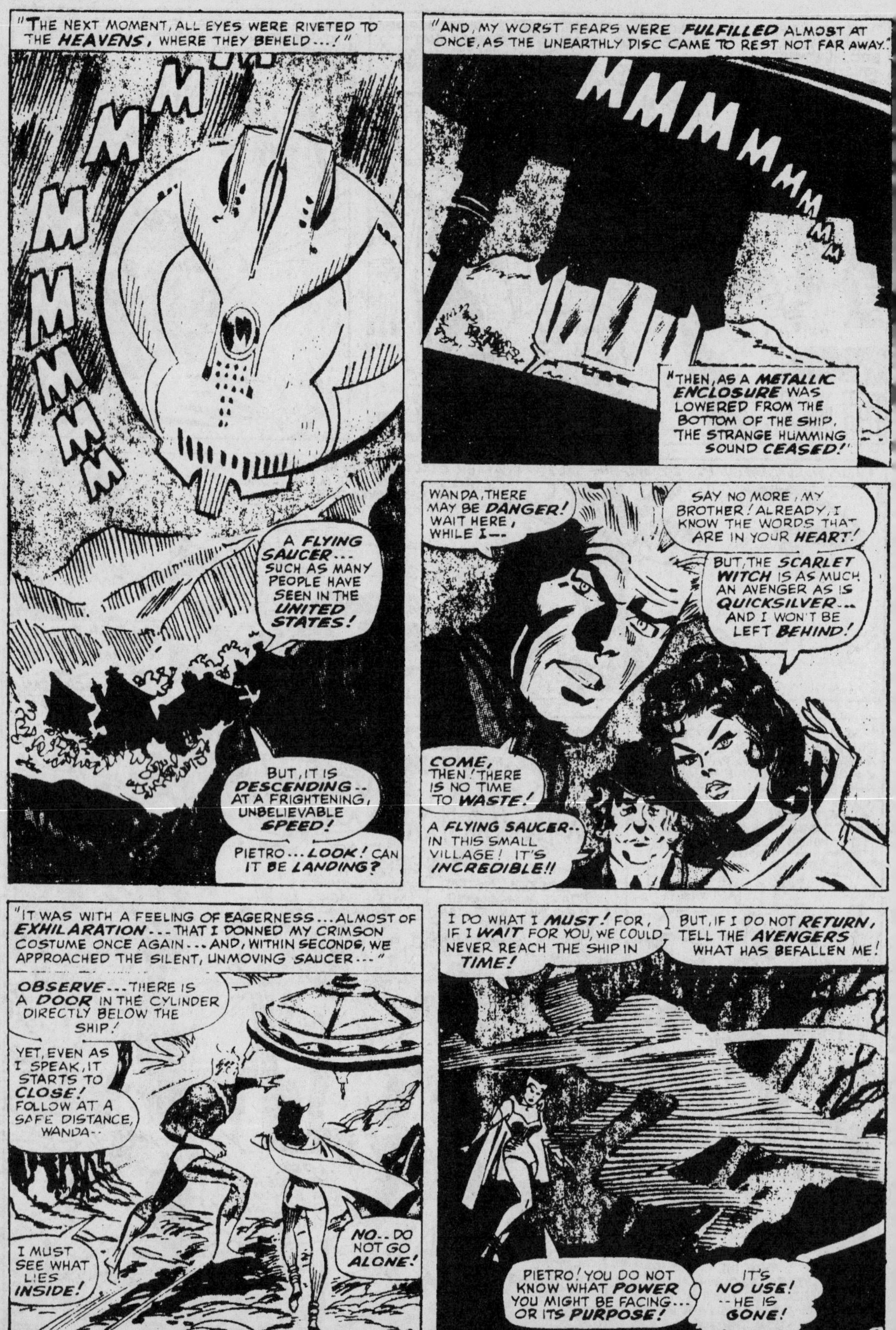
"THE NEXT MOMENT, ALL EYES WERE RIVETED TO THE HEAVENS, WHERE THEY BEHELD...!"
MMMMMMMMM
A FLYING SAUCER... SUCH AS MANY PEOPLE HAVE SEEN IN THE UNITED STATES!
BUT, IT IS DESCENDING.. AT A FRIGHTENING, UNBELIEVABLE SPEED!
PIETRO... LOOK! CAN IT BE LANDING?
"AND, MY WORST FEARS WERE FULFILLED ALMOST AT ONCE, AS THE UNEARTHLY DISC CAME TO REST NOT FAR AWAY."
MMMMMMMMM
"THEN, AS A METALLIC ENCLOSURE WAS LOWERED FROM THE BOTTOM OF THE SHIP, THE STRANGE HUMMING SOUND CEASED!"
WANDA, THERE MAY BE DANGER! WAIT HERE, WHILE I--
SAY NO MORE, MY BROTHER! ALREADY, I KNOW THE WORDS THAT ARE IN YOUR HEART!
BUT, THE SCARLET WITCH IS AS MUCH AN AVENGER AS IS QUICKSILVER... AND I WON'T BE LEFT BEHIND!
COME, THEN! THERE IS NO TIME TO WASTE!
A FLYING SAUCER.. IN THIS SMALL VILLAGE! IT'S INCREDIBLE!!
"IT WAS WITH A FEELING OF EAGERNESS... ALMOST OF EXHILARATION... THAT I DONNED MY CRIMSON COSTUME ONCE AGAIN... AND, WITHIN SECONDS, WE APPROACHED THE SILENT, UNMOVING SAUCER..."
OBSERVE... THERE IS A DOOR IN THE CYLINDER DIRECTLY BELOW THE SHIP!
YET, EVEN AS I SPEAK, IT STARTS TO CLOSE! FOLLOW AT A SAFE DISTANCE, WANDA--
I MUST SEE WHAT LIES INSIDE!
NO.. DO NOT GO ALONE!
I DO WHAT I MUST! FOR, IF I WAIT FOR YOU, WE COULD NEVER REACH THE SHIP IN TIME!
BUT, IF I DO NOT RETURN, TELL THE AVENGERS WHAT HAS BEFALLEN ME!
PIETRO! YOU DO NOT KNOW WHAT POWER YOU MIGHT BE FACING... OR ITS PURPOSE!
IT'S NO USE! --HE IS GONE!
3.

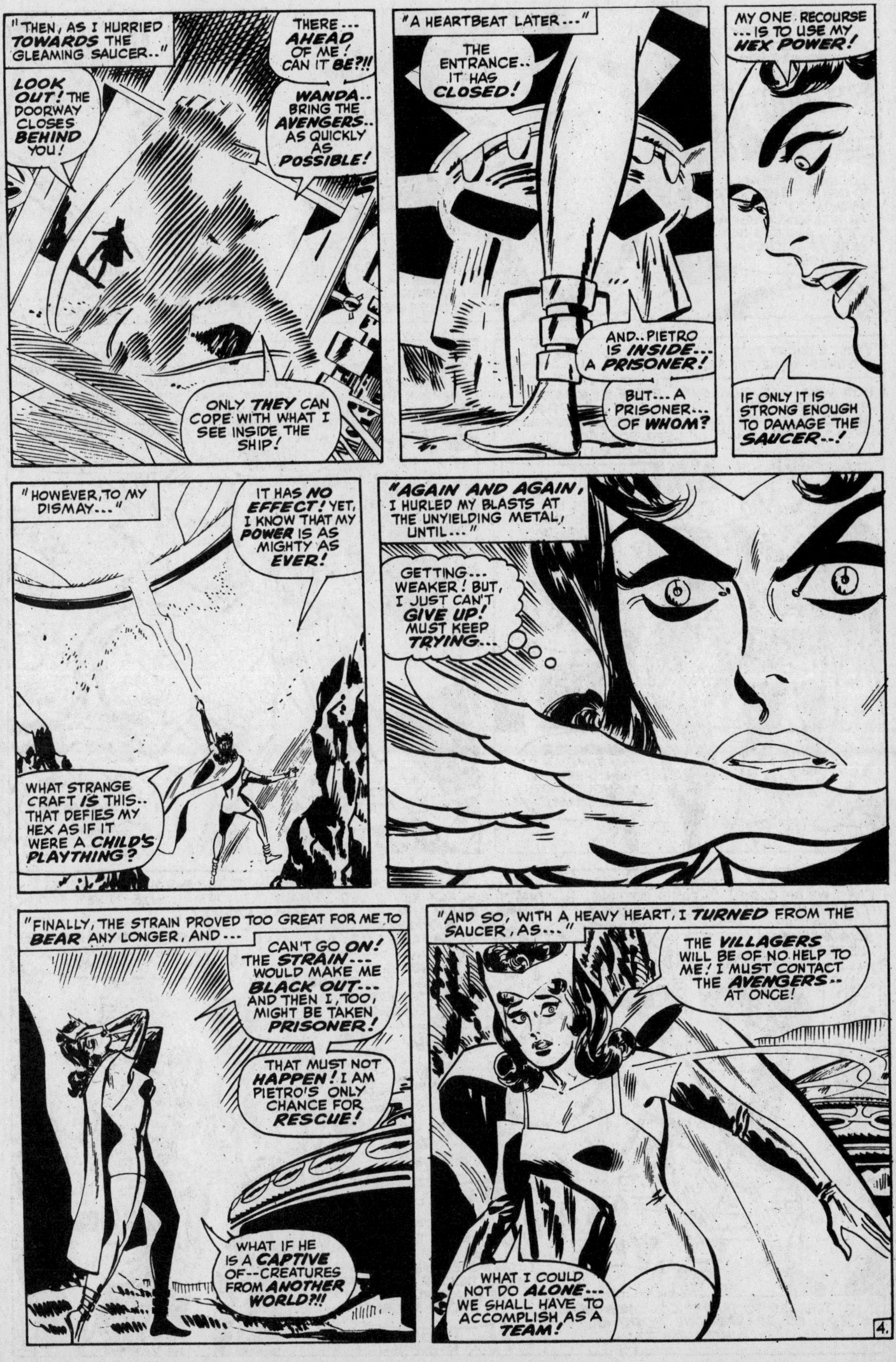
"THEN, AS I HURRIED TOWARDS THE GLEAMING SAUCER.."
THERE... AHEAD OF ME! CAN IT BE?!!
LOOK OUT! THE DOORWAY CLOSES BEHIND YOU!
WANDA.. BRING THE AVENGERS.. AS QUICKLY AS POSSIBLE!
ONLY THEY CAN COPE WITH WHAT I SEE INSIDE THE SHIP!
"A HEARTBEAT LATER..."
THE ENTRANCE.. IT HAS CLOSED!
AND..PIETRO IS INSIDE... A PRISONER!
BUT... A PRISONER... OF WHOM?
MY ONE RECOURSE ...IS TO USE MY HEX POWER!
IF ONLY IT IS STRONG ENOUGH TO DAMAGE THE SAUCER--!
"HOWEVER, TO MY DISMAY..."
IT HAS NO EFFECT! YET, I KNOW THAT MY POWER IS AS MIGHTY AS EVER!
WHAT STRANGE CRAFT IS THIS.. THAT DEFIES MY HEX AS IF IT WERE A CHILD'S PLAYTHING?
"AGAIN AND AGAIN, I HURLED MY BLASTS AT THE UNYIELDING METAL, UNTIL..."
GETTING... WEAKER! BUT, I JUST CAN'T GIVE UP! MUST KEEP TRYING...
"FINALLY, THE STRAIN PROVED TOO GREAT FOR ME TO BEAR ANY LONGER, AND ---
CAN'T GO ON! THE STRAIN--- WOULD MAKE ME BLACK OUT--- AND THEN I, TOO, MIGHT BE TAKEN PRISONER!
THAT MUST NOT HAPPEN! I AM PIETRO'S ONLY CHANCE FOR RESCUE!
WHAT IF HE IS A CAPTIVE OF--CREATURES FROM ANOTHER WORLD?!!
"AND SO, WITH A HEAVY HEART, I TURNED FROM THE SAUCER, AS..."
THE VILLAGERS WILL BE OF NO HELP TO ME! I MUST CONTACT THE AVENGERS-- AT ONCE!
WHAT I COULD NOT DO ALONE--- WE SHALL HAVE TO ACCOMPLISH AS A TEAM!
4.

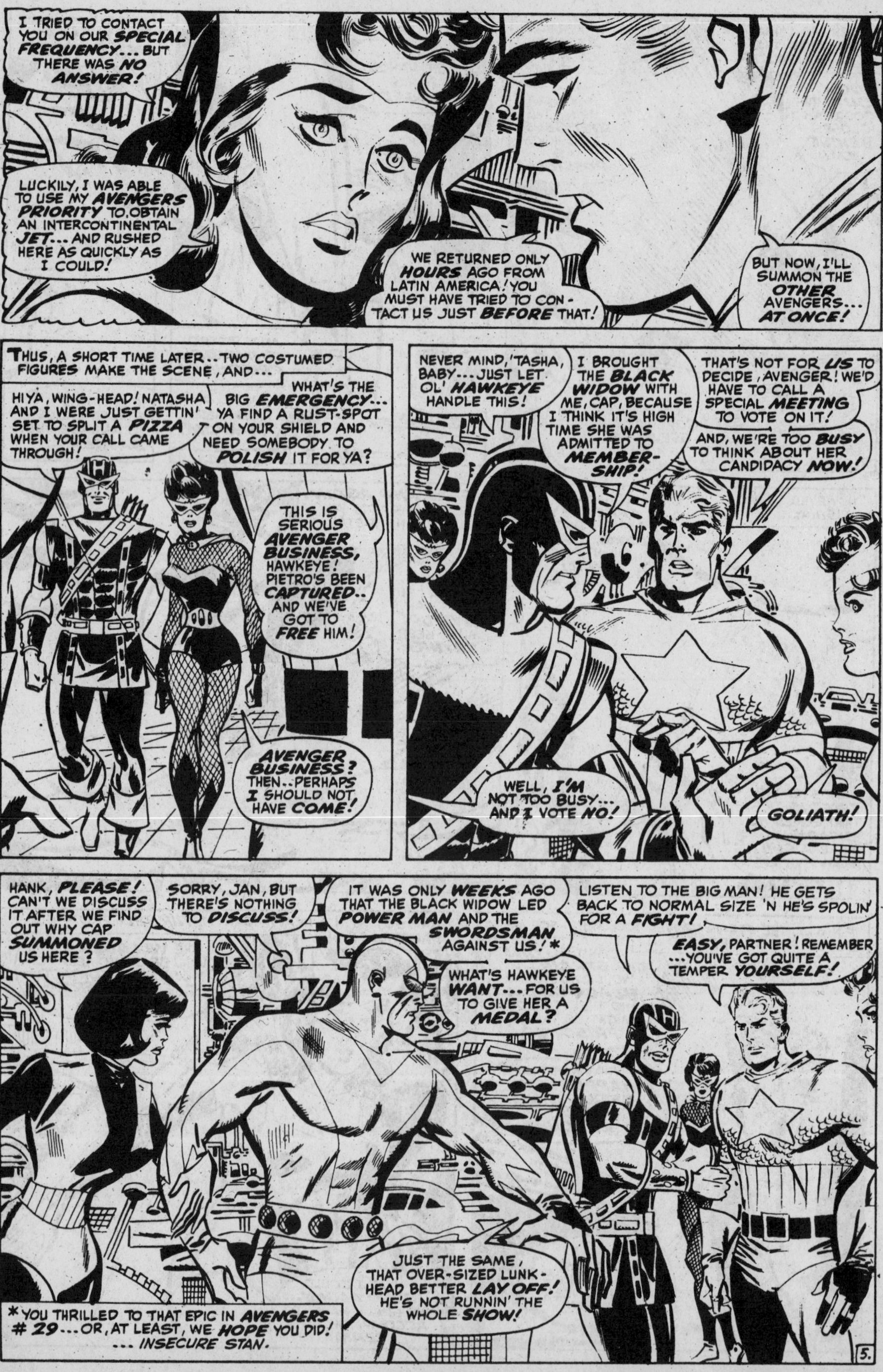

I TRIED TO CONTACT YOU ON OUR SPECIAL FREQUENCY... BUT THERE WAS NO ANSWER!
LUCKILY, I WAS ABLE TO USE MY AVENGERS PRIORITY TO OBTAIN AN INTERCONTINENTAL JET... AND RUSHED HERE AS QUICKLY AS I COULD!
WE RETURNED ONLY HOURS AGO FROM LATIN AMERICA! YOU MUST HAVE TRIED TO CONTACT US JUST BEFORE THAT!
BUT NOW, I'LL SUMMON THE OTHER AVENGERS... AT ONCE!
THUS, A SHORT TIME LATER.. TWO COSTUMED FIGURES MAKE THE SCENE, AND...
HIYA, WING-HEAD! NATASHA AND I WERE JUST GETTIN' SET TO SPLIT A PIZZA WHEN YOUR CALL CAME THROUGH!
WHAT'S THE BIG EMERGENCY... YA FIND A RUST-SPOT ON YOUR SHIELD AND NEED SOMEBODY TO POLISH IT FOR YA?
THIS IS SERIOUS AVENGER BUSINESS, HAWKEYE! PIETRO'S BEEN CAPTURED.. AND WE'VE GOT TO FREE HIM!
AVENGER BUSINESS? THEN.. PERHAPS I SHOULD NOT HAVE COME!
NEVER MIND, 'TASHA, BABY... JUST LET OL' HAWKEYE HANDLE THIS!
I BROUGHT THE BLACK WIDOW WITH ME, CAP, BECAUSE I THINK IT'S HIGH TIME SHE WAS ADMITTED TO MEMBERSHIP!
THAT'S NOT FOR US TO DECIDE, AVENGER! WE'D HAVE TO CALL A SPECIAL MEETING TO VOTE ON IT!
AND, WE'RE TOO BUSY TO THINK ABOUT HER CANDIDACY NOW!
WELL, I'M NOT TOO BUSY... AND I VOTE NO!
GOLIATH!
HANK, PLEASE! CAN'T WE DISCUSS IT AFTER WE FIND OUT WHY CAP SUMMONED US HERE?
SORRY, JAN, BUT THERE'S NOTHING TO DISCUSS!
IT WAS ONLY WEEKS AGO THAT THE BLACK WIDOW LED POWER MAN AND THE SWORDSMAN AGAINST US!*
WHAT'S HAWKEYE WANT... FOR US TO GIVE HER A MEDAL?
LISTEN TO THE BIG MAN! HE GETS BACK TO NORMAL SIZE 'N HE'S SPOLIN' FOR A FIGHT!
EASY, PARTNER! REMEMBER ...YOU'VE GOT QUITE A TEMPER YOURSELF!
JUST THE SAME, THAT OVER-SIZED LUNKHEAD BETTER LAY OFF! HE'S NOT RUNNIN' THE WHOLE SHOW!
*YOU THRILLED TO THAT EPIC IN AVENGERS # 29... OR, AT LEAST, WE HOPE YOU DID! ... INSECURE STAN.
5.

HE HAS A POINT, HANK! THERE'S NO REASON FOR YOU TO GET SO UPSET!

PERHAPS YOU'RE RIGHT, JAN...WE'LL TAKE THE WHOLE MATTER UP SOME OTHER TIME!

JUST THE SAME, AS ONE OF THE ORIGINAL AVENGERS, I DON'T CARE TO SEE IT TURN INTO A REST HOME FOR REFORMED SUPER-VILLAINS!

GOLIATH, I'VE HAD IT UP TO HERE WITH YOUR HARPIN' ABOUT HOW LONG YOU'VE BEEN AN AVENGER!

WHAT I WANNA KNOW IS, WHERE WERE YOU FOR THOSE BLASTED MONTHS THAT THE REST OF US WERE KEEPIN' THE AVENGERS FROM BEIN' JUST A NAME IN A HISTORY BOOK?

YOU TALK PRETTY BIG, FOR A GUY WHO SPENDS MOST OF HIS TIME TAKIN' VACATIONS!

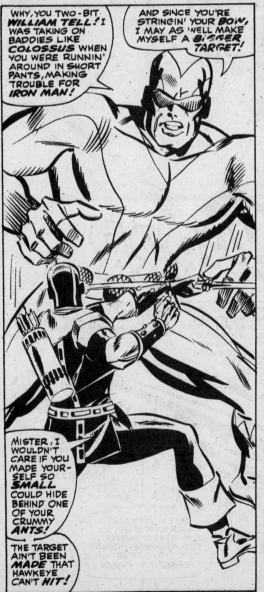

WHY, YOU TWO-BIT WILLIAM TELL! I WAS TAKING ON BADDIES LIKE COLOSSUS WHEN YOU WERE RUNNIN' AROUND IN SHORT PANTS, MAKING TROUBLE FOR IRON MAN!

AND SINCE YOU'RE STRINGIN' YOUR BOW, I MAY AS WELL MAKE MYSELF A BIGGER TARGET!

MISTER, I WOULDN'T CARE IF YOU MADE YOUR-SELF SO SMALL COULD HIDE BEHIND ONE OF YOUR CRUMMY ANTS! THE TARGET AIN'T BEEN MADE THAT HAWKEYE CAN'T HIT!

BUT, JUST AS THE POWERFUL PAIR PREPARE TO CLASH...

NOW HOLD IT RIGHT THERE, HENRY PYM! ENOUGH IS ENOUGH! CAP DIDN'T SEND OUT AN EMERGENCY CALL JUST SO YOU TWO COULD ROUGH-HOUSE!

MAYBE NOT, BUT I'M TIRED OF THAT REFUGEE FROM A ROBIN HOOD MOVIE THROWIN' HIS WEIGHT AROUND JUST BECAUSE HE CAN SHOOT A FEW ARROWS!

IF IT'S MY ARCHERY THAT'S BOTHERIN' YA, BIG MAN, I'LL BE GLAD TO DUKE IT OUT WITH YA...ANY TIME YOU SAY!

COOL OFF, HAWKEYE! WE'VE ALL BEEN UNDER A STRAIN LATELY, BATTLING THE LIVING LASER! LET'S NOT TAKE IT OUT ON EACH OTHER!

YOU CALLED IT, CAP! JUST KEEP THAT JOKER OFF MY BACK!

ONE OF THESE DAYS, BIG MOUTH, CAP WON'T BE AROUND TO PROTECT YOU!

6.

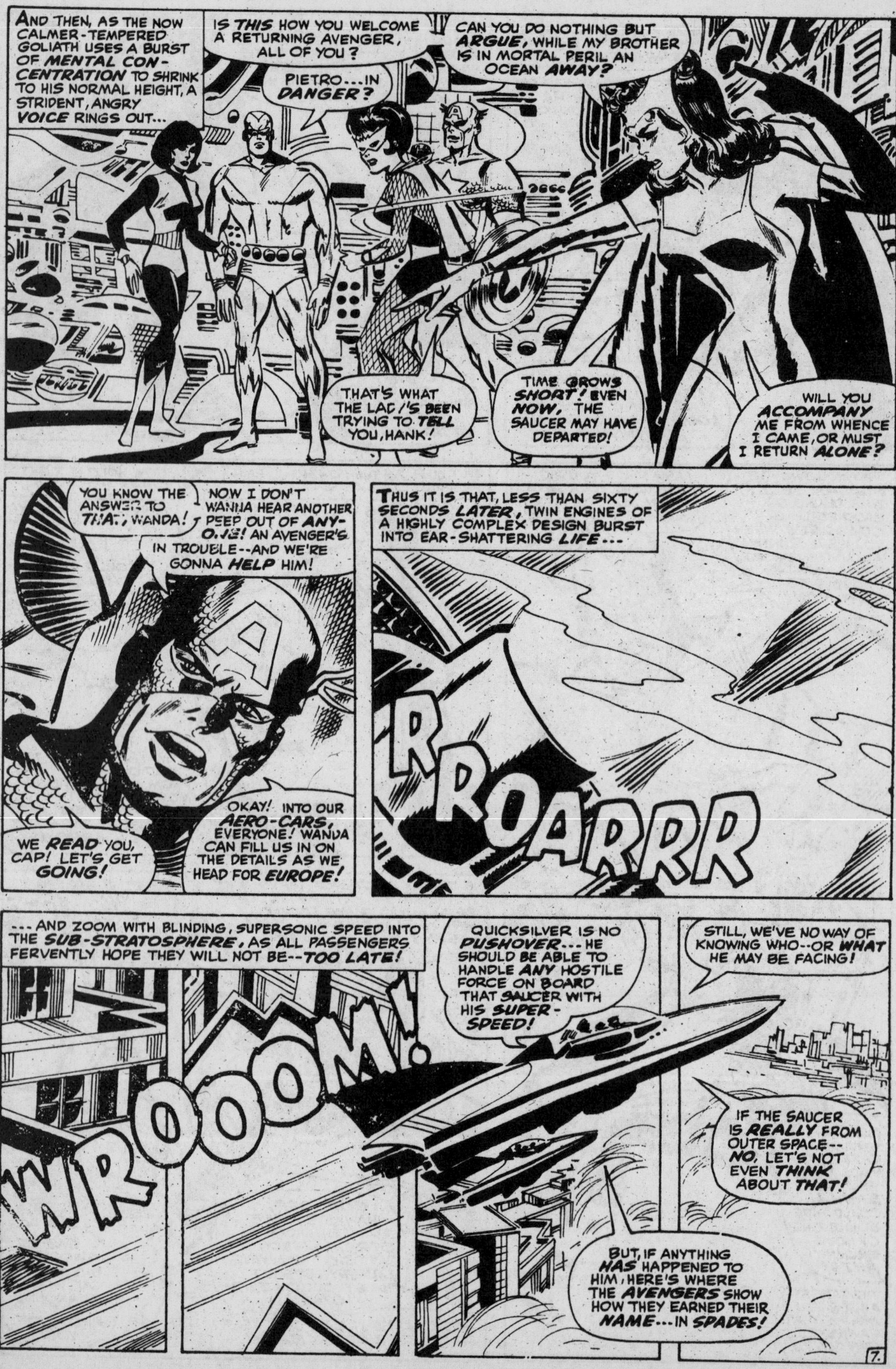
AND THEN, AS THE NOW CALMER-TEMPERED GOLIATH USES A BURST OF MENTAL CONCENTRATION TO SHRINK TO HIS NORMAL HEIGHT, A STRIDENT, ANGRY VOICE RINGS OUT...
IS THIS HOW YOU WELCOME A RETURNING AVENGER, ALL OF YOU?
PIETRO...IN DANGER?
CAN YOU DO NOTHING BUT ARGUE, WHILE MY BROTHER IS IN MORTAL PERIL AN OCEAN AWAY?
THAT'S WHAT THE LADY'S BEEN TRYING TO TELL YOU, HANK!
TIME GROWS SHORT! EVEN NOW, THE SAUCER MAY HAVE DEPARTED!
WILL YOU ACCOMPANY ME FROM WHENCE I CAME, OR MUST I RETURN ALONE?
YOU KNOW THE ANSWER TO THAT, WANDA!
NOW I DON'T WANNA HEAR ANOTHER PEEP OUT OF ANYONE! AN AVENGER'S IN TROUBLE--AND WE'RE GONNA HELP HIM!
WE READ YOU, CAP! LET'S GET GOING!
OKAY! INTO OUR AERO-CARS, EVERYONE! WANDA CAN FILL US IN ON THE DETAILS AS WE HEAD FOR EUROPE!
THUS IT IS THAT, LESS THAN SIXTY SECONDS LATER, TWIN ENGINES OF A HIGHLY COMPLEX DESIGN BURST INTO EAR-SHATTERING LIFE...
RROARRR
...AND ZOOM WITH BLINDING, SUPERSONIC SPEED INTO THE SUB-STRATOSPHERE, AS ALL PASSENGERS FERVENTLY HOPE THEY WILL NOT BE--TOO LATE!
WROOOOM!
QUICKSILVER IS NO PUSHOVER...HE SHOULD BE ABLE TO HANDLE ANY HOSTILE FORCE ON BOARD THAT SAUCER WITH HIS SUPER-SPEED!
STILL, WE'VE NO WAY OF KNOWING WHO--OR WHAT HE MAY BE FACING!
IF THE SAUCER IS REALLY FROM OUTER SPACE--NO, LET'S NOT EVEN THINK ABOUT THAT!
BUT, IF ANYTHING HAS HAPPENED TO HIM, HERE'S WHERE THE AVENGERS SHOW HOW THEY EARNED THEIR NAME...IN SPADES!
7.

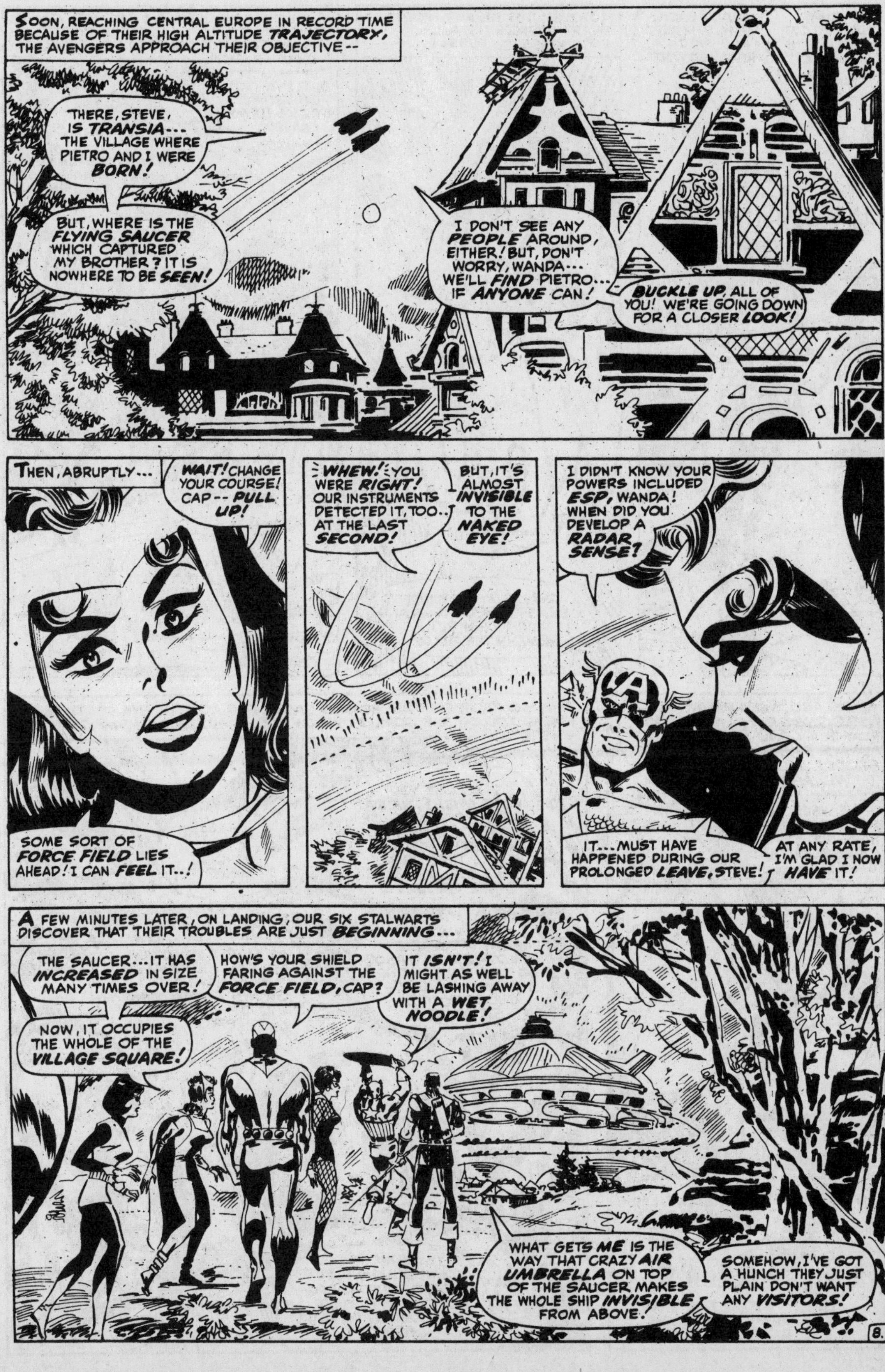
SOON, REACHING CENTRAL EUROPE IN RECORD TIME BECAUSE OF THEIR HIGH ALTITUDE TRAJECTORY, THE AVENGERS APPROACH THEIR OBJECTIVE--
THERE, STEVE, IS TRANSIA... THE VILLAGE WHERE PIETRO AND I WERE BORN!
BUT, WHERE IS THE FLYING SAUCER WHICH CAPTURED MY BROTHER? IT IS NOWHERE TO BE SEEN!
I DON'T SEE ANY PEOPLE AROUND, EITHER! BUT, DON'T WORRY, WANDA... WE'LL FIND PIETRO... IF ANYONE CAN!
BUCKLE UP, ALL OF YOU! WE'RE GOING DOWN FOR A CLOSER LOOK!
THEN, ABRUPTLY...
WAIT! CHANGE YOUR COURSE! CAP -- PULL UP!
SOME SORT OF FORCE FIELD LIES AHEAD! I CAN FEEL IT..!
WHEW! YOU WERE RIGHT! OUR INSTRUMENTS DETECTED IT, TOO.. AT THE LAST SECOND!
BUT, IT'S ALMOST INVISIBLE TO THE NAKED EYE!
I DIDN'T KNOW YOUR POWERS INCLUDED ESP, WANDA! WHEN DID YOU DEVELOP A RADAR SENSE?
IT... MUST HAVE HAPPENED DURING OUR PROLONGED LEAVE, STEVE!
AT ANY RATE, I'M GLAD I NOW HAVE IT!
A FEW MINUTES LATER, ON LANDING, OUR SIX STALWARTS DISCOVER THAT THEIR TROUBLES ARE JUST BEGINNING...
THE SAUCER... IT HAS INCREASED IN SIZE MANY TIMES OVER!
NOW, IT OCCUPIES THE WHOLE OF THE VILLAGE SQUARE!
HOW'S YOUR SHIELD FARING AGAINST THE FORCE FIELD, CAP?
IT ISN'T! I MIGHT AS WELL BE LASHING AWAY WITH A WET NOODLE!
WHAT GETS ME IS THE WAY THAT CRAZY AIR UMBRELLA ON TOP OF THE SAUCER MAKES THE WHOLE SHIP INVISIBLE FROM ABOVE.
SOMEHOW, I'VE GOT A HUNCH THEY JUST PLAIN DON'T WANT ANY VISITORS!
8.

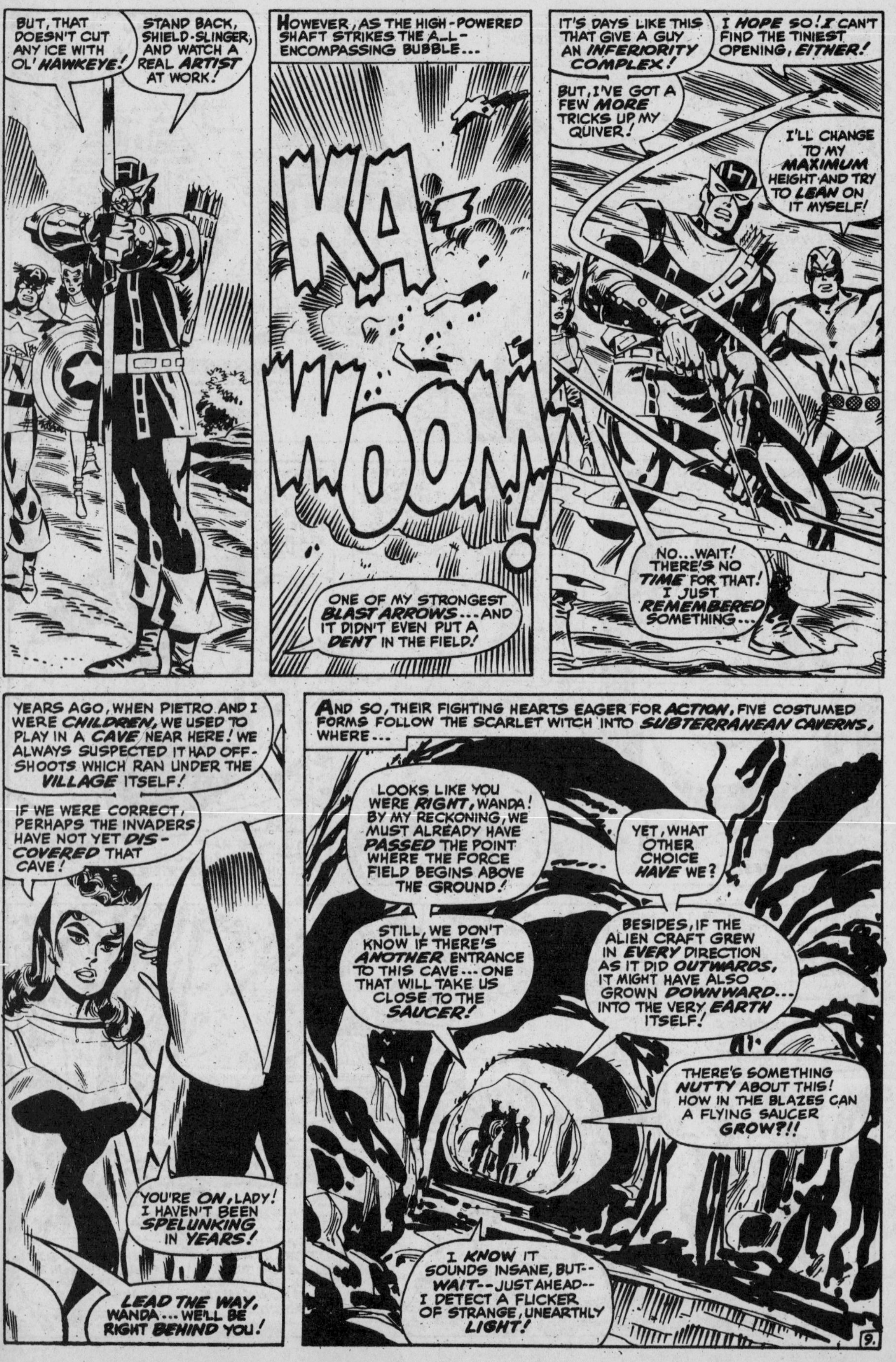

BUT, THAT DOESN'T CUT ANY ICE WITH OL' HAWKEYE!
STAND BACK, SHIELD-SLINGER, AND WATCH A REAL ARTIST AT WORK!
HOWEVER, AS THE HIGH-POWERED SHAFT STRIKES THE ALL-ENCOMPASSING BUBBLE...
KA-WOOM!
ONE OF MY STRONGEST BLAST ARROWS... AND IT DIDN'T EVEN PUT A DENT IN THE FIELD!
IT'S DAYS LIKE THIS THAT GIVE A GUY AN INFERIORITY COMPLEX!
I HOPE SO! I CAN'T FIND THE TINIEST OPENING, EITHER!
BUT, I'VE GOT A FEW MORE TRICKS UP MY QUIVER!
I'LL CHANGE TO MY MAXIMUM HEIGHT AND TRY TO LEAN ON IT MYSELF!
NO...WAIT! THERE'S NO TIME FOR THAT! I JUST REMEMBERED SOMETHING...
YEARS AGO, WHEN PIETRO AND I WERE CHILDREN, WE USED TO PLAY IN A CAVE NEAR HERE! WE ALWAYS SUSPECTED IT HAD OFF-SHOOTS WHICH RAN UNDER THE VILLAGE ITSELF!
IF WE WERE CORRECT, PERHAPS THE INVADERS HAVE NOT YET DISCOVERED THAT CAVE!
YOU'RE ON, LADY! I HAVEN'T BEEN SPELUNKING IN YEARS!
LEAD THE WAY, WANDA... WE'LL BE RIGHT BEHIND YOU!
AND SO, THEIR FIGHTING HEARTS EAGER FOR ACTION, FIVE COSTUMED FORMS FOLLOW THE SCARLET WITCH INTO SUBTERRANEAN CAVERNS, WHERE...
LOOKS LIKE YOU WERE RIGHT, WANDA! BY MY RECKONING, WE MUST ALREADY HAVE PASSED THE POINT WHERE THE FORCE FIELD BEGINS ABOVE THE GROUND!
YET, WHAT OTHER CHOICE HAVE WE?
STILL, WE DON'T KNOW IF THERE'S ANOTHER ENTRANCE TO THIS CAVE... ONE THAT WILL TAKE US CLOSE TO THE SAUCER!
BESIDES, IF THE ALIEN CRAFT GREW IN EVERY DIRECTION AS IT DID OUTWARDS, IT MIGHT HAVE ALSO GROWN DOWNWARD... INTO THE VERY EARTH ITSELF!
THERE'S SOMETHING NUTTY ABOUT THIS! HOW IN THE BLAZES CAN A FLYING SAUCER GROW?!!
I KNOW IT SOUNDS INSANE, BUT-- WAIT--JUST AHEAD-- I DETECT A FLICKER OF STRANGE, UNEARTHLY LIGHT!
9.

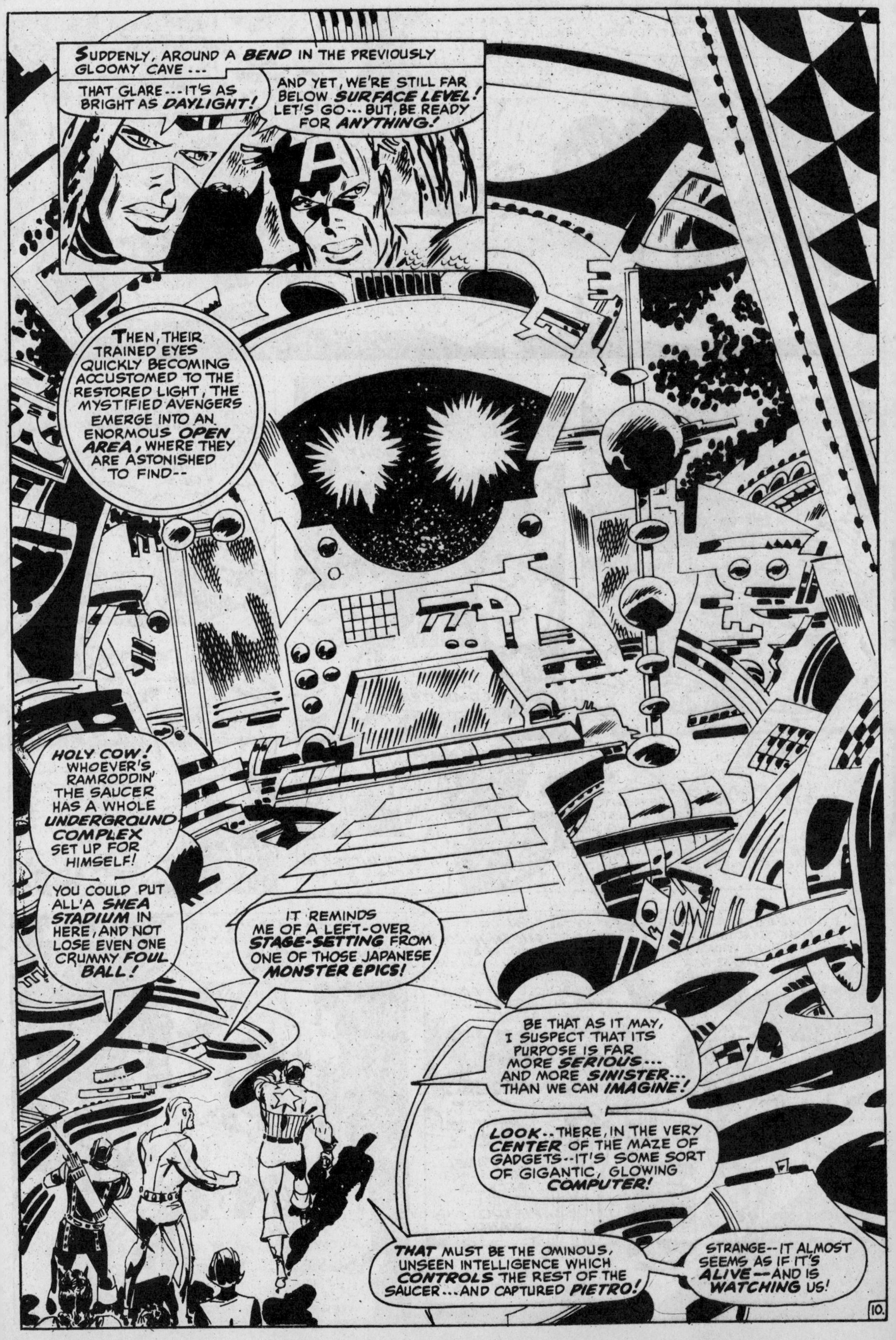
SUDDENLY, AROUND A BEND IN THE PREVIOUSLY GLOOMY CAVE ---
THAT GLARE --- IT'S AS BRIGHT AS DAYLIGHT!
AND YET, WE'RE STILL FAR BELOW SURFACE LEVEL! LET'S GO --- BUT, BE READY FOR ANYTHING!
THEN, THEIR TRAINED EYES QUICKLY BECOMING ACCUSTOMED TO THE RESTORED LIGHT, THE MYSTIFIED AVENGERS EMERGE INTO AN ENORMOUS OPEN AREA, WHERE THEY ARE ASTONISHED TO FIND--
HOLY COW! WHOEVER'S RAMRODDIN' THE SAUCER HAS A WHOLE UNDERGROUND COMPLEX SET UP FOR HIMSELF!
YOU COULD PUT ALL'A SHEA STADIUM IN HERE, AND NOT LOSE EVEN ONE CRUMMY FOUL BALL!
IT REMINDS ME OF A LEFT-OVER STAGE-SETTING FROM ONE OF THOSE JAPANESE MONSTER EPICS!
BE THAT AS IT MAY, I SUSPECT THAT ITS PURPOSE IS FAR MORE SERIOUS... AND MORE SINISTER... THAN WE CAN IMAGINE!
LOOK.. THERE, IN THE VERY CENTER OF THE MAZE OF GADGETS--IT'S SOME SORT OF GIGANTIC, GLOWING COMPUTER!
THAT MUST BE THE OMINOUS, UNSEEN INTELLIGENCE WHICH CONTROLS THE REST OF THE SAUCER... AND CAPTURED PIETRO!
STRANGE--IT ALMOST SEEMS AS IF IT'S ALIVE--AND IS WATCHING US!
10.

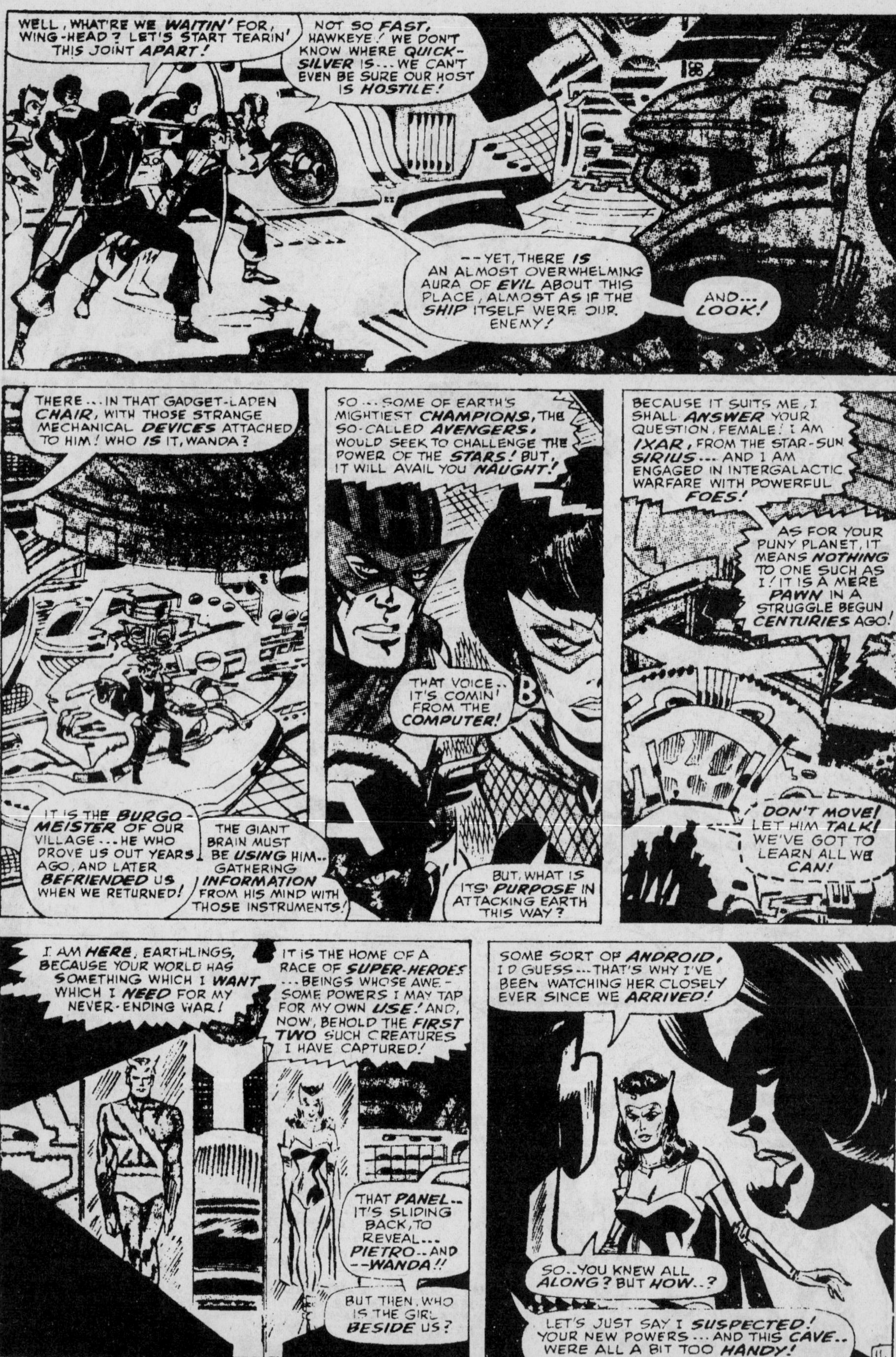
WELL, WHAT'RE WE WAITIN' FOR, WING-HEAD? LET'S START TEARIN' THIS JOINT APART!
NOT SO FAST, HAWKEYE! WE DON'T KNOW WHERE QUICK-SILVER IS... WE CAN'T EVEN BE SURE OUR HOST IS HOSTILE!
--YET, THERE IS AN ALMOST OVERWHELMING AURA OF EVIL ABOUT THIS PLACE, ALMOST AS IF THE SHIP ITSELF WERE OUR ENEMY!
AND... LOOK!
THERE... IN THAT GADGET-LADEN CHAIR, WITH THOSE STRANGE MECHANICAL DEVICES ATTACHED TO HIM! WHO IS IT, WANDA?
IT IS THE BURGO-MEISTER OF OUR VILLAGE... HE WHO DROVE US OUT YEARS AGO, AND LATER BEFRIENDED US WHEN WE RETURNED!
THE GIANT BRAIN MUST BE USING HIM.. GATHERING INFORMATION FROM HIS MIND WITH THOSE INSTRUMENTS!
SO... SOME OF EARTH'S MIGHTIEST CHAMPIONS, THE SO-CALLED AVENGERS, WOULD SEEK TO CHALLENGE THE POWER OF THE STARS! BUT, IT WILL AVAIL YOU NAUGHT!
THAT VOICE.. IT'S COMIN' FROM THE COMPUTER!
BUT, WHAT IS ITS' PURPOSE IN ATTACKING EARTH THIS WAY?
BECAUSE IT SUITS ME, I SHALL ANSWER YOUR QUESTION, FEMALE! I AM IXAR, FROM THE STAR-SUN SIRIUS... AND I AM ENGAGED IN INTERGALACTIC WARFARE WITH POWERFUL FOES!
AS FOR YOUR PUNY PLANET, IT MEANS NOTHING TO ONE SUCH AS I! IT IS A MERE PAWN IN A STRUGGLE BEGUN CENTURIES AGO!
DON'T MOVE! LET HIM TALK! WE'VE GOT TO LEARN ALL WE CAN!
I AM HERE, EARTHLINGS, BECAUSE YOUR WORLD HAS SOMETHING WHICH I WANT WHICH I NEED FOR MY NEVER-ENDING WAR!
IT IS THE HOME OF A RACE OF SUPER-HEROES... BEINGS WHOSE AWE-SOME POWERS I MAY TAP FOR MY OWN USE! AND, NOW, BEHOLD THE FIRST TWO SUCH CREATURES I HAVE CAPTURED!
THAT PANEL-- IT'S SLIDING BACK, TO REVEAL... PIETRO--AND --WANDA!!
BUT THEN, WHO IS THE GIRL BESIDE US?
SOME SORT OF ANDROID, I'D GUESS... THAT'S WHY I'VE BEEN WATCHING HER CLOSELY EVER SINCE WE ARRIVED!
SO.. YOU KNEW ALL ALONG? BUT HOW..?
LET'S JUST SAY I SUSPECTED! YOUR NEW POWERS... AND THIS CAVE.. WERE ALL A BIT TOO HANDY!
11.

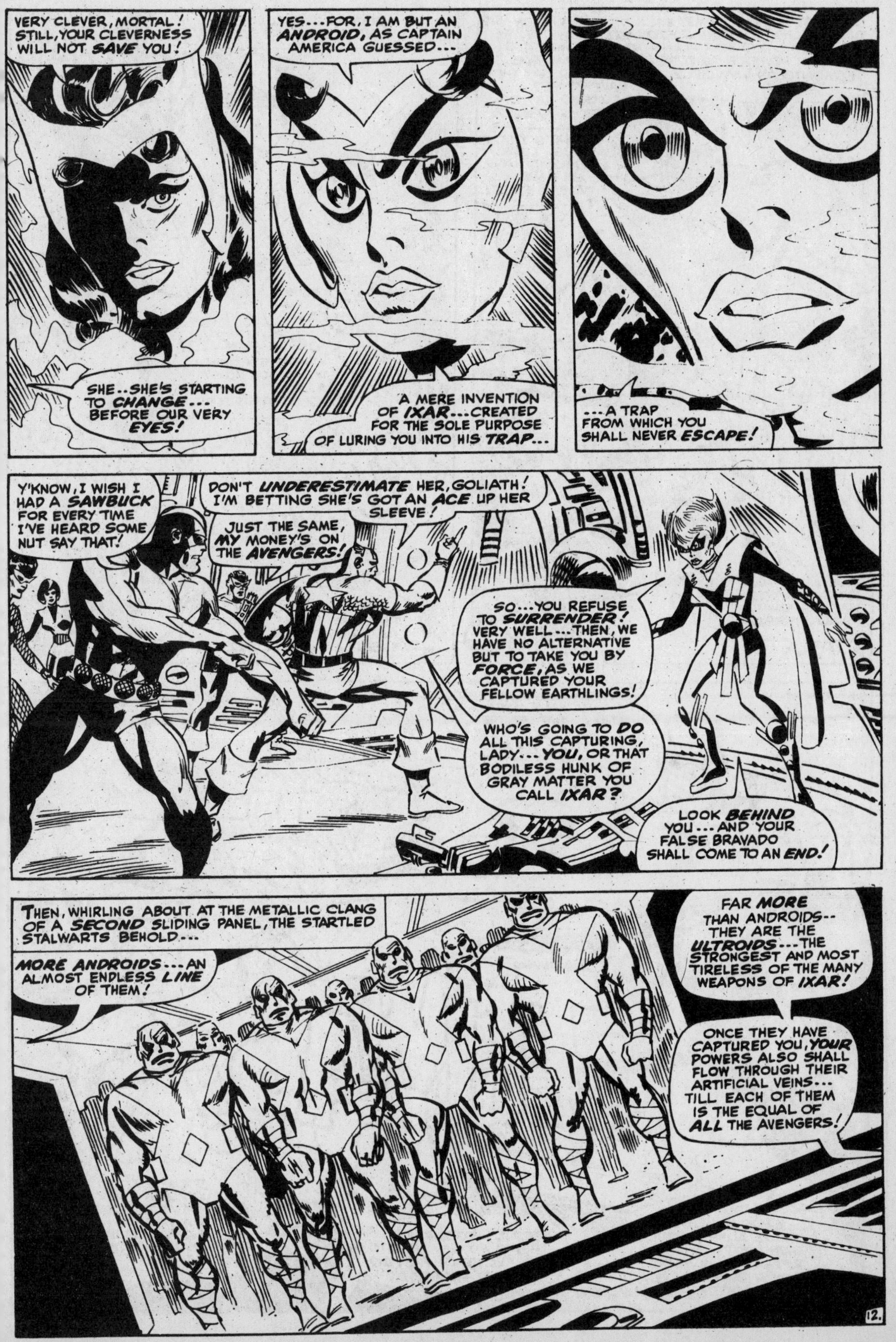
VERY CLEVER, MORTAL! STILL, YOUR CLEVERNESS WILL NOT SAVE YOU!
SHE..SHE'S STARTING TO CHANGE... BEFORE OUR VERY EYES!
YES...FOR, I AM BUT AN ANDROID, AS CAPTAIN AMERICA GUESSED...
A MERE INVENTION OF IXAR...CREATED FOR THE SOLE PURPOSE OF LURING YOU INTO HIS TRAP...
...A TRAP FROM WHICH YOU SHALL NEVER ESCAPE!
Y'KNOW, I WISH I HAD A SAWBUCK FOR EVERY TIME I'VE HEARD SOME NUT SAY THAT!
DON'T UNDERESTIMATE HER, GOLIATH! I'M BETTING SHE'S GOT AN ACE UP HER SLEEVE!
JUST THE SAME, MY MONEY'S ON THE AVENGERS!
SO...YOU REFUSE TO SURRENDER! VERY WELL...THEN, WE HAVE NO ALTERNATIVE BUT TO TAKE YOU BY FORCE, AS WE CAPTURED YOUR FELLOW EARTHLINGS!
WHO'S GOING TO DO ALL THIS CAPTURING, LADY...YOU, OR THAT BODILESS HUNK OF GRAY MATTER YOU CALL IXAR?
LOOK BEHIND YOU...AND YOUR FALSE BRAVADO SHALL COME TO AN END!
THEN, WHIRLING ABOUT AT THE METALLIC CLANG OF A SECOND SLIDING PANEL, THE STARTLED STALWARTS BEHOLD---
MORE ANDROIDS...AN ALMOST ENDLESS LINE OF THEM!
FAR MORE THAN ANDROIDS-- THEY ARE THE ULTROIDS---THE STRONGEST AND MOST TIRELESS OF THE MANY WEAPONS OF IXAR!
ONCE THEY HAVE CAPTURED YOU, YOUR POWERS ALSO SHALL FLOW THROUGH THEIR ARTIFICIAL VEINS...TILL EACH OF THEM IS THE EQUAL OF ALL THE AVENGERS!

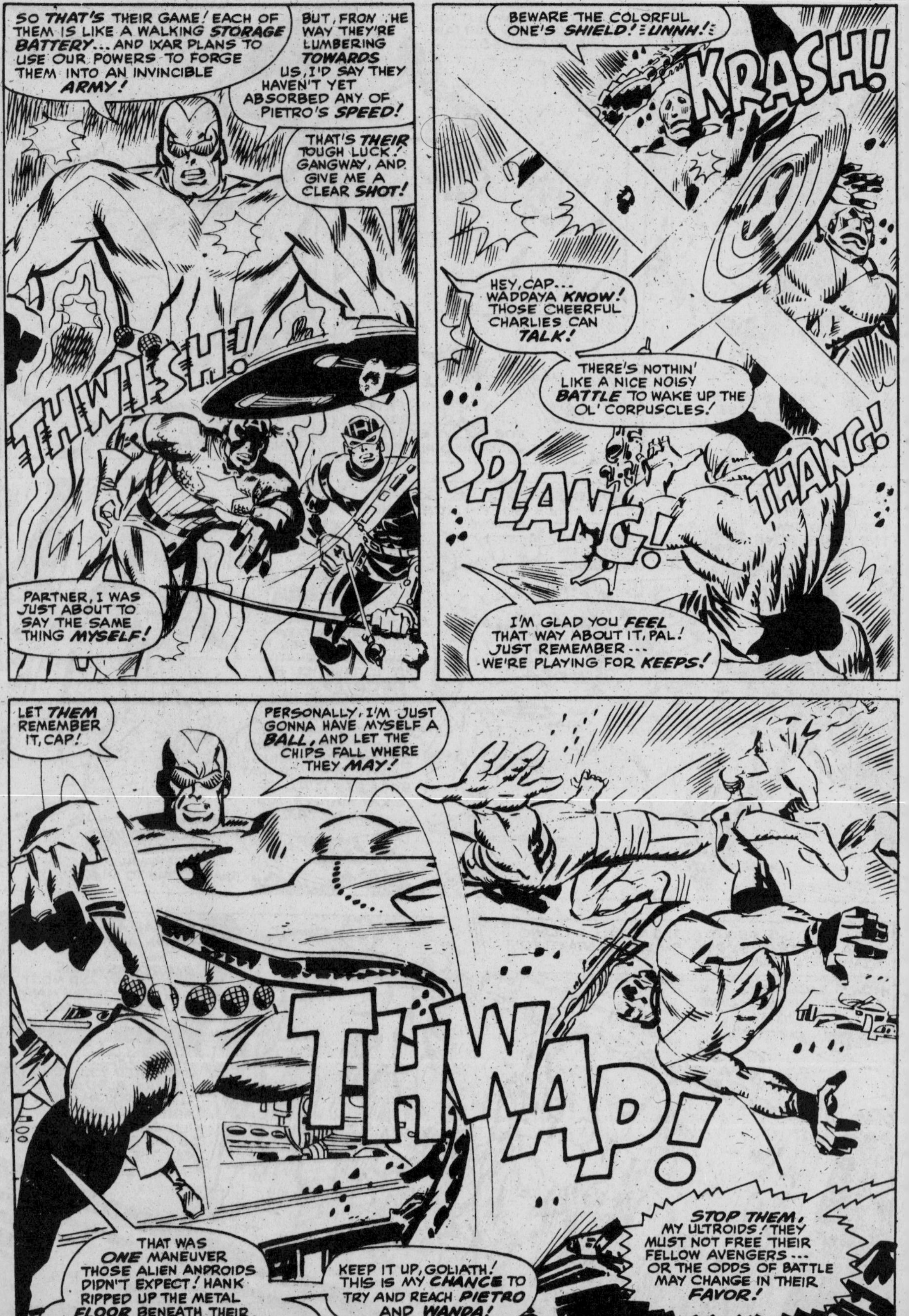
SO THAT'S THEIR GAME! EACH OF THEM IS LIKE A WALKING STORAGE BATTERY... AND IXAR PLANS TO USE OUR POWERS TO FORGE THEM INTO AN INVINCIBLE ARMY!
BUT, FROM THE WAY THEY'RE LUMBERING TOWARDS US, I'D SAY THEY HAVEN'T YET ABSORBED ANY OF PIETRO'S SPEED!
THAT'S THEIR TOUGH LUCK. GANGWAY, AND GIVE ME A CLEAR SHOT!
THWISH!
PARTNER, I WAS JUST ABOUT TO SAY THE SAME THING MYSELF!
BEWARE THE COLORFUL ONE'S SHIELD! UNNH!
KRASH!
HEY, CAP... WADDAYA KNOW! THOSE CHEERFUL CHARLIES CAN TALK!
THERE'S NOTHIN' LIKE A NICE NOISY BATTLE TO WAKE UP THE OL' CORPUSCLES!
SPLANG!
THANG!
I'M GLAD YOU FEEL THAT WAY ABOUT IT, PAL! JUST REMEMBER... WE'RE PLAYING FOR KEEPS!
LET THEM REMEMBER IT, CAP!
PERSONALLY, I'M JUST GONNA HAVE MYSELF A BALL, AND LET THE CHIPS FALL WHERE THEY MAY!
THWAP!
THAT WAS ONE MANEUVER THOSE ALIEN ANDROIDS DIDN'T EXPECT! HANK RIPPED UP THE METAL FLOOR BENEATH THEIR FEET... AND SENT THEM SPRAWLING!
KEEP IT UP, GOLIATH! THIS IS MY CHANCE TO TRY AND REACH PIETRO AND WANDA!
STOP THEM, MY ULTROIDS! THEY MUST NOT FREE THEIR FELLOW AVENGERS... OR THE ODDS OF BATTLE MAY CHANGE IN THEIR FAVOR!
13.

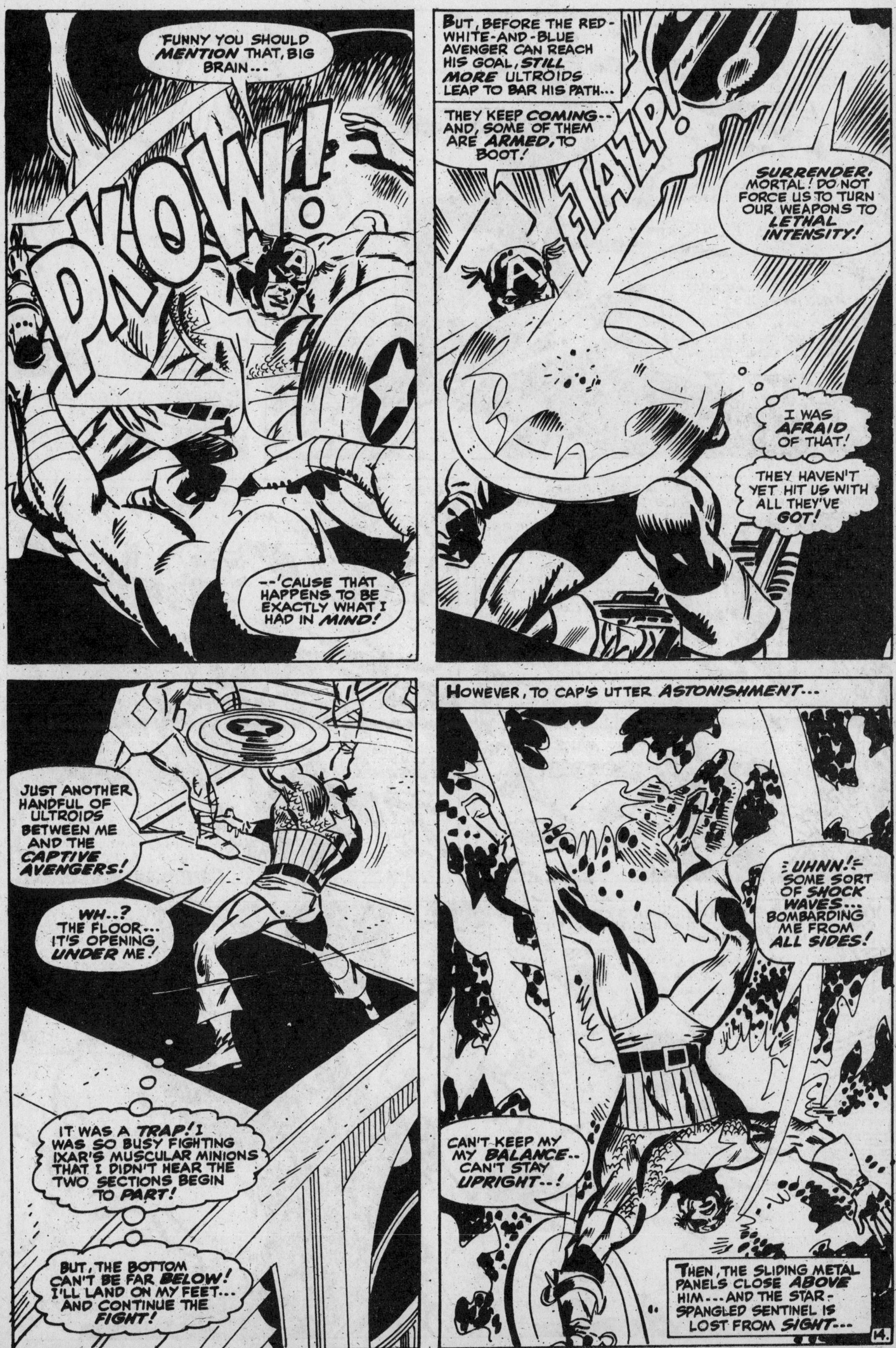
FUNNY YOU SHOULD MENTION THAT, BIG BRAIN...
PKOW!
--'CAUSE THAT HAPPENS TO BE EXACTLY WHAT I HAD IN MIND!
BUT, BEFORE THE RED-WHITE-AND-BLUE AVENGER CAN REACH HIS GOAL, STILL MORE ULTROIDS LEAP TO BAR HIS PATH...
THEY KEEP COMING-- AND, SOME OF THEM ARE ARMED, TO BOOT!
FTAZZP!
SURRENDER, MORTAL! DO NOT FORCE US TO TURN OUR WEAPONS TO LETHAL INTENSITY!
I WAS AFRAID OF THAT!
THEY HAVEN'T YET HIT US WITH ALL THEY'VE GOT!
JUST ANOTHER HANDFUL OF ULTROIDS BETWEEN ME AND THE CAPTIVE AVENGERS!
WH..? THE FLOOR... IT'S OPENING UNDER ME!
IT WAS A TRAP! I WAS SO BUSY FIGHTING IXAR'S MUSCULAR MINIONS THAT I DIDN'T HEAR THE TWO SECTIONS BEGIN TO PART!
BUT, THE BOTTOM CAN'T BE FAR BELOW! I'LL LAND ON MY FEET... AND CONTINUE THE FIGHT!
HOWEVER, TO CAP'S UTTER ASTONISHMENT...
UHNN! SOME SORT OF SHOCK WAVES... BOMBARDING ME FROM ALL SIDES!
CAN'T KEEP MY MY BALANCE.. CAN'T STAY UPRIGHT--!
THEN, THE SLIDING METAL PANELS CLOSE ABOVE HIM... AND THE STAR-SPANGLED SENTINEL IS LOST FROM SIGHT...
14.

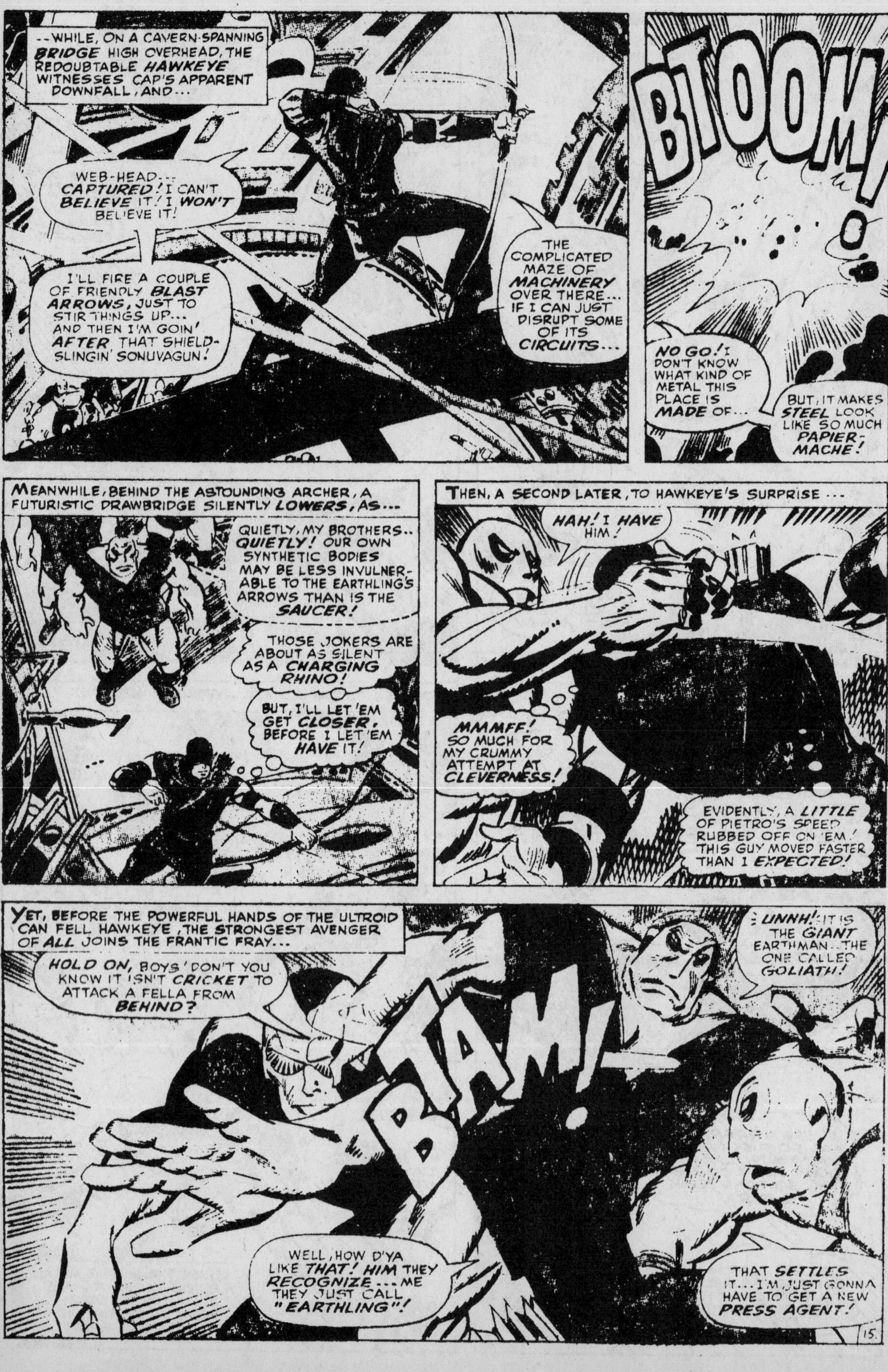

--WHILE, ON A CAVERN-SPANNING BRIDGE HIGH OVERHEAD, THE REDOUBTABLE HAWKEYE WITNESSES CAP'S APPARENT DOWNFALL, AND...
WEB-HEAD--- CAPTURED! I CAN'T BELIEVE IT! I WON'T BELIEVE IT!
I'LL FIRE A COUPLE OF FRIENDLY BLAST ARROWS, JUST TO STIR THINGS UP... AND THEN I'M GOIN' AFTER THAT SHIELD-SLINGIN' SONUVAGUN!
THE COMPLICATED MAZE OF MACHINERY OVER THERE... IF I CAN JUST DISRUPT SOME OF ITS CIRCUITS...
BTOOM!
NO GO! I DON'T KNOW WHAT KIND OF METAL THIS PLACE IS MADE OF...
BUT, IT MAKES STEEL LOOK LIKE SO MUCH PAPIER-MACHE!
MEANWHILE, BEHIND THE ASTOUNDING ARCHER, A FUTURISTIC DRAWBRIDGE SILENTLY LOWERS, AS...
QUIETLY, MY BROTHERS.. QUIETLY! OUR OWN SYNTHETIC BODIES MAY BE LESS INVULNERABLE TO THE EARTHLING'S ARROWS THAN IS THE SAUCER!
THOSE JOKERS ARE ABOUT AS SILENT AS A CHARGING RHINO!
BUT, I'LL LET 'EM GET CLOSER, BEFORE I LET 'EM HAVE IT!
...
THEN, A SECOND LATER, TO HAWKEYE'S SURPRISE ...
HAH! I HAVE HIM!
MMMFF! SO MUCH FOR MY CRUMMY ATTEMPT AT CLEVERNESS!
EVIDENTLY, A LITTLE OF PIETRO'S SPEED RUBBED OFF ON 'EM! THIS GUY MOVED FASTER THAN I EXPECTED!
YET, BEFORE THE POWERFUL HANDS OF THE ULTROID CAN FELL HAWKEYE, THE STRONGEST AVENGER OF ALL JOINS THE FRANTIC FRAY...
HOLD ON, BOYS! DON'T YOU KNOW IT ISN'T CRICKET TO ATTACK A FELLA FROM BEHIND?
UNNH! IT IS THE GIANT EARTHMAN.. THE ONE CALLED GOLIATH!
BTAM!
WELL, HOW D'YA LIKE THAT! HIM THEY RECOGNIZE ... ME THEY JUST CALL "EARTHLING"!
THAT SETTLES IT... I'M JUST GONNA HAVE TO GET A NEW PRESS AGENT!

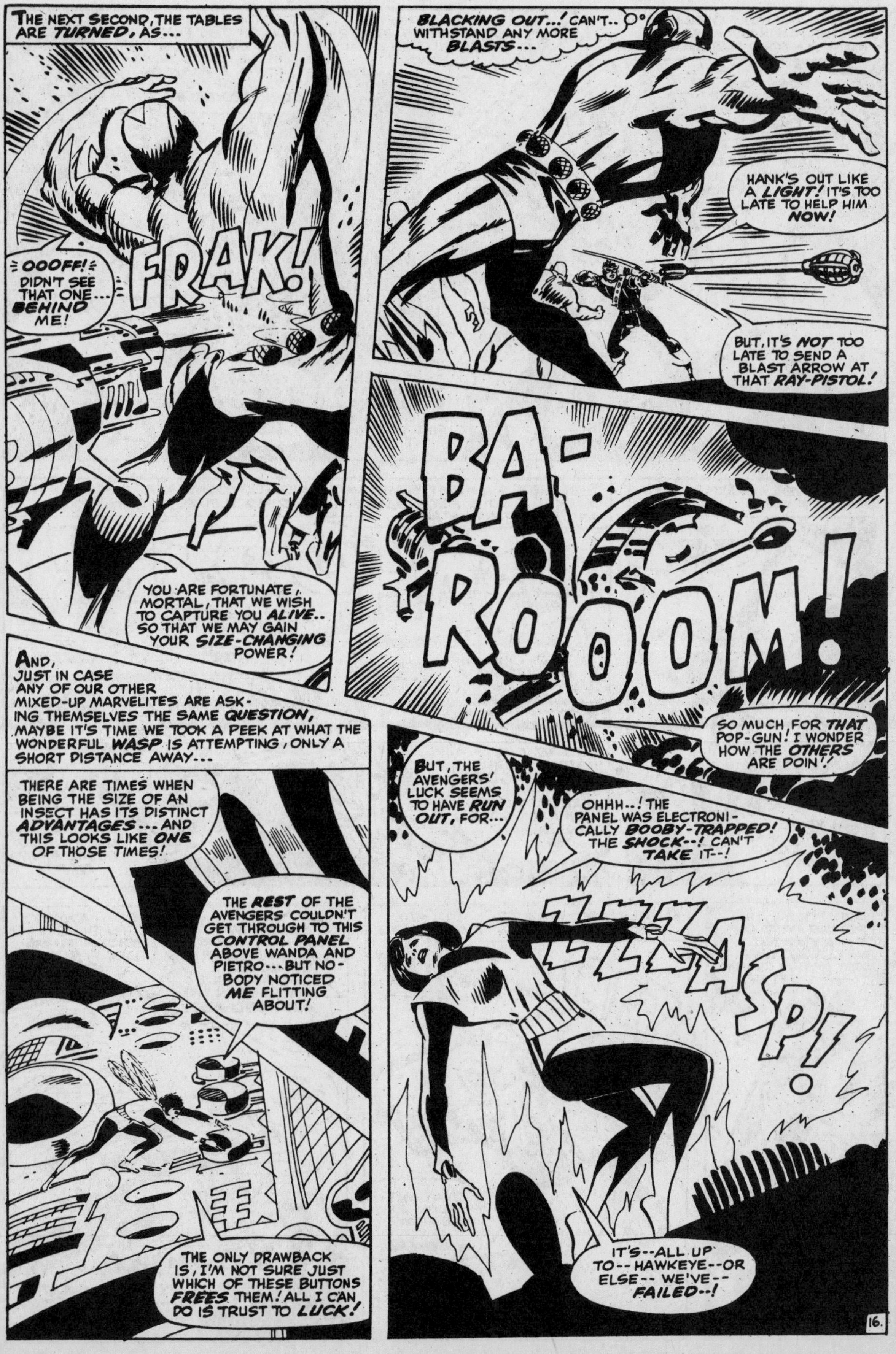
THE NEXT SECOND, THE TABLES ARE TURNED, AS...
OOOFF! DIDN'T SEE THAT ONE... BEHIND ME!
FRAK!
YOU ARE FORTUNATE, MORTAL, THAT WE WISH TO CAPTURE YOU ALIVE.. SO THAT WE MAY GAIN YOUR SIZE-CHANGING POWER!
BLACKING OUT..! CAN'T.. WITHSTAND ANY MORE BLASTS...
HANK'S OUT LIKE A LIGHT! IT'S TOO LATE TO HELP HIM NOW!
BUT, IT'S NOT TOO LATE TO SEND A BLAST ARROW AT THAT RAY-PISTOL!
BA-ROOOM!
SO MUCH FOR THAT POP-GUN! I WONDER HOW THE OTHERS ARE DOIN'!
AND, JUST IN CASE ANY OF OUR OTHER MIXED-UP MARVELITES ARE ASKING THEMSELVES THE SAME QUESTION, MAYBE IT'S TIME WE TOOK A PEEK AT WHAT THE WONDERFUL WASP IS ATTEMPTING, ONLY A SHORT DISTANCE AWAY...
THERE ARE TIMES WHEN BEING THE SIZE OF AN INSECT HAS ITS DISTINCT ADVANTAGES... AND THIS LOOKS LIKE ONE OF THOSE TIMES!
THE REST OF THE AVENGERS COULDN'T GET THROUGH TO THIS CONTROL PANEL ABOVE WANDA AND PIETRO... BUT NOBODY NOTICED ME FLITTING ABOUT!
THE ONLY DRAWBACK IS, I'M NOT SURE JUST WHICH OF THESE BUTTONS FREES THEM! ALL I CAN DO IS TRUST TO LUCK!
BUT, THE AVENGERS' LUCK SEEMS TO HAVE RUN OUT, FOR...
OHHH..! THE PANEL WAS ELECTRONICALLY BOOBY-TRAPPED! THE SHOCK--! CAN'T TAKE IT--!
ZZZZASP!
IT'S--ALL UP TO--HAWKEYE--OR ELSE-- WE'VE-- FAILED--!
16.

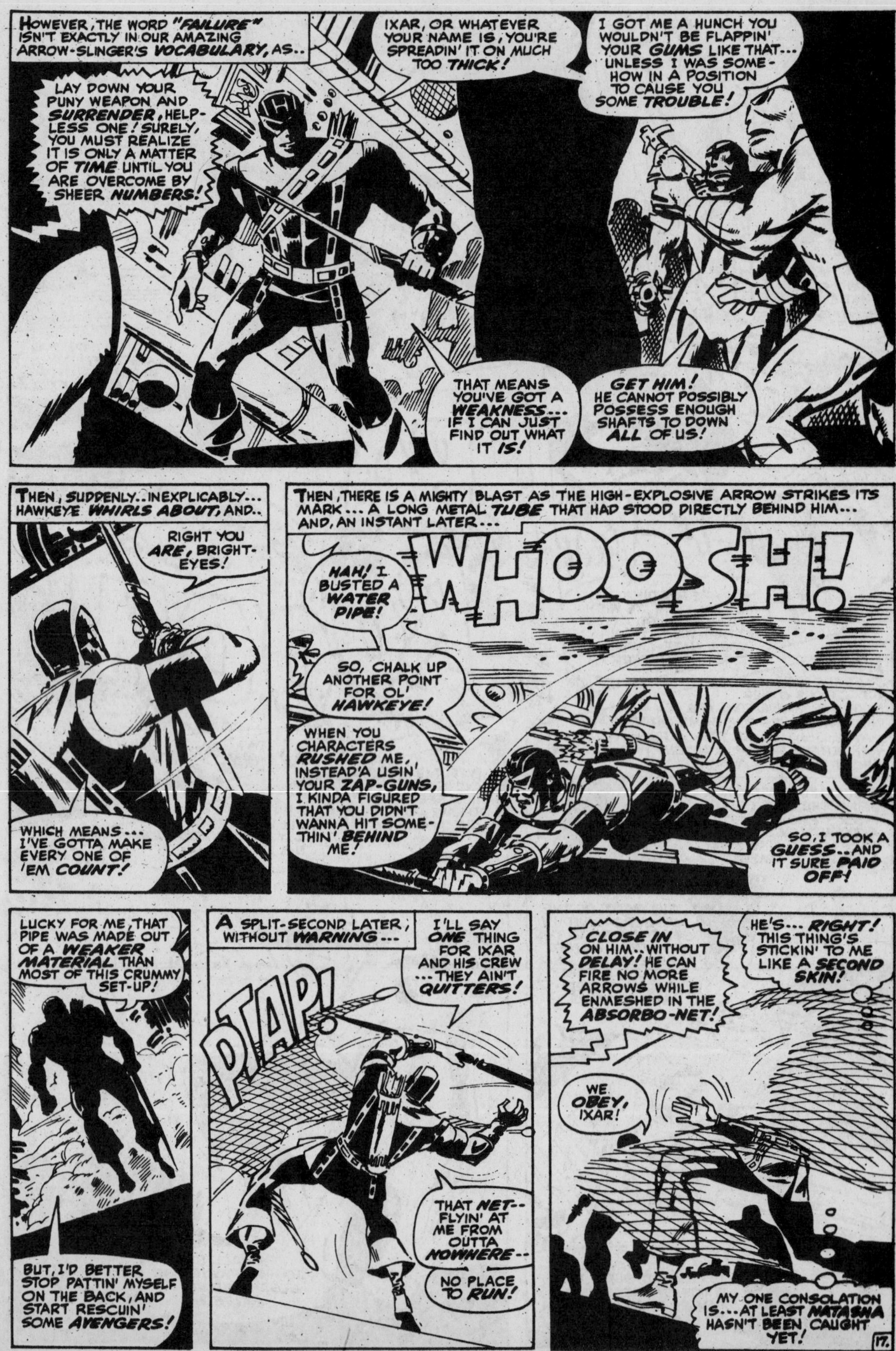
HOWEVER, THE WORD "FAILURE" ISN'T EXACTLY IN OUR AMAZING ARROW-SLINGER'S VOCABULARY, AS..
LAY DOWN YOUR PUNY WEAPON AND SURRENDER, HELPLESS ONE! SURELY, YOU MUST REALIZE IT IS ONLY A MATTER OF TIME UNTIL YOU ARE OVERCOME BY SHEER NUMBERS!
IXAR, OR WHATEVER YOUR NAME IS, YOU'RE SPREADIN' IT ON MUCH TOO THICK!
I GOT ME A HUNCH YOU WOULDN'T BE FLAPPIN' YOUR GUMS LIKE THAT... UNLESS I WAS SOMEHOW IN A POSITION TO CAUSE YOU SOME TROUBLE!
THAT MEANS YOU'VE GOT A WEAKNESS... IF I CAN JUST FIND OUT WHAT IT IS!
GET HIM! HE CANNOT POSSIBLY POSSESS ENOUGH SHAFTS TO DOWN ALL OF US!
THEN, SUDDENLY..INEXPLICABLY... HAWKEYE WHIRLS ABOUT, AND..
RIGHT YOU ARE, BRIGHT-EYES!
WHICH MEANS... I'VE GOTTA MAKE EVERY ONE OF 'EM COUNT!
THEN, THERE IS A MIGHTY BLAST AS THE HIGH-EXPLOSIVE ARROW STRIKES ITS MARK... A LONG METAL TUBE THAT HAD STOOD DIRECTLY BEHIND HIM... AND, AN INSTANT LATER...
WHOOSH!
HAH! I BUSTED A WATER PIPE!
SO, CHALK UP ANOTHER POINT FOR OL' HAWKEYE!
WHEN YOU CHARACTERS RUSHED ME, INSTEAD'A USIN' YOUR ZAP-GUNS, I KINDA FIGURED THAT YOU DIDN'T WANNA HIT SOMETHIN' BEHIND ME!
SO, I TOOK A GUESS..AND IT SURE PAID OFF!
LUCKY FOR ME, THAT PIPE WAS MADE OUT OF A WEAKER MATERIAL THAN MOST OF THIS CRUMMY SET-UP!
BUT, I'D BETTER STOP PATTIN' MYSELF ON THE BACK, AND START RESCUIN' SOME AVENGERS!
A SPLIT-SECOND LATER, WITHOUT WARNING...
I'LL SAY ONE THING FOR IXAR AND HIS CREW ...THEY AIN'T QUITTERS!
PTAP!
THAT NET-- FLYIN' AT ME FROM OUTTA NOWHERE--
NO PLACE TO RUN!
CLOSE IN ON HIM..WITHOUT DELAY! HE CAN FIRE NO MORE ARROWS WHILE ENMESHED IN THE ABSORBO-NET!
HE'S... RIGHT! THIS THING'S STICKIN' TO ME LIKE A SECOND SKIN!
WE OBEY, IXAR!
MY ONE CONSOLATION IS...AT LEAST NATASHA HASN'T BEEN CAUGHT YET!

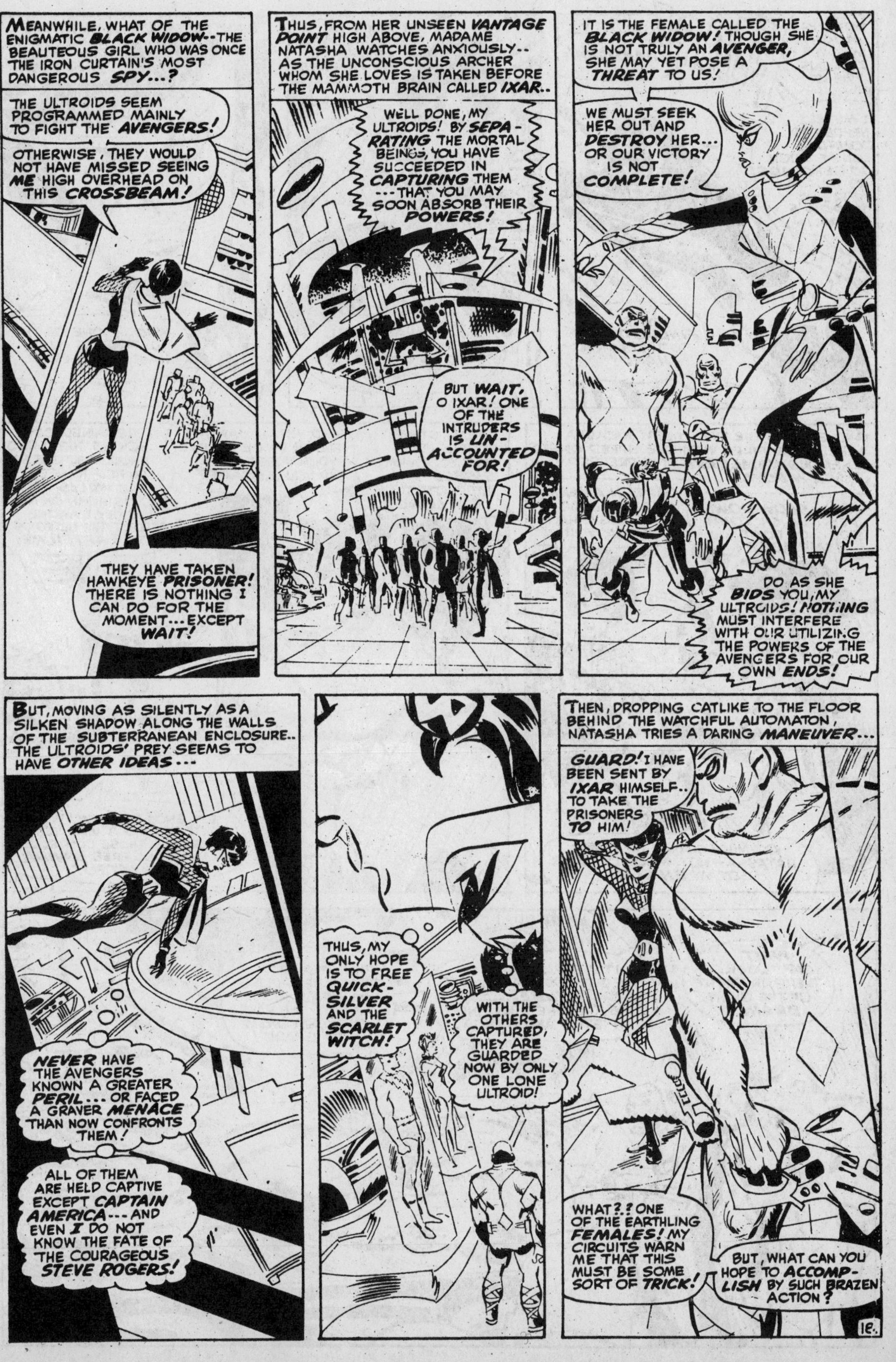
MEANWHILE, WHAT OF THE ENIGMATIC BLACK WIDOW--THE BEAUTEOUS GIRL WHO WAS ONCE THE IRON CURTAIN'S MOST DANGEROUS SPY...?
THE ULTROIDS SEEM PROGRAMMED MAINLY TO FIGHT THE AVENGERS!
OTHERWISE, THEY WOULD NOT HAVE MISSED SEEING ME HIGH OVERHEAD ON THIS CROSSBEAM!
THEY HAVE TAKEN HAWKEYE PRISONER! THERE IS NOTHING I CAN DO FOR THE MOMENT... EXCEPT WAIT!
THUS, FROM HER UNSEEN VANTAGE POINT HIGH ABOVE, MADAME NATASHA WATCHES ANXIOUSLY-- AS THE UNCONSCIOUS ARCHER WHOM SHE LOVES IS TAKEN BEFORE THE MAMMOTH BRAIN CALLED IXAR..
WELL DONE, MY ULTROIDS! BY SEPA-RATING THE MORTAL BEINGS, YOU HAVE SUCCEEDED IN CAPTURING THEM ---THAT YOU MAY SOON ABSORB THEIR POWERS!
BUT WAIT, O IXAR! ONE OF THE INTRUDERS IS UN-ACCOUNTED FOR!
IT IS THE FEMALE CALLED THE BLACK WIDOW! THOUGH SHE IS NOT TRULY AN AVENGER, SHE MAY YET POSE A THREAT TO US!
WE MUST SEEK HER OUT AND DESTROY HER... OR OUR VICTORY IS NOT COMPLETE!
DO AS SHE BIDS YOU, MY ULTROIDS! NOTHING MUST INTERFERE WITH OUR UTILIZING THE POWERS OF THE AVENGERS FOR OUR OWN ENDS!
BUT, MOVING AS SILENTLY AS A SILKEN SHADOW ALONG THE WALLS OF THE SUBTERRANEAN ENCLOSURE.. THE ULTROIDS' PREY SEEMS TO HAVE OTHER IDEAS---
NEVER HAVE THE AVENGERS KNOWN A GREATER PERIL... OR FACED A GRAVER MENACE THAN NOW CONFRONTS THEM!
ALL OF THEM ARE HELD CAPTIVE EXCEPT CAPTAIN AMERICA--- AND EVEN I DO NOT KNOW THE FATE OF THE COURAGEOUS STEVE ROGERS!
THUS, MY ONLY HOPE IS TO FREE QUICK-SILVER AND THE SCARLET WITCH!
WITH THE OTHERS CAPTURED, THEY ARE GUARDED NOW BY ONLY ONE LONE ULTROID!
THEN, DROPPING CATLIKE TO THE FLOOR BEHIND THE WATCHFUL AUTOMATON, NATASHA TRIES A DARING MANEUVER...
GUARD! I HAVE BEEN SENT BY IXAR HIMSELF.. TO TAKE THE PRISONERS TO HIM!
WHAT?? ONE OF THE EARTHLING FEMALES! MY CIRCUITS WARN ME THAT THIS MUST BE SOME SORT OF TRICK!
BUT, WHAT CAN YOU HOPE TO ACCOMP-LISH BY SUCH BRAZEN ACTION?
12.

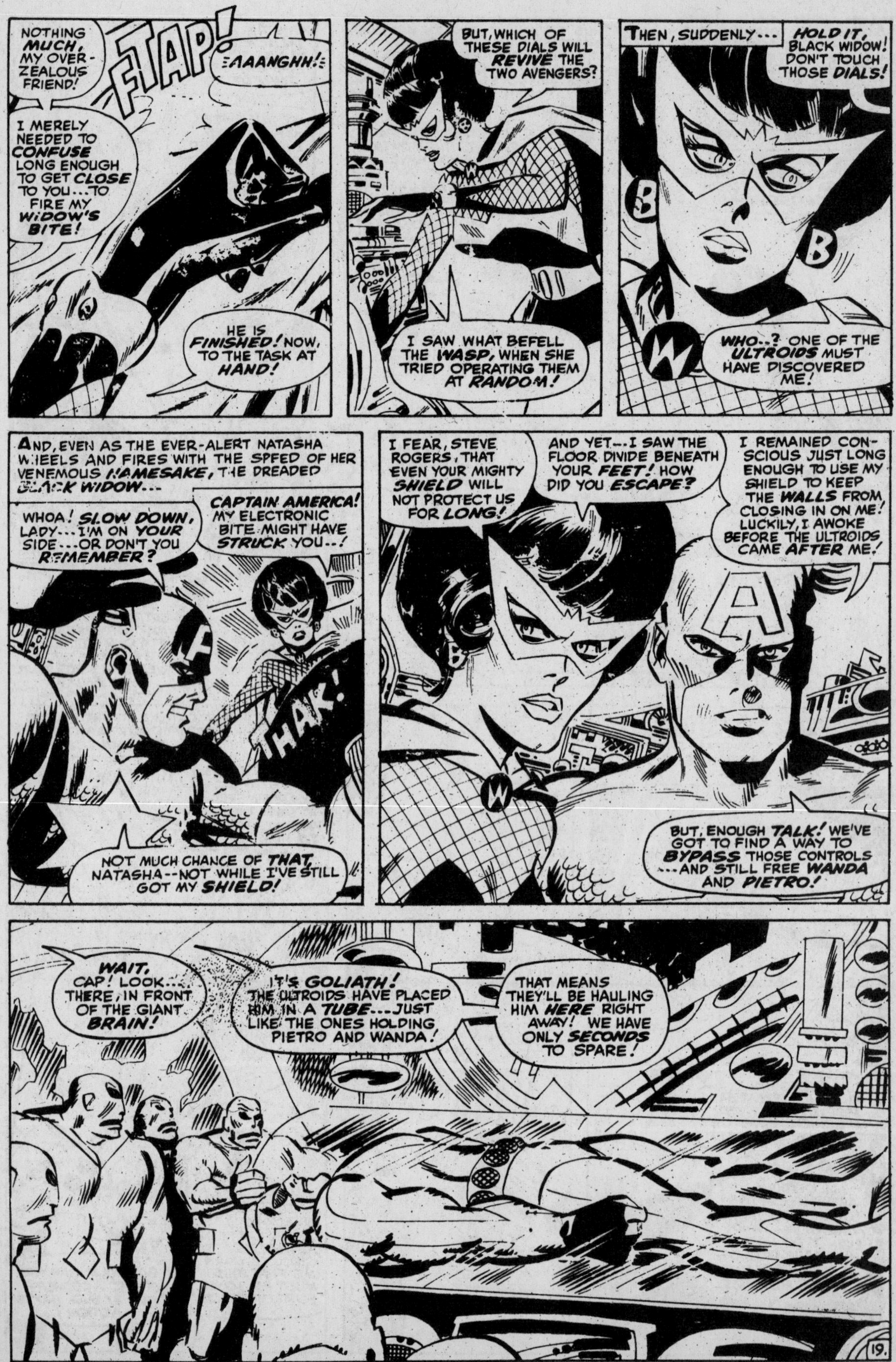
NOTHING MUCH, MY OVER-ZEALOUS FRIEND!
FTAP!
AAANGHH!
I MERELY NEEDED TO CONFUSE LONG ENOUGH TO GET CLOSE TO YOU... TO FIRE MY WIDOW'S BITE!
HE IS FINISHED! NOW, TO THE TASK AT HAND!
BUT, WHICH OF THESE DIALS WILL REVIVE THE TWO AVENGERS?
I SAW WHAT BEFELL THE WASP, WHEN SHE TRIED OPERATING THEM AT RANDOM!
THEN, SUDDENLY...
HOLD IT, BLACK WIDOW! DON'T TOUCH THOSE DIALS!
WHO..? ONE OF THE ULTROIDS MUST HAVE DISCOVERED ME!
AND, EVEN AS THE EVER-ALERT NATASHA WHEELS AND FIRES WITH THE SPEED OF HER VENEMOUS NAMESAKE, THE DREADED BLACK WIDOW...
WHOA! SLOW DOWN, LADY... I'M ON YOUR SIDE... OR DON'T YOU REMEMBER?
CAPTAIN AMERICA! MY ELECTRONIC BITE MIGHT HAVE STRUCK YOU...!
THAK!
NOT MUCH CHANCE OF THAT, NATASHA--NOT WHILE I'VE STILL GOT MY SHIELD!
I FEAR, STEVE ROGERS, THAT EVEN YOUR MIGHTY SHIELD WILL NOT PROTECT US FOR LONG!
AND YET--I SAW THE FLOOR DIVIDE BENEATH YOUR FEET! HOW DID YOU ESCAPE?
I REMAINED CONSCIOUS JUST LONG ENOUGH TO USE MY SHIELD TO KEEP THE WALLS FROM CLOSING IN ON ME! LUCKILY, I AWOKE BEFORE THE ULTROIDS CAME AFTER ME!
BUT, ENOUGH TALK! WE'VE GOT TO FIND A WAY TO BYPASS THOSE CONTROLS ...AND STILL FREE WANDA AND PIETRO!
WAIT, CAP! LOOK... THERE, IN FRONT OF THE GIANT BRAIN!
IT'S GOLIATH! THE ULTROIDS HAVE PLACED HIM IN A TUBE...JUST LIKE THE ONES HOLDING PIETRO AND WANDA!
THAT MEANS THEY'LL BE HAULING HIM HERE RIGHT AWAY! WE HAVE ONLY SECONDS TO SPARE!

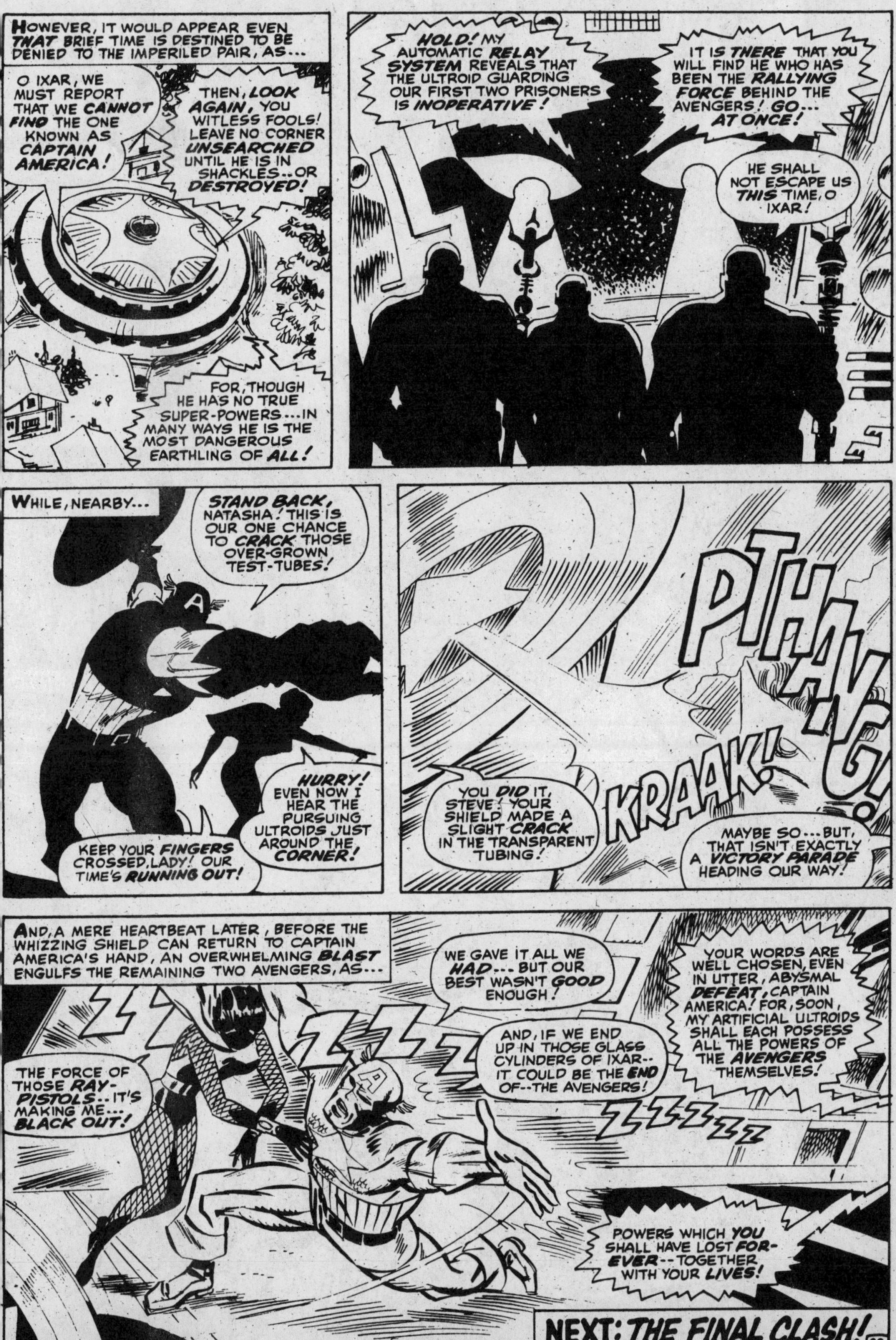

HOWEVER, IT WOULD APPEAR EVEN THAT BRIEF TIME IS DESTINED TO BE DENIED TO THE IMPERILED PAIR, AS...
O IXAR, WE MUST REPORT THAT WE CANNOT FIND THE ONE KNOWN AS CAPTAIN AMERICA!
THEN, LOOK AGAIN, YOU WITLESS FOOLS! LEAVE NO CORNER UNSEARCHED UNTIL HE IS IN SHACKLES..OR DESTROYED!
FOR, THOUGH HE HAS NO TRUE SUPER-POWERS...IN MANY WAYS HE IS THE MOST DANGEROUS EARTHLING OF ALL!
HOLD! MY AUTOMATIC RELAY SYSTEM REVEALS THAT THE ULTROID GUARDING OUR FIRST TWO PRISONERS IS INOPERATIVE!
IT IS THERE THAT YOU WILL FIND HE WHO HAS BEEN THE RALLYING FORCE BEHIND THE AVENGERS! GO... AT ONCE!
HE SHALL NOT ESCAPE US THIS TIME, O IXAR!
WHILE, NEARBY...
STAND BACK, NATASHA! THIS IS OUR ONE CHANCE TO CRACK THOSE OVER-GROWN TEST-TUBES!
HURRY! EVEN NOW I HEAR THE PURSUING ULTROIDS JUST AROUND THE CORNER!
KEEP YOUR FINGERS CROSSED, LADY! OUR TIME'S RUNNING OUT!
PTHANG!
KRAAK!
YOU DID IT, STEVE! YOUR SHIELD MADE A SLIGHT CRACK IN THE TRANSPARENT TUBING!
MAYBE SO...BUT, THAT ISN'T EXACTLY A VICTORY PARADE HEADING OUR WAY!
AND, A MERE HEARTBEAT LATER, BEFORE THE WHIZZING SHIELD CAN RETURN TO CAPTAIN AMERICA'S HAND, AN OVERWHELMING BLAST ENGULFS THE REMAINING TWO AVENGERS, AS...
WE GAVE IT ALL WE HAD...BUT OUR BEST WASN'T GOOD ENOUGH!
THE FORCE OF THOSE RAY-PISTOLS..IT'S MAKING ME... BLACK OUT!
AND, IF WE END UP IN THOSE GLASS CYLINDERS OF IXAR-- IT COULD BE THE END OF--THE AVENGERS!
YOUR WORDS ARE WELL CHOSEN, EVEN IN UTTER, ABYSMAL DEFEAT, CAPTAIN AMERICA! FOR, SOON, MY ARTIFICIAL ULTROIDS SHALL EACH POSSESS ALL THE POWERS OF THE AVENGERS THEMSELVES!
POWERS WHICH YOU SHALL HAVE LOST FOR-EVER--TOGETHER WITH YOUR LIVES!
NEXT: THE FINAL CLASH!
20.

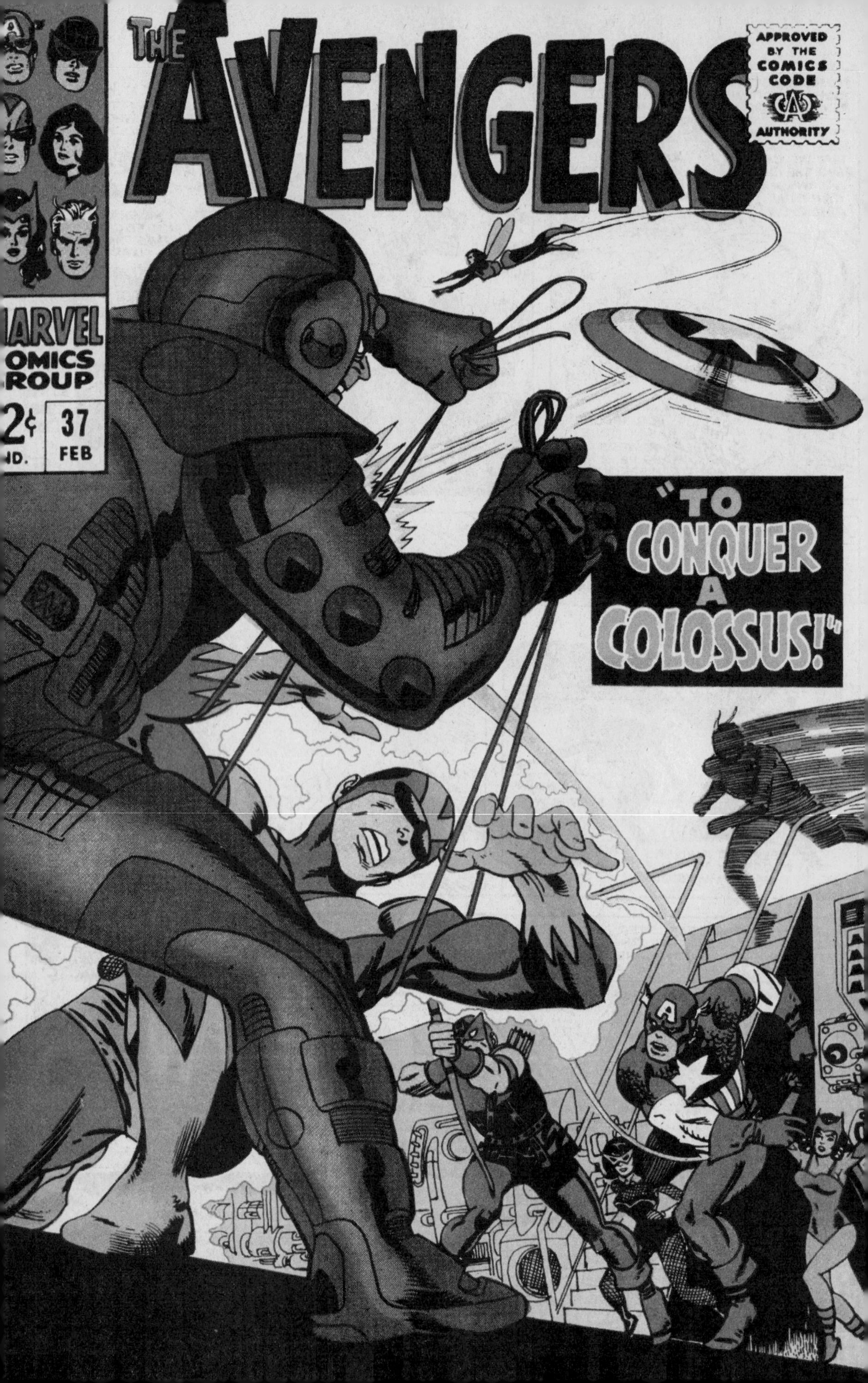
THE AVENGERS
APPROVED BY THE COMICS CODE AUTHORITY
MARVEL COMICS GROUP
12¢ IND.
37 FEB
"TO CONQUER A COLOSSUS!"

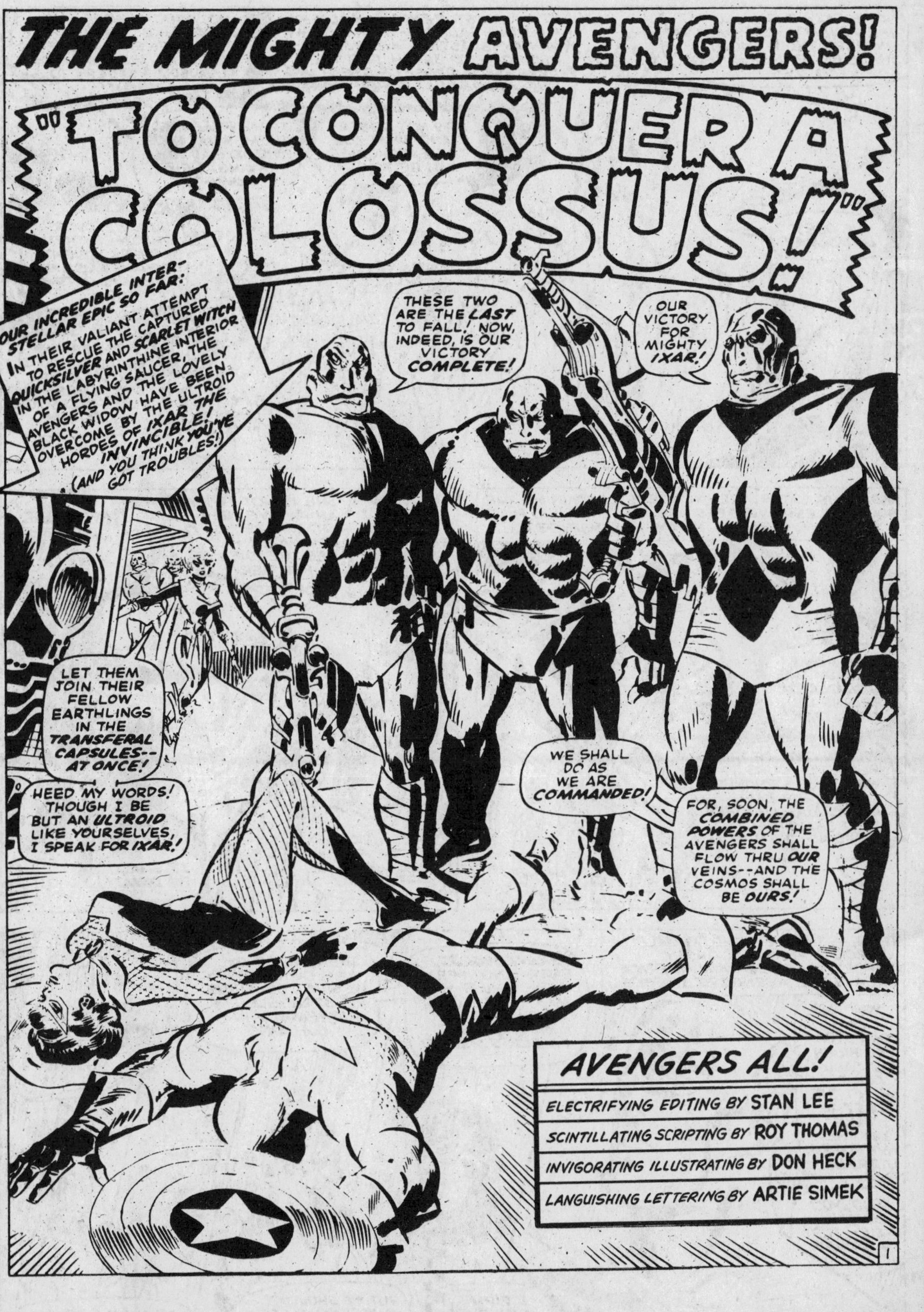
THE MIGHTY AVENGERS!
"TO CONQUER A COLOSSUS!"
OUR INCREDIBLE INTER-STELLAR EPIC SO FAR: IN THEIR VALIANT ATTEMPT TO RESCUE THE CAPTURED QUICKSILVER AND SCARLET WITCH IN THE LABYRINTHINE INTERIOR OF A FLYING SAUCER, THE AVENGERS AND THE LOVELY BLACK WIDOW HAVE BEEN OVERCOME BY THE ULTROID HORDES OF IXAR THE INVINCIBLE! (AND YOU THINK YOU'VE GOT TROUBLES!)
THESE TWO ARE THE LAST TO FALL! NOW, INDEED, IS OUR VICTORY COMPLETE!
OUR VICTORY FOR MIGHTY IXAR!
LET THEM JOIN THEIR FELLOW EARTHLINGS IN THE TRANSFERAL CAPSULES--AT ONCE!
HEED MY WORDS! THOUGH I BE BUT AN ULTROID LIKE YOURSELVES, I SPEAK FOR IXAR!
WE SHALL DO AS WE ARE COMMANDED!
FOR, SOON, THE COMBINED POWERS OF THE AVENGERS SHALL FLOW THRU OUR VEINS--AND THE COSMOS SHALL BE OURS!
AVENGERS ALL!
ELECTRIFYING EDITING BY STAN LEE
SCINTILLATING SCRIPTING BY ROY THOMAS
INVIGORATING ILLUSTRATING BY DON HECK
LANGUISHING LETTERING BY ARTIE SIMEK
1

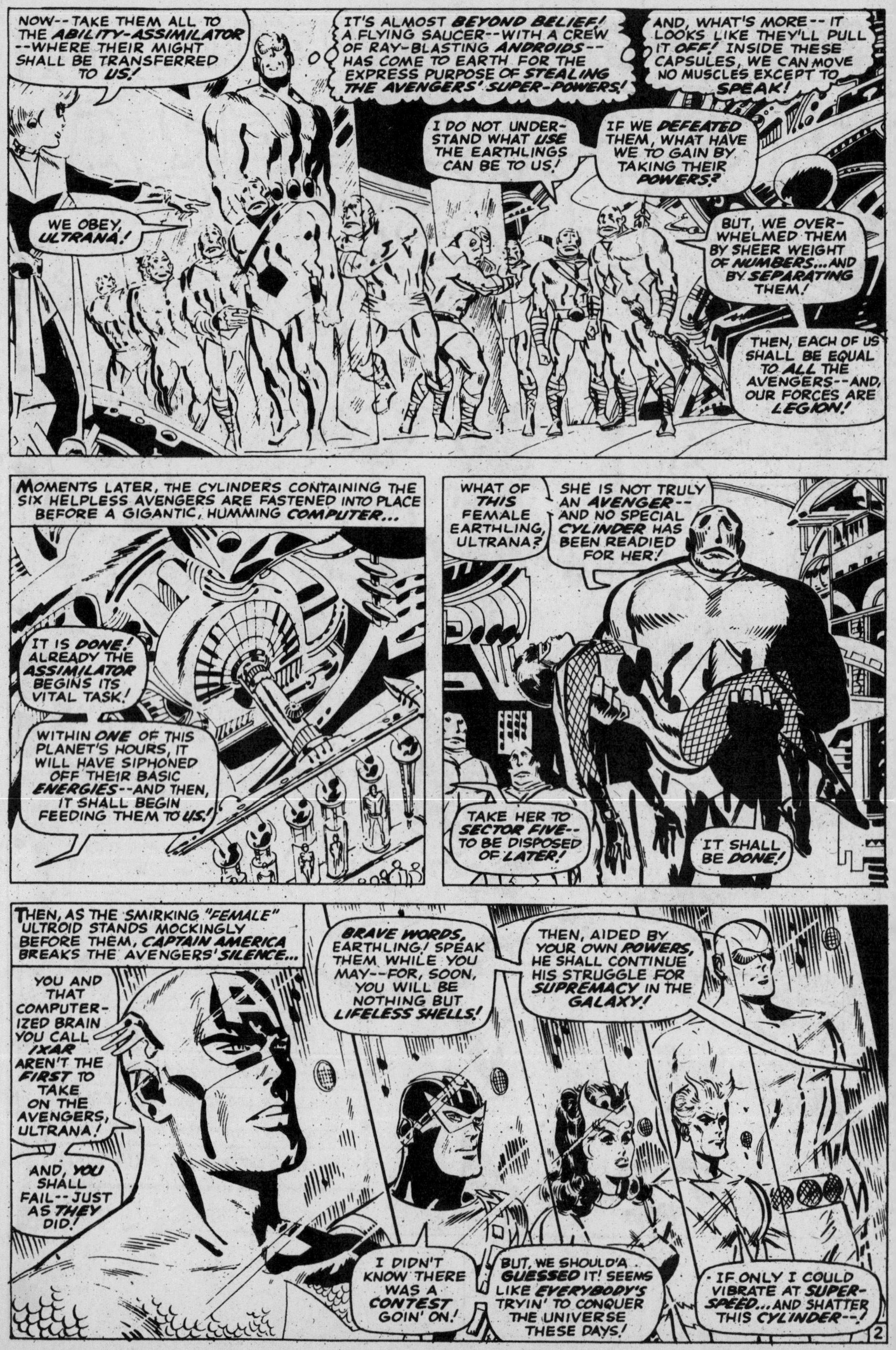
NOW--TAKE THEM ALL TO THE ABILITY-ASSIMILATOR--WHERE THEIR MIGHT SHALL BE TRANSFERRED TO US!
WE OBEY, ULTRANA!
IT'S ALMOST BEYOND BELIEF! A FLYING SAUCER--WITH A CREW OF RAY-BLASTING ANDROIDS--HAS COME TO EARTH FOR THE EXPRESS PURPOSE OF STEALING THE AVENGERS' SUPER-POWERS!
AND, WHAT'S MORE--IT LOOKS LIKE THEY'LL PULL IT OFF! INSIDE THESE CAPSULES, WE CAN MOVE NO MUSCLES EXCEPT TO SPEAK!
I DO NOT UNDERSTAND WHAT USE THE EARTHLINGS CAN BE TO US!
IF WE DEFEATED THEM, WHAT HAVE WE TO GAIN BY TAKING THEIR POWERS?
BUT, WE OVERWHELMED THEM BY SHEER WEIGHT OF NUMBERS...AND BY SEPARATING THEM!
THEN, EACH OF US SHALL BE EQUAL TO ALL THE AVENGERS--AND, OUR FORCES ARE LEGION!
MOMENTS LATER, THE CYLINDERS CONTAINING THE SIX HELPLESS AVENGERS ARE FASTENED INTO PLACE BEFORE A GIGANTIC, HUMMING COMPUTER...
IT IS DONE! ALREADY THE ASSIMILATOR BEGINS ITS VITAL TASK!
WITHIN ONE OF THIS PLANET'S HOURS, IT WILL HAVE SIPHONED OFF THEIR BASIC ENERGIES--AND THEN, IT SHALL BEGIN FEEDING THEM TO US!
WHAT OF THIS FEMALE EARTHLING, ULTRANA?
SHE IS NOT TRULY AN AVENGER--AND NO SPECIAL CYLINDER HAS BEEN READIED FOR HER!
TAKE HER TO SECTOR FIVE--TO BE DISPOSED OF LATER!
IT SHALL BE DONE!
THEN, AS THE SMIRKING "FEMALE" ULTROID STANDS MOCKINGLY BEFORE THEM, CAPTAIN AMERICA BREAKS THE AVENGERS' SILENCE...
YOU AND THAT COMPUTERIZED BRAIN YOU CALL IXAR AREN'T THE FIRST TO TAKE ON THE AVENGERS, ULTRANA!
AND, YOU SHALL FAIL--JUST AS THEY DID!
BRAVE WORDS, EARTHLING! SPEAK THEM WHILE YOU MAY--FOR, SOON, YOU WILL BE NOTHING BUT LIFELESS SHELLS!
THEN, AIDED BY YOUR OWN POWERS, HE SHALL CONTINUE HIS STRUGGLE FOR SUPREMACY IN THE GALAXY!
I DIDN'T KNOW THERE WAS A CONTEST GOIN' ON!
BUT, WE SHOULD'A GUESSED IT! SEEMS LIKE EVERYBODY'S TRYIN' TO CONQUER THE UNIVERSE THESE DAYS!
IF ONLY I COULD VIBRATE AT SUPER-SPEED...AND SHATTER THIS CYLINDER--!
2

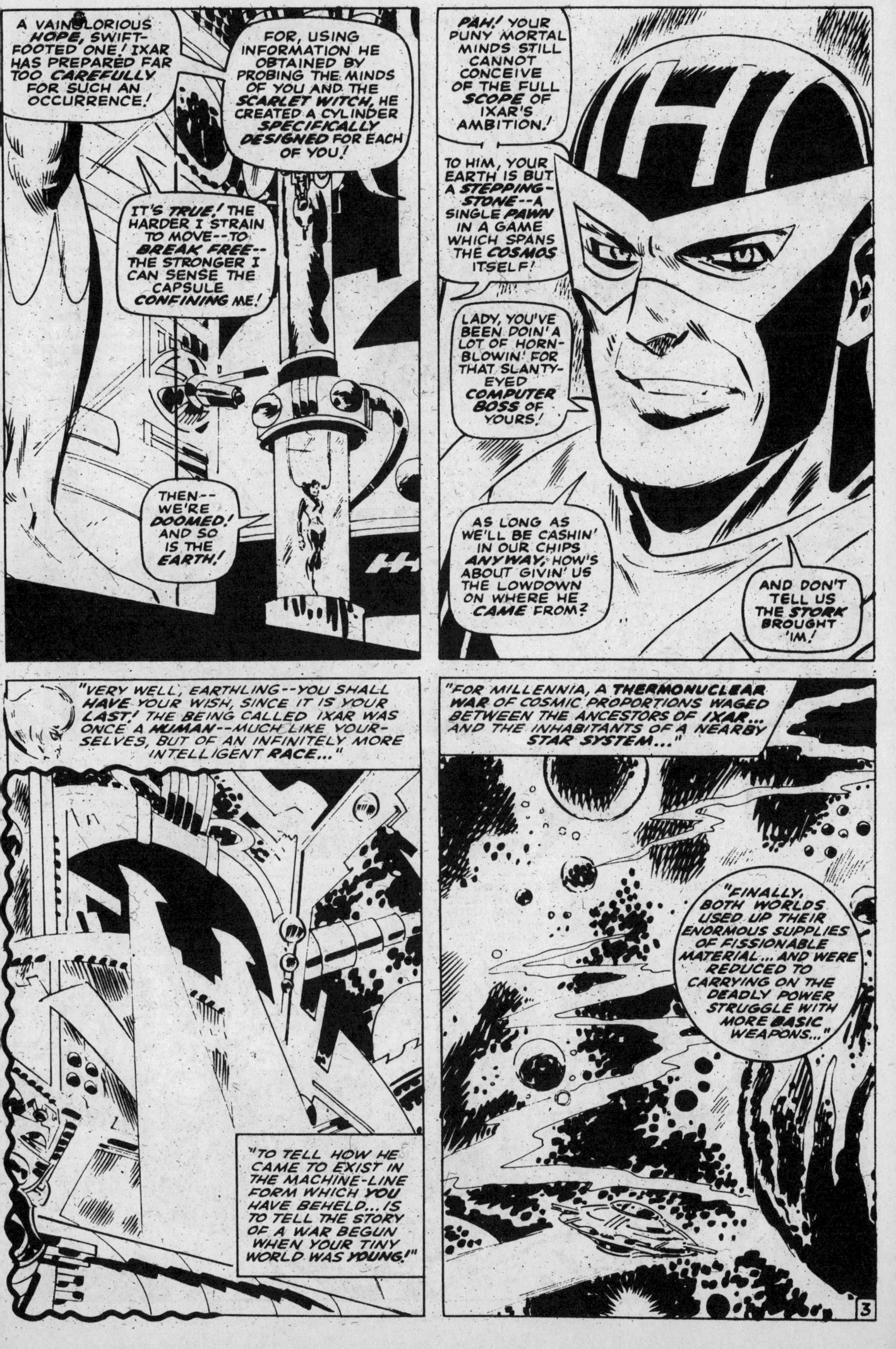
A VAINGLORIOUS HOPE, SWIFT-FOOTED ONE! IXAR HAS PREPARED FAR TOO CAREFULLY FOR SUCH AN OCCURRENCE!
FOR, USING INFORMATION HE OBTAINED BY PROBING THE MINDS OF YOU AND THE SCARLET WITCH, HE CREATED A CYLINDER SPECIFICALLY DESIGNED FOR EACH OF YOU!
IT'S TRUE! THE HARDER I STRAIN TO MOVE--TO BREAK FREE--THE STRONGER I CAN SENSE THE CAPSULE CONFINING ME!
THEN--WE'RE DOOMED! AND SO IS THE EARTH!
PAH! YOUR PUNY MORTAL MINDS STILL CANNOT CONCEIVE OF THE FULL SCOPE OF IXAR'S AMBITION!
TO HIM, YOUR EARTH IS BUT A STEPPING-STONE--A SINGLE PAWN IN A GAME WHICH SPANS THE COSMOS ITSELF!
LADY, YOU'VE BEEN DOIN' A LOT OF HORN-BLOWIN' FOR THAT SLANTY-EYED COMPUTER BOSS OF YOURS!
AS LONG AS WE'LL BE CASHIN' IN OUR CHIPS ANYWAY, HOW'S ABOUT GIVIN' US THE LOWDOWN ON WHERE HE CAME FROM?
AND DON'T TELL US THE STORK BROUGHT 'IM!
"VERY WELL, EARTHLING--YOU SHALL HAVE YOUR WISH, SINCE IT IS YOUR LAST! THE BEING CALLED IXAR WAS ONCE A HUMAN--MUCH LIKE YOURSELVES, BUT OF AN INFINITELY MORE INTELLIGENT RACE..."
"TO TELL HOW HE CAME TO EXIST IN THE MACHINE-LINE FORM WHICH YOU HAVE BEHELD... IS TO TELL THE STORY OF A WAR BEGUN WHEN YOUR TINY WORLD WAS YOUNG!"
"FOR MILLENNIA, A THERMONUCLEAR WAR OF COSMIC PROPORTIONS WAGED BETWEEN THE ANCESTORS OF IXAR... AND THE INHABITANTS OF A NEARBY STAR SYSTEM..."
"FINALLY, BOTH WORLDS USED UP THEIR ENORMOUS SUPPLIES OF FISSIONABLE MATERIAL... AND WERE REDUCED TO CARRYING ON THE DEADLY POWER STRUGGLE WITH MORE BASIC WEAPONS..."
3

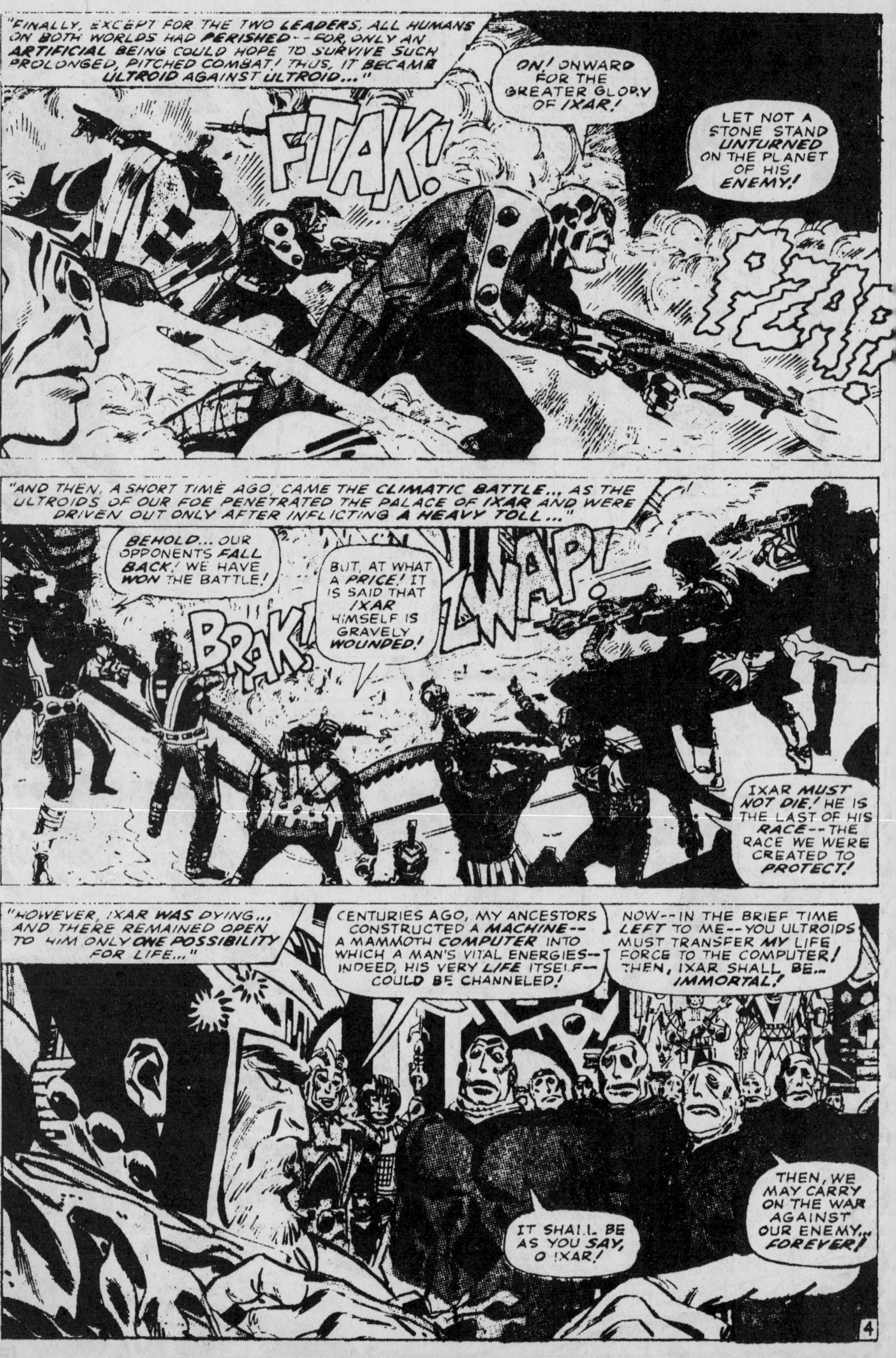
"FINALLY, EXCEPT FOR THE TWO LEADERS, ALL HUMANS ON BOTH WORLDS HAD PERISHED--FOR, ONLY AN ARTIFICIAL BEING COULD HOPE TO SURVIVE SUCH PROLONGED, PITCHED COMBAT! THUS, IT BECAME ULTROID AGAINST ULTROID..."
ON! ONWARD FOR THE GREATER GLORY OF IXAR!
LET NOT A STONE STAND UNTURNED ON THE PLANET OF HIS ENEMY!
FTAK!
"AND THEN, A SHORT TIME AGO, CAME THE CLIMATIC BATTLE... AS THE ULTROIDS OF OUR FOE PENETRATED THE PALACE OF IXAR AND WERE DRIVEN OUT ONLY AFTER INFLICTING A HEAVY TOLL..."
BEHOLD... OUR OPPONENTS FALL BACK! WE HAVE WON THE BATTLE!
BUT, AT WHAT A PRICE! IT IS SAID THAT IXAR HIMSELF IS GRAVELY WOUNDED!
IXAR MUST NOT DIE! HE IS THE LAST OF HIS RACE--THE RACE WE WERE CREATED TO PROTECT!
"HOWEVER, IXAR WAS DYING... AND THERE REMAINED OPEN TO HIM ONLY ONE POSSIBILITY FOR LIFE..."
CENTURIES AGO, MY ANCESTORS CONSTRUCTED A MACHINE--A MAMMOTH COMPUTER INTO WHICH A MAN'S VITAL ENERGIES--INDEED, HIS VERY LIFE ITSELF--COULD BE CHANNELED!
NOW--IN THE BRIEF TIME LEFT TO ME--YOU ULTROIDS MUST TRANSFER MY LIFE FORCE TO THE COMPUTER! THEN, IXAR SHALL BE... IMMORTAL!
IT SHALL BE AS YOU SAY, O IXAR!
THEN, WE MAY CARRY ON THE WAR AGAINST OUR ENEMY... FOREVER!
4

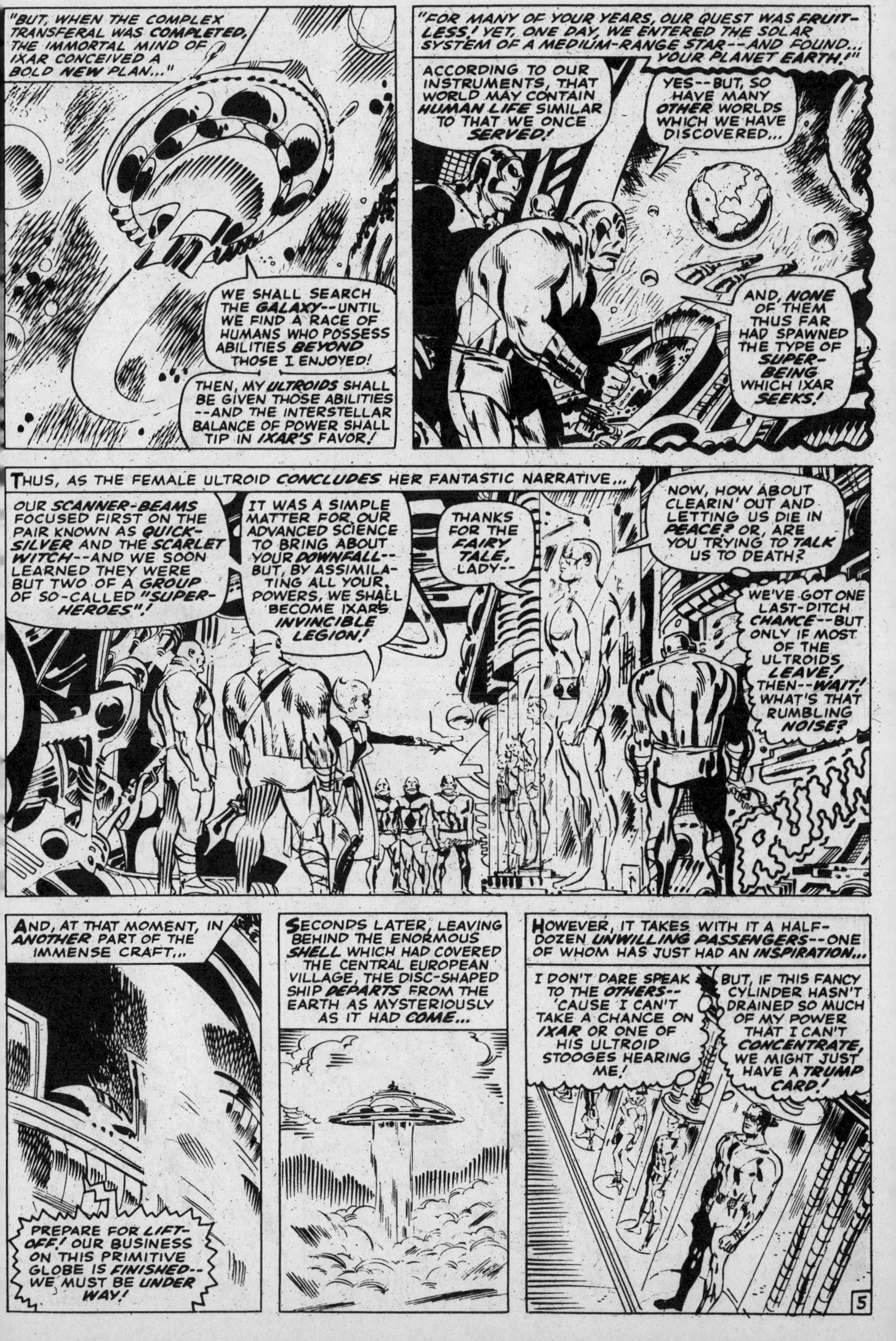
"BUT, WHEN THE COMPLEX TRANSFERAL WAS COMPLETED, THE IMMORTAL MIND OF IXAR CONCEIVED A BOLD NEW PLAN..."
WE SHALL SEARCH THE GALAXY--UNTIL WE FIND A RACE OF HUMANS WHO POSSESS ABILITIES BEYOND THOSE I ENJOYED!
THEN, MY ULTROIDS SHALL BE GIVEN THOSE ABILITIES --AND THE INTERSTELLAR BALANCE OF POWER SHALL TIP IN IXAR'S FAVOR!
"FOR MANY OF YOUR YEARS, OUR QUEST WAS FRUITLESS! YET, ONE DAY, WE ENTERED THE SOLAR SYSTEM OF A MEDIUM-RANGE STAR--AND FOUND... YOUR PLANET EARTH!"
ACCORDING TO OUR INSTRUMENTS, THAT WORLD MAY CONTAIN HUMAN LIFE SIMILAR TO THAT WE ONCE SERVED!
YES--BUT, SO HAVE MANY OTHER WORLDS WHICH WE HAVE DISCOVERED...
AND, NONE OF THEM THUS FAR HAD SPAWNED THE TYPE OF SUPER-BEING WHICH IXAR SEEKS!
THUS, AS THE FEMALE ULTROID CONCLUDES HER FANTASTIC NARRATIVE...
OUR SCANNER-BEAMS FOCUSED FIRST ON THE PAIR KNOWN AS QUICKSILVER AND THE SCARLET WITCH--AND WE SOON LEARNED THEY WERE BUT TWO OF A GROUP OF SO-CALLED "SUPER-HEROES"!
IT WAS A SIMPLE MATTER FOR OUR ADVANCED SCIENCE TO BRING ABOUT YOUR DOWNFALL--BUT, BY ASSIMILATING ALL YOUR POWERS, WE SHALL BECOME IXAR'S INVINCIBLE LEGION!
THANKS FOR THE FAIRY TALE, LADY--
NOW, HOW ABOUT CLEARIN' OUT AND LETTING US DIE IN PEACE? OR, ARE YOU TRYING TO TALK US TO DEATH?
WE'VE GOT ONE LAST-DITCH CHANCE--BUT ONLY IF MOST OF THE ULTROIDS LEAVE! THEN--WAIT! WHAT'S THAT RUMBLING NOISE?
AND, AT THAT MOMENT, IN ANOTHER PART OF THE IMMENSE CRAFT...
PREPARE FOR LIFT-OFF! OUR BUSINESS ON THIS PRIMITIVE GLOBE IS FINISHED--WE MUST BE UNDER WAY!
SECONDS LATER, LEAVING BEHIND THE ENORMOUS SHELL WHICH HAD COVERED THE CENTRAL EUROPEAN VILLAGE, THE DISC-SHAPED SHIP DEPARTS FROM THE EARTH AS MYSTERIOUSLY AS IT HAD COME...
HOWEVER, IT TAKES WITH IT A HALF-DOZEN UNWILLING PASSENGERS--ONE OF WHOM HAS JUST HAD AN INSPIRATION...
I DON'T DARE SPEAK TO THE OTHERS--'CAUSE I CAN'T TAKE A CHANCE ON IXAR OR ONE OF HIS ULTROID STOOGES HEARING ME!
BUT, IF THIS FANCY CYLINDER HASN'T DRAINED SO MUCH OF MY POWER THAT I CAN'T CONCENTRATE, WE MIGHT JUST HAVE A TRUMP CARD!
5

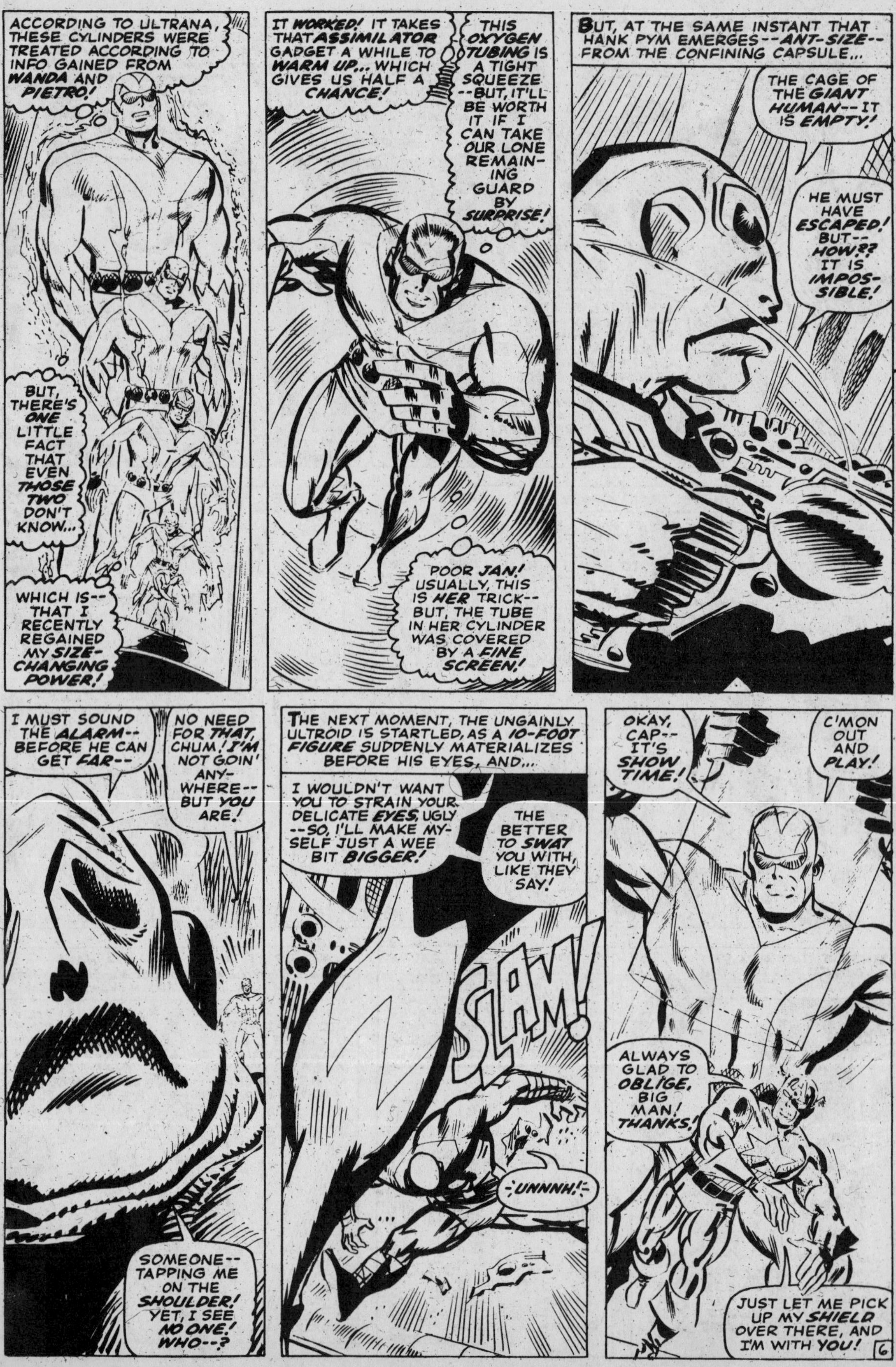
ACCORDING TO ULTRANA, THESE CYLINDERS WERE TREATED ACCORDING TO INFO GAINED FROM WANDA AND PIETRO!
BUT, THERE'S ONE LITTLE FACT THAT EVEN THOSE TWO DON'T KNOW...
WHICH IS-- THAT I RECENTLY REGAINED MY SIZE-CHANGING POWER!
IT WORKED! IT TAKES THAT ASSIMILATOR GADGET A WHILE TO WARM UP... WHICH GIVES US HALF A CHANCE!
THIS OXYGEN TUBING IS A TIGHT SQUEEZE --BUT, IT'LL BE WORTH IT IF I CAN TAKE OUR LONE REMAINING GUARD BY SURPRISE!
POOR JAN! USUALLY, THIS IS HER TRICK-- BUT, THE TUBE IN HER CYLINDER WAS COVERED BY A FINE SCREEN!
BUT, AT THE SAME INSTANT THAT HANK PYM EMERGES--ANT-SIZE-- FROM THE CONFINING CAPSULE...
THE CAGE OF THE GIANT HUMAN-- IT IS EMPTY!
HE MUST HAVE ESCAPED! BUT-- HOW?? IT IS IMPOSSIBLE!
I MUST SOUND THE ALARM-- BEFORE HE CAN GET FAR--
NO NEED FOR THAT, CHUM! I'M NOT GOIN' ANYWHERE-- BUT YOU ARE!
SOMEONE-- TAPPING ME ON THE SHOULDER! YET, I SEE NO ONE! WHO--?
THE NEXT MOMENT, THE UNGAINLY ULTROID IS STARTLED, AS A 10-FOOT FIGURE SUDDENLY MATERIALIZES BEFORE HIS EYES, AND...
I WOULDN'T WANT YOU TO STRAIN YOUR DELICATE EYES, UGLY --SO, I'LL MAKE MYSELF JUST A WEE BIT BIGGER!
THE BETTER TO SWAT YOU WITH, LIKE THEY SAY!
SLAM!
UNNNH!
OKAY, CAP-- IT'S SHOW TIME!
C'MON OUT AND PLAY!
ALWAYS GLAD TO OBLIGE, BIG MAN! THANKS!
JUST LET ME PICK UP MY SHIELD OVER THERE, AND I'M WITH YOU!
6

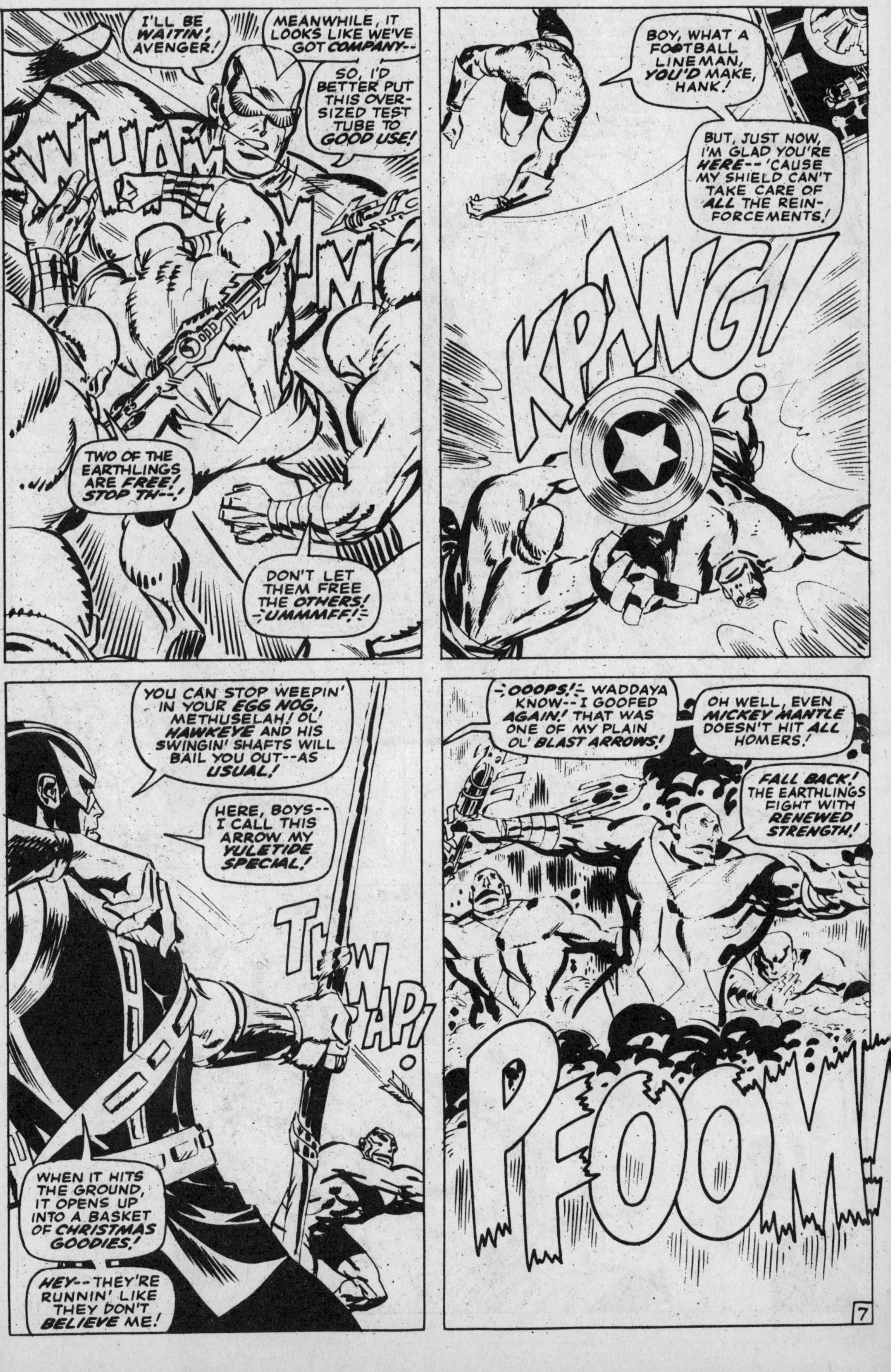
I'LL BE WAITIN', AVENGER!
MEANWHILE, IT LOOKS LIKE WE'VE GOT COMPANY--
SO, I'D BETTER PUT THIS OVER-SIZED TEST TUBE TO GOOD USE!
WHAM
TWO OF THE EARTHLINGS ARE FREE! STOP TH--!
DON'T LET THEM FREE THE OTHERS! -UMMMFF!-
BOY, WHAT A FOOTBALL LINEMAN, YOU'D MAKE, HANK!
BUT, JUST NOW, I'M GLAD YOU'RE HERE--'CAUSE MY SHIELD CAN'T TAKE CARE OF ALL THE REIN-FORCEMENTS!
KPANG!
YOU CAN STOP WEEPIN' IN YOUR EGG NOG, METHUSELAH! OL' HAWKEYE AND HIS SWINGIN' SHAFTS WILL BAIL YOU OUT--AS USUAL!
HERE, BOYS-- I CALL THIS ARROW MY YULETIDE SPECIAL!
THWAP!
WHEN IT HITS THE GROUND, IT OPENS UP INTO A BASKET OF CHRISTMAS GOODIES!
HEY--THEY'RE RUNNIN' LIKE THEY DON'T BELIEVE ME!
-OOOPS!- WADDAYA KNOW--I GOOFED AGAIN! THAT WAS ONE OF MY PLAIN OL' BLAST ARROWS!
OH WELL, EVEN MICKEY MANTLE DOESN'T HIT ALL HOMERS!
FALL BACK! THE EARTHLINGS FIGHT WITH RENEWED STRENGTH!
PFOOM!

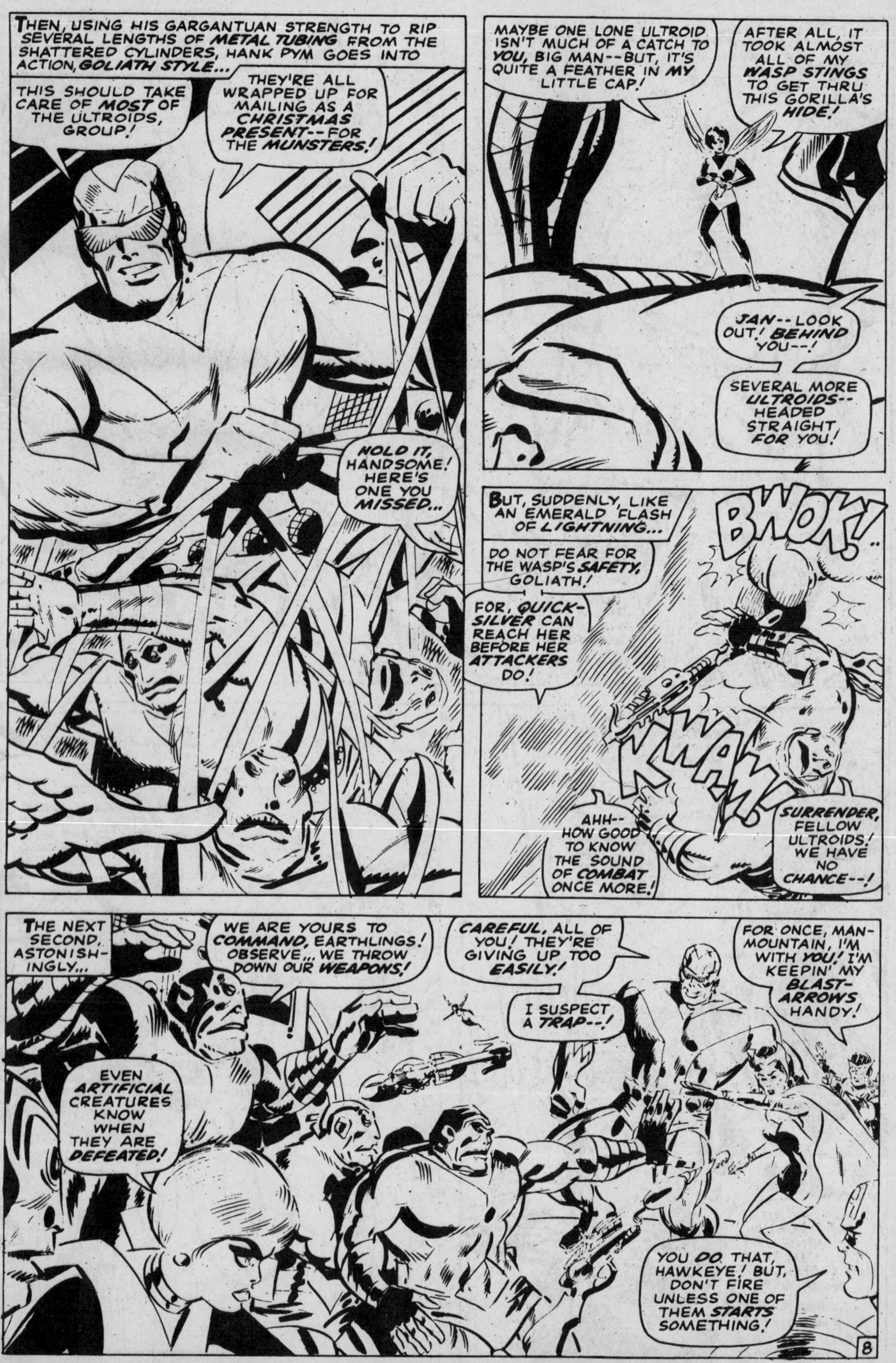
THEN, USING HIS GARGANTUAN STRENGTH TO RIP SEVERAL LENGTHS OF METAL TUBING FROM THE SHATTERED CYLINDERS, HANK PYM GOES INTO ACTION, GOLIATH STYLE...
THIS SHOULD TAKE CARE OF MOST OF THE ULTROIDS, GROUP!
THEY'RE ALL WRAPPED UP FOR MAILING AS A CHRISTMAS PRESENT--FOR THE MUNSTERS!
HOLD IT, HANDSOME! HERE'S ONE YOU MISSED...
MAYBE ONE LONE ULTROID ISN'T MUCH OF A CATCH TO YOU, BIG MAN--BUT, IT'S QUITE A FEATHER IN MY LITTLE CAP!
AFTER ALL, IT TOOK ALMOST ALL OF MY WASP STINGS TO GET THRU THIS GORILLA'S HIDE!
JAN--LOOK OUT! BEHIND YOU--!
SEVERAL MORE ULTROIDS--HEADED STRAIGHT FOR YOU!
BUT, SUDDENLY, LIKE AN EMERALD FLASH OF LIGHTNING...
DO NOT FEAR FOR THE WASP'S SAFETY, GOLIATH!
FOR, QUICKSILVER CAN REACH HER BEFORE HER ATTACKERS DO!
BWOK!
KWAM!
AHH--HOW GOOD TO KNOW THE SOUND OF COMBAT ONCE MORE!
SURRENDER, FELLOW ULTROIDS! WE HAVE NO CHANCE--!
THE NEXT SECOND, ASTONISHINGLY...
WE ARE YOURS TO COMMAND, EARTHLINGS! OBSERVE... WE THROW DOWN OUR WEAPONS!
EVEN ARTIFICIAL CREATURES KNOW WHEN THEY ARE DEFEATED!
CAREFUL, ALL OF YOU! THEY'RE GIVING UP TOO EASILY!
I SUSPECT A TRAP--!
FOR ONCE, MAN-MOUNTAIN, I'M WITH YOU! I'M KEEPIN' MY BLAST-ARROWS HANDY!
YOU DO THAT, HAWKEYE! BUT, DON'T FIRE UNLESS ONE OF THEM STARTS SOMETHING!

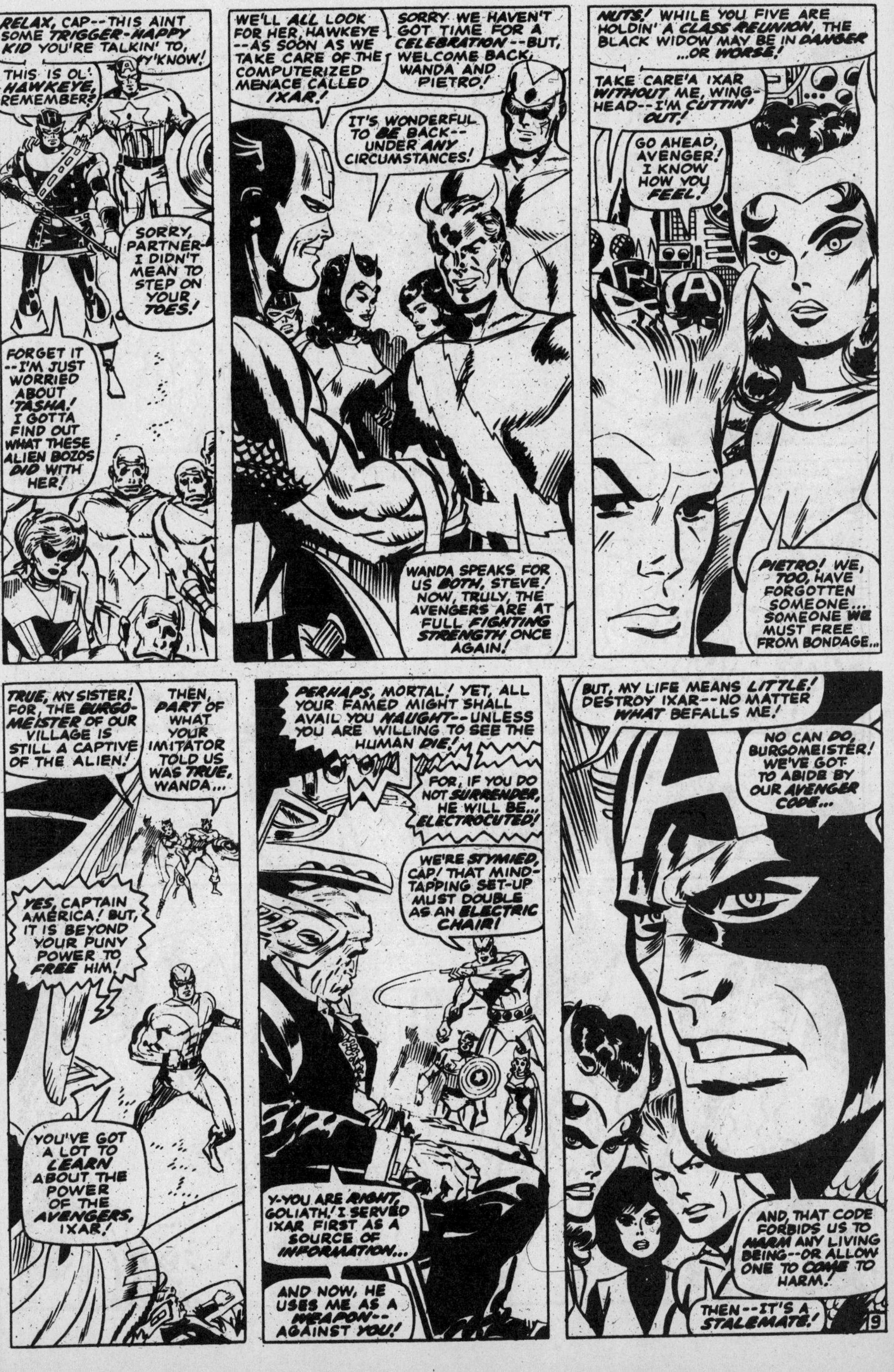
RELAX, CAP--THIS AINT SOME TRIGGER-HAPPY KID YOU'RE TALKIN' TO, Y'KNOW!
THIS IS OL' HAWKEYE, REMEMBER?
SORRY, PARTNER--I DIDN'T MEAN TO STEP ON YOUR TOES!
FORGET IT--I'M JUST WORRIED ABOUT 'TASHA! I GOTTA FIND OUT WHAT THESE ALIEN BOZOS DID WITH HER!
WE'LL ALL LOOK FOR HER, HAWKEYE--AS SOON AS WE TAKE CARE OF THE COMPUTERIZED MENACE CALLED IXAR!
SORRY WE HAVEN'T GOT TIME FOR A CELEBRATION--BUT, WELCOME BACK, WANDA AND PIETRO!
IT'S WONDERFUL TO BE BACK--UNDER ANY CIRCUMSTANCES!
WANDA SPEAKS FOR US BOTH, STEVE! NOW, TRULY, THE AVENGERS ARE AT FULL FIGHTING STRENGTH ONCE AGAIN!
NUTS! WHILE YOU FIVE ARE HOLDIN' A CLASS REUNION, THE BLACK WIDOW MAY BE IN DANGER ...OR WORSE!
TAKE CARE'A IXAR WITHOUT ME, WING-HEAD--I'M CUTTIN' OUT!
GO AHEAD, AVENGER! I KNOW HOW YOU FEEL!
PIETRO! WE, TOO, HAVE FORGOTTEN SOMEONE... SOMEONE WE MUST FREE FROM BONDAGE...
TRUE, MY SISTER! FOR, THE BURGO-MEISTER OF OUR VILLAGE IS STILL A CAPTIVE OF THE ALIEN!
THEN, PART OF WHAT YOUR IMITATOR TOLD US WAS TRUE, WANDA...
YES, CAPTAIN AMERICA! BUT, IT IS BEYOND YOUR PUNY POWER TO FREE HIM!
YOU'VE GOT A LOT TO LEARN ABOUT THE POWER OF THE AVENGERS, IXAR!
PERHAPS, MORTAL! YET, ALL YOUR FAMED MIGHT SHALL AVAIL YOU NAUGHT--UNLESS YOU ARE WILLING TO SEE THE HUMAN DIE!
FOR, IF YOU DO NOT SURRENDER, HE WILL BE... ELECTROCUTED!
WE'RE STYMIED, CAP! THAT MIND-TAPPING SET-UP MUST DOUBLE AS AN ELECTRIC CHAIR!
Y-YOU ARE RIGHT, GOLIATH! I SERVED IXAR FIRST AS A SOURCE OF INFORMATION...
AND NOW, HE USES ME AS A WEAPON--AGAINST YOU!
BUT, MY LIFE MEANS LITTLE! DESTROY IXAR--NO MATTER WHAT BEFALLS ME!
NO CAN DO, BURGOMEISTER! WE'VE GOT TO ABIDE BY OUR AVENGER CODE...
AND, THAT CODE FORBIDS US TO HARM ANY LIVING BEING--OR ALLOW ONE TO COME TO HARM!
THEN--IT'S A STALEMATE!

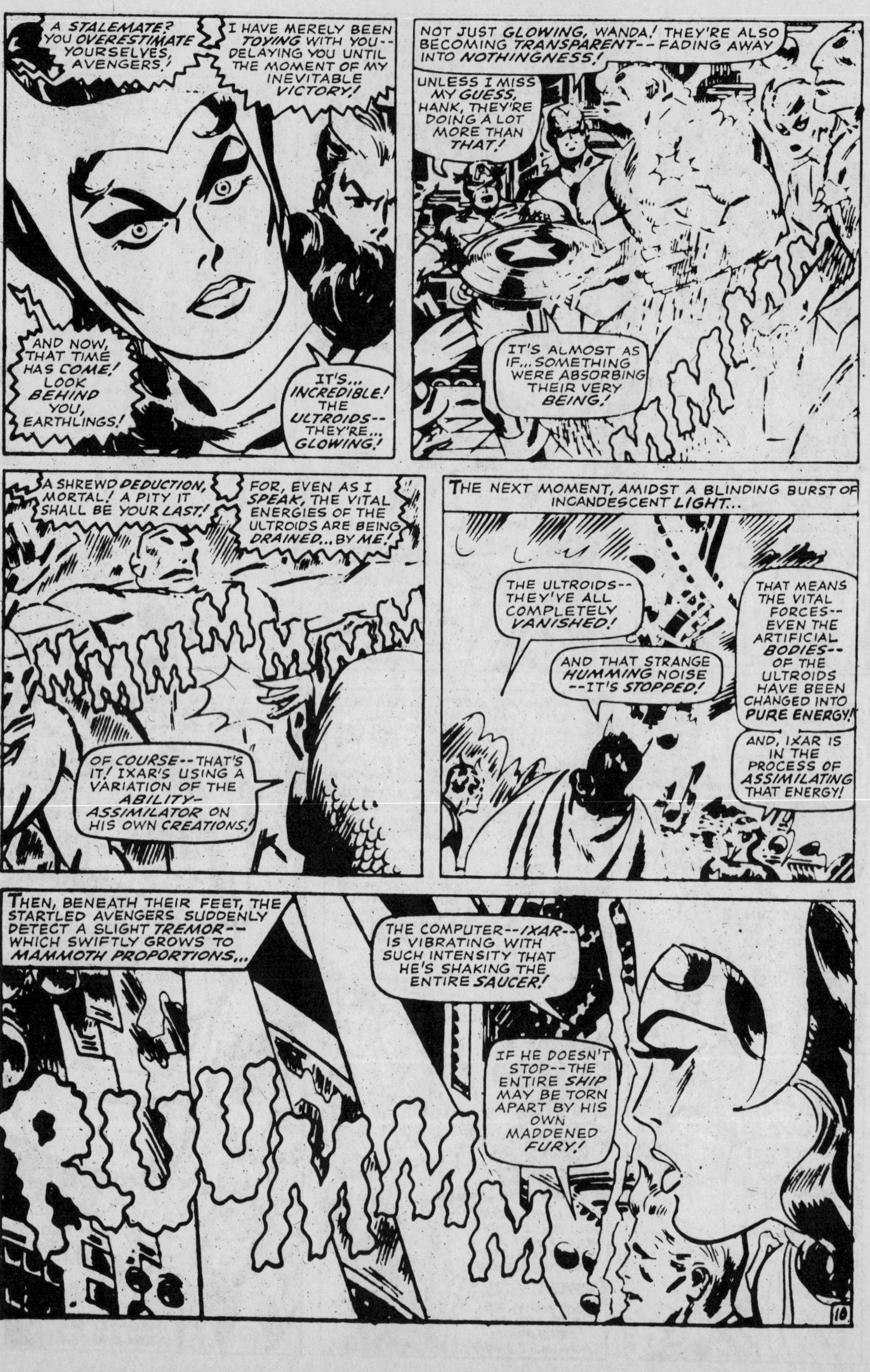
A STALEMATE? YOU OVERESTIMATE YOURSELVES, AVENGERS!
I HAVE MERELY BEEN TOYING WITH YOU-- DELAYING YOU UNTIL THE MOMENT OF MY INEVITABLE VICTORY!
AND NOW, THAT TIME HAS COME! LOOK BEHIND YOU, EARTHLINGS!
IT'S... INCREDIBLE! THE ULTROIDS-- THEY'RE... GLOWING!
NOT JUST GLOWING, WANDA! THEY'RE ALSO BECOMING TRANSPARENT-- FADING AWAY INTO NOTHINGNESS!
UNLESS I MISS MY GUESS, HANK, THEY'RE DOING A LOT MORE THAN THAT!
IT'S ALMOST AS IF... SOMETHING WERE ABSORBING THEIR VERY BEING!
A SHREWD DEDUCTION, MORTAL! A PITY IT SHALL BE YOUR LAST!
FOR, EVEN AS I SPEAK, THE VITAL ENERGIES OF THE ULTROIDS ARE BEING DRAINED... BY ME!
MMMMMMMMM
OF COURSE-- THAT'S IT! IXAR'S USING A VARIATION OF THE ABILITY-ASSIMILATOR ON HIS OWN CREATIONS!
THE NEXT MOMENT, AMIDST A BLINDING BURST OF INCANDESCENT LIGHT...
THE ULTROIDS-- THEY'VE ALL COMPLETELY VANISHED!
AND THAT STRANGE HUMMING NOISE --IT'S STOPPED!
THAT MEANS THE VITAL FORCES-- EVEN THE ARTIFICIAL BODIES-- OF THE ULTROIDS HAVE BEEN CHANGED INTO PURE ENERGY!
AND, IXAR IS IN THE PROCESS OF ASSIMILATING THAT ENERGY!
THEN, BENEATH THEIR FEET, THE STARTLED AVENGERS SUDDENLY DETECT A SLIGHT TREMOR-- WHICH SWIFTLY GROWS TO MAMMOTH PROPORTIONS...
THE COMPUTER--IXAR-- IS VIBRATING WITH SUCH INTENSITY THAT HE'S SHAKING THE ENTIRE SAUCER!
IF HE DOESN'T STOP--THE ENTIRE SHIP MAY BE TORN APART BY HIS OWN MADDENED FURY!
RUMMM
10

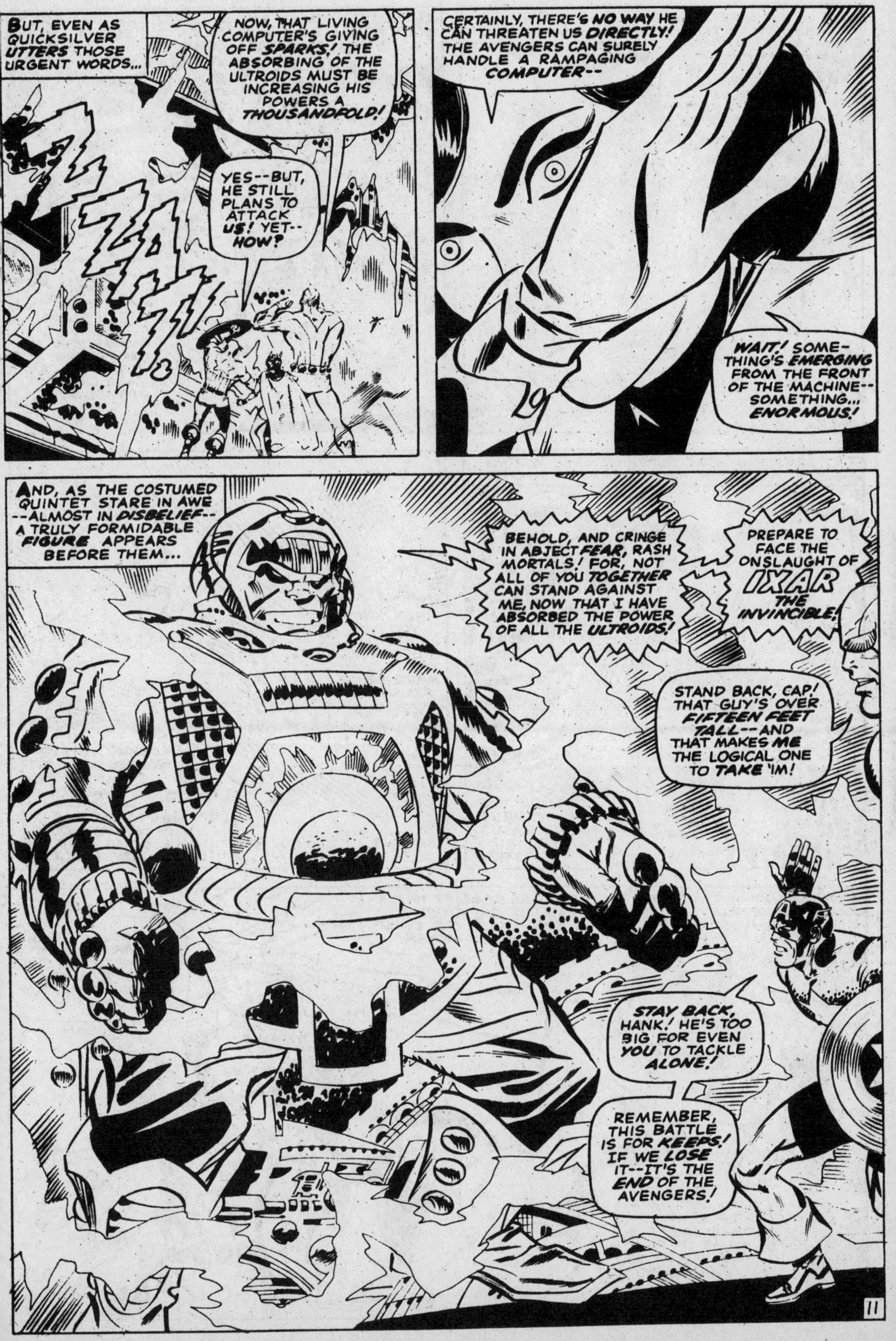
BUT, EVEN AS QUICKSILVER UTTERS THOSE URGENT WORDS...
NOW, THAT LIVING COMPUTER'S GIVING OFF SPARKS! THE ABSORBING OF THE ULTROIDS MUST BE INCREASING HIS POWERS A THOUSANDFOLD!
YES--BUT, HE STILL PLANS TO ATTACK US! YET-- HOW?
ZZATT
CERTAINLY, THERE'S NO WAY HE CAN THREATEN US DIRECTLY! THE AVENGERS CAN SURELY HANDLE A RAMPAGING COMPUTER--
WAIT! SOMETHING'S EMERGING FROM THE FRONT OF THE MACHINE-- SOMETHING... ENORMOUS!
AND, AS THE COSTUMED QUINTET STARE IN AWE --ALMOST IN DISBELIEF-- A TRULY FORMIDABLE FIGURE APPEARS BEFORE THEM...
BEHOLD, AND CRINGE IN ABJECT FEAR, RASH MORTALS! FOR, NOT ALL OF YOU TOGETHER CAN STAND AGAINST ME, NOW THAT I HAVE ABSORBED THE POWER OF ALL THE ULTROIDS!
PREPARE TO FACE THE ONSLAUGHT OF IXAR THE INVINCIBLE!
STAND BACK, CAP! THAT GUY'S OVER FIFTEEN FEET TALL--AND THAT MAKES ME THE LOGICAL ONE TO TAKE 'IM!
STAY BACK, HANK! HE'S TOO BIG FOR EVEN YOU TO TACKLE ALONE!
REMEMBER, THIS BATTLE IS FOR KEEPS! IF WE LOSE IT--IT'S THE END OF THE AVENGERS!
11

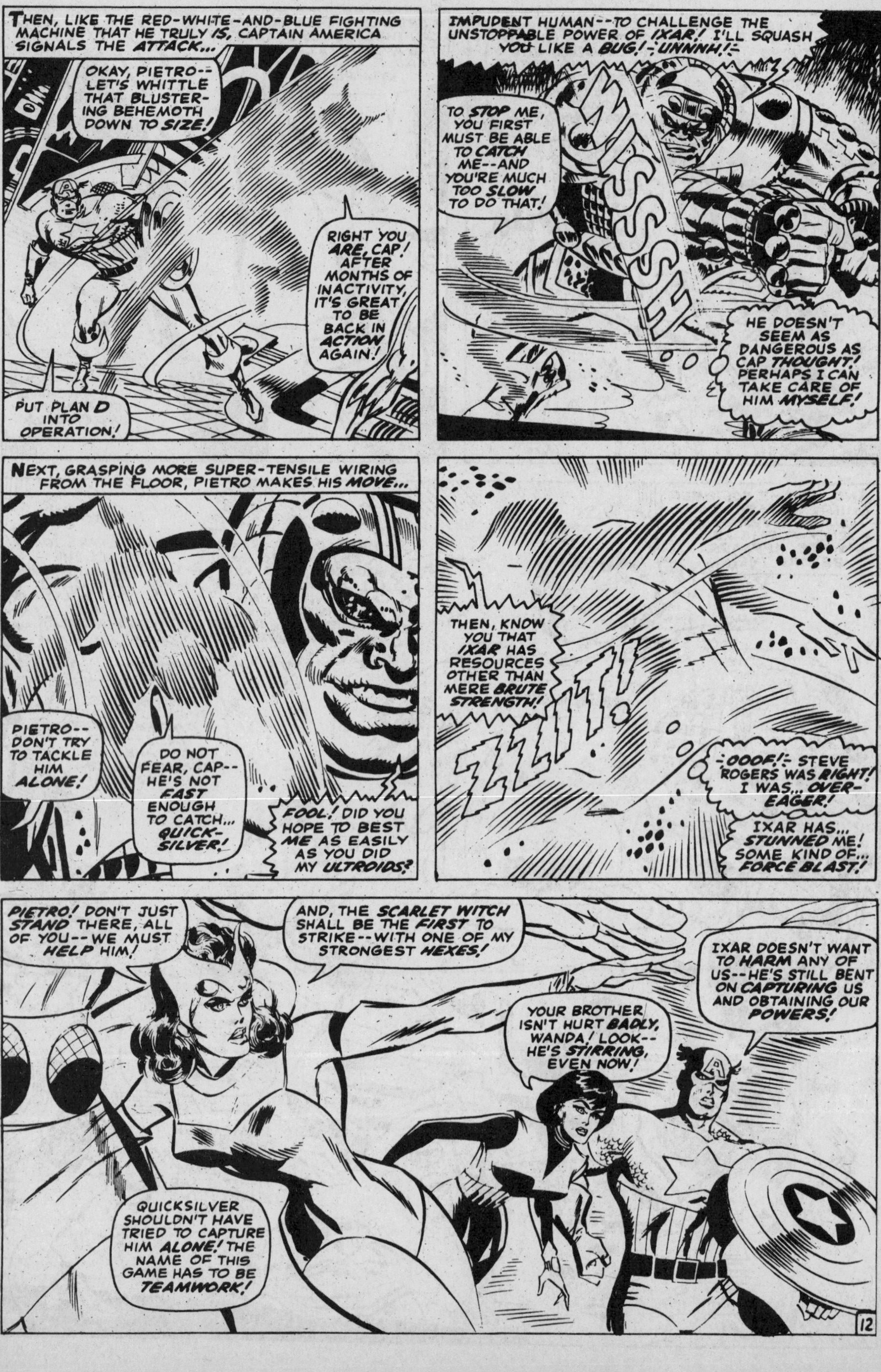

THEN, LIKE THE RED-WHITE-AND-BLUE FIGHTING MACHINE THAT HE TRULY IS, CAPTAIN AMERICA SIGNALS THE ATTACK...
OKAY, PIETRO-- LET'S WHITTLE THAT BLUSTERING BEHEMOTH DOWN TO SIZE!
RIGHT YOU ARE, CAP! AFTER MONTHS OF INACTIVITY, IT'S GREAT TO BE BACK IN ACTION AGAIN!
PUT PLAN D INTO OPERATION!
IMPUDENT HUMAN--TO CHALLENGE THE UNSTOPPABLE POWER OF IXAR! I'LL SQUASH YOU LIKE A BUG! -UNNNH!-
TO STOP ME, YOU FIRST MUST BE ABLE TO CATCH ME--AND YOU'RE MUCH TOO SLOW TO DO THAT!
WHISSH
HE DOESN'T SEEM AS DANGEROUS AS CAP THOUGHT! PERHAPS I CAN TAKE CARE OF HIM MYSELF!
NEXT, GRASPING MORE SUPER-TENSILE WIRING FROM THE FLOOR, PIETRO MAKES HIS MOVE...
PIETRO-- DON'T TRY TO TACKLE HIM ALONE!
DO NOT FEAR, CAP-- HE'S NOT FAST ENOUGH TO CATCH... QUICKSILVER!
FOOL! DID YOU HOPE TO BEST ME AS EASILY AS YOU DID MY ULTROIDS?
THEN, KNOW YOU THAT IXAR HAS RESOURCES OTHER THAN MERE BRUTE STRENGTH!
ZZZIT!
-OOOF!- STEVE ROGERS WAS RIGHT! I WAS... OVER-EAGER!
IXAR HAS... STUNNED ME! SOME KIND OF... FORCE BLAST!
PIETRO! DON'T JUST STAND THERE, ALL OF YOU--WE MUST HELP HIM!
AND, THE SCARLET WITCH SHALL BE THE FIRST TO STRIKE--WITH ONE OF MY STRONGEST HEXES!
IXAR DOESN'T WANT TO HARM ANY OF US--HE'S STILL BENT ON CAPTURING US AND OBTAINING OUR POWERS!
YOUR BROTHER ISN'T HURT BADLY, WANDA! LOOK-- HE'S STIRRING, EVEN NOW!
QUICKSILVER SHOULDN'T HAVE TRIED TO CAPTURE HIM ALONE! THE NAME OF THIS GAME HAS TO BE TEAMWORK!

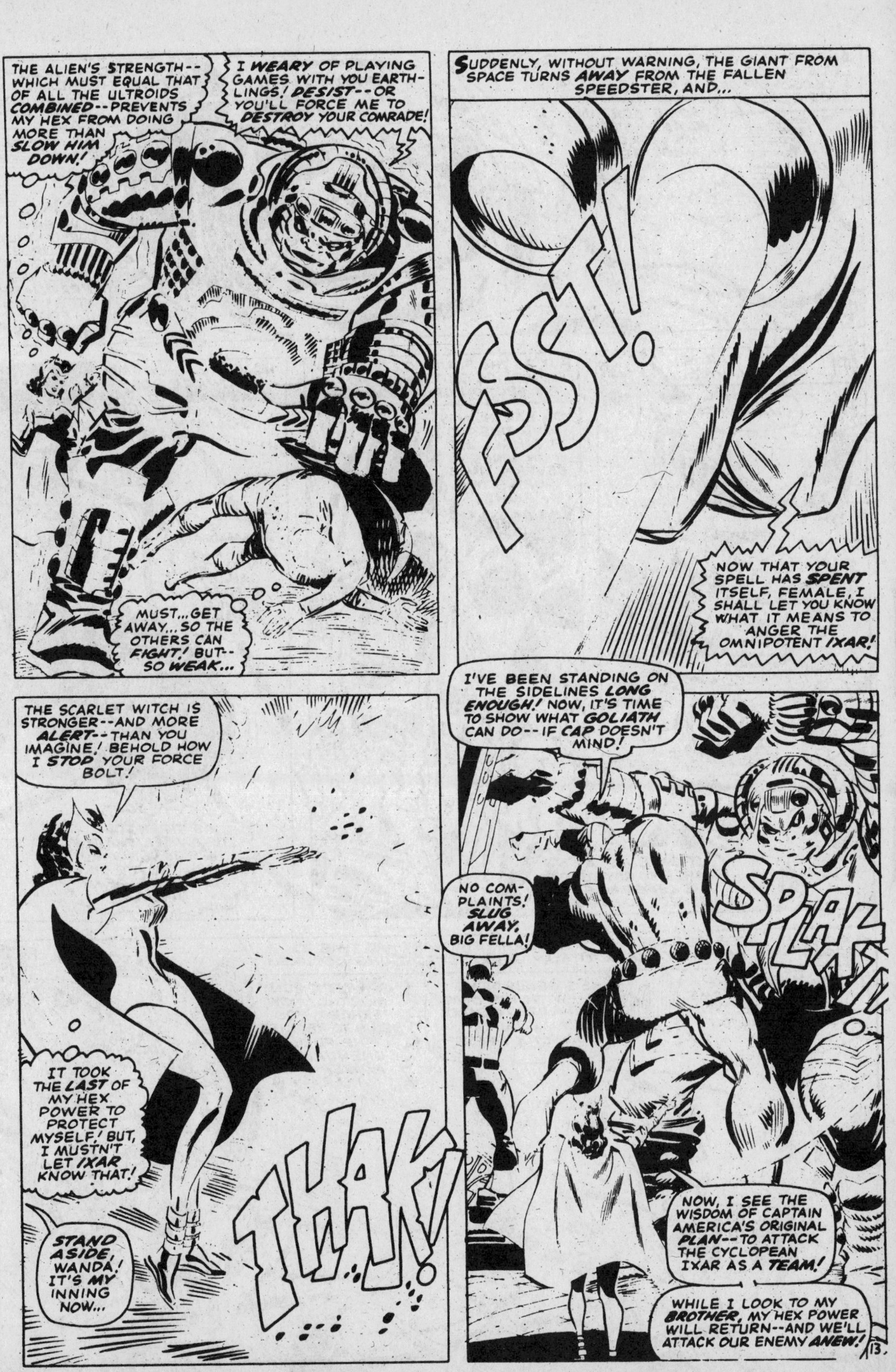
THE ALIEN'S STRENGTH--WHICH MUST EQUAL THAT OF ALL THE ULTROIDS COMBINED--PREVENTS MY HEX FROM DOING MORE THAN SLOW HIM DOWN!
I WEARY OF PLAYING GAMES WITH YOU EARTHLINGS! DESIST--OR YOU'LL FORCE ME TO DESTROY YOUR COMRADE!
MUST...GET AWAY...SO THE OTHERS CAN FIGHT! BUT--SO WEAK...
SUDDENLY, WITHOUT WARNING, THE GIANT FROM SPACE TURNS AWAY FROM THE FALLEN SPEEDSTER, AND...
FSST!
NOW THAT YOUR SPELL HAS SPENT ITSELF, FEMALE, I SHALL LET YOU KNOW WHAT IT MEANS TO ANGER THE OMNIPOTENT IXAR!
THE SCARLET WITCH IS STRONGER--AND MORE ALERT--THAN YOU IMAGINE! BEHOLD HOW I STOP YOUR FORCE BOLT!
IT TOOK THE LAST OF MY HEX POWER TO PROTECT MYSELF! BUT, I MUSTN'T LET IXAR KNOW THAT!
STAND ASIDE, WANDA! IT'S MY INNING NOW...
THAK!
I'VE BEEN STANDING ON THE SIDELINES LONG ENOUGH! NOW, IT'S TIME TO SHOW WHAT GOLIATH CAN DO--IF CAP DOESN'T MIND!
NO COMPLAINTS! SLUG AWAY, BIG FELLA!
SPLAK
NOW, I SEE THE WISDOM OF CAPTAIN AMERICA'S ORIGINAL PLAN--TO ATTACK THE CYCLOPEAN IXAR AS A TEAM!
WHILE I LOOK TO MY BROTHER, MY HEX POWER WILL RETURN--AND WE'LL ATTACK OUR ENEMY ANEW!
13

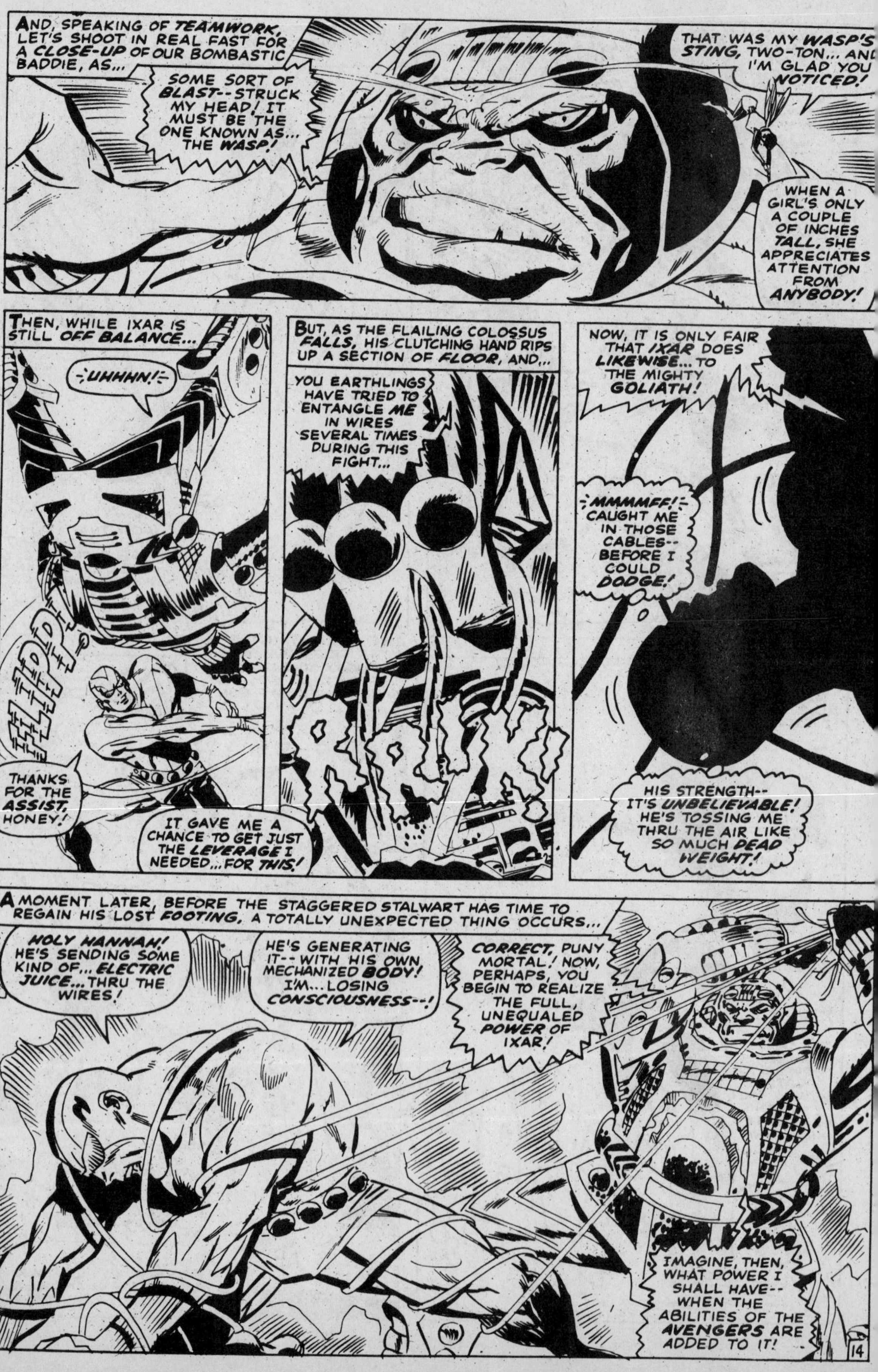

AND, SPEAKING OF TEAMWORK, LET'S SHOOT IN REAL FAST FOR A CLOSE-UP OF OUR BOMBASTIC BADDIE, AS...
SOME SORT OF BLAST-- STRUCK MY HEAD! IT MUST BE THE ONE KNOWN AS... THE WASP!
THAT WAS MY WASP'S STING, TWO-TON... AND I'M GLAD YOU NOTICED!
WHEN A GIRL'S ONLY A COUPLE OF INCHES TALL, SHE APPRECIATES ATTENTION FROM ANYBODY!
THEN, WHILE IXAR IS STILL OFF BALANCE...
UHHHN!
FLIPP
THANKS FOR THE ASSIST, HONEY!
IT GAVE ME A CHANCE TO GET JUST THE LEVERAGE I NEEDED... FOR THIS!
BUT, AS THE FLAILING COLOSSUS FALLS, HIS CLUTCHING HAND RIPS UP A SECTION OF FLOOR, AND...
YOU EARTHLINGS HAVE TRIED TO ENTANGLE ME IN WIRES SEVERAL TIMES DURING THIS FIGHT...
NOW, IT IS ONLY FAIR THAT IXAR DOES LIKEWISE... TO THE MIGHTY GOLIATH!
MMMMFF! CAUGHT ME IN THOSE CABLES-- BEFORE I COULD DODGE!
HIS STRENGTH-- IT'S UNBELIEVABLE! HE'S TOSSING ME THRU THE AIR LIKE SO MUCH DEAD WEIGHT!
A MOMENT LATER, BEFORE THE STAGGERED STALWART HAS TIME TO REGAIN HIS LOST FOOTING, A TOTALLY UNEXPECTED THING OCCURS...
HOLY HANNAH! HE'S SENDING SOME KIND OF... ELECTRIC JUICE... THRU THE WIRES!
HE'S GENERATING IT-- WITH HIS OWN MECHANIZED BODY! I'M... LOSING CONSCIOUSNESS--!
CORRECT, PUNY MORTAL! NOW, PERHAPS, YOU BEGIN TO REALIZE THE FULL, UNEQUALED POWER OF IXAR!
IMAGINE, THEN, WHAT POWER I SHALL HAVE-- WHEN THE ABILITIES OF THE AVENGERS ARE ADDED TO IT!
14

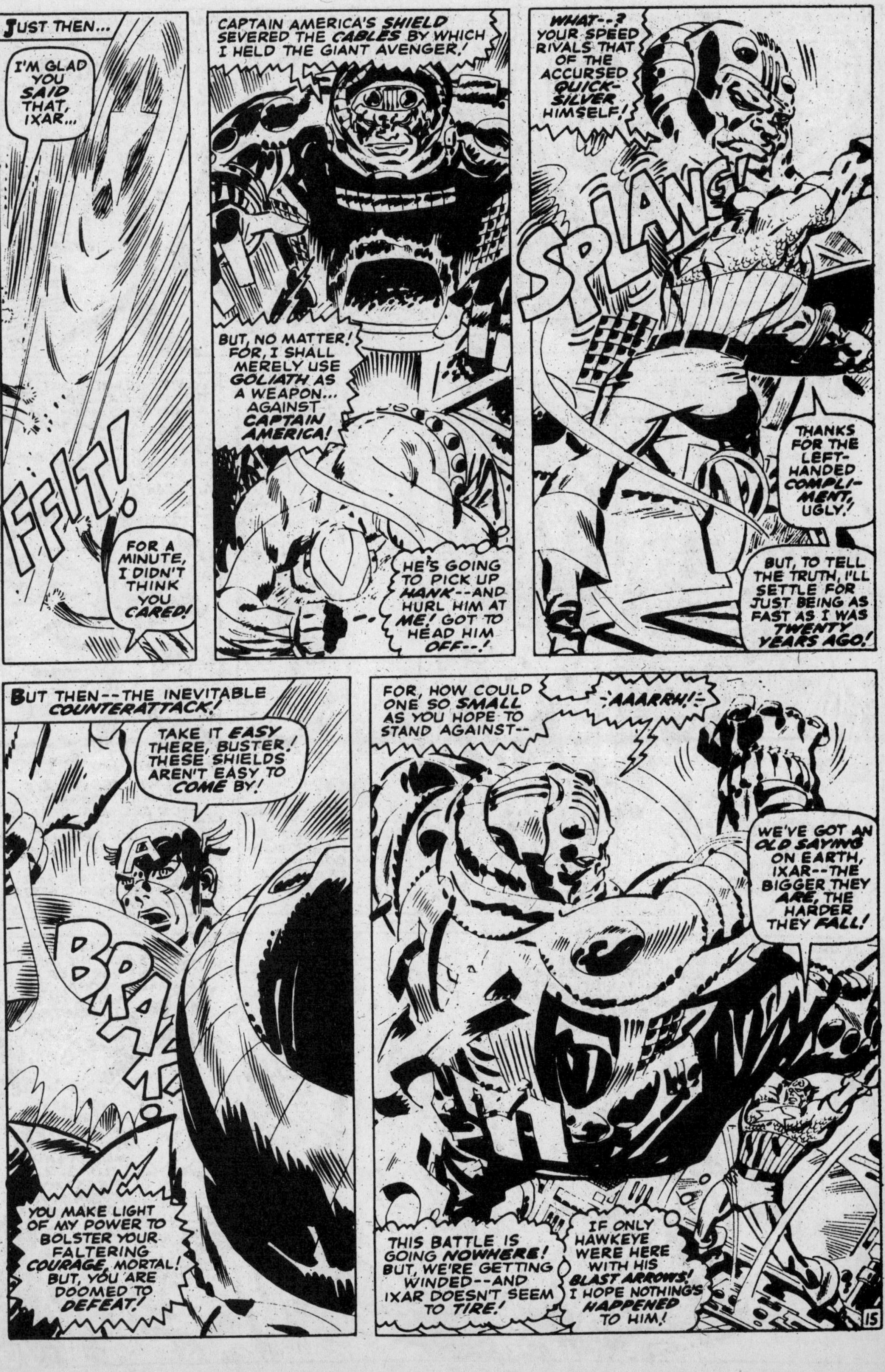

JUST THEN...
I'M GLAD YOU SAID THAT, IXAR...
FFIT!
FOR A MINUTE, I DIDN'T THINK YOU CARED!
CAPTAIN AMERICA'S SHIELD SEVERED THE CABLES BY WHICH I HELD THE GIANT AVENGER!
BUT, NO MATTER! FOR, I SHALL MERELY USE GOLIATH AS A WEAPON... AGAINST CAPTAIN AMERICA!
HE'S GOING TO PICK UP HANK--AND HURL HIM AT ME! GOT TO HEAD HIM OFF--!
WHAT--? YOUR SPEED RIVALS THAT OF THE ACCURSED QUICK-SILVER HIMSELF!
SPLANG!
THANKS FOR THE LEFT-HANDED COMPLI-MENT, UGLY!
BUT, TO TELL THE TRUTH, I'LL SETTLE FOR JUST BEING AS FAST AS I WAS TWENTY YEARS AGO!
BUT THEN--THE INEVITABLE COUNTERATTACK!
TAKE IT EASY THERE, BUSTER! THESE SHIELDS AREN'T EASY TO COME BY!
BRAK
YOU MAKE LIGHT OF MY POWER TO BOLSTER YOUR FALTERING COURAGE, MORTAL! BUT, YOU ARE DOOMED TO DEFEAT!
FOR, HOW COULD ONE SO SMALL AS YOU HOPE TO STAND AGAINST--
AAARRH!
WE'VE GOT AN OLD SAYING ON EARTH, IXAR--THE BIGGER THEY ARE, THE HARDER THEY FALL!
THIS BATTLE IS GOING NOWHERE! BUT, WE'RE GETTING WINDED--AND IXAR DOESN'T SEEM TO TIRE!
IF ONLY HAWKEYE WERE HERE WITH HIS BLAST ARROWS! I HOPE NOTHING'S HAPPENED TO HIM!
15

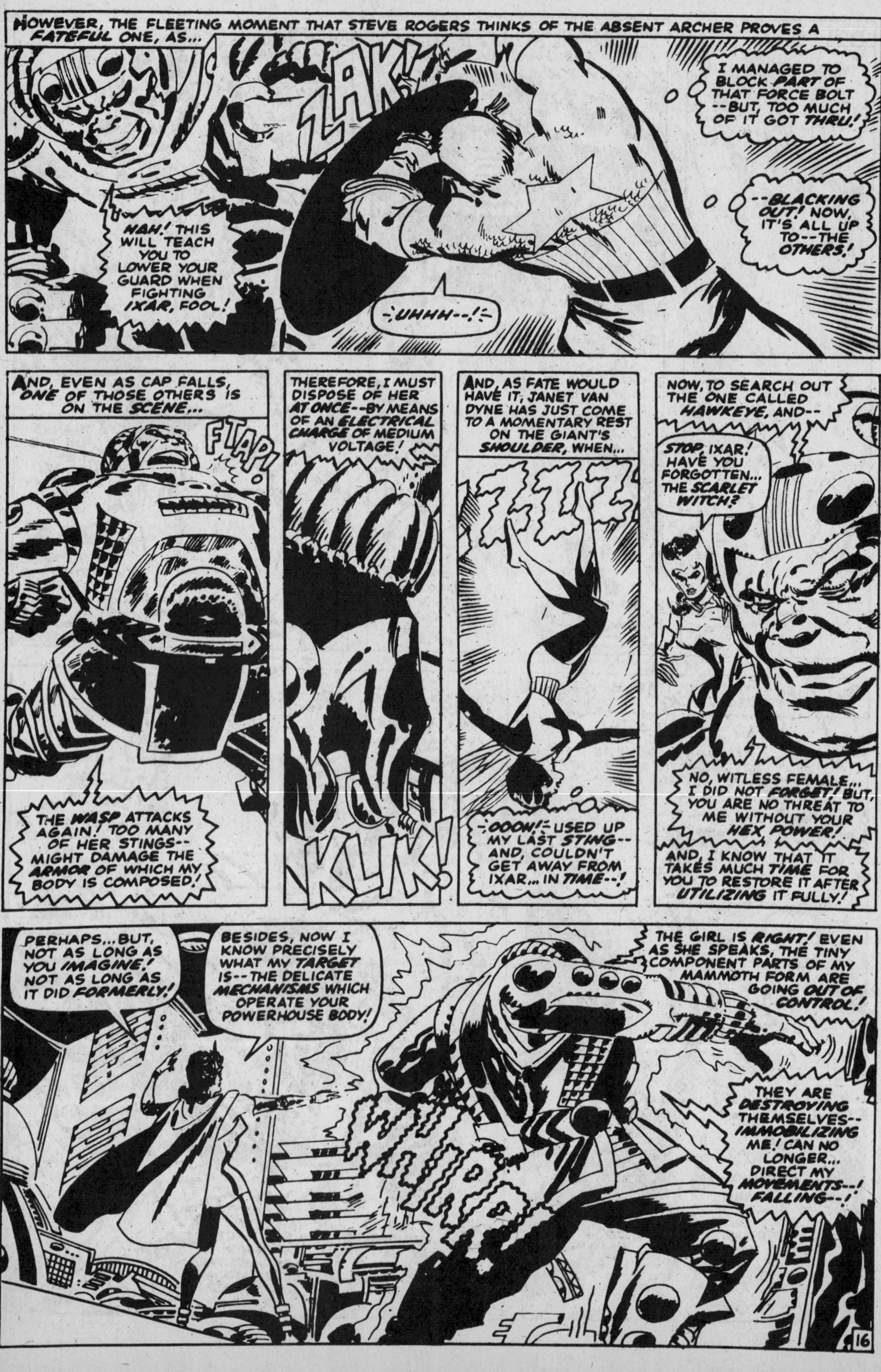

HOWEVER, THE FLEETING MOMENT THAT STEVE ROGERS THINKS OF THE ABSENT ARCHER PROVES A FATEFUL ONE, AS...
ZAK!
I MANAGED TO BLOCK PART OF THAT FORCE BOLT --BUT, TOO MUCH OF IT GOT THRU!
NAH! THIS WILL TEACH YOU TO LOWER YOUR GUARD WHEN FIGHTING IXAR, FOOL!
--BLACKING OUT! NOW, IT'S ALL UP TO--THE OTHERS!
-UHHH--!-
AND, EVEN AS CAP FALLS, ONE OF THOSE OTHERS IS ON THE SCENE...
FTAP!
THE WASP ATTACKS AGAIN! TOO MANY OF HER STINGS--MIGHT DAMAGE THE ARMOR OF WHICH MY BODY IS COMPOSED!
THEREFORE, I MUST DISPOSE OF HER AT ONCE--BY MEANS OF AN ELECTRICAL CHARGE OF MEDIUM VOLTAGE!
KLIK!
AND, AS FATE WOULD HAVE IT, JANET VAN DYNE HAS JUST COME TO A MOMENTARY REST ON THE GIANT'S SHOULDER, WHEN...
ZZZZ
-OOOW!- USED UP MY LAST STING--AND, COULDN'T GET AWAY FROM IXAR... IN TIME--!
NOW, TO SEARCH OUT THE ONE CALLED HAWKEYE, AND--
STOP, IXAR! HAVE YOU FORGOTTEN... THE SCARLET WITCH?
NO, WITLESS FEMALE... I DID NOT FORGET! BUT, YOU ARE NO THREAT TO ME WITHOUT YOUR HEX POWER!
AND, I KNOW THAT IT TAKES MUCH TIME FOR YOU TO RESTORE IT AFTER UTILIZING IT FULLY!
PERHAPS... BUT, NOT AS LONG AS YOU IMAGINE! NOT AS LONG AS IT DID FORMERLY!
BESIDES, NOW I KNOW PRECISELY WHAT MY TARGET IS--THE DELICATE MECHANISMS WHICH OPERATE YOUR POWERHOUSE BODY!
THE GIRL IS RIGHT! EVEN AS SHE SPEAKS, THE TINY COMPONENT PARTS OF MY MAMMOTH FORM ARE GOING OUT OF CONTROL!
THEY ARE DESTROYING THEMSELVES--IMMOBILIZING ME! CAN NO LONGER... DIRECT MY MOVEMENTS--! FALLING--!
WHAP

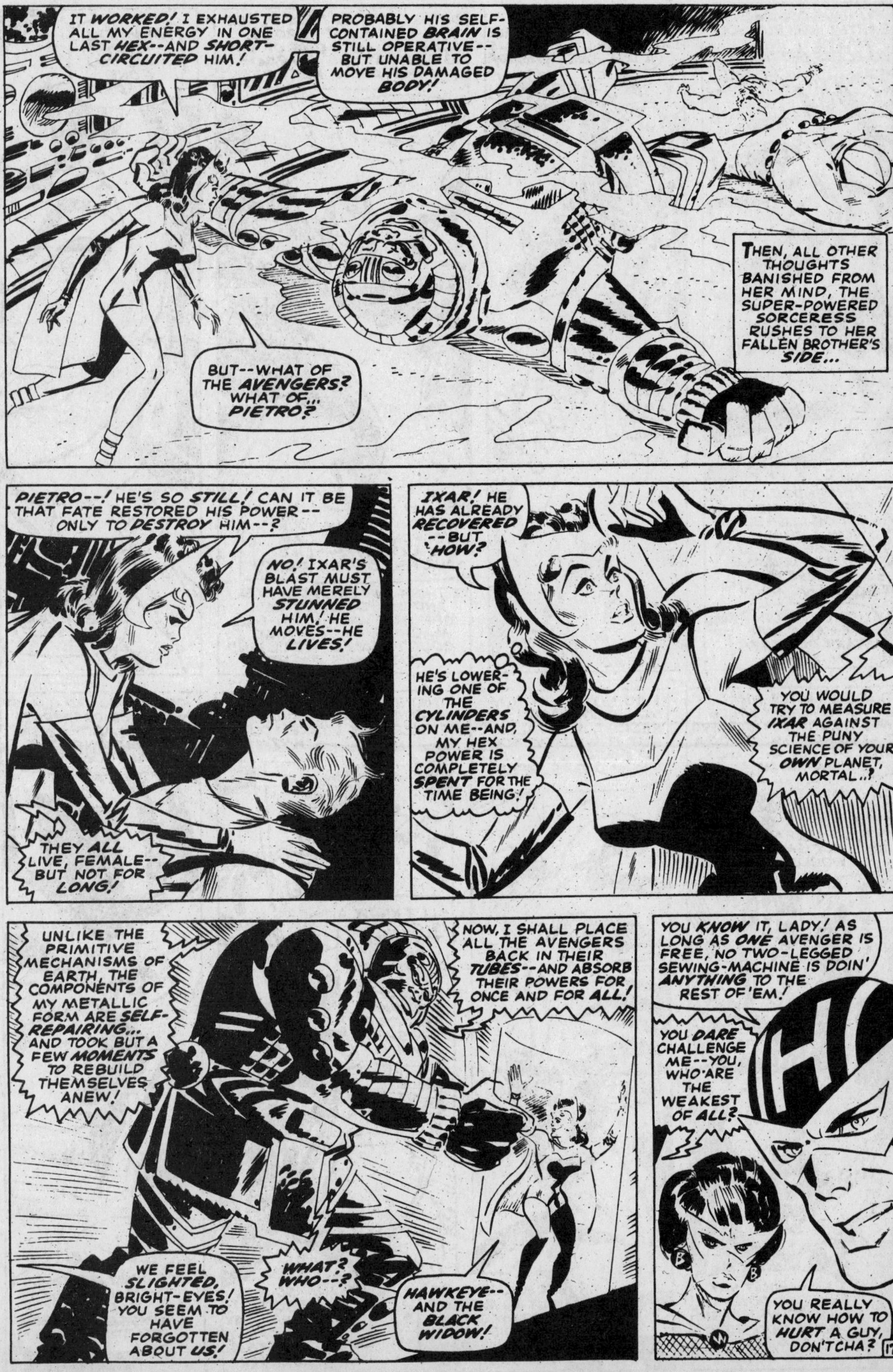
IT WORKED! I EXHAUSTED ALL MY ENERGY IN ONE LAST HEX--AND SHORT-CIRCUITED HIM!
PROBABLY HIS SELF-CONTAINED BRAIN IS STILL OPERATIVE--BUT UNABLE TO MOVE HIS DAMAGED BODY!
BUT--WHAT OF THE AVENGERS? WHAT OF... PIETRO?
THEN, ALL OTHER THOUGHTS BANISHED FROM HER MIND, THE SUPER-POWERED SORCERESS RUSHES TO HER FALLEN BROTHER'S SIDE...
PIETRO--! HE'S SO STILL! CAN IT BE THAT FATE RESTORED HIS POWER--ONLY TO DESTROY HIM--?
NO! IXAR'S BLAST MUST HAVE MERELY STUNNED HIM! HE MOVES--HE LIVES!
THEY ALL LIVE, FEMALE--BUT NOT FOR LONG!
IXAR! HE HAS ALREADY RECOVERED--BUT HOW?
HE'S LOWERING ONE OF THE CYLINDERS ON ME--AND, MY HEX POWER IS COMPLETELY SPENT FOR THE TIME BEING!
YOU WOULD TRY TO MEASURE IXAR AGAINST THE PUNY SCIENCE OF YOUR OWN PLANET, MORTAL..?
UNLIKE THE PRIMITIVE MECHANISMS OF EARTH, THE COMPONENTS OF MY METALLIC FORM ARE SELF-REPAIRING... AND TOOK BUT A FEW MOMENTS TO REBUILD THEMSELVES ANEW!
NOW, I SHALL PLACE ALL THE AVENGERS BACK IN THEIR TUBES--AND ABSORB THEIR POWERS FOR ONCE AND FOR ALL!
WE FEEL SLIGHTED, BRIGHT-EYES! YOU SEEM TO HAVE FORGOTTEN ABOUT US!
WHAT? WHO--?
HAWKEYE--AND THE BLACK WIDOW!
YOU KNOW IT, LADY! AS LONG AS ONE AVENGER IS FREE, NO TWO-LEGGED SEWING-MACHINE IS DOIN' ANYTHING TO THE REST OF 'EM!
YOU DARE CHALLENGE ME--YOU, WHO ARE THE WEAKEST OF ALL?
YOU REALLY KNOW HOW TO HURT A GUY, DON'TCHA?

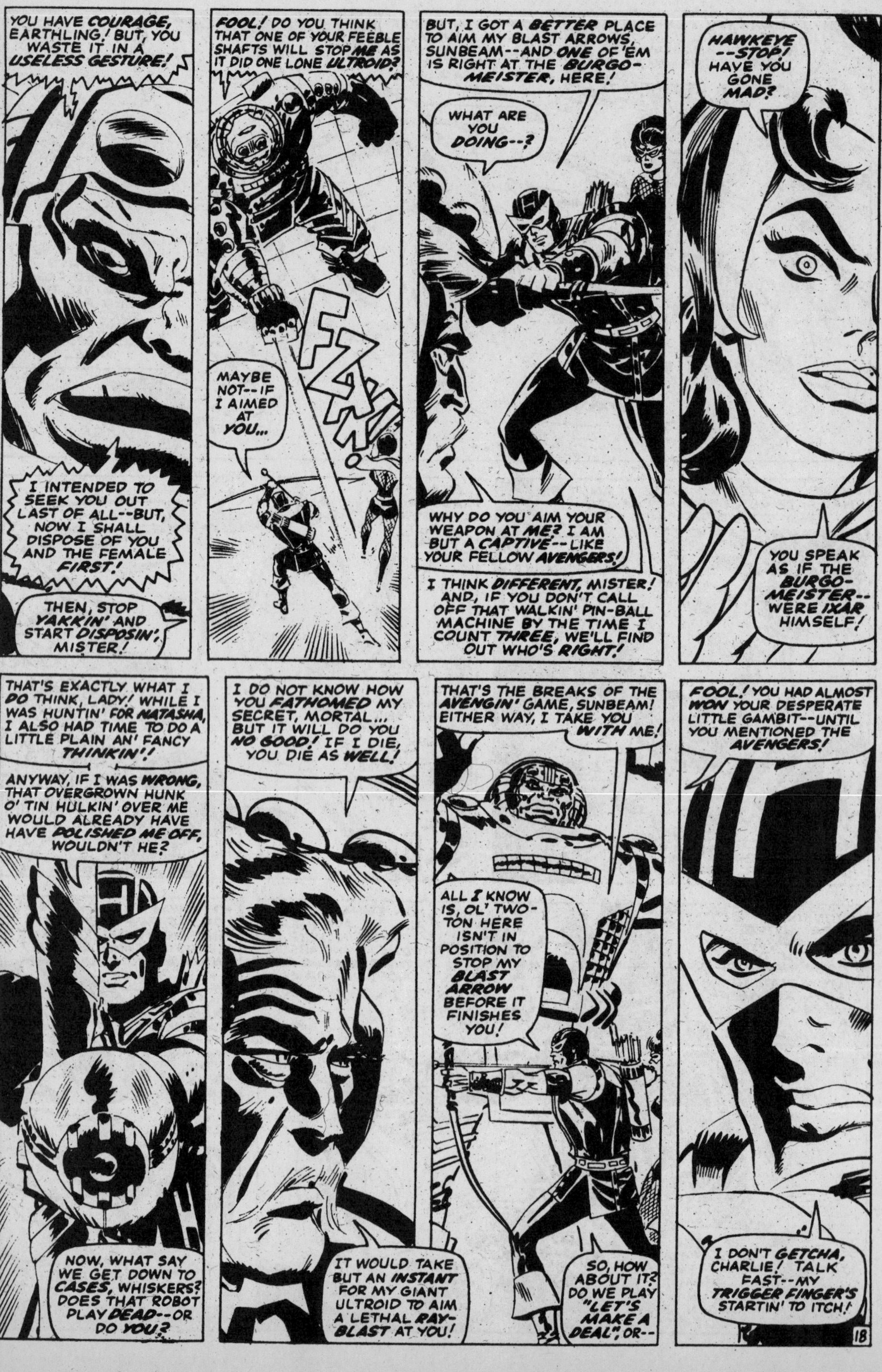

YOU HAVE COURAGE, EARTHLING! BUT, YOU WASTE IT IN A USELESS GESTURE!
I INTENDED TO SEEK YOU OUT LAST OF ALL--BUT, NOW I SHALL DISPOSE OF YOU AND THE FEMALE FIRST!
THEN, STOP YAKKIN' AND START DISPOSIN', MISTER!
FOOL! DO YOU THINK THAT ONE OF YOUR FEEBLE SHAFTS WILL STOP ME AS IT DID ONE LONE ULTROID?
FZZAK!
MAYBE NOT--IF I AIMED AT YOU...
BUT, I GOT A BETTER PLACE TO AIM MY BLAST ARROWS, SUNBEAM--AND ONE OF 'EM IS RIGHT AT THE BURGO-MEISTER, HERE!
WHAT ARE YOU DOING--?
WHY DO YOU AIM YOUR WEAPON AT ME? I AM BUT A CAPTIVE--LIKE YOUR FELLOW AVENGERS!
I THINK DIFFERENT, MISTER! AND, IF YOU DON'T CALL OFF THAT WALKIN' PIN-BALL MACHINE BY THE TIME I COUNT THREE, WE'LL FIND OUT WHO'S RIGHT!
HAWKEYE --STOP! HAVE YOU GONE MAD?
YOU SPEAK AS IF THE BURGO-MEISTER--WERE IXAR HIMSELF!
THAT'S EXACTLY WHAT I DO THINK, LADY! WHILE I WAS HUNTIN' FOR NATASHA, I ALSO HAD TIME TO DO A LITTLE PLAIN AN' FANCY THINKIN'!
ANYWAY, IF I WAS WRONG, THAT OVERGROWN HUNK O' TIN HULKIN' OVER ME WOULD ALREADY HAVE HAVE POLISHED ME OFF, WOULDN'T HE?
NOW, WHAT SAY WE GET DOWN TO CASES, WHISKERS? DOES THAT ROBOT PLAY DEAD--OR DO YOU?
I DO NOT KNOW HOW YOU FATHOMED MY SECRET, MORTAL... BUT IT WILL DO YOU NO GOOD! IF I DIE, YOU DIE AS WELL!
IT WOULD TAKE BUT AN INSTANT FOR MY GIANT ULTROID TO AIM A LETHAL RAY-BLAST AT YOU!
THAT'S THE BREAKS OF THE AVENGIN' GAME, SUNBEAM! EITHER WAY, I TAKE YOU WITH ME!
ALL I KNOW IS, OL' TWO-TON HERE ISN'T IN POSITION TO STOP MY BLAST ARROW BEFORE IT FINISHES YOU!
SO, HOW ABOUT IT? DO WE PLAY "LET'S MAKE A DEAL", OR--
FOOL! YOU HAD ALMOST WON YOUR DESPERATE LITTLE GAMBIT--UNTIL YOU MENTIONED THE AVENGERS!
I DON'T GETCHA, CHARLIE! TALK FAST--MY TRIGGER FINGER'S STARTIN' TO ITCH!

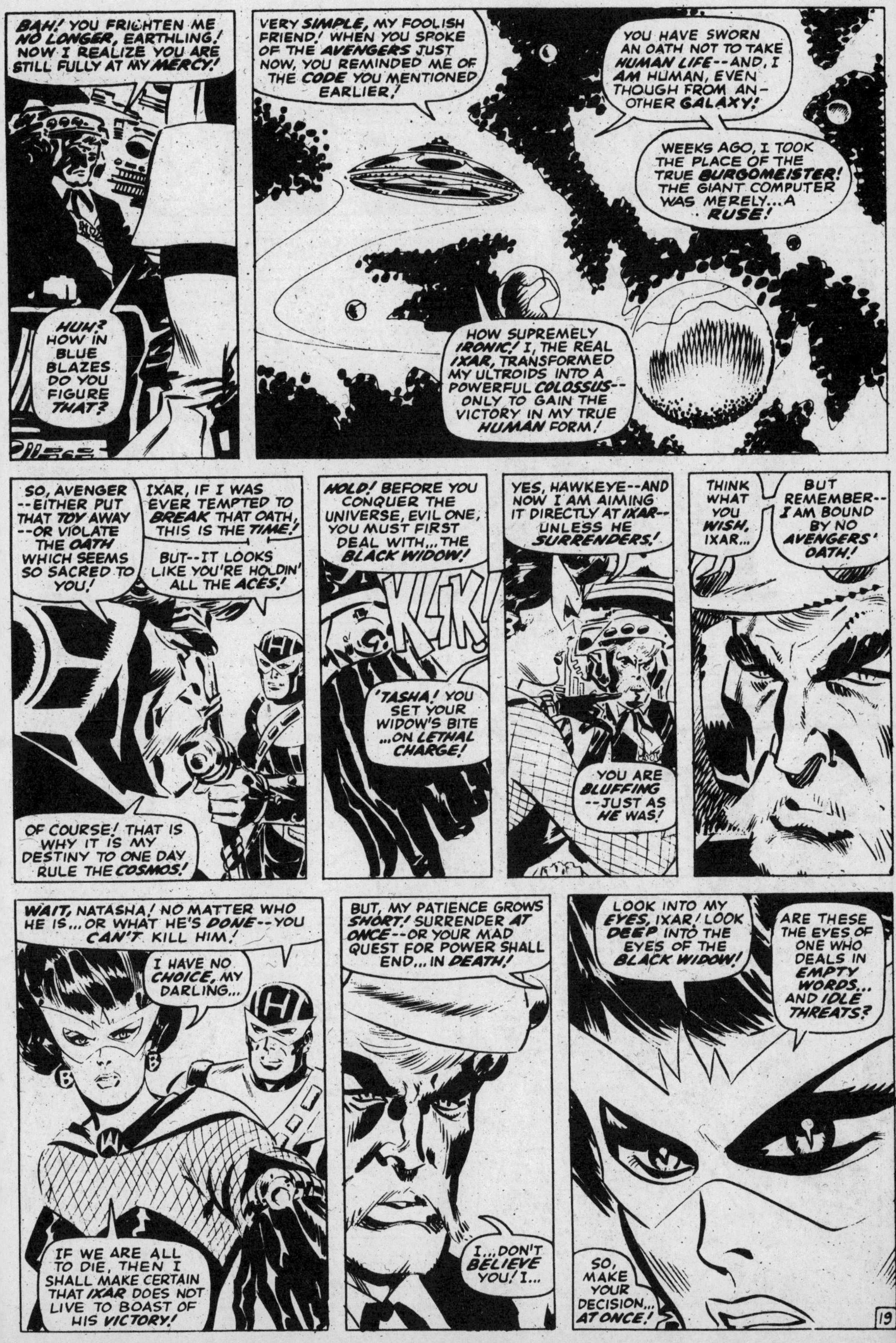
BAH! YOU FRIGHTEN ME NO LONGER, EARTHLING! NOW I REALIZE YOU ARE STILL FULLY AT MY MERCY!
HUH? HOW IN BLUE BLAZES DO YOU FIGURE THAT?
VERY SIMPLE, MY FOOLISH FRIEND! WHEN YOU SPOKE OF THE AVENGERS JUST NOW, YOU REMINDED ME OF THE CODE YOU MENTIONED EARLIER!
YOU HAVE SWORN AN OATH NOT TO TAKE HUMAN LIFE--AND, I AM HUMAN, EVEN THOUGH FROM ANOTHER GALAXY!
WEEKS AGO, I TOOK THE PLACE OF THE TRUE BURGOMEISTER! THE GIANT COMPUTER WAS MERELY... A RUSE!
HOW SUPREMELY IRONIC! I, THE REAL IXAR, TRANSFORMED MY ULTROIDS INTO A POWERFUL COLOSSUS--ONLY TO GAIN THE VICTORY IN MY TRUE HUMAN FORM!
SO, AVENGER --EITHER PUT THAT TOY AWAY --OR VIOLATE THE OATH WHICH SEEMS SO SACRED TO YOU!
IXAR, IF I WAS EVER TEMPTED TO BREAK THAT OATH, THIS IS THE TIME!
BUT--IT LOOKS LIKE YOU'RE HOLDIN' ALL THE ACES!
OF COURSE! THAT IS WHY IT IS MY DESTINY TO ONE DAY RULE THE COSMOS!
HOLD! BEFORE YOU CONQUER THE UNIVERSE, EVIL ONE, YOU MUST FIRST DEAL WITH... THE BLACK WIDOW!
KLIK!
'TASHA! YOU SET YOUR WIDOW'S BITE ...ON LETHAL CHARGE!
YES, HAWKEYE--AND NOW I AM AIMING IT DIRECTLY AT IXAR--UNLESS HE SURRENDERS!
YOU ARE BLUFFING --JUST AS HE WAS!
THINK WHAT YOU WISH, IXAR...
BUT REMEMBER-- I AM BOUND BY NO AVENGERS' OATH!
WAIT, NATASHA! NO MATTER WHO HE IS... OR WHAT HE'S DONE--YOU CAN'T KILL HIM!
I HAVE NO CHOICE, MY DARLING...
IF WE ARE ALL TO DIE, THEN I SHALL MAKE CERTAIN THAT IXAR DOES NOT LIVE TO BOAST OF HIS VICTORY!
BUT, MY PATIENCE GROWS SHORT! SURRENDER AT ONCE--OR YOUR MAD QUEST FOR POWER SHALL END... IN DEATH!
I... DON'T BELIEVE YOU! I...
LOOK INTO MY EYES, IXAR! LOOK DEEP INTO THE EYES OF THE BLACK WIDOW!
ARE THESE THE EYES OF ONE WHO DEALS IN EMPTY WORDS... AND IDLE THREATS?
SO, MAKE YOUR DECISION... AT ONCE!
19

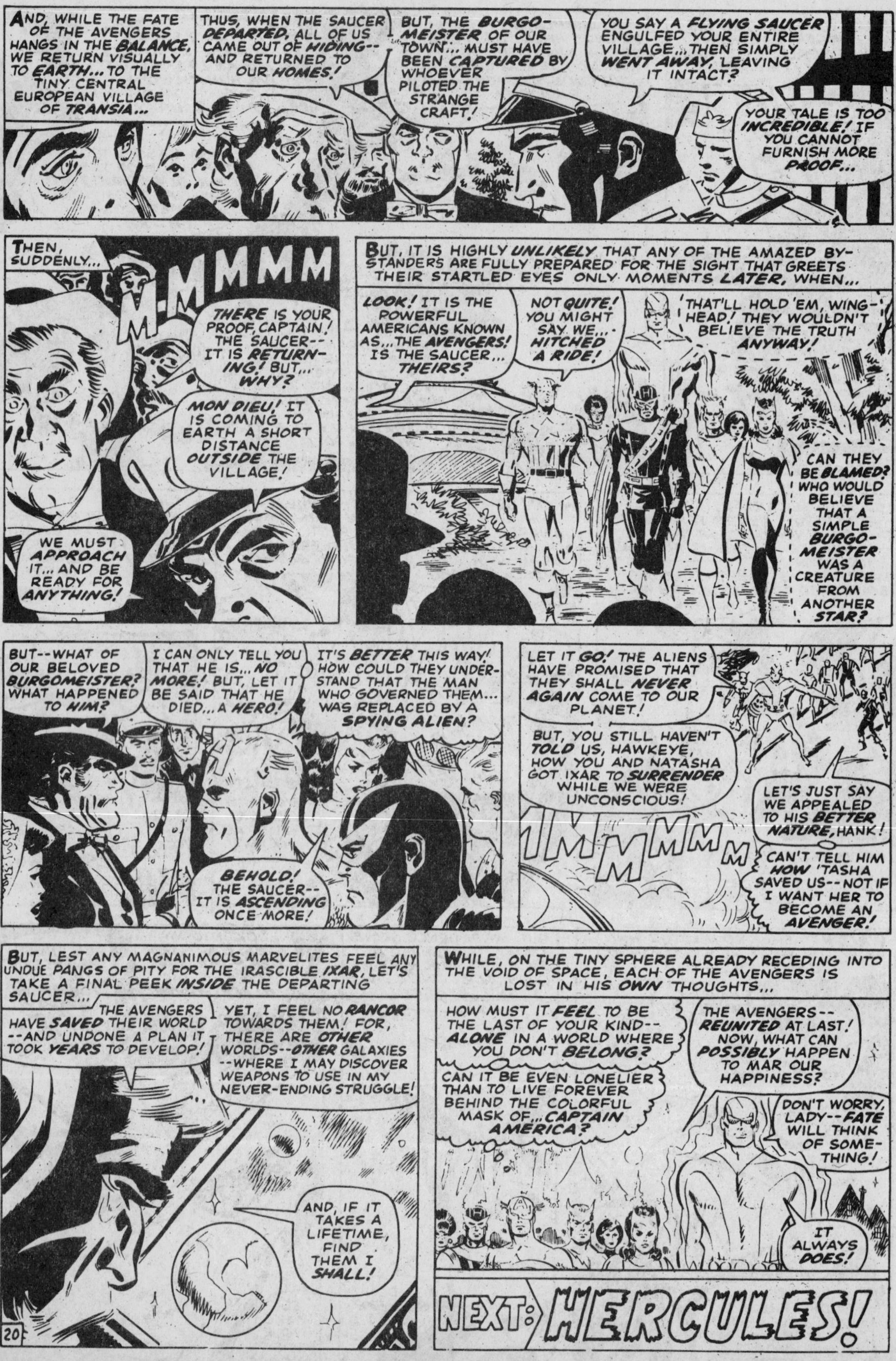
AND, WHILE THE FATE OF THE AVENGERS HANGS IN THE BALANCE, WE RETURN VISUALLY TO EARTH... TO THE TINY CENTRAL EUROPEAN VILLAGE OF TRANSIA...
THUS, WHEN THE SAUCER DEPARTED, ALL OF US CAME OUT OF HIDING-- AND RETURNED TO OUR HOMES!
BUT, THE BURGO-MEISTER OF OUR TOWN... MUST HAVE BEEN CAPTURED BY WHOEVER PILOTED THE STRANGE CRAFT!
YOU SAY A FLYING SAUCER ENGULFED YOUR ENTIRE VILLAGE... THEN SIMPLY WENT AWAY, LEAVING IT INTACT?
YOUR TALE IS TOO INCREDIBLE! IF YOU CANNOT FURNISH MORE PROOF...
THEN, SUDDENLY...
M-MMMMM
THERE IS YOUR PROOF, CAPTAIN! THE SAUCER-- IT IS RETURNING! BUT... WHY?
MON DIEU! IT IS COMING TO EARTH A SHORT DISTANCE OUTSIDE THE VILLAGE!
WE MUST APPROACH IT... AND BE READY FOR ANYTHING!
BUT, IT IS HIGHLY UNLIKELY THAT ANY OF THE AMAZED BY-STANDERS ARE FULLY PREPARED FOR THE SIGHT THAT GREETS THEIR STARTLED EYES ONLY MOMENTS LATER, WHEN...
LOOK! IT IS THE POWERFUL AMERICANS KNOWN AS... THE AVENGERS! IS THE SAUCER... THEIRS?
NOT QUITE! YOU MIGHT SAY WE... HITCHED A RIDE!
THAT'LL HOLD 'EM, WING-HEAD! THEY WOULDN'T BELIEVE THE TRUTH ANYWAY!
CAN THEY BE BLAMED? WHO WOULD BELIEVE THAT A SIMPLE BURGO-MEISTER WAS A CREATURE FROM ANOTHER STAR?
BUT--WHAT OF OUR BELOVED BURGOMEISTER? WHAT HAPPENED TO HIM?
I CAN ONLY TELL YOU THAT HE IS... NO MORE! BUT, LET IT BE SAID THAT HE DIED... A HERO!
IT'S BETTER THIS WAY! HOW COULD THEY UNDER-STAND THAT THE MAN WHO GOVERNED THEM... WAS REPLACED BY A SPYING ALIEN?
BEHOLD! THE SAUCER-- IT IS ASCENDING ONCE MORE!
LET IT GO! THE ALIENS HAVE PROMISED THAT THEY SHALL NEVER AGAIN COME TO OUR PLANET!
BUT, YOU STILL HAVEN'T TOLD US, HAWKEYE, HOW YOU AND NATASHA GOT IXAR TO SURRENDER WHILE WE WERE UNCONSCIOUS!
LET'S JUST SAY WE APPEALED TO HIS BETTER NATURE, HANK!
MMMMMMM
CAN'T TELL HIM HOW 'TASHA SAVED US--NOT IF I WANT HER TO BECOME AN AVENGER!
BUT, LEST ANY MAGNANIMOUS MARVELITES FEEL ANY UNDUE PANGS OF PITY FOR THE IRASCIBLE IXAR, LET'S TAKE A FINAL PEEK INSIDE THE DEPARTING SAUCER...
THE AVENGERS HAVE SAVED THEIR WORLD --AND UNDONE A PLAN IT TOOK YEARS TO DEVELOP!
YET, I FEEL NO RANCOR TOWARDS THEM! FOR, THERE ARE OTHER WORLDS--OTHER GALAXIES --WHERE I MAY DISCOVER WEAPONS TO USE IN MY NEVER-ENDING STRUGGLE!
AND, IF IT TAKES A LIFETIME, FIND THEM I SHALL!
WHILE, ON THE TINY SPHERE ALREADY RECEDING INTO THE VOID OF SPACE, EACH OF THE AVENGERS IS LOST IN HIS OWN THOUGHTS...
HOW MUST IT FEEL TO BE THE LAST OF YOUR KIND-- ALONE IN A WORLD WHERE YOU DON'T BELONG?
CAN IT BE EVEN LONELIER THAN TO LIVE FOREVER BEHIND THE COLORFUL MASK OF... CAPTAIN AMERICA?
THE AVENGERS-- REUNITED AT LAST! NOW, WHAT CAN POSSIBLY HAPPEN TO MAR OUR HAPPINESS?
DON'T WORRY, LADY--FATE WILL THINK OF SOME-THING!
IT ALWAYS DOES!
NEXT: HERCULES!
20

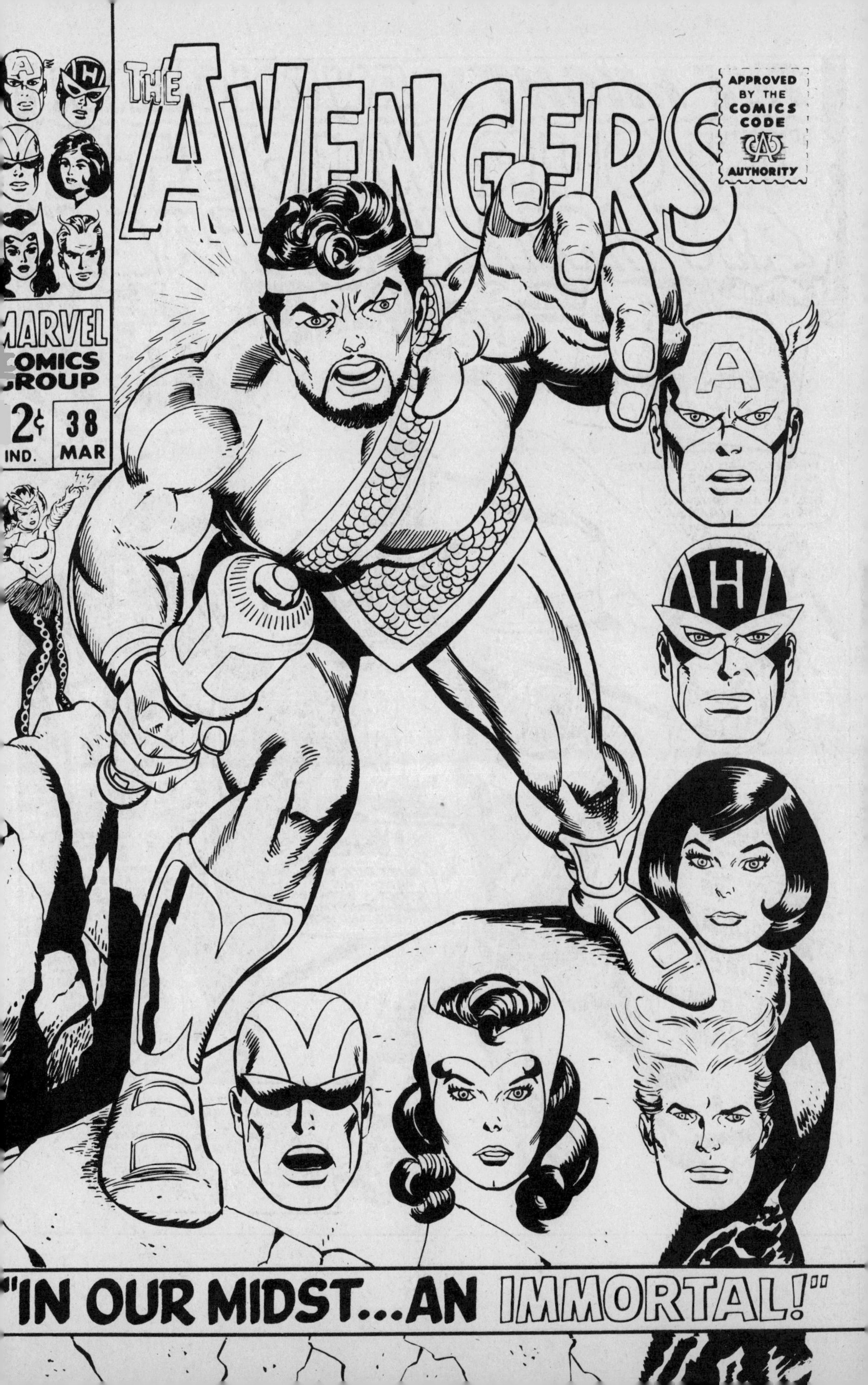
THE AVENGERS
APPROVED BY THE COMICS CODE AUTHORITY
MARVEL COMICS GROUP
12¢ IND.
38 MAR
"IN OUR MIDST...AN IMMORTAL!"

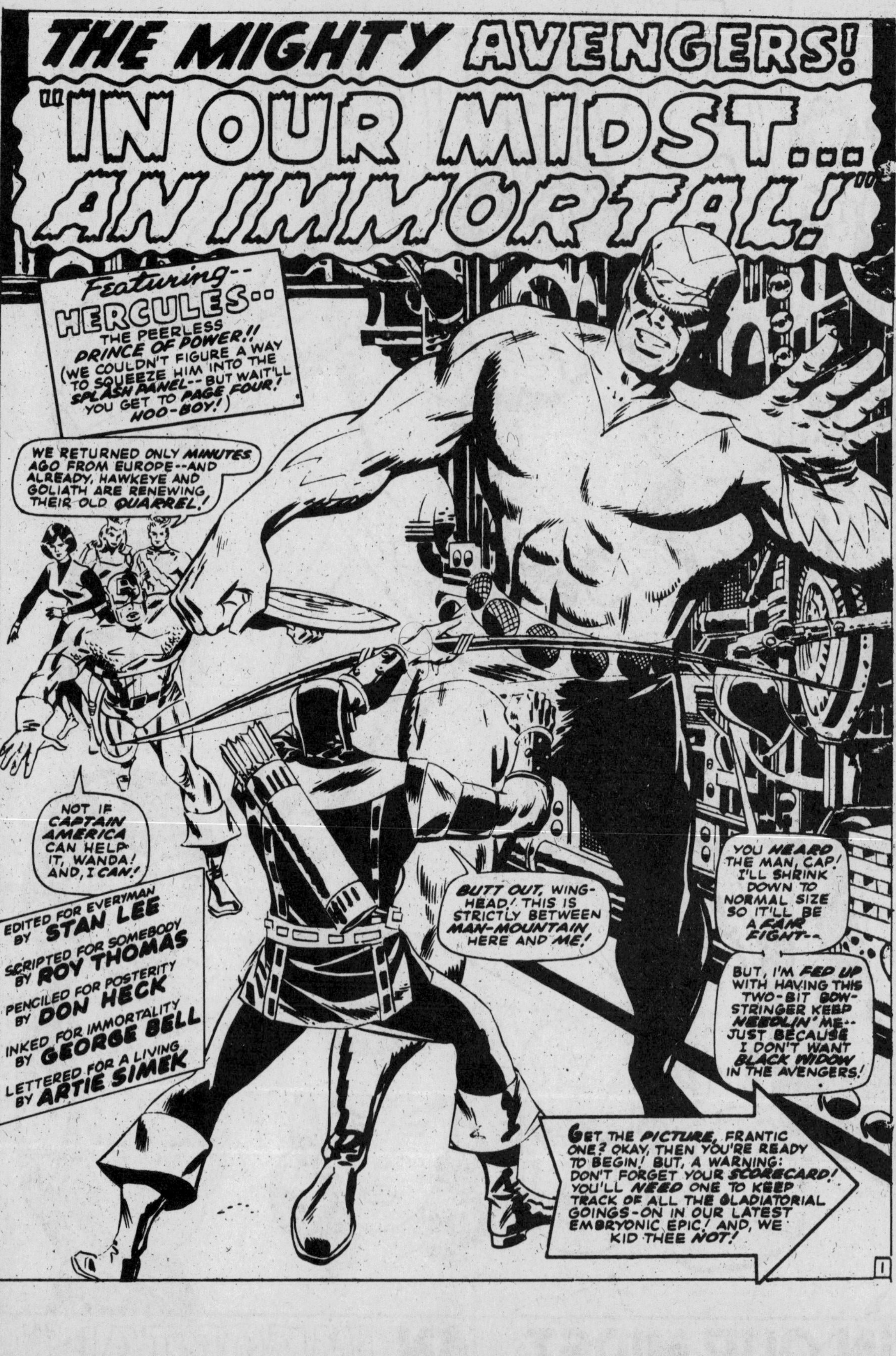

THE MIGHTY AVENGERS!
"IN OUR MIDST... AN IMMORTAL!"
Featuring-- HERCULES.. THE PEERLESS PRINCE OF POWER!! (WE COULDN'T FIGURE A WAY TO SQUEEZE HIM INTO THE SPLASH PANEL-- BUT WAIT'LL YOU GET TO PAGE FOUR! HOO-BOY!)
WE RETURNED ONLY MINUTES AGO FROM EUROPE--AND ALREADY, HAWKEYE AND GOLIATH ARE RENEWING THEIR OLD QUARREL!
NOT IF CAPTAIN AMERICA CAN HELP IT, WANDA! AND, I CAN!
BUTT OUT, WING-HEAD! THIS IS STRICTLY BETWEEN MAN-MOUNTAIN HERE AND ME!
YOU HEARD THE MAN, CAP! I'LL SHRINK DOWN TO NORMAL SIZE SO IT'LL BE A FAIR FIGHT--
BUT, I'M FED UP WITH HAVING THIS TWO-BIT BOW-STRINGER KEEP NEEDLIN' ME.. JUST BECAUSE I DON'T WANT BLACK WIDOW IN THE AVENGERS!
EDITED FOR EVERYMAN BY STAN LEE
SCRIPTED FOR SOMEBODY BY ROY THOMAS
PENCILED FOR POSTERITY BY DON HECK
INKED FOR IMMORTALITY BY GEORGE BELL
LETTERED FOR A LIVING BY ARTIE SIMEK
GET THE PICTURE, FRANTIC ONE? OKAY, THEN YOU'RE READY TO BEGIN! BUT, A WARNING: DON'T FORGET YOUR SCORECARD! YOU'LL NEED ONE TO KEEP TRACK OF ALL THE GLADIATORIAL GOINGS-ON IN OUR LATEST EMBRYONIC EPIC! AND, WE KID THEE NOT!
1

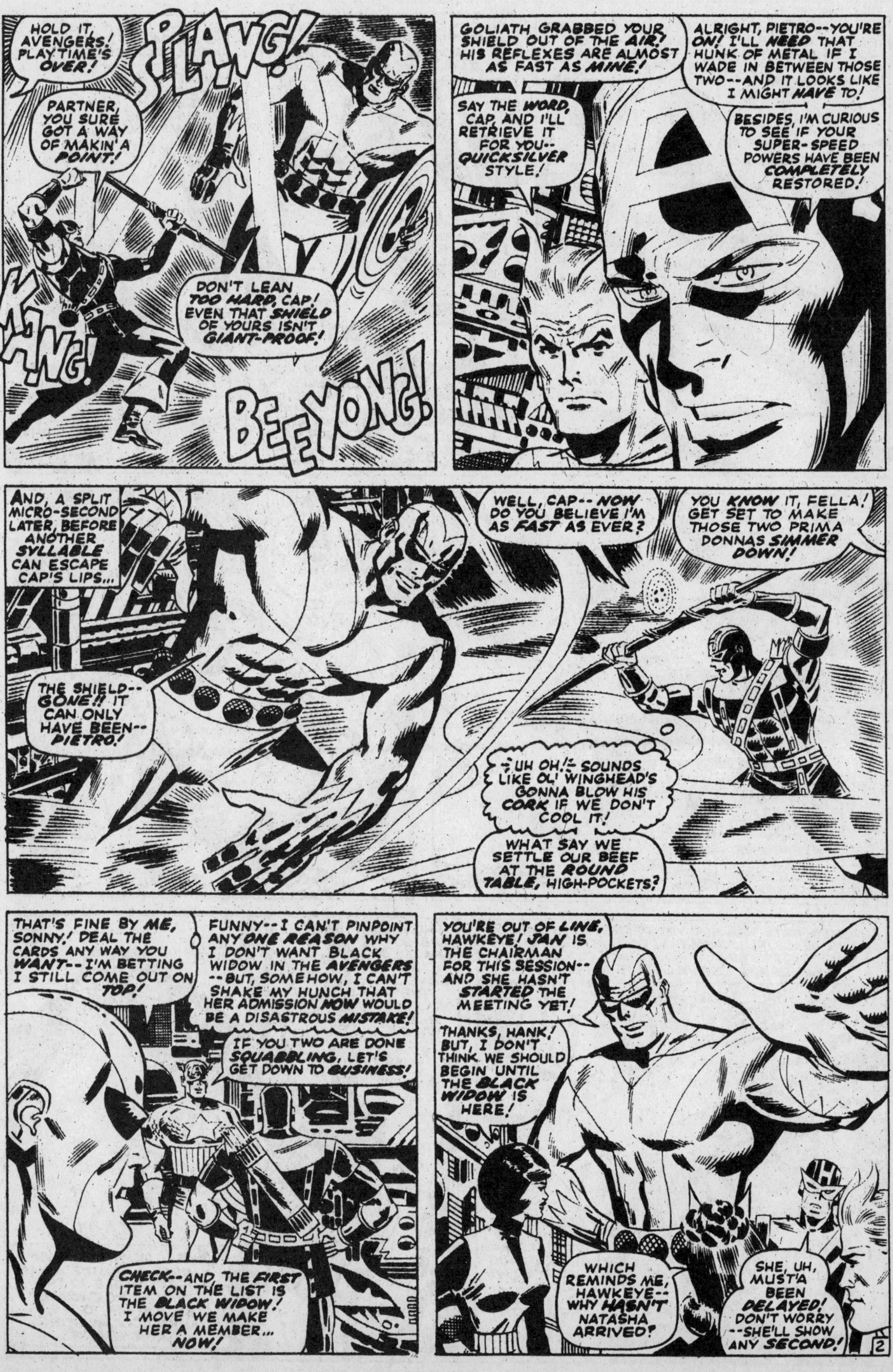
HOLD IT, AVENGERS! PLAYTIME'S OVER!
SPLANG!
PARTNER, YOU SURE GOT A WAY OF MAKIN' A POINT!
KANG!
DON'T LEAN TOO HARD, CAP! EVEN THAT SHIELD OF YOURS ISN'T GIANT-PROOF!
BEEYONG!
GOLIATH GRABBED YOUR SHIELD OUT OF THE AIR! HIS REFLEXES ARE ALMOST AS FAST AS MINE!
SAY THE WORD, CAP, AND I'LL RETRIEVE IT FOR YOU-- QUICKSILVER STYLE!
ALRIGHT, PIETRO--YOU'RE ON! I'LL NEED THAT HUNK OF METAL IF I WADE IN BETWEEN THOSE TWO--AND IT LOOKS LIKE I MIGHT HAVE TO!
BESIDES, I'M CURIOUS TO SEE IF YOUR SUPER-SPEED POWERS HAVE BEEN COMPLETELY RESTORED!
AND, A SPLIT MICRO-SECOND LATER, BEFORE ANOTHER SYLLABLE CAN ESCAPE CAP'S LIPS...
THE SHIELD-- GONE!! IT CAN ONLY HAVE BEEN-- PIETRO!
WELL, CAP-- NOW DO YOU BELIEVE I'M AS FAST AS EVER?
YOU KNOW IT, FELLA! GET SET TO MAKE THOSE TWO PRIMA DONNAS SIMMER DOWN!
UH OH! SOUNDS LIKE OL' WINGHEAD'S GONNA BLOW HIS CORK IF WE DON'T COOL IT!
WHAT SAY WE SETTLE OUR BEEF AT THE ROUND TABLE, HIGH-POCKETS?
THAT'S FINE BY ME, SONNY! DEAL THE CARDS ANY WAY YOU WANT--I'M BETTING I STILL COME OUT ON TOP!
FUNNY--I CAN'T PINPOINT ANY ONE REASON WHY I DON'T WANT BLACK WIDOW IN THE AVENGERS --BUT, SOMEHOW, I CAN'T SHAKE MY HUNCH THAT HER ADMISSION NOW WOULD BE A DISASTROUS MISTAKE!
IF YOU TWO ARE DONE SQUABBLING, LET'S GET DOWN TO BUSINESS!
CHECK--AND THE FIRST ITEM ON THE LIST IS THE BLACK WIDOW! I MOVE WE MAKE HER A MEMBER... NOW!
YOU'RE OUT OF LINE, HAWKEYE! JAN IS THE CHAIRMAN FOR THIS SESSION-- AND SHE HASN'T STARTED THE MEETING YET!
THANKS, HANK! BUT, I DON'T THINK WE SHOULD BEGIN UNTIL THE BLACK WIDOW IS HERE!
WHICH REMINDS ME, HAWKEYE-- WHY HASN'T NATASHA ARRIVED?
SHE, UH, MUST'A BEEN DELAYED! DON'T WORRY --SHE'LL SHOW ANY SECOND!
2

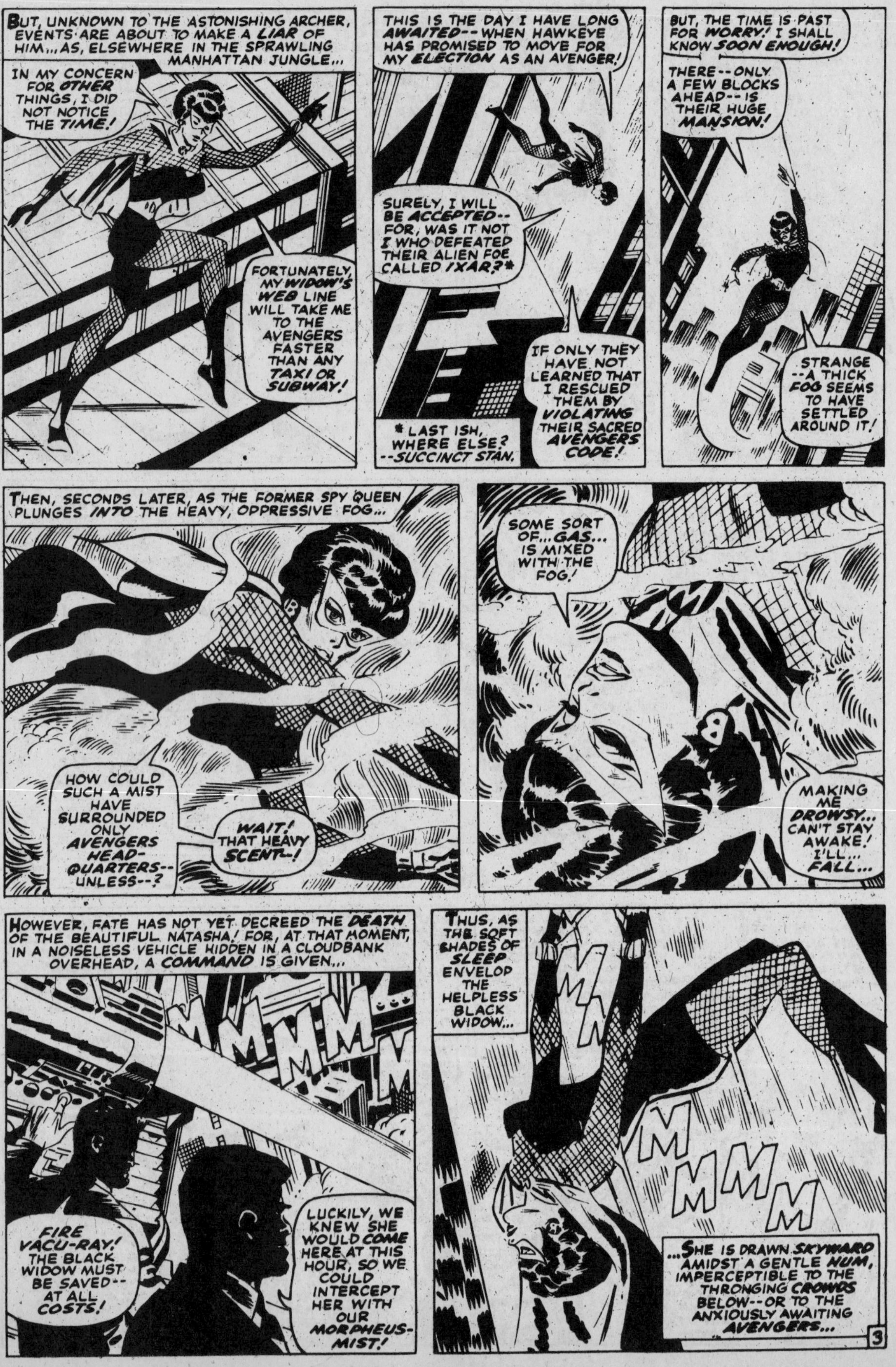
BUT, UNKNOWN TO THE ASTONISHING ARCHER, EVENTS ARE ABOUT TO MAKE A LIAR OF HIM... AS, ELSEWHERE IN THE SPRAWLING MANHATTAN JUNGLE...
IN MY CONCERN FOR OTHER THINGS, I DID NOT NOTICE THE TIME!
FORTUNATELY, MY WIDOW'S WEB LINE WILL TAKE ME TO THE AVENGERS FASTER THAN ANY TAXI OR SUBWAY!
THIS IS THE DAY I HAVE LONG AWAITED-- WHEN HAWKEYE HAS PROMISED TO MOVE FOR MY ELECTION AS AN AVENGER!
SURELY, I WILL BE ACCEPTED-- FOR, WAS IT NOT I WHO DEFEATED THEIR ALIEN FOE CALLED IXAR?*
IF ONLY THEY HAVE NOT LEARNED THAT I RESCUED THEM BY VIOLATING THEIR SACRED AVENGERS CODE!
* LAST ISH, WHERE ELSE? --SUCCINCT STAN.
BUT, THE TIME IS PAST FOR WORRY! I SHALL KNOW SOON ENOUGH!
THERE-- ONLY A FEW BLOCKS AHEAD-- IS THEIR HUGE MANSION!
STRANGE --A THICK FOG SEEMS TO HAVE SETTLED AROUND IT!
THEN, SECONDS LATER, AS THE FORMER SPY QUEEN PLUNGES INTO THE HEAVY, OPPRESSIVE FOG...
HOW COULD SUCH A MIST HAVE SURROUNDED ONLY AVENGERS HEAD-QUARTERS-- UNLESS--?
WAIT! THAT HEAVY SCENT--!
SOME SORT OF... GAS... IS MIXED WITH THE FOG!
MAKING ME DROWSY... CAN'T STAY AWAKE! I'LL... FALL...
HOWEVER, FATE HAS NOT YET DECREED THE DEATH OF THE BEAUTIFUL NATASHA! FOR, AT THAT MOMENT, IN A NOISELESS VEHICLE HIDDEN IN A CLOUDBANK OVERHEAD, A COMMAND IS GIVEN...
MMMMM
FIRE VACU-RAY! THE BLACK WIDOW MUST BE SAVED-- AT ALL COSTS!
LUCKILY, WE KNEW SHE WOULD COME HERE AT THIS HOUR, SO WE COULD INTERCEPT HER WITH OUR MORPHEUS-MIST!
THUS, AS THE SOFT SHADES OF SLEEP ENVELOP THE HELPLESS BLACK WIDOW...
MMMMMM
...SHE IS DRAWN SKYWARD AMIDST A GENTLE HUM, IMPERCEPTIBLE TO THE THRONGING CROWDS BELOW-- OR TO THE ANXIOUSLY AWAITING AVENGERS...

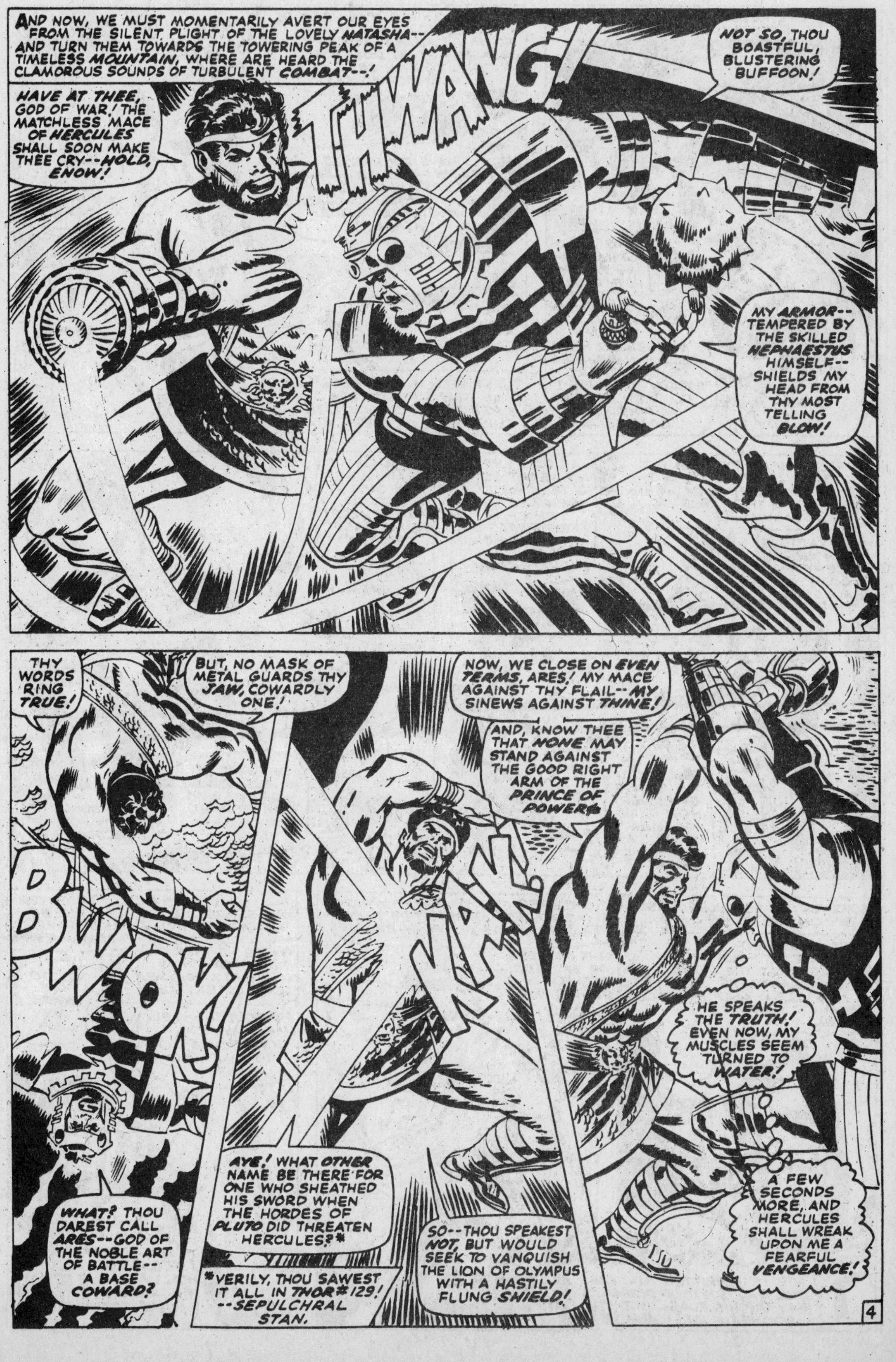
AND NOW, WE MUST MOMENTARILY AVERT OUR EYES FROM THE SILENT PLIGHT OF THE LOVELY NATASHA-- AND TURN THEM TOWARDS THE TOWERING PEAK OF A TIMELESS MOUNTAIN, WHERE ARE HEARD THE CLAMOROUS SOUNDS OF TURBULENT COMBAT--!
HAVE AT THEE, GOD OF WAR! THE MATCHLESS MACE OF HERCULES SHALL SOON MAKE THEE CRY--HOLD, ENOW!
THWANG!
NOT SO, THOU BOASTFUL, BLUSTERING BUFFOON!
MY ARMOR-- TEMPERED BY THE SKILLED HEPHAESTUS HIMSELF-- SHIELDS MY HEAD FROM THY MOST TELLING BLOW!
THY WORDS RING TRUE!
BUT, NO MASK OF METAL GUARDS THY JAW, COWARDLY ONE!
WHAT? THOU DAREST CALL ARES--GOD OF THE NOBLE ART OF BATTLE-- A BASE COWARD?
AYE! WHAT OTHER NAME BE THERE FOR ONE WHO SHEATHED HIS SWORD WHEN THE HORDES OF PLUTO DID THREATEN HERCULES?*
*VERILY, THOU SAWEST IT ALL IN THOR #129! --SEPULCHRAL STAN.
NOW, WE CLOSE ON EVEN TERMS, ARES! MY MACE AGAINST THY FLAIL--MY SINEWS AGAINST THINE!
AND, KNOW THEE THAT NONE MAY STAND AGAINST THE GOOD RIGHT ARM OF THE PRINCE OF POWER!
SO--THOU SPEAKEST NOT, BUT WOULD SEEK TO VANQUISH THE LION OF OLYMPUS WITH A HASTILY FLUNG SHIELD!
HE SPEAKS THE TRUTH! EVEN NOW, MY MUSCLES SEEM TURNED TO WATER!
A FEW SECONDS MORE, AND HERCULES SHALL WREAK UPON ME A FEARFUL VENGEANCE!
4

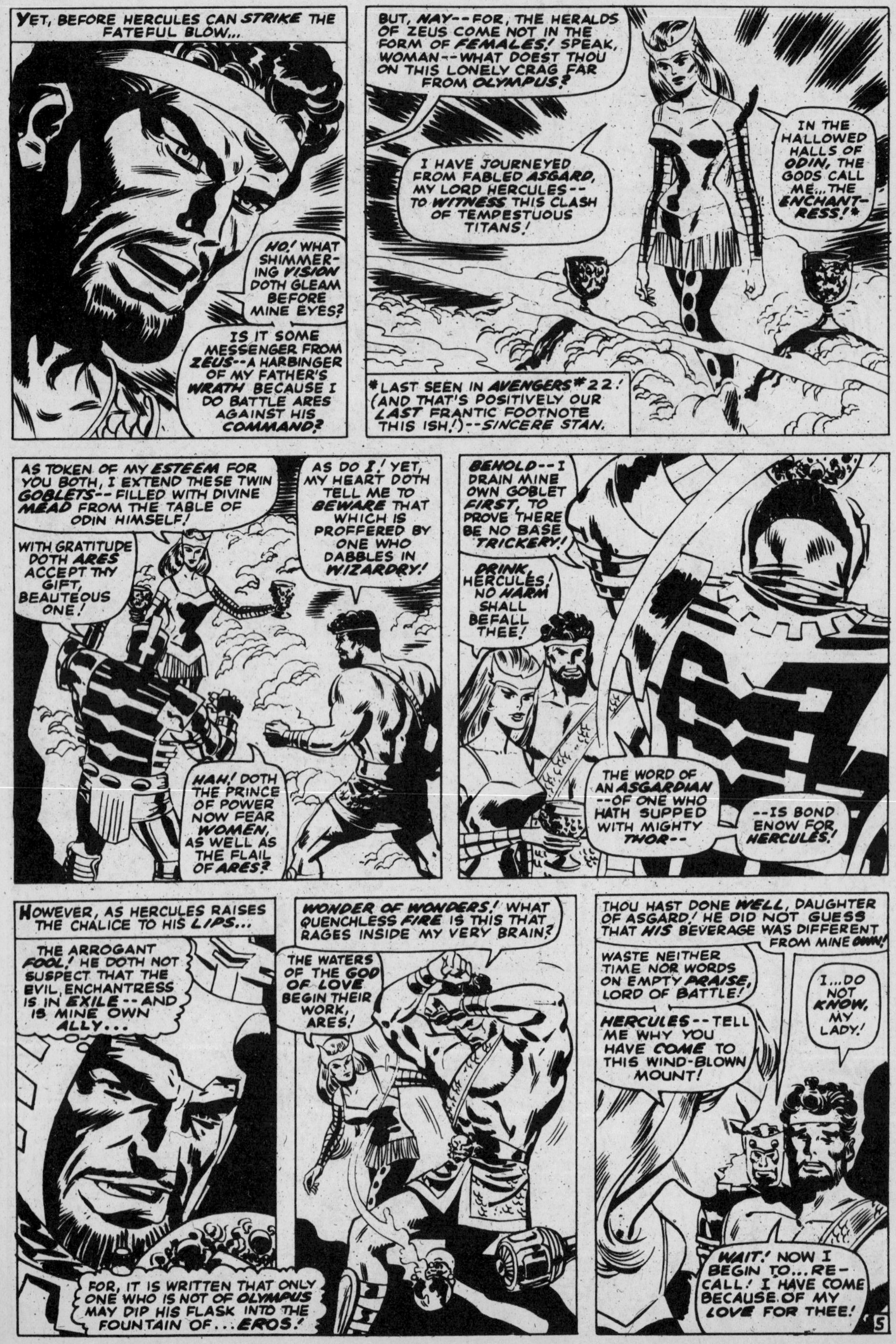
YET, BEFORE HERCULES CAN STRIKE THE FATEFUL BLOW...
HO! WHAT SHIMMERING VISION DOTH GLEAM BEFORE MINE EYES?
IS IT SOME MESSENGER FROM ZEUS--A HARBINGER OF MY FATHER'S WRATH BECAUSE I DO BATTLE ARES AGAINST HIS COMMAND?
BUT, NAY--FOR, THE HERALDS OF ZEUS COME NOT IN THE FORM OF FEMALES! SPEAK, WOMAN--WHAT DOEST THOU ON THIS LONELY CRAG FAR FROM OLYMPUS?
I HAVE JOURNEYED FROM FABLED ASGARD, MY LORD HERCULES--TO WITNESS THIS CLASH OF TEMPESTUOUS TITANS!
IN THE HALLOWED HALLS OF ODIN, THE GODS CALL ME... THE ENCHANTRESS!*
*LAST SEEN IN AVENGERS #22! (AND THAT'S POSITIVELY OUR LAST FRANTIC FOOTNOTE THIS ISH!)--SINCERE STAN.
AS TOKEN OF MY ESTEEM FOR YOU BOTH, I EXTEND THESE TWIN GOBLETS--FILLED WITH DIVINE MEAD FROM THE TABLE OF ODIN HIMSELF!
WITH GRATITUDE DOTH ARES ACCEPT THY GIFT, BEAUTEOUS ONE!
AS DO I! YET, MY HEART DOTH TELL ME TO BEWARE THAT WHICH IS PROFFERED BY ONE WHO DABBLES IN WIZARDRY!
HAH! DOTH THE PRINCE OF POWER NOW FEAR WOMEN, AS WELL AS THE FLAIL OF ARES?
BEHOLD--I DRAIN MINE OWN GOBLET FIRST, TO PROVE THERE BE NO BASE TRICKERY!
DRINK, HERCULES! NO HARM SHALL BEFALL THEE!
THE WORD OF AN ASGARDIAN--OF ONE WHO HATH SUPPED WITH MIGHTY THOR--
--IS BOND ENOW FOR HERCULES!
HOWEVER, AS HERCULES RAISES THE CHALICE TO HIS LIPS...
THE ARROGANT FOOL! HE DOTH NOT SUSPECT THAT THE EVIL ENCHANTRESS IS IN EXILE--AND IS MINE OWN ALLY...
FOR, IT IS WRITTEN THAT ONLY ONE WHO IS NOT OF OLYMPUS MAY DIP HIS FLASK INTO THE FOUNTAIN OF... EROS!
WONDER OF WONDERS! WHAT QUENCHLESS FIRE IS THIS THAT RAGES INSIDE MY VERY BRAIN?
THE WATERS OF THE GOD OF LOVE BEGIN THEIR WORK, ARES!
THOU HAST DONE WELL, DAUGHTER OF ASGARD! HE DID NOT GUESS THAT HIS BEVERAGE WAS DIFFERENT FROM MINE OWN!
WASTE NEITHER TIME NOR WORDS ON EMPTY PRAISE, LORD OF BATTLE!
HERCULES--TELL ME WHY YOU HAVE COME TO THIS WIND-BLOWN MOUNT!
I...DO NOT KNOW, MY LADY!
WAIT! NOW I BEGIN TO...RE-CALL! I HAVE COME BECAUSE OF MY LOVE FOR THEE!
5

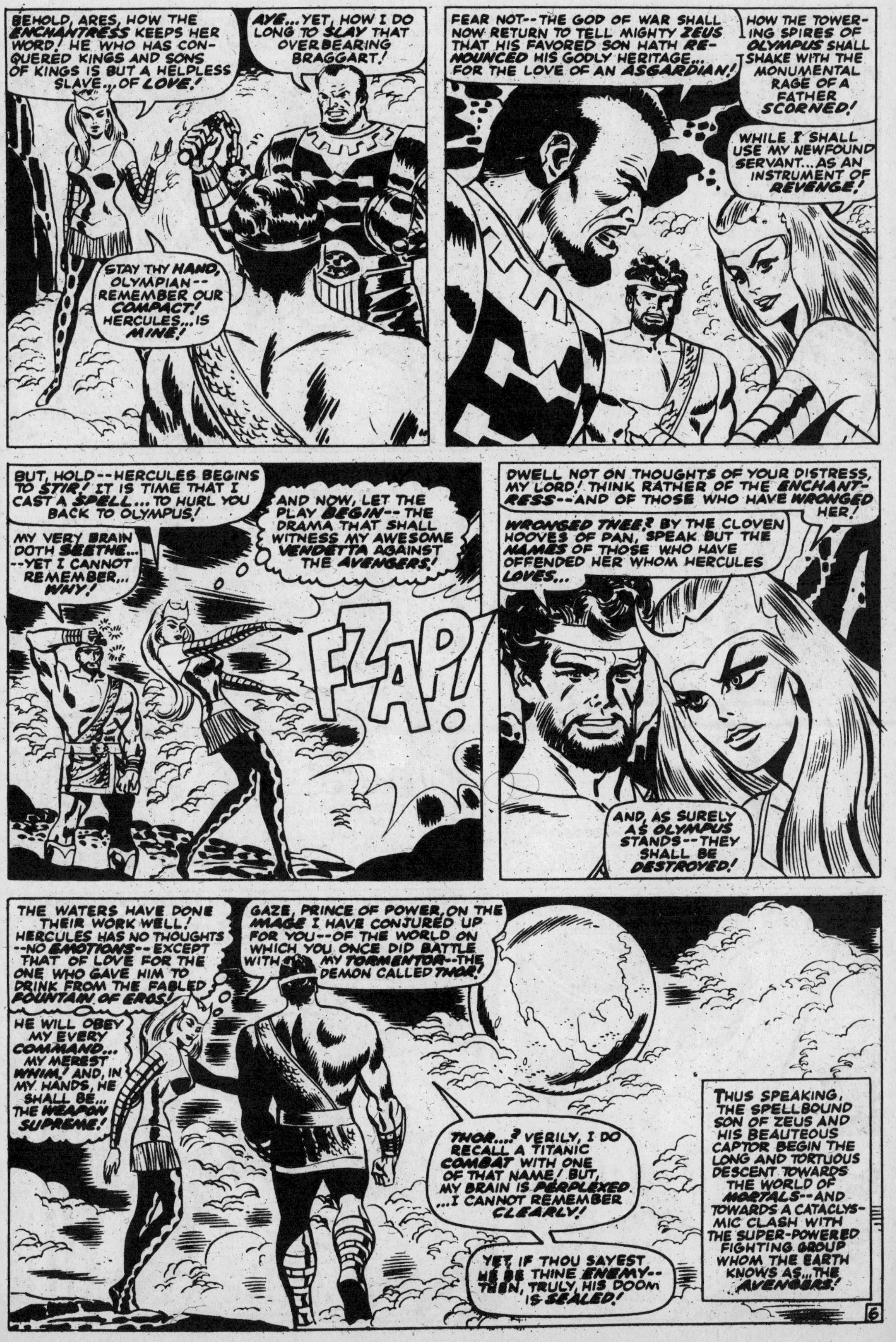
BEHOLD, ARES, HOW THE ENCHANTRESS KEEPS HER WORD! HE WHO HAS CONQUERED KINGS AND SONS OF KINGS IS BUT A HELPLESS SLAVE... OF LOVE!
AYE... YET, HOW I DO LONG TO SLAY THAT OVERBEARING BRAGGART!
STAY THY HAND, OLYMPIAN-- REMEMBER OUR COMPACT! HERCULES... IS MINE!
FEAR NOT-- THE GOD OF WAR SHALL NOW RETURN TO TELL MIGHTY ZEUS THAT HIS FAVORED SON HATH RENOUNCED HIS GODLY HERITAGE... FOR THE LOVE OF AN ASGARDIAN!
HOW THE TOWERING SPIRES OF OLYMPUS SHALL SHAKE WITH THE MONUMENTAL RAGE OF A FATHER SCORNED!
WHILE I SHALL USE MY NEWFOUND SERVANT... AS AN INSTRUMENT OF REVENGE!
BUT, HOLD-- HERCULES BEGINS TO STIR! IT IS TIME THAT I CAST A SPELL... TO HURL YOU BACK TO OLYMPUS!
MY VERY BRAIN DOTH SEETHE... --YET I CANNOT REMEMBER... WHY!
AND NOW, LET THE PLAY BEGIN-- THE DRAMA THAT SHALL WITNESS MY AWESOME VENDETTA AGAINST THE AVENGERS!
FZAP!
DWELL NOT ON THOUGHTS OF YOUR DISTRESS, MY LORD! THINK RATHER OF THE ENCHANTRESS-- AND OF THOSE WHO HAVE WRONGED HER!
WRONGED THEE? BY THE CLOVEN HOOVES OF PAN, SPEAK BUT THE NAMES OF THOSE WHO HAVE OFFENDED HER WHOM HERCULES LOVES...
AND, AS SURELY AS OLYMPUS STANDS-- THEY SHALL BE DESTROYED!
THE WATERS HAVE DONE THEIR WORK WELL! HERCULES HAS NO THOUGHTS --NO EMOTIONS-- EXCEPT THAT OF LOVE FOR THE ONE WHO GAVE HIM TO DRINK FROM THE FABLED FOUNTAIN OF EROS!
HE WILL OBEY MY EVERY COMMAND... MY MEREST WHIM! AND, IN MY HANDS, HE SHALL BE... THE WEAPON SUPREME!
GAZE, PRINCE OF POWER, ON THE IMAGE I HAVE CONJURED UP FOR YOU-- OF THE WORLD ON WHICH YOU ONCE DID BATTLE WITH MY TORMENTOR-- THE DEMON CALLED THOR!
THOR...? VERILY, I DO RECALL A TITANIC COMBAT WITH ONE OF THAT NAME! BUT, MY BRAIN IS PERPLEXED ...I CANNOT REMEMBER CLEARLY!
YET IF THOU SAYEST HE BE THINE ENEMY-- THEN, TRULY, HIS DOOM IS SEALED!
THUS SPEAKING, THE SPELLBOUND SON OF ZEUS AND HIS BEAUTEOUS CAPTOR BEGIN THE LONG AND TORTUOUS DESCENT TOWARDS THE WORLD OF MORTALS-- AND TOWARDS A CATACLYSMIC CLASH WITH THE SUPER-POWERED FIGHTING GROUP WHOM THE EARTH KNOWS AS... THE AVENGERS!
6

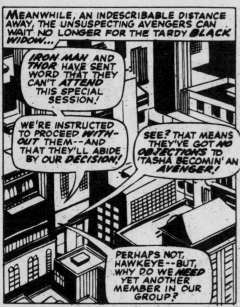

MEANWHILE, AN INDESCRIBABLE DISTANCE AWAY, THE UNSUSPECTING AVENGERS CAN WAIT NO LONGER FOR THE TARDY *BLACK WIDOW...*

IRON MAN AND THOR HAVE SENT WORD THAT THEY CAN'T *ATTEND* THIS SPECIAL SESSION!

WE'RE INSTRUCTED TO PROCEED *WITHOUT* THEM--AND THAT THEY'LL ABIDE BY OUR *DECISION!*

SEE? THAT MEANS THEY'VE GOT *NO* OBJECTIONS TO 'TASHA BECOMIN' AN *AVENGER!*

PERHAPS NOT, HAWKEYE--BUT, WHY DO WE *NEED* YET ANOTHER MEMBER IN OUR GROUP?

BECAUSE I *SAY SO,* THAT'S WHY, PIETRO! ARE *YOU* GONNA START BUGGIN' ME THE SAME WAY *MAN-MOUNTAIN* IS?

SIMMER DOWN, PARTNER! BEFORE WE *VOTE* ON ADMITTING THE BLACK WIDOW, WE HAVE TO CONSIDER EVERY ANGLE!

HOW ABOUT *THIS* FOR AN ANGLE, CAP? I'M GETTING *HUNGRY!*

NUTS! BY THE TIME WE GET AROUND TO LETTIN' 'TASHA *JOIN,* SHE'LL BE OLD ENOUGH TO *RETIRE!*

I AGREE WITH *JAN,* HAWKEYE! PERHAPS A LITTLE FOOD-- AND A LITTLE *TIME*--ARE WHAT WE NEED TO CONSIDER OUR DECISION!

BESIDES, DURING OUR DINNER, THE *BLACK WIDOW* MAY ARRIVE TO SPEAK ON HER OWN BEHALF!

OKAY, YA TALKED ME *INTO* IT! WE CAN GRAB A COUPLE'A *BURGERS* ACROSS THE STREET!

BUT THEN, WE GOTTA GET DOWN TO *CASES!*

AGREED! MEETING RECESSED!

SOON, LEAVING ONE OF THEIR NUMBER BEHIND IN CASE OF *EMERGENCY,* A DISCREETLY DISGUISED QUINTET DESCENDS TO *STREET LEVEL...*

AS *OFFICER-OF-THE-DAY,* IT'S MY DUTY TO MONITOR ALL OUR INCOMING *INFORMATION!*

I'VE ASKED *JARVIS,* THE BUTLER, TO FIX ME A HAM-AND-CHEESE *SANDWICH* TO TIDE ME OVER!

ONLY *NATASHA* AND I KNOW THAT SHE DEFEATED *IXAR* BY THREATENING HIS *LIFE*--SOMETHING THE OTHERS WOULDN'T GO FOR!

IS *THAT* WHY SHE HASN'T SHOWN? DOES SHE FIGURE SHE ISN'T *WORTHY* TO BE AN AVENGER?

BUT, UNKNOWN TO HAWKEYE, THE *TRUE* REASON FOR THE BLACK WIDOW'S LATENESS IS OF A LESS *SUBTLE* NATURE...

WHERE *AM* I? OH YES-- NOW I *REMEMBER!* THAT GAS... PUT ME TO *SLEEP!*

I'M INSIDE SOME HUGE *CHAMBER*-- AND, MY CAPTORS ARE STANDING RIGHT *BESIDE* ME!

SUDDENLY, WITH THE SPEED OF HER VENOMOUS *NAMESAKE,* THE FABULOUS FEMME *STRIKES--!*

UH OH! *LOOK OUT,* JOE! SHE'S *AWAKE*--AND MAD AS A *HORNET!*

YOU'RE TELLIN' *ME!* COOL IT, LADY--YOU GOT US ALL *WRONG!*

NO, FOOL--RATHER, IT IS *YOU* WHO ARE WRONG--IF YOU THINK THE LIKES OF YOU CAN HOLD THE *BLACK WIDOW!*

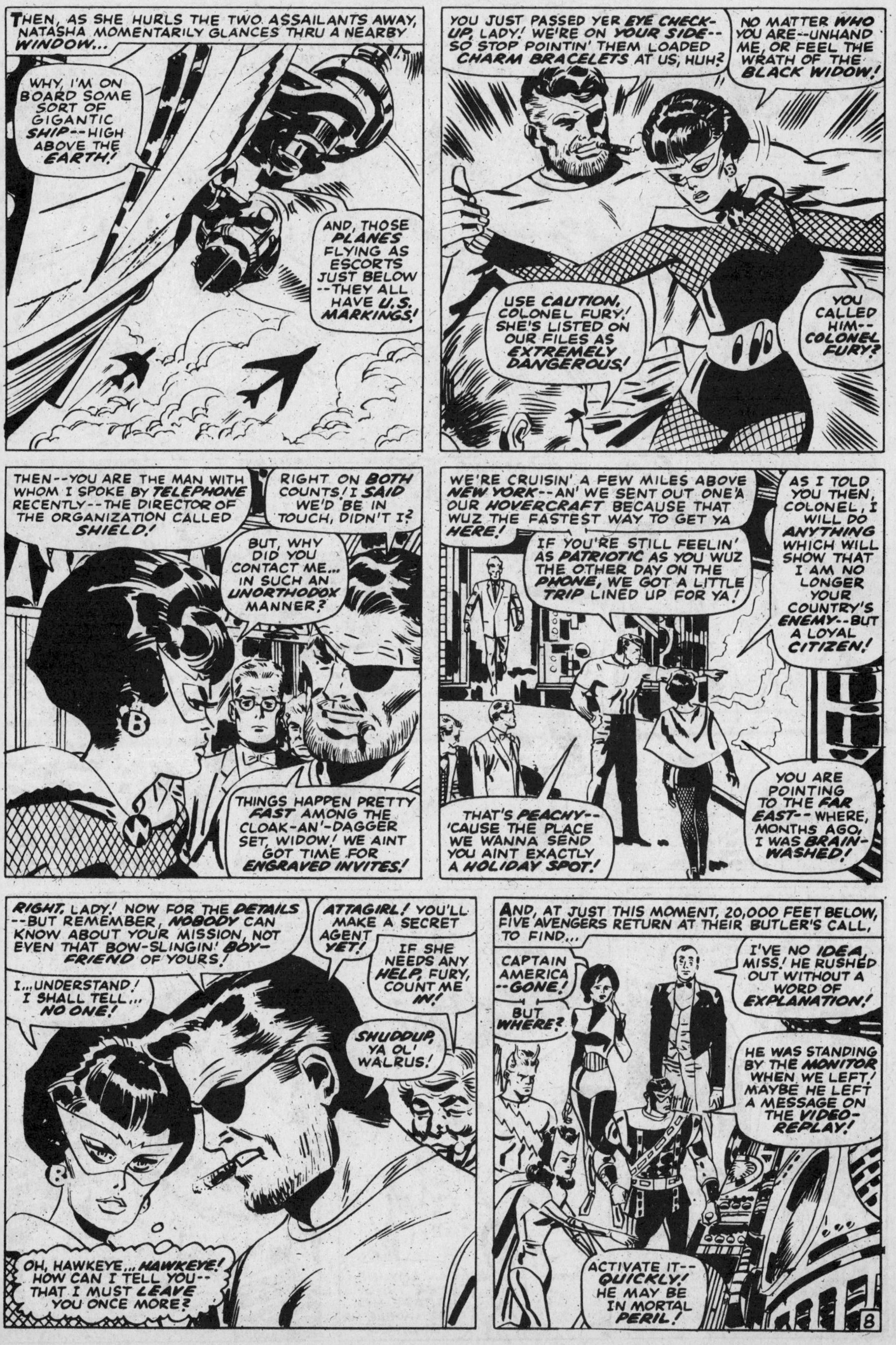
THEN, AS SHE HURLS THE TWO ASSAILANTS AWAY, NATASHA MOMENTARILY GLANCES THRU A NEARBY WINDOW...
WHY, I'M ON BOARD SOME SORT OF GIGANTIC SHIP--HIGH ABOVE THE EARTH!
AND, THOSE PLANES FLYING AS ESCORTS JUST BELOW --THEY ALL HAVE U.S. MARKINGS!
YOU JUST PASSED YER EYE CHECK-UP, LADY! WE'RE ON YOUR SIDE--SO STOP POINTIN' THEM LOADED CHARM BRACELETS AT US, HUH?
NO MATTER WHO YOU ARE--UNHAND ME, OR FEEL THE WRATH OF THE BLACK WIDOW!
USE CAUTION, COLONEL FURY! SHE'S LISTED ON OUR FILES AS EXTREMELY DANGEROUS!
YOU CALLED HIM--COLONEL FURY?
THEN--YOU ARE THE MAN WITH WHOM I SPOKE BY TELEPHONE RECENTLY--THE DIRECTOR OF THE ORGANIZATION CALLED SHIELD!
RIGHT ON BOTH COUNTS! I SAID WE'D BE IN TOUCH, DIDN'T I?
BUT, WHY DID YOU CONTACT ME... IN SUCH AN UNORTHODOX MANNER?
THINGS HAPPEN PRETTY FAST AMONG THE CLOAK-AN'-DAGGER SET, WIDOW! WE AINT GOT TIME FOR ENGRAVED INVITES!
WE'RE CRUISIN' A FEW MILES ABOVE NEW YORK--AN' WE SENT OUT ONE'A OUR HOVERCRAFT BECAUSE THAT WUZ THE FASTEST WAY TO GET YA HERE!
IF YOU'RE STILL FEELIN' AS PATRIOTIC AS YOU WUZ THE OTHER DAY ON THE PHONE, WE GOT A LITTLE TRIP LINED UP FOR YA!
AS I TOLD YOU THEN, COLONEL, I WILL DO ANYTHING WHICH WILL SHOW THAT I AM NO LONGER YOUR COUNTRY'S ENEMY--BUT A LOYAL CITIZEN!
YOU ARE POINTING TO THE FAR EAST--WHERE, MONTHS AGO, I WAS BRAIN-WASHED!
THAT'S PEACHY--'CAUSE THE PLACE WE WANNA SEND YOU AINT EXACTLY A HOLIDAY SPOT!
RIGHT, LADY! NOW FOR THE DETAILS--BUT REMEMBER, NOBODY CAN KNOW ABOUT YOUR MISSION, NOT EVEN THAT BOW-SLINGIN' BOY-FRIEND OF YOURS!
I...UNDERSTAND! I SHALL TELL... NO ONE!
ATTAGIRL! YOU'LL MAKE A SECRET AGENT YET!
IF SHE NEEDS ANY HELP, FURY, COUNT ME IN!
SHUDDUP, YA OL' WALRUS!
OH, HAWKEYE... HAWKEYE! HOW CAN I TELL YOU--THAT I MUST LEAVE YOU ONCE MORE?
AND, AT JUST THIS MOMENT, 20,000 FEET BELOW, FIVE AVENGERS RETURN AT THEIR BUTLER'S CALL, TO FIND...
CAPTAIN AMERICA--GONE!
BUT WHERE?
I'VE NO IDEA, MISS! HE RUSHED OUT WITHOUT A WORD OF EXPLANATION!
HE WAS STANDING BY THE MONITOR WHEN WE LEFT! MAYBE HE LEFT A MESSAGE ON THE VIDEO-REPLAY!
ACTIVATE IT--QUICKLY! HE MAY BE IN MORTAL PERIL!
8

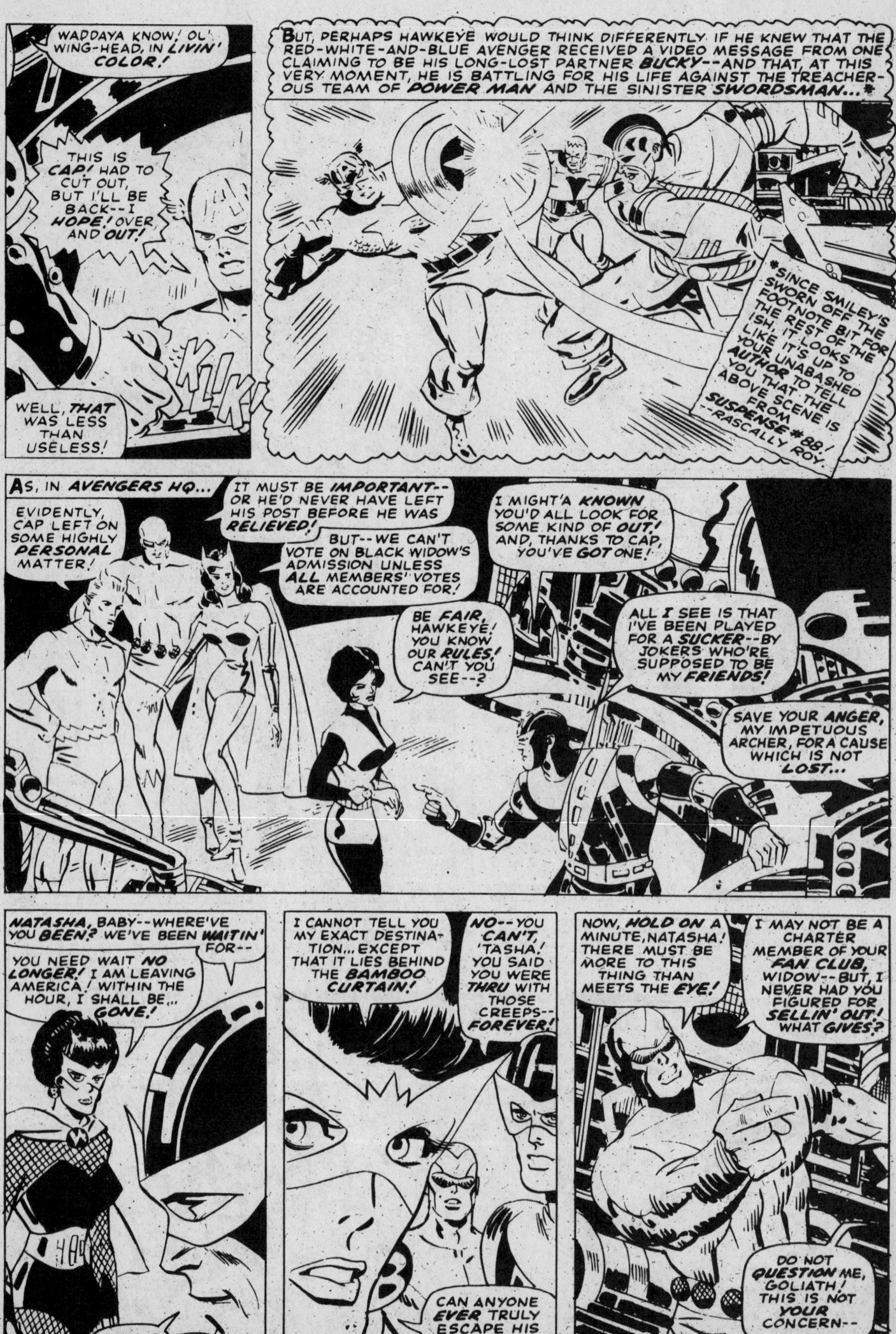
WADDAYA KNOW! OL' WING-HEAD, IN LIVIN' COLOR!
THIS IS CAP! HAD TO CUT OUT, BUT I'LL BE BACK--I HOPE! OVER AND OUT!
KLIK!
WELL, THAT WAS LESS THAN USELESS!
BUT, PERHAPS HAWKEYE WOULD THINK DIFFERENTLY IF HE KNEW THAT THE RED-WHITE-AND-BLUE AVENGER RECEIVED A VIDEO MESSAGE FROM ONE CLAIMING TO BE HIS LONG-LOST PARTNER BUCKY--AND THAT, AT THIS VERY MOMENT, HE IS BATTLING FOR HIS LIFE AGAINST THE TREACHEROUS TEAM OF POWER MAN AND THE SINISTER SWORDSMAN...*
*SINCE SMILEY'S SWORN OFF THE FOOTNOTE BIT FOR THE REST OF THE ISH, IT LOOKS LIKE IT'S UP TO YOUR UNABASHED AUTHOR TO TELL YOU THAT THE ABOVE SCENE IS FROM SUSPENSE #88! --RASCALLY ROY.
AS, IN AVENGERS HQ...
EVIDENTLY, CAP LEFT ON SOME HIGHLY PERSONAL MATTER!
IT MUST BE IMPORTANT--OR HE'D NEVER HAVE LEFT HIS POST BEFORE HE WAS RELIEVED!
BUT--WE CAN'T VOTE ON BLACK WIDOW'S ADMISSION UNLESS ALL MEMBERS' VOTES ARE ACCOUNTED FOR!
I MIGHT'A KNOWN YOU'D ALL LOOK FOR SOME KIND OF OUT! AND, THANKS TO CAP, YOU'VE GOT ONE!
BE FAIR, HAWKEYE! YOU KNOW OUR RULES! CAN'T YOU SEE--?
ALL I SEE IS THAT I'VE BEEN PLAYED FOR A SUCKER--BY JOKERS WHO'RE SUPPOSED TO BE MY FRIENDS!
SAVE YOUR ANGER, MY IMPETUOUS ARCHER, FOR A CAUSE WHICH IS NOT LOST...
NATASHA, BABY--WHERE'VE YOU BEEN? WE'VE BEEN WAITIN' FOR--
YOU NEED WAIT NO LONGER! I AM LEAVING AMERICA! WITHIN THE HOUR, I SHALL BE... GONE!
GONE? WHERE?
I CANNOT TELL YOU MY EXACT DESTINATION... EXCEPT THAT IT LIES BEHIND THE BAMBOO CURTAIN!
NO--YOU CAN'T, 'TASHA! YOU SAID YOU WERE THRU WITH THOSE CREEPS--FOREVER!
CAN ANYONE EVER TRULY ESCAPE HIS PAST--WHILE HE YET LIVES?
NOW, HOLD ON A MINUTE, NATASHA! THERE MUST BE MORE TO THIS THING THAN MEETS THE EYE!
I MAY NOT BE A CHARTER MEMBER OF YOUR FAN CLUB, WIDOW--BUT, I NEVER HAD YOU FIGURED FOR SELLIN' OUT! WHAT GIVES?
DO NOT QUESTION ME, GOLIATH! THIS IS NOT YOUR CONCERN--
9

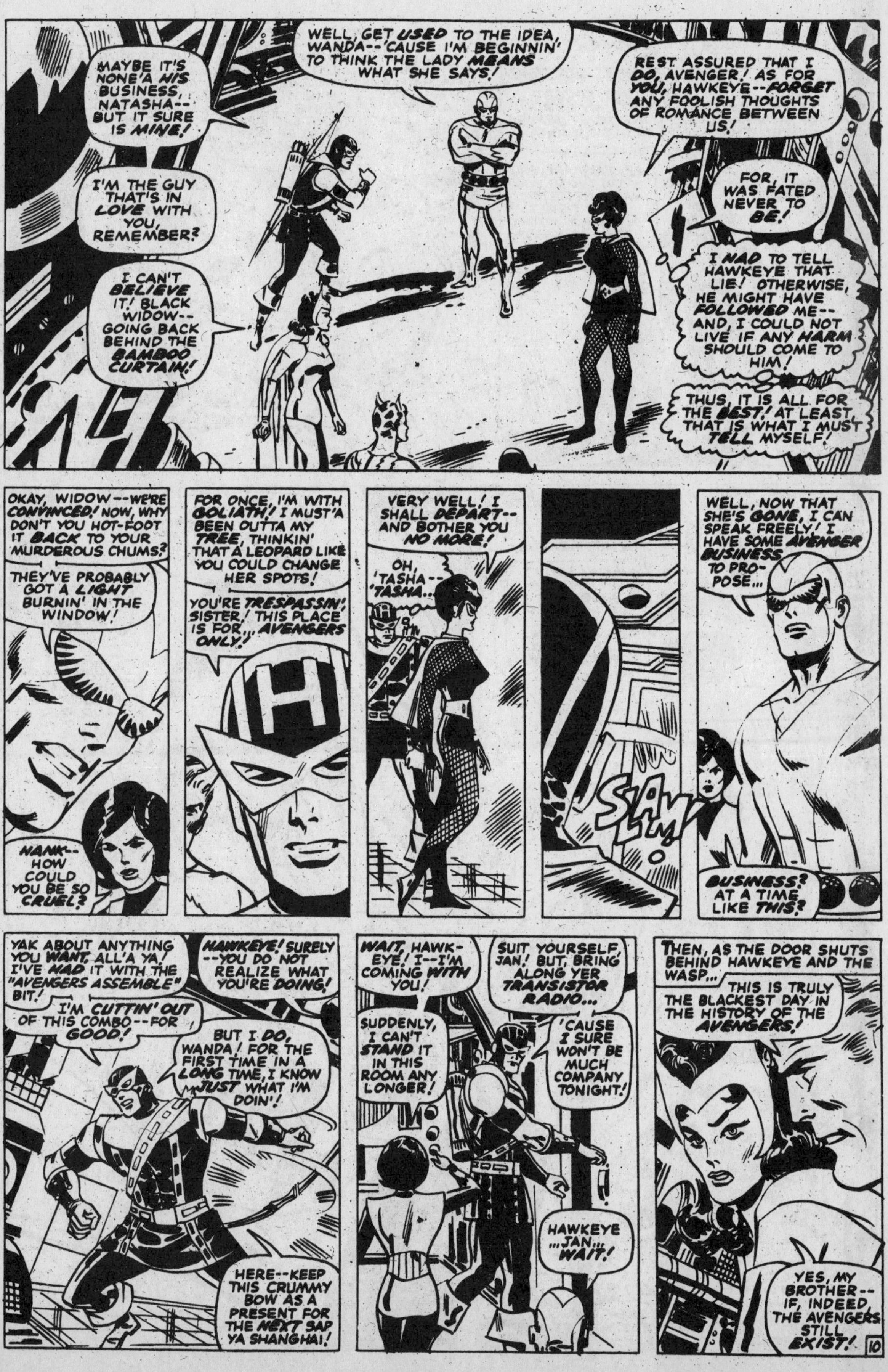
MAYBE IT'S NONE'A HIS BUSINESS, NATASHA--BUT IT SURE IS MINE!
WELL, GET USED TO THE IDEA, WANDA--'CAUSE I'M BEGINNIN' TO THINK THE LADY MEANS WHAT SHE SAYS!
REST ASSURED THAT I DO, AVENGER! AS FOR YOU, HAWKEYE--FORGET ANY FOOLISH THOUGHTS OF ROMANCE BETWEEN US!
I'M THE GUY THAT'S IN LOVE WITH YOU, REMEMBER?
FOR, IT WAS FATED NEVER TO BE!
I HAD TO TELL HAWKEYE THAT LIE! OTHERWISE, HE MIGHT HAVE FOLLOWED ME--AND, I COULD NOT LIVE IF ANY HARM SHOULD COME TO HIM!
I CAN'T BELIEVE IT! BLACK WIDOW--GOING BACK BEHIND THE BAMBOO CURTAIN!
THUS, IT IS ALL FOR THE BEST! AT LEAST, THAT IS WHAT I MUST TELL MYSELF!
OKAY, WIDOW--WE'RE CONVINCED! NOW, WHY DON'T YOU HOT-FOOT IT BACK TO YOUR MURDEROUS CHUMS?
THEY'VE PROBABLY GOT A LIGHT BURNIN' IN THE WINDOW!
HANK--HOW COULD YOU BE SO CRUEL?
FOR ONCE, I'M WITH GOLIATH! I MUST'A BEEN OUTTA MY TREE, THINKIN' THAT A LEOPARD LIKE YOU COULD CHANGE HER SPOTS!
YOU'RE TRESPASSIN', SISTER! THIS PLACE IS FOR... AVENGERS ONLY!
VERY WELL! I SHALL DEPART--AND BOTHER YOU NO MORE!
OH, 'TASHA--'TASHA...
SLAM
WELL, NOW THAT SHE'S GONE, I CAN SPEAK FREELY! I HAVE SOME AVENGER BUSINESS TO PROPOSE...
BUSINESS? AT A TIME LIKE THIS?
YAK ABOUT ANYTHING YOU WANT, ALL'A YA! I'VE HAD IT WITH THE "AVENGERS ASSEMBLE" BIT!
I'M CUTTIN' OUT OF THIS COMBO--FOR GOOD!
HAWKEYE! SURELY--YOU DO NOT REALIZE WHAT YOU'RE DOING!
BUT I DO, WANDA! FOR THE FIRST TIME IN A LONG TIME, I KNOW JUST WHAT I'M DOIN'!
HERE--KEEP THIS CRUMMY BOW AS A PRESENT FOR THE NEXT SAP YA SHANGHAI!
WAIT, HAWKEYE! I--I'M COMING WITH YOU!
SUDDENLY, I CAN'T STAND IT IN THIS ROOM ANY LONGER!
SUIT YOURSELF, JAN! BUT, BRING ALONG YER TRANSISTOR RADIO...
'CAUSE I SURE WON'T BE MUCH COMPANY TONIGHT!
HAWKEYE ...JAN... WAIT!
THEN, AS THE DOOR SHUTS BEHIND HAWKEYE AND THE WASP...
THIS IS TRULY THE BLACKEST DAY IN THE HISTORY OF THE AVENGERS!
YES, MY BROTHER--IF, INDEED, THE AVENGERS STILL EXIST!

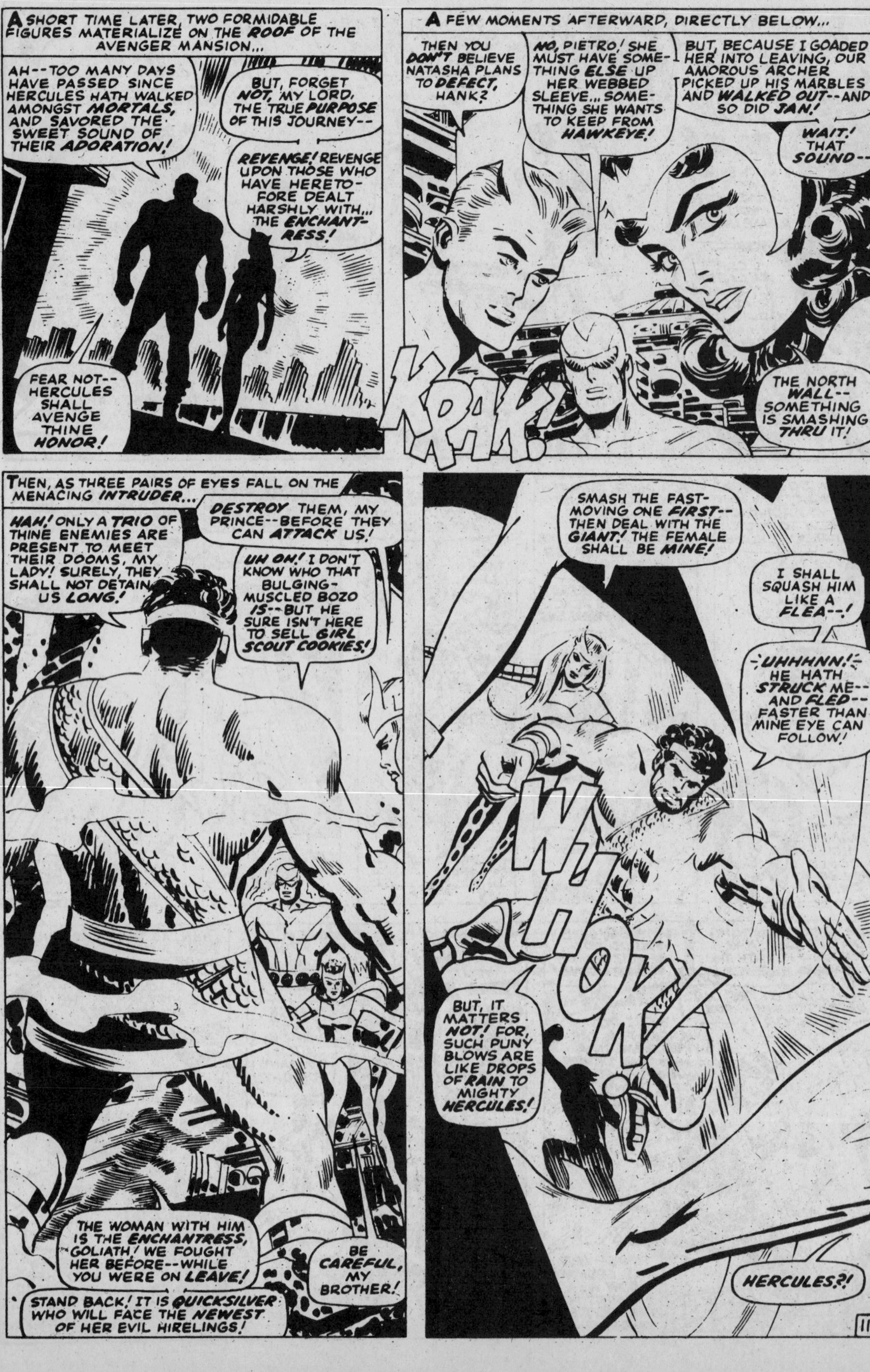
A SHORT TIME LATER, TWO FORMIDABLE FIGURES MATERIALIZE ON THE ROOF OF THE AVENGER MANSION...
AH--TOO MANY DAYS HAVE PASSED SINCE HERCULES HATH WALKED AMONGST MORTALS, AND SAVORED THE SWEET SOUND OF THEIR ADORATION!
BUT, FORGET NOT, MY LORD, THE TRUE PURPOSE OF THIS JOURNEY--
REVENGE! REVENGE UPON THOSE WHO HAVE HERETOFORE DEALT HARSHLY WITH... THE ENCHANTRESS!
FEAR NOT--HERCULES SHALL AVENGE THINE HONOR!
A FEW MOMENTS AFTERWARD, DIRECTLY BELOW...
THEN YOU DON'T BELIEVE NATASHA PLANS TO DEFECT, HANK?
NO, PIETRO! SHE MUST HAVE SOMETHING ELSE UP HER WEBBED SLEEVE... SOMETHING SHE WANTS TO KEEP FROM HAWKEYE!
BUT, BECAUSE I GOADED HER INTO LEAVING, OUR AMOROUS ARCHER PICKED UP HIS MARBLES AND WALKED OUT--AND SO DID JAN!
WAIT! THAT SOUND--
KRAK!
THE NORTH WALL--SOMETHING IS SMASHING THRU IT!
THEN, AS THREE PAIRS OF EYES FALL ON THE MENACING INTRUDER...
HAH! ONLY A TRIO OF THINE ENEMIES ARE PRESENT TO MEET THEIR DOOMS, MY LADY! SURELY, THEY SHALL NOT DETAIN US LONG!
DESTROY THEM, MY PRINCE--BEFORE THEY CAN ATTACK US!
UH OH! I DON'T KNOW WHO THAT BULGING-MUSCLED BOZO IS--BUT HE SURE ISN'T HERE TO SELL GIRL SCOUT COOKIES!
THE WOMAN WITH HIM IS THE ENCHANTRESS, GOLIATH! WE FOUGHT HER BEFORE--WHILE YOU WERE ON LEAVE!
BE CAREFUL, MY BROTHER!
STAND BACK! IT IS QUICKSILVER WHO WILL FACE THE NEWEST OF HER EVIL HIRELINGS!
SMASH THE FAST-MOVING ONE FIRST--THEN DEAL WITH THE GIANT! THE FEMALE SHALL BE MINE!
I SHALL SQUASH HIM LIKE A FLEA--!
UHHHHNN! HE HATH STRUCK ME--AND FLED--FASTER THAN MINE EYE CAN FOLLOW!
WHOK!
BUT, IT MATTERS NOT! FOR, SUCH PUNY BLOWS ARE LIKE DROPS OF RAIN TO MIGHTY HERCULES!
HERCULES?!
11

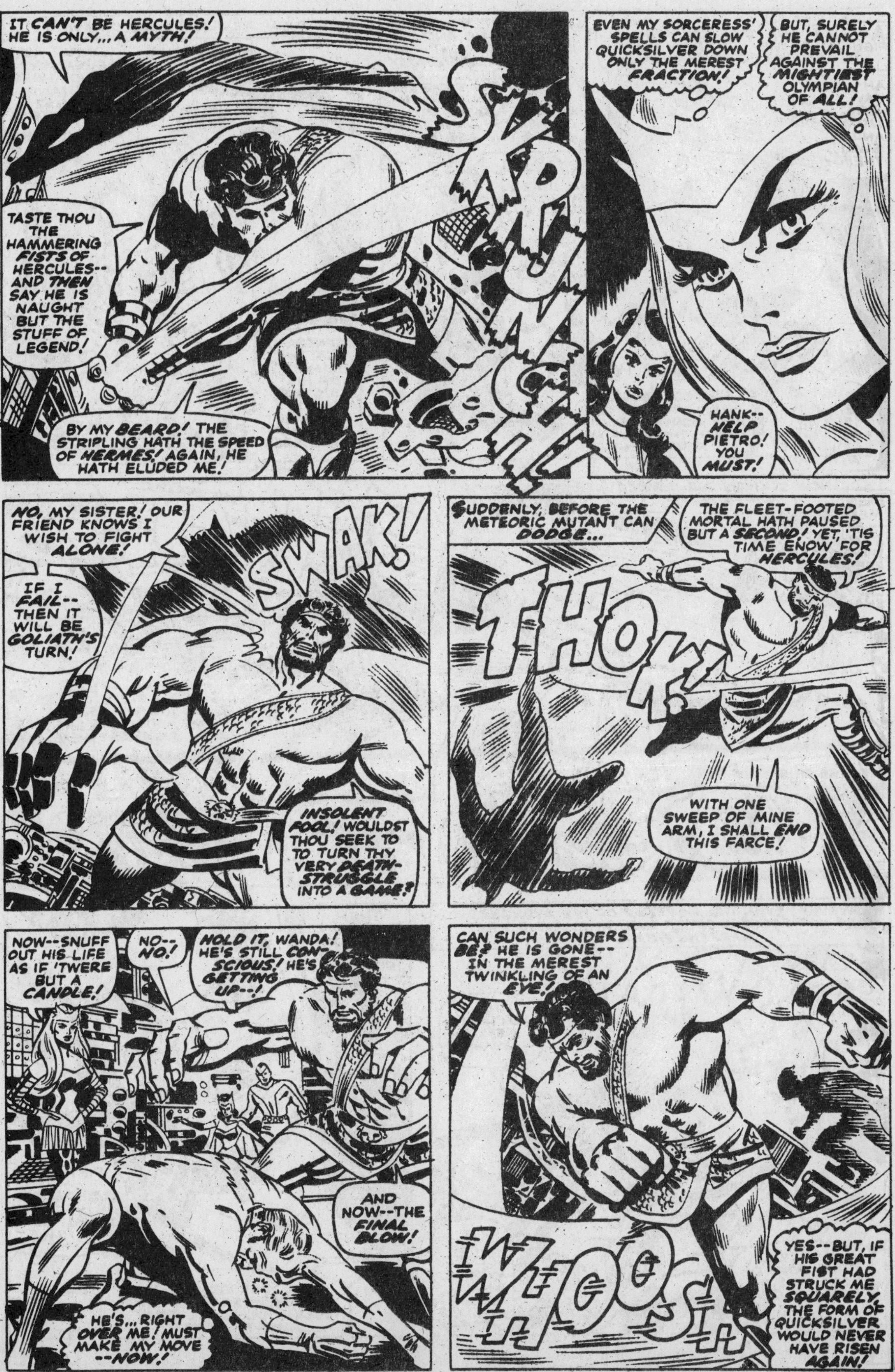
IT CAN'T BE HERCULES! HE IS ONLY... A MYTH!
TASTE THOU THE HAMMERING FISTS OF HERCULES-- AND THEN SAY HE IS NAUGHT BUT THE STUFF OF LEGEND!
SKRUNCH!
BY MY BEARD! THE STRIPLING HATH THE SPEED OF HERMES! AGAIN, HE HATH ELUDED ME!
EVEN MY SORCERESS' SPELLS CAN SLOW QUICKSILVER DOWN ONLY THE MEREST FRACTION!
BUT, SURELY HE CANNOT PREVAIL AGAINST THE MIGHTIEST OLYMPIAN OF ALL!
HANK-- HELP PIETRO! YOU MUST!
NO, MY SISTER! OUR FRIEND KNOWS I WISH TO FIGHT ALONE!
IF I FAIL-- THEN IT WILL BE GOLIATH'S TURN!
SWAK!
INSOLENT FOOL! WOULDST THOU SEEK TO TO TURN THY VERY DEATH-STRUGGLE INTO A GAME?
SUDDENLY, BEFORE THE METEORIC MUTANT CAN DODGE...
THE FLEET-FOOTED MORTAL HATH PAUSED BUT A SECOND! YET, 'TIS TIME ENOW FOR HERCULES!
THOK!
WITH ONE SWEEP OF MINE ARM, I SHALL END THIS FARCE!
NOW--SNUFF OUT HIS LIFE AS IF 'TWERE BUT A CANDLE!
NO-- NO!
HOLD IT, WANDA! HE'S STILL CONSCIOUS! HE'S GETTING UP--!
AND NOW--THE FINAL BLOW!
HE'S... RIGHT OVER ME! MUST MAKE MY MOVE --NOW!
CAN SUCH WONDERS BE? HE IS GONE-- IN THE MEREST TWINKLING OF AN EYE!
WHOOSH
YES--BUT, IF HIS GREAT FIST HAD STRUCK ME SQUARELY, THE FORM OF QUICKSILVER WOULD NEVER HAVE RISEN AGAIN!

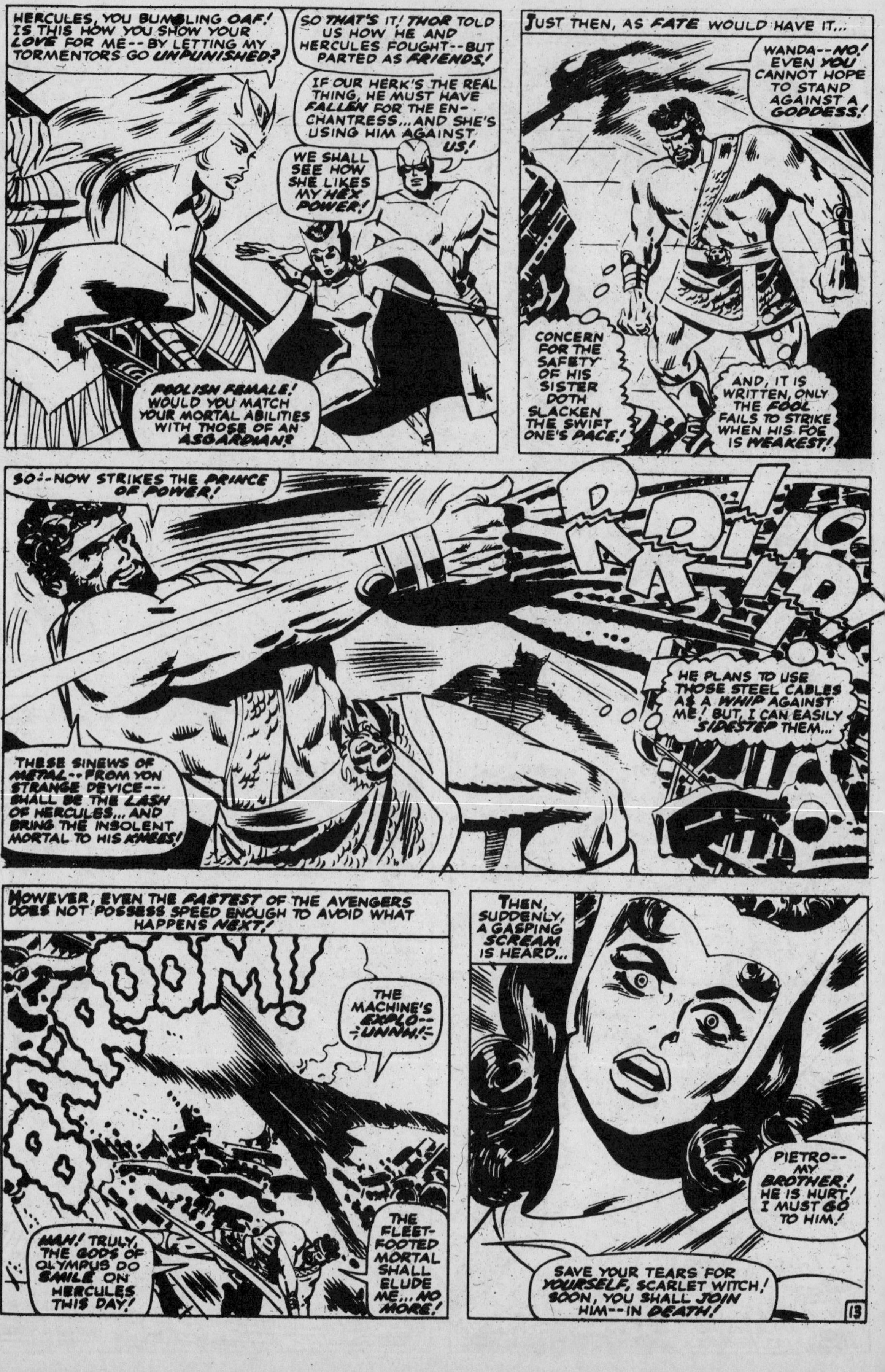

HERCULES, YOU BUMBLING OAF! IS THIS HOW YOU SHOW YOUR LOVE FOR ME--BY LETTING MY TORMENTORS GO UNPUNISHED?
SO THAT'S IT! THOR TOLD US HOW HE AND HERCULES FOUGHT--BUT PARTED AS FRIENDS!
IF OUR HERK'S THE REAL THING, HE MUST HAVE FALLEN FOR THE ENCHANTRESS... AND SHE'S USING HIM AGAINST US!
WE SHALL SEE HOW SHE LIKES MY HEX POWER!
FOOLISH FEMALE! WOULD YOU MATCH YOUR MORTAL ABILITIES WITH THOSE OF AN ASGARDIAN?
JUST THEN, AS FATE WOULD HAVE IT...
WANDA--NO! EVEN YOU CANNOT HOPE TO STAND AGAINST A GODDESS!
CONCERN FOR THE SAFETY OF HIS SISTER DOTH SLACKEN THE SWIFT ONE'S PACE!
AND, IT IS WRITTEN, ONLY THE FOOL FAILS TO STRIKE WHEN HIS FOE IS WEAKEST!
SO--NOW STRIKES THE PRINCE OF POWER!
RRIIIP!
HE PLANS TO USE THOSE STEEL CABLES AS A WHIP AGAINST ME! BUT, I CAN EASILY SIDESTEP THEM...
THESE SINEWS OF METAL--FROM YON STRANGE DEVICE--SHALL BE THE LASH OF HERCULES... AND BRING THE INSOLENT MORTAL TO HIS KNEES!
HOWEVER, EVEN THE FASTEST OF THE AVENGERS DOES NOT POSSESS SPEED ENOUGH TO AVOID WHAT HAPPENS NEXT!
BAROOM!
THE MACHINE'S EXPLO--UNNH!
MAN! TRULY, THE GODS OF OLYMPUS DO SMILE ON HERCULES THIS DAY!
THE FLEET-FOOTED MORTAL SHALL ELUDE ME... NO MORE!
THEN, SUDDENLY, A GASPING SCREAM IS HEARD...
PIETRO--MY BROTHER! HE IS HURT! I MUST GO TO HIM!
SAVE YOUR TEARS FOR YOURSELF, SCARLET WITCH! SOON, YOU SHALL JOIN HIM--IN DEATH!
13

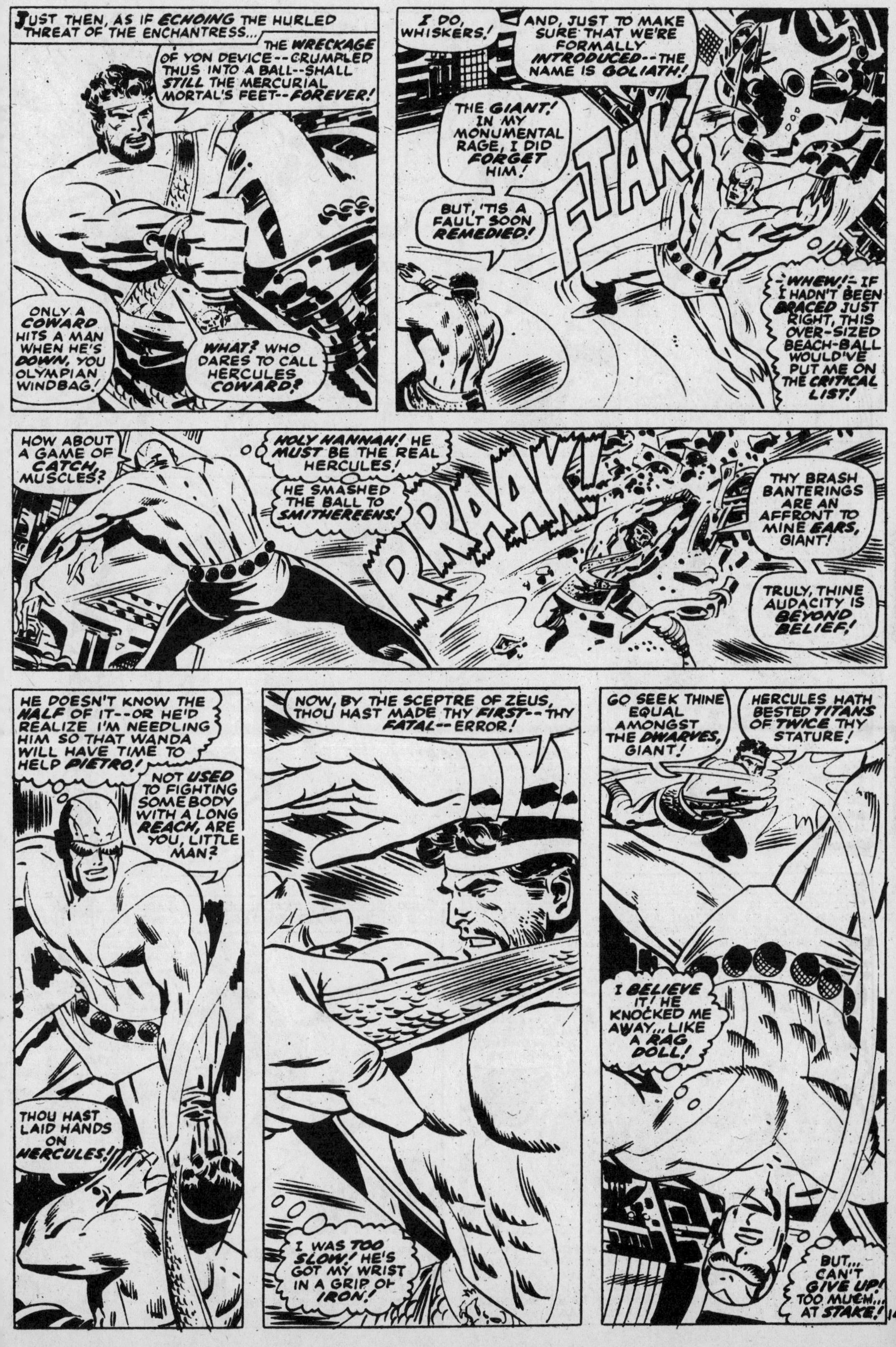
JUST THEN, AS IF ECHOING THE HURLED THREAT OF THE ENCHANTRESS...
THE WRECKAGE OF YON DEVICE--CRUMPLED THUS INTO A BALL--SHALL STILL THE MERCURIAL MORTAL'S FEET--FOREVER!
ONLY A COWARD HITS A MAN WHEN HE'S DOWN, YOU OLYMPIAN WINDBAG!
WHAT? WHO DARES TO CALL HERCULES COWARD?
I DO, WHISKERS!
AND, JUST TO MAKE SURE THAT WE'RE FORMALLY INTRODUCED--THE NAME IS GOLIATH!
THE GIANT! IN MY MONUMENTAL RAGE, I DID FORGET HIM!
BUT, 'TIS A FAULT SOON REMEDIED!
FTAK!
-WHEW!- IF I HADN'T BEEN BRACED JUST RIGHT, THIS OVER-SIZED BEACH-BALL WOULD'VE PUT ME ON THE CRITICAL LIST!
HOW ABOUT A GAME OF CATCH, MUSCLES?
HOLY HANNAH! HE MUST BE THE REAL HERCULES!
HE SMASHED THE BALL TO SMITHEREENS!
RRAAK!
THY BRASH BANTERINGS ARE AN AFFRONT TO MINE EARS, GIANT!
TRULY, THINE AUDACITY IS BEYOND BELIEF!
HE DOESN'T KNOW THE HALF OF IT--OR HE'D REALIZE I'M NEEDLING HIM SO THAT WANDA WILL HAVE TIME TO HELP PIETRO!
NOT USED TO FIGHTING SOMEBODY WITH A LONG REACH, ARE YOU, LITTLE MAN?
THOU HAST LAID HANDS ON HERCULES!
NOW, BY THE SCEPTRE OF ZEUS, THOU HAST MADE THY FIRST--THY FATAL--ERROR!
I WAS TOO SLOW! HE'S GOT MY WRIST IN A GRIP OF IRON!
GO SEEK THINE EQUAL AMONGST THE DWARVES, GIANT!
HERCULES HATH BESTED TITANS OF TWICE THY STATURE!
I BELIEVE IT! HE KNOCKED ME AWAY... LIKE A RAG DOLL!
BUT... CAN'T GIVE UP! TOO MUCH... AT STAKE!

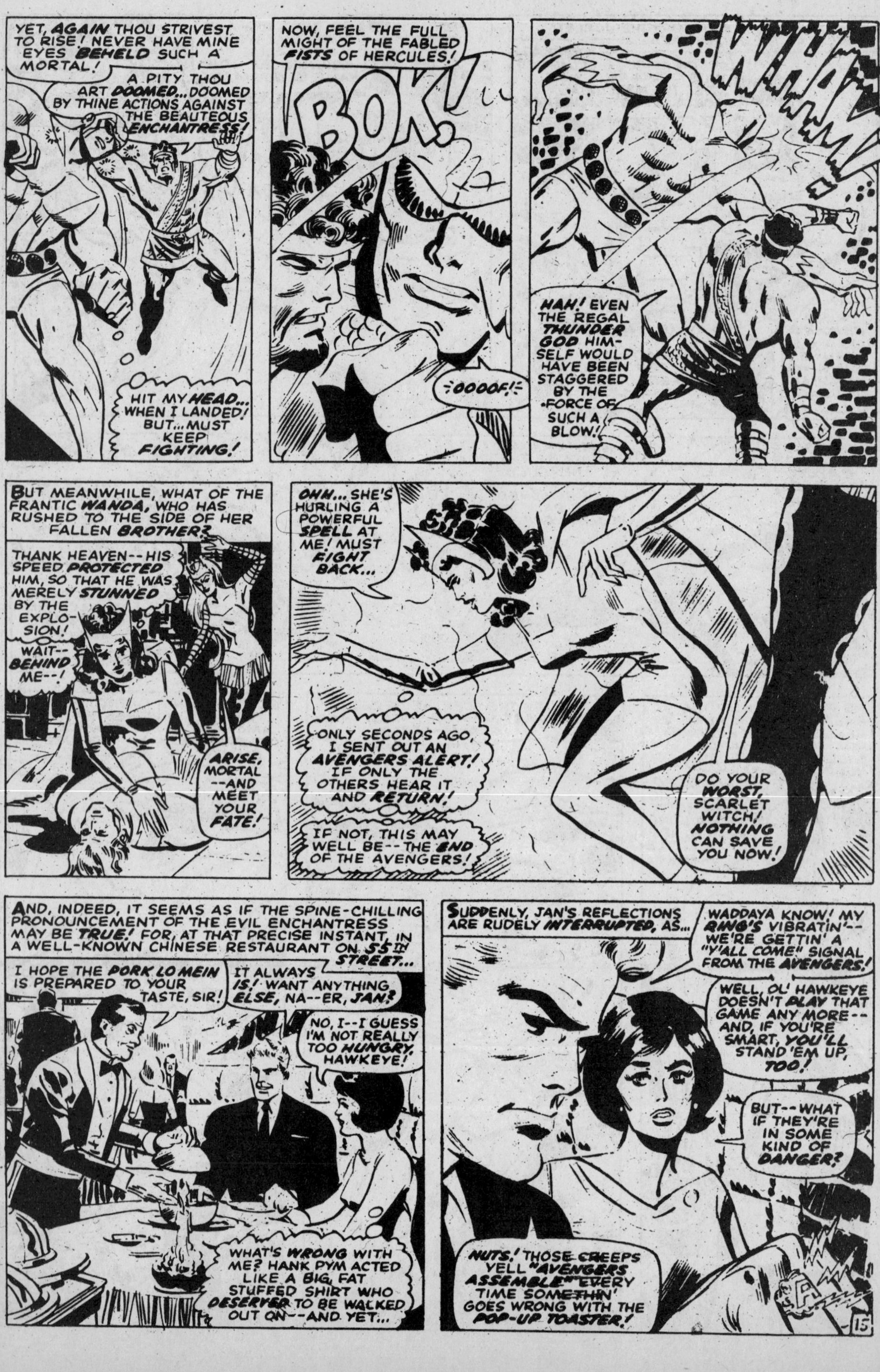
YET, AGAIN THOU STRIVEST TO RISE! NEVER HAVE MINE EYES BEHELD SUCH A MORTAL!
A PITY THOU ART DOOMED... DOOMED BY THINE ACTIONS AGAINST THE BEAUTEOUS ENCHANTRESS!
HIT MY HEAD... WHEN I LANDED! BUT... MUST KEEP FIGHTING!
NOW, FEEL THE FULL MIGHT OF THE FABLED FISTS OF HERCULES!
BOK!
OOOOF!
WHAM
HAH! EVEN THE REGAL THUNDER GOD HIMSELF WOULD HAVE BEEN STAGGERED BY THE FORCE OF SUCH A BLOW!
BUT MEANWHILE, WHAT OF THE FRANTIC WANDA, WHO HAS RUSHED TO THE SIDE OF HER FALLEN BROTHER?
THANK HEAVEN--HIS SPEED PROTECTED HIM, SO THAT HE WAS MERELY STUNNED BY THE EXPLOSION!
WAIT-- BEHIND ME--!
ARISE, MORTAL --AND MEET YOUR FATE!
OHH... SHE'S HURLING A POWERFUL SPELL AT ME! MUST FIGHT BACK...
ONLY SECONDS AGO, I SENT OUT AN AVENGERS ALERT! IF ONLY THE OTHERS HEAR IT AND RETURN!
IF NOT, THIS MAY WELL BE-- THE END OF THE AVENGERS!
DO YOUR WORST, SCARLET WITCH! NOTHING CAN SAVE YOU NOW!
AND, INDEED, IT SEEMS AS IF THE SPINE-CHILLING PRONOUNCEMENT OF THE EVIL ENCHANTRESS MAY BE TRUE! FOR, AT THAT PRECISE INSTANT, IN A WELL-KNOWN CHINESE RESTAURANT ON 55TH STREET...
I HOPE THE PORK LO MEIN IS PREPARED TO YOUR TASTE, SIR!
IT ALWAYS IS! WANT ANYTHING ELSE, NA--ER, JAN?
NO, I--I GUESS I'M NOT REALLY TOO HUNGRY, HAWKEYE!
WHAT'S WRONG WITH ME? HANK PYM ACTED LIKE A BIG, FAT STUFFED SHIRT WHO DESERVES TO BE WALKED OUT ON--AND YET...
SUDDENLY, JAN'S REFLECTIONS ARE RUDELY INTERRUPTED, AS...
WADDAYA KNOW! MY RING'S VIBRATIN'-- WE'RE GETTIN' A "Y'ALL COME" SIGNAL FROM THE AVENGERS!
WELL, OL' HAWKEYE DOESN'T PLAY THAT GAME ANY MORE-- AND, IF YOU'RE SMART, YOU'LL STAND 'EM UP, TOO!
BUT--WHAT IF THEY'RE IN SOME KIND OF DANGER?
NUTS! THOSE CREEPS YELL "AVENGERS ASSEMBLE" EVERY TIME SOMETHIN' GOES WRONG WITH THE POP-UP TOASTER!
15

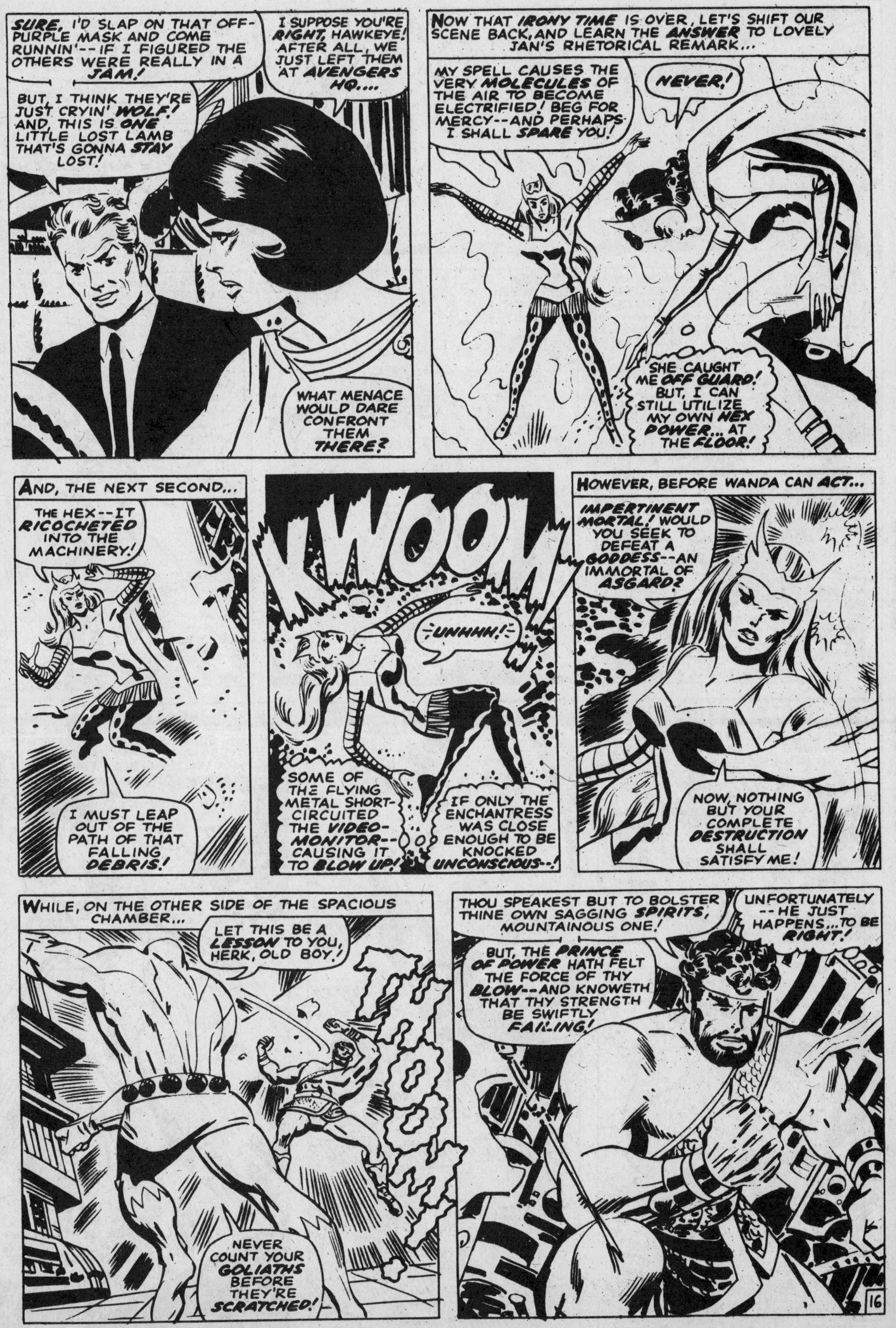
SURE, I'D SLAP ON THAT OFF-PURPLE MASK AND COME RUNNIN'--IF I FIGURED THE OTHERS WERE REALLY IN A JAM!
I SUPPOSE YOU'RE RIGHT, HAWKEYE! AFTER ALL, WE JUST LEFT THEM AT AVENGERS HQ....
BUT, I THINK THEY'RE JUST CRYIN' WOLF! AND, THIS IS ONE LITTLE LOST LAMB THAT'S GONNA STAY LOST!
WHAT MENACE WOULD DARE CONFRONT THEM THERE?
NOW THAT IRONY TIME IS OVER, LET'S SHIFT OUR SCENE BACK, AND LEARN THE ANSWER TO LOVELY JAN'S RHETORICAL REMARK...
MY SPELL CAUSES THE VERY MOLECULES OF THE AIR TO BECOME ELECTRIFIED! BEG FOR MERCY--AND PERHAPS I SHALL SPARE YOU!
NEVER!
SHE CAUGHT ME OFF GUARD! BUT, I CAN STILL UTILIZE MY OWN HEX POWER... AT THE FLOOR!
AND, THE NEXT SECOND...
THE HEX--IT RICOCHETED INTO THE MACHINERY!
I MUST LEAP OUT OF THE PATH OF THAT FALLING DEBRIS!
KWOOM
UNHHH!
SOME OF THE FLYING METAL SHORT-CIRCUITED THE VIDEO-MONITOR--CAUSING IT TO BLOW UP!
IF ONLY THE ENCHANTRESS WAS CLOSE ENOUGH TO BE KNOCKED UNCONSCIOUS--!
HOWEVER, BEFORE WANDA CAN ACT...
IMPERTINENT MORTAL! WOULD YOU SEEK TO DEFEAT A GODDESS--AN IMMORTAL OF ASGARD?
NOW, NOTHING BUT YOUR COMPLETE DESTRUCTION SHALL SATISFY ME!
WHILE, ON THE OTHER SIDE OF THE SPACIOUS CHAMBER...
LET THIS BE A LESSON TO YOU, HERK, OLD BOY!
THOOM
NEVER COUNT YOUR GOLIATHS BEFORE THEY'RE SCRATCHED!
THOU SPEAKEST BUT TO BOLSTER THINE OWN SAGGING SPIRITS, MOUNTAINOUS ONE!
UNFORTUNATELY--HE JUST HAPPENS... TO BE RIGHT!
BUT, THE PRINCE OF POWER HATH FELT THE FORCE OF THY BLOW--AND KNOWETH THAT THY STRENGTH BE SWIFTLY FAILING!
16

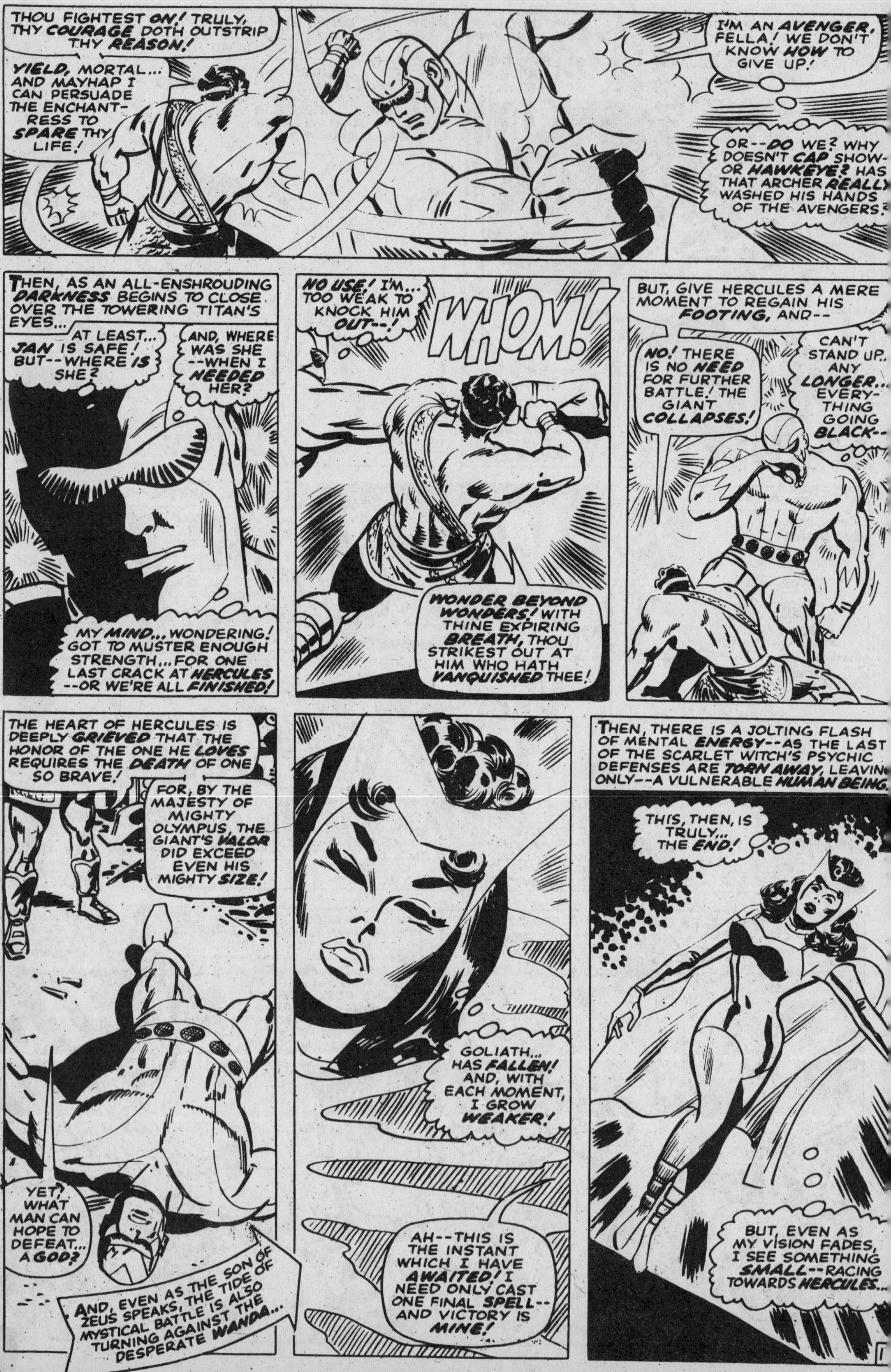
THOU FIGHTEST ON! TRULY, THY COURAGE DOTH OUTSTRIP THY REASON!
YIELD, MORTAL... AND MAYHAP I CAN PERSUADE THE ENCHANTRESS TO SPARE THY LIFE!
I'M AN AVENGER, FELLA! WE DON'T KNOW HOW TO GIVE UP!
OR--DO WE? WHY DOESN'T CAP SHOW-- OR HAWKEYE? HAS THAT ARCHER REALLY WASHED HIS HANDS OF THE AVENGERS?
THEN, AS AN ALL-ENSHROUDING DARKNESS BEGINS TO CLOSE OVER THE TOWERING TITAN'S EYES...
AT LEAST... JAN IS SAFE! BUT--WHERE IS SHE?
AND, WHERE WAS SHE --WHEN I NEEDED HER?
MY MIND... WONDERING! GOT TO MUSTER ENOUGH STRENGTH... FOR ONE LAST CRACK AT HERCULES --OR WE'RE ALL FINISHED!
NO USE! I'M... TOO WEAK TO KNOCK HIM OUT--!
WHOM!
WONDER BEYOND WONDERS! WITH THINE EXPIRING BREATH, THOU STRIKEST OUT AT HIM WHO HATH VANQUISHED THEE!
BUT, GIVE HERCULES A MERE MOMENT TO REGAIN HIS FOOTING, AND--
NO! THERE IS NO NEED FOR FURTHER BATTLE! THE GIANT COLLAPSES!
CAN'T STAND UP... ANY LONGER... EVERY-THING GOING BLACK--
THE HEART OF HERCULES IS DEEPLY GRIEVED THAT THE HONOR OF THE ONE HE LOVES REQUIRES THE DEATH OF ONE SO BRAVE!
FOR, BY THE MAJESTY OF MIGHTY OLYMPUS, THE GIANT'S VALOR DID EXCEED EVEN HIS MIGHTY SIZE!
YET! WHAT MAN CAN HOPE TO DEFEAT... A GOD?
AND, EVEN AS THE SON OF ZEUS SPEAKS, THE TIDE OF MYSTICAL BATTLE IS ALSO TURNING AGAINST THE DESPERATE WANDA...
GOLIATH... HAS FALLEN! AND, WITH EACH MOMENT, I GROW WEAKER!
AH--THIS IS THE INSTANT WHICH I HAVE AWAITED! I NEED ONLY CAST ONE FINAL SPELL-- AND VICTORY IS MINE!
THEN, THERE IS A JOLTING FLASH OF MENTAL ENERGY--AS THE LAST OF THE SCARLET WITCH'S PSYCHIC DEFENSES ARE TORN AWAY, LEAVING ONLY--A VULNERABLE HUMAN BEING.
THIS, THEN, IS TRULY... THE END!
BUT, EVEN AS MY VISION FADES, I SEE SOMETHING SMALL--RACING TOWARDS HERCULES...

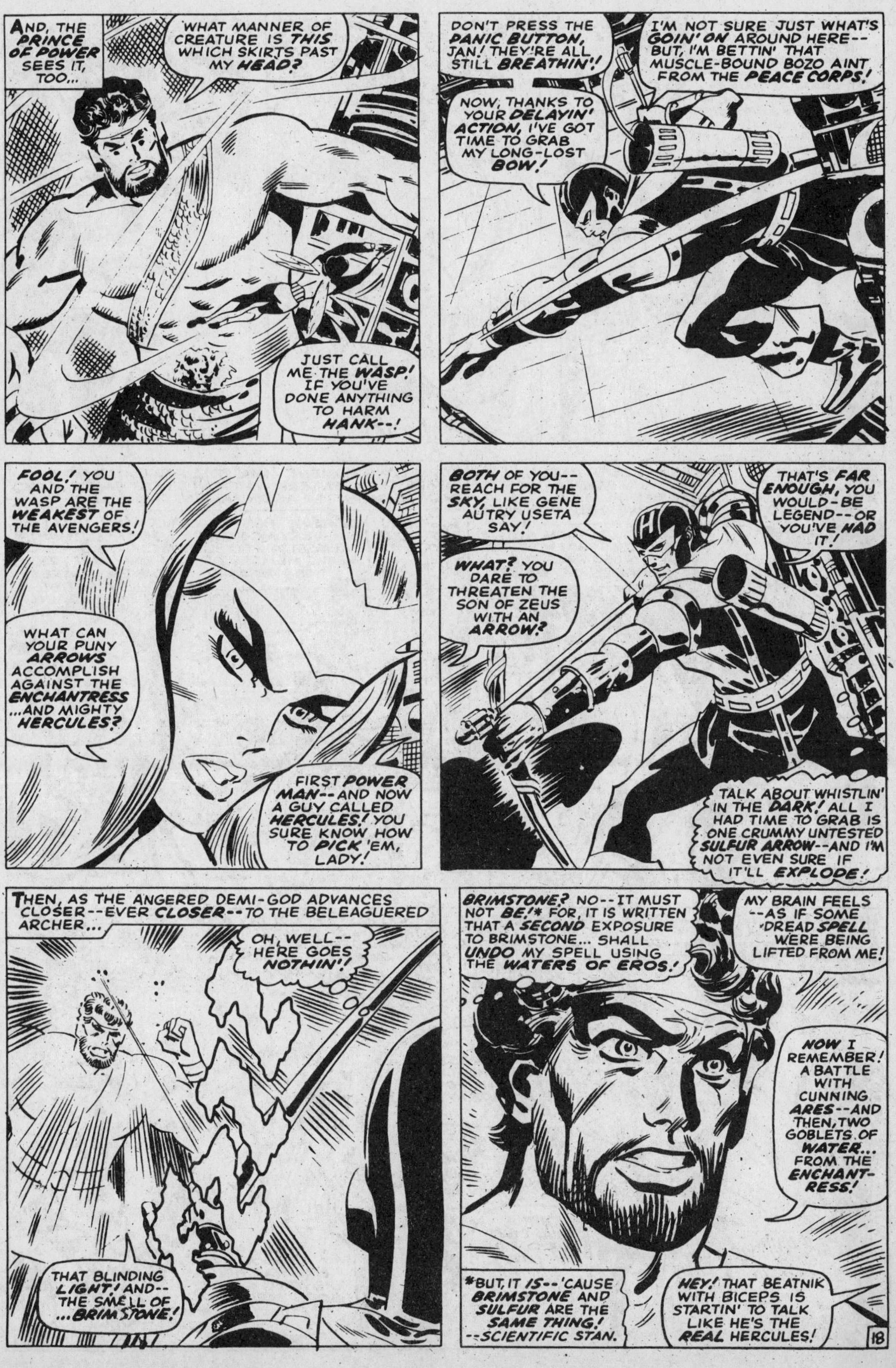
AND, THE PRINCE OF POWER SEES IT, TOO...
WHAT MANNER OF CREATURE IS THIS WHICH SKIRTS PAST MY HEAD?
JUST CALL ME THE WASP! IF YOU'VE DONE ANYTHING TO HARM HANK--!
DON'T PRESS THE PANIC BUTTON, JAN! THEY'RE ALL STILL BREATHIN'!
I'M NOT SURE JUST WHAT'S GOIN' ON AROUND HERE--BUT, I'M BETTIN' THAT MUSCLE-BOUND BOZO AINT FROM THE PEACE CORPS!
NOW, THANKS TO YOUR DELAYIN' ACTION, I'VE GOT TIME TO GRAB MY LONG-LOST BOW!
FOOL! YOU AND THE WASP ARE THE WEAKEST OF THE AVENGERS!
WHAT CAN YOUR PUNY ARROWS ACCOMPLISH AGAINST THE ENCHANTRESS ...AND MIGHTY HERCULES?
FIRST POWER MAN--AND NOW A GUY CALLED HERCULES! YOU SURE KNOW HOW TO PICK 'EM, LADY!
BOTH OF YOU--REACH FOR THE SKY, LIKE GENE AUTRY USETA SAY!
THAT'S FAR ENOUGH, YOU WOULD-BE LEGEND--OR YOU'VE HAD IT!
WHAT? YOU DARE TO THREATEN THE SON OF ZEUS WITH AN ARROW?
TALK ABOUT WHISTLIN' IN THE DARK! ALL I HAD TIME TO GRAB IS ONE CRUMMY UNTESTED SULFUR ARROW--AND I'M NOT EVEN SURE IF IT'LL EXPLODE!
THEN, AS THE ANGERED DEMI-GOD ADVANCES CLOSER--EVER CLOSER--TO THE BELEAGUERED ARCHER...
OH, WELL--HERE GOES NOTHIN'!
THAT BLINDING LIGHT! AND--THE SMELL OF ...BRIMSTONE!
BRIMSTONE? NO--IT MUST NOT BE!* FOR, IT IS WRITTEN THAT A SECOND EXPOSURE TO BRIMSTONE... SHALL UNDO MY SPELL USING THE WATERS OF EROS!
MY BRAIN FEELS--AS IF SOME DREAD SPELL WERE BEING LIFTED FROM ME!
NOW I REMEMBER! A BATTLE WITH CUNNING ARES--AND THEN, TWO GOBLETS OF WATER... FROM THE ENCHANTRESS!
*BUT, IT IS--'CAUSE BRIMSTONE AND SULFUR ARE THE SAME THING! --SCIENTIFIC STAN.
HEY! THAT BEATNIK WITH BICEPS IS STARTIN' TO TALK LIKE HE'S THE REAL HERCULES!
18

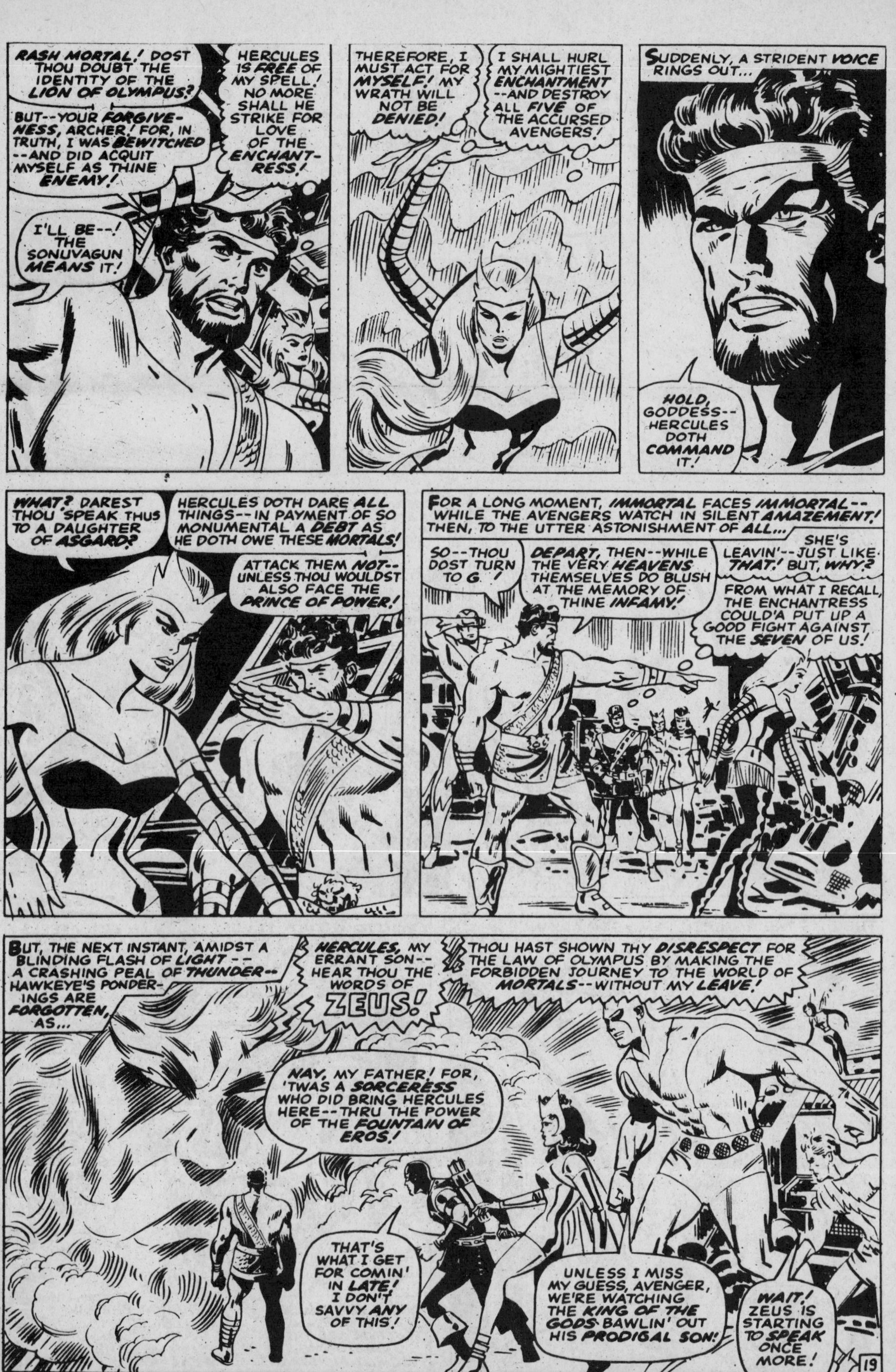
RASH MORTAL! DOST THOU DOUBT THE IDENTITY OF THE LION OF OLYMPUS?
BUT--YOUR FORGIVENESS, ARCHER! FOR, IN TRUTH, I WAS BEWITCHED --AND DID ACQUIT MYSELF AS THINE ENEMY!
HERCULES IS FREE OF MY SPELL! NO MORE SHALL HE STRIKE FOR LOVE OF THE ENCHANTRESS!
I'LL BE--! THE SONUVAGUN MEANS IT!
THEREFORE, I MUST ACT FOR MYSELF! MY WRATH WILL NOT BE DENIED!
I SHALL HURL MY MIGHTIEST ENCHANTMENT --AND DESTROY ALL FIVE OF THE ACCURSED AVENGERS!
SUDDENLY, A STRIDENT VOICE RINGS OUT...
HOLD, GODDESS-- HERCULES DOTH COMMAND IT!
WHAT? DAREST THOU SPEAK THUS TO A DAUGHTER OF ASGARD?
HERCULES DOTH DARE ALL THINGS--IN PAYMENT OF SO MONUMENTAL A DEBT AS HE DOTH OWE THESE MORTALS!
ATTACK THEM NOT-- UNLESS THOU WOULDST ALSO FACE THE PRINCE OF POWER!
FOR A LONG MOMENT, IMMORTAL FACES IMMORTAL-- WHILE THE AVENGERS WATCH IN SILENT AMAZEMENT! THEN, TO THE UTTER ASTONISHMENT OF ALL...
SO--THOU DOST TURN TO G !
DEPART, THEN--WHILE THE VERY HEAVENS THEMSELVES DO BLUSH AT THE MEMORY OF THINE INFAMY!
SHE'S LEAVIN'--JUST LIKE THAT! BUT, WHY?
FROM WHAT I RECALL, THE ENCHANTRESS COULD'A PUT UP A GOOD FIGHT AGAINST THE SEVEN OF US!
BUT, THE NEXT INSTANT, AMIDST A BLINDING FLASH OF LIGHT -- A CRASHING PEAL OF THUNDER-- HAWKEYE'S PONDERINGS ARE FORGOTTEN, AS...
HERCULES, MY ERRANT SON-- HEAR THOU THE WORDS OF ZEUS!
THOU HAST SHOWN THY DISRESPECT FOR THE LAW OF OLYMPUS BY MAKING THE FORBIDDEN JOURNEY TO THE WORLD OF MORTALS--WITHOUT MY LEAVE!
NAY, MY FATHER! FOR, 'TWAS A SORCERESS WHO DID BRING HERCULES HERE--THRU THE POWER OF THE FOUNTAIN OF EROS!
THAT'S WHAT I GET FOR COMIN' IN LATE! I DON'T SAVVY ANY OF THIS!
UNLESS I MISS MY GUESS, AVENGER, WE'RE WATCHING THE KING OF THE GODS BAWLIN' OUT HIS PRODIGAL SON!
WAIT! ZEUS IS STARTING TO SPEAK ONCE MORE!
19

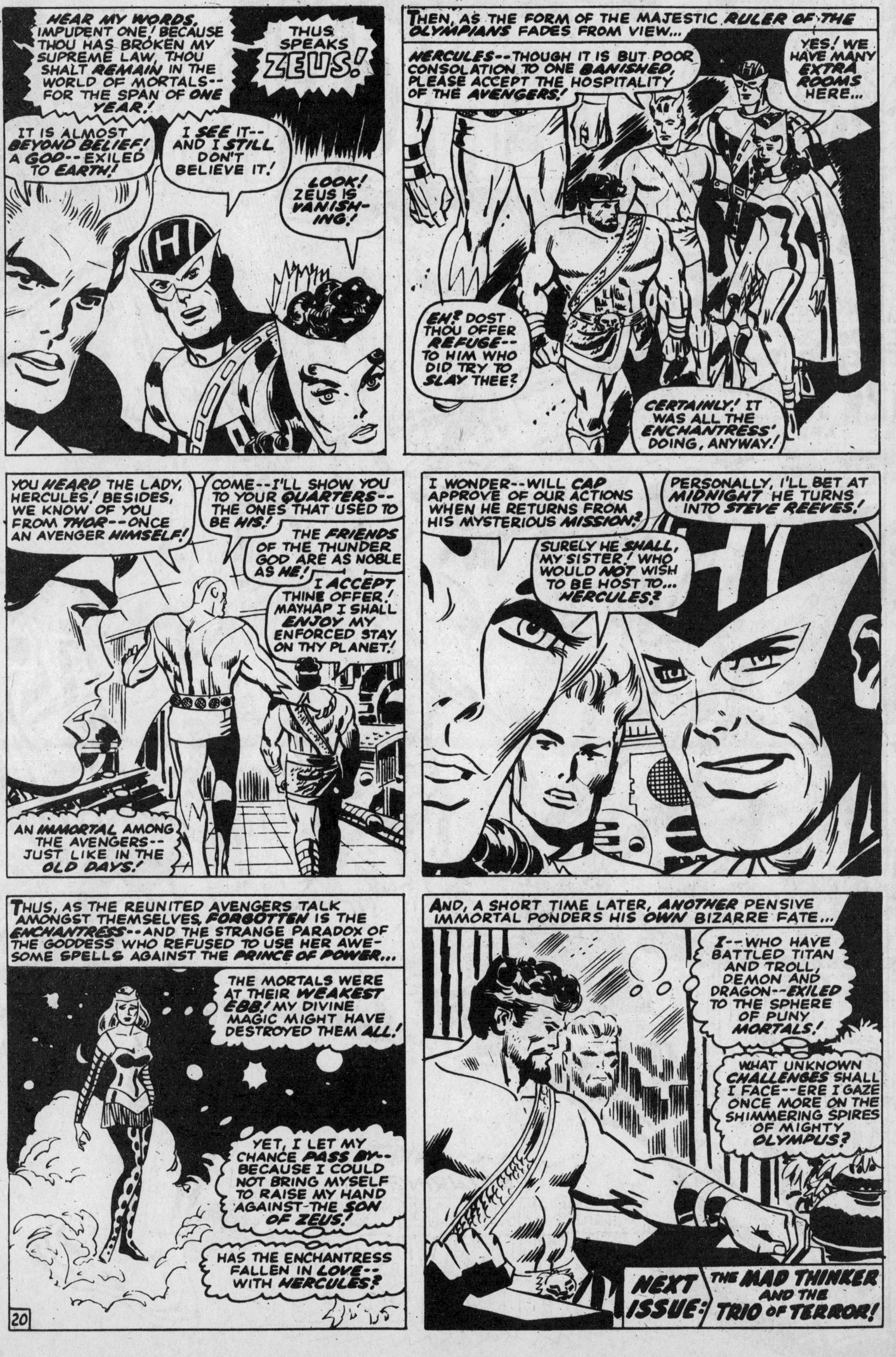
HEAR MY WORDS, IMPUDENT ONE! BECAUSE THOU HAS BROKEN MY SUPREME LAW, THOU SHALT REMAIN IN THE WORLD OF MORTALS-- FOR THE SPAN OF ONE YEAR!
THUS SPEAKS ZEUS!
IT IS ALMOST BEYOND BELIEF! A GOD--EXILED TO EARTH!
I SEE IT-- AND I STILL DON'T BELIEVE IT!
LOOK! ZEUS IS VANISH-ING!
THEN, AS THE FORM OF THE MAJESTIC RULER OF THE OLYMPIANS FADES FROM VIEW...
HERCULES--THOUGH IT IS BUT POOR CONSOLATION TO ONE BANISHED, PLEASE ACCEPT THE HOSPITALITY OF THE AVENGERS!
YES! WE HAVE MANY EXTRA ROOMS HERE...
EH? DOST THOU OFFER REFUGE-- TO HIM WHO DID TRY TO SLAY THEE?
CERTAINLY! IT WAS ALL THE ENCHANTRESS' DOING, ANYWAY!
YOU HEARD THE LADY, HERCULES! BESIDES, WE KNOW OF YOU FROM THOR--ONCE AN AVENGER HIMSELF!
COME--I'LL SHOW YOU TO YOUR QUARTERS-- THE ONES THAT USED TO BE HIS!
THE FRIENDS OF THE THUNDER GOD ARE AS NOBLE AS HE!
I ACCEPT THINE OFFER! MAYHAP I SHALL ENJOY MY ENFORCED STAY ON THY PLANET!
AN IMMORTAL AMONG THE AVENGERS-- JUST LIKE IN THE OLD DAYS!
I WONDER--WILL CAP APPROVE OF OUR ACTIONS WHEN HE RETURNS FROM HIS MYSTERIOUS MISSION?
PERSONALLY, I'LL BET AT MIDNIGHT HE TURNS INTO STEVE REEVES!
SURELY HE SHALL, MY SISTER! WHO WOULD NOT WISH TO BE HOST TO... HERCULES?
THUS, AS THE REUNITED AVENGERS TALK AMONGST THEMSELVES, FORGOTTEN IS THE ENCHANTRESS--AND THE STRANGE PARADOX OF THE GODDESS WHO REFUSED TO USE HER AWE-SOME SPELLS AGAINST THE PRINCE OF POWER...
THE MORTALS WERE AT THEIR WEAKEST EBB! MY DIVINE MAGIC MIGHT HAVE DESTROYED THEM ALL!
YET, I LET MY CHANCE PASS BY-- BECAUSE I COULD NOT BRING MYSELF TO RAISE MY HAND AGAINST THE SON OF ZEUS!
HAS THE ENCHANTRESS FALLEN IN LOVE-- WITH HERCULES?
AND, A SHORT TIME LATER, ANOTHER PENSIVE IMMORTAL PONDERS HIS OWN BIZARRE FATE...
I--WHO HAVE BATTLED TITAN AND TROLL, DEMON AND DRAGON--EXILED TO THE SPHERE OF PUNY MORTALS!
WHAT UNKNOWN CHALLENGES SHALL I FACE--ERE I GAZE ONCE MORE ON THE SHIMMERING SPIRES OF MIGHTY OLYMPUS?
NEXT ISSUE: THE MAD THINKER AND THE TRIO OF TERROR!

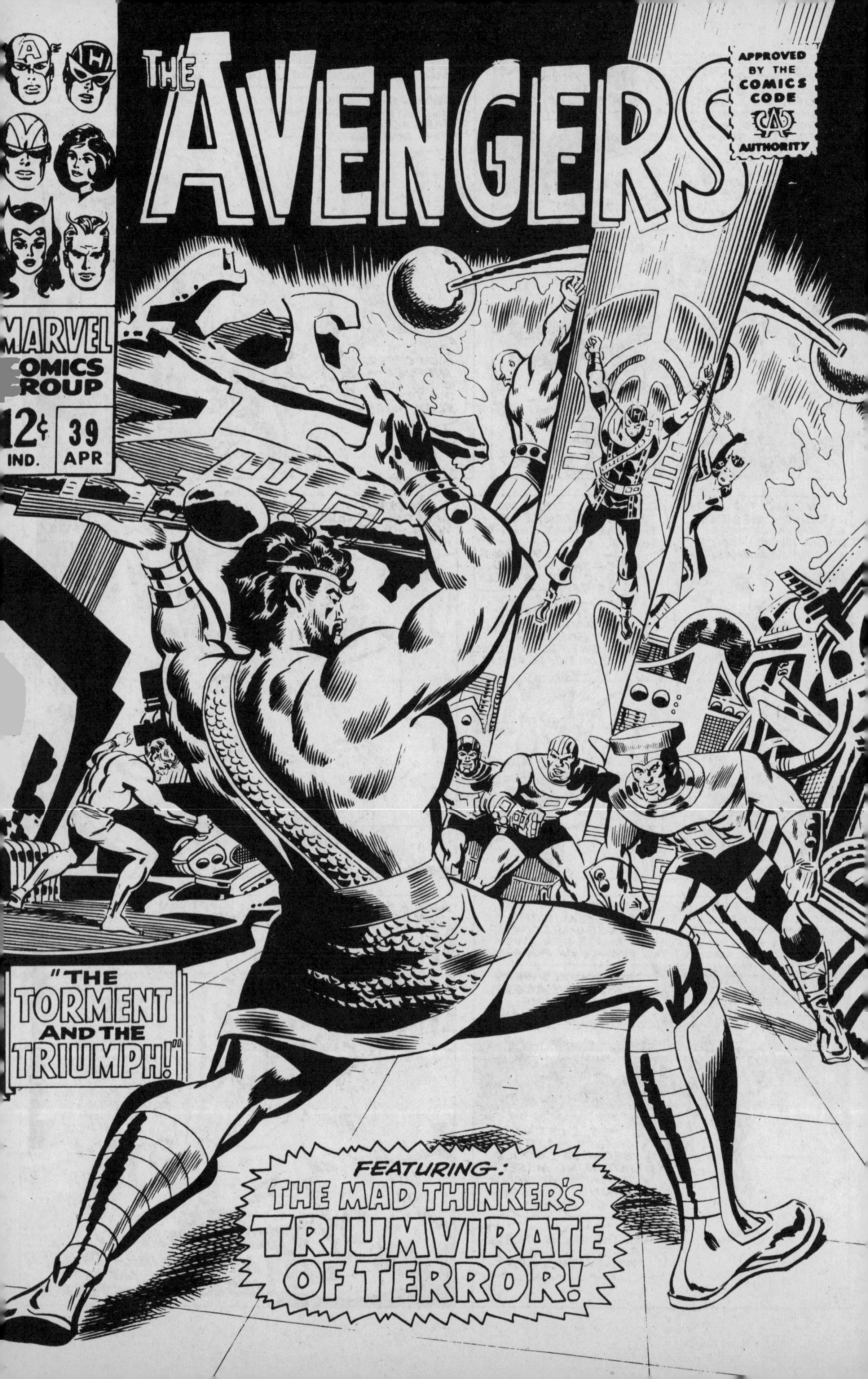

THE AVENGERS
APPROVED BY THE COMICS CODE AUTHORITY
MARVEL COMICS GROUP
12¢ IND.
39 APR
"THE TORMENT AND THE TRIUMPH!"
FEATURING-: THE MAD THINKER'S TRIUMVIRATE OF TERROR!

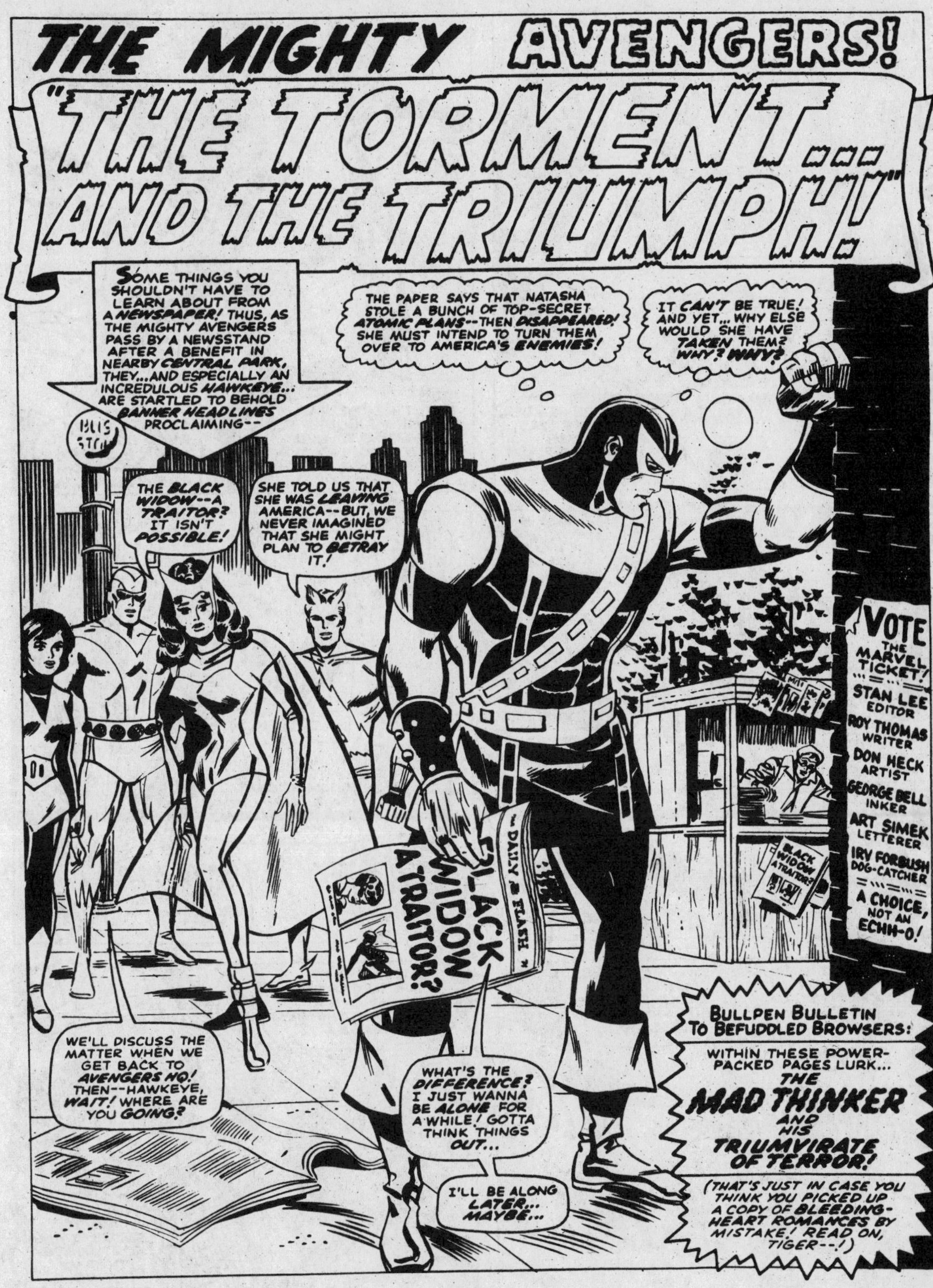
THE MIGHTY AVENGERS!
"THE TORMENT... AND THE TRIUMPH!"
SOME THINGS YOU SHOULDN'T HAVE TO LEARN ABOUT FROM A NEWSPAPER! THUS, AS THE MIGHTY AVENGERS PASS BY A NEWSSTAND AFTER A BENEFIT IN NEARBY CENTRAL PARK, THEY...AND ESPECIALLY AN INCREDULOUS HAWKEYE... ARE STARTLED TO BEHOLD BANNER HEADLINES PROCLAIMING--
THE PAPER SAYS THAT NATASHA STOLE A BUNCH OF TOP-SECRET ATOMIC PLANS--THEN DISAPPEARED! SHE MUST INTEND TO TURN THEM OVER TO AMERICA'S ENEMIES!
IT CAN'T BE TRUE! AND YET... WHY ELSE WOULD SHE HAVE TAKEN THEM? WHY? WHY?
THE BLACK WIDOW--A TRAITOR? IT ISN'T POSSIBLE!
SHE TOLD US THAT SHE WAS LEAVING AMERICA--BUT, WE NEVER IMAGINED THAT SHE MIGHT PLAN TO BETRAY IT!
VOTE THE MARVEL TICKET! STAN LEE EDITOR ROY THOMAS WRITER DON HECK ARTIST GEORGE BELL INKER ART SIMEK LETTERER IRV FORBUSH DOG-CATCHER A CHOICE, NOT AN ECHH-O!
DAILY FLASH
BLACK WIDOW A TRAITOR?
BLACK WIDOW A TRAITOR?
WE'LL DISCUSS THE MATTER WHEN WE GET BACK TO AVENGERS HQ! THEN--HAWKEYE, WAIT! WHERE ARE YOU GOING?
WHAT'S THE DIFFERENCE? I JUST WANNA BE ALONE FOR A WHILE! GOTTA THINK THINGS OUT...
I'LL BE ALONG LATER... MAYBE...
BULLPEN BULLETIN TO BEFUDDLED BROWSERS: WITHIN THESE POWER-PACKED PAGES LURK... THE MAD THINKER AND HIS TRIUMVIRATE OF TERROR!
(THAT'S JUST IN CASE YOU THINK YOU PICKED UP A COPY OF BLEEDING-HEART ROMANCES BY MISTAKE! READ ON, TIGER--!)

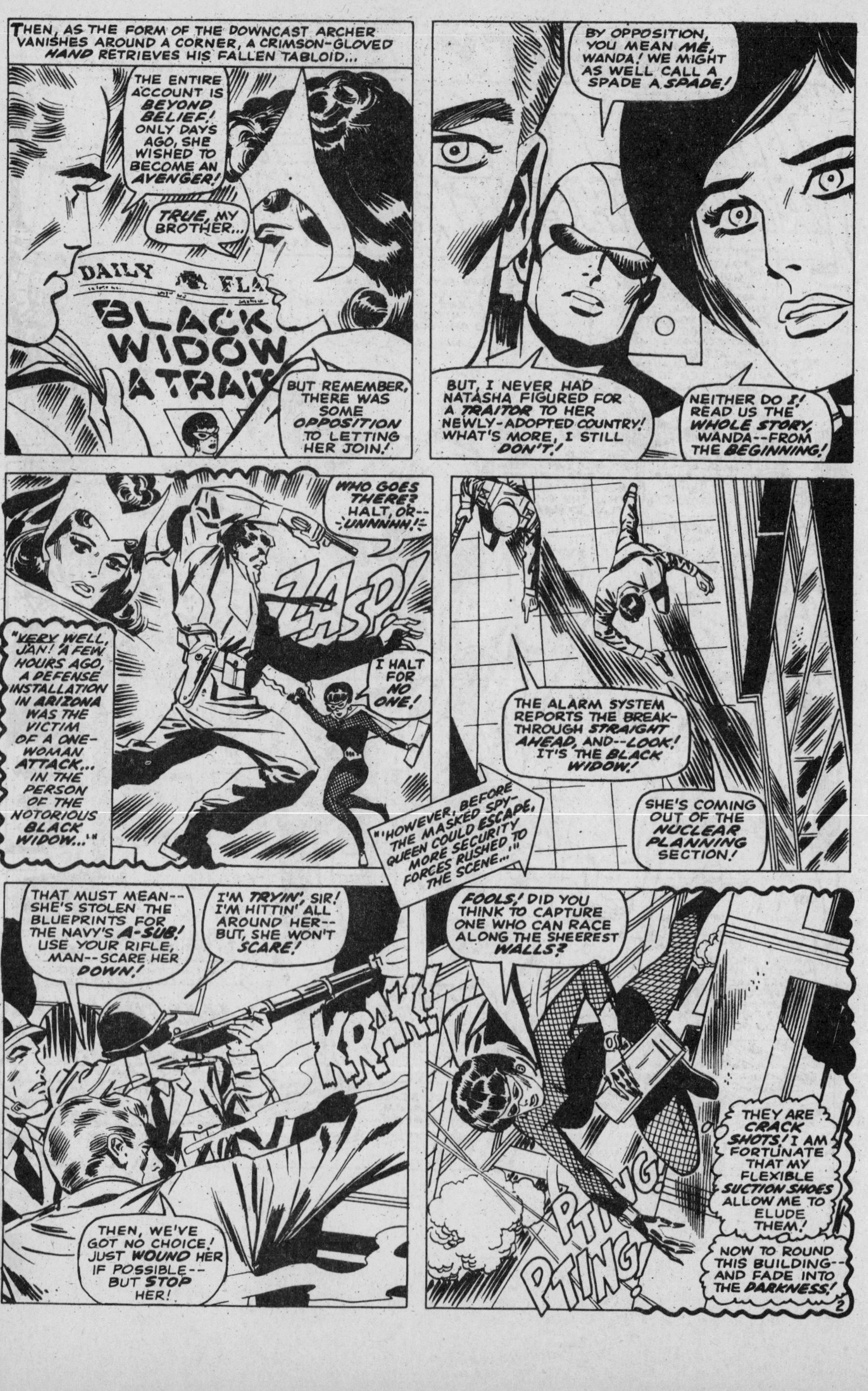

THEN, AS THE FORM OF THE DOWNCAST ARCHER VANISHES AROUND A CORNER, A CRIMSON-GLOVED HAND RETRIEVES HIS FALLEN TABLOID...
THE ENTIRE ACCOUNT IS BEYOND BELIEF! ONLY DAYS AGO, SHE WISHED TO BECOME AN AVENGER!
TRUE, MY BROTHER...
DAILY
BLACK WIDOW A TRAI
BUT REMEMBER, THERE WAS SOME OPPOSITION TO LETTING HER JOIN!
BY OPPOSITION, YOU MEAN ME, WANDA! WE MIGHT AS WELL CALL A SPADE A SPADE!
BUT, I NEVER HAD NATASHA FIGURED FOR A TRAITOR TO HER NEWLY-ADOPTED COUNTRY! WHAT'S MORE, I STILL DON'T!
NEITHER DO I! READ US THE WHOLE STORY, WANDA--FROM THE BEGINNING!
"VERY WELL, JAN! A FEW HOURS AGO, A DEFENSE INSTALLATION IN ARIZONA WAS THE VICTIM OF A ONE-WOMAN ATTACK... IN THE PERSON OF THE NOTORIOUS BLACK WIDOW..."
WHO GOES THERE? HALT, OR-- UNNNHH!
ZASP!
I HALT FOR NO ONE!
"HOWEVER, BEFORE THE MASKED SPY-QUEEN COULD ESCAPE, MORE SECURITY FORCES RUSHED TO THE SCENE..."
THE ALARM SYSTEM REPORTS THE BREAK-THROUGH STRAIGHT AHEAD, AND--LOOK! IT'S THE BLACK WIDOW!
SHE'S COMING OUT OF THE NUCLEAR PLANNING SECTION!
THAT MUST MEAN-- SHE'S STOLEN THE BLUEPRINTS FOR THE NAVY'S A-SUB! USE YOUR RIFLE, MAN--SCARE HER DOWN!
I'M TRYIN', SIR! I'M HITTIN' ALL AROUND HER-- BUT, SHE WON'T SCARE!
KRAK!
THEN, WE'VE GOT NO CHOICE! JUST WOUND HER IF POSSIBLE-- BUT STOP HER!
FOOLS! DID YOU THINK TO CAPTURE ONE WHO CAN RACE ALONG THE SHEEREST WALLS?
PTING!
PTING!
THEY ARE CRACK SHOTS! I AM FORTUNATE THAT MY FLEXIBLE SUCTION SHOES ALLOW ME TO ELUDE THEM!
NOW TO ROUND THIS BUILDING-- AND FADE INTO THE DARKNESS!

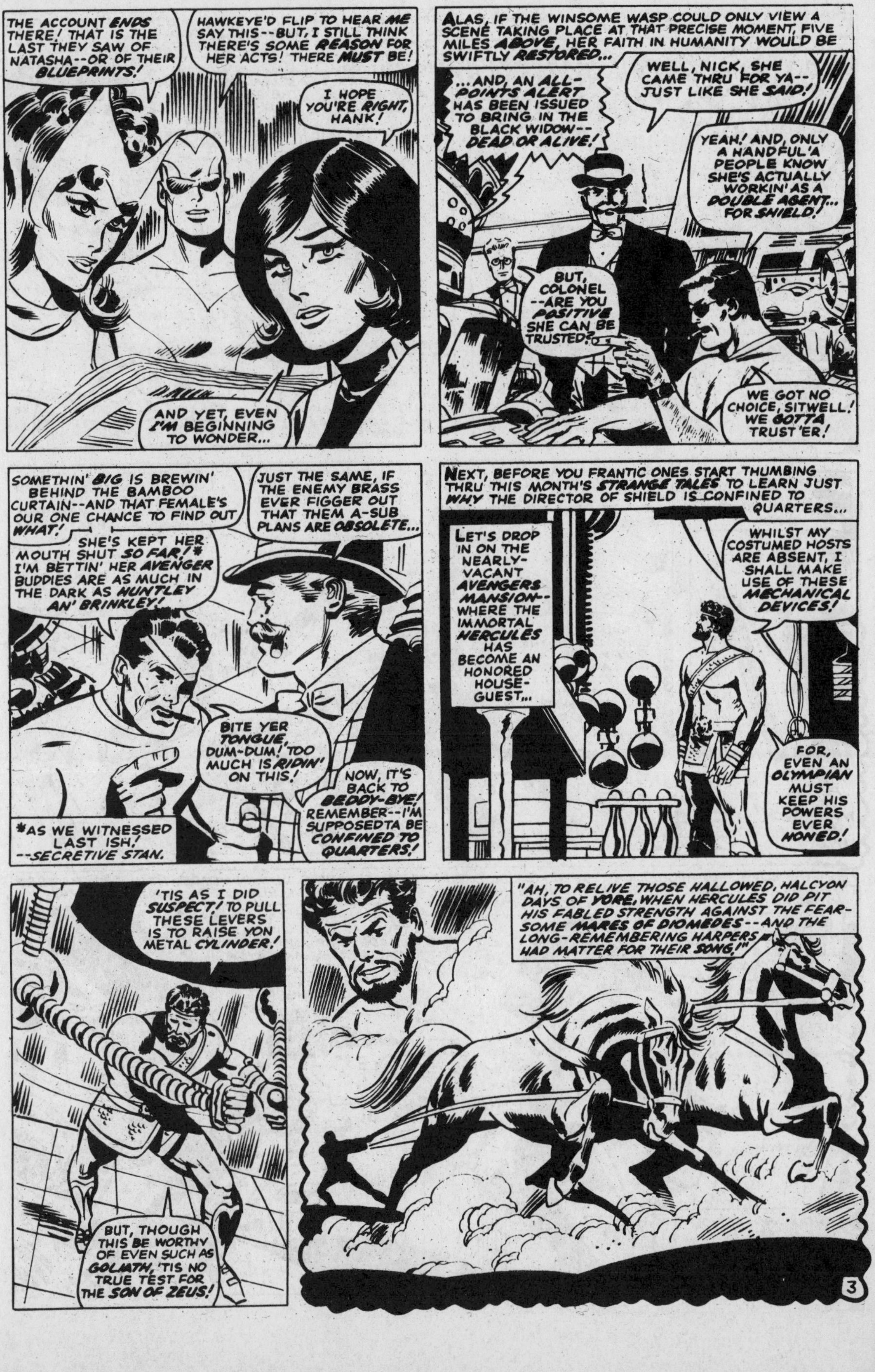
THE ACCOUNT ENDS THERE! THAT IS THE LAST THEY SAW OF NATASHA--OR OF THEIR BLUEPRINTS!
HAWKEYE'D FLIP TO HEAR ME SAY THIS--BUT, I STILL THINK THERE'S SOME REASON FOR HER ACTS! THERE MUST BE!
I HOPE YOU'RE RIGHT, HANK!
AND YET, EVEN I'M BEGINNING TO WONDER...
ALAS, IF THE WINSOME WASP COULD ONLY VIEW A SCENE TAKING PLACE AT THAT PRECISE MOMENT, FIVE MILES ABOVE, HER FAITH IN HUMANITY WOULD BE SWIFTLY RESTORED...
...AND, AN ALL-POINTS ALERT HAS BEEN ISSUED TO BRING IN THE BLACK WIDOW--DEAD OR ALIVE!
WELL, NICK, SHE CAME THRU FOR YA--JUST LIKE SHE SAID!
YEAH! AND, ONLY A HANDFUL'A PEOPLE KNOW SHE'S ACTUALLY WORKIN' AS A DOUBLE AGENT... FOR SHIELD!
BUT, COLONEL--ARE YOU POSITIVE SHE CAN BE TRUSTED?
WE GOT NO CHOICE, SITWELL! WE GOTTA TRUST 'ER!
SOMETHIN' BIG IS BREWIN' BEHIND THE BAMBOO CURTAIN--AND THAT FEMALE'S OUR ONE CHANCE TO FIND OUT WHAT!
JUST THE SAME, IF THE ENEMY BRASS EVER FIGGER OUT THAT THEM A-SUB PLANS ARE OBSOLETE...
SHE'S KEPT HER MOUTH SHUT SO FAR!* I'M BETTIN' HER AVENGER BUDDIES ARE AS MUCH IN THE DARK AS HUNTLEY AN' BRINKLEY!
BITE YER TONGUE, DUM-DUM! TOO MUCH IS RIDIN' ON THIS!
NOW, IT'S BACK TO BEDDY-BYE! REMEMBER--I'M SUPPOSEDTA BE CONFINED TO QUARTERS!
*AS WE WITNESSED LAST ISH! --SECRETIVE STAN.
NEXT, BEFORE YOU FRANTIC ONES START THUMBING THRU THIS MONTH'S STRANGE TALES TO LEARN JUST WHY THE DIRECTOR OF SHIELD IS CONFINED TO QUARTERS...
LET'S DROP IN ON THE NEARLY-VACANT AVENGERS MANSION--WHERE THE IMMORTAL HERCULES HAS BECOME AN HONORED HOUSE-GUEST...
WHILST MY COSTUMED HOSTS ARE ABSENT, I SHALL MAKE USE OF THESE MECHANICAL DEVICES!
FOR, EVEN AN OLYMPIAN MUST KEEP HIS POWERS EVER HONED!
'TIS AS I DID SUSPECT! TO PULL THESE LEVERS IS TO RAISE YON METAL CYLINDER!
BUT, THOUGH THIS BE WORTHY OF EVEN SUCH AS GOLIATH, 'TIS NO TRUE TEST FOR THE SON OF ZEUS!
"AH, TO RELIVE THOSE HALLOWED, HALCYON DAYS OF YORE, WHEN HERCULES DID PIT HIS FABLED STRENGTH AGAINST THE FEARSOME MARES OF DIOMEDES--AND THE LONG-REMEMBERING HARPERS HAD MATTER FOR THEIR SONG!"
3

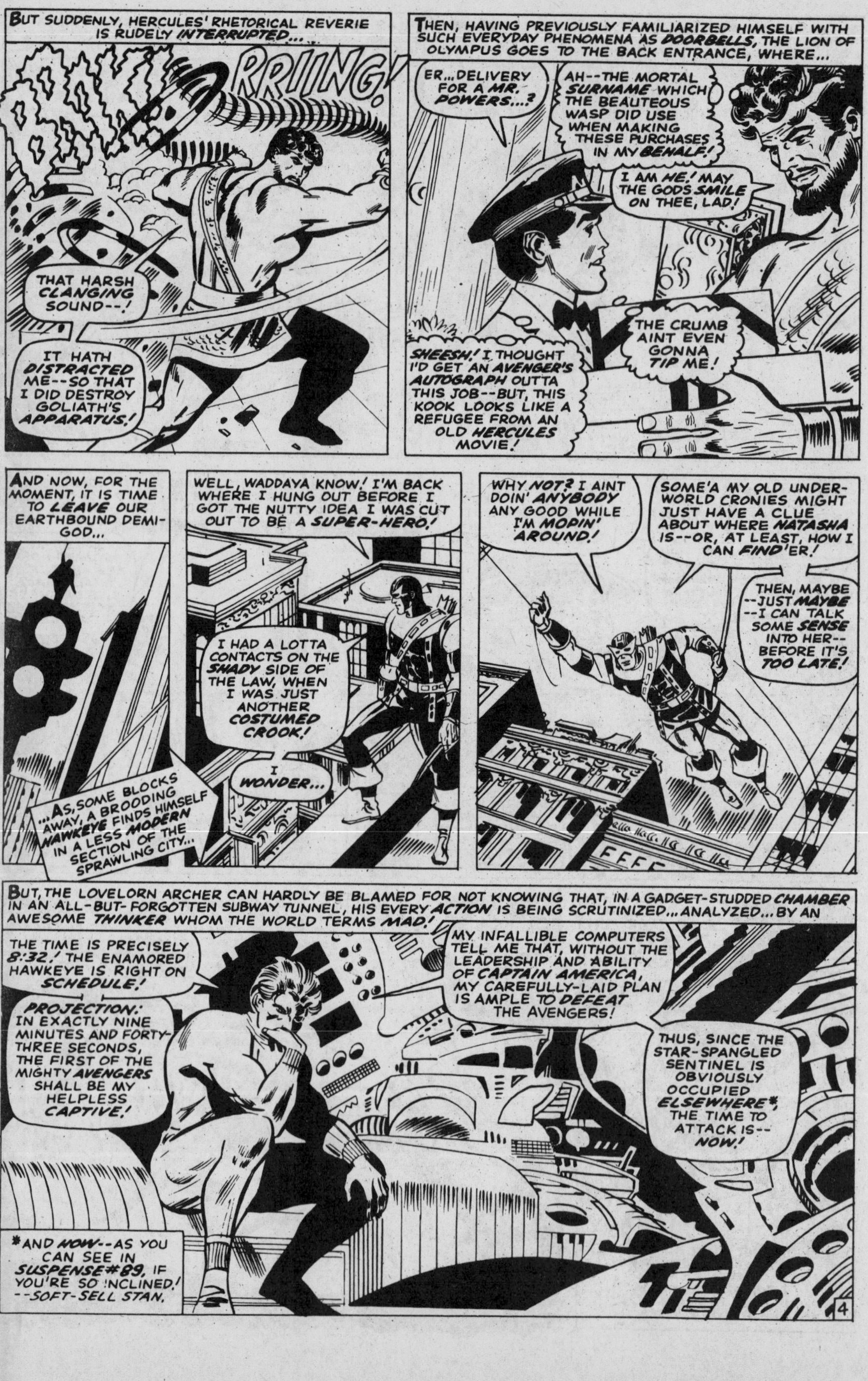
BUT SUDDENLY, HERCULES' RHETORICAL REVERIE IS RUDELY INTERRUPTED...
BAKK
RRIING!
THAT HARSH CLANGING SOUND--!
IT HATH DISTRACTED ME--SO THAT I DID DESTROY GOLIATH'S APPARATUS!
THEN, HAVING PREVIOUSLY FAMILIARIZED HIMSELF WITH SUCH EVERYDAY PHENOMENA AS DOORBELLS, THE LION OF OLYMPUS GOES TO THE BACK ENTRANCE, WHERE...
ER...DELIVERY FOR A MR. POWERS...?
AH--THE MORTAL SURNAME WHICH THE BEAUTEOUS WASP DID USE WHEN MAKING THESE PURCHASES IN MY BEHALF!
I AM HE! MAY THE GODS SMILE ON THEE, LAD!
THE CRUMB AINT EVEN GONNA TIP ME!
SHEESH! I THOUGHT I'D GET AN AVENGER'S AUTOGRAPH OUTTA THIS JOB--BUT, THIS KOOK LOOKS LIKE A REFUGEE FROM AN OLD HERCULES MOVIE!
AND NOW, FOR THE MOMENT, IT IS TIME TO LEAVE OUR EARTHBOUND DEMI-GOD...
...AS, SOME BLOCKS AWAY, A BROODING HAWKEYE FINDS HIMSELF IN A LESS MODERN SECTION OF THE SPRAWLING CITY...
WELL, WADDAYA KNOW! I'M BACK WHERE I HUNG OUT BEFORE I GOT THE NUTTY IDEA I WAS CUT OUT TO BE A SUPER-HERO!
I HAD A LOTTA CONTACTS ON THE SHADY SIDE OF THE LAW, WHEN I WAS JUST ANOTHER COSTUMED CROOK!
I WONDER...
WHY NOT? I AINT DOIN' ANYBODY ANY GOOD WHILE I'M MOPIN' AROUND!
SOME'A MY OLD UNDER-WORLD CRONIES MIGHT JUST HAVE A CLUE ABOUT WHERE NATASHA IS--OR, AT LEAST, HOW I CAN FIND'ER!
THEN, MAYBE --JUST MAYBE --I CAN TALK SOME SENSE INTO HER-- BEFORE IT'S TOO LATE!
BUT, THE LOVELORN ARCHER CAN HARDLY BE BLAMED FOR NOT KNOWING THAT, IN A GADGET-STUDDED CHAMBER IN AN ALL-BUT-FORGOTTEN SUBWAY TUNNEL, HIS EVERY ACTION IS BEING SCRUTINIZED... ANALYZED... BY AN AWESOME THINKER WHOM THE WORLD TERMS MAD!
THE TIME IS PRECISELY 8:32! THE ENAMORED HAWKEYE IS RIGHT ON SCHEDULE!
PROJECTION: IN EXACTLY NINE MINUTES AND FORTY-THREE SECONDS, THE FIRST OF THE MIGHTY AVENGERS SHALL BE MY HELPLESS CAPTIVE!
MY INFALLIBLE COMPUTERS TELL ME THAT, WITHOUT THE LEADERSHIP AND ABILITY OF CAPTAIN AMERICA, MY CAREFULLY-LAID PLAN IS AMPLE TO DEFEAT THE AVENGERS!
THUS, SINCE THE STAR-SPANGLED SENTINEL IS OBVIOUSLY OCCUPIED ELSEWHERE*, THE TIME TO ATTACK IS-- NOW!
*AND NOW--AS YOU CAN SEE IN SUSPENSE #89, IF YOU'RE SO INCLINED! --SOFT-SELL STAN.
4

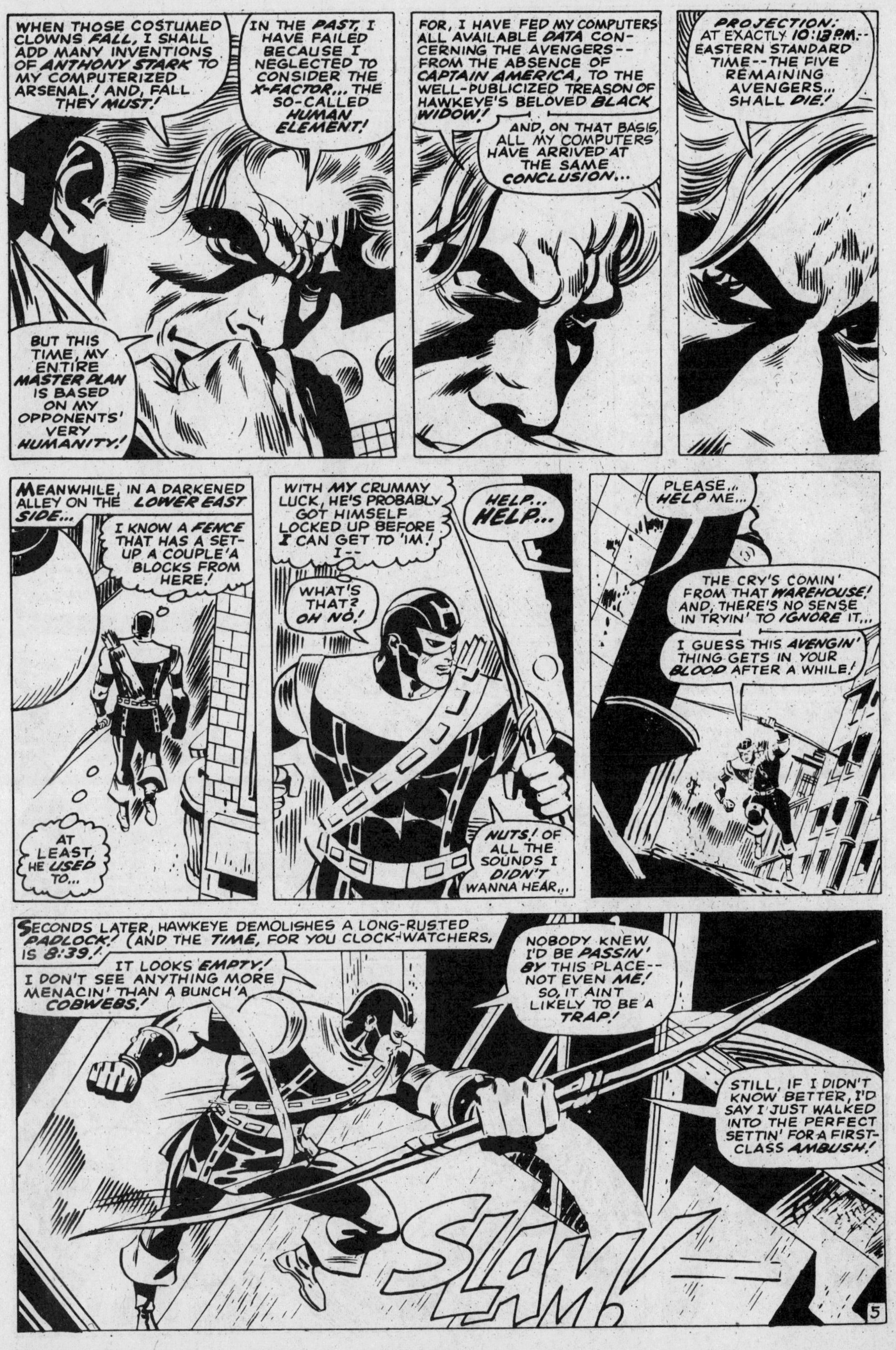

WHEN THOSE COSTUMED CLOWNS FALL, I SHALL ADD MANY INVENTIONS OF ANTHONY STARK TO MY COMPUTERIZED ARSENAL! AND, FALL THEY MUST!
IN THE PAST, I HAVE FAILED BECAUSE I NEGLECTED TO CONSIDER THE X-FACTOR... THE SO-CALLED HUMAN ELEMENT!
BUT THIS TIME, MY ENTIRE MASTER PLAN IS BASED ON MY OPPONENTS' VERY HUMANITY!
FOR, I HAVE FED MY COMPUTERS ALL AVAILABLE DATA CONCERNING THE AVENGERS-- FROM THE ABSENCE OF CAPTAIN AMERICA, TO THE WELL-PUBLICIZED TREASON OF HAWKEYE'S BELOVED BLACK WIDOW!
AND, ON THAT BASIS, ALL MY COMPUTERS HAVE ARRIVED AT THE SAME CONCLUSION...
PROJECTION: AT EXACTLY 10:13 P.M.-- EASTERN STANDARD TIME--THE FIVE REMAINING AVENGERS... SHALL DIE!
MEANWHILE, IN A DARKENED ALLEY ON THE LOWER EAST SIDE...
I KNOW A FENCE THAT HAS A SET-UP A COUPLE'A BLOCKS FROM HERE!
AT LEAST, HE USED TO...
WITH MY CRUMMY LUCK, HE'S PROBABLY GOT HIMSELF LOCKED UP BEFORE I CAN GET TO 'IM! I--
HELP... HELP...
WHAT'S THAT? OH NO!
NUTS! OF ALL THE SOUNDS I DIDN'T WANNA HEAR...
PLEASE... HELP ME...
THE CRY'S COMIN' FROM THAT WAREHOUSE! AND, THERE'S NO SENSE IN TRYIN' TO IGNORE IT...
I GUESS THIS AVENGIN' THING GETS IN YOUR BLOOD AFTER A WHILE!
SECONDS LATER, HAWKEYE DEMOLISHES A LONG-RUSTED PADLOCK! (AND THE TIME, FOR YOU CLOCK-WATCHERS, IS 8:39.)
IT LOOKS EMPTY! I DON'T SEE ANYTHING MORE MENACIN' THAN A BUNCH'A COBWEBS!
NOBODY KNEW I'D BE PASSIN' BY THIS PLACE-- NOT EVEN ME! SO, IT AINT LIKELY TO BE A TRAP!
STILL, IF I DIDN'T KNOW BETTER, I'D SAY I JUST WALKED INTO THE PERFECT SETTIN' FOR A FIRST-CLASS AMBUSH!
SLAM!

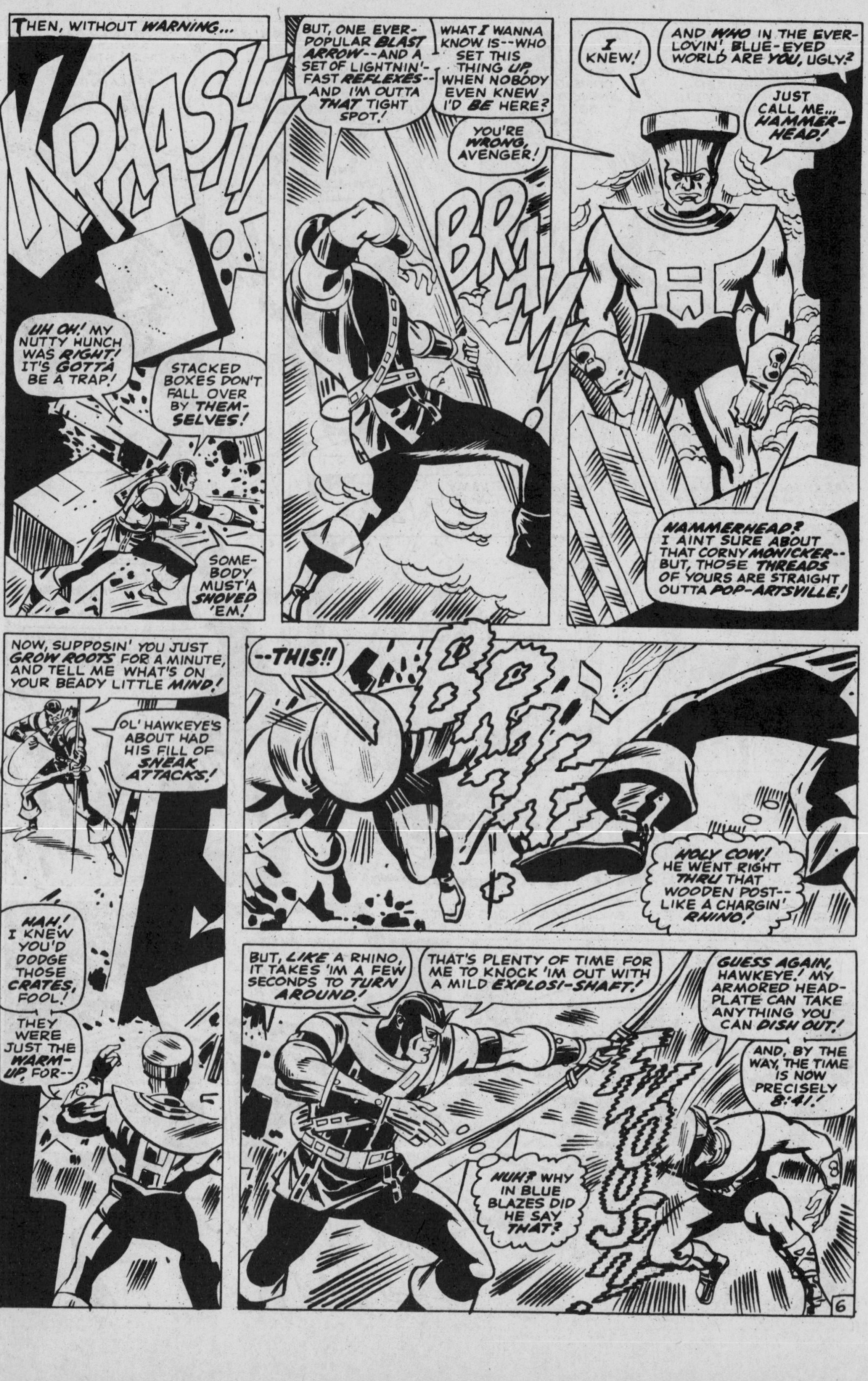
THEN, WITHOUT WARNING...
KRAASH!
UH OH! MY NUTTY HUNCH WAS RIGHT! IT'S GOTTA BE A TRAP!
STACKED BOXES DON'T FALL OVER BY THEMSELVES!
SOMEBODY MUST'A SHOVED 'EM!
BUT, ONE EVER-POPULAR BLAST ARROW--AND A SET OF LIGHTNIN'-FAST REFLEXES--AND I'M OUTTA THAT TIGHT SPOT!
WHAT I WANNA KNOW IS--WHO SET THIS THING UP, WHEN NOBODY EVEN KNEW I'D BE HERE?
YOU'RE WRONG, AVENGER!
BRAM
I KNEW!
AND WHO IN THE EVER-LOVIN', BLUE-EYED WORLD ARE YOU, UGLY?
JUST CALL ME... HAMMERHEAD!
HAMMERHEAD? I AINT SURE ABOUT THAT CORNY MONICKER--BUT, THOSE THREADS OF YOURS ARE STRAIGHT OUTTA POP-ARTSVILLE!
NOW, SUPPOSIN' YOU JUST GROW ROOTS FOR A MINUTE, AND TELL ME WHAT'S ON YOUR BEADY LITTLE MIND!
OL' HAWKEYE'S ABOUT HAD HIS FILL OF SNEAK ATTACKS!
HAH! I KNEW YOU'D DODGE THOSE CRATES, FOOL!
THEY WERE JUST THE WARM-UP, FOR--
--THIS!!
HOLY COW! HE WENT RIGHT THRU THAT WOODEN POST--LIKE A CHARGIN' RHINO!
BUT, LIKE A RHINO, IT TAKES 'IM A FEW SECONDS TO TURN AROUND!
THAT'S PLENTY OF TIME FOR ME TO KNOCK 'IM OUT WITH A MILD EXPLOSI-SHAFT!
GUESS AGAIN, HAWKEYE! MY ARMORED HEADPLATE CAN TAKE ANYTHING YOU CAN DISH OUT!
AND, BY THE WAY, THE TIME IS NOW PRECISELY 8:41!
HUH? WHY IN BLUE BLAZES DID HE SAY THAT?
6

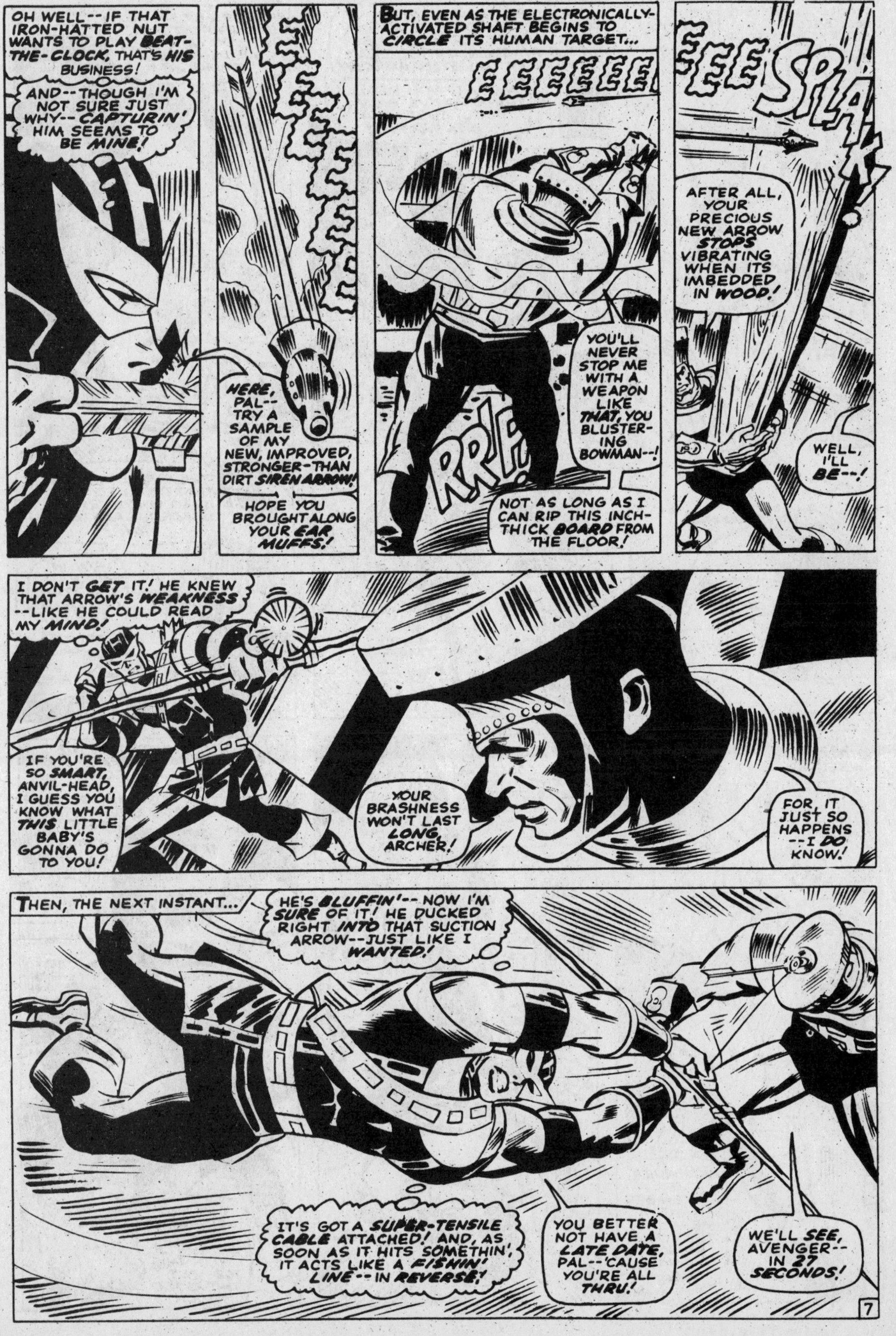

OH WELL--IF THAT IRON-HATTED NUT WANTS TO PLAY BEAT-THE-CLOCK, THAT'S HIS BUSINESS!
AND--THOUGH I'M NOT SURE JUST WHY--CAPTURIN' HIM SEEMS TO BE MINE!
EEEEEEE
HERE, PAL--TRY A SAMPLE OF MY NEW, IMPROVED, STRONGER-THAN DIRT SIREN ARROW!
HOPE YOU BROUGHT ALONG YOUR EAR MUFFS!
BUT, EVEN AS THE ELECTRONICALLY-ACTIVATED SHAFT BEGINS TO CIRCLE ITS HUMAN TARGET...
EEEEEEE
YOU'LL NEVER STOP ME WITH A WEAPON LIKE THAT, YOU BLUSTERING BOWMAN--!
RRIP!
NOT AS LONG AS I CAN RIP THIS INCH-THICK BOARD FROM THE FLOOR!
EEE SPLAK!
AFTER ALL, YOUR PRECIOUS NEW ARROW STOPS VIBRATING WHEN ITS IMBEDDED IN WOOD!
WELL, I'LL BE--!
I DON'T GET IT! HE KNEW THAT ARROW'S WEAKNESS--LIKE HE COULD READ MY MIND!
IF YOU'RE SO SMART, ANVIL-HEAD, I GUESS YOU KNOW WHAT THIS LITTLE BABY'S GONNA DO TO YOU!
YOUR BRASHNESS WON'T LAST LONG, ARCHER!
FOR, IT JUST SO HAPPENS--I DO KNOW!
THEN, THE NEXT INSTANT...
HE'S BLUFFIN'--NOW I'M SURE OF IT! HE DUCKED RIGHT INTO THAT SUCTION ARROW--JUST LIKE I WANTED!
IT'S GOT A SUPER-TENSILE CABLE ATTACHED! AND, AS SOON AS IT HITS SOMETHIN', IT ACTS LIKE A FISHIN' LINE--IN REVERSE!
YOU BETTER NOT HAVE A LATE DATE, PAL--'CAUSE YOU'RE ALL THRU!
WE'LL SEE, AVENGER--IN 27 SECONDS!

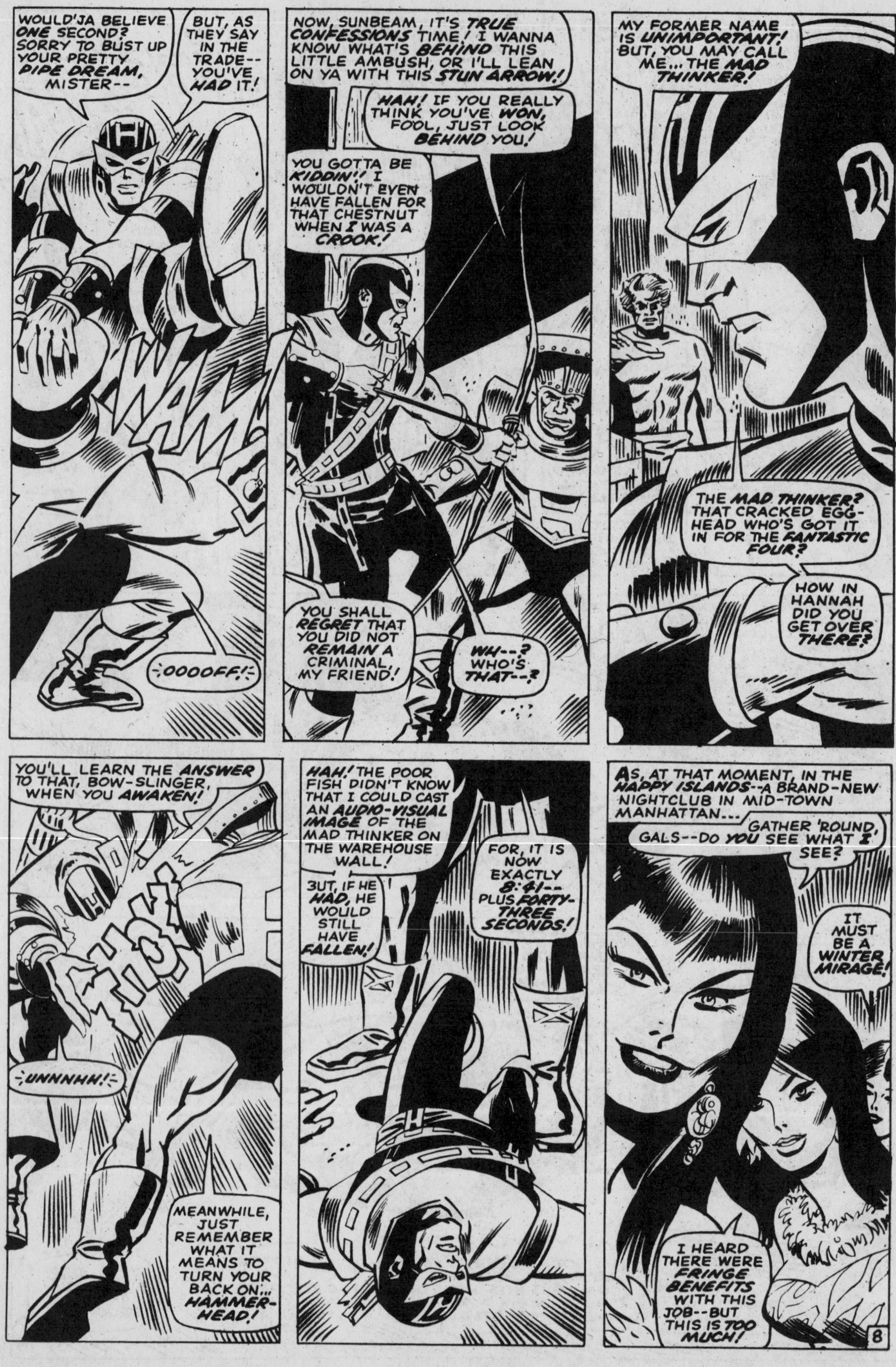
WOULD'JA BELIEVE ONE SECOND? SORRY TO BUST UP YOUR PRETTY PIPE DREAM, MISTER--
BUT, AS THEY SAY IN THE TRADE--YOU'VE HAD IT!
WAM
OOOOFF!
NOW, SUNBEAM, IT'S TRUE CONFESSIONS TIME! I WANNA KNOW WHAT'S BEHIND THIS LITTLE AMBUSH, OR I'LL LEAN ON YA WITH THIS STUN ARROW!
HAH! IF YOU REALLY THINK YOU'VE WON, FOOL, JUST LOOK BEHIND YOU!
YOU GOTTA BE KIDDIN'! I WOULDN'T EVEN HAVE FALLEN FOR THAT CHESTNUT WHEN I WAS A CROOK!
YOU SHALL REGRET THAT YOU DID NOT REMAIN A CRIMINAL, MY FRIEND!
WH--? WHO'S THAT--?
MY FORMER NAME IS UNIMPORTANT! BUT, YOU MAY CALL ME... THE MAD THINKER!
THE MAD THINKER? THAT CRACKED EGG-HEAD WHO'S GOT IT IN FOR THE FANTASTIC FOUR?
HOW IN HANNAH DID YOU GET OVER THERE?
YOU'LL LEARN THE ANSWER TO THAT, BOW-SLINGER, WHEN YOU AWAKEN!
THOK
UNNNHH!
MEANWHILE, JUST REMEMBER WHAT IT MEANS TO TURN YOUR BACK ON... HAMMER-HEAD!
HAH! THE POOR FISH DIDN'T KNOW THAT I COULD CAST AN AUDIO-VISUAL IMAGE OF THE MAD THINKER ON THE WAREHOUSE WALL!
BUT, IF HE HAD, HE WOULD STILL HAVE FALLEN!
FOR, IT IS NOW EXACTLY 8:41--PLUS FORTY-THREE SECONDS!
AS, AT THAT MOMENT, IN THE HAPPY ISLANDS--A BRAND-NEW NIGHTCLUB IN MID-TOWN MANHATTAN...
GATHER 'ROUND, GALS--DO YOU SEE WHAT I SEE?
IT MUST BE A WINTER MIRAGE!
I HEARD THERE WERE FRINGE BENEFITS WITH THIS JOB--BUT THIS IS TOO MUCH!
8

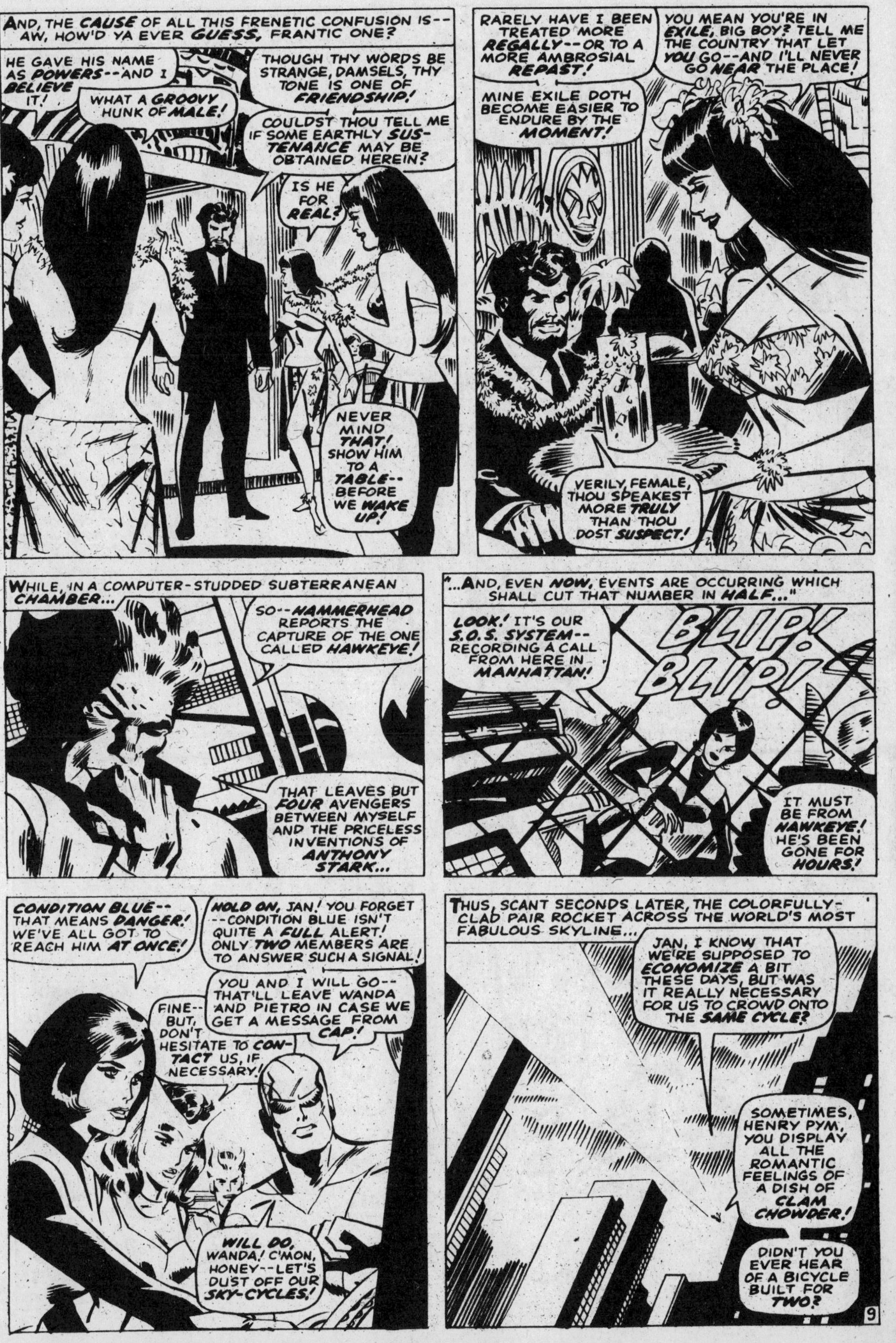

AND, THE CAUSE OF ALL THIS FRENETIC CONFUSION IS-- AW, HOW'D YA EVER GUESS, FRANTIC ONE?
HE GAVE HIS NAME AS POWERS--AND I BELIEVE IT!
WHAT A GROOVY HUNK OF MALE!
THOUGH THY WORDS BE STRANGE, DAMSELS, THY TONE IS ONE OF FRIENDSHIP!
COULDST THOU TELL ME IF SOME EARTHLY SUSTENANCE MAY BE OBTAINED HEREIN?
IS HE FOR REAL?
NEVER MIND THAT! SHOW HIM TO A TABLE--BEFORE WE WAKE UP!
RARELY HAVE I BEEN TREATED MORE REGALLY--OR TO A MORE AMBROSIAL REPAST!
YOU MEAN YOU'RE IN EXILE, BIG BOY? TELL ME THE COUNTRY THAT LET YOU GO--AND I'LL NEVER GO NEAR THE PLACE!
MINE EXILE DOTH BECOME EASIER TO ENDURE BY THE MOMENT!
VERILY, FEMALE, THOU SPEAKEST MORE TRULY THAN THOU DOST SUSPECT!
WHILE, IN A COMPUTER-STUDDED SUBTERRANEAN CHAMBER...
SO--HAMMERHEAD REPORTS THE CAPTURE OF THE ONE CALLED HAWKEYE!
THAT LEAVES BUT FOUR AVENGERS BETWEEN MYSELF AND THE PRICELESS INVENTIONS OF ANTHONY STARK...
"...AND, EVEN NOW, EVENTS ARE OCCURRING WHICH SHALL CUT THAT NUMBER IN HALF..."
LOOK! IT'S OUR S.O.S. SYSTEM--RECORDING A CALL FROM HERE IN MANHATTAN!
BLIP! BLIP!
IT MUST BE FROM HAWKEYE! HE'S BEEN GONE FOR HOURS!
CONDITION BLUE--THAT MEANS DANGER! WE'VE ALL GOT TO REACH HIM AT ONCE!
HOLD ON, JAN! YOU FORGET--CONDITION BLUE ISN'T QUITE A FULL ALERT! ONLY TWO MEMBERS ARE TO ANSWER SUCH A SIGNAL!
YOU AND I WILL GO--THAT'LL LEAVE WANDA AND PIETRO IN CASE WE GET A MESSAGE FROM CAP!
FINE--BUT, DON'T HESITATE TO CONTACT US, IF NECESSARY!
WILL DO, WANDA! C'MON, HONEY--LET'S DUST OFF OUR SKY-CYCLES!
THUS, SCANT SECONDS LATER, THE COLORFULLY-CLAD PAIR ROCKET ACROSS THE WORLD'S MOST FABULOUS SKYLINE...
JAN, I KNOW THAT WE'RE SUPPOSED TO ECONOMIZE A BIT THESE DAYS, BUT WAS IT REALLY NECESSARY FOR US TO CROWD ONTO THE SAME CYCLE?
SOMETIMES, HENRY PYM, YOU DISPLAY ALL THE ROMANTIC FEELINGS OF A DISH OF CLAM CHOWDER!
DIDN'T YOU EVER HEAR OF A BICYCLE BUILT FOR TWO?

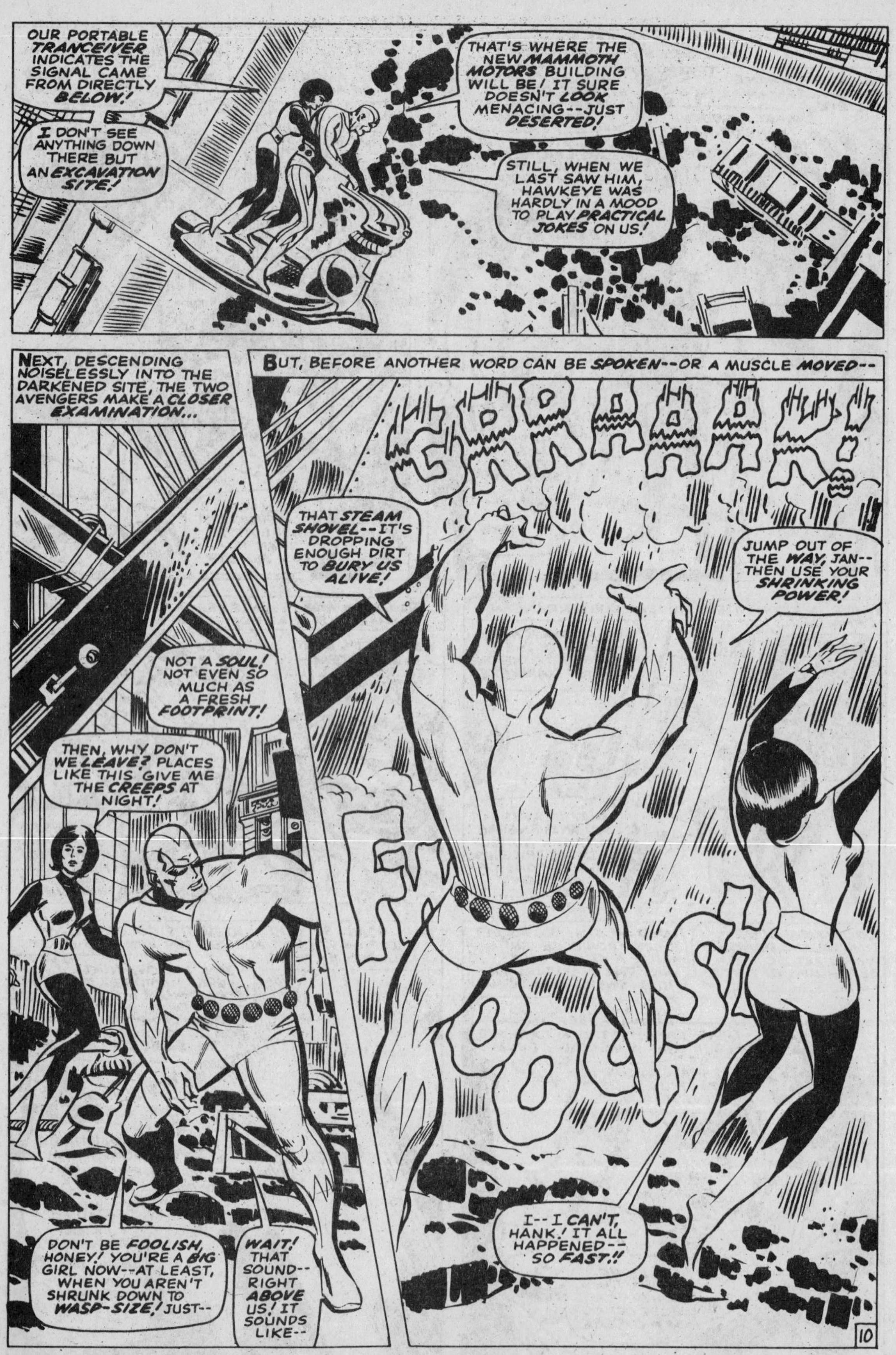

OUR PORTABLE TRANCEIVER INDICATES THE SIGNAL CAME FROM DIRECTLY BELOW!
I DON'T SEE ANYTHING DOWN THERE BUT AN EXCAVATION SITE!
THAT'S WHERE THE NEW MAMMOTH MOTORS BUILDING WILL BE! IT SURE DOESN'T LOOK MENACING--JUST DESERTED!
STILL, WHEN WE LAST SAW HIM, HAWKEYE WAS HARDLY IN A MOOD TO PLAY PRACTICAL JOKES ON US!
NEXT, DESCENDING NOISELESSLY INTO THE DARKENED SITE, THE TWO AVENGERS MAKE A CLOSER EXAMINATION...
NOT A SOUL! NOT EVEN SO MUCH AS A FRESH FOOTPRINT!
THEN, WHY DON'T WE LEAVE? PLACES LIKE THIS GIVE ME THE CREEPS AT NIGHT!
DON'T BE FOOLISH, HONEY! YOU'RE A BIG GIRL NOW--AT LEAST, WHEN YOU AREN'T SHRUNK DOWN TO WASP-SIZE! JUST--
WAIT! THAT SOUND--RIGHT ABOVE US! IT SOUNDS LIKE--
BUT, BEFORE ANOTHER WORD CAN BE SPOKEN--OR A MUSCLE MOVED--
GRRAAAK!
THAT STEAM SHOVEL--IT'S DROPPING ENOUGH DIRT TO BURY US ALIVE!
JUMP OUT OF THE WAY, JAN--THEN USE YOUR SHRINKING POWER!
I--I CAN'T, HANK! IT ALL HAPPENED--SO FAST!!
10

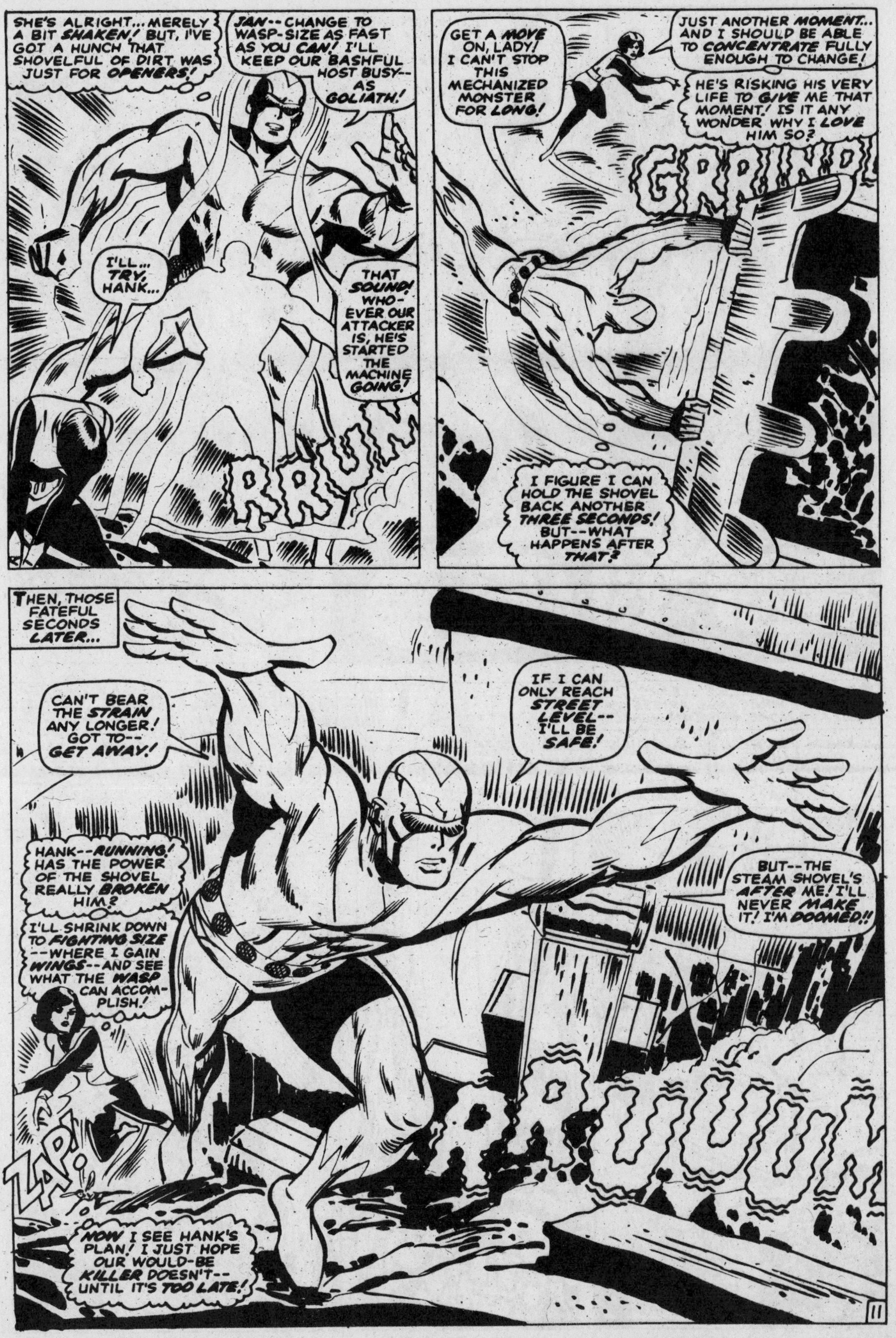
SHE'S ALRIGHT... MERELY A BIT SHAKEN! BUT, I'VE GOT A HUNCH THAT SHOVELFUL OF DIRT WAS JUST FOR OPENERS!
JAN--CHANGE TO WASP-SIZE AS FAST AS YOU CAN! I'LL KEEP OUR BASHFUL HOST BUSY--AS GOLIATH!
I'LL... TRY, HANK...
THAT SOUND! WHO-EVER OUR ATTACKER IS, HE'S STARTED THE MACHINE GOING!
RRUM
GET A MOVE ON, LADY! I CAN'T STOP THIS MECHANIZED MONSTER FOR LONG!
JUST ANOTHER MOMENT... AND I SHOULD BE ABLE TO CONCENTRATE FULLY ENOUGH TO CHANGE!
HE'S RISKING HIS VERY LIFE TO GIVE ME THAT MOMENT! IS IT ANY WONDER WHY I LOVE HIM SO?
GRRIND
I FIGURE I CAN HOLD THE SHOVEL BACK ANOTHER THREE SECONDS! BUT--WHAT HAPPENS AFTER THAT?
THEN, THOSE FATEFUL SECONDS LATER...
CAN'T BEAR THE STRAIN ANY LONGER! GOT TO--GET AWAY!
IF I CAN ONLY REACH STREET LEVEL--I'LL BE SAFE!
HANK--RUNNING! HAS THE POWER OF THE SHOVEL REALLY BROKEN HIM?
I'LL SHRINK DOWN TO FIGHTING SIZE--WHERE I GAIN WINGS--AND SEE WHAT THE WASP CAN ACCOMPLISH!
BUT--THE STEAM SHOVEL'S AFTER ME! I'LL NEVER MAKE IT! I'M DOOMED!!
RRUUUM
ZAP!
NOW I SEE HANK'S PLAN! I JUST HOPE OUR WOULD-BE KILLER DOESN'T--UNTIL IT'S TOO LATE!
11

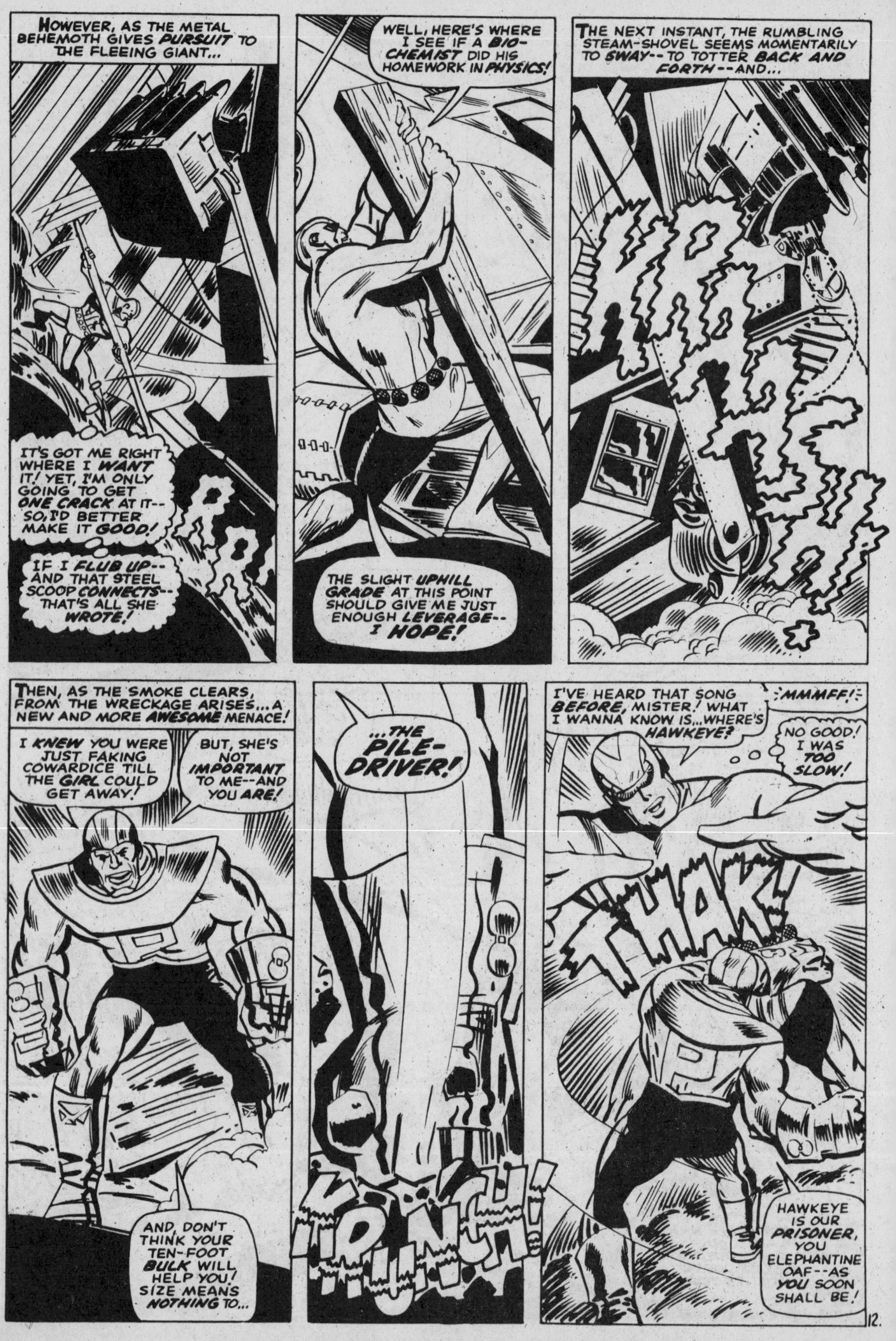
HOWEVER, AS THE METAL BEHEMOTH GIVES PURSUIT TO THE FLEEING GIANT...
IT'S GOT ME RIGHT WHERE I WANT IT! YET, I'M ONLY GOING TO GET ONE CRACK AT IT-- SO, I'D BETTER MAKE IT GOOD!
IF I FLUB UP-- AND THAT STEEL SCOOP CONNECTS-- THAT'S ALL SHE WROTE!
WELL, HERE'S WHERE I SEE IF A BIO-CHEMIST DID HIS HOMEWORK IN PHYSICS!
THE SLIGHT UPHILL GRADE AT THIS POINT SHOULD GIVE ME JUST ENOUGH LEVERAGE-- I HOPE!
THE NEXT INSTANT, THE RUMBLING STEAM-SHOVEL SEEMS MOMENTARILY TO SWAY-- TO TOTTER BACK AND FORTH --AND...
THEN, AS THE SMOKE CLEARS, FROM THE WRECKAGE ARISES... A NEW AND MORE AWESOME MENACE!
I KNEW YOU WERE JUST FAKING COWARDICE TILL THE GIRL COULD GET AWAY!
BUT, SHE'S NOT IMPORTANT TO ME--AND YOU ARE!
AND, DON'T THINK YOUR TEN-FOOT BULK WILL HELP YOU! SIZE MEANS NOTHING TO...
...THE PILE-DRIVER!
I'VE HEARD THAT SONG BEFORE, MISTER! WHAT I WANNA KNOW IS... WHERE'S HAWKEYE?
MMMFF!
NO GOOD! I WAS TOO SLOW!
THAK!
HAWKEYE IS OUR PRISONER, YOU ELEPHANTINE OAF--AS YOU SOON SHALL BE!

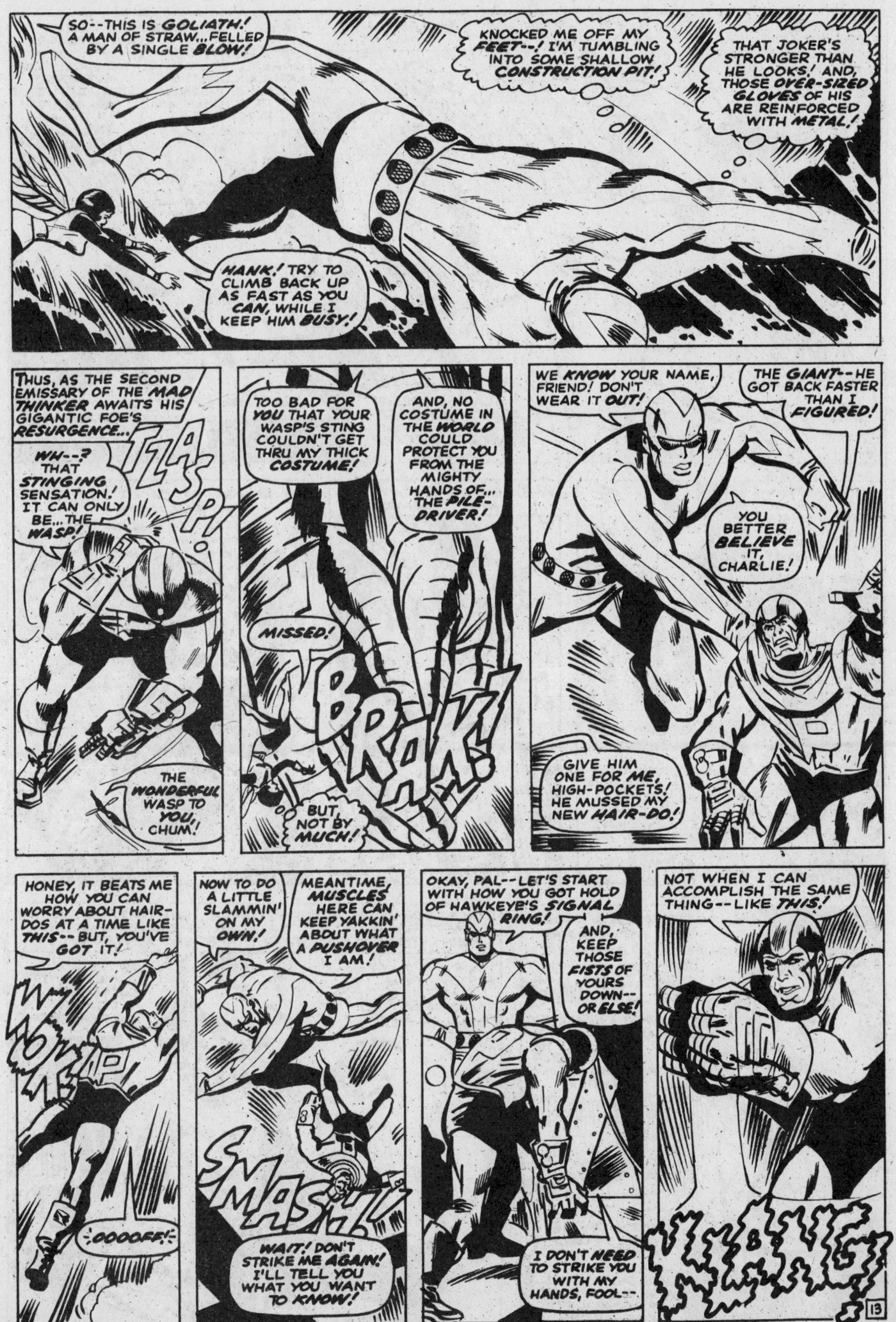

SO--THIS IS GOLIATH! A MAN OF STRAW...FELLED BY A SINGLE BLOW!
KNOCKED ME OFF MY FEET--! I'M TUMBLING INTO SOME SHALLOW CONSTRUCTION PIT!
THAT JOKER'S STRONGER THAN HE LOOKS! AND, THOSE OVER-SIZED GLOVES OF HIS ARE REINFORCED WITH METAL!
HANK! TRY TO CLIMB BACK UP AS FAST AS YOU CAN, WHILE I KEEP HIM BUSY!
THUS, AS THE SECOND EMISSARY OF THE MAD THINKER AWAITS HIS GIGANTIC FOE'S RESURGENCE...
TZZASP!
WH--? THAT STINGING SENSATION! IT CAN ONLY BE...THE WASP!
THE WONDERFUL WASP TO YOU, CHUM!
TOO BAD FOR YOU THAT YOUR WASP'S STING COULDN'T GET THRU MY THICK COSTUME!
AND, NO COSTUME IN THE WORLD COULD PROTECT YOU FROM THE MIGHTY HANDS OF... THE PILE-DRIVER!
MISSED!
BRAK!
BUT, NOT BY MUCH!
WE KNOW YOUR NAME, FRIEND! DON'T WEAR IT OUT!
THE GIANT--HE GOT BACK FASTER THAN I FIGURED!
YOU BETTER BELIEVE IT, CHARLIE!
GIVE HIM ONE FOR ME, HIGH-POCKETS! HE MUSSED MY NEW HAIR-DO!
HONEY, IT BEATS ME HOW YOU CAN WORRY ABOUT HAIR-DOS AT A TIME LIKE THIS--BUT, YOU'VE GOT IT!
WOK!
OOOOFF!
NOW TO DO A LITTLE SLAMMIN' ON MY OWN!
MEANTIME, MUSCLES HERE CAN KEEP YAKKIN' ABOUT WHAT A PUSHOVER I AM!
SMASH!
WAIT! DON'T STRIKE ME AGAIN! I'LL TELL YOU WHAT YOU WANT TO KNOW!
OKAY, PAL--LET'S START WITH HOW YOU GOT HOLD OF HAWKEYE'S SIGNAL RING!
AND, KEEP THOSE FISTS OF YOURS DOWN--OR ELSE!
I DON'T NEED TO STRIKE YOU WITH MY HANDS, FOOL--
NOT WHEN I CAN ACCOMPLISH THE SAME THING--LIKE THIS!
KLANG!
13

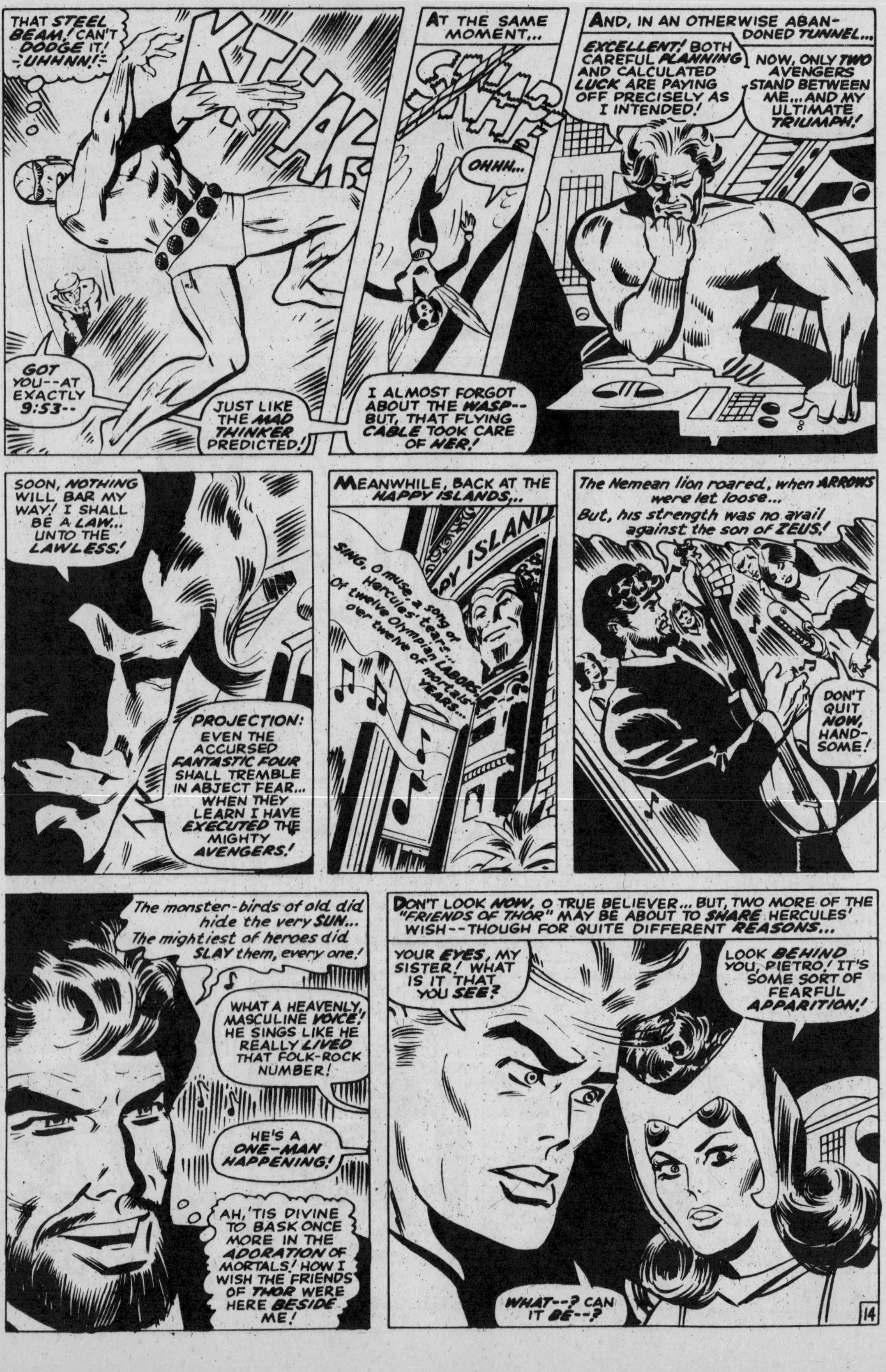
THAT STEEL BEAM! CAN'T DODGE IT! --UHHNN!--
KTHAK!
GOT YOU--AT EXACTLY 9:53--
JUST LIKE THE MAD THINKER PREDICTED!
AT THE SAME MOMENT...
SNAP!
OHHH...
I ALMOST FORGOT ABOUT THE WASP--BUT, THAT FLYING CABLE TOOK CARE OF HER!
AND, IN AN OTHERWISE ABANDONED TUNNEL...
EXCELLENT! BOTH CAREFUL PLANNING AND CALCULATED LUCK ARE PAYING OFF PRECISELY AS I INTENDED!
NOW, ONLY TWO AVENGERS STAND BETWEEN ME...AND MY ULTIMATE TRIUMPH!
SOON, NOTHING WILL BAR MY WAY! I SHALL BE A LAW... UNTO THE LAWLESS!
PROJECTION: EVEN THE ACCURSED FANTASTIC FOUR SHALL TREMBLE IN ABJECT FEAR... WHEN THEY LEARN I HAVE EXECUTED THE MIGHTY AVENGERS!
MEANWHILE, BACK AT THE HAPPY ISLANDS...
PY ISLAND
SING, O muse, a song of Hercules' tears... Of twelve Olympian LABORS, o'er twelve of mortals' YEARS...
The Nemean lion roared, when ARROWS were let loose... But, his strength was no avail against the son of ZEUS!
DON'T QUIT NOW, HANDSOME!
The monster-birds of old did hide the very SUN... The mightiest of heroes did SLAY them, every one!
WHAT A HEAVENLY, MASCULINE VOICE! HE SINGS LIKE HE REALLY LIVED THAT FOLK-ROCK NUMBER!
HE'S A ONE-MAN HAPPENING!
AH, 'TIS DIVINE TO BASK ONCE MORE IN THE ADORATION OF MORTALS! HOW I WISH THE FRIENDS OF THOR WERE HERE BESIDE ME!
DON'T LOOK NOW, O TRUE BELIEVER... BUT, TWO MORE OF THE "FRIENDS OF THOR" MAY BE ABOUT TO SHARE HERCULES' WISH--THOUGH FOR QUITE DIFFERENT REASONS...
YOUR EYES, MY SISTER! WHAT IS IT THAT YOU SEE?
LOOK BEHIND YOU, PIETRO! IT'S SOME SORT OF FEARFUL APPARITION!
WHAT--? CAN IT BE--?
14

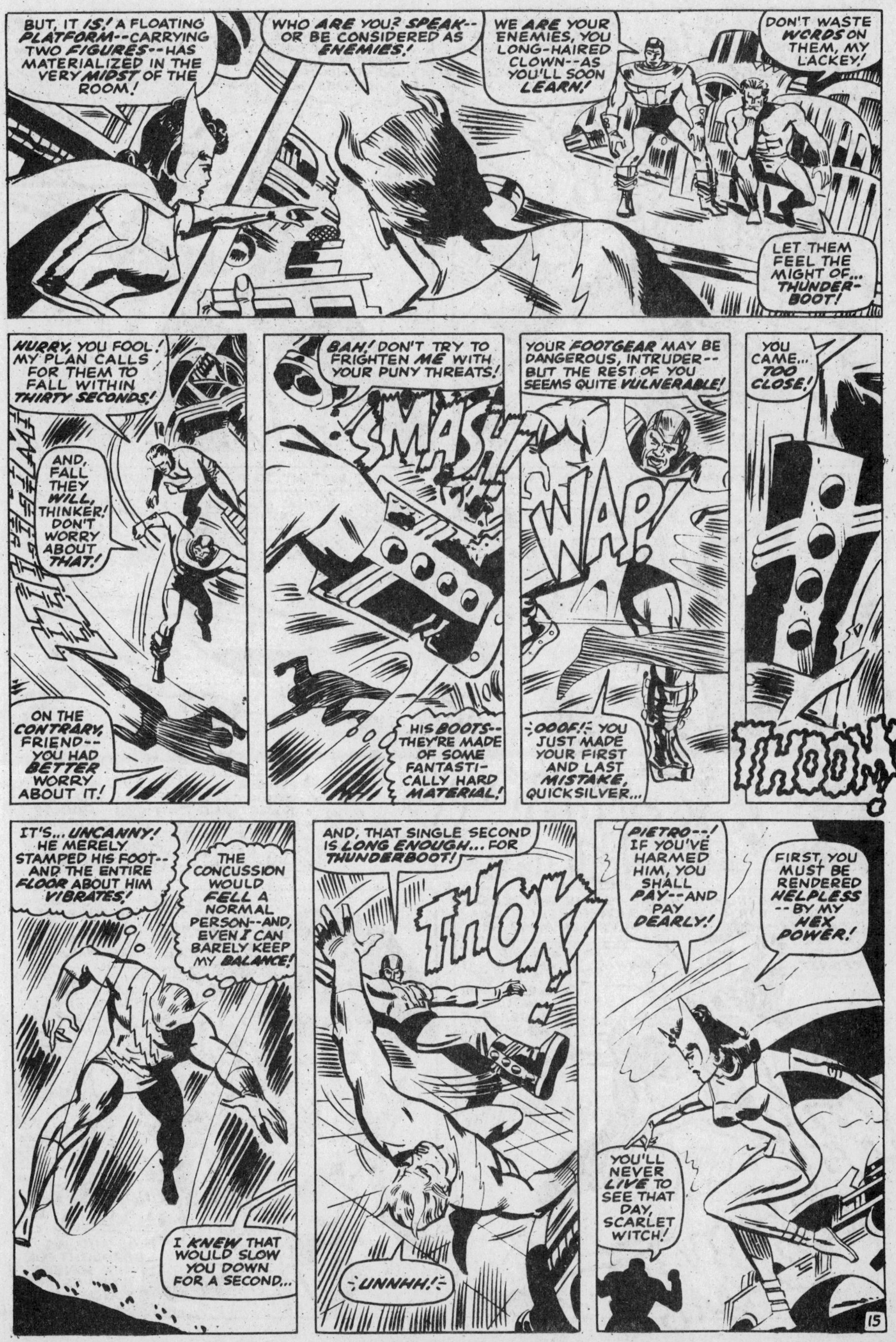
BUT, IT IS! A FLOATING PLATFORM--CARRYING TWO FIGURES--HAS MATERIALIZED IN THE VERY MIDST OF THE ROOM!
WHO ARE YOU? SPEAK--OR BE CONSIDERED AS ENEMIES!
WE ARE YOUR ENEMIES, YOU LONG-HAIRED CLOWN--AS YOU'LL SOON LEARN!
DON'T WASTE WORDS ON THEM, MY LACKEY!
LET THEM FEEL THE MIGHT OF... THUNDER-BOOT!
HURRY, YOU FOOL! MY PLAN CALLS FOR THEM TO FALL WITHIN THIRTY SECONDS!
AND, FALL THEY WILL, THINKER! DON'T WORRY ABOUT THAT!
ON THE CONTRARY, FRIEND--YOU HAD BETTER WORRY ABOUT IT!
BAH! DON'T TRY TO FRIGHTEN ME WITH YOUR PUNY THREATS!
SMASH!
HIS BOOTS--THEY'RE MADE OF SOME FANTASTI-CALLY HARD MATERIAL!
YOUR FOOTGEAR MAY BE DANGEROUS, INTRUDER--BUT THE REST OF YOU SEEMS QUITE VULNERABLE!
WAP!
OOOF!--YOU JUST MADE YOUR FIRST AND LAST MISTAKE, QUICKSILVER...
YOU CAME... TOO CLOSE!
THOOM!
IT'S... UNCANNY! HE MERELY STAMPED HIS FOOT--AND THE ENTIRE FLOOR ABOUT HIM VIBRATES!
THE CONCUSSION WOULD FELL A NORMAL PERSON--AND, EVEN I CAN BARELY KEEP MY BALANCE!
I KNEW THAT WOULD SLOW YOU DOWN FOR A SECOND...
AND, THAT SINGLE SECOND IS LONG ENOUGH... FOR THUNDERBOOT!
THOK!
UNNHH!
PIETRO--! IF YOU'VE HARMED HIM, YOU SHALL PAY--AND PAY DEARLY!
FIRST, YOU MUST BE RENDERED HELPLESS--BY MY HEX POWER!
YOU'LL NEVER LIVE TO SEE THAT DAY, SCARLET WITCH!

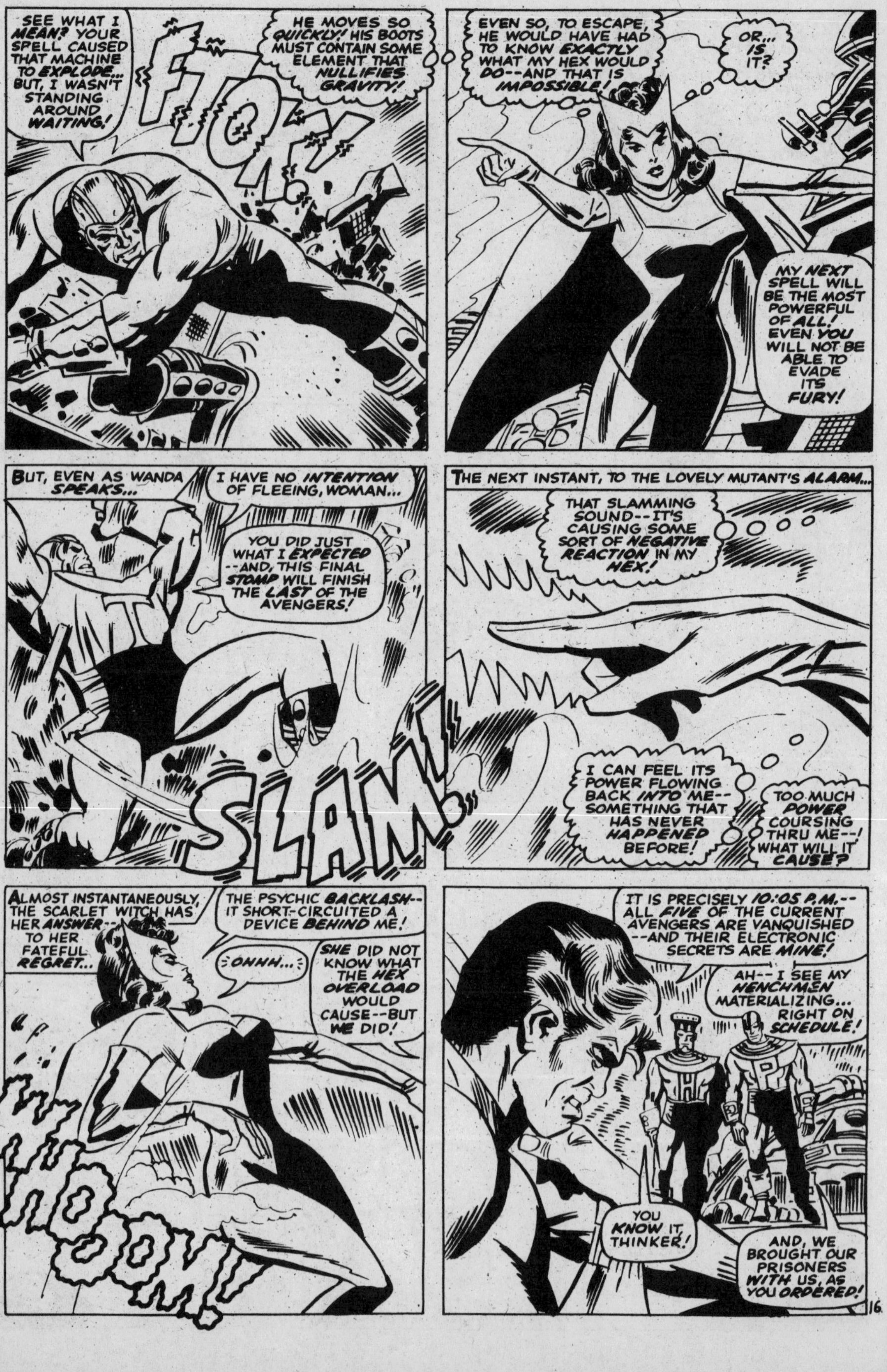
SEE WHAT I MEAN? YOUR SPELL CAUSED THAT MACHINE TO EXPLODE... BUT, I WASN'T STANDING AROUND WAITING!
FTOOM
HE MOVES SO QUICKLY! HIS BOOTS MUST CONTAIN SOME ELEMENT THAT NULLIFIES GRAVITY!
EVEN SO, TO ESCAPE, HE WOULD HAVE HAD TO KNOW EXACTLY WHAT MY HEX WOULD DO--AND THAT IS IMPOSSIBLE!
OR... IS IT?
MY NEXT SPELL WILL BE THE MOST POWERFUL OF ALL! EVEN YOU WILL NOT BE ABLE TO EVADE ITS FURY!
BUT, EVEN AS WANDA SPEAKS...
I HAVE NO INTENTION OF FLEEING, WOMAN...
YOU DID JUST WHAT I EXPECTED --AND, THIS FINAL STOMP WILL FINISH THE LAST OF THE AVENGERS!
SLAM!
THE NEXT INSTANT, TO THE LOVELY MUTANT'S ALARM...
THAT SLAMMING SOUND--IT'S CAUSING SOME SORT OF NEGATIVE REACTION IN MY HEX!
I CAN FEEL ITS POWER FLOWING BACK INTO ME--SOMETHING THAT HAS NEVER HAPPENED BEFORE!
TOO MUCH POWER COURSING THRU ME--! WHAT WILL IT CAUSE?
ALMOST INSTANTANEOUSLY, THE SCARLET WITCH HAS HER ANSWER--TO HER FATEFUL REGRET...
THE PSYCHIC BACKLASH--IT SHORT-CIRCUITED A DEVICE BEHIND ME!
ONHH...
SHE DID NOT KNOW WHAT THE HEX OVERLOAD WOULD CAUSE--BUT WE DID!
WHOOM!
IT IS PRECISELY 10:05 P.M.--ALL FIVE OF THE CURRENT AVENGERS ARE VANQUISHED --AND THEIR ELECTRONIC SECRETS ARE MINE!
AH--I SEE MY HENCHMEN MATERIALIZING... RIGHT ON SCHEDULE!
YOU KNOW IT, THINKER!
AND, WE BROUGHT OUR PRISONERS WITH US, AS YOU ORDERED!
16

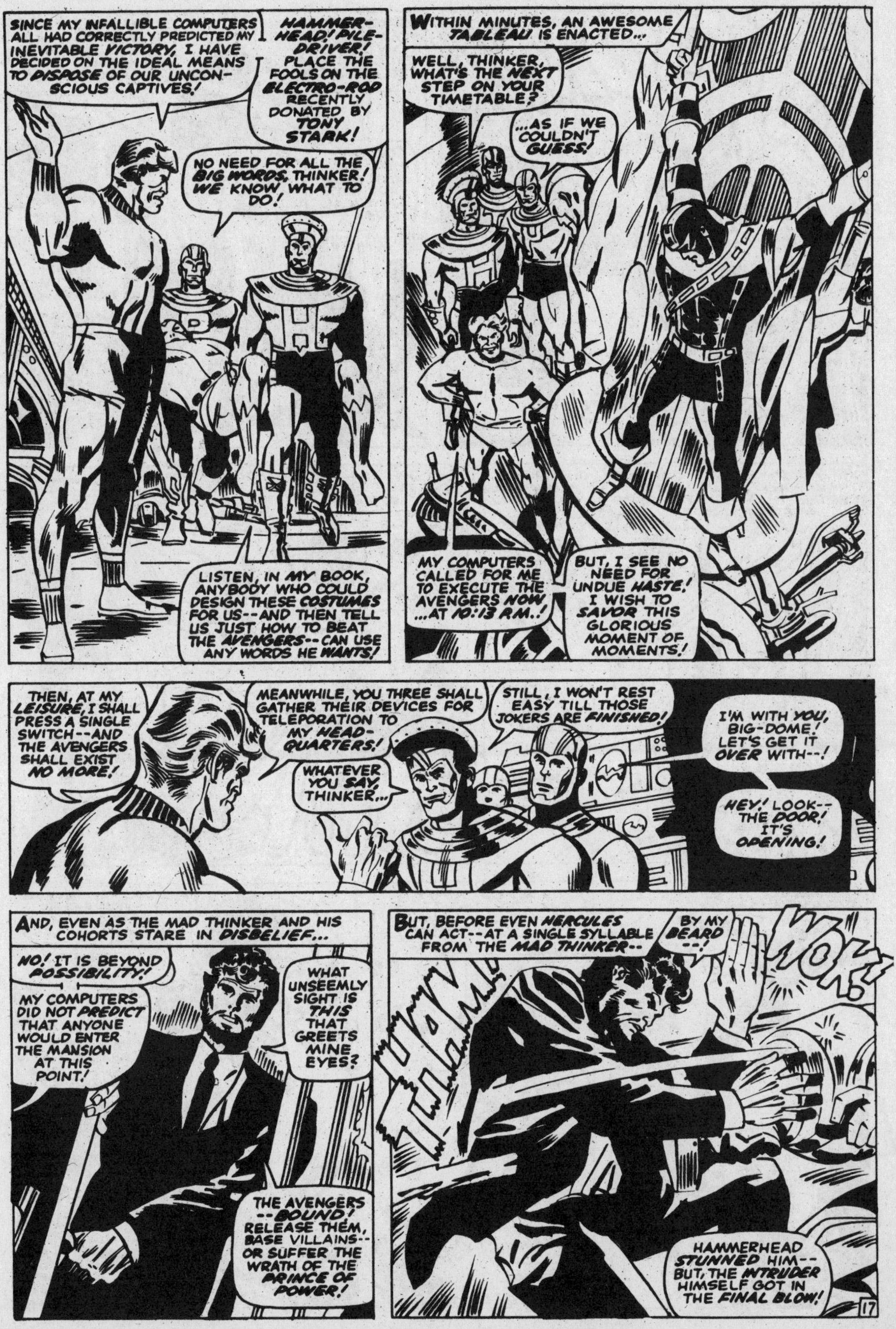
SINCE MY INFALLIBLE COMPUTERS ALL HAD CORRECTLY PREDICTED MY INEVITABLE VICTORY, I HAVE DECIDED ON THE IDEAL MEANS TO DISPOSE OF OUR UNCONSCIOUS CAPTIVES!
HAMMERHEAD! PILE-DRIVER! PLACE THE FOOLS ON THE ELECTRO-ROD RECENTLY DONATED BY TONY STARK!
NO NEED FOR ALL THE BIG WORDS, THINKER! WE KNOW, WHAT TO DO!
LISTEN, IN MY BOOK, ANYBODY WHO COULD DESIGN THESE COSTUMES FOR US--AND THEN TELL US JUST HOW TO BEAT THE AVENGERS--CAN USE ANY WORDS HE WANTS!
WITHIN MINUTES, AN AWESOME TABLEAU IS ENACTED...
WELL, THINKER, WHAT'S THE NEXT STEP ON YOUR TIMETABLE?
...AS IF WE COULDN'T GUESS!
MY COMPUTERS CALLED FOR ME TO EXECUTE THE AVENGERS NOW ...AT 10:13 P.M.!
BUT, I SEE NO NEED FOR UNDUE HASTE! I WISH TO SAVOR THIS GLORIOUS MOMENT OF MOMENTS!
THEN, AT MY LEISURE, I SHALL PRESS A SINGLE SWITCH--AND THE AVENGERS SHALL EXIST NO MORE!
MEANWHILE, YOU THREE SHALL GATHER THEIR DEVICES FOR TELEPORATION TO MY HEAD-QUARTERS!
WHATEVER YOU SAY, THINKER...
STILL, I WON'T REST EASY TILL THOSE JOKERS ARE FINISHED!
I'M WITH YOU, BIG-DOME! LET'S GET IT OVER WITH--!
HEY! LOOK--THE DOOR! IT'S OPENING!
AND, EVEN AS THE MAD THINKER AND HIS COHORTS STARE IN DISBELIEF...
NO! IT IS BEYOND POSSIBILITY!
MY COMPUTERS DID NOT PREDICT THAT ANYONE WOULD ENTER THE MANSION AT THIS POINT!
WHAT UNSEEMLY SIGHT IS THIS THAT GREETS MINE EYES?
THE AVENGERS--BOUND! RELEASE THEM, BASE VILLAINS--OR SUFFER THE WRATH OF THE PRINCE OF POWER!
BUT, BEFORE EVEN HERCULES CAN ACT--AT A SINGLE SYLLABLE FROM THE MAD THINKER--
BY MY BEARD--!
WOK!
THAM!
HAMMERHEAD STUNNED HIM--BUT, THE INTRUDER HIMSELF GOT IN THE FINAL BLOW!
17

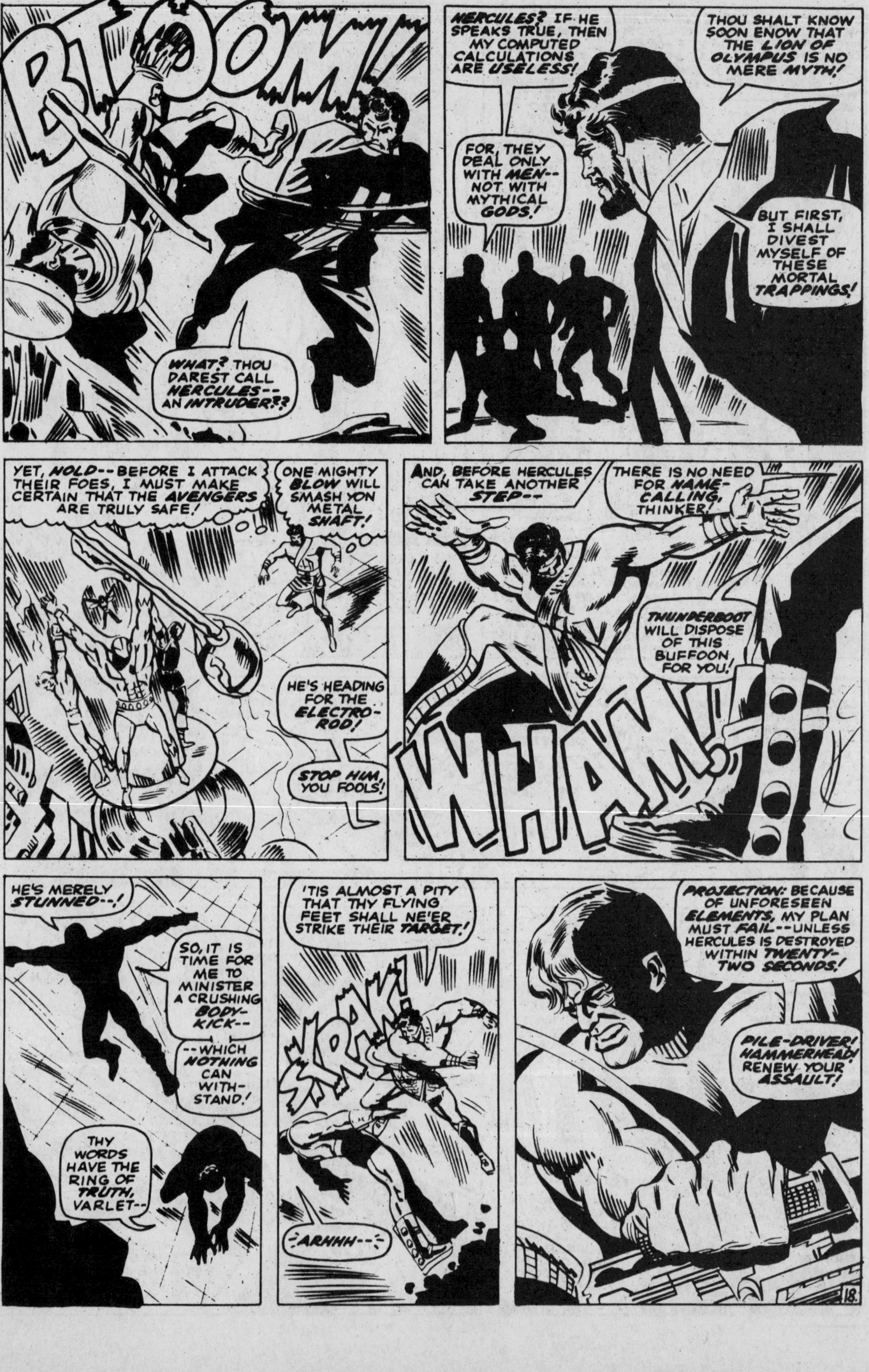
BTOOM!
WHAT? THOU DAREST CALL HERCULES-- AN INTRUDER?!?
HERCULES? IF HE SPEAKS TRUE, THEN MY COMPUTED CALCULATIONS ARE USELESS!
FOR, THEY DEAL ONLY WITH MEN-- NOT WITH MYTHICAL GODS!
THOU SHALT KNOW SOON ENOW THAT THE LION OF OLYMPUS IS NO MERE MYTH!
BUT FIRST, I SHALL DIVEST MYSELF OF THESE MORTAL TRAPPINGS!
YET, HOLD-- BEFORE I ATTACK THEIR FOES, I MUST MAKE CERTAIN THAT THE AVENGERS ARE TRULY SAFE!
ONE MIGHTY BLOW WILL SMASH YON METAL SHAFT!
HE'S HEADING FOR THE ELECTRO-ROD!
STOP HIM, YOU FOOLS!
AND, BEFORE HERCULES CAN TAKE ANOTHER STEP--
THERE IS NO NEED FOR NAME-CALLING, THINKER!
THUNDERBOOT WILL DISPOSE OF THIS BUFFOON FOR YOU!
WHAM!
HE'S MERELY STUNNED--!
SO, IT IS TIME FOR ME TO MINISTER A CRUSHING BODY-KICK--
--WHICH NOTHING CAN WITH-STAND!
THY WORDS HAVE THE RING OF TRUTH, VARLET--
'TIS ALMOST A PITY THAT THY FLYING FEET SHALL NE'ER STRIKE THEIR TARGET!
SPRAK!
ARHHH--
PROJECTION: BECAUSE OF UNFORESEEN ELEMENTS, MY PLAN MUST FAIL--UNLESS HERCULES IS DESTROYED WITHIN TWENTY-TWO SECONDS!
PILE-DRIVER! HAMMERHEAD! RENEW YOUR ASSAULT!
18

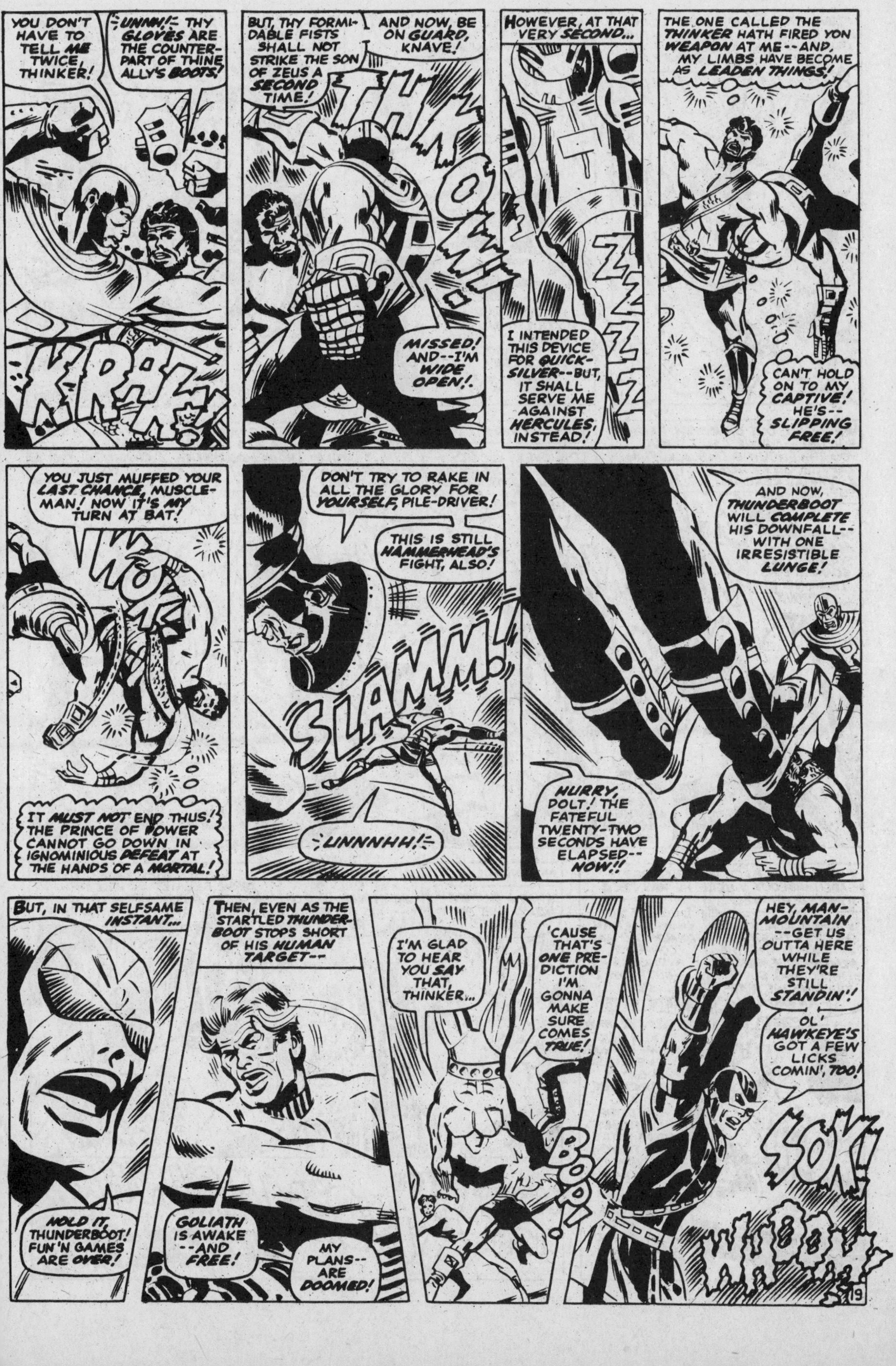

YOU DON'T HAVE TO TELL ME TWICE, THINKER!
UNNH!-- THY GLOVES ARE THE COUNTERPART OF THINE ALLY'S BOOTS!
KRAK!
BUT, THY FORMIDABLE FISTS SHALL NOT STRIKE THE SON OF ZEUS A SECOND TIME!
AND NOW, BE ON GUARD, KNAVE!
THWOOM!
MISSED! AND--I'M WIDE OPEN!.
HOWEVER, AT THAT VERY SECOND...
ZZZZZ
I INTENDED THIS DEVICE FOR QUICKSILVER--BUT, IT SHALL SERVE ME AGAINST HERCULES, INSTEAD!
THE ONE CALLED THE THINKER HATH FIRED YON WEAPON AT ME--AND, MY LIMBS HAVE BECOME AS LEADEN THINGS!
CAN'T HOLD ON TO MY CAPTIVE! HE'S--SLIPPING FREE!
YOU JUST MUFFED YOUR LAST CHANCE, MUSCLE-MAN! NOW IT'S MY TURN AT BAT!
WOK
IT MUST NOT END THUS! THE PRINCE OF POWER CANNOT GO DOWN IN IGNOMINIOUS DEFEAT AT THE HANDS OF A MORTAL!
DON'T TRY TO RAKE IN ALL THE GLORY FOR YOURSELF, PILE-DRIVER!
THIS IS STILL HAMMERHEAD'S FIGHT, ALSO!
SLAMM!
UNNNHH!
AND NOW, THUNDERBOOT WILL COMPLETE HIS DOWNFALL--WITH ONE IRRESISTIBLE LUNGE!
HURRY, DOLT! THE FATEFUL TWENTY-TWO SECONDS HAVE ELAPSED--NOW!!
BUT, IN THAT SELFSAME INSTANT...
HOLD IT, THUNDERBOOT! FUN 'N GAMES ARE OVER!
THEN, EVEN AS THE STARTLED THUNDERBOOT STOPS SHORT OF HIS HUMAN TARGET--
GOLIATH IS AWAKE--AND FREE!
MY PLANS--ARE DOOMED!
I'M GLAD TO HEAR YOU SAY THAT, THINKER...
'CAUSE THAT'S ONE PREDICTION I'M GONNA MAKE SURE COMES TRUE!
BOP!
HEY, MAN-MOUNTAIN--GET US OUTTA HERE WHILE THEY'RE STILL STANDIN'!
OL' HAWKEYE'S GOT A FEW LICKS COMIN', TOO!
SOK!
WHOOM!

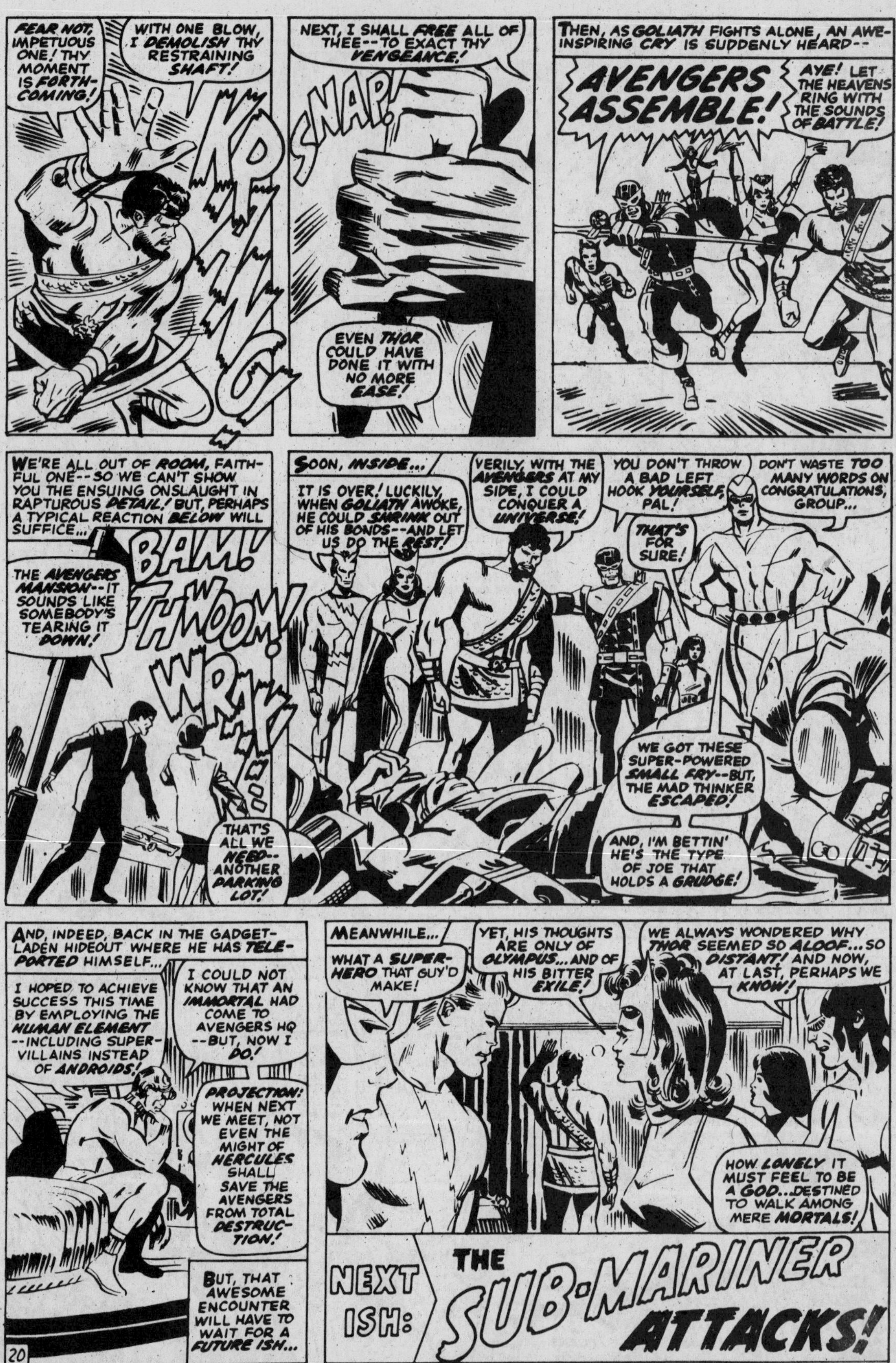
FEAR NOT, IMPETUOUS ONE! THY MOMENT IS FORTH-COMING!
WITH ONE BLOW, I DEMOLISH THY RESTRAINING SHAFT!
KRANG!
NEXT, I SHALL FREE ALL OF THEE--TO EXACT THY VENGEANCE!
SNAP!
EVEN THOR COULD HAVE DONE IT WITH NO MORE EASE!
THEN, AS GOLIATH FIGHTS ALONE, AN AWE-INSPIRING CRY IS SUDDENLY HEARD--
AVENGERS ASSEMBLE!
AYE! LET THE HEAVENS RING WITH THE SOUNDS OF BATTLE!
WE'RE ALL OUT OF ROOM, FAITH-FUL ONE--SO WE CAN'T SHOW YOU THE ENSUING ONSLAUGHT IN RAPTUROUS DETAIL! BUT, PERHAPS A TYPICAL REACTION BELOW WILL SUFFICE...
BAM!
THWOOM!
WRAK!
THE AVENGERS MANSION--IT SOUNDS LIKE SOMEBODY'S TEARING IT DOWN!
THAT'S ALL WE NEED--ANOTHER PARKING LOT!
SOON, INSIDE...
IT IS OVER! LUCKILY, WHEN GOLIATH AWOKE, HE COULD SHRINK OUT OF HIS BONDS--AND LET US DO THE REST!
VERILY, WITH THE AVENGERS AT MY SIDE, I COULD CONQUER A UNIVERSE!
YOU DON'T THROW A BAD LEFT HOOK YOURSELF, PAL!
THAT'S FOR SURE!
DON'T WASTE TOO MANY WORDS ON CONGRATULATIONS, GROUP...
WE GOT THESE SUPER-POWERED SMALL FRY--BUT, THE MAD THINKER ESCAPED!
AND, I'M BETTIN' HE'S THE TYPE OF JOE THAT HOLDS A GRUDGE!
AND, INDEED, BACK IN THE GADGET-LADEN HIDEOUT WHERE HE HAS TELE-PORTED HIMSELF...
I HOPED TO ACHIEVE SUCCESS THIS TIME BY EMPLOYING THE HUMAN ELEMENT --INCLUDING SUPER-VILLAINS INSTEAD OF ANDROIDS!
I COULD NOT KNOW THAT AN IMMORTAL HAD COME TO AVENGERS HQ --BUT, NOW I DO!
PROJECTION: WHEN NEXT WE MEET, NOT EVEN THE MIGHT OF HERCULES SHALL SAVE THE AVENGERS FROM TOTAL DESTRUC-TION!
BUT, THAT AWESOME ENCOUNTER WILL HAVE TO WAIT FOR A FUTURE ISH...
MEANWHILE...
WHAT A SUPER-HERO THAT GUY'D MAKE!
YET, HIS THOUGHTS ARE ONLY OF OLYMPUS... AND OF HIS BITTER EXILE!
WE ALWAYS WONDERED WHY THOR SEEMED SO ALOOF... SO DISTANT! AND NOW, AT LAST, PERHAPS WE KNOW!
HOW LONELY IT MUST FEEL TO BE A GOD...DESTINED TO WALK AMONG MERE MORTALS!
NEXT ISH: THE SUB-MARINER ATTACKS!
20

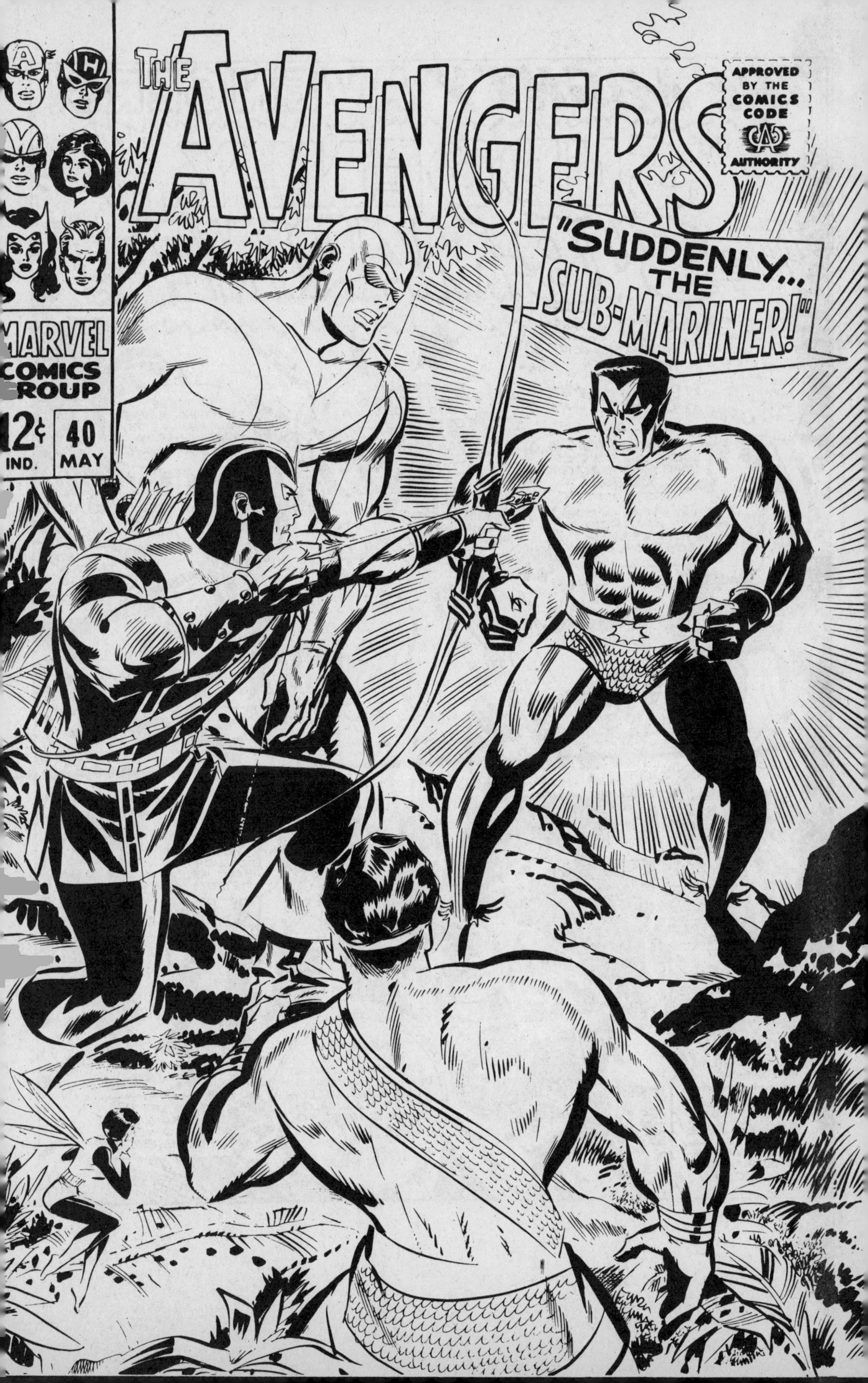

THE AVENGERS
APPROVED BY THE COMICS CODE AUTHORITY
"SUDDENLY... THE SUB-MARINER!"
MARVEL COMICS GROUP
12¢ IND.
40 MAY

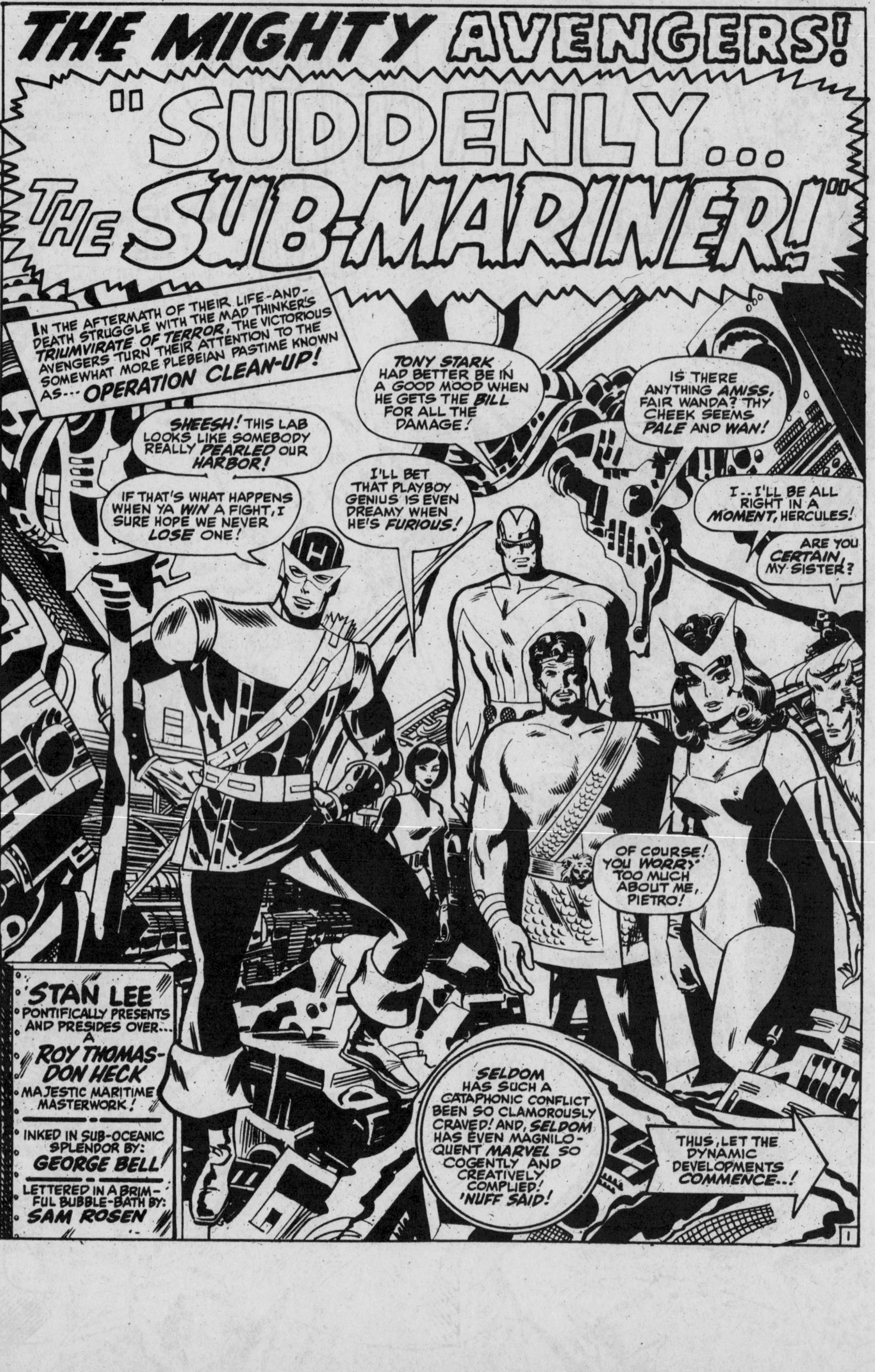
THE MIGHTY AVENGERS!
"SUDDENLY... THE SUB-MARINER!"
IN THE AFTERMATH OF THEIR LIFE-AND-DEATH STRUGGLE WITH THE MAD THINKER'S TRIUMVIRATE OF TERROR, THE VICTORIOUS AVENGERS TURN THEIR ATTENTION TO THE SOMEWHAT MORE PLEBEIAN PASTIME KNOWN AS... OPERATION CLEAN-UP!
SHEESH! THIS LAB LOOKS LIKE SOMEBODY REALLY PEARLED OUR HARBOR!
IF THAT'S WHAT HAPPENS WHEN YA WIN A FIGHT, I SURE HOPE WE NEVER LOSE ONE!
TONY STARK HAD BETTER BE IN A GOOD MOOD WHEN HE GETS THE BILL FOR ALL THE DAMAGE!
I'LL BET THAT PLAYBOY GENIUS IS EVEN DREAMY WHEN HE'S FURIOUS!
IS THERE ANYTHING AMISS, FAIR WANDA? THY CHEEK SEEMS PALE AND WAN!
I.. I'LL BE ALL RIGHT IN A MOMENT, HERCULES!
ARE YOU CERTAIN, MY SISTER?
OF COURSE! YOU WORRY TOO MUCH ABOUT ME, PIETRO!
STAN LEE PONTIFICALLY PRESENTS AND PRESIDES OVER... A ROY THOMAS-DON HECK MAJESTIC MARITIME MASTERWORK!
INKED IN SUB-OCEANIC SPLENDOR BY: GEORGE BELL
LETTERED IN A BRIM-FUL BUBBLE-BATH BY: SAM ROSEN
SELDOM HAS SUCH A CATAPHONIC CONFLICT BEEN SO CLAMOROUSLY CRAVED! AND, SELDOM HAS EVEN MAGNILOQUENT MARVEL SO COGENTLY AND CREATIVELY COMPLIED! 'NUFF SAID!
THUS, LET THE DYNAMIC DEVELOPMENTS COMMENCE..!
1

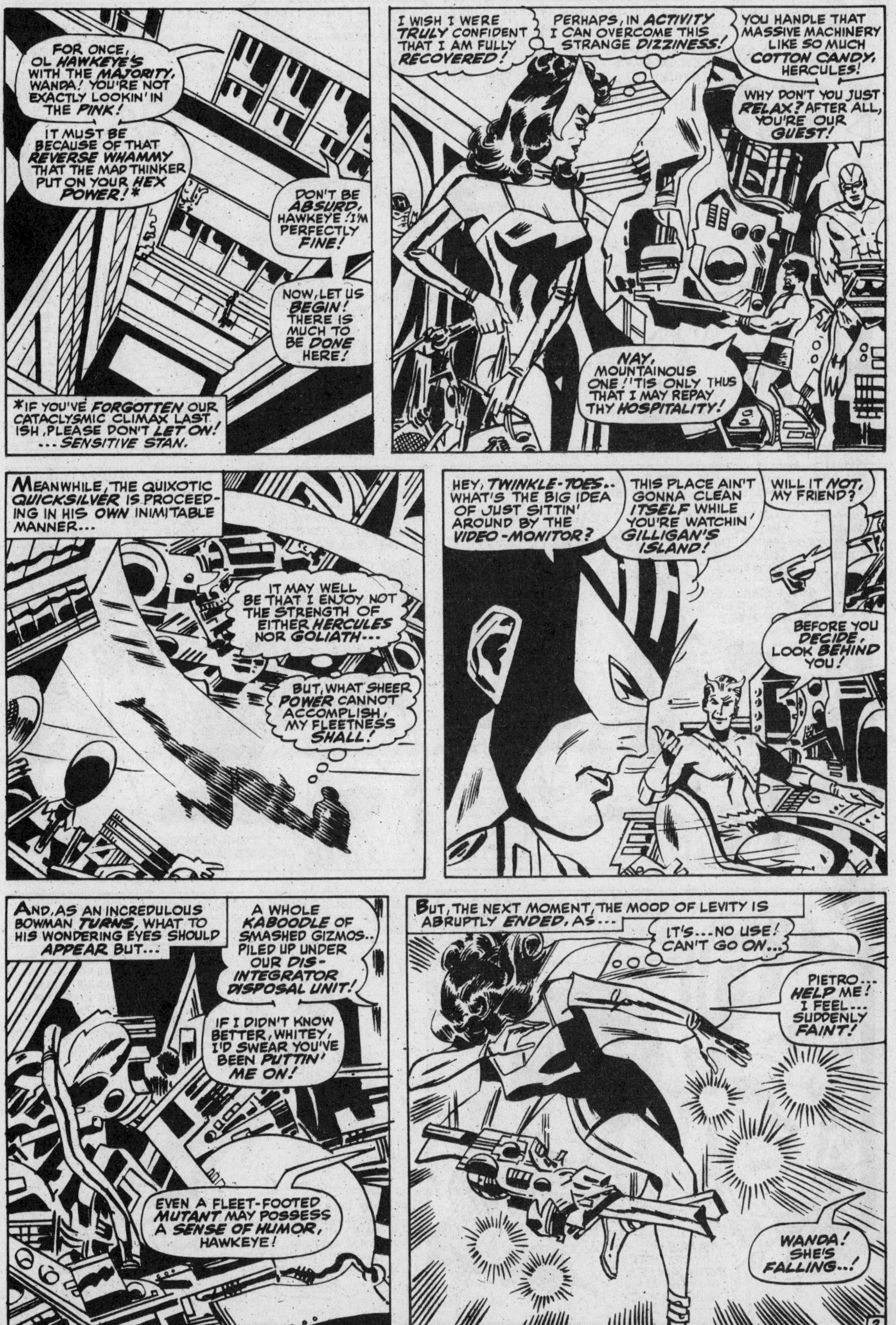

FOR ONCE, OL HAWKEYE'S WITH THE MAJORITY, WANDA! YOU'RE NOT EXACTLY LOOKIN' IN THE PINK!
IT MUST BE BECAUSE OF THAT REVERSE WHAMMY THAT THE MAD THINKER PUT ON YOUR HEX POWER!*
DON'T BE ABSURD, HAWKEYE! I'M PERFECTLY FINE!
NOW, LET US BEGIN! THERE IS MUCH TO BE DONE HERE!
*IF YOU'VE FORGOTTEN OUR CATACLYSMIC CLIMAX LAST ISH, PLEASE DON'T LET ON! ...SENSITIVE STAN.
I WISH I WERE TRULY CONFIDENT THAT I AM FULLY RECOVERED!
PERHAPS, IN ACTIVITY I CAN OVERCOME THIS STRANGE DIZZINESS!
YOU HANDLE THAT MASSIVE MACHINERY LIKE SO MUCH COTTON CANDY, HERCULES!
WHY DON'T YOU JUST RELAX? AFTER ALL, YOU'RE OUR GUEST!
NAY, MOUNTAINOUS ONE! 'TIS ONLY THUS THAT I MAY REPAY THY HOSPITALITY!
MEANWHILE, THE QUIXOTIC QUICKSILVER IS PROCEEDING IN HIS OWN INIMITABLE MANNER...
IT MAY WELL BE THAT I ENJOY NOT THE STRENGTH OF EITHER HERCULES NOR GOLIATH...
BUT, WHAT SHEER POWER CANNOT ACCOMPLISH, MY FLEETNESS SHALL!
HEY, TWINKLE-TOES.. WHAT'S THE BIG IDEA OF JUST SITTIN' AROUND BY THE VIDEO-MONITOR?
THIS PLACE AIN'T GONNA CLEAN ITSELF WHILE YOU'RE WATCHIN' GILLIGAN'S ISLAND!
WILL IT NOT, MY FRIEND?
BEFORE YOU DECIDE, LOOK BEHIND YOU!
AND, AS AN INCREDULOUS BOWMAN TURNS, WHAT TO HIS WONDERING EYES SHOULD APPEAR BUT...
A WHOLE KABOODLE OF SMASHED GIZMOS.. PILED UP UNDER OUR DIS-INTEGRATOR DISPOSAL UNIT!
IF I DIDN'T KNOW BETTER, WHITEY, I'D SWEAR YOU'VE BEEN PUTTIN' ME ON!
EVEN A FLEET-FOOTED MUTANT MAY POSSESS A SENSE OF HUMOR, HAWKEYE!
BUT, THE NEXT MOMENT, THE MOOD OF LEVITY IS ABRUPTLY ENDED, AS...
IT'S... NO USE! CAN'T GO ON...
PIETRO... HELP ME! I FEEL... SUDDENLY FAINT!
WANDA! SHE'S FALLING...!
2.

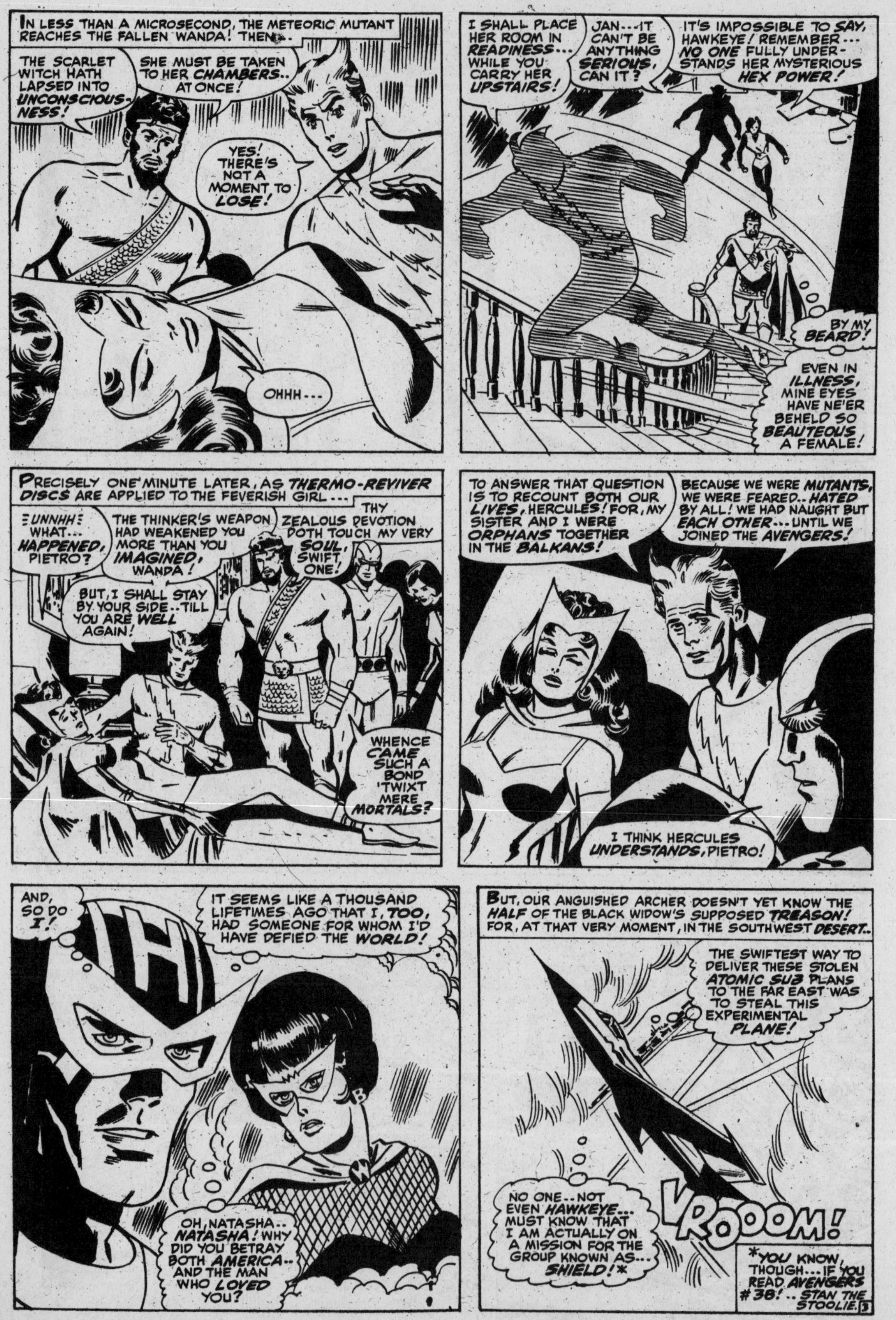

IN LESS THAN A MICROSECOND, THE METEORIC MUTANT REACHES THE FALLEN WANDA! THEN...
THE SCARLET WITCH HATH LAPSED INTO UNCONSCIOUSNESS!
SHE MUST BE TAKEN TO HER CHAMBERS.. AT ONCE!
YES! THERE'S NOT A MOMENT TO LOSE!
OHHH...
I SHALL PLACE HER ROOM IN READINESS... WHILE YOU CARRY HER UPSTAIRS!
JAN...IT CAN'T BE ANYTHING SERIOUS, CAN IT?
IT'S IMPOSSIBLE TO SAY, HAWKEYE! REMEMBER... NO ONE FULLY UNDERSTANDS HER MYSTERIOUS HEX POWER!
BY MY BEARD!
EVEN IN ILLNESS, MINE EYES HAVE NE'ER BEHELD SO BEAUTEOUS A FEMALE!
PRECISELY ONE MINUTE LATER, AS THERMO-REVIVER DISCS ARE APPLIED TO THE FEVERISH GIRL...
UNNHH! WHAT... HAPPENED, PIETRO?
THE THINKER'S WEAPON HAD WEAKENED YOU MORE THAN YOU IMAGINED, WANDA!
THY ZEALOUS DEVOTION DOTH TOUCH MY VERY SOUL, SWIFT ONE!
BUT, I SHALL STAY BY YOUR SIDE..TILL YOU ARE WELL AGAIN!
WHENCE CAME SUCH A BOND 'TWIXT MERE MORTALS?
TO ANSWER THAT QUESTION IS TO RECOUNT BOTH OUR LIVES, HERCULES! FOR, MY SISTER AND I WERE ORPHANS TOGETHER IN THE BALKANS!
BECAUSE WE WERE MUTANTS, WE WERE FEARED.. HATED BY ALL! WE HAD NAUGHT BUT EACH OTHER... UNTIL WE JOINED THE AVENGERS!
I THINK HERCULES UNDERSTANDS, PIETRO!
AND, SO DO I!
IT SEEMS LIKE A THOUSAND LIFETIMES AGO THAT I, TOO, HAD SOMEONE FOR WHOM I'D HAVE DEFIED THE WORLD!
OH, NATASHA.. NATASHA! WHY DID YOU BETRAY BOTH AMERICA.. AND THE MAN WHO LOVED YOU?
BUT, OUR ANGUISHED ARCHER DOESN'T YET KNOW THE HALF OF THE BLACK WIDOW'S SUPPOSED TREASON! FOR, AT THAT VERY MOMENT, IN THE SOUTHWEST DESERT..
THE SWIFTEST WAY TO DELIVER THESE STOLEN ATOMIC SUB PLANS TO THE FAR EAST WAS TO STEAL THIS EXPERIMENTAL PLANE!
VROOOM!
NO ONE..NOT EVEN HAWKEYE... MUST KNOW THAT I AM ACTUALLY ON A MISSION FOR THE GROUP KNOWN AS... SHIELD!*
*YOU KNOW, THOUGH... IF YOU READ AVENGERS #38!.. STAN THE STOOLIE.
3

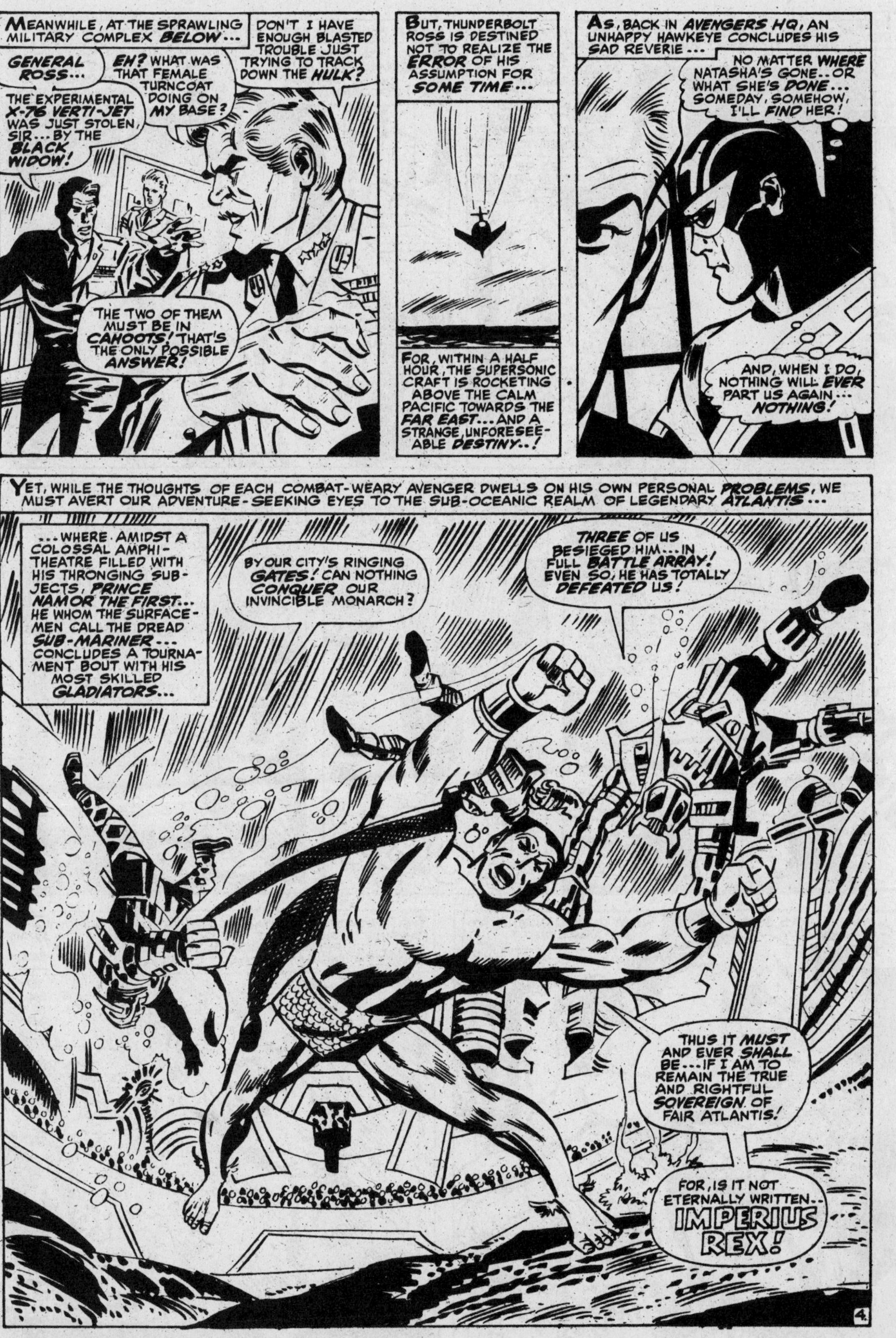
MEANWHILE, AT THE SPRAWLING MILITARY COMPLEX BELOW...
GENERAL ROSS... THE EXPERIMENTAL X-76 VERTI-JET WAS JUST STOLEN, SIR... BY THE BLACK WIDOW!
EH? WHAT WAS THAT FEMALE TURNCOAT DOING ON MY BASE?
DON'T I HAVE ENOUGH BLASTED TROUBLE JUST TRYING TO TRACK DOWN THE HULK?
THE TWO OF THEM MUST BE IN CAHOOTS! THAT'S THE ONLY POSSIBLE ANSWER!
BUT, THUNDERBOLT ROSS IS DESTINED NOT TO REALIZE THE ERROR OF HIS ASSUMPTION FOR SOME TIME...
FOR, WITHIN A HALF HOUR, THE SUPERSONIC CRAFT IS ROCKETING ABOVE THE CALM PACIFIC TOWARDS THE FAR EAST... AND A STRANGE, UNFORESEEABLE DESTINY..!
AS, BACK IN AVENGERS HQ, AN UNHAPPY HAWKEYE CONCLUDES HIS SAD REVERIE...
NO MATTER WHERE NATASHA'S GONE... OR WHAT SHE'S DONE... SOMEDAY, SOMEHOW, I'LL FIND HER!
AND, WHEN I DO, NOTHING WILL EVER PART US AGAIN... NOTHING!
YET, WHILE THE THOUGHTS OF EACH COMBAT-WEARY AVENGER DWELLS ON HIS OWN PERSONAL PROBLEMS, WE MUST AVERT OUR ADVENTURE-SEEKING EYES TO THE SUB-OCEANIC REALM OF LEGENDARY ATLANTIS...
...WHERE AMIDST A COLOSSAL AMPHITHEATRE FILLED WITH HIS THRONGING SUBJECTS, PRINCE NAMOR THE FIRST... HE WHOM THE SURFACE-MEN CALL THE DREAD SUB-MARINER... CONCLUDES A TOURNAMENT BOUT WITH HIS MOST SKILLED GLADIATORS...
BY OUR CITY'S RINGING GATES! CAN NOTHING CONQUER OUR INVINCIBLE MONARCH?
THREE OF US BESIEGED HIM... IN FULL BATTLE ARRAY! EVEN SO, HE HAS TOTALLY DEFEATED US!
THUS IT MUST AND EVER SHALL BE... IF I AM TO REMAIN THE TRUE AND RIGHTFUL SOVEREIGN OF FAIR ATLANTIS!
FOR, IS IT NOT ETERNALLY WRITTEN.. IMPERIUS REX!
4

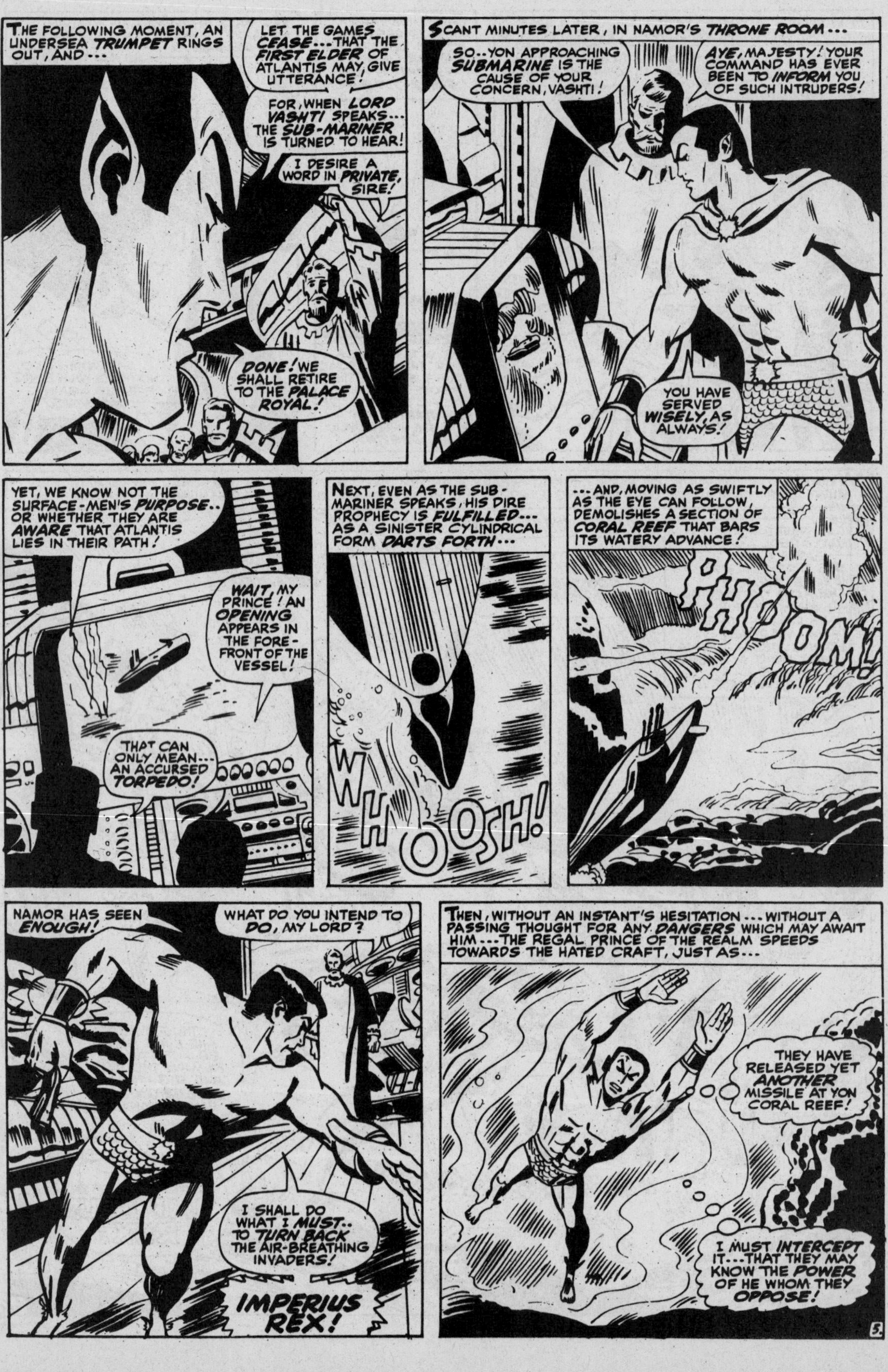
THE FOLLOWING MOMENT, AN UNDERSEA TRUMPET RINGS OUT, AND...
LET THE GAMES CEASE... THAT THE FIRST ELDER OF ATLANTIS MAY GIVE UTTERANCE!
FOR, WHEN LORD VASHTI SPEAKS... THE SUB-MARINER IS TURNED TO HEAR!
I DESIRE A WORD IN PRIVATE, SIRE!
DONE! WE SHALL RETIRE TO THE PALACE ROYAL!
SCANT MINUTES LATER, IN NAMOR'S THRONE ROOM...
SO.. YON APPROACHING SUBMARINE IS THE CAUSE OF YOUR CONCERN, VASHTI!
AYE, MAJESTY! YOUR COMMAND HAS EVER BEEN TO INFORM YOU OF SUCH INTRUDERS!
YOU HAVE SERVED WISELY, AS ALWAYS!
YET, WE KNOW NOT THE SURFACE-MEN'S PURPOSE.. OR WHETHER THEY ARE AWARE THAT ATLANTIS LIES IN THEIR PATH!
WAIT, MY PRINCE! AN OPENING APPEARS IN THE FORE-FRONT OF THE VESSEL!
THAT CAN ONLY MEAN... AN ACCURSED TORPEDO!
NEXT, EVEN AS THE SUB-MARINER SPEAKS, HIS DIRE PROPHECY IS FULFILLED... AS A SINISTER CYLINDRICAL FORM DARTS FORTH...
WHOOSH!
...AND, MOVING AS SWIFTLY AS THE EYE CAN FOLLOW, DEMOLISHES A SECTION OF CORAL REEF THAT BARS ITS WATERY ADVANCE!
PHOOOM!
NAMOR HAS SEEN ENOUGH!
WHAT DO YOU INTEND TO DO, MY LORD?
I SHALL DO WHAT I MUST.. TO TURN BACK THE AIR-BREATHING INVADERS!
IMPERIUS REX!
THEN, WITHOUT AN INSTANT'S HESITATION... WITHOUT A PASSING THOUGHT FOR ANY DANGERS WHICH MAY AWAIT HIM... THE REGAL PRINCE OF THE REALM SPEEDS TOWARDS THE HATED CRAFT, JUST AS...
THEY HAVE RELEASED YET ANOTHER MISSILE AT YON CORAL REEF!
I MUST INTERCEPT IT... THAT THEY MAY KNOW THE POWER OF HE WHOM THEY OPPOSE!
5.

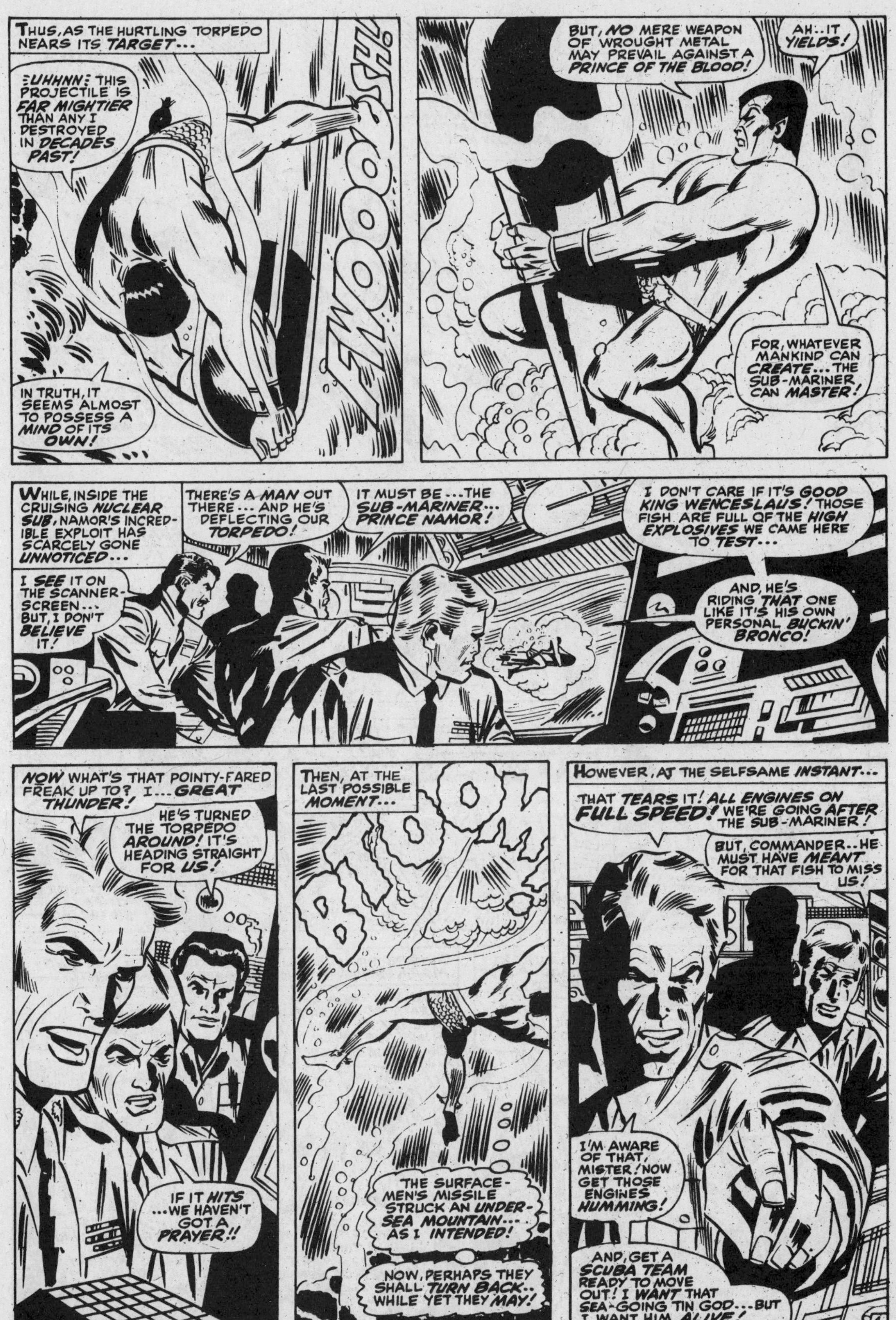
THUS, AS THE HURTLING TORPEDO NEARS ITS TARGET...
UHHNN! THIS PROJECTILE IS FAR MIGHTIER THAN ANY I DESTROYED IN DECADES PAST!
THSWOOOOM
IN TRUTH, IT SEEMS ALMOST TO POSSESS A MIND OF ITS OWN!
BUT, NO MERE WEAPON OF WROUGHT METAL MAY PREVAIL AGAINST A PRINCE OF THE BLOOD!
AH..IT YIELDS!
FOR, WHATEVER MANKIND CAN CREATE...THE SUB-MARINER CAN MASTER!
WHILE, INSIDE THE CRUISING NUCLEAR SUB, NAMOR'S INCREDIBLE EXPLOIT HAS SCARCELY GONE UNNOTICED...
THERE'S A MAN OUT THERE... AND HE'S DEFLECTING OUR TORPEDO!
IT MUST BE ...THE SUB-MARINER... PRINCE NAMOR!
I DON'T CARE IF IT'S GOOD KING WENCESLAUS! THOSE FISH ARE FULL OF THE HIGH EXPLOSIVES WE CAME HERE TO TEST...
I SEE IT ON THE SCANNER-SCREEN... BUT, I DON'T BELIEVE IT!
AND, HE'S RIDING THAT ONE LIKE IT'S HIS OWN PERSONAL BUCKIN' BRONCO!
NOW WHAT'S THAT POINTY-EARED FREAK UP TO? I... GREAT THUNDER!
HE'S TURNED THE TORPEDO AROUND! IT'S HEADING STRAIGHT FOR US!
IF IT HITS ...WE HAVEN'T GOT A PRAYER!!
THEN, AT THE LAST POSSIBLE MOMENT...
BLOOOM
THE SURFACE-MEN'S MISSILE STRUCK AN UNDERSEA MOUNTAIN... AS I INTENDED!
NOW, PERHAPS THEY SHALL TURN BACK.. WHILE YET THEY MAY!
HOWEVER, AT THE SELFSAME INSTANT...
THAT TEARS IT! ALL ENGINES ON FULL SPEED! WE'RE GOING AFTER THE SUB-MARINER!
BUT, COMMANDER..HE MUST HAVE MEANT FOR THAT FISH TO MISS US!
I'M AWARE OF THAT, MISTER! NOW GET THOSE ENGINES HUMMING!
AND, GET A SCUBA TEAM READY TO MOVE OUT! I WANT THAT SEA-GOING TIN GOD...BUT I WANT HIM ALIVE!
6.

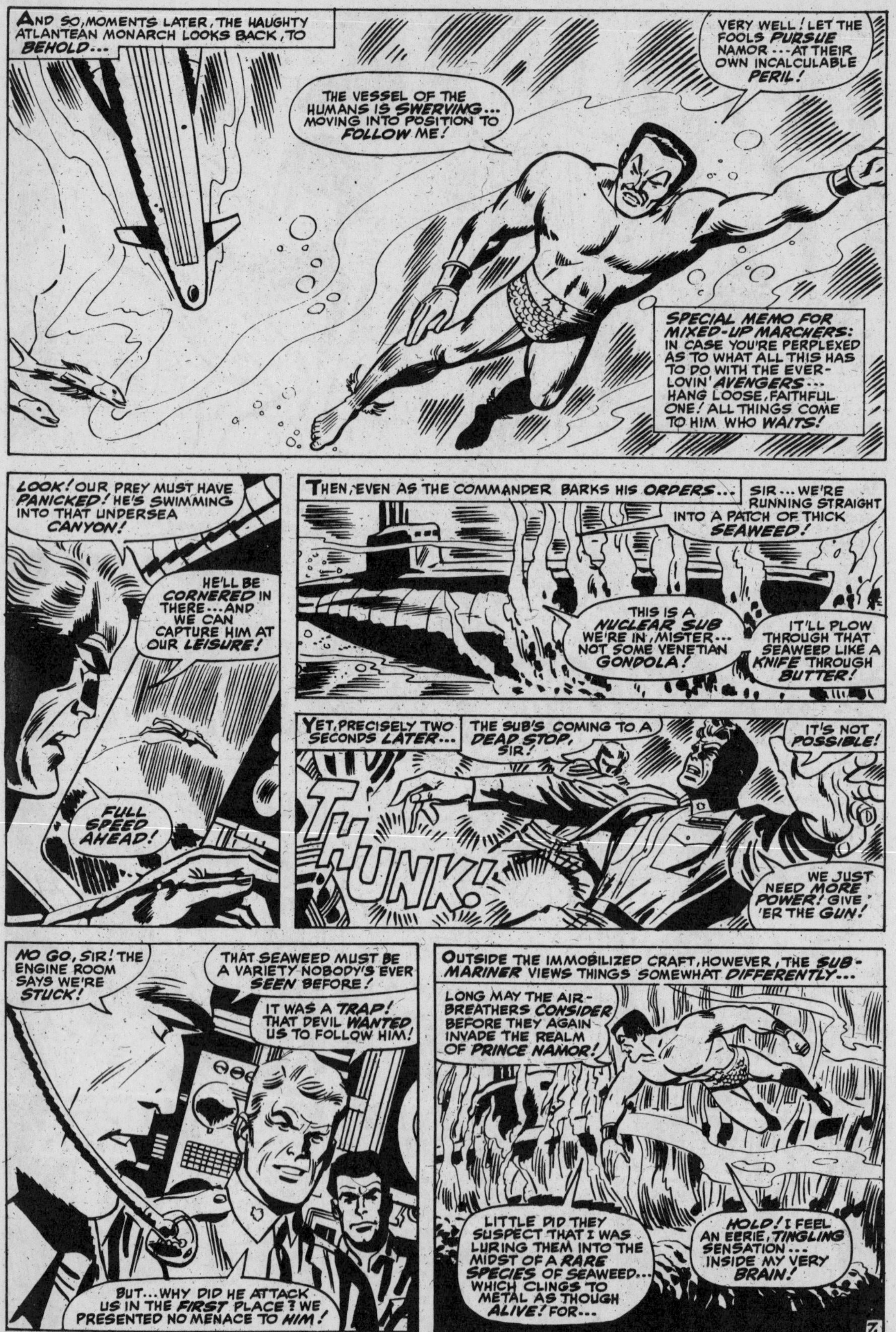
AND SO, MOMENTS LATER, THE HAUGHTY ATLANTEAN MONARCH LOOKS BACK, TO BEHOLD...
THE VESSEL OF THE HUMANS IS SWERVING... MOVING INTO POSITION TO FOLLOW ME!
VERY WELL! LET THE FOOLS PURSUE NAMOR ---AT THEIR OWN INCALCULABLE PERIL!
SPECIAL MEMO FOR MIXED-UP MARCHERS: IN CASE YOU'RE PERPLEXED AS TO WHAT ALL THIS HAS TO DO WITH THE EVER-LOVIN' AVENGERS--- HANG LOOSE, FAITHFUL ONE! ALL THINGS COME TO HIM WHO WAITS!
LOOK! OUR PREY MUST HAVE PANICKED! HE'S SWIMMING INTO THAT UNDERSEA CANYON!
HE'LL BE CORNERED IN THERE...AND WE CAN CAPTURE HIM AT OUR LEISURE!
FULL SPEED AHEAD!
THEN, EVEN AS THE COMMANDER BARKS HIS ORDERS...
SIR... WE'RE RUNNING STRAIGHT INTO A PATCH OF THICK SEAWEED!
THIS IS A NUCLEAR SUB WE'RE IN, MISTER... NOT SOME VENETIAN GONDOLA!
IT'LL PLOW THROUGH THAT SEAWEED LIKE A KNIFE THROUGH BUTTER!
YET, PRECISELY TWO SECONDS LATER...
THE SUB'S COMING TO A DEAD STOP, SIR!
IT'S NOT POSSIBLE!
THUNK!
WE JUST NEED MORE POWER! GIVE 'ER THE GUN!
NO GO, SIR! THE ENGINE ROOM SAYS WE'RE STUCK!
THAT SEAWEED MUST BE A VARIETY NOBODY'S EVER SEEN BEFORE!
IT WAS A TRAP! THAT DEVIL WANTED US TO FOLLOW HIM!
BUT...WHY DID HE ATTACK US IN THE FIRST PLACE? WE PRESENTED NO MENACE TO HIM!
OUTSIDE THE IMMOBILIZED CRAFT, HOWEVER, THE SUB-MARINER VIEWS THINGS SOMEWHAT DIFFERENTLY...
LONG MAY THE AIR-BREATHERS CONSIDER BEFORE THEY AGAIN INVADE THE REALM OF PRINCE NAMOR!
LITTLE DID THEY SUSPECT THAT I WAS LURING THEM INTO THE MIDST OF A RARE SPECIES OF SEAWEED... WHICH CLINGS TO METAL AS THOUGH ALIVE! FOR...
HOLD! I FEEL AN EERIE, TINGLING SENSATION... INSIDE MY VERY BRAIN!
7.

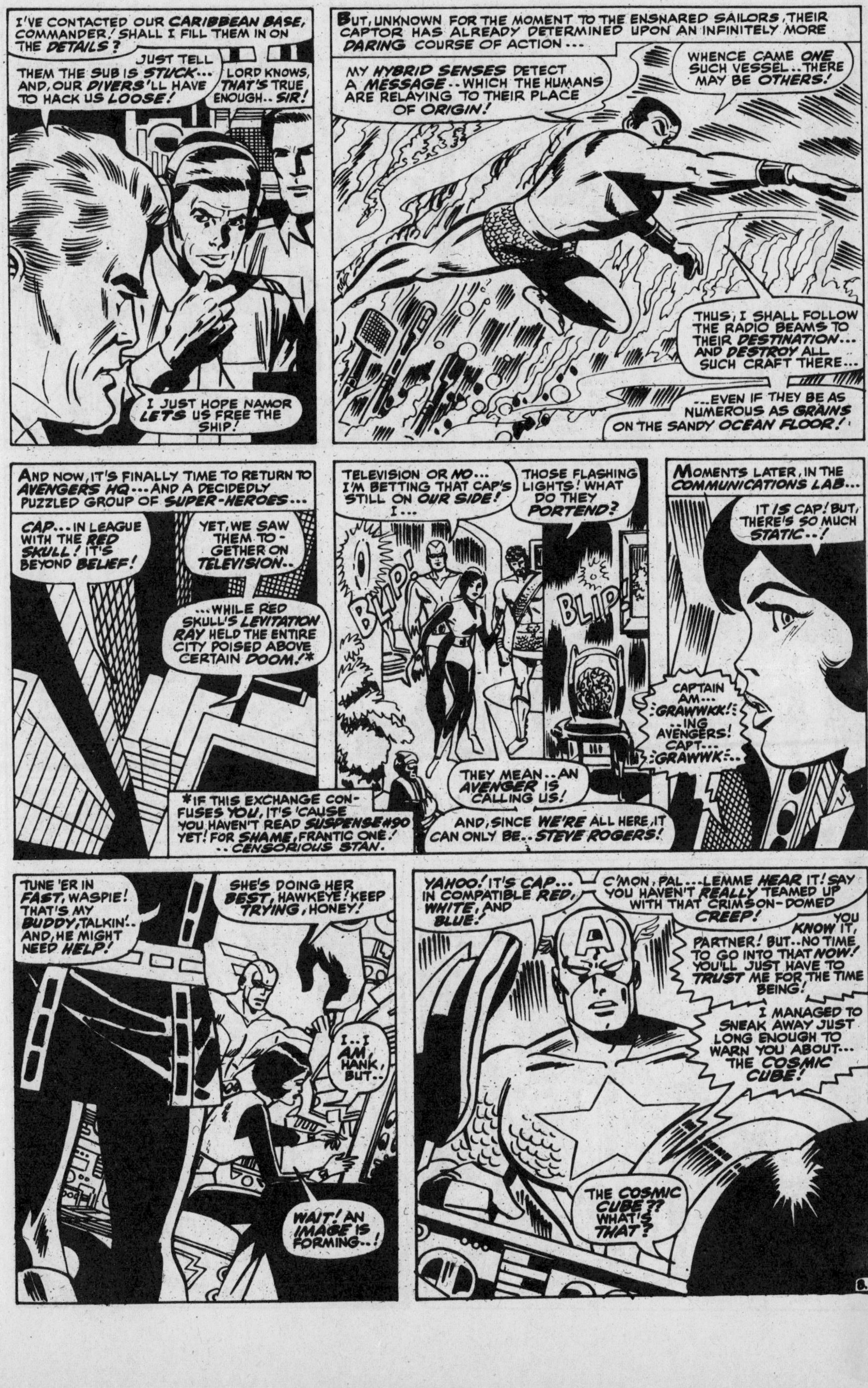
I'VE CONTACTED OUR CARIBBEAN BASE, COMMANDER! SHALL I FILL THEM IN ON THE DETAILS?
JUST TELL THEM THE SUB IS STUCK... AND, OUR DIVERS'LL HAVE TO HACK US LOOSE!
LORD KNOWS, THAT'S TRUE ENOUGH.. SIR!
I JUST HOPE NAMOR LETS US FREE THE SHIP!
BUT, UNKNOWN FOR THE MOMENT TO THE ENSNARED SAILORS, THEIR CAPTOR HAS ALREADY DETERMINED UPON AN INFINITELY MORE DARING COURSE OF ACTION...
MY HYBRID SENSES DETECT A MESSAGE.. WHICH THE HUMANS ARE RELAYING TO THEIR PLACE OF ORIGIN!
WHENCE CAME ONE SUCH VESSEL.. THERE MAY BE OTHERS!
THUS, I SHALL FOLLOW THE RADIO BEAMS TO THEIR DESTINATION... AND DESTROY ALL SUCH CRAFT THERE...
...EVEN IF THEY BE AS NUMEROUS AS GRAINS ON THE SANDY OCEAN FLOOR!
AND NOW, IT'S FINALLY TIME TO RETURN TO AVENGERS HQ... AND A DECIDEDLY PUZZLED GROUP OF SUPER-HEROES...
CAP... IN LEAGUE WITH THE RED SKULL! IT'S BEYOND BELIEF!
YET, WE SAW THEM TOGETHER ON TELEVISION..
...WHILE RED SKULL'S LEVITATION RAY HELD THE ENTIRE CITY POISED ABOVE CERTAIN DOOM!*
*IF THIS EXCHANGE CONFUSES YOU, IT'S 'CAUSE YOU HAVEN'T READ SUSPENSE #90 YET! FOR SHAME, FRANTIC ONE! ..CENSORIOUS STAN.
TELEVISION OR NO... I'M BETTING THAT CAP'S STILL ON OUR SIDE! I...
THOSE FLASHING LIGHTS! WHAT DO THEY PORTEND?
BLIP!
BLIP!
THEY MEAN.. AN AVENGER IS CALLING US!
AND, SINCE WE'RE ALL HERE, IT CAN ONLY BE.. STEVE ROGERS!
MOMENTS LATER, IN THE COMMUNICATIONS LAB...
IT IS CAP! BUT, THERE'S SO MUCH STATIC..!
CAPTAIN AM... GRAWWKK!.. ..ING AVENGERS! CAPT... GRAWWK!..
TUNE 'ER IN FAST, WASPIE! THAT'S MY BUDDY, TALKIN'.. AND, HE MIGHT NEED HELP!
SHE'S DOING HER BEST, HAWKEYE! KEEP TRYING, HONEY!
I.. I AM, HANK, BUT..
WAIT! AN IMAGE IS FORMING..!
YAHOO! IT'S CAP... IN COMPATIBLE RED, WHITE, AND BLUE!
C'MON, PAL... LEMME HEAR IT! SAY YOU HAVEN'T REALLY TEAMED UP WITH THAT CRIMSON-DOMED CREEP!
YOU KNOW IT, PARTNER! BUT.. NO TIME TO GO INTO THAT NOW! YOU'LL JUST HAVE TO TRUST ME FOR THE TIME BEING!
I MANAGED TO SNEAK AWAY JUST LONG ENOUGH TO WARN YOU ABOUT... THE COSMIC CUBE!
THE COSMIC CUBE?? WHAT'S THAT?
8.

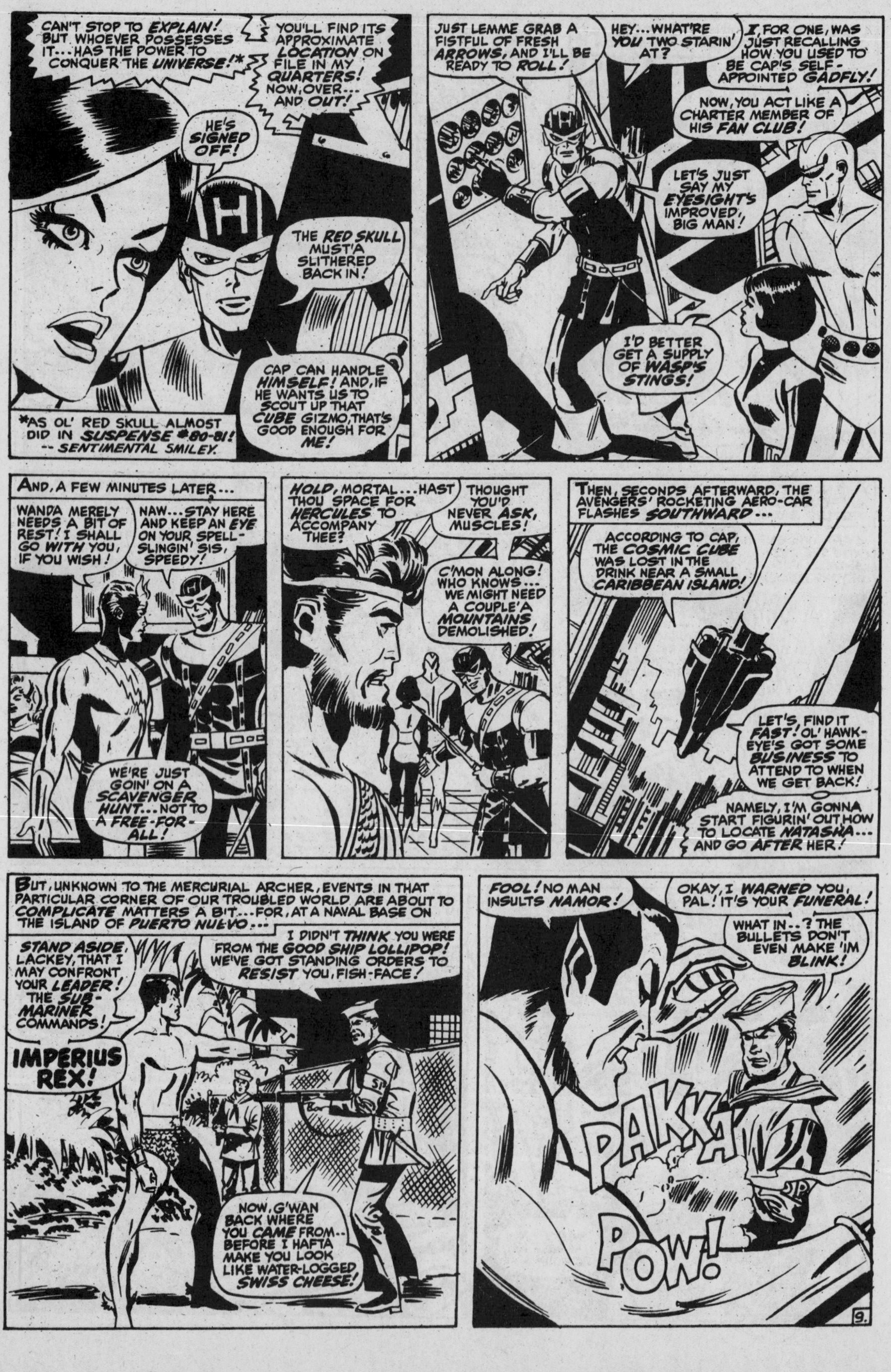
CAN'T STOP TO EXPLAIN! BUT WHOEVER POSSESSES IT... HAS THE POWER TO CONQUER THE UNIVERSE!*
YOU'LL FIND ITS APPROXIMATE LOCATION ON FILE IN MY QUARTERS! NOW, OVER... AND OUT!
HE'S SIGNED OFF!
THE RED SKULL MUST'A SLITHERED BACK IN!
CAP CAN HANDLE HIMSELF! AND, IF HE WANTS US TO SCOUT UP THAT CUBE GIZMO, THAT'S GOOD ENOUGH FOR ME!
*AS OL' RED SKULL ALMOST DID IN SUSPENSE #80-81! -- SENTIMENTAL SMILEY.
JUST LEMME GRAB A FISTFUL OF FRESH ARROWS, AND I'LL BE READY TO ROLL!
HEY... WHAT'RE YOU TWO STARIN' AT?
I, FOR ONE, WAS JUST RECALLING HOW YOU USED TO BE CAP'S SELF-APPOINTED GADFLY!
NOW, YOU ACT LIKE A CHARTER MEMBER OF HIS FAN CLUB!
LET'S JUST SAY MY EYESIGHT'S IMPROVED, BIG MAN!
I'D BETTER GET A SUPPLY OF WASP'S STINGS!
AND, A FEW MINUTES LATER...
WANDA MERELY NEEDS A BIT OF REST! I SHALL GO WITH YOU, IF YOU WISH!
NAW... STAY HERE AND KEEP AN EYE ON YOUR SPELL-SLINGIN' SIS, SPEEDY!
WE'RE JUST GOIN' ON A SCAVENGER HUNT... NOT TO A FREE-FOR-ALL!
HOLD, MORTAL... HAST THOU SPACE FOR HERCULES TO ACCOMPANY THEE?
THOUGHT YOU'D NEVER ASK, MUSCLES!
C'MON ALONG! WHO KNOWS... WE MIGHT NEED A COUPLE'A MOUNTAINS DEMOLISHED!
THEN, SECONDS AFTERWARD, THE AVENGERS' ROCKETING AERO-CAR FLASHES SOUTHWARD...
ACCORDING TO CAP, THE COSMIC CUBE WAS LOST IN THE DRINK NEAR A SMALL CARIBBEAN ISLAND!
LET'S FIND IT FAST! OL' HAWK-EYE'S GOT SOME BUSINESS TO ATTEND TO WHEN WE GET BACK!
NAMELY, I'M GONNA START FIGURIN' OUT HOW TO LOCATE NATASHA... AND GO AFTER HER!
BUT, UNKNOWN TO THE MERCURIAL ARCHER, EVENTS IN THAT PARTICULAR CORNER OF OUR TROUBLED WORLD ARE ABOUT TO COMPLICATE MATTERS A BIT... FOR, AT A NAVAL BASE ON THE ISLAND OF PUERTO NUEVO...
STAND ASIDE, LACKEY, THAT I MAY CONFRONT YOUR LEADER! THE SUB-MARINER COMMANDS!
I DIDN'T THINK YOU WERE FROM THE GOOD SHIP LOLLIPOP! WE'VE GOT STANDING ORDERS TO RESIST YOU, FISH-FACE!
IMPERIUS REX!
NOW, G'WAN BACK WHERE YOU CAME FROM-- BEFORE I HAFTA MAKE YOU LOOK LIKE WATER-LOGGED SWISS CHEESE!
FOOL! NO MAN INSULTS NAMOR!
OKAY, I WARNED YOU, PAL! IT'S YOUR FUNERAL!
WHAT IN..? THE BULLETS DON'T EVEN MAKE 'IM BLINK!
PAKKA
POW!
9.

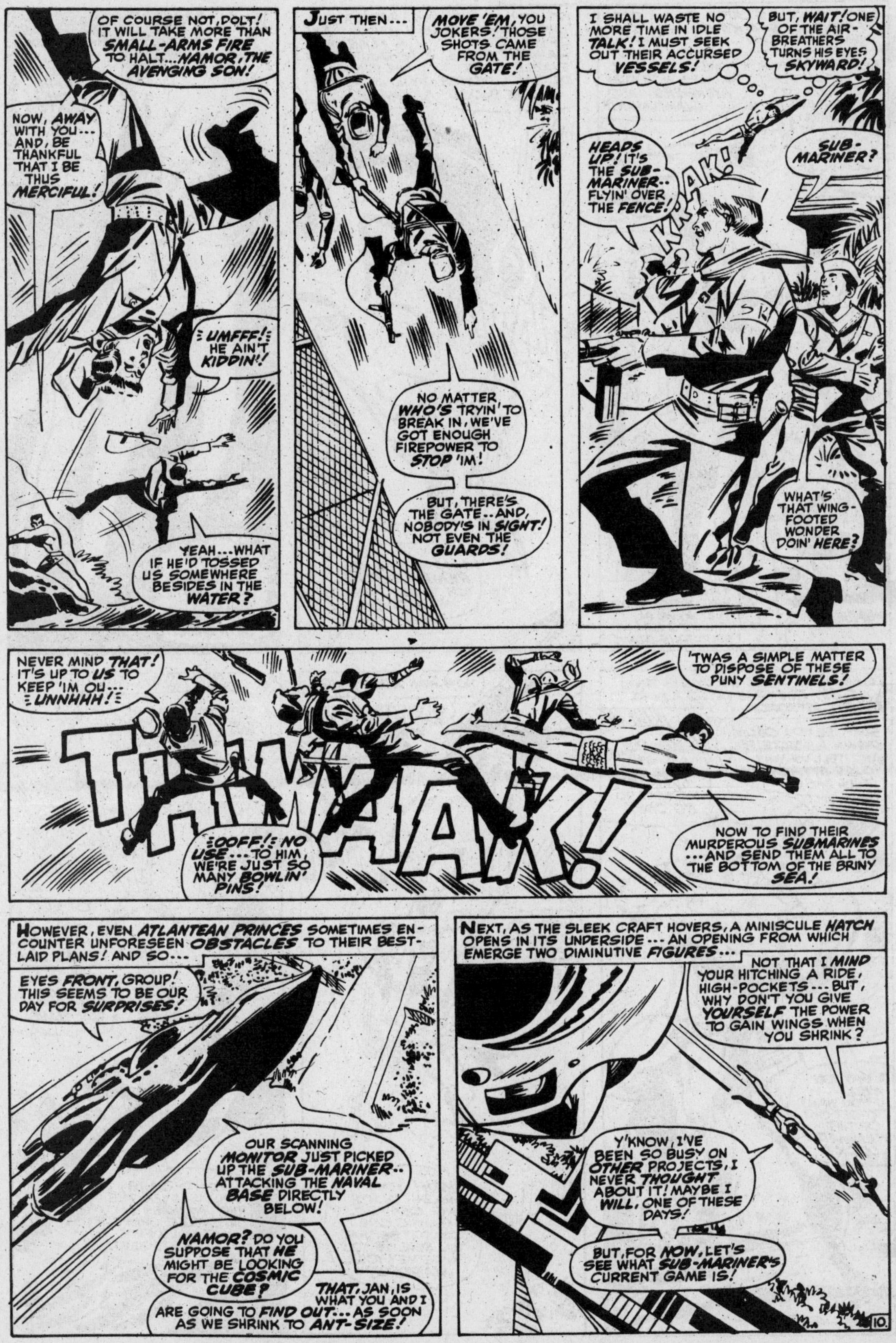
OF COURSE NOT, DOLT! IT WILL TAKE MORE THAN SMALL-ARMS FIRE TO HALT... NAMOR, THE AVENGING SON!
NOW, AWAY WITH YOU... AND, BE THANKFUL THAT I BE THUS MERCIFUL!
UMFFF! HE AIN'T KIDDIN'!
YEAH... WHAT IF HE'D TOSSED US SOMEWHERE BESIDES IN THE WATER?
JUST THEN...
MOVE 'EM, YOU JOKERS! THOSE SHOTS CAME FROM THE GATE!
NO MATTER WHO'S TRYIN' TO BREAK IN, WE'VE GOT ENOUGH FIREPOWER TO STOP 'IM!
BUT, THERE'S THE GATE.. AND, NOBODY'S IN SIGHT! NOT EVEN THE GUARDS!
I SHALL WASTE NO MORE TIME IN IDLE TALK! I MUST SEEK OUT THEIR ACCURSED VESSELS!
BUT, WAIT! ONE OF THE AIR-BREATHERS TURNS HIS EYES SKYWARD!
HEADS UP! IT'S THE SUB-MARINER.. FLYIN' OVER THE FENCE!
KRAAK!
SUB-MARINER?
WHAT'S THAT WING-FOOTED WONDER DOIN' HERE?
NEVER MIND THAT! IT'S UP TO US TO KEEP 'IM OU... UNNHHH!
THWAAK!
OOFF! NO USE... TO HIM, WE'RE JUST SO MANY BOWLIN' PINS!
'TWAS A SIMPLE MATTER TO DISPOSE OF THESE PUNY SENTINELS!
NOW TO FIND THEIR MURDEROUS SUBMARINES ...AND SEND THEM ALL TO THE BOTTOM OF THE BRINY SEA!
HOWEVER, EVEN ATLANTEAN PRINCES SOMETIMES ENCOUNTER UNFORESEEN OBSTACLES TO THEIR BEST-LAID PLANS! AND SO...
EYES FRONT, GROUP! THIS SEEMS TO BE OUR DAY FOR SURPRISES!
OUR SCANNING MONITOR JUST PICKED UP THE SUB-MARINER.. ATTACKING THE NAVAL BASE DIRECTLY BELOW!
NAMOR? DO YOU SUPPOSE THAT HE MIGHT BE LOOKING FOR THE COSMIC CUBE?
THAT, JAN, IS WHAT YOU AND I ARE GOING TO FIND OUT... AS SOON AS WE SHRINK TO ANT-SIZE!
NEXT, AS THE SLEEK CRAFT HOVERS, A MINISCULE HATCH OPENS IN ITS UNDERSIDE... AN OPENING FROM WHICH EMERGE TWO DIMINUTIVE FIGURES...
NOT THAT I MIND YOUR HITCHING A RIDE, HIGH-POCKETS... BUT, WHY DON'T YOU GIVE YOURSELF THE POWER TO GAIN WINGS WHEN YOU SHRINK?
Y'KNOW, I'VE BEEN SO BUSY ON OTHER PROJECTS, I NEVER THOUGHT ABOUT IT! MAYBE I WILL, ONE OF THESE DAYS!
BUT, FOR NOW, LET'S SEE WHAT SUB-MARINER'S CURRENT GAME IS!
10.

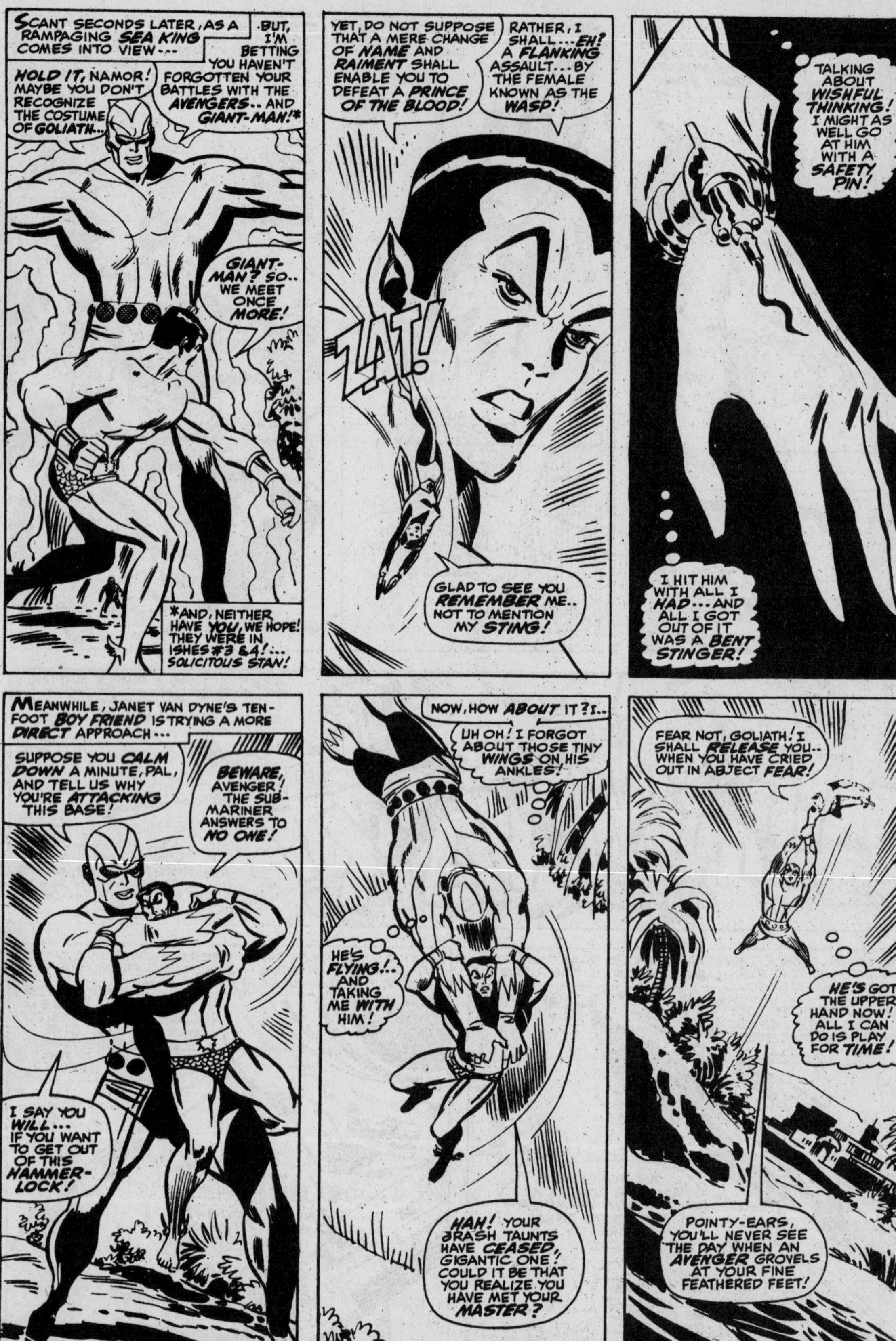
SCANT SECONDS LATER, AS A RAMPAGING SEA KING COMES INTO VIEW---
HOLD IT, NAMOR! MAYBE YOU DON'T RECOGNIZE THE COSTUME OF GOLIATH...
BUT, I'M BETTING YOU HAVEN'T FORGOTTEN YOUR BATTLES WITH THE AVENGERS.. AND GIANT-MAN!*
GIANT-MAN? SO.. WE MEET ONCE MORE!
*AND, NEITHER HAVE YOU, WE HOPE! THEY WERE IN ISHES #3 &4!... SOLICITOUS STAN!
YET, DO NOT SUPPOSE THAT A MERE CHANGE OF NAME AND RAIMENT SHALL ENABLE YOU TO DEFEAT A PRINCE OF THE BLOOD!
RATHER, I SHALL... EH? A FLANKING ASSAULT... BY THE FEMALE KNOWN AS THE WASP!
ZAT!
GLAD TO SEE YOU REMEMBER ME.. NOT TO MENTION MY STING!
TALKING ABOUT WISHFUL THINKING! I MIGHT AS WELL GO AT HIM WITH A SAFETY PIN!
I HIT HIM WITH ALL I HAD... AND ALL I GOT OUT OF IT WAS A BENT STINGER!
MEANWHILE, JANET VAN DYNE'S TEN-FOOT BOY FRIEND IS TRYING A MORE DIRECT APPROACH...
SUPPOSE YOU CALM DOWN A MINUTE, PAL, AND TELL US WHY YOU'RE ATTACKING THIS BASE!
BEWARE, AVENGER! THE SUB-MARINER ANSWERS TO NO ONE!
I SAY YOU WILL... IF YOU WANT TO GET OUT OF THIS HAMMER-LOCK!
NOW, HOW ABOUT IT? I...
UH OH! I FORGOT ABOUT THOSE TINY WINGS ON HIS ANKLES!
HE'S FLYING!.. AND TAKING ME WITH HIM!
HAH! YOUR BRASH TAUNTS HAVE CEASED, GIGANTIC ONE! COULD IT BE THAT YOU REALIZE YOU HAVE MET YOUR MASTER?
FEAR NOT, GOLIATH! I SHALL RELEASE YOU.. WHEN YOU HAVE CRIED OUT IN ABJECT FEAR!
HE'S GOT THE UPPER HAND NOW! ALL I CAN DO IS PLAY FOR TIME!
POINTY-EARS, YOU'LL NEVER SEE THE DAY WHEN AN AVENGER GROVELS AT YOUR FINE FEATHERED FEET!
11.

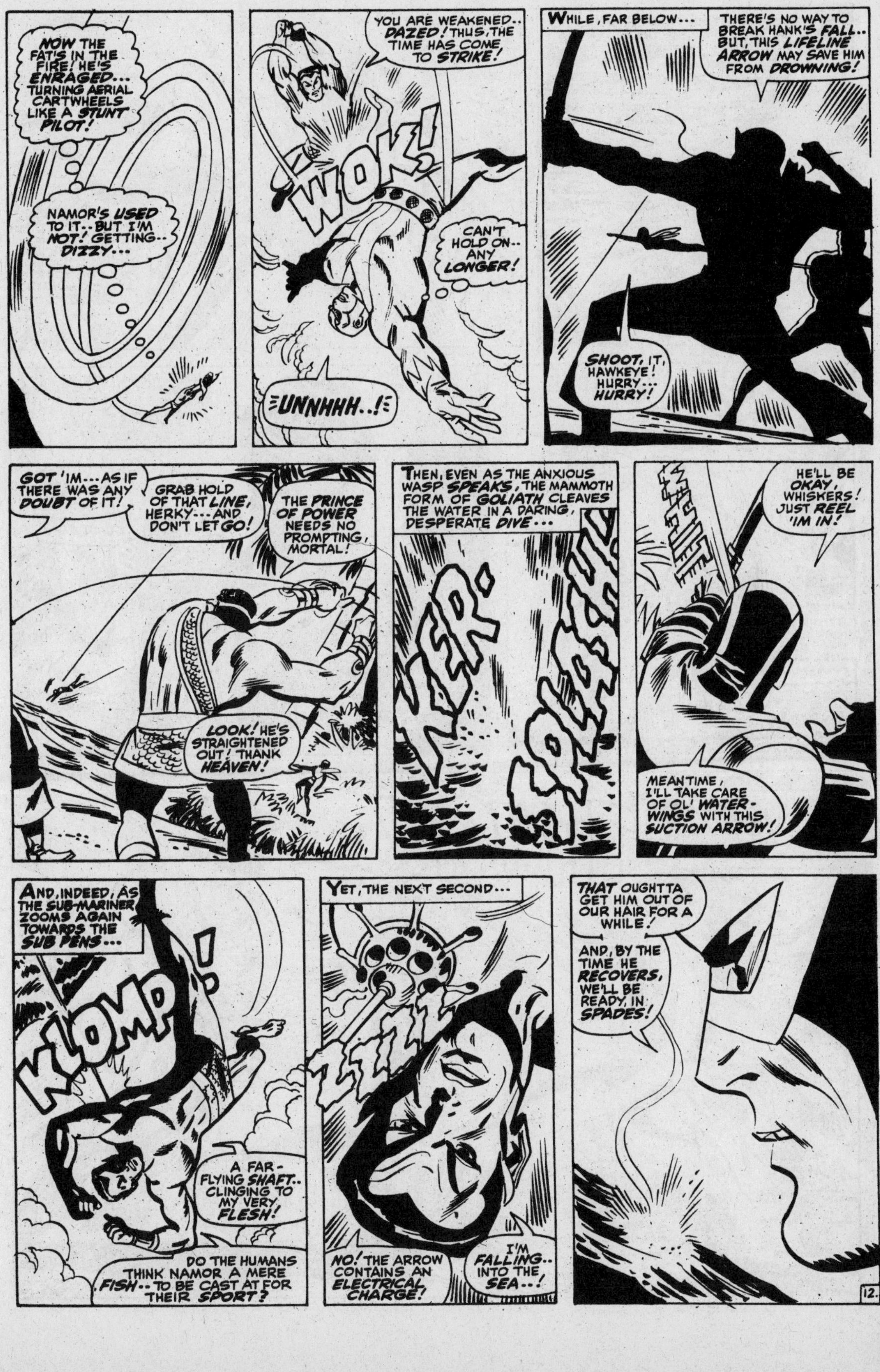
NOW THE FAT'S IN THE FIRE! HE'S ENRAGED... TURNING AERIAL CARTWHEELS LIKE A STUNT PILOT!
NAMOR'S USED TO IT.. BUT I'M NOT! GETTING.. DIZZY...
YOU ARE WEAKENED.. DAZED! THUS, THE TIME HAS COME TO STRIKE!
WOK!
CAN'T HOLD ON.. ANY LONGER!
UNNHHH..!
WHILE, FAR BELOW...
THERE'S NO WAY TO BREAK HANK'S FALL.. BUT, THIS LIFELINE ARROW MAY SAVE HIM FROM DROWNING!
SHOOT, IT, HAWKEYE! HURRY... HURRY!
GOT 'IM... AS IF THERE WAS ANY DOUBT OF IT!
GRAB HOLD OF THAT LINE, HERKY... AND DON'T LET GO!
THE PRINCE OF POWER NEEDS NO PROMPTING, MORTAL!
LOOK! HE'S STRAIGHTENED OUT! THANK HEAVEN!
THEN, EVEN AS THE ANXIOUS WASP SPEAKS, THE MAMMOTH FORM OF GOLIATH CLEAVES THE WATER IN A DARING, DESPERATE DIVE...
HE'LL BE OKAY, WHISKERS! JUST REEL 'IM IN!
MEANTIME, I'LL TAKE CARE OF OL' WATER-WINGS WITH THIS SUCTION ARROW!
AND, INDEED, AS THE SUB-MARINER ZOOMS AGAIN TOWARDS THE SUB PENS...
KLOMP!
A FAR-FLYING SHAFT.. CLINGING TO MY VERY FLESH!
DO THE HUMANS THINK NAMOR A MERE FISH.. TO BE CAST AT FOR THEIR SPORT?
YET, THE NEXT SECOND...
ZZZZT
NO! THE ARROW CONTAINS AN ELECTRICAL CHARGE!
I'M FALLING.. INTO THE SEA..!
THAT OUGHTTA GET HIM OUT OF OUR HAIR FOR A WHILE!
AND, BY THE TIME HE RECOVERS, WE'LL BE READY, IN SPADES!
12.

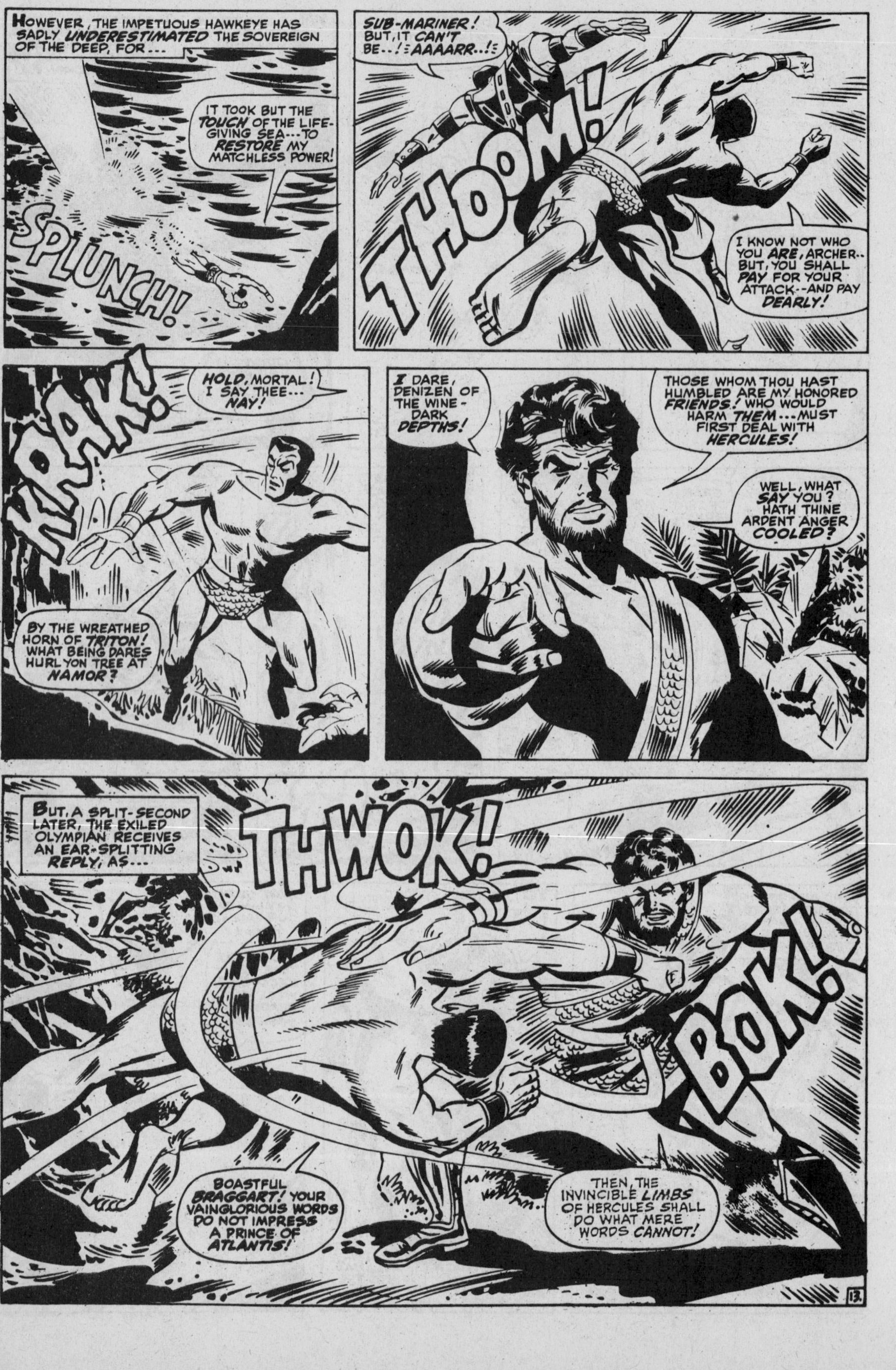
HOWEVER, THE IMPETUOUS HAWKEYE HAS SADLY UNDERESTIMATED THE SOVEREIGN OF THE DEEP, FOR...
IT TOOK BUT THE TOUCH OF THE LIFE-GIVING SEA--TO RESTORE MY MATCHLESS POWER!
SPLUNCH!
SUB-MARINER! BUT, IT CAN'T BE..!--AAAARR..!
THOOM!
I KNOW NOT WHO YOU ARE, ARCHER.. BUT, YOU SHALL PAY FOR YOUR ATTACK--AND PAY DEARLY!
KRAK!
HOLD, MORTAL! I SAY THEE--- NAY!
BY THE WREATHED HORN OF TRITON! WHAT BEING DARES HURL YON TREE AT NAMOR?
I DARE, DENIZEN OF THE WINE-DARK DEPTHS!
THOSE WHOM THOU HAST HUMBLED ARE MY HONORED FRIENDS! WHO WOULD HARM THEM---MUST FIRST DEAL WITH HERCULES!
WELL, WHAT SAY YOU? HATH THINE ARDENT ANGER COOLED?
BUT, A SPLIT-SECOND LATER, THE EXILED OLYMPIAN RECEIVES AN EAR-SPLITTING REPLY, AS...
THWOK!
BOK!
BOASTFUL BRAGGART! YOUR VAINGLORIOUS WORDS DO NOT IMPRESS A PRINCE OF ATLANTIS!
THEN, THE INVINCIBLE LIMBS OF HERCULES SHALL DO WHAT MERE WORDS CANNOT!
13.

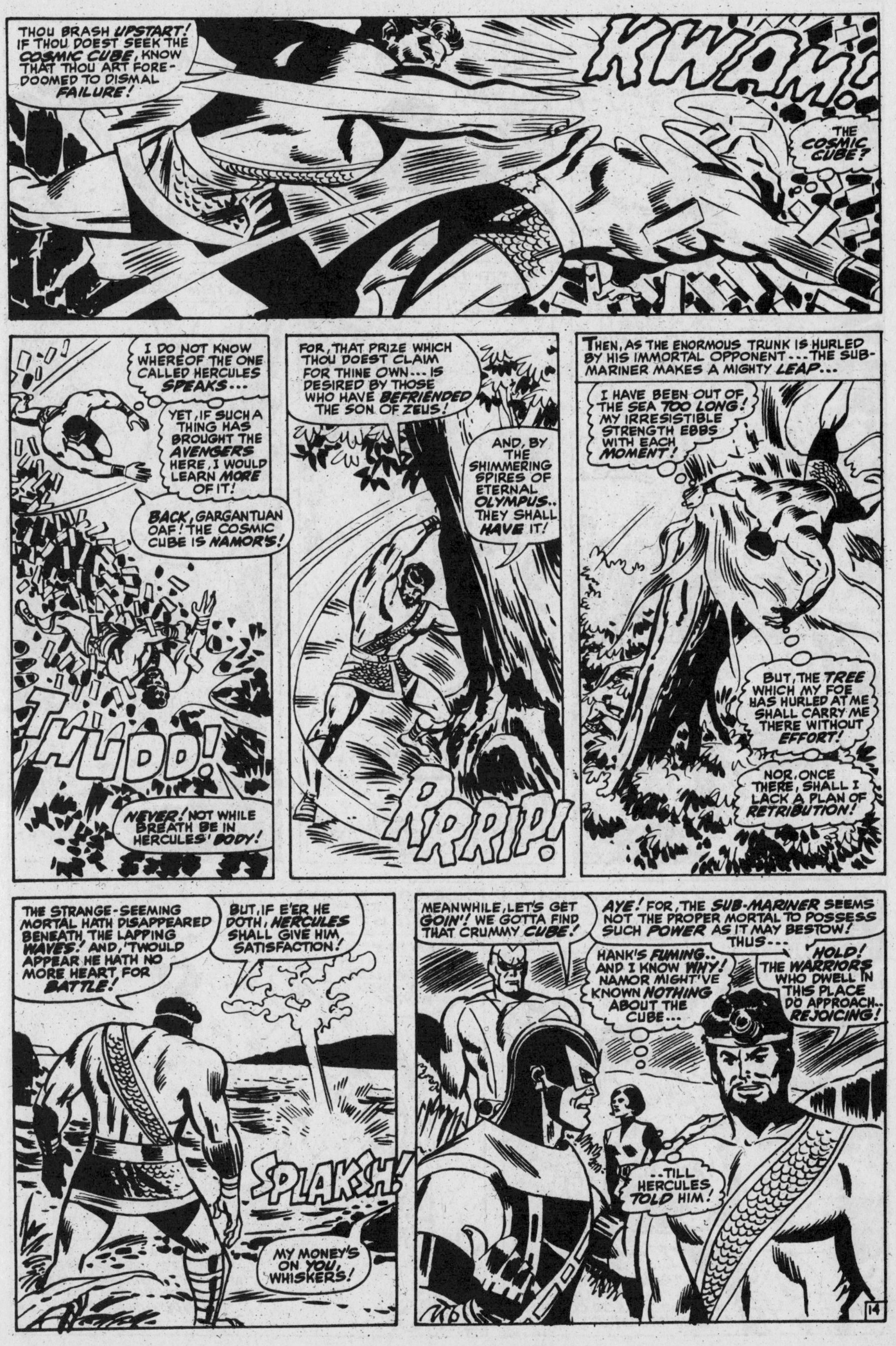
THOU BRASH UPSTART! IF THOU DOEST SEEK THE COSMIC CUBE, KNOW THAT THOU ART FORE-DOOMED TO DISMAL FAILURE!
KWAM!
THE COSMIC CUBE?
I DO NOT KNOW WHEREOF THE ONE CALLED HERCULES SPEAKS...
YET, IF SUCH A THING HAS BROUGHT THE AVENGERS HERE, I WOULD LEARN MORE OF IT!
BACK, GARGANTUAN OAF! THE COSMIC CUBE IS NAMOR'S!
THUDD!
NEVER! NOT WHILE BREATH BE IN HERCULES' BODY!
FOR, THAT PRIZE WHICH THOU DOEST CLAIM FOR THINE OWN... IS DESIRED BY THOSE WHO HAVE BEFRIENDED THE SON OF ZEUS!
AND, BY THE SHIMMERING SPIRES OF ETERNAL OLYMPUS.. THEY SHALL HAVE IT!
RRRIP!
THEN, AS THE ENORMOUS TRUNK IS HURLED BY HIS IMMORTAL OPPONENT---THE SUB-MARINER MAKES A MIGHTY LEAP...
I HAVE BEEN OUT OF THE SEA TOO LONG! MY IRRESISTIBLE STRENGTH EBBS WITH EACH MOMENT!
BUT, THE TREE WHICH MY FOE HAS HURLED AT ME SHALL CARRY ME THERE WITHOUT EFFORT!
NOR, ONCE THERE, SHALL I LACK A PLAN OF RETRIBUTION!
THE STRANGE-SEEMING MORTAL HATH DISAPPEARED BENEATH THE LAPPING WAVES! AND, 'TWOULD APPEAR HE HATH NO MORE HEART FOR BATTLE!
BUT, IF E'ER HE DOTH, HERCULES SHALL GIVE HIM SATISFACTION!
SPLAKSH!
MY MONEY'S ON YOU, WHISKERS!
MEANWHILE, LET'S GET GOIN'! WE GOTTA FIND THAT CRUMMY CUBE!
AYE! FOR THE SUB-MARINER SEEMS NOT THE PROPER MORTAL TO POSSESS SUCH POWER AS IT MAY BESTOW! THUS---
HANK'S FUMING.. AND I KNOW WHY! NAMOR MIGHT'VE KNOWN NOTHING ABOUT THE CUBE...
HOLD! THE WARRIORS WHO DWELL IN THIS PLACE DO APPROACH.. REJOICING!
--TILL HERCULES TOLD HIM!
14

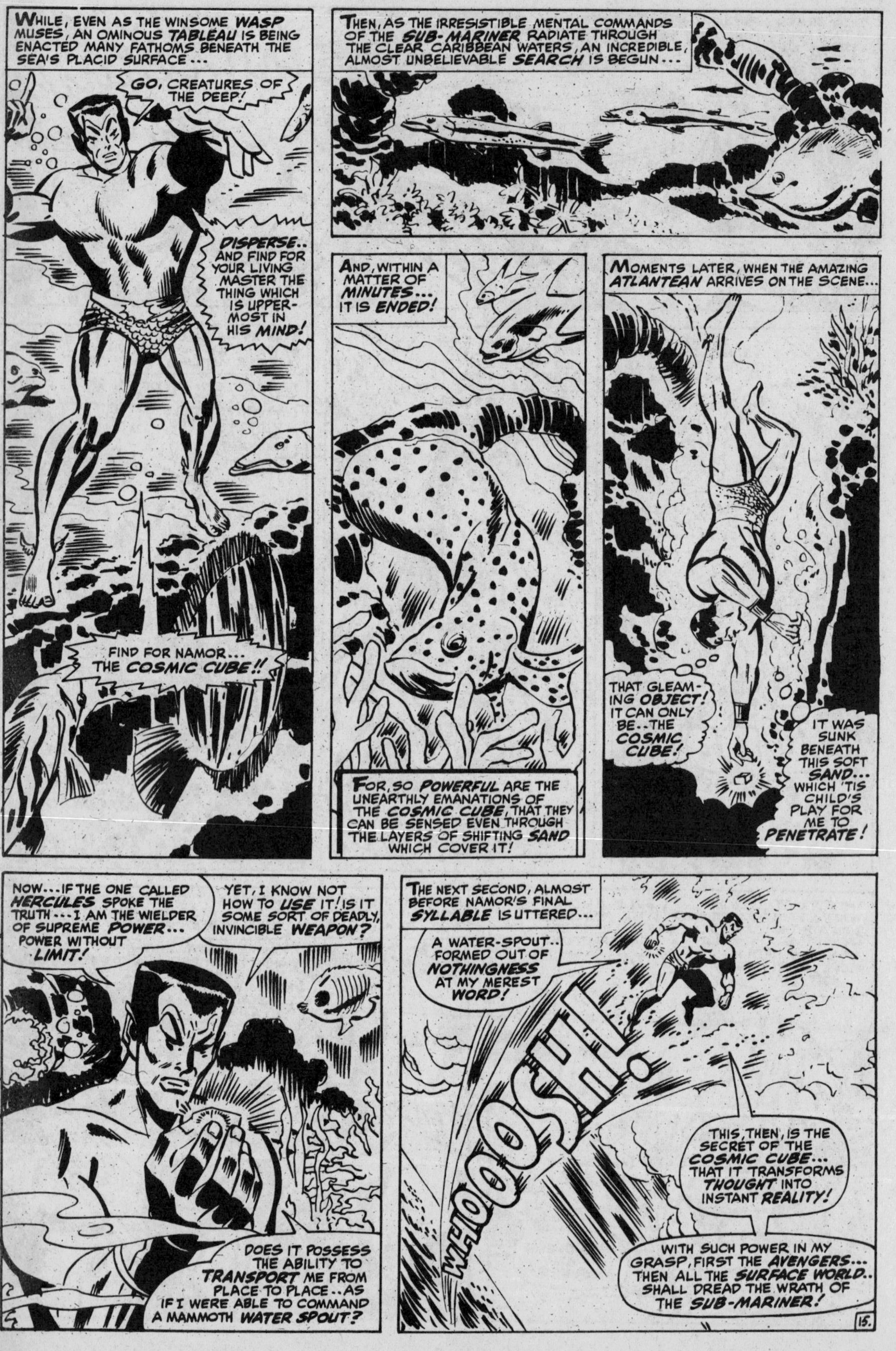
While, even as the winsome Wasp muses, an ominous tableau is being enacted many fathoms beneath the sea's placid surface...
Go, creatures of the deep!
Disperse.. and find for your living master the thing which is uppermost in his mind!
Find for Namor... the Cosmic Cube!!
Then, as the irresistible mental commands of the Sub-Mariner radiate through the clear Caribbean waters, an incredible, almost unbelievable search is begun...
And, within a matter of minutes... it is ended!
For, so powerful are the unearthly emanations of the Cosmic Cube, that they can be sensed even through the layers of shifting sand which cover it!
Moments later, when the amazing Atlantean arrives on the scene...
That gleaming object! It can only be.. the Cosmic Cube!
It was sunk beneath this soft sand... which 'tis child's play for me to penetrate!
Now... if the one called Hercules spoke the truth... I am the wielder of supreme power... power without limit!
Yet, I know not how to use it! Is it some sort of deadly, invincible weapon?
Does it possess the ability to transport me from place to place.. as if I were able to command a mammoth water spout?
The next second, almost before Namor's final syllable is uttered...
A water-spout.. formed out of nothingness at my merest word!
WHOOOOSH!
This, then, is the secret of the Cosmic Cube... that it transforms thought into instant reality!
With such power in my grasp, first the Avengers... then all the surface world.. shall dread the wrath of the Sub-Mariner!
15.

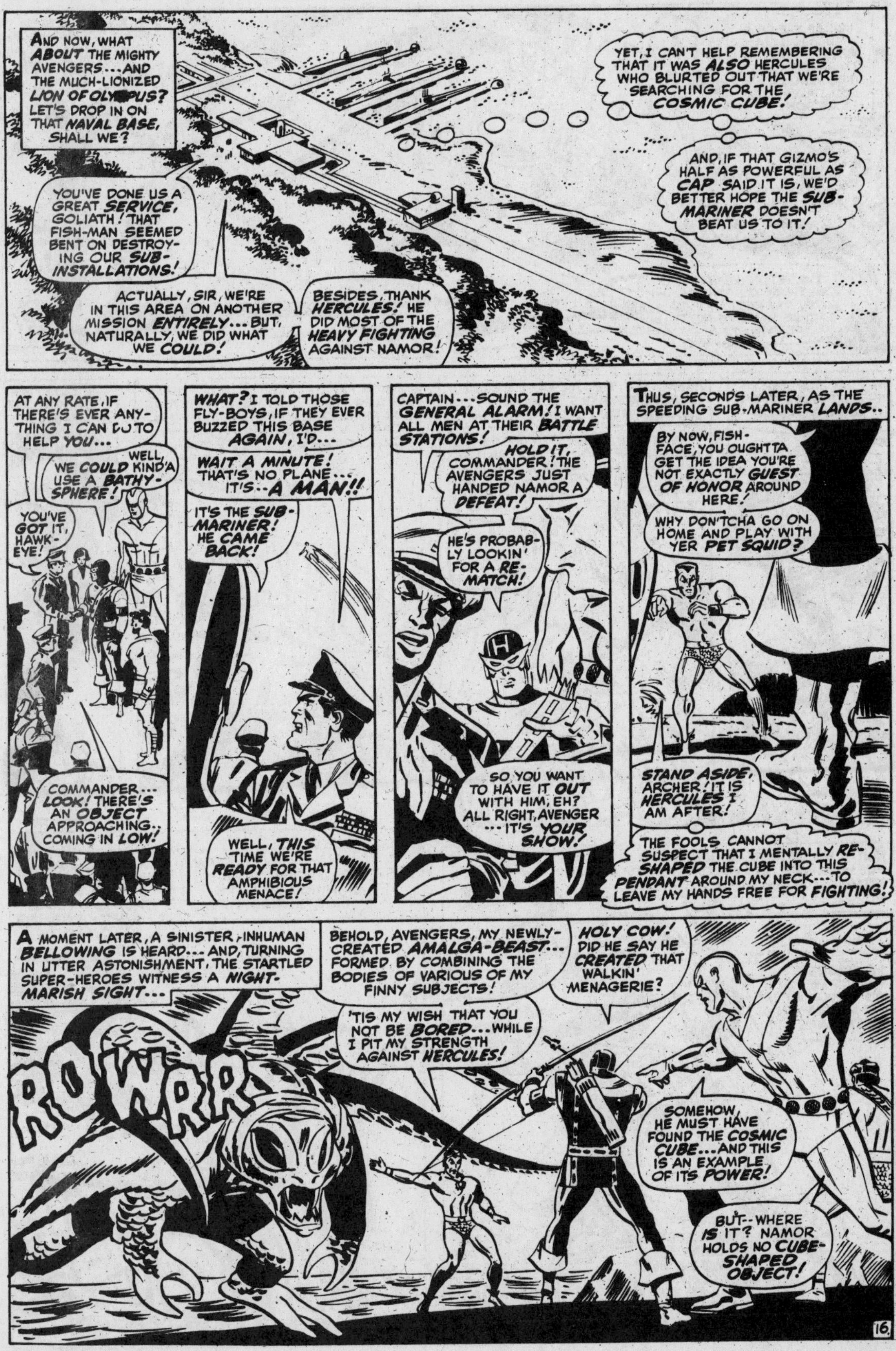

AND NOW, WHAT ABOUT THE MIGHTY AVENGERS... AND THE MUCH-LIONIZED LION OF OLYMPUS? LET'S DROP IN ON THAT NAVAL BASE, SHALL WE?
YET, I CAN'T HELP REMEMBERING THAT IT WAS ALSO HERCULES WHO BLURTED OUT THAT WE'RE SEARCHING FOR THE COSMIC CUBE!
AND, IF THAT GIZMO'S HALF AS POWERFUL AS CAP SAID IT IS, WE'D BETTER HOPE THE SUB-MARINER DOESN'T BEAT US TO IT!
YOU'VE DONE US A GREAT SERVICE, GOLIATH! THAT FISH-MAN SEEMED BENT ON DESTROYING OUR SUB-INSTALLATIONS!
ACTUALLY, SIR, WE'RE IN THIS AREA ON ANOTHER MISSION ENTIRELY... BUT, NATURALLY, WE DID WHAT WE COULD!
BESIDES, THANK HERCULES! HE DID MOST OF THE HEAVY FIGHTING AGAINST NAMOR!
AT ANY RATE, IF THERE'S EVER ANYTHING I CAN DO TO HELP YOU...
WELL, WE COULD KIND'A USE A BATHYSPHERE!
YOU'VE GOT IT, HAWKEYE!
COMMANDER... LOOK! THERE'S AN OBJECT APPROACHING.. COMING IN LOW!
WHAT? I TOLD THOSE FLY-BOYS, IF THEY EVER BUZZED THIS BASE AGAIN, I'D...
WAIT A MINUTE! THAT'S NO PLANE... IT'S--A MAN!!
IT'S THE SUB-MARINER! HE CAME BACK!
WELL, THIS TIME WE'RE READY FOR THAT AMPHIBIOUS MENACE!
CAPTAIN... SOUND THE GENERAL ALARM! I WANT ALL MEN AT THEIR BATTLE STATIONS!
HOLD IT, COMMANDER! THE AVENGERS JUST HANDED NAMOR A DEFEAT!
HE'S PROBABLY LOOKIN' FOR A RE-MATCH!
SO YOU WANT TO HAVE IT OUT WITH HIM, EH? ALL RIGHT, AVENGER... IT'S YOUR SHOW!
THUS, SECONDS LATER, AS THE SPEEDING SUB-MARINER LANDS..
BY NOW, FISH-FACE, YOU OUGHTTA GET THE IDEA YOU'RE NOT EXACTLY GUEST OF HONOR AROUND HERE!
WHY DON'TCHA GO ON HOME AND PLAY WITH YER PET SQUID?
STAND ASIDE, ARCHER! IT IS HERCULES I AM AFTER!
THE FOOLS CANNOT SUSPECT THAT I MENTALLY RE-SHAPED THE CUBE INTO THIS PENDANT AROUND MY NECK---TO LEAVE MY HANDS FREE FOR FIGHTING!
A MOMENT LATER, A SINISTER, INHUMAN BELLOWING IS HEARD... AND, TURNING IN UTTER ASTONISHMENT, THE STARTLED SUPER-HEROES WITNESS A NIGHTMARISH SIGHT...
BEHOLD, AVENGERS, MY NEWLY-CREATED AMALGA-BEAST... FORMED BY COMBINING THE BODIES OF VARIOUS OF MY FINNY SUBJECTS!
'TIS MY WISH THAT YOU NOT BE BORED... WHILE I PIT MY STRENGTH AGAINST HERCULES!
HOLY COW! DID HE SAY HE CREATED THAT WALKIN' MENAGERIE?
ROWRR
SOMEHOW, HE MUST HAVE FOUND THE COSMIC CUBE... AND THIS IS AN EXAMPLE OF ITS POWER!
BUT--WHERE IS IT? NAMOR HOLDS NO CUBE-SHAPED OBJECT!
16.

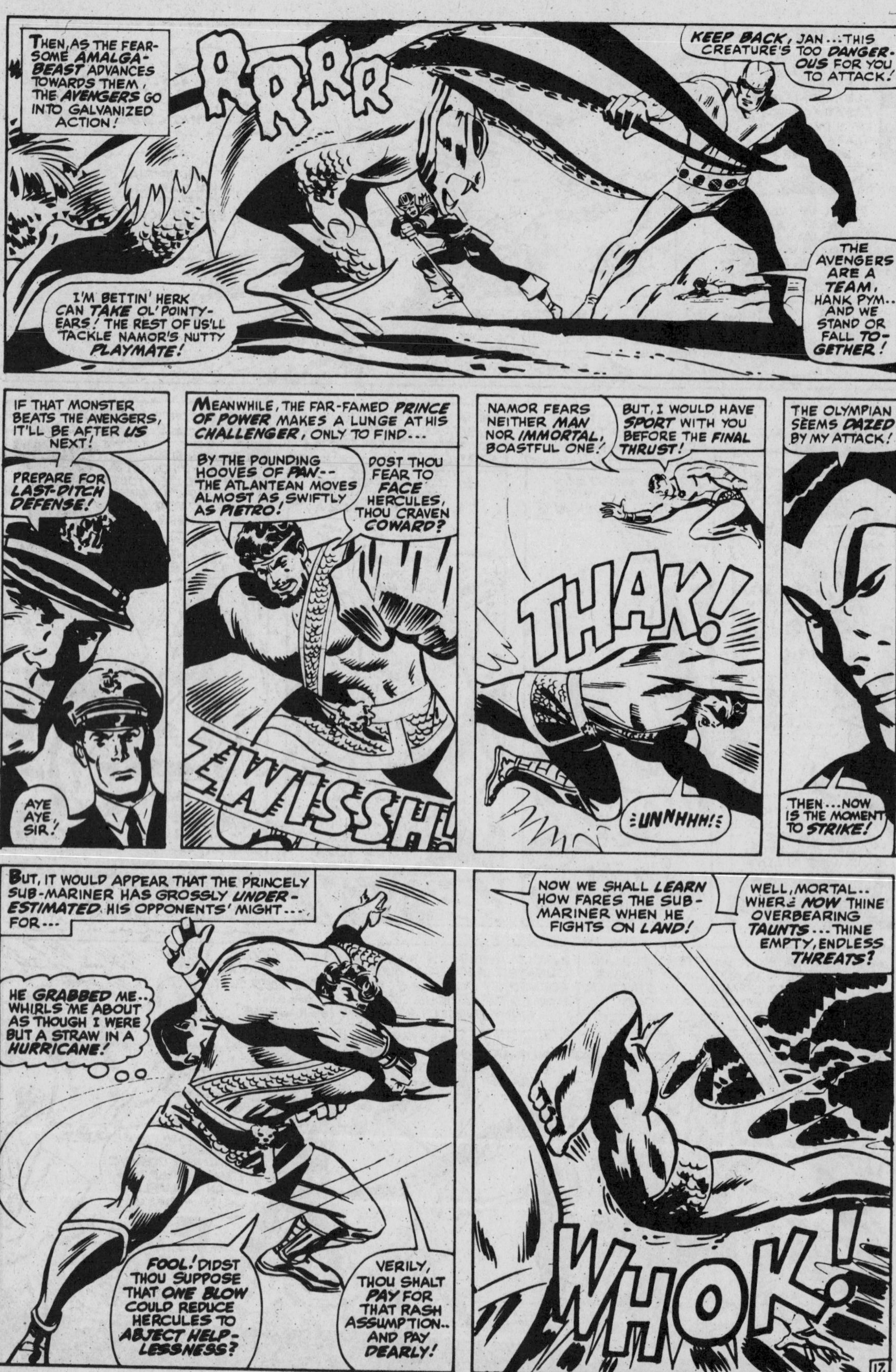
THEN, AS THE FEARSOME AMALGA-BEAST ADVANCES TOWARDS THEM, THE AVENGERS GO INTO GALVANIZED ACTION!
RRRR
KEEP BACK, JAN...THIS CREATURE'S TOO DANGEROUS FOR YOU TO ATTACK!
I'M BETTIN' HERK CAN TAKE OL' POINTY-EARS! THE REST OF US'LL TACKLE NAMOR'S NUTTY PLAYMATE!
THE AVENGERS ARE A TEAM, HANK PYM.. AND WE STAND OR FALL TOGETHER!
IF THAT MONSTER BEATS THE AVENGERS, IT'LL BE AFTER US NEXT!
PREPARE FOR LAST-DITCH DEFENSE!
AYE AYE, SIR!
MEANWHILE, THE FAR-FAMED PRINCE OF POWER MAKES A LUNGE AT HIS CHALLENGER, ONLY TO FIND...
BY THE POUNDING HOOVES OF PAN-- THE ATLANTEAN MOVES ALMOST AS SWIFTLY AS PIETRO!
DOST THOU FEAR TO FACE HERCULES, THOU CRAVEN COWARD?
ZWISSH!
NAMOR FEARS NEITHER MAN NOR IMMORTAL, BOASTFUL ONE!
BUT, I WOULD HAVE SPORT WITH YOU BEFORE THE FINAL THRUST!
THAK!
UNNHHH!
THE OLYMPIAN SEEMS DAZED BY MY ATTACK!
THEN...NOW IS THE MOMENT TO STRIKE!
BUT, IT WOULD APPEAR THAT THE PRINCELY SUB-MARINER HAS GROSSLY UNDERESTIMATED HIS OPPONENTS' MIGHT... FOR...
HE GRABBED ME... WHIRLS ME ABOUT AS THOUGH I WERE BUT A STRAW IN A HURRICANE!
FOOL! DIDST THOU SUPPOSE THAT ONE BLOW COULD REDUCE HERCULES TO ABJECT HELPLESSNESS?
VERILY, THOU SHALT PAY FOR THAT RASH ASSUMPTION.. AND PAY DEARLY!
NOW WE SHALL LEARN HOW FARES THE SUB-MARINER WHEN HE FIGHTS ON LAND!
WELL, MORTAL... WHERE NOW THINE OVERBEARING TAUNTS...THINE EMPTY, ENDLESS THREATS?
WHOK!
17.

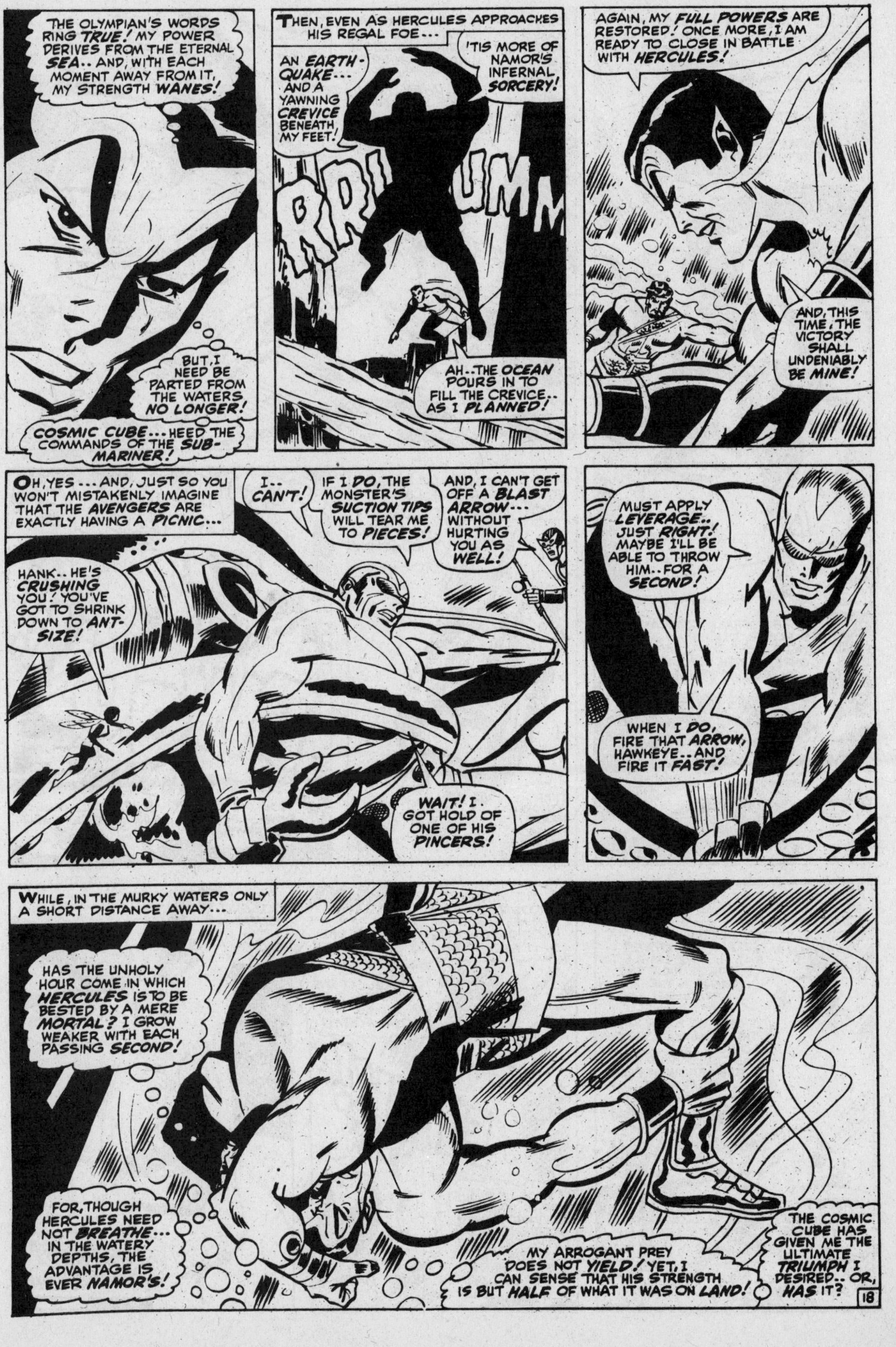
THE OLYMPIAN'S WORDS RING TRUE! MY POWER DERIVES FROM THE ETERNAL SEA.. AND, WITH EACH MOMENT AWAY FROM IT, MY STRENGTH WANES!
BUT, I NEED BE PARTED FROM THE WATERS NO LONGER!
COSMIC CUBE... HEED THE COMMANDS OF THE SUB-MARINER!
THEN, EVEN AS HERCULES APPROACHES HIS REGAL FOE...
AN EARTH-QUAKE... AND A YAWNING CREVICE BENEATH MY FEET!
'TIS MORE OF NAMOR'S INFERNAL SORCERY!
RRRUMM
AH..THE OCEAN POURS IN TO FILL THE CREVICE.. AS I PLANNED!
AGAIN, MY FULL POWERS ARE RESTORED! ONCE MORE, I AM READY TO CLOSE IN BATTLE WITH HERCULES!
AND, THIS TIME, THE VICTORY SHALL UNDENIABLY BE MINE!
OH, YES ... AND, JUST SO YOU WON'T MISTAKENLY IMAGINE THAT THE AVENGERS ARE EXACTLY HAVING A PICNIC...
I.. CAN'T!
IF I DO, THE MONSTER'S SUCTION TIPS WILL TEAR ME TO PIECES!
AND, I CAN'T GET OFF A BLAST ARROW--- WITHOUT HURTING YOU AS WELL!
HANK.. HE'S CRUSHING YOU! YOU'VE GOT TO SHRINK DOWN TO ANT-SIZE!
WAIT! I. GOT HOLD OF ONE OF HIS PINCERS!
MUST APPLY LEVERAGE.. JUST RIGHT! MAYBE I'LL BE ABLE TO THROW HIM.. FOR A SECOND!
WHEN I DO, FIRE THAT ARROW, HAWKEYE.. AND FIRE IT FAST!
WHILE, IN THE MURKY WATERS ONLY A SHORT DISTANCE AWAY...
HAS THE UNHOLY HOUR COME IN WHICH HERCULES IS TO BE BESTED BY A MERE MORTAL? I GROW WEAKER WITH EACH PASSING SECOND!
FOR, THOUGH HERCULES NEED NOT BREATHE... IN THE WATERY DEPTHS, THE ADVANTAGE IS EVER NAMOR'S!
MY ARROGANT PREY DOES NOT YIELD! YET, I CAN SENSE THAT HIS STRENGTH IS BUT HALF OF WHAT IT WAS ON LAND!
THE COSMIC CUBE HAS GIVEN ME THE ULTIMATE TRIUMPH I DESIRED.. OR, HAS IT?
18

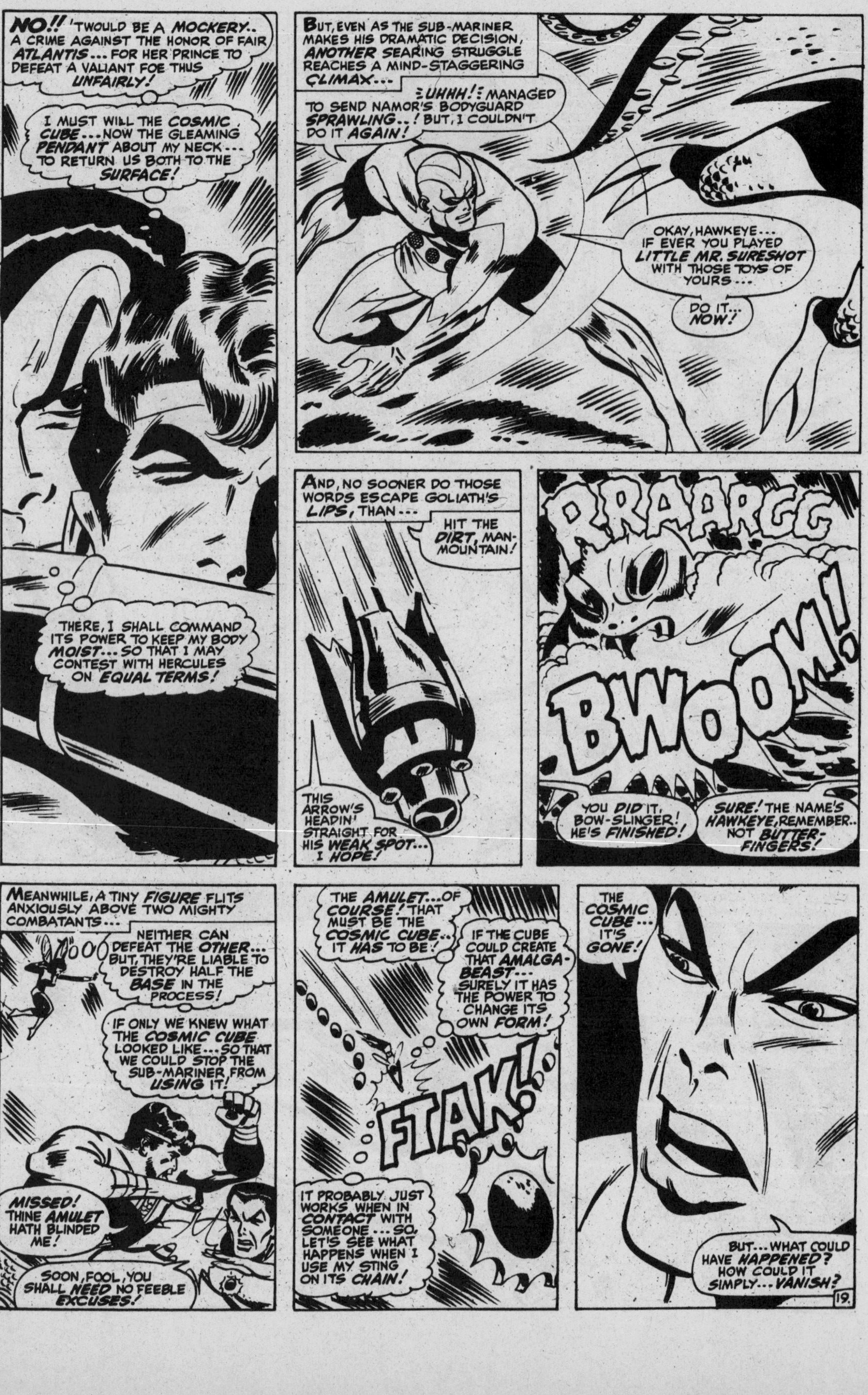

NO!! 'TWOULD BE A MOCKERY.. A CRIME AGAINST THE HONOR OF FAIR ATLANTIS... FOR HER PRINCE TO DEFEAT A VALIANT FOE THUS UNFAIRLY!
I MUST WILL THE COSMIC CUBE... NOW THE GLEAMING PENDANT ABOUT MY NECK... TO RETURN US BOTH TO THE SURFACE!
THERE, I SHALL COMMAND ITS POWER TO KEEP MY BODY MOIST... SO THAT I MAY CONTEST WITH HERCULES ON EQUAL TERMS!
BUT, EVEN AS THE SUB-MARINER MAKES HIS DRAMATIC DECISION, ANOTHER SEARING STRUGGLE REACHES A MIND-STAGGERING CLIMAX...
UHHH! MANAGED TO SEND NAMOR'S BODYGUARD SPRAWLING..! BUT, I COULDN'T DO IT AGAIN!
OKAY, HAWKEYE... IF EVER YOU PLAYED LITTLE MR. SURESHOT WITH THOSE TOYS OF YOURS...
DO IT... NOW!
AND, NO SOONER DO THOSE WORDS ESCAPE GOLIATH'S LIPS, THAN...
HIT THE DIRT, MAN-MOUNTAIN!
THIS ARROW'S HEADIN' STRAIGHT FOR HIS WEAK SPOT... I HOPE!
RRAARGG
BWOOM!
YOU DID IT, BOW-SLINGER! HE'S FINISHED!
SURE! THE NAME'S HAWKEYE, REMEMBER.. NOT BUTTER-FINGERS!
MEANWHILE, A TINY FIGURE FLITS ANXIOUSLY ABOVE TWO MIGHTY COMBATANTS...
NEITHER CAN DEFEAT THE OTHER... BUT, THEY'RE LIABLE TO DESTROY HALF THE BASE IN THE PROCESS!
IF ONLY WE KNEW WHAT THE COSMIC CUBE LOOKED LIKE... SO THAT WE COULD STOP THE SUB-MARINER FROM USING IT!
MISSED! THINE AMULET HATH BLINDED ME!
SOON, FOOL, YOU SHALL NEED NO FEEBLE EXCUSES!
THE AMULET... OF COURSE! THAT MUST BE THE COSMIC CUBE.. IT HAS TO BE!
IF THE CUBE COULD CREATE THAT AMALGA-BEAST SURELY IT HAS THE POWER TO CHANGE ITS OWN FORM!
FTAK!
IT PROBABLY JUST WORKS WHEN IN CONTACT WITH SOMEONE... SO, LET'S SEE WHAT HAPPENS WHEN I USE MY STING ON ITS CHAIN!
THE COSMIC CUBE... IT'S GONE!
BUT... WHAT COULD HAVE HAPPENED? HOW COULD IT SIMPLY... VANISH?
19.

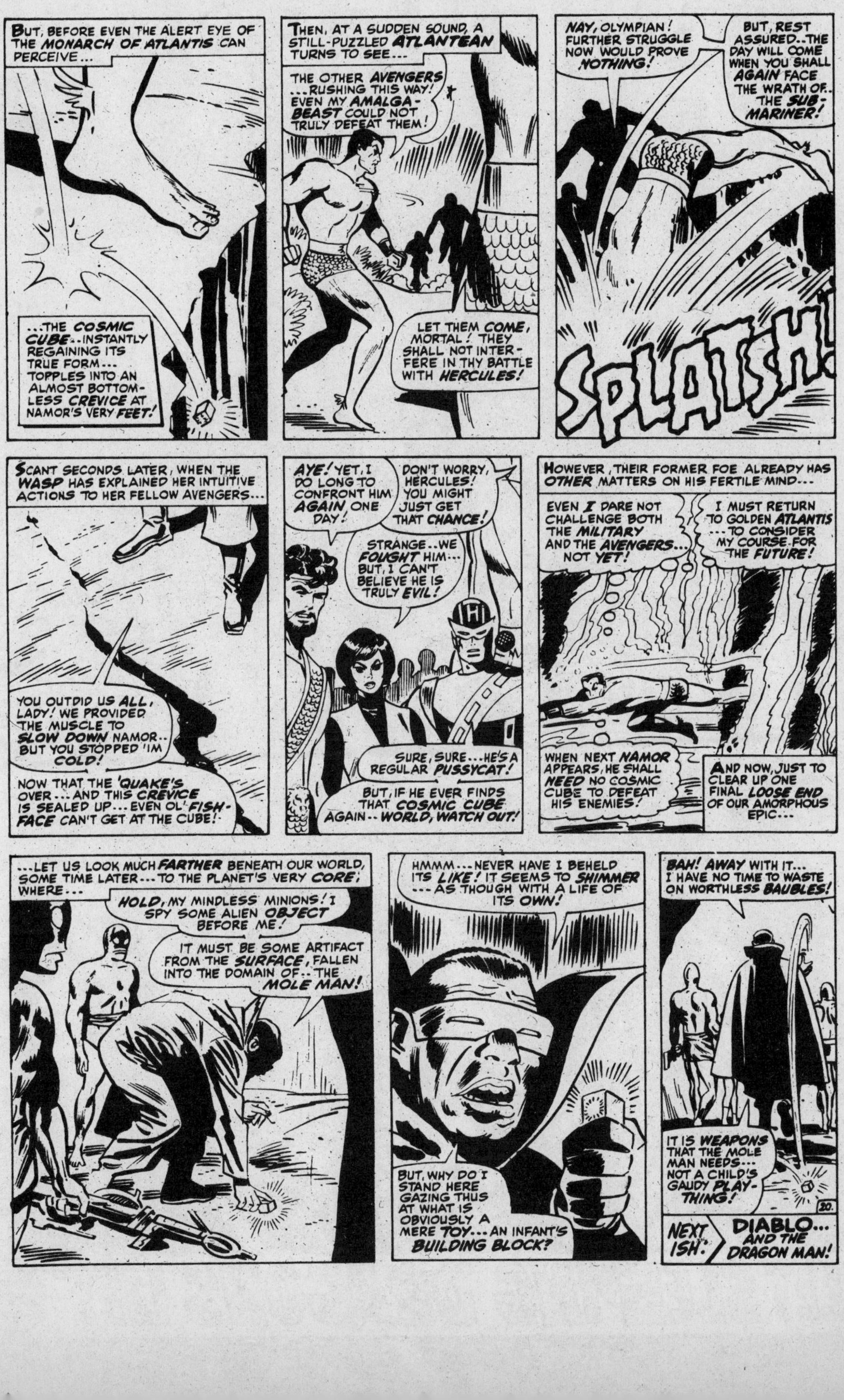

BUT, BEFORE EVEN THE ALERT EYE OF THE MONARCH OF ATLANTIS CAN PERCEIVE...
...THE COSMIC CUBE...INSTANTLY REGAINING ITS TRUE FORM...TOPPLES INTO AN ALMOST BOTTOMLESS CREVICE AT NAMOR'S VERY FEET!
THEN, AT A SUDDEN SOUND, A STILL-PUZZLED ATLANTEAN TURNS TO SEE...
THE OTHER AVENGERS...RUSHING THIS WAY! EVEN MY AMALGA-BEAST COULD NOT TRULY DEFEAT THEM!
LET THEM COME, MORTAL! THEY SHALL NOT INTERFERE IN THY BATTLE WITH HERCULES!
NAY, OLYMPIAN! FURTHER STRUGGLE NOW WOULD PROVE NOTHING!
BUT, REST ASSURED..THE DAY WILL COME WHEN YOU SHALL AGAIN FACE THE WRATH OF.. THE SUB-MARINER!
SPLATSH!
SCANT SECONDS LATER, WHEN THE WASP HAS EXPLAINED HER INTUITIVE ACTIONS TO HER FELLOW AVENGERS...
YOU OUTDID US ALL, LADY! WE PROVIDED THE MUSCLE TO SLOW DOWN NAMOR.. BUT YOU STOPPED 'IM COLD!
NOW THAT THE 'QUAKE'S OVER...AND THIS CREVICE IS SEALED UP...EVEN OL' FISH-FACE CAN'T GET AT THE CUBE!
AYE! YET, I DO LONG TO CONFRONT HIM AGAIN ONE DAY!
DON'T WORRY, HERCULES! YOU MIGHT JUST GET THAT CHANCE!
STRANGE..WE FOUGHT HIM... BUT, I CAN'T BELIEVE HE IS TRULY EVIL!
SURE, SURE...HE'S A REGULAR PUSSYCAT!
BUT, IF HE EVER FINDS THAT COSMIC CUBE AGAIN--WORLD, WATCH OUT!
HOWEVER, THEIR FORMER FOE ALREADY HAS OTHER MATTERS ON HIS FERTILE MIND...
EVEN I DARE NOT CHALLENGE BOTH THE MILITARY AND THE AVENGERS... NOT YET!
I MUST RETURN TO GOLDEN ATLANTIS ...TO CONSIDER MY COURSE FOR THE FUTURE!
WHEN NEXT NAMOR APPEARS, HE SHALL NEED NO COSMIC CUBE TO DEFEAT HIS ENEMIES!
AND NOW, JUST TO CLEAR UP ONE FINAL LOOSE END OF OUR AMORPHOUS EPIC...
...LET US LOOK MUCH FARTHER BENEATH OUR WORLD, SOME TIME LATER---TO THE PLANET'S VERY CORE, WHERE...
HOLD, MY MINDLESS MINIONS! I SPY SOME ALIEN OBJECT BEFORE ME!
IT MUST BE SOME ARTIFACT FROM THE SURFACE, FALLEN INTO THE DOMAIN OF.. THE MOLE MAN!
HMMM...NEVER HAVE I BEHELD ITS LIKE! IT SEEMS TO SHIMMER ---AS THOUGH WITH A LIFE OF ITS OWN!
BUT, WHY DO I STAND HERE GAZING THUS AT WHAT IS OBVIOUSLY A MERE TOY...AN INFANT'S BUILDING BLOCK?
BAH! AWAY WITH IT... I HAVE NO TIME TO WASTE ON WORTHLESS BAUBLES!
IT IS WEAPONS THAT THE MOLE MAN NEEDS... NOT A CHILD'S GAUDY PLAYTHING!
20.
NEXT ISH. DIABLO... AND THE DRAGON MAN!

THE AVENGERS
APPROVED BY THE COMICS CODE AUTHORITY
MARVEL COMICS GROUP
41 JUNE
FEATURING: DIABLO AND THE EVER-DELIGHTFUL DRAGON MAN!
"LET SLEEPING DRAGONS LIE!"

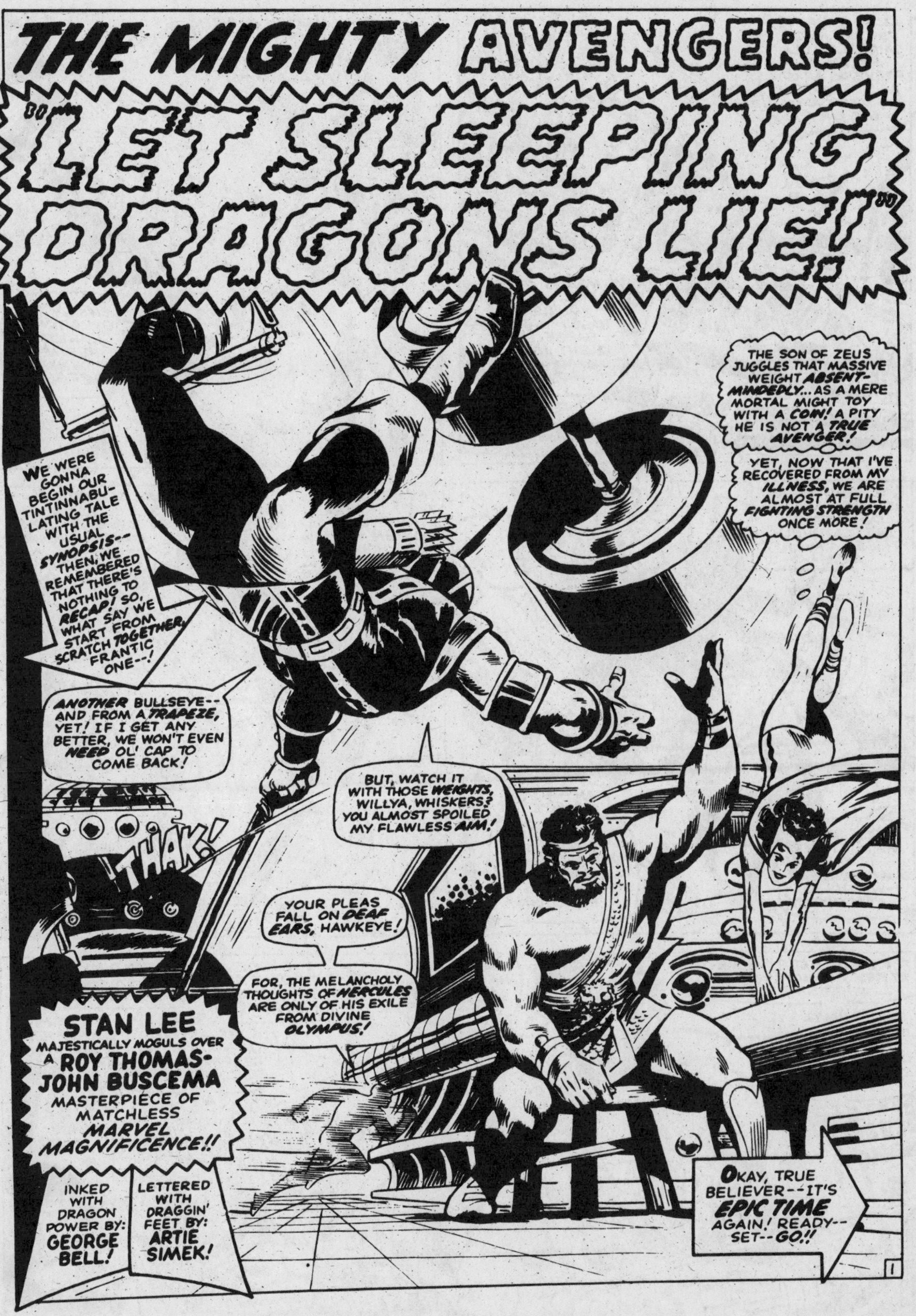
THE MIGHTY AVENGERS!
"LET SLEEPING DRAGONS LIE!"
WE WERE GONNA BEGIN OUR TINTINNABULATING TALE WITH THE USUAL SYNOPSIS-- THEN, WE REMEMBERED THAT THERE'S NOTHING TO RECAP! SO, WHAT SAY WE START FROM SCRATCH TOGETHER, FRANTIC ONE--!
THE SON OF ZEUS JUGGLES THAT MASSIVE WEIGHT ABSENT-MINDEDLY... AS A MERE MORTAL MIGHT TOY WITH A COIN! A PITY HE IS NOT A TRUE AVENGER!
YET, NOW THAT I'VE RECOVERED FROM MY ILLNESS, WE ARE ALMOST AT FULL FIGHTING STRENGTH ONCE MORE!
ANOTHER BULLSEYE-- AND FROM A TRAPEZE, YET! IF I GET ANY BETTER, WE WON'T EVEN NEED OL' CAP TO COME BACK!
BUT, WATCH IT WITH THOSE WEIGHTS, WILLYA, WHISKERS? YOU ALMOST SPOILED MY FLAWLESS AIM!
THAK!
YOUR PLEAS FALL ON DEAF EARS, HAWKEYE!
FOR, THE MELANCHOLY THOUGHTS OF HERCULES ARE ONLY OF HIS EXILE FROM DIVINE OLYMPUS!
STAN LEE MAJESTICALLY MOGULS OVER A ROY THOMAS-JOHN BUSCEMA MASTERPIECE OF MATCHLESS MARVEL MAGNIFICENCE!!
INKED WITH DRAGON POWER BY: GEORGE BELL!
LETTERED WITH DRAGGIN' FEET BY: ARTIE SIMEK!
OKAY, TRUE BELIEVER--IT'S EPIC TIME AGAIN! READY-- SET--GO!!
1

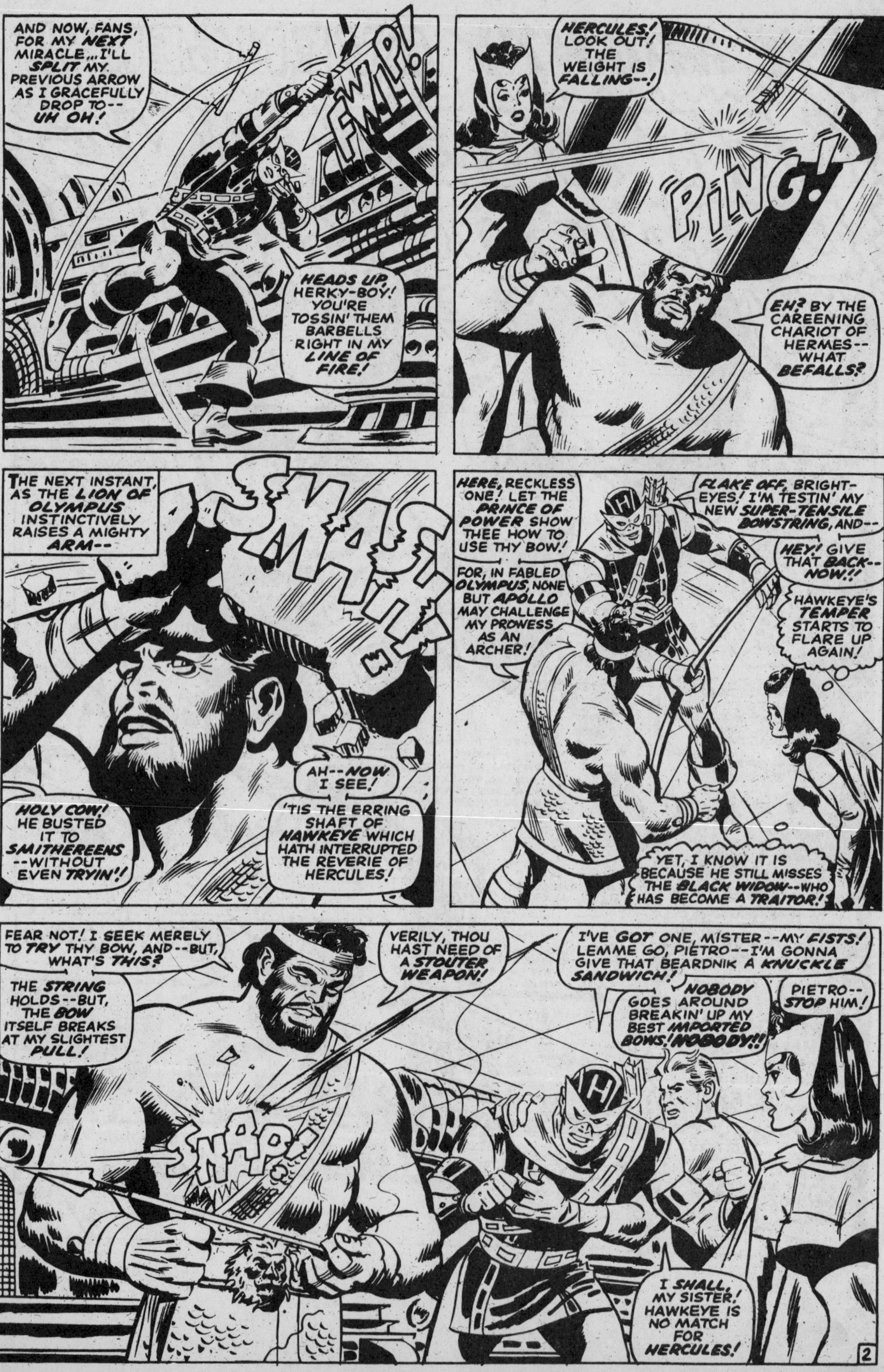
AND NOW, FANS, FOR MY NEXT MIRACLE... I'LL SPLIT MY PREVIOUS ARROW AS I GRACEFULLY DROP TO-- UH OH!
FWIP!
HEADS UP, HERKY-BOY! YOU'RE TOSSIN' THEM BARBELLS RIGHT IN MY LINE OF FIRE!
HERCULES! LOOK OUT! THE WEIGHT IS FALLING--!
PING!
EH? BY THE CAREENING CHARIOT OF HERMES-- WHAT BEFALLS?
THE NEXT INSTANT, AS THE LION OF OLYMPUS INSTINCTIVELY RAISES A MIGHTY ARM--
SMASH!
AH--NOW I SEE!
'TIS THE ERRING SHAFT OF HAWKEYE WHICH HATH INTERRUPTED THE REVERIE OF HERCULES!
HOLY COW! HE BUSTED IT TO SMITHEREENS --WITHOUT EVEN TRYIN'!
HERE, RECKLESS ONE! LET THE PRINCE OF POWER SHOW THEE HOW TO USE THY BOW!
FOR, IN FABLED OLYMPUS, NONE BUT APOLLO MAY CHALLENGE MY PROWESS AS AN ARCHER!
FLAKE OFF, BRIGHT-EYES! I'M TESTIN' MY NEW SUPER-TENSILE BOWSTRING, AND--
HEY! GIVE THAT BACK--NOW!!
HAWKEYE'S TEMPER STARTS TO FLARE UP AGAIN!
YET, I KNOW IT IS BECAUSE HE STILL MISSES THE BLACK WIDOW--WHO HAS BECOME A TRAITOR!
FEAR NOT! I SEEK MERELY TO TRY THY BOW, AND--BUT, WHAT'S THIS?
THE STRING HOLDS--BUT, THE BOW ITSELF BREAKS AT MY SLIGHTEST PULL!
SNAP!
VERILY, THOU HAST NEED OF A STOUTER WEAPON!
I'VE GOT ONE, MISTER--MY FISTS! LEMME GO, PIETRO--I'M GONNA GIVE THAT BEARDNIK A KNUCKLE SANDWICH!
NOBODY GOES AROUND BREAKIN' UP MY BEST IMPORTED BOWS! NOBODY!!
PIETRO-- STOP HIM!
I SHALL, MY SISTER! HAWKEYE IS NO MATCH FOR HERCULES!

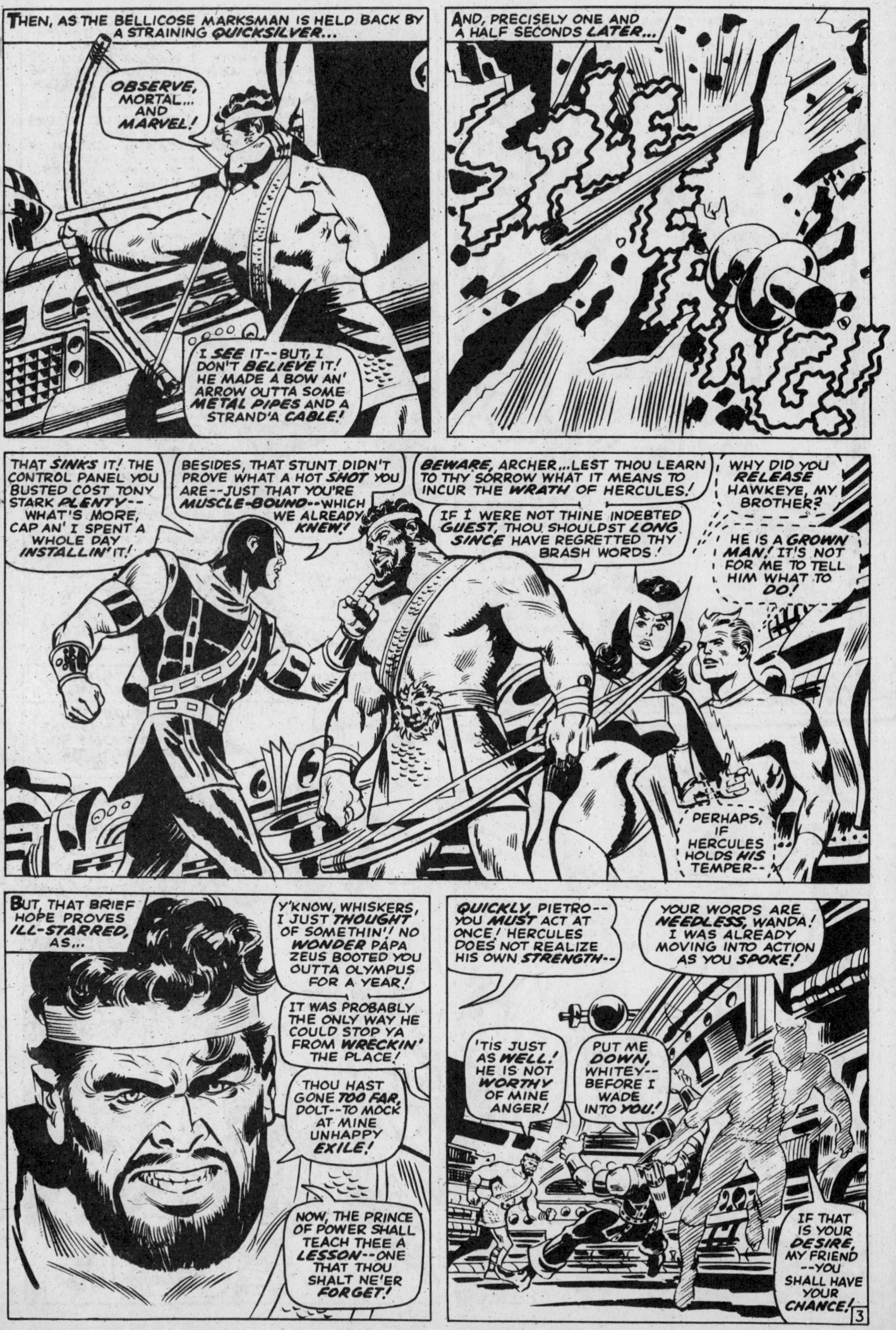

THEN, AS THE BELLICOSE MARKSMAN IS HELD BACK BY A STRAINING QUICKSILVER...
OBSERVE, MORTAL... AND MARVEL!
I SEE IT--BUT, I DON'T BELIEVE IT! HE MADE A BOW AN' ARROW OUTTA SOME METAL PIPES AND A STRAND'A CABLE!
AND, PRECISELY ONE AND A HALF SECONDS LATER...
THAT SINKS IT! THE CONTROL PANEL YOU BUSTED COST TONY STARK PLENTY-- WHAT'S MORE, CAP AN' I SPENT A WHOLE DAY INSTALLIN' IT!
BESIDES, THAT STUNT DIDN'T PROVE WHAT A HOT SHOT YOU ARE--JUST THAT YOU'RE MUSCLE-BOUND--WHICH WE ALREADY KNEW!
BEWARE, ARCHER...LEST THOU LEARN TO THY SORROW WHAT IT MEANS TO INCUR THE WRATH OF HERCULES!
IF I WERE NOT THINE INDEBTED GUEST, THOU SHOULDST LONG SINCE HAVE REGRETTED THY BRASH WORDS!
WHY DID YOU RELEASE HAWKEYE, MY BROTHER?
HE IS A GROWN MAN! IT'S NOT FOR ME TO TELL HIM WHAT TO DO!
PERHAPS, IF HERCULES HOLDS HIS TEMPER--
BUT, THAT BRIEF HOPE PROVES ILL-STARRED, AS...
Y'KNOW, WHISKERS, I JUST THOUGHT OF SOMETHIN'! NO WONDER PAPA ZEUS BOOTED YOU OUTTA OLYMPUS FOR A YEAR!
IT WAS PROBABLY THE ONLY WAY HE COULD STOP YA FROM WRECKIN' THE PLACE!
THOU HAST GONE TOO FAR, DOLT--TO MOCK AT MINE UNHAPPY EXILE!
NOW, THE PRINCE OF POWER SHALL TEACH THEE A LESSON--ONE THAT THOU SHALT NE'ER FORGET!
QUICKLY, PIETRO--YOU MUST ACT AT ONCE! HERCULES DOES NOT REALIZE HIS OWN STRENGTH--
YOUR WORDS ARE NEEDLESS, WANDA! I WAS ALREADY MOVING INTO ACTION AS YOU SPOKE!
'TIS JUST AS WELL! HE IS NOT WORTHY OF MINE ANGER!
PUT ME DOWN, WHITEY--BEFORE I WADE INTO YOU!
IF THAT IS YOUR DESIRE, MY FRIEND --YOU SHALL HAVE YOUR CHANCE!
3

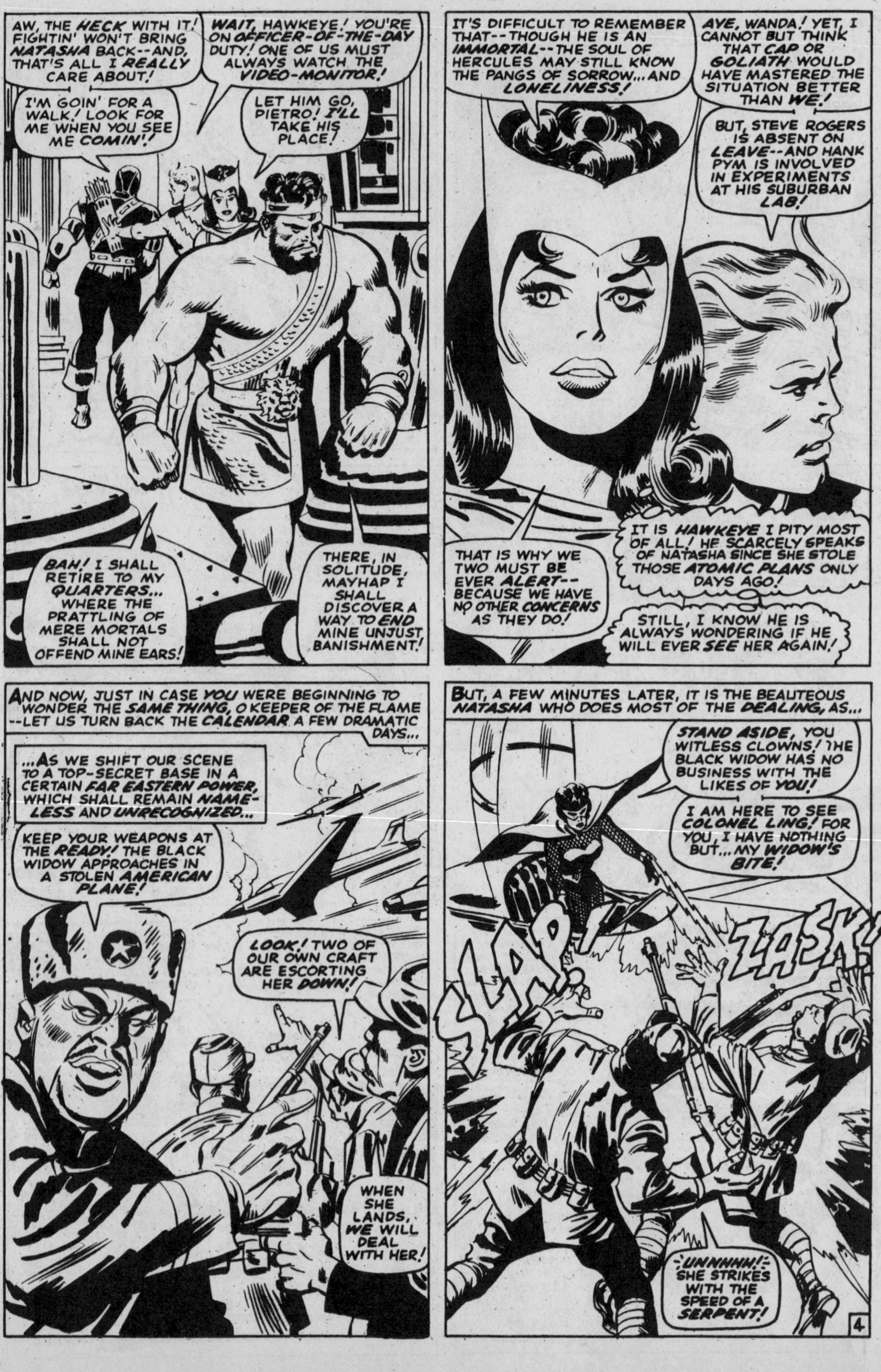

AW, THE HECK WITH IT! FIGHTIN' WON'T BRING NATASHA BACK--AND, THAT'S ALL I REALLY CARE ABOUT!
I'M GOIN' FOR A WALK! LOOK FOR ME WHEN YOU SEE ME COMIN'!
WAIT, HAWKEYE! YOU'RE ON OFFICER-OF-THE-DAY DUTY! ONE OF US MUST ALWAYS WATCH THE VIDEO-MONITOR!
LET HIM GO, PIETRO! I'LL TAKE HIS PLACE!
BAH! I SHALL RETIRE TO MY QUARTERS... WHERE THE PRATTLING OF MERE MORTALS SHALL NOT OFFEND MINE EARS!
THERE, IN SOLITUDE, MAYHAP I SHALL DISCOVER A WAY TO END MINE UNJUST BANISHMENT!
IT'S DIFFICULT TO REMEMBER THAT--THOUGH HE IS AN IMMORTAL--THE SOUL OF HERCULES MAY STILL KNOW THE PANGS OF SORROW... AND LONELINESS!
AYE, WANDA! YET, I CANNOT BUT THINK THAT CAP OR GOLIATH WOULD HAVE MASTERED THE SITUATION BETTER THAN WE!
BUT, STEVE ROGERS IS ABSENT ON LEAVE--AND HANK PYM IS INVOLVED IN EXPERIMENTS AT HIS SUBURBAN LAB!
THAT IS WHY WE TWO MUST BE EVER ALERT--BECAUSE WE HAVE NO OTHER CONCERNS AS THEY DO!
IT IS HAWKEYE I PITY MOST OF ALL! HE SCARCELY SPEAKS OF NATASHA SINCE SHE STOLE THOSE ATOMIC PLANS ONLY DAYS AGO!
STILL, I KNOW HE IS ALWAYS WONDERING IF HE WILL EVER SEE HER AGAIN!
AND NOW, JUST IN CASE YOU WERE BEGINNING TO WONDER THE SAME THING, O KEEPER OF THE FLAME --LET US TURN BACK THE CALENDAR A FEW DRAMATIC DAYS...
...AS WE SHIFT OUR SCENE TO A TOP-SECRET BASE IN A CERTAIN FAR EASTERN POWER, WHICH SHALL REMAIN NAME-LESS AND UNRECOGNIZED...
KEEP YOUR WEAPONS AT THE READY! THE BLACK WIDOW APPROACHES IN A STOLEN AMERICAN PLANE!
LOOK! TWO OF OUR OWN CRAFT ARE ESCORTING HER DOWN!
WHEN SHE LANDS, WE WILL DEAL WITH HER!
BUT, A FEW MINUTES LATER, IT IS THE BEAUTEOUS NATASHA WHO DOES MOST OF THE DEALING, AS...
STAND ASIDE, YOU WITLESS CLOWNS! THE BLACK WIDOW HAS NO BUSINESS WITH THE LIKES OF YOU!
I AM HERE TO SEE COLONEL LING! FOR YOU, I HAVE NOTHING BUT... MY WIDOW'S BITE!
SLAP!
ZASK!
UNNHHH! SHE STRIKES WITH THE SPEED OF A SERPENT!
4

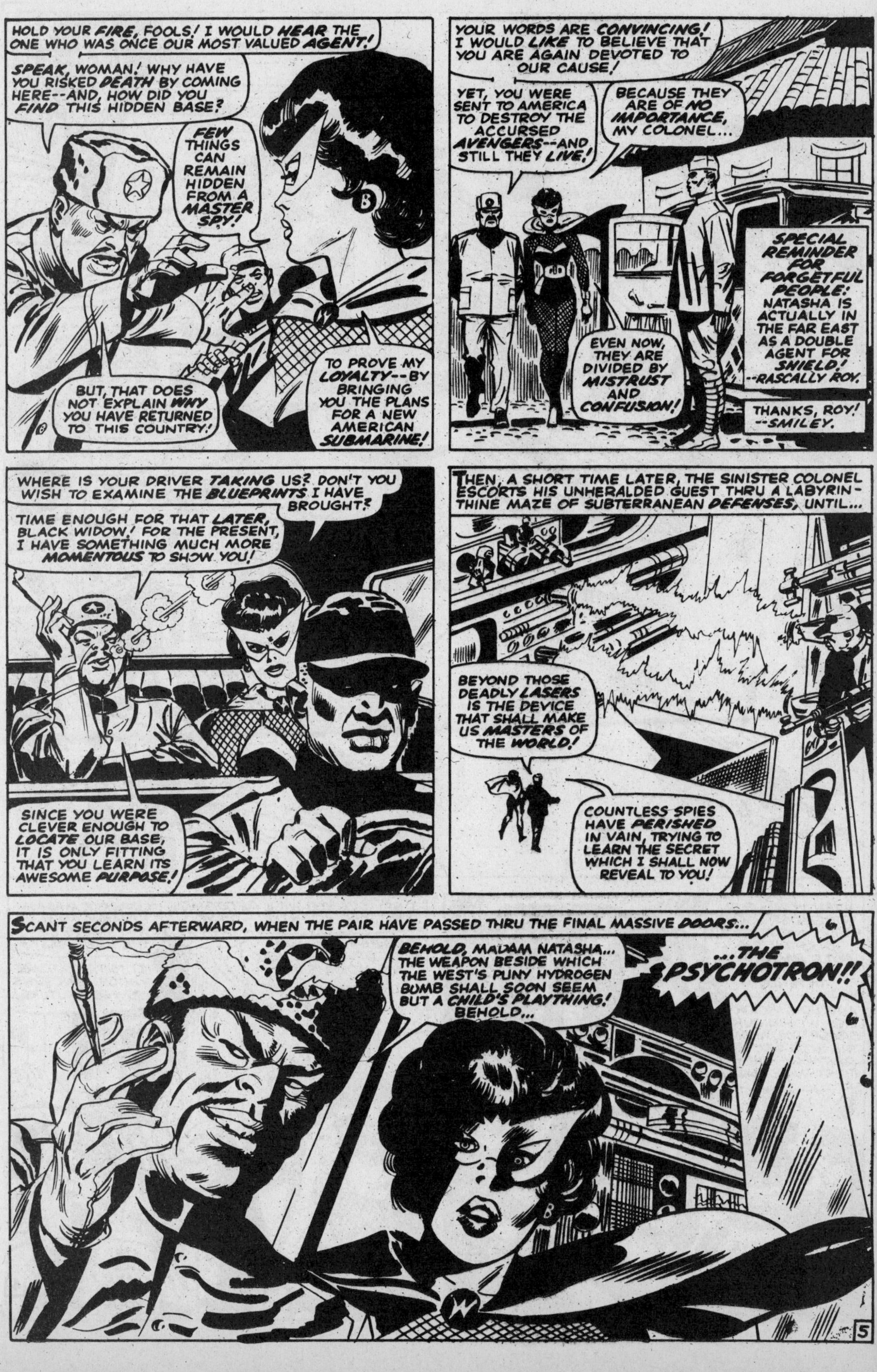
HOLD YOUR FIRE, FOOLS! I WOULD HEAR THE ONE WHO WAS ONCE OUR MOST VALUED AGENT!
SPEAK, WOMAN! WHY HAVE YOU RISKED DEATH BY COMING HERE--AND, HOW DID YOU FIND THIS HIDDEN BASE?
FEW THINGS CAN REMAIN HIDDEN FROM A MASTER SPY!
BUT, THAT DOES NOT EXPLAIN WHY YOU HAVE RETURNED TO THIS COUNTRY!
TO PROVE MY LOYALTY--BY BRINGING YOU THE PLANS FOR A NEW AMERICAN SUBMARINE!
YOUR WORDS ARE CONVINCING! I WOULD LIKE TO BELIEVE THAT YOU ARE AGAIN DEVOTED TO OUR CAUSE!
YET, YOU WERE SENT TO AMERICA TO DESTROY THE ACCURSED AVENGERS--AND STILL THEY LIVE!
BECAUSE THEY ARE OF NO IMPORTANCE, MY COLONEL...
EVEN NOW, THEY ARE DIVIDED BY MISTRUST AND CONFUSION!
SPECIAL REMINDER FOR FORGETFUL PEOPLE: NATASHA IS ACTUALLY IN THE FAR EAST AS A DOUBLE AGENT FOR SHIELD! --RASCALLY ROY.
THANKS, ROY! --SMILEY.
WHERE IS YOUR DRIVER TAKING US? DON'T YOU WISH TO EXAMINE THE BLUEPRINTS I HAVE BROUGHT?
TIME ENOUGH FOR THAT LATER, BLACK WIDOW! FOR THE PRESENT, I HAVE SOMETHING MUCH MORE MOMENTOUS TO SHOW YOU!
SINCE YOU WERE CLEVER ENOUGH TO LOCATE OUR BASE, IT IS ONLY FITTING THAT YOU LEARN ITS AWESOME PURPOSE!
THEN, A SHORT TIME LATER, THE SINISTER COLONEL ESCORTS HIS UNHERALDED GUEST THRU A LABYRINTHINE MAZE OF SUBTERRANEAN DEFENSES, UNTIL...
BEYOND THOSE DEADLY LASERS IS THE DEVICE THAT SHALL MAKE US MASTERS OF THE WORLD!
COUNTLESS SPIES HAVE PERISHED IN VAIN, TRYING TO LEARN THE SECRET WHICH I SHALL NOW REVEAL TO YOU!
SCANT SECONDS AFTERWARD, WHEN THE PAIR HAVE PASSED THRU THE FINAL MASSIVE DOORS...
BEHOLD, MADAM NATASHA... THE WEAPON BESIDE WHICH THE WEST'S PUNY HYDROGEN BOMB SHALL SOON SEEM BUT A CHILD'S PLAYTHING! BEHOLD...
...THE PSYCHOTRON!!
5

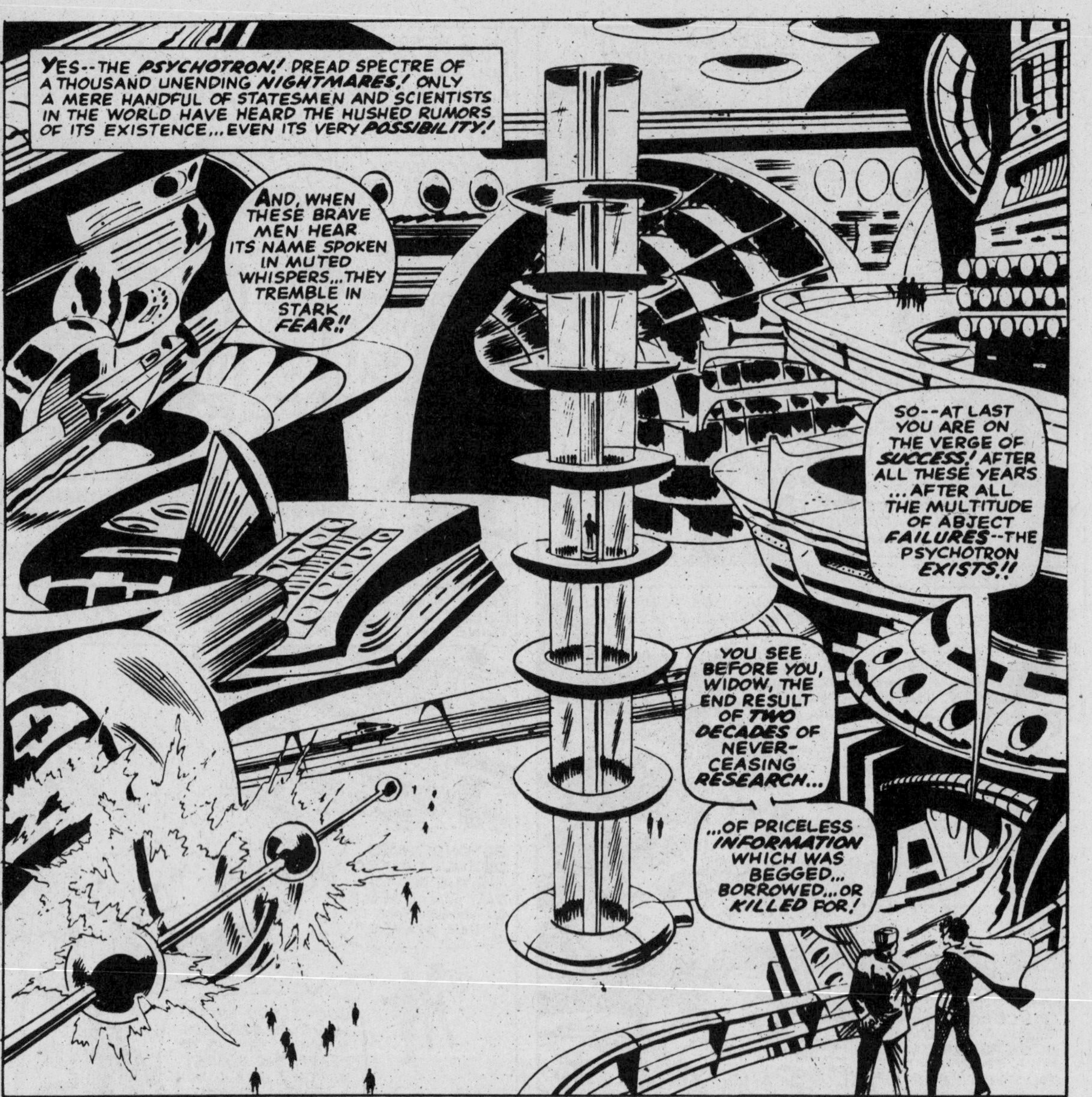
YES--THE PSYCHOTRON! DREAD SPECTRE OF A THOUSAND UNENDING NIGHTMARES! ONLY A MERE HANDFUL OF STATESMEN AND SCIENTISTS IN THE WORLD HAVE HEARD THE HUSHED RUMORS OF ITS EXISTENCE... EVEN ITS VERY POSSIBILITY!
AND, WHEN THESE BRAVE MEN HEAR ITS NAME SPOKEN IN MUTED WHISPERS... THEY TREMBLE IN STARK FEAR!!
SO--AT LAST YOU ARE ON THE VERGE OF SUCCESS! AFTER ALL THESE YEARS ...AFTER ALL THE MULTITUDE OF ABJECT FAILURES--THE PSYCHOTRON EXISTS!!
YOU SEE BEFORE YOU, WIDOW, THE END RESULT OF TWO DECADES OF NEVER-CEASING RESEARCH...
...OF PRICELESS INFORMATION WHICH WAS BEGGED... BORROWED... OR KILLED FOR!

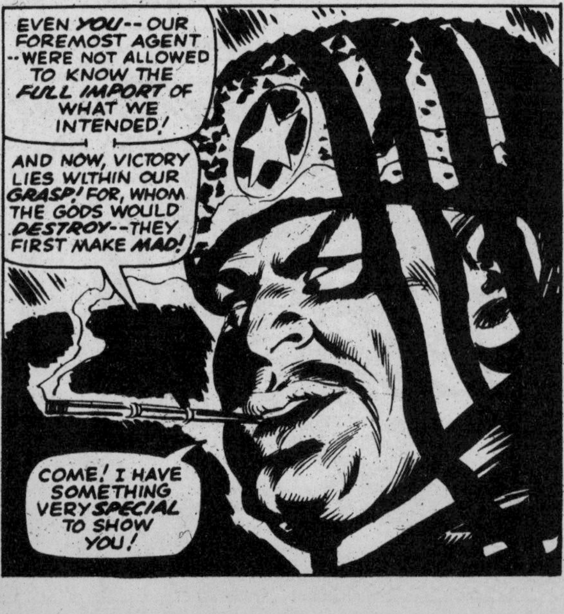
EVEN YOU--OUR FOREMOST AGENT --WERE NOT ALLOWED TO KNOW THE FULL IMPORT OF WHAT WE INTENDED!
AND NOW, VICTORY LIES WITHIN OUR GRASP! FOR, WHOM THE GODS WOULD DESTROY--THEY FIRST MAKE MAD!
COME! I HAVE SOMETHING VERY SPECIAL TO SHOW YOU!

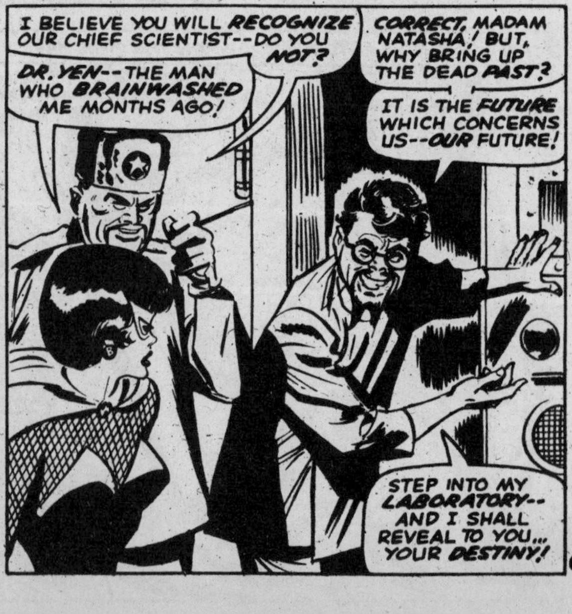
I BELIEVE YOU WILL RECOGNIZE OUR CHIEF SCIENTIST--DO YOU NOT?
DR. YEN--THE MAN WHO BRAINWASHED ME MONTHS AGO!
CORRECT, MADAM NATASHA! BUT, WHY BRING UP THE DEAD PAST?
IT IS THE FUTURE WHICH CONCERNS US--OUR FUTURE!
STEP INTO MY LABORATORY-- AND I SHALL REVEAL TO YOU... YOUR DESTINY!

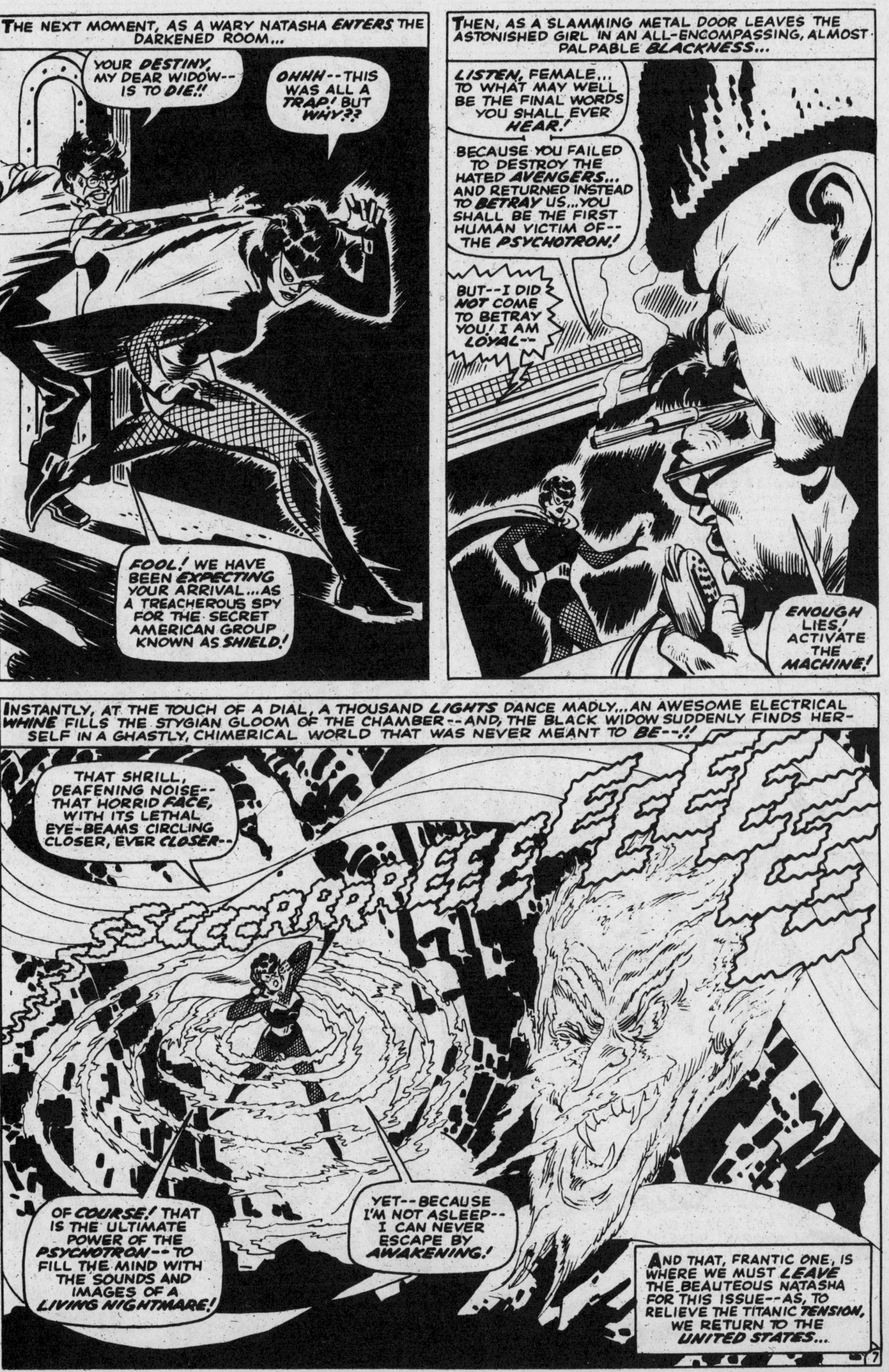

THE NEXT MOMENT, AS A WARY NATASHA ENTERS THE DARKENED ROOM...
YOUR DESTINY, MY DEAR WIDOW-- IS TO DIE!!
OHHH--THIS WAS ALL A TRAP! BUT WHY??
FOOL! WE HAVE BEEN EXPECTING YOUR ARRIVAL...AS A TREACHEROUS SPY FOR THE SECRET AMERICAN GROUP KNOWN AS SHIELD!
THEN, AS A SLAMMING METAL DOOR LEAVES THE ASTONISHED GIRL IN AN ALL-ENCOMPASSING, ALMOST PALPABLE BLACKNESS...
LISTEN, FEMALE... TO WHAT MAY WELL BE THE FINAL WORDS YOU SHALL EVER HEAR!
BECAUSE YOU FAILED TO DESTROY THE HATED AVENGERS... AND RETURNED INSTEAD TO BETRAY US...YOU SHALL BE THE FIRST HUMAN VICTIM OF-- THE PSYCHOTRON!
BUT--I DID NOT COME TO BETRAY YOU! I AM LOYAL--
ENOUGH LIES! ACTIVATE THE MACHINE!
INSTANTLY, AT THE TOUCH OF A DIAL, A THOUSAND LIGHTS DANCE MADLY...AN AWESOME ELECTRICAL WHINE FILLS THE STYGIAN GLOOM OF THE CHAMBER--AND, THE BLACK WIDOW SUDDENLY FINDS HERSELF IN A GHASTLY, CHIMERICAL WORLD THAT WAS NEVER MEANT TO BE--!!
THAT SHRILL, DEAFENING NOISE-- THAT HORRID FACE, WITH ITS LETHAL EYE-BEAMS CIRCLING CLOSER, EVER CLOSER--
SCCRRREEEEEE
OF COURSE! THAT IS THE ULTIMATE POWER OF THE PSYCHOTRON--TO FILL THE MIND WITH THE SOUNDS AND IMAGES OF A LIVING NIGHTMARE!
YET--BECAUSE I'M NOT ASLEEP-- I CAN NEVER ESCAPE BY AWAKENING!
AND THAT, FRANTIC ONE, IS WHERE WE MUST LEAVE THE BEAUTEOUS NATASHA FOR THIS ISSUE--AS, TO RELIEVE THE TITANIC TENSION, WE RETURN TO THE UNITED STATES...
7

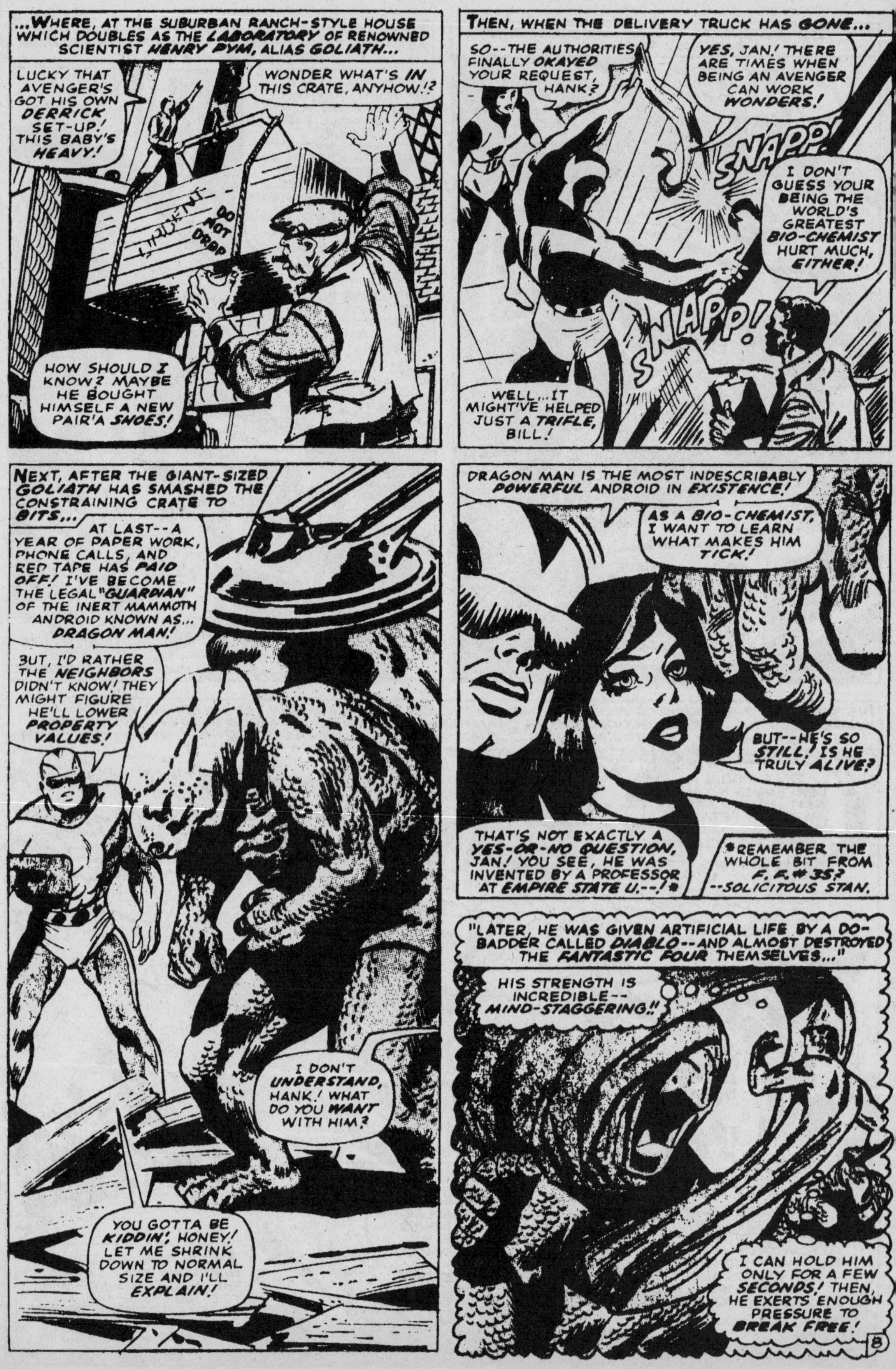
...WHERE, AT THE SUBURBAN RANCH-STYLE HOUSE WHICH DOUBLES AS THE LABORATORY OF RENOWNED SCIENTIST HENRY PYM, ALIAS GOLIATH...
LUCKY THAT AVENGER'S GOT HIS OWN DERRICK SET-UP! THIS BABY'S HEAVY!
WONDER WHAT'S IN THIS CRATE, ANYHOW!?
URGENT
DO NOT DROP
HOW SHOULD I KNOW? MAYBE HE BOUGHT HIMSELF A NEW PAIR'A SHOES!
THEN, WHEN THE DELIVERY TRUCK HAS GONE...
SO--THE AUTHORITIES FINALLY OKAYED YOUR REQUEST, HANK?
YES, JAN! THERE ARE TIMES WHEN BEING AN AVENGER CAN WORK WONDERS!
SNAPP!
I DON'T GUESS YOUR BEING THE WORLD'S GREATEST BIO-CHEMIST HURT MUCH, EITHER!
SNAPP!
WELL...IT MIGHT'VE HELPED JUST A TRIFLE, BILL!
NEXT, AFTER THE GIANT-SIZED GOLIATH HAS SMASHED THE CONSTRAINING CRATE TO BITS...
AT LAST--A YEAR OF PAPER WORK, PHONE CALLS, AND RED TAPE HAS PAID OFF! I'VE BECOME THE LEGAL "GUARDIAN" OF THE INERT MAMMOTH ANDROID KNOWN AS... DRAGON MAN!
BUT, I'D RATHER THE NEIGHBORS DIDN'T KNOW! THEY MIGHT FIGURE HE'LL LOWER PROPERTY VALUES!
I DON'T UNDERSTAND, HANK! WHAT DO YOU WANT WITH HIM?
YOU GOTTA BE KIDDIN', HONEY! LET ME SHRINK DOWN TO NORMAL SIZE AND I'LL EXPLAIN!
DRAGON MAN IS THE MOST INDESCRIBABLY POWERFUL ANDROID IN EXISTENCE!
AS A BIO-CHEMIST, I WANT TO LEARN WHAT MAKES HIM TICK!
BUT--HE'S SO STILL! IS HE TRULY ALIVE?
THAT'S NOT EXACTLY A YES-OR-NO QUESTION, JAN! YOU SEE, HE WAS INVENTED BY A PROFESSOR AT EMPIRE STATE U.--!*
*REMEMBER THE WHOLE BIT FROM F.F. #35? --SOLICITOUS STAN.
"LATER, HE WAS GIVEN ARTIFICIAL LIFE BY A DO-BADDER CALLED DIABLO--AND ALMOST DESTROYED THE FANTASTIC FOUR THEMSELVES..."
HIS STRENGTH IS INCREDIBLE--MIND-STAGGERING!!
I CAN HOLD HIM ONLY FOR A FEW SECONDS! THEN, HE EXERTS ENOUGH PRESSURE TO BREAK FREE!
8

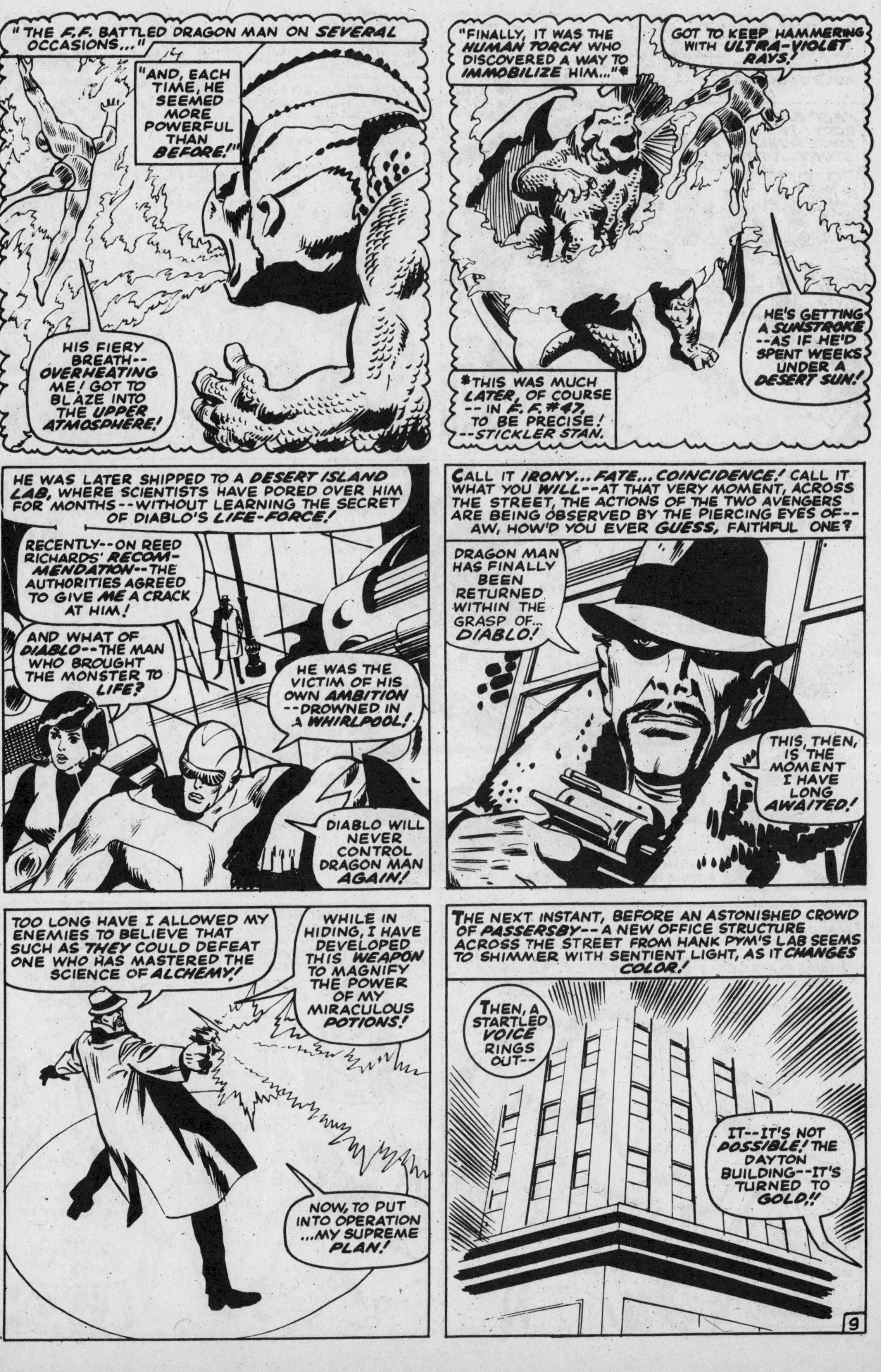
"THE F.F. BATTLED DRAGON MAN ON SEVERAL OCCASIONS..."
"AND, EACH TIME, HE SEEMED MORE POWERFUL THAN BEFORE!"
HIS FIERY BREATH--OVERHEATING ME! GOT TO BLAZE INTO THE UPPER ATMOSPHERE!
"FINALLY, IT WAS THE HUMAN TORCH WHO DISCOVERED A WAY TO IMMOBILIZE HIM..."*
GOT TO KEEP HAMMERING WITH ULTRA-VIOLET RAYS!
HE'S GETTING A SUNSTROKE --AS IF HE'D SPENT WEEKS UNDER A DESERT SUN!
*THIS WAS MUCH LATER, OF COURSE -- IN F.F. #47, TO BE PRECISE! --STICKLER STAN.
HE WAS LATER SHIPPED TO A DESERT ISLAND LAB, WHERE SCIENTISTS HAVE PORED OVER HIM FOR MONTHS--WITHOUT LEARNING THE SECRET OF DIABLO'S LIFE-FORCE!
RECENTLY--ON REED RICHARDS' RECOMMENDATION--THE AUTHORITIES AGREED TO GIVE ME A CRACK AT HIM!
AND WHAT OF DIABLO--THE MAN WHO BROUGHT THE MONSTER TO LIFE?
HE WAS THE VICTIM OF HIS OWN AMBITION --DROWNED IN A WHIRLPOOL!
DIABLO WILL NEVER CONTROL DRAGON MAN AGAIN!
CALL IT IRONY... FATE... COINCIDENCE! CALL IT WHAT YOU WILL--AT THAT VERY MOMENT, ACROSS THE STREET, THE ACTIONS OF THE TWO AVENGERS ARE BEING OBSERVED BY THE PIERCING EYES OF-- AW, HOW'D YOU EVER GUESS, FAITHFUL ONE?
DRAGON MAN HAS FINALLY BEEN RETURNED WITHIN THE GRASP OF... DIABLO!
THIS, THEN, IS THE MOMENT I HAVE LONG AWAITED!
TOO LONG HAVE I ALLOWED MY ENEMIES TO BELIEVE THAT SUCH AS THEY COULD DEFEAT ONE WHO HAS MASTERED THE SCIENCE OF ALCHEMY!
WHILE IN HIDING, I HAVE DEVELOPED THIS WEAPON TO MAGNIFY THE POWER OF MY MIRACULOUS POTIONS!
NOW, TO PUT INTO OPERATION ...MY SUPREME PLAN!
THE NEXT INSTANT, BEFORE AN ASTONISHED CROWD OF PASSERSBY--A NEW OFFICE STRUCTURE ACROSS THE STREET FROM HANK PYM'S LAB SEEMS TO SHIMMER WITH SENTIENT LIGHT, AS IT CHANGES COLOR!
THEN, A STARTLED VOICE RINGS OUT--
IT--IT'S NOT POSSIBLE! THE DAYTON BUILDING--IT'S TURNED TO GOLD!!
9

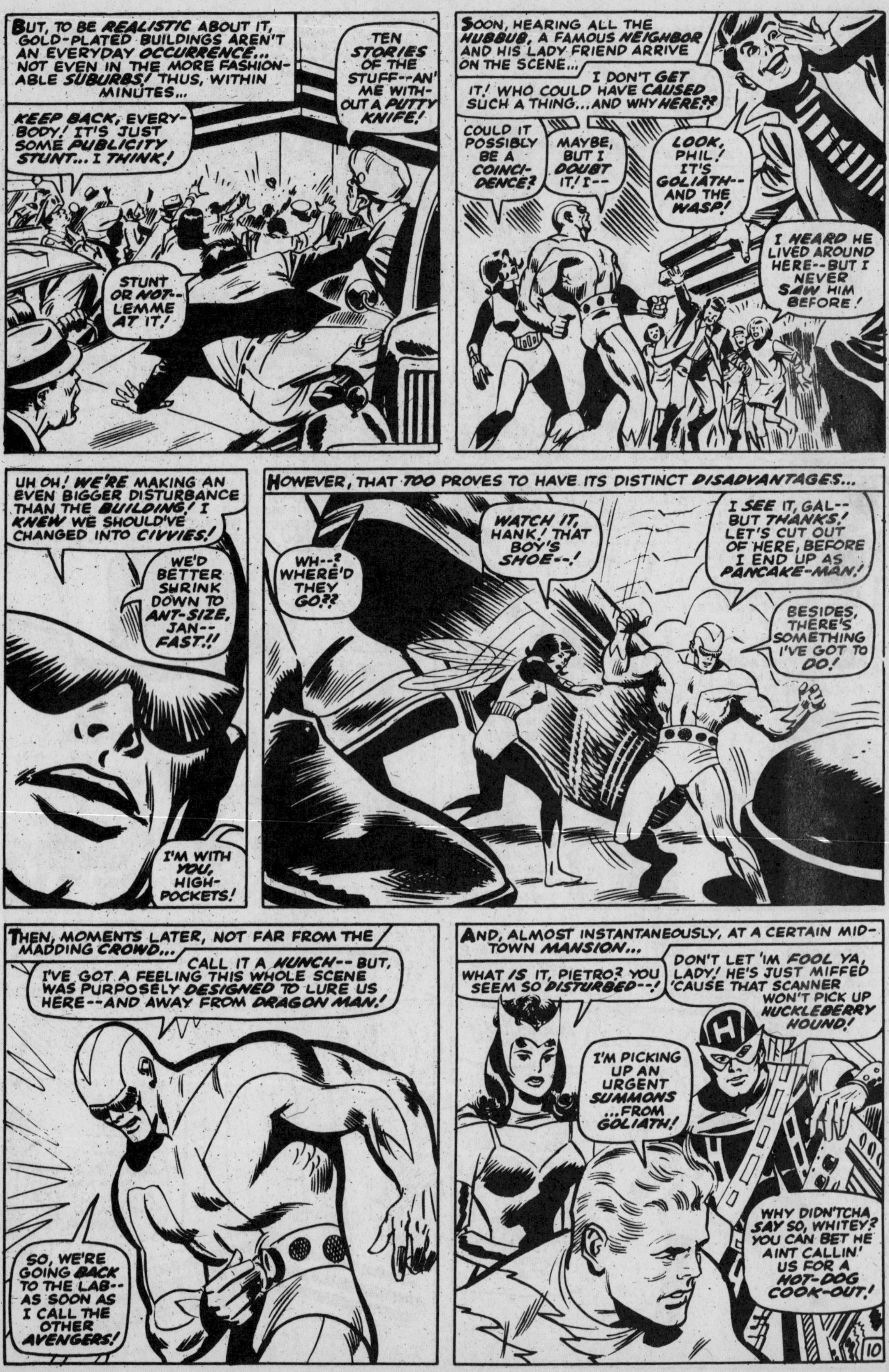

BUT, TO BE REALISTIC ABOUT IT, GOLD-PLATED BUILDINGS AREN'T AN EVERYDAY OCCURRENCE... NOT EVEN IN THE MORE FASHIONABLE SUBURBS! THUS, WITHIN MINUTES...
TEN STORIES OF THE STUFF--AN' ME WITHOUT A PUTTY KNIFE!
KEEP BACK, EVERYBODY! IT'S JUST SOME PUBLICITY STUNT... I THINK!
STUNT OR NOT--LEMME AT IT!
SOON, HEARING ALL THE HUBBUB, A FAMOUS NEIGHBOR AND HIS LADY FRIEND ARRIVE ON THE SCENE...
I DON'T GET IT! WHO COULD HAVE CAUSED SUCH A THING... AND WHY HERE??
COULD IT POSSIBLY BE A COINCIDENCE?
MAYBE, BUT I DOUBT IT! I--
LOOK, PHIL! IT'S GOLIATH--AND THE WASP!
I HEARD HE LIVED AROUND HERE--BUT I NEVER SAW HIM BEFORE!
UH OH! WE'RE MAKING AN EVEN BIGGER DISTURBANCE THAN THE BUILDING! I KNEW WE SHOULD'VE CHANGED INTO CIVVIES!
WE'D BETTER SHRINK DOWN TO ANT-SIZE, JAN--FAST!!
I'M WITH YOU, HIGH-POCKETS!
HOWEVER, THAT TOO PROVES TO HAVE ITS DISTINCT DISADVANTAGES...
WH--? WHERE'D THEY GO??
WATCH IT, HANK! THAT BOY'S SHOE--!
I SEE IT, GAL--BUT THANKS! LET'S CUT OUT OF HERE, BEFORE I END UP AS PANCAKE-MAN!
BESIDES, THERE'S SOMETHING I'VE GOT TO DO!
THEN, MOMENTS LATER, NOT FAR FROM THE MADDING CROWD...
CALL IT A HUNCH--BUT, I'VE GOT A FEELING THIS WHOLE SCENE WAS PURPOSELY DESIGNED TO LURE US HERE--AND AWAY FROM DRAGON MAN!
SO, WE'RE GOING BACK TO THE LAB--AS SOON AS I CALL THE OTHER AVENGERS!
AND, ALMOST INSTANTANEOUSLY, AT A CERTAIN MID-TOWN MANSION...
WHAT IS IT, PIETRO? YOU SEEM SO DISTURBED--!
DON'T LET 'IM FOOL YA, LADY! HE'S JUST MIFFED 'CAUSE THAT SCANNER WON'T PICK UP HUCKLEBERRY HOUND!
I'M PICKING UP AN URGENT SUMMONS ...FROM GOLIATH!
WHY DIDN'TCHA SAY SO, WHITEY? YOU CAN BET HE AINT CALLIN' US FOR A HOT-DOG COOK-OUT!
10

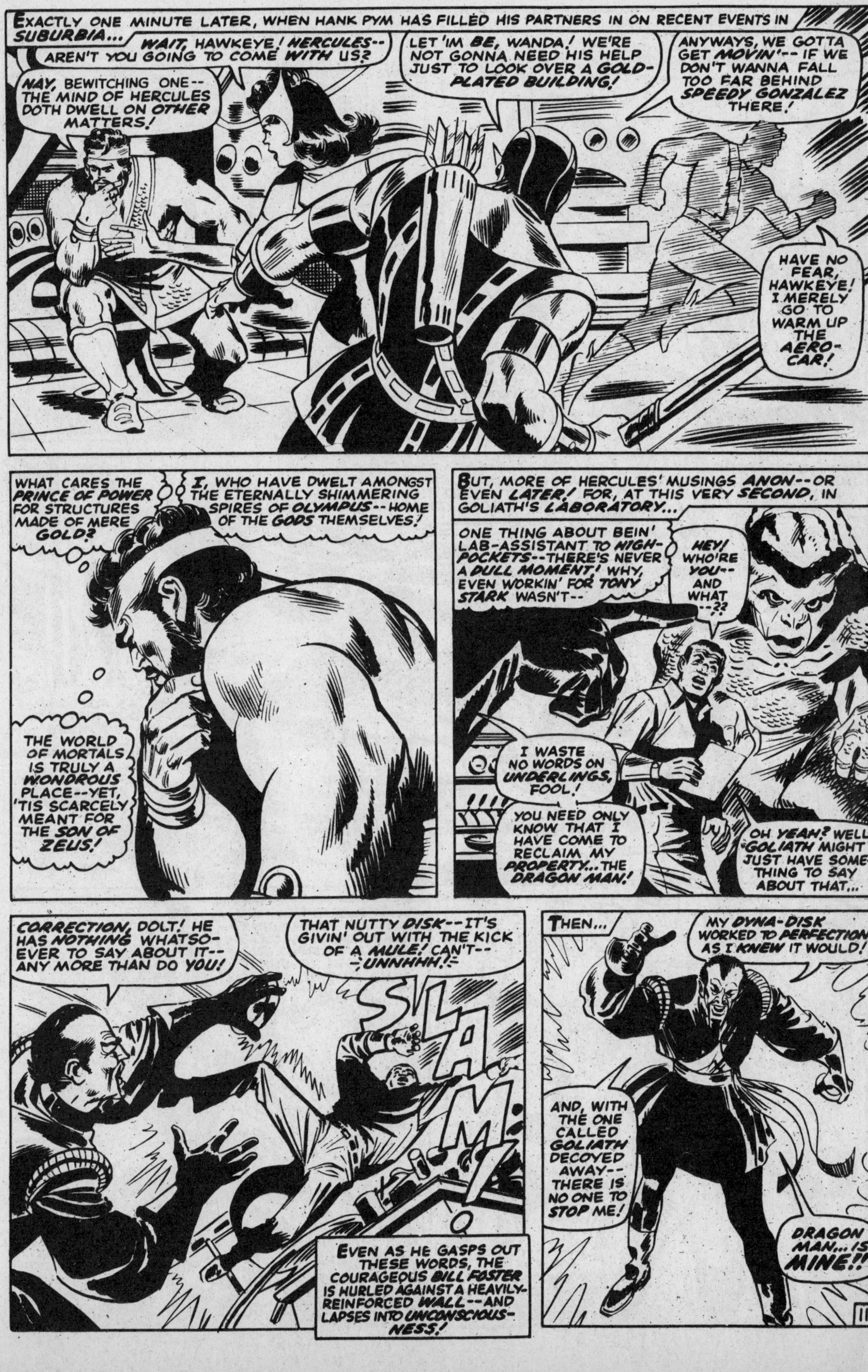
EXACTLY ONE MINUTE LATER, WHEN HANK PYM HAS FILLED HIS PARTNERS IN ON RECENT EVENTS IN SUBURBIA...
WAIT, HAWKEYE! HERCULES-- AREN'T YOU GOING TO COME WITH US?
NAY, BEWITCHING ONE-- THE MIND OF HERCULES DOTH DWELL ON OTHER MATTERS!
LET 'IM BE, WANDA! WE'RE NOT GONNA NEED HIS HELP JUST TO LOOK OVER A GOLD-PLATED BUILDING!
ANYWAYS, WE GOTTA GET MOVIN'-- IF WE DON'T WANNA FALL TOO FAR BEHIND SPEEDY GONZALEZ THERE!
HAVE NO FEAR, HAWKEYE! I MERELY GO TO WARM UP THE AERO-CAR!
WHAT CARES THE PRINCE OF POWER FOR STRUCTURES MADE OF MERE GOLD?
I, WHO HAVE DWELT AMONGST THE ETERNALLY SHIMMERING SPIRES OF OLYMPUS--HOME OF THE GODS THEMSELVES!
THE WORLD OF MORTALS IS TRULY A WONDROUS PLACE--YET, 'TIS SCARCELY MEANT FOR THE SON OF ZEUS!
BUT, MORE OF HERCULES' MUSINGS ANON--OR EVEN LATER! FOR, AT THIS VERY SECOND, IN GOLIATH'S LABORATORY...
ONE THING ABOUT BEIN' LAB-ASSISTANT TO HIGH-POCKETS--THERE'S NEVER A DULL MOMENT! WHY, EVEN WORKIN' FOR TONY STARK WASN'T--
HEY! WHO'RE YOU-- AND WHAT--??
I WASTE NO WORDS ON UNDERLINGS, FOOL!
YOU NEED ONLY KNOW THAT I HAVE COME TO RECLAIM MY PROPERTY... THE DRAGON MAN!
OH YEAH? WELL, GOLIATH MIGHT JUST HAVE SOME-THING TO SAY ABOUT THAT...
CORRECTION, DOLT! HE HAS NOTHING WHATSO-EVER TO SAY ABOUT IT-- ANY MORE THAN DO YOU!
THAT NUTTY DISK--IT'S GIVIN' OUT WITH THE KICK OF A MULE! CAN'T-- --UNNHHH!--
SLAM!
EVEN AS HE GASPS OUT THESE WORDS, THE COURAGEOUS BILL FOSTER IS HURLED AGAINST A HEAVILY-REINFORCED WALL--AND LAPSES INTO UNCONSCIOUS-NESS!
THEN...
MY DYNA-DISK WORKED TO PERFECTION, AS I KNEW IT WOULD!
AND, WITH THE ONE CALLED GOLIATH DECOYED AWAY-- THERE IS NO ONE TO STOP ME!
DRAGON MAN... IS MINE!!
11

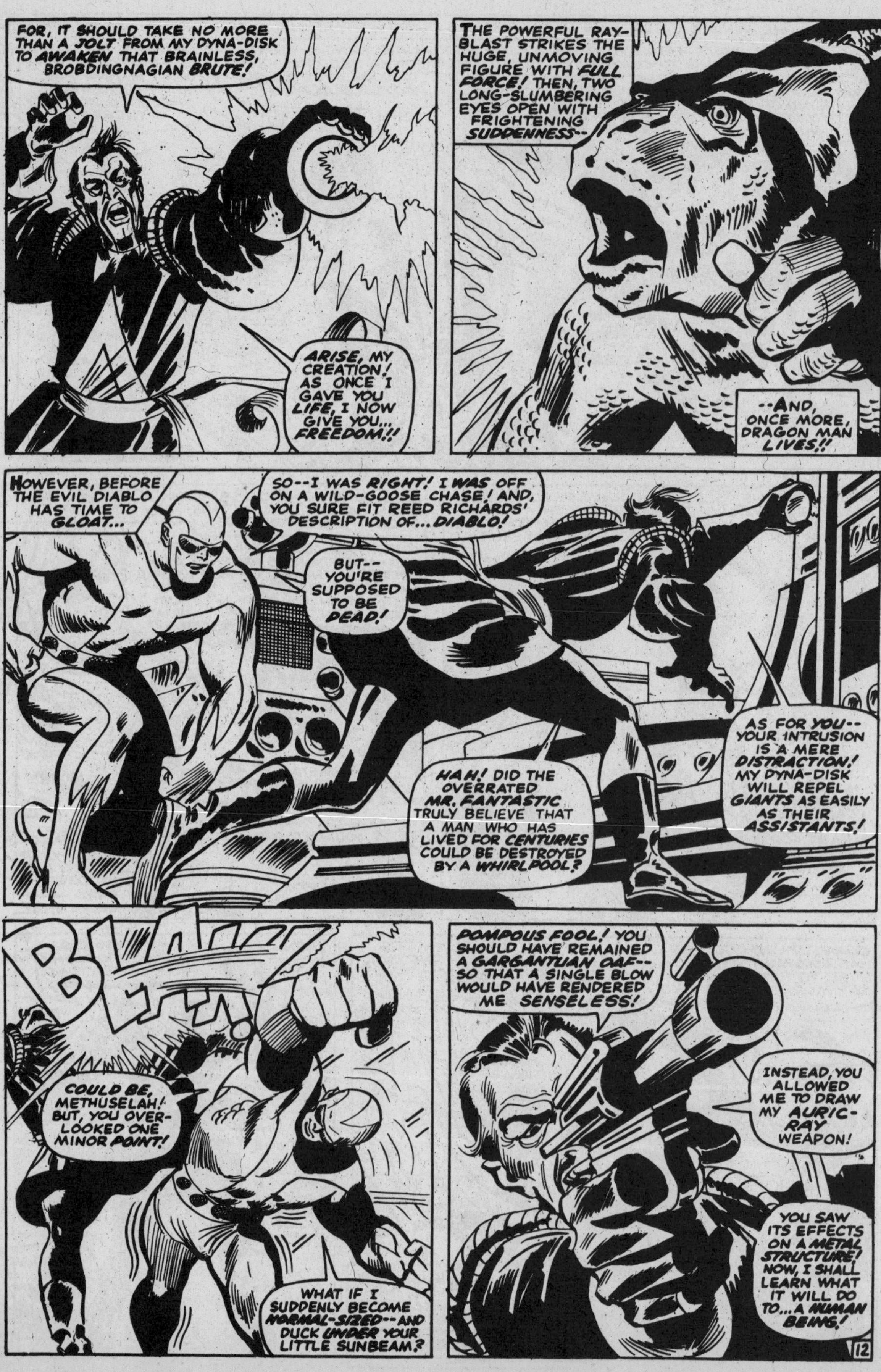
FOR, IT SHOULD TAKE NO MORE THAN A JOLT FROM MY DYNA-DISK TO AWAKEN THAT BRAINLESS, BROBDINGNAGIAN BRUTE!
ARISE, MY CREATION! AS ONCE I GAVE YOU LIFE, I NOW GIVE YOU... FREEDOM!!
THE POWERFUL RAY-BLAST STRIKES THE HUGE, UNMOVING FIGURE WITH FULL FORCE! THEN, TWO LONG-SLUMBERING EYES OPEN WITH FRIGHTENING SUDDENNESS--
--AND, ONCE MORE, DRAGON MAN LIVES!!
HOWEVER, BEFORE THE EVIL DIABLO HAS TIME TO GLOAT...
SO--I WAS RIGHT! I WAS OFF ON A WILD-GOOSE CHASE! AND, YOU SURE FIT REED RICHARDS' DESCRIPTION OF... DIABLO!
BUT--YOU'RE SUPPOSED TO BE DEAD!
HAH! DID THE OVERRATED MR. FANTASTIC TRULY BELIEVE THAT A MAN WHO HAS LIVED FOR CENTURIES COULD BE DESTROYED BY A WHIRLPOOL?
AS FOR YOU--YOUR INTRUSION IS A MERE DISTRACTION! MY DYNA-DISK WILL REPEL GIANTS AS EASILY AS THEIR ASSISTANTS!
BLAM!
COULD BE, METHUSELAH! BUT, YOU OVER-LOOKED ONE MINOR POINT!
WHAT IF I SUDDENLY BECOME NORMAL-SIZED--AND DUCK UNDER YOUR LITTLE SUNBEAM?
POMPOUS FOOL! YOU SHOULD HAVE REMAINED A GARGANTUAN OAF--SO THAT A SINGLE BLOW WOULD HAVE RENDERED ME SENSELESS!
INSTEAD, YOU ALLOWED ME TO DRAW MY AURIC-RAY WEAPON!
YOU SAW ITS EFFECTS ON A METAL STRUCTURE! NOW, I SHALL LEARN WHAT IT WILL DO TO... A HUMAN BEING!
12

TO TELL THE *TRUTH,* FRIEND...

I'D JUST AS SOON YOU DIDN'T *FIND OUT!*

THE *WASP!!*

I WAS *CARELESS!* I SHOULD HAVE KNOWN YOU WOULD NOT BE FAR FROM *GOLIATH!*

THWIIP!

BUT, YOU ELIMINATED ONLY *ONE* OF MY *WEAPONS!*

I STILL HAVE... MY *DYNA-DISK!*

OHHHH--!

IT'S LIKE BEING STRUCK BY A *SOLID OBJECT!* I'M...*FALLING--!*

THEN, AS THE STRICKEN GIRL PLUMMETS *DOWNWARD...*

YOU'LL *PAY* FOR THAT, DIABLO! IF SHE'S *INJURED--!*

YOUR THREAT IS *EMPTY,* GOLIATH!

FOR, THE *DRAGON MAN* NOW LIVES --AND OBEYS THE COMMANDS OF THE ONE WHO *REVIVED* HIM!

AND, MY *COMMAND* IS --TO *KILL!!*

I'LL ADMIT HE *LOOKS* LIKE SOMETHING OUT OF *KING KONG--*

BUT, I'VE JUST GOT *YOUR WORD* FOR HOW *TOUGH* HE IS!

RRRR

I'M WHISTLING IN THE *DARK!* THAT MONSTER'S ALL *MUSCLE!*

GOT TO *CHARGE* HIM-- GET IN THE FIRST *BLOW!*

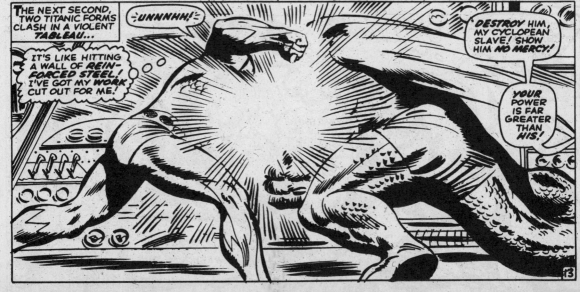

THE NEXT SECOND, TWO TITANIC FORMS CLASH IN A VIOLENT *TABLEAU...*

-UNNNHH!

IT'S LIKE HITTING A WALL OF *REINFORCED STEEL!* I'VE GOT MY *WORK* CUT OUT FOR ME!

DESTROY HIM, MY CYCLOPEAN *SLAVE!* SHOW HIM *NO MERCY!*

YOUR *POWER* IS FAR GREATER THAN *HIS!*

13

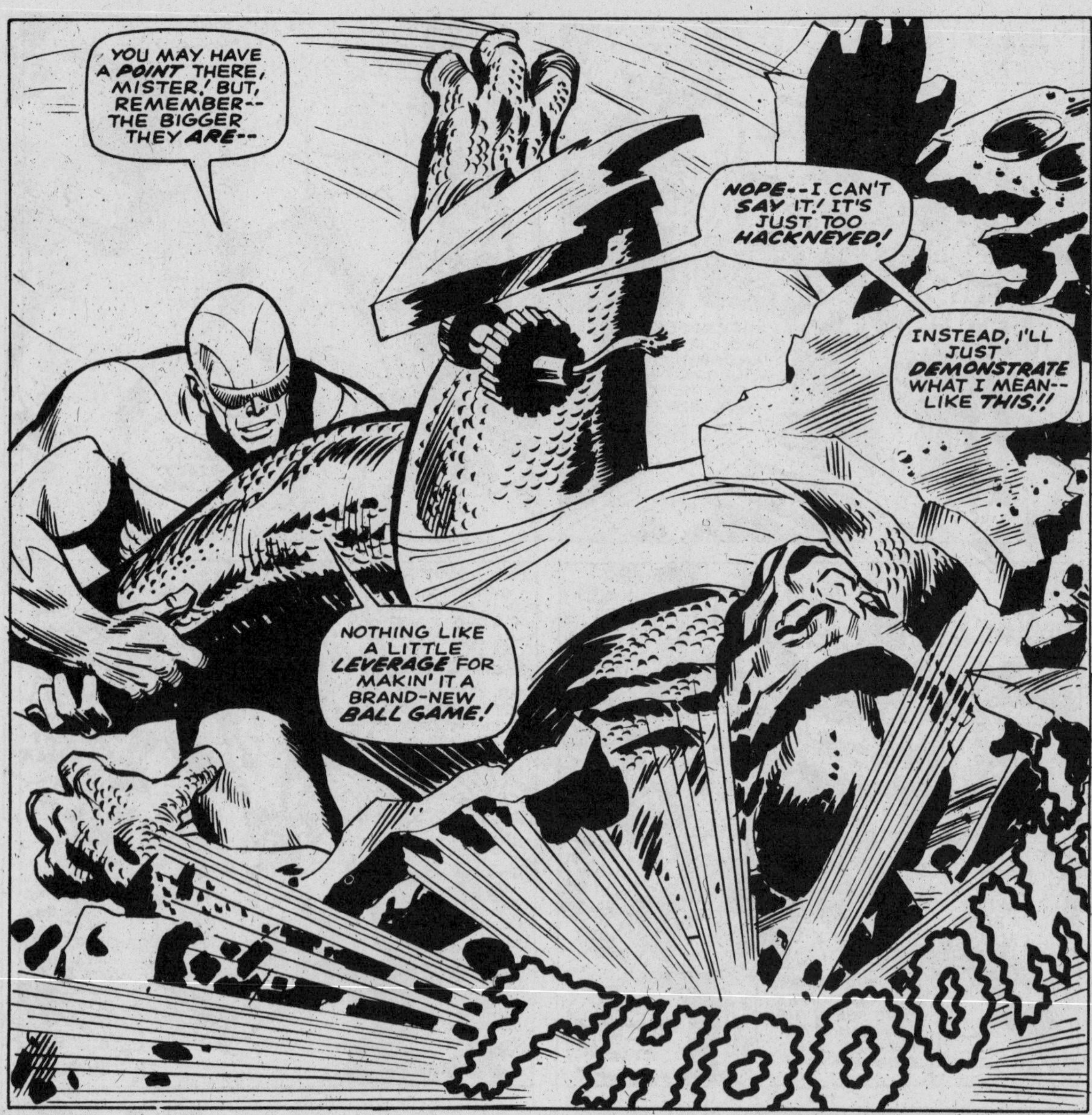
YOU MAY HAVE A POINT THERE, MISTER! BUT, REMEMBER-- THE BIGGER THEY ARE--
NOPE--I CAN'T SAY IT! IT'S JUST TOO HACKNEYED!
INSTEAD, I'LL JUST DEMONSTRATE WHAT I MEAN-- LIKE THIS!!
NOTHING LIKE A LITTLE LEVERAGE FOR MAKIN' IT A BRAND-NEW BALL GAME!
THOOOM

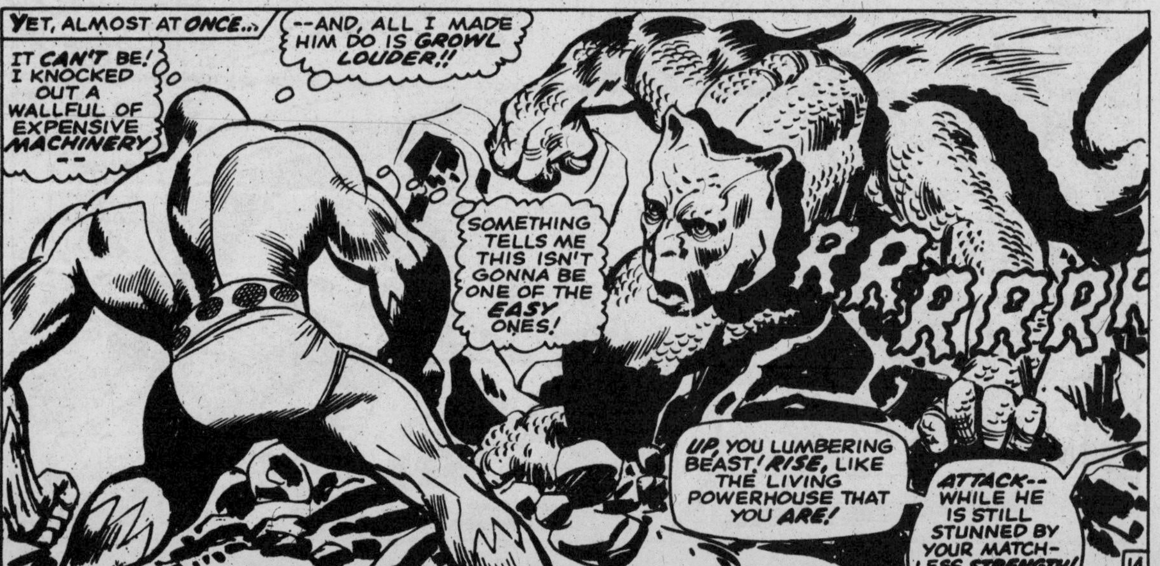
YET, ALMOST AT ONCE...
IT CAN'T BE! I KNOCKED OUT A WALLFUL OF EXPENSIVE MACHINERY--
--AND, ALL I MADE HIM DO IS GROWL LOUDER!!
SOMETHING TELLS ME THIS ISN'T GONNA BE ONE OF THE EASY ONES!
RRRRR
UP, YOU LUMBERING BEAST! RISE, LIKE THE LIVING POWERHOUSE THAT YOU ARE!
ATTACK-- WHILE HE IS STILL STUNNED BY YOUR MATCH-LESS STRENGTH!

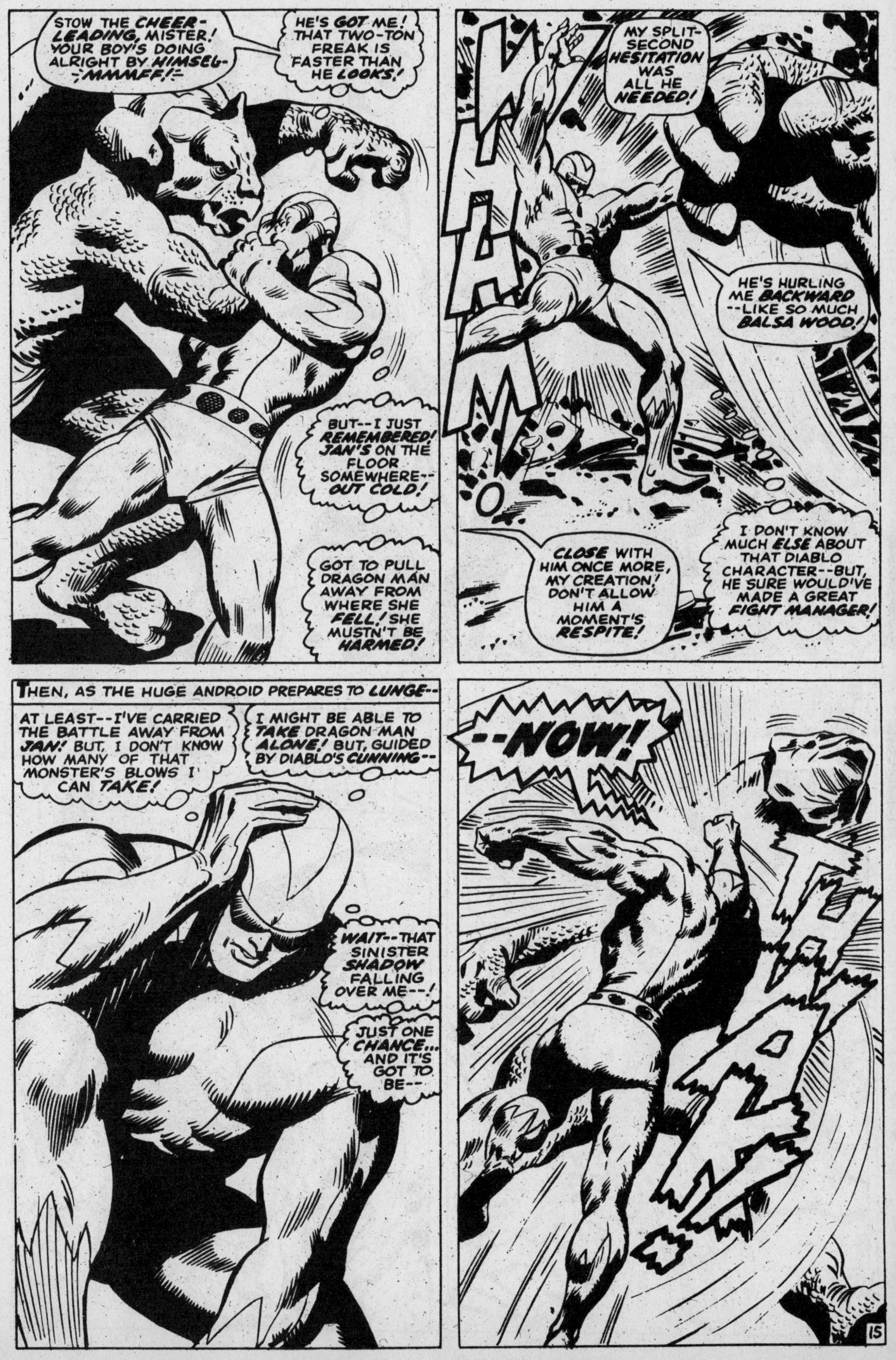
STOW THE CHEER-LEADING, MISTER! YOUR BOY'S DOING ALRIGHT BY HIMSELF--MMMFF!
HE'S GOT ME! THAT TWO-TON FREAK IS FASTER THAN HE LOOKS!
BUT--I JUST REMEMBERED! JAN'S ON THE FLOOR SOMEWHERE--OUT COLD!
GOT TO PULL DRAGON MAN AWAY FROM WHERE SHE FELL! SHE MUSTN'T BE HARMED!
WHAM
MY SPLIT-SECOND HESITATION WAS ALL HE NEEDED!
HE'S HURLING ME BACKWARD --LIKE SO MUCH BALSA WOOD!
CLOSE WITH HIM ONCE MORE, MY CREATION! DON'T ALLOW HIM A MOMENT'S RESPITE!
I DON'T KNOW MUCH ELSE ABOUT THAT DIABLO CHARACTER--BUT, HE SURE WOULD'VE MADE A GREAT FIGHT MANAGER!
THEN, AS THE HUGE ANDROID PREPARES TO LUNGE--
AT LEAST--I'VE CARRIED THE BATTLE AWAY FROM JAN! BUT, I DON'T KNOW HOW MANY OF THAT MONSTER'S BLOWS I CAN TAKE!
I MIGHT BE ABLE TO TAKE DRAGON MAN ALONE! BUT, GUIDED BY DIABLO'S CUNNING--
WAIT--THAT SINISTER SHADOW FALLING OVER ME--!
JUST ONE CHANCE... AND IT'S GOT TO BE--
--NOW!
THWAK
15

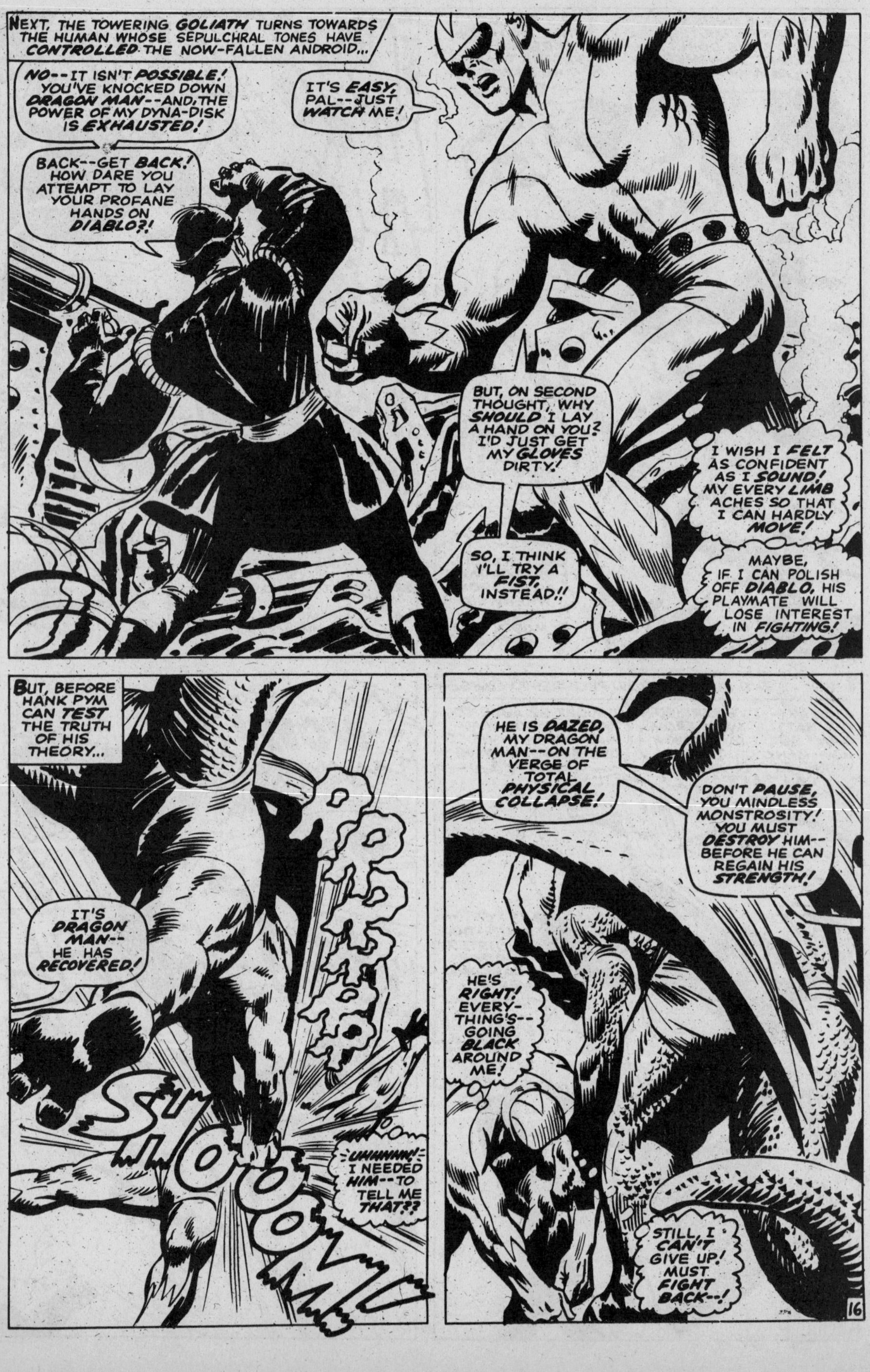
NEXT, THE TOWERING GOLIATH TURNS TOWARDS THE HUMAN WHOSE SEPULCHRAL TONES HAVE CONTROLLED THE NOW-FALLEN ANDROID...
NO--IT ISN'T POSSIBLE! YOU'VE KNOCKED DOWN DRAGON MAN--AND, THE POWER OF MY DYNA-DISK IS EXHAUSTED!
IT'S EASY, PAL--JUST WATCH ME!
BACK--GET BACK! HOW DARE YOU ATTEMPT TO LAY YOUR PROFANE HANDS ON DIABLO?!
BUT, ON SECOND THOUGHT, WHY SHOULD I LAY A HAND ON YOU? I'D JUST GET MY GLOVES DIRTY!
SO, I THINK I'LL TRY A FIST, INSTEAD!!
I WISH I FELT AS CONFIDENT AS I SOUND! MY EVERY LIMB ACHES SO THAT I CAN HARDLY MOVE!
MAYBE, IF I CAN POLISH OFF DIABLO, HIS PLAYMATE WILL LOSE INTEREST IN FIGHTING!
BUT, BEFORE HANK PYM CAN TEST THE TRUTH OF HIS THEORY...
IT'S DRAGON MAN--HE HAS RECOVERED!
SHOOOOM!
UNHHHH! I NEEDED HIM--TO TELL ME THAT??
HE IS DAZED, MY DRAGON MAN--ON THE VERGE OF TOTAL PHYSICAL COLLAPSE!
DON'T PAUSE, YOU MINDLESS MONSTROSITY! YOU MUST DESTROY HIM--BEFORE HE CAN REGAIN HIS STRENGTH!
HE'S RIGHT! EVERYTHING'S--GOING BLACK AROUND ME!
STILL, I CAN'T GIVE UP! MUST FIGHT BACK--!
16

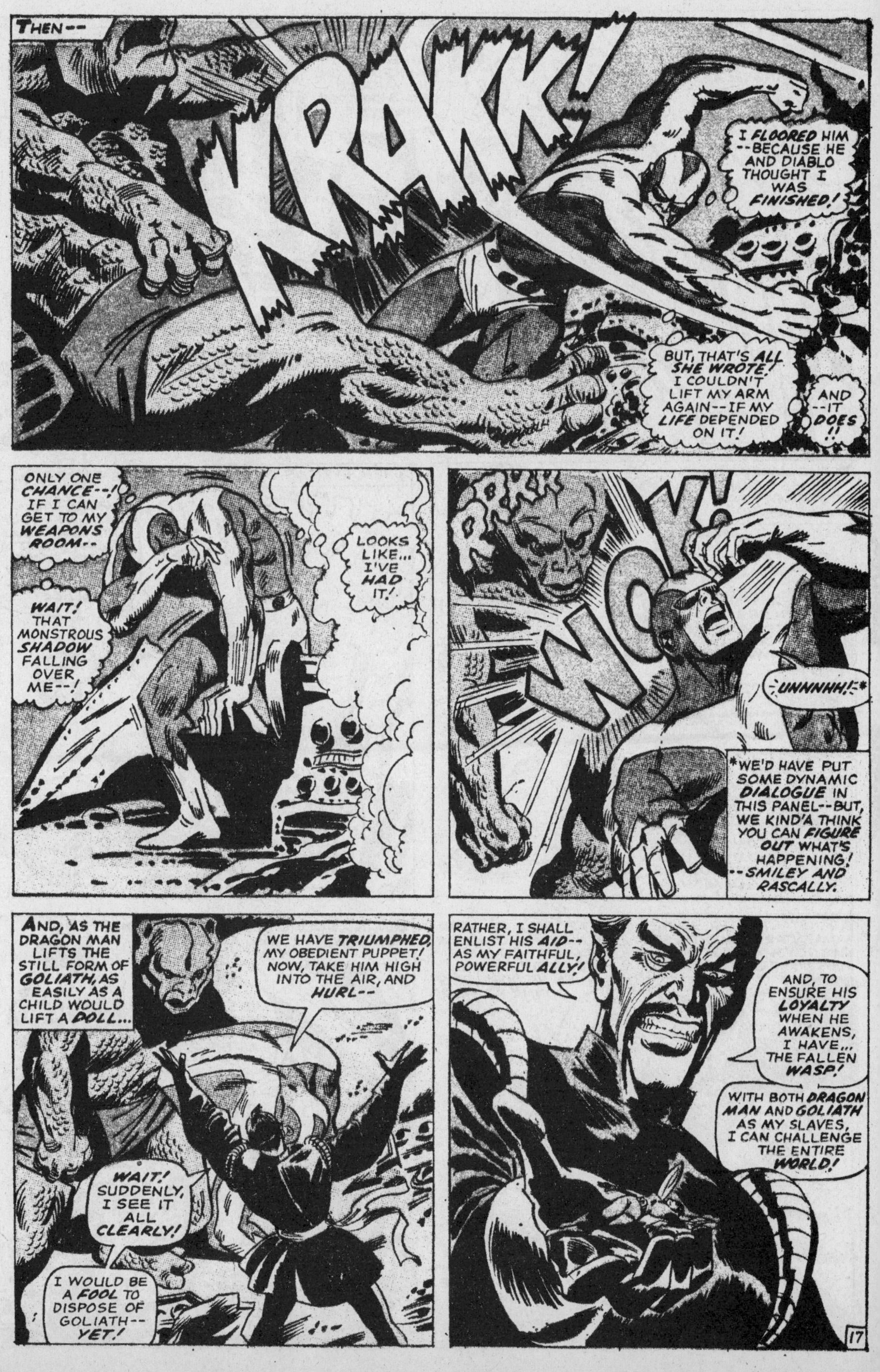
THEN--
KRAKK!
I FLOORED HIM --BECAUSE HE AND DIABLO THOUGHT I WAS FINISHED!
BUT, THAT'S ALL SHE WROTE! I COULDN'T LIFT MY ARM AGAIN--IF MY LIFE DEPENDED ON IT!
AND --IT DOES!!
ONLY ONE CHANCE--! IF I CAN GET TO MY WEAPONS ROOM--
LOOKS LIKE... I'VE HAD IT!
WAIT! THAT MONSTROUS SHADOW FALLING OVER ME--!
WOK!
UNNNHH!*
*WE'D HAVE PUT SOME DYNAMIC DIALOGUE IN THIS PANEL--BUT, WE KIND'A THINK YOU CAN FIGURE OUT WHAT'S HAPPENING! --SMILEY AND RASCALLY.
AND, AS THE DRAGON MAN LIFTS THE STILL FORM OF GOLIATH, AS EASILY AS A CHILD WOULD LIFT A DOLL...
WE HAVE TRIUMPHED, MY OBEDIENT PUPPET! NOW, TAKE HIM HIGH INTO THE AIR, AND HURL--
WAIT! SUDDENLY, I SEE IT ALL CLEARLY!
I WOULD BE A FOOL TO DISPOSE OF GOLIATH-- YET!
RATHER, I SHALL ENLIST HIS AID-- AS MY FAITHFUL, POWERFUL ALLY!
AND, TO ENSURE HIS LOYALTY WHEN HE AWAKENS, I HAVE... THE FALLEN WASP!
WITH BOTH DRAGON MAN AND GOLIATH AS MY SLAVES, I CAN CHALLENGE THE ENTIRE WORLD!
17

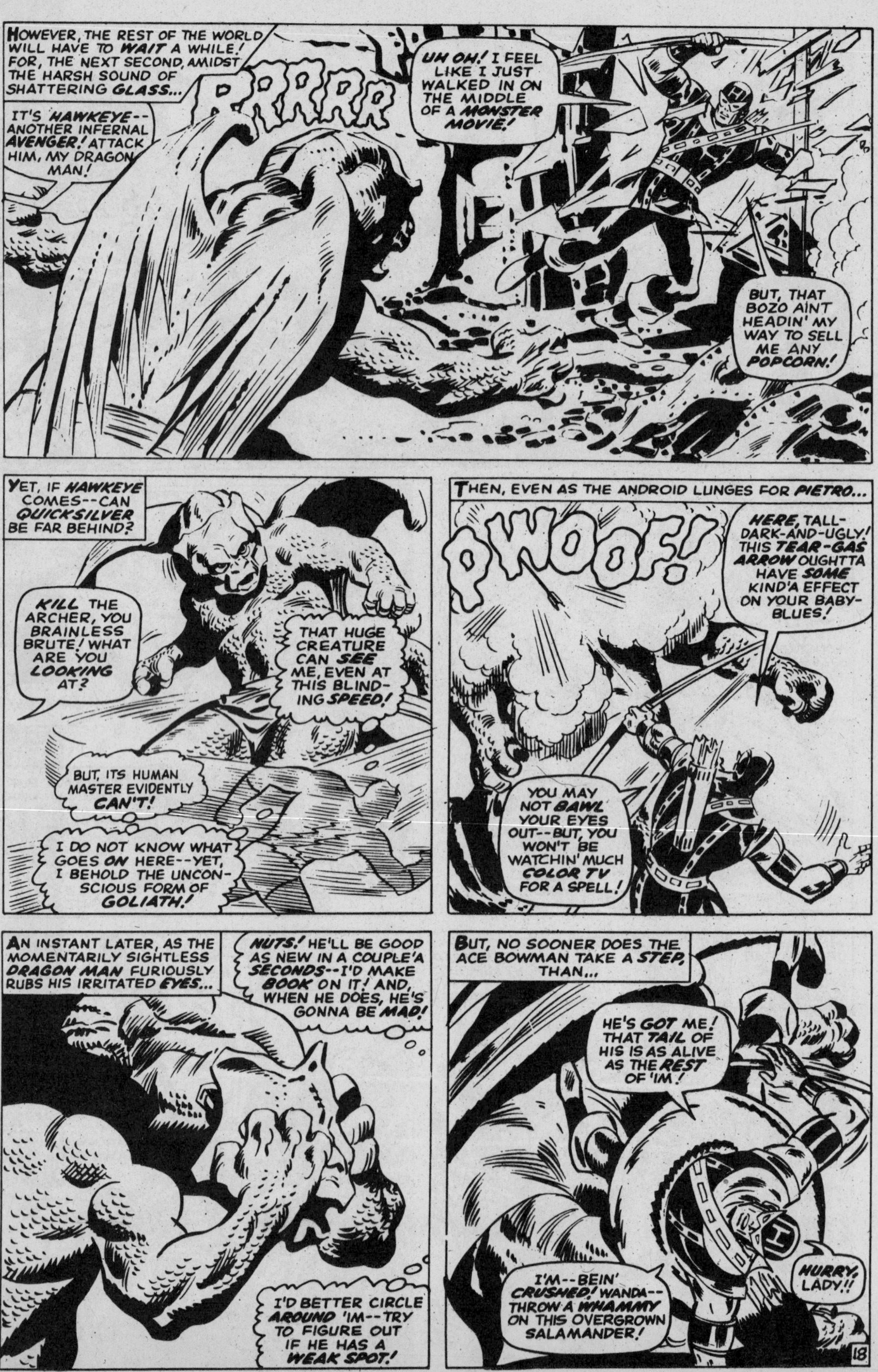
HOWEVER, THE REST OF THE WORLD WILL HAVE TO WAIT A WHILE! FOR, THE NEXT SECOND, AMIDST THE HARSH SOUND OF SHATTERING GLASS...
RRRRR
IT'S HAWKEYE-- ANOTHER INFERNAL AVENGER! ATTACK HIM, MY DRAGON MAN!
UH OH! I FEEL LIKE I JUST WALKED IN ON THE MIDDLE OF A MONSTER MOVIE!
BUT, THAT BOZO AINT HEADIN' MY WAY TO SELL ME ANY POPCORN!
YET, IF HAWKEYE COMES--CAN QUICKSILVER BE FAR BEHIND?
KILL THE ARCHER, YOU BRAINLESS BRUTE! WHAT ARE YOU LOOKING AT?
THAT HUGE CREATURE CAN SEE ME, EVEN AT THIS BLINDING SPEED!
BUT, ITS HUMAN MASTER EVIDENTLY CAN'T!
I DO NOT KNOW WHAT GOES ON HERE--YET, I BEHOLD THE UNCONSCIOUS FORM OF GOLIATH!
THEN, EVEN AS THE ANDROID LUNGES FOR PIETRO...
PWOOF!
HERE, TALL-DARK-AND-UGLY! THIS TEAR-GAS ARROW OUGHTTA HAVE SOME KIND'A EFFECT ON YOUR BABY-BLUES!
YOU MAY NOT BAWL YOUR EYES OUT--BUT, YOU WON'T BE WATCHIN' MUCH COLOR TV FOR A SPELL!
AN INSTANT LATER, AS THE MOMENTARILY SIGHTLESS DRAGON MAN FURIOUSLY RUBS HIS IRRITATED EYES...
NUTS! HE'LL BE GOOD AS NEW IN A COUPLE'A SECONDS--I'D MAKE BOOK ON IT! AND, WHEN HE DOES, HE'S GONNA BE MAD!
I'D BETTER CIRCLE AROUND 'IM--TRY TO FIGURE OUT IF HE HAS A WEAK SPOT!
BUT, NO SOONER DOES THE ACE BOWMAN TAKE A STEP, THAN...
HE'S GOT ME! THAT TAIL OF HIS IS AS ALIVE AS THE REST OF 'IM!
I'M--BEIN' CRUSHED! WANDA-- THROW A WHAMMY ON THIS OVERGROWN SALAMANDER!
HURRY, LADY!!
18

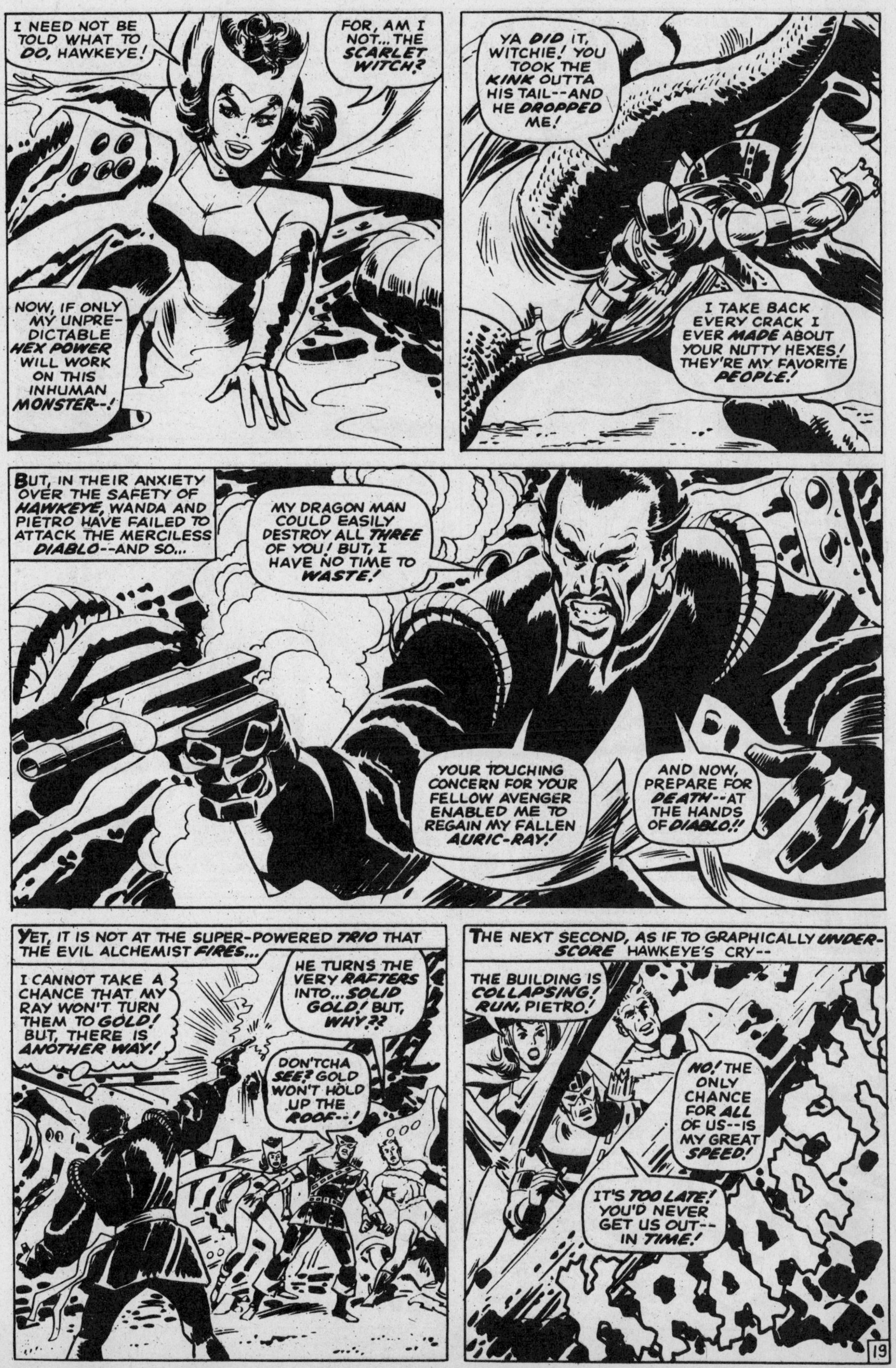

I NEED NOT BE TOLD WHAT TO DO, HAWKEYE!
FOR, AM I NOT... THE SCARLET WITCH?
NOW, IF ONLY MY UNPRE-DICTABLE HEX POWER WILL WORK ON THIS INHUMAN MONSTER--!
YA DID IT, WITCHIE! YOU TOOK THE KINK OUTTA HIS TAIL--AND HE DROPPED ME!
I TAKE BACK EVERY CRACK I EVER MADE ABOUT YOUR NUTTY HEXES! THEY'RE MY FAVORITE PEOPLE!
BUT, IN THEIR ANXIETY OVER THE SAFETY OF HAWKEYE, WANDA AND PIETRO HAVE FAILED TO ATTACK THE MERCILESS DIABLO--AND SO...
MY DRAGON MAN COULD EASILY DESTROY ALL THREE OF YOU! BUT, I HAVE NO TIME TO WASTE!
YOUR TOUCHING CONCERN FOR YOUR FELLOW AVENGER ENABLED ME TO REGAIN MY FALLEN AURIC-RAY!
AND NOW, PREPARE FOR DEATH--AT THE HANDS OF DIABLO!!
YET, IT IS NOT AT THE SUPER-POWERED TRIO THAT THE EVIL ALCHEMIST FIRES...
I CANNOT TAKE A CHANCE THAT MY RAY WON'T TURN THEM TO GOLD! BUT, THERE IS ANOTHER WAY!
HE TURNS THE VERY RAFTERS INTO...SOLID GOLD! BUT, WHY??
DON'TCHA SEE? GOLD WON'T HOLD UP THE ROOF--!
THE NEXT SECOND, AS IF TO GRAPHICALLY UNDER-SCORE HAWKEYE'S CRY--
THE BUILDING IS COLLAPSING! RUN, PIETRO!
NO! THE ONLY CHANCE FOR ALL OF US--IS MY GREAT SPEED!
IT'S TOO LATE! YOU'D NEVER GET US OUT--IN TIME!
19

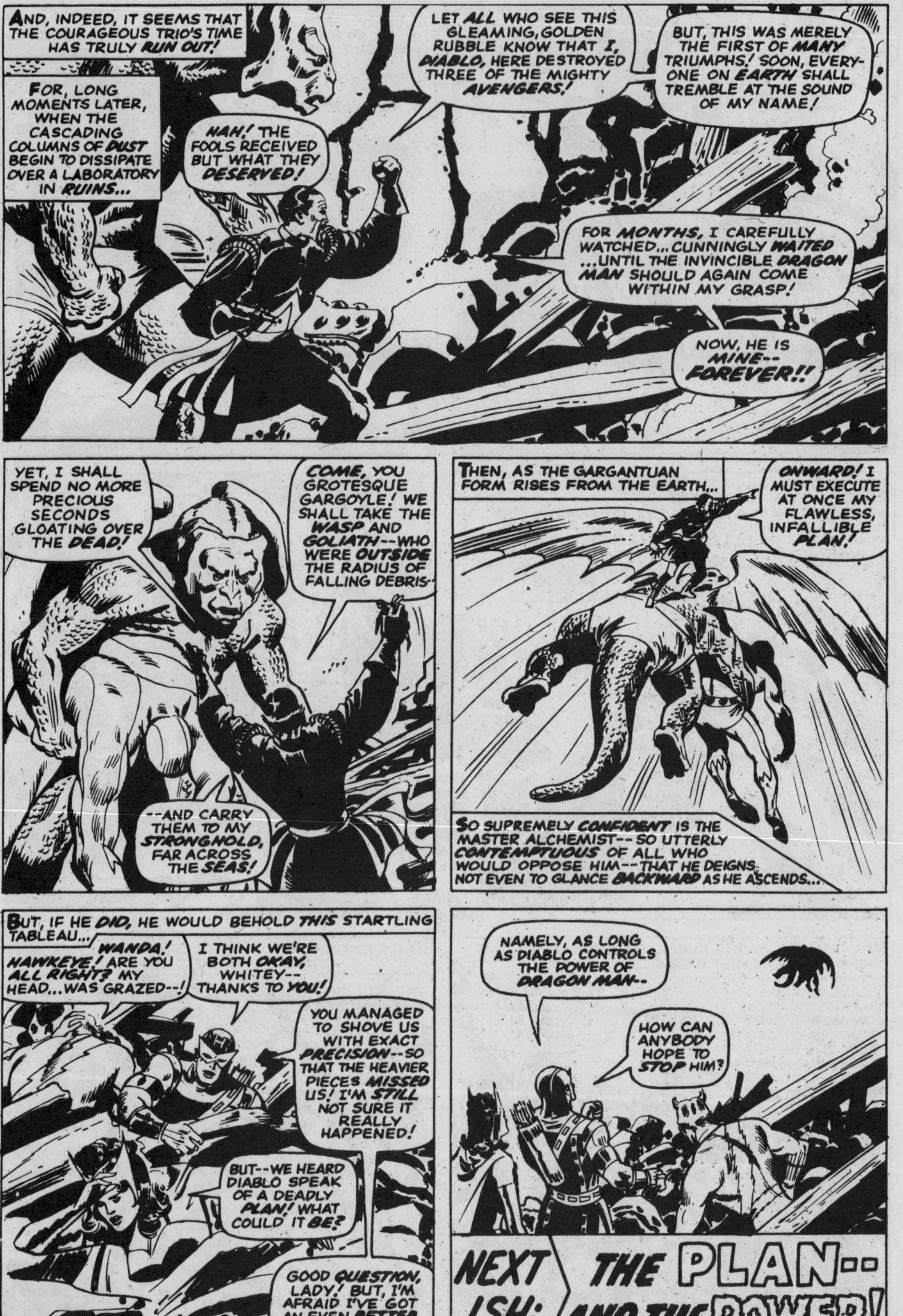

AND, INDEED, IT SEEMS THAT THE COURAGEOUS TRIO'S TIME HAS TRULY RUN OUT!
FOR, LONG MOMENTS LATER, WHEN THE CASCADING COLUMNS OF DUST BEGIN TO DISSIPATE OVER A LABORATORY IN RUINS...
NAH! THE FOOLS RECEIVED BUT WHAT THEY DESERVED!
LET ALL WHO SEE THIS GLEAMING, GOLDEN RUBBLE KNOW THAT I, DIABLO, HERE DESTROYED THREE OF THE MIGHTY AVENGERS!
BUT, THIS WAS MERELY THE FIRST OF MANY TRIUMPHS! SOON, EVERY-ONE ON EARTH SHALL TREMBLE AT THE SOUND OF MY NAME!
FOR MONTHS, I CAREFULLY WATCHED... CUNNINGLY WAITED ...UNTIL THE INVINCIBLE DRAGON MAN SHOULD AGAIN COME WITHIN MY GRASP!
NOW, HE IS MINE-- FOREVER!!
YET, I SHALL SPEND NO MORE PRECIOUS SECONDS GLOATING OVER THE DEAD!
COME, YOU GROTESQUE GARGOYLE! WE SHALL TAKE THE WASP AND GOLIATH--WHO WERE OUTSIDE THE RADIUS OF FALLING DEBRIS-
--AND CARRY THEM TO MY STRONGHOLD, FAR ACROSS THE SEAS!
THEN, AS THE GARGANTUAN FORM RISES FROM THE EARTH...
ONWARD! I MUST EXECUTE AT ONCE MY FLAWLESS, INFALLIBLE PLAN!
SO SUPREMELY CONFIDENT IS THE MASTER ALCHEMIST-- SO UTTERLY CONTEMPTUOUS OF ALL WHO WOULD OPPOSE HIM--THAT HE DEIGNS NOT EVEN TO GLANCE BACKWARD AS HE ASCENDS...
BUT, IF HE DID, HE WOULD BEHOLD THIS STARTLING TABLEAU...
WANDA! HAWKEYE! ARE YOU ALL RIGHT? MY HEAD...WAS GRAZED--!
I THINK WE'RE BOTH OKAY, WHITEY-- THANKS TO YOU!
YOU MANAGED TO SHOVE US WITH EXACT PRECISION--SO THAT THE HEAVIER PIECES MISSED US! I'M STILL NOT SURE IT REALLY HAPPENED!
BUT--WE HEARD DIABLO SPEAK OF A DEADLY PLAN! WHAT COULD IT BE?
GOOD QUESTION, LADY! BUT, I'M AFRAID I'VE GOT AN EVEN BETTER ONE...
NAMELY, AS LONG AS DIABLO CONTROLS THE POWER OF DRAGON MAN--
HOW CAN ANYBODY HOPE TO STOP HIM?
NEXT ISH: THE PLAN-- AND THE POWER!
20

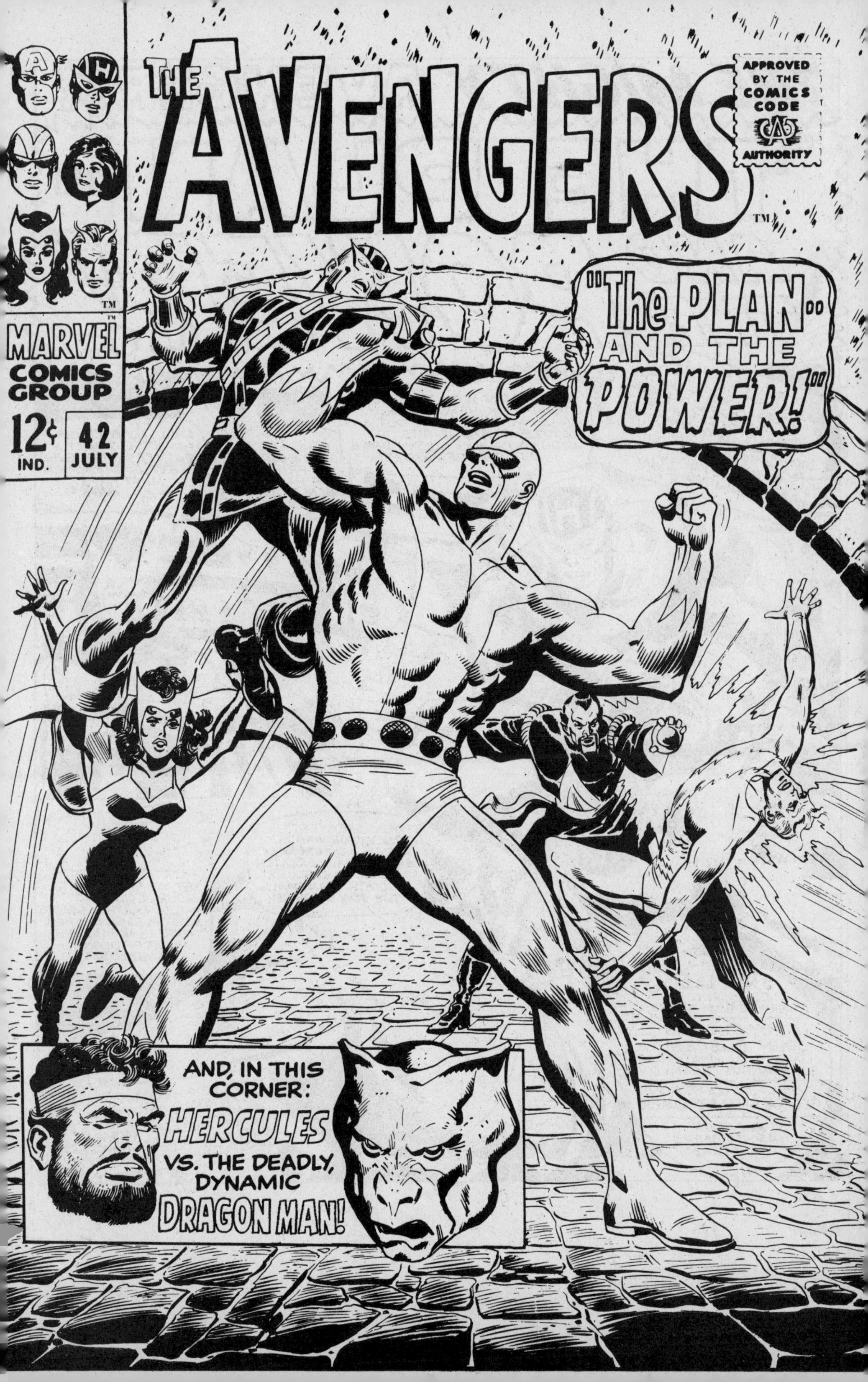
THE AVENGERS
TM
APPROVED BY THE COMICS CODE AUTHORITY
MARVEL COMICS GROUP
12¢ IND.
42 JULY
"The PLAN.. AND THE POWER!"
AND, IN THIS CORNER:
HERCULES
VS. THE DEADLY, DYNAMIC
DRAGON MAN!

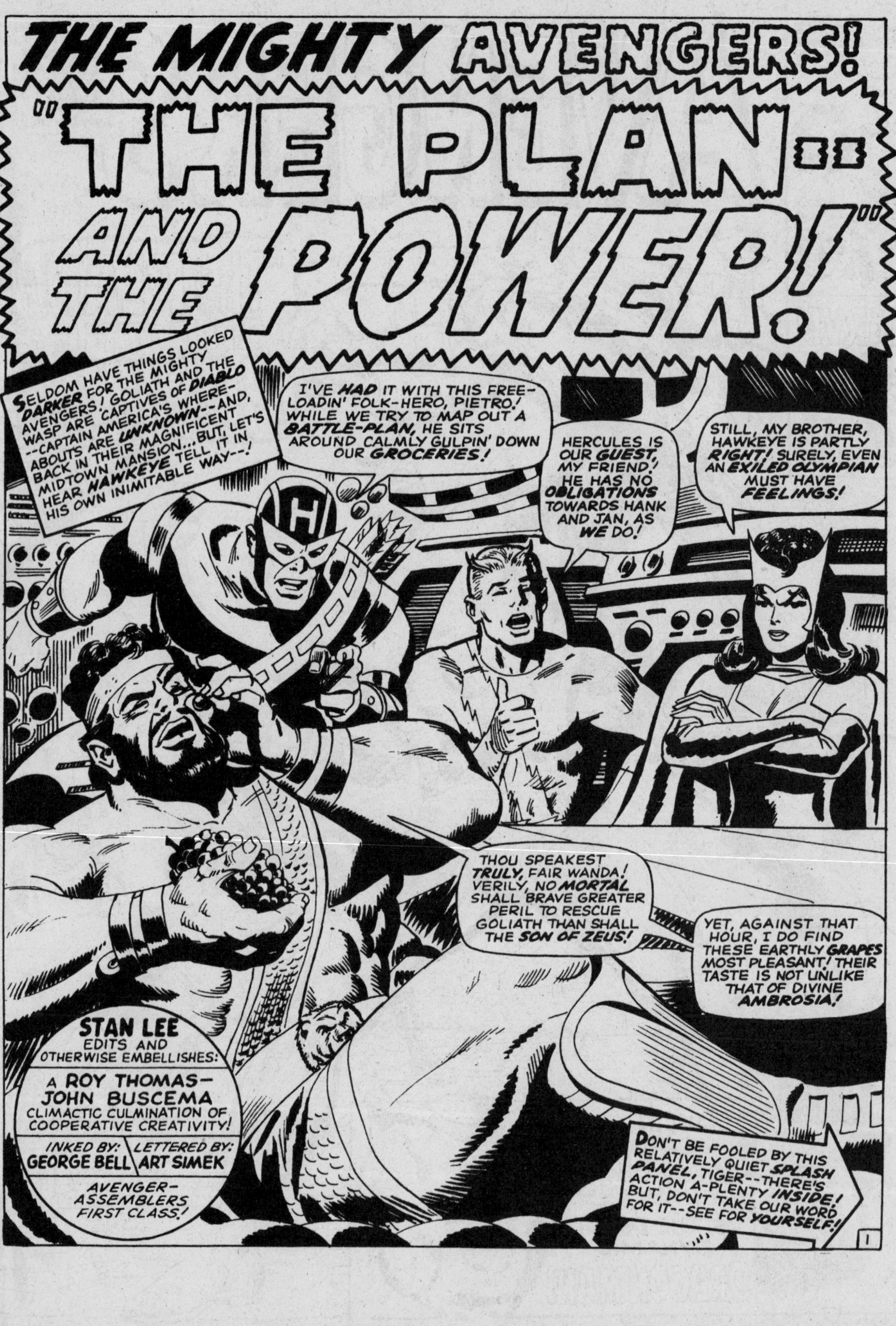
THE MIGHTY AVENGERS!
"THE PLAN.. AND THE POWER!"
SELDOM HAVE THINGS LOOKED DARKER FOR THE MIGHTY AVENGERS! GOLIATH AND THE WASP ARE CAPTIVES OF DIABLO --CAPTAIN AMERICA'S WHERE-ABOUTS ARE UNKNOWN--AND, BACK IN THEIR MAGNIFICENT MIDTOWN MANSION... BUT, LET'S HEAR HAWKEYE TELL IT IN HIS OWN INIMITABLE WAY--!
I'VE HAD IT WITH THIS FREE-LOADIN' FOLK-HERO, PIETRO! WHILE WE TRY TO MAP OUT A BATTLE-PLAN, HE SITS AROUND CALMLY GULPIN' DOWN OUR GROCERIES!
HERCULES IS OUR GUEST, MY FRIEND! HE HAS NO OBLIGATIONS TOWARDS HANK AND JAN, AS WE DO!
STILL, MY BROTHER, HAWKEYE IS PARTLY RIGHT! SURELY, EVEN AN EXILED OLYMPIAN MUST HAVE FEELINGS!
THOU SPEAKEST TRULY, FAIR WANDA! VERILY, NO MORTAL SHALL BRAVE GREATER PERIL TO RESCUE GOLIATH THAN SHALL THE SON OF ZEUS!
YET, AGAINST THAT HOUR, I DO FIND THESE EARTHLY GRAPES MOST PLEASANT! THEIR TASTE IS NOT UNLIKE THAT OF DIVINE AMBROSIA!
STAN LEE EDITS AND OTHERWISE EMBELLISHES:
A ROY THOMAS-JOHN BUSCEMA CLIMACTIC CULMINATION OF COOPERATIVE CREATIVITY!
INKED BY: GEORGE BELL
LETTERED BY: ART SIMEK
AVENGER-ASSEMBLERS FIRST CLASS!
DON'T BE FOOLED BY THIS RELATIVELY QUIET SPLASH PANEL, TIGER--THERE'S ACTION A-PLENTY INSIDE! BUT, DON'T TAKE OUR WORD FOR IT--SEE FOR YOURSELF!
1

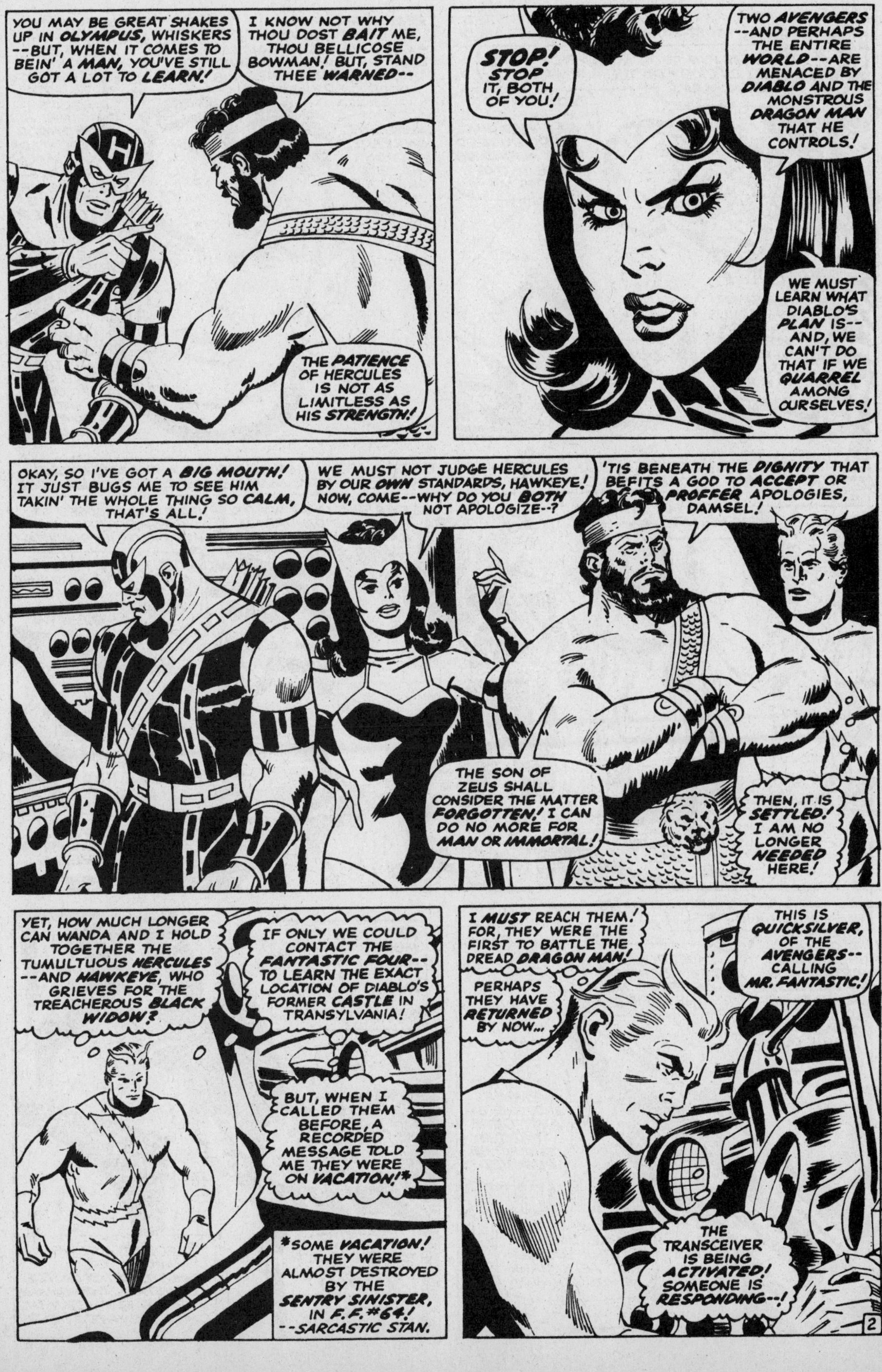
YOU MAY BE GREAT SHAKES UP IN OLYMPUS, WHISKERS --BUT, WHEN IT COMES TO BEIN' A MAN, YOU'VE STILL GOT A LOT TO LEARN!
I KNOW NOT WHY THOU DOST BAIT ME, THOU BELLICOSE BOWMAN! BUT, STAND THEE WARNED--
THE PATIENCE OF HERCULES IS NOT AS LIMITLESS AS HIS STRENGTH!
STOP! STOP IT, BOTH OF YOU!
TWO AVENGERS --AND PERHAPS THE ENTIRE WORLD--ARE MENACED BY DIABLO AND THE MONSTROUS DRAGON MAN THAT HE CONTROLS!
WE MUST LEARN WHAT DIABLO'S PLAN IS-- AND, WE CAN'T DO THAT IF WE QUARREL AMONG OURSELVES!
OKAY, SO I'VE GOT A BIG MOUTH! IT JUST BUGS ME TO SEE HIM TAKIN' THE WHOLE THING SO CALM, THAT'S ALL!
WE MUST NOT JUDGE HERCULES BY OUR OWN STANDARDS, HAWKEYE! NOW, COME--WHY DO YOU BOTH NOT APOLOGIZE--?
'TIS BENEATH THE DIGNITY THAT BEFITS A GOD TO ACCEPT OR PROFFER APOLOGIES, DAMSEL!
THE SON OF ZEUS SHALL CONSIDER THE MATTER FORGOTTEN! I CAN DO NO MORE FOR MAN OR IMMORTAL!
THEN, IT IS SETTLED! I AM NO LONGER NEEDED HERE!
YET, HOW MUCH LONGER CAN WANDA AND I HOLD TOGETHER THE TUMULTUOUS HERCULES --AND HAWKEYE, WHO GRIEVES FOR THE TREACHEROUS BLACK WIDOW?
IF ONLY WE COULD CONTACT THE FANTASTIC FOUR-- TO LEARN THE EXACT LOCATION OF DIABLO'S FORMER CASTLE IN TRANSYLVANIA!
BUT, WHEN I CALLED THEM BEFORE, A RECORDED MESSAGE TOLD ME THEY WERE ON VACATION!*
*SOME VACATION! THEY WERE ALMOST DESTROYED BY THE SENTRY SINISTER, IN F.F. #64! --SARCASTIC STAN.
I MUST REACH THEM! FOR, THEY WERE THE FIRST TO BATTLE THE DREAD DRAGON MAN!
PERHAPS THEY HAVE RETURNED BY NOW...
THIS IS QUICKSILVER, OF THE AVENGERS-- CALLING MR. FANTASTIC!
THE TRANSCEIVER IS BEING ACTIVATED! SOMEONE IS RESPONDING--!
2

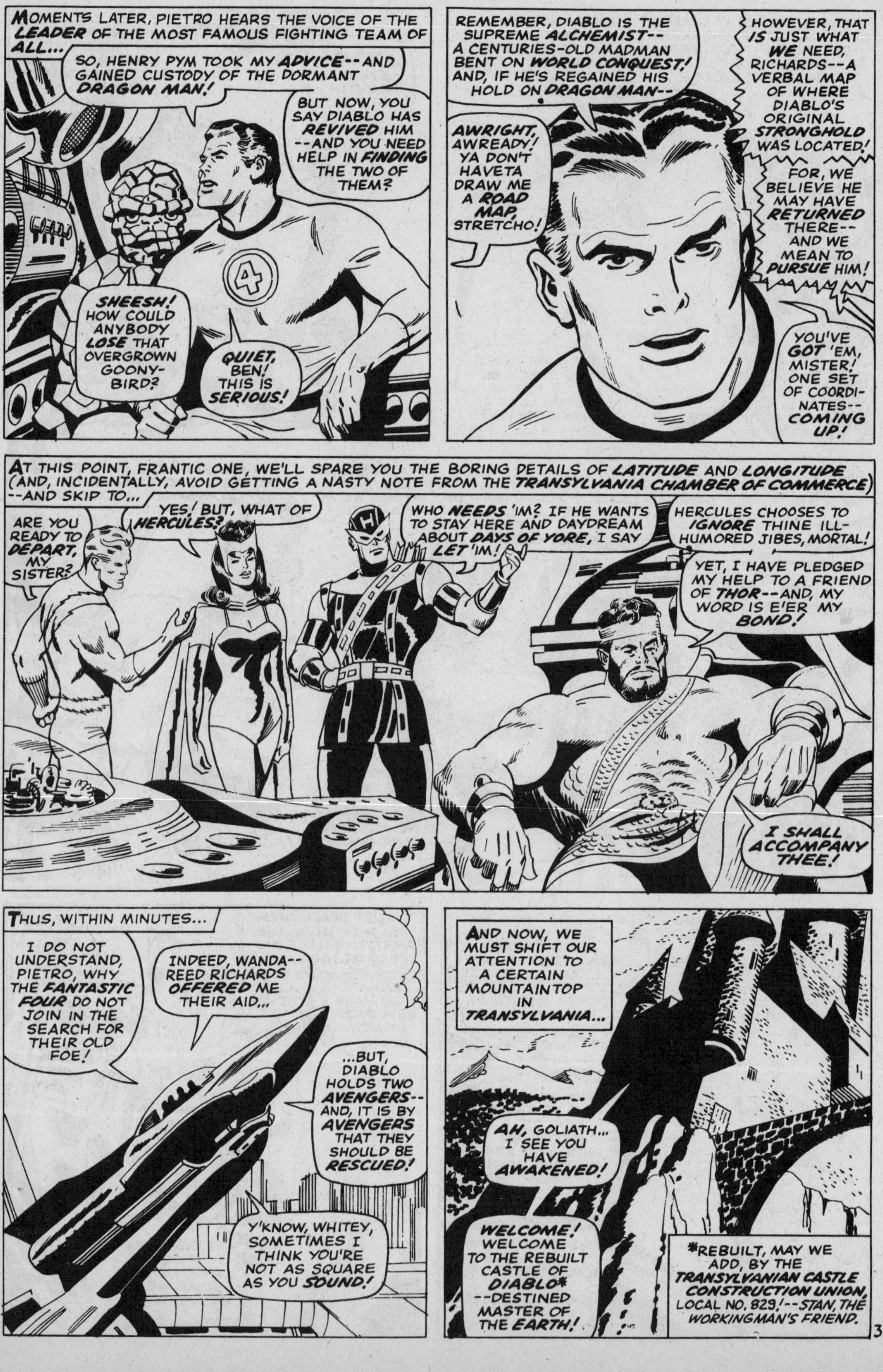
MOMENTS LATER, PIETRO HEARS THE VOICE OF THE LEADER OF THE MOST FAMOUS FIGHTING TEAM OF ALL...
SO, HENRY PYM TOOK MY ADVICE--AND GAINED CUSTODY OF THE DORMANT DRAGON MAN!
BUT NOW, YOU SAY DIABLO HAS REVIVED HIM --AND YOU NEED HELP IN FINDING THE TWO OF THEM?
SHEESH! HOW COULD ANYBODY LOSE THAT OVERGROWN GOONY-BIRD?
QUIET, BEN! THIS IS SERIOUS!
REMEMBER, DIABLO IS THE SUPREME ALCHEMIST--A CENTURIES-OLD MADMAN BENT ON WORLD CONQUEST! AND, IF HE'S REGAINED HIS HOLD ON DRAGON MAN--
AWRIGHT, AWREADY! YA DON'T HAVETA DRAW ME A ROAD MAP, STRETCHO!
HOWEVER, THAT IS JUST WHAT WE NEED, RICHARDS--A VERBAL MAP OF WHERE DIABLO'S ORIGINAL STRONGHOLD WAS LOCATED!
FOR, WE BELIEVE HE MAY HAVE RETURNED THERE--AND WE MEAN TO PURSUE HIM!
YOU'VE GOT 'EM, MISTER! ONE SET OF COORDI-NATES--COMING UP!
AT THIS POINT, FRANTIC ONE, WE'LL SPARE YOU THE BORING DETAILS OF LATITUDE AND LONGITUDE (AND, INCIDENTALLY, AVOID GETTING A NASTY NOTE FROM THE TRANSYLVANIA CHAMBER OF COMMERCE) --AND SKIP TO...
ARE YOU READY TO DEPART, MY SISTER?
YES! BUT, WHAT OF HERCULES?
WHO NEEDS 'IM? IF HE WANTS TO STAY HERE AND DAYDREAM ABOUT DAYS OF YORE, I SAY LET 'IM!
HERCULES CHOOSES TO IGNORE THINE ILL-HUMORED JIBES, MORTAL!
YET, I HAVE PLEDGED MY HELP TO A FRIEND OF THOR--AND, MY WORD IS E'ER MY BOND!
I SHALL ACCOMPANY THEE!
THUS, WITHIN MINUTES...
I DO NOT UNDERSTAND, PIETRO, WHY THE FANTASTIC FOUR DO NOT JOIN IN THE SEARCH FOR THEIR OLD FOE!
INDEED, WANDA--REED RICHARDS OFFERED ME THEIR AID...
...BUT, DIABLO HOLDS TWO AVENGERS--AND, IT IS BY AVENGERS THAT THEY SHOULD BE RESCUED!
Y'KNOW, WHITEY, SOMETIMES I THINK YOU'RE NOT AS SQUARE AS YOU SOUND!
AND NOW, WE MUST SHIFT OUR ATTENTION TO A CERTAIN MOUNTAINTOP IN TRANSYLVANIA...
AH, GOLIATH... I SEE YOU HAVE AWAKENED!
WELCOME! WELCOME TO THE REBUILT CASTLE OF DIABLO* --DESTINED MASTER OF THE EARTH!
*REBUILT, MAY WE ADD, BY THE TRANSYLVANIAN CASTLE CONSTRUCTION UNION, LOCAL NO. 829!--STAN, THE WORKINGMAN'S FRIEND.
3

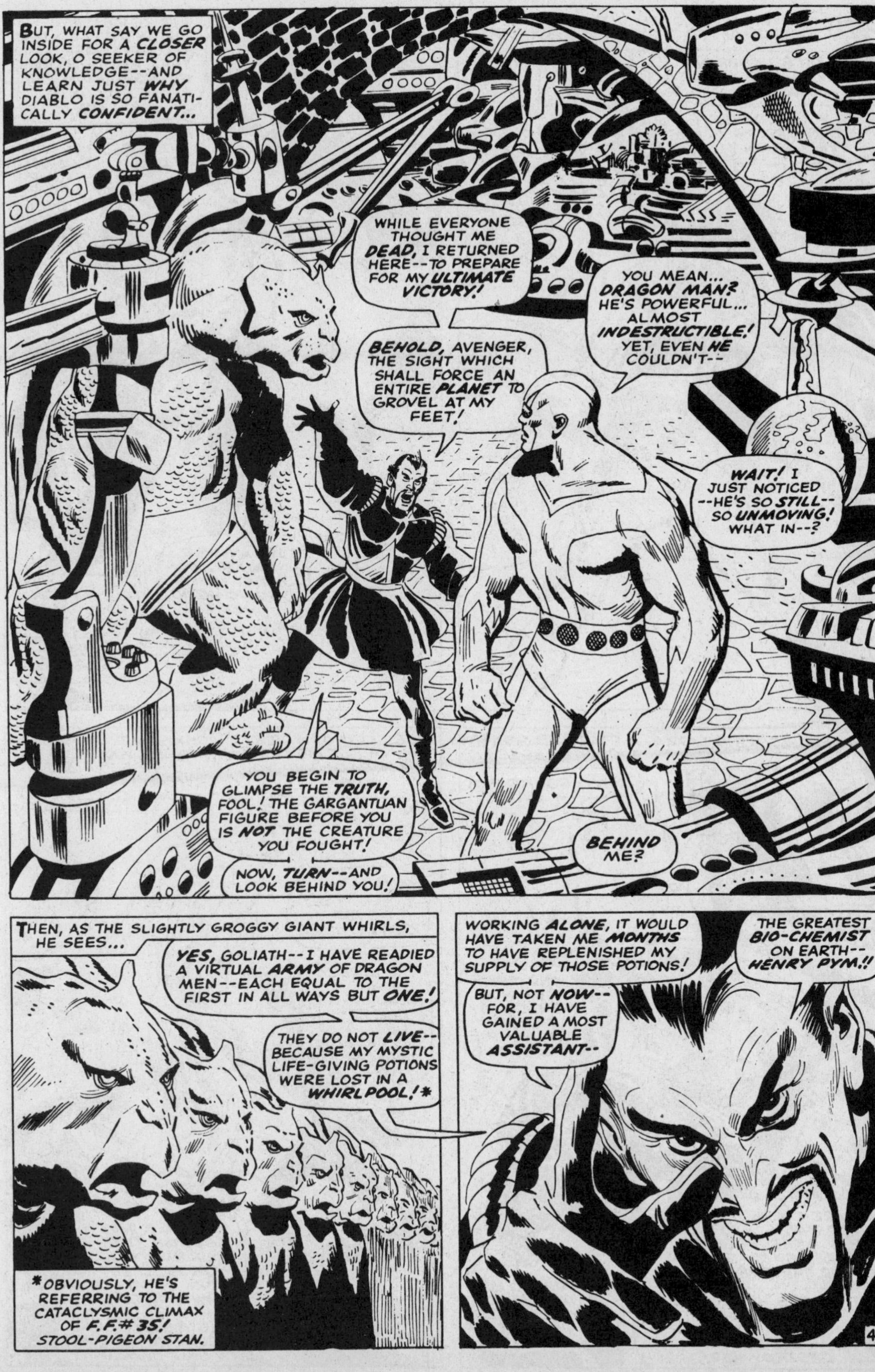

BUT, WHAT SAY WE GO INSIDE FOR A CLOSER LOOK, O SEEKER OF KNOWLEDGE--AND LEARN JUST WHY DIABLO IS SO FANATICALLY CONFIDENT...
WHILE EVERYONE THOUGHT ME DEAD, I RETURNED HERE--TO PREPARE FOR MY ULTIMATE VICTORY!
BEHOLD, AVENGER, THE SIGHT WHICH SHALL FORCE AN ENTIRE PLANET TO GROVEL AT MY FEET!
YOU MEAN... DRAGON MAN? HE'S POWERFUL... ALMOST INDESTRUCTIBLE! YET, EVEN HE COULDN'T--
WAIT! I JUST NOTICED --HE'S SO STILL--SO UNMOVING! WHAT IN--?
YOU BEGIN TO GLIMPSE THE TRUTH, FOOL! THE GARGANTUAN FIGURE BEFORE YOU IS NOT THE CREATURE YOU FOUGHT!
NOW, TURN--AND LOOK BEHIND YOU!
BEHIND ME?
THEN, AS THE SLIGHTLY GROGGY GIANT WHIRLS, HE SEES...
YES, GOLIATH--I HAVE READIED A VIRTUAL ARMY OF DRAGON MEN--EACH EQUAL TO THE FIRST IN ALL WAYS BUT ONE!
THEY DO NOT LIVE--BECAUSE MY MYSTIC LIFE-GIVING POTIONS WERE LOST IN A WHIRLPOOL!*
*OBVIOUSLY, HE'S REFERRING TO THE CATACLYSMIC CLIMAX OF F.F. #35! STOOL-PIGEON STAN.
WORKING ALONE, IT WOULD HAVE TAKEN ME MONTHS TO HAVE REPLENISHED MY SUPPLY OF THOSE POTIONS!
BUT, NOT NOW--FOR, I HAVE GAINED A MOST VALUABLE ASSISTANT--
THE GREATEST BIO-CHEMIST ON EARTH--HENRY PYM!!

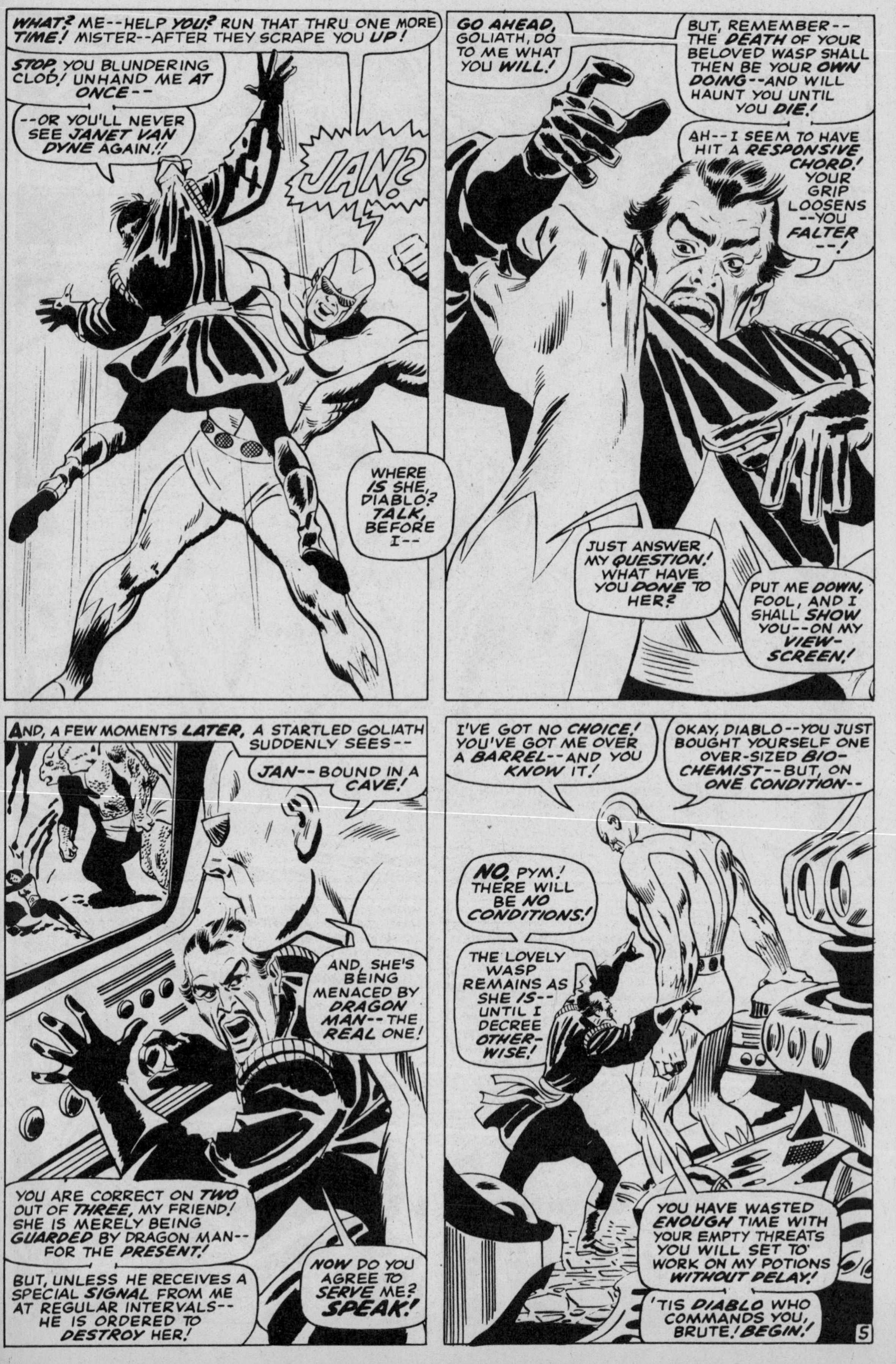
WHAT? ME--HELP YOU? RUN THAT THRU ONE MORE TIME! MISTER--AFTER THEY SCRAPE YOU UP!
STOP, YOU BLUNDERING CLOD! UNHAND ME AT ONCE--
--OR YOU'LL NEVER SEE JANET VAN DYNE AGAIN!!
JAN?
WHERE IS SHE, DIABLO? TALK, BEFORE I--
GO AHEAD, GOLIATH, DO TO ME WHAT YOU WILL!
BUT, REMEMBER--THE DEATH OF YOUR BELOVED WASP SHALL THEN BE YOUR OWN DOING--AND WILL HAUNT YOU UNTIL YOU DIE!
AH--I SEEM TO HAVE HIT A RESPONSIVE CHORD! YOUR GRIP LOOSENS--YOU FALTER--!
JUST ANSWER MY QUESTION! WHAT HAVE YOU DONE TO HER?
PUT ME DOWN, FOOL, AND I SHALL SHOW YOU--ON MY VIEW-SCREEN!
AND, A FEW MOMENTS LATER, A STARTLED GOLIATH SUDDENLY SEES--
JAN--BOUND IN A CAVE!
AND, SHE'S BEING MENACED BY DRAGON MAN--THE REAL ONE!
YOU ARE CORRECT ON TWO OUT OF THREE, MY FRIEND! SHE IS MERELY BEING GUARDED BY DRAGON MAN--FOR THE PRESENT!
BUT, UNLESS HE RECEIVES A SPECIAL SIGNAL FROM ME AT REGULAR INTERVALS--HE IS ORDERED TO DESTROY HER!
NOW DO YOU AGREE TO SERVE ME? SPEAK!
I'VE GOT NO CHOICE! YOU'VE GOT ME OVER A BARREL--AND YOU KNOW IT!
OKAY, DIABLO--YOU JUST BOUGHT YOURSELF ONE OVER-SIZED BIO-CHEMIST--BUT, ON ONE CONDITION--
NO, PYM! THERE WILL BE NO CONDITIONS!
THE LOVELY WASP REMAINS AS SHE IS--UNTIL I DECREE OTHER-WISE!
YOU HAVE WASTED ENOUGH TIME WITH YOUR EMPTY THREATS YOU WILL SET TO WORK ON MY POTIONS WITHOUT DELAY!
'TIS DIABLO WHO COMMANDS YOU, BRUTE! BEGIN!
5

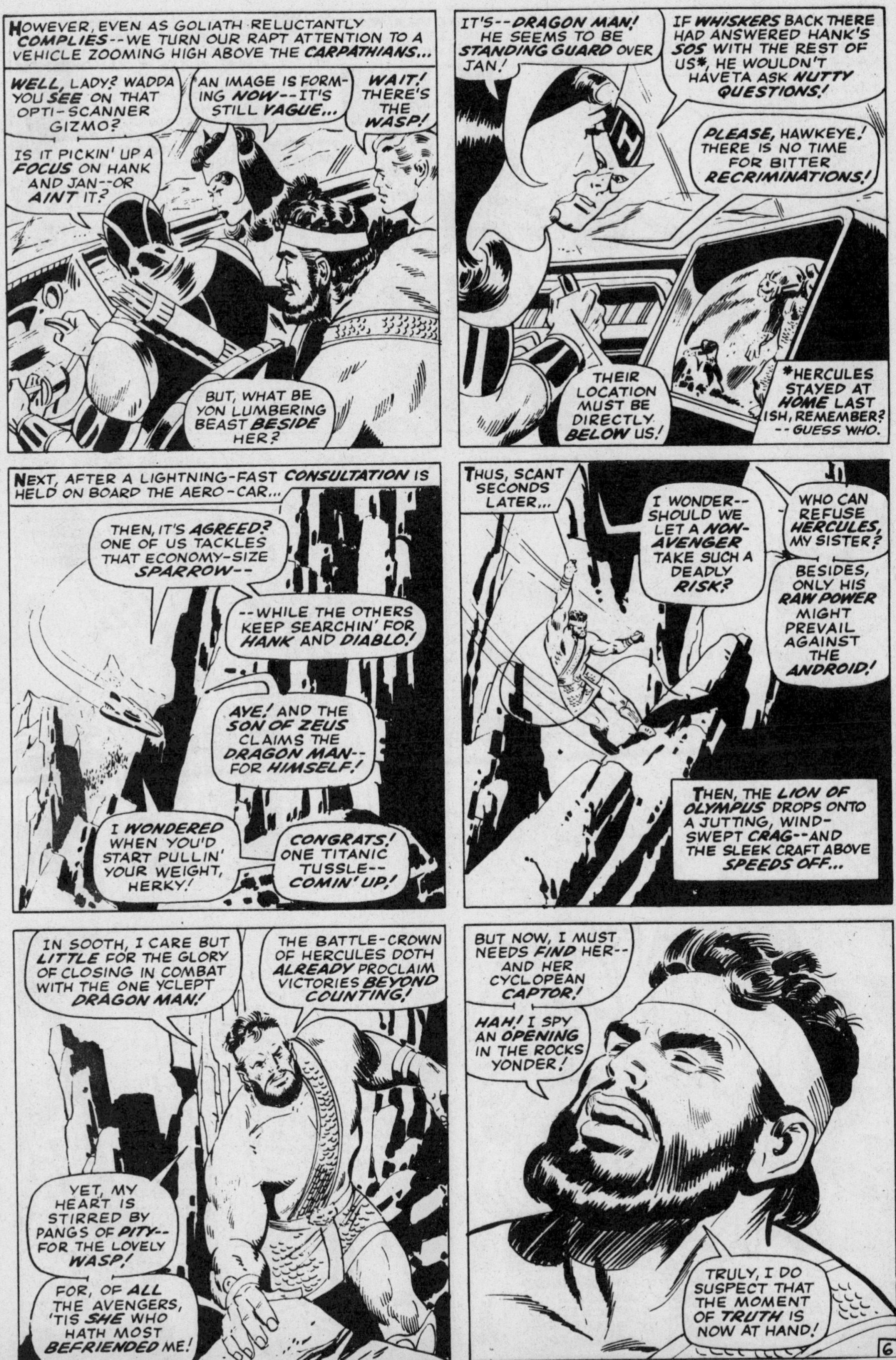
HOWEVER, EVEN AS GOLIATH RELUCTANTLY COMPLIES--WE TURN OUR RAPT ATTENTION TO A VEHICLE ZOOMING HIGH ABOVE THE CARPATHIANS...
WELL, LADY? WADDA YOU SEE ON THAT OPTI-SCANNER GIZMO?
IS IT PICKIN' UP A FOCUS ON HANK AND JAN--OR AINT IT?
AN IMAGE IS FORMING NOW--IT'S STILL VAGUE...
WAIT! THERE'S THE WASP!
BUT, WHAT BE YON LUMBERING BEAST BESIDE HER?
IT'S--DRAGON MAN! HE SEEMS TO BE STANDING GUARD OVER JAN!
IF WHISKERS BACK THERE HAD ANSWERED HANK'S SOS WITH THE REST OF US*, HE WOULDN'T HAVETA ASK NUTTY QUESTIONS!
PLEASE, HAWKEYE! THERE IS NO TIME FOR BITTER RECRIMINATIONS!
THEIR LOCATION MUST BE DIRECTLY BELOW US!
*HERCULES STAYED AT HOME LAST ISH, REMEMBER? --GUESS WHO.
NEXT, AFTER A LIGHTNING-FAST CONSULTATION IS HELD ON BOARD THE AERO-CAR...
THEN, IT'S AGREED? ONE OF US TACKLES THAT ECONOMY-SIZE SPARROW--
--WHILE THE OTHERS KEEP SEARCHIN' FOR HANK AND DIABLO!
AYE! AND THE SON OF ZEUS CLAIMS THE DRAGON MAN--FOR HIMSELF!
I WONDERED WHEN YOU'D START PULLIN' YOUR WEIGHT, HERKY!
CONGRATS! ONE TITANIC TUSSLE--COMIN' UP!
THUS, SCANT SECONDS LATER...
I WONDER--SHOULD WE LET A NON-AVENGER TAKE SUCH A DEADLY RISK?
WHO CAN REFUSE HERCULES, MY SISTER?
BESIDES, ONLY HIS RAW POWER MIGHT PREVAIL AGAINST THE ANDROID!
THEN, THE LION OF OLYMPUS DROPS ONTO A JUTTING, WIND-SWEPT CRAG--AND THE SLEEK CRAFT ABOVE SPEEDS OFF...
IN SOOTH, I CARE BUT LITTLE FOR THE GLORY OF CLOSING IN COMBAT WITH THE ONE YCLEPT DRAGON MAN!
THE BATTLE-CROWN OF HERCULES DOTH ALREADY PROCLAIM VICTORIES BEYOND COUNTING!
YET, MY HEART IS STIRRED BY PANGS OF PITY--FOR THE LOVELY WASP!
FOR, OF ALL THE AVENGERS, 'TIS SHE WHO HATH MOST BEFRIENDED ME!
BUT NOW, I MUST NEEDS FIND HER--AND HER CYCLOPEAN CAPTOR!
HAH! I SPY AN OPENING IN THE ROCKS YONDER!
TRULY, I DO SUSPECT THAT THE MOMENT OF TRUTH IS NOW AT HAND!
6

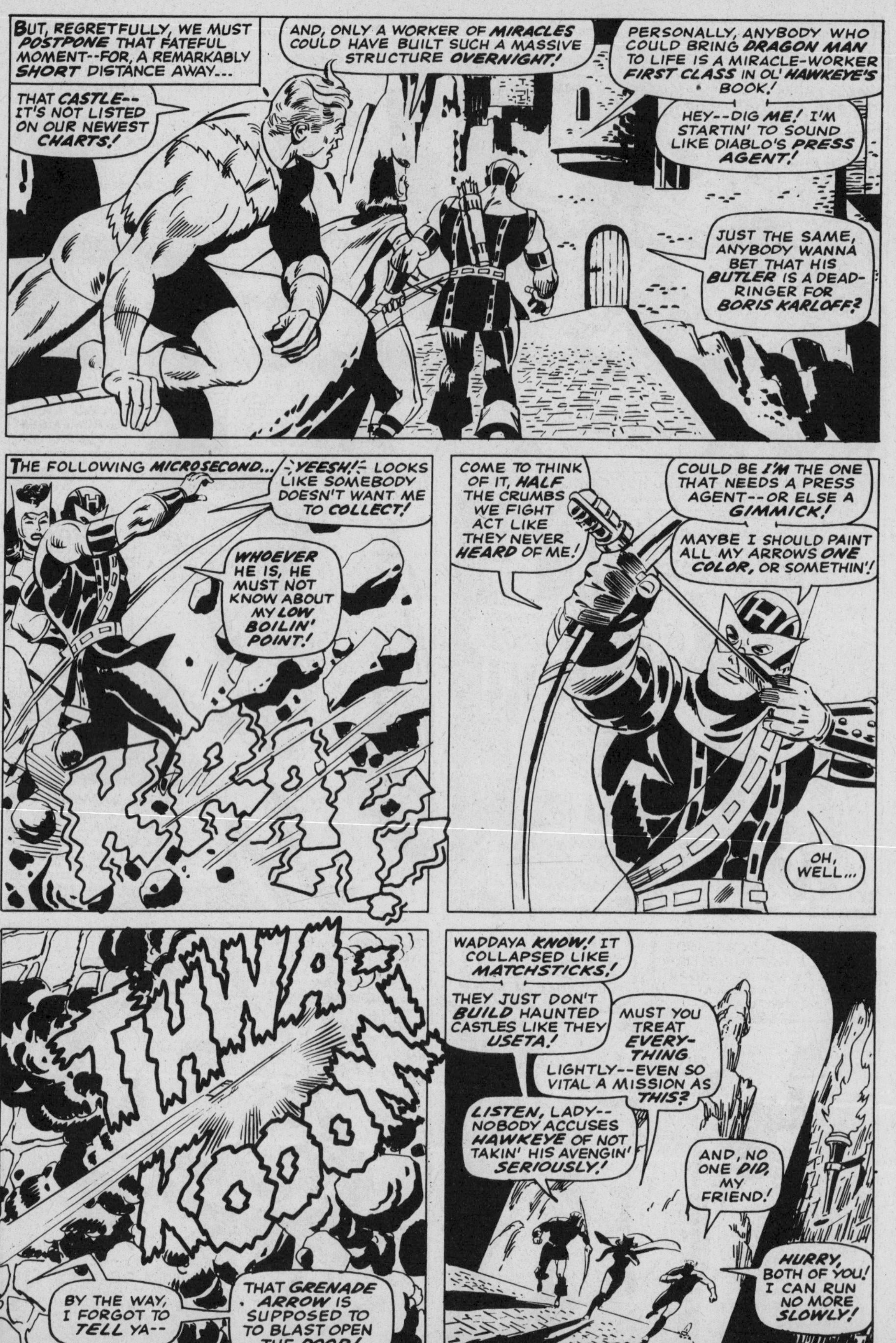

BUT, REGRETFULLY, WE MUST POSTPONE THAT FATEFUL MOMENT--FOR, A REMARKABLY SHORT DISTANCE AWAY...
THAT CASTLE-- IT'S NOT LISTED ON OUR NEWEST CHARTS!
AND, ONLY A WORKER OF MIRACLES COULD HAVE BUILT SUCH A MASSIVE STRUCTURE OVERNIGHT!
PERSONALLY, ANYBODY WHO COULD BRING DRAGON MAN TO LIFE IS A MIRACLE-WORKER FIRST CLASS IN OL' HAWKEYE'S BOOK!
HEY--DIG ME! I'M STARTIN' TO SOUND LIKE DIABLO'S PRESS AGENT!
JUST THE SAME, ANYBODY WANNA BET THAT HIS BUTLER IS A DEAD-RINGER FOR BORIS KARLOFF?
THE FOLLOWING MICROSECOND...
-YEESH!- LOOKS LIKE SOMEBODY DOESN'T WANT ME TO COLLECT!
WHOEVER HE IS, HE MUST NOT KNOW ABOUT MY LOW BOILIN' POINT!
COME TO THINK OF IT, HALF THE CRUMBS WE FIGHT ACT LIKE THEY NEVER HEARD OF ME!
COULD BE I'M THE ONE THAT NEEDS A PRESS AGENT--OR ELSE A GIMMICK!
MAYBE I SHOULD PAINT ALL MY ARROWS ONE COLOR, OR SOMETHIN'!
OH, WELL...
THWAKOOM
BY THE WAY, I FORGOT TO TELL YA--
THAT GRENADE ARROW IS SUPPOSED TO TO BLAST OPEN THE DOOR!
WADDAYA KNOW! IT COLLAPSED LIKE MATCHSTICKS!
THEY JUST DON'T BUILD HAUNTED CASTLES LIKE THEY USETA!
MUST YOU TREAT EVERY-THING LIGHTLY--EVEN SO VITAL A MISSION AS THIS?
LISTEN, LADY-- NOBODY ACCUSES HAWKEYE OF NOT TAKIN' HIS AVENGIN' SERIOUSLY!
AND, NO ONE DID, MY FRIEND!
HURRY, BOTH OF YOU! I CAN RUN NO MORE SLOWLY!
7

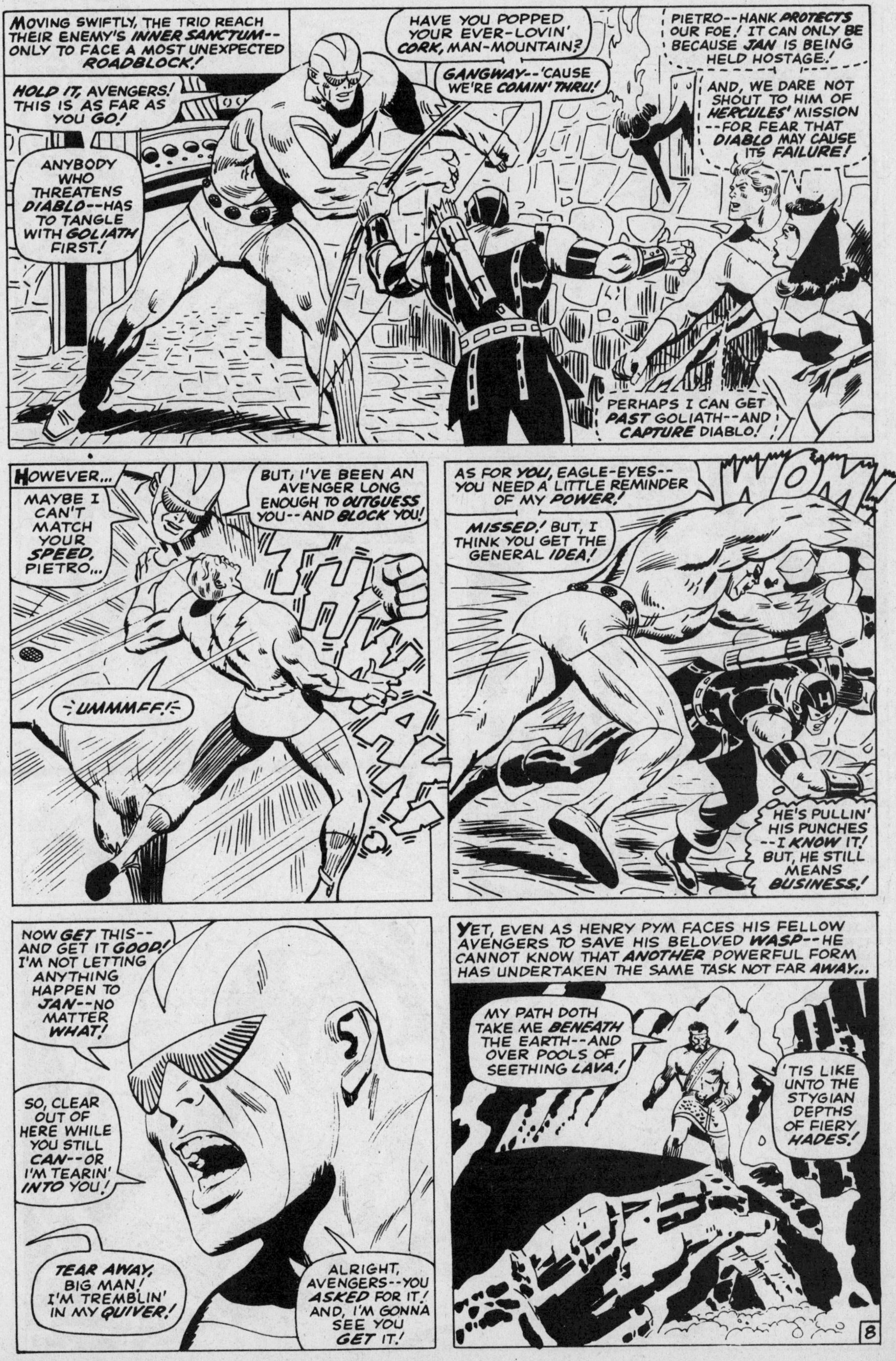

MOVING SWIFTLY, THE TRIO REACH THEIR ENEMY'S INNER SANCTUM--ONLY TO FACE A MOST UNEXPECTED ROADBLOCK!
HOLD IT, AVENGERS! THIS IS AS FAR AS YOU GO!
ANYBODY WHO THREATENS DIABLO--HAS TO TANGLE WITH GOLIATH FIRST!
HAVE YOU POPPED YOUR EVER-LOVIN' CORK, MAN-MOUNTAIN?
GANGWAY--'CAUSE WE'RE COMIN' THRU!
PIETRO--HANK PROTECTS OUR FOE! IT CAN ONLY BE BECAUSE JAN IS BEING HELD HOSTAGE!
AND, WE DARE NOT SHOUT TO HIM OF HERCULES' MISSION--FOR FEAR THAT DIABLO MAY CAUSE ITS FAILURE!
PERHAPS I CAN GET PAST GOLIATH--AND CAPTURE DIABLO!
HOWEVER...
MAYBE I CAN'T MATCH YOUR SPEED, PIETRO...
BUT, I'VE BEEN AN AVENGER LONG ENOUGH TO OUTGUESS YOU--AND BLOCK YOU!
THWAK!
UMMMFF!
AS FOR YOU, EAGLE-EYES--YOU NEED A LITTLE REMINDER OF MY POWER!
WOM!
MISSED! BUT, I THINK YOU GET THE GENERAL IDEA!
HE'S PULLIN' HIS PUNCHES--I KNOW IT! BUT, HE STILL MEANS BUSINESS!
NOW GET THIS--AND GET IT GOOD! I'M NOT LETTING ANYTHING HAPPEN TO JAN--NO MATTER WHAT!
SO, CLEAR OUT OF HERE WHILE YOU STILL CAN--OR I'M TEARIN' INTO YOU!
TEAR AWAY, BIG MAN! I'M TREMBLIN' IN MY QUIVER!
ALRIGHT, AVENGERS--YOU ASKED FOR IT! AND, I'M GONNA SEE YOU GET IT!
YET, EVEN AS HENRY PYM FACES HIS FELLOW AVENGERS TO SAVE HIS BELOVED WASP--HE CANNOT KNOW THAT ANOTHER POWERFUL FORM HAS UNDERTAKEN THE SAME TASK NOT FAR AWAY...
MY PATH DOTH TAKE ME BENEATH THE EARTH--AND OVER POOLS OF SEETHING LAVA!
'TIS LIKE UNTO THE STYGIAN DEPTHS OF FIERY HADES!
8

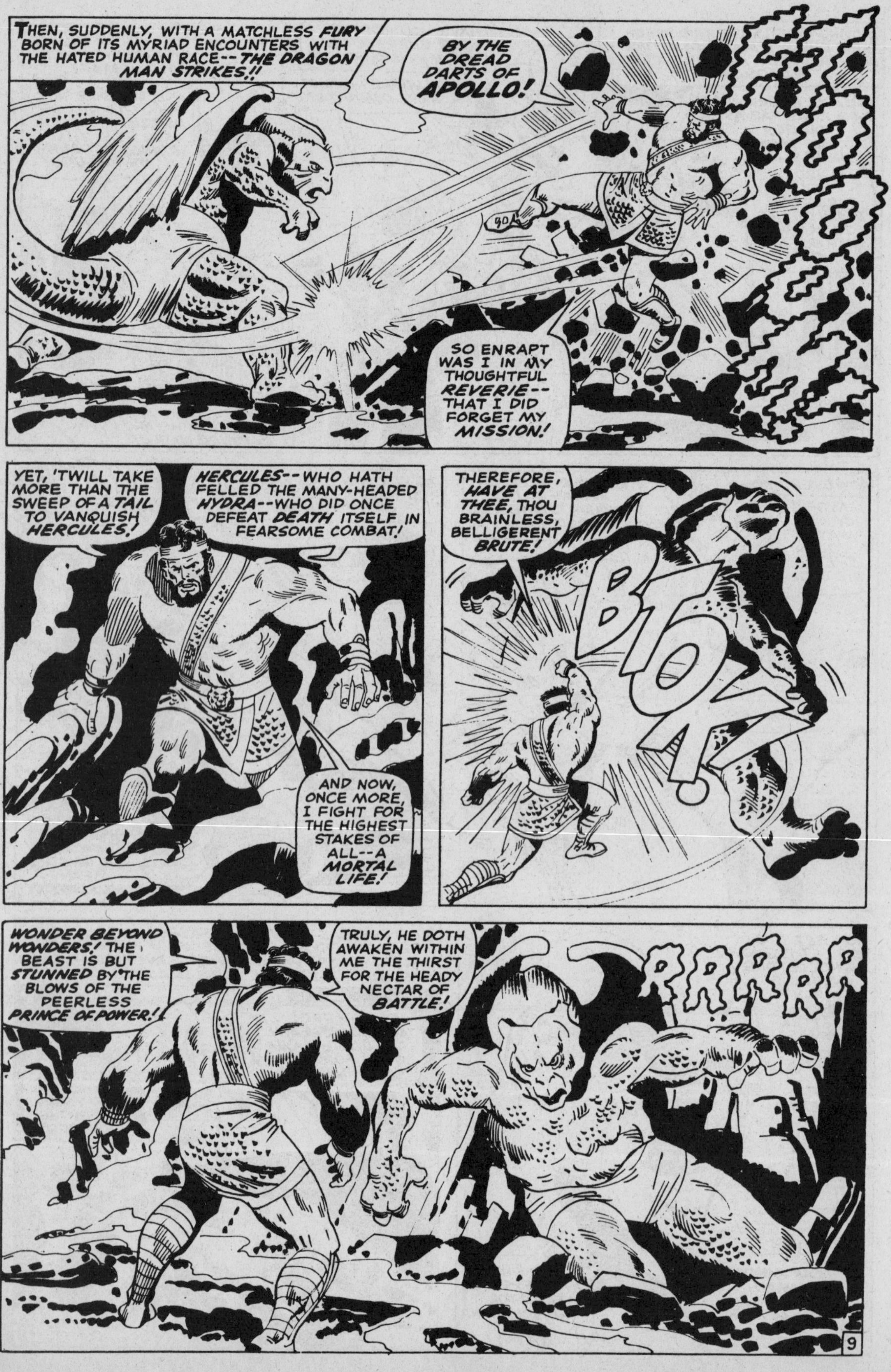
THEN, SUDDENLY, WITH A MATCHLESS FURY BORN OF ITS MYRIAD ENCOUNTERS WITH THE HATED HUMAN RACE--THE DRAGON MAN STRIKES!!
BY THE DREAD DARTS OF APOLLO!
SO ENRAPT WAS I IN MY THOUGHTFUL REVERIE--THAT I DID FORGET MY MISSION!
YET, 'TWILL TAKE MORE THAN THE SWEEP OF A TAIL TO VANQUISH HERCULES!
HERCULES--WHO HATH FELLED THE MANY-HEADED HYDRA--WHO DID ONCE DEFEAT DEATH ITSELF IN FEARSOME COMBAT!
AND NOW, ONCE MORE, I FIGHT FOR THE HIGHEST STAKES OF ALL--A MORTAL LIFE!
THEREFORE, HAVE AT THEE, THOU BRAINLESS, BELLIGERENT BRUTE!
BTOK!
WONDER BEYOND WONDERS! THE BEAST IS BUT STUNNED BY THE BLOWS OF THE PEERLESS PRINCE OF POWER!
TRULY, HE DOTH AWAKEN WITHIN ME THE THIRST FOR THE HEADY NECTAR OF BATTLE!
RRRRR
9

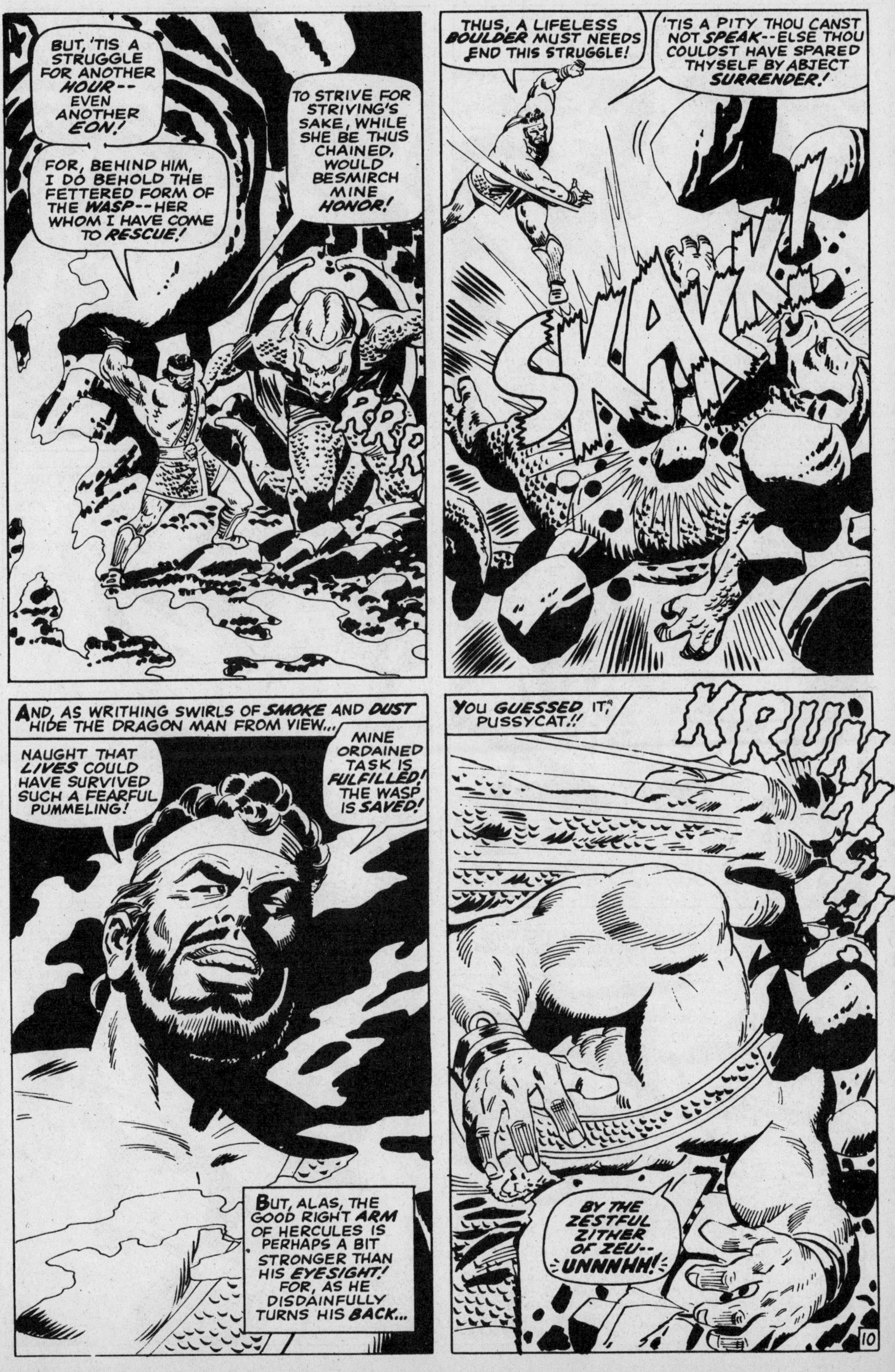
BUT, 'TIS A STRUGGLE FOR ANOTHER HOUR-- EVEN ANOTHER EON!
FOR, BEHIND HIM, I DO BEHOLD THE FETTERED FORM OF THE WASP--HER WHOM I HAVE COME TO RESCUE!
TO STRIVE FOR STRIVING'S SAKE, WHILE SHE BE THUS CHAINED, WOULD BESMIRCH MINE HONOR!
THUS, A LIFELESS BOULDER MUST NEEDS END THIS STRUGGLE!
'TIS A PITY THOU CANST NOT SPEAK--ELSE THOU COULDST HAVE SPARED THYSELF BY ABJECT SURRENDER!
SKAKK!
AND, AS WRITHING SWIRLS OF SMOKE AND DUST HIDE THE DRAGON MAN FROM VIEW...
NAUGHT THAT LIVES COULD HAVE SURVIVED SUCH A FEARFUL PUMMELING!
MINE ORDAINED TASK IS FULFILLED! THE WASP IS SAVED!
BUT, ALAS, THE GOOD RIGHT ARM OF HERCULES IS PERHAPS A BIT STRONGER THAN HIS EYESIGHT! FOR, AS HE DISDAINFULLY TURNS HIS BACK...
YOU GUESSED IT, PUSSYCAT!!
KRUNCH
BY THE ZESTFUL ZITHER OF ZEU-- UNNNHH!
10

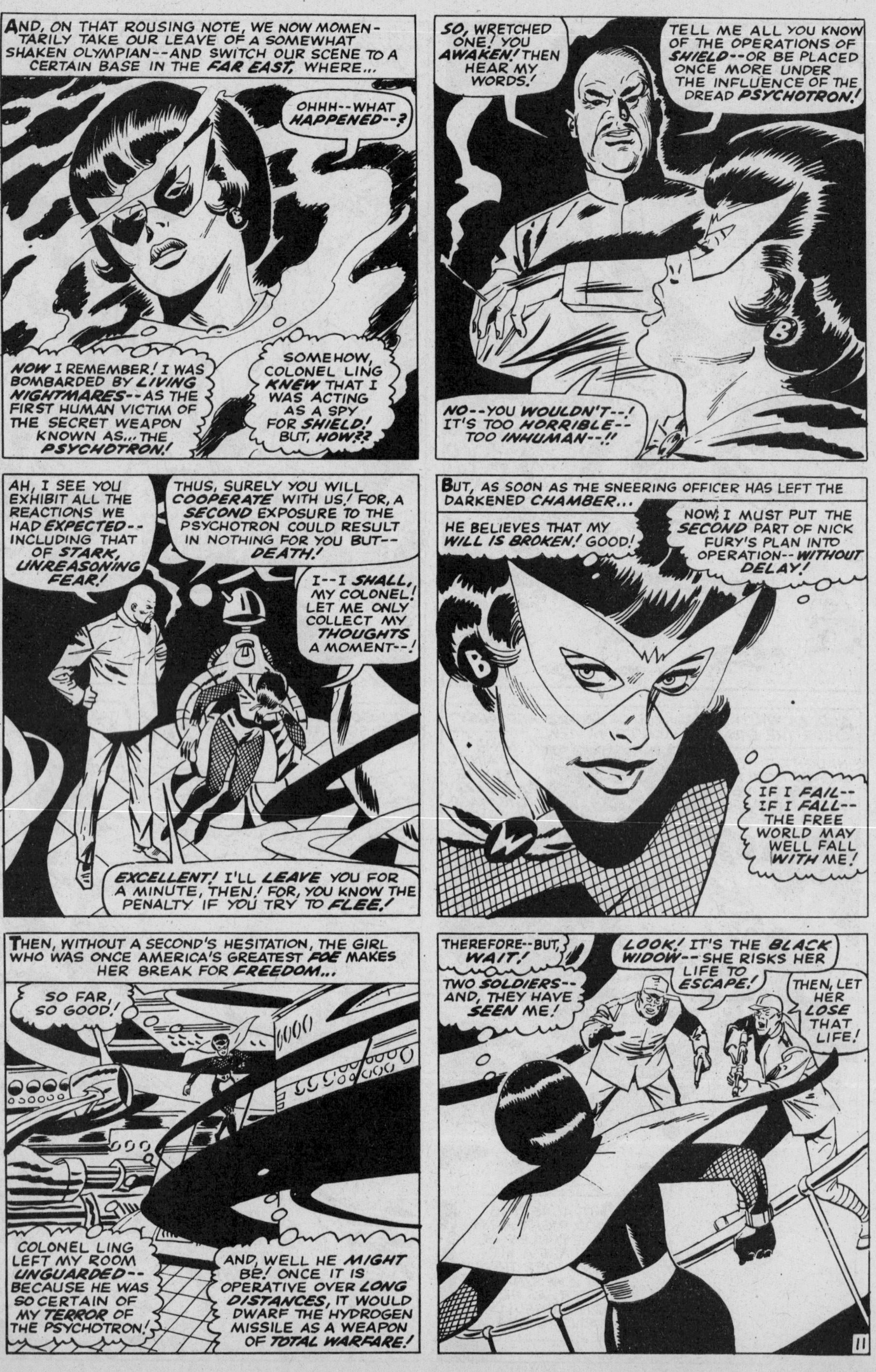
AND, ON THAT ROUSING NOTE, WE NOW MOMENTARILY TAKE OUR LEAVE OF A SOMEWHAT SHAKEN OLYMPIAN--AND SWITCH OUR SCENE TO A CERTAIN BASE IN THE FAR EAST, WHERE...
OHHH--WHAT HAPPENED--?
NOW I REMEMBER! I WAS BOMBARDED BY LIVING NIGHTMARES--AS THE FIRST HUMAN VICTIM OF THE SECRET WEAPON KNOWN AS... THE PSYCHOTRON!
SOMEHOW, COLONEL LING KNEW THAT I WAS ACTING AS A SPY FOR SHIELD! BUT, HOW??
SO, WRETCHED ONE! YOU AWAKEN! THEN HEAR MY WORDS!
TELL ME ALL YOU KNOW OF THE OPERATIONS OF SHIELD--OR BE PLACED ONCE MORE UNDER THE INFLUENCE OF THE DREAD PSYCHOTRON!
NO--YOU WOULDN'T--! IT'S TOO HORRIBLE--TOO INHUMAN--!!
AH, I SEE YOU EXHIBIT ALL THE REACTIONS WE HAD EXPECTED--INCLUDING THAT OF STARK, UNREASONING FEAR!
THUS, SURELY YOU WILL COOPERATE WITH US! FOR, A SECOND EXPOSURE TO THE PSYCHOTRON COULD RESULT IN NOTHING FOR YOU BUT--DEATH!
I--I SHALL, MY COLONEL! LET ME ONLY COLLECT MY THOUGHTS A MOMENT--!
EXCELLENT! I'LL LEAVE YOU FOR A MINUTE, THEN! FOR, YOU KNOW THE PENALTY IF YOU TRY TO FLEE!
BUT, AS SOON AS THE SNEERING OFFICER HAS LEFT THE DARKENED CHAMBER...
HE BELIEVES THAT MY WILL IS BROKEN! GOOD!
NOW, I MUST PUT THE SECOND PART OF NICK FURY'S PLAN INTO OPERATION--WITHOUT DELAY!
IF I FAIL--IF I FALL--THE FREE WORLD MAY WELL FALL WITH ME!
THEN, WITHOUT A SECOND'S HESITATION, THE GIRL WHO WAS ONCE AMERICA'S GREATEST FOE MAKES HER BREAK FOR FREEDOM...
SO FAR, SO GOOD!
COLONEL LING LEFT MY ROOM UNGUARDED--BECAUSE HE WAS SO CERTAIN OF MY TERROR OF THE PSYCHOTRON!
AND, WELL HE MIGHT BE! ONCE IT IS OPERATIVE OVER LONG DISTANCES, IT WOULD DWARF THE HYDROGEN MISSILE AS A WEAPON OF TOTAL WARFARE!
THEREFORE--BUT, WAIT!
TWO SOLDIERS--AND, THEY HAVE SEEN ME!
LOOK! IT'S THE BLACK WIDOW--SHE RISKS HER LIFE TO ESCAPE!
THEN, LET HER LOSE THAT LIFE!
11

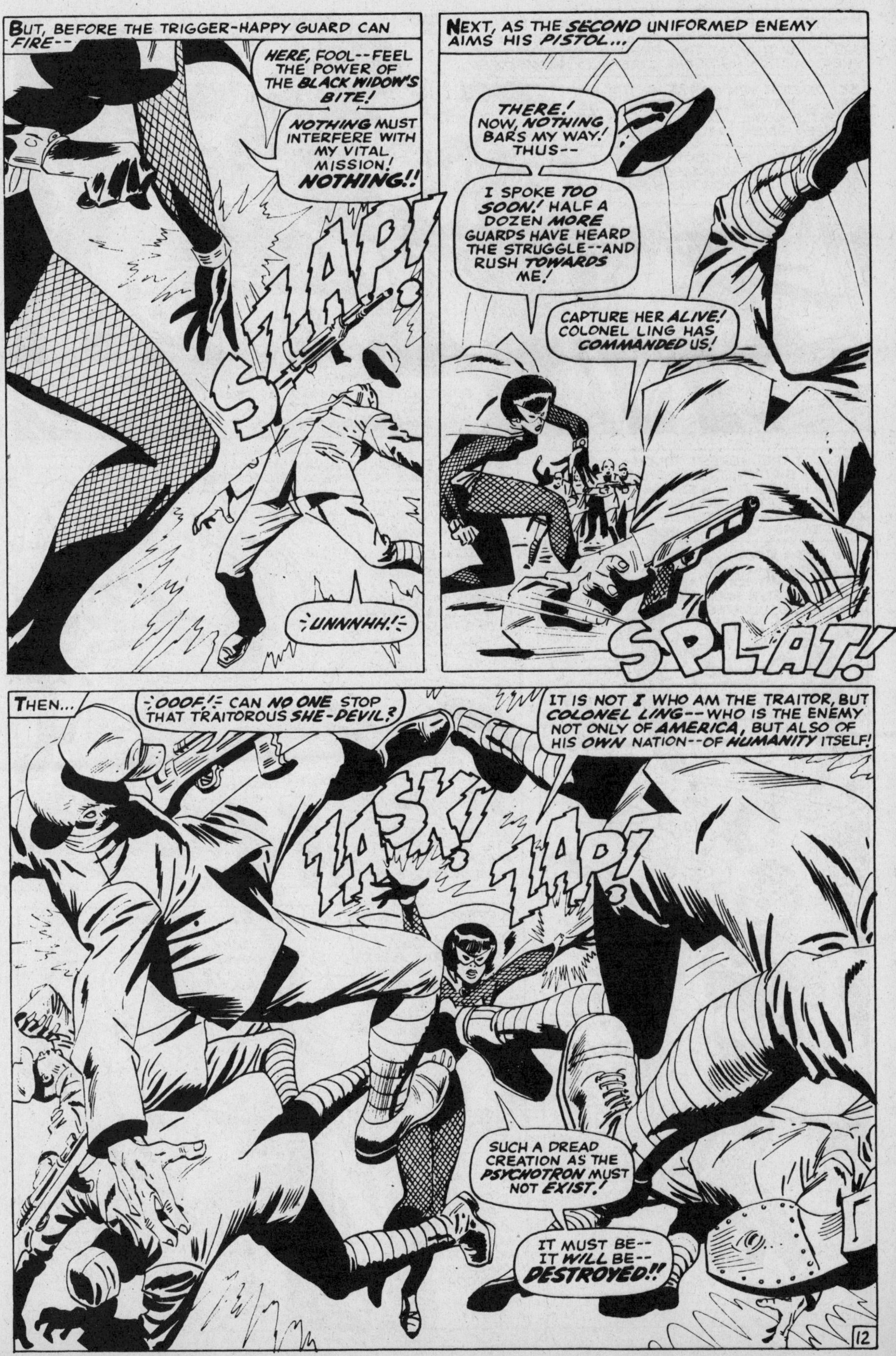

BUT, BEFORE THE TRIGGER-HAPPY GUARD CAN FIRE--
HERE, FOOL--FEEL THE POWER OF THE BLACK WIDOW'S BITE!
NOTHING MUST INTERFERE WITH MY VITAL MISSION! NOTHING!!
ZAP!
S
UNNNHH!
NEXT, AS THE SECOND UNIFORMED ENEMY AIMS HIS PISTOL...
THERE! NOW, NOTHING BARS MY WAY! THUS--
I SPOKE TOO SOON! HALF A DOZEN MORE GUARDS HAVE HEARD THE STRUGGLE--AND RUSH TOWARDS ME!
CAPTURE HER ALIVE! COLONEL LING HAS COMMANDED US!
SPLAT!
THEN...
OOOF! CAN NO ONE STOP THAT TRAITOROUS SHE-DEVIL?
IT IS NOT I WHO AM THE TRAITOR, BUT COLONEL LING--WHO IS THE ENEMY NOT ONLY OF AMERICA, BUT ALSO OF HIS OWN NATION--OF HUMANITY ITSELF!
ZASK!
ZAP!
SUCH A DREAD CREATION AS THE PSYCHOTRON MUST NOT EXIST!
IT MUST BE--IT WILL BE--DESTROYED!!
12

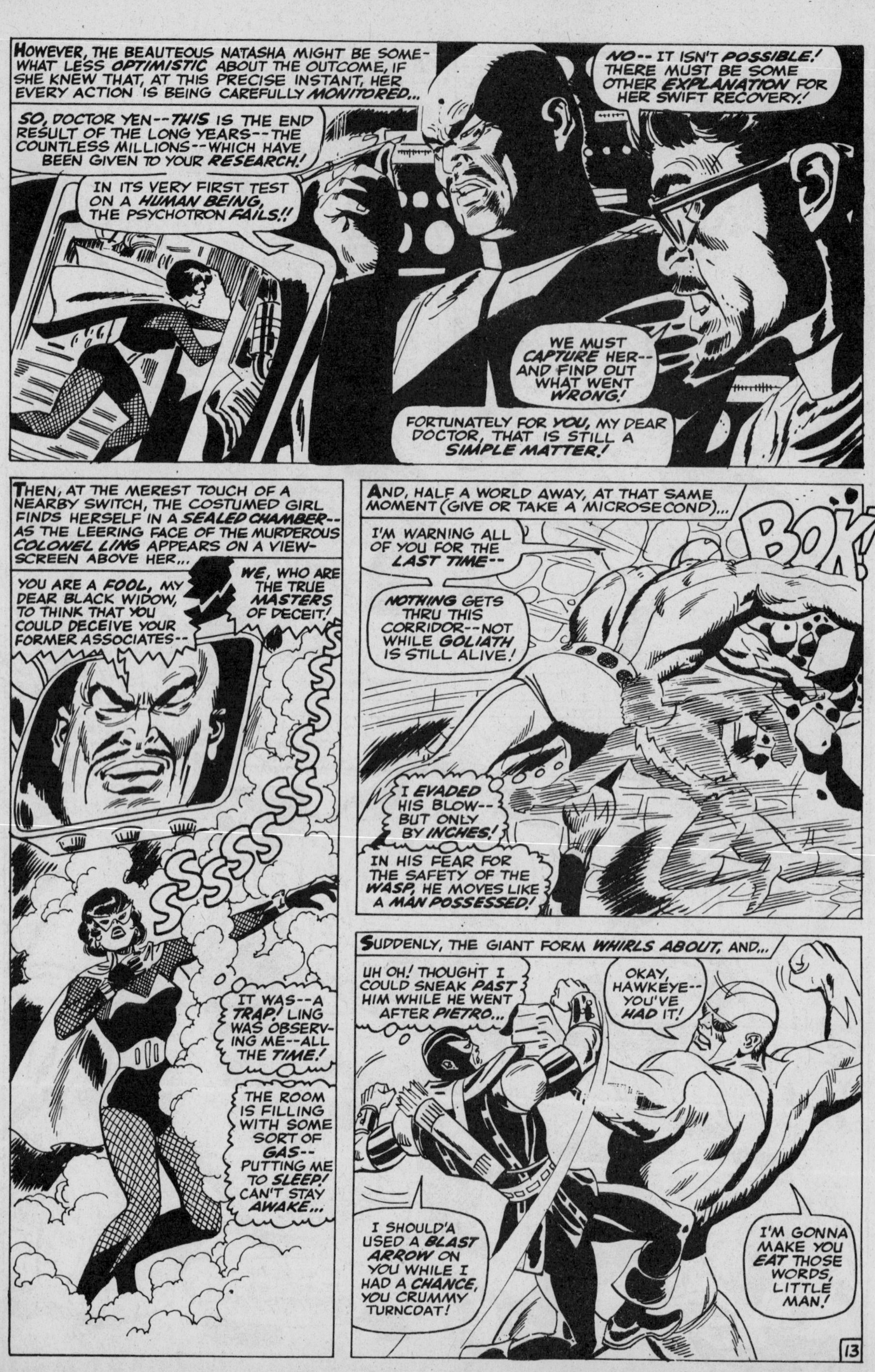
HOWEVER, THE BEAUTEOUS NATASHA MIGHT BE SOMEWHAT LESS OPTIMISTIC ABOUT THE OUTCOME, IF SHE KNEW THAT, AT THIS PRECISE INSTANT, HER EVERY ACTION IS BEING CAREFULLY MONITORED...
SO, DOCTOR YEN--THIS IS THE END RESULT OF THE LONG YEARS--THE COUNTLESS MILLIONS--WHICH HAVE BEEN GIVEN TO YOUR RESEARCH!
IN ITS VERY FIRST TEST ON A HUMAN BEING, THE PSYCHOTRON FAILS!!
NO--IT ISN'T POSSIBLE! THERE MUST BE SOME OTHER EXPLANATION FOR HER SWIFT RECOVERY!
WE MUST CAPTURE HER--AND FIND OUT WHAT WENT WRONG!
FORTUNATELY FOR YOU, MY DEAR DOCTOR, THAT IS STILL A SIMPLE MATTER!
THEN, AT THE MEREST TOUCH OF A NEARBY SWITCH, THE COSTUMED GIRL FINDS HERSELF IN A SEALED CHAMBER--AS THE LEERING FACE OF THE MURDEROUS COLONEL LING APPEARS ON A VIEW-SCREEN ABOVE HER...
YOU ARE A FOOL, MY DEAR BLACK WIDOW, TO THINK THAT YOU COULD DECEIVE YOUR FORMER ASSOCIATES--
WE, WHO ARE THE TRUE MASTERS OF DECEIT!
SSSSSSSSSSSSSS
IT WAS--A TRAP! LING WAS OBSERVING ME--ALL THE TIME!
THE ROOM IS FILLING WITH SOME SORT OF GAS--PUTTING ME TO SLEEP! CAN'T STAY AWAKE...
AND, HALF A WORLD AWAY, AT THAT SAME MOMENT (GIVE OR TAKE A MICROSECOND)...
BOK!
I'M WARNING ALL OF YOU FOR THE LAST TIME--
NOTHING GETS THRU THIS CORRIDOR--NOT WHILE GOLIATH IS STILL ALIVE!
I EVADED HIS BLOW--BUT ONLY BY INCHES!
IN HIS FEAR FOR THE SAFETY OF THE WASP, HE MOVES LIKE A MAN POSSESSED!
SUDDENLY, THE GIANT FORM WHIRLS ABOUT, AND...
UH OH! THOUGHT I COULD SNEAK PAST HIM WHILE HE WENT AFTER PIETRO...
OKAY, HAWKEYE--YOU'VE HAD IT!
I SHOULD'A USED A BLAST ARROW ON YOU WHILE I HAD A CHANCE, YOU CRUMMY TURNCOAT!
I'M GONNA MAKE YOU EAT THOSE WORDS, LITTLE MAN!
13

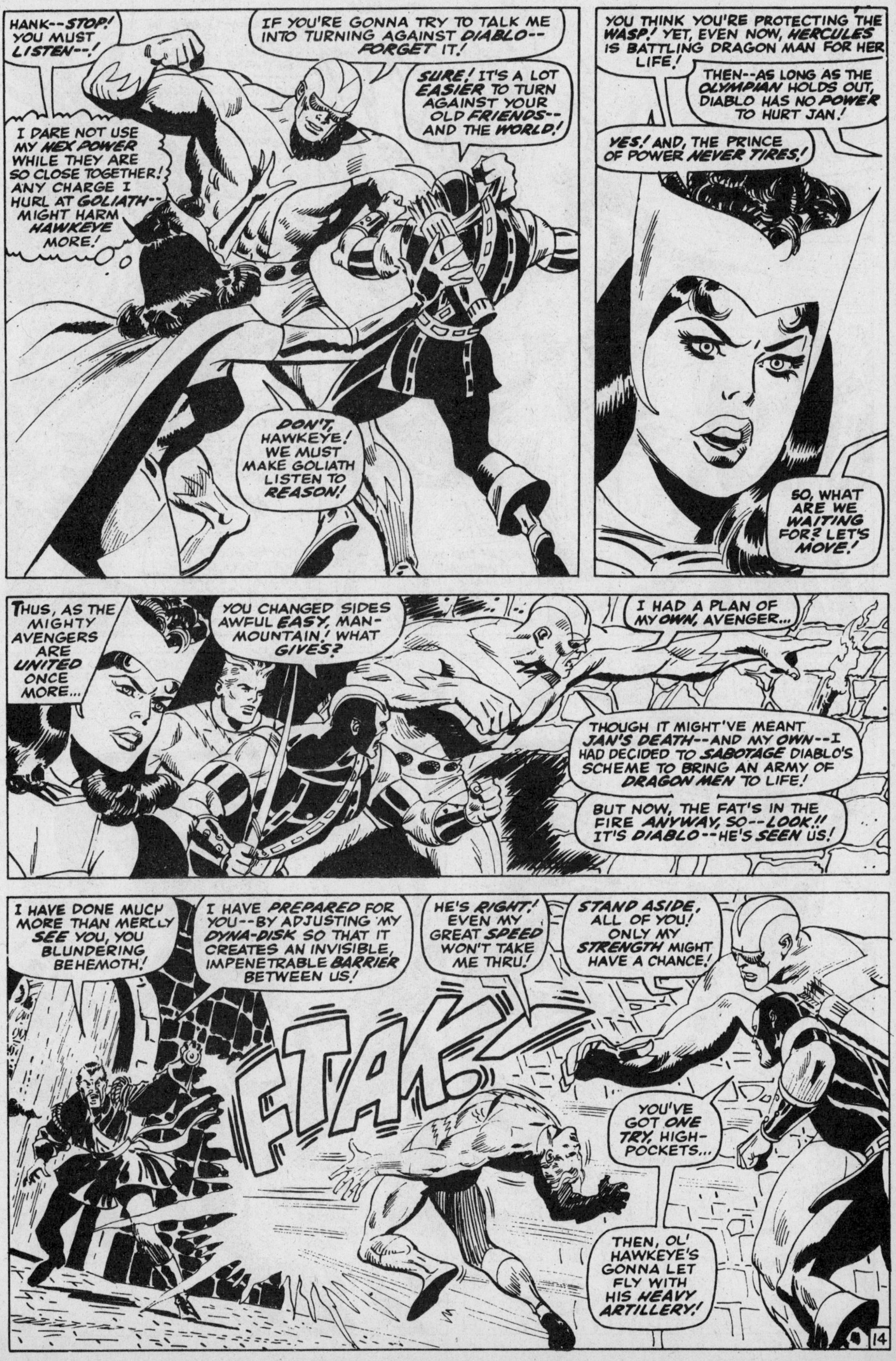

HANK--STOP! YOU MUST LISTEN--!
IF YOU'RE GONNA TRY TO TALK ME INTO TURNING AGAINST DIABLO-- FORGET IT!
SURE! IT'S A LOT EASIER TO TURN AGAINST YOUR OLD FRIENDS-- AND THE WORLD!
I DARE NOT USE MY HEX POWER WHILE THEY ARE SO CLOSE TOGETHER! ANY CHARGE I HURL AT GOLIATH-- MIGHT HARM HAWKEYE MORE!
DON'T, HAWKEYE! WE MUST MAKE GOLIATH LISTEN TO REASON!
YOU THINK YOU'RE PROTECTING THE WASP! YET, EVEN NOW, HERCULES IS BATTLING DRAGON MAN FOR HER LIFE!
THEN--AS LONG AS THE OLYMPIAN HOLDS OUT, DIABLO HAS NO POWER TO HURT JAN!
YES! AND, THE PRINCE OF POWER NEVER TIRES!
SO, WHAT ARE WE WAITING FOR? LET'S MOVE!
THUS, AS THE MIGHTY AVENGERS ARE UNITED ONCE MORE...
YOU CHANGED SIDES AWFUL EASY, MAN-MOUNTAIN! WHAT GIVES?
I HAD A PLAN OF MY OWN, AVENGER...
THOUGH IT MIGHT'VE MEANT JAN'S DEATH--AND MY OWN--I HAD DECIDED TO SABOTAGE DIABLO'S SCHEME TO BRING AN ARMY OF DRAGON MEN TO LIFE!
BUT NOW, THE FAT'S IN THE FIRE ANYWAY, SO--LOOK!! IT'S DIABLO--HE'S SEEN US!
I HAVE DONE MUCH MORE THAN MERELY SEE YOU, YOU BLUNDERING BEHEMOTH!
I HAVE PREPARED FOR YOU--BY ADJUSTING MY DYNA-DISK SO THAT IT CREATES AN INVISIBLE, IMPENETRABLE BARRIER BETWEEN US!
HE'S RIGHT! EVEN MY GREAT SPEED WON'T TAKE ME THRU!
STAND ASIDE, ALL OF YOU! ONLY MY STRENGTH MIGHT HAVE A CHANCE!
FTAK
YOU'VE GOT ONE TRY, HIGH-POCKETS...
THEN, OL' HAWKEYE'S GONNA LET FLY WITH HIS HEAVY ARTILLERY!
14

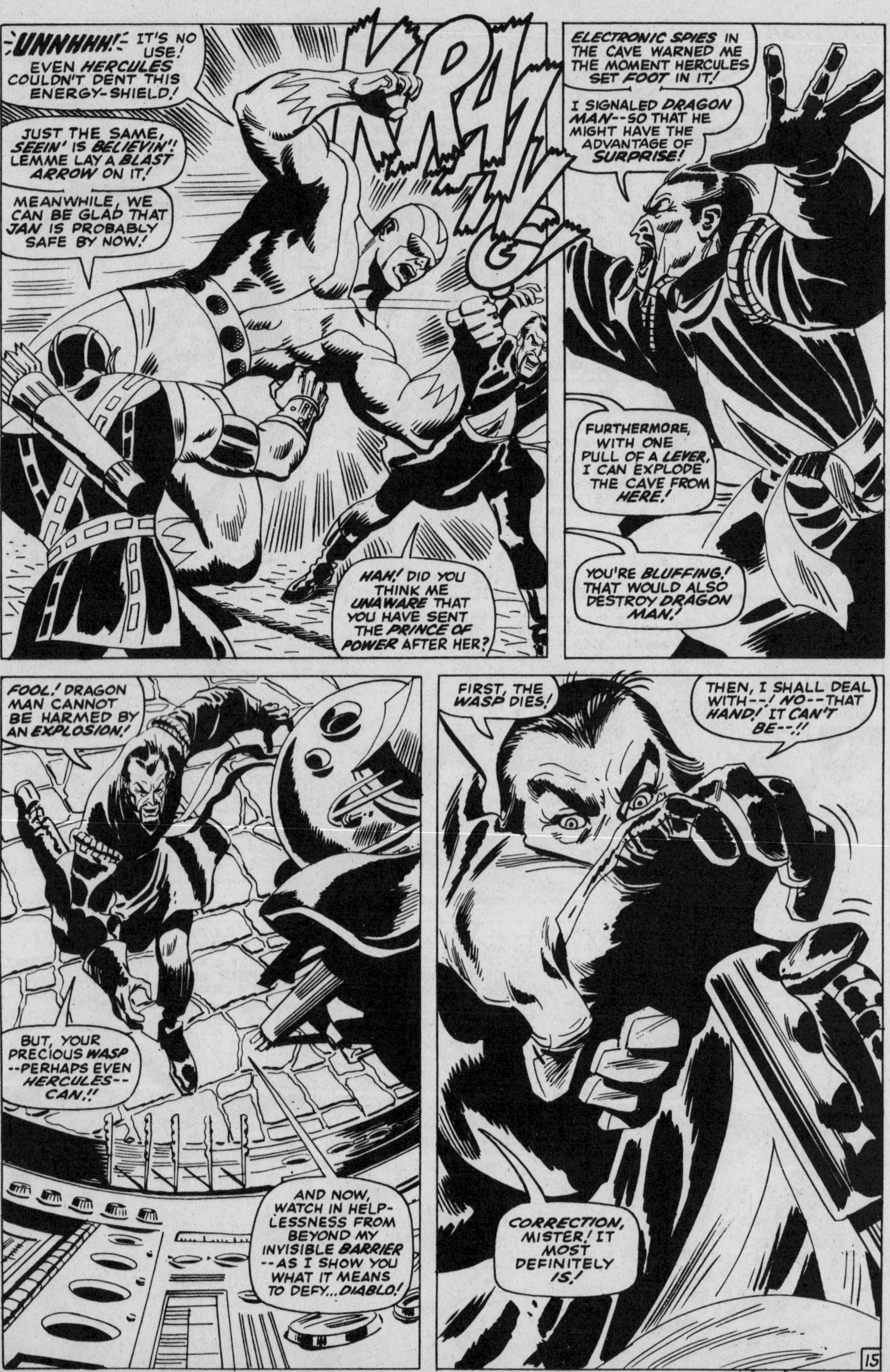
UNNHHH! IT'S NO USE! EVEN HERCULES COULDN'T DENT THIS ENERGY-SHIELD!
JUST THE SAME, SEEIN' IS BELIEVIN'! LEMME LAY A BLAST ARROW ON IT!
MEANWHILE, WE CAN BE GLAD THAT JAN IS PROBABLY SAFE BY NOW!
KRAAANG
HAH! DID YOU THINK ME UNAWARE THAT YOU HAVE SENT THE PRINCE OF POWER AFTER HER?
ELECTRONIC SPIES IN THE CAVE WARNED ME THE MOMENT HERCULES SET FOOT IN IT!
I SIGNALED DRAGON MAN--SO THAT HE MIGHT HAVE THE ADVANTAGE OF SURPRISE!
FURTHERMORE, WITH ONE PULL OF A LEVER, I CAN EXPLODE THE CAVE FROM HERE!
YOU'RE BLUFFING! THAT WOULD ALSO DESTROY DRAGON MAN!
FOOL! DRAGON MAN CANNOT BE HARMED BY AN EXPLOSION!
BUT, YOUR PRECIOUS WASP --PERHAPS EVEN HERCULES-- CAN!!
AND NOW, WATCH IN HELP-LESSNESS FROM BEYOND MY INVISIBLE BARRIER --AS I SHOW YOU WHAT IT MEANS TO DEFY...DIABLO!
FIRST, THE WASP DIES!
THEN, I SHALL DEAL WITH--! NO--THAT HAND! IT CAN'T BE--!!
CORRECTION, MISTER! IT MOST DEFINITELY IS!

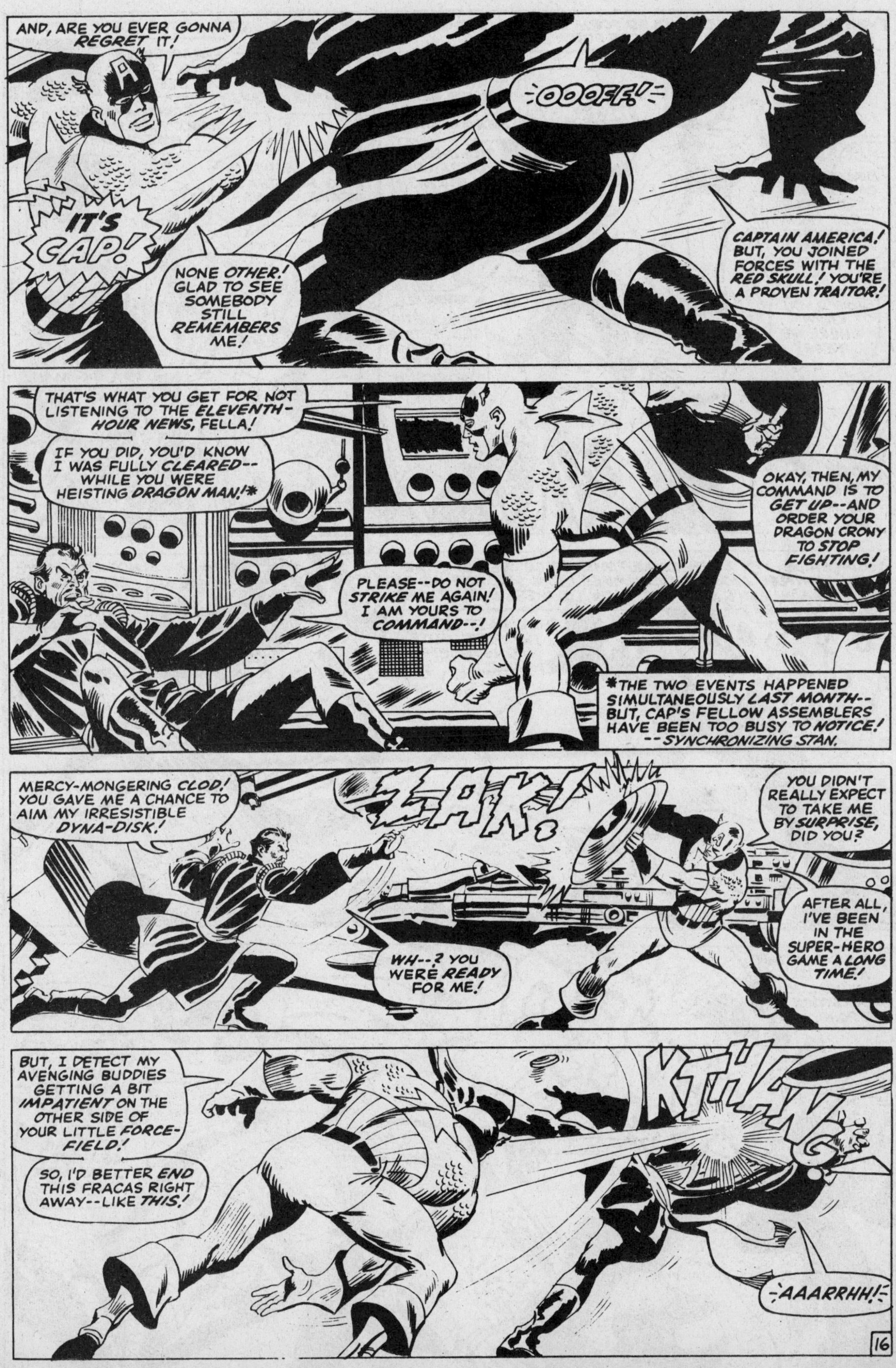
AND, ARE YOU EVER GONNA REGRET IT!
OOOFF!
IT'S CAP!
NONE OTHER! GLAD TO SEE SOMEBODY STILL REMEMBERS ME!
CAPTAIN AMERICA! BUT, YOU JOINED FORCES WITH THE RED SKULL! YOU'RE A PROVEN TRAITOR!
THAT'S WHAT YOU GET FOR NOT LISTENING TO THE ELEVENTH-HOUR NEWS, FELLA!
IF YOU DID, YOU'D KNOW I WAS FULLY CLEARED-- WHILE YOU WERE HEISTING DRAGON MAN!*
OKAY, THEN, MY COMMAND IS TO GET UP--AND ORDER YOUR DRAGON CRONY TO STOP FIGHTING!
PLEASE--DO NOT STRIKE ME AGAIN! I AM YOURS TO COMMAND--!
*THE TWO EVENTS HAPPENED SIMULTANEOUSLY LAST MONTH-- BUT, CAP'S FELLOW ASSEMBLERS HAVE BEEN TOO BUSY TO NOTICE! --SYNCHRONIZING STAN.
MERCY-MONGERING CLOD! YOU GAVE ME A CHANCE TO AIM MY IRRESISTIBLE DYNA-DISK!
ZAK!
YOU DIDN'T REALLY EXPECT TO TAKE ME BY SURPRISE, DID YOU?
WH--? YOU WERE READY FOR ME!
AFTER ALL, I'VE BEEN IN THE SUPER-HERO GAME A LONG TIME!
BUT, I DETECT MY AVENGING BUDDIES GETTING A BIT IMPATIENT ON THE OTHER SIDE OF YOUR LITTLE FORCE-FIELD!
SO, I'D BETTER END THIS FRACAS RIGHT AWAY--LIKE THIS!
KTHANG
AAARRHH!
16

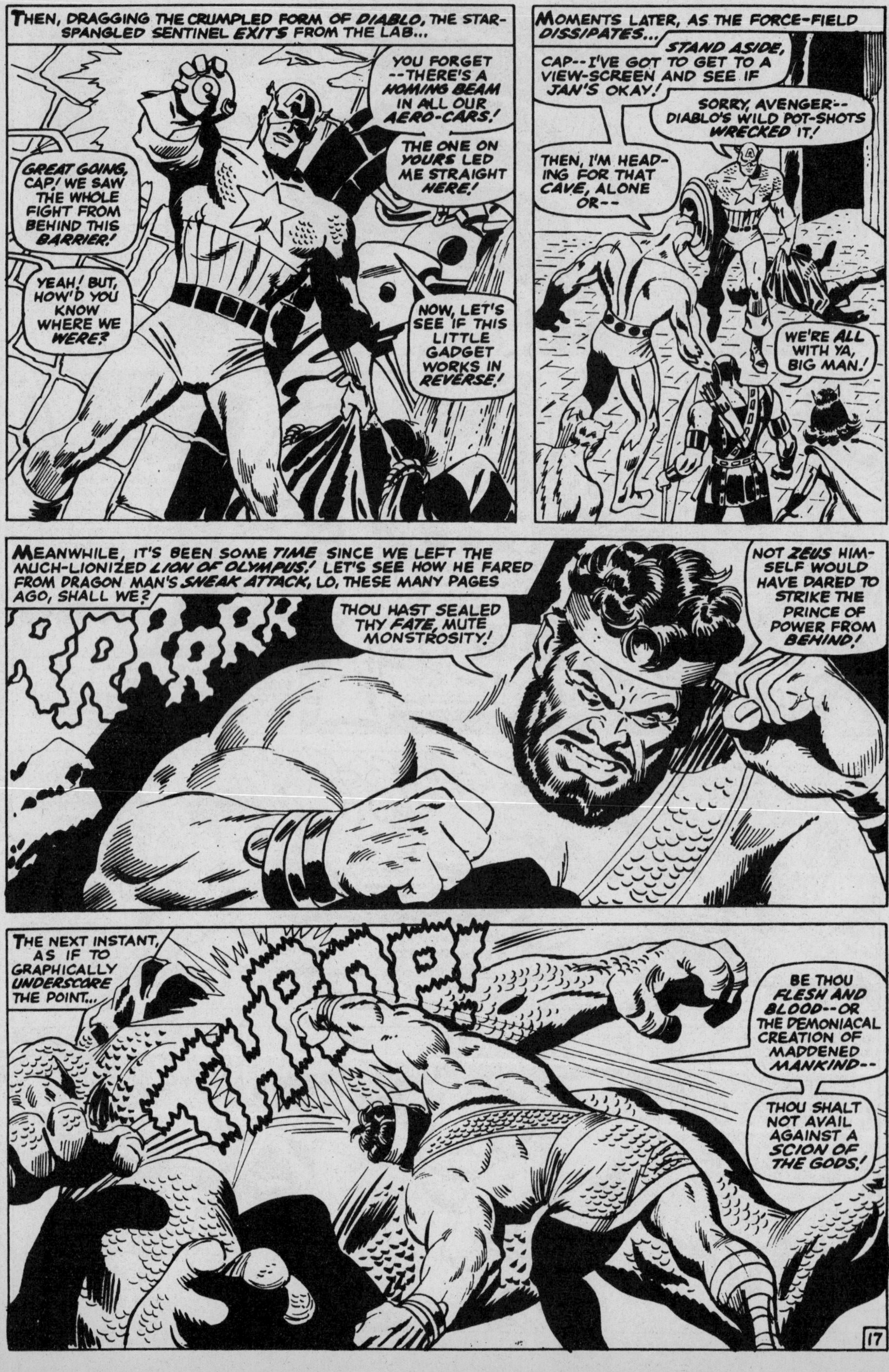
THEN, DRAGGING THE CRUMPLED FORM OF DIABLO, THE STAR-SPANGLED SENTINEL EXITS FROM THE LAB...
GREAT GOING, CAP! WE SAW THE WHOLE FIGHT FROM BEHIND THIS BARRIER!
YEAH! BUT, HOW'D YOU KNOW WHERE WE WERE?
YOU FORGET --THERE'S A HOMING BEAM IN ALL OUR AERO-CARS!
THE ONE ON YOURS LED ME STRAIGHT HERE!
NOW, LET'S SEE IF THIS LITTLE GADGET WORKS IN REVERSE!
MOMENTS LATER, AS THE FORCE-FIELD DISSIPATES...
STAND ASIDE, CAP--I'VE GOT TO GET TO A VIEW-SCREEN AND SEE IF JAN'S OKAY!
SORRY, AVENGER--DIABLO'S WILD POT-SHOTS WRECKED IT!
THEN, I'M HEADING FOR THAT CAVE, ALONE OR--
WE'RE ALL WITH YA, BIG MAN!
MEANWHILE, IT'S BEEN SOME TIME SINCE WE LEFT THE MUCH-LIONIZED LION OF OLYMPUS! LET'S SEE HOW HE FARED FROM DRAGON MAN'S SNEAK ATTACK, LO, THESE MANY PAGES AGO, SHALL WE?
RARRR
THOU HAST SEALED THY FATE, MUTE MONSTROSITY!
NOT ZEUS HIMSELF WOULD HAVE DARED TO STRIKE THE PRINCE OF POWER FROM BEHIND!
THE NEXT INSTANT, AS IF TO GRAPHICALLY UNDERSCORE THE POINT...
THPOOM!
BE THOU FLESH AND BLOOD--OR THE DEMONIACAL CREATION OF MADDENED MANKIND--
THOU SHALT NOT AVAIL AGAINST A SCION OF THE GODS!
17

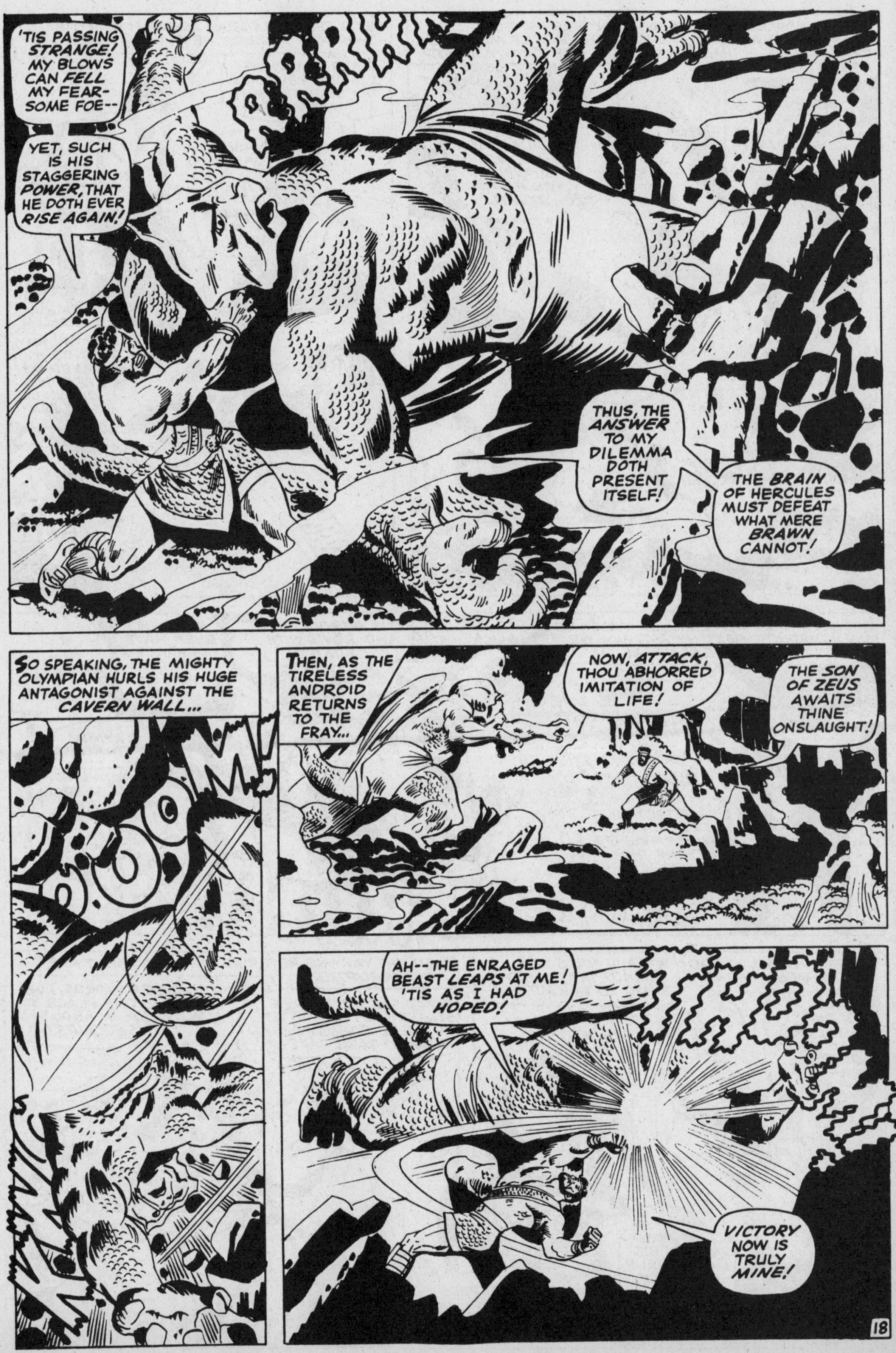
'TIS PASSING STRANGE! MY BLOWS CAN FELL MY FEARSOME FOE--
YET, SUCH IS HIS STAGGERING POWER, THAT HE DOTH EVER RISE AGAIN!
THUS, THE ANSWER TO MY DILEMMA DOTH PRESENT ITSELF!
THE BRAIN OF HERCULES MUST DEFEAT WHAT MERE BRAWN CANNOT!
SO SPEAKING, THE MIGHTY OLYMPIAN HURLS HIS HUGE ANTAGONIST AGAINST THE CAVERN WALL...
BOOOM!
THEN, AS THE TIRELESS ANDROID RETURNS TO THE FRAY...
NOW, ATTACK, THOU ABHORRED IMITATION OF LIFE!
THE SON OF ZEUS AWAITS THINE ONSLAUGHT!
AH--THE ENRAGED BEAST LEAPS AT ME! 'TIS AS I HAD HOPED!
VICTORY NOW IS TRULY MINE!
18

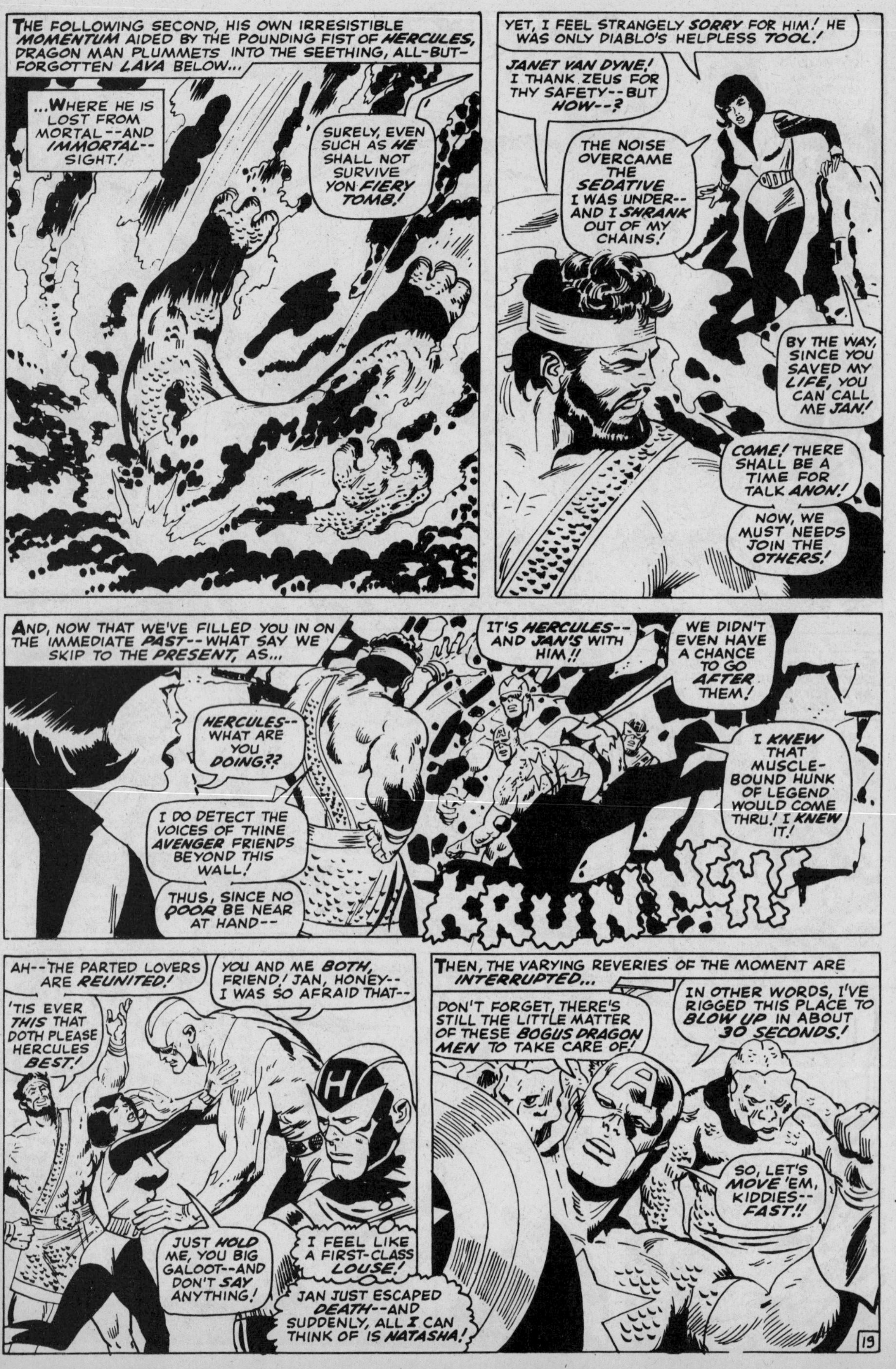
THE FOLLOWING SECOND, HIS OWN IRRESISTIBLE MOMENTUM AIDED BY THE POUNDING FIST OF HERCULES, DRAGON MAN PLUMMETS INTO THE SEETHING, ALL-BUT-FORGOTTEN LAVA BELOW...
...WHERE HE IS LOST FROM MORTAL--AND IMMORTAL--SIGHT!
SURELY, EVEN SUCH AS HE SHALL NOT SURVIVE YON FIERY TOMB!
YET, I FEEL STRANGELY SORRY FOR HIM! HE WAS ONLY DIABLO'S HELPLESS TOOL!
JANET VAN DYNE! I THANK ZEUS FOR THY SAFETY--BUT HOW--?
THE NOISE OVERCAME THE SEDATIVE I WAS UNDER--AND I SHRANK OUT OF MY CHAINS!
BY THE WAY, SINCE YOU SAVED MY LIFE, YOU CAN CALL ME JAN!
COME! THERE SHALL BE A TIME FOR TALK ANON!
NOW, WE MUST NEEDS JOIN THE OTHERS!
AND, NOW THAT WE'VE FILLED YOU IN ON THE IMMEDIATE PAST--WHAT SAY WE SKIP TO THE PRESENT, AS...
HERCULES--WHAT ARE YOU DOING??
I DO DETECT THE VOICES OF THINE AVENGER FRIENDS BEYOND THIS WALL!
THUS, SINCE NO DOOR BE NEAR AT HAND--
IT'S HERCULES--AND JAN'S WITH HIM!!
WE DIDN'T EVEN HAVE A CHANCE TO GO AFTER THEM!
I KNEW THAT MUSCLE-BOUND HUNK OF LEGEND WOULD COME THRU! I KNEW IT!
KRUNNCH!
AH--THE PARTED LOVERS ARE REUNITED!
'TIS EVER THIS THAT DOTH PLEASE HERCULES BEST!
YOU AND ME BOTH, FRIEND! JAN, HONEY--I WAS SO AFRAID THAT--
JUST HOLD ME, YOU BIG GALOOT--AND DON'T SAY ANYTHING!
I FEEL LIKE A FIRST-CLASS LOUSE!
JAN JUST ESCAPED DEATH--AND SUDDENLY, ALL I CAN THINK OF IS NATASHA!
THEN, THE VARYING REVERIES OF THE MOMENT ARE INTERRUPTED...
DON'T FORGET, THERE'S STILL THE LITTLE MATTER OF THESE BOGUS DRAGON MEN TO TAKE CARE OF!
IN OTHER WORDS, I'VE RIGGED THIS PLACE TO BLOW UP IN ABOUT 30 SECONDS!
SO, LET'S MOVE 'EM, KIDDIES--FAST!!
19

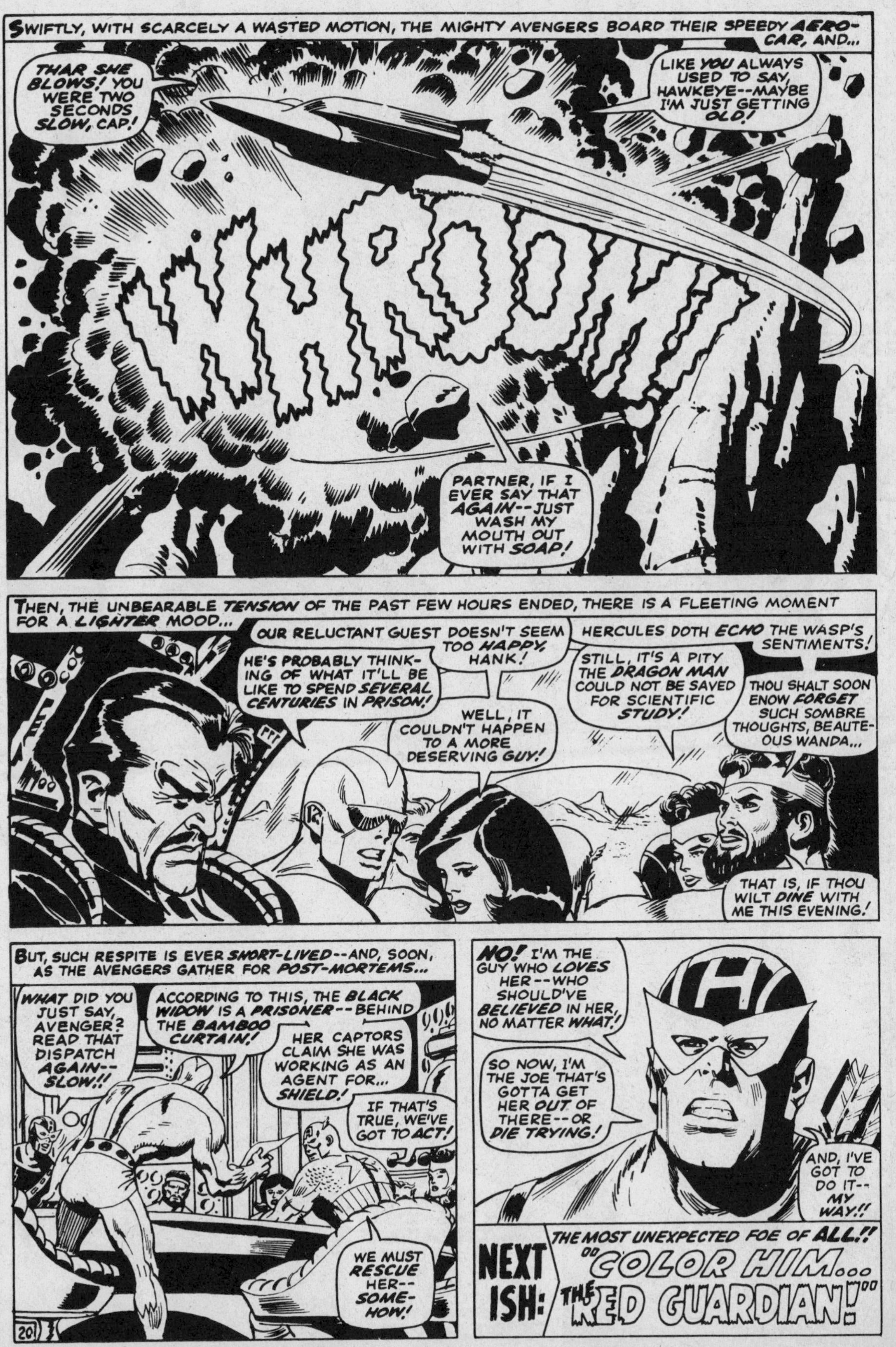
SWIFTLY, WITH SCARCELY A WASTED MOTION, THE MIGHTY AVENGERS BOARD THEIR SPEEDY AERO-CAR, AND...
THAR SHE BLOWS! YOU WERE TWO SECONDS SLOW, CAP!
LIKE YOU ALWAYS USED TO SAY, HAWKEYE--MAYBE I'M JUST GETTING OLD!
WHROOM!
PARTNER, IF I EVER SAY THAT AGAIN--JUST WASH MY MOUTH OUT WITH SOAP!
THEN, THE UNBEARABLE TENSION OF THE PAST FEW HOURS ENDED, THERE IS A FLEETING MOMENT FOR A LIGHTER MOOD...
OUR RELUCTANT GUEST DOESN'T SEEM TOO HAPPY, HANK!
HE'S PROBABLY THINKING OF WHAT IT'LL BE LIKE TO SPEND SEVERAL CENTURIES IN PRISON!
WELL, IT COULDN'T HAPPEN TO A MORE DESERVING GUY!
HERCULES DOTH ECHO THE WASP'S SENTIMENTS!
STILL, IT'S A PITY THE DRAGON MAN COULD NOT BE SAVED FOR SCIENTIFIC STUDY!
THOU SHALT SOON ENOW FORGET SUCH SOMBRE THOUGHTS, BEAUTEOUS WANDA...
THAT IS, IF THOU WILT DINE WITH ME THIS EVENING!
BUT, SUCH RESPITE IS EVER SHORT-LIVED--AND, SOON, AS THE AVENGERS GATHER FOR POST-MORTEMS...
WHAT DID YOU JUST SAY, AVENGER? READ THAT DISPATCH AGAIN--SLOW!!
ACCORDING TO THIS, THE BLACK WIDOW IS A PRISONER--BEHIND THE BAMBOO CURTAIN!
HER CAPTORS CLAIM SHE WAS WORKING AS AN AGENT FOR... SHIELD!
IF THAT'S TRUE, WE'VE GOT TO ACT!
WE MUST RESCUE HER--SOME-HOW!
20
NO! I'M THE GUY WHO LOVES HER--WHO SHOULD'VE BELIEVED IN HER, NO MATTER WHAT!
SO NOW, I'M THE JOE THAT'S GOTTA GET HER OUT OF THERE--OR DIE TRYING!
AND, I'VE GOT TO DO IT--MY WAY!!
NEXT ISH:
THE MOST UNEXPECTED FOE OF ALL!!
"COLOR HIM... THE RED GUARDIAN!"

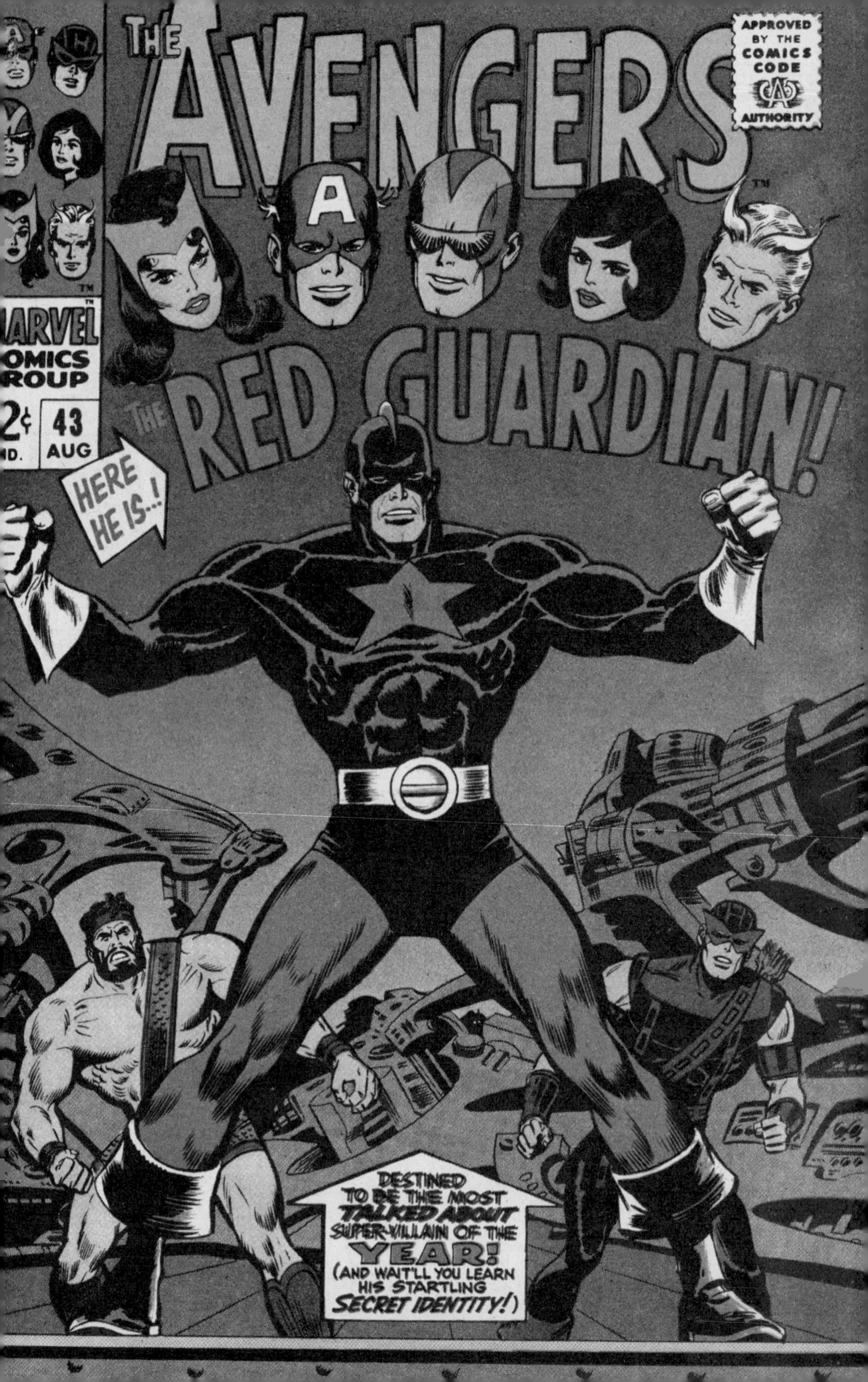
THE AVENGERS
APPROVED BY THE COMICS CODE AUTHORITY
MARVEL COMICS GROUP
43 AUG
THE RED GUARDIAN!
HERE HE IS..!
DESTINED TO BE THE MOST TALKED ABOUT SUPER-VILLAIN OF THE YEAR!
(AND WAIT'LL YOU LEARN HIS STARTLING SECRET IDENTITY!)

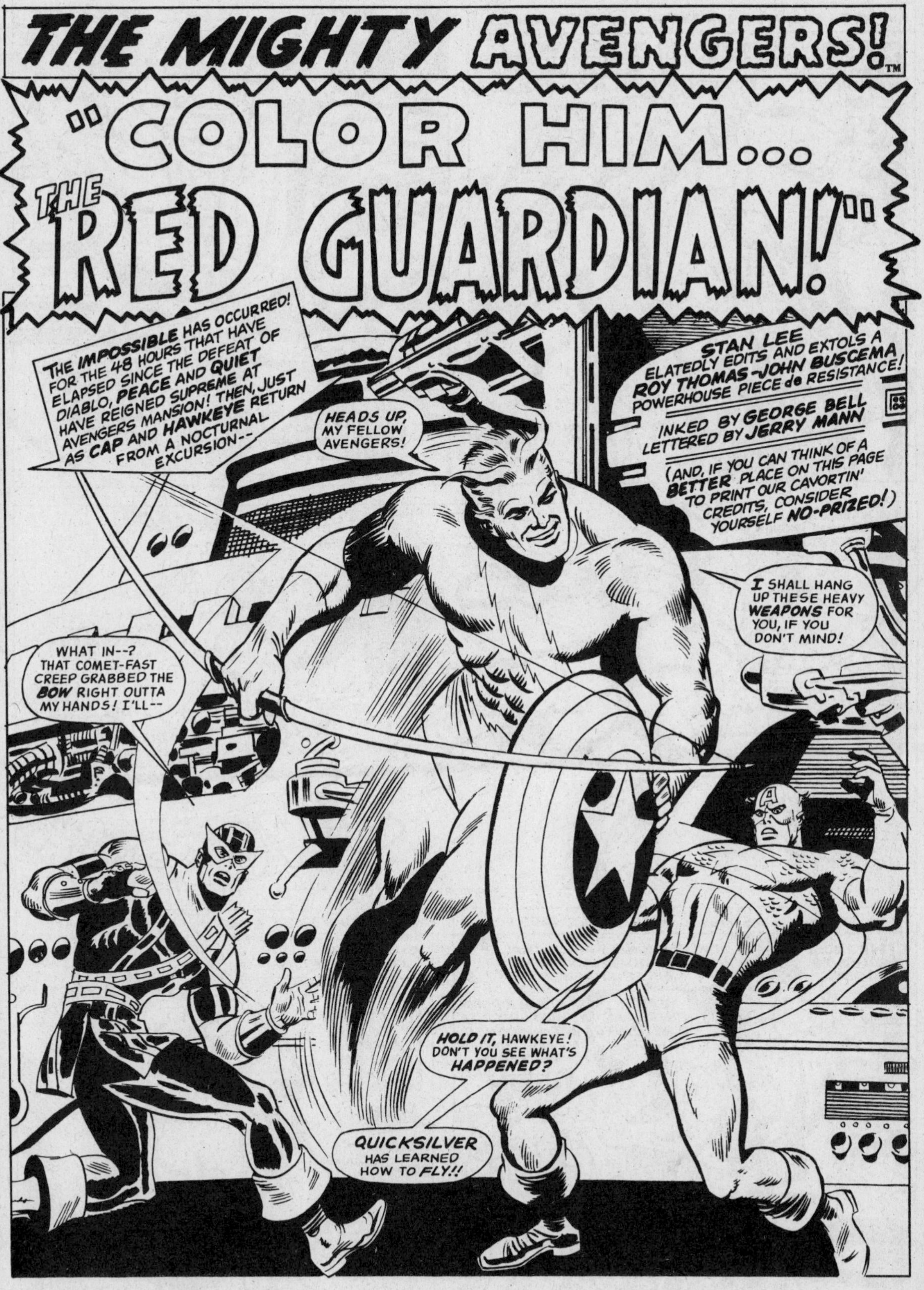
THE MIGHTY AVENGERS!™
"COLOR HIM... THE RED GUARDIAN!"
THE IMPOSSIBLE HAS OCCURRED! FOR THE 48 HOURS THAT HAVE ELAPSED SINCE THE DEFEAT OF DIABLO, PEACE AND QUIET HAVE REIGNED SUPREME AT AVENGERS MANSION! THEN, JUST AS CAP AND HAWKEYE RETURN FROM A NOCTURNAL EXCURSION--
STAN LEE ELATEDLY EDITS AND EXTOLS A ROY THOMAS-JOHN BUSCEMA POWERHOUSE PIECE de RESISTANCE!
INKED BY GEORGE BELL
LETTERED BY JERRY MANN
(AND, IF YOU CAN THINK OF A BETTER PLACE ON THIS PAGE TO PRINT OUR CAVORTIN' CREDITS, CONSIDER YOURSELF NO-PRIZED!)
HEADS UP, MY FELLOW AVENGERS!
I SHALL HANG UP THESE HEAVY WEAPONS FOR YOU, IF YOU DON'T MIND!
WHAT IN--? THAT COMET-FAST CREEP GRABBED THE BOW RIGHT OUTTA MY HANDS! I'LL--
HOLD IT, HAWKEYE! DON'T YOU SEE WHAT'S HAPPENED?
QUICKSILVER HAS LEARNED HOW TO FLY!!

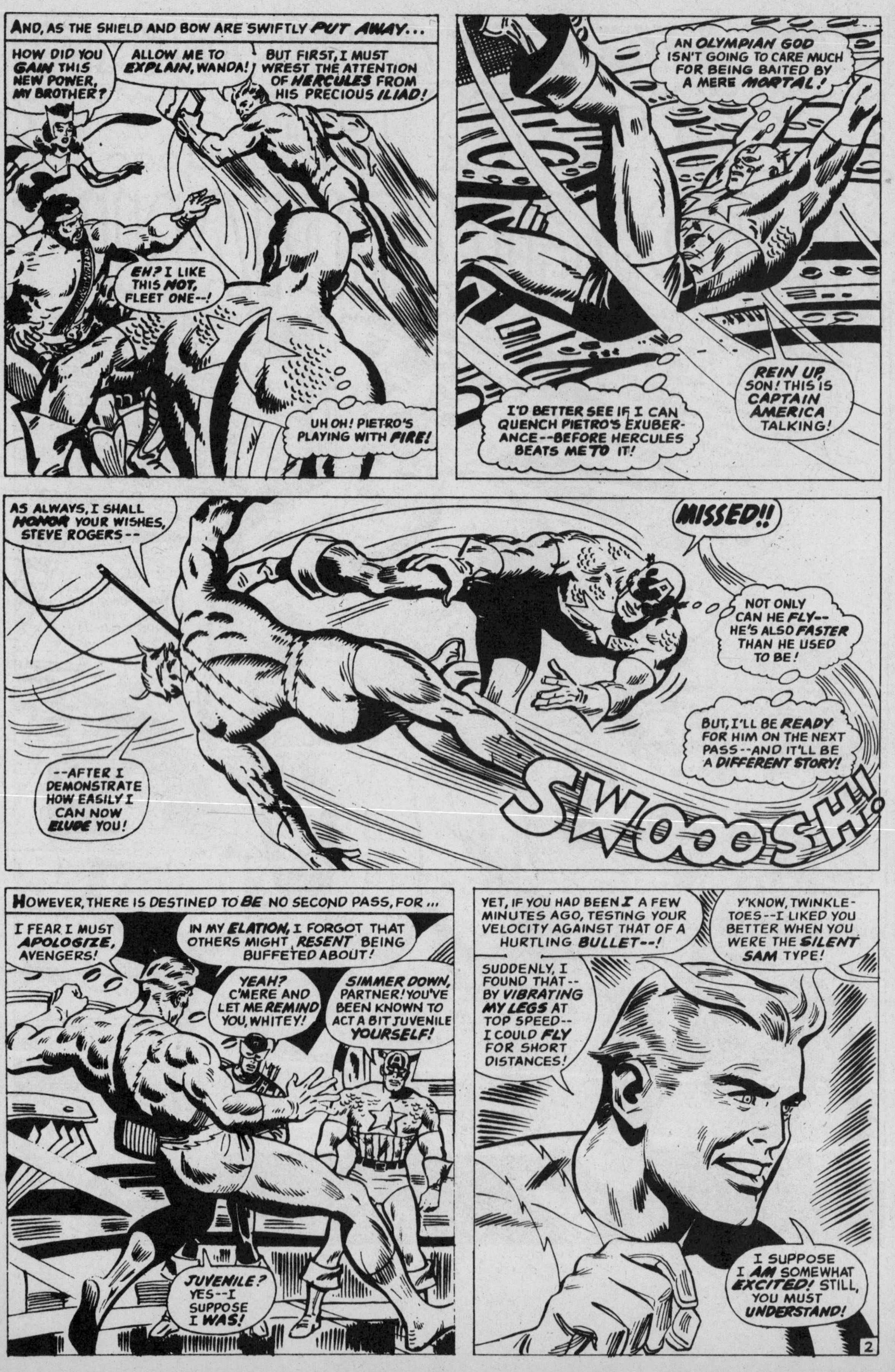
AND, AS THE SHIELD AND BOW ARE SWIFTLY PUT AWAY...
HOW DID YOU GAIN THIS NEW POWER, MY BROTHER?
ALLOW ME TO EXPLAIN, WANDA!
BUT FIRST, I MUST WREST THE ATTENTION OF HERCULES FROM HIS PRECIOUS ILIAD!
EH? I LIKE THIS NOT, FLEET ONE--!
UH OH! PIETRO'S PLAYING WITH FIRE!
AN OLYMPIAN GOD ISN'T GOING TO CARE MUCH FOR BEING BAITED BY A MERE MORTAL!
I'D BETTER SEE IF I CAN QUENCH PIETRO'S EXUBERANCE--BEFORE HERCULES BEATS ME TO IT!
REIN UP, SON! THIS IS CAPTAIN AMERICA TALKING!
AS ALWAYS, I SHALL HONOR YOUR WISHES, STEVE ROGERS--
--AFTER I DEMONSTRATE HOW EASILY I CAN NOW ELUDE YOU!
MISSED!!
NOT ONLY CAN HE FLY-- HE'S ALSO FASTER THAN HE USED TO BE!
BUT, I'LL BE READY FOR HIM ON THE NEXT PASS--AND IT'LL BE A DIFFERENT STORY!
SWOOOSH!
HOWEVER, THERE IS DESTINED TO BE NO SECOND PASS, FOR...
I FEAR I MUST APOLOGIZE, AVENGERS!
IN MY ELATION, I FORGOT THAT OTHERS MIGHT RESENT BEING BUFFETED ABOUT!
YEAH? C'MERE AND LET ME REMIND YOU, WHITEY!
SIMMER DOWN, PARTNER! YOU'VE BEEN KNOWN TO ACT A BIT JUVENILE YOURSELF!
JUVENILE? YES--I SUPPOSE I WAS!
YET, IF YOU HAD BEEN I A FEW MINUTES AGO, TESTING YOUR VELOCITY AGAINST THAT OF A HURTLING BULLET--!
SUDDENLY, I FOUND THAT-- BY VIBRATING MY LEGS AT TOP SPEED-- I COULD FLY FOR SHORT DISTANCES!
Y'KNOW, TWINKLE-TOES--I LIKED YOU BETTER WHEN YOU WERE THE SILENT SAM TYPE!
I SUPPOSE I AM SOMEWHAT EXCITED! STILL, YOU MUST UNDERSTAND!
2

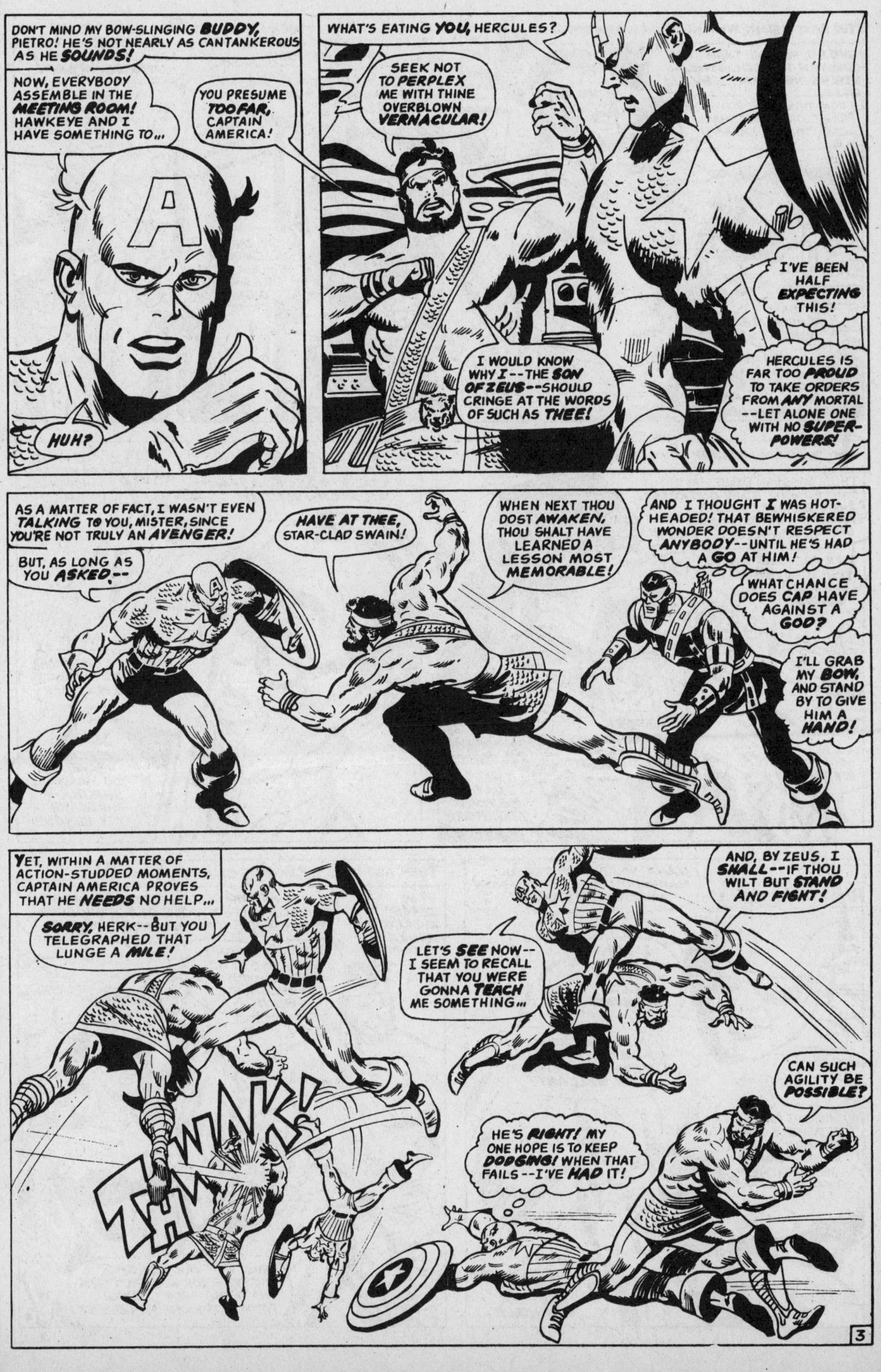

DON'T MIND MY BOW-SLINGING BUDDY, PIETRO! HE'S NOT NEARLY AS CANTANKEROUS AS HE SOUNDS!
NOW, EVERYBODY ASSEMBLE IN THE MEETING ROOM! HAWKEYE AND I HAVE SOMETHING TO...
YOU PRESUME TOO FAR, CAPTAIN AMERICA!
HUH?
WHAT'S EATING YOU, HERCULES?
SEEK NOT TO PERPLEX ME WITH THINE OVERBLOWN VERNACULAR!
I WOULD KNOW WHY I--THE SON OF ZEUS--SHOULD CRINGE AT THE WORDS OF SUCH AS THEE!
I'VE BEEN HALF EXPECTING THIS!
HERCULES IS FAR TOO PROUD TO TAKE ORDERS FROM ANY MORTAL --LET ALONE ONE WITH NO SUPER-POWERS!
AS A MATTER OF FACT, I WASN'T EVEN TALKING TO YOU, MISTER, SINCE YOU'RE NOT TRULY AN AVENGER!
BUT, AS LONG AS YOU ASKED,--
HAVE AT THEE, STAR-CLAD SWAIN!
WHEN NEXT THOU DOST AWAKEN, THOU SHALT HAVE LEARNED A LESSON MOST MEMORABLE!
AND I THOUGHT I WAS HOT-HEADED! THAT BEWHISKERED WONDER DOESN'T RESPECT ANYBODY--UNTIL HE'S HAD A GO AT HIM!
WHAT CHANCE DOES CAP HAVE AGAINST A GOD?
I'LL GRAB MY BOW, AND STAND BY TO GIVE HIM A HAND!
YET, WITHIN A MATTER OF ACTION-STUDDED MOMENTS, CAPTAIN AMERICA PROVES THAT HE NEEDS NO HELP...
SORRY, HERK--BUT YOU TELEGRAPHED THAT LUNGE A MILE!
THWAK!
LET'S SEE NOW-- I SEEM TO RECALL THAT YOU WERE GONNA TEACH ME SOMETHING...
AND, BY ZEUS, I SHALL--IF THOU WILT BUT STAND AND FIGHT!
CAN SUCH AGILITY BE POSSIBLE?
HE'S RIGHT! MY ONE HOPE IS TO KEEP DODGING! WHEN THAT FAILS--I'VE HAD IT!

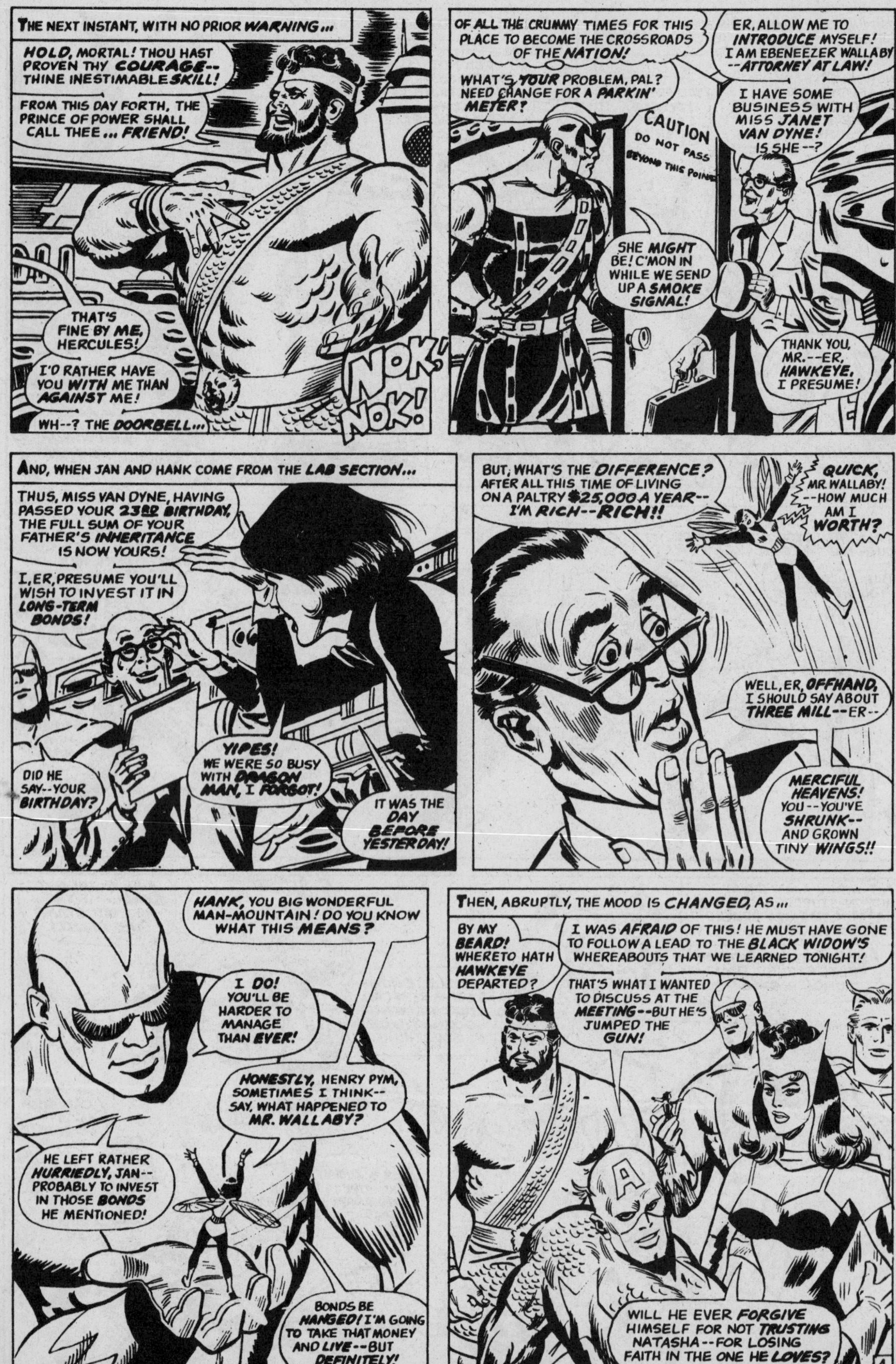
THE NEXT INSTANT, WITH NO PRIOR WARNING...
HOLD, MORTAL! THOU HAST PROVEN THY COURAGE-- THINE INESTIMABLE SKILL!
FROM THIS DAY FORTH, THE PRINCE OF POWER SHALL CALL THEE... FRIEND!
THAT'S FINE BY ME, HERCULES!
I'D RATHER HAVE YOU WITH ME THAN AGAINST ME!
WH--? THE DOORBELL...
NOK! NOK!
OF ALL THE CRUMMY TIMES FOR THIS PLACE TO BECOME THE CROSSROADS OF THE NATION!
WHAT'S YOUR PROBLEM, PAL? NEED CHANGE FOR A PARKIN' METER?
ER, ALLOW ME TO INTRODUCE MYSELF! I AM EBENEEZER WALLABY --ATTORNEY AT LAW!
I HAVE SOME BUSINESS WITH MISS JANET VAN DYNE! IS SHE --?
CAUTION DO NOT PASS BEYOND THIS POINT
SHE MIGHT BE! C'MON IN WHILE WE SEND UP A SMOKE SIGNAL!
THANK YOU, MR.--ER, HAWKEYE, I PRESUME!
AND, WHEN JAN AND HANK COME FROM THE LAB SECTION...
THUS, MISS VAN DYNE, HAVING PASSED YOUR 23RD BIRTHDAY, THE FULL SUM OF YOUR FATHER'S INHERITANCE IS NOW YOURS!
I, ER, PRESUME YOU'LL WISH TO INVEST IT IN LONG-TERM BONDS!
DID HE SAY--YOUR BIRTHDAY?
YIPES! WE WERE SO BUSY WITH DRAGON MAN, I FORGOT!
IT WAS THE DAY BEFORE YESTERDAY!
BUT, WHAT'S THE DIFFERENCE? AFTER ALL THIS TIME OF LIVING ON A PALTRY $25,000 A YEAR-- I'M RICH--RICH!!
QUICK, MR. WALLABY! --HOW MUCH AM I WORTH?
WELL, ER, OFFHAND, I SHOULD SAY ABOUT THREE MILL--ER--
MERCIFUL HEAVENS! YOU--YOU'VE SHRUNK-- AND GROWN TINY WINGS!!
HANK, YOU BIG WONDERFUL MAN-MOUNTAIN! DO YOU KNOW WHAT THIS MEANS?
I DO! YOU'LL BE HARDER TO MANAGE THAN EVER!
HONESTLY, HENRY PYM, SOMETIMES I THINK-- SAY, WHAT HAPPENED TO MR. WALLABY?
HE LEFT RATHER HURRIEDLY, JAN-- PROBABLY TO INVEST IN THOSE BONDS HE MENTIONED!
BONDS BE HANGED! I'M GOING TO TAKE THAT MONEY AND LIVE--BUT DEFINITELY!
THEN, ABRUPTLY, THE MOOD IS CHANGED, AS...
BY MY BEARD! WHERETO HATH HAWKEYE DEPARTED?
I WAS AFRAID OF THIS! HE MUST HAVE GONE TO FOLLOW A LEAD TO THE BLACK WIDOW'S WHEREABOUTS THAT WE LEARNED TONIGHT!
THAT'S WHAT I WANTED TO DISCUSS AT THE MEETING--BUT HE'S JUMPED THE GUN!
WILL HE EVER FORGIVE HIMSELF FOR NOT TRUSTING NATASHA--FOR LOSING FAITH IN THE ONE HE LOVES?
4

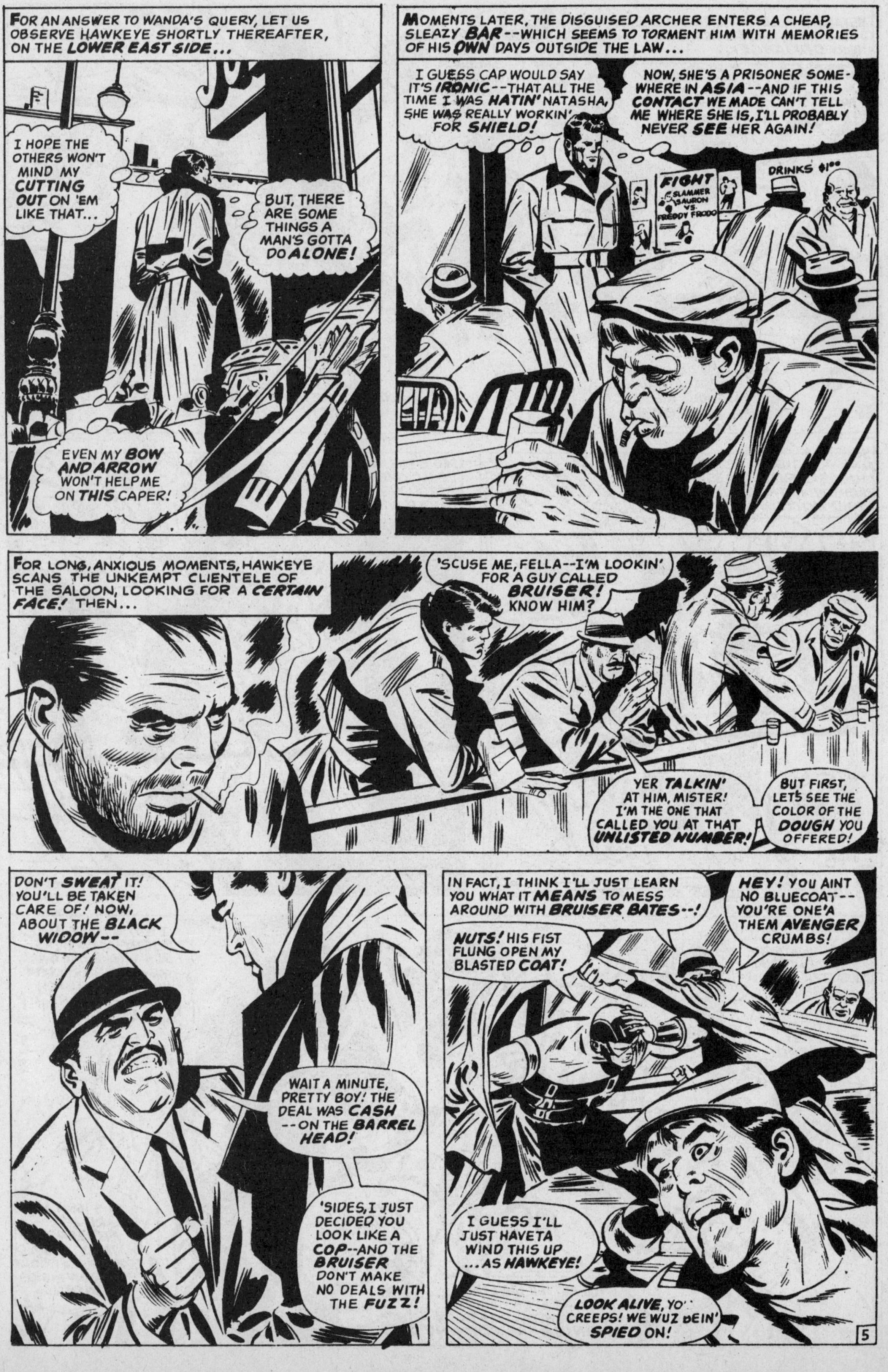
FOR AN ANSWER TO WANDA'S QUERY, LET US OBSERVE HAWKEYE SHORTLY THEREAFTER, ON THE LOWER EAST SIDE...
I HOPE THE OTHERS WON'T MIND MY CUTTING OUT ON 'EM LIKE THAT...
BUT, THERE ARE SOME THINGS A MAN'S GOTTA DO ALONE!
EVEN MY BOW AND ARROW WON'T HELP ME ON THIS CAPER!
MOMENTS LATER, THE DISGUISED ARCHER ENTERS A CHEAP, SLEAZY BAR--WHICH SEEMS TO TORMENT HIM WITH MEMORIES OF HIS OWN DAYS OUTSIDE THE LAW...
I GUESS CAP WOULD SAY IT'S IRONIC--THAT ALL THE TIME I WAS HATIN' NATASHA, SHE WAS REALLY WORKIN' FOR SHIELD!
NOW, SHE'S A PRISONER SOMEWHERE IN ASIA--AND IF THIS CONTACT WE MADE CAN'T TELL ME WHERE SHE IS, I'LL PROBABLY NEVER SEE HER AGAIN!
FIGHT SLAMMER SAURON VS. FREDDY FRODO
DRINKS $1.00
FOR LONG, ANXIOUS MOMENTS, HAWKEYE SCANS THE UNKEMPT CLIENTELE OF THE SALOON, LOOKING FOR A CERTAIN FACE! THEN...
'SCUSE ME, FELLA--I'M LOOKIN' FOR A GUY CALLED BRUISER! KNOW HIM?
YER TALKIN' AT HIM, MISTER! I'M THE ONE THAT CALLED YOU AT THAT UNLISTED NUMBER!
BUT FIRST, LET'S SEE THE COLOR OF THE DOUGH YOU OFFERED!
DON'T SWEAT IT! YOU'LL BE TAKEN CARE OF! NOW, ABOUT THE BLACK WIDOW--
WAIT A MINUTE, PRETTY BOY! THE DEAL WAS CASH--ON THE BARREL HEAD!
'SIDES, I JUST DECIDED YOU LOOK LIKE A COP--AND THE BRUISER DON'T MAKE NO DEALS WITH THE FUZZ!
IN FACT, I THINK I'LL JUST LEARN YOU WHAT IT MEANS TO MESS AROUND WITH BRUISER BATES--!
HEY! YOU AINT NO BLUECOAT--YOU'RE ONE'A THEM AVENGER CRUMBS!
NUTS! HIS FIST FLUNG OPEN MY BLASTED COAT!
I GUESS I'LL JUST HAVETA WIND THIS UP ...AS HAWKEYE!
LOOK ALIVE, YO' CREEPS! WE WUZ BEIN' SPIED ON!
5

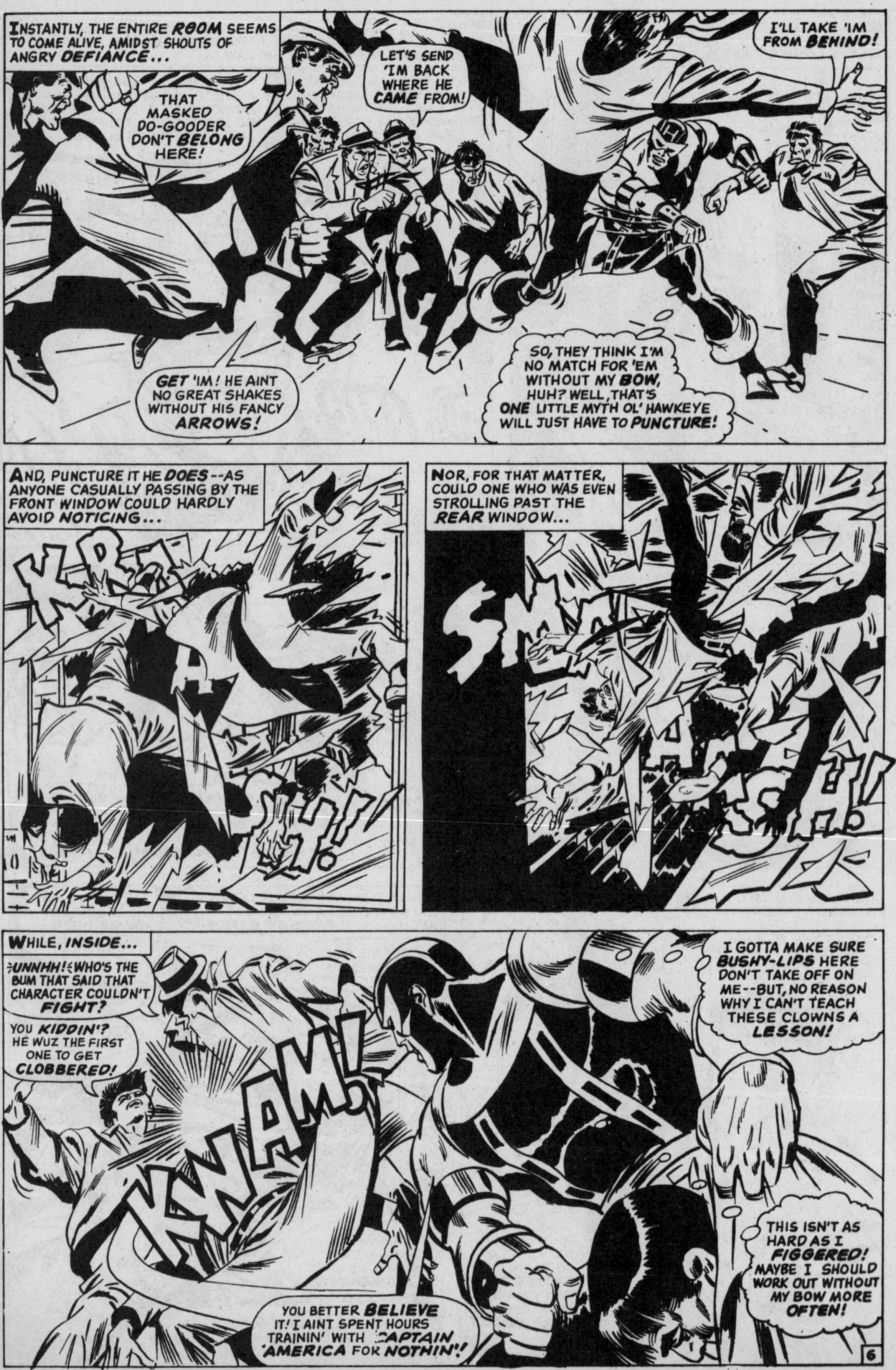

INSTANTLY, THE ENTIRE ROOM SEEMS TO COME ALIVE, AMIDST SHOUTS OF ANGRY DEFIANCE...
THAT MASKED DO-GOODER DON'T BELONG HERE!
LET'S SEND 'IM BACK WHERE HE CAME FROM!
I'LL TAKE 'IM FROM BEHIND!
GET 'IM! HE AINT NO GREAT SHAKES WITHOUT HIS FANCY ARROWS!
SO, THEY THINK I'M NO MATCH FOR 'EM WITHOUT MY BOW, HUH? WELL, THAT'S ONE LITTLE MYTH OL' HAWKEYE WILL JUST HAVE TO PUNCTURE!
AND, PUNCTURE IT HE DOES--AS ANYONE CASUALLY PASSING BY THE FRONT WINDOW COULD HARDLY AVOID NOTICING...
NOR, FOR THAT MATTER, COULD ONE WHO WAS EVEN STROLLING PAST THE REAR WINDOW...
WHILE, INSIDE...
UNNHH! WHO'S THE BUM THAT SAID THAT CHARACTER COULDN'T FIGHT?
YOU KIDDIN'? HE WUZ THE FIRST ONE TO GET CLOBBERED!
I GOTTA MAKE SURE BUSHY-LIPS HERE DON'T TAKE OFF ON ME--BUT, NO REASON WHY I CAN'T TEACH THESE CLOWNS A LESSON!
KWAM!
THIS ISN'T AS HARD AS I FIGGERED! MAYBE I SHOULD WORK OUT WITHOUT MY BOW MORE OFTEN!
YOU BETTER BELIEVE IT! I AINT SPENT HOURS TRAININ' WITH CAPTAIN AMERICA FOR NOTHIN'!
6

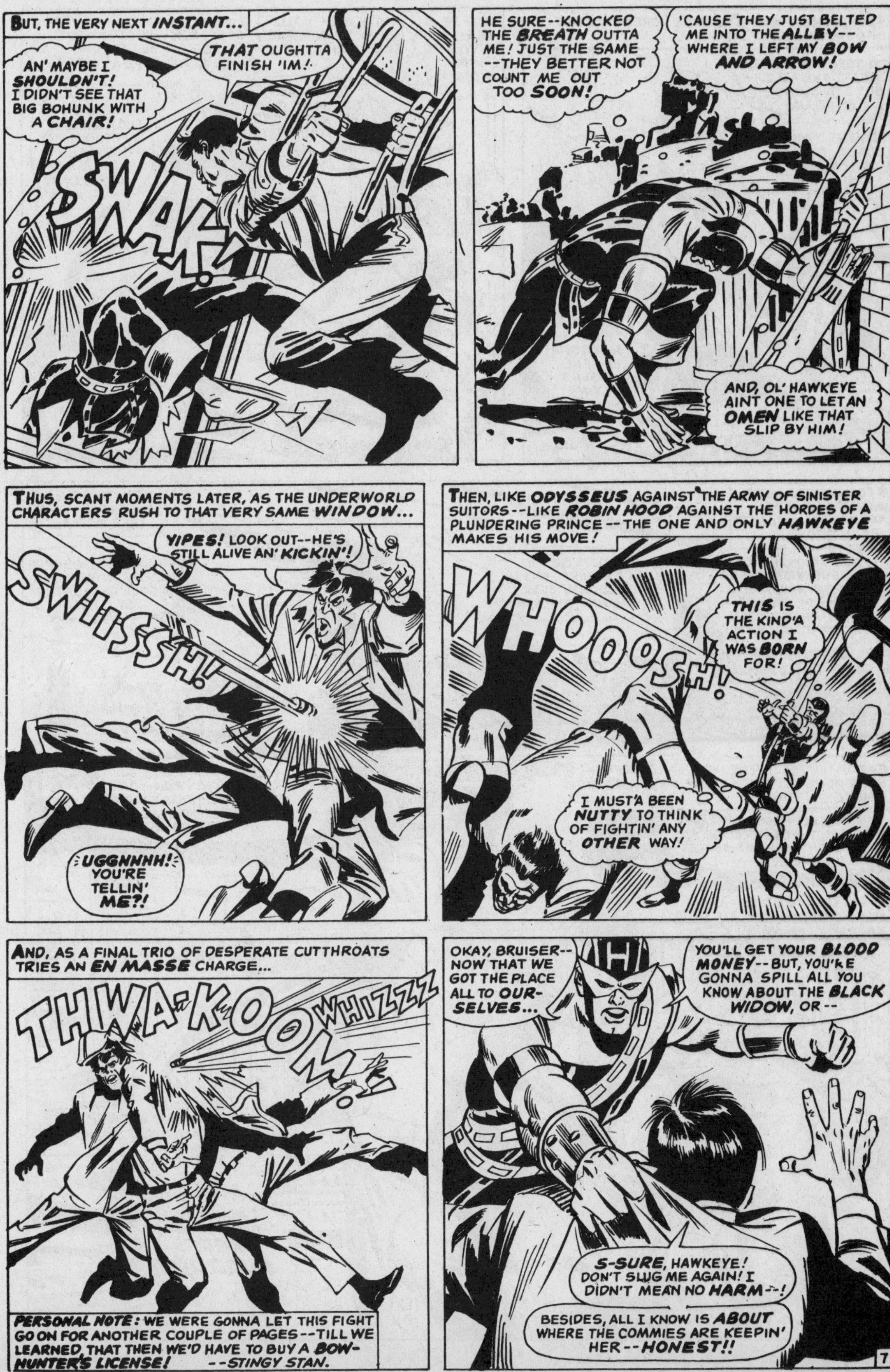
BUT, THE VERY NEXT INSTANT...
AN' MAYBE I SHOULDN'T! I DIDN'T SEE THAT BIG BOHUNK WITH A CHAIR!
THAT OUGHTTA FINISH 'IM!
SWAK!
HE SURE--KNOCKED THE BREATH OUTTA ME! JUST THE SAME --THEY BETTER NOT COUNT ME OUT TOO SOON!
'CAUSE THEY JUST BELTED ME INTO THE ALLEY-- WHERE I LEFT MY BOW AND ARROW!
AND, OL' HAWKEYE AINT ONE TO LET AN OMEN LIKE THAT SLIP BY HIM!
THUS, SCANT MOMENTS LATER, AS THE UNDERWORLD CHARACTERS RUSH TO THAT VERY SAME WINDOW...
YIPES! LOOK OUT--HE'S STILL ALIVE AN' KICKIN'!
SWIISSH!
UGGNNNH! YOU'RE TELLIN' ME?!
THEN, LIKE ODYSSEUS AGAINST THE ARMY OF SINISTER SUITORS--LIKE ROBIN HOOD AGAINST THE HORDES OF A PLUNDERING PRINCE--THE ONE AND ONLY HAWKEYE MAKES HIS MOVE!
WHOOOOSH!
THIS IS THE KIND'A ACTION I WAS BORN FOR!
I MUST'A BEEN NUTTY TO THINK OF FIGHTIN' ANY OTHER WAY!
AND, AS A FINAL TRIO OF DESPERATE CUTTHROATS TRIES AN EN MASSE CHARGE...
THWA-KOOM!
WHIZZZ
PERSONAL NOTE: WE WERE GONNA LET THIS FIGHT GO ON FOR ANOTHER COUPLE OF PAGES--TILL WE LEARNED THAT THEN WE'D HAVE TO BUY A BOW-HUNTER'S LICENSE! --STINGY STAN.
OKAY, BRUISER-- NOW THAT WE GOT THE PLACE ALL TO OURSELVES...
YOU'LL GET YOUR BLOOD MONEY--BUT, YOU'RE GONNA SPILL ALL YOU KNOW ABOUT THE BLACK WIDOW, OR--
S-SURE, HAWKEYE! DON'T SLUG ME AGAIN! I DIDN'T MEAN NO HARM--!
BESIDES, ALL I KNOW IS ABOUT WHERE THE COMMIES ARE KEEPIN' HER--HONEST!!

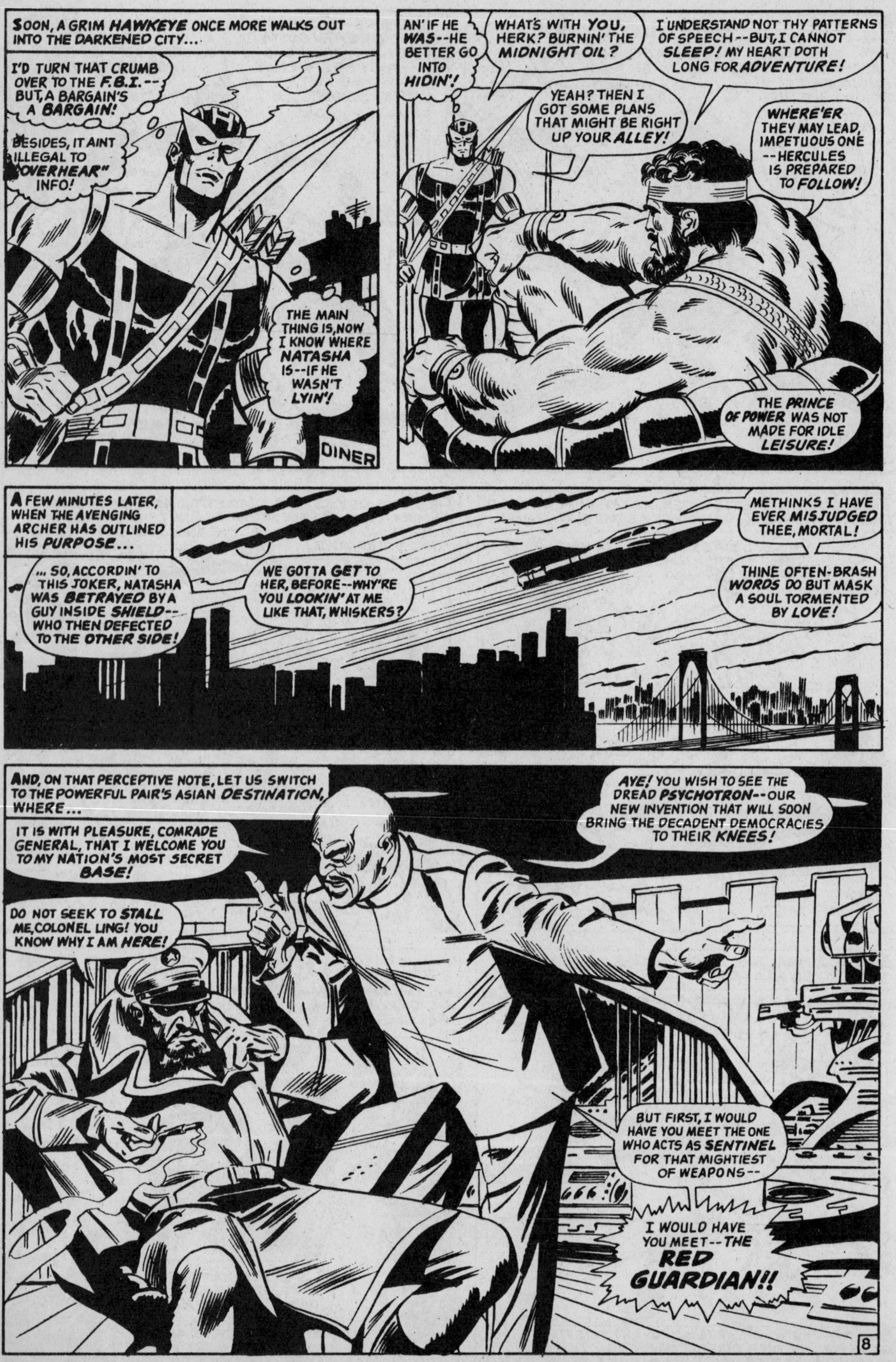
SOON, A GRIM HAWKEYE ONCE MORE WALKS OUT INTO THE DARKENED CITY...
I'D TURN THAT CRUMB OVER TO THE F.B.I.-- BUT, A BARGAIN'S A BARGAIN!
BESIDES, IT AINT ILLEGAL TO "OVERHEAR" INFO!
THE MAIN THING IS, NOW I KNOW WHERE NATASHA IS--IF HE WASN'T LYIN'!
DINER
AN' IF HE WAS--HE BETTER GO INTO HIDIN'!
WHAT'S WITH YOU, HERK? BURNIN' THE MIDNIGHT OIL?
I UNDERSTAND NOT THY PATTERNS OF SPEECH--BUT, I CANNOT SLEEP! MY HEART DOTH LONG FOR ADVENTURE!
YEAH? THEN I GOT SOME PLANS THAT MIGHT BE RIGHT UP YOUR ALLEY!
WHERE'ER THEY MAY LEAD, IMPETUOUS ONE --HERCULES IS PREPARED TO FOLLOW!
THE PRINCE OF POWER WAS NOT MADE FOR IDLE LEISURE!
A FEW MINUTES LATER, WHEN THE AVENGING ARCHER HAS OUTLINED HIS PURPOSE...
...SO, ACCORDIN' TO THIS JOKER, NATASHA WAS BETRAYED BY A GUY INSIDE SHIELD-- WHO THEN DEFECTED TO THE OTHER SIDE!
WE GOTTA GET TO HER, BEFORE--WHY'RE YOU LOOKIN' AT ME LIKE THAT, WHISKERS?
METHINKS I HAVE EVER MISJUDGED THEE, MORTAL!
THINE OFTEN-BRASH WORDS DO BUT MASK A SOUL TORMENTED BY LOVE!
AND, ON THAT PERCEPTIVE NOTE, LET US SWITCH TO THE POWERFUL PAIR'S ASIAN DESTINATION, WHERE...
IT IS WITH PLEASURE, COMRADE GENERAL, THAT I WELCOME YOU TO MY NATION'S MOST SECRET BASE!
DO NOT SEEK TO STALL ME, COLONEL LING! YOU KNOW WHY I AM HERE!
AYE! YOU WISH TO SEE THE DREAD PSYCHOTRON--OUR NEW INVENTION THAT WILL SOON BRING THE DECADENT DEMOCRACIES TO THEIR KNEES!
BUT FIRST, I WOULD HAVE YOU MEET THE ONE WHO ACTS AS SENTINEL FOR THAT MIGHTIEST OF WEAPONS--
I WOULD HAVE YOU MEET--THE RED GUARDIAN!!

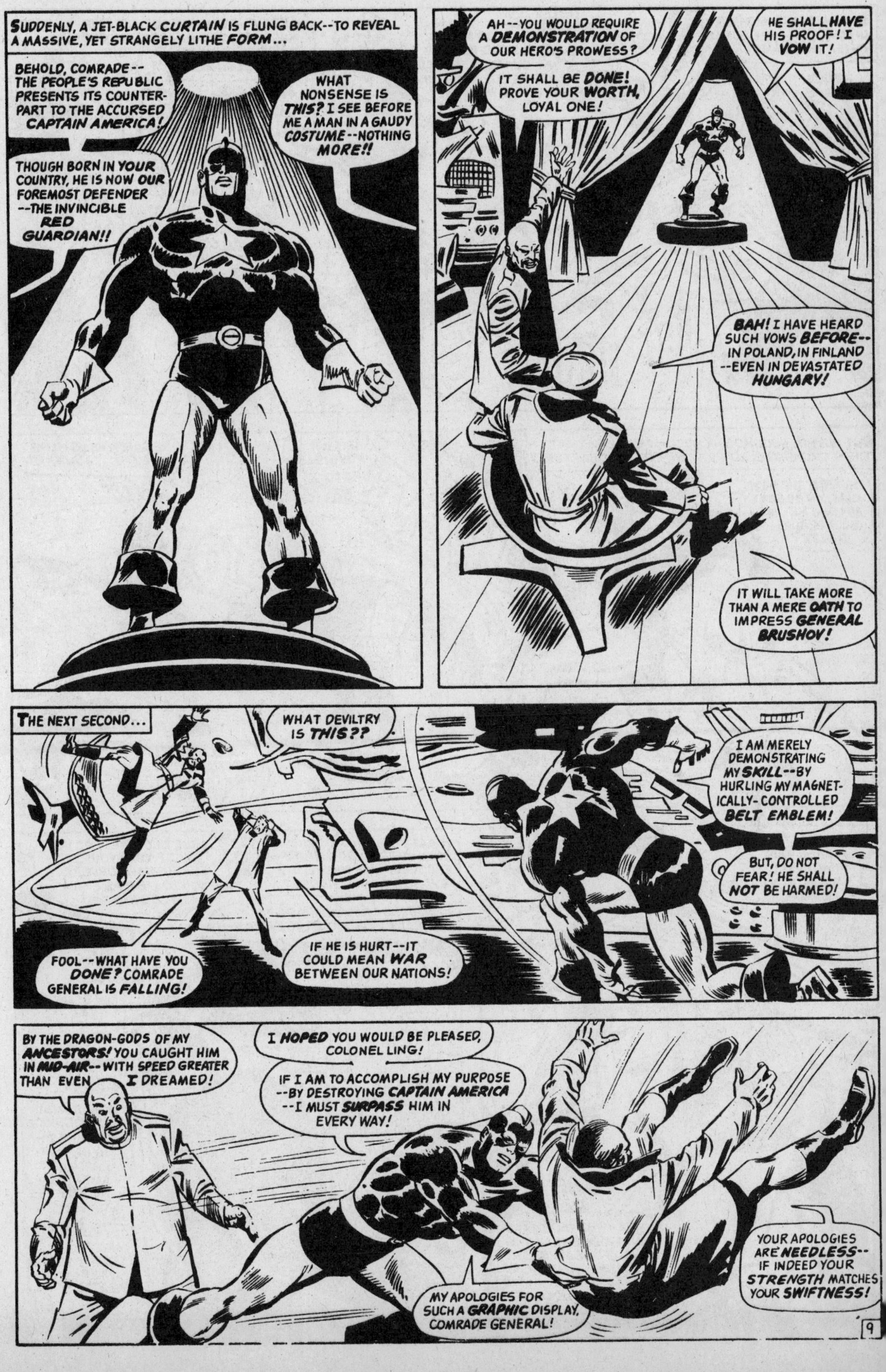
SUDDENLY, A JET-BLACK CURTAIN IS FLUNG BACK--TO REVEAL A MASSIVE, YET STRANGELY LITHE FORM...
BEHOLD, COMRADE-- THE PEOPLE'S REPUBLIC PRESENTS ITS COUNTER-PART TO THE ACCURSED CAPTAIN AMERICA!
WHAT NONSENSE IS THIS? I SEE BEFORE ME A MAN IN A GAUDY COSTUME--NOTHING MORE!!
THOUGH BORN IN YOUR COUNTRY, HE IS NOW OUR FOREMOST DEFENDER --THE INVINCIBLE RED GUARDIAN!!
AH--YOU WOULD REQUIRE A DEMONSTRATION OF OUR HERO'S PROWESS?
IT SHALL BE DONE! PROVE YOUR WORTH, LOYAL ONE!
HE SHALL HAVE HIS PROOF! I VOW IT!
BAH! I HAVE HEARD SUCH VOWS BEFORE-- IN POLAND, IN FINLAND --EVEN IN DEVASTATED HUNGARY!
IT WILL TAKE MORE THAN A MERE OATH TO IMPRESS GENERAL BRUSHOV!
THE NEXT SECOND...
WHAT DEVILTRY IS THIS??
I AM MERELY DEMONSTRATING MY SKILL--BY HURLING MY MAGNET-ICALLY-CONTROLLED BELT EMBLEM!
BUT, DO NOT FEAR! HE SHALL NOT BE HARMED!
FOOL--WHAT HAVE YOU DONE? COMRADE GENERAL IS FALLING!
IF HE IS HURT--IT COULD MEAN WAR BETWEEN OUR NATIONS!
BY THE DRAGON-GODS OF MY ANCESTORS! YOU CAUGHT HIM IN MID-AIR--WITH SPEED GREATER THAN EVEN I DREAMED!
I HOPED YOU WOULD BE PLEASED, COLONEL LING!
IF I AM TO ACCOMPLISH MY PURPOSE --BY DESTROYING CAPTAIN AMERICA --I MUST SURPASS HIM IN EVERY WAY!
MY APOLOGIES FOR SUCH A GRAPHIC DISPLAY, COMRADE GENERAL!
YOUR APOLOGIES ARE NEEDLESS-- IF INDEED YOUR STRENGTH MATCHES YOUR SWIFTNESS!
9

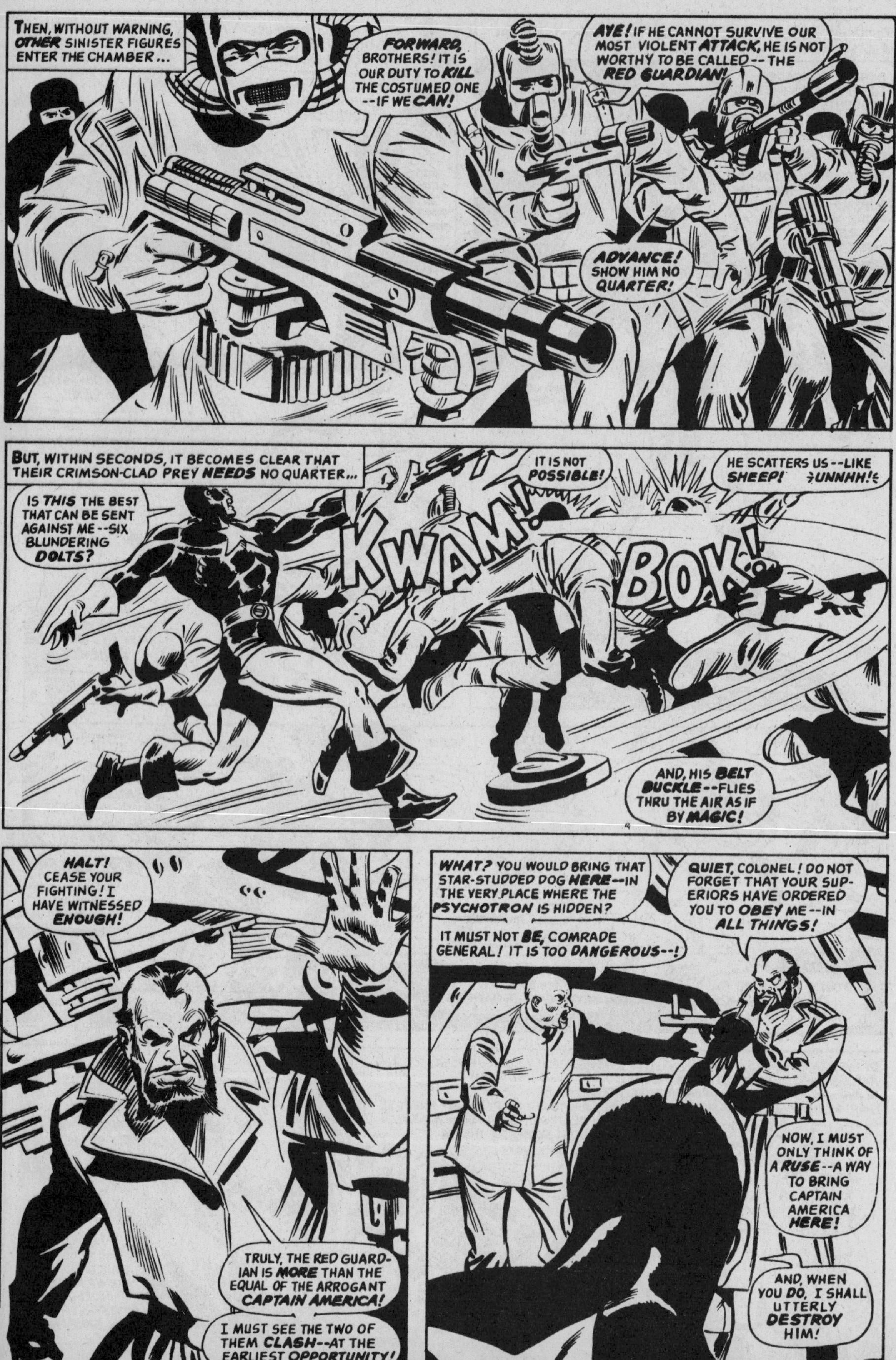
THEN, WITHOUT WARNING, OTHER SINISTER FIGURES ENTER THE CHAMBER...
FORWARD, BROTHERS! IT IS OUR DUTY TO KILL THE COSTUMED ONE --IF WE CAN!
AYE! IF HE CANNOT SURVIVE OUR MOST VIOLENT ATTACK, HE IS NOT WORTHY TO BE CALLED-- THE RED GUARDIAN!
ADVANCE! SHOW HIM NO QUARTER!
BUT, WITHIN SECONDS, IT BECOMES CLEAR THAT THEIR CRIMSON-CLAD PREY NEEDS NO QUARTER...
IS THIS THE BEST THAT CAN BE SENT AGAINST ME --SIX BLUNDERING DOLTS?
IT IS NOT POSSIBLE!
HE SCATTERS US --LIKE SHEEP! UNNHH!
KWAM!
BOK!
AND, HIS BELT BUCKLE --FLIES THRU THE AIR AS IF BY MAGIC!
HALT! CEASE YOUR FIGHTING! I HAVE WITNESSED ENOUGH!
TRULY, THE RED GUARDIAN IS MORE THAN THE EQUAL OF THE ARROGANT CAPTAIN AMERICA!
I MUST SEE THE TWO OF THEM CLASH--AT THE EARLIEST OPPORTUNITY!
WHAT? YOU WOULD BRING THAT STAR-STUDDED DOG HERE--IN THE VERY PLACE WHERE THE PSYCHOTRON IS HIDDEN?
IT MUST NOT BE, COMRADE GENERAL! IT IS TOO DANGEROUS--!
QUIET, COLONEL! DO NOT FORGET THAT YOUR SUPERIORS HAVE ORDERED YOU TO OBEY ME --IN ALL THINGS!
NOW, I MUST ONLY THINK OF A RUSE --A WAY TO BRING CAPTAIN AMERICA HERE!
AND, WHEN YOU DO, I SHALL UTTERLY DESTROY HIM!
10

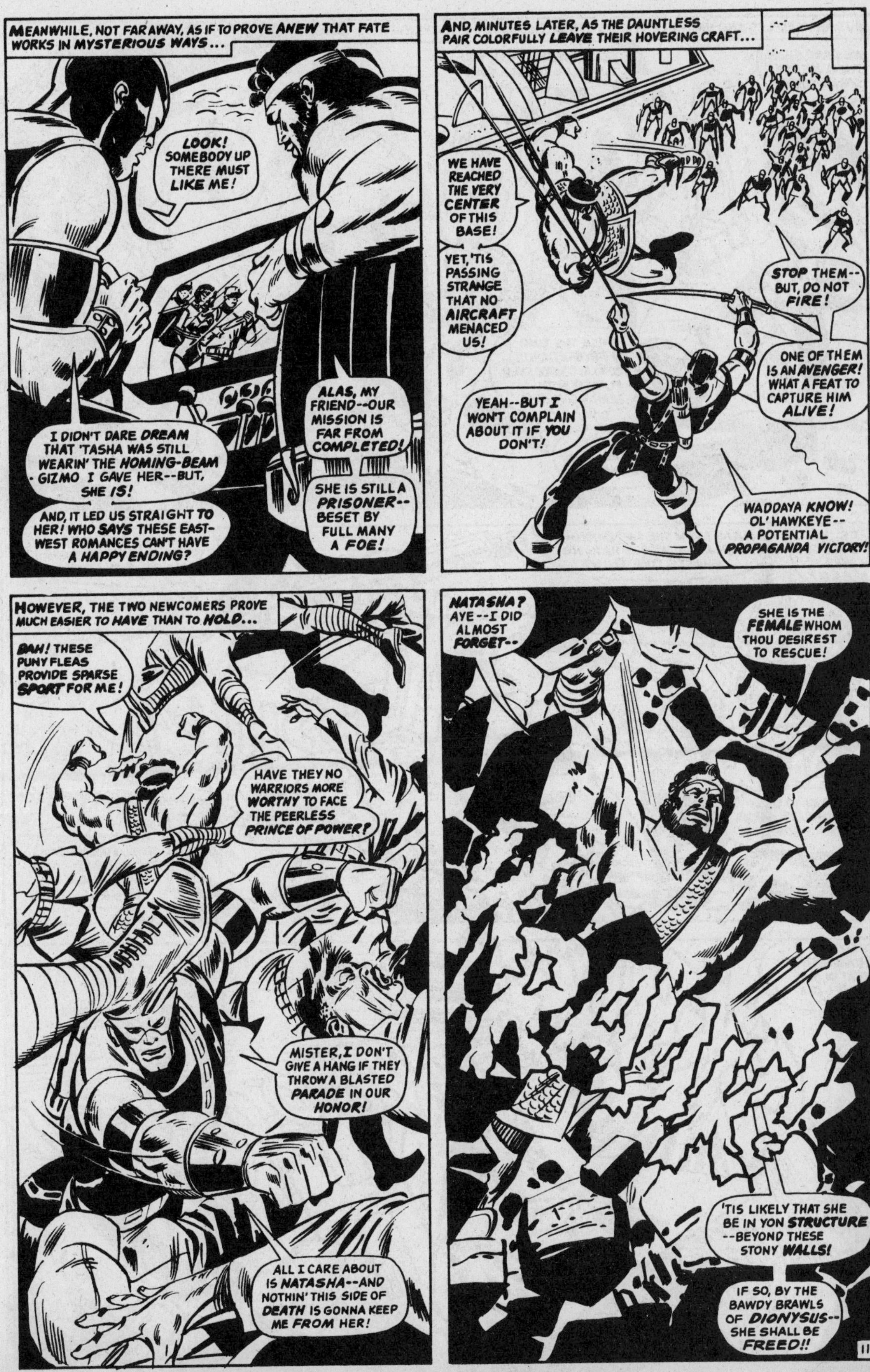
MEANWHILE, NOT FAR AWAY, AS IF TO PROVE ANEW THAT FATE WORKS IN MYSTERIOUS WAYS...
LOOK! SOMEBODY UP THERE MUST LIKE ME!
I DIDN'T DARE DREAM THAT 'TASHA WAS STILL WEARIN' THE HOMING-BEAM GIZMO I GAVE HER--BUT, SHE IS!
AND, IT LED US STRAIGHT TO HER! WHO SAYS THESE EAST-WEST ROMANCES CAN'T HAVE A HAPPY ENDING?
ALAS, MY FRIEND--OUR MISSION IS FAR FROM COMPLETED!
SHE IS STILL A PRISONER--BESET BY FULL MANY A FOE!
AND, MINUTES LATER, AS THE DAUNTLESS PAIR COLORFULLY LEAVE THEIR HOVERING CRAFT...
WE HAVE REACHED THE VERY CENTER OF THIS BASE!
YET, 'TIS PASSING STRANGE THAT NO AIRCRAFT MENACED US!
YEAH--BUT I WON'T COMPLAIN ABOUT IT IF YOU DON'T!
STOP THEM--BUT, DO NOT FIRE!
ONE OF THEM IS AN AVENGER! WHAT A FEAT TO CAPTURE HIM ALIVE!
WADDAYA KNOW! OL' HAWKEYE--A POTENTIAL PROPAGANDA VICTORY!
HOWEVER, THE TWO NEWCOMERS PROVE MUCH EASIER TO HAVE THAN TO HOLD...
BAH! THESE PUNY FLEAS PROVIDE SPARSE SPORT FOR ME!
HAVE THEY NO WARRIORS MORE WORTHY TO FACE THE PEERLESS PRINCE OF POWER?
MISTER, I DON'T GIVE A HANG IF THEY THROW A BLASTED PARADE IN OUR HONOR!
ALL I CARE ABOUT IS NATASHA--AND NOTHIN' THIS SIDE OF DEATH IS GONNA KEEP ME FROM HER!
NATASHA? AYE--I DID ALMOST FORGET--
SHE IS THE FEMALE WHOM THOU DESIREST TO RESCUE!
'TIS LIKELY THAT SHE BE IN YON STRUCTURE--BEYOND THESE STONY WALLS!
IF SO, BY THE BAWDY BRAWLS OF DIONYSUS--SHE SHALL BE FREED!!

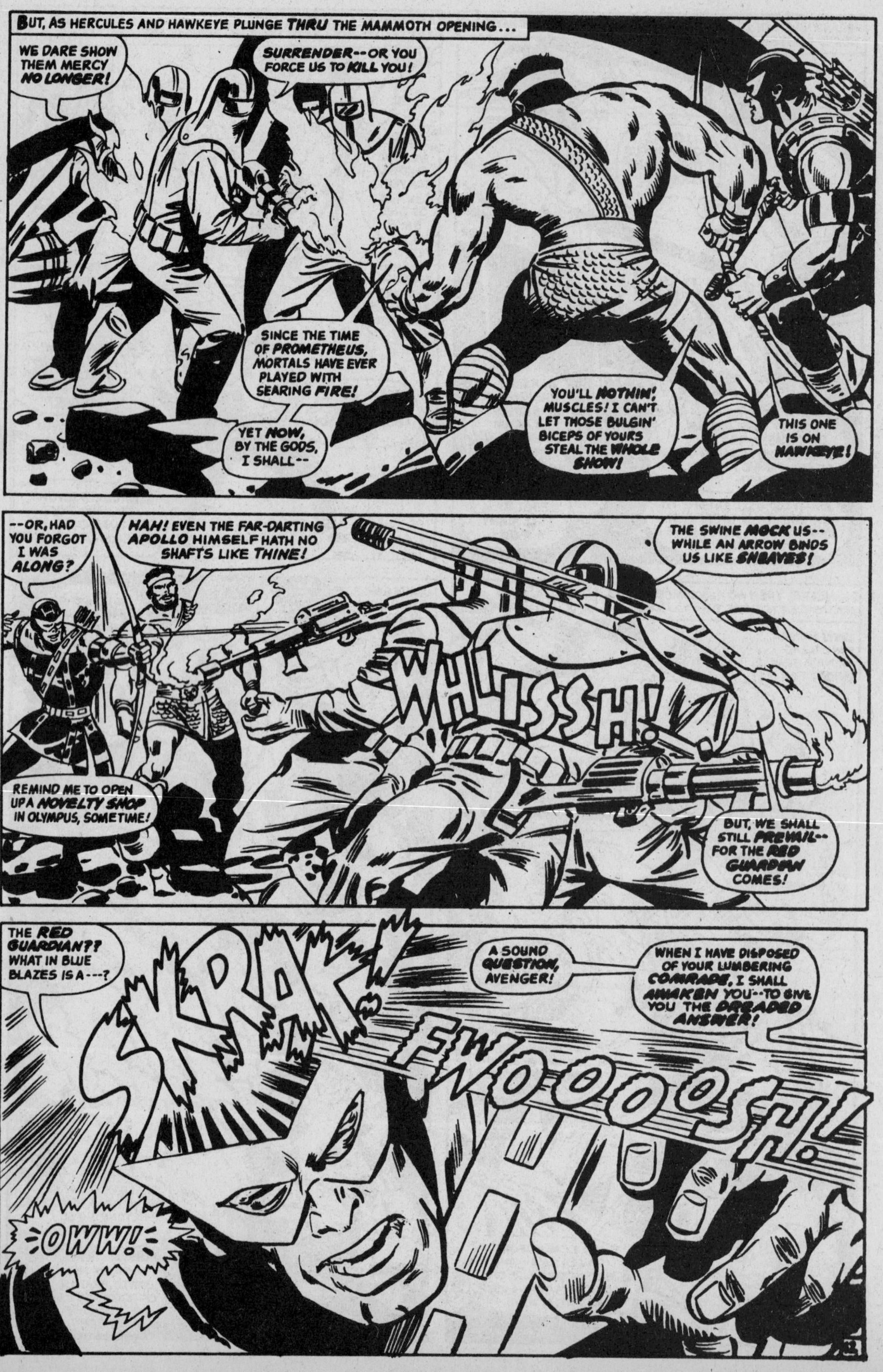
BUT, AS HERCULES AND HAWKEYE PLUNGE THRU THE MAMMOTH OPENING...
WE DARE SHOW THEM MERCY NO LONGER!
SURRENDER--OR YOU FORCE US TO KILL YOU!
SINCE THE TIME OF PROMETHEUS, MORTALS HAVE EVER PLAYED WITH SEARING FIRE!
YET NOW, BY THE GODS, I SHALL--
YOU'LL NOTHIN', MUSCLES! I CAN'T LET THOSE BULGIN' BICEPS OF YOURS STEAL THE WHOLE SHOW!
THIS ONE IS ON HAWKEYE!
--OR, HAD YOU FORGOT I WAS ALONG?
HAH! EVEN THE FAR-DARTING APOLLO HIMSELF HATH NO SHAFTS LIKE THINE!
THE SWINE MOCK US--WHILE AN ARROW BINDS US LIKE SHEAVES!
WHIISSH!
REMIND ME TO OPEN UP A NOVELTY SHOP IN OLYMPUS, SOMETIME!
BUT, WE SHALL STILL PREVAIL--FOR THE RED GUARDIAN COMES!
THE RED GUARDIAN?? WHAT IN BLUE BLAZES IS A---?
SKRAK!
A SOUND QUESTION, AVENGER!
WHEN I HAVE DISPOSED OF YOUR LUMBERING COMRADE, I SHALL AWAKEN YOU--TO GIVE YOU THE DREADED ANSWER!
FWOOOOSH!
OWW!

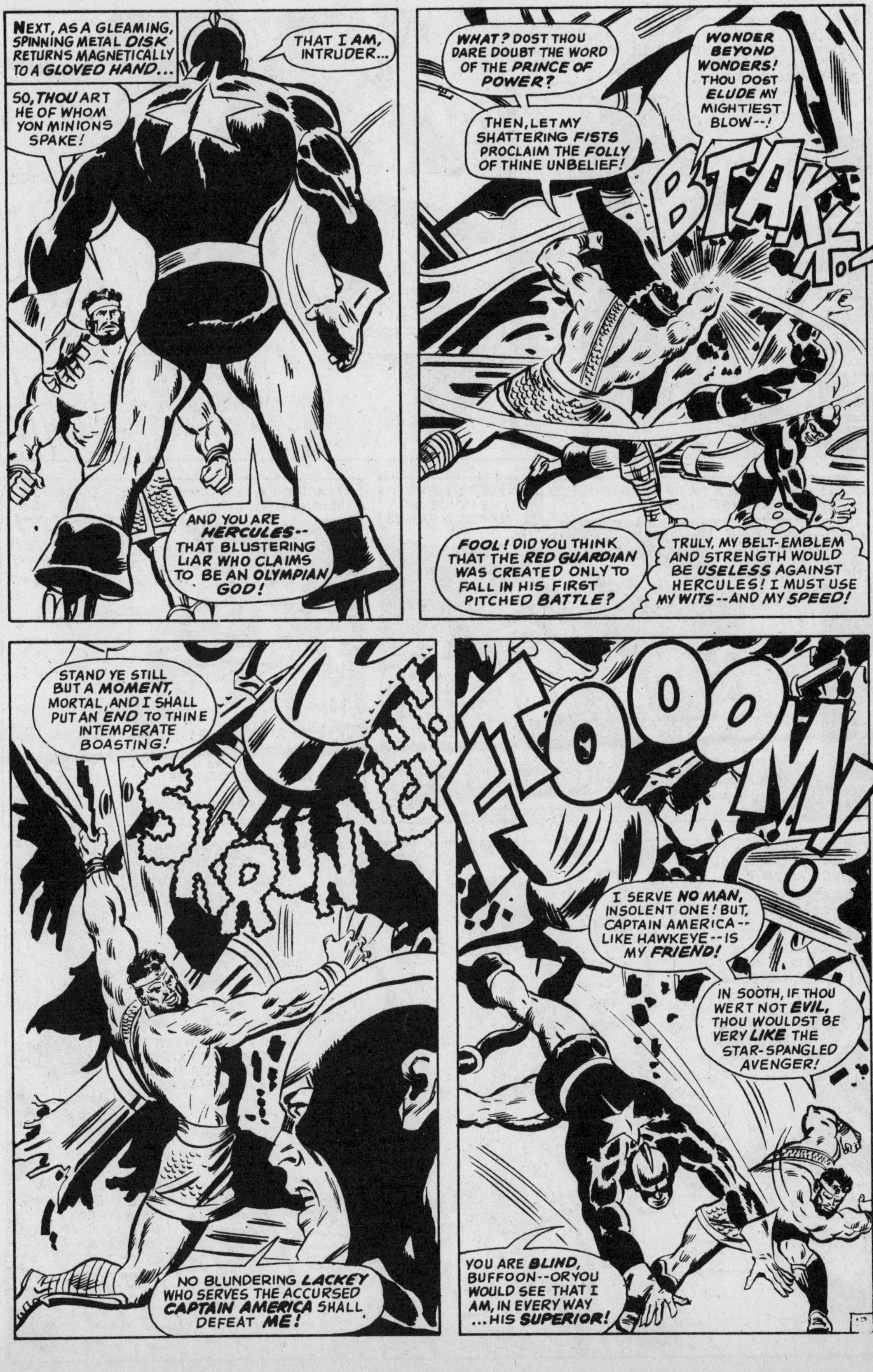
NEXT, AS A GLEAMING, SPINNING METAL DISK RETURNS MAGNETICALLY TO A GLOVED HAND...
THAT I AM, INTRUDER...
SO, THOU ART HE OF WHOM YON MINIONS SPAKE!
AND YOU ARE HERCULES-- THAT BLUSTERING LIAR WHO CLAIMS TO BE AN OLYMPIAN GOD!
WHAT? DOST THOU DARE DOUBT THE WORD OF THE PRINCE OF POWER?
THEN, LET MY SHATTERING FISTS PROCLAIM THE FOLLY OF THINE UNBELIEF!
WONDER BEYOND WONDERS! THOU DOST ELUDE MY MIGHTIEST BLOW--!
BTAKK!
FOOL! DID YOU THINK THAT THE RED GUARDIAN WAS CREATED ONLY TO FALL IN HIS FIRST PITCHED BATTLE?
TRULY, MY BELT-EMBLEM AND STRENGTH WOULD BE USELESS AGAINST HERCULES! I MUST USE MY WITS--AND MY SPEED!
STAND YE STILL BUT A MOMENT, MORTAL, AND I SHALL PUT AN END TO THINE INTEMPERATE BOASTING!
SKRUNCH!
NO BLUNDERING LACKEY WHO SERVES THE ACCURSED CAPTAIN AMERICA SHALL DEFEAT ME!
FTOOOM!
I SERVE NO MAN, INSOLENT ONE! BUT, CAPTAIN AMERICA -- LIKE HAWKEYE -- IS MY FRIEND!
IN SOOTH, IF THOU WERT NOT EVIL, THOU WOULDST BE VERY LIKE THE STAR-SPANGLED AVENGER!
YOU ARE BLIND, BUFFOON--OR YOU WOULD SEE THAT I AM, IN EVERY WAY ...HIS SUPERIOR!

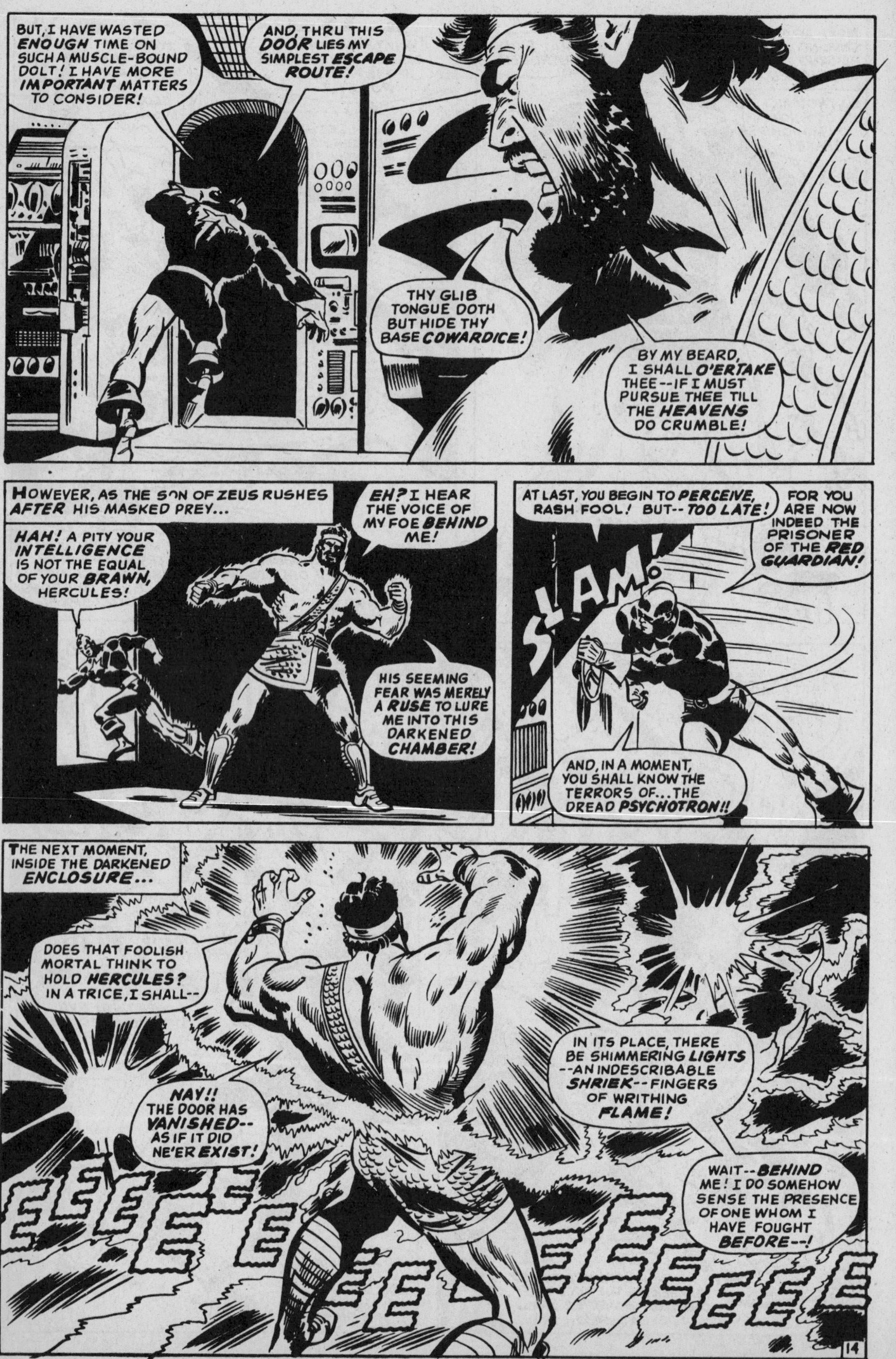
BUT, I HAVE WASTED ENOUGH TIME ON SUCH A MUSCLE-BOUND DOLT! I HAVE MORE IMPORTANT MATTERS TO CONSIDER!
AND, THRU THIS DOOR LIES MY SIMPLEST ESCAPE ROUTE!
THY GLIB TONGUE DOTH BUT HIDE THY BASE COWARDICE!
BY MY BEARD, I SHALL O'ERTAKE THEE--IF I MUST PURSUE THEE TILL THE HEAVENS DO CRUMBLE!
HOWEVER, AS THE SON OF ZEUS RUSHES AFTER HIS MASKED PREY...
HAH! A PITY YOUR INTELLIGENCE IS NOT THE EQUAL OF YOUR BRAWN, HERCULES!
EH? I HEAR THE VOICE OF MY FOE BEHIND ME!
HIS SEEMING FEAR WAS MERELY A RUSE TO LURE ME INTO THIS DARKENED CHAMBER!
AT LAST, YOU BEGIN TO PERCEIVE, RASH FOOL! BUT--TOO LATE!
FOR YOU ARE NOW INDEED THE PRISONER OF THE RED GUARDIAN!
SLAM!
AND, IN A MOMENT, YOU SHALL KNOW THE TERRORS OF... THE DREAD PSYCHOTRON!!
THE NEXT MOMENT, INSIDE THE DARKENED ENCLOSURE...
DOES THAT FOOLISH MORTAL THINK TO HOLD HERCULES? IN A TRICE, I SHALL--
NAY!! THE DOOR HAS VANISHED--AS IF IT DID NE'ER EXIST!
IN ITS PLACE, THERE BE SHIMMERING LIGHTS--AN INDESCRIBABLE SHRIEK--FINGERS OF WRITHING FLAME!
EEEEEEEEEEEEEEEEEEEE
WAIT--BEHIND ME! I DO SOMEHOW SENSE THE PRESENCE OF ONE WHOM I HAVE FOUGHT BEFORE--!
14

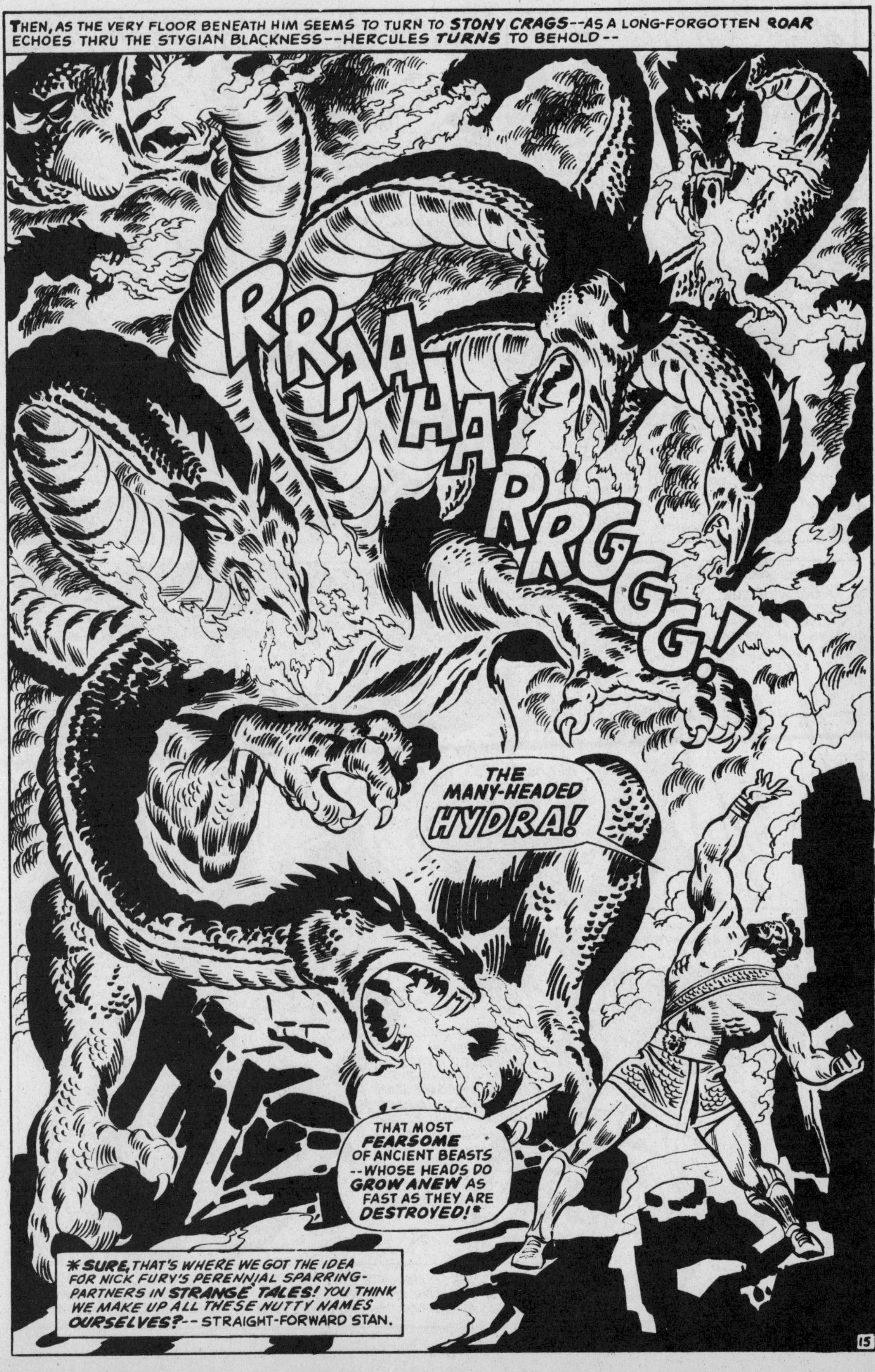
THEN, AS THE VERY FLOOR BENEATH HIM SEEMS TO TURN TO STONY CRAGS--AS A LONG-FORGOTTEN ROAR ECHOES THRU THE STYGIAN BLACKNESS--HERCULES TURNS TO BEHOLD--
RRAAHAARRGGG!
THE MANY-HEADED HYDRA!
THAT MOST FEARSOME OF ANCIENT BEASTS --WHOSE HEADS DO GROW ANEW AS FAST AS THEY ARE DESTROYED!*
*SURE, THAT'S WHERE WE GOT THE IDEA FOR NICK FURY'S PERENNIAL SPARRING-PARTNERS IN STRANGE TALES! YOU THINK WE MAKE UP ALL THESE NUTTY NAMES OURSELVES?-- STRAIGHT-FORWARD STAN.

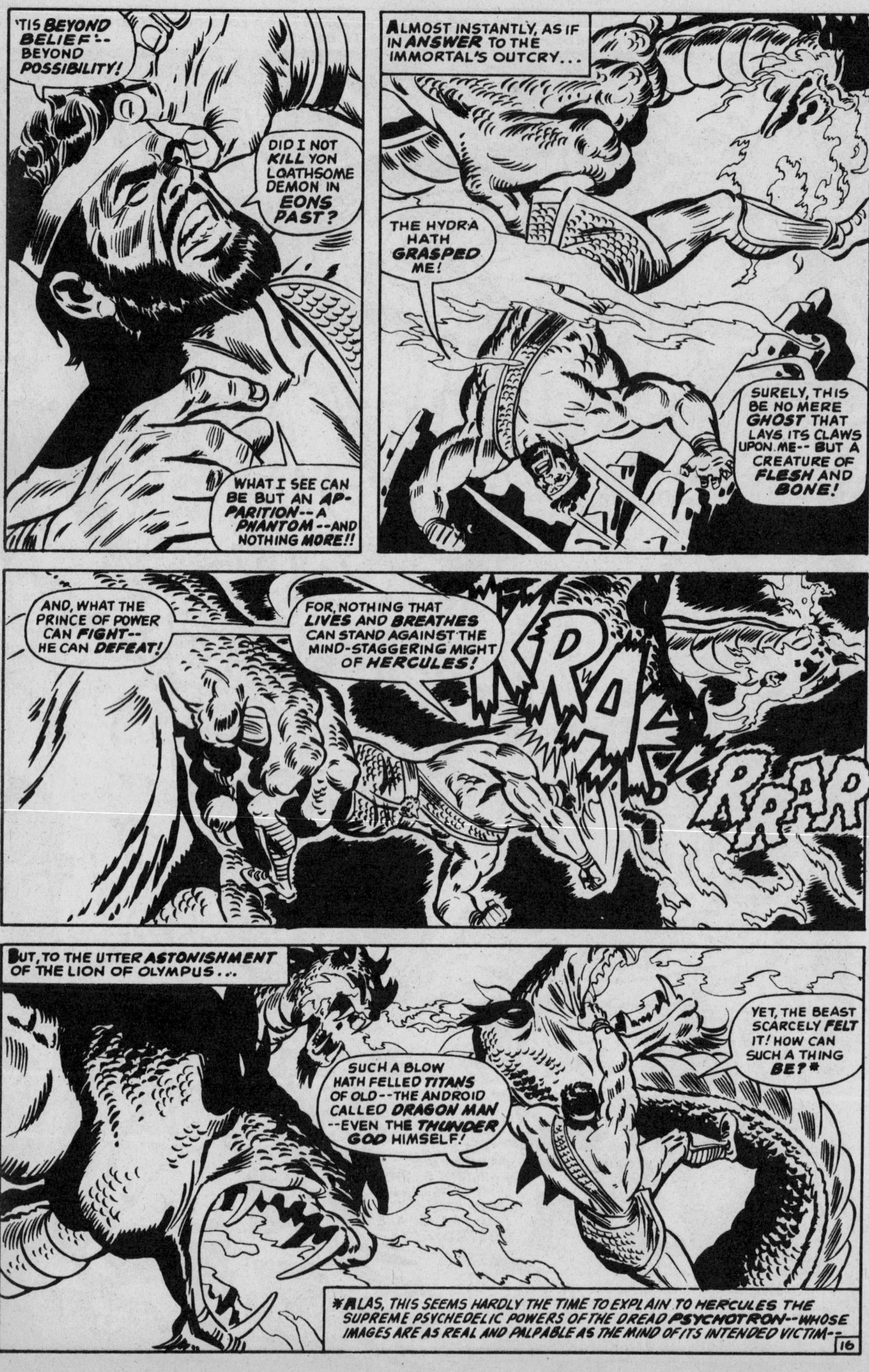

'TIS BEYOND BELIEF-- BEYOND POSSIBILITY!
DID I NOT KILL YON LOATHSOME DEMON IN EONS PAST?
WHAT I SEE CAN BE BUT AN APPARITION-- A PHANTOM --AND NOTHING MORE!!
ALMOST INSTANTLY, AS IF IN ANSWER TO THE IMMORTAL'S OUTCRY...
THE HYDRA HATH GRASPED ME!
SURELY, THIS BE NO MERE GHOST THAT LAYS ITS CLAWS UPON ME-- BUT A CREATURE OF FLESH AND BONE!
AND, WHAT THE PRINCE OF POWER CAN FIGHT-- HE CAN DEFEAT!
FOR, NOTHING THAT LIVES AND BREATHES CAN STAND AGAINST THE MIND-STAGGERING MIGHT OF HERCULES!
KRAAA
RRAR
BUT, TO THE UTTER ASTONISHMENT OF THE LION OF OLYMPUS...
SUCH A BLOW HATH FELLED TITANS OF OLD--THE ANDROID CALLED DRAGON MAN --EVEN THE THUNDER GOD HIMSELF!
YET, THE BEAST SCARCELY FELT IT! HOW CAN SUCH A THING BE?*
*ALAS, THIS SEEMS HARDLY THE TIME TO EXPLAIN TO HERCULES THE SUPREME PSYCHEDELIC POWERS OF THE DREAD PSYCHOTRON--WHOSE IMAGES ARE AS REAL AND PALPABLE AS THE MIND OF ITS INTENDED VICTIM--
16

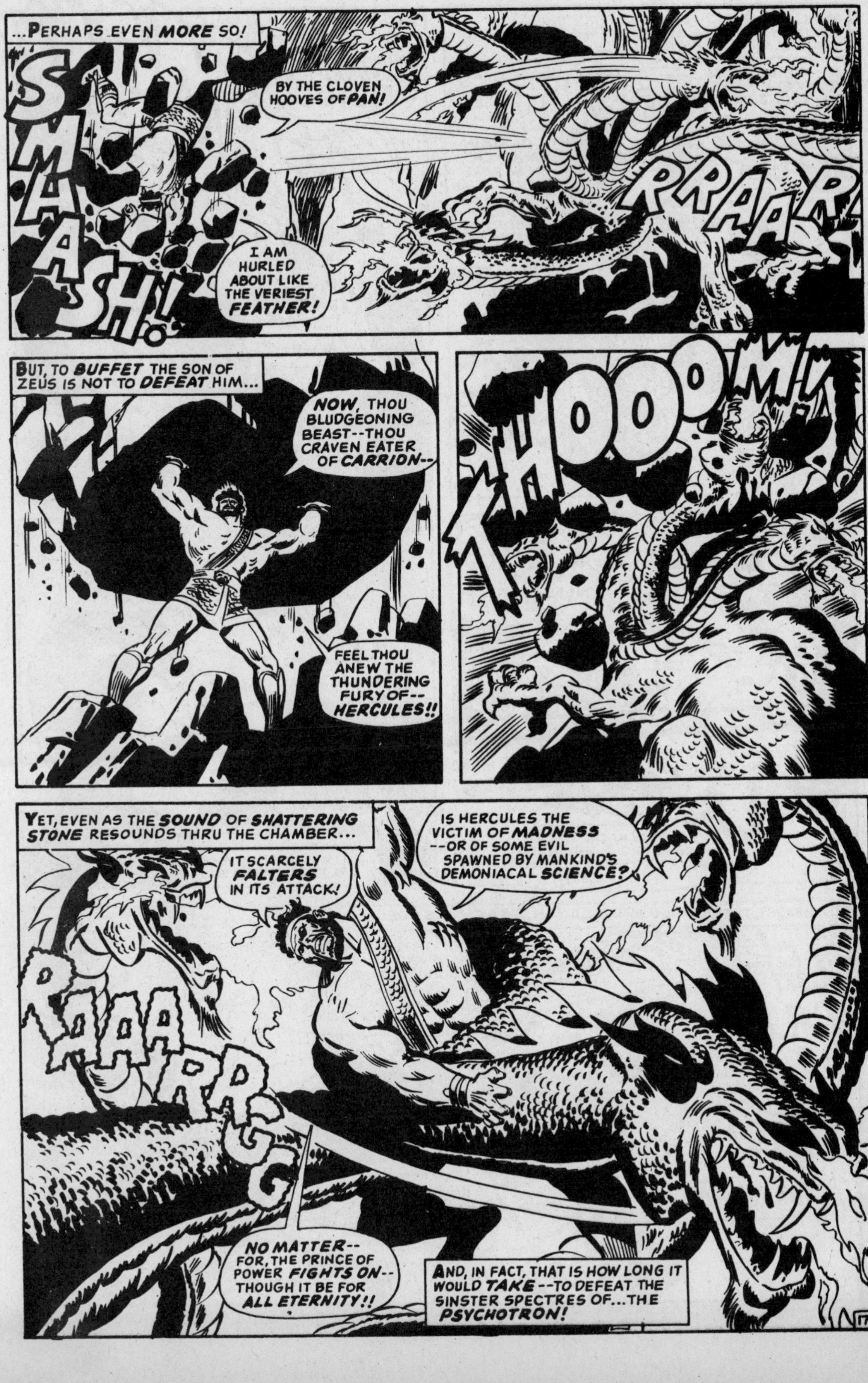
...PERHAPS EVEN MORE SO!
SMAASH!
BY THE CLOVEN HOOVES OF PAN!
I AM HURLED ABOUT LIKE THE VERIEST FEATHER!
RRAAR!
BUT, TO BUFFET THE SON OF ZEUS IS NOT TO DEFEAT HIM...
NOW, THOU BLUDGEONING BEAST--THOU CRAVEN EATER OF CARRION--
FEEL THOU ANEW THE THUNDERING FURY OF--HERCULES!!
WHOOOM!
YET, EVEN AS THE SOUND OF SHATTERING STONE RESOUNDS THRU THE CHAMBER...
IT SCARCELY FALTERS IN ITS ATTACK!
IS HERCULES THE VICTIM OF MADNESS--OR OF SOME EVIL SPAWNED BY MANKIND'S DEMONIACAL SCIENCE?
RAAARRGG
NO MATTER--FOR, THE PRINCE OF POWER FIGHTS ON--THOUGH IT BE FOR ALL ETERNITY!!
AND, IN FACT, THAT IS HOW LONG IT WOULD TAKE--TO DEFEAT THE SINSTER SPECTRES OF...THE PSYCHOTRON!
17

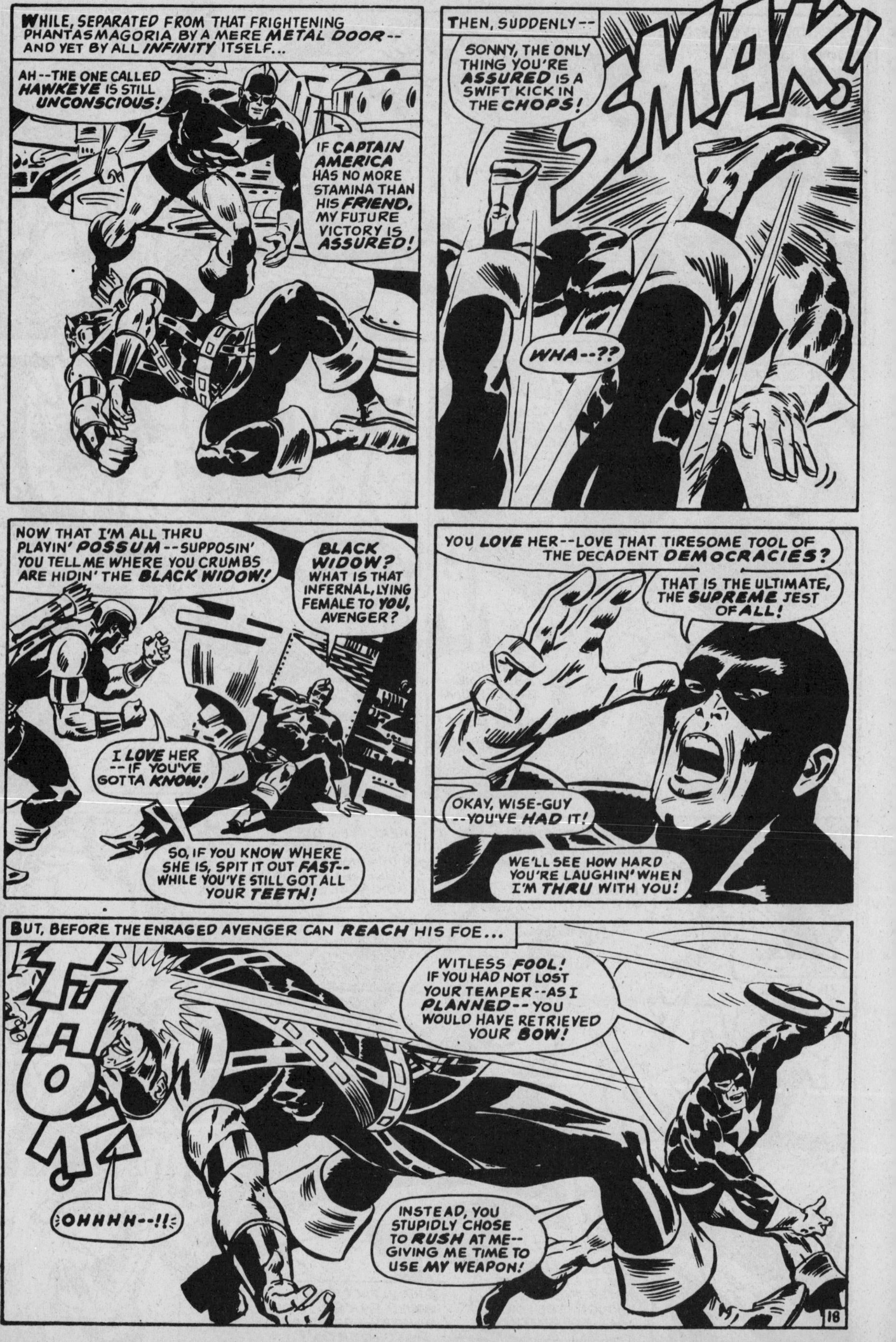

WHILE, SEPARATED FROM THAT FRIGHTENING PHANTASMAGORIA BY A MERE METAL DOOR -- AND YET BY ALL INFINITY ITSELF...
AH -- THE ONE CALLED HAWKEYE IS STILL UNCONSCIOUS!
IF CAPTAIN AMERICA HAS NO MORE STAMINA THAN HIS FRIEND, MY FUTURE VICTORY IS ASSURED!
THEN, SUDDENLY --
SONNY, THE ONLY THING YOU'RE ASSURED IS A SWIFT KICK IN THE CHOPS!
SMAK!
WHA--??
NOW THAT I'M ALL THRU PLAYIN' POSSUM -- SUPPOSIN' YOU TELL ME WHERE YOU CRUMBS ARE HIDIN' THE BLACK WIDOW!
BLACK WIDOW? WHAT IS THAT INFERNAL, LYING FEMALE TO YOU, AVENGER?
I LOVE HER -- IF YOU'VE GOTTA KNOW!
SO, IF YOU KNOW WHERE SHE IS, SPIT IT OUT FAST -- WHILE YOU'VE STILL GOT ALL YOUR TEETH!
YOU LOVE HER -- LOVE THAT TIRESOME TOOL OF THE DECADENT DEMOCRACIES?
THAT IS THE ULTIMATE, THE SUPREME JEST OF ALL!
OKAY, WISE-GUY -- YOU'VE HAD IT!
WE'LL SEE HOW HARD YOU'RE LAUGHIN' WHEN I'M THRU WITH YOU!
BUT, BEFORE THE ENRAGED AVENGER CAN REACH HIS FOE...
THOK
WITLESS FOOL! IF YOU HAD NOT LOST YOUR TEMPER -- AS I PLANNED -- YOU WOULD HAVE RETRIEVED YOUR BOW!
OHHHH--!!
INSTEAD, YOU STUPIDLY CHOSE TO RUSH AT ME -- GIVING ME TIME TO USE MY WEAPON!
18

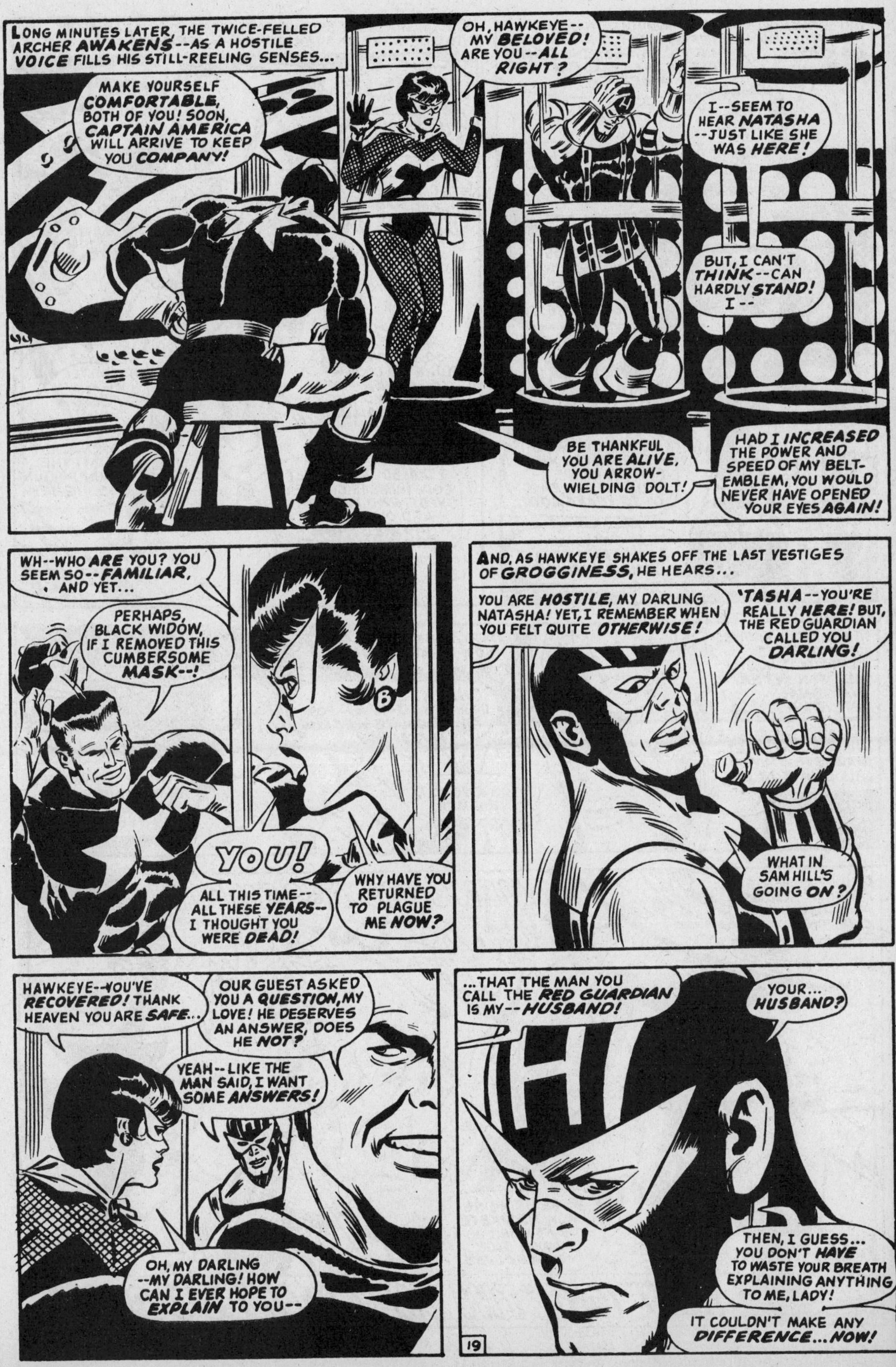
LONG MINUTES LATER, THE TWICE-FELLED ARCHER AWAKENS--AS A HOSTILE VOICE FILLS HIS STILL-REELING SENSES...
MAKE YOURSELF COMFORTABLE, BOTH OF YOU! SOON, CAPTAIN AMERICA WILL ARRIVE TO KEEP YOU COMPANY!
OH, HAWKEYE-- MY BELOVED! ARE YOU--ALL RIGHT?
I--SEEM TO HEAR NATASHA --JUST LIKE SHE WAS HERE!
BUT, I CAN'T THINK--CAN HARDLY STAND! I--
BE THANKFUL YOU ARE ALIVE, YOU ARROW-WIELDING DOLT!
HAD I INCREASED THE POWER AND SPEED OF MY BELT-EMBLEM, YOU WOULD NEVER HAVE OPENED YOUR EYES AGAIN!
WH--WHO ARE YOU? YOU SEEM SO--FAMILIAR, AND YET...
PERHAPS, BLACK WIDOW, IF I REMOVED THIS CUMBERSOME MASK--!
YOU!
ALL THIS TIME-- ALL THESE YEARS-- I THOUGHT YOU WERE DEAD!
WHY HAVE YOU RETURNED TO PLAGUE ME NOW?
AND, AS HAWKEYE SHAKES OFF THE LAST VESTIGES OF GROGGINESS, HE HEARS...
YOU ARE HOSTILE, MY DARLING NATASHA! YET, I REMEMBER WHEN YOU FELT QUITE OTHERWISE!
'TASHA--YOU'RE REALLY HERE! BUT, THE RED GUARDIAN CALLED YOU DARLING!
WHAT IN SAM HILL'S GOING ON?
HAWKEYE--YOU'VE RECOVERED! THANK HEAVEN YOU ARE SAFE...
OUR GUEST ASKED YOU A QUESTION, MY LOVE! HE DESERVES AN ANSWER, DOES HE NOT?
YEAH--LIKE THE MAN SAID, I WANT SOME ANSWERS!
OH, MY DARLING --MY DARLING! HOW CAN I EVER HOPE TO EXPLAIN TO YOU--
...THAT THE MAN YOU CALL THE RED GUARDIAN IS MY--HUSBAND!
YOUR... HUSBAND?
THEN, I GUESS... YOU DON'T HAVE TO WASTE YOUR BREATH EXPLAINING ANYTHING TO ME, LADY!
IT COULDN'T MAKE ANY DIFFERENCE...NOW!
19

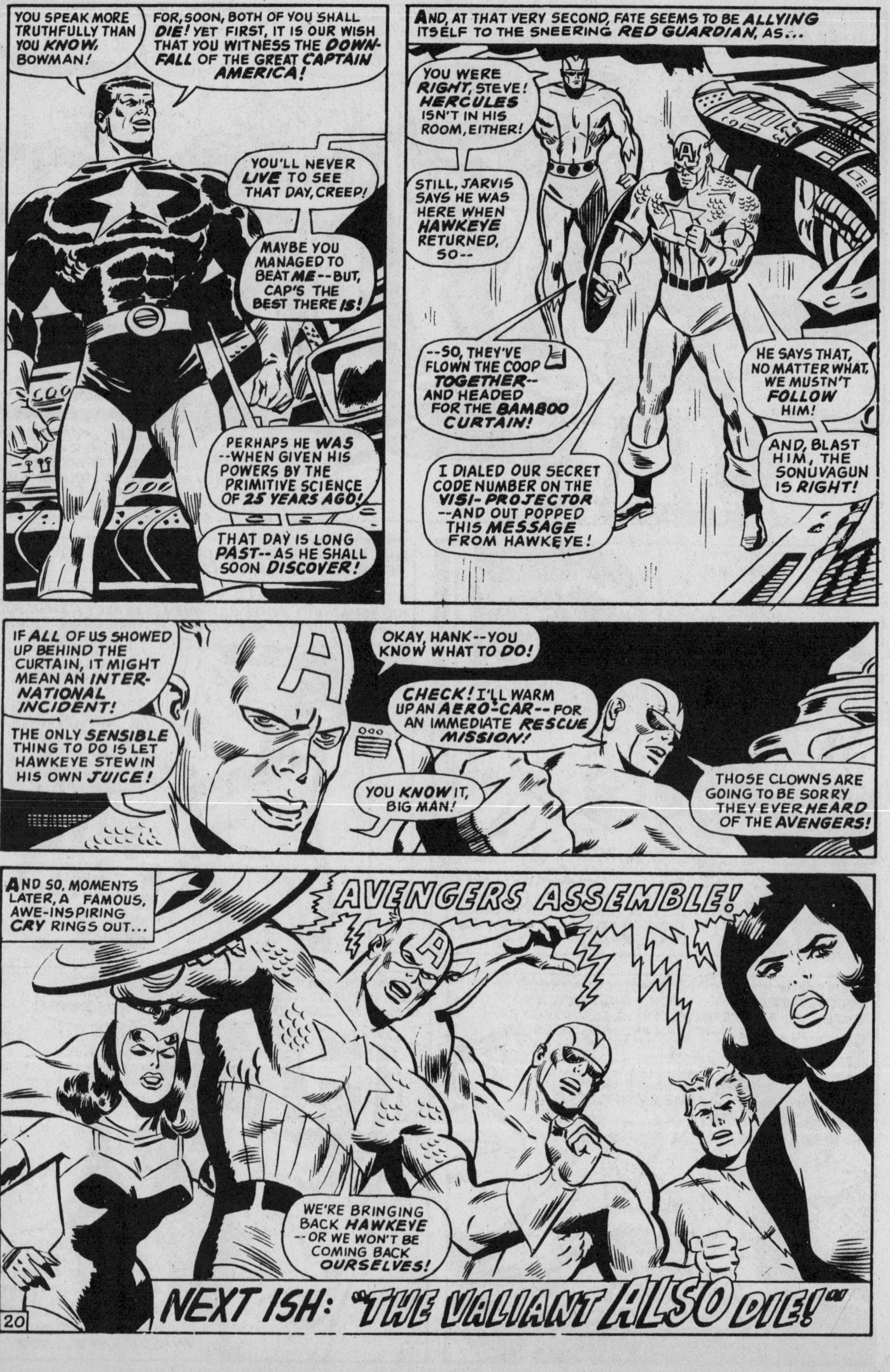
YOU SPEAK MORE TRUTHFULLY THAN YOU KNOW, BOWMAN!
FOR, SOON, BOTH OF YOU SHALL DIE! YET FIRST, IT IS OUR WISH THAT YOU WITNESS THE DOWN-FALL OF THE GREAT CAPTAIN AMERICA!
YOU'LL NEVER LIVE TO SEE THAT DAY, CREEP!
MAYBE YOU MANAGED TO BEAT ME--BUT, CAP'S THE BEST THERE IS!
PERHAPS HE WAS --WHEN GIVEN HIS POWERS BY THE PRIMITIVE SCIENCE OF 25 YEARS AGO!
THAT DAY IS LONG PAST--AS HE SHALL SOON DISCOVER!
AND, AT THAT VERY SECOND, FATE SEEMS TO BE ALLYING ITSELF TO THE SNEERING RED GUARDIAN, AS...
YOU WERE RIGHT, STEVE! HERCULES ISN'T IN HIS ROOM, EITHER!
STILL, JARVIS SAYS HE WAS HERE WHEN HAWKEYE RETURNED, SO--
--SO, THEY'VE FLOWN THE COOP TOGETHER--AND HEADED FOR THE BAMBOO CURTAIN!
I DIALED OUR SECRET CODE NUMBER ON THE VISI-PROJECTOR --AND OUT POPPED THIS MESSAGE FROM HAWKEYE!
HE SAYS THAT, NO MATTER WHAT, WE MUSTN'T FOLLOW HIM!
AND, BLAST HIM, THE SONUVAGUN IS RIGHT!
IF ALL OF US SHOWED UP BEHIND THE CURTAIN, IT MIGHT MEAN AN INTER-NATIONAL INCIDENT!
THE ONLY SENSIBLE THING TO DO IS LET HAWKEYE STEW IN HIS OWN JUICE!
OKAY, HANK--YOU KNOW WHAT TO DO!
CHECK! I'LL WARM UP AN AERO-CAR--FOR AN IMMEDIATE RESCUE MISSION!
YOU KNOW IT, BIG MAN!
THOSE CLOWNS ARE GOING TO BE SORRY THEY EVER HEARD OF THE AVENGERS!
AND SO, MOMENTS LATER, A FAMOUS, AWE-INSPIRING CRY RINGS OUT...
AVENGERS ASSEMBLE!
WE'RE BRINGING BACK HAWKEYE --OR WE WON'T BE COMING BACK OURSELVES!
NEXT ISH: "THE VALIANT ALSO DIE!"
20

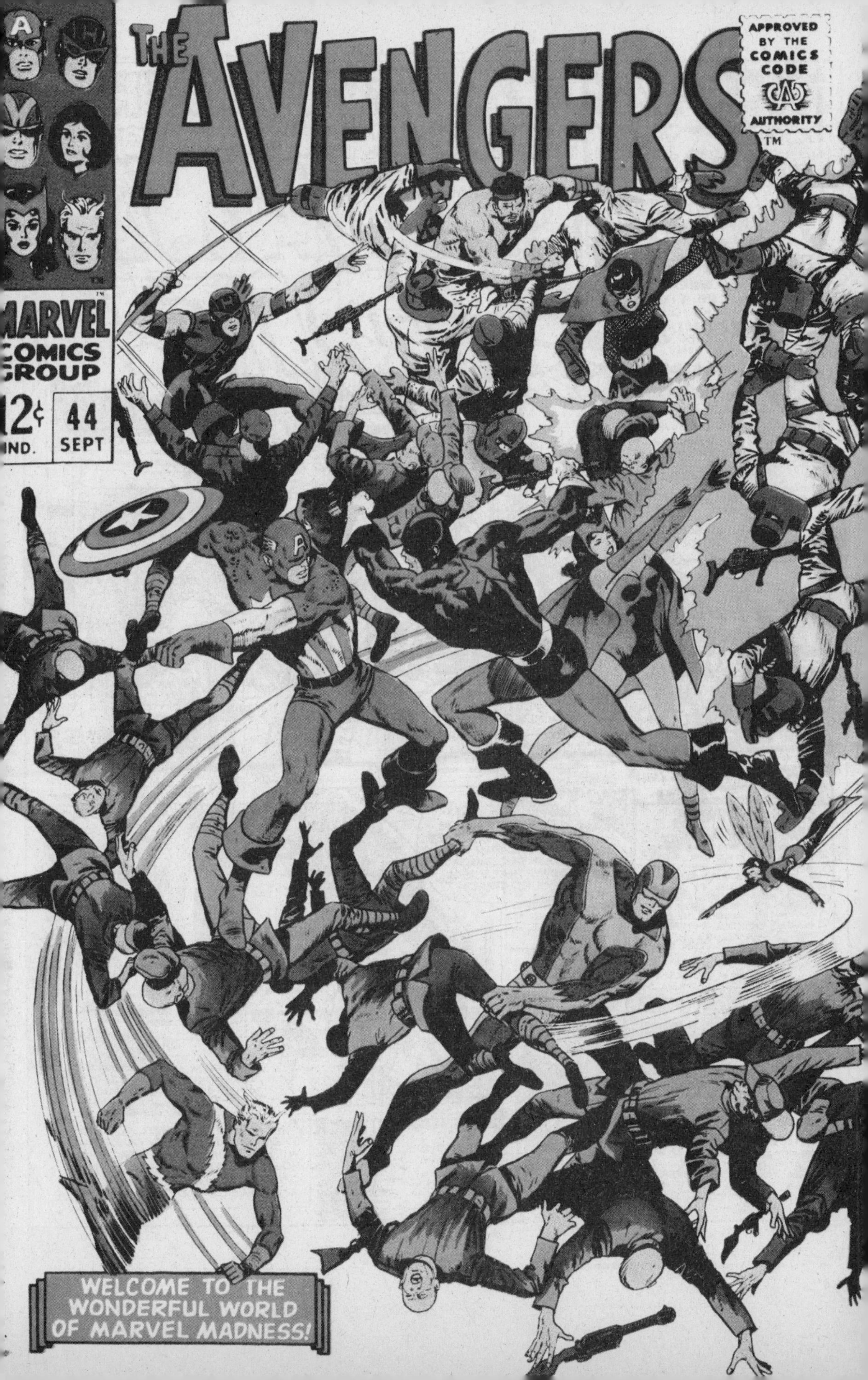
THE AVENGERS
APPROVED BY THE COMICS CODE CA AUTHORITY
TM
MARVEL COMICS GROUP
12¢ IND.
44 SEPT
WELCOME TO THE WONDERFUL WORLD OF MARVEL MADNESS!

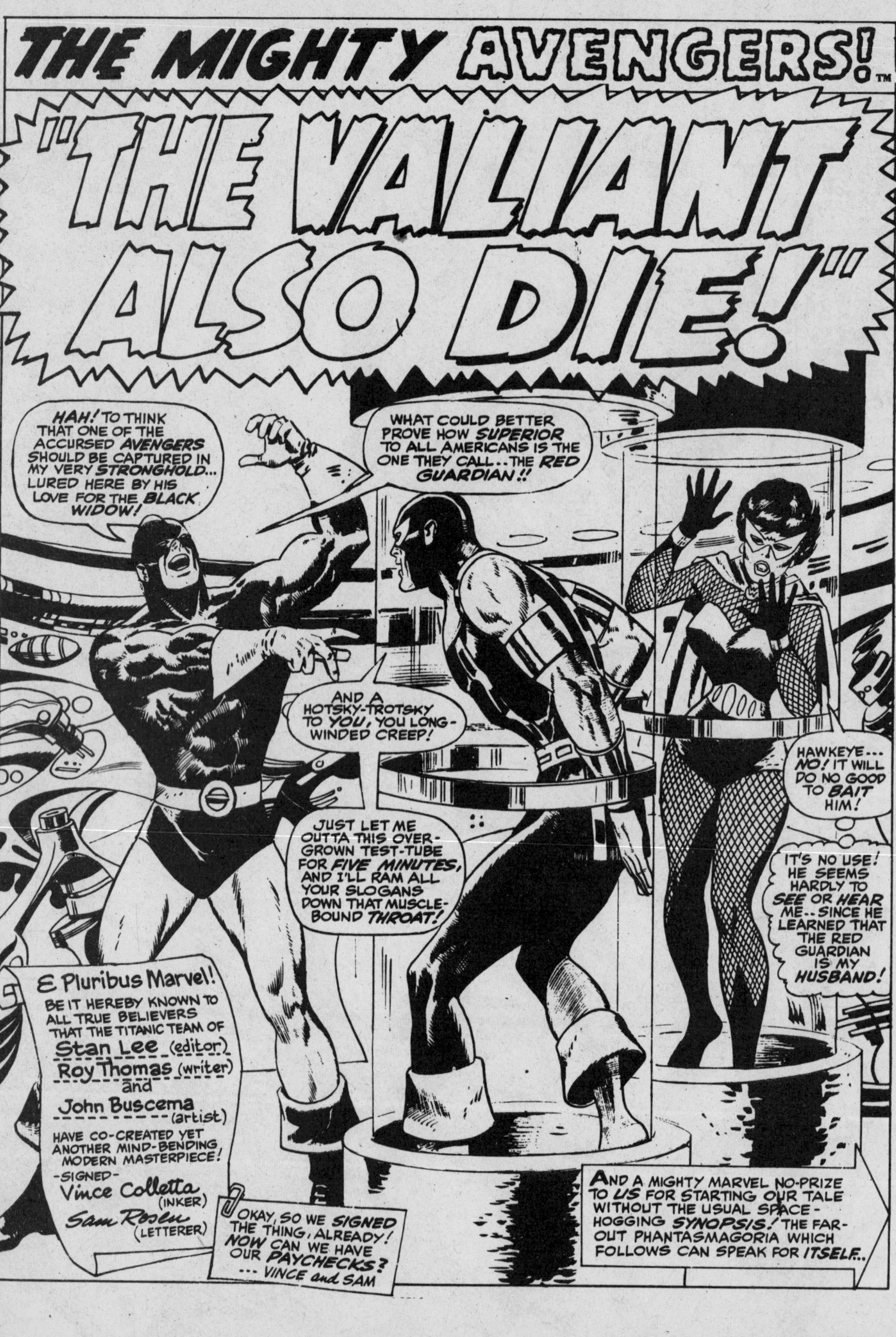
THE MIGHTY AVENGERS!™
"THE VALIANT ALSO DIE!"
HAH! TO THINK THAT ONE OF THE ACCURSED AVENGERS SHOULD BE CAPTURED IN MY VERY STRONGHOLD... LURED HERE BY HIS LOVE FOR THE BLACK WIDOW!
WHAT COULD BETTER PROVE HOW SUPERIOR TO ALL AMERICANS IS THE ONE THEY CALL.. THE RED GUARDIAN!!
AND A HOTSKY-TROTSKY TO YOU, YOU LONG-WINDED CREEP!
JUST LET ME OUTTA THIS OVER-GROWN TEST-TUBE FOR FIVE MINUTES, AND I'LL RAM ALL YOUR SLOGANS DOWN THAT MUSCLE-BOUND THROAT!
HAWKEYE... NO! IT WILL DO NO GOOD TO BAIT HIM!
IT'S NO USE! HE SEEMS HARDLY TO SEE OR HEAR ME.. SINCE HE LEARNED THAT THE RED GUARDIAN IS MY HUSBAND!
E Pluribus Marvel! BE IT HEREBY KNOWN TO ALL TRUE BELIEVERS THAT THE TITANIC TEAM OF Stan Lee (editor) Roy Thomas (writer) and John Buscema (artist) HAVE CO-CREATED YET ANOTHER MIND-BENDING MODERN MASTERPIECE! -SIGNED- Vince Colletta (INKER) Sam Rosen (LETTERER)
OKAY, SO WE SIGNED THE THING, ALREADY! NOW CAN WE HAVE OUR PAYCHECKS? ... VINCE and SAM
AND A MIGHTY MARVEL NO-PRIZE TO US FOR STARTING OUR TALE WITHOUT THE USUAL SPACE-HOGGING SYNOPSIS! THE FAR-OUT PHANTASMAGORIA WHICH FOLLOWS CAN SPEAK FOR ITSELF..

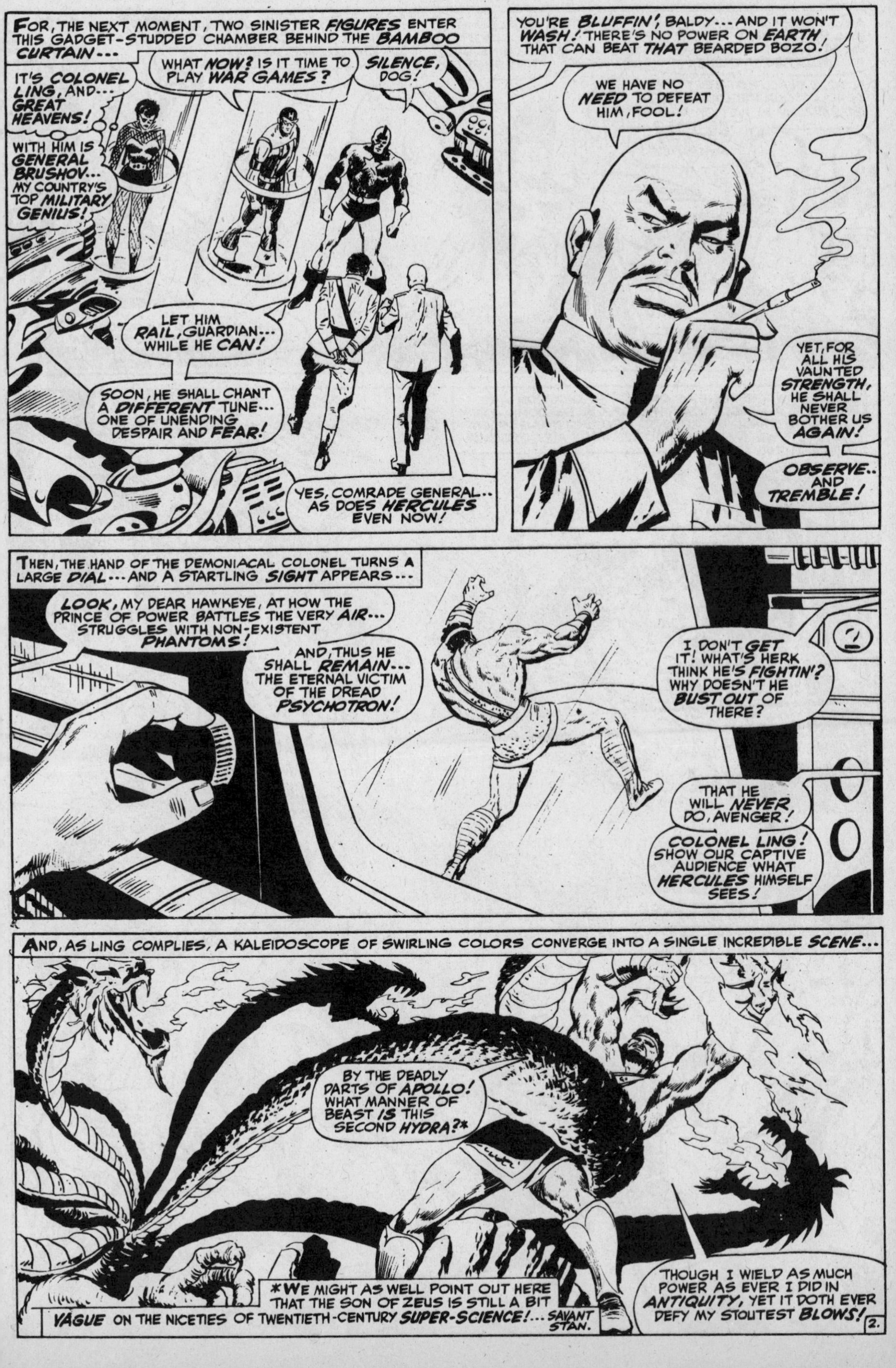
FOR, THE NEXT MOMENT, TWO SINISTER FIGURES ENTER THIS GADGET-STUDDED CHAMBER BEHIND THE BAMBOO CURTAIN...
IT'S COLONEL LING, AND... GREAT HEAVENS!
WITH HIM IS GENERAL BRUSHOV... MY COUNTRY'S TOP MILITARY GENIUS!
WHAT NOW? IS IT TIME TO PLAY WAR GAMES?
SILENCE, DOG!
LET HIM RAIL, GUARDIAN... WHILE HE CAN!
SOON, HE SHALL CHANT A DIFFERENT TUNE... ONE OF UNENDING DESPAIR AND FEAR!
YES, COMRADE GENERAL... AS DOES HERCULES EVEN NOW!
YOU'RE BLUFFIN', BALDY... AND IT WON'T WASH! THERE'S NO POWER ON EARTH THAT CAN BEAT THAT BEARDED BOZO!
WE HAVE NO NEED TO DEFEAT HIM, FOOL!
YET, FOR ALL HIS VAUNTED STRENGTH, HE SHALL NEVER BOTHER US AGAIN!
OBSERVE.. AND TREMBLE!
THEN, THE HAND OF THE DEMONIACAL COLONEL TURNS A LARGE DIAL... AND A STARTLING SIGHT APPEARS...
LOOK, MY DEAR HAWKEYE, AT HOW THE PRINCE OF POWER BATTLES THE VERY AIR... STRUGGLES WITH NON-EXISTENT PHANTOMS!
AND, THUS HE SHALL REMAIN... THE ETERNAL VICTIM OF THE DREAD PSYCHOTRON!
I DON'T GET IT! WHAT'S HERK THINK HE'S FIGHTIN'? WHY DOESN'T HE BUST OUT OF THERE?
THAT HE WILL NEVER DO, AVENGER!
COLONEL LING! SHOW OUR CAPTIVE AUDIENCE WHAT HERCULES HIMSELF SEES!
AND, AS LING COMPLIES, A KALEIDOSCOPE OF SWIRLING COLORS CONVERGE INTO A SINGLE INCREDIBLE SCENE...
BY THE DEADLY DARTS OF APOLLO! WHAT MANNER OF BEAST IS THIS SECOND HYDRA?*
THOUGH I WIELD AS MUCH POWER AS EVER I DID IN ANTIQUITY, YET IT DOTH EVER DEFY MY STOUTEST BLOWS!
*WE MIGHT AS WELL POINT OUT HERE THAT THE SON OF ZEUS IS STILL A BIT VAGUE ON THE NICETIES OF TWENTIETH-CENTURY SUPER-SCIENCE!... SAVANT STAN.
2.

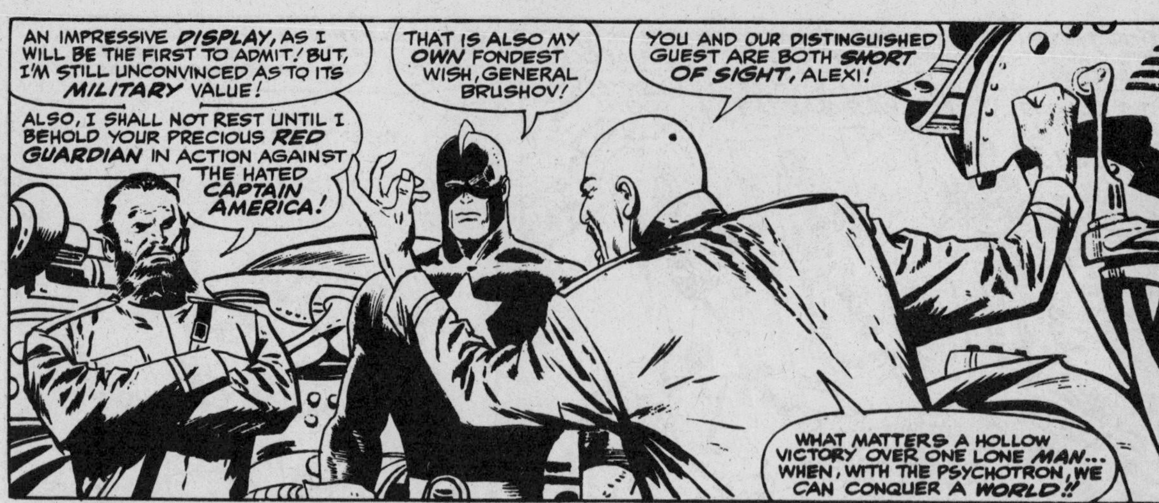

AN IMPRESSIVE DISPLAY, AS I WILL BE THE FIRST TO ADMIT! BUT, I'M STILL UNCONVINCED AS TO ITS MILITARY VALUE!
ALSO, I SHALL NOT REST UNTIL I BEHOLD YOUR PRECIOUS RED GUARDIAN IN ACTION AGAINST THE HATED CAPTAIN AMERICA!
THAT IS ALSO MY OWN FONDEST WISH, GENERAL BRUSHOV!
YOU AND OUR DISTINGUISHED GUEST ARE BOTH SHORT OF SIGHT, ALEXI!
WHAT MATTERS A HOLLOW VICTORY OVER ONE LONE MAN... WHEN, WITH THE PSYCHOTRON, WE CAN CONQUER A WORLD!!

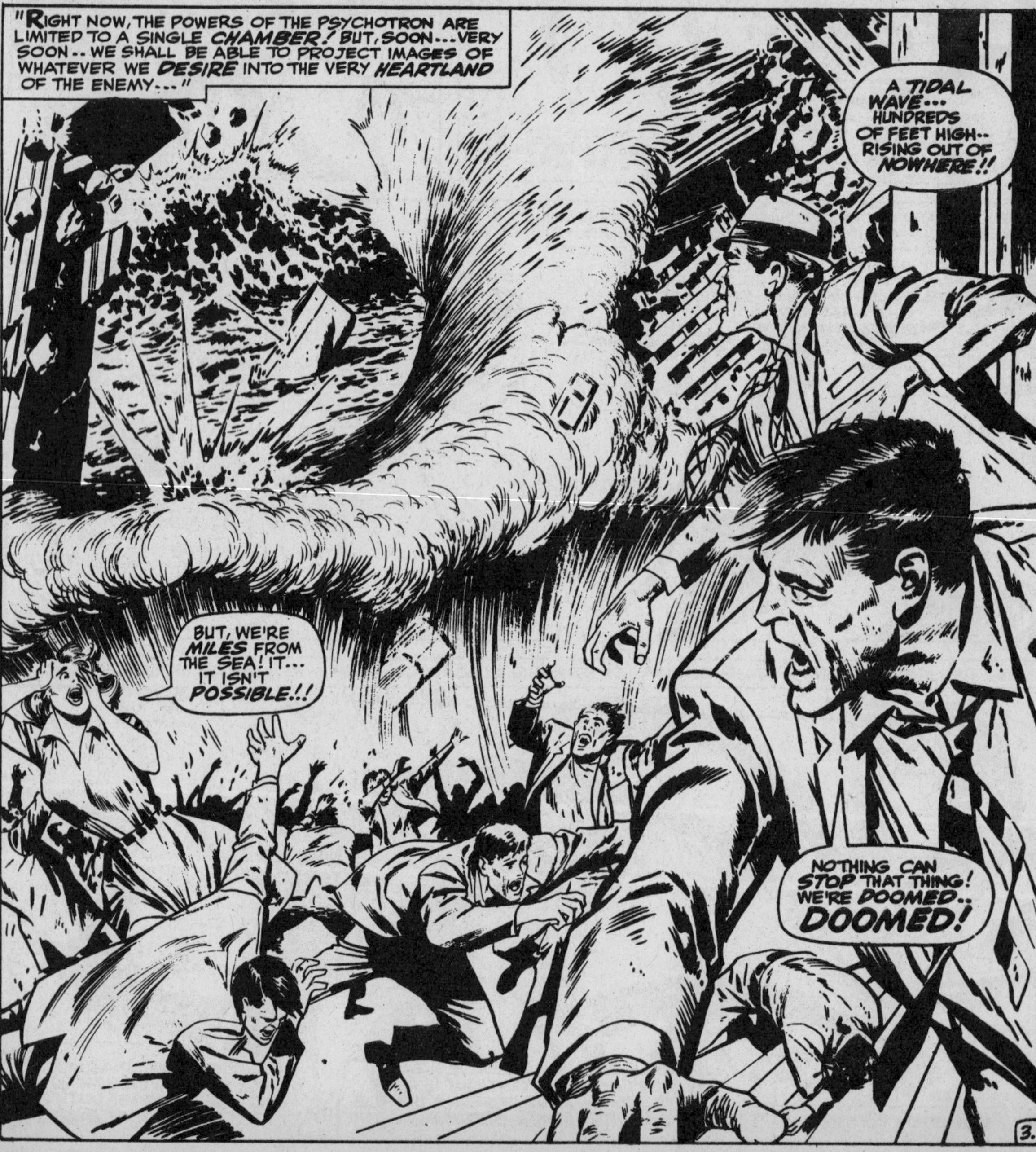

"RIGHT NOW, THE POWERS OF THE PSYCHOTRON ARE LIMITED TO A SINGLE CHAMBER! BUT, SOON... VERY SOON.. WE SHALL BE ABLE TO PROJECT IMAGES OF WHATEVER WE DESIRE INTO THE VERY HEARTLAND OF THE ENEMY..."
A TIDAL WAVE... HUNDREDS OF FEET HIGH-- RISING OUT OF NOWHERE!!
BUT, WE'RE MILES FROM THE SEA! IT... IT ISN'T POSSIBLE!!
NOTHING CAN STOP THAT THING! WE'RE DOOMED.. DOOMED!
3.

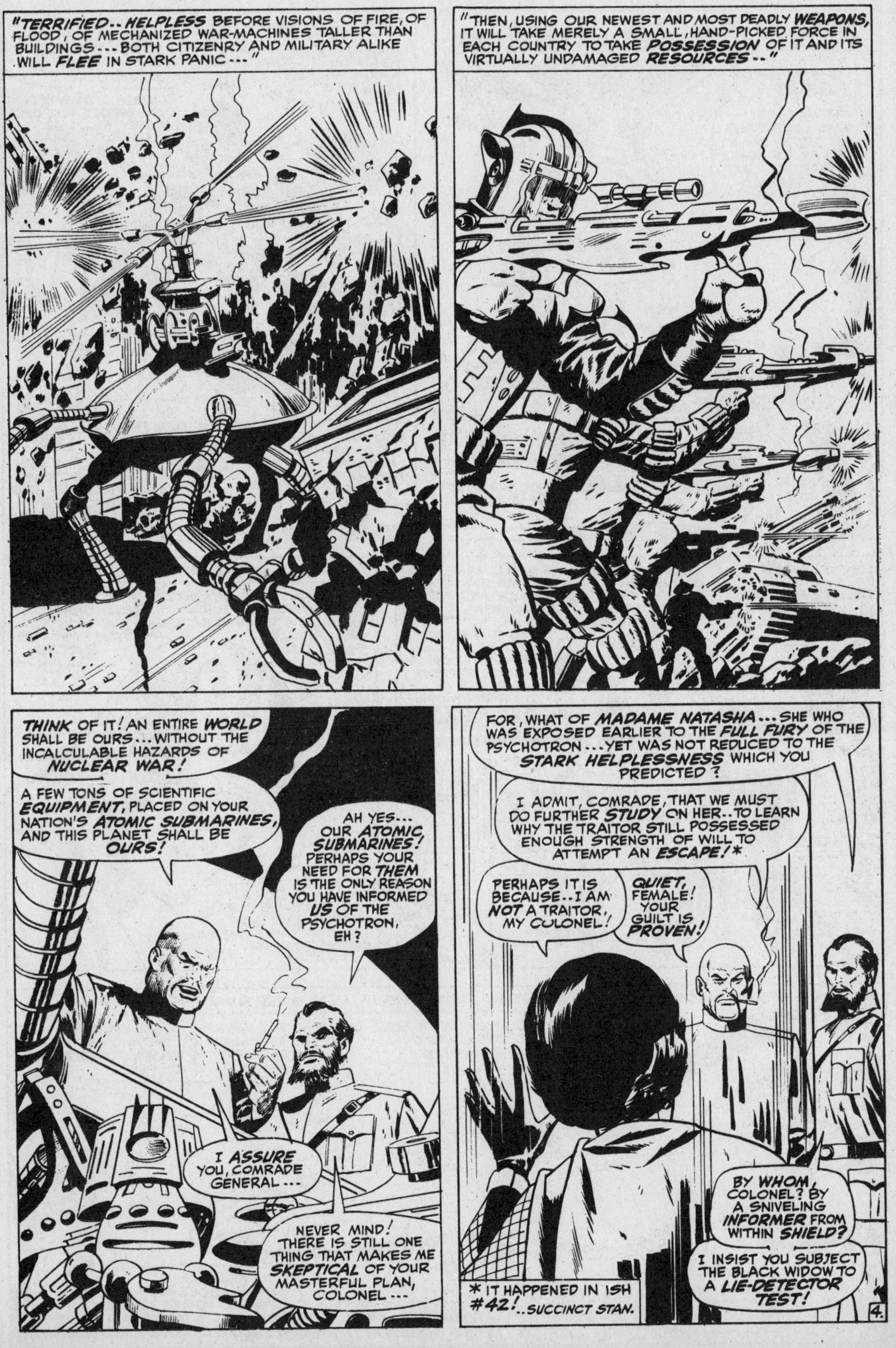
"TERRIFIED.. HELPLESS BEFORE VISIONS OF FIRE, OF FLOOD, OF MECHANIZED WAR-MACHINES TALLER THAN BUILDINGS--- BOTH CITIZENRY AND MILITARY ALIKE WILL FLEE IN STARK PANIC---"
"THEN, USING OUR NEWEST AND MOST DEADLY WEAPONS, IT WILL TAKE MERELY A SMALL, HAND-PICKED FORCE IN EACH COUNTRY TO TAKE POSSESSION OF IT AND ITS VIRTUALLY UNDAMAGED RESOURCES--"
THINK OF IT! AN ENTIRE WORLD SHALL BE OURS... WITHOUT THE INCALCULABLE HAZARDS OF NUCLEAR WAR!
A FEW TONS OF SCIENTIFIC EQUIPMENT, PLACED ON YOUR NATION'S ATOMIC SUBMARINES, AND THIS PLANET SHALL BE OURS!
AH YES... OUR ATOMIC SUBMARINES! PERHAPS YOUR NEED FOR THEM IS THE ONLY REASON YOU HAVE INFORMED US OF THE PSYCHOTRON, EH?
I ASSURE YOU, COMRADE GENERAL---
NEVER MIND! THERE IS STILL ONE THING THAT MAKES ME SKEPTICAL OF YOUR MASTERFUL PLAN, COLONEL---
FOR, WHAT OF MADAME NATASHA... SHE WHO WAS EXPOSED EARLIER TO THE FULL FURY OF THE PSYCHOTRON...YET WAS NOT REDUCED TO THE STARK HELPLESSNESS WHICH YOU PREDICTED?
I ADMIT, COMRADE, THAT WE MUST DO FURTHER STUDY ON HER..TO LEARN WHY THE TRAITOR STILL POSSESSED ENOUGH STRENGTH OF WILL TO ATTEMPT AN ESCAPE!*
PERHAPS IT IS BECAUSE..I AM NOT A TRAITOR, MY COLONEL!
QUIET, FEMALE! YOUR GUILT IS PROVEN!
BY WHOM, COLONEL? BY A SNIVELING INFORMER FROM WITHIN SHIELD?
I INSIST YOU SUBJECT THE BLACK WIDOW TO A LIE-DETECTOR TEST!
*IT HAPPENED IN ISH #42!..SUCCINCT STAN.
4.

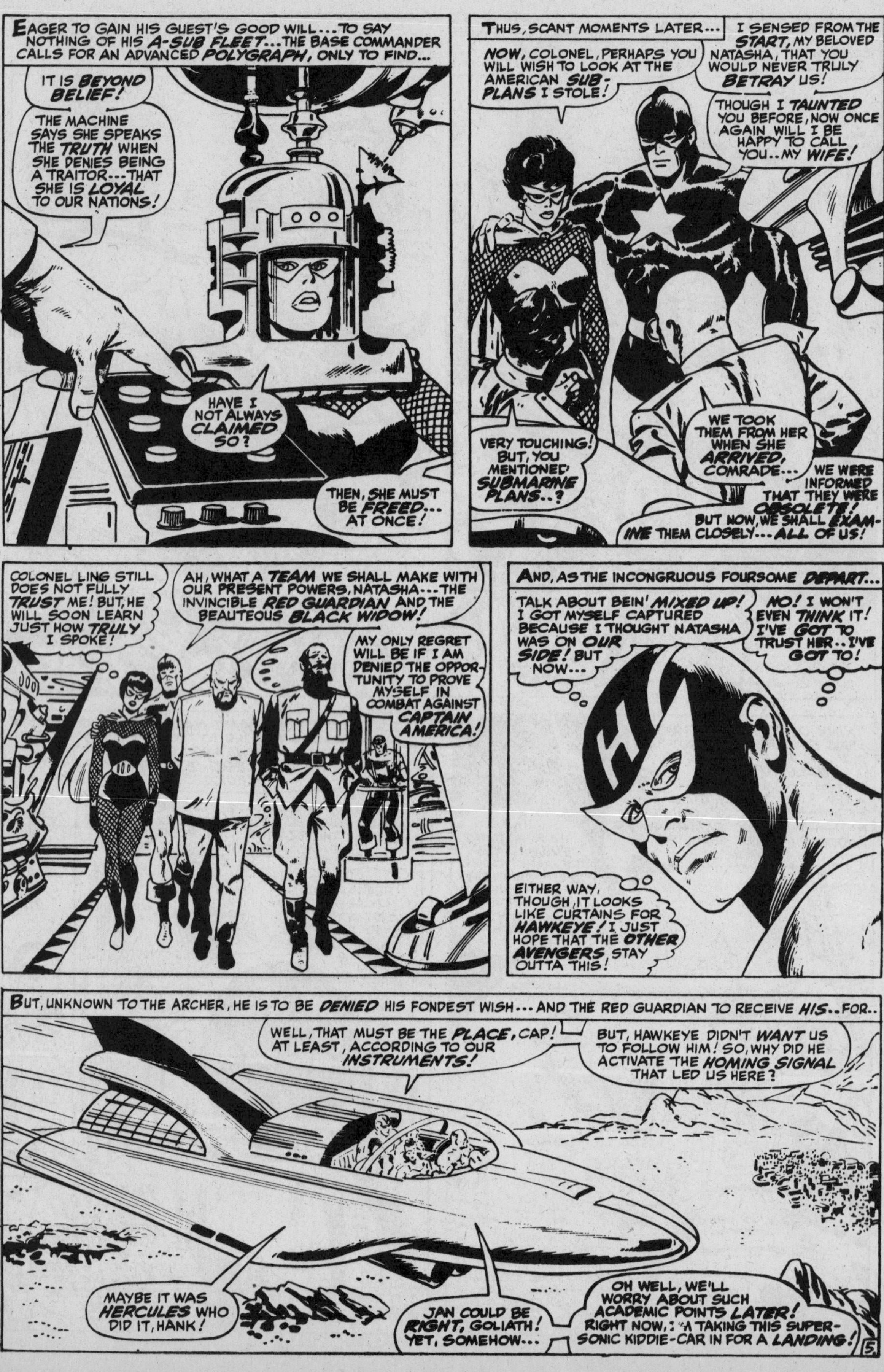
EAGER TO GAIN HIS GUEST'S GOOD WILL...TO SAY NOTHING OF HIS A-SUB FLEET...THE BASE COMMANDER CALLS FOR AN ADVANCED POLYGRAPH, ONLY TO FIND...
IT IS BEYOND BELIEF!
THE MACHINE SAYS SHE SPEAKS THE TRUTH WHEN SHE DENIES BEING A TRAITOR---THAT SHE IS LOYAL TO OUR NATIONS!
HAVE I NOT ALWAYS CLAIMED SO?
THEN, SHE MUST BE FREED... AT ONCE!
THUS, SCANT MOMENTS LATER...
NOW, COLONEL, PERHAPS YOU WILL WISH TO LOOK AT THE AMERICAN SUB-PLANS I STOLE!
I SENSED FROM THE START, MY BELOVED NATASHA, THAT YOU WOULD NEVER TRULY BETRAY US!
THOUGH I TAUNTED YOU BEFORE, NOW ONCE AGAIN WILL I BE HAPPY TO CALL YOU.. MY WIFE!
VERY TOUCHING! BUT, YOU MENTIONED SUBMARINE PLANS..?
WE TOOK THEM FROM HER WHEN SHE ARRIVED, COMRADE...
WE WERE INFORMED THAT THEY WERE OBSOLETE! BUT NOW, WE SHALL EXAMINE THEM CLOSELY...ALL OF US!
COLONEL LING STILL DOES NOT FULLY TRUST ME! BUT, HE WILL SOON LEARN JUST HOW TRULY I SPOKE!
AH, WHAT A TEAM WE SHALL MAKE WITH OUR PRESENT POWERS, NATASHA---THE INVINCIBLE RED GUARDIAN AND THE BEAUTEOUS BLACK WIDOW!
MY ONLY REGRET WILL BE IF I AM DENIED THE OPPORTUNITY TO PROVE MYSELF IN COMBAT AGAINST CAPTAIN AMERICA!
AND, AS THE INCONGRUOUS FOURSOME DEPART...
TALK ABOUT BEIN' MIXED UP! I GOT MYSELF CAPTURED BECAUSE I THOUGHT NATASHA WAS ON OUR SIDE! BUT NOW...
NO! I WON'T EVEN THINK IT! I'VE GOT TO TRUST HER..I'VE GOT TO!
EITHER WAY, THOUGH, IT LOOKS LIKE CURTAINS FOR HAWKEYE! I JUST HOPE THAT THE OTHER AVENGERS STAY OUTTA THIS!
BUT, UNKNOWN TO THE ARCHER, HE IS TO BE DENIED HIS FONDEST WISH...AND THE RED GUARDIAN TO RECEIVE HIS..FOR..
WELL, THAT MUST BE THE PLACE, CAP! AT LEAST, ACCORDING TO OUR INSTRUMENTS!
BUT, HAWKEYE DIDN'T WANT US TO FOLLOW HIM! SO, WHY DID HE ACTIVATE THE HOMING SIGNAL THAT LED US HERE?
MAYBE IT WAS HERCULES WHO DID IT, HANK!
JAN COULD BE RIGHT, GOLIATH! YET, SOMEHOW...
OH WELL, WE'LL WORRY ABOUT SUCH ACADEMIC POINTS LATER! RIGHT NOW, I'M TAKING THIS SUPER-SONIC KIDDIE-CAR IN FOR A LANDING!
5

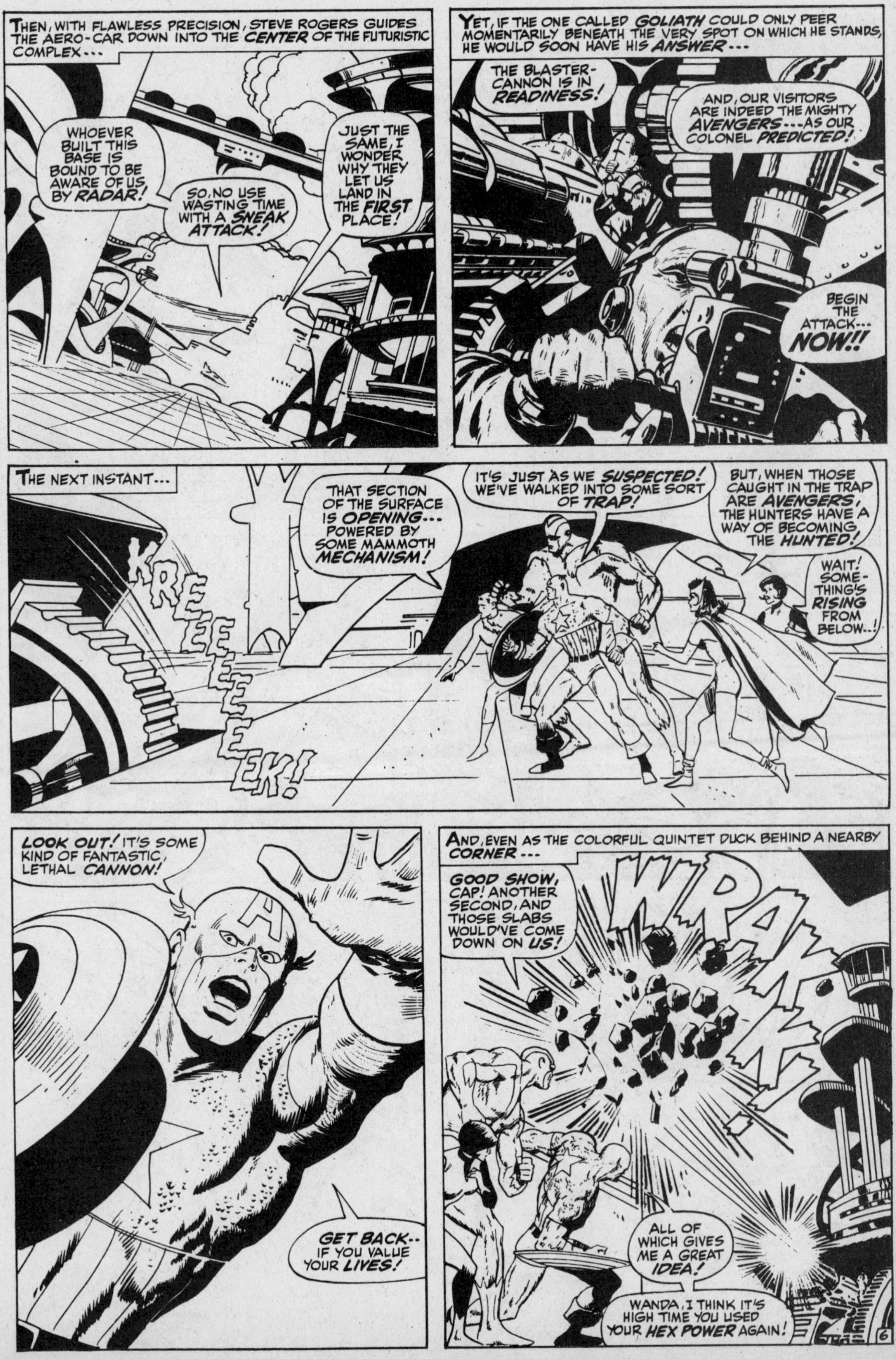
THEN, WITH FLAWLESS PRECISION, STEVE ROGERS GUIDES THE AERO-CAR DOWN INTO THE CENTER OF THE FUTURISTIC COMPLEX...
WHOEVER BUILT THIS BASE IS BOUND TO BE AWARE OF US BY RADAR!
SO, NO USE WASTING TIME WITH A SNEAK ATTACK!
JUST THE SAME, I WONDER WHY THEY LET US LAND IN THE FIRST PLACE!
YET, IF THE ONE CALLED GOLIATH COULD ONLY PEER MOMENTARILY BENEATH THE VERY SPOT ON WHICH HE STANDS, HE WOULD SOON HAVE HIS ANSWER...
THE BLASTER-CANNON IS IN READINESS!
AND, OUR VISITORS ARE INDEED THE MIGHTY AVENGERS...AS OUR COLONEL PREDICTED!
BEGIN THE ATTACK... NOW!!
THE NEXT INSTANT...
KREEEEEEEEK!
THAT SECTION OF THE SURFACE IS OPENING... POWERED BY SOME MAMMOTH MECHANISM!
IT'S JUST AS WE SUSPECTED! WE'VE WALKED INTO SOME SORT OF TRAP!
BUT, WHEN THOSE CAUGHT IN THE TRAP ARE AVENGERS, THE HUNTERS HAVE A WAY OF BECOMING THE HUNTED!
WAIT! SOME-THING'S RISING FROM BELOW..!
LOOK OUT! IT'S SOME KIND OF FANTASTIC, LETHAL CANNON!
GET BACK.. IF YOU VALUE YOUR LIVES!
AND, EVEN AS THE COLORFUL QUINTET DUCK BEHIND A NEARBY CORNER...
GOOD SHOW, CAP! ANOTHER SECOND, AND THOSE SLABS WOULD'VE COME DOWN ON US!
WRAK!
ALL OF WHICH GIVES ME A GREAT IDEA!
WANDA, I THINK IT'S HIGH TIME YOU USED YOUR HEX POWER AGAIN!
6

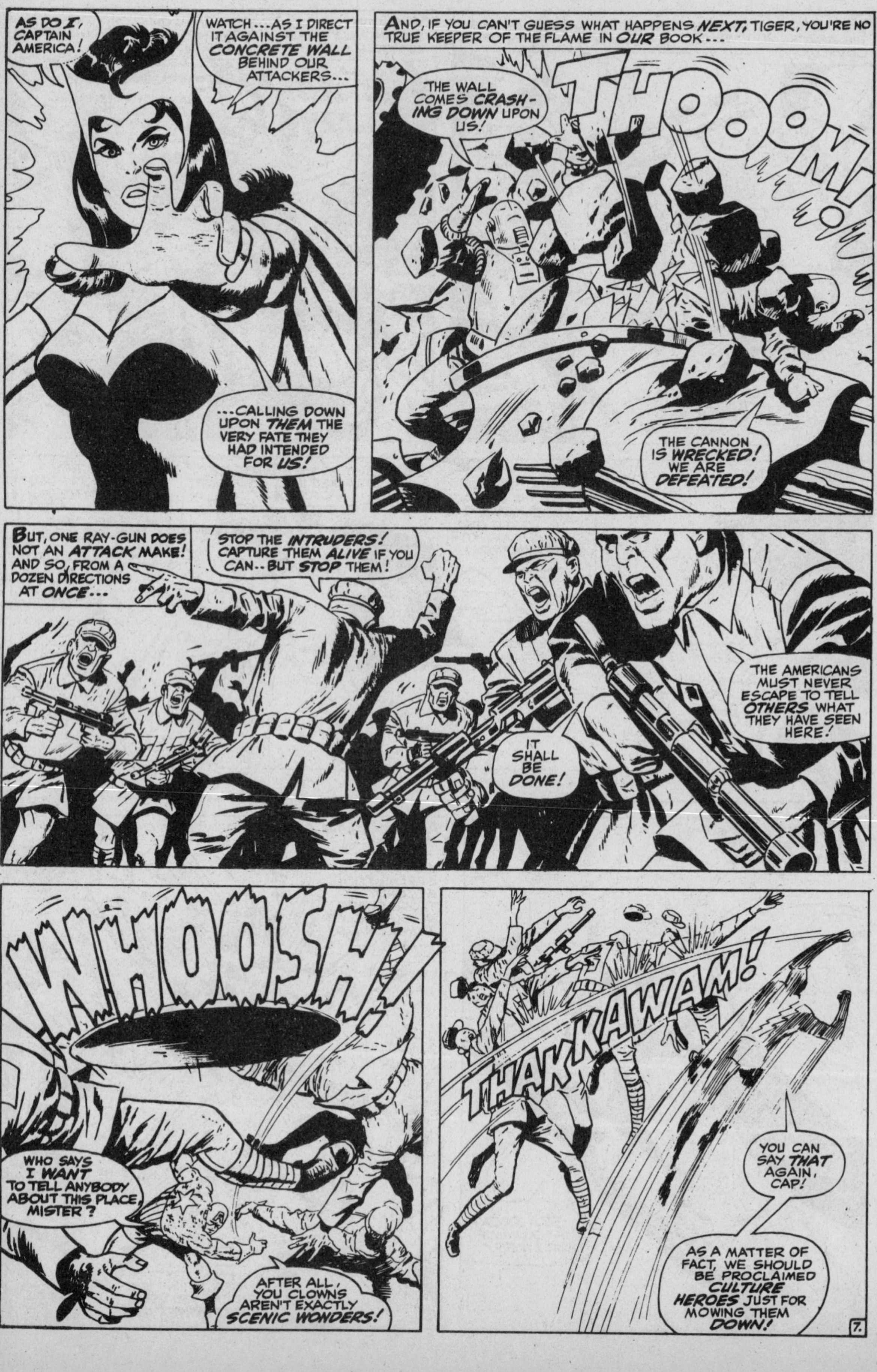
AS DO I, CAPTAIN AMERICA!
WATCH... AS I DIRECT IT AGAINST THE CONCRETE WALL BEHIND OUR ATTACKERS...
...CALLING DOWN UPON THEM THE VERY FATE THEY HAD INTENDED FOR US!
AND, IF YOU CAN'T GUESS WHAT HAPPENS NEXT, TIGER, YOU'RE NO TRUE KEEPER OF THE FLAME IN OUR BOOK...
THE WALL COMES CRASHING DOWN UPON US!
THOOOM!
THE CANNON IS WRECKED! WE ARE DEFEATED!
BUT, ONE RAY-GUN DOES NOT AN ATTACK MAKE! AND SO, FROM A DOZEN DIRECTIONS AT ONCE...
STOP THE INTRUDERS! CAPTURE THEM ALIVE IF YOU CAN.. BUT STOP THEM!
THE AMERICANS MUST NEVER ESCAPE TO TELL OTHERS WHAT THEY HAVE SEEN HERE!
IT SHALL BE DONE!
WHOOSH!
WHO SAYS I WANT TO TELL ANYBODY ABOUT THIS PLACE, MISTER?
AFTER ALL, YOU CLOWNS AREN'T EXACTLY SCENIC WONDERS!
THAKKAWAM!
YOU CAN SAY THAT AGAIN, CAP!
AS A MATTER OF FACT, WE SHOULD BE PROCLAIMED CULTURE HEROES JUST FOR MOWING THEM DOWN!
7.

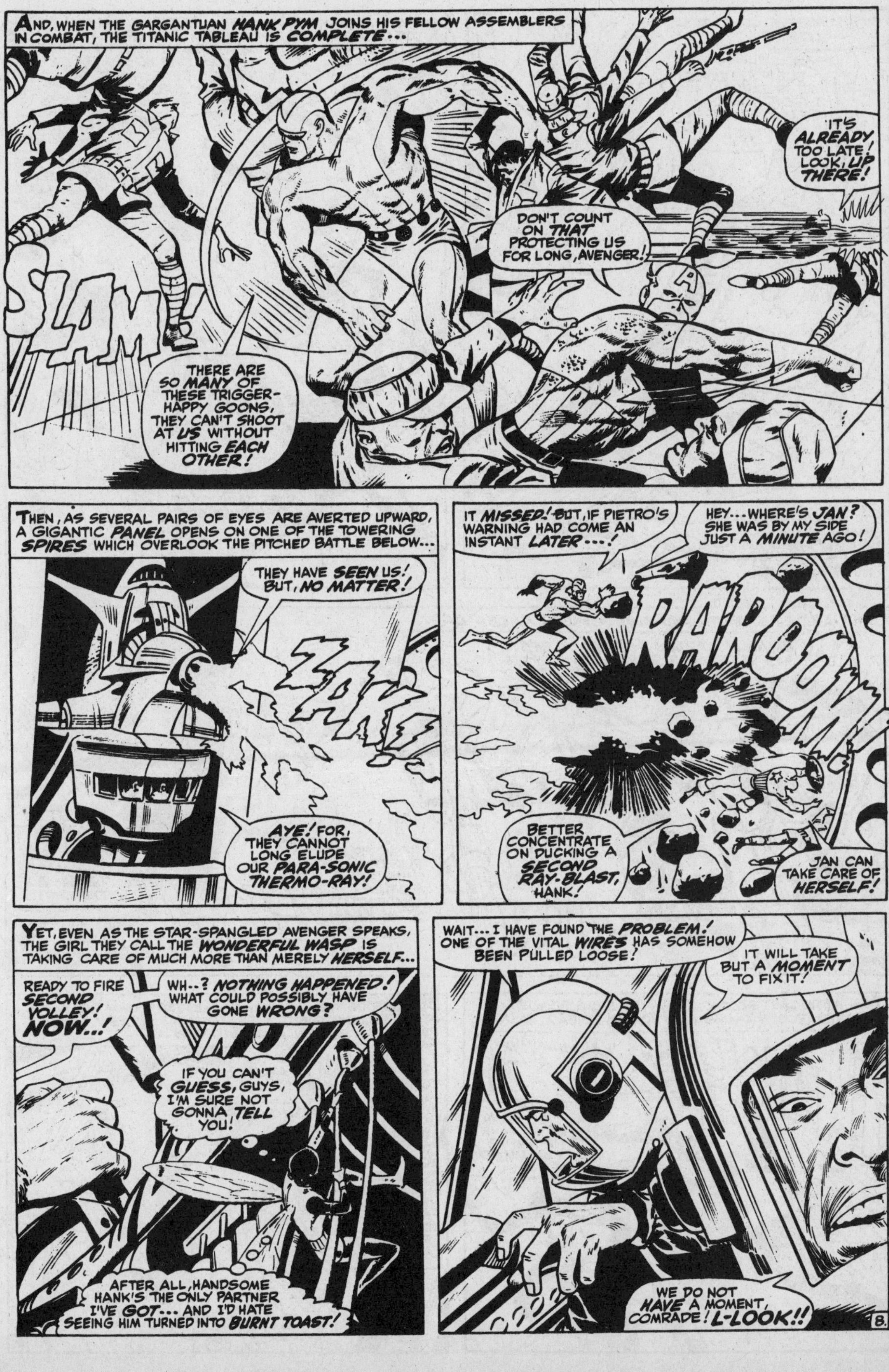
AND, WHEN THE GARGANTUAN HANK PYM JOINS HIS FELLOW ASSEMBLERS IN COMBAT, THE TITANIC TABLEAU IS COMPLETE...
IT'S ALREADY TOO LATE! LOOK, UP THERE!
DON'T COUNT ON THAT PROTECTING US FOR LONG, AVENGER!
SLAM!
THERE ARE SO MANY OF THESE TRIGGER-HAPPY GOONS, THEY CAN'T SHOOT AT US WITHOUT HITTING EACH OTHER!
THEN, AS SEVERAL PAIRS OF EYES ARE AVERTED UPWARD, A GIGANTIC PANEL OPENS ON ONE OF THE TOWERING SPIRES WHICH OVERLOOK THE PITCHED BATTLE BELOW...
THEY HAVE SEEN US! BUT, NO MATTER!
ZAK!
AYE! FOR, THEY CANNOT LONG ELUDE OUR PARA-SONIC THERMO-RAY!
IT MISSED! BUT, IF PIETRO'S WARNING HAD COME AN INSTANT LATER...!
HEY... WHERE'S JAN? SHE WAS BY MY SIDE JUST A MINUTE AGO!
RAROOM!!
BETTER CONCENTRATE ON DUCKING A SECOND RAY-BLAST, HANK!
JAN CAN TAKE CARE OF HERSELF!
YET, EVEN AS THE STAR-SPANGLED AVENGER SPEAKS, THE GIRL THEY CALL THE WONDERFUL WASP IS TAKING CARE OF MUCH MORE THAN MERELY HERSELF...
READY TO FIRE SECOND VOLLEY! NOW..!
WH..? NOTHING HAPPENED! WHAT COULD POSSIBLY HAVE GONE WRONG?
IF YOU CAN'T GUESS, GUYS, I'M SURE NOT GONNA TELL YOU!
AFTER ALL, HANDSOME HANK'S THE ONLY PARTNER I'VE GOT... AND I'D HATE SEEING HIM TURNED INTO BURNT TOAST!
WAIT... I HAVE FOUND THE PROBLEM! ONE OF THE VITAL WIRES HAS SOMEHOW BEEN PULLED LOOSE!
IT WILL TAKE BUT A MOMENT TO FIX IT!
WE DO NOT HAVE A MOMENT, COMRADE! L-LOOK!!

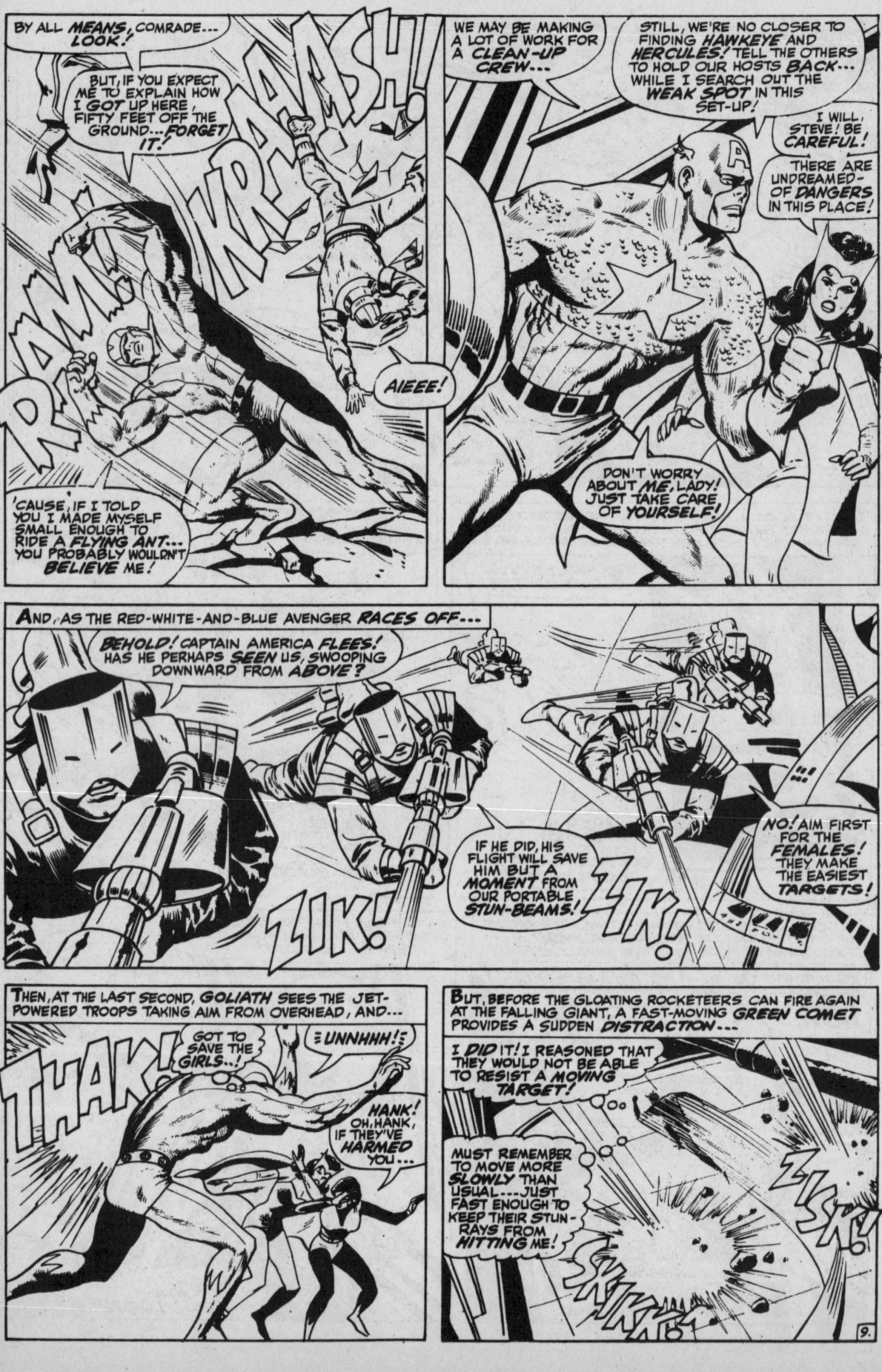
BY ALL MEANS, COMRADE... LOOK!
BUT, IF YOU EXPECT ME TO EXPLAIN HOW I GOT UP HERE, FIFTY FEET OFF THE GROUND... FORGET IT!
KRAASH!
RAM!
AIEEE!
'CAUSE, IF I TOLD YOU I MADE MYSELF SMALL ENOUGH TO RIDE A FLYING ANT... YOU PROBABLY WOULDN'T BELIEVE ME!
WE MAY BE MAKING A LOT OF WORK FOR A CLEAN-UP CREW...
STILL, WE'RE NO CLOSER TO FINDING HAWKEYE AND HERCULES! TELL THE OTHERS TO HOLD OUR HOSTS BACK... WHILE I SEARCH OUT THE WEAK SPOT IN THIS SET-UP!
I WILL, STEVE! BE CAREFUL!
THERE ARE UNDREAMED-OF DANGERS IN THIS PLACE!
DON'T WORRY ABOUT ME, LADY! JUST TAKE CARE OF YOURSELF!
AND, AS THE RED-WHITE-AND-BLUE AVENGER RACES OFF...
BEHOLD! CAPTAIN AMERICA FLEES! HAS HE PERHAPS SEEN US, SWOOPING DOWNWARD FROM ABOVE?
IF HE DID, HIS FLIGHT WILL SAVE HIM BUT A MOMENT FROM OUR PORTABLE STUN-BEAMS!
NO! AIM FIRST FOR THE FEMALES! THEY MAKE THE EASIEST TARGETS!
ZIK!
ZIK!
THEN, AT THE LAST SECOND, GOLIATH SEES THE JET-POWERED TROOPS TAKING AIM FROM OVERHEAD, AND...
THAK!
GOT TO SAVE THE GIRLS..!
UNNHHH!
HANK! OH, HANK, IF THEY'VE HARMED YOU...
BUT, BEFORE THE GLOATING ROCKETEERS CAN FIRE AGAIN AT THE FALLING GIANT, A FAST-MOVING GREEN COMET PROVIDES A SUDDEN DISTRACTION...
I DID IT! I REASONED THAT THEY WOULD NOT BE ABLE TO RESIST A MOVING TARGET!
MUST REMEMBER TO MOVE MORE SLOWLY THAN USUAL... JUST FAST ENOUGH TO KEEP THEIR STUN-RAYS FROM HITTING ME!
ZISK!
SKIKK!
9.

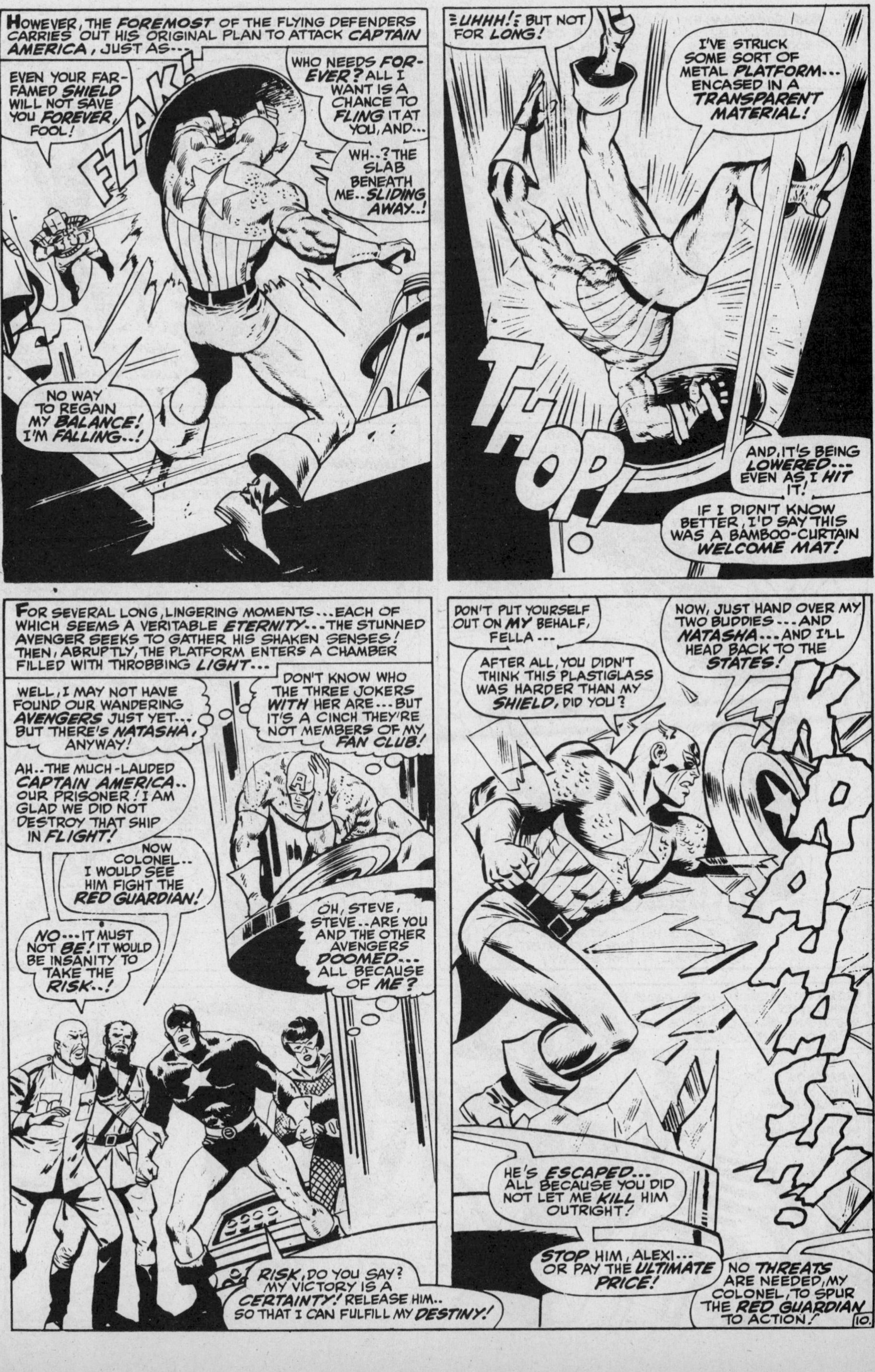
HOWEVER, THE FOREMOST OF THE FLYING DEFENDERS CARRIES OUT HIS ORIGINAL PLAN TO ATTACK CAPTAIN AMERICA, JUST AS...
EVEN YOUR FAR-FAMED SHIELD WILL NOT SAVE YOU FOREVER, FOOL!
FZAK!
WHO NEEDS FOREVER? ALL I WANT IS A CHANCE TO FLING IT AT YOU, AND...
WH..? THE SLAB BENEATH ME..SLIDING AWAY..!
NO WAY TO REGAIN MY BALANCE! I'M FALLING..!
UHHH! BUT NOT FOR LONG!
I'VE STRUCK SOME SORT OF METAL PLATFORM... ENCASED IN A TRANSPARENT MATERIAL!
THOP!
AND, IT'S BEING LOWERED... EVEN AS I HIT IT!
IF I DIDN'T KNOW BETTER, I'D SAY THIS WAS A BAMBOO-CURTAIN WELCOME MAT!
FOR SEVERAL LONG, LINGERING MOMENTS... EACH OF WHICH SEEMS A VERITABLE ETERNITY... THE STUNNED AVENGER SEEKS TO GATHER HIS SHAKEN SENSES! THEN, ABRUPTLY, THE PLATFORM ENTERS A CHAMBER FILLED WITH THROBBING LIGHT...
WELL, I MAY NOT HAVE FOUND OUR WANDERING AVENGERS JUST YET... BUT THERE'S NATASHA, ANYWAY!
DON'T KNOW WHO THE THREE JOKERS WITH HER ARE... BUT IT'S A CINCH THEY'RE NOT MEMBERS OF MY FAN CLUB!
AH..THE MUCH-LAUDED CAPTAIN AMERICA.. OUR PRISONER! I AM GLAD WE DID NOT DESTROY THAT SHIP IN FLIGHT!
NOW COLONEL.. I WOULD SEE HIM FIGHT THE RED GUARDIAN!
NO... IT MUST NOT BE! IT WOULD BE INSANITY TO TAKE THE RISK..!
OH, STEVE, STEVE..ARE YOU AND THE OTHER AVENGERS DOOMED... ALL BECAUSE OF ME?
RISK, DO YOU SAY? MY VICTORY IS A CERTAINTY! RELEASE HIM.. SO THAT I CAN FULFILL MY DESTINY!
DON'T PUT YOURSELF OUT ON MY BEHALF, FELLA...
AFTER ALL, YOU DIDN'T THINK THIS PLASTIGLASS WAS HARDER THAN MY SHIELD, DID YOU?
NOW, JUST HAND OVER MY TWO BUDDIES... AND NATASHA... AND I'LL HEAD BACK TO THE STATES!
KRAASH!
HE'S ESCAPED... ALL BECAUSE YOU DID NOT LET ME KILL HIM OUTRIGHT!
STOP HIM, ALEXI... OR PAY THE ULTIMATE PRICE!
NO THREATS ARE NEEDED, MY COLONEL, TO SPUR THE RED GUARDIAN TO ACTION!
10.

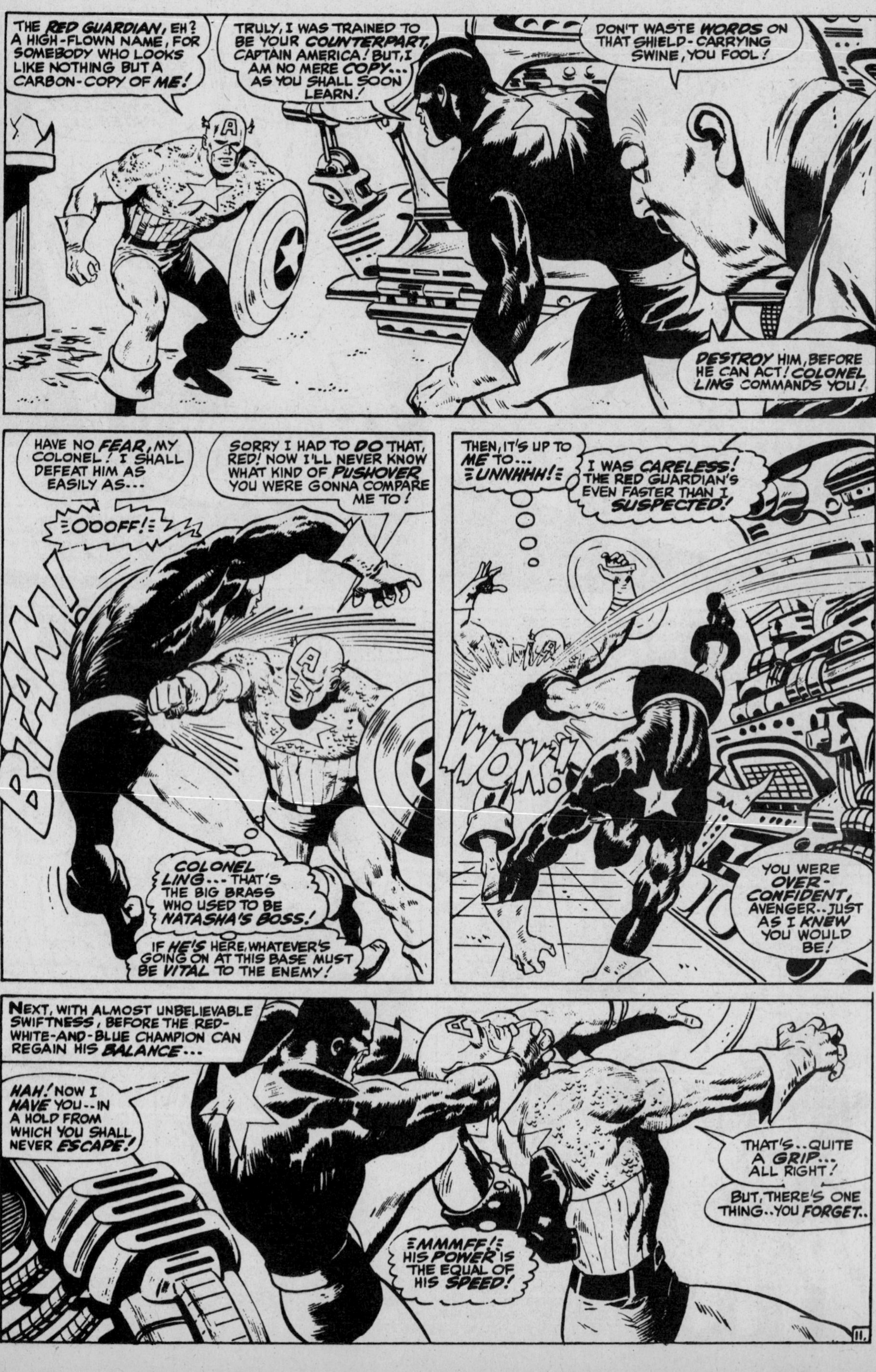

THE RED GUARDIAN, EH? A HIGH-FLOWN NAME, FOR SOMEBODY WHO LOOKS LIKE NOTHING BUT A CARBON-COPY OF ME!
TRULY, I WAS TRAINED TO BE YOUR COUNTERPART, CAPTAIN AMERICA! BUT, I AM NO MERE COPY... AS YOU SHALL SOON LEARN!
DON'T WASTE WORDS ON THAT SHIELD-CARRYING SWINE, YOU FOOL!
DESTROY HIM, BEFORE HE CAN ACT! COLONEL LING COMMANDS YOU!
HAVE NO FEAR, MY COLONEL! I SHALL DEFEAT HIM AS EASILY AS...
OOOFF!
SORRY I HAD TO DO THAT, RED! NOW I'LL NEVER KNOW WHAT KIND OF PUSHOVER YOU WERE GONNA COMPARE ME TO!
BTAM!
COLONEL LING... THAT'S THE BIG BRASS WHO USED TO BE NATASHA'S BOSS!
IF HE'S HERE, WHATEVER'S GOING ON AT THIS BASE MUST BE VITAL TO THE ENEMY!
THEN, IT'S UP TO ME TO... UNNHHH!
I WAS CARELESS! THE RED GUARDIAN'S EVEN FASTER THAN I SUSPECTED!
WOK!
YOU WERE OVER-CONFIDENT, AVENGER.. JUST AS I KNEW YOU WOULD BE!
NEXT, WITH ALMOST UNBELIEVABLE SWIFTNESS, BEFORE THE RED-WHITE-AND-BLUE CHAMPION CAN REGAIN HIS BALANCE...
HAH! NOW I HAVE YOU--IN A HOLD FROM WHICH YOU SHALL NEVER ESCAPE!
THAT'S.. QUITE A GRIP... ALL RIGHT!
BUT, THERE'S ONE THING.. YOU FORGET..
MMMFF! HIS POWER IS THE EQUAL OF HIS SPEED!
11.

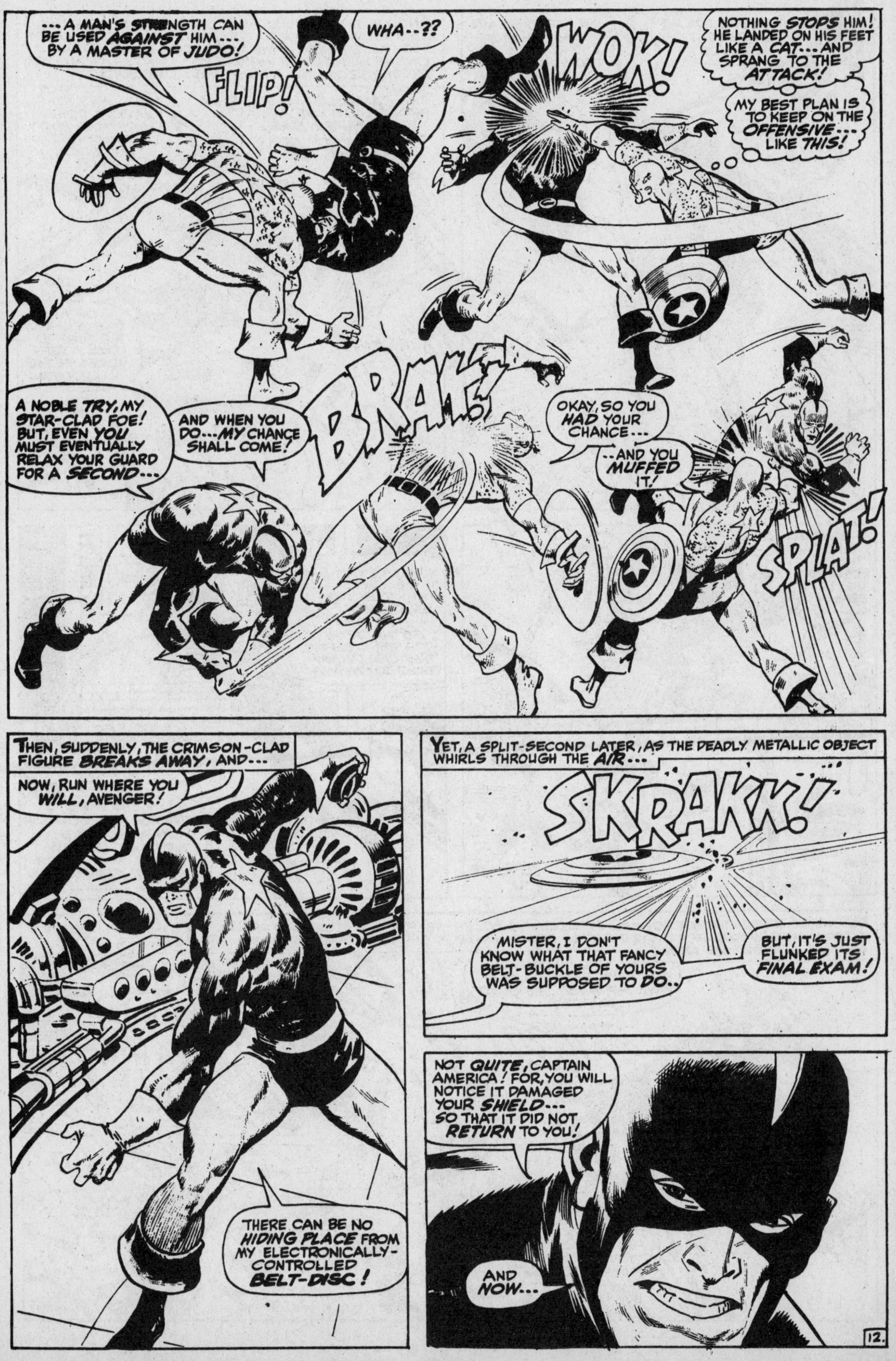

...A MAN'S STRENGTH CAN BE USED AGAINST HIM ... BY A MASTER OF JUDO!
FLIP!
WHA--??
WOK!
NOTHING STOPS HIM! HE LANDED ON HIS FEET LIKE A CAT... AND SPRANG TO THE ATTACK!
MY BEST PLAN IS TO KEEP ON THE OFFENSIVE... LIKE THIS!
A NOBLE TRY, MY STAR-CLAD FOE! BUT, EVEN YOU MUST EVENTUALLY RELAX YOUR GUARD FOR A SECOND...
AND WHEN YOU DO... MY CHANCE SHALL COME!
BRAK!
OKAY, SO YOU HAD YOUR CHANCE...
..AND YOU MUFFED IT!
SPLAT!
THEN, SUDDENLY, THE CRIMSON-CLAD FIGURE BREAKS AWAY, AND...
NOW, RUN WHERE YOU WILL, AVENGER!
THERE CAN BE NO HIDING PLACE FROM MY ELECTRONICALLY-CONTROLLED BELT-DISC!
YET, A SPLIT-SECOND LATER, AS THE DEADLY METALLIC OBJECT WHIRLS THROUGH THE AIR...
SKRAKK!
MISTER, I DON'T KNOW WHAT THAT FANCY BELT-BUCKLE OF YOURS WAS SUPPOSED TO DO..
BUT, IT'S JUST FLUNKED ITS FINAL EXAM!
NOT QUITE, CAPTAIN AMERICA! FOR, YOU WILL NOTICE IT DAMAGED YOUR SHIELD... SO THAT IT DID NOT RETURN TO YOU!
AND NOW...
12.

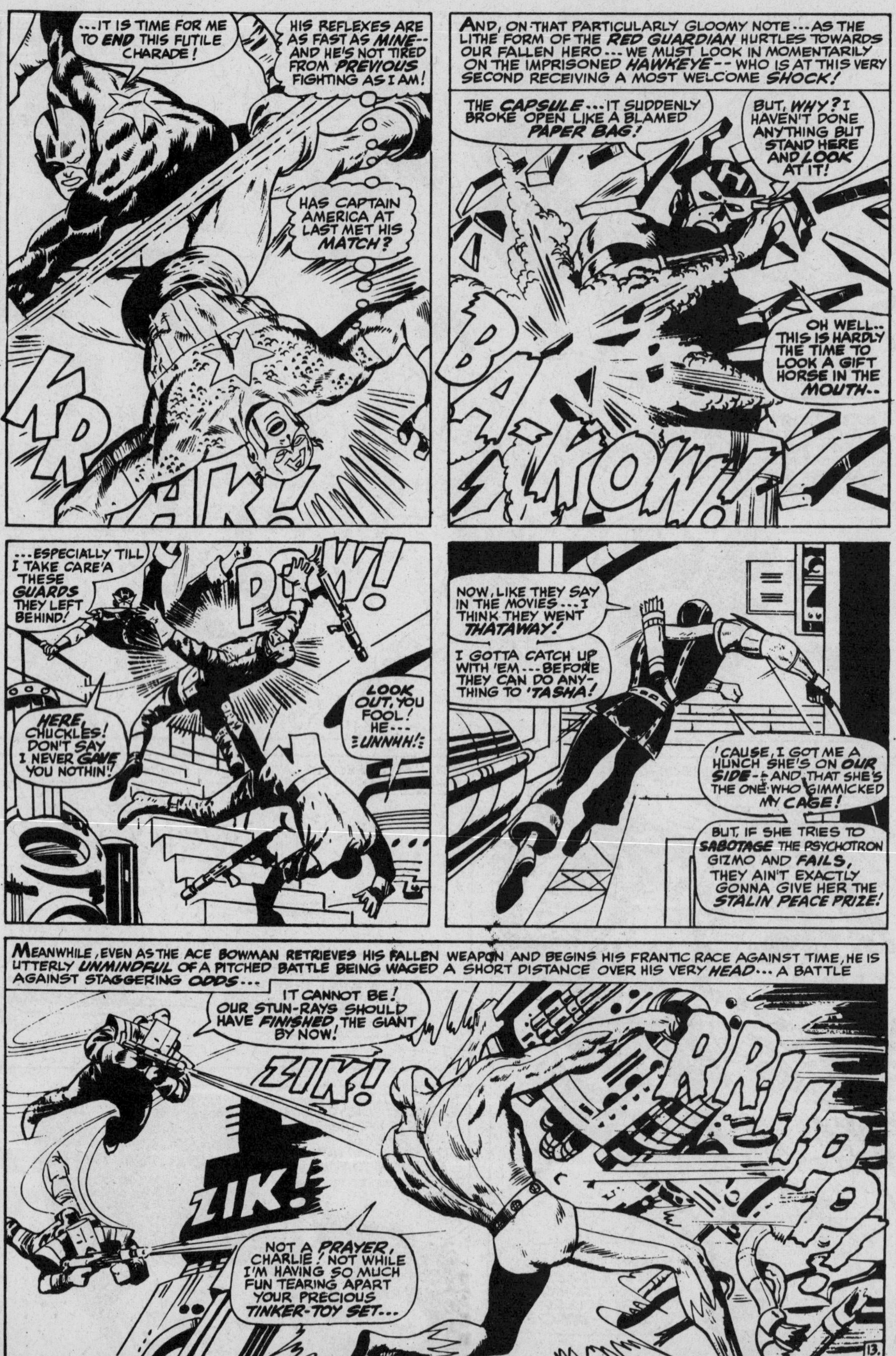
...IT IS TIME FOR ME TO END THIS FUTILE CHARADE!
HIS REFLEXES ARE AS FAST AS MINE-- AND HE'S NOT TIRED FROM PREVIOUS FIGHTING AS I AM!
HAS CAPTAIN AMERICA AT LAST MET HIS MATCH?
KRAK!
AND, ON THAT PARTICULARLY GLOOMY NOTE... AS THE LITHE FORM OF THE RED GUARDIAN HURTLES TOWARDS OUR FALLEN HERO... WE MUST LOOK IN MOMENTARILY ON THE IMPRISONED HAWKEYE-- WHO IS AT THIS VERY SECOND RECEIVING A MOST WELCOME SHOCK!
THE CAPSULE... IT SUDDENLY BROKE OPEN LIKE A BLAMED PAPER BAG!
BUT, WHY? I HAVEN'T DONE ANYTHING BUT STAND HERE AND LOOK AT IT!
OH WELL.. THIS IS HARDLY THE TIME TO LOOK A GIFT HORSE IN THE MOUTH..
BA-KOW!
...ESPECIALLY TILL I TAKE CARE'A THESE GUARDS THEY LEFT BEHIND!
POW!
HERE, CHUCKLES! DON'T SAY I NEVER GAVE YOU NOTHIN'!
LOOK OUT, YOU FOOL! HE--- UNNHH!
NOW, LIKE THEY SAY IN THE MOVIES... I THINK THEY WENT THATAWAY!
I GOTTA CATCH UP WITH 'EM---BEFORE THEY CAN DO ANYTHING TO 'TASHA!
'CAUSE, I GOT ME A HUNCH SHE'S ON OUR SIDE-- AND THAT SHE'S THE ONE WHO GIMMICKED MY CAGE!
BUT, IF SHE TRIES TO SABOTAGE THE PSYCHOTRON GIZMO AND FAILS, THEY AIN'T EXACTLY GONNA GIVE HER THE STALIN PEACE PRIZE!
MEANWHILE, EVEN AS THE ACE BOWMAN RETRIEVES HIS FALLEN WEAPON AND BEGINS HIS FRANTIC RACE AGAINST TIME, HE IS UTTERLY UNMINDFUL OF A PITCHED BATTLE BEING WAGED A SHORT DISTANCE OVER HIS VERY HEAD... A BATTLE AGAINST STAGGERING ODDS...
IT CANNOT BE! OUR STUN-RAYS SHOULD HAVE FINISHED THE GIANT BY NOW!
ZIK!
ZIK!
RRIPP
NOT A PRAYER, CHARLIE! NOT WHILE I'M HAVING SO MUCH FUN TEARING APART YOUR PRECIOUS TINKER-TOY SET...
13.

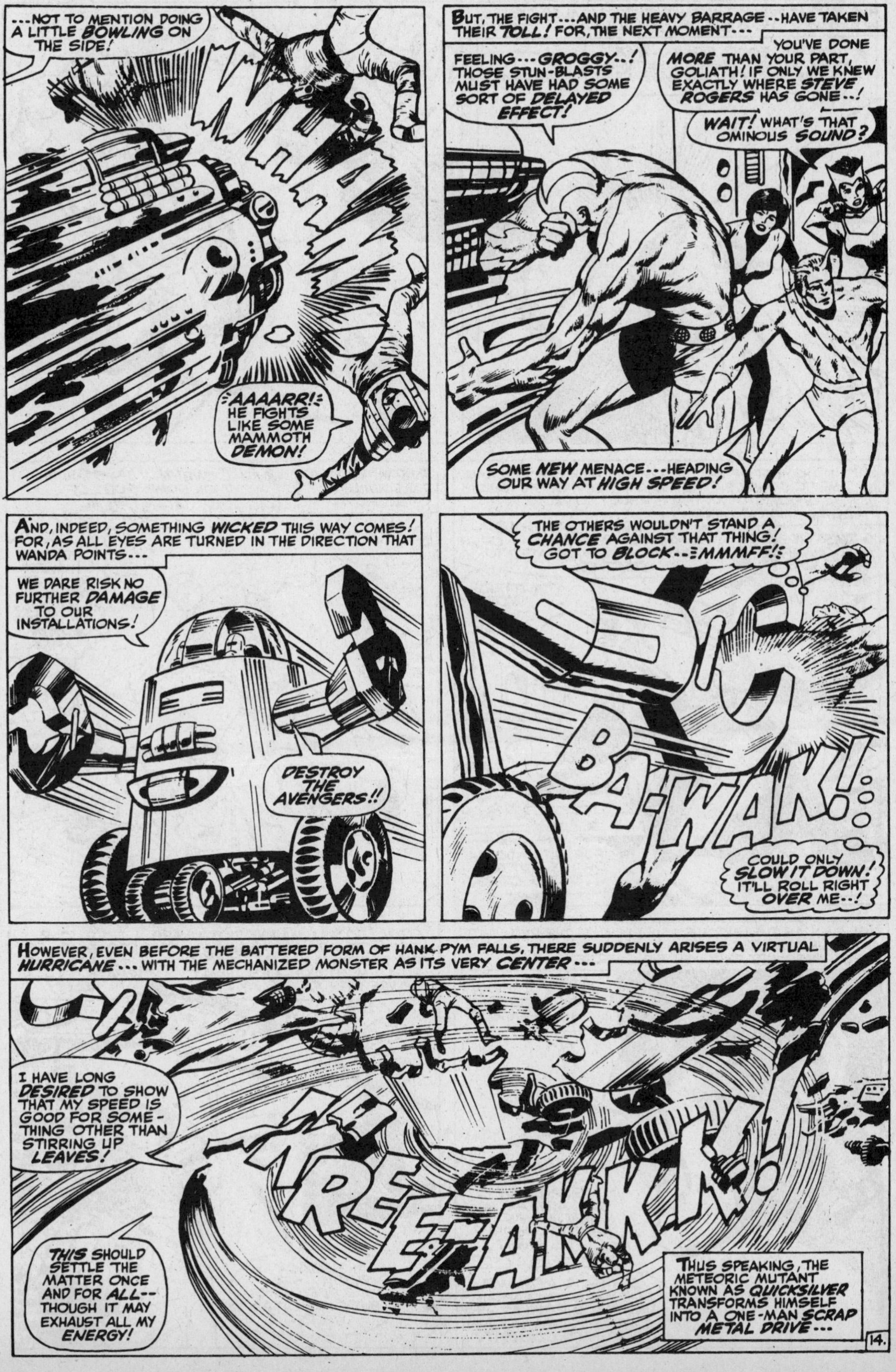

...NOT TO MENTION DOING A LITTLE BOWLING ON THE SIDE!
WHAM
AAAARR! HE FIGHTS LIKE SOME MAMMOTH DEMON!
BUT, THE FIGHT...AND THE HEAVY BARRAGE--HAVE TAKEN THEIR TOLL! FOR, THE NEXT MOMENT---
FEELING...GROGGY--! THOSE STUN-BLASTS MUST HAVE HAD SOME SORT OF DELAYED EFFECT!
YOU'VE DONE MORE THAN YOUR PART, GOLIATH! IF ONLY WE KNEW EXACTLY WHERE STEVE ROGERS HAS GONE--!
WAIT! WHAT'S THAT OMINOUS SOUND?
SOME NEW MENACE---HEADING OUR WAY AT HIGH SPEED!
AND, INDEED, SOMETHING WICKED THIS WAY COMES! FOR, AS ALL EYES ARE TURNED IN THE DIRECTION THAT WANDA POINTS---
WE DARE RISK NO FURTHER DAMAGE TO OUR INSTALLATIONS!
DESTROY THE AVENGERS!!
THE OTHERS WOULDN'T STAND A CHANCE AGAINST THAT THING! GOT TO BLOCK--MMMFF!--
BA-WAK!
COULD ONLY SLOW IT DOWN! IT'LL ROLL RIGHT OVER ME--!
HOWEVER, EVEN BEFORE THE BATTERED FORM OF HANK PYM FALLS, THERE SUDDENLY ARISES A VIRTUAL HURRICANE...WITH THE MECHANIZED MONSTER AS ITS VERY CENTER---
I HAVE LONG DESIRED TO SHOW THAT MY SPEED IS GOOD FOR SOMETHING OTHER THAN STIRRING UP LEAVES!
KREE-AKKK!
THIS SHOULD SETTLE THE MATTER ONCE AND FOR ALL--THOUGH IT MAY EXHAUST ALL MY ENERGY!
THUS SPEAKING, THE METEORIC MUTANT KNOWN AS QUICKSILVER TRANSFORMS HIMSELF INTO A ONE-MAN SCRAP METAL DRIVE---

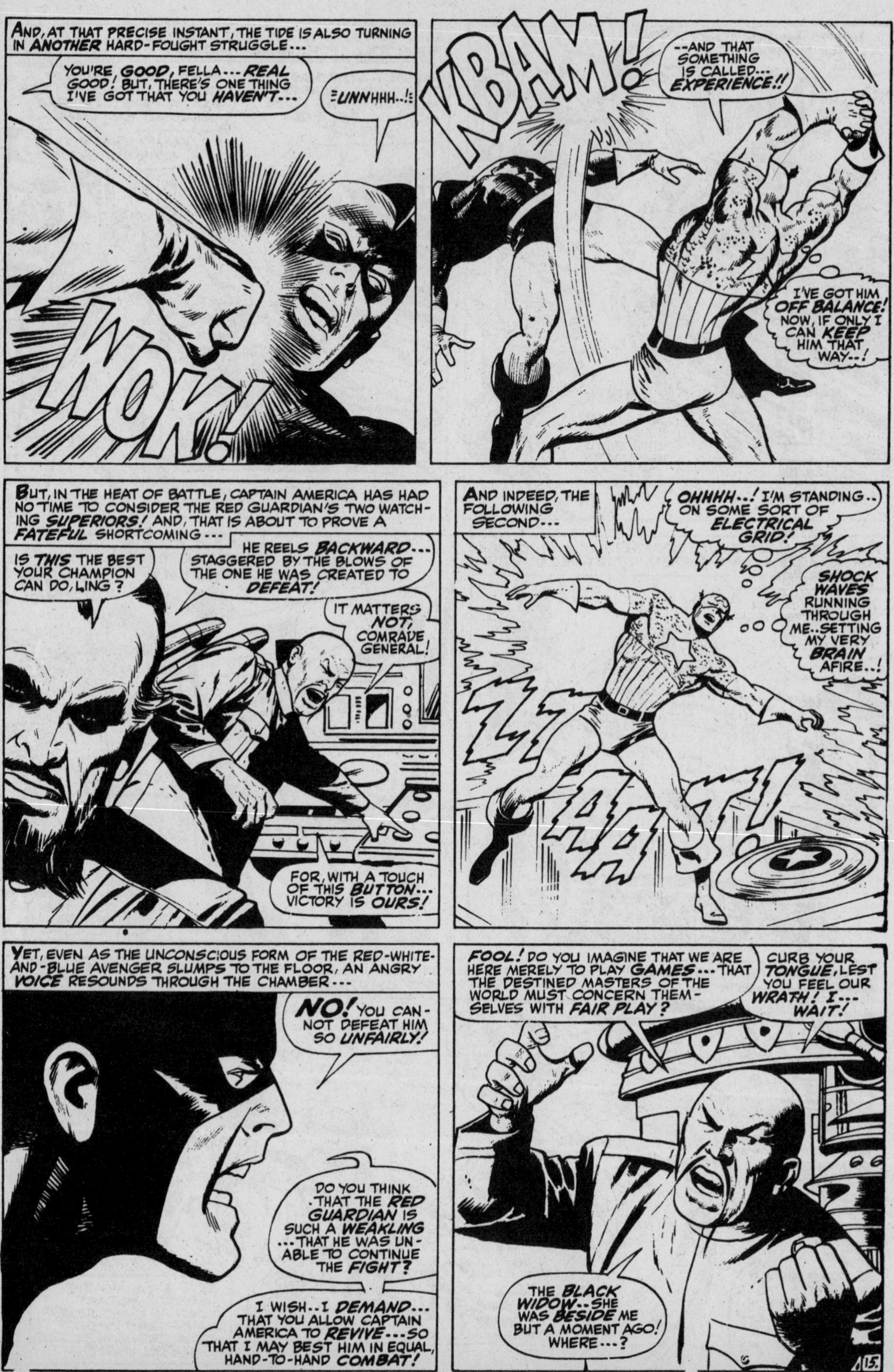

AND, AT THAT PRECISE INSTANT, THE TIDE IS ALSO TURNING IN ANOTHER HARD-FOUGHT STRUGGLE...
YOU'RE GOOD, FELLA... REAL GOOD! BUT, THERE'S ONE THING I'VE GOT THAT YOU HAVEN'T...
UNNHHH..!
WOK!
KBAM!
--AND THAT SOMETHING IS CALLED... EXPERIENCE!!
I'VE GOT HIM OFF BALANCE! NOW, IF ONLY I CAN KEEP HIM THAT WAY..!
BUT, IN THE HEAT OF BATTLE, CAPTAIN AMERICA HAS HAD NO TIME TO CONSIDER THE RED GUARDIAN'S TWO WATCHING SUPERIORS! AND, THAT IS ABOUT TO PROVE A FATEFUL SHORTCOMING...
IS THIS THE BEST YOUR CHAMPION CAN DO, LING?
HE REELS BACKWARD... STAGGERED BY THE BLOWS OF THE ONE HE WAS CREATED TO DEFEAT!
IT MATTERS NOT, COMRADE GENERAL!
FOR, WITH A TOUCH OF THIS BUTTON... VICTORY IS OURS!
AND INDEED, THE FOLLOWING SECOND...
OHHHH..! I'M STANDING.. ON SOME SORT OF ELECTRICAL GRID!
SHOCK WAVES RUNNING THROUGH ME..SETTING MY VERY BRAIN AFIRE..!
ZZAAAT!
YET, EVEN AS THE UNCONSCIOUS FORM OF THE RED-WHITE-AND-BLUE AVENGER SLUMPS TO THE FLOOR, AN ANGRY VOICE RESOUNDS THROUGH THE CHAMBER...
NO! YOU CANNOT DEFEAT HIM SO UNFAIRLY!
DO YOU THINK THAT THE RED GUARDIAN IS SUCH A WEAKLING ...THAT HE WAS UNABLE TO CONTINUE THE FIGHT?
I WISH..I DEMAND... THAT YOU ALLOW CAPTAIN AMERICA TO REVIVE...SO THAT I MAY BEST HIM IN EQUAL, HAND-TO-HAND COMBAT!
FOOL! DO YOU IMAGINE THAT WE ARE HERE MERELY TO PLAY GAMES... THAT THE DESTINED MASTERS OF THE WORLD MUST CONCERN THEMSELVES WITH FAIR PLAY?
CURB YOUR TONGUE, LEST YOU FEEL OUR WRATH! I... WAIT!
THE BLACK WIDOW.. SHE WAS BESIDE ME BUT A MOMENT AGO! WHERE...?
15.

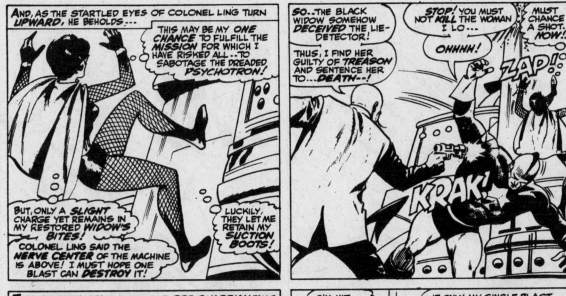

AND, AS THE STARTLED EYES OF COLONEL LING TURN *UPWARD*, HE BEHOLDS---

THIS MAY BE MY *ONE CHANCE* TO FULFILL THE *MISSION* FOR WHICH I HAVE RISKED ALL--TO SABOTAGE THE DREADED *PSYCHOTRON!*

BUT, ONLY A *SLIGHT CHARGE* YET REMAINS IN MY RESTORED *WIDOW'S BITES!* COLONEL LING SAID THE *NERVE CENTER* OF THE MACHINE IS ABOVE! I MUST HOPE ONE BLAST CAN *DESTROY* IT!

LUCKILY, THEY LET ME RETAIN MY *SUCTION BOOTS!*

SO..THE BLACK WIDOW SOMEHOW *DECEIVED* THE LIE-DETECTOR!

THUS, I FIND HER *GUILTY* OF *TREASON* AND SENTENCE HER TO...*DEATH--!*

STOP! YOU MUST NOT *KILL* THE WOMAN I LO--!

OHHHH!

MUST CHANCE A SHOT...*NOW!!*

ZAP!

KRAK!

THEN, AS THE MORTALLY WOUNDED *RED GUARDIAN* FALLS, A GUN IS ONCE MORE LEVELED AT *MADAME NATASHA*...

BUT, THE NEXT MOMENT, FROM OUT OF *NOWHERE* COMES A SPEEDING *SHAFT!*

SOMETHING STRUCK ME FROM *BEHIND..!*

WHAM!

BRAK!

≡MMMFF!≡

YET, IT WAS *TOO LATE!* THE BLACK WIDOW IS *DOOMED!!*

I'M *HIT..* FALLING!

IF ONLY MY *SINGLE BLAST*--- ACCOMPLISHED ITS *PURPOSE...*

I'VE GOT TO *BREAK* 'TASHA'S FALL! I'VE *GOT* TO!!

IF THOSE RATS HAVE *KILLED* HER, THEY'LL *PAY* FOR IT! I *SWEAR* THEY WILL!

BUT, ABRUPTLY, ALL THOUGHTS OF PERSONAL VENGEANCE ARE *FORGOTTEN*..AS A POWERFUL, ALMOST-FORGOTTEN *FORM* BURSTS THROUGH SEVERAL INCHES OF TEMPERED *STEEL* ---

THE INDESTRUCTIBLE *HYDRA* HATH SUDDENLY FADED FROM VIEW!

THROOM

THEN, 'TWAS BUT SOME *TRICKERY*-- AN *ILLUSION*... AS I DID *SUSPECT!*

I AM *FREE!* YET, FROM WHENCE THE *FLAMES* THAT I SEE BEFORE ME? ARE THEY *TOO* A MIRAGE?

I WISH THEY *WERE*, WHISKERS!

THIS ISN'T EXACTLY THE TIME FOR *DETAILS*, BUT OUR HOST'S LITTLE POPGUN MUST'A HIT SOMETHIN' *FLAMMABLE!*

CAP, OVER THERE, LOOKS LIKE HE'S JUST *STUNNED!* HOIST HIM OVER YOUR SHOULDER AND *LET'S GO!*

WHAT OF THE *BLACK WIDOW*... SHE WHOM WE DID COME HERE TO *RESCUE?* SHE DOTH SEEM SO *LIFELESS..*

SHE'S STILL *BREATHIN'!* BUT, IF WE DON'T GET OUTTA HERE *FAST*...

16.

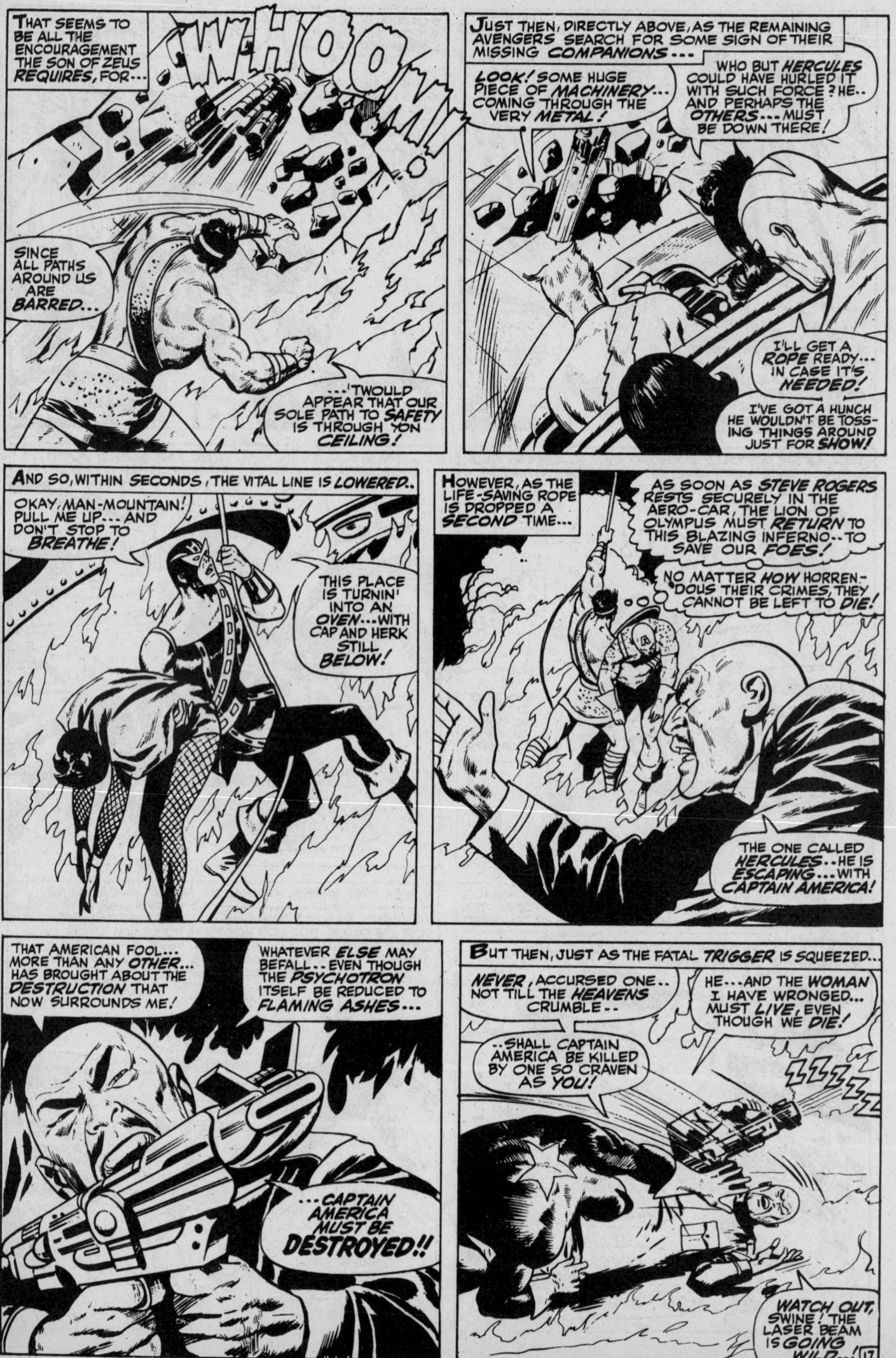
THAT SEEMS TO BE ALL THE ENCOURAGEMENT THE SON OF ZEUS REQUIRES, FOR...
WHOOOM!!
SINCE ALL PATHS AROUND US ARE BARRED...
...'TWOULD APPEAR THAT OUR SOLE PATH TO SAFETY IS THROUGH YON CEILING!
JUST THEN, DIRECTLY ABOVE, AS THE REMAINING AVENGERS SEARCH FOR SOME SIGN OF THEIR MISSING COMPANIONS...
LOOK! SOME HUGE PIECE OF MACHINERY... COMING THROUGH THE VERY METAL!
WHO BUT HERCULES COULD HAVE HURLED IT WITH SUCH FORCE? HE.. AND PERHAPS THE OTHERS... MUST BE DOWN THERE!
I'LL GET A ROPE READY... IN CASE IT'S NEEDED!
I'VE GOT A HUNCH HE WOULDN'T BE TOSSING THINGS AROUND JUST FOR SHOW!
AND SO, WITHIN SECONDS, THE VITAL LINE IS LOWERED..
OKAY, MAN-MOUNTAIN! PULL ME UP... AND DON'T STOP TO BREATHE!
THIS PLACE IS TURNIN' INTO AN OVEN... WITH CAP AND HERK STILL BELOW!
HOWEVER, AS THE LIFE-SAVING ROPE IS DROPPED A SECOND TIME...
AS SOON AS STEVE ROGERS RESTS SECURELY IN THE AERO-CAR, THE LION OF OLYMPUS MUST RETURN TO THIS BLAZING INFERNO--TO SAVE OUR FOES!
NO MATTER HOW HORRENDOUS THEIR CRIMES, THEY CANNOT BE LEFT TO DIE!
THE ONE CALLED HERCULES... HE IS ESCAPING... WITH CAPTAIN AMERICA!
THAT AMERICAN FOOL... MORE THAN ANY OTHER... HAS BROUGHT ABOUT THE DESTRUCTION THAT NOW SURROUNDS ME!
WHATEVER ELSE MAY BEFALL.. EVEN THOUGH THE PSYCHOTRON ITSELF BE REDUCED TO FLAMING ASHES...
...CAPTAIN AMERICA MUST BE DESTROYED!!
BUT THEN, JUST AS THE FATAL TRIGGER IS SQUEEZED...
NEVER, ACCURSED ONE.. NOT TILL THE HEAVENS CRUMBLE--
..SHALL CAPTAIN AMERICA BE KILLED BY ONE SO CRAVEN AS YOU!
HE... AND THE WOMAN I HAVE WRONGED... MUST LIVE, EVEN THOUGH WE DIE!
WATCH OUT, SWINE! THE LASER BEAM IS GOING WILD..!

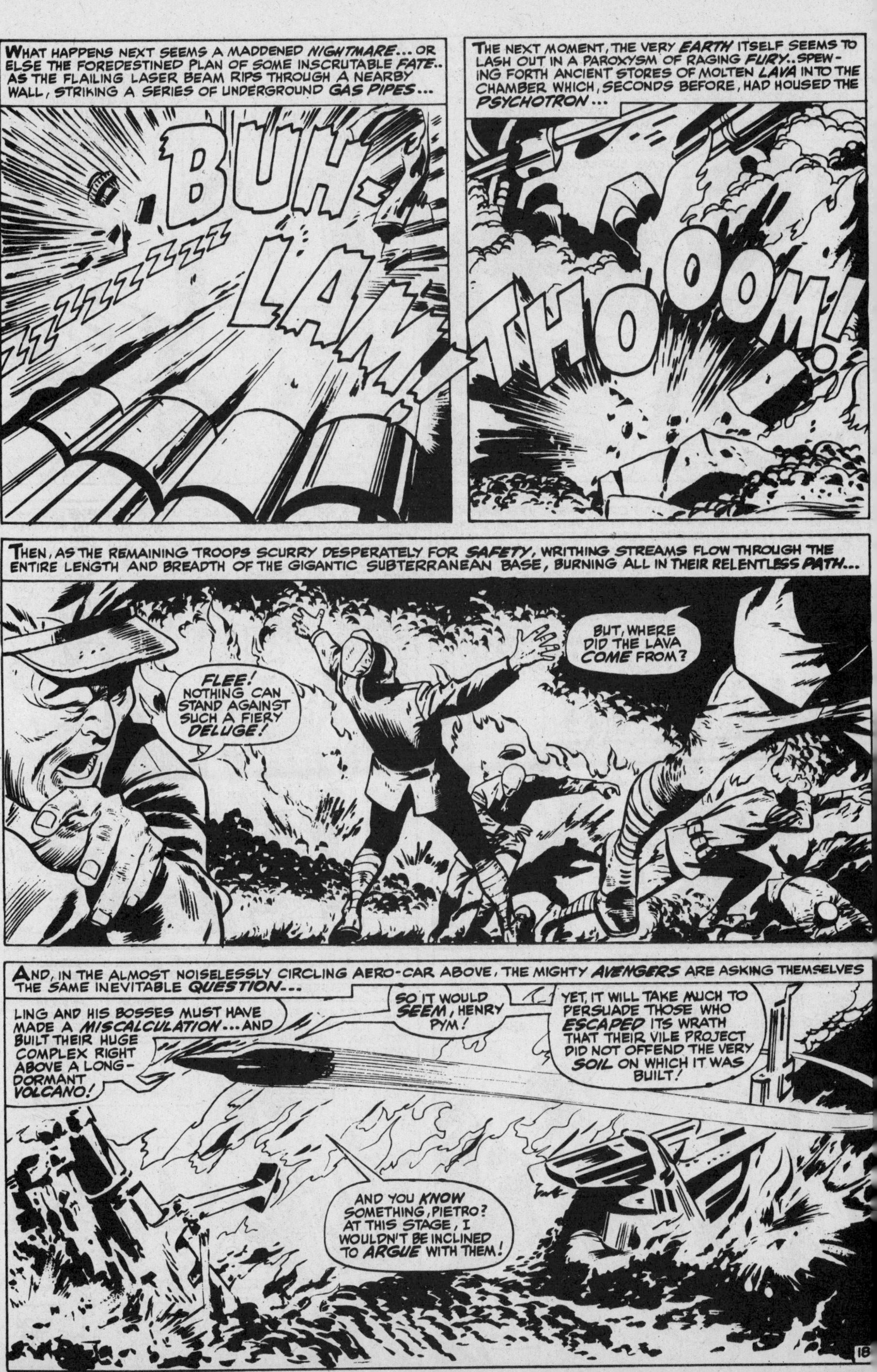
WHAT HAPPENS NEXT SEEMS A MADDENED NIGHTMARE... OR ELSE THE FOREDESTINED PLAN OF SOME INSCRUTABLE FATE.. AS THE FLAILING LASER BEAM RIPS THROUGH A NEARBY WALL, STRIKING A SERIES OF UNDERGROUND GAS PIPES...
ZZZZZZZZZ
BUH-LAM!
THE NEXT MOMENT, THE VERY EARTH ITSELF SEEMS TO LASH OUT IN A PAROXYSM OF RAGING FURY.. SPEWING FORTH ANCIENT STORES OF MOLTEN LAVA INTO THE CHAMBER WHICH, SECONDS BEFORE, HAD HOUSED THE PSYCHOTRON...
THOOOM!
THEN, AS THE REMAINING TROOPS SCURRY DESPERATELY FOR SAFETY, WRITHING STREAMS FLOW THROUGH THE ENTIRE LENGTH AND BREADTH OF THE GIGANTIC SUBTERRANEAN BASE, BURNING ALL IN THEIR RELENTLESS PATH...
FLEE! NOTHING CAN STAND AGAINST SUCH A FIERY DELUGE!
BUT, WHERE DID THE LAVA COME FROM?
AND, IN THE ALMOST NOISELESSLY CIRCLING AERO-CAR ABOVE, THE MIGHTY AVENGERS ARE ASKING THEMSELVES THE SAME INEVITABLE QUESTION...
LING AND HIS BOSSES MUST HAVE MADE A MISCALCULATION... AND BUILT THEIR HUGE COMPLEX RIGHT ABOVE A LONG-DORMANT VOLCANO!
SO IT WOULD SEEM, HENRY PYM!
YET, IT WILL TAKE MUCH TO PERSUADE THOSE WHO ESCAPED ITS WRATH THAT THEIR VILE PROJECT DID NOT OFFEND THE VERY SOIL ON WHICH IT WAS BUILT!
AND YOU KNOW SOMETHING, PIETRO? AT THIS STAGE, I WOULDN'T BE INCLINED TO ARGUE WITH THEM!
18

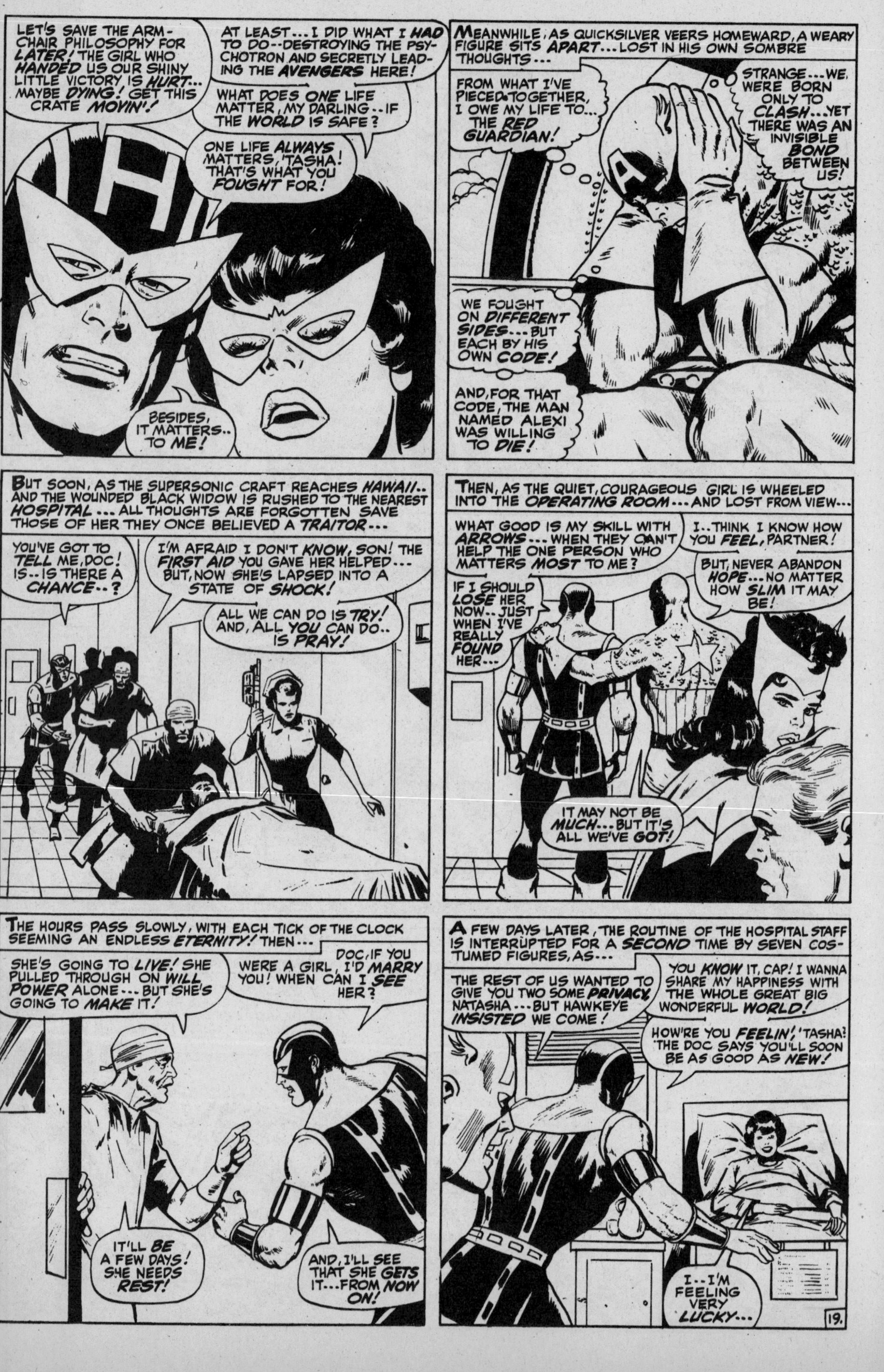
LET'S SAVE THE ARM-CHAIR PHILOSOPHY FOR LATER! THE GIRL WHO HANDED US OUR SHINY LITTLE VICTORY IS HURT... MAYBE DYING! GET THIS CRATE MOVIN'!
AT LEAST... I DID WHAT I HAD TO DO--DESTROYING THE PSYCHOTRON AND SECRETLY LEADING THE AVENGERS HERE!
WHAT DOES ONE LIFE MATTER, MY DARLING.. IF THE WORLD IS SAFE?
ONE LIFE ALWAYS MATTERS, 'TASHA! THAT'S WHAT YOU FOUGHT FOR!
BESIDES, IT MATTERS.. TO ME!
MEANWHILE, AS QUICKSILVER VEERS HOMEWARD, A WEARY FIGURE SITS APART... LOST IN HIS OWN SOMBRE THOUGHTS...
FROM WHAT I'VE PIECED TOGETHER, I OWE MY LIFE TO... THE RED GUARDIAN!
STRANGE... WE WERE BORN ONLY TO CLASH... YET THERE WAS AN INVISIBLE BOND BETWEEN US!
WE FOUGHT ON DIFFERENT SIDES... BUT EACH BY HIS OWN CODE!
AND, FOR THAT CODE, THE MAN NAMED ALEXI WAS WILLING TO DIE!
BUT SOON, AS THE SUPERSONIC CRAFT REACHES HAWAII.. AND THE WOUNDED BLACK WIDOW IS RUSHED TO THE NEAREST HOSPITAL... ALL THOUGHTS ARE FORGOTTEN SAVE THOSE OF HER THEY ONCE BELIEVED A TRAITOR...
YOU'VE GOT TO TELL ME, DOC! IS-- IS THERE A CHANCE--?
I'M AFRAID I DON'T KNOW, SON! THE FIRST AID YOU GAVE HER HELPED... BUT, NOW SHE'S LAPSED INTO A STATE OF SHOCK!
ALL WE CAN DO IS TRY! AND, ALL YOU CAN DO.. IS PRAY!
THEN, AS THE QUIET, COURAGEOUS GIRL IS WHEELED INTO THE OPERATING ROOM... AND LOST FROM VIEW...
WHAT GOOD IS MY SKILL WITH ARROWS... WHEN THEY CAN'T HELP THE ONE PERSON WHO MATTERS MOST TO ME?
IF I SHOULD LOSE HER NOW.. JUST WHEN I'VE REALLY FOUND HER...
I.. THINK I KNOW HOW YOU FEEL, PARTNER!
BUT, NEVER ABANDON HOPE... NO MATTER HOW SLIM IT MAY BE!
IT MAY NOT BE MUCH... BUT IT'S ALL WE'VE GOT!
THE HOURS PASS SLOWLY, WITH EACH TICK OF THE CLOCK SEEMING AN ENDLESS ETERNITY! THEN...
SHE'S GOING TO LIVE! SHE PULLED THROUGH ON WILL POWER ALONE... BUT SHE'S GOING TO MAKE IT!
DOC, IF YOU WERE A GIRL, I'D MARRY YOU! WHEN CAN I SEE HER?
IT'LL BE A FEW DAYS! SHE NEEDS REST!
AND, I'LL SEE THAT SHE GETS IT... FROM NOW ON!
A FEW DAYS LATER, THE ROUTINE OF THE HOSPITAL STAFF IS INTERRUPTED FOR A SECOND TIME BY SEVEN COSTUMED FIGURES, AS...
THE REST OF US WANTED TO GIVE YOU TWO SOME PRIVACY, NATASHA... BUT HAWKEYE INSISTED WE COME!
YOU KNOW IT, CAP! I WANNA SHARE MY HAPPINESS WITH THE WHOLE GREAT BIG WONDERFUL WORLD!
HOW'RE YOU FEELIN', 'TASHA? THE DOC SAYS YOU'LL SOON BE AS GOOD AS NEW!
I-- I'M FEELING VERY LUCKY...
19.

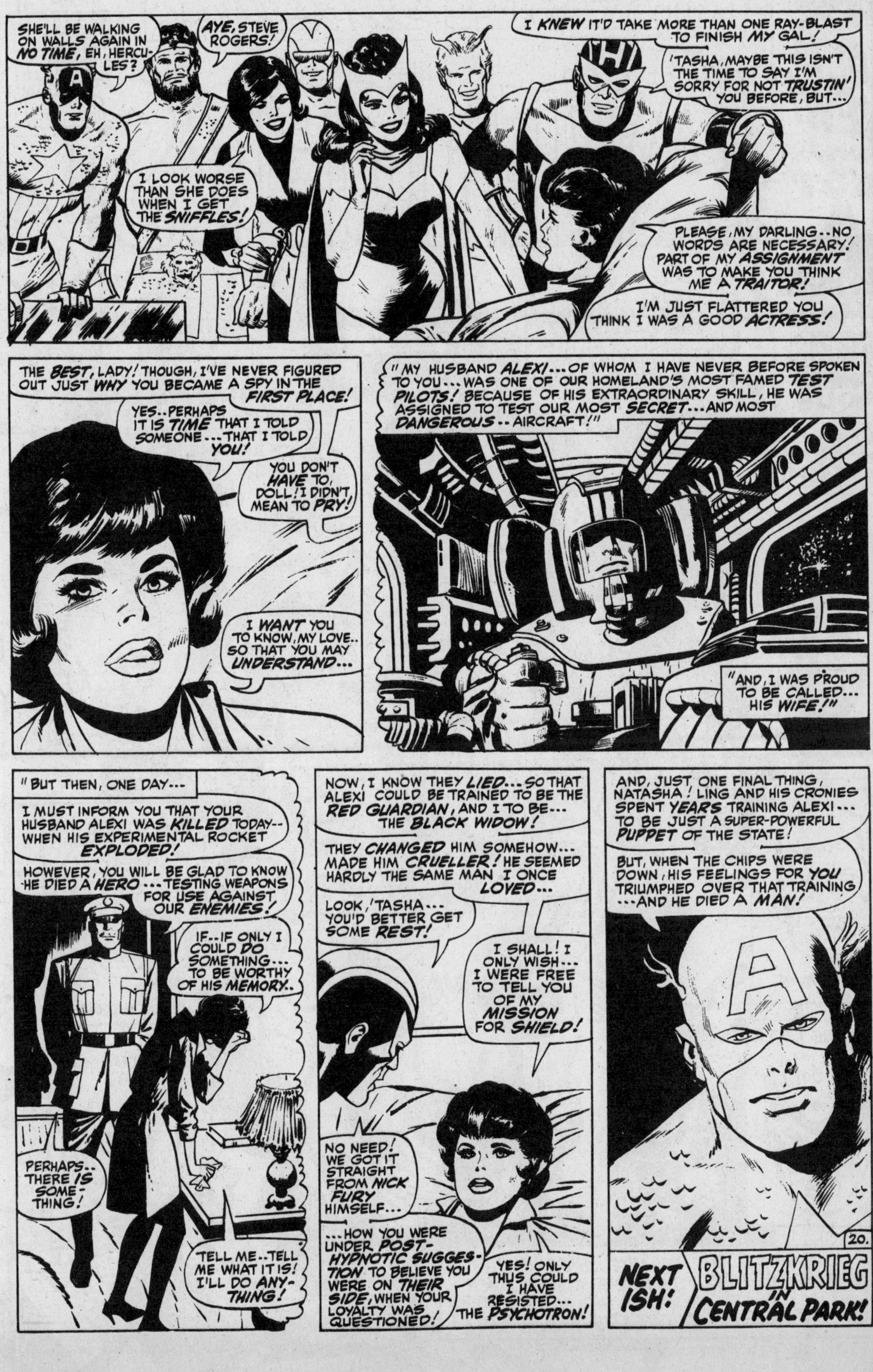

SHE'LL BE WALKING ON WALLS AGAIN IN NO TIME, EH, HERCU-LES?
AYE, STEVE ROGERS!
I LOOK WORSE THAN SHE DOES WHEN I GET THE SNIFFLES!
I KNEW IT'D TAKE MORE THAN ONE RAY-BLAST TO FINISH MY GAL!
'TASHA, MAYBE THIS ISN'T THE TIME TO SAY I'M SORRY FOR NOT TRUSTIN' YOU BEFORE, BUT...
PLEASE, MY DARLING.. NO WORDS ARE NECESSARY! PART OF MY ASSIGNMENT WAS TO MAKE YOU THINK ME A TRAITOR!
I'M JUST FLATTERED YOU THINK I WAS A GOOD ACTRESS!
THE BEST, LADY! THOUGH, I'VE NEVER FIGURED OUT JUST WHY YOU BECAME A SPY IN THE FIRST PLACE!
YES.. PERHAPS IT IS TIME THAT I TOLD SOMEONE... THAT I TOLD YOU!
YOU DON'T HAVE TO, DOLL! I DIDN'T MEAN TO PRY!
I WANT YOU TO KNOW, MY LOVE.. SO THAT YOU MAY UNDERSTAND...
"MY HUSBAND ALEXI... OF WHOM I HAVE NEVER BEFORE SPOKEN TO YOU... WAS ONE OF OUR HOMELAND'S MOST FAMED TEST PILOTS! BECAUSE OF HIS EXTRAORDINARY SKILL, HE WAS ASSIGNED TO TEST OUR MOST SECRET... AND MOST DANGEROUS.. AIRCRAFT!"
"AND, I WAS PROUD TO BE CALLED... HIS WIFE!"
"BUT THEN, ONE DAY...
I MUST INFORM YOU THAT YOUR HUSBAND ALEXI WAS KILLED TODAY-- WHEN HIS EXPERIMENTAL ROCKET EXPLODED!
HOWEVER, YOU WILL BE GLAD TO KNOW HE DIED A HERO... TESTING WEAPONS FOR USE AGAINST OUR ENEMIES!
IF.. IF ONLY I COULD DO SOMETHING... TO BE WORTHY OF HIS MEMORY..
PERHAPS.. THERE IS SOME-THING!
TELL ME.. TELL ME WHAT IT IS! I'LL DO ANY-THING!
NOW, I KNOW THEY LIED... SO THAT ALEXI COULD BE TRAINED TO BE THE RED GUARDIAN, AND I TO BE... THE BLACK WIDOW!
THEY CHANGED HIM SOMEHOW... MADE HIM CRUELLER! HE SEEMED HARDLY THE SAME MAN I ONCE LOVED...
LOOK, 'TASHA... YOU'D BETTER GET SOME REST!
I SHALL! I ONLY WISH... I WERE FREE TO TELL YOU OF MY MISSION FOR SHIELD!
NO NEED! WE GOT IT STRAIGHT FROM NICK FURY HIMSELF...
...HOW YOU WERE UNDER POST-HYPNOTIC SUGGES-TION TO BELIEVE YOU WERE ON THEIR SIDE, WHEN YOUR LOYALTY WAS QUESTIONED!
YES! ONLY THUS COULD I HAVE RESISTED... THE PSYCHOTRON!
AND, JUST ONE FINAL THING, NATASHA! LING AND HIS CRONIES SPENT YEARS TRAINING ALEXI... TO BE JUST A SUPER-POWERFUL PUPPET OF THE STATE!
BUT, WHEN THE CHIPS WERE DOWN, HIS FEELINGS FOR YOU TRIUMPHED OVER THAT TRAINING ...AND HE DIED A MAN!
20.
NEXT ISH!
BLITZKRIEG IN CENTRAL PARK!

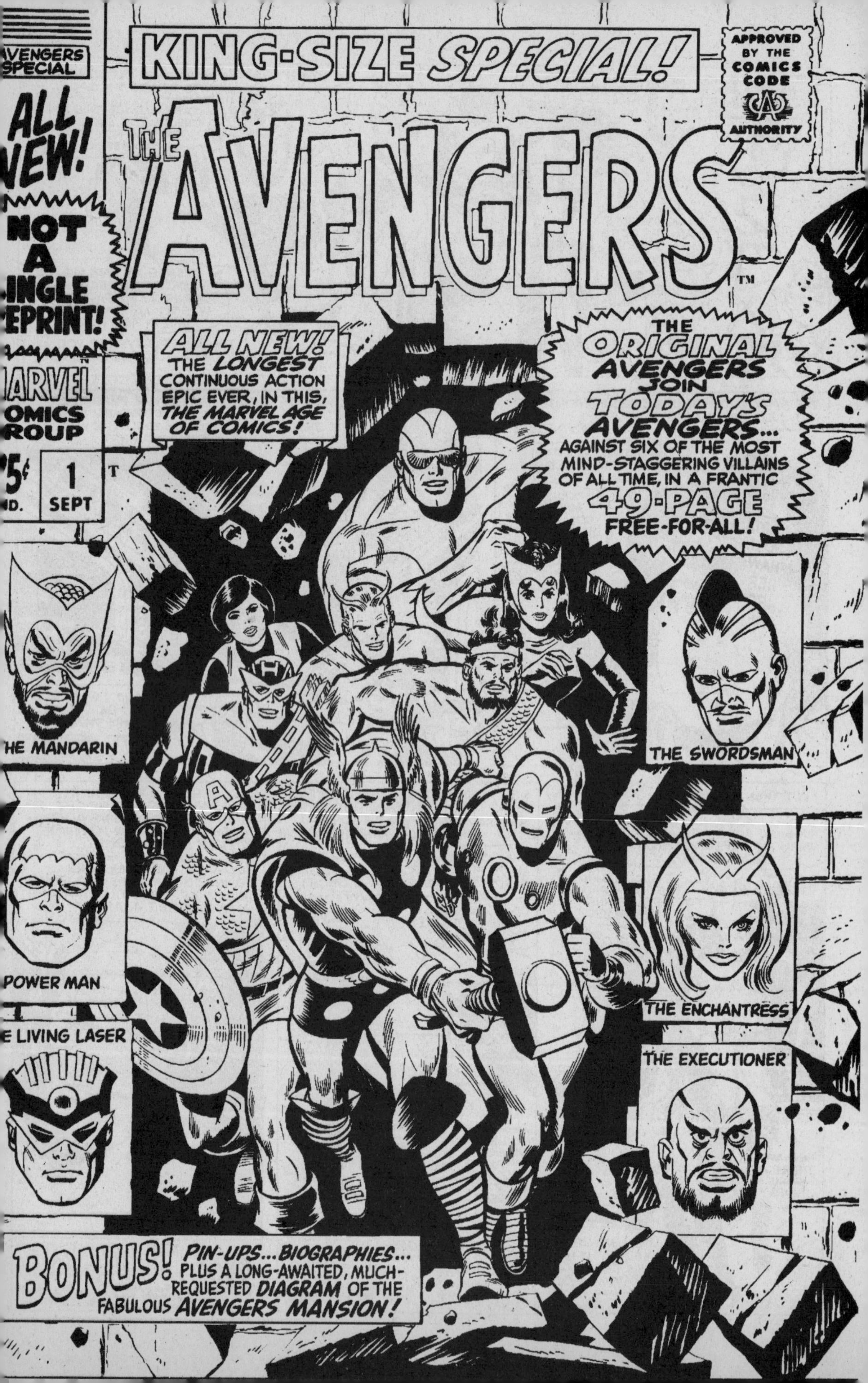
AVENGERS SPECIAL
KING-SIZE SPECIAL!
APPROVED BY THE COMICS CODE AUTHORITY
ALL NEW!
NOT A INGLE EPRINT!
MARVEL OMICS ROUP
5¢
1 SEPT
THE AVENGERS
ALL NEW! THE LONGEST CONTINUOUS ACTION EPIC EVER, IN THIS, THE MARVEL AGE OF COMICS!
THE ORIGINAL AVENGERS JOIN TODAY'S AVENGERS... AGAINST SIX OF THE MOST MIND-STAGGERING VILLAINS OF ALL TIME, IN A FRANTIC 49-PAGE FREE-FOR-ALL!
THE MANDARIN
THE SWORDSMAN
POWER MAN
THE ENCHANTRESS
E LIVING LASER
THE EXECUTIONER
BONUS! PIN-UPS...BIOGRAPHIES... PLUS A LONG-AWAITED, MUCH-REQUESTED DIAGRAM OF THE FABULOUS AVENGERS MANSION!

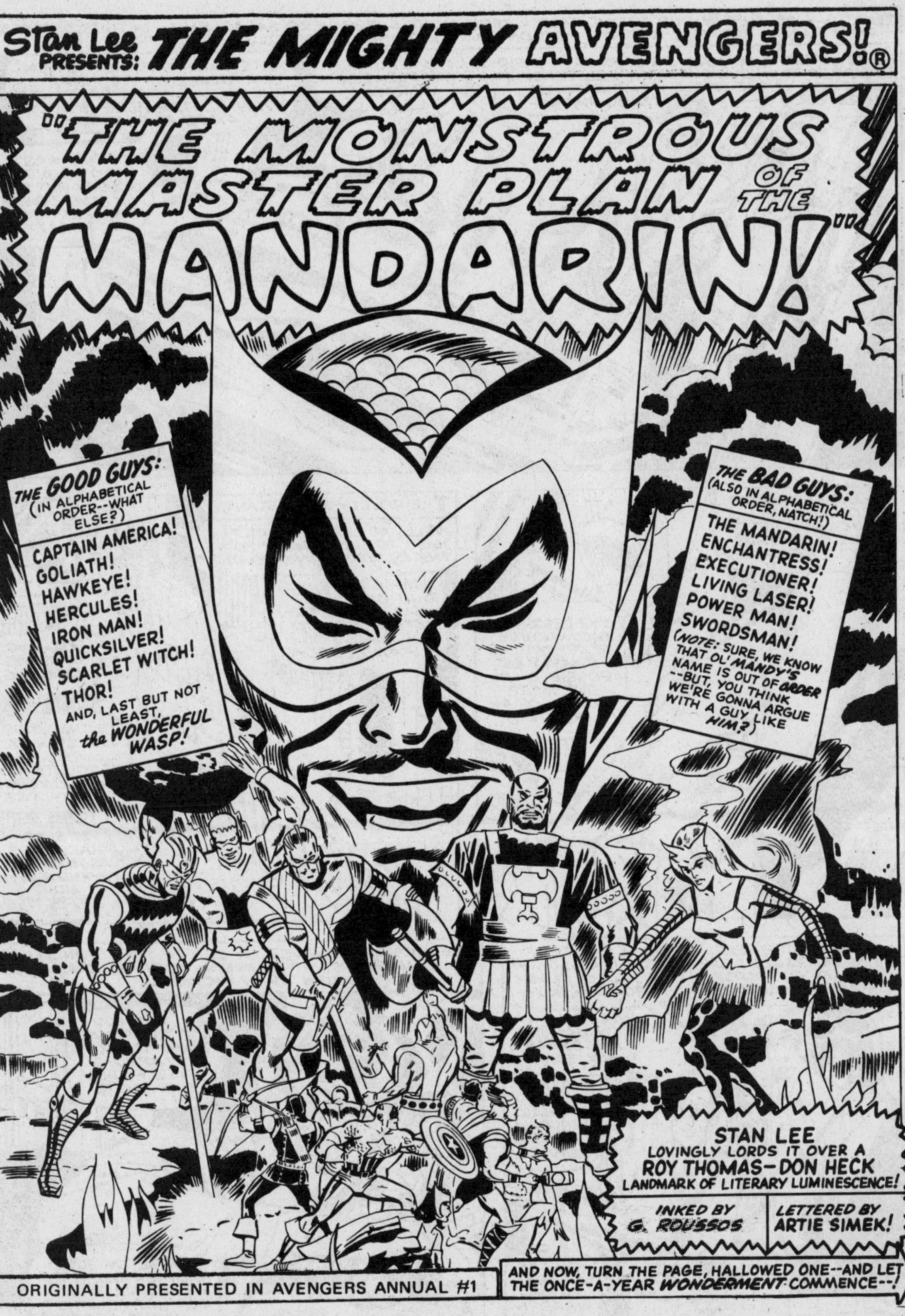
Stan Lee PRESENTS: THE MIGHTY AVENGERS!®
"THE MONSTROUS MASTER PLAN OF THE MANDARIN!"
THE GOOD GUYS: (IN ALPHABETICAL ORDER--WHAT ELSE?)
CAPTAIN AMERICA! GOLIATH! HAWKEYE! HERCULES! IRON MAN! QUICKSILVER! SCARLET WITCH! THOR! AND, LAST BUT NOT LEAST, the WONDERFUL WASP!
THE BAD GUYS: (ALSO IN ALPHABETICAL ORDER, NATCH!)
THE MANDARIN! ENCHANTRESS! EXECUTIONER! LIVING LASER! POWER MAN! SWORDSMAN! (NOTE: SURE, WE KNOW THAT OL' MANDY'S NAME IS OUT OF ORDER --BUT, YOU THINK WE'RE GONNA ARGUE WITH A GUY LIKE HIM?)
STAN LEE LOVINGLY LORDS IT OVER A ROY THOMAS–DON HECK LANDMARK OF LITERARY LUMINESCENCE!
INKED BY G. ROUSSOS
LETTERED BY ARTIE SIMEK!
ORIGINALLY PRESENTED IN AVENGERS ANNUAL #1
AND NOW, TURN THE PAGE, HALLOWED ONE--AND LET THE ONCE-A-YEAR WONDERMENT COMMENCE--!

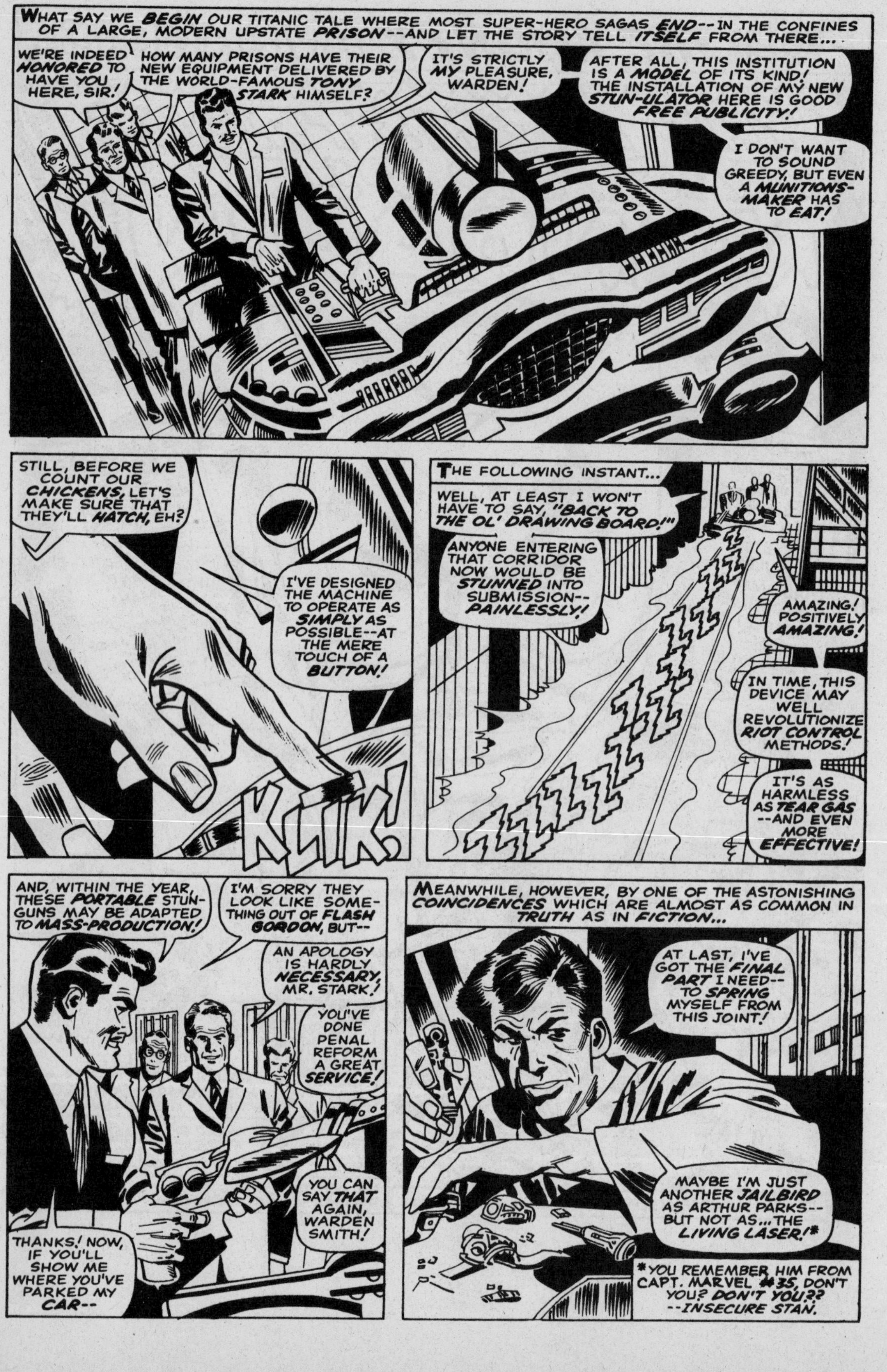
WHAT SAY WE BEGIN OUR TITANIC TALE WHERE MOST SUPER-HERO SAGAS END--IN THE CONFINES OF A LARGE, MODERN UPSTATE PRISON--AND LET THE STORY TELL ITSELF FROM THERE...
WE'RE INDEED HONORED TO HAVE YOU HERE, SIR!
HOW MANY PRISONS HAVE THEIR NEW EQUIPMENT DELIVERED BY THE WORLD-FAMOUS TONY STARK HIMSELF?
IT'S STRICTLY MY PLEASURE, WARDEN!
AFTER ALL, THIS INSTITUTION IS A MODEL OF ITS KIND! THE INSTALLATION OF MY NEW STUN-ULATOR HERE IS GOOD FREE PUBLICITY!
I DON'T WANT TO SOUND GREEDY, BUT EVEN A MUNITIONS-MAKER HAS TO EAT!
STILL, BEFORE WE COUNT OUR CHICKENS, LET'S MAKE SURE THAT THEY'LL HATCH, EH?
I'VE DESIGNED THE MACHINE TO OPERATE AS SIMPLY AS POSSIBLE--AT THE MERE TOUCH OF A BUTTON!
KLIK!
THE FOLLOWING INSTANT...
WELL, AT LEAST I WON'T HAVE TO SAY, "BACK TO THE OL' DRAWING BOARD!"
ANYONE ENTERING THAT CORRIDOR NOW WOULD BE STUNNED INTO SUBMISSION--PAINLESSLY!
AMAZING! POSITIVELY AMAZING!
IN TIME, THIS DEVICE MAY WELL REVOLUTIONIZE RIOT CONTROL METHODS!
IT'S AS HARMLESS AS TEAR GAS--AND EVEN MORE EFFECTIVE!
AND, WITHIN THE YEAR, THESE PORTABLE STUN-GUNS MAY BE ADAPTED TO MASS-PRODUCTION!
I'M SORRY THEY LOOK LIKE SOMETHING OUT OF FLASH GORDON, BUT--
AN APOLOGY IS HARDLY NECESSARY, MR. STARK!
YOU'VE DONE PENAL REFORM A GREAT SERVICE!
YOU CAN SAY THAT AGAIN, WARDEN SMITH!
THANKS! NOW, IF YOU'LL SHOW ME WHERE YOU'VE PARKED MY CAR--
MEANWHILE, HOWEVER, BY ONE OF THE ASTONISHING COINCIDENCES WHICH ARE ALMOST AS COMMON IN TRUTH AS IN FICTION...
AT LAST, I'VE GOT THE FINAL PART I NEED--TO SPRING MYSELF FROM THIS JOINT!
MAYBE I'M JUST ANOTHER JAILBIRD AS ARTHUR PARKS--BUT NOT AS...THE LIVING LASER!*
*YOU REMEMBER HIM FROM CAPT. MARVEL #35, DON'T YOU? DON'T YOU?? --INSECURE STAN.

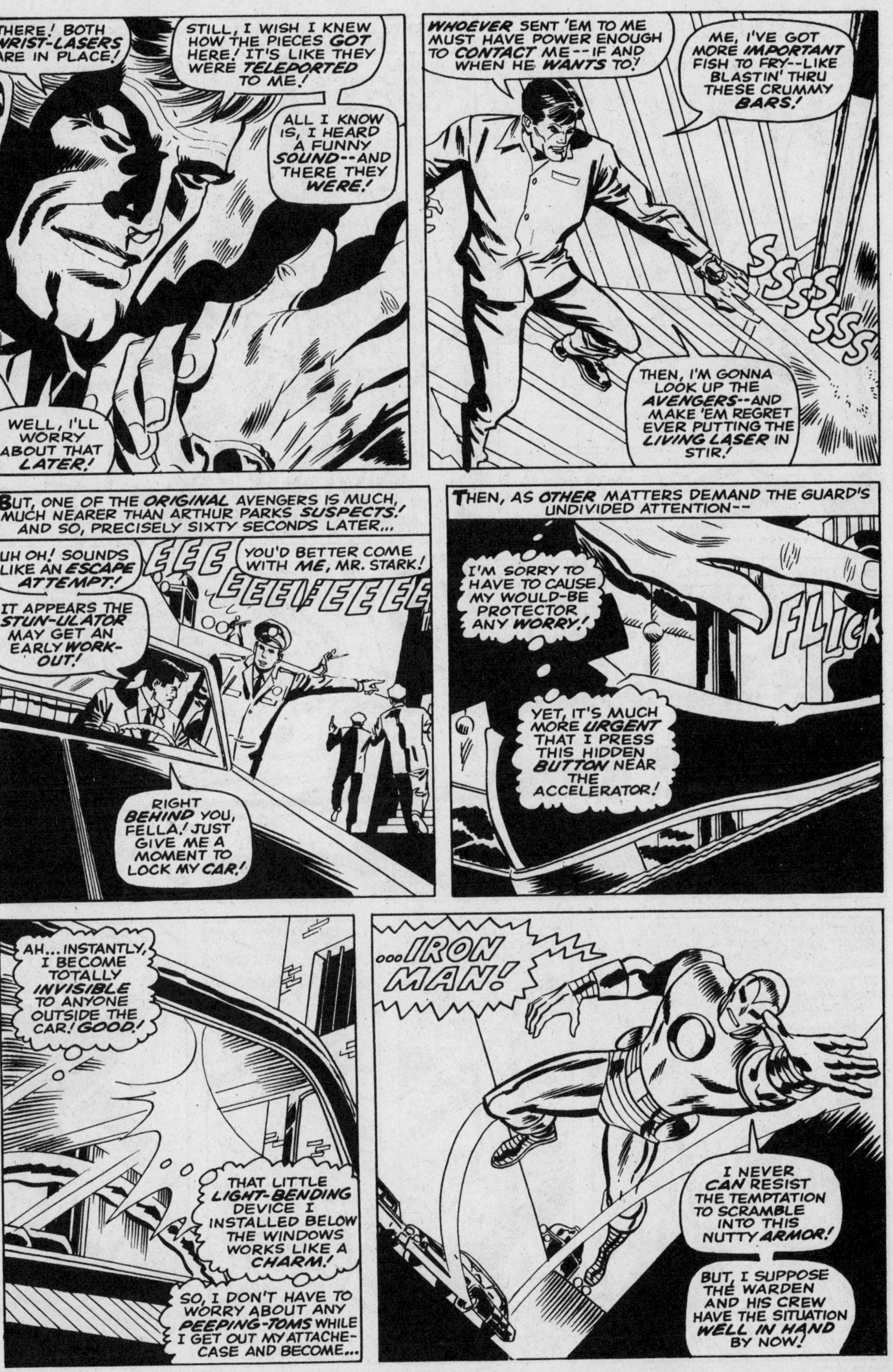
THERE! BOTH WRIST-LASERS ARE IN PLACE!
STILL, I WISH I KNEW HOW THE PIECES GOT HERE! IT'S LIKE THEY WERE TELEPORTED TO ME!
ALL I KNOW IS, I HEARD A FUNNY SOUND--AND THERE THEY WERE!
WELL, I'LL WORRY ABOUT THAT LATER!
WHOEVER SENT 'EM TO ME MUST HAVE POWER ENOUGH TO CONTACT ME--IF AND WHEN HE WANTS TO!
ME, I'VE GOT MORE IMPORTANT FISH TO FRY--LIKE BLASTIN' THRU THESE CRUMMY BARS!
SSSSSSSS
THEN, I'M GONNA LOOK UP THE AVENGERS--AND MAKE 'EM REGRET EVER PUTTING THE LIVING LASER IN STIR!
BUT, ONE OF THE ORIGINAL AVENGERS IS MUCH, MUCH NEARER THAN ARTHUR PARKS SUSPECTS! AND SO, PRECISELY SIXTY SECONDS LATER...
UH OH! SOUNDS LIKE AN ESCAPE ATTEMPT!
EEE EEEIEEEE
YOU'D BETTER COME WITH ME, MR. STARK!
IT APPEARS THE STUN-ULATOR MAY GET AN EARLY WORK-OUT!
RIGHT BEHIND YOU, FELLA! JUST GIVE ME A MOMENT TO LOCK MY CAR!
THEN, AS OTHER MATTERS DEMAND THE GUARD'S UNDIVIDED ATTENTION--
I'M SORRY TO HAVE TO CAUSE MY WOULD-BE PROTECTOR ANY WORRY!
FLICK
YET, IT'S MUCH MORE URGENT THAT I PRESS THIS HIDDEN BUTTON NEAR THE ACCELERATOR!
AH...INSTANTLY, I BECOME TOTALLY INVISIBLE TO ANYONE OUTSIDE THE CAR! GOOD!
THAT LITTLE LIGHT-BENDING DEVICE I INSTALLED BELOW THE WINDOWS WORKS LIKE A CHARM!
SO, I DON'T HAVE TO WORRY ABOUT ANY PEEPING-TOMS WHILE I GET OUT MY ATTACHE-CASE AND BECOME...
...IRON MAN!
I NEVER CAN RESIST THE TEMPTATION TO SCRAMBLE INTO THIS NUTTY ARMOR!
BUT, I SUPPOSE THE WARDEN AND HIS CREW HAVE THE SITUATION WELL IN HAND BY NOW!

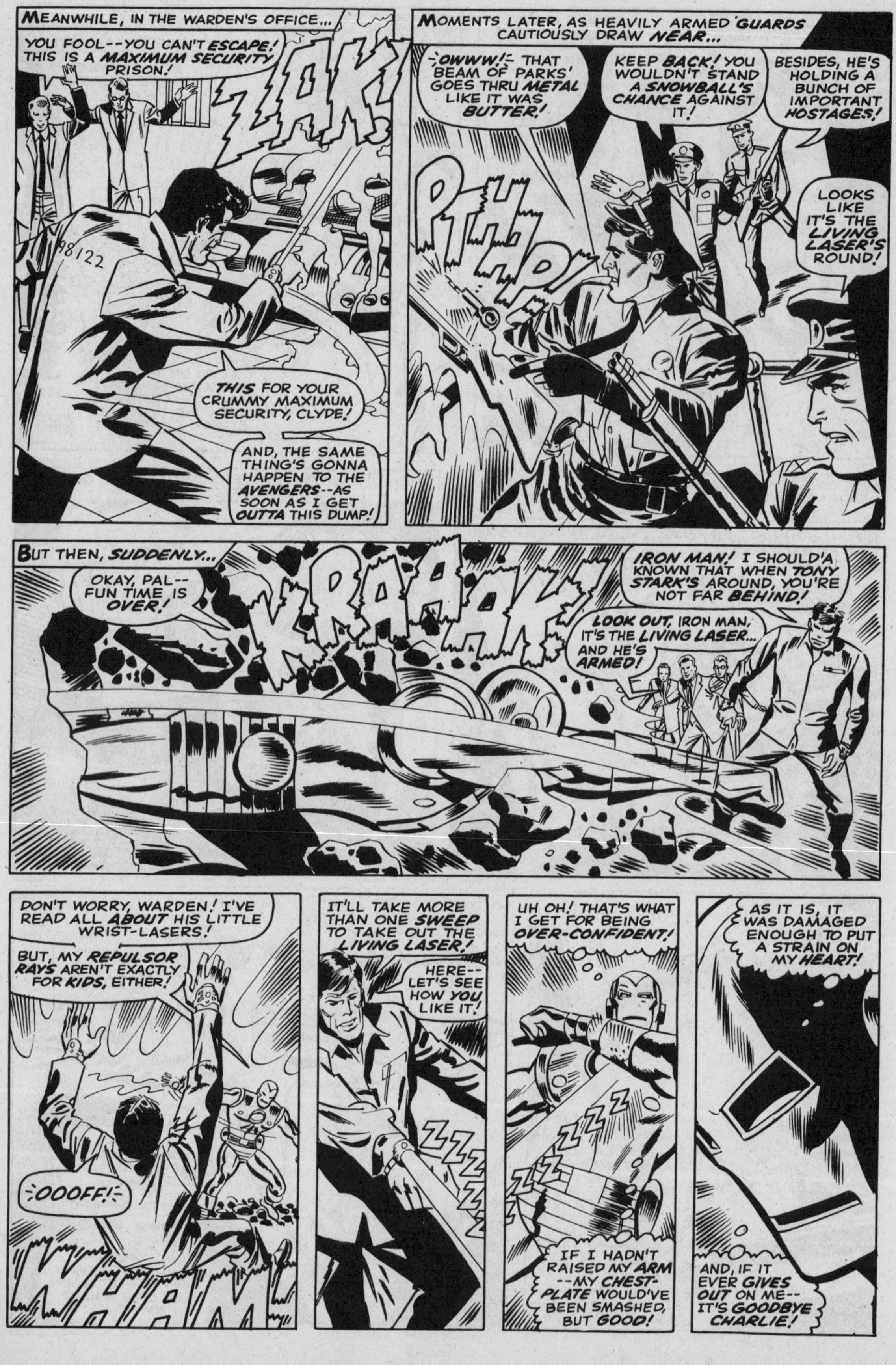
MEANWHILE, IN THE WARDEN'S OFFICE...
YOU FOOL--YOU CAN'T ESCAPE! THIS IS A MAXIMUM SECURITY PRISON!
ZAK!
98122
THIS FOR YOUR CRUMMY MAXIMUM SECURITY, CLYDE!
AND, THE SAME THING'S GONNA HAPPEN TO THE AVENGERS--AS SOON AS I GET OUTTA THIS DUMP!
MOMENTS LATER, AS HEAVILY ARMED GUARDS CAUTIOUSLY DRAW NEAR...
-OWWW!- THAT BEAM OF PARKS' GOES THRU METAL LIKE IT WAS BUTTER!
KEEP BACK! YOU WOULDN'T STAND A SNOWBALL'S CHANCE AGAINST IT!
BESIDES, HE'S HOLDING A BUNCH OF IMPORTANT HOSTAGES!
PTHAP!
LOOKS LIKE IT'S THE LIVING LASER'S ROUND!
BUT THEN, SUDDENLY...
OKAY, PAL--FUN TIME IS OVER!
KRAAAK!
IRON MAN! I SHOULD'A KNOWN THAT WHEN TONY STARK'S AROUND, YOU'RE NOT FAR BEHIND!
LOOK OUT, IRON MAN, IT'S THE LIVING LASER... AND HE'S ARMED!
DON'T WORRY, WARDEN! I'VE READ ALL ABOUT HIS LITTLE WRIST-LASERS!
BUT, MY REPULSOR RAYS AREN'T EXACTLY FOR KIDS, EITHER!
-OOOFF!-
WHAM!
IT'LL TAKE MORE THAN ONE SWEEP TO TAKE OUT THE LIVING LASER!
HERE--LET'S SEE HOW YOU LIKE IT!
ZZZZ
UH OH! THAT'S WHAT I GET FOR BEING OVER-CONFIDENT!
IF I HADN'T RAISED MY ARM--MY CHEST-PLATE WOULD'VE BEEN SMASHED, BUT GOOD!
AS IT IS, IT WAS DAMAGED ENOUGH TO PUT A STRAIN ON MY HEART!
AND, IF IT EVER GIVES OUT ON ME--IT'S GOODBYE CHARLIE!

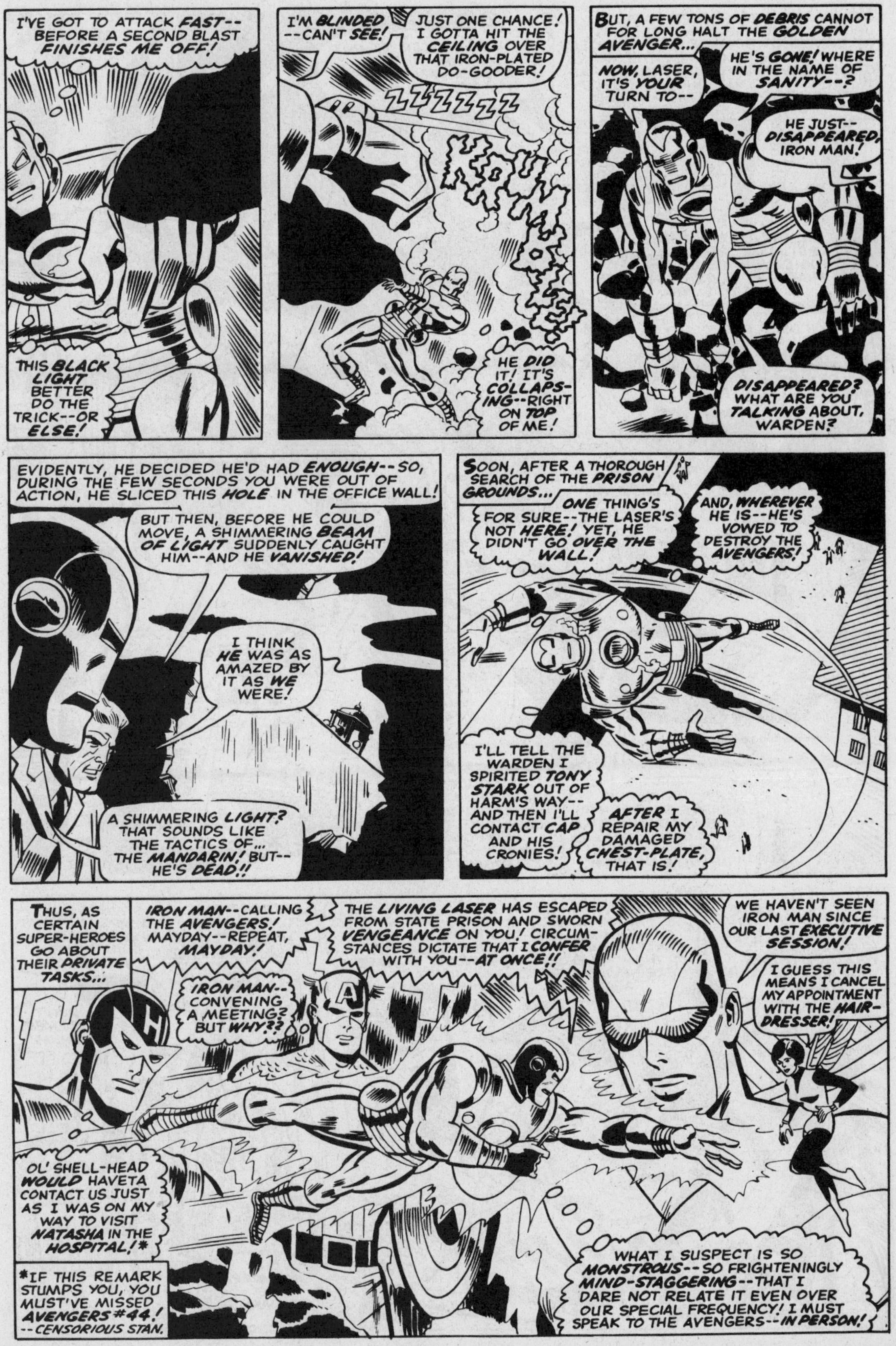
I'VE GOT TO ATTACK FAST-- BEFORE A SECOND BLAST FINISHES ME OFF!
THIS BLACK LIGHT BETTER DO THE TRICK--OR ELSE!
I'M BLINDED --CAN'T SEE!
JUST ONE CHANCE! I GOTTA HIT THE CEILING OVER THAT IRON-PLATED DO-GOODER!
ZZZZZZZ
KRUUMMPHH
HE DID IT! IT'S COLLAPSING--RIGHT ON TOP OF ME!
BUT, A FEW TONS OF DEBRIS CANNOT FOR LONG HALT THE GOLDEN AVENGER...
NOW, LASER, IT'S YOUR TURN TO--
HE'S GONE! WHERE IN THE NAME OF SANITY--?
HE JUST--DISAPPEARED, IRON MAN!
DISAPPEARED? WHAT ARE YOU TALKING ABOUT, WARDEN?
EVIDENTLY, HE DECIDED HE'D HAD ENOUGH--SO, DURING THE FEW SECONDS YOU WERE OUT OF ACTION, HE SLICED THIS HOLE IN THE OFFICE WALL!
BUT THEN, BEFORE HE COULD MOVE, A SHIMMERING BEAM OF LIGHT SUDDENLY CAUGHT HIM--AND HE VANISHED!
I THINK HE WAS AS AMAZED BY IT AS WE WERE!
A SHIMMERING LIGHT? THAT SOUNDS LIKE THE TACTICS OF... THE MANDARIN! BUT--HE'S DEAD!!
SOON, AFTER A THOROUGH SEARCH OF THE PRISON GROUNDS...
ONE THING'S FOR SURE--THE LASER'S NOT HERE! YET, HE DIDN'T GO OVER THE WALL!
AND, WHEREVER HE IS--HE'S VOWED TO DESTROY THE AVENGERS!
I'LL TELL THE WARDEN I SPIRITED TONY STARK OUT OF HARM'S WAY--AND THEN I'LL CONTACT CAP AND HIS CRONIES!
AFTER I REPAIR MY DAMAGED CHEST-PLATE, THAT IS!
THUS, AS CERTAIN SUPER-HEROES GO ABOUT THEIR PRIVATE TASKS...
IRON MAN--CALLING THE AVENGERS! MAYDAY--REPEAT, MAYDAY!
THE LIVING LASER HAS ESCAPED FROM STATE PRISON AND SWORN VENGEANCE ON YOU! CIRCUMSTANCES DICTATE THAT I CONFER WITH YOU--AT ONCE!!
WE HAVEN'T SEEN IRON MAN SINCE OUR LAST EXECUTIVE SESSION!
I GUESS THIS MEANS I CANCEL MY APPOINTMENT WITH THE HAIRDRESSER!
IRON MAN--CONVENING A MEETING? BUT WHY??
OL' SHELL-HEAD WOULD HAVETA CONTACT US JUST AS I WAS ON MY WAY TO VISIT NATASHA IN THE HOSPITAL!*
*IF THIS REMARK STUMPS YOU, YOU MUST'VE MISSED AVENGERS #44! --CENSORIOUS STAN.
WHAT I SUSPECT IS SO MONSTROUS--SO FRIGHTENINGLY MIND-STAGGERING--THAT I DARE NOT RELATE IT EVEN OVER OUR SPECIAL FREQUENCY! I MUST SPEAK TO THE AVENGERS--IN PERSON!

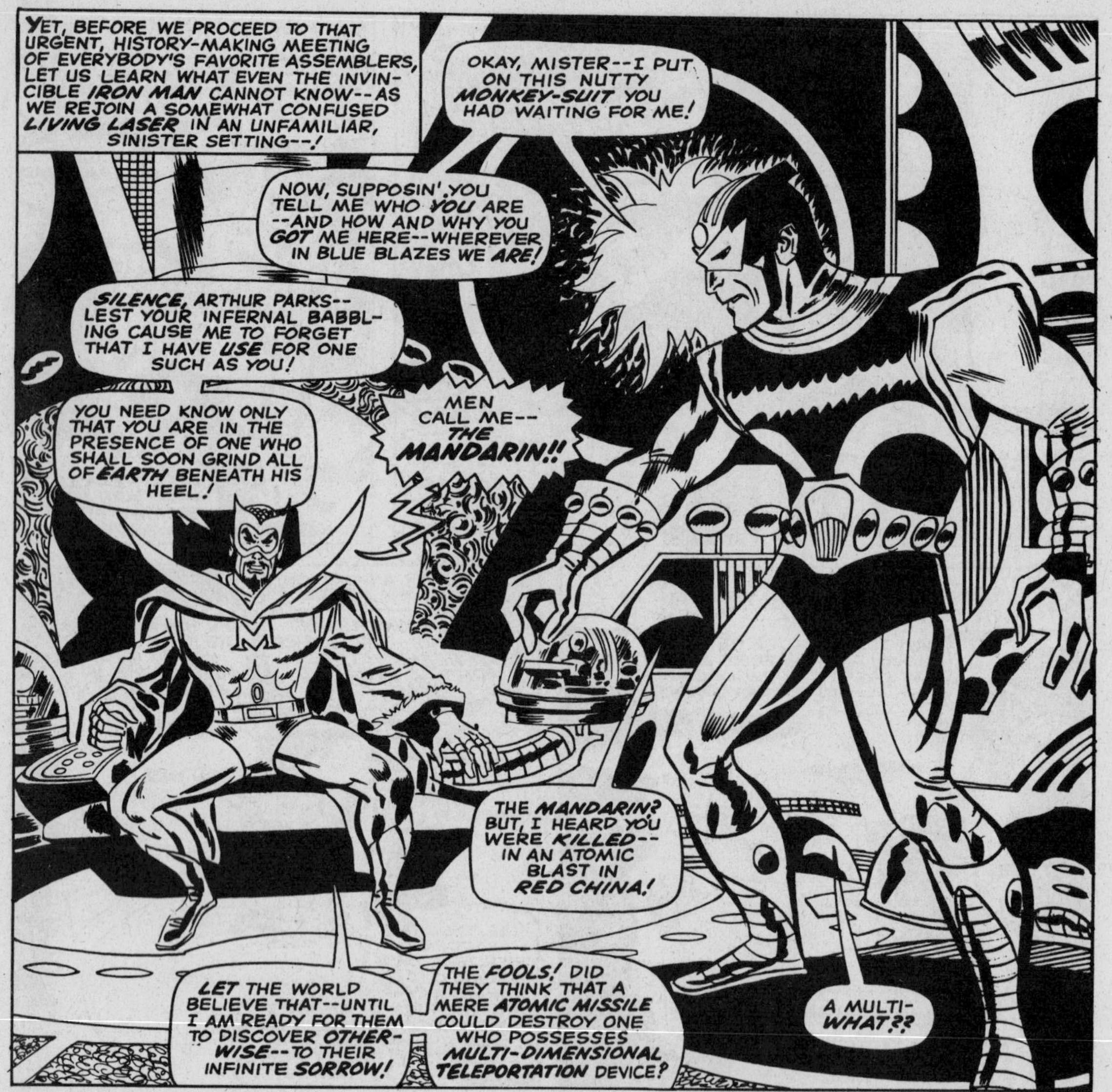
YET, BEFORE WE PROCEED TO THAT URGENT, HISTORY-MAKING MEETING OF EVERYBODY'S FAVORITE ASSEMBLERS, LET US LEARN WHAT EVEN THE INVINCIBLE IRON MAN CANNOT KNOW--AS WE REJOIN A SOMEWHAT CONFUSED LIVING LASER IN AN UNFAMILIAR, SINISTER SETTING--!
OKAY, MISTER--I PUT ON THIS NUTTY MONKEY-SUIT YOU HAD WAITING FOR ME!
NOW, SUPPOSIN' YOU TELL ME WHO YOU ARE --AND HOW AND WHY YOU GOT ME HERE--WHEREVER IN BLUE BLAZES WE ARE!
SILENCE, ARTHUR PARKS--LEST YOUR INFERNAL BABBLING CAUSE ME TO FORGET THAT I HAVE USE FOR ONE SUCH AS YOU!
YOU NEED KNOW ONLY THAT YOU ARE IN THE PRESENCE OF ONE WHO SHALL SOON GRIND ALL OF EARTH BENEATH HIS HEEL!
MEN CALL ME--THE MANDARIN!!
THE MANDARIN? BUT, I HEARD YOU WERE KILLED--IN AN ATOMIC BLAST IN RED CHINA!
LET THE WORLD BELIEVE THAT--UNTIL I AM READY FOR THEM TO DISCOVER OTHERWISE--TO THEIR INFINITE SORROW!
THE FOOLS! DID THEY THINK THAT A MERE ATOMIC MISSILE COULD DESTROY ONE WHO POSSESSES MULTI-DIMENSIONAL TELEPORTATION DEVICE?
A MULTI-WHAT??

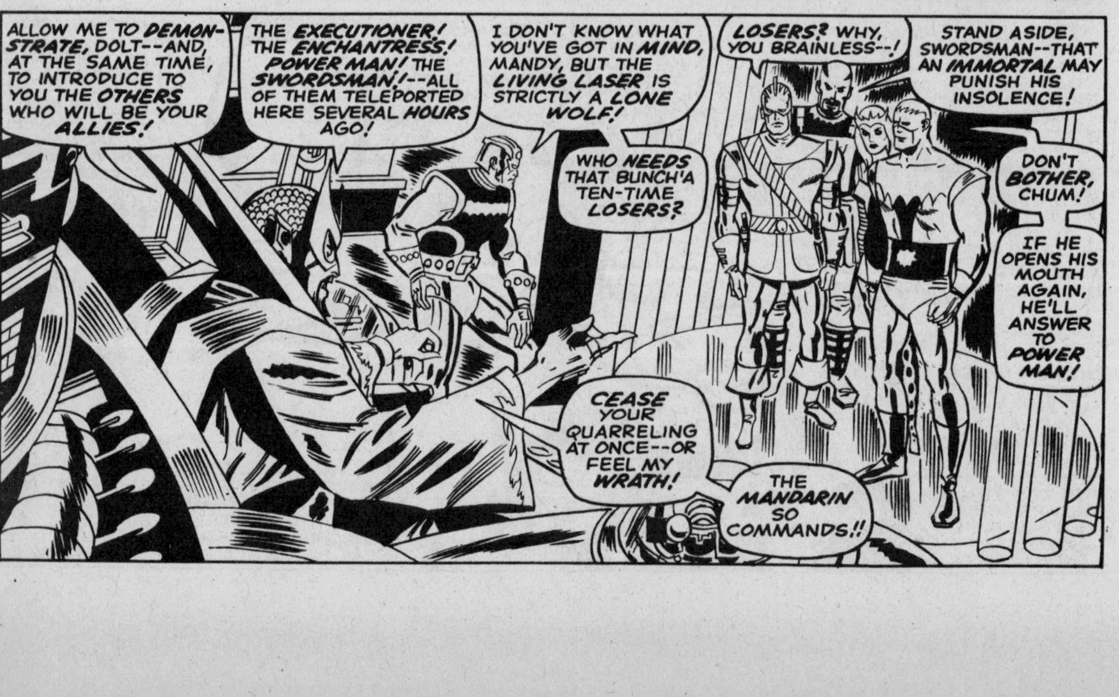
ALLOW ME TO DEMONSTRATE, DOLT--AND, AT THE SAME TIME, TO INTRODUCE TO YOU THE OTHERS WHO WILL BE YOUR ALLIES!
THE EXECUTIONER! THE ENCHANTRESS! POWER MAN! THE SWORDSMAN!--ALL OF THEM TELEPORTED HERE SEVERAL HOURS AGO!
I DON'T KNOW WHAT YOU'VE GOT IN MIND, MANDY, BUT THE LIVING LASER IS STRICTLY A LONE WOLF!
WHO NEEDS THAT BUNCH'A TEN-TIME LOSERS?
LOSERS? WHY, YOU BRAINLESS--!
STAND ASIDE, SWORDSMAN--THAT AN IMMORTAL MAY PUNISH HIS INSOLENCE!
DON'T BOTHER, CHUM!
IF HE OPENS HIS MOUTH AGAIN, HE'LL ANSWER TO POWER MAN!
CEASE YOUR QUARRELING AT ONCE--OR FEEL MY WRATH!
THE MANDARIN SO COMMANDS!!

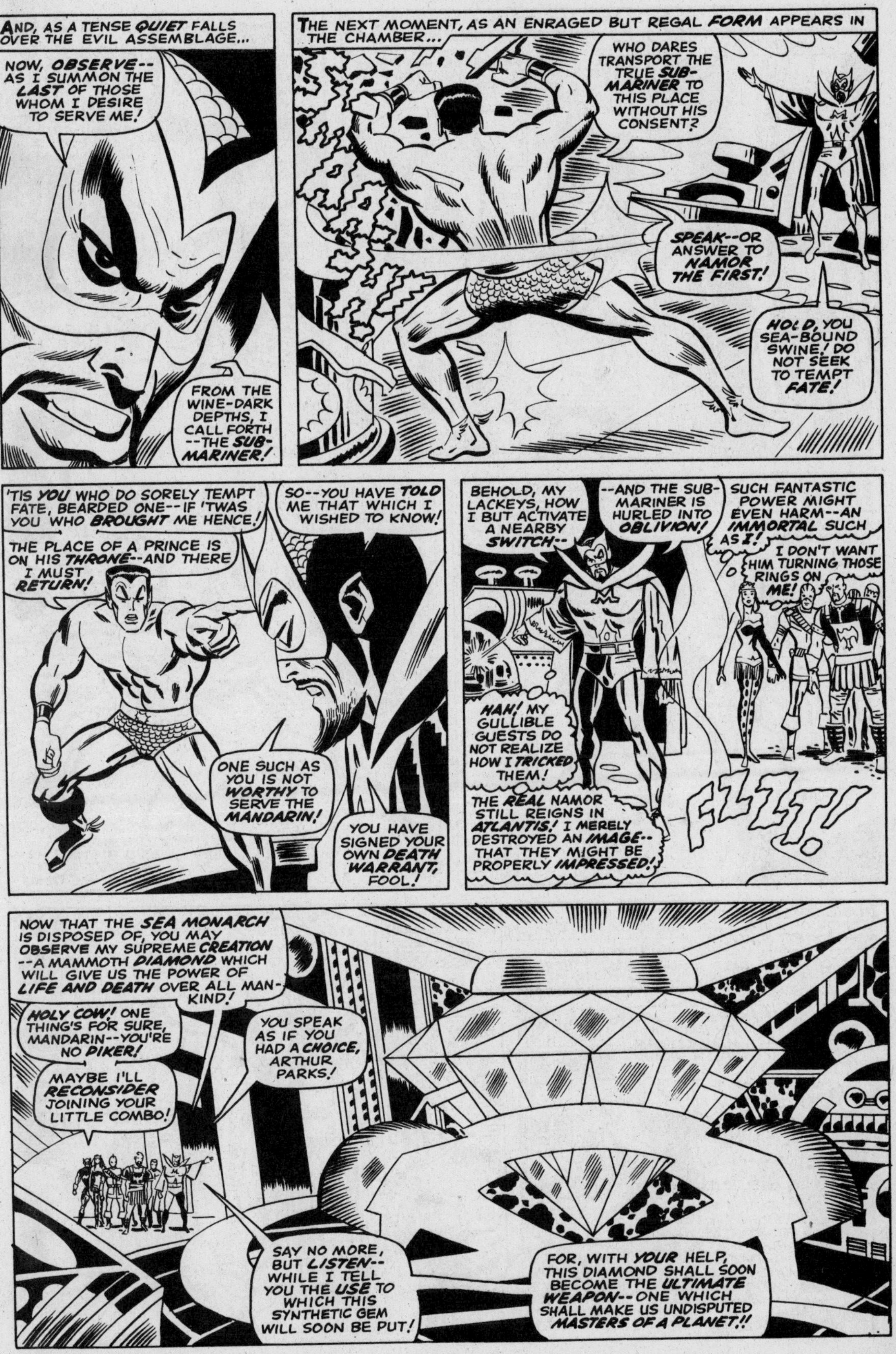
AND, AS A TENSE QUIET FALLS OVER THE EVIL ASSEMBLAGE...
NOW, OBSERVE--AS I SUMMON THE LAST OF THOSE WHOM I DESIRE TO SERVE ME!
FROM THE WINE-DARK DEPTHS, I CALL FORTH --THE SUB-MARINER!
THE NEXT MOMENT, AS AN ENRAGED BUT REGAL FORM APPEARS IN THE CHAMBER...
WHO DARES TRANSPORT THE TRUE SUB-MARINER TO THIS PLACE WITHOUT HIS CONSENT?
SPEAK--OR ANSWER TO NAMOR THE FIRST!
HOLD, YOU SEA-BOUND SWINE! DO NOT SEEK TO TEMPT FATE!
'TIS YOU WHO DO SORELY TEMPT FATE, BEARDED ONE--IF 'TWAS YOU WHO BROUGHT ME HENCE!
THE PLACE OF A PRINCE IS ON HIS THRONE--AND THERE I MUST RETURN!
SO--YOU HAVE TOLD ME THAT WHICH I WISHED TO KNOW!
ONE SUCH AS YOU IS NOT WORTHY TO SERVE THE MANDARIN!
YOU HAVE SIGNED YOUR OWN DEATH WARRANT, FOOL!
BEHOLD, MY LACKEYS, HOW I BUT ACTIVATE A NEARBY SWITCH--
--AND THE SUB-MARINER IS HURLED INTO OBLIVION!
SUCH FANTASTIC POWER MIGHT EVEN HARM--AN IMMORTAL SUCH AS I!
I DON'T WANT HIM TURNING THOSE RINGS ON ME!
HAH! MY GULLIBLE GUESTS DO NOT REALIZE HOW I TRICKED THEM!
THE REAL NAMOR STILL REIGNS IN ATLANTIS! I MERELY DESTROYED AN IMAGE--THAT THEY MIGHT BE PROPERLY IMPRESSED!
FZZT!
NOW THAT THE SEA MONARCH IS DISPOSED OF, YOU MAY OBSERVE MY SUPREME CREATION--A MAMMOTH DIAMOND WHICH WILL GIVE US THE POWER OF LIFE AND DEATH OVER ALL MAN-KIND!
HOLY COW! ONE THING'S FOR SURE, MANDARIN--YOU'RE NO PIKER!
MAYBE I'LL RECONSIDER JOINING YOUR LITTLE COMBO!
YOU SPEAK AS IF YOU HAD A CHOICE, ARTHUR PARKS!
SAY NO MORE, BUT LISTEN--WHILE I TELL YOU THE USE TO WHICH THIS SYNTHETIC GEM WILL SOON BE PUT!
FOR, WITH YOUR HELP, THIS DIAMOND SHALL SOON BECOME THE ULTIMATE WEAPON--ONE WHICH SHALL MAKE US UNDISPUTED MASTERS OF A PLANET!!

MEANWHILE, AT NEW YORK'S FAR-FAMED *AVENGERS* MANSION...

WHY, *NO*, SIR -- THE AVENGERS HAVEN'T *ARRIVED* YET!

WILL YOU HAVE A SPOT OF *TEA* WHILE YOU'RE WAITING, SIR?

ER, NO, THANK YOU, JARVIS!

I'LL JUST WAIT IN THE *MEETING ROOM!*

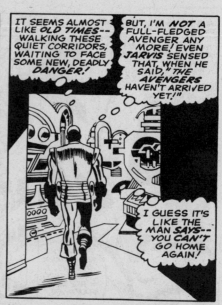

IT SEEMS ALMOST LIKE *OLD TIMES* -- WALKING THESE *QUIET* CORRIDORS, WAITING TO FACE SOME NEW, DEADLY *DANGER!*

BUT, I'M *NOT* A *FULL-FLEDGED* AVENGER ANY MORE! EVEN *JARVIS* SENSED THAT, WHEN HE SAID, "THE *AVENGERS* HAVEN'T ARRIVED YET!"

I GUESS IT'S LIKE THE MAN *SAYS* -- YOU *CAN'T* GO HOME AGAIN!

*SUDDENLY, THE GLEAMING GLADIATOR'S REVERIE IS SHARPLY *INTERRUPTED*...*

HOLD, SIRRAH! THE *PRINCE OF POWER* COMMANDS!

HUH? WHAT IN HOLY HANNAH--?

SO -- THOU WOULDST ENGAGE ME IN FUTILE *STRUGGLE!*

THEN, HAVE *AT* THEE, IRON-CLAD ONE! NE'ERMORE SHALT THOU INVADE THE *SANCTUARY* OF THE *AVENGERS!*

K-TANG!

MISTER, I HELPED *FOUND* THE *AVENGERS!* WHO IN THE NAME OF WILL SHAKESPEARE ARE *YOU?*

IT'S NO USE! HE'S HITTING MY *HELMET* SO HARD, HE CAN'T *HEAR* ME!

IN THE STREET BELOW, THE CLAMOROUS SOUNDS OF BATTLE ARE HEARD BY TWO OF *NEW YORK'S FINEST*...

WAIT, CHARLIE! JUST WHERE DO YOU THINK *YOU'RE* GOING?

DIDN'T YOU HEAR THAT *NOISE?* THERE'S A *FIGHT* -- IN THE AVENGERS MANSION!

SURE, I HEARD IT! HALF OF *MANHATTAN* MUST'A HEARD IT!

BUT, IF YOU WEREN'T A TWO-DAY *ROOKIE*, YOU'D KNOW THAT PLACE IS *OFF LIMITS* -- LIKE THE *U.N.* AND THE *BAXTER BUILDING!*

BESIDES, SOMEBODY JUST FLEW IN THAT *WINDOW* WHO CAN SETTLE ANY FIGHT!

AND, AT THAT VERY MOMENT, *INSIDE*...

IRON MAN! HERCULES!

LET THIS FOOL-HARDY CLASH BE AT AN *END!*

THOR! WHAT ARE *YOU* DOING HERE?

GREETINGS, GOD OF THUNDER! HAST THOU COME TO WATCH ME *THRASH* YON VILLAIN?

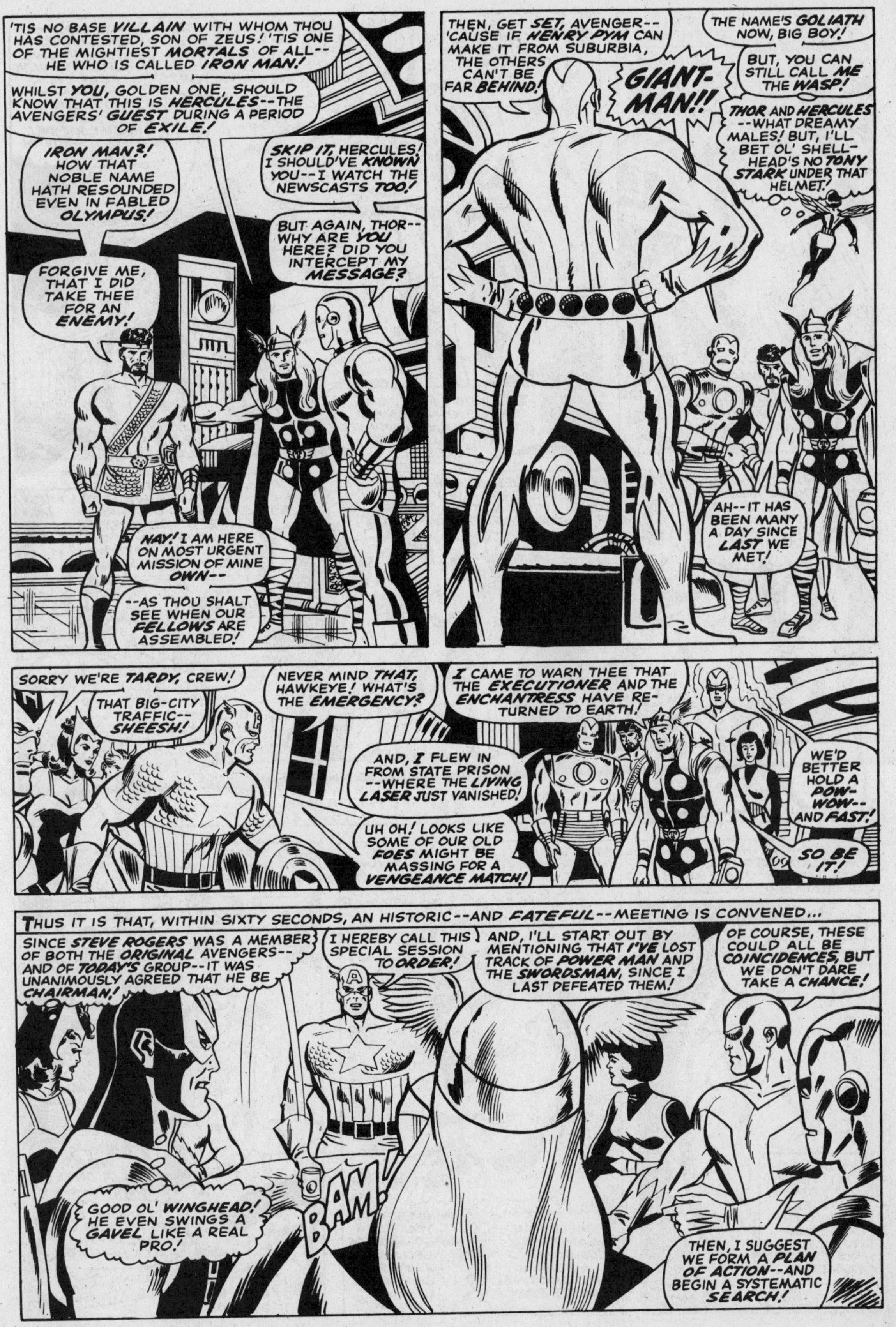

'TIS NO BASE VILLAIN WITH WHOM THOU HAS CONTESTED, SON OF ZEUS! 'TIS ONE OF THE MIGHTIEST MORTALS OF ALL-- HE WHO IS CALLED IRON MAN!
WHILST YOU, GOLDEN ONE, SHOULD KNOW THAT THIS IS HERCULES--THE AVENGERS' GUEST DURING A PERIOD OF EXILE!
IRON MAN?! HOW THAT NOBLE NAME HATH RESOUNDED EVEN IN FABLED OLYMPUS!
SKIP IT, HERCULES! I SHOULD'VE KNOWN YOU--I WATCH THE NEWSCASTS TOO!
FORGIVE ME, THAT I DID TAKE THEE FOR AN ENEMY!
BUT AGAIN, THOR--WHY ARE YOU HERE? DID YOU INTERCEPT MY MESSAGE?
NAY! I AM HERE ON MOST URGENT MISSION OF MINE OWN--
--AS THOU SHALT SEE WHEN OUR FELLOWS ARE ASSEMBLED!
THEN, GET SET, AVENGER--'CAUSE IF HENRY PYM CAN MAKE IT FROM SUBURBIA, THE OTHERS CAN'T BE FAR BEHIND!
GIANT-MAN!!
THE NAME'S GOLIATH NOW, BIG BOY!
BUT, YOU CAN STILL CALL ME THE WASP!
THOR AND HERCULES --WHAT DREAMY MALES! BUT, I'LL BET OL' SHELL-HEAD'S NO TONY STARK UNDER THAT HELMET!
AH--IT HAS BEEN MANY A DAY SINCE LAST WE MET!
SORRY WE'RE TARDY, CREW!
THAT BIG-CITY TRAFFIC--SHEESH!
NEVER MIND THAT, HAWKEYE! WHAT'S THE EMERGENCY?
I CAME TO WARN THEE THAT THE EXECUTIONER AND THE ENCHANTRESS HAVE RETURNED TO EARTH!
AND, I FLEW IN FROM STATE PRISON --WHERE THE LIVING LASER JUST VANISHED!
UH OH! LOOKS LIKE SOME OF OUR OLD FOES MIGHT BE MASSING FOR A VENGEANCE MATCH!
WE'D BETTER HOLD A POW-WOW--AND FAST!
SO BE IT!
THUS IT IS THAT, WITHIN SIXTY SECONDS, AN HISTORIC--AND FATEFUL--MEETING IS CONVENED...
SINCE STEVE ROGERS WAS A MEMBER OF BOTH THE ORIGINAL AVENGERS--AND OF TODAY'S GROUP--IT WAS UNANIMOUSLY AGREED THAT HE BE CHAIRMAN!
I HEREBY CALL THIS SPECIAL SESSION TO ORDER!
BAM!
GOOD OL' WINGHEAD! HE EVEN SWINGS A GAVEL LIKE A REAL PRO!
AND, I'LL START OUT BY MENTIONING THAT I'VE LOST TRACK OF POWER MAN AND THE SWORDSMAN, SINCE I LAST DEFEATED THEM!
OF COURSE, THESE COULD ALL BE COINCIDENCES, BUT WE DON'T DARE TAKE A CHANCE!
THEN, I SUGGEST WE FORM A PLAN OF ACTION--AND BEGIN A SYSTEMATIC SEARCH!

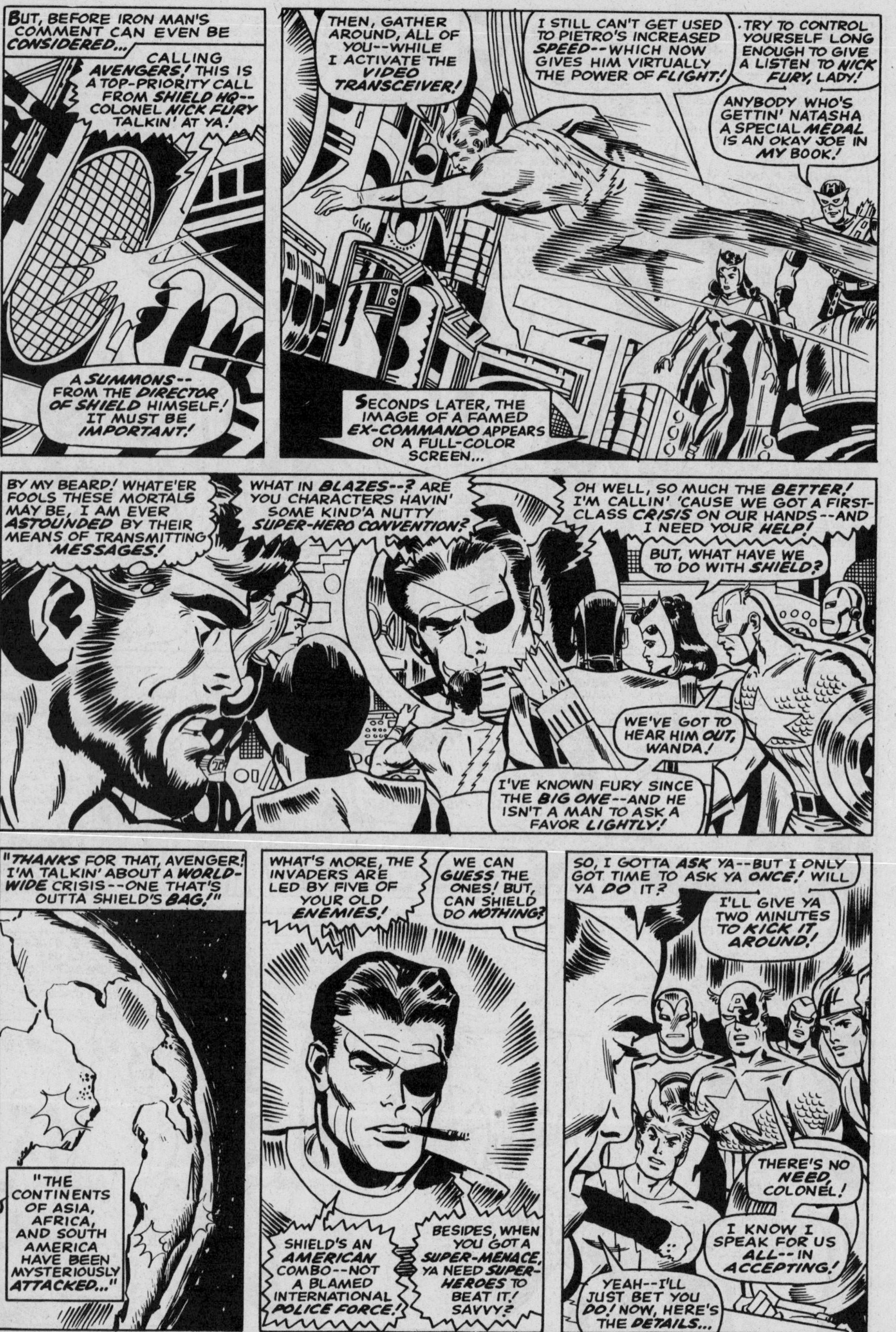
BUT, BEFORE IRON MAN'S COMMENT CAN EVEN BE CONSIDERED...
CALLING AVENGERS! THIS IS A TOP-PRIORITY CALL FROM SHIELD HQ-- COLONEL NICK FURY TALKIN' AT YA!
A SUMMONS-- FROM THE DIRECTOR OF SHIELD HIMSELF! IT MUST BE IMPORTANT!
THEN, GATHER AROUND, ALL OF YOU--WHILE I ACTIVATE THE VIDEO TRANSCEIVER!
I STILL CAN'T GET USED TO PIETRO'S INCREASED SPEED--WHICH NOW GIVES HIM VIRTUALLY THE POWER OF FLIGHT!
TRY TO CONTROL YOURSELF LONG ENOUGH TO GIVE A LISTEN TO NICK FURY, LADY!
ANYBODY WHO'S GETTIN' NATASHA A SPECIAL MEDAL IS AN OKAY JOE IN MY BOOK!
SECONDS LATER, THE IMAGE OF A FAMED EX-COMMANDO APPEARS ON A FULL-COLOR SCREEN...
BY MY BEARD! WHATE'ER FOOLS THESE MORTALS MAY BE, I AM EVER ASTOUNDED BY THEIR MEANS OF TRANSMITTING MESSAGES!
WHAT IN BLAZES--? ARE YOU CHARACTERS HAVIN' SOME KIND'A NUTTY SUPER-HERO CONVENTION?
OH WELL, SO MUCH THE BETTER! I'M CALLIN' 'CAUSE WE GOT A FIRST-CLASS CRISIS ON OUR HANDS--AND I NEED YOUR HELP!
BUT, WHAT HAVE WE TO DO WITH SHIELD?
WE'VE GOT TO HEAR HIM OUT, WANDA!
I'VE KNOWN FURY SINCE THE BIG ONE--AND HE ISN'T A MAN TO ASK A FAVOR LIGHTLY!
"THANKS FOR THAT, AVENGER! I'M TALKIN' ABOUT A WORLD-WIDE CRISIS--ONE THAT'S OUTTA SHIELD'S BAG!"
"THE CONTINENTS OF ASIA, AFRICA, AND SOUTH AMERICA HAVE BEEN MYSTERIOUSLY ATTACKED..."
WHAT'S MORE, THE INVADERS ARE LED BY FIVE OF YOUR OLD ENEMIES!
WE CAN GUESS THE ONES! BUT, CAN SHIELD DO NOTHING?
SHIELD'S AN AMERICAN COMBO--NOT A BLAMED INTERNATIONAL POLICE FORCE!
BESIDES, WHEN YOU GOT A SUPER-MENACE, YA NEED SUPER-HEROES TO BEAT IT! SAVVY?
SO, I GOTTA ASK YA--BUT I ONLY GOT TIME TO ASK YA ONCE! WILL YA DO IT?
I'LL GIVE YA TWO MINUTES TO KICK IT AROUND!
THERE'S NO NEED, COLONEL!
I KNOW I SPEAK FOR US ALL--IN ACCEPTING!
YEAH--I'LL JUST BET YOU DO! NOW, HERE'S THE DETAILS...

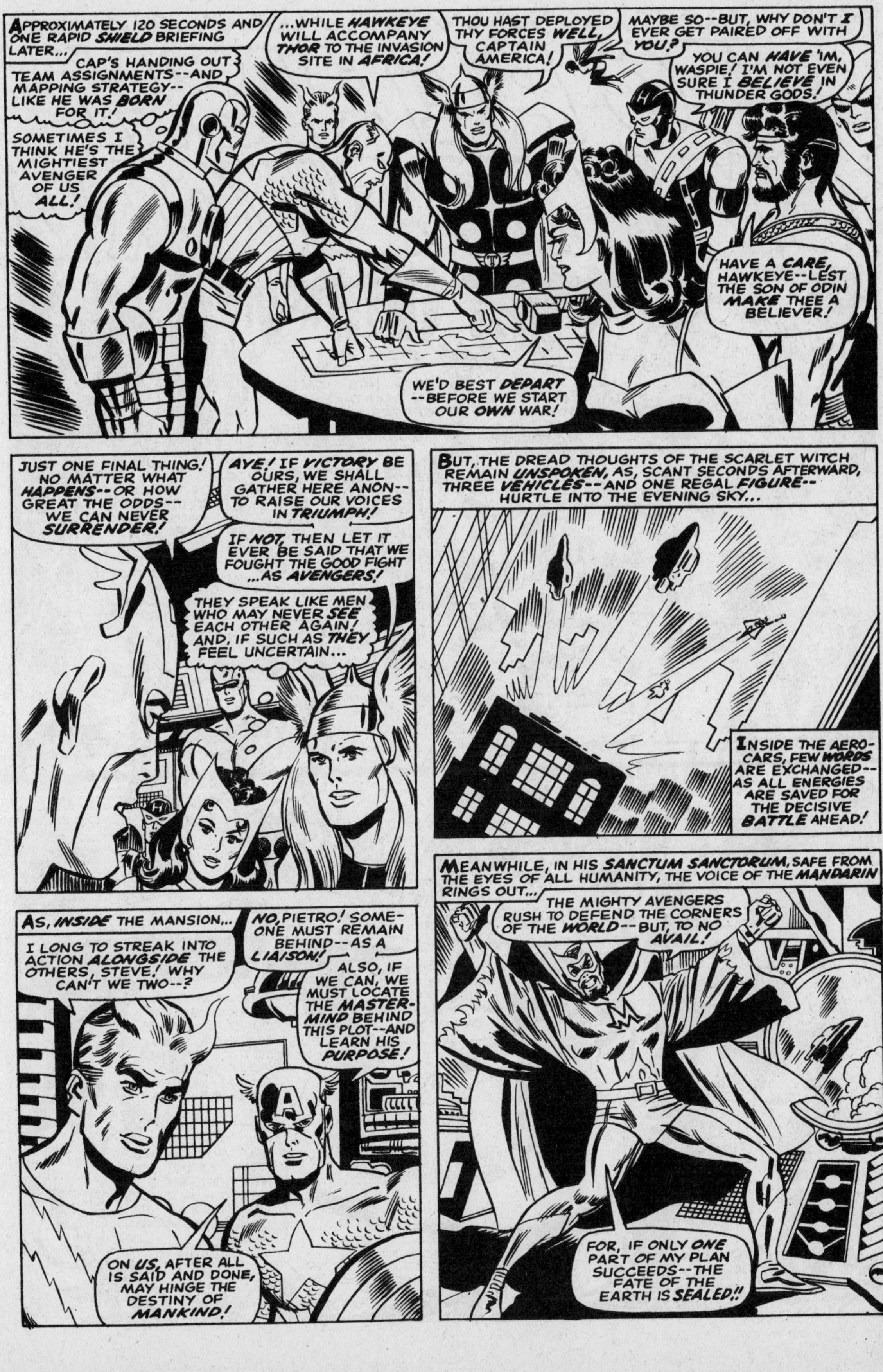
APPROXIMATELY 120 SECONDS AND ONE RAPID SHIELD BRIEFING LATER...
CAP'S HANDING OUT TEAM ASSIGNMENTS--AND MAPPING STRATEGY--LIKE HE WAS BORN FOR IT!
SOMETIMES I THINK HE'S THE MIGHTIEST AVENGER OF US ALL!
...WHILE HAWKEYE WILL ACCOMPANY THOR TO THE INVASION SITE IN AFRICA!
THOU HAST DEPLOYED THY FORCES WELL, CAPTAIN AMERICA!
MAYBE SO--BUT, WHY DON'T I EVER GET PAIRED OFF WITH YOU?
YOU CAN HAVE 'IM, WASPIE! I'M NOT EVEN SURE I BELIEVE IN THUNDER GODS!
HAVE A CARE, HAWKEYE--LEST THE SON OF ODIN MAKE THEE A BELIEVER!
WE'D BEST DEPART --BEFORE WE START OUR OWN WAR!
JUST ONE FINAL THING! NO MATTER WHAT HAPPENS--OR HOW GREAT THE ODDS--WE CAN NEVER SURRENDER!
AYE! IF VICTORY BE OURS, WE SHALL GATHER HERE ANON--TO RAISE OUR VOICES IN TRIUMPH!
IF NOT, THEN LET IT EVER BE SAID THAT WE FOUGHT THE GOOD FIGHT ...AS AVENGERS!
THEY SPEAK LIKE MEN WHO MAY NEVER SEE EACH OTHER AGAIN! AND, IF SUCH AS THEY FEEL UNCERTAIN...
BUT, THE DREAD THOUGHTS OF THE SCARLET WITCH REMAIN UNSPOKEN, AS, SCANT SECONDS AFTERWARD, THREE VEHICLES--AND ONE REGAL FIGURE--HURTLE INTO THE EVENING SKY...
INSIDE THE AERO-CARS, FEW WORDS ARE EXCHANGED--AS ALL ENERGIES ARE SAVED FOR THE DECISIVE BATTLE AHEAD!
AS, INSIDE THE MANSION...
I LONG TO STREAK INTO ACTION ALONGSIDE THE OTHERS, STEVE! WHY CAN'T WE TWO--?
NO, PIETRO! SOME-ONE MUST REMAIN BEHIND--AS A LIAISON!
ALSO, IF WE CAN, WE MUST LOCATE THE MASTER-MIND BEHIND THIS PLOT--AND LEARN HIS PURPOSE!
ON US, AFTER ALL IS SAID AND DONE, MAY HINGE THE DESTINY OF MANKIND!
MEANWHILE, IN HIS SANCTUM SANCTORUM, SAFE FROM THE EYES OF ALL HUMANITY, THE VOICE OF THE MANDARIN RINGS OUT...
THE MIGHTY AVENGERS RUSH TO DEFEND THE CORNERS OF THE WORLD--BUT, TO NO AVAIL!
FOR, IF ONLY ONE PART OF MY PLAN SUCCEEDS--THE FATE OF THE EARTH IS SEALED!!

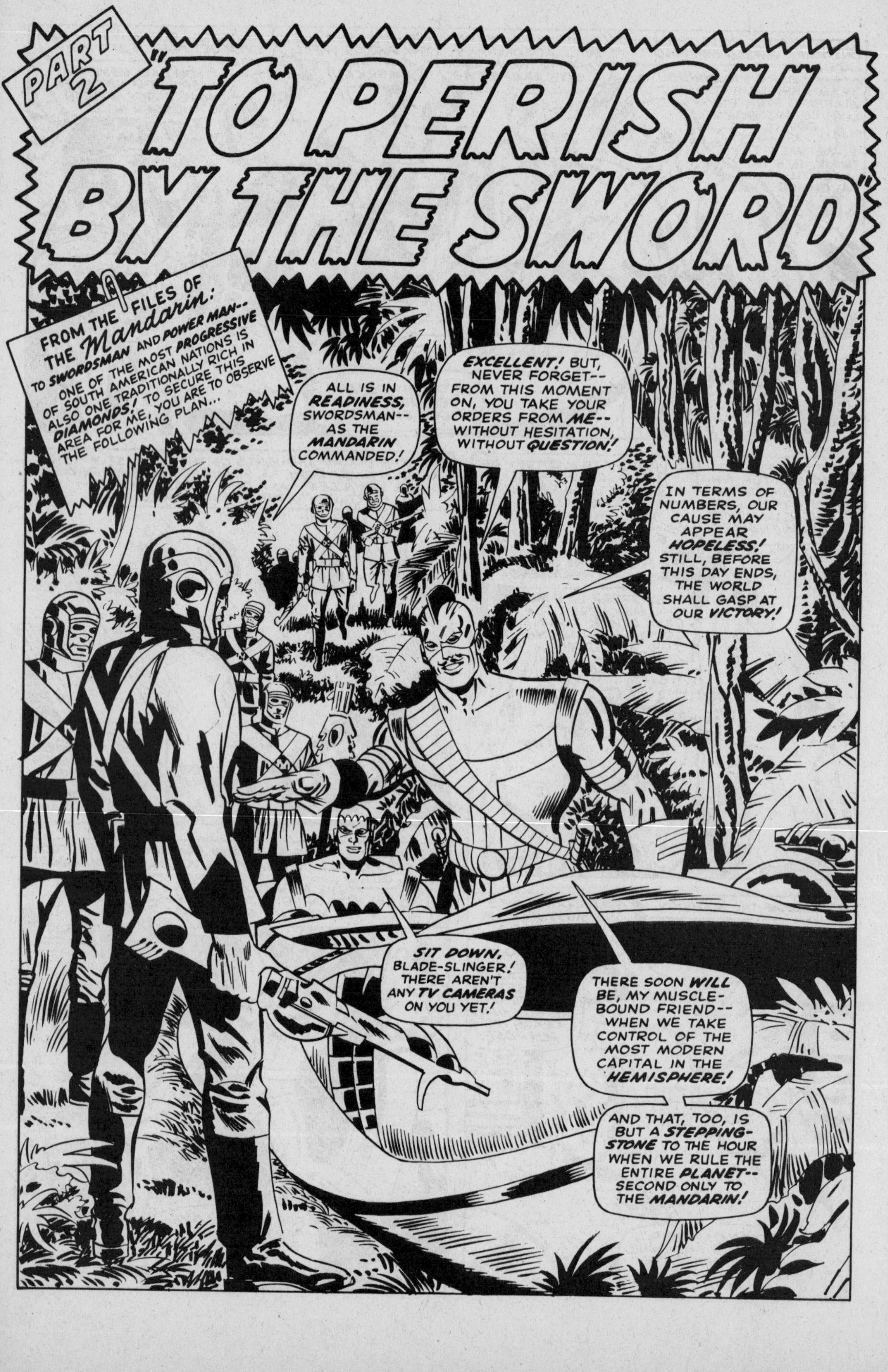
PART 2
"TO PERISH BY THE SWORD"
FROM THE FILES OF THE Mandarin: TO SWORDSMAN AND POWER MAN-- ONE OF THE MOST PROGRESSIVE OF SOUTH AMERICAN NATIONS IS ALSO ONE TRADITIONALLY RICH IN DIAMONDS! TO SECURE THIS AREA FOR ME, YOU ARE TO OBSERVE THE FOLLOWING PLAN...
ALL IS IN READINESS, SWORDSMAN-- AS THE MANDARIN COMMANDED!
EXCELLENT! BUT, NEVER FORGET-- FROM THIS MOMENT ON, YOU TAKE YOUR ORDERS FROM ME-- WITHOUT HESITATION, WITHOUT QUESTION!
IN TERMS OF NUMBERS, OUR CAUSE MAY APPEAR HOPELESS! STILL, BEFORE THIS DAY ENDS, THE WORLD SHALL GASP AT OUR VICTORY!
SIT DOWN, BLADE-SLINGER! THERE AREN'T ANY TV CAMERAS ON YOU YET!
THERE SOON WILL BE, MY MUSCLE-BOUND FRIEND-- WHEN WE TAKE CONTROL OF THE MOST MODERN CAPITAL IN THE HEMISPHERE!
AND THAT, TOO, IS BUT A STEPPING-STONE TO THE HOUR WHEN WE RULE THE ENTIRE PLANET-- SECOND ONLY TO THE MANDARIN!

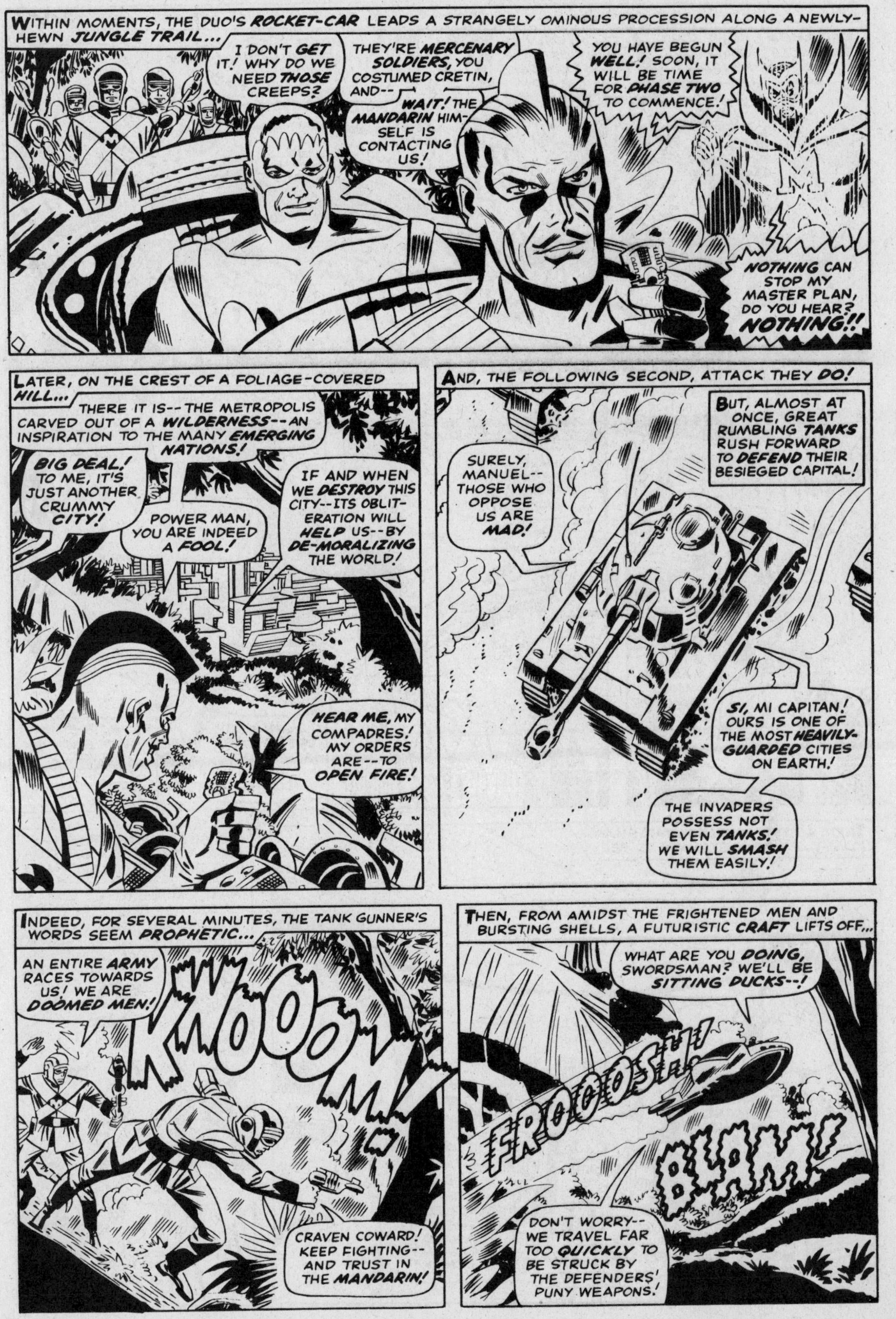

WITHIN MOMENTS, THE DUO'S ROCKET-CAR LEADS A STRANGELY OMINOUS PROCESSION ALONG A NEWLY-HEWN JUNGLE TRAIL...
I DON'T GET IT! WHY DO WE NEED THOSE CREEPS?
THEY'RE MERCENARY SOLDIERS, YOU COSTUMED CRETIN, AND--
WAIT! THE MANDARIN HIMSELF IS CONTACTING US!
YOU HAVE BEGUN WELL! SOON, IT WILL BE TIME FOR PHASE TWO TO COMMENCE!
NOTHING CAN STOP MY MASTER PLAN, DO YOU HEAR? NOTHING!!
LATER, ON THE CREST OF A FOLIAGE-COVERED HILL...
THERE IT IS--THE METROPOLIS CARVED OUT OF A WILDERNESS--AN INSPIRATION TO THE MANY EMERGING NATIONS!
BIG DEAL! TO ME, IT'S JUST ANOTHER CRUMMY CITY!
IF AND WHEN WE DESTROY THIS CITY--ITS OBLITERATION WILL HELP US--BY DE-MORALIZING THE WORLD!
POWER MAN, YOU ARE INDEED A FOOL!
HEAR ME, MY COMPADRES! MY ORDERS ARE--TO OPEN FIRE!
AND, THE FOLLOWING SECOND, ATTACK THEY DO!
BUT, ALMOST AT ONCE, GREAT RUMBLING TANKS RUSH FORWARD TO DEFEND THEIR BESIEGED CAPITAL!
SURELY, MANUEL--THOSE WHO OPPOSE US ARE MAD!
SI, MI CAPITAN! OURS IS ONE OF THE MOST HEAVILY-GUARDED CITIES ON EARTH!
THE INVADERS POSSESS NOT EVEN TANKS! WE WILL SMASH THEM EASILY!
INDEED, FOR SEVERAL MINUTES, THE TANK GUNNER'S WORDS SEEM PROPHETIC...
AN ENTIRE ARMY RACES TOWARDS US! WE ARE DOOMED MEN!
KWOOOOM!
CRAVEN COWARD! KEEP FIGHTING--AND TRUST IN THE MANDARIN!
THEN, FROM AMIDST THE FRIGHTENED MEN AND BURSTING SHELLS, A FUTURISTIC CRAFT LIFTS OFF...
WHAT ARE YOU DOING, SWORDSMAN? WE'LL BE SITTING DUCKS--!
FROOOSH!
BLAM!
DON'T WORRY--WE TRAVEL FAR TOO QUICKLY TO BE STRUCK BY THE DEFENDERS' PUNY WEAPONS!

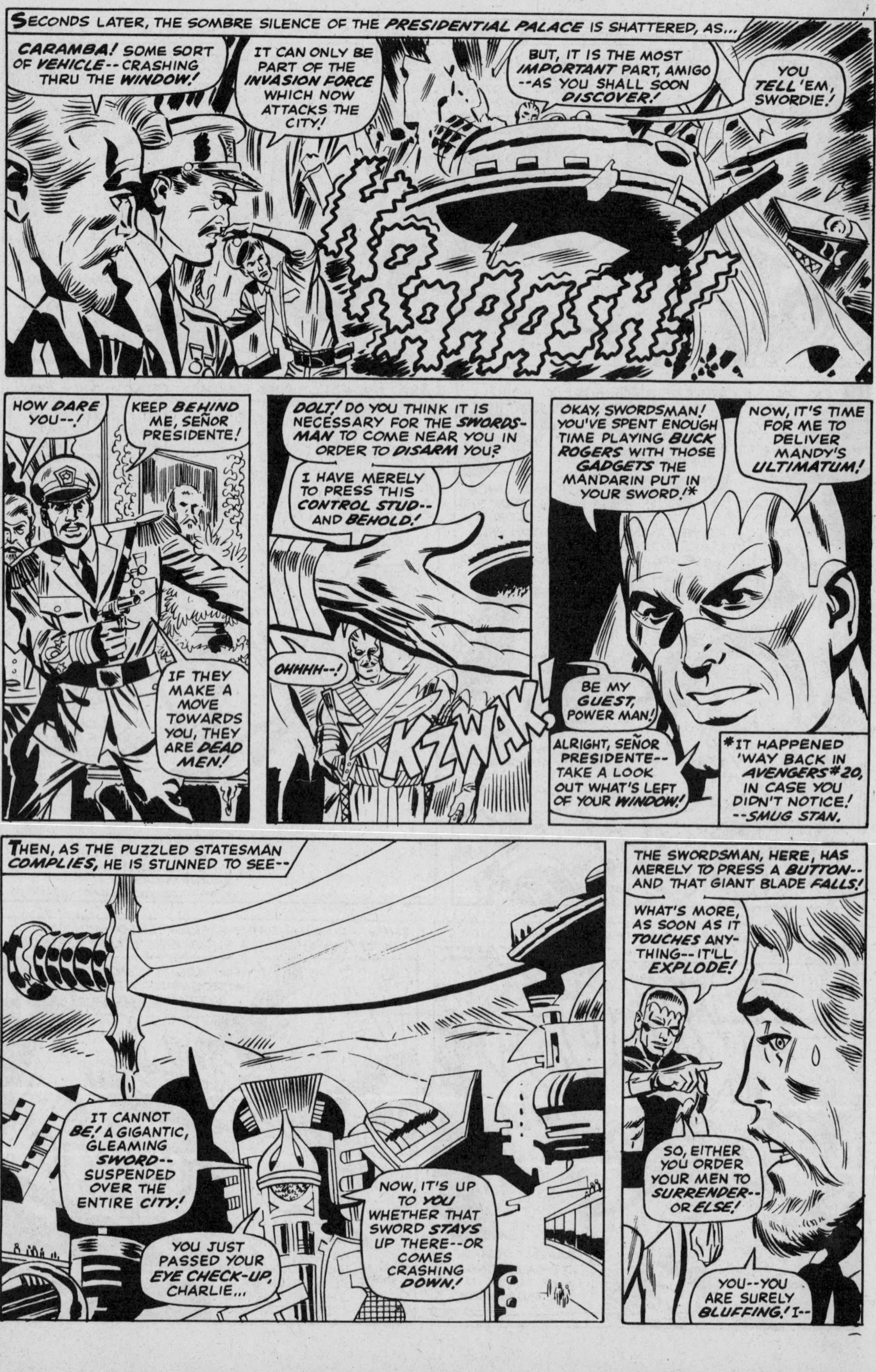
SECONDS LATER, THE SOMBRE SILENCE OF THE PRESIDENTIAL PALACE IS SHATTERED, AS...
CARAMBA! SOME SORT OF VEHICLE--CRASHING THRU THE WINDOW!
IT CAN ONLY BE PART OF THE INVASION FORCE WHICH NOW ATTACKS THE CITY!
BUT, IT IS THE MOST IMPORTANT PART, AMIGO --AS YOU SHALL SOON DISCOVER!
YOU TELL 'EM, SWORDIE!
KRAASH!
HOW DARE YOU--!
KEEP BEHIND ME, SEÑOR PRESIDENTE!
IF THEY MAKE A MOVE TOWARDS YOU, THEY ARE DEAD MEN!
DOLT! DO YOU THINK IT IS NECESSARY FOR THE SWORDSMAN TO COME NEAR YOU IN ORDER TO DISARM YOU?
I HAVE MERELY TO PRESS THIS CONTROL STUD--AND BEHOLD!
OHHHH--!
KZWAK!
OKAY, SWORDSMAN! YOU'VE SPENT ENOUGH TIME PLAYING BUCK ROGERS WITH THOSE GADGETS THE MANDARIN PUT IN YOUR SWORD!*
NOW, IT'S TIME FOR ME TO DELIVER MANDY'S ULTIMATUM!
BE MY GUEST, POWER MAN!
ALRIGHT, SEÑOR PRESIDENTE--TAKE A LOOK OUT WHAT'S LEFT OF YOUR WINDOW!
*IT HAPPENED 'WAY BACK IN AVENGERS #20, IN CASE YOU DIDN'T NOTICE! --SMUG STAN.
THEN, AS THE PUZZLED STATESMAN COMPLIES, HE IS STUNNED TO SEE--
IT CANNOT BE! A GIGANTIC, GLEAMING SWORD--SUSPENDED OVER THE ENTIRE CITY!
YOU JUST PASSED YOUR EYE CHECK-UP, CHARLIE...
NOW, IT'S UP TO YOU WHETHER THAT SWORD STAYS UP THERE--OR COMES CRASHING DOWN!
THE SWORDSMAN, HERE, HAS MERELY TO PRESS A BUTTON--AND THAT GIANT BLADE FALLS!
WHAT'S MORE, AS SOON AS IT TOUCHES ANYTHING--IT'LL EXPLODE!
SO, EITHER YOU ORDER YOUR MEN TO SURRENDER--OR ELSE!
YOU--YOU ARE SURELY BLUFFING! I--

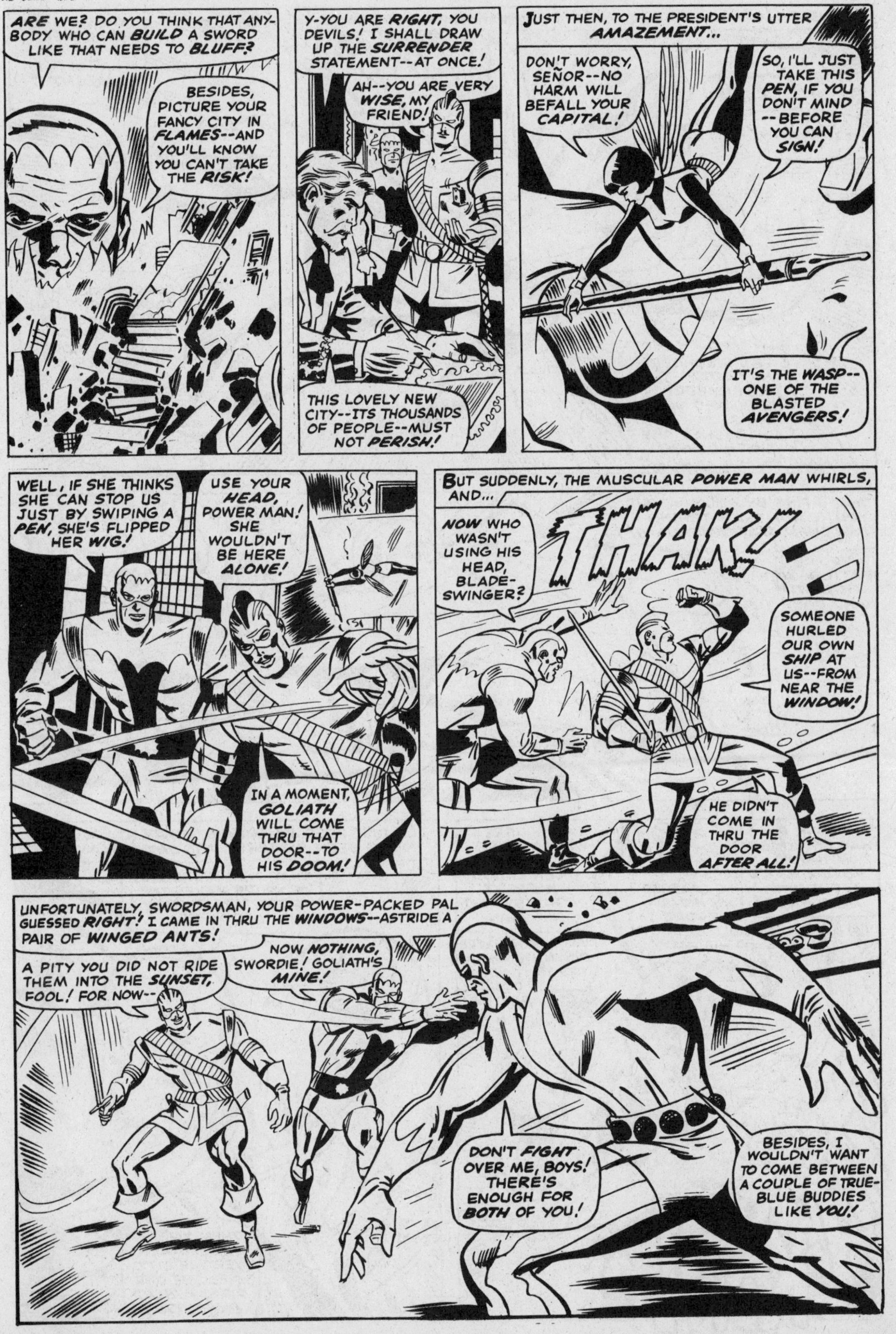
ARE WE? DO YOU THINK THAT ANYBODY WHO CAN BUILD A SWORD LIKE THAT NEEDS TO BLUFF?
BESIDES, PICTURE YOUR FANCY CITY IN FLAMES--AND YOU'LL KNOW YOU CAN'T TAKE THE RISK!
Y-YOU ARE RIGHT, YOU DEVILS! I SHALL DRAW UP THE SURRENDER STATEMENT--AT ONCE!
AH--YOU ARE VERY WISE, MY FRIEND!
THIS LOVELY NEW CITY--ITS THOUSANDS OF PEOPLE--MUST NOT PERISH!
JUST THEN, TO THE PRESIDENT'S UTTER AMAZEMENT...
DON'T WORRY, SEÑOR--NO HARM WILL BEFALL YOUR CAPITAL!
SO, I'LL JUST TAKE THIS PEN, IF YOU DON'T MIND --BEFORE YOU CAN SIGN!
IT'S THE WASP-- ONE OF THE BLASTED AVENGERS!
WELL, IF SHE THINKS SHE CAN STOP US JUST BY SWIPING A PEN, SHE'S FLIPPED HER WIG!
USE YOUR HEAD, POWER MAN! SHE WOULDN'T BE HERE ALONE!
IN A MOMENT, GOLIATH WILL COME THRU THAT DOOR--TO HIS DOOM!
BUT SUDDENLY, THE MUSCULAR POWER MAN WHIRLS, AND...
NOW WHO WASN'T USING HIS HEAD, BLADE-SWINGER?
THAK!
SOMEONE HURLED OUR OWN SHIP AT US--FROM NEAR THE WINDOW!
HE DIDN'T COME IN THRU THE DOOR AFTER ALL!
UNFORTUNATELY, SWORDSMAN, YOUR POWER-PACKED PAL GUESSED RIGHT! I CAME IN THRU THE WINDOWS--ASTRIDE A PAIR OF WINGED ANTS!
A PITY YOU DID NOT RIDE THEM INTO THE SUNSET, FOOL! FOR NOW--
NOW NOTHING, SWORDIE! GOLIATH'S MINE!
DON'T FIGHT OVER ME, BOYS! THERE'S ENOUGH FOR BOTH OF YOU!
BESIDES, I WOULDN'T WANT TO COME BETWEEN A COUPLE OF TRUE-BLUE BUDDIES LIKE YOU!

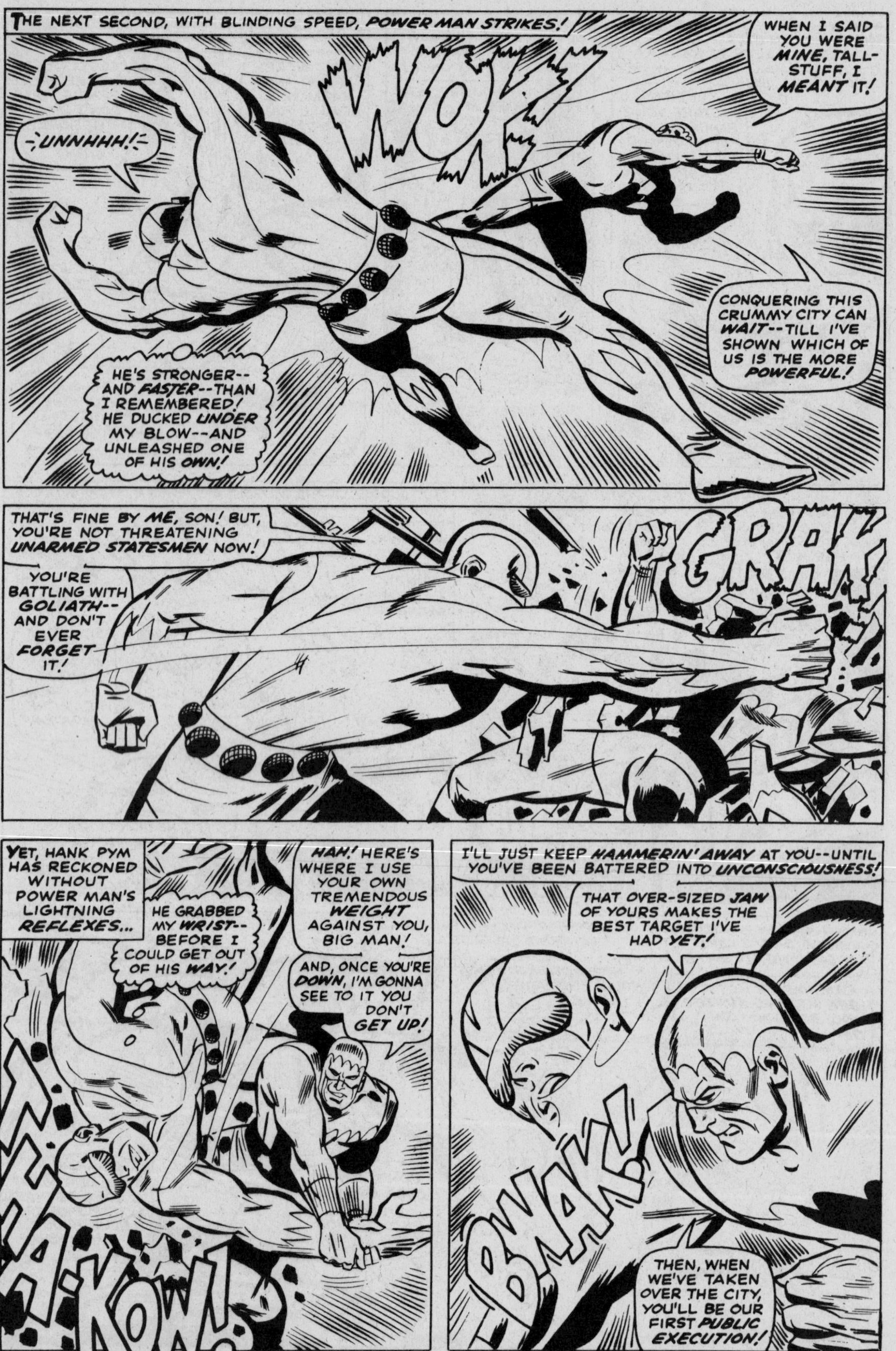
THE NEXT SECOND, WITH BLINDING SPEED, POWER MAN STRIKES!
WHEN I SAID YOU WERE MINE, TALL-STUFF, I MEANT IT!
WOK
-UNNHHH!-
CONQUERING THIS CRUMMY CITY CAN WAIT--TILL I'VE SHOWN WHICH OF US IS THE MORE POWERFUL!
HE'S STRONGER--AND FASTER--THAN I REMEMBERED! HE DUCKED UNDER MY BLOW--AND UNLEASHED ONE OF HIS OWN!
THAT'S FINE BY ME, SON! BUT, YOU'RE NOT THREATENING UNARMED STATESMEN NOW!
GRAK
YOU'RE BATTLING WITH GOLIATH--AND DON'T EVER FORGET IT!
YET, HANK PYM HAS RECKONED WITHOUT POWER MAN'S LIGHTNING REFLEXES...
HE GRABBED MY WRIST--BEFORE I COULD GET OUT OF HIS WAY!
HAH! HERE'S WHERE I USE YOUR OWN TREMENDOUS WEIGHT AGAINST YOU, BIG MAN!
AND, ONCE YOU'RE DOWN, I'M GONNA SEE TO IT YOU DON'T GET UP!
THA-KOW!
I'LL JUST KEEP HAMMERIN' AWAY AT YOU--UNTIL YOU'VE BEEN BATTERED INTO UNCONSCIOUSNESS!
THAT OVER-SIZED JAW OF YOURS MAKES THE BEST TARGET I'VE HAD YET!
BWAK!
THEN, WHEN WE'VE TAKEN OVER THE CITY, YOU'LL BE OUR FIRST PUBLIC EXECUTION!

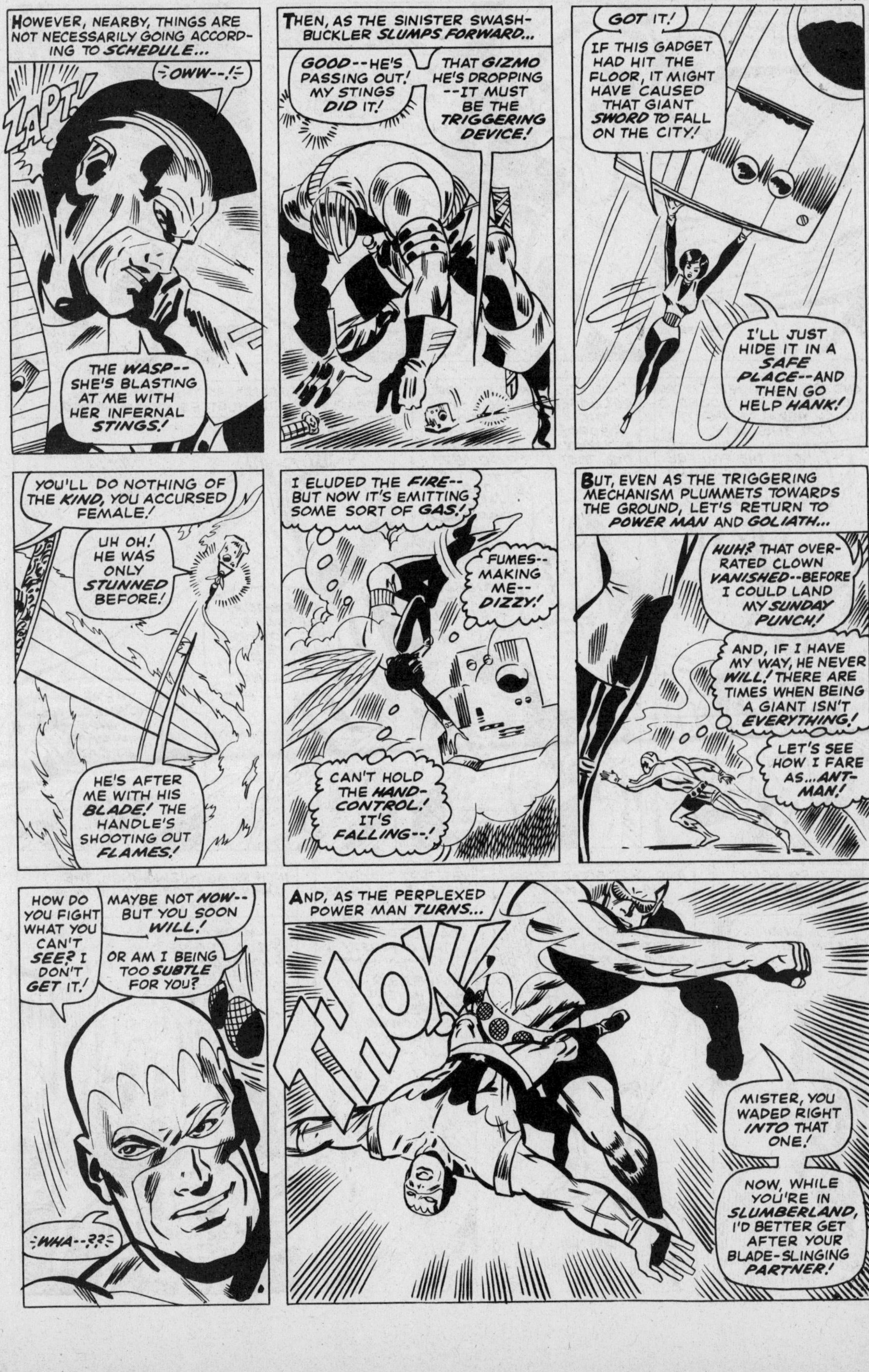
HOWEVER, NEARBY, THINGS ARE NOT NECESSARILY GOING ACCORDING TO SCHEDULE...
ZAPT!
OWW--!
THE WASP--SHE'S BLASTING AT ME WITH HER INFERNAL STINGS!
THEN, AS THE SINISTER SWASHBUCKLER SLUMPS FORWARD...
GOOD--HE'S PASSING OUT! MY STINGS DID IT!
THAT GIZMO HE'S DROPPING--IT MUST BE THE TRIGGERING DEVICE!
GOT IT!
IF THIS GADGET HAD HIT THE FLOOR, IT MIGHT HAVE CAUSED THAT GIANT SWORD TO FALL ON THE CITY!
I'LL JUST HIDE IT IN A SAFE PLACE--AND THEN GO HELP HANK!
YOU'LL DO NOTHING OF THE KIND, YOU ACCURSED FEMALE!
UH OH! HE WAS ONLY STUNNED BEFORE!
HE'S AFTER ME WITH HIS BLADE! THE HANDLE'S SHOOTING OUT FLAMES!
I ELUDED THE FIRE--BUT NOW IT'S EMITTING SOME SORT OF GAS!
FUMES--MAKING ME--DIZZY!
CAN'T HOLD THE HAND-CONTROL! IT'S FALLING--!
BUT, EVEN AS THE TRIGGERING MECHANISM PLUMMETS TOWARDS THE GROUND, LET'S RETURN TO POWER MAN AND GOLIATH...
HUH? THAT OVER-RATED CLOWN VANISHED--BEFORE I COULD LAND MY SUNDAY PUNCH!
AND, IF I HAVE MY WAY, HE NEVER WILL! THERE ARE TIMES WHEN BEING A GIANT ISN'T EVERYTHING!
LET'S SEE HOW I FARE AS...ANT-MAN!
HOW DO YOU FIGHT WHAT YOU CAN'T SEE? I DON'T GET IT!
MAYBE NOT NOW--BUT YOU SOON WILL!
OR AM I BEING TOO SUBTLE FOR YOU?
WHA--??
AND, AS THE PERPLEXED POWER MAN TURNS...
THOK!
MISTER, YOU WADED RIGHT INTO THAT ONE!
NOW, WHILE YOU'RE IN SLUMBERLAND, I'D BETTER GET AFTER YOUR BLADE-SLINGING PARTNER!

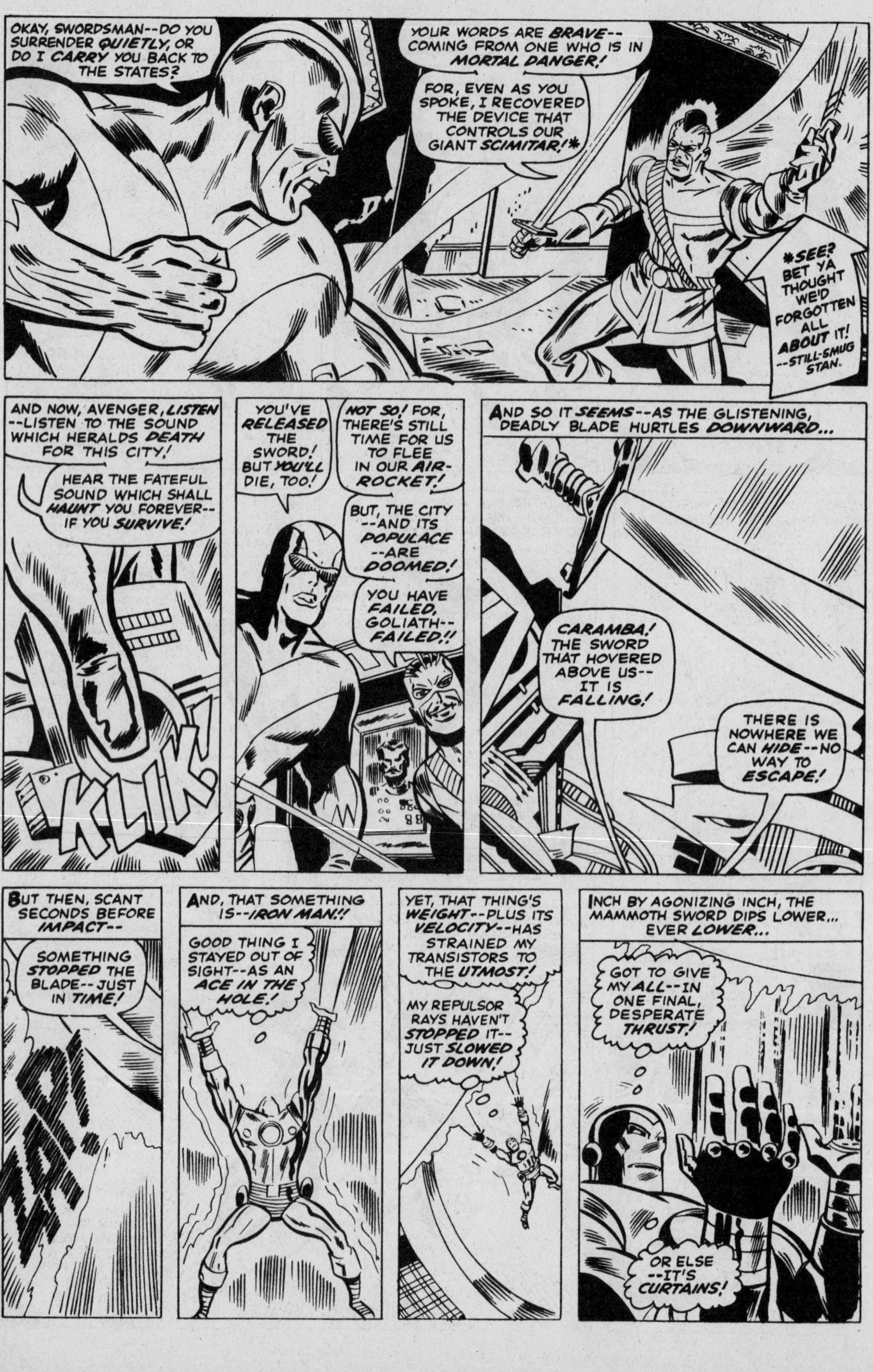
OKAY, SWORDSMAN--DO YOU SURRENDER QUIETLY, OR DO I CARRY YOU BACK TO THE STATES?
YOUR WORDS ARE BRAVE-- COMING FROM ONE WHO IS IN MORTAL DANGER!
FOR, EVEN AS YOU SPOKE, I RECOVERED THE DEVICE THAT CONTROLS OUR GIANT SCIMITAR!*
*SEE? BET YA THOUGHT WE'D FORGOTTEN ALL ABOUT IT! --STILL-SMUG STAN.
AND NOW, AVENGER, LISTEN --LISTEN TO THE SOUND WHICH HERALDS DEATH FOR THIS CITY!
HEAR THE FATEFUL SOUND WHICH SHALL HAUNT YOU FOREVER-- IF YOU SURVIVE!
KLIK!
YOU'VE RELEASED THE SWORD! BUT YOU'LL DIE, TOO!
NOT SO! FOR, THERE'S STILL TIME FOR US TO FLEE IN OUR AIR-ROCKET!
BUT, THE CITY --AND ITS POPULACE --ARE DOOMED!
YOU HAVE FAILED, GOLIATH-- FAILED!!
AND SO IT SEEMS--AS THE GLISTENING, DEADLY BLADE HURTLES DOWNWARD...
CARAMBA! THE SWORD THAT HOVERED ABOVE US-- IT IS FALLING!
THERE IS NOWHERE WE CAN HIDE--NO WAY TO ESCAPE!
BUT THEN, SCANT SECONDS BEFORE IMPACT--
SOMETHING STOPPED THE BLADE--JUST IN TIME!
ZAPP!
AND, THAT SOMETHING IS--IRON MAN!!
GOOD THING I STAYED OUT OF SIGHT--AS AN ACE IN THE HOLE!
YET, THAT THING'S WEIGHT--PLUS ITS VELOCITY--HAS STRAINED MY TRANSISTORS TO THE UTMOST!
MY REPULSOR RAYS HAVEN'T STOPPED IT-- JUST SLOWED IT DOWN!
INCH BY AGONIZING INCH, THE MAMMOTH SWORD DIPS LOWER... EVER LOWER...
GOT TO GIVE MY ALL--IN ONE FINAL, DESPERATE THRUST!
OR ELSE --IT'S CURTAINS!

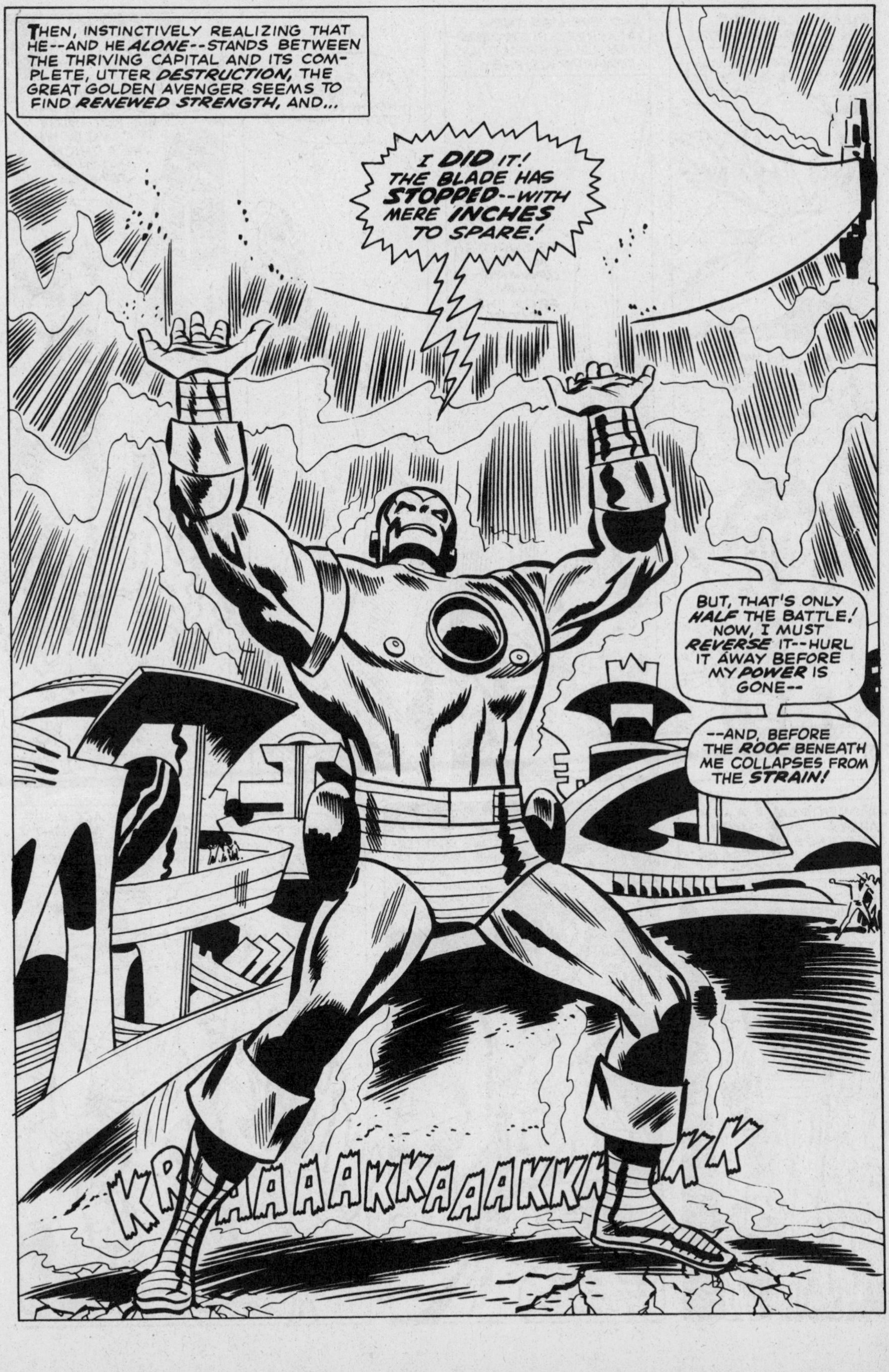
THEN, INSTINCTIVELY REALIZING THAT HE--AND HE ALONE--STANDS BETWEEN THE THRIVING CAPITAL AND ITS COMPLETE, UTTER DESTRUCTION, THE GREAT GOLDEN AVENGER SEEMS TO FIND RENEWED STRENGTH, AND...
I DID IT! THE BLADE HAS STOPPED--WITH MERE INCHES TO SPARE!
BUT, THAT'S ONLY HALF THE BATTLE! NOW, I MUST REVERSE IT--HURL IT AWAY BEFORE MY POWER IS GONE--
--AND, BEFORE THE ROOF BENEATH ME COLLAPSES FROM THE STRAIN!
KRAAAAKKAAAAKKKKK

MEANWHILE, IN THE NEARBY *PRESIDENTIAL PALACE*... GO, IRON MAN-- *GO*!! YOU'VE GOT TO DO IT--YOU'VE GOT TO!

GOLIATH WAS A *FOOL* TO TAKE HIS EYES OFF ME! *WHATEVER* HAPPENS--HE SHALL *DIE*!

AND, EVEN AS THE TREACHEROUS *SWORDS-MAN* MOVES STEALTHILY TOWARDS HIS PREY...

THE SWORD'S MOVING *UPWARD*--AWAY FROM THE *CITY*!

IT'S *GAINING SPEED*! NOTHING CAN STOP IT *NOW*!

THANK *HEAVEN*! IT *EXPLODED*--BUT NOT UNTIL IT CAME DOWN IN A THICK PATCH OF *JUNGLE*!

WOOM!

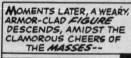

MOMENTS LATER, A WEARY, ARMOR-CLAD *FIGURE* DESCENDS, AMIDST THE CLAMOROUS CHEERS OF THE *MASSES*--

BUT, HE IS FAR TOO *EXHAUSTED* TO NOTICE-- OR CARE...

AS...

ONE SHATTER-ING SWOOP OF MY LETHAL SWORD--AND REVENGE WILL BE *MINE*!

I JUST REMEMBERED-- WHERE'S THE *WASP*? I HAVEN'T SEEN HER SINCE--

JAN--WHERE ARE YOU? DO YOU *HEAR* ME?

SURE THING, BIG MAN-- LUCKILY FOR *YOU*!

THE GIANT'S ACCURSED *PARTNER*! I THOUGHT I HAD TAKEN CARE OF HER WITH MY BLADE'S *NERVE GAS*!

WHAM!

OH, YOU *DID*, HUH?

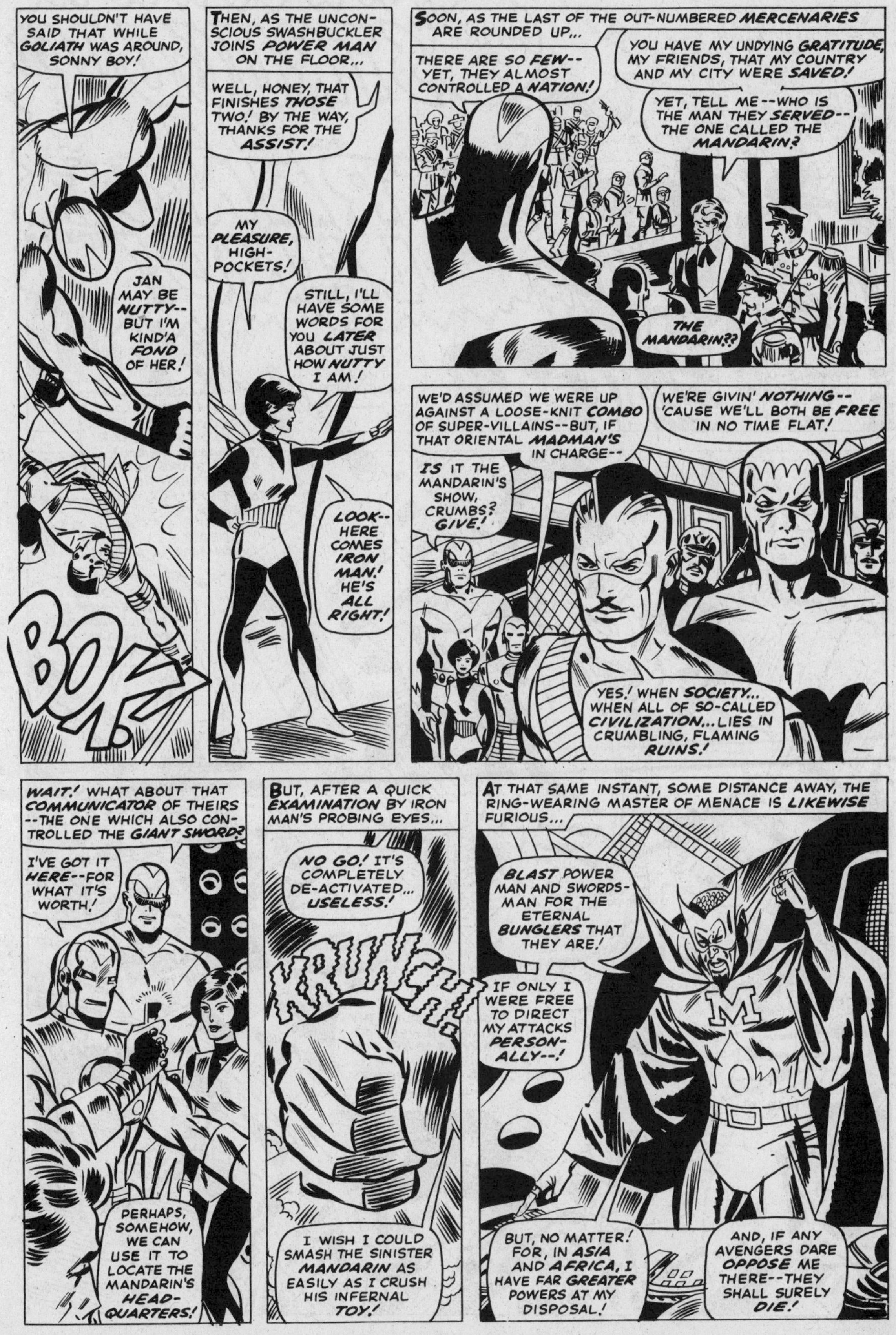

YOU SHOULDN'T HAVE SAID THAT WHILE GOLIATH WAS AROUND, SONNY BOY!
JAN MAY BE NUTTY-- BUT I'M KIND'A FOND OF HER!
BOK!
THEN, AS THE UNCONSCIOUS SWASHBUCKLER JOINS POWER MAN ON THE FLOOR...
WELL, HONEY, THAT FINISHES THOSE TWO! BY THE WAY, THANKS FOR THE ASSIST!
MY PLEASURE, HIGH-POCKETS!
STILL, I'LL HAVE SOME WORDS FOR YOU LATER ABOUT JUST HOW NUTTY I AM!
LOOK-- HERE COMES IRON MAN! HE'S ALL RIGHT!
SOON, AS THE LAST OF THE OUT-NUMBERED MERCENARIES ARE ROUNDED UP...
THERE ARE SO FEW-- YET, THEY ALMOST CONTROLLED A NATION!
YOU HAVE MY UNDYING GRATITUDE, MY FRIENDS, THAT MY COUNTRY AND MY CITY WERE SAVED!
YET, TELL ME--WHO IS THE MAN THEY SERVED-- THE ONE CALLED THE MANDARIN?
THE MANDARIN??
WE'D ASSUMED WE WERE UP AGAINST A LOOSE-KNIT COMBO OF SUPER-VILLAINS--BUT, IF THAT ORIENTAL MADMAN'S IN CHARGE--
IS IT THE MANDARIN'S SHOW, CRUMBS? GIVE!
WE'RE GIVIN' NOTHING-- 'CAUSE WE'LL BOTH BE FREE IN NO TIME FLAT!
YES! WHEN SOCIETY... WHEN ALL OF SO-CALLED CIVILIZATION... LIES IN CRUMBLING, FLAMING RUINS!
WAIT! WHAT ABOUT THAT COMMUNICATOR OF THEIRS --THE ONE WHICH ALSO CONTROLLED THE GIANT SWORD?
I'VE GOT IT HERE--FOR WHAT IT'S WORTH!
PERHAPS, SOMEHOW, WE CAN USE IT TO LOCATE THE MANDARIN'S HEAD-QUARTERS!
BUT, AFTER A QUICK EXAMINATION BY IRON MAN'S PROBING EYES...
NO GO! IT'S COMPLETELY DE-ACTIVATED... USELESS!
KRUNCH!
I WISH I COULD SMASH THE SINISTER MANDARIN AS EASILY AS I CRUSH HIS INFERNAL TOY!
AT THAT SAME INSTANT, SOME DISTANCE AWAY, THE RING-WEARING MASTER OF MENACE IS LIKEWISE FURIOUS...
BLAST POWER MAN AND SWORDSMAN FOR THE ETERNAL BUNGLERS THAT THEY ARE!
IF ONLY I WERE FREE TO DIRECT MY ATTACKS PERSON-ALLY--!
BUT, NO MATTER! FOR, IN ASIA AND AFRICA, I HAVE FAR GREATER POWERS AT MY DISPOSAL!
AND, IF ANY AVENGERS DARE OPPOSE ME THERE--THEY SHALL SURELY DIE!

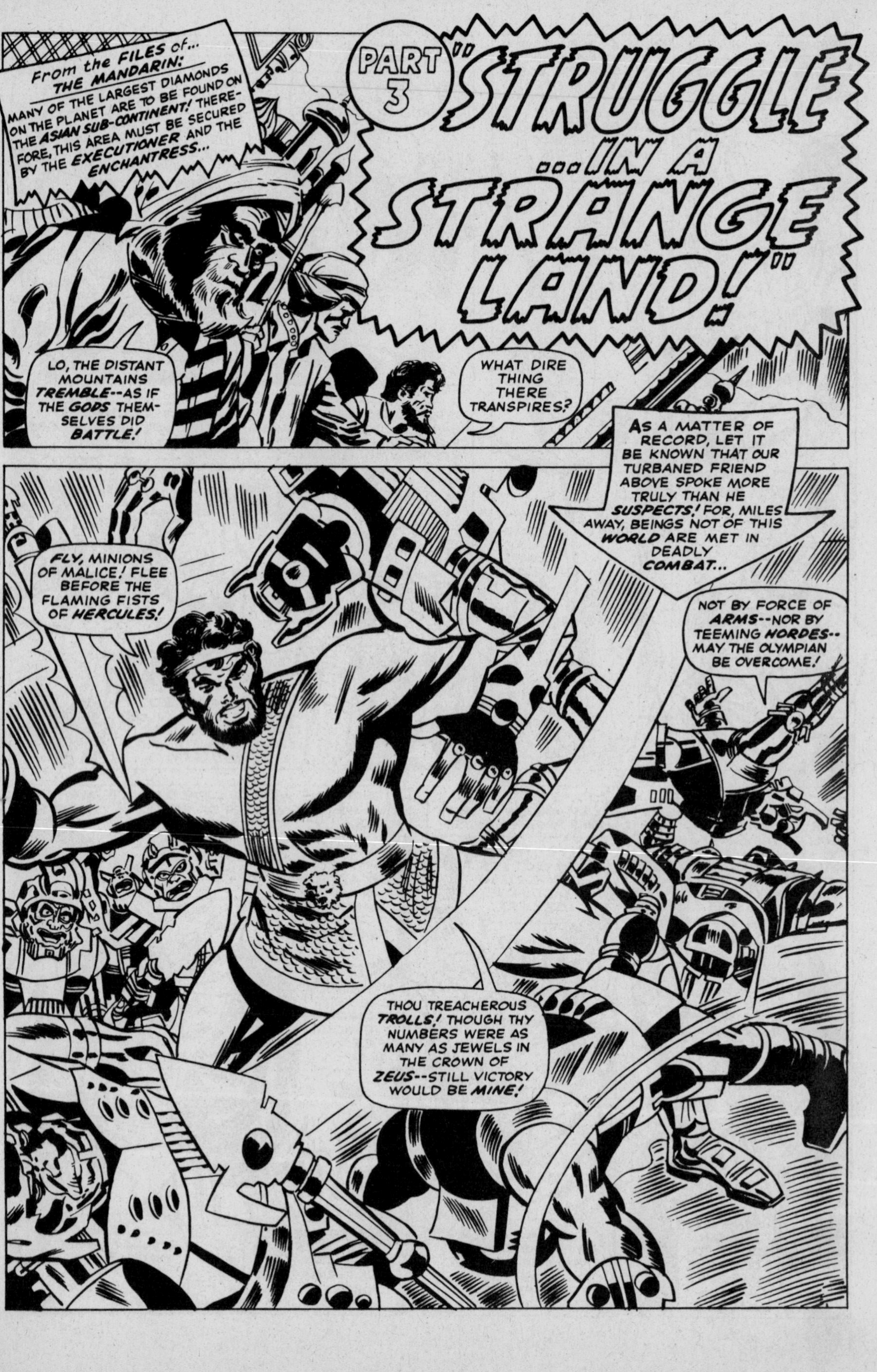
From the FILES of... THE MANDARIN:
MANY OF THE LARGEST DIAMONDS ON THE PLANET ARE TO BE FOUND ON THE ASIAN SUB-CONTINENT! THEREFORE, THIS AREA MUST BE SECURED BY THE EXECUTIONER AND THE ENCHANTRESS...
PART 3
"STRUGGLE ...IN A STRANGE LAND!"
LO, THE DISTANT MOUNTAINS TREMBLE--AS IF THE GODS THEMSELVES DID BATTLE!
WHAT DIRE THING THERE TRANSPIRES?
AS A MATTER OF RECORD, LET IT BE KNOWN THAT OUR TURBANED FRIEND ABOVE SPOKE MORE TRULY THAN HE SUSPECTS! FOR, MILES AWAY, BEINGS NOT OF THIS WORLD ARE MET IN DEADLY COMBAT...
FLY, MINIONS OF MALICE! FLEE BEFORE THE FLAMING FISTS OF HERCULES!
NOT BY FORCE OF ARMS--NOR BY TEEMING HORDES--MAY THE OLYMPIAN BE OVERCOME!
THOU TREACHEROUS TROLLS! THOUGH THY NUMBERS WERE AS MANY AS JEWELS IN THE CROWN OF ZEUS--STILL VICTORY WOULD BE MINE!

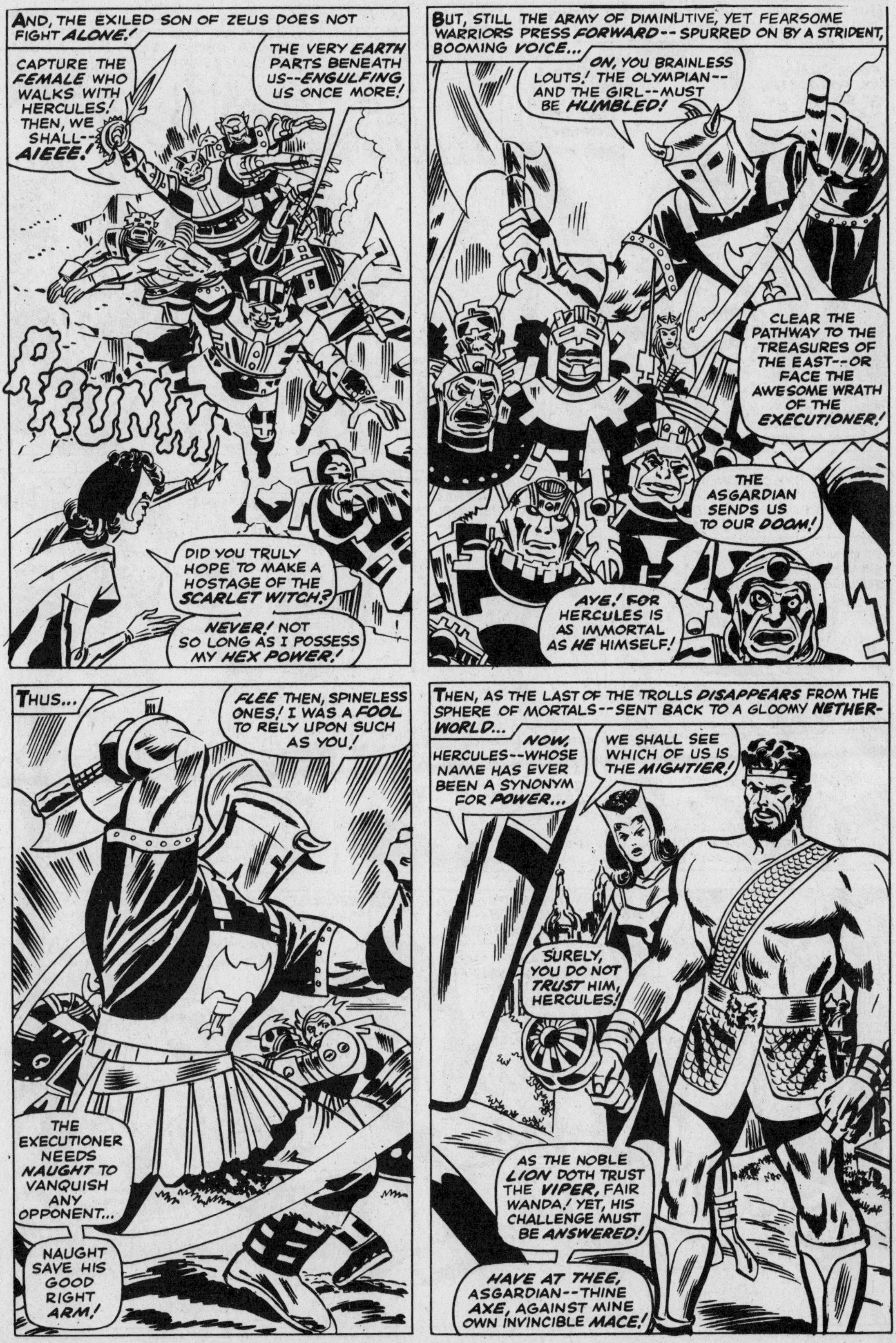
AND, THE EXILED SON OF ZEUS DOES NOT FIGHT ALONE!
CAPTURE THE FEMALE WHO WALKS WITH HERCULES! THEN, WE SHALL-- AIEEE!
THE VERY EARTH PARTS BENEATH US--ENGULFING US ONCE MORE!
RRUMM
DID YOU TRULY HOPE TO MAKE A HOSTAGE OF THE SCARLET WITCH?
NEVER! NOT SO LONG AS I POSSESS MY HEX POWER!
BUT, STILL THE ARMY OF DIMINUTIVE, YET FEARSOME WARRIORS PRESS FORWARD--SPURRED ON BY A STRIDENT, BOOMING VOICE...
ON, YOU BRAINLESS LOUTS! THE OLYMPIAN--AND THE GIRL--MUST BE HUMBLED!
CLEAR THE PATHWAY TO THE TREASURES OF THE EAST--OR FACE THE AWESOME WRATH OF THE EXECUTIONER!
THE ASGARDIAN SENDS US TO OUR DOOM!
AYE! FOR HERCULES IS AS IMMORTAL AS HE HIMSELF!
THUS...
FLEE THEN, SPINELESS ONES! I WAS A FOOL TO RELY UPON SUCH AS YOU!
THE EXECUTIONER NEEDS NAUGHT TO VANQUISH ANY OPPONENT...
NAUGHT SAVE HIS GOOD RIGHT ARM!
THEN, AS THE LAST OF THE TROLLS DISAPPEARS FROM THE SPHERE OF MORTALS--SENT BACK TO A GLOOMY NETHER-WORLD...
NOW, HERCULES--WHOSE NAME HAS EVER BEEN A SYNONYM FOR POWER...
WE SHALL SEE WHICH OF US IS THE MIGHTIER!
SURELY, YOU DO NOT TRUST HIM, HERCULES!
AS THE NOBLE LION DOTH TRUST THE VIPER, FAIR WANDA! YET, HIS CHALLENGE MUST BE ANSWERED!
HAVE AT THEE, ASGARDIAN--THINE AXE, AGAINST MINE OWN INVINCIBLE MACE!

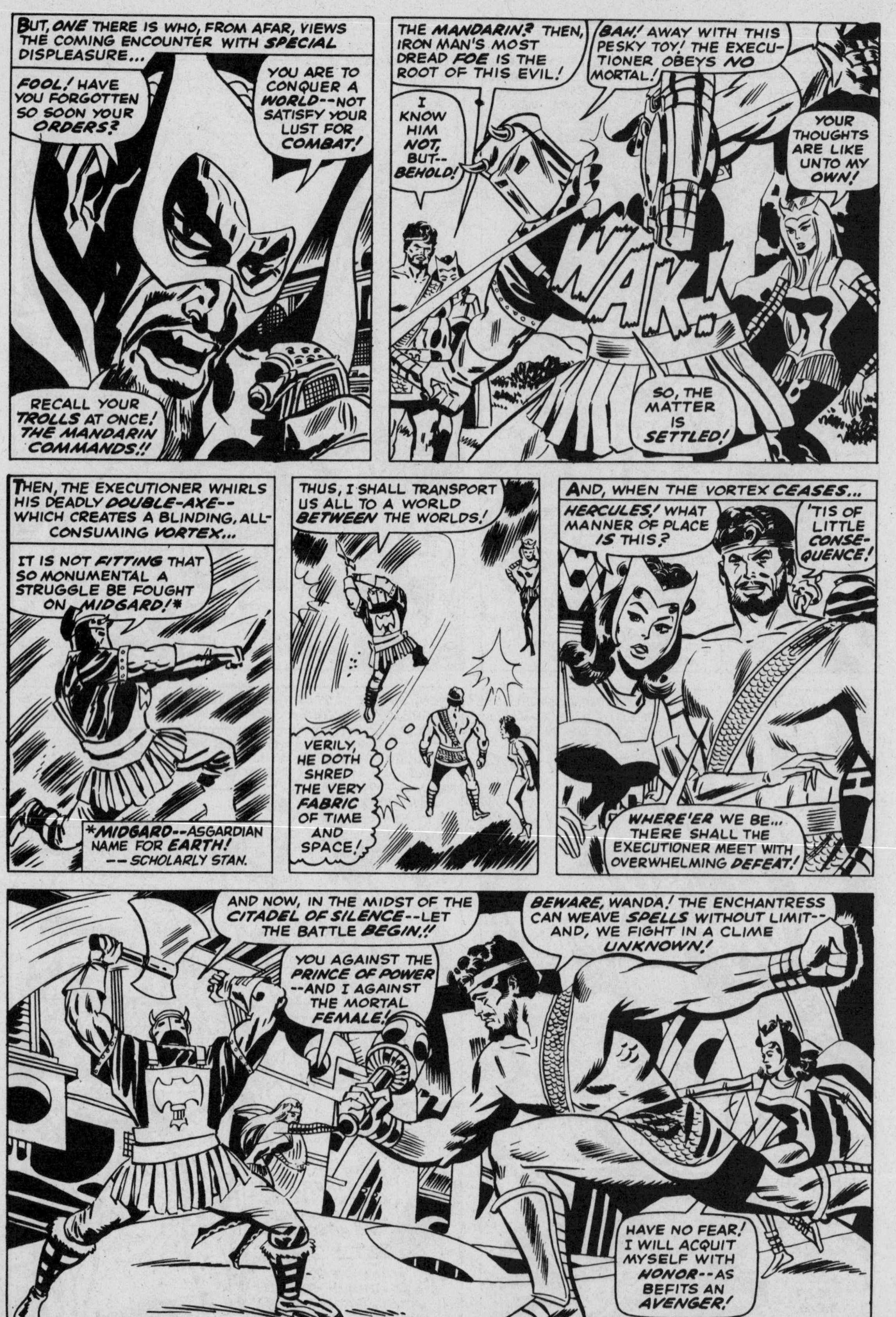

BUT, ONE THERE IS WHO, FROM AFAR, VIEWS THE COMING ENCOUNTER WITH SPECIAL DISPLEASURE...
FOOL! HAVE YOU FORGOTTEN SO SOON YOUR ORDERS?
YOU ARE TO CONQUER A WORLD--NOT SATISFY YOUR LUST FOR COMBAT!
RECALL YOUR TROLLS AT ONCE! THE MANDARIN COMMANDS!!
THE MANDARIN? THEN, IRON MAN'S MOST DREAD FOE IS THE ROOT OF THIS EVIL!
I KNOW HIM NOT, BUT-- BEHOLD!
BAH! AWAY WITH THIS PESKY TOY! THE EXECUTIONER OBEYS NO MORTAL!
YOUR THOUGHTS ARE LIKE UNTO MY OWN!
WAK!
SO, THE MATTER IS SETTLED!
THEN, THE EXECUTIONER WHIRLS HIS DEADLY DOUBLE-AXE-- WHICH CREATES A BLINDING, ALL-CONSUMING VORTEX...
IT IS NOT FITTING THAT SO MONUMENTAL A STRUGGLE BE FOUGHT ON MIDGARD!*
*MIDGARD--ASGARDIAN NAME FOR EARTH! --SCHOLARLY STAN.
THUS, I SHALL TRANSPORT US ALL TO A WORLD BETWEEN THE WORLDS!
VERILY, HE DOTH SHRED THE VERY FABRIC OF TIME AND SPACE!
AND, WHEN THE VORTEX CEASES...
HERCULES! WHAT MANNER OF PLACE IS THIS?
'TIS OF LITTLE CONSE-QUENCE!
WHERE'ER WE BE... THERE SHALL THE EXECUTIONER MEET WITH OVERWHELMING DEFEAT!
AND NOW, IN THE MIDST OF THE CITADEL OF SILENCE--LET THE BATTLE BEGIN!!
YOU AGAINST THE PRINCE OF POWER --AND I AGAINST THE MORTAL FEMALE!
BEWARE, WANDA! THE ENCHANTRESS CAN WEAVE SPELLS WITHOUT LIMIT-- AND, WE FIGHT IN A CLIME UNKNOWN!
HAVE NO FEAR! I WILL ACQUIT MYSELF WITH HONOR--AS BEFITS AN AVENGER!

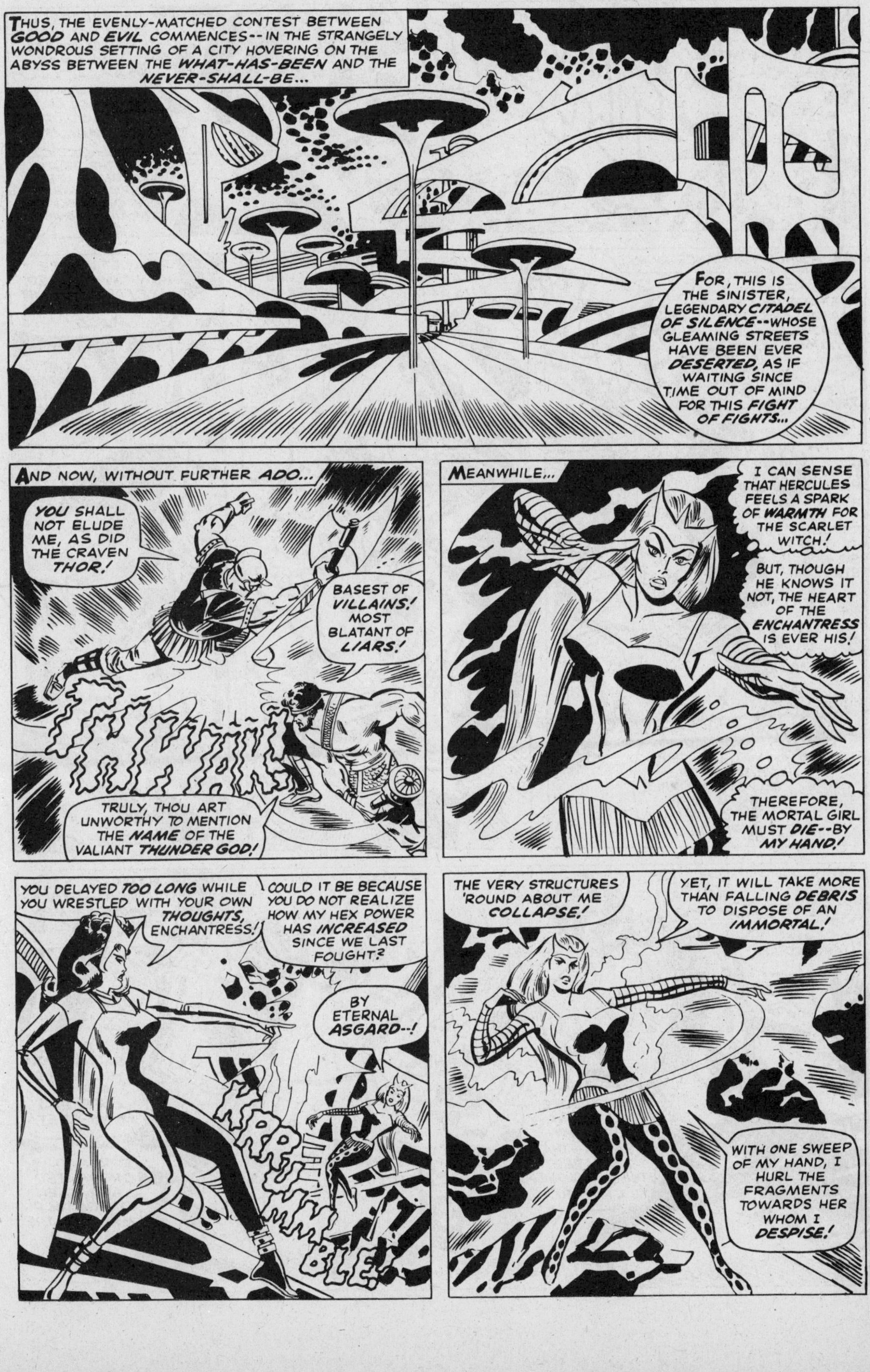
THUS, THE EVENLY-MATCHED CONTEST BETWEEN GOOD AND EVIL COMMENCES--IN THE STRANGELY WONDROUS SETTING OF A CITY HOVERING ON THE ABYSS BETWEEN THE WHAT-HAS-BEEN AND THE NEVER-SHALL-BE...
FOR, THIS IS THE SINISTER, LEGENDARY CITADEL OF SILENCE--WHOSE GLEAMING STREETS HAVE BEEN EVER DESERTED, AS IF WAITING SINCE TIME OUT OF MIND FOR THIS FIGHT OF FIGHTS...
AND NOW, WITHOUT FURTHER ADO...
YOU SHALL NOT ELUDE ME, AS DID THE CRAVEN THOR!
BASEST OF VILLAINS! MOST BLATANT OF LIARS!
THHAKK
TRULY, THOU ART UNWORTHY TO MENTION THE NAME OF THE VALIANT THUNDER GOD!
MEANWHILE...
I CAN SENSE THAT HERCULES FEELS A SPARK OF WARMTH FOR THE SCARLET WITCH!
BUT, THOUGH HE KNOWS IT NOT, THE HEART OF THE ENCHANTRESS IS EVER HIS!
THEREFORE, THE MORTAL GIRL MUST DIE--BY MY HAND!
YOU DELAYED TOO LONG WHILE YOU WRESTLED WITH YOUR OWN THOUGHTS, ENCHANTRESS!
COULD IT BE BECAUSE YOU DO NOT REALIZE HOW MY HEX POWER HAS INCREASED SINCE WE LAST FOUGHT?
BY ETERNAL ASGARD--!
KRRUMMBLE!
THE VERY STRUCTURES 'ROUND ABOUT ME COLLAPSE!
YET, IT WILL TAKE MORE THAN FALLING DEBRIS TO DISPOSE OF AN IMMORTAL!
WITH ONE SWEEP OF MY HAND, I HURL THE FRAGMENTS TOWARDS HER WHOM I DESPISE!

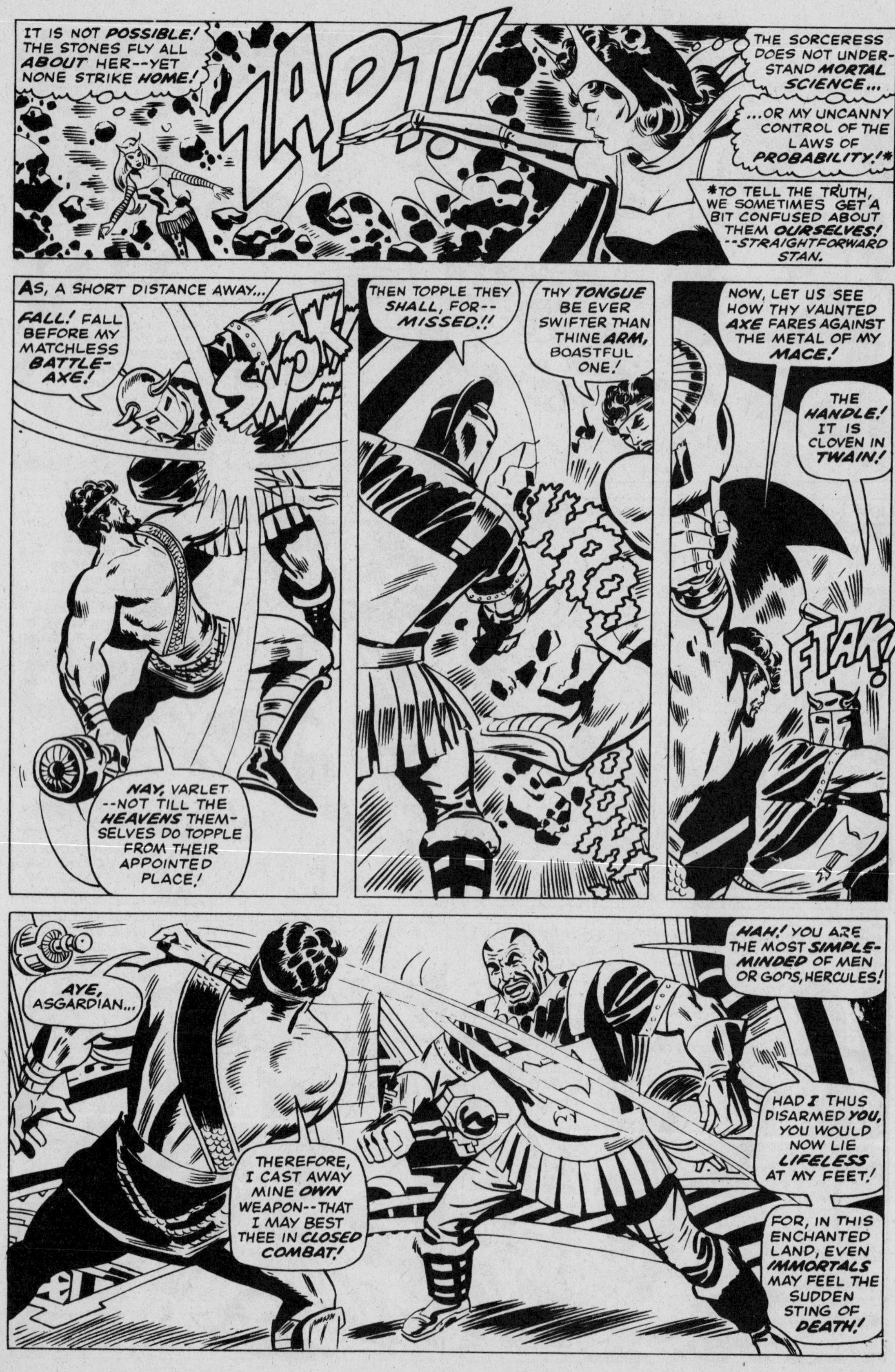
IT IS NOT POSSIBLE! THE STONES FLY ALL ABOUT HER--YET NONE STRIKE HOME!
ZAPT!
THE SORCERESS DOES NOT UNDERSTAND MORTAL SCIENCE...
...OR MY UNCANNY CONTROL OF THE LAWS OF PROBABILITY!*
*TO TELL THE TRUTH, WE SOMETIMES GET A BIT CONFUSED ABOUT THEM OURSELVES! --STRAIGHTFORWARD STAN.
AS, A SHORT DISTANCE AWAY...
FALL! FALL BEFORE MY MATCHLESS BATTLE-AXE!
SWOK!
NAY, VARLET --NOT TILL THE HEAVENS THEMSELVES DO TOPPLE FROM THEIR APPOINTED PLACE!
THEN TOPPLE THEY SHALL, FOR--MISSED!!
THY TONGUE BE EVER SWIFTER THAN THINE ARM, BOASTFUL ONE!
NOW, LET US SEE HOW THY VAUNTED AXE FARES AGAINST THE METAL OF MY MACE!
THE HANDLE! IT IS CLOVEN IN TWAIN!
FTAK!
AYE, ASGARDIAN...
THEREFORE, I CAST AWAY MINE OWN WEAPON--THAT I MAY BEST THEE IN CLOSED COMBAT!
HAH! YOU ARE THE MOST SIMPLE-MINDED OF MEN OR GODS, HERCULES!
HAD I THUS DISARMED YOU, YOU WOULD NOW LIE LIFELESS AT MY FEET!
FOR, IN THIS ENCHANTED LAND, EVEN IMMORTALS MAY FEEL THE SUDDEN STING OF DEATH!

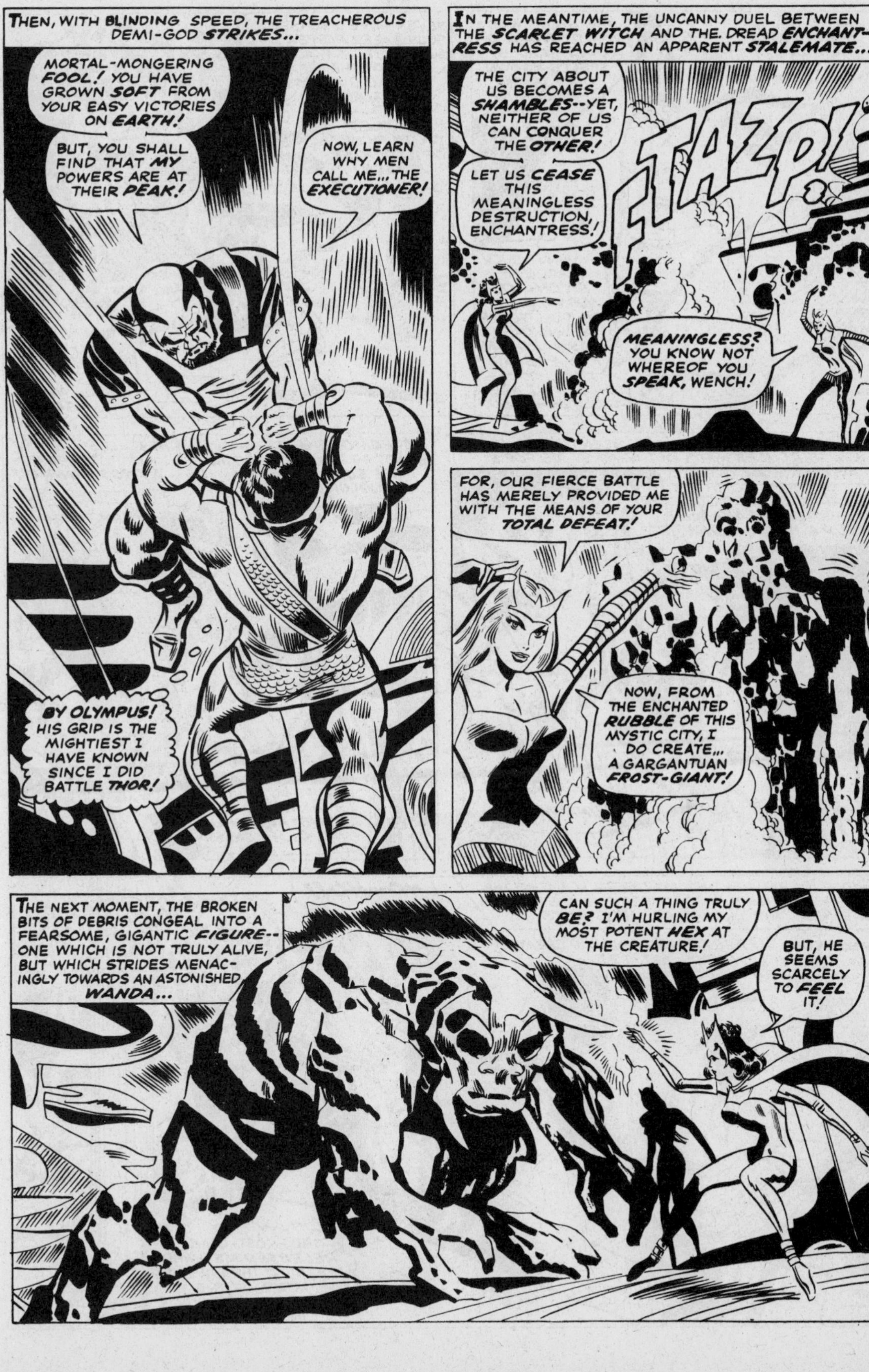
THEN, WITH BLINDING SPEED, THE TREACHEROUS DEMI-GOD STRIKES...
MORTAL-MONGERING FOOL! YOU HAVE GROWN SOFT FROM YOUR EASY VICTORIES ON EARTH!
BUT, YOU SHALL FIND THAT MY POWERS ARE AT THEIR PEAK!
NOW, LEARN WHY MEN CALL ME... THE EXECUTIONER!
BY OLYMPUS! HIS GRIP IS THE MIGHTIEST I HAVE KNOWN SINCE I DID BATTLE THOR!
IN THE MEANTIME, THE UNCANNY DUEL BETWEEN THE SCARLET WITCH AND THE DREAD ENCHANTRESS HAS REACHED AN APPARENT STALEMATE...
THE CITY ABOUT US BECOMES A SHAMBLES--YET, NEITHER OF US CAN CONQUER THE OTHER!
LET US CEASE THIS MEANINGLESS DESTRUCTION, ENCHANTRESS!
FTAZP!
MEANINGLESS? YOU KNOW NOT WHEREOF YOU SPEAK, WENCH!
FOR, OUR FIERCE BATTLE HAS MERELY PROVIDED ME WITH THE MEANS OF YOUR TOTAL DEFEAT!
NOW, FROM THE ENCHANTED RUBBLE OF THIS MYSTIC CITY, I DO CREATE... A GARGANTUAN FROST-GIANT!
THE NEXT MOMENT, THE BROKEN BITS OF DEBRIS CONGEAL INTO A FEARSOME, GIGANTIC FIGURE-- ONE WHICH IS NOT TRULY ALIVE, BUT WHICH STRIDES MENACINGLY TOWARDS AN ASTONISHED WANDA...
CAN SUCH A THING TRULY BE? I'M HURLING MY MOST POTENT HEX AT THE CREATURE!
BUT, HE SEEMS SCARCELY TO FEEL IT!

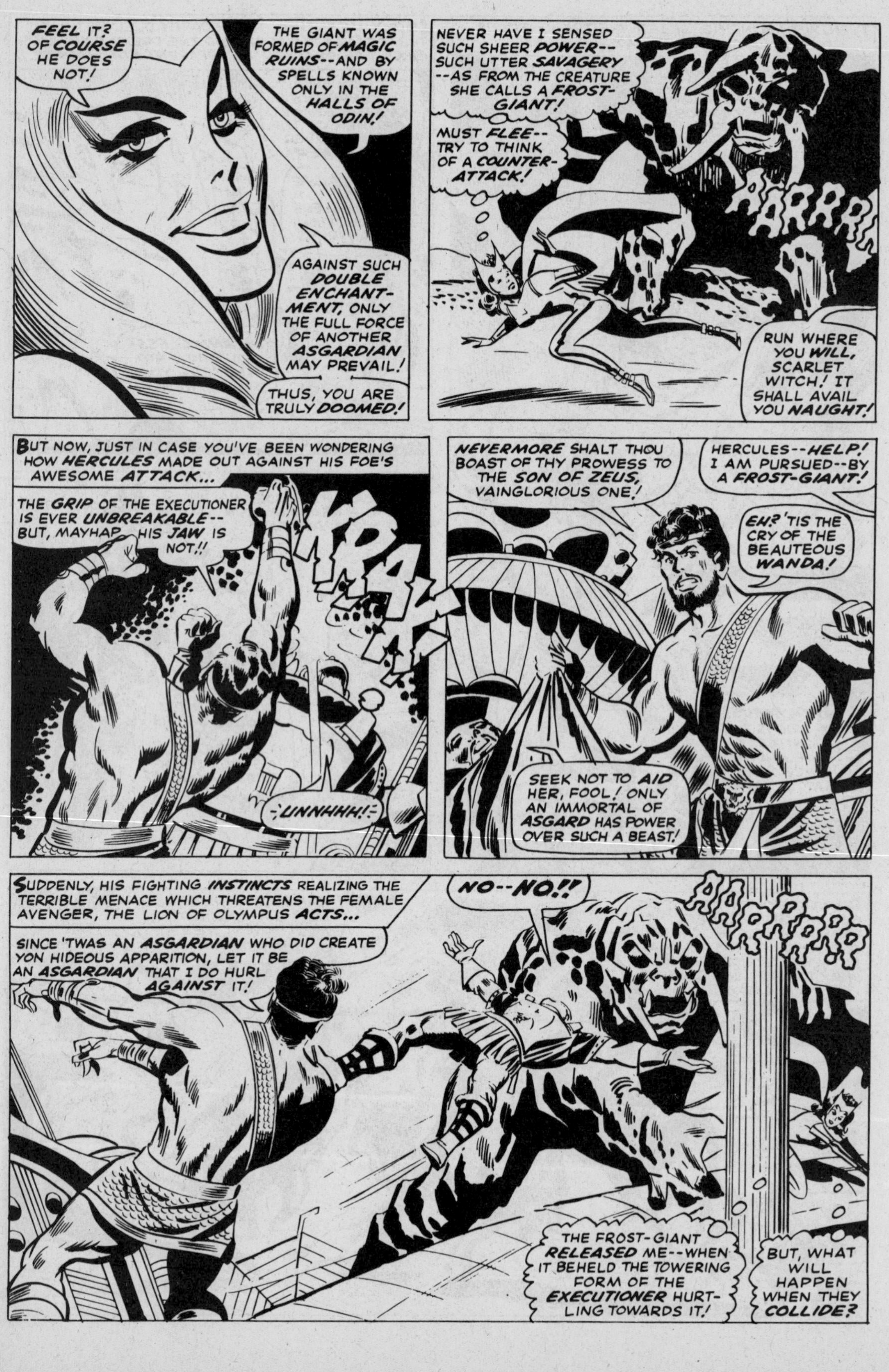
FEEL IT? OF COURSE HE DOES NOT!
THE GIANT WAS FORMED OF MAGIC RUINS--AND BY SPELLS KNOWN ONLY IN THE HALLS OF ODIN!
AGAINST SUCH DOUBLE ENCHANTMENT, ONLY THE FULL FORCE OF ANOTHER ASGARDIAN MAY PREVAIL!
THUS, YOU ARE TRULY DOOMED!
NEVER HAVE I SENSED SUCH SHEER POWER--SUCH UTTER SAVAGERY--AS FROM THE CREATURE SHE CALLS A FROST-GIANT!
MUST FLEE--TRY TO THINK OF A COUNTER-ATTACK!
ARRRR
RUN WHERE YOU WILL, SCARLET WITCH! IT SHALL AVAIL YOU NAUGHT!
BUT NOW, JUST IN CASE YOU'VE BEEN WONDERING HOW HERCULES MADE OUT AGAINST HIS FOE'S AWESOME ATTACK...
THE GRIP OF THE EXECUTIONER IS EVER UNBREAKABLE--BUT, MAYHAP, HIS JAW IS NOT!!
KRAAK
UNNHHH!
NEVERMORE SHALT THOU BOAST OF THY PROWESS TO THE SON OF ZEUS, VAINGLORIOUS ONE!
HERCULES--HELP! I AM PURSUED--BY A FROST-GIANT!
EH? 'TIS THE CRY OF THE BEAUTEOUS WANDA!
SEEK NOT TO AID HER, FOOL! ONLY AN IMMORTAL OF ASGARD HAS POWER OVER SUCH A BEAST!
SUDDENLY, HIS FIGHTING INSTINCTS REALIZING THE TERRIBLE MENACE WHICH THREATENS THE FEMALE AVENGER, THE LION OF OLYMPUS ACTS...
SINCE 'TWAS AN ASGARDIAN WHO DID CREATE YON HIDEOUS APPARITION, LET IT BE AN ASGARDIAN THAT I DO HURL AGAINST IT!
NO--NO!!
AARRRRR
THE FROST-GIANT RELEASED ME--WHEN IT BEHELD THE TOWERING FORM OF THE EXECUTIONER HURTLING TOWARDS IT!
BUT, WHAT WILL HAPPEN WHEN THEY COLLIDE?

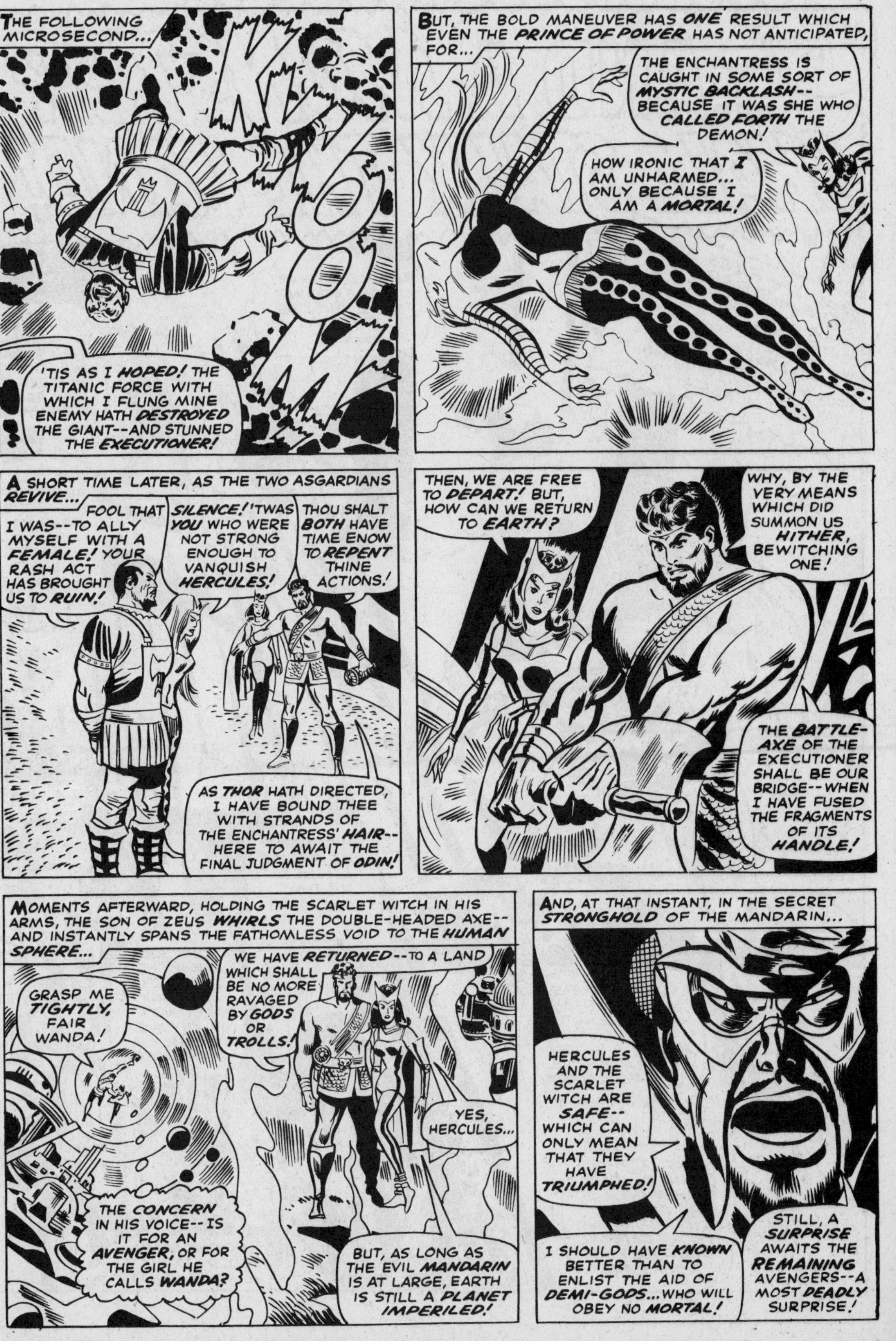
THE FOLLOWING MICROSECOND...
KA-BOOM
'TIS AS I HOPED! THE TITANIC FORCE WITH WHICH I FLUNG MINE ENEMY HATH DESTROYED THE GIANT--AND STUNNED THE EXECUTIONER!
BUT, THE BOLD MANEUVER HAS ONE RESULT WHICH EVEN THE PRINCE OF POWER HAS NOT ANTICIPATED, FOR...
THE ENCHANTRESS IS CAUGHT IN SOME SORT OF MYSTIC BACKLASH--BECAUSE IT WAS SHE WHO CALLED FORTH THE DEMON!
HOW IRONIC THAT I AM UNHARMED... ONLY BECAUSE I AM A MORTAL!
A SHORT TIME LATER, AS THE TWO ASGARDIANS REVIVE...
FOOL THAT I WAS--TO ALLY MYSELF WITH A FEMALE! YOUR RASH ACT HAS BROUGHT US TO RUIN!
SILENCE! 'TWAS YOU WHO WERE NOT STRONG ENOUGH TO VANQUISH HERCULES!
THOU SHALT BOTH HAVE TIME ENOW TO REPENT THINE ACTIONS!
AS THOR HATH DIRECTED, I HAVE BOUND THEE WITH STRANDS OF THE ENCHANTRESS' HAIR--HERE TO AWAIT THE FINAL JUDGMENT OF ODIN!
THEN, WE ARE FREE TO DEPART! BUT, HOW CAN WE RETURN TO EARTH?
WHY, BY THE VERY MEANS WHICH DID SUMMON US HITHER, BEWITCHING ONE!
THE BATTLE-AXE OF THE EXECUTIONER SHALL BE OUR BRIDGE--WHEN I HAVE FUSED THE FRAGMENTS OF ITS HANDLE!
MOMENTS AFTERWARD, HOLDING THE SCARLET WITCH IN HIS ARMS, THE SON OF ZEUS WHIRLS THE DOUBLE-HEADED AXE--AND INSTANTLY SPANS THE FATHOMLESS VOID TO THE HUMAN SPHERE...
GRASP ME TIGHTLY, FAIR WANDA!
WE HAVE RETURNED--TO A LAND WHICH SHALL BE NO MORE RAVAGED BY GODS OR TROLLS!
YES, HERCULES...
THE CONCERN IN HIS VOICE--IS IT FOR AN AVENGER, OR FOR THE GIRL HE CALLS WANDA?
BUT, AS LONG AS THE EVIL MANDARIN IS AT LARGE, EARTH IS STILL A PLANET IMPERILED!
AND, AT THAT INSTANT, IN THE SECRET STRONGHOLD OF THE MANDARIN...
HERCULES AND THE SCARLET WITCH ARE SAFE--WHICH CAN ONLY MEAN THAT THEY HAVE TRIUMPHED!
I SHOULD HAVE KNOWN BETTER THAN TO ENLIST THE AID OF DEMI-GODS... WHO WILL OBEY NO MORTAL!
STILL, A SURPRISE AWAITS THE REMAINING AVENGERS--A MOST DEADLY SURPRISE!

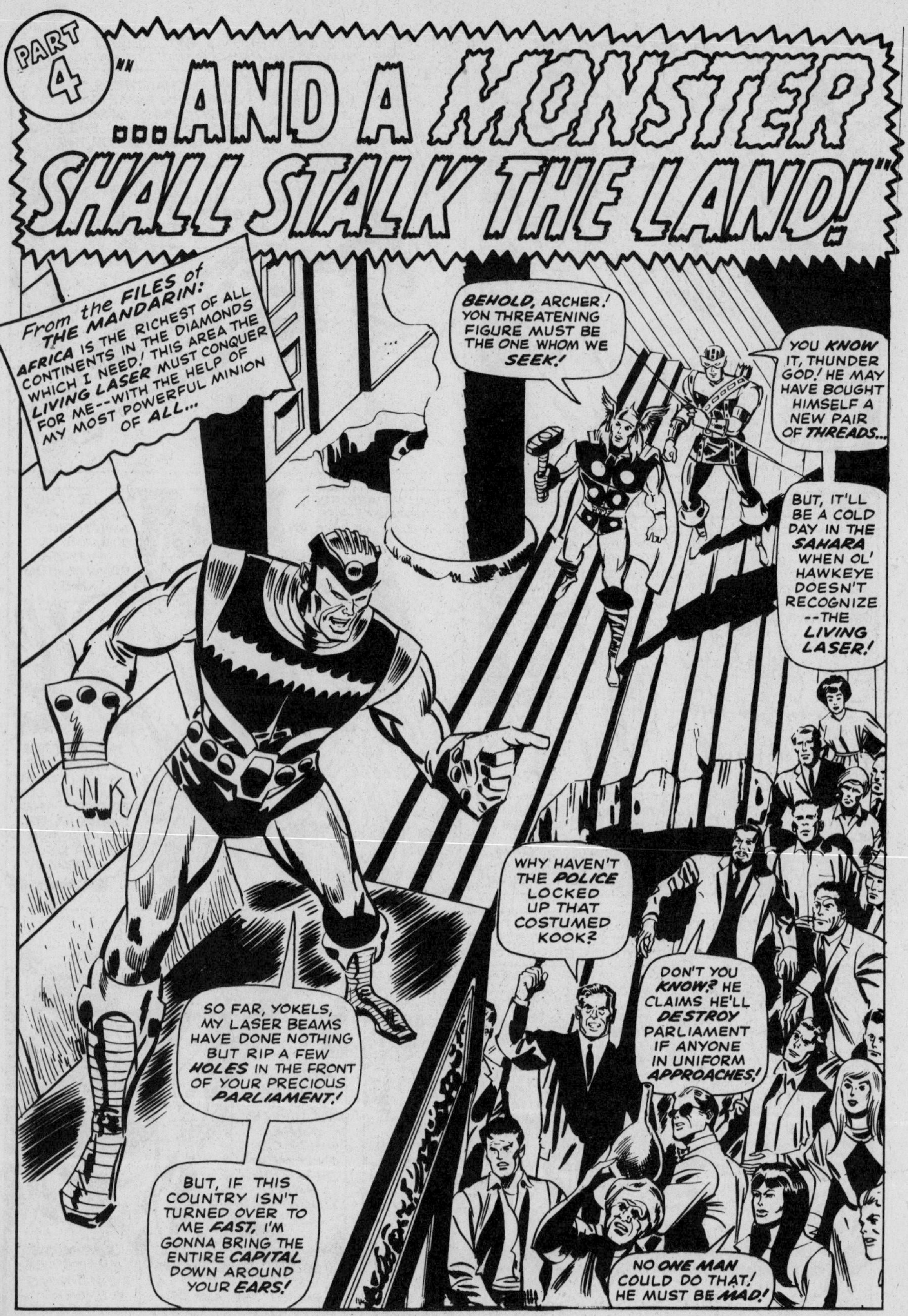

PART 4
"...AND A MONSTER SHALL STALK THE LAND!"
From the FILES of THE MANDARIN: AFRICA IS THE RICHEST OF ALL CONTINENTS IN THE DIAMONDS WHICH I NEED! THIS AREA THE LIVING LASER MUST CONQUER FOR ME--WITH THE HELP OF MY MOST POWERFUL MINION OF ALL...
BEHOLD, ARCHER! YON THREATENING FIGURE MUST BE THE ONE WHOM WE SEEK!
YOU KNOW IT, THUNDER GOD! HE MAY HAVE BOUGHT HIMSELF A NEW PAIR OF THREADS...
BUT, IT'LL BE A COLD DAY IN THE SAHARA WHEN OL' HAWKEYE DOESN'T RECOGNIZE --THE LIVING LASER!
WHY HAVEN'T THE POLICE LOCKED UP THAT COSTUMED KOOK?
DON'T YOU KNOW? HE CLAIMS HE'LL DESTROY PARLIAMENT IF ANYONE IN UNIFORM APPROACHES!
SO FAR, YOKELS, MY LASER BEAMS HAVE DONE NOTHING BUT RIP A FEW HOLES IN THE FRONT OF YOUR PRECIOUS PARLIAMENT!
BUT, IF THIS COUNTRY ISN'T TURNED OVER TO ME FAST, I'M GONNA BRING THE ENTIRE CAPITAL DOWN AROUND YOUR EARS!
NO ONE MAN COULD DO THAT! HE MUST BE MAD!

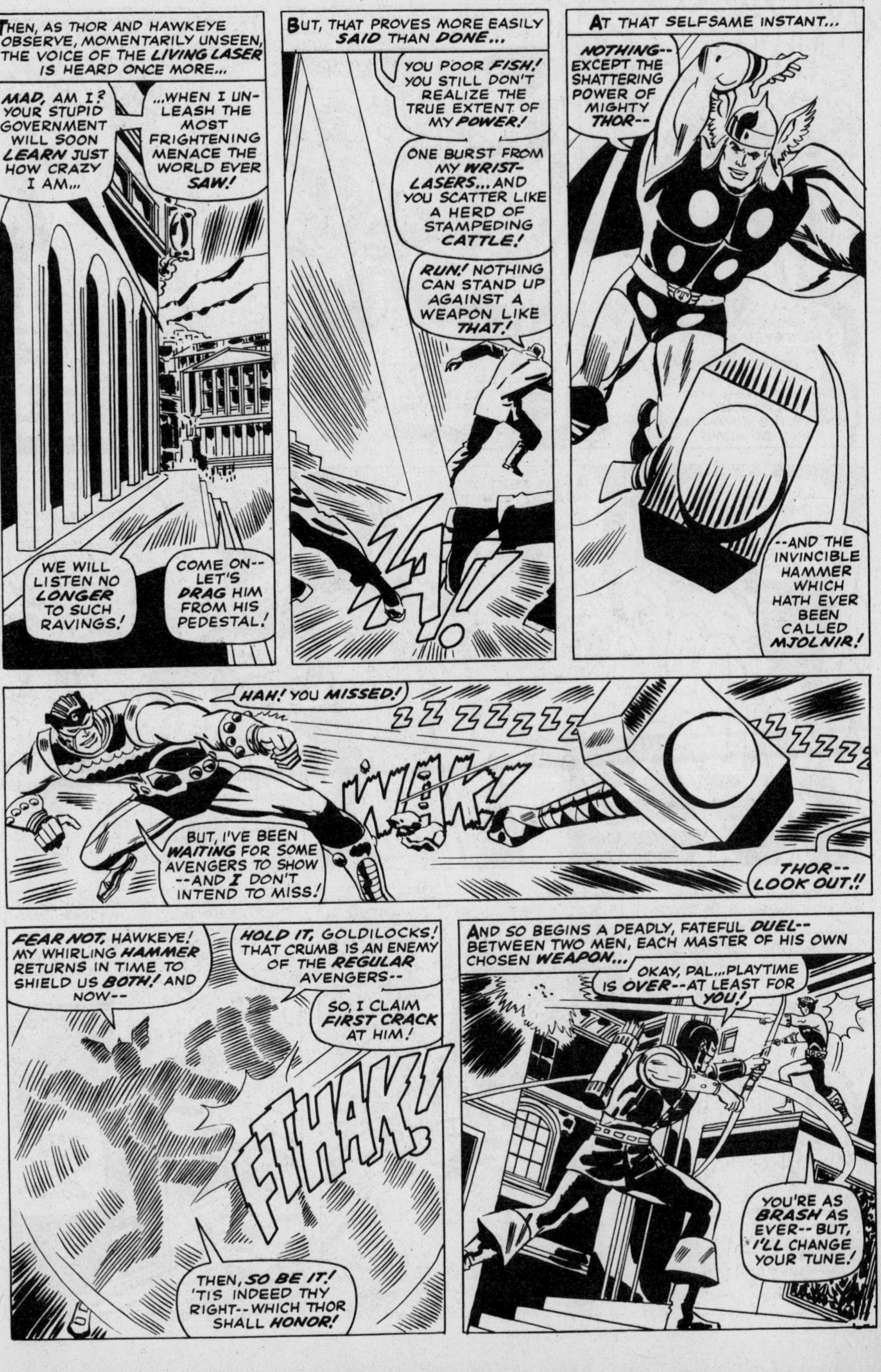
THEN, AS THOR AND HAWKEYE OBSERVE, MOMENTARILY UNSEEN, THE VOICE OF THE LIVING LASER IS HEARD ONCE MORE...
MAD, AM I? YOUR STUPID GOVERNMENT WILL SOON LEARN JUST HOW CRAZY I AM...
...WHEN I UNLEASH THE MOST FRIGHTENING MENACE THE WORLD EVER SAW!
WE WILL LISTEN NO LONGER TO SUCH RAVINGS!
COME ON-- LET'S DRAG HIM FROM HIS PEDESTAL!
BUT, THAT PROVES MORE EASILY SAID THAN DONE...
YOU POOR FISH! YOU STILL DON'T REALIZE THE TRUE EXTENT OF MY POWER!
ONE BURST FROM MY WRIST-LASERS... AND YOU SCATTER LIKE A HERD OF STAMPEDING CATTLE!
RUN! NOTHING CAN STAND UP AGAINST A WEAPON LIKE THAT!
ZAT!
AT THAT SELFSAME INSTANT...
NOTHING-- EXCEPT THE SHATTERING POWER OF MIGHTY THOR--
--AND THE INVINCIBLE HAMMER WHICH HATH EVER BEEN CALLED MJOLNIR!
HAH! YOU MISSED!
ZZZZZZZ
WAK!
ZZZZZ
BUT, I'VE BEEN WAITING FOR SOME AVENGERS TO SHOW --AND I DON'T INTEND TO MISS!
THOR-- LOOK OUT!!
FEAR NOT, HAWKEYE! MY WHIRLING HAMMER RETURNS IN TIME TO SHIELD US BOTH! AND NOW--
HOLD IT, GOLDILOCKS! THAT CRUMB IS AN ENEMY OF THE REGULAR AVENGERS--
SO, I CLAIM FIRST CRACK AT HIM!
FTHAK!
THEN, SO BE IT! 'TIS INDEED THY RIGHT--WHICH THOR SHALL HONOR!
AND SO BEGINS A DEADLY, FATEFUL DUEL-- BETWEEN TWO MEN, EACH MASTER OF HIS OWN CHOSEN WEAPON...
OKAY, PAL...PLAYTIME IS OVER--AT LEAST FOR YOU!
YOU'RE AS BRASH AS EVER-- BUT, I'LL CHANGE YOUR TUNE!

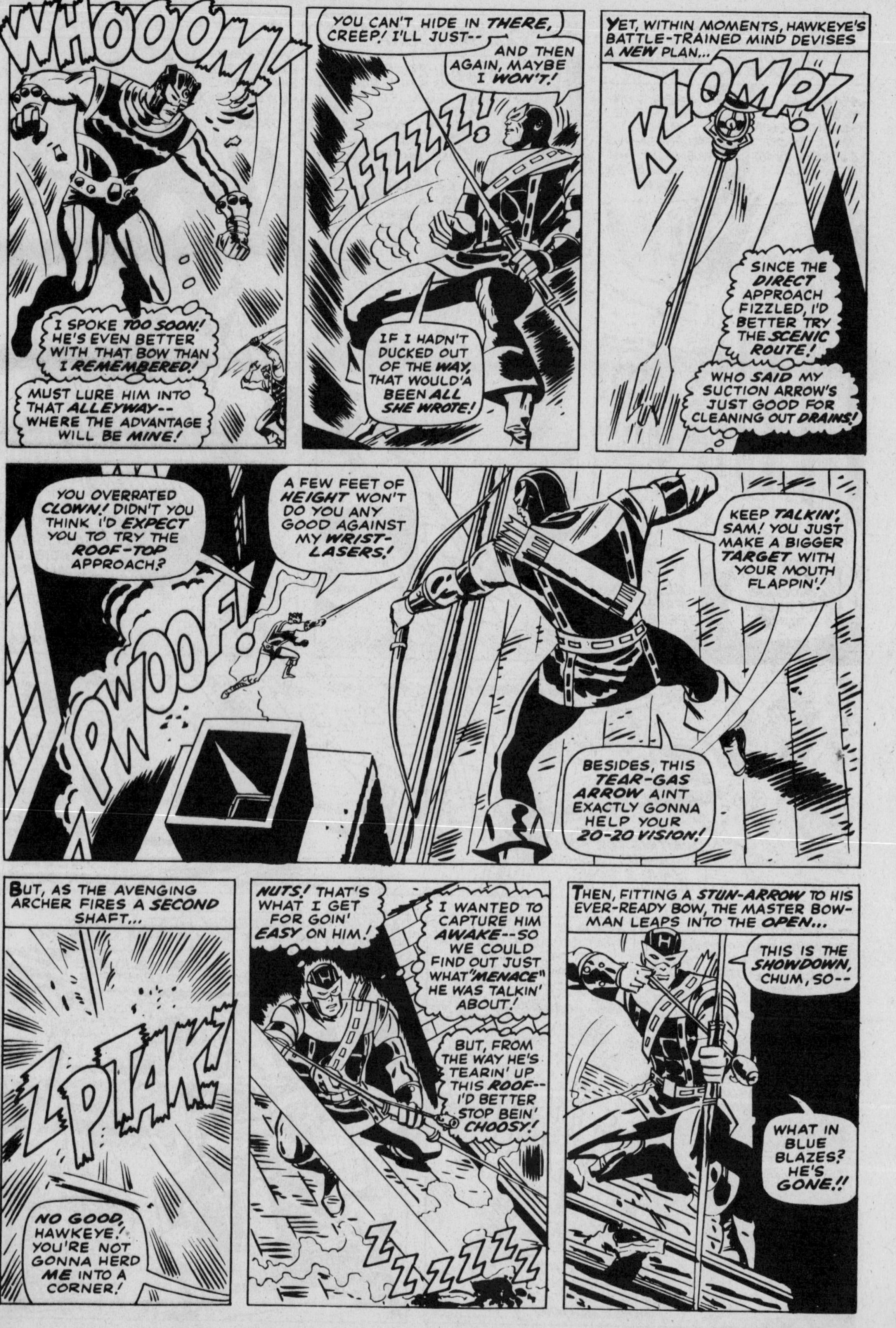
WHOOOM!
I SPOKE TOO SOON! HE'S EVEN BETTER WITH THAT BOW THAN I REMEMBERED!
MUST LURE HIM INTO THAT ALLEYWAY-- WHERE THE ADVANTAGE WILL BE MINE!
YOU CAN'T HIDE IN THERE, CREEP! I'LL JUST--
AND THEN AGAIN, MAYBE I WON'T!
FZZZZ!
IF I HADN'T DUCKED OUT OF THE WAY, THAT WOULD'A BEEN ALL SHE WROTE!
YET, WITHIN MOMENTS, HAWKEYE'S BATTLE-TRAINED MIND DEVISES A NEW PLAN...
KLOMP!
SINCE THE DIRECT APPROACH FIZZLED, I'D BETTER TRY THE SCENIC ROUTE!
WHO SAID MY SUCTION ARROW'S JUST GOOD FOR CLEANING OUT DRAINS!
YOU OVERRATED CLOWN! DIDN'T YOU THINK I'D EXPECT YOU TO TRY THE ROOF-TOP APPROACH?
A FEW FEET OF HEIGHT WON'T DO YOU ANY GOOD AGAINST MY WRIST-LASERS!
PWOOF!
KEEP TALKIN', SAM! YOU JUST MAKE A BIGGER TARGET WITH YOUR MOUTH FLAPPIN'!
BESIDES, THIS TEAR-GAS ARROW AINT EXACTLY GONNA HELP YOUR 20-20 VISION!
BUT, AS THE AVENGING ARCHER FIRES A SECOND SHAFT...
ZPTAK!
NO GOOD, HAWKEYE! YOU'RE NOT GONNA HERD ME INTO A CORNER!
NUTS! THAT'S WHAT I GET FOR GOIN' EASY ON HIM!
I WANTED TO CAPTURE HIM AWAKE--SO WE COULD FIND OUT JUST WHAT "MENACE" HE WAS TALKIN' ABOUT!
BUT, FROM THE WAY HE'S TEARIN' UP THIS ROOF-- I'D BETTER STOP BEIN' CHOOSY!
ZZZZZZZ
THEN, FITTING A STUN-ARROW TO HIS EVER-READY BOW, THE MASTER BOW-MAN LEAPS INTO THE OPEN...
THIS IS THE SHOWDOWN, CHUM, SO--
WHAT IN BLUE BLAZES? HE'S GONE!!

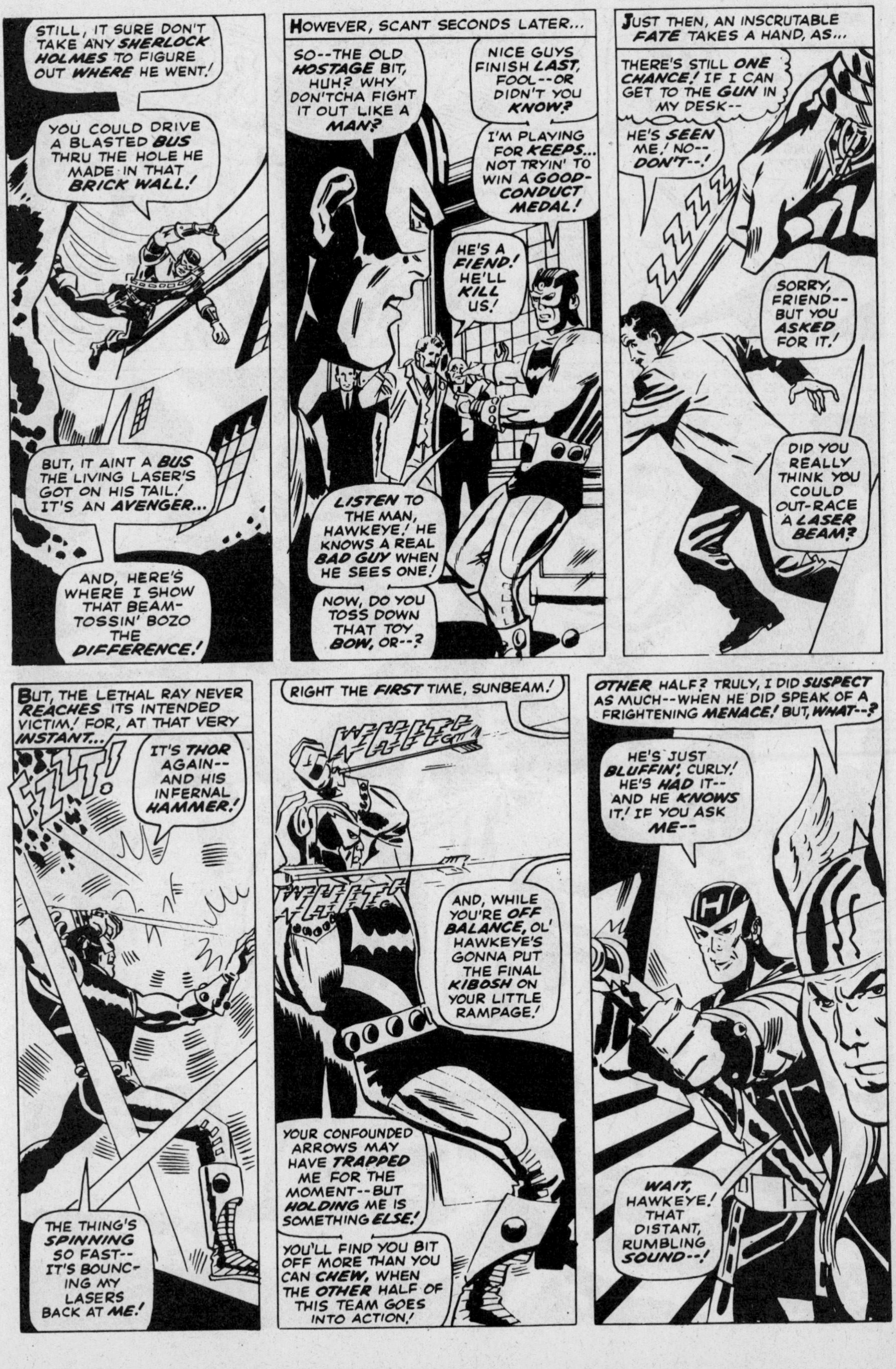
STILL, IT SURE DON'T TAKE ANY SHERLOCK HOLMES TO FIGURE OUT WHERE HE WENT!
YOU COULD DRIVE A BLASTED BUS THRU THE HOLE HE MADE IN THAT BRICK WALL!
BUT, IT AINT A BUS THE LIVING LASER'S GOT ON HIS TAIL! IT'S AN AVENGER...
AND, HERE'S WHERE I SHOW THAT BEAM-TOSSIN' BOZO THE DIFFERENCE!
HOWEVER, SCANT SECONDS LATER...
SO--THE OLD HOSTAGE BIT, HUH? WHY DON'TCHA FIGHT IT OUT LIKE A MAN?
NICE GUYS FINISH LAST, FOOL--OR DIDN'T YOU KNOW?
I'M PLAYING FOR KEEPS... NOT TRYIN' TO WIN A GOOD-CONDUCT MEDAL!
HE'S A FIEND! HE'LL KILL US!
LISTEN TO THE MAN, HAWKEYE! HE KNOWS A REAL BAD GUY WHEN HE SEES ONE!
NOW, DO YOU TOSS DOWN THAT TOY BOW, OR--?
JUST THEN, AN INSCRUTABLE FATE TAKES A HAND, AS...
THERE'S STILL ONE CHANCE! IF I CAN GET TO THE GUN IN MY DESK--
HE'S SEEN ME! NO--DON'T--!
ZZZZZ
SORRY, FRIEND--BUT YOU ASKED FOR IT!
DID YOU REALLY THINK YOU COULD OUT-RACE A LASER BEAM?
BUT, THE LETHAL RAY NEVER REACHES ITS INTENDED VICTIM! FOR, AT THAT VERY INSTANT...
FZZT!
IT'S THOR AGAIN--AND HIS INFERNAL HAMMER!
THE THING'S SPINNING SO FAST--IT'S BOUNCING MY LASERS BACK AT ME!
RIGHT THE FIRST TIME, SUNBEAM!
AND, WHILE YOU'RE OFF BALANCE, OL' HAWKEYE'S GONNA PUT THE FINAL KIBOSH ON YOUR LITTLE RAMPAGE!
YOUR CONFOUNDED ARROWS MAY HAVE TRAPPED ME FOR THE MOMENT--BUT HOLDING ME IS SOMETHING ELSE!
YOU'LL FIND YOU BIT OFF MORE THAN YOU CAN CHEW, WHEN THE OTHER HALF OF THIS TEAM GOES INTO ACTION!
OTHER HALF? TRULY, I DID SUSPECT AS MUCH--WHEN HE DID SPEAK OF A FRIGHTENING MENACE! BUT, WHAT--?
HE'S JUST BLUFFIN', CURLY! HE'S HAD IT--AND HE KNOWS IT! IF YOU ASK ME--
WAIT, HAWKEYE! THAT DISTANT, RUMBLING SOUND--!

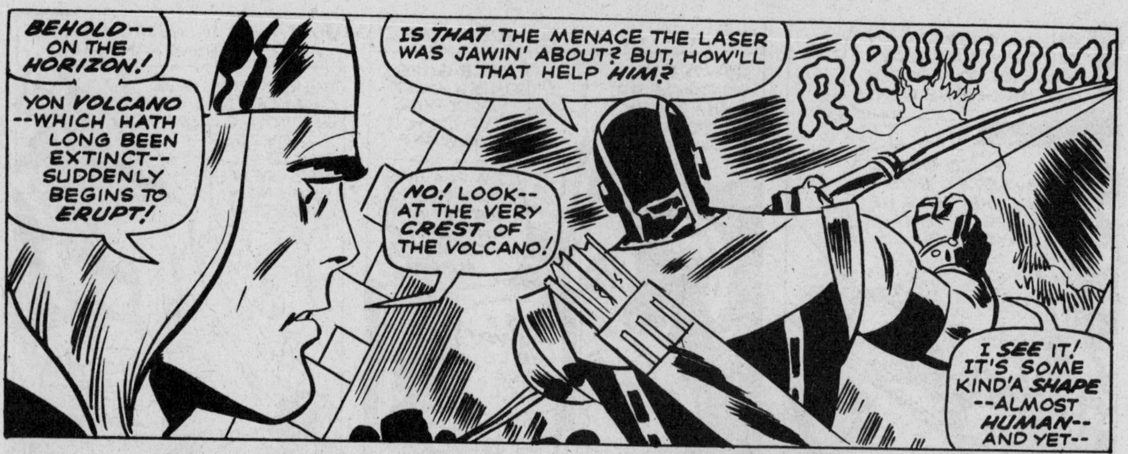
BEHOLD-- ON THE HORIZON!
YON VOLCANO --WHICH HATH LONG BEEN EXTINCT-- SUDDENLY BEGINS TO ERUPT!
IS THAT THE MENACE THE LASER WAS JAWIN' ABOUT? BUT, HOW'LL THAT HELP HIM?
RRUUUM
NO! LOOK-- AT THE VERY CREST OF THE VOLCANO!
I SEE IT! IT'S SOME KIND'A SHAPE --ALMOST HUMAN-- AND YET--

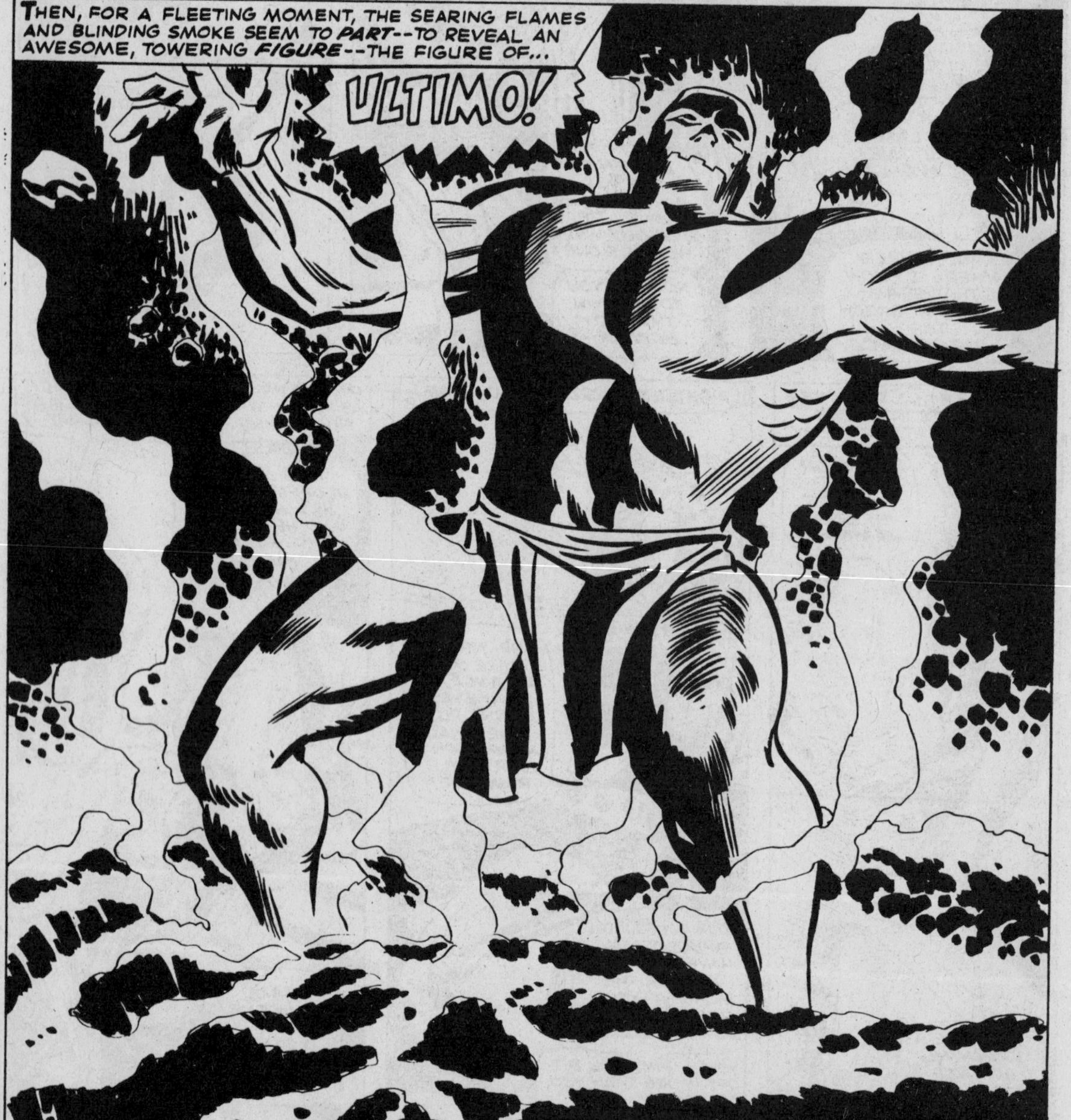
THEN, FOR A FLEETING MOMENT, THE SEARING FLAMES AND BLINDING SMOKE SEEM TO PART--TO REVEAL AN AWESOME, TOWERING FIGURE--THE FIGURE OF...
ULTIMO!

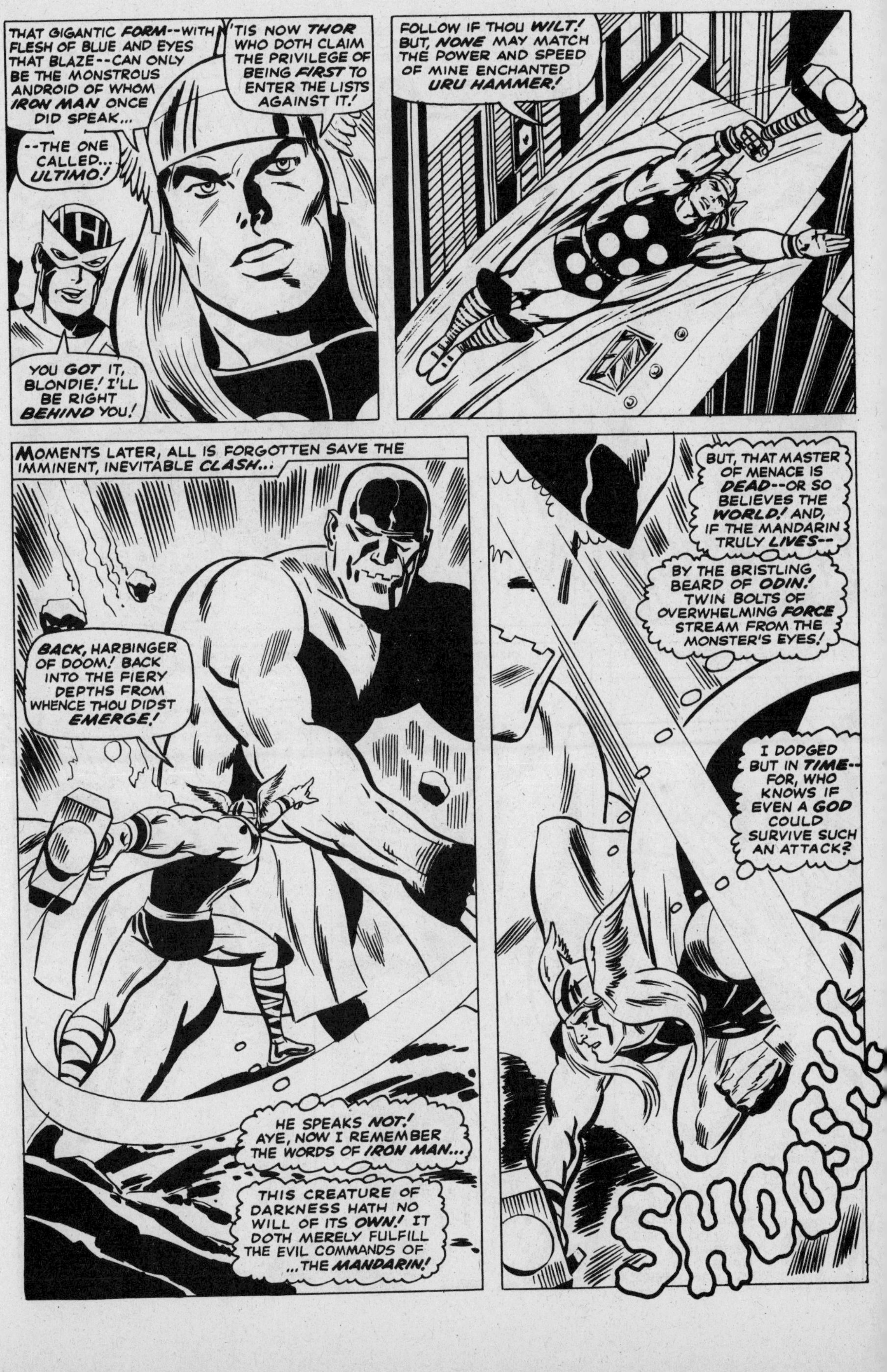
THAT GIGANTIC FORM--WITH FLESH OF BLUE AND EYES THAT BLAZE--CAN ONLY BE THE MONSTROUS ANDROID OF WHOM IRON MAN ONCE DID SPEAK...
--THE ONE CALLED... ULTIMO!
'TIS NOW THOR WHO DOTH CLAIM THE PRIVILEGE OF BEING FIRST TO ENTER THE LISTS AGAINST IT!
YOU GOT IT, BLONDIE! I'LL BE RIGHT BEHIND YOU!
FOLLOW IF THOU WILT! BUT, NONE MAY MATCH THE POWER AND SPEED OF MINE ENCHANTED URU HAMMER!
MOMENTS LATER, ALL IS FORGOTTEN SAVE THE IMMINENT, INEVITABLE CLASH...
BACK, HARBINGER OF DOOM! BACK INTO THE FIERY DEPTHS FROM WHENCE THOU DIDST EMERGE!
HE SPEAKS NOT! AYE, NOW I REMEMBER THE WORDS OF IRON MAN...
THIS CREATURE OF DARKNESS HATH NO WILL OF ITS OWN! IT DOTH MERELY FULFILL THE EVIL COMMANDS OF ...THE MANDARIN!
BUT, THAT MASTER OF MENACE IS DEAD--OR SO BELIEVES THE WORLD! AND, IF THE MANDARIN TRULY LIVES--
BY THE BRISTLING BEARD OF ODIN! TWIN BOLTS OF OVERWHELMING FORCE STREAM FROM THE MONSTER'S EYES!
I DODGED BUT IN TIME-- FOR, WHO KNOWS IF EVEN A GOD COULD SURVIVE SUCH AN ATTACK?
SHOOSH!

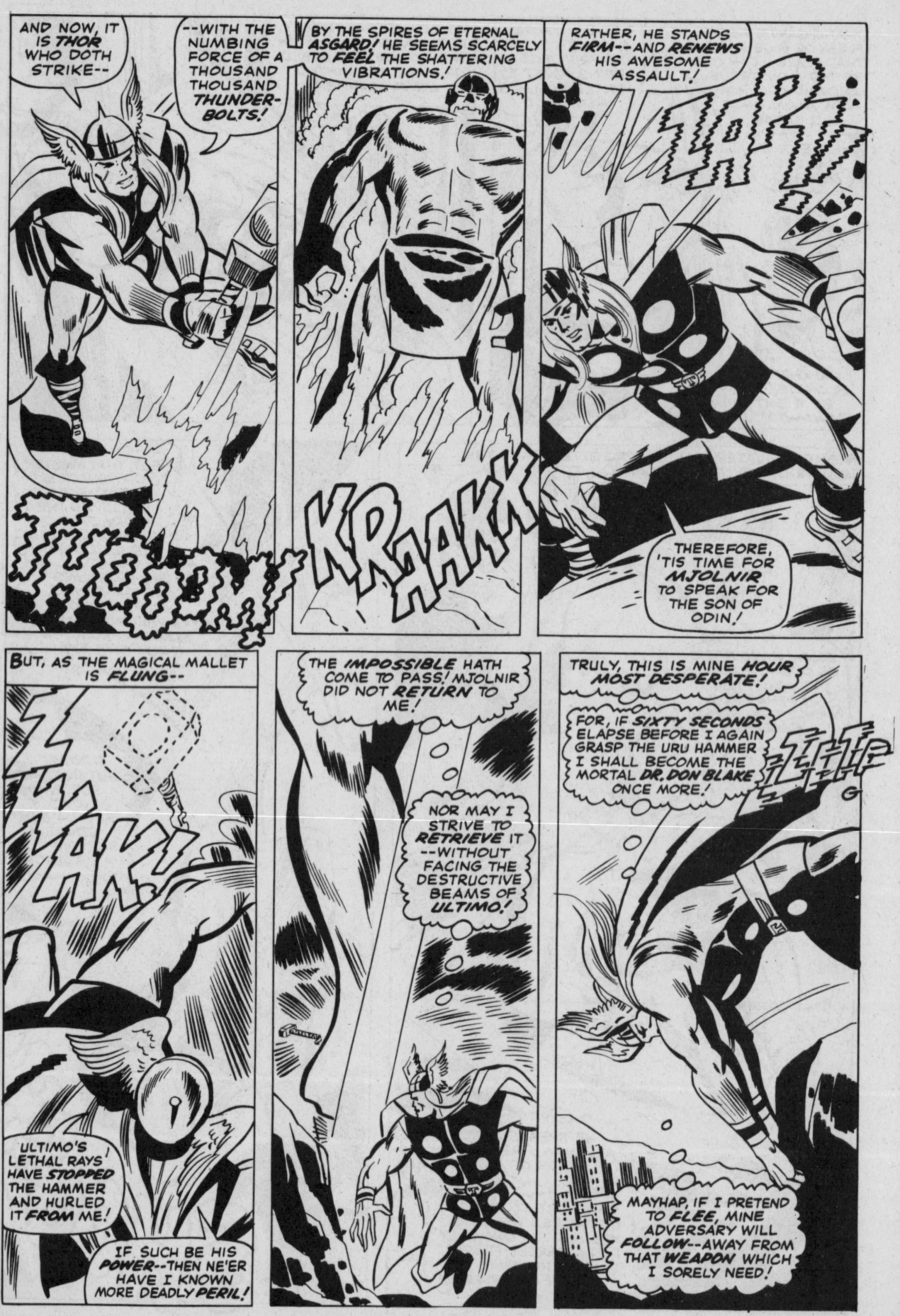
AND NOW, IT IS THOR WHO DOTH STRIKE--
--WITH THE NUMBING FORCE OF A THOUSAND THOUSAND THUNDER-BOLTS!
THOOOM!
BY THE SPIRES OF ETERNAL ASGARD! HE SEEMS SCARCELY TO FEEL THE SHATTERING VIBRATIONS!
KRAAKK
RATHER, HE STANDS FIRM--AND RENEWS HIS AWESOME ASSAULT!
ZAP!
THEREFORE, 'TIS TIME FOR MJOLNIR TO SPEAK FOR THE SON OF ODIN!
BUT, AS THE MAGICAL MALLET IS FLUNG--
ZWAKK!
ULTIMO'S LETHAL RAYS HAVE STOPPED THE HAMMER AND HURLED IT FROM ME!
IF SUCH BE HIS POWER--THEN NE'ER HAVE I KNOWN MORE DEADLY PERIL!
THE IMPOSSIBLE HATH COME TO PASS! MJOLNIR DID NOT RETURN TO ME!
NOR MAY I STRIVE TO RETRIEVE IT --WITHOUT FACING THE DESTRUCTIVE BEAMS OF ULTIMO!
TRULY, THIS IS MINE HOUR MOST DESPERATE!
FOR, IF SIXTY SECONDS ELAPSE BEFORE I AGAIN GRASP THE URU HAMMER I SHALL BECOME THE MORTAL DR. DON BLAKE ONCE MORE!
MAYHAP, IF I PRETEND TO FLEE, MINE ADVERSARY WILL FOLLOW--AWAY FROM THAT WEAPON WHICH I SORELY NEED!

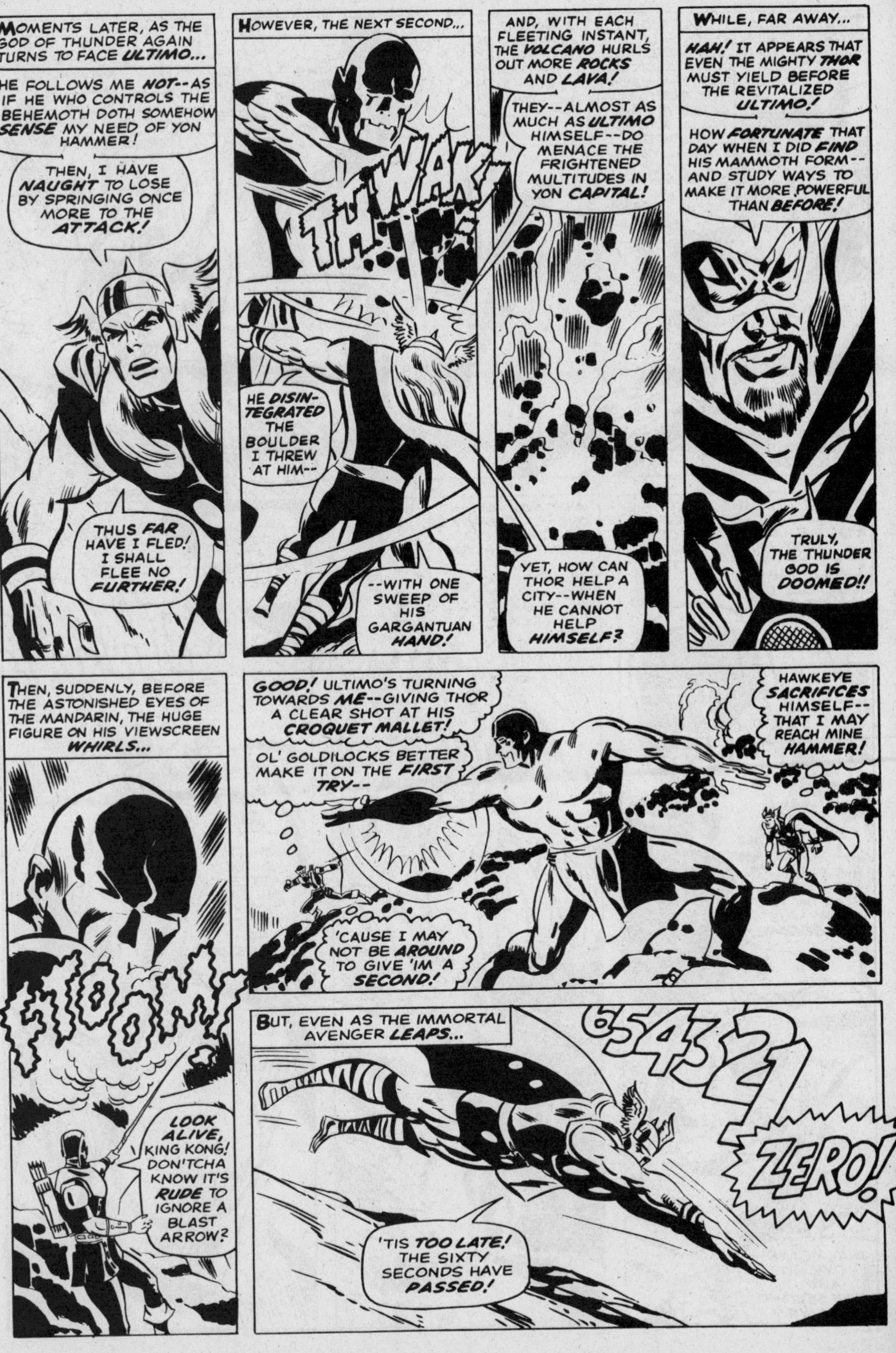
MOMENTS LATER, AS THE GOD OF THUNDER AGAIN TURNS TO FACE ULTIMO...
HE FOLLOWS ME NOT--AS IF HE WHO CONTROLS THE BEHEMOTH DOTH SOMEHOW SENSE MY NEED OF YON HAMMER!
THEN, I HAVE NAUGHT TO LOSE BY SPRINGING ONCE MORE TO THE ATTACK!
THUS FAR HAVE I FLED! I SHALL FLEE NO FURTHER!
HOWEVER, THE NEXT SECOND...
THWAK!
HE DISINTEGRATED THE BOULDER I THREW AT HIM--
--WITH ONE SWEEP OF HIS GARGANTUAN HAND!
AND, WITH EACH FLEETING INSTANT, THE VOLCANO HURLS OUT MORE ROCKS AND LAVA!
THEY--ALMOST AS MUCH AS ULTIMO HIMSELF--DO MENACE THE FRIGHTENED MULTITUDES IN YON CAPITAL!
YET, HOW CAN THOR HELP A CITY--WHEN HE CANNOT HELP HIMSELF?
WHILE, FAR AWAY...
HAH! IT APPEARS THAT EVEN THE MIGHTY THOR MUST YIELD BEFORE THE REVITALIZED ULTIMO!
HOW FORTUNATE THAT DAY WHEN I DID FIND HIS MAMMOTH FORM--AND STUDY WAYS TO MAKE IT MORE POWERFUL THAN BEFORE!
TRULY, THE THUNDER GOD IS DOOMED!!
THEN, SUDDENLY, BEFORE THE ASTONISHED EYES OF THE MANDARIN, THE HUGE FIGURE ON HIS VIEWSCREEN WHIRLS...
FTOOM!
LOOK ALIVE, KING KONG! DON'TCHA KNOW IT'S RUDE TO IGNORE A BLAST ARROW?
GOOD! ULTIMO'S TURNING TOWARDS ME--GIVING THOR A CLEAR SHOT AT HIS CROQUET MALLET!
OL' GOLDILOCKS BETTER MAKE IT ON THE FIRST TRY--
'CAUSE I MAY NOT BE AROUND TO GIVE 'IM A SECOND!
HAWKEYE SACRIFICES HIMSELF--THAT I MAY REACH MINE HAMMER!
BUT, EVEN AS THE IMMORTAL AVENGER LEAPS...
6 5 4 3 2 1
ZERO!
'TIS TOO LATE! THE SIXTY SECONDS HAVE PASSED!

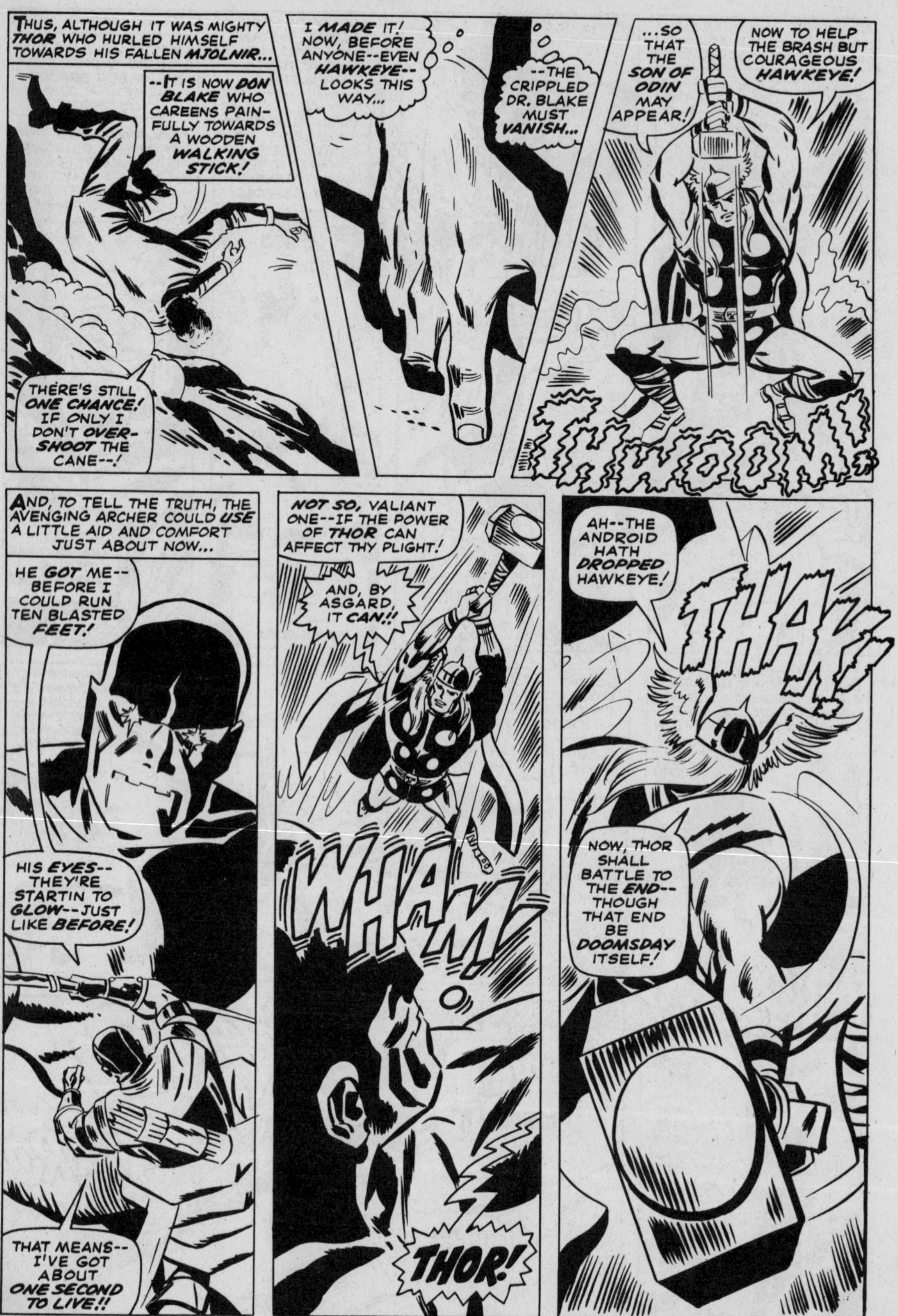
THUS, ALTHOUGH IT WAS MIGHTY THOR WHO HURLED HIMSELF TOWARDS HIS FALLEN MJOLNIR...
--IT IS NOW DON BLAKE WHO CAREENS PAINFULLY TOWARDS A WOODEN WALKING STICK!
THERE'S STILL ONE CHANCE! IF ONLY I DON'T OVERSHOOT THE CANE--!
I MADE IT! NOW, BEFORE ANYONE--EVEN HAWKEYE--LOOKS THIS WAY...
--THE CRIPPLED DR. BLAKE MUST VANISH...
...SO THAT THE SON OF ODIN MAY APPEAR!
NOW TO HELP THE BRASH BUT COURAGEOUS HAWKEYE!
THWOOM!
AND, TO TELL THE TRUTH, THE AVENGING ARCHER COULD USE A LITTLE AID AND COMFORT JUST ABOUT NOW...
HE GOT ME--BEFORE I COULD RUN TEN BLASTED FEET!
HIS EYES--THEY'RE STARTIN TO GLOW--JUST LIKE BEFORE!
THAT MEANS--I'VE GOT ABOUT ONE SECOND TO LIVE!!
NOT SO, VALIANT ONE--IF THE POWER OF THOR CAN AFFECT THY PLIGHT!
AND, BY ASGARD, IT CAN!!
WHAM
THOR!
AH--THE ANDROID HATH DROPPED HAWKEYE!
THAK!
NOW, THOR SHALL BATTLE TO THE END--THOUGH THAT END BE DOOMSDAY ITSELF!

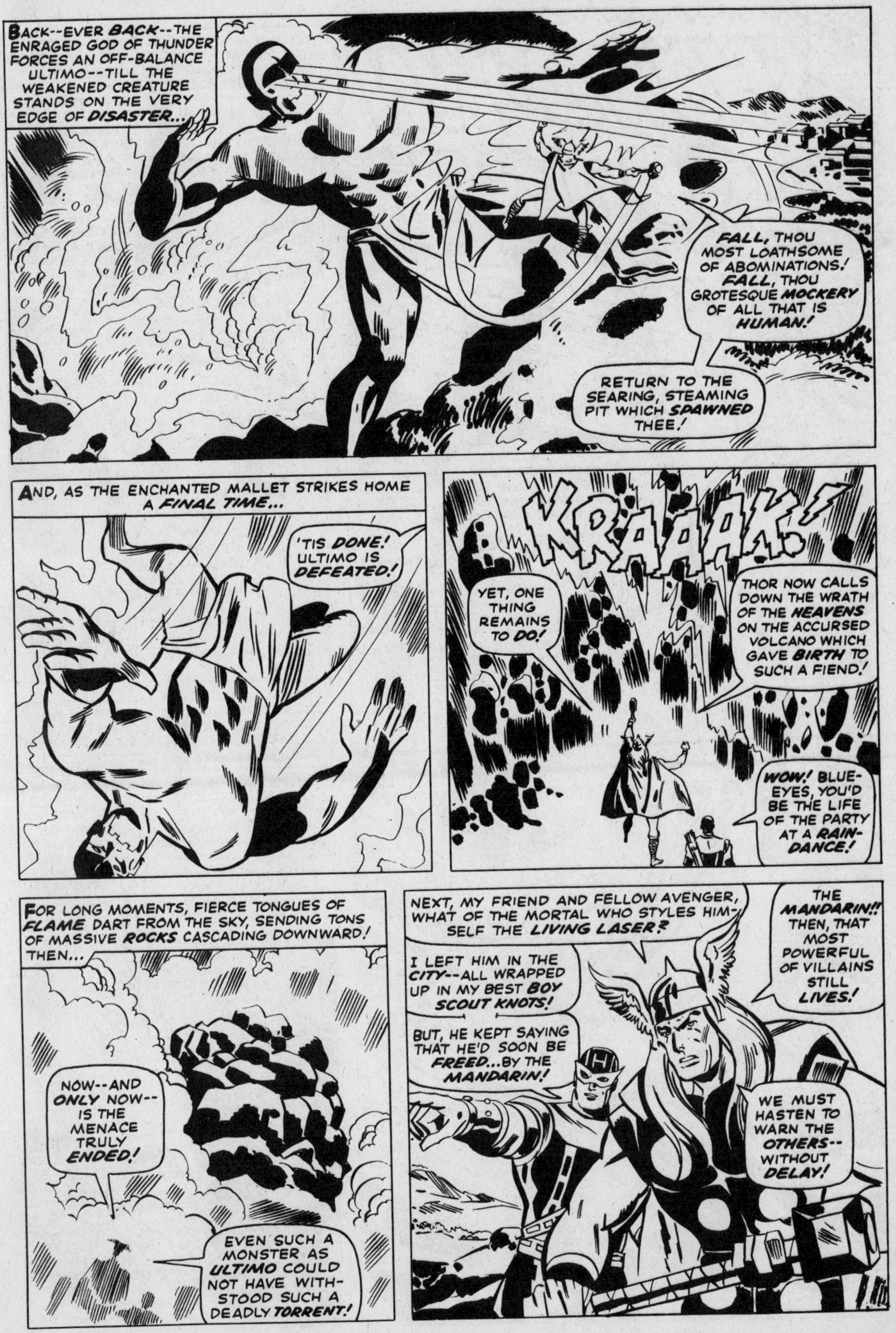
BACK--EVER BACK--THE ENRAGED GOD OF THUNDER FORCES AN OFF-BALANCE ULTIMO--TILL THE WEAKENED CREATURE STANDS ON THE VERY EDGE OF DISASTER...
FALL, THOU MOST LOATHSOME OF ABOMINATIONS! FALL, THOU GROTESQUE MOCKERY OF ALL THAT IS HUMAN!
RETURN TO THE SEARING, STEAMING PIT WHICH SPAWNED THEE!
AND, AS THE ENCHANTED MALLET STRIKES HOME A FINAL TIME...
'TIS DONE! ULTIMO IS DEFEATED!
KRAAAK!
YET, ONE THING REMAINS TO DO!
THOR NOW CALLS DOWN THE WRATH OF THE HEAVENS ON THE ACCURSED VOLCANO WHICH GAVE BIRTH TO SUCH A FIEND!
WOW! BLUE-EYES, YOU'D BE THE LIFE OF THE PARTY AT A RAIN-DANCE!
FOR LONG MOMENTS, FIERCE TONGUES OF FLAME DART FROM THE SKY, SENDING TONS OF MASSIVE ROCKS CASCADING DOWNWARD! THEN...
NOW--AND ONLY NOW--IS THE MENACE TRULY ENDED!
EVEN SUCH A MONSTER AS ULTIMO COULD NOT HAVE WITH-STOOD SUCH A DEADLY TORRENT!
NEXT, MY FRIEND AND FELLOW AVENGER, WHAT OF THE MORTAL WHO STYLES HIM-SELF THE LIVING LASER?
I LEFT HIM IN THE CITY--ALL WRAPPED UP IN MY BEST BOY SCOUT KNOTS!
BUT, HE KEPT SAYING THAT HE'D SOON BE FREED...BY THE MANDARIN!
THE MANDARIN!! THEN, THAT MOST POWERFUL OF VILLAINS STILL LIVES!
WE MUST HASTEN TO WARN THE OTHERS--WITHOUT DELAY!

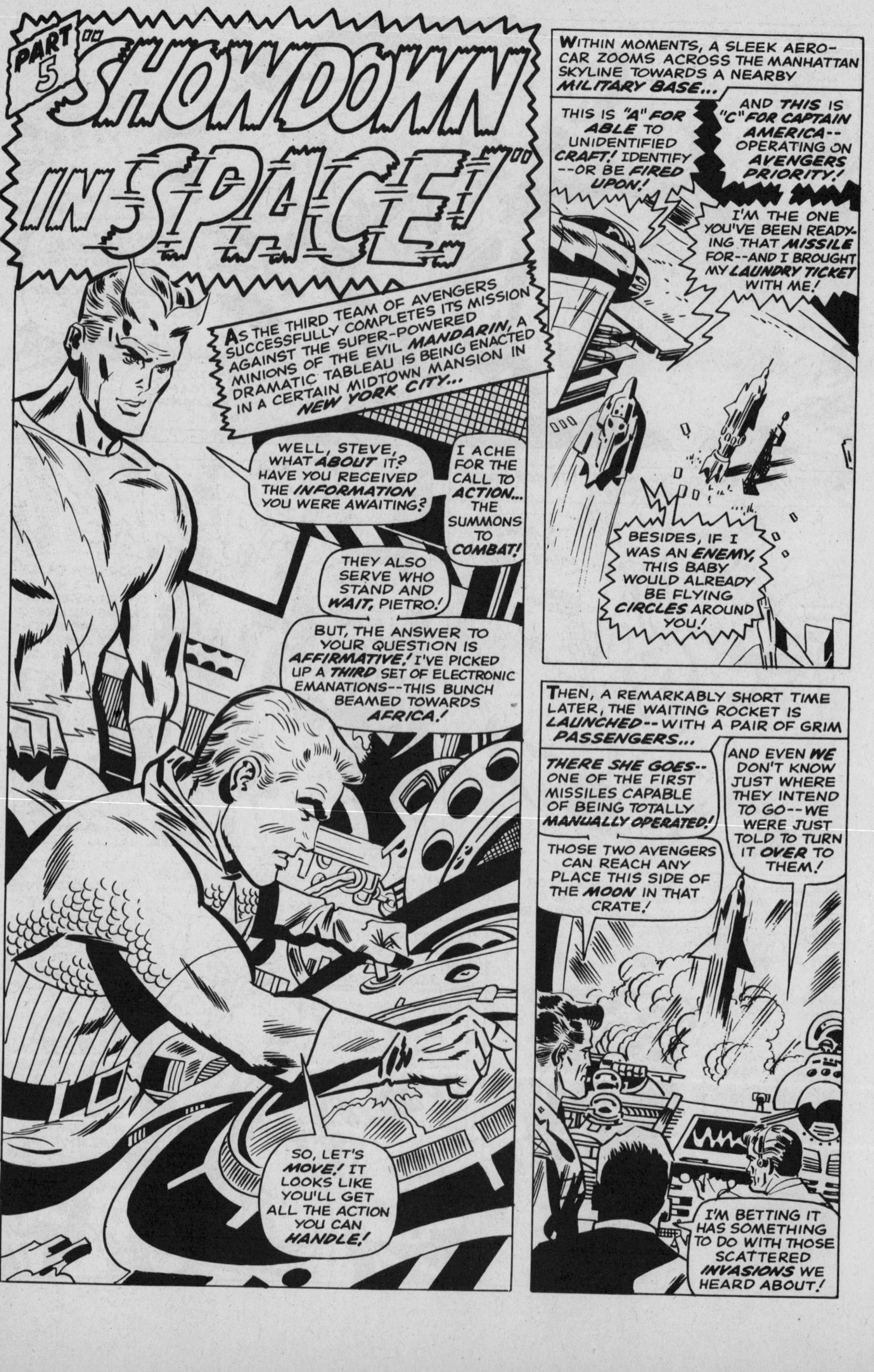
PART 5
"SHOWDOWN IN SPACE!"
AS THE THIRD TEAM OF AVENGERS SUCCESSFULLY COMPLETES ITS MISSION AGAINST THE SUPER-POWERED MINIONS OF THE EVIL MANDARIN, A DRAMATIC TABLEAU IS BEING ENACTED IN A CERTAIN MIDTOWN MANSION IN NEW YORK CITY...
WELL, STEVE, WHAT ABOUT IT? HAVE YOU RECEIVED THE INFORMATION YOU WERE AWAITING?
I ACHE FOR THE CALL TO ACTION... THE SUMMONS TO COMBAT!
THEY ALSO SERVE WHO STAND AND WAIT, PIETRO!
BUT, THE ANSWER TO YOUR QUESTION IS AFFIRMATIVE! I'VE PICKED UP A THIRD SET OF ELECTRONIC EMANATIONS--THIS BUNCH BEAMED TOWARDS AFRICA!
SO, LET'S MOVE! IT LOOKS LIKE YOU'LL GET ALL THE ACTION YOU CAN HANDLE!
WITHIN MOMENTS, A SLEEK AERO-CAR ZOOMS ACROSS THE MANHATTAN SKYLINE TOWARDS A NEARBY MILITARY BASE...
THIS IS "A" FOR ABLE TO UNIDENTIFIED CRAFT! IDENTIFY --OR BE FIRED UPON!
AND THIS IS "C" FOR CAPTAIN AMERICA-- OPERATING ON AVENGERS PRIORITY!
I'M THE ONE YOU'VE BEEN READYING THAT MISSILE FOR--AND I BROUGHT MY LAUNDRY TICKET WITH ME!
BESIDES, IF I WAS AN ENEMY, THIS BABY WOULD ALREADY BE FLYING CIRCLES AROUND YOU!
THEN, A REMARKABLY SHORT TIME LATER, THE WAITING ROCKET IS LAUNCHED-- WITH A PAIR OF GRIM PASSENGERS...
THERE SHE GOES-- ONE OF THE FIRST MISSILES CAPABLE OF BEING TOTALLY MANUALLY OPERATED!
AND EVEN WE DON'T KNOW JUST WHERE THEY INTEND TO GO--WE WERE JUST TOLD TO TURN IT OVER TO THEM!
THOSE TWO AVENGERS CAN REACH ANY PLACE THIS SIDE OF THE MOON IN THAT CRATE!
I'M BETTING IT HAS SOMETHING TO DO WITH THOSE SCATTERED INVASIONS WE HEARD ABOUT!

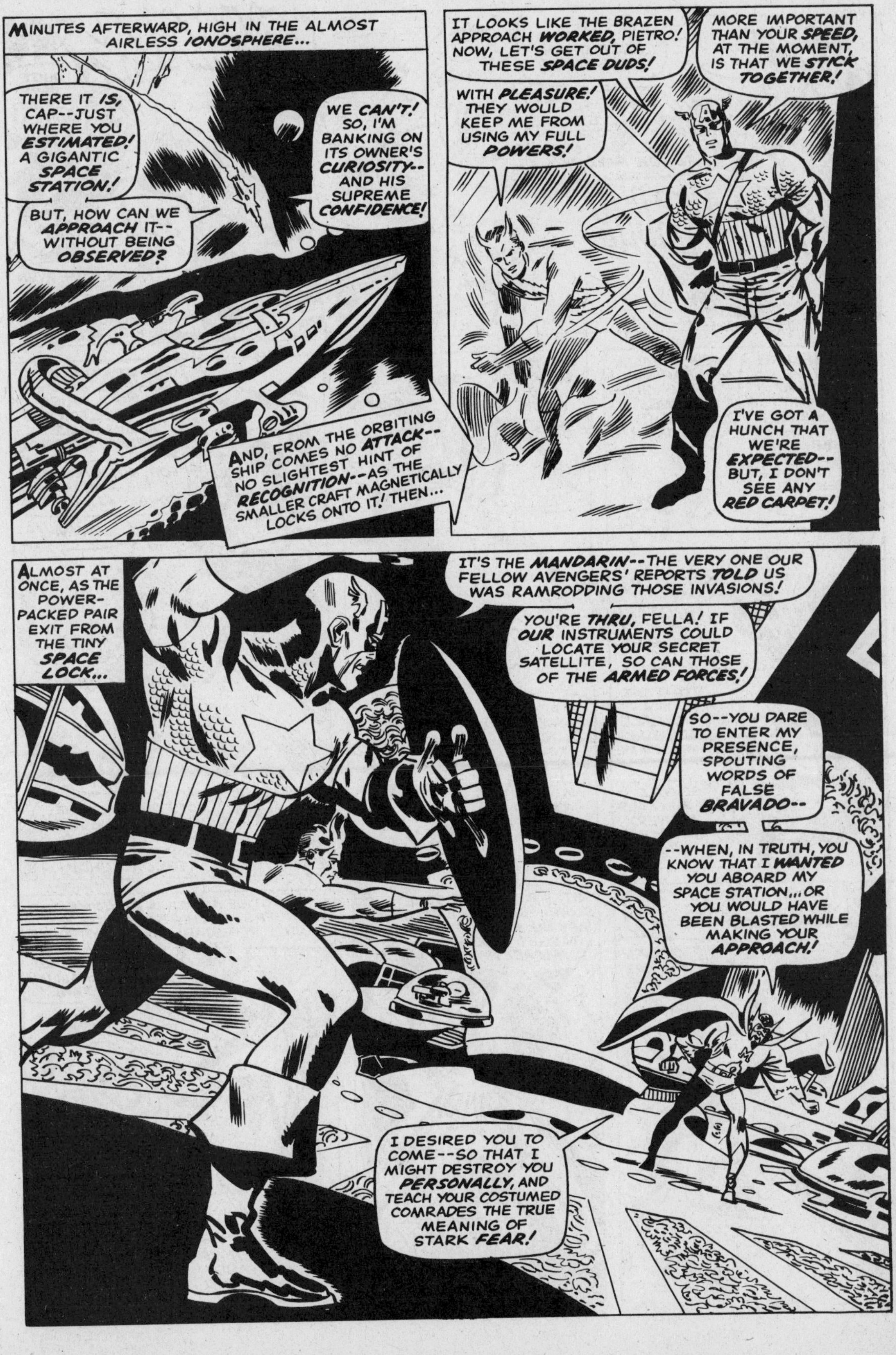
MINUTES AFTERWARD, HIGH IN THE ALMOST AIRLESS IONOSPHERE...
THERE IT IS, CAP--JUST WHERE YOU ESTIMATED! A GIGANTIC SPACE STATION!
BUT, HOW CAN WE APPROACH IT--WITHOUT BEING OBSERVED?
WE CAN'T! SO, I'M BANKING ON ITS OWNER'S CURIOSITY--AND HIS SUPREME CONFIDENCE!
AND, FROM THE ORBITING SHIP COMES NO ATTACK--NO SLIGHTEST HINT OF RECOGNITION--AS THE SMALLER CRAFT MAGNETICALLY LOCKS ONTO IT! THEN...
IT LOOKS LIKE THE BRAZEN APPROACH WORKED, PIETRO! NOW, LET'S GET OUT OF THESE SPACE DUDS!
WITH PLEASURE! THEY WOULD KEEP ME FROM USING MY FULL POWERS!
MORE IMPORTANT THAN YOUR SPEED, AT THE MOMENT, IS THAT WE STICK TOGETHER!
I'VE GOT A HUNCH THAT WE'RE EXPECTED--BUT, I DON'T SEE ANY RED CARPET!
ALMOST AT ONCE, AS THE POWER-PACKED PAIR EXIT FROM THE TINY SPACE LOCK...
IT'S THE MANDARIN--THE VERY ONE OUR FELLOW AVENGERS' REPORTS TOLD US WAS RAMRODDING THOSE INVASIONS!
YOU'RE THRU, FELLA! IF OUR INSTRUMENTS COULD LOCATE YOUR SECRET SATELLITE, SO CAN THOSE OF THE ARMED FORCES!
SO--YOU DARE TO ENTER MY PRESENCE, SPOUTING WORDS OF FALSE BRAVADO--
--WHEN, IN TRUTH, YOU KNOW THAT I WANTED YOU ABOARD MY SPACE STATION...OR YOU WOULD HAVE BEEN BLASTED WHILE MAKING YOUR APPROACH!
I DESIRED YOU TO COME--SO THAT I MIGHT DESTROY YOU PERSONALLY, AND TEACH YOUR COSTUMED COMRADES THE TRUE MEANING OF STARK FEAR!

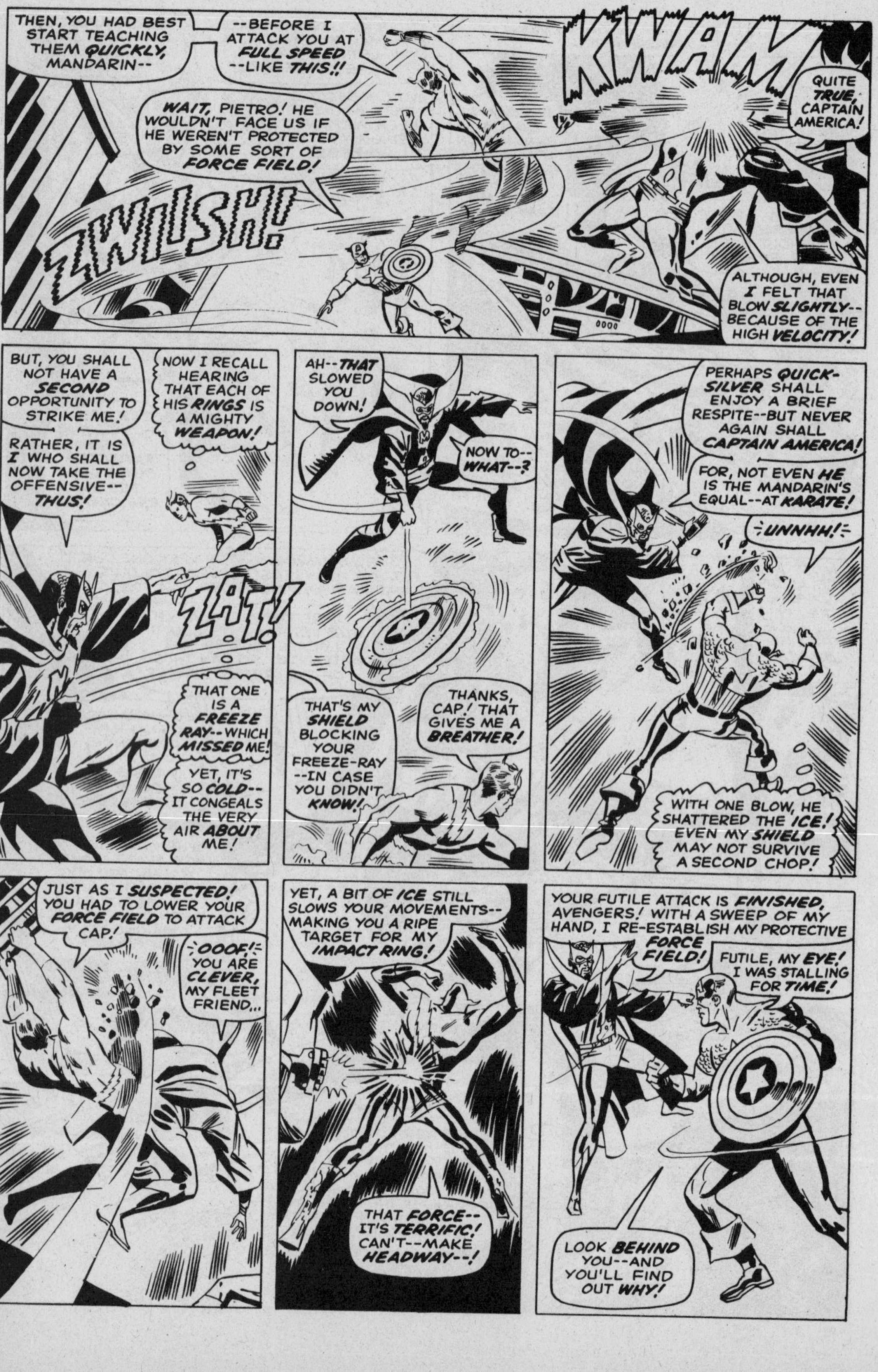
THEN, YOU HAD BEST START TEACHING THEM QUICKLY, MANDARIN--
--BEFORE I ATTACK YOU AT FULL SPEED --LIKE THIS!!
WAIT, PIETRO! HE WOULDN'T FACE US IF HE WEREN'T PROTECTED BY SOME SORT OF FORCE FIELD!
ZWISH!
KWAM
QUITE TRUE, CAPTAIN AMERICA!
ALTHOUGH, EVEN I FELT THAT BLOW SLIGHTLY--BECAUSE OF THE HIGH VELOCITY!
BUT, YOU SHALL NOT HAVE A SECOND OPPORTUNITY TO STRIKE ME!
NOW I RECALL HEARING THAT EACH OF HIS RINGS IS A MIGHTY WEAPON!
RATHER, IT IS I WHO SHALL NOW TAKE THE OFFENSIVE--THUS!
ZAT!
THAT ONE IS A FREEZE RAY--WHICH MISSED ME!
YET, IT'S SO COLD--IT CONGEALS THE VERY AIR ABOUT ME!
AH--THAT SLOWED YOU DOWN!
NOW TO--WHAT--?
THAT'S MY SHIELD BLOCKING YOUR FREEZE-RAY --IN CASE YOU DIDN'T KNOW!
THANKS, CAP! THAT GIVES ME A BREATHER!
PERHAPS QUICK-SILVER SHALL ENJOY A BRIEF RESPITE--BUT NEVER AGAIN SHALL CAPTAIN AMERICA!
FOR, NOT EVEN HE IS THE MANDARIN'S EQUAL--AT KARATE!
UNNHH!
WITH ONE BLOW, HE SHATTERED THE ICE! EVEN MY SHIELD MAY NOT SURVIVE A SECOND CHOP!
JUST AS I SUSPECTED! YOU HAD TO LOWER YOUR FORCE FIELD TO ATTACK CAP!
OOOF! YOU ARE CLEVER, MY FLEET FRIEND...
YET, A BIT OF ICE STILL SLOWS YOUR MOVEMENTS--MAKING YOU A RIPE TARGET FOR MY IMPACT RING!
THAT FORCE--IT'S TERRIFIC! CAN'T--MAKE HEADWAY--!
YOUR FUTILE ATTACK IS FINISHED, AVENGERS! WITH A SWEEP OF MY HAND, I RE-ESTABLISH MY PROTECTIVE FORCE FIELD!
FUTILE, MY EYE! I WAS STALLING FOR TIME!
LOOK BEHIND YOU--AND YOU'LL FIND OUT WHY!

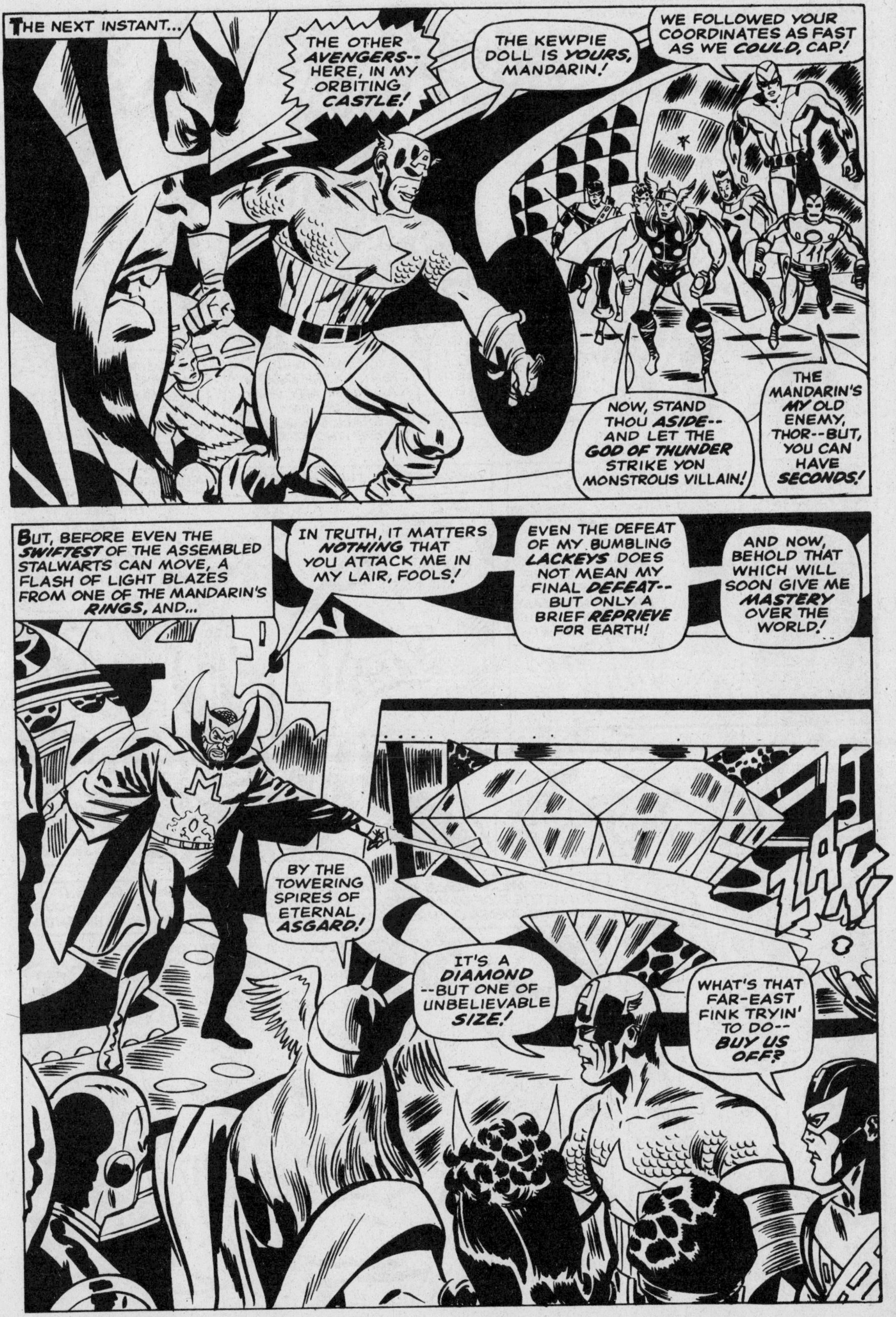
THE NEXT INSTANT...
THE OTHER AVENGERS-- HERE, IN MY ORBITING CASTLE!
THE KEWPIE DOLL IS YOURS, MANDARIN!
WE FOLLOWED YOUR COORDINATES AS FAST AS WE COULD, CAP!
NOW, STAND THOU ASIDE-- AND LET THE GOD OF THUNDER STRIKE YON MONSTROUS VILLAIN!
THE MANDARIN'S MY OLD ENEMY, THOR--BUT, YOU CAN HAVE SECONDS!
BUT, BEFORE EVEN THE SWIFTEST OF THE ASSEMBLED STALWARTS CAN MOVE, A FLASH OF LIGHT BLAZES FROM ONE OF THE MANDARIN'S RINGS, AND...
IN TRUTH, IT MATTERS NOTHING THAT YOU ATTACK ME IN MY LAIR, FOOLS!
EVEN THE DEFEAT OF MY BUMBLING LACKEYS DOES NOT MEAN MY FINAL DEFEAT-- BUT ONLY A BRIEF REPRIEVE FOR EARTH!
AND NOW, BEHOLD THAT WHICH WILL SOON GIVE ME MASTERY OVER THE WORLD!
ZZAK
BY THE TOWERING SPIRES OF ETERNAL ASGARD!
IT'S A DIAMOND --BUT ONE OF UNBELIEVABLE SIZE!
WHAT'S THAT FAR-EAST FINK TRYIN' TO DO-- BUY US OFF?

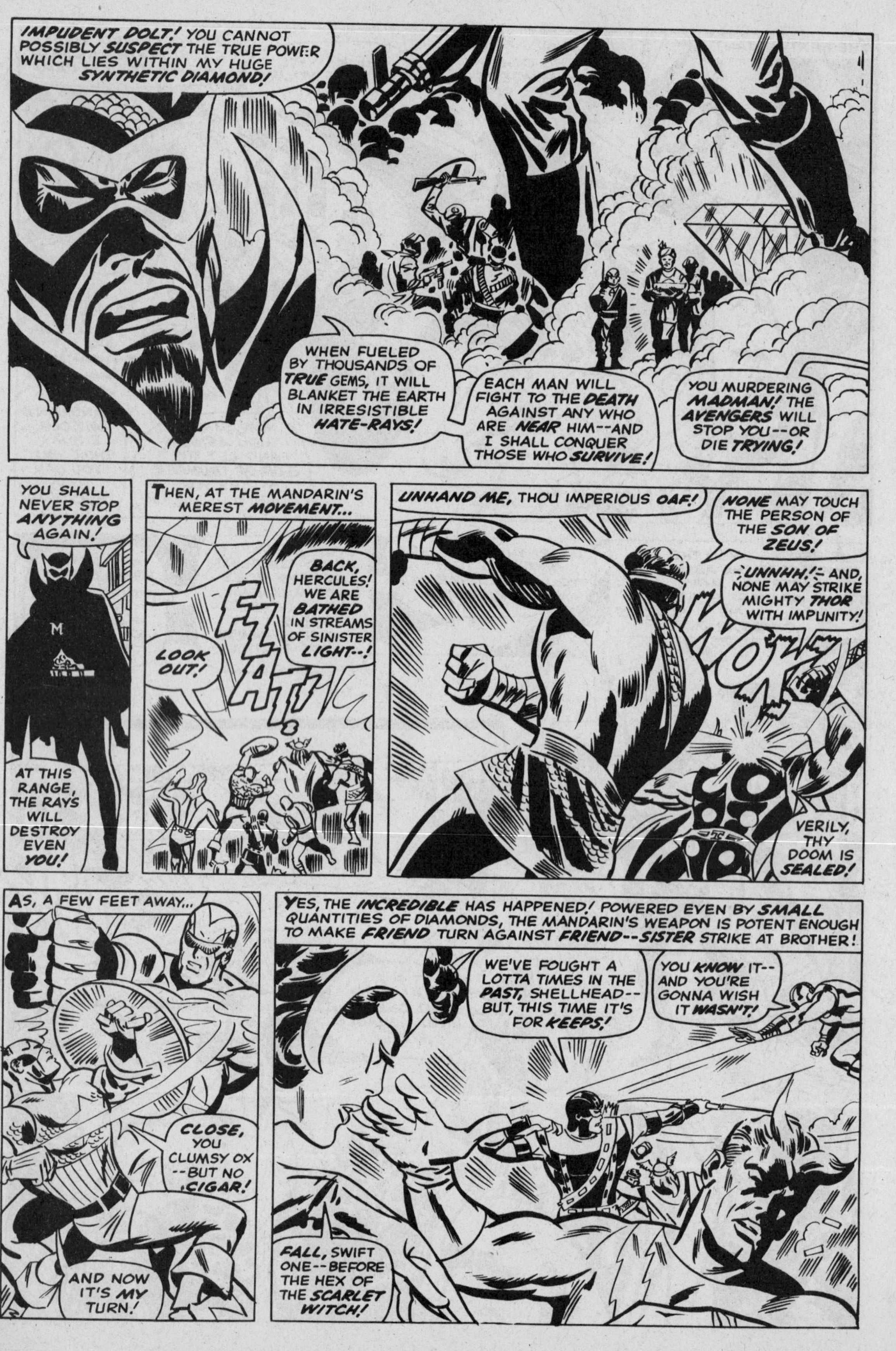

IMPUDENT DOLT! YOU CANNOT POSSIBLY SUSPECT THE TRUE POWER WHICH LIES WITHIN MY HUGE SYNTHETIC DIAMOND!
WHEN FUELED BY THOUSANDS OF TRUE GEMS, IT WILL BLANKET THE EARTH IN IRRESISTIBLE HATE-RAYS!
EACH MAN WILL FIGHT TO THE DEATH AGAINST ANY WHO ARE NEAR HIM--AND I SHALL CONQUER THOSE WHO SURVIVE!
YOU MURDERING MADMAN! THE AVENGERS WILL STOP YOU--OR DIE TRYING!
YOU SHALL NEVER STOP ANYTHING AGAIN!
AT THIS RANGE, THE RAYS WILL DESTROY EVEN YOU!
THEN, AT THE MANDARIN'S MEREST MOVEMENT...
BACK, HERCULES! WE ARE BATHED IN STREAMS OF SINISTER LIGHT--!
LOOK OUT!
FLAT!
UNHAND ME, THOU IMPERIOUS OAF!
NONE MAY TOUCH THE PERSON OF THE SON OF ZEUS!
-UNNHH!- AND, NONE MAY STRIKE MIGHTY THOR WITH IMPUNITY!
WOK
VERILY, THY DOOM IS SEALED!
AS, A FEW FEET AWAY...
CLOSE, YOU CLUMSY OX --BUT NO CIGAR!
AND NOW IT'S MY TURN!
YES, THE INCREDIBLE HAS HAPPENED! POWERED EVEN BY SMALL QUANTITIES OF DIAMONDS, THE MANDARIN'S WEAPON IS POTENT ENOUGH TO MAKE FRIEND TURN AGAINST FRIEND--SISTER STRIKE AT BROTHER!
WE'VE FOUGHT A LOTTA TIMES IN THE PAST, SHELLHEAD--BUT, THIS TIME IT'S FOR KEEPS!
YOU KNOW IT--AND YOU'RE GONNA WISH IT WASN'T!
FALL, SWIFT ONE--BEFORE THE HEX OF THE SCARLET WITCH!

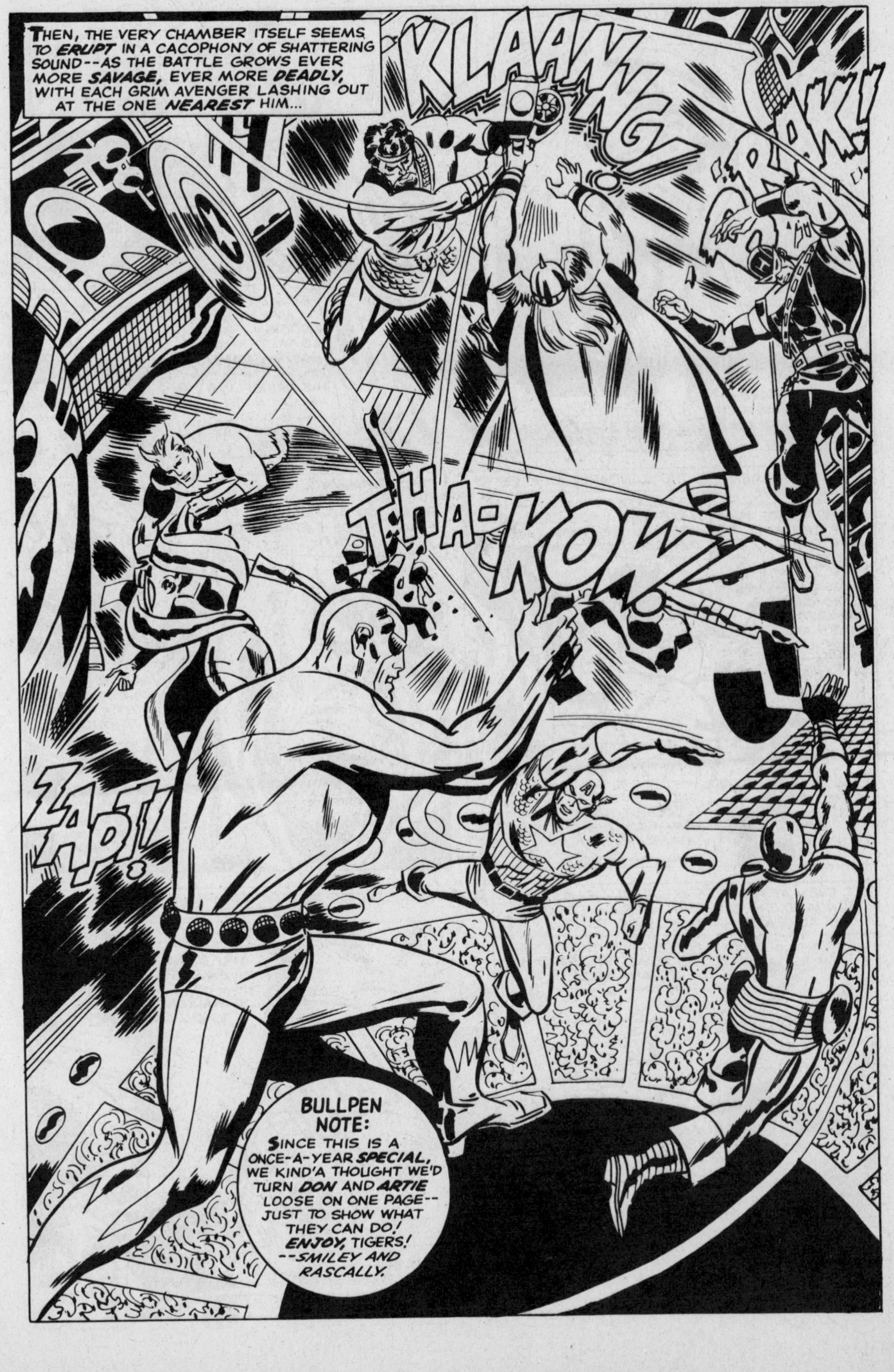
THEN, THE VERY CHAMBER ITSELF SEEMS TO ERUPT IN A CACOPHONY OF SHATTERING SOUND--AS THE BATTLE GROWS EVER MORE SAVAGE, EVER MORE DEADLY, WITH EACH GRIM AVENGER LASHING OUT AT THE ONE NEAREST HIM...
KLAANNG!
KRAK!
THA-KOW!
ZAPT!
BULLPEN NOTE:
SINCE THIS IS A ONCE-A-YEAR SPECIAL, WE KIND'A THOUGHT WE'D TURN DON AND ARTIE LOOSE ON ONE PAGE-- JUST TO SHOW WHAT THEY CAN DO! ENJOY, TIGERS! --SMILEY AND RASCALLY.

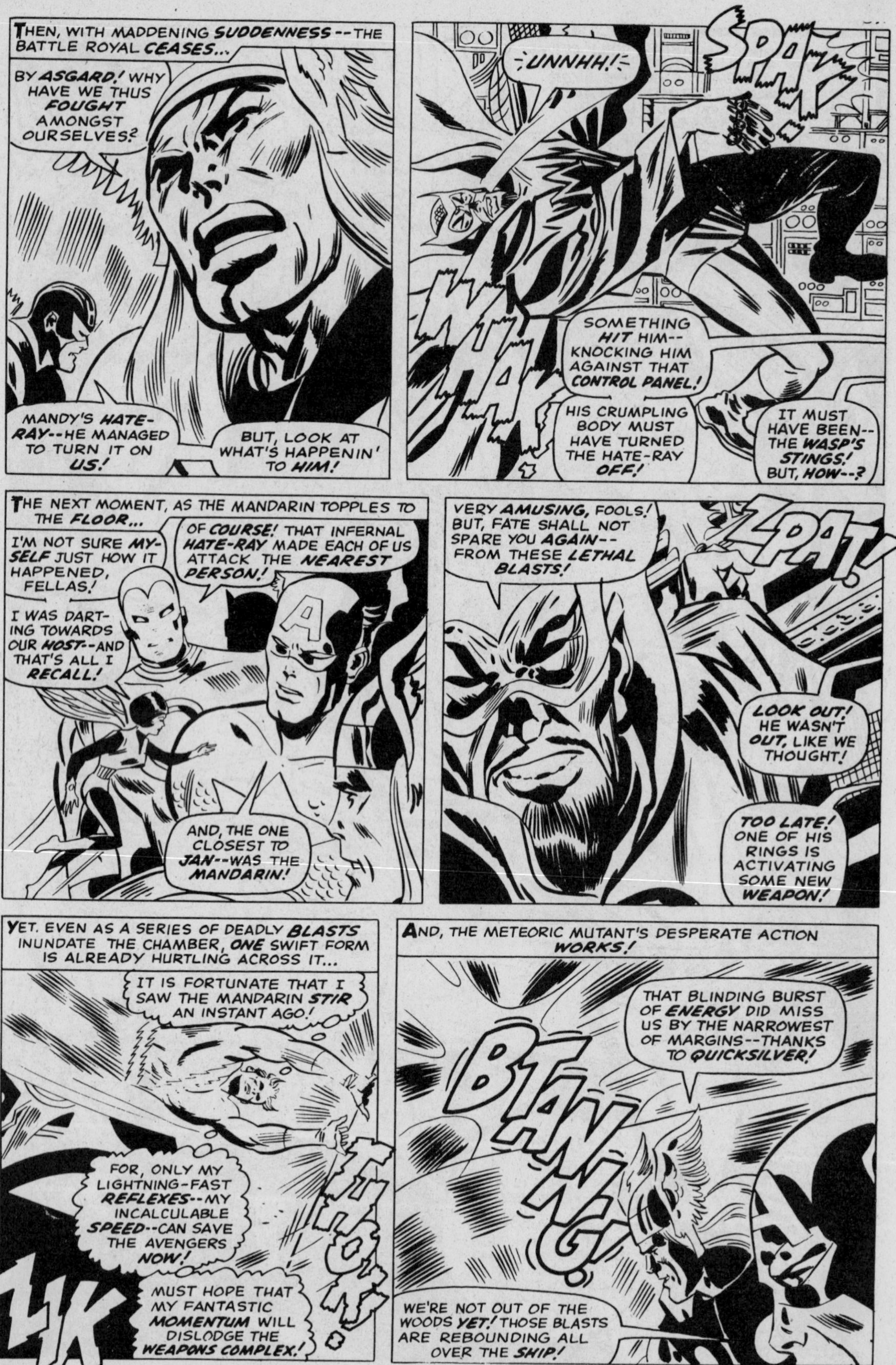
THEN, WITH MADDENING SUDDENNESS--THE BATTLE ROYAL CEASES...
BY ASGARD! WHY HAVE WE THUS FOUGHT AMONGST OURSELVES?
MANDY'S HATE-RAY--HE MANAGED TO TURN IT ON US!
BUT, LOOK AT WHAT'S HAPPENIN' TO HIM!
UNNHH!
SPAK
WHAK
SOMETHING HIT HIM--KNOCKING HIM AGAINST THAT CONTROL PANEL!
HIS CRUMPLING BODY MUST HAVE TURNED THE HATE-RAY OFF!
IT MUST HAVE BEEN--THE WASP'S STINGS! BUT, HOW--?
THE NEXT MOMENT, AS THE MANDARIN TOPPLES TO THE FLOOR...
I'M NOT SURE MYSELF JUST HOW IT HAPPENED, FELLAS!
OF COURSE! THAT INFERNAL HATE-RAY MADE EACH OF US ATTACK THE NEAREST PERSON!
I WAS DARTING TOWARDS OUR HOST--AND THAT'S ALL I RECALL!
AND, THE ONE CLOSEST TO JAN--WAS THE MANDARIN!
VERY AMUSING, FOOLS! BUT, FATE SHALL NOT SPARE YOU AGAIN--FROM THESE LETHAL BLASTS!
ZPAT!
LOOK OUT! HE WASN'T OUT, LIKE WE THOUGHT!
TOO LATE! ONE OF HIS RINGS IS ACTIVATING SOME NEW WEAPON!
YET, EVEN AS A SERIES OF DEADLY BLASTS INUNDATE THE CHAMBER, ONE SWIFT FORM IS ALREADY HURTLING ACROSS IT...
IT IS FORTUNATE THAT I SAW THE MANDARIN STIR AN INSTANT AGO!
FOR, ONLY MY LIGHTNING-FAST REFLEXES--MY INCALCULABLE SPEED--CAN SAVE THE AVENGERS NOW!
MUST HOPE THAT MY FANTASTIC MOMENTUM WILL DISLODGE THE WEAPONS COMPLEX!
ZIK
THOOK!
AND, THE METEORIC MUTANT'S DESPERATE ACTION WORKS!
THAT BLINDING BURST OF ENERGY DID MISS US BY THE NARROWEST OF MARGINS--THANKS TO QUICKSILVER!
BTANNG!
WE'RE NOT OUT OF THE WOODS YET! THOSE BLASTS ARE REBOUNDING ALL OVER THE SHIP!

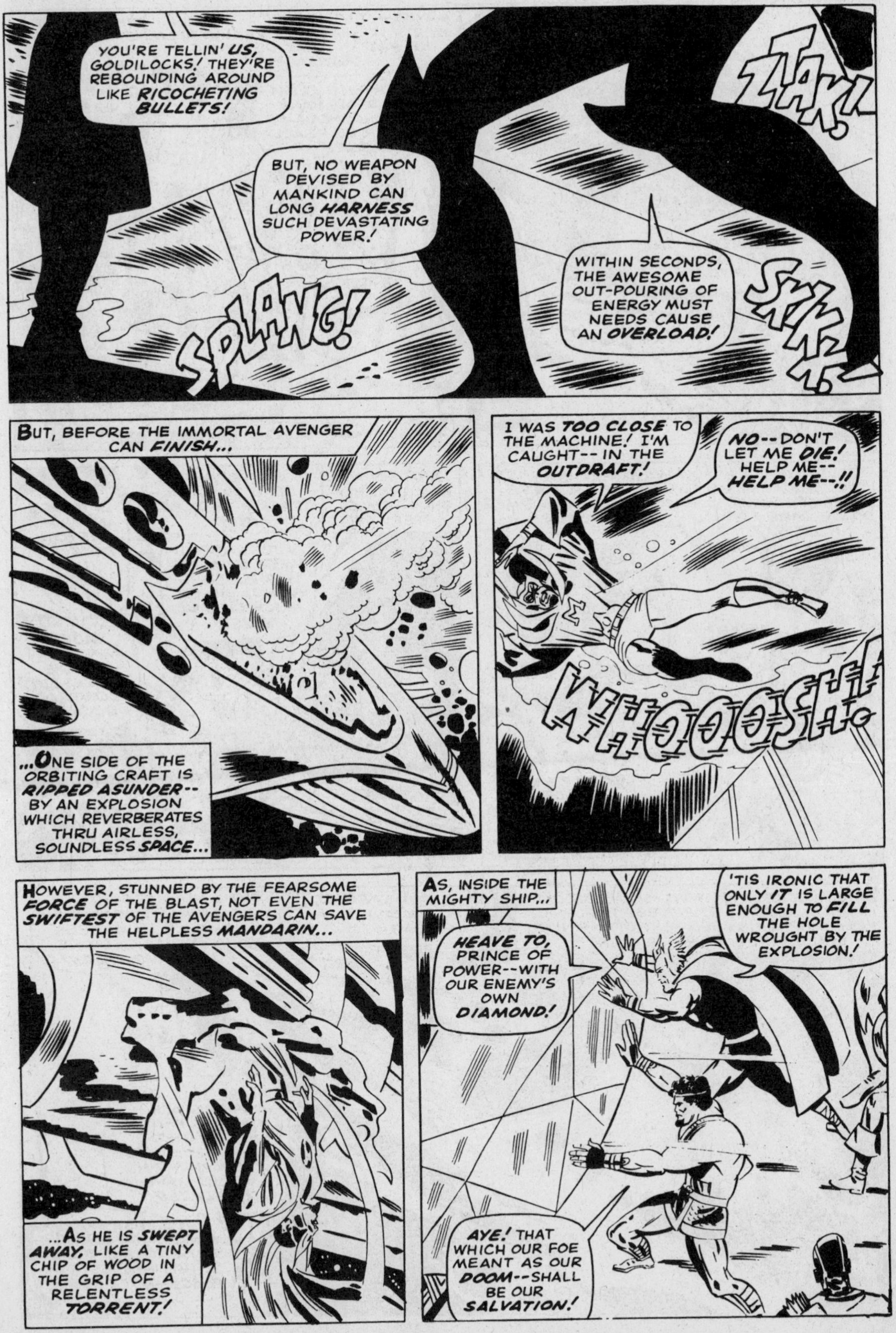
YOU'RE TELLIN' US, GOLDILOCKS! THEY'RE REBOUNDING AROUND LIKE RICOCHETING BULLETS!
ZZAK!
BUT, NO WEAPON DEVISED BY MANKIND CAN LONG HARNESS SUCH DEVASTATING POWER!
WITHIN SECONDS, THE AWESOME OUT-POURING OF ENERGY MUST NEEDS CAUSE AN OVERLOAD!
SPLANG!
SKKK!
BUT, BEFORE THE IMMORTAL AVENGER CAN FINISH...
...ONE SIDE OF THE ORBITING CRAFT IS RIPPED ASUNDER-- BY AN EXPLOSION WHICH REVERBERATES THRU AIRLESS, SOUNDLESS SPACE...
I WAS TOO CLOSE TO THE MACHINE! I'M CAUGHT-- IN THE OUTDRAFT!
NO--DON'T LET ME DIE! HELP ME-- HELP ME--!!
WHOOOSH!
HOWEVER, STUNNED BY THE FEARSOME FORCE OF THE BLAST, NOT EVEN THE SWIFTEST OF THE AVENGERS CAN SAVE THE HELPLESS MANDARIN...
...AS HE IS SWEPT AWAY, LIKE A TINY CHIP OF WOOD IN THE GRIP OF A RELENTLESS TORRENT!
AS, INSIDE THE MIGHTY SHIP...
HEAVE TO, PRINCE OF POWER--WITH OUR ENEMY'S OWN DIAMOND!
'TIS IRONIC THAT ONLY IT IS LARGE ENOUGH TO FILL THE HOLE WROUGHT BY THE EXPLOSION!
AYE! THAT WHICH OUR FOE MEANT AS OUR DOOM--SHALL BE OUR SALVATION!

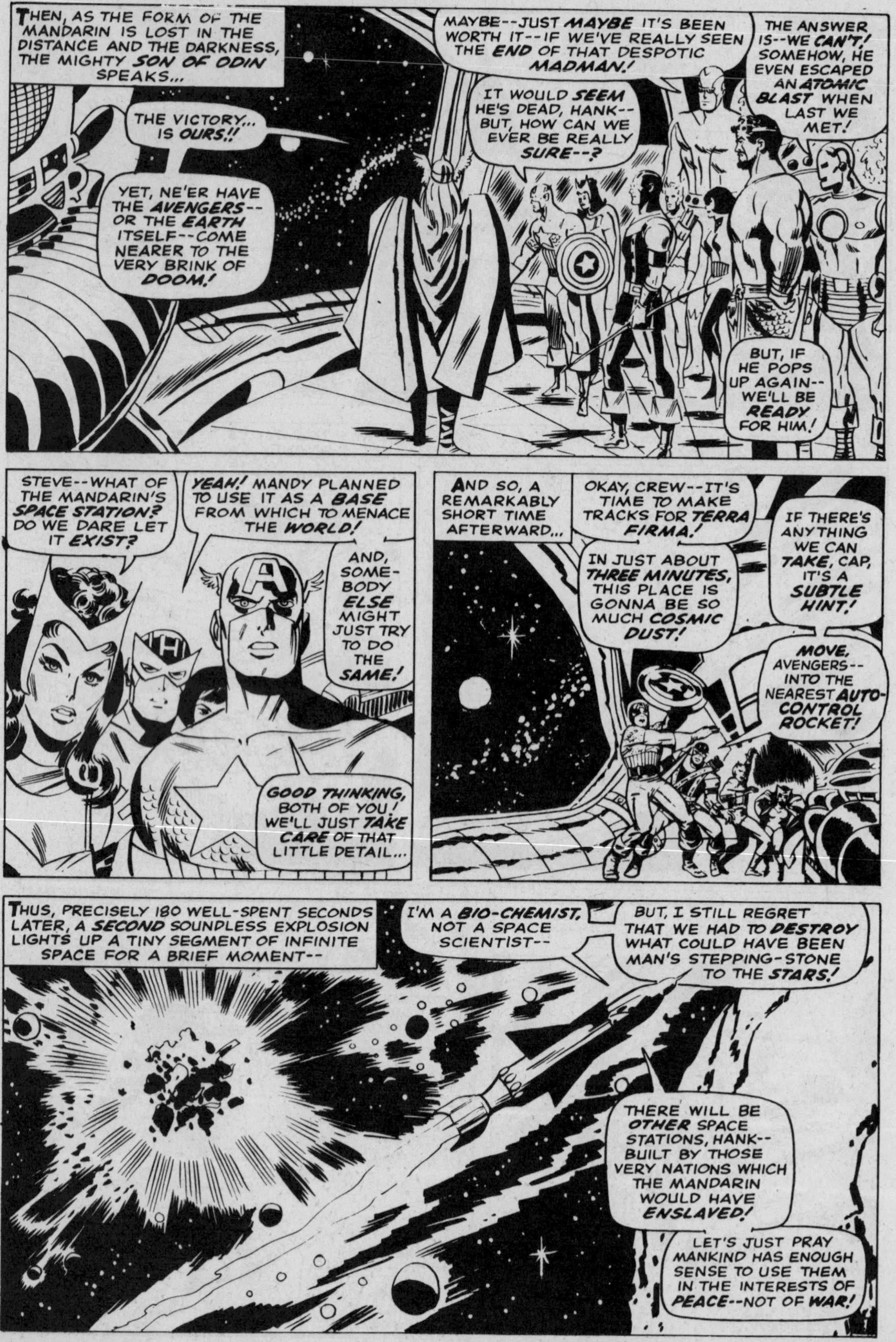
THEN, AS THE FORM OF THE MANDARIN IS LOST IN THE DISTANCE AND THE DARKNESS, THE MIGHTY SON OF ODIN SPEAKS...
THE VICTORY... IS OURS!!
YET, NE'ER HAVE THE AVENGERS--OR THE EARTH ITSELF--COME NEARER TO THE VERY BRINK OF DOOM!
MAYBE--JUST MAYBE IT'S BEEN WORTH IT--IF WE'VE REALLY SEEN THE END OF THAT DESPOTIC MADMAN!
IT WOULD SEEM HE'S DEAD, HANK--BUT, HOW CAN WE EVER BE REALLY SURE--?
THE ANSWER IS--WE CAN'T! SOMEHOW, HE EVEN ESCAPED AN ATOMIC BLAST WHEN LAST WE MET!
BUT, IF HE POPS UP AGAIN--WE'LL BE READY FOR HIM!
STEVE--WHAT OF THE MANDARIN'S SPACE STATION? DO WE DARE LET IT EXIST?
YEAH! MANDY PLANNED TO USE IT AS A BASE FROM WHICH TO MENACE THE WORLD!
AND, SOMEBODY ELSE MIGHT JUST TRY TO DO THE SAME!
GOOD THINKING, BOTH OF YOU! WE'LL JUST TAKE CARE OF THAT LITTLE DETAIL...
AND SO, A REMARKABLY SHORT TIME AFTERWARD...
OKAY, CREW--IT'S TIME TO MAKE TRACKS FOR TERRA FIRMA!
IN JUST ABOUT THREE MINUTES, THIS PLACE IS GONNA BE SO MUCH COSMIC DUST!
IF THERE'S ANYTHING WE CAN TAKE, CAP, IT'S A SUBTLE HINT!
MOVE, AVENGERS--INTO THE NEAREST AUTO-CONTROL ROCKET!
THUS, PRECISELY 180 WELL-SPENT SECONDS LATER, A SECOND SOUNDLESS EXPLOSION LIGHTS UP A TINY SEGMENT OF INFINITE SPACE FOR A BRIEF MOMENT--
I'M A BIO-CHEMIST, NOT A SPACE SCIENTIST--
BUT, I STILL REGRET THAT WE HAD TO DESTROY WHAT COULD HAVE BEEN MAN'S STEPPING-STONE TO THE STARS!
THERE WILL BE OTHER SPACE STATIONS, HANK--BUILT BY THOSE VERY NATIONS WHICH THE MANDARIN WOULD HAVE ENSLAVED!
LET'S JUST PRAY MANKIND HAS ENOUGH SENSE TO USE THEM IN THE INTERESTS OF PEACE--NOT OF WAR!

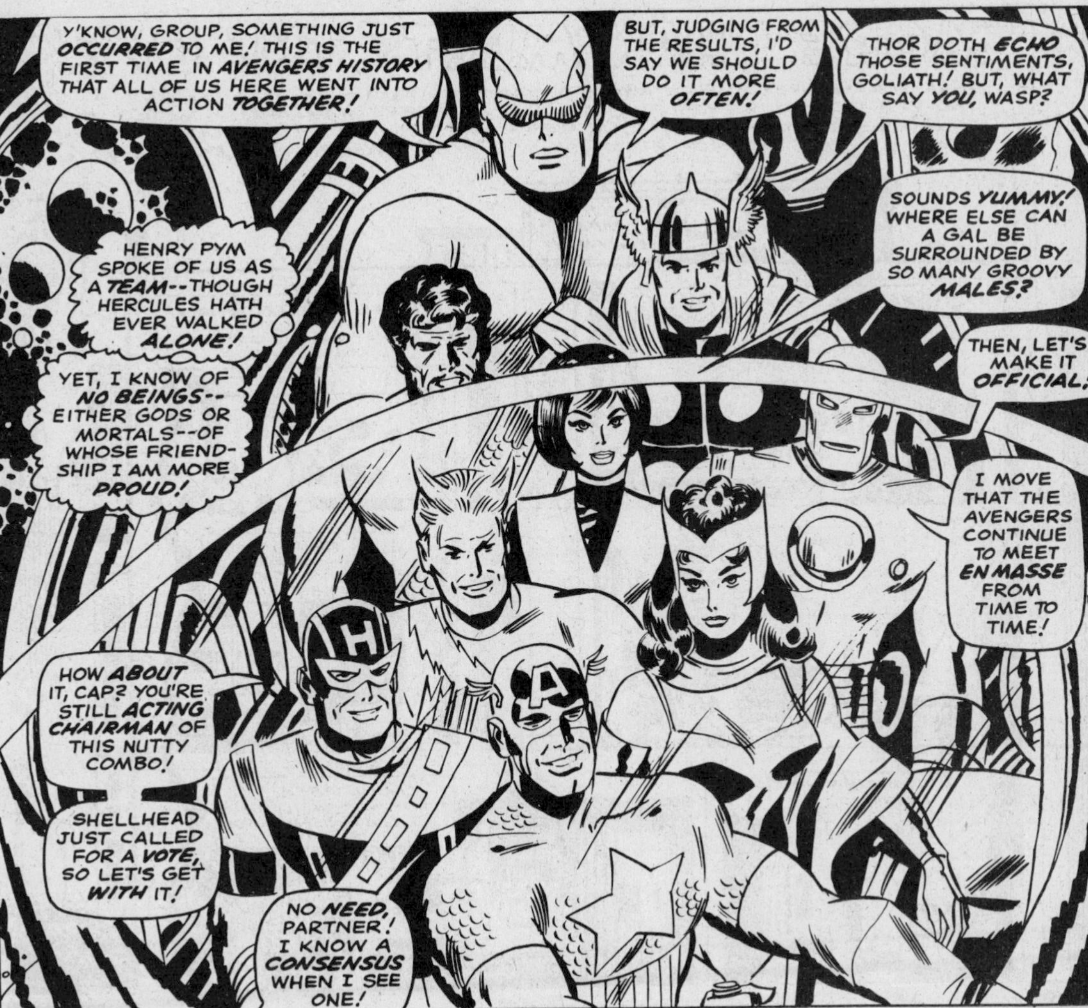
Y'KNOW, GROUP, SOMETHING JUST OCCURRED TO ME! THIS IS THE FIRST TIME IN AVENGERS HISTORY THAT ALL OF US HERE WENT INTO ACTION TOGETHER!
BUT, JUDGING FROM THE RESULTS, I'D SAY WE SHOULD DO IT MORE OFTEN!
THOR DOTH ECHO THOSE SENTIMENTS, GOLIATH! BUT, WHAT SAY YOU, WASP?
SOUNDS YUMMY! WHERE ELSE CAN A GAL BE SURROUNDED BY SO MANY GROOVY MALES?
HENRY PYM SPOKE OF US AS A TEAM--THOUGH HERCULES HATH EVER WALKED ALONE!
YET, I KNOW OF NO BEINGS--EITHER GODS OR MORTALS--OF WHOSE FRIENDSHIP I AM MORE PROUD!
THEN, LET'S MAKE IT OFFICIAL!
I MOVE THAT THE AVENGERS CONTINUE TO MEET EN MASSE FROM TIME TO TIME!
HOW ABOUT IT, CAP? YOU'RE STILL ACTING CHAIRMAN OF THIS NUTTY COMBO!
SHELLHEAD JUST CALLED FOR A VOTE, SO LET'S GET WITH IT!
NO NEED, PARTNER! I KNOW A CONSENSUS WHEN I SEE ONE!

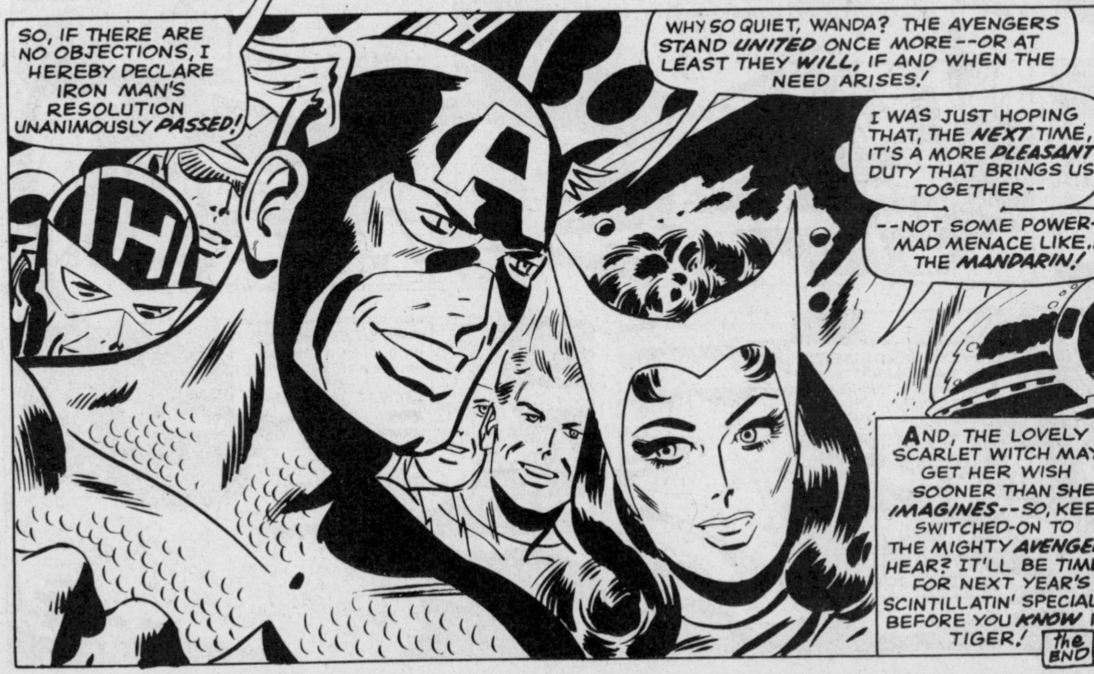
SO, IF THERE ARE NO OBJECTIONS, I HEREBY DECLARE IRON MAN'S RESOLUTION UNANIMOUSLY PASSED!
WHY SO QUIET, WANDA? THE AVENGERS STAND UNITED ONCE MORE--OR AT LEAST THEY WILL, IF AND WHEN THE NEED ARISES!
I WAS JUST HOPING THAT, THE NEXT TIME, IT'S A MORE PLEASANT DUTY THAT BRINGS US TOGETHER--
--NOT SOME POWER-MAD MENACE LIKE... THE MANDARIN!
AND, THE LOVELY SCARLET WITCH MAY GET HER WISH SOONER THAN SHE IMAGINES--SO, KEEP SWITCHED-ON TO THE MIGHTY AVENGERS, HEAR? IT'LL BE TIME FOR NEXT YEAR'S SCINTILLATIN' SPECIALS BEFORE YOU KNOW IT, TIGER!
THE END

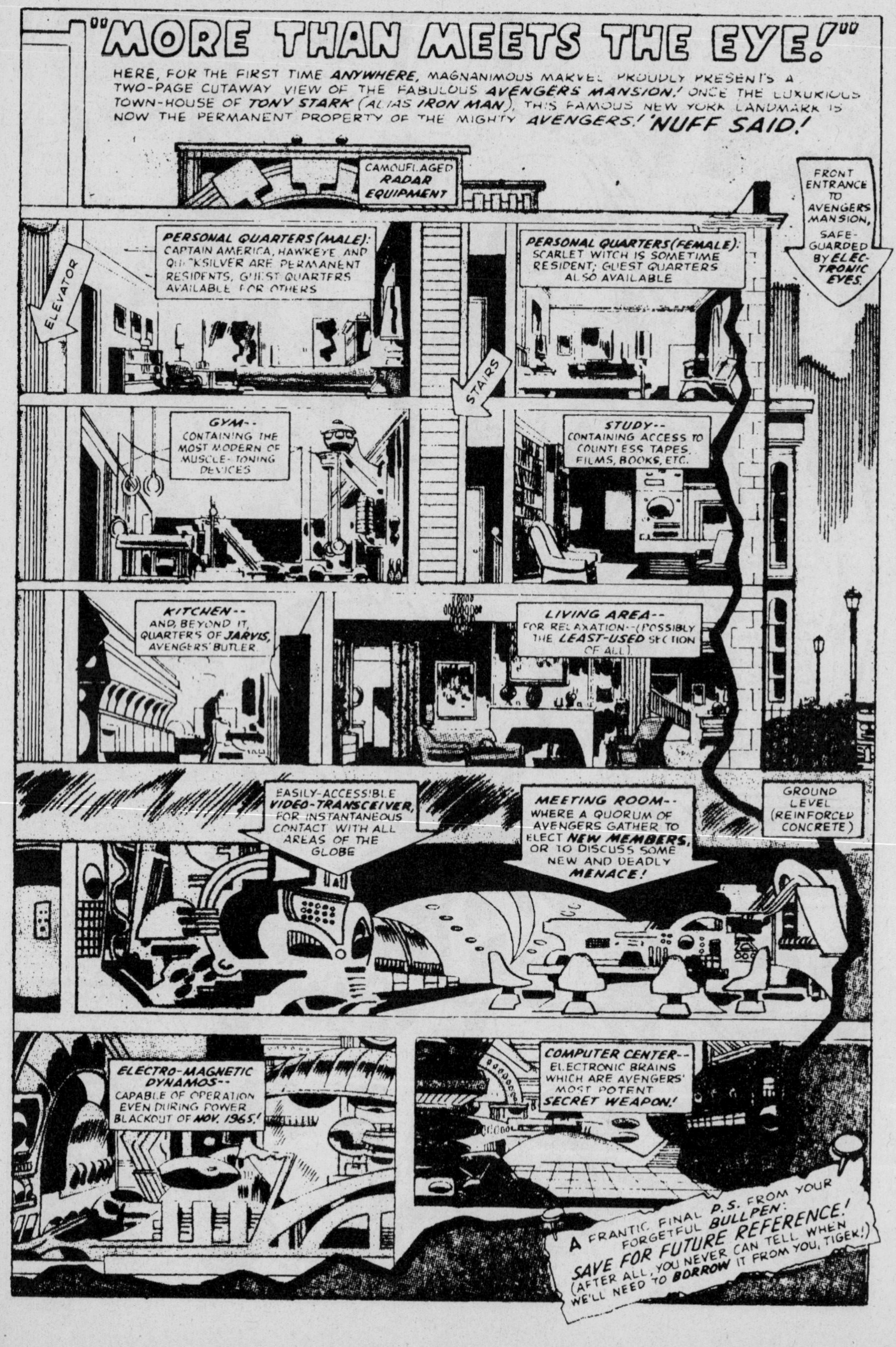
"MORE THAN MEETS THE EYE!"
HERE, FOR THE FIRST TIME ANYWHERE, MAGNANIMOUS MARVEL PROUDLY PRESENTS A TWO-PAGE CUTAWAY VIEW OF THE FABULOUS AVENGERS MANSION! ONCE THE LUXURIOUS TOWN-HOUSE OF TONY STARK (ALIAS IRON MAN), THIS FAMOUS NEW YORK LANDMARK IS NOW THE PERMANENT PROPERTY OF THE MIGHTY AVENGERS! 'NUFF SAID!
CAMOUFLAGED RADAR EQUIPMENT
FRONT ENTRANCE TO AVENGERS MANSION, SAFE-GUARDED BY ELECTRONIC EYES.
PERSONAL QUARTERS (MALE): CAPTAIN AMERICA, HAWKEYE, AND QUICKSILVER ARE PERMANENT RESIDENTS, GUEST QUARTERS AVAILABLE FOR OTHERS
PERSONAL QUARTERS (FEMALE): SCARLET WITCH IS SOMETIME RESIDENT; GUEST QUARTERS ALSO AVAILABLE
ELEVATOR
STAIRS
GYM-- CONTAINING THE MOST MODERN OF MUSCLE-TONING DEVICES
STUDY-- CONTAINING ACCESS TO COUNTLESS TAPES, FILMS, BOOKS, ETC.
KITCHEN-- AND, BEYOND IT, QUARTERS OF JARVIS, AVENGERS' BUTLER
LIVING AREA-- FOR RELAXATION--(POSSIBLY THE LEAST-USED SECTION OF ALL).
EASILY-ACCESSIBLE VIDEO-TRANSCEIVER, FOR INSTANTANEOUS CONTACT WITH ALL AREAS OF THE GLOBE
MEETING ROOM-- WHERE A QUORUM OF AVENGERS GATHER TO ELECT NEW MEMBERS, OR TO DISCUSS SOME NEW AND DEADLY MENACE!
GROUND LEVEL (REINFORCED CONCRETE)
ELECTRO-MAGNETIC DYNAMOS-- CAPABLE OF OPERATION EVEN DURING POWER BLACKOUT OF NOV. 1965!
COMPUTER CENTER-- ELECTRONIC BRAINS WHICH ARE AVENGERS' MOST POTENT SECRET WEAPON!
A FRANTIC FINAL P.S. FROM YOUR FORGETFUL BULLPEN: SAVE FOR FUTURE REFERENCE! (AFTER ALL, YOU NEVER CAN TELL WHEN WE'LL NEED TO BORROW IT FROM YOU, TIGER!)

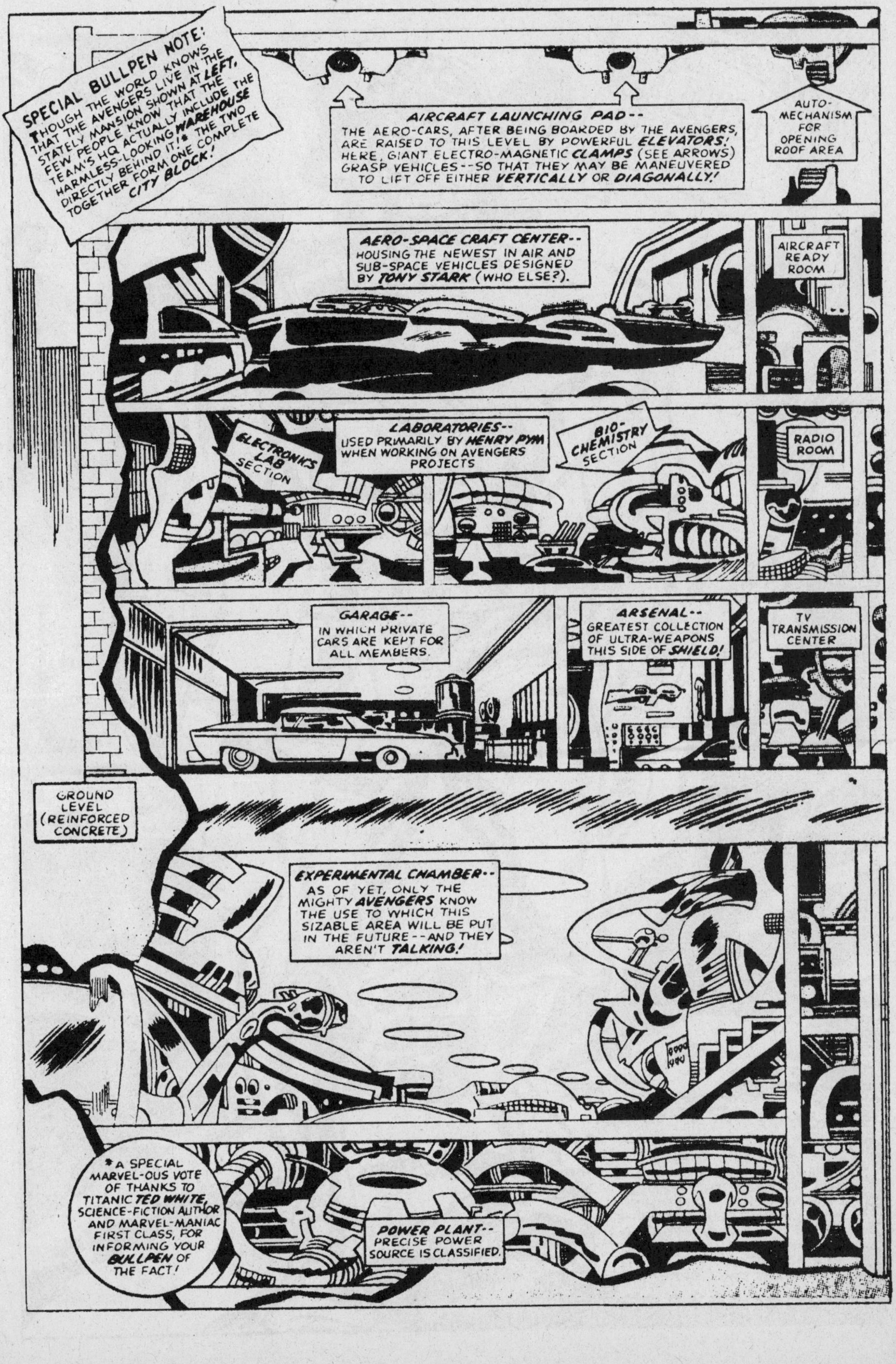
SPECIAL BULLPEN NOTE: THOUGH THE WORLD KNOWS THAT THE AVENGERS LIVE IN THE STATELY MANSION SHOWN AT LEFT, FEW PEOPLE KNOW THAT THE TEAM'S HQ ACTUALLY INCLUDE THE HARMLESS-LOOKING WAREHOUSE DIRECTLY BEHIND IT!* THE TWO TOGETHER FORM ONE COMPLETE CITY BLOCK!
AIRCRAFT LAUNCHING PAD-- THE AERO-CARS, AFTER BEING BOARDED BY THE AVENGERS, ARE RAISED TO THIS LEVEL BY POWERFUL ELEVATORS! HERE, GIANT ELECTRO-MAGNETIC CLAMPS (SEE ARROWS) GRASP VEHICLES--SO THAT THEY MAY BE MANEUVERED TO LIFT OFF EITHER VERTICALLY OR DIAGONALLY!
AUTO-MECHANISM FOR OPENING ROOF AREA
AERO-SPACE CRAFT CENTER-- HOUSING THE NEWEST IN AIR AND SUB-SPACE VEHICLES DESIGNED BY TONY STARK (WHO ELSE?).
AIRCRAFT READY ROOM
ELECTRONICS LAB SECTION
LABORATORIES-- USED PRIMARILY BY HENRY PYM WHEN WORKING ON AVENGERS PROJECTS
BIO-CHEMISTRY SECTION
RADIO ROOM
GARAGE-- IN WHICH PRIVATE CARS ARE KEPT FOR ALL MEMBERS.
ARSENAL-- GREATEST COLLECTION OF ULTRA-WEAPONS THIS SIDE OF SHIELD!
TV TRANSMISSION CENTER
GROUND LEVEL (REINFORCED CONCRETE)
EXPERIMENTAL CHAMBER-- AS OF YET, ONLY THE MIGHTY AVENGERS KNOW THE USE TO WHICH THIS SIZABLE AREA WILL BE PUT IN THE FUTURE--AND THEY AREN'T TALKING!
*A SPECIAL MARVEL-OUS VOTE OF THANKS TO TITANIC TED WHITE, SCIENCE-FICTION AUTHOR AND MARVEL-MANIAC FIRST CLASS, FOR INFORMING YOUR BULLPEN OF THE FACT!
POWER PLANT-- PRECISE POWER SOURCE IS CLASSIFIED.

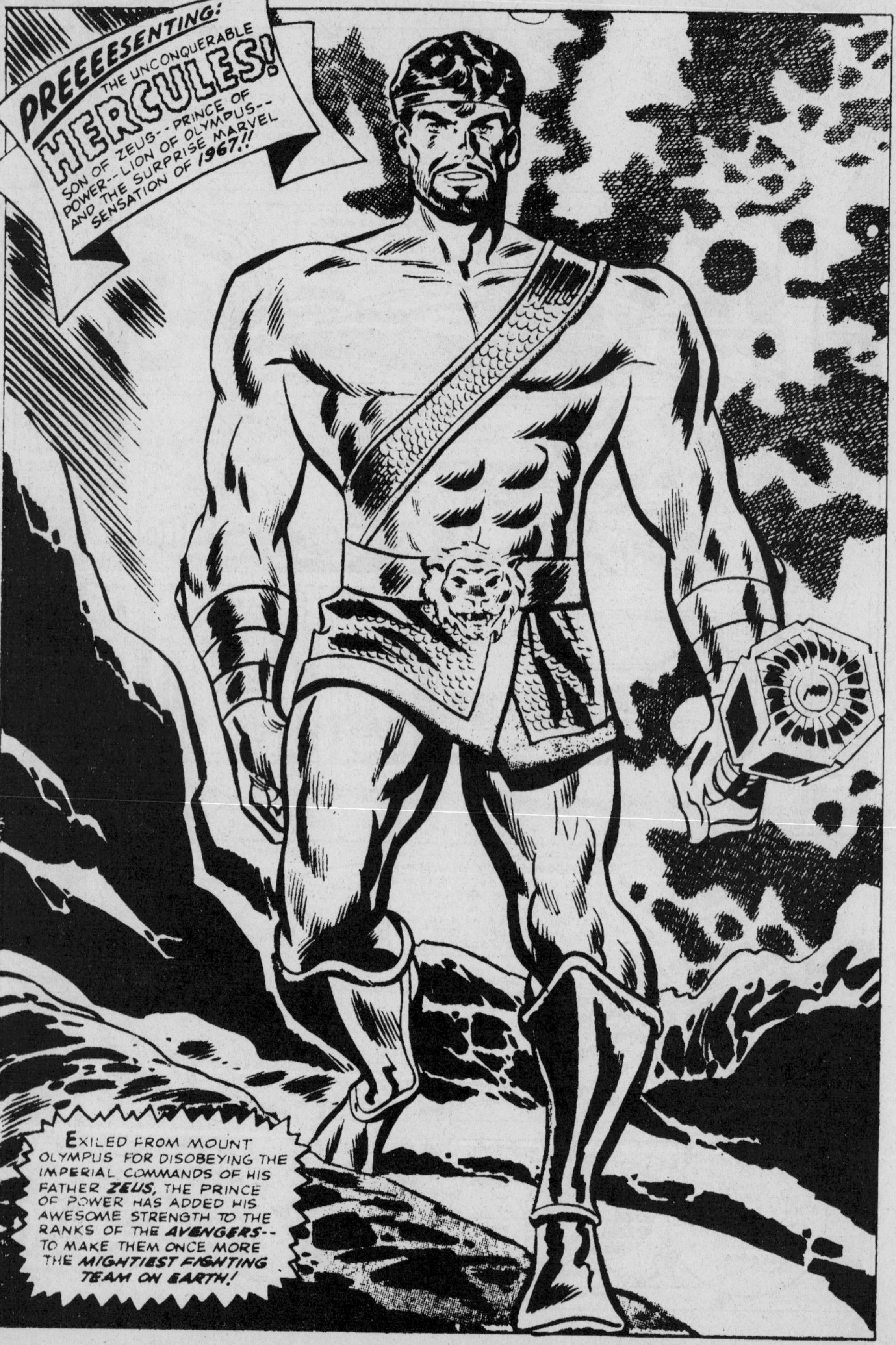
PREEEEESENTING:
THE UNCONQUERABLE
HERCULES!
SON OF ZEUS-- PRINCE OF POWER-- LION OF OLYMPUS-- AND THE SURPRISE MARVEL SENSATION OF 1967!!
EXILED FROM MOUNT OLYMPUS FOR DISOBEYING THE IMPERIAL COMMANDS OF HIS FATHER ZEUS, THE PRINCE OF POWER HAS ADDED HIS AWESOME STRENGTH TO THE RANKS OF THE AVENGERS-- TO MAKE THEM ONCE MORE THE MIGHTIEST FIGHTING TEAM ON EARTH!

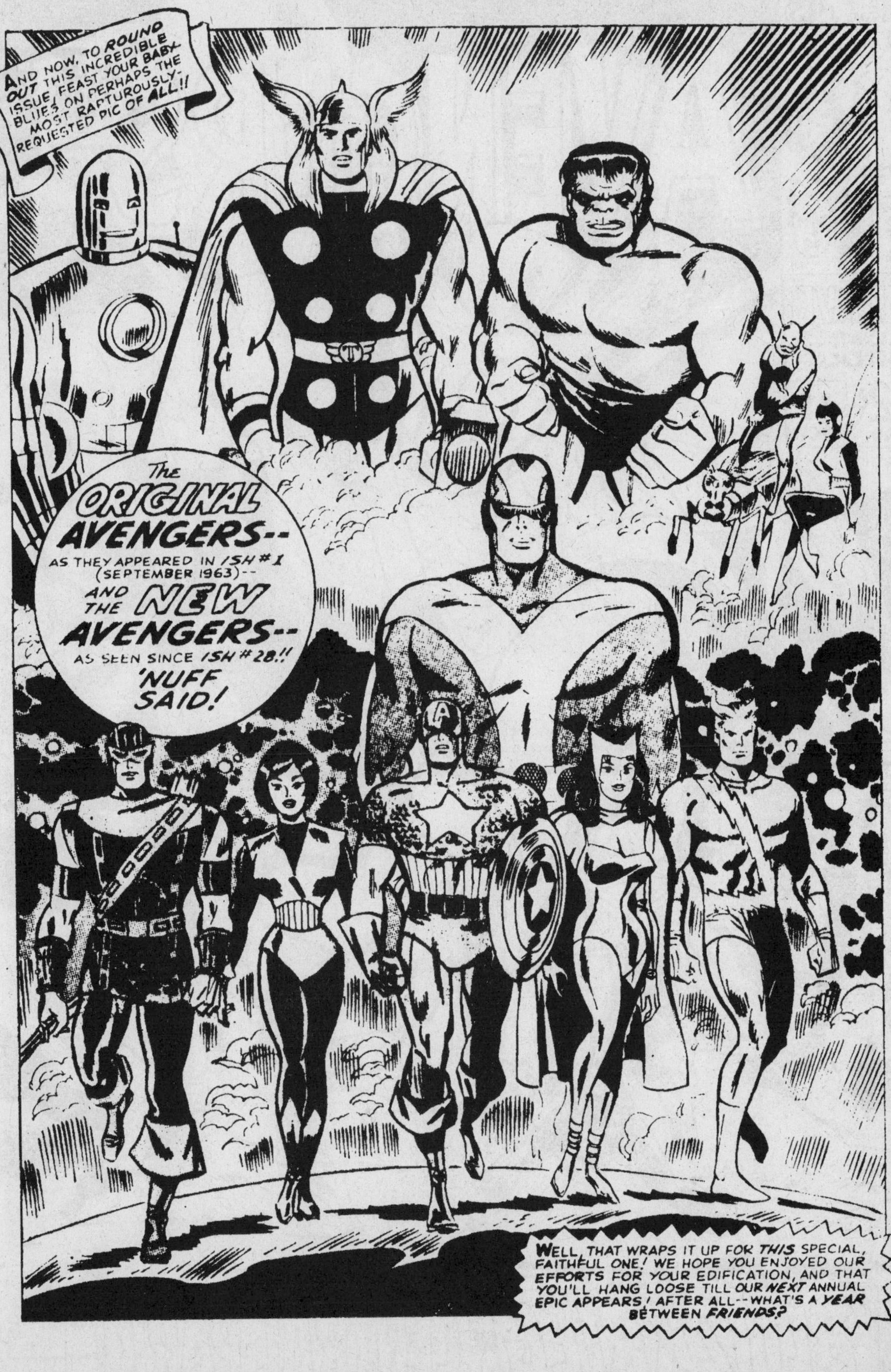
AND NOW, TO ROUND OUT THIS INCREDIBLE ISSUE, FEAST YOUR BABY BLUES ON PERHAPS THE MOST RAPTUROUSLY-REQUESTED PIC OF ALL!!
THE ORIGINAL AVENGERS-- AS THEY APPEARED IN ISH #1 (SEPTEMBER 1963)-- AND THE NEW AVENGERS-- AS SEEN SINCE ISH #28!! 'NUFF SAID!
WELL, THAT WRAPS IT UP FOR THIS SPECIAL, FAITHFUL ONE! WE HOPE YOU ENJOYED OUR EFFORTS FOR YOUR EDIFICATION, AND THAT YOU'LL HANG LOOSE TILL OUR NEXT ANNUAL EPIC APPEARS! AFTER ALL--WHAT'S A YEAR BETWEEN FRIENDS?

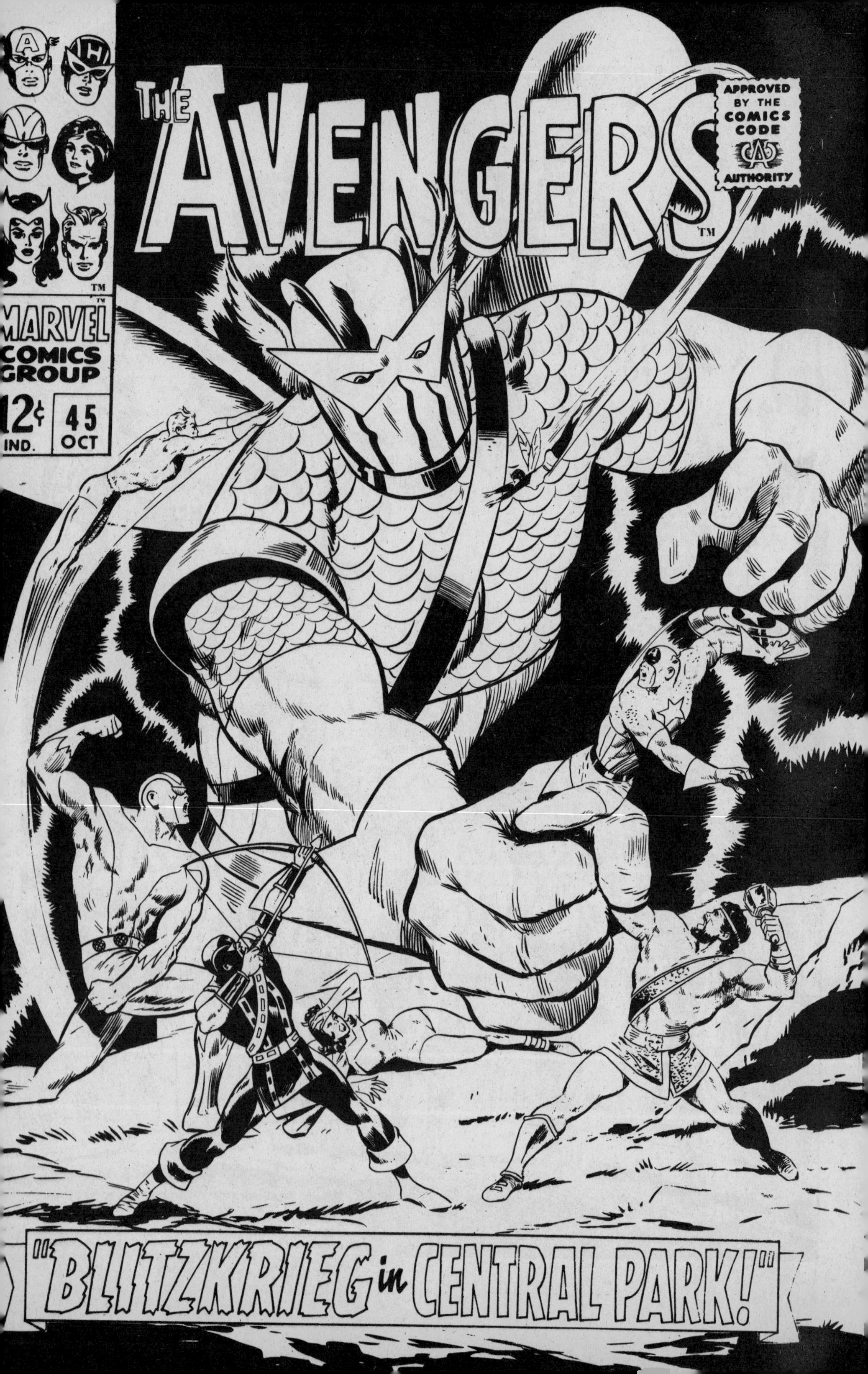
THE AVENGERS™
APPROVED BY THE COMICS CODE CA AUTHORITY
MARVEL COMICS GROUP
12¢ IND.
45 OCT
"BLITZKRIEG in CENTRAL PARK!"

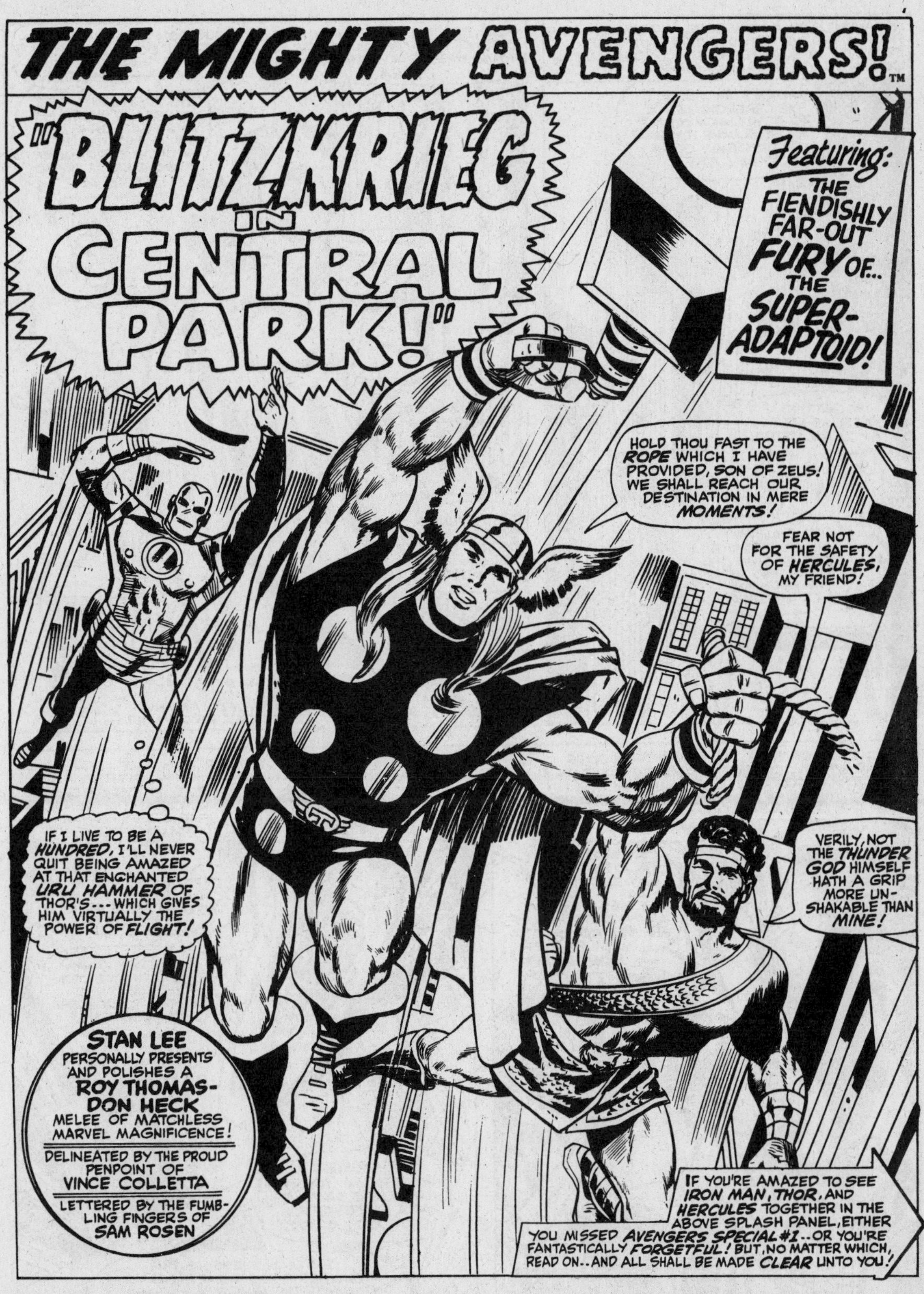
THE MIGHTY AVENGERS!™
"BLITZKRIEG IN CENTRAL PARK!"
Featuring: THE FIENDISHLY FAR-OUT FURY OF... THE SUPER-ADAPTOID!
HOLD THOU FAST TO THE ROPE WHICH I HAVE PROVIDED, SON OF ZEUS! WE SHALL REACH OUR DESTINATION IN MERE MOMENTS!
FEAR NOT FOR THE SAFETY OF HERCULES, MY FRIEND!
IF I LIVE TO BE A HUNDRED, I'LL NEVER QUIT BEING AMAZED AT THAT ENCHANTED URU HAMMER OF THOR'S... WHICH GIVES HIM VIRTUALLY THE POWER OF FLIGHT!
VERILY, NOT THE THUNDER GOD HIMSELF HATH A GRIP MORE UN-SHAKABLE THAN MINE!
STAN LEE PERSONALLY PRESENTS AND POLISHES A ROY THOMAS-DON HECK MELEE OF MATCHLESS MARVEL MAGNIFICENCE!
DELINEATED BY THE PROUD PENPOINT OF VINCE COLLETTA
LETTERED BY THE FUMB-LING FINGERS OF SAM ROSEN
IF YOU'RE AMAZED TO SEE IRON MAN, THOR, AND HERCULES TOGETHER IN THE ABOVE SPLASH PANEL, EITHER YOU MISSED AVENGERS SPECIAL #1..OR YOU'RE FANTASTICALLY FORGETFUL! BUT, NO MATTER WHICH, READ ON.. AND ALL SHALL BE MADE CLEAR UNTO YOU!

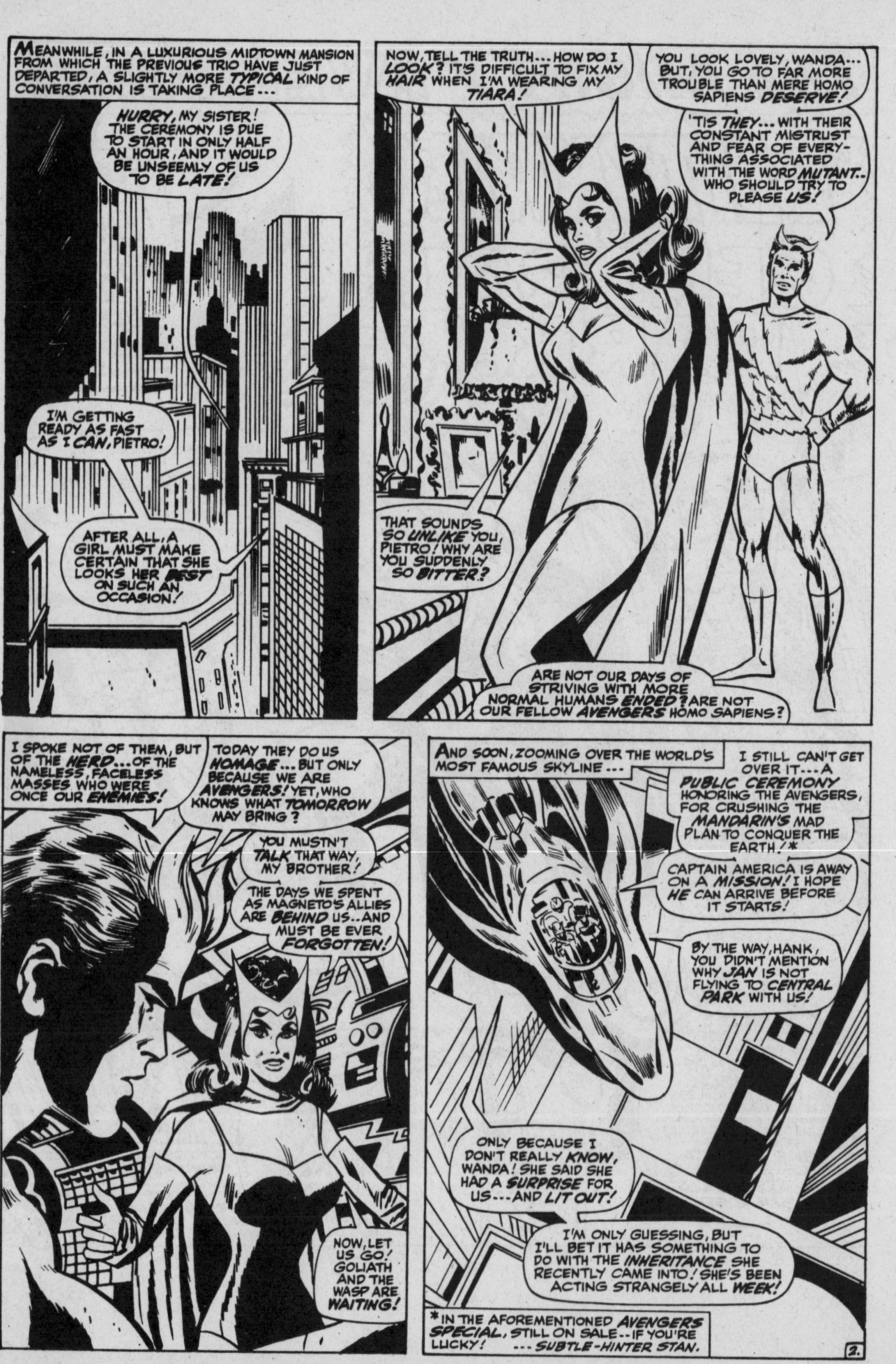
MEANWHILE, IN A LUXURIOUS MIDTOWN MANSION FROM WHICH THE PREVIOUS TRIO HAVE JUST DEPARTED, A SLIGHTLY MORE TYPICAL KIND OF CONVERSATION IS TAKING PLACE...
HURRY, MY SISTER! THE CEREMONY IS DUE TO START IN ONLY HALF AN HOUR, AND IT WOULD BE UNSEEMLY OF US TO BE LATE!
I'M GETTING READY AS FAST AS I CAN, PIETRO!
AFTER ALL, A GIRL MUST MAKE CERTAIN THAT SHE LOOKS HER BEST ON SUCH AN OCCASION!
NOW, TELL THE TRUTH... HOW DO I LOOK? IT'S DIFFICULT TO FIX MY HAIR WHEN I'M WEARING MY TIARA!
YOU LOOK LOVELY, WANDA... BUT, YOU GO TO FAR MORE TROUBLE THAN MERE HOMO SAPIENS DESERVE!
'TIS THEY... WITH THEIR CONSTANT MISTRUST AND FEAR OF EVERYTHING ASSOCIATED WITH THE WORD MUTANT... WHO SHOULD TRY TO PLEASE US!
THAT SOUNDS SO UNLIKE YOU, PIETRO! WHY ARE YOU SUDDENLY SO BITTER?
ARE NOT OUR DAYS OF STRIVING WITH MORE NORMAL HUMANS ENDED? ARE NOT OUR FELLOW AVENGERS HOMO SAPIENS?
I SPOKE NOT OF THEM, BUT OF THE HERD... OF THE NAMELESS, FACELESS MASSES WHO WERE ONCE OUR ENEMIES!
TODAY THEY DO US HOMAGE... BUT ONLY BECAUSE WE ARE AVENGERS! YET, WHO KNOWS WHAT TOMORROW MAY BRING?
YOU MUSTN'T TALK THAT WAY, MY BROTHER!
THE DAYS WE SPENT AS MAGNETO'S ALLIES ARE BEHIND US.. AND MUST BE EVER FORGOTTEN!
NOW, LET US GO! GOLIATH AND THE WASP ARE WAITING!
AND SOON, ZOOMING OVER THE WORLD'S MOST FAMOUS SKYLINE...
I STILL CAN'T GET OVER IT--- A PUBLIC CEREMONY HONORING THE AVENGERS, FOR CRUSHING THE MANDARIN'S MAD PLAN TO CONQUER THE EARTH!*
CAPTAIN AMERICA IS AWAY ON A MISSION! I HOPE HE CAN ARRIVE BEFORE IT STARTS!
BY THE WAY, HANK, YOU DIDN'T MENTION WHY JAN IS NOT FLYING TO CENTRAL PARK WITH US!
ONLY BECAUSE I DON'T REALLY KNOW, WANDA! SHE SAID SHE HAD A SURPRISE FOR US--- AND LIT OUT!
I'M ONLY GUESSING, BUT I'LL BET IT HAS SOMETHING TO DO WITH THE INHERITANCE SHE RECENTLY CAME INTO! SHE'S BEEN ACTING STRANGELY ALL WEEK!
*IN THE AFOREMENTIONED AVENGERS SPECIAL, STILL ON SALE-- IF YOU'RE LUCKY! --- SUBTLE-HINTER STAN.
2.

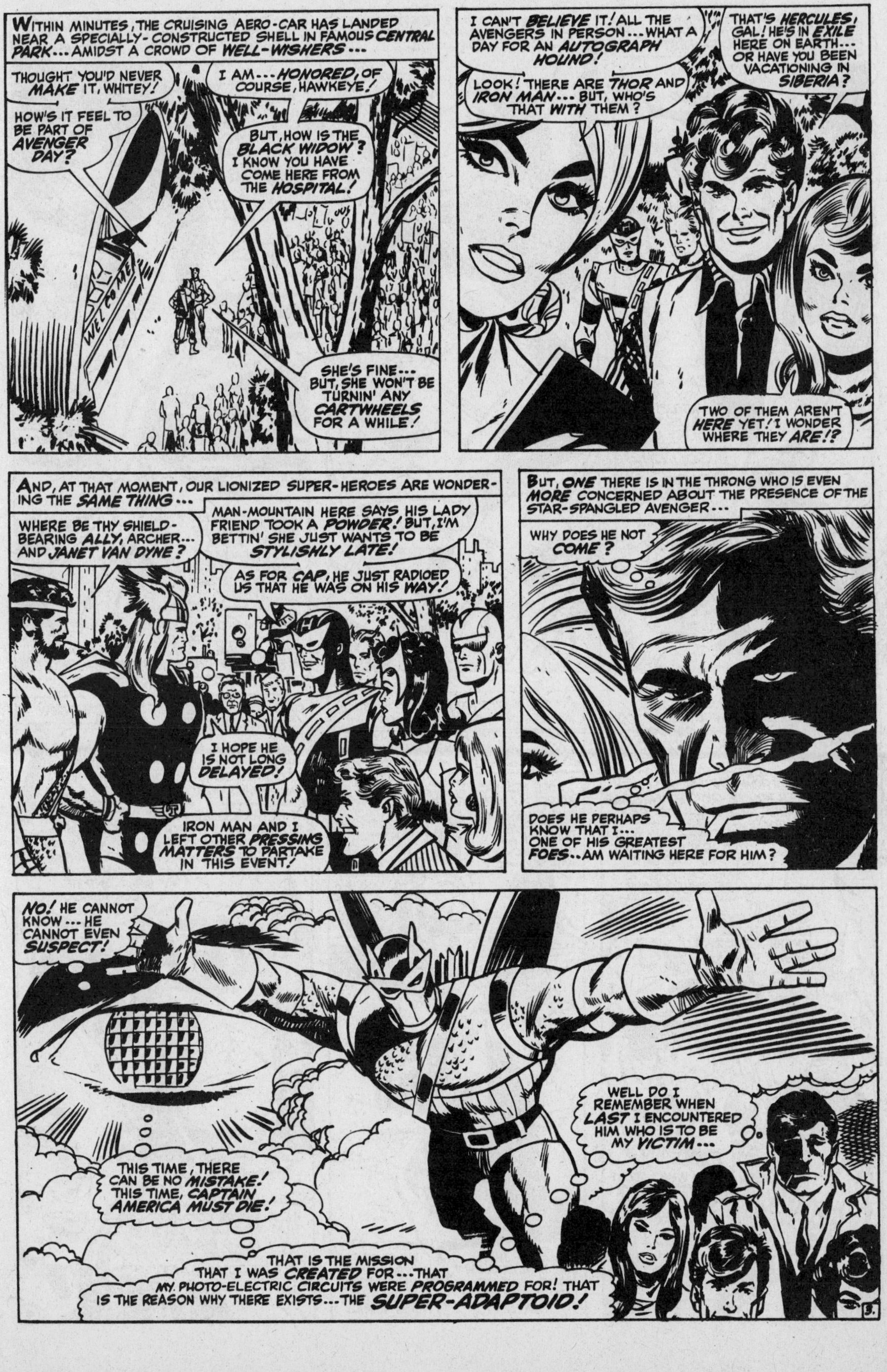

WITHIN MINUTES, THE CRUISING AERO-CAR HAS LANDED NEAR A SPECIALLY-CONSTRUCTED SHELL IN FAMOUS CENTRAL PARK... AMIDST A CROWD OF WELL-WISHERS...
THOUGHT YOU'D NEVER MAKE IT, WHITEY!
HOW'S IT FEEL TO BE PART OF AVENGER DAY?
I AM... HONORED, OF COURSE, HAWKEYE!
BUT, HOW IS THE BLACK WIDOW? I KNOW YOU HAVE COME HERE FROM THE HOSPITAL!
SHE'S FINE... BUT, SHE WON'T BE TURNIN' ANY CARTWHEELS FOR A WHILE!
WELCOME
I CAN'T BELIEVE IT! ALL THE AVENGERS IN PERSON... WHAT A DAY FOR AN AUTOGRAPH HOUND!
LOOK! THERE ARE THOR AND IRON MAN... BUT, WHO'S THAT WITH THEM?
THAT'S HERCULES, GAL! HE'S IN EXILE HERE ON EARTH... OR HAVE YOU BEEN VACATIONING IN SIBERIA?
TWO OF THEM AREN'T HERE YET! I WONDER WHERE THEY ARE!?
AND, AT THAT MOMENT, OUR LIONIZED SUPER-HEROES ARE WONDERING THE SAME THING...
WHERE BE THY SHIELD-BEARING ALLY, ARCHER... AND JANET VAN DYNE?
MAN-MOUNTAIN HERE SAYS HIS LADY FRIEND TOOK A POWDER! BUT, I'M BETTIN' SHE JUST WANTS TO BE STYLISHLY LATE!
AS FOR CAP, HE JUST RADIOED US THAT HE WAS ON HIS WAY!
I HOPE HE IS NOT LONG DELAYED!
IRON MAN AND I LEFT OTHER PRESSING MATTERS TO PARTAKE IN THIS EVENT!
BUT, ONE THERE IS IN THE THRONG WHO IS EVEN MORE CONCERNED ABOUT THE PRESENCE OF THE STAR-SPANGLED AVENGER...
WHY DOES HE NOT COME?
DOES HE PERHAPS KNOW THAT I... ONE OF HIS GREATEST FOES.. AM WAITING HERE FOR HIM?
NO! HE CANNOT KNOW... HE CANNOT EVEN SUSPECT!
WELL DO I REMEMBER WHEN LAST I ENCOUNTERED HIM WHO IS TO BE MY VICTIM...
THIS TIME, THERE CAN BE NO MISTAKE! THIS TIME, CAPTAIN AMERICA MUST DIE!
THAT IS THE MISSION THAT I WAS CREATED FOR... THAT MY PHOTO-ELECTRIC CIRCUITS WERE PROGRAMMED FOR! THAT IS THE REASON WHY THERE EXISTS... THE SUPER-ADAPTOID!
3.

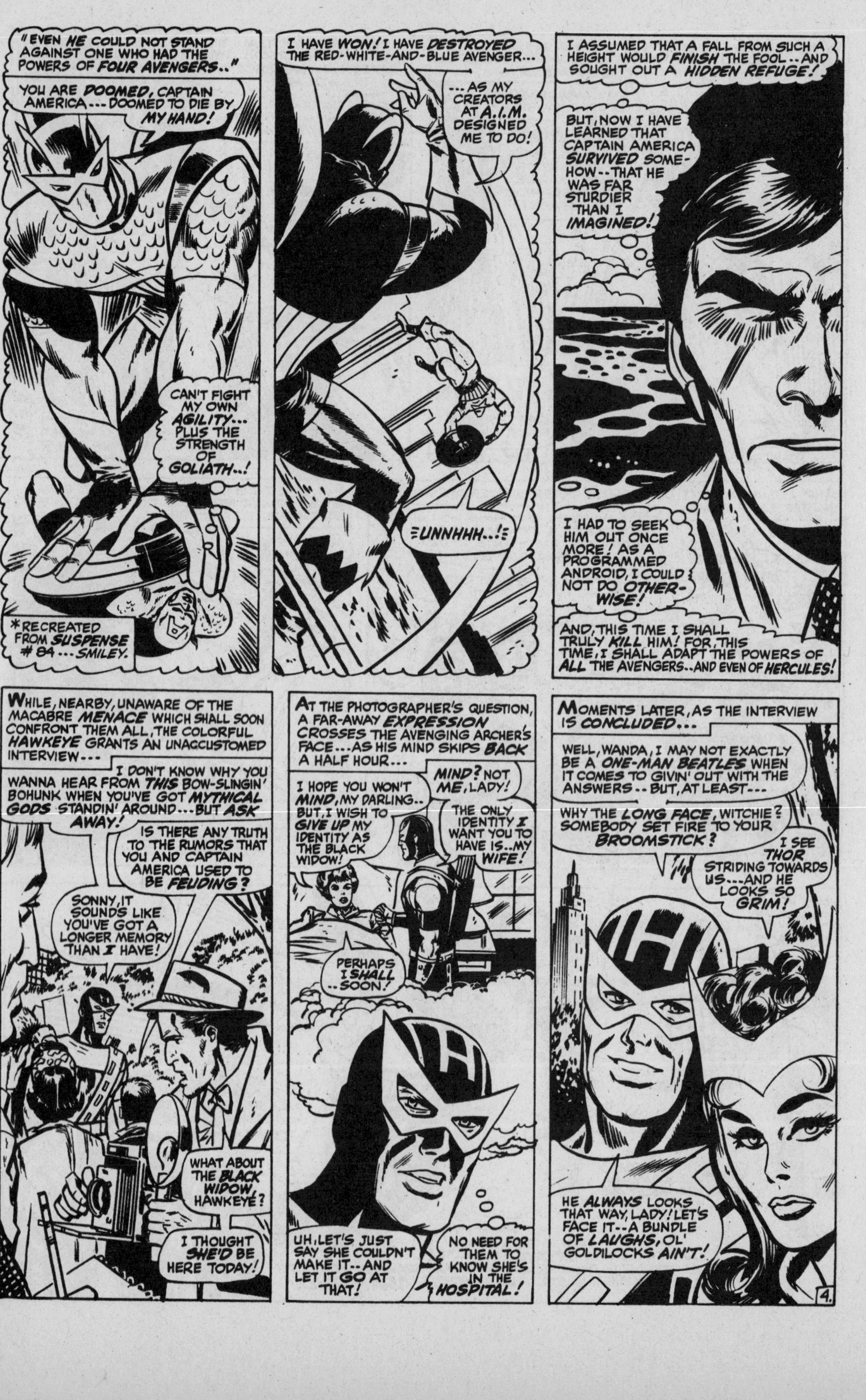

"EVEN HE COULD NOT STAND AGAINST ONE WHO HAD THE POWERS OF FOUR AVENGERS.."
YOU ARE DOOMED, CAPTAIN AMERICA--- DOOMED TO DIE BY MY HAND!
CAN'T FIGHT MY OWN AGILITY... PLUS THE STRENGTH OF GOLIATH..!
*RECREATED FROM SUSPENSE # 84 ... SMILEY.
I HAVE WON! I HAVE DESTROYED THE RED-WHITE-AND-BLUE AVENGER...
...AS MY CREATORS AT A.I.M. DESIGNED ME TO DO!
UNNHHH..!
I ASSUMED THAT A FALL FROM SUCH A HEIGHT WOULD FINISH THE FOOL...AND SOUGHT OUT A HIDDEN REFUGE!
BUT, NOW I HAVE LEARNED THAT CAPTAIN AMERICA SURVIVED SOME-HOW--THAT HE WAS FAR STURDIER THAN I IMAGINED!
I HAD TO SEEK HIM OUT ONCE MORE! AS A PROGRAMMED ANDROID, I COULD NOT DO OTHER-WISE!
AND, THIS TIME I SHALL TRULY KILL HIM! FOR, THIS TIME, I SHALL ADAPT THE POWERS OF ALL THE AVENGERS..AND EVEN OF HERCULES!
WHILE, NEARBY, UNAWARE OF THE MACABRE MENACE WHICH SHALL SOON CONFRONT THEM ALL, THE COLORFUL HAWKEYE GRANTS AN UNACCUSTOMED INTERVIEW---
I DON'T KNOW WHY YOU WANNA HEAR FROM THIS BOW-SLINGIN' BOHUNK WHEN YOU'VE GOT MYTHICAL GODS STANDIN' AROUND---BUT ASK AWAY!
IS THERE ANY TRUTH TO THE RUMORS THAT YOU AND CAPTAIN AMERICA USED TO BE FEUDING?
SONNY, IT SOUNDS LIKE YOU'VE GOT A LONGER MEMORY THAN I HAVE!
WHAT ABOUT THE BLACK WIDOW, HAWKEYE?
I THOUGHT SHE'D BE HERE TODAY!
AT THE PHOTOGRAPHER'S QUESTION, A FAR-AWAY EXPRESSION CROSSES THE AVENGING ARCHER'S FACE...AS HIS MIND SKIPS BACK A HALF HOUR...
I HOPE YOU WON'T MIND, MY DARLING.. BUT, I WISH TO GIVE UP MY IDENTITY AS THE BLACK WIDOW!
MIND? NOT ME, LADY!
THE ONLY IDENTITY I WANT YOU TO HAVE IS..MY WIFE!
PERHAPS I SHALL ..SOON!
UH, LET'S JUST SAY SHE COULDN'T MAKE IT--AND LET IT GO AT THAT!
NO NEED FOR THEM TO KNOW SHE'S IN THE HOSPITAL!
MOMENTS LATER, AS THE INTERVIEW IS CONCLUDED...
WELL, WANDA, I MAY NOT EXACTLY BE A ONE-MAN BEATLES WHEN IT COMES TO GIVIN' OUT WITH THE ANSWERS.. BUT, AT LEAST---
WHY THE LONG FACE, WITCHIE? SOMEBODY SET FIRE TO YOUR BROOMSTICK?
I SEE THOR STRIDING TOWARDS US---AND HE LOOKS SO GRIM!
HE ALWAYS LOOKS THAT WAY, LADY! LET'S FACE IT--A BUNDLE OF LAUGHS, OL' GOLDILOCKS AIN'T!
4.

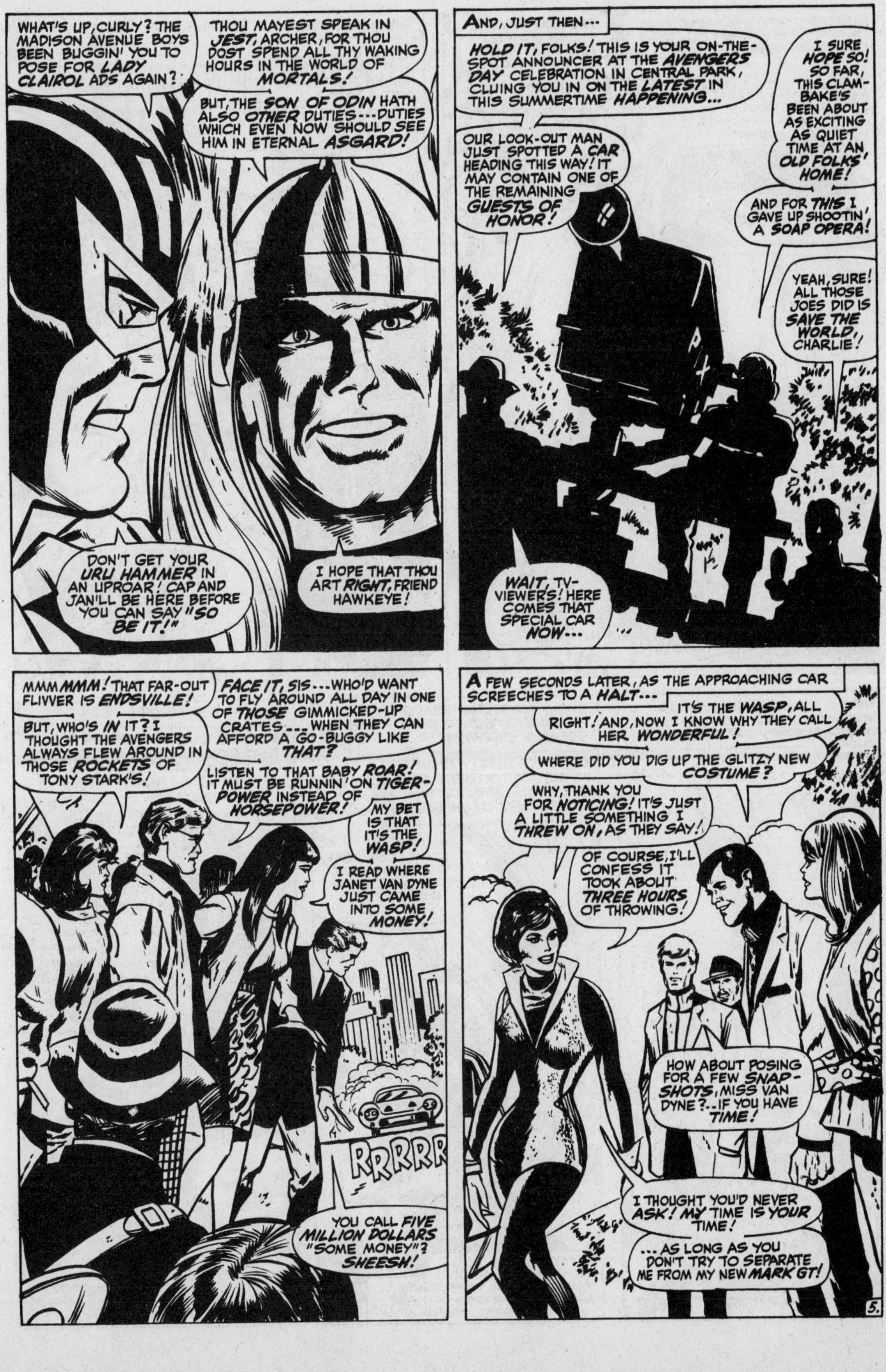
WHAT'S UP, CURLY? THE MADISON AVENUE BOYS BEEN BUGGIN' YOU TO POSE FOR LADY CLAIROL ADS AGAIN?
THOU MAYEST SPEAK IN JEST, ARCHER, FOR THOU DOST SPEND ALL THY WAKING HOURS IN THE WORLD OF MORTALS!
BUT, THE SON OF ODIN HATH ALSO OTHER DUTIES---DUTIES WHICH EVEN NOW SHOULD SEE HIM IN ETERNAL ASGARD!
DON'T GET YOUR URU HAMMER IN AN UPROAR! CAP AND JAN'LL BE HERE BEFORE YOU CAN SAY "SO BE IT!"
I HOPE THAT THOU ART RIGHT, FRIEND HAWKEYE!
AND, JUST THEN...
HOLD IT, FOLKS! THIS IS YOUR ON-THE-SPOT ANNOUNCER AT THE AVENGERS DAY CELEBRATION IN CENTRAL PARK, CLUING YOU IN ON THE LATEST IN THIS SUMMERTIME HAPPENING...
I SURE HOPE SO! SO FAR, THIS CLAM-BAKE'S BEEN ABOUT AS EXCITING AS QUIET TIME AT AN OLD FOLKS' HOME!
OUR LOOK-OUT MAN JUST SPOTTED A CAR HEADING THIS WAY! IT MAY CONTAIN ONE OF THE REMAINING GUESTS OF HONOR!
AND FOR THIS I GAVE UP SHOOTIN' A SOAP OPERA!
YEAH, SURE! ALL THOSE JOES DID IS SAVE THE WORLD, CHARLIE!
WAIT, TV-VIEWERS! HERE COMES THAT SPECIAL CAR NOW...
MMMMMM! THAT FAR-OUT FLIVVER IS ENDSVILLE!
BUT, WHO'S IN IT? I THOUGHT THE AVENGERS ALWAYS FLEW AROUND IN THOSE ROCKETS OF TONY STARK'S!
FACE IT, SIS...WHO'D WANT TO FLY AROUND ALL DAY IN ONE OF THOSE GIMMICKED-UP CRATES---WHEN THEY CAN AFFORD A GO-BUGGY LIKE THAT?
LISTEN TO THAT BABY ROAR! IT MUST BE RUNNIN' ON TIGER-POWER INSTEAD OF HORSEPOWER!
MY BET IS THAT IT'S THE WASP!
I READ WHERE JANET VAN DYNE JUST CAME INTO SOME MONEY!
RRRRR
YOU CALL FIVE MILLION DOLLARS "SOME MONEY"? SHEESH!
A FEW SECONDS LATER, AS THE APPROACHING CAR SCREECHES TO A HALT...
IT'S THE WASP, ALL RIGHT! AND, NOW I KNOW WHY THEY CALL HER WONDERFUL!
WHERE DID YOU DIG UP THE GLITZY NEW COSTUME?
WHY, THANK YOU FOR NOTICING! IT'S JUST A LITTLE SOMETHING I THREW ON, AS THEY SAY!
OF COURSE, I'LL CONFESS IT TOOK ABOUT THREE HOURS OF THROWING!
HOW ABOUT POSING FOR A FEW SNAP-SHOTS, MISS VAN DYNE?..IF YOU HAVE TIME!
I THOUGHT YOU'D NEVER ASK! MY TIME IS YOUR TIME!
...AS LONG AS YOU DON'T TRY TO SEPARATE ME FROM MY NEW MARK GT!
5.

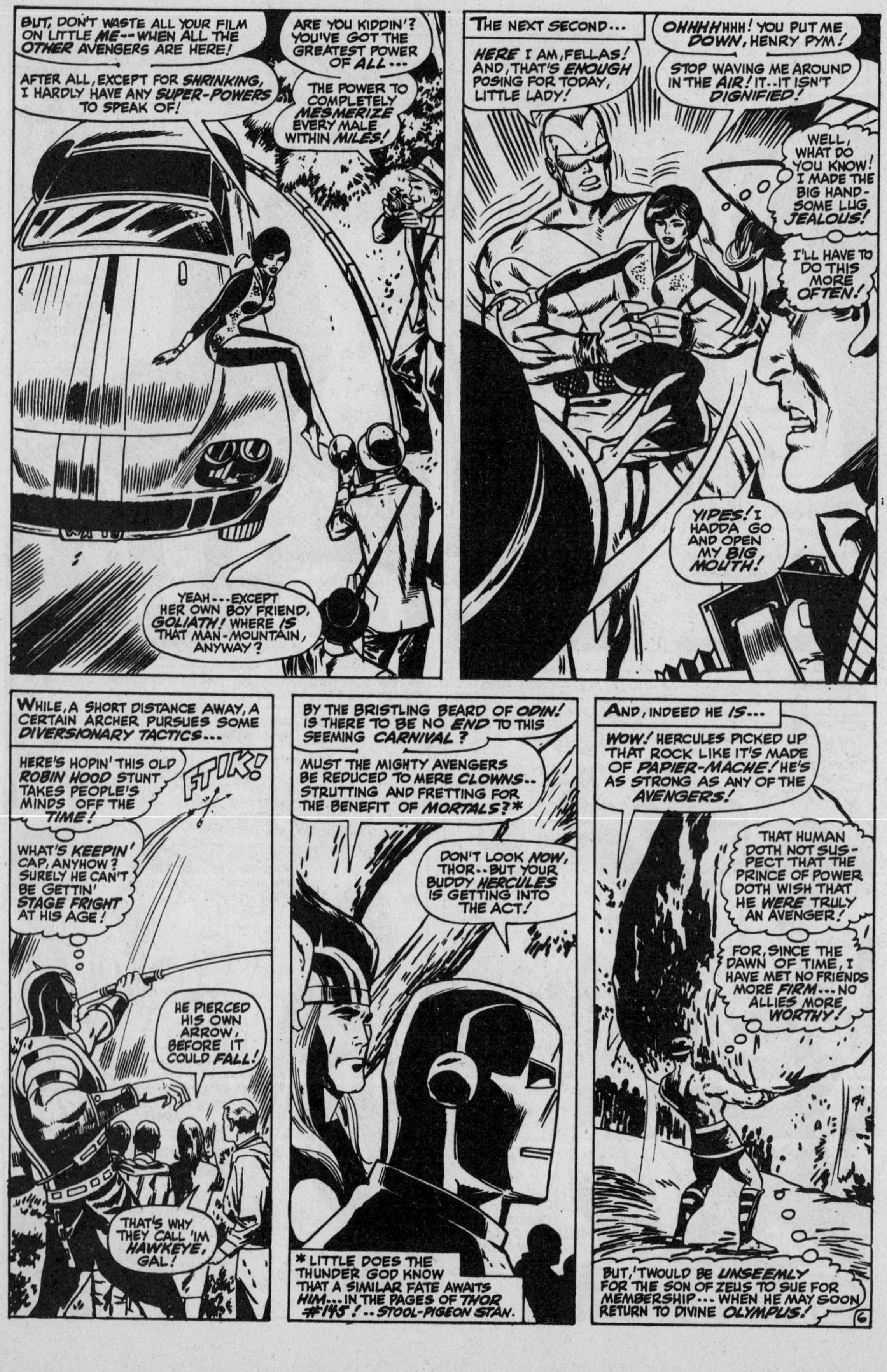
BUT, DON'T WASTE ALL YOUR FILM ON LITTLE ME-- WHEN ALL THE OTHER AVENGERS ARE HERE!
AFTER ALL, EXCEPT FOR SHRINKING, I HARDLY HAVE ANY SUPER-POWERS TO SPEAK OF!
ARE YOU KIDDIN'? YOU'VE GOT THE GREATEST POWER OF ALL...
THE POWER TO COMPLETELY MESMERIZE EVERY MALE WITHIN MILES!
YEAH...EXCEPT HER OWN BOY FRIEND, GOLIATH! WHERE IS THAT MAN-MOUNTAIN, ANYWAY?
THE NEXT SECOND...
HERE I AM, FELLAS! AND, THAT'S ENOUGH POSING FOR TODAY, LITTLE LADY!
OHHHHHHH! YOU PUT ME DOWN, HENRY PYM!
STOP WAVING ME AROUND IN THE AIR! IT..IT ISN'T DIGNIFIED!
WELL, WHAT DO YOU KNOW! I MADE THE BIG HAND-SOME LUG JEALOUS!
I'LL HAVE TO DO THIS MORE OFTEN!
YIPES! I HADDA GO AND OPEN MY BIG MOUTH!
WHILE, A SHORT DISTANCE AWAY, A CERTAIN ARCHER PURSUES SOME DIVERSIONARY TACTICS...
HERE'S HOPIN' THIS OLD ROBIN HOOD STUNT TAKES PEOPLE'S MINDS OFF THE TIME!
FTIK!
WHAT'S KEEPIN' CAP, ANYHOW? SURELY HE CAN'T BE GETTIN' STAGE FRIGHT AT HIS AGE!
HE PIERCED HIS OWN ARROW, BEFORE IT COULD FALL!
THAT'S WHY THEY CALL 'IM HAWKEYE, GAL!
BY THE BRISTLING BEARD OF ODIN! IS THERE TO BE NO END TO THIS SEEMING CARNIVAL?
MUST THE MIGHTY AVENGERS BE REDUCED TO MERE CLOWNS.. STRUTTING AND FRETTING FOR THE BENEFIT OF MORTALS?*
DON'T LOOK NOW, THOR..BUT YOUR BUDDY HERCULES IS GETTING INTO THE ACT!
*LITTLE DOES THE THUNDER GOD KNOW THAT A SIMILAR FATE AWAITS HIM...IN THE PAGES OF THOR #145!..STOOL-PIGEON STAN.
AND, INDEED HE IS...
WOW! HERCULES PICKED UP THAT ROCK LIKE IT'S MADE OF PAPIER-MACHE! HE'S AS STRONG AS ANY OF THE AVENGERS!
THAT HUMAN DOTH NOT SUS-PECT THAT THE PRINCE OF POWER DOTH WISH THAT HE WERE TRULY AN AVENGER!
FOR, SINCE THE DAWN OF TIME, I HAVE MET NO FRIENDS MORE FIRM...NO ALLIES MORE WORTHY!
BUT, 'TWOULD BE UNSEEMLY FOR THE SON OF ZEUS TO SUE FOR MEMBERSHIP...WHEN HE MAY SOON RETURN TO DIVINE OLYMPUS!
6

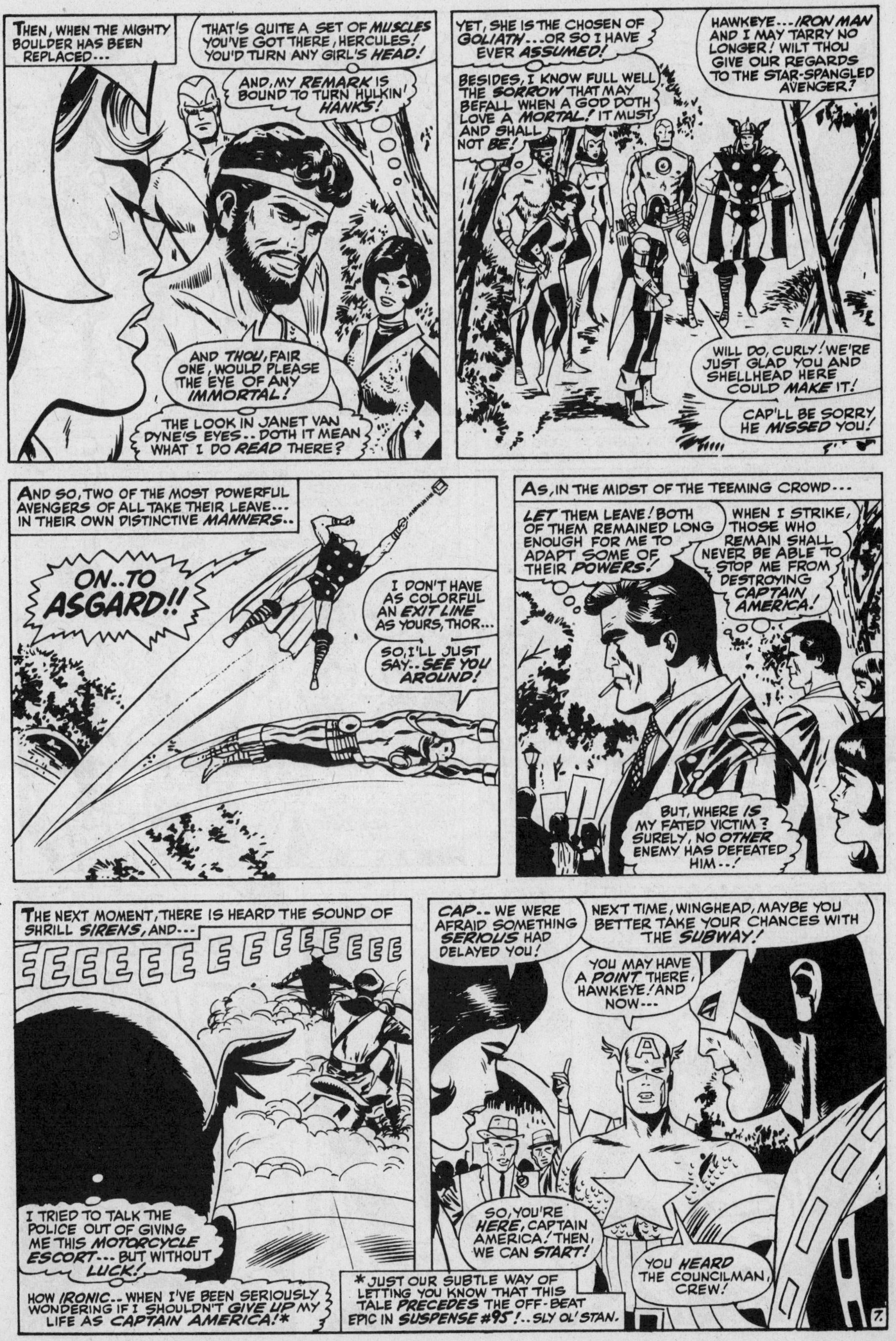
THEN, WHEN THE MIGHTY BOULDER HAS BEEN REPLACED...
THAT'S QUITE A SET OF MUSCLES YOU'VE GOT THERE, HERCULES! YOU'D TURN ANY GIRL'S HEAD!
AND, MY REMARK IS BOUND TO TURN HULKIN' HANKS!
AND THOU, FAIR ONE, WOULD PLEASE THE EYE OF ANY IMMORTAL!
THE LOOK IN JANET VAN DYNE'S EYES.. DOTH IT MEAN WHAT I DO READ THERE?
YET, SHE IS THE CHOSEN OF GOLIATH...OR SO I HAVE EVER ASSUMED!
BESIDES, I KNOW FULL WELL THE SORROW THAT MAY BEFALL WHEN A GOD DOTH LOVE A MORTAL! IT MUST AND SHALL NOT BE!
HAWKEYE...IRON MAN AND I MAY TARRY NO LONGER! WILT THOU GIVE OUR REGARDS TO THE STAR-SPANGLED AVENGER?
WILL DO, CURLY! WE'RE JUST GLAD YOU AND SHELLHEAD HERE COULD MAKE IT!
CAP'LL BE SORRY HE MISSED YOU!
AND SO, TWO OF THE MOST POWERFUL AVENGERS OF ALL TAKE THEIR LEAVE... IN THEIR OWN DISTINCTIVE MANNERS..
ON..TO ASGARD!!
I DON'T HAVE AS COLORFUL AN EXIT LINE AS YOURS, THOR...
SO, I'LL JUST SAY.. SEE YOU AROUND!
AS, IN THE MIDST OF THE TEEMING CROWD...
LET THEM LEAVE! BOTH OF THEM REMAINED LONG ENOUGH FOR ME TO ADAPT SOME OF THEIR POWERS!
WHEN I STRIKE, THOSE WHO REMAIN SHALL NEVER BE ABLE TO STOP ME FROM DESTROYING CAPTAIN AMERICA!
BUT, WHERE IS MY FATED VICTIM? SURELY, NO OTHER ENEMY HAS DEFEATED HIM..!
THE NEXT MOMENT, THERE IS HEARD THE SOUND OF SHRILL SIRENS, AND...
EEEEEEEEEEEEEE
I TRIED TO TALK THE POLICE OUT OF GIVING ME THIS MOTORCYCLE ESCORT... BUT WITHOUT LUCK!
HOW IRONIC.. WHEN I'VE BEEN SERIOUSLY WONDERING IF I SHOULDN'T GIVE UP MY LIFE AS CAPTAIN AMERICA!*
CAP.. WE WERE AFRAID SOMETHING SERIOUS HAD DELAYED YOU!
NEXT TIME, WINGHEAD, MAYBE YOU BETTER TAKE YOUR CHANCES WITH THE SUBWAY!
YOU MAY HAVE A POINT THERE, HAWKEYE! AND NOW---
SO, YOU'RE HERE, CAPTAIN AMERICA! THEN, WE CAN START!
YOU HEARD THE COUNCILMAN, CREW!
*JUST OUR SUBTLE WAY OF LETTING YOU KNOW THAT THIS TALE PRECEDES THE OFF-BEAT EPIC IN SUSPENSE #95!.. SLY OL' STAN.
7.

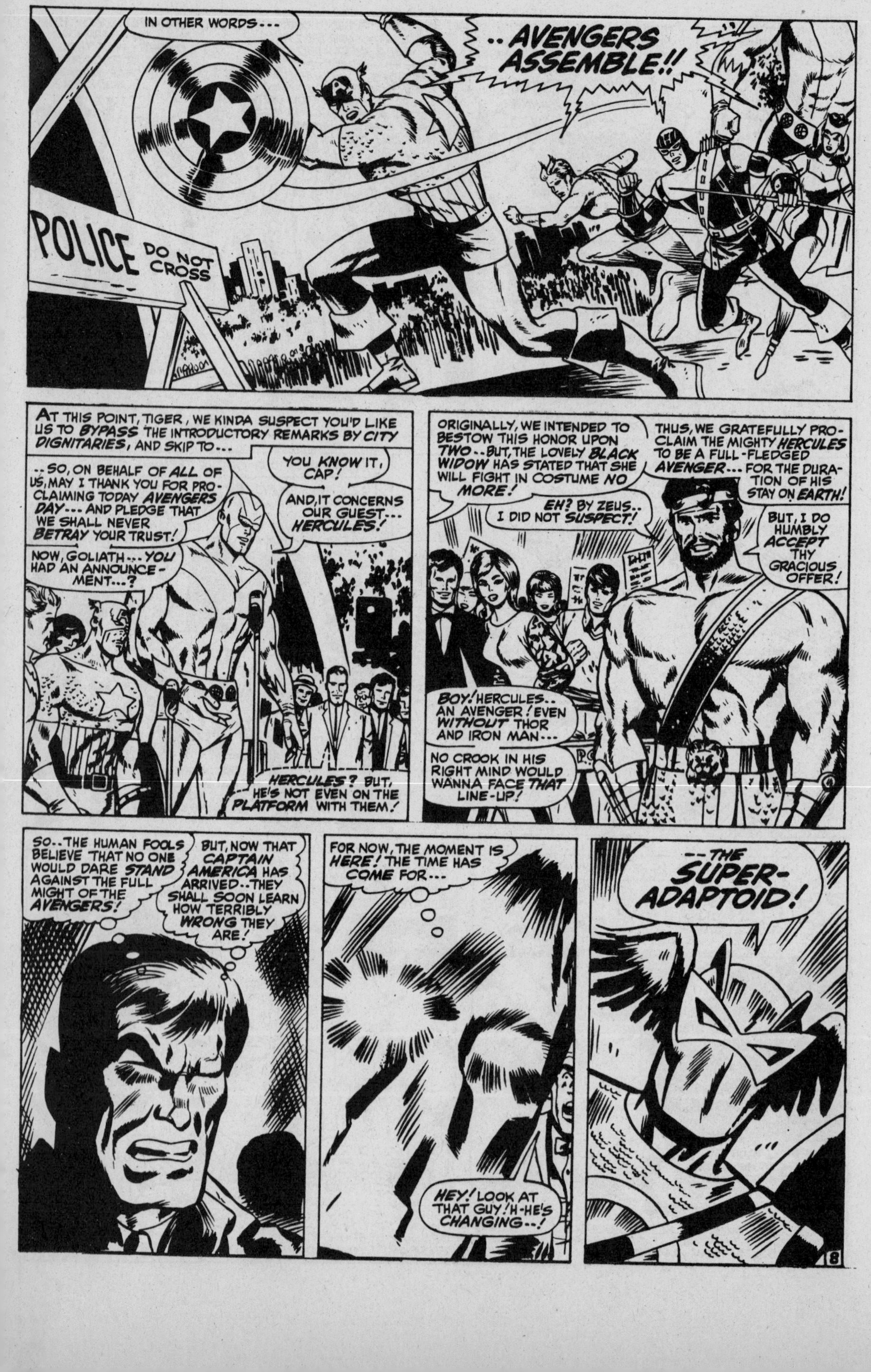
IN OTHER WORDS...
..AVENGERS ASSEMBLE!!
POLICE DO NOT CROSS
AT THIS POINT, TIGER, WE KINDA SUSPECT YOU'D LIKE US TO BYPASS THE INTRODUCTORY REMARKS BY CITY DIGNITARIES, AND SKIP TO...
--SO, ON BEHALF OF ALL OF US, MAY I THANK YOU FOR PROCLAIMING TODAY AVENGERS DAY--- AND PLEDGE THAT WE SHALL NEVER BETRAY YOUR TRUST!
YOU KNOW IT, CAP!
NOW, GOLIATH... YOU HAD AN ANNOUNCEMENT...?
AND, IT CONCERNS OUR GUEST--- HERCULES!
HERCULES? BUT, HE'S NOT EVEN ON THE PLATFORM WITH THEM!
ORIGINALLY, WE INTENDED TO BESTOW THIS HONOR UPON TWO..BUT, THE LOVELY BLACK WIDOW HAS STATED THAT SHE WILL FIGHT IN COSTUME NO MORE!
THUS, WE GRATEFULLY PROCLAIM THE MIGHTY HERCULES TO BE A FULL-FLEDGED AVENGER... FOR THE DURATION OF HIS STAY ON EARTH!
EH? BY ZEUS.. I DID NOT SUSPECT!
BUT, I DO HUMBLY ACCEPT THY GRACIOUS OFFER!
BOY! HERCULES.. AN AVENGER! EVEN WITHOUT THOR AND IRON MAN...
NO CROOK IN HIS RIGHT MIND WOULD WANNA FACE THAT LINE-UP!
SO..THE HUMAN FOOLS BELIEVE THAT NO ONE WOULD DARE STAND AGAINST THE FULL MIGHT OF THE AVENGERS!
BUT, NOW THAT CAPTAIN AMERICA HAS ARRIVED..THEY SHALL SOON LEARN HOW TERRIBLY WRONG THEY ARE!
FOR NOW, THE MOMENT IS HERE! THE TIME HAS COME FOR...
HEY! LOOK AT THAT GUY! H-HE'S CHANGING--!
--THE SUPER-ADAPTOID!
8

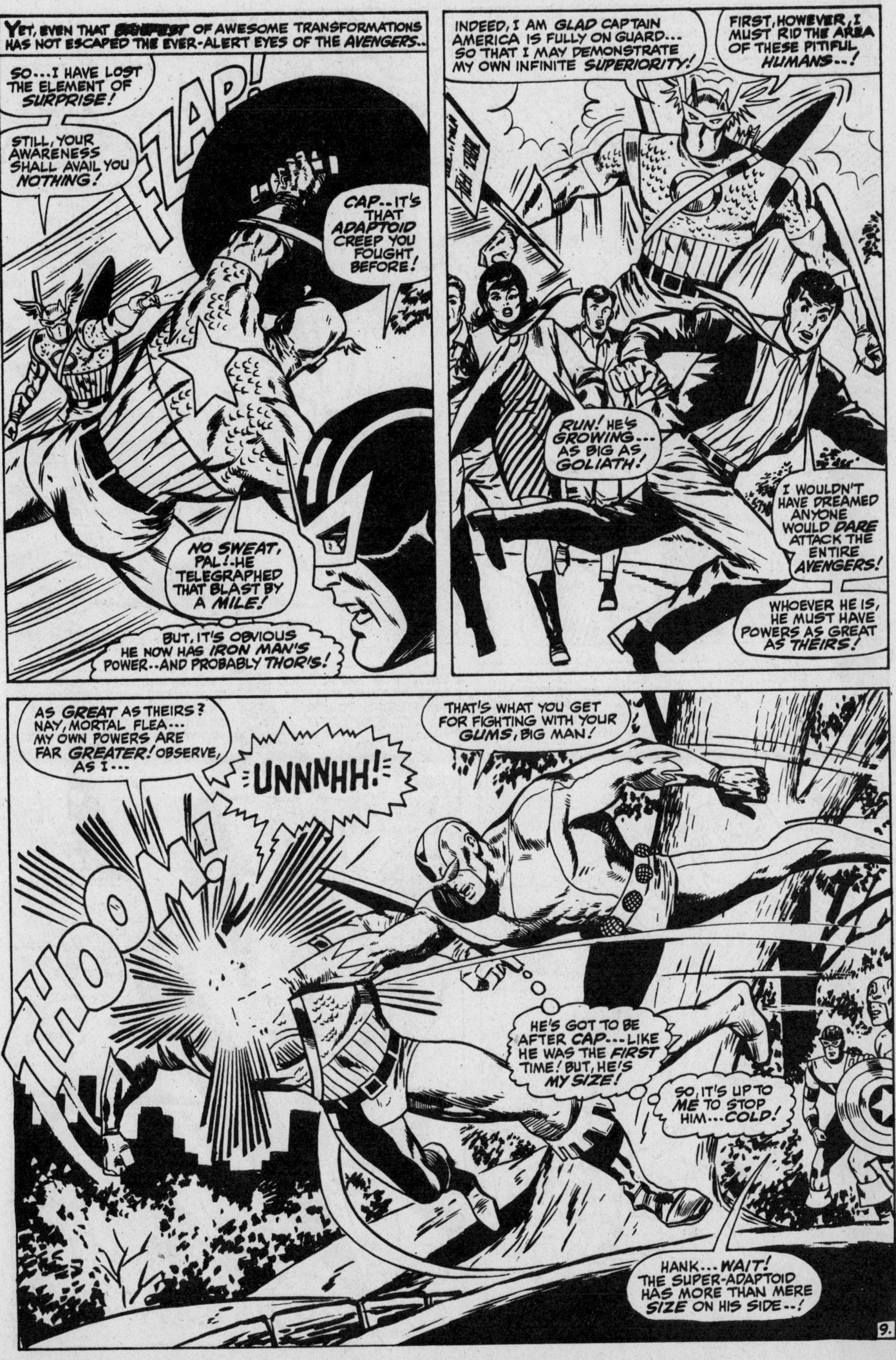

YET, EVEN THAT BRIEFEST OF AWESOME TRANSFORMATIONS HAS NOT ESCAPED THE EVER-ALERT EYES OF THE AVENGERS..
SO...I HAVE LOST THE ELEMENT OF SURPRISE!
STILL, YOUR AWARENESS SHALL AVAIL YOU NOTHING!
FZAP!
CAP..IT'S THAT ADAPTOID CREEP YOU FOUGHT BEFORE!
NO SWEAT, PAL!..HE TELEGRAPHED THAT BLAST BY A MILE!
BUT, IT'S OBVIOUS HE NOW HAS IRON MAN'S POWER..AND PROBABLY THOR'S!
INDEED, I AM GLAD CAPTAIN AMERICA IS FULLY ON GUARD... SO THAT I MAY DEMONSTRATE MY OWN INFINITE SUPERIORITY!
FIRST, HOWEVER, I MUST RID THE AREA OF THESE PITIFUL HUMANS..!
RUN! HE'S GROWING... AS BIG AS GOLIATH!
I WOULDN'T HAVE DREAMED ANYONE WOULD DARE ATTACK THE ENTIRE AVENGERS!
WHOEVER HE IS, HE MUST HAVE POWERS AS GREAT AS THEIRS!
AS GREAT AS THEIRS? NAY, MORTAL FLEA... MY OWN POWERS ARE FAR GREATER! OBSERVE, AS I...
UNNNHH!
THOOM!
THAT'S WHAT YOU GET FOR FIGHTING WITH YOUR GUMS, BIG MAN!
HE'S GOT TO BE AFTER CAP...LIKE HE WAS THE FIRST TIME! BUT, HE'S MY SIZE!
SO, IT'S UP TO ME TO STOP HIM...COLD!
HANK...WAIT! THE SUPER-ADAPTOID HAS MORE THAN MERE SIZE ON HIS SIDE..!

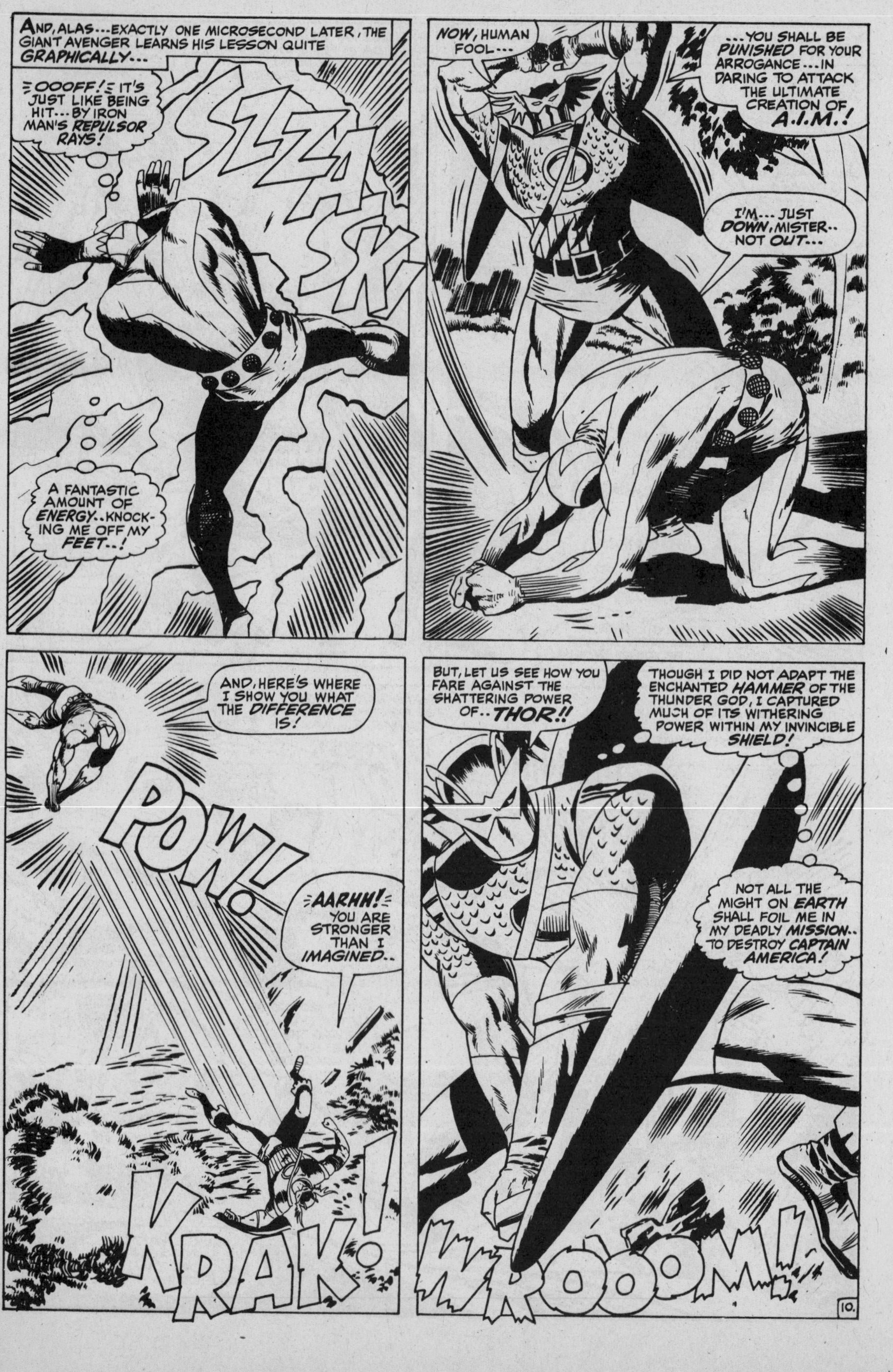
AND, ALAS...EXACTLY ONE MICROSECOND LATER, THE GIANT AVENGER LEARNS HIS LESSON QUITE GRAPHICALLY...
OOOFF! IT'S JUST LIKE BEING HIT...BY IRON MAN'S REPULSOR RAYS!
SZZZASK
A FANTASTIC AMOUNT OF ENERGY..KNOCKING ME OFF MY FEET..!
NOW, HUMAN FOOL...
...YOU SHALL BE PUNISHED FOR YOUR ARROGANCE...IN DARING TO ATTACK THE ULTIMATE CREATION OF A.I.M.!
I'M... JUST DOWN, MISTER.. NOT OUT...
AND, HERE'S WHERE I SHOW YOU WHAT THE DIFFERENCE IS!
POW!
AARHH! YOU ARE STRONGER THAN I IMAGINED..
KRAK!
BUT, LET US SEE HOW YOU FARE AGAINST THE SHATTERING POWER OF..THOR!!
THOUGH I DID NOT ADAPT THE ENCHANTED HAMMER OF THE THUNDER GOD, I CAPTURED MUCH OF ITS WITHERING POWER WITHIN MY INVINCIBLE SHIELD!
NOT ALL THE MIGHT ON EARTH SHALL FOIL ME IN MY DEADLY MISSION.. TO DESTROY CAPTAIN AMERICA!
WROOOM!
10.

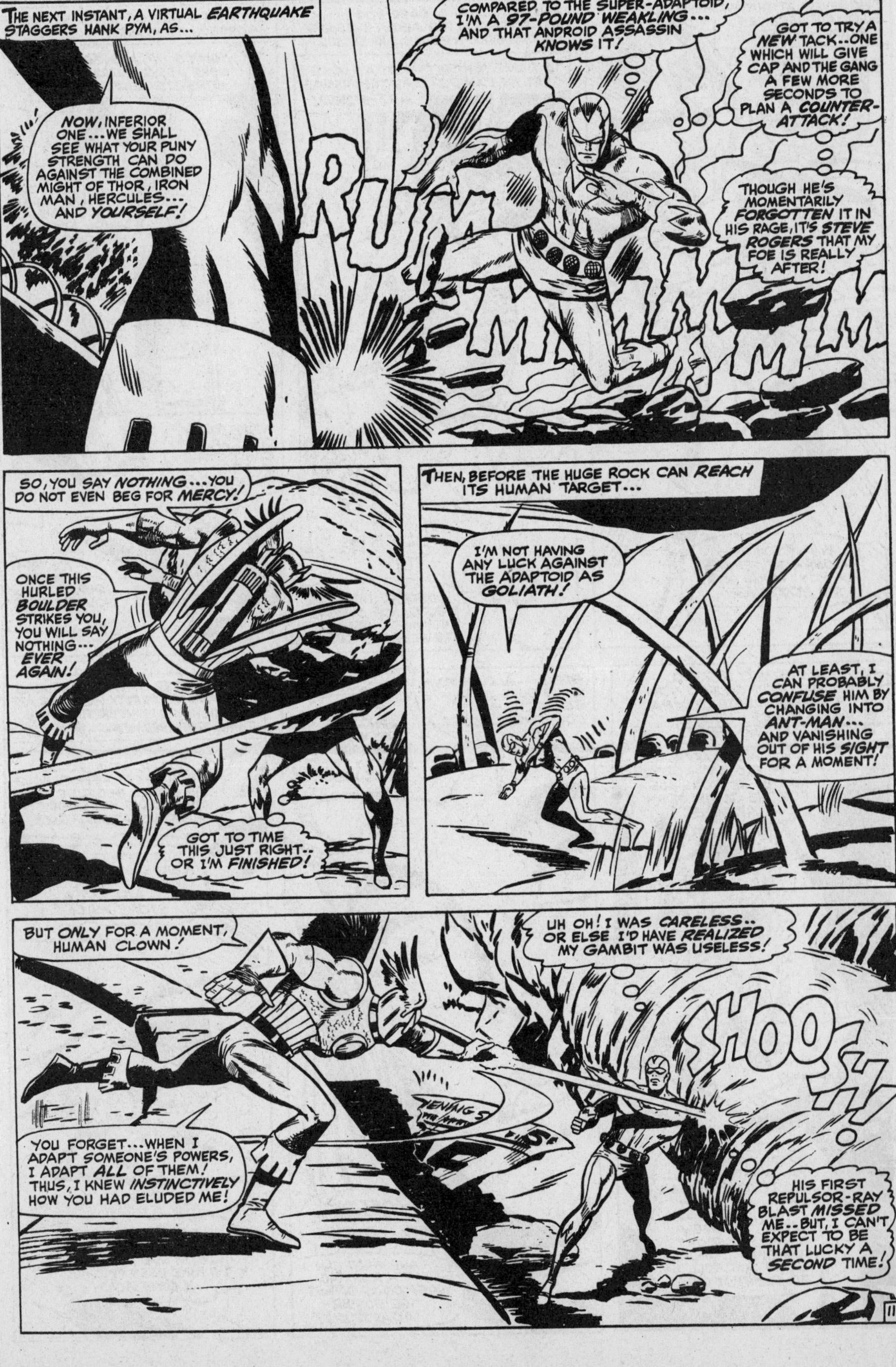

THE NEXT INSTANT, A VIRTUAL EARTHQUAKE STAGGERS HANK PYM, AS...
NOW, INFERIOR ONE... WE SHALL SEE WHAT YOUR PUNY STRENGTH CAN DO AGAINST THE COMBINED MIGHT OF THOR, IRON MAN, HERCULES... AND YOURSELF!
COMPARED TO THE SUPER-ADAPTOID, I'M A 97-POUND WEAKLING... AND THAT ANDROID ASSASSIN KNOWS IT!
GOT TO TRY A NEW TACK.. ONE WHICH WILL GIVE CAP AND THE GANG A FEW MORE SECONDS TO PLAN A COUNTER-ATTACK!
THOUGH HE'S MOMENTARILY FORGOTTEN IT IN HIS RAGE, IT'S STEVE ROGERS THAT MY FOE IS REALLY AFTER!
RUMMMMMMM
SO, YOU SAY NOTHING... YOU DO NOT EVEN BEG FOR MERCY!
ONCE THIS HURLED BOULDER STRIKES YOU, YOU WILL SAY NOTHING... EVER AGAIN!
GOT TO TIME THIS JUST RIGHT.. OR I'M FINISHED!
THEN, BEFORE THE HUGE ROCK CAN REACH ITS HUMAN TARGET...
I'M NOT HAVING ANY LUCK AGAINST THE ADAPTOID AS GOLIATH!
AT LEAST, I CAN PROBABLY CONFUSE HIM BY CHANGING INTO ANT-MAN... AND VANISHING OUT OF HIS SIGHT FOR A MOMENT!
BUT ONLY FOR A MOMENT, HUMAN CLOWN!
YOU FORGET... WHEN I ADAPT SOMEONE'S POWERS, I ADAPT ALL OF THEM! THUS, I KNEW INSTINCTIVELY HOW YOU HAD ELUDED ME!
UH OH! I WAS CARELESS.. OR ELSE I'D HAVE REALIZED MY GAMBIT WAS USELESS!
SHOOSH!
HIS FIRST REPULSOR-RAY BLAST MISSED ME.. BUT, I CAN'T EXPECT TO BE THAT LUCKY A SECOND TIME!

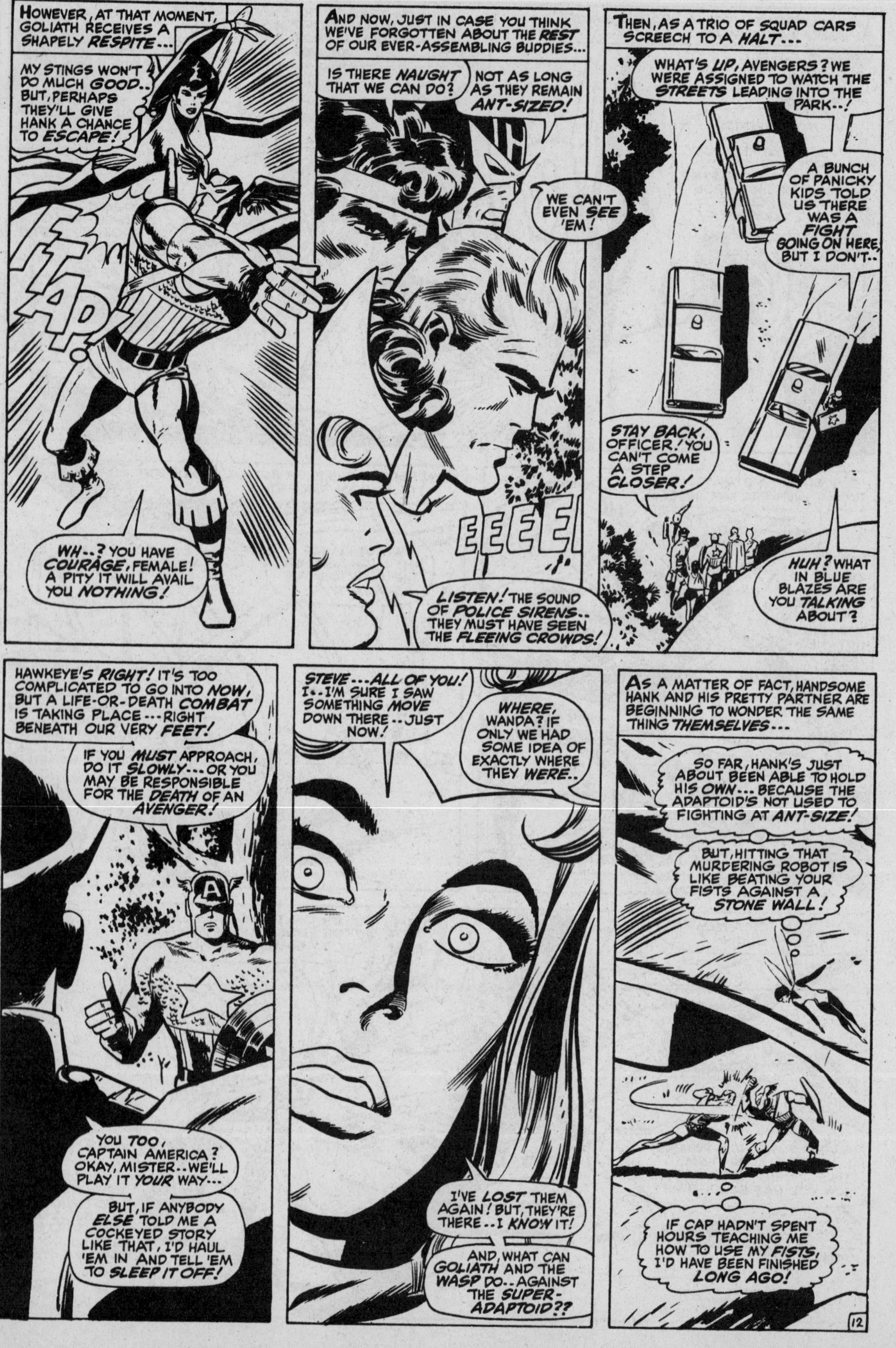
HOWEVER, AT THAT MOMENT, GOLIATH RECEIVES A SHAPELY RESPITE...
MY STINGS WON'T DO MUCH GOOD.. BUT, PERHAPS THEY'LL GIVE HANK A CHANCE TO ESCAPE!
FFTAP!
WH..? YOU HAVE COURAGE, FEMALE! A PITY IT WILL AVAIL YOU NOTHING!
AND NOW, JUST IN CASE YOU THINK WE'VE FORGOTTEN ABOUT THE REST OF OUR EVER-ASSEMBLING BUDDIES...
IS THERE NAUGHT THAT WE CAN DO?
NOT AS LONG AS THEY REMAIN ANT-SIZED!
WE CAN'T EVEN SEE 'EM!
EEEEE
LISTEN! THE SOUND OF POLICE SIRENS.. THEY MUST HAVE SEEN THE FLEEING CROWDS!
THEN, AS A TRIO OF SQUAD CARS SCREECH TO A HALT...
WHAT'S UP, AVENGERS? WE WERE ASSIGNED TO WATCH THE STREETS LEADING INTO THE PARK..!
A BUNCH OF PANICKY KIDS TOLD US THERE WAS A FIGHT GOING ON HERE, BUT I DON'T..
STAY BACK, OFFICER! YOU CAN'T COME A STEP CLOSER!
HUH? WHAT IN BLUE BLAZES ARE YOU TALKING ABOUT?
HAWKEYE'S RIGHT! IT'S TOO COMPLICATED TO GO INTO NOW, BUT A LIFE-OR-DEATH COMBAT IS TAKING PLACE---RIGHT BENEATH OUR VERY FEET!
IF YOU MUST APPROACH, DO IT SLOWLY... OR YOU MAY BE RESPONSIBLE FOR THE DEATH OF AN AVENGER!
YOU TOO, CAPTAIN AMERICA? OKAY, MISTER.. WE'LL PLAY IT YOUR WAY...
BUT, IF ANYBODY ELSE TOLD ME A COCKEYED STORY LIKE THAT, I'D HAUL 'EM IN AND TELL 'EM TO SLEEP IT OFF!
STEVE...ALL OF YOU! I..I'M SURE I SAW SOMETHING MOVE DOWN THERE..JUST NOW!
WHERE, WANDA? IF ONLY WE HAD SOME IDEA OF EXACTLY WHERE THEY WERE..
I'VE LOST THEM AGAIN! BUT, THEY'RE THERE..I KNOW IT!
AND, WHAT CAN GOLIATH AND THE WASP DO.. AGAINST THE SUPER-ADAPTOID??
AS A MATTER OF FACT, HANDSOME HANK AND HIS PRETTY PARTNER ARE BEGINNING TO WONDER THE SAME THING THEMSELVES...
SO FAR, HANK'S JUST ABOUT BEEN ABLE TO HOLD HIS OWN... BECAUSE THE ADAPTOID'S NOT USED TO FIGHTING AT ANT-SIZE!
BUT, HITTING THAT MURDERING ROBOT IS LIKE BEATING YOUR FISTS AGAINST A STONE WALL!
IF CAP HADN'T SPENT HOURS TEACHING ME HOW TO USE MY FISTS, I'D HAVE BEEN FINISHED LONG AGO!
12

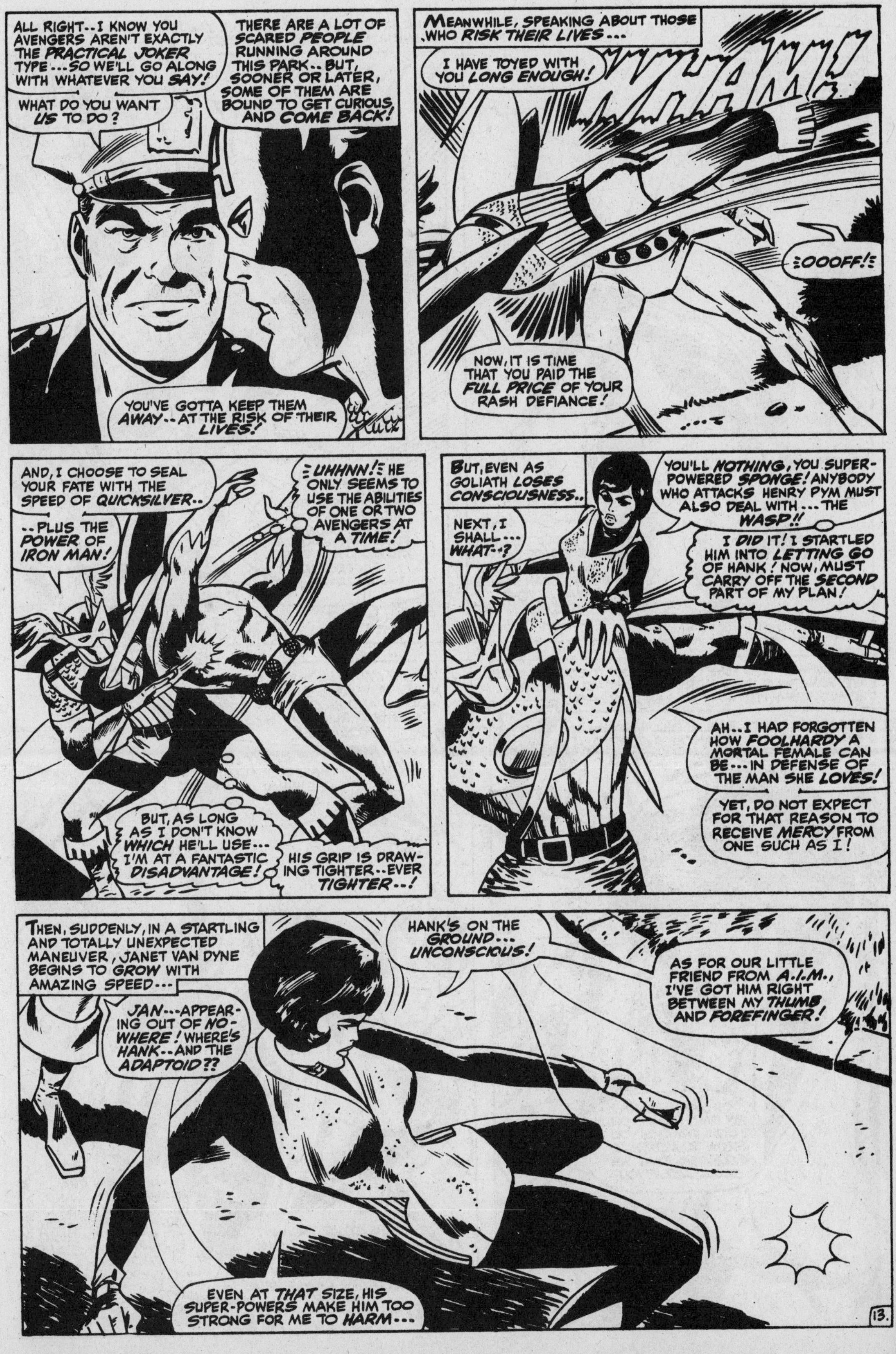
ALL RIGHT--I KNOW YOU AVENGERS AREN'T EXACTLY THE PRACTICAL JOKER TYPE ... SO WE'LL GO ALONG WITH WHATEVER YOU SAY!
WHAT DO YOU WANT US TO DO?
THERE ARE A LOT OF SCARED PEOPLE RUNNING AROUND THIS PARK.. BUT, SOONER OR LATER, SOME OF THEM ARE BOUND TO GET CURIOUS AND COME BACK!
YOU'VE GOTTA KEEP THEM AWAY--AT THE RISK OF THEIR LIVES!
MEANWHILE, SPEAKING ABOUT THOSE WHO RISK THEIR LIVES ...
I HAVE TOYED WITH YOU LONG ENOUGH!
WHAM!
OOOFF!
NOW, IT IS TIME THAT YOU PAID THE FULL PRICE OF YOUR RASH DEFIANCE!
AND, I CHOOSE TO SEAL YOUR FATE WITH THE SPEED OF QUICKSILVER..
..PLUS THE POWER OF IRON MAN!
UHHNN! HE ONLY SEEMS TO USE THE ABILITIES OF ONE OR TWO AVENGERS AT A TIME!
BUT, AS LONG AS I DON'T KNOW WHICH HE'LL USE... I'M AT A FANTASTIC DISADVANTAGE!
HIS GRIP IS DRAWING TIGHTER..EVER TIGHTER--!
BUT, EVEN AS GOLIATH LOSES CONSCIOUSNESS..
NEXT, I SHALL ... WHAT--?
YOU'LL NOTHING, YOU SUPER-POWERED SPONGE! ANYBODY WHO ATTACKS HENRY PYM MUST ALSO DEAL WITH ... THE WASP!!
I DID IT! I STARTLED HIM INTO LETTING GO OF HANK! NOW, MUST CARRY OFF THE SECOND PART OF MY PLAN!
AH..I HAD FORGOTTEN HOW FOOLHARDY A MORTAL FEMALE CAN BE ... IN DEFENSE OF THE MAN SHE LOVES!
YET, DO NOT EXPECT FOR THAT REASON TO RECEIVE MERCY FROM ONE SUCH AS I!
THEN, SUDDENLY, IN A STARTLING AND TOTALLY UNEXPECTED MANEUVER, JANET VAN DYNE BEGINS TO GROW WITH AMAZING SPEED ...
JAN---APPEARING OUT OF NOWHERE! WHERE'S HANK..AND THE ADAPTOID??
HANK'S ON THE GROUND... UNCONSCIOUS!
AS FOR OUR LITTLE FRIEND FROM A.I.M., I'VE GOT HIM RIGHT BETWEEN MY THUMB AND FOREFINGER!
EVEN AT THAT SIZE, HIS SUPER-POWERS MAKE HIM TOO STRONG FOR ME TO HARM ...
13.

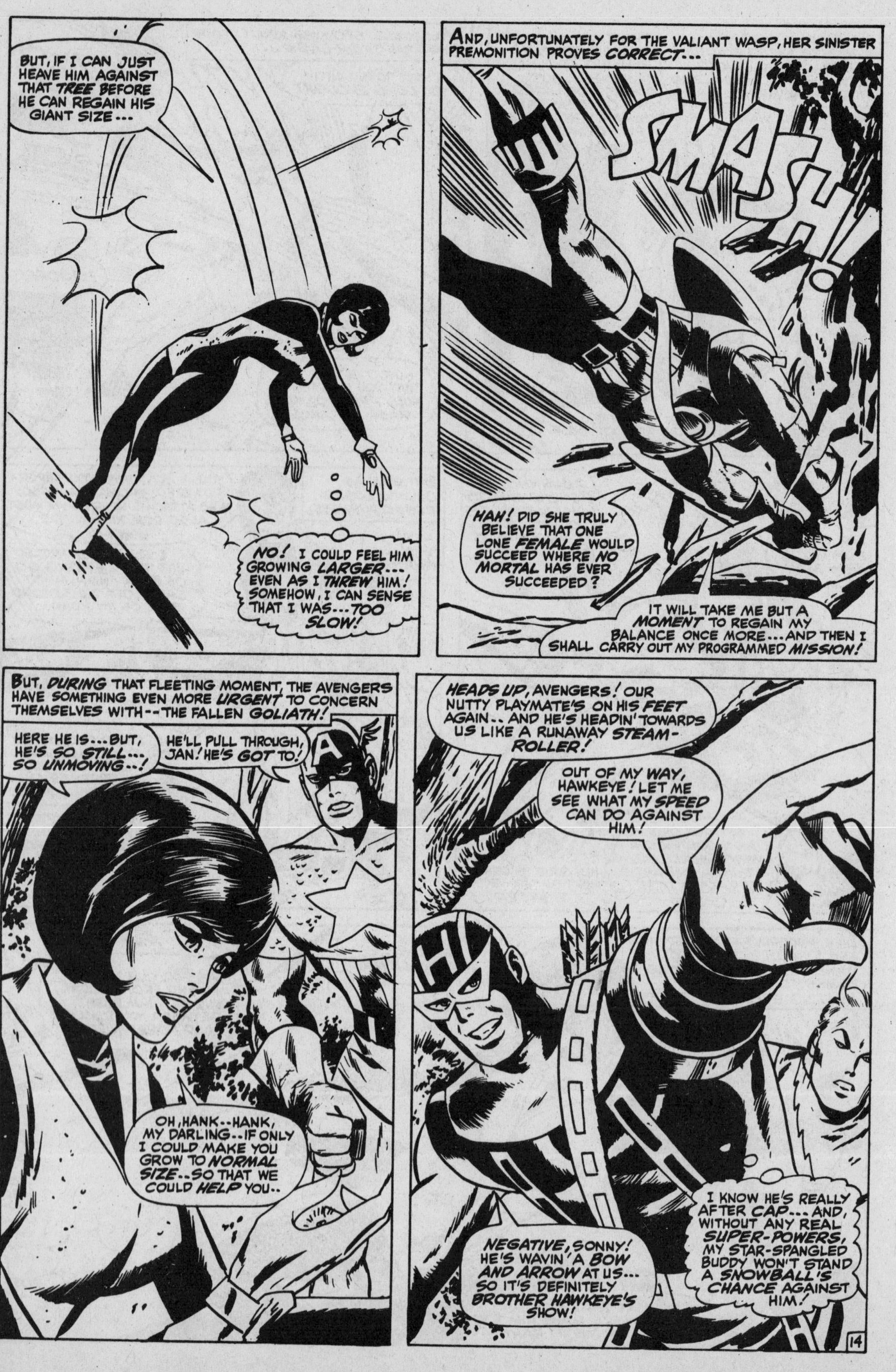

BUT, IF I CAN JUST HEAVE HIM AGAINST THAT TREE BEFORE HE CAN REGAIN HIS GIANT SIZE...
NO! I COULD FEEL HIM GROWING LARGER... EVEN AS I THREW HIM! SOMEHOW, I CAN SENSE THAT I WAS... TOO SLOW!
AND, UNFORTUNATELY FOR THE VALIANT WASP, HER SINISTER PREMONITION PROVES CORRECT...
SMASH!
HAH! DID SHE TRULY BELIEVE THAT ONE LONE FEMALE WOULD SUCCEED WHERE NO MORTAL HAS EVER SUCCEEDED?
IT WILL TAKE ME BUT A MOMENT TO REGAIN MY BALANCE ONCE MORE... AND THEN I SHALL CARRY OUT MY PROGRAMMED MISSION!
BUT, DURING THAT FLEETING MOMENT, THE AVENGERS HAVE SOMETHING EVEN MORE URGENT TO CONCERN THEMSELVES WITH--THE FALLEN GOLIATH!
HERE HE IS... BUT, HE'S SO STILL... SO UNMOVING..!
HE'LL PULL THROUGH, JAN! HE'S GOT TO!
OH, HANK--HANK, MY DARLING.. IF ONLY I COULD MAKE YOU GROW TO NORMAL SIZE.. SO THAT WE COULD HELP YOU..
HEADS UP, AVENGERS! OUR NUTTY PLAYMATE'S ON HIS FEET AGAIN.. AND HE'S HEADIN' TOWARDS US LIKE A RUNAWAY STEAM-ROLLER!
OUT OF MY WAY, HAWKEYE! LET ME SEE WHAT MY SPEED CAN DO AGAINST HIM!
NEGATIVE, SONNY! HE'S WAVIN' A BOW AND ARROW AT US... SO IT'S DEFINITELY BROTHER HAWKEYE'S SHOW!
I KNOW HE'S REALLY AFTER CAP... AND, WITHOUT ANY REAL SUPER-POWERS, MY STAR-SPANGLED BUDDY WON'T STAND A SNOWBALL'S CHANCE AGAINST HIM!
14

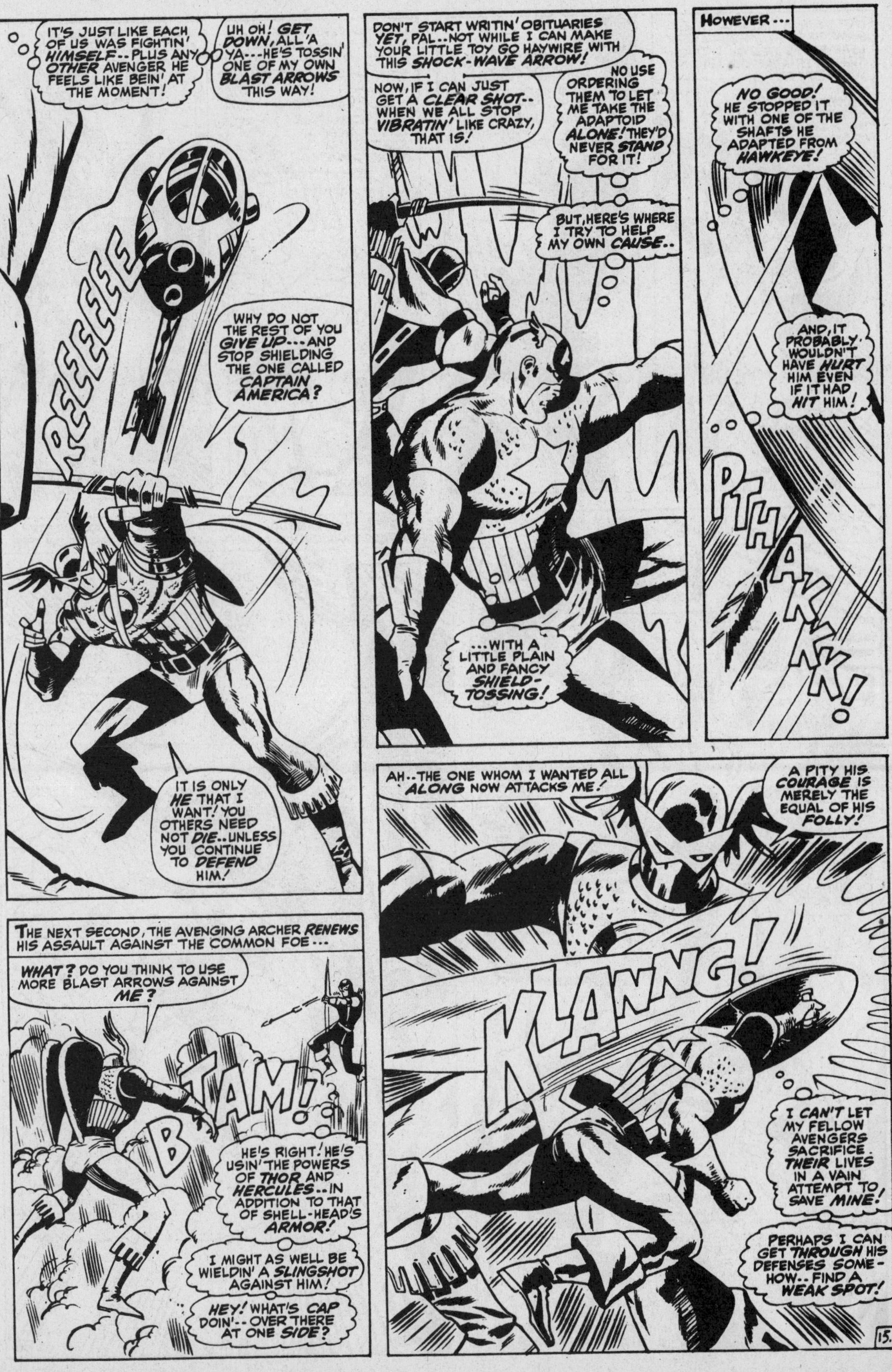
IT'S JUST LIKE EACH OF US WAS FIGHTIN' HIMSELF--PLUS ANY OTHER AVENGER HE FEELS LIKE BEIN' AT THE MOMENT!
UH OH! GET DOWN, ALL 'A YA--HE'S TOSSIN' ONE OF MY OWN BLAST ARROWS THIS WAY!
REEEEEE
WHY DO NOT THE REST OF YOU GIVE UP--AND STOP SHIELDING THE ONE CALLED CAPTAIN AMERICA?
IT IS ONLY HE THAT I WANT! YOU OTHERS NEED NOT DIE..UNLESS YOU CONTINUE TO DEFEND HIM!
DON'T START WRITIN' OBITUARIES YET, PAL..NOT WHILE I CAN MAKE YOUR LITTLE TOY GO HAYWIRE WITH THIS SHOCK-WAVE ARROW!
NOW, IF I CAN JUST GET A CLEAR SHOT.. WHEN WE ALL STOP VIBRATIN' LIKE CRAZY, THAT IS!
NO USE ORDERING THEM TO LET ME TAKE THE ADAPTOID ALONE! THEY'D NEVER STAND FOR IT!
BUT, HERE'S WHERE I TRY TO HELP MY OWN CAUSE..
...WITH A LITTLE PLAIN AND FANCY SHIELD-TOSSING!
HOWEVER...
NO GOOD! HE STOPPED IT WITH ONE OF THE SHAFTS HE ADAPTED FROM HAWKEYE!
AND, IT PROBABLY WOULDN'T HAVE HURT HIM EVEN IF IT HAD HIT HIM!
PTHAKKK!
THE NEXT SECOND, THE AVENGING ARCHER RENEWS HIS ASSAULT AGAINST THE COMMON FOE...
WHAT? DO YOU THINK TO USE MORE BLAST ARROWS AGAINST ME?
BTAM!
HE'S RIGHT! HE'S USIN' THE POWERS OF THOR AND HERCULES..IN ADDITION TO THAT OF SHELL-HEAD'S ARMOR!
I MIGHT AS WELL BE WIELDIN' A SLINGSHOT AGAINST HIM!
HEY! WHAT'S CAP DOIN'-- OVER THERE AT ONE SIDE?
AH..THE ONE WHOM I WANTED ALL ALONG NOW ATTACKS ME!
A PITY HIS COURAGE IS MERELY THE EQUAL OF HIS FOLLY!
KLANNG!
I CAN'T LET MY FELLOW AVENGERS SACRIFICE THEIR LIVES IN A VAIN ATTEMPT TO SAVE MINE!
PERHAPS I CAN GET THROUGH HIS DEFENSES SOME-HOW.. FIND A WEAK SPOT!
15.

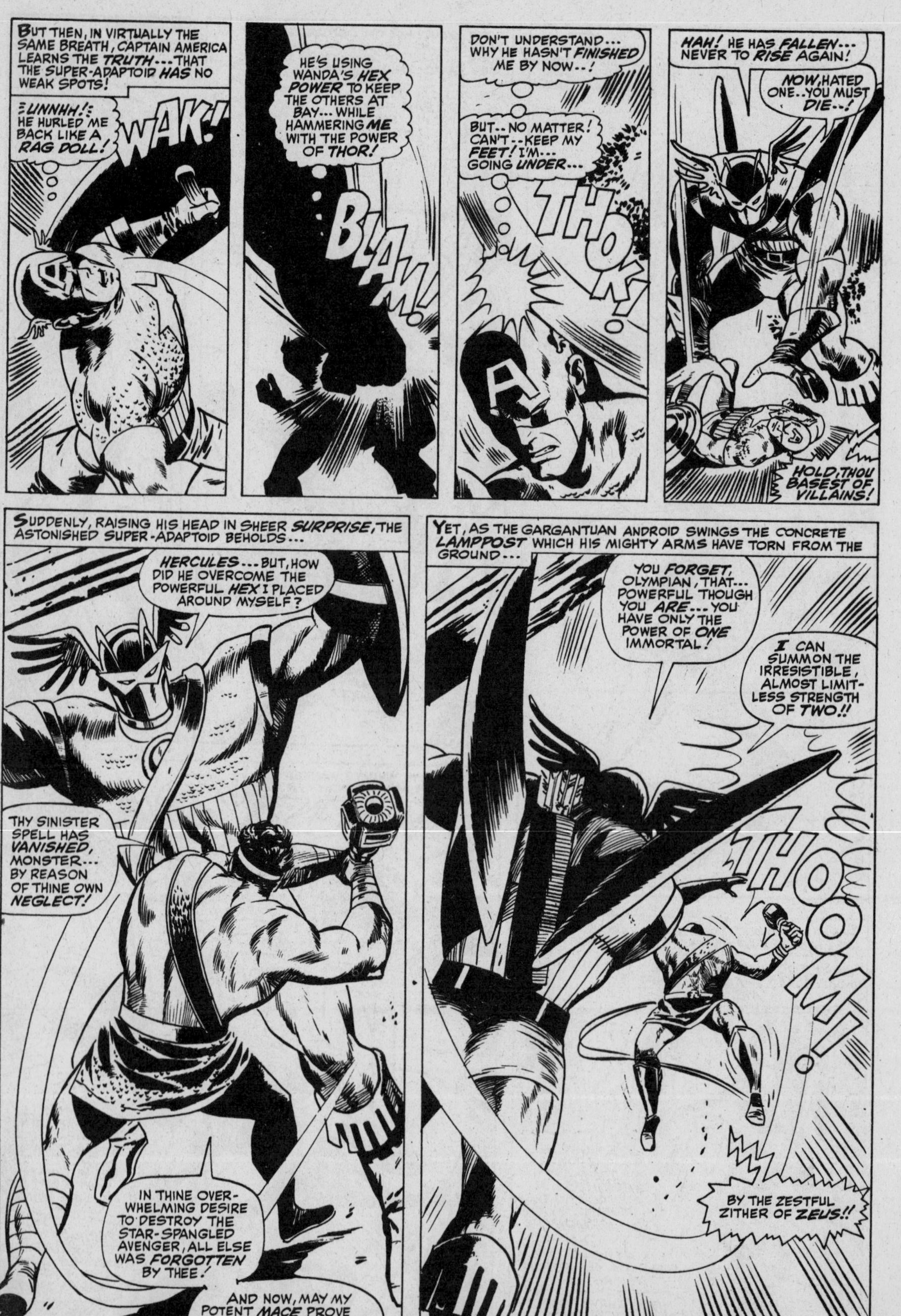

BUT THEN, IN VIRTUALLY THE SAME BREATH, CAPTAIN AMERICA LEARNS THE TRUTH--- THAT THE SUPER-ADAPTOID HAS NO WEAK SPOTS!
UNNHH!: HE HURLED ME BACK LIKE A RAG DOLL!
WAK!
HE'S USING WANDA'S HEX POWER TO KEEP THE OTHERS AT BAY... WHILE HAMMERING ME WITH THE POWER OF THOR!
BLAM!
DON'T UNDERSTAND... WHY HE HASN'T FINISHED ME BY NOW--!
BUT--NO MATTER! CAN'T--KEEP MY FEET! I'M... GOING UNDER...
THOK!
HAH! HE HAS FALLEN... NEVER TO RISE AGAIN!
NOW, HATED ONE.. YOU MUST DIE--!
HOLD, THOU BASEST OF VILLAINS!
SUDDENLY, RAISING HIS HEAD IN SHEER SURPRISE, THE ASTONISHED SUPER-ADAPTOID BEHOLDS...
HERCULES... BUT, HOW DID HE OVERCOME THE POWERFUL HEX I PLACED AROUND MYSELF?
THY SINISTER SPELL HAS VANISHED, MONSTER... BY REASON OF THINE OWN NEGLECT!
IN THINE OVER-WHELMING DESIRE TO DESTROY THE STAR-SPANGLED AVENGER, ALL ELSE WAS FORGOTTEN BY THEE!
AND NOW, MAY MY POTENT MACE PROVE THAT YON MISTAKE WAS THY FATEFUL UNDOING!
YET, AS THE GARGANTUAN ANDROID SWINGS THE CONCRETE LAMPPOST WHICH HIS MIGHTY ARMS HAVE TORN FROM THE GROUND...
YOU FORGET, OLYMPIAN, THAT... POWERFUL THOUGH YOU ARE... YOU HAVE ONLY THE POWER OF ONE IMMORTAL!
I CAN SUMMON THE IRRESISTIBLE, ALMOST LIMIT-LESS STRENGTH OF TWO!!
THOOM!
BY THE ZESTFUL ZITHER OF ZEUS!!
16

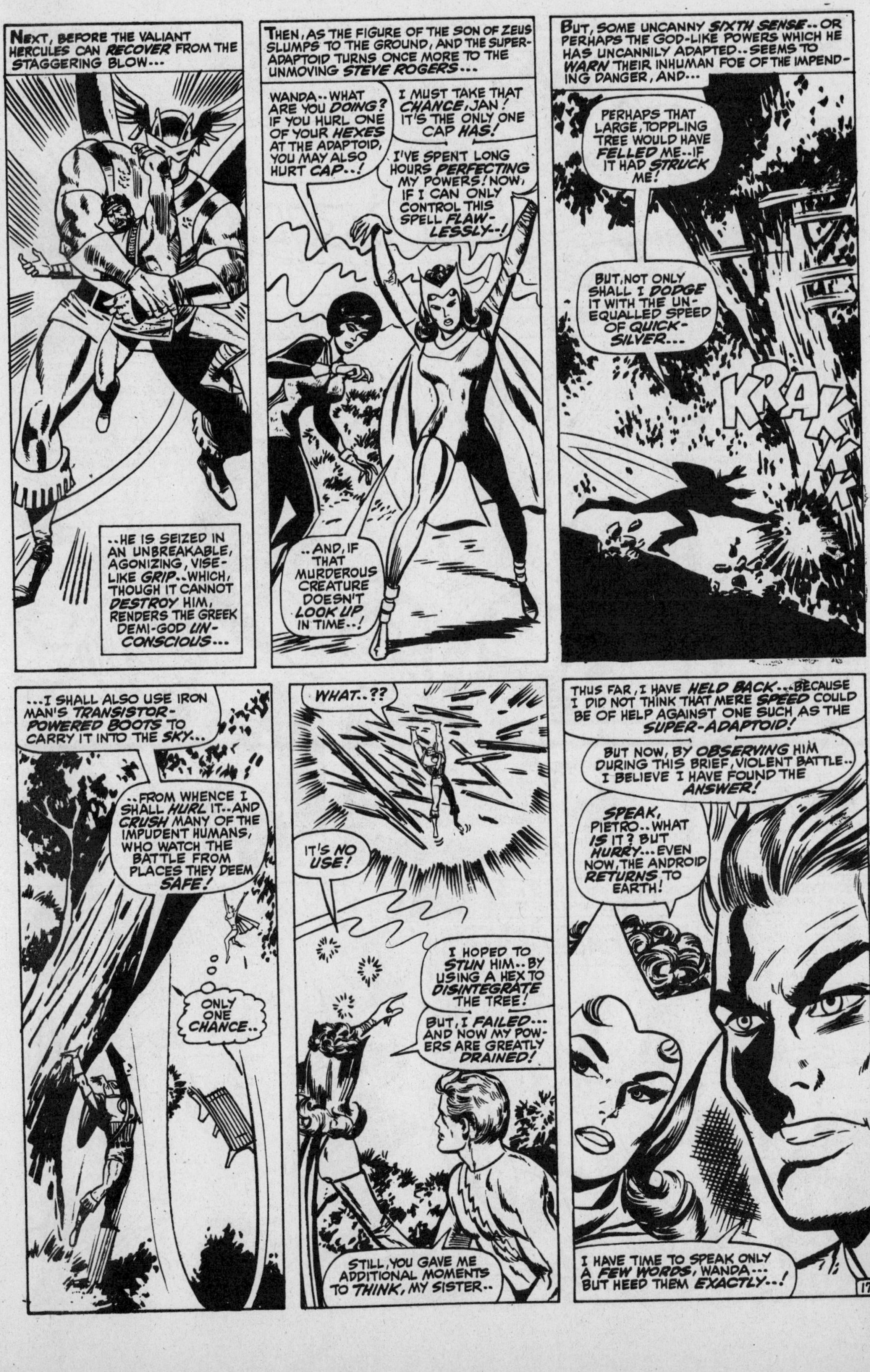

NEXT, BEFORE THE VALIANT HERCULES CAN RECOVER FROM THE STAGGERING BLOW...
..HE IS SEIZED IN AN UNBREAKABLE, AGONIZING, VISE-LIKE GRIP..WHICH, THOUGH IT CANNOT DESTROY HIM, RENDERS THE GREEK DEMI-GOD UN-CONSCIOUS...
THEN, AS THE FIGURE OF THE SON OF ZEUS SLUMPS TO THE GROUND, AND THE SUPER-ADAPTOID TURNS ONCE MORE TO THE UNMOVING STEVE ROGERS...
WANDA..WHAT ARE YOU DOING? IF YOU HURL ONE OF YOUR HEXES AT THE ADAPTOID, YOU MAY ALSO HURT CAP..!
I MUST TAKE THAT CHANCE, JAN! IT'S THE ONLY ONE CAP HAS!
I'VE SPENT LONG HOURS PERFECTING MY POWERS! NOW, IF I CAN ONLY CONTROL THIS SPELL FLAW-LESSLY--!
..AND, IF THAT MURDEROUS CREATURE DOESN'T LOOK UP IN TIME..!
BUT, SOME UNCANNY SIXTH SENSE..OR PERHAPS THE GOD-LIKE POWERS WHICH HE HAS UNCANNILY ADAPTED..SEEMS TO WARN THEIR INHUMAN FOE OF THE IMPENDING DANGER, AND...
PERHAPS THAT LARGE, TOPPLING TREE WOULD HAVE FELLED ME..IF IT HAD STRUCK ME!
BUT, NOT ONLY SHALL I DODGE IT WITH THE UN-EQUALLED SPEED OF QUICK-SILVER...
KRAKKKK
...I SHALL ALSO USE IRON MAN'S TRANSISTOR-POWERED BOOTS TO CARRY IT INTO THE SKY...
..FROM WHENCE I SHALL HURL IT..AND CRUSH MANY OF THE IMPUDENT HUMANS, WHO WATCH THE BATTLE FROM PLACES THEY DEEM SAFE!
ONLY ONE CHANCE..
WHAT..??
IT'S NO USE!
I HOPED TO STUN HIM..BY USING A HEX TO DISINTEGRATE THE TREE!
BUT, I FAILED... AND NOW MY POW-ERS ARE GREATLY DRAINED!
STILL, YOU GAVE ME ADDITIONAL MOMENTS TO THINK, MY SISTER..
THUS FAR, I HAVE HELD BACK...BECAUSE I DID NOT THINK THAT MERE SPEED COULD BE OF HELP AGAINST ONE SUCH AS THE SUPER-ADAPTOID!
BUT NOW, BY OBSERVING HIM DURING THIS BRIEF, VIOLENT BATTLE.. I BELIEVE I HAVE FOUND THE ANSWER!
SPEAK, PIETRO..WHAT IS IT? BUT HURRY...EVEN NOW, THE ANDROID RETURNS TO EARTH!
I HAVE TIME TO SPEAK ONLY A FEW WORDS, WANDA... BUT HEED THEM EXACTLY..!
17

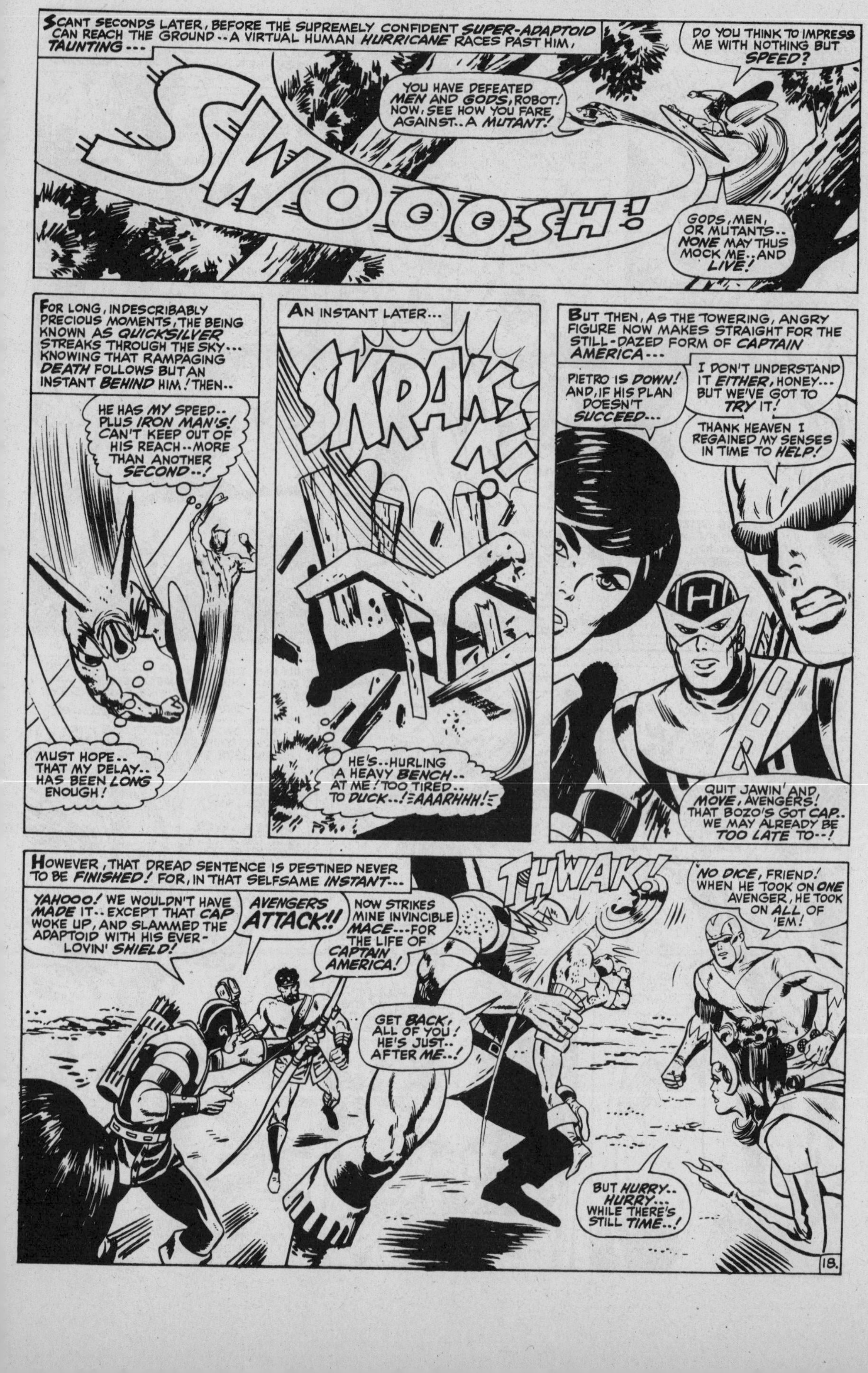
SCANT SECONDS LATER, BEFORE THE SUPREMELY CONFIDENT SUPER-ADAPTOID CAN REACH THE GROUND.. A VIRTUAL HUMAN HURRICANE RACES PAST HIM, TAUNTING...
YOU HAVE DEFEATED MEN AND GODS, ROBOT! NOW, SEE HOW YOU FARE AGAINST.. A MUTANT!
DO YOU THINK TO IMPRESS ME WITH NOTHING BUT SPEED?
SWOOOSH!
GODS, MEN, OR MUTANTS.. NONE MAY THUS MOCK ME.. AND LIVE!
FOR LONG, INDESCRIBABLY PRECIOUS MOMENTS, THE BEING KNOWN AS QUICKSILVER STREAKS THROUGH THE SKY... KNOWING THAT RAMPAGING DEATH FOLLOWS BUT AN INSTANT BEHIND HIM! THEN..
HE HAS MY SPEED.. PLUS IRON MAN'S! CAN'T KEEP OUT OF HIS REACH.. MORE THAN ANOTHER SECOND..!
MUST HOPE.. THAT MY DELAY.. HAS BEEN LONG ENOUGH!
AN INSTANT LATER...
SKRAK-K!
HE'S..HURLING A HEAVY BENCH.. AT ME! TOO TIRED.. TO DUCK..! AAARHHH!
BUT THEN, AS THE TOWERING, ANGRY FIGURE NOW MAKES STRAIGHT FOR THE STILL-DAZED FORM OF CAPTAIN AMERICA...
PIETRO IS DOWN! AND, IF HIS PLAN DOESN'T SUCCEED...
I DON'T UNDERSTAND IT EITHER, HONEY... BUT WE'VE GOT TO TRY IT!
THANK HEAVEN I REGAINED MY SENSES IN TIME TO HELP!
QUIT JAWIN' AND MOVE, AVENGERS! THAT BOZO'S GOT CAP.. WE MAY ALREADY BE TOO LATE TO--!
HOWEVER, THAT DREAD SENTENCE IS DESTINED NEVER TO BE FINISHED! FOR, IN THAT SELFSAME INSTANT...
THWAK!
YAHOOO! WE WOULDN'T HAVE MADE IT.. EXCEPT THAT CAP WOKE UP, AND SLAMMED THE ADAPTOID WITH HIS EVER-LOVIN' SHIELD!
AVENGERS ATTACK!!
NOW STRIKES MINE INVINCIBLE MACE...FOR THE LIFE OF CAPTAIN AMERICA!
GET BACK, ALL OF YOU! HE'S JUST.. AFTER ME..!
NO DICE, FRIEND! WHEN HE TOOK ON ONE AVENGER, HE TOOK ON ALL OF 'EM!
BUT HURRY.. HURRY... WHILE THERE'S STILL TIME..!
18.

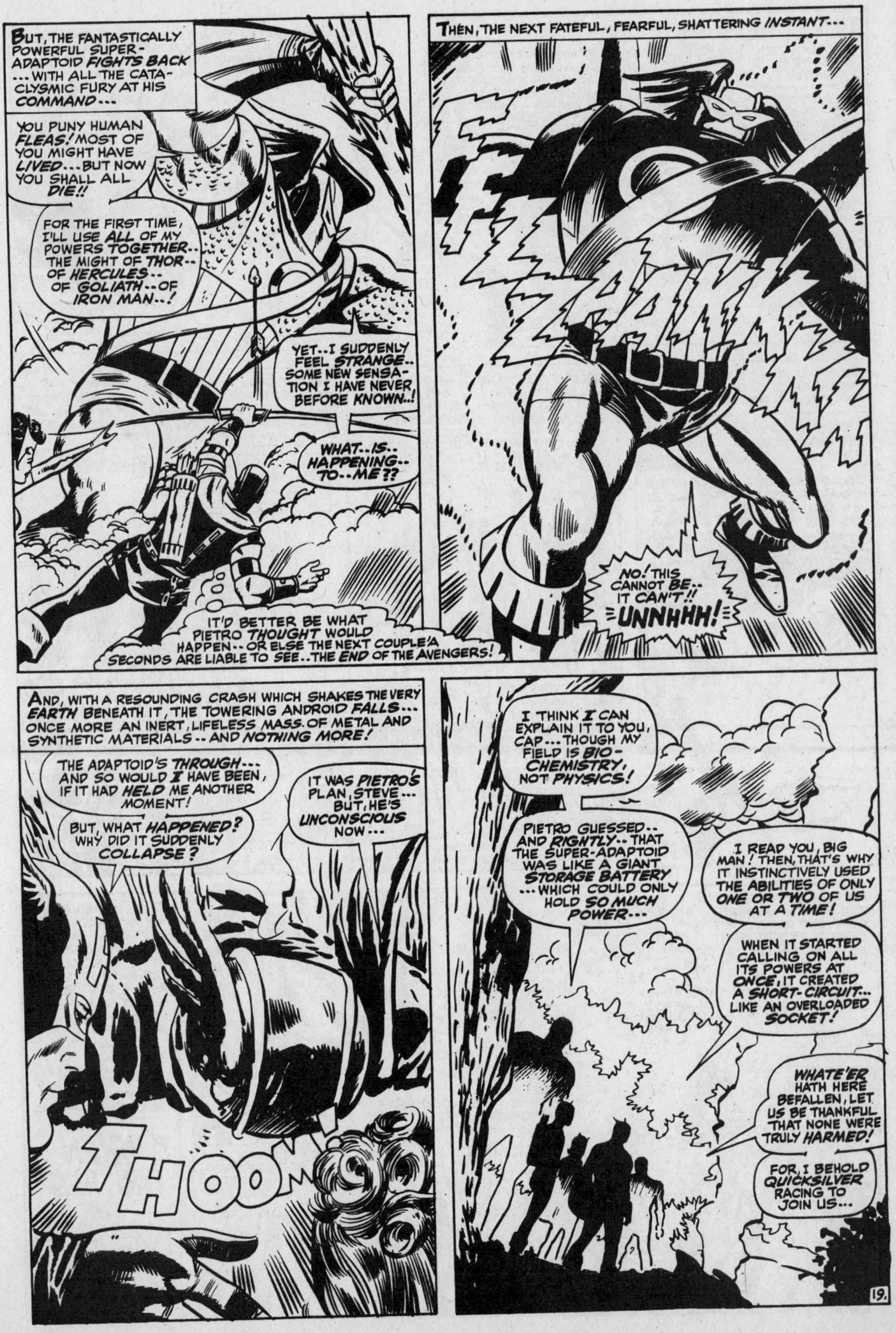
BUT, THE FANTASTICALLY POWERFUL SUPER-ADAPTOID FIGHTS BACK ...WITH ALL THE CATACLYSMIC FURY AT HIS COMMAND...
YOU PUNY HUMAN FLEAS! MOST OF YOU MIGHT HAVE LIVED...BUT NOW YOU SHALL ALL DIE!!
FOR THE FIRST TIME, I'LL USE ALL OF MY POWERS TOGETHER.. THE MIGHT OF THOR-- OF HERCULES-- OF GOLIATH--OF IRON MAN--!
YET..I SUDDENLY FEEL STRANGE.. SOME NEW SENSATION I HAVE NEVER BEFORE KNOWN..!
WHAT..IS.. HAPPENING-- TO--ME??
IT'D BETTER BE WHAT PIETRO THOUGHT WOULD HAPPEN--OR ELSE THE NEXT COUPLE'A SECONDS ARE LIABLE TO SEE..THE END OF THE AVENGERS!
THEN, THE NEXT FATEFUL, FEARFUL, SHATTERING INSTANT...
FZZAKK
NO! THIS CANNOT BE.. IT CAN'T!! UNNHHH!
AND, WITH A RESOUNDING CRASH WHICH SHAKES THE VERY EARTH BENEATH IT, THE TOWERING ANDROID FALLS... ONCE MORE AN INERT, LIFELESS MASS OF METAL AND SYNTHETIC MATERIALS--AND NOTHING MORE!
THE ADAPTOID'S THROUGH... AND SO WOULD I HAVE BEEN, IF IT HAD HELD ME ANOTHER MOMENT!
BUT, WHAT HAPPENED? WHY DID IT SUDDENLY COLLAPSE?
IT WAS PIETRO'S PLAN, STEVE... BUT, HE'S UNCONSCIOUS NOW...
THOOM
I THINK I CAN EXPLAIN IT TO YOU, CAP...THOUGH MY FIELD IS BIO-CHEMISTRY, NOT PHYSICS!
PIETRO GUESSED.. AND RIGHTLY.. THAT THE SUPER-ADAPTOID WAS LIKE A GIANT STORAGE BATTERY ...WHICH COULD ONLY HOLD SO MUCH POWER...
I READ YOU, BIG MAN! THEN, THAT'S WHY IT INSTINCTIVELY USED THE ABILITIES OF ONLY ONE OR TWO OF US AT A TIME!
WHEN IT STARTED CALLING ON ALL ITS POWERS AT ONCE, IT CREATED A SHORT-CIRCUIT... LIKE AN OVERLOADED SOCKET!
WHATE'ER HATH HERE BEFALLEN, LET US BE THANKFUL THAT NONE WERE TRULY HARMED!
FOR, I BEHOLD QUICKSILVER RACING TO JOIN US...

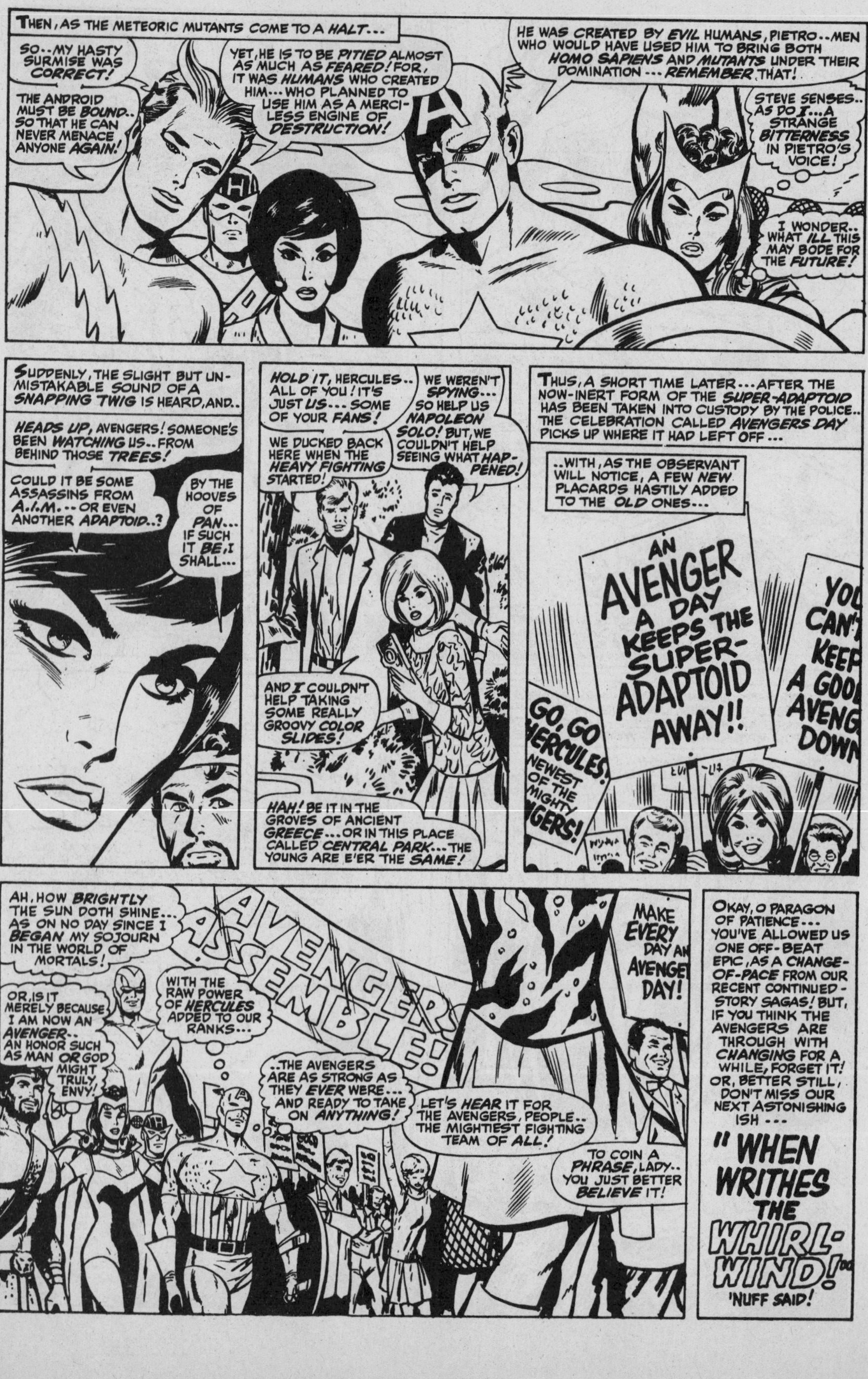

THEN, AS THE METEORIC MUTANTS COME TO A HALT...
SO.. MY HASTY SURMISE WAS CORRECT!
THE ANDROID MUST BE BOUND.. SO THAT HE CAN NEVER MENACE ANYONE AGAIN!
YET, HE IS TO BE PITIED ALMOST AS MUCH AS FEARED! FOR, IT WAS HUMANS WHO CREATED HIM... WHO PLANNED TO USE HIM AS A MERCILESS ENGINE OF DESTRUCTION!
HE WAS CREATED BY EVIL HUMANS, PIETRO.. MEN WHO WOULD HAVE USED HIM TO BRING BOTH HOMO SAPIENS AND MUTANTS UNDER THEIR DOMINATION -- REMEMBER THAT!
STEVE SENSES.. AS DO I... A STRANGE BITTERNESS IN PIETRO'S VOICE!
I WONDER.. WHAT ILL THIS MAY BODE FOR THE FUTURE!
SUDDENLY, THE SLIGHT BUT UNMISTAKABLE SOUND OF A SNAPPING TWIG IS HEARD, AND..
HEADS UP, AVENGERS! SOMEONE'S BEEN WATCHING US.. FROM BEHIND THOSE TREES!
COULD IT BE SOME ASSASSINS FROM A.I.M.-- OR EVEN ANOTHER ADAPTOID..?
BY THE HOOVES OF PAN... IF SUCH IT BE, I SHALL...
HOLD IT, HERCULES.. ALL OF YOU! IT'S JUST US... SOME OF YOUR FANS!
WE WEREN'T SPYING... SO HELP US NAPOLEON SOLO! BUT, WE COULDN'T HELP SEEING WHAT HAPPENED!
WE DUCKED BACK HERE WHEN THE HEAVY FIGHTING STARTED!
AND I COULDN'T HELP TAKING SOME REALLY GROOVY COLOR SLIDES!
HAH! BE IT IN THE GROVES OF ANCIENT GREECE... OR IN THIS PLACE CALLED CENTRAL PARK... THE YOUNG ARE E'ER THE SAME!
THUS, A SHORT TIME LATER... AFTER THE NOW-INERT FORM OF THE SUPER-ADAPTOID HAS BEEN TAKEN INTO CUSTODY BY THE POLICE.. THE CELEBRATION CALLED AVENGERS DAY PICKS UP WHERE IT HAD LEFT OFF...
..WITH, AS THE OBSERVANT WILL NOTICE, A FEW NEW PLACARDS HASTILY ADDED TO THE OLD ONES...
AN AVENGER A DAY KEEPS THE SUPER-ADAPTOID AWAY!!
GO, GO HERCULES! NEWEST OF THE MIGHTY [A]VENGERS!
YOU CAN'T KEEP A GOO[D] AVENG[ER] DOWN
AH, HOW BRIGHTLY THE SUN DOTH SHINE... AS ON NO DAY SINCE I BEGAN MY SOJOURN IN THE WORLD OF MORTALS!
AVENGERS ASSEMBLE!
MAKE EVERY DAY AN AVENGER DAY!
OR, IS IT MERELY BECAUSE I AM NOW AN AVENGER.. AN HONOR SUCH AS MAN OR GOD MIGHT TRULY ENVY!
WITH THE RAW POWER OF HERCULES ADDED TO OUR RANKS...
..THE AVENGERS ARE AS STRONG AS THEY EVER WERE... AND READY TO TAKE ON ANYTHING!
LET'S HEAR IT FOR THE AVENGERS, PEOPLE.. THE MIGHTIEST FIGHTING TEAM OF ALL!
TO COIN A PHRASE, LADY.. YOU JUST BETTER BELIEVE IT!
OKAY, O PARAGON OF PATIENCE... YOU'VE ALLOWED US ONE OFF-BEAT EPIC, AS A CHANGE-OF-PACE FROM OUR RECENT CONTINUED-STORY SAGAS! BUT, IF YOU THINK THE AVENGERS ARE THROUGH WITH CHANGING FOR A WHILE, FORGET IT! OR, BETTER STILL, DON'T MISS OUR NEXT ASTONISHING ISH ---
"WHEN WRITHES THE WHIRLWIND!"
'NUFF SAID!

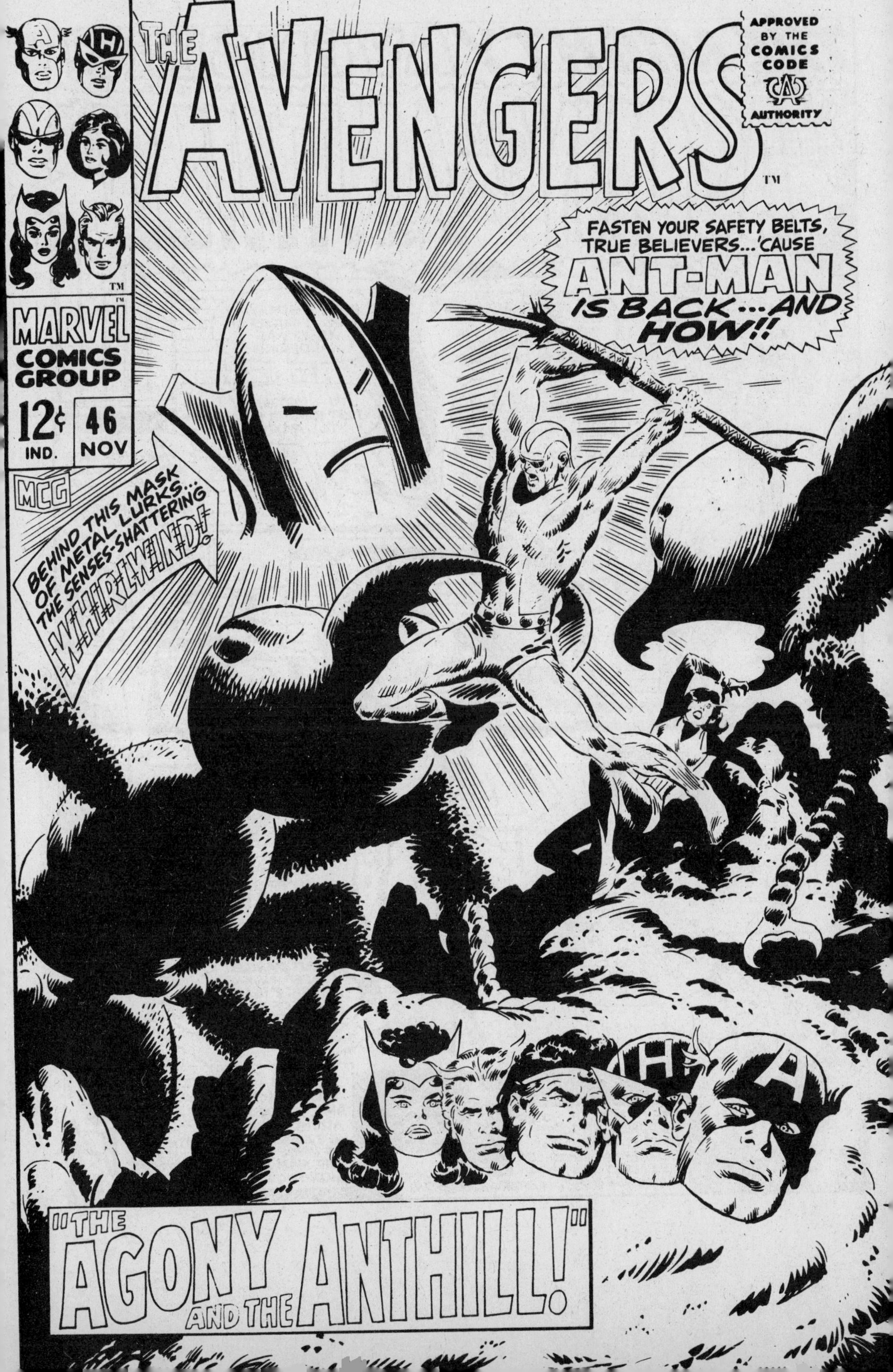
THE AVENGERS
APPROVED BY THE COMICS CODE CA AUTHORITY
MARVEL COMICS GROUP
12¢ IND.
46 NOV
MCG
FASTEN YOUR SAFETY BELTS, TRUE BELIEVERS...'CAUSE ANT-MAN IS BACK...AND HOW!!
BEHIND THIS MASK OF METAL LURKS... THE SENSES-SHATTERING WHIRLWIND!
"THE AGONY AND THE ANTHILL!"

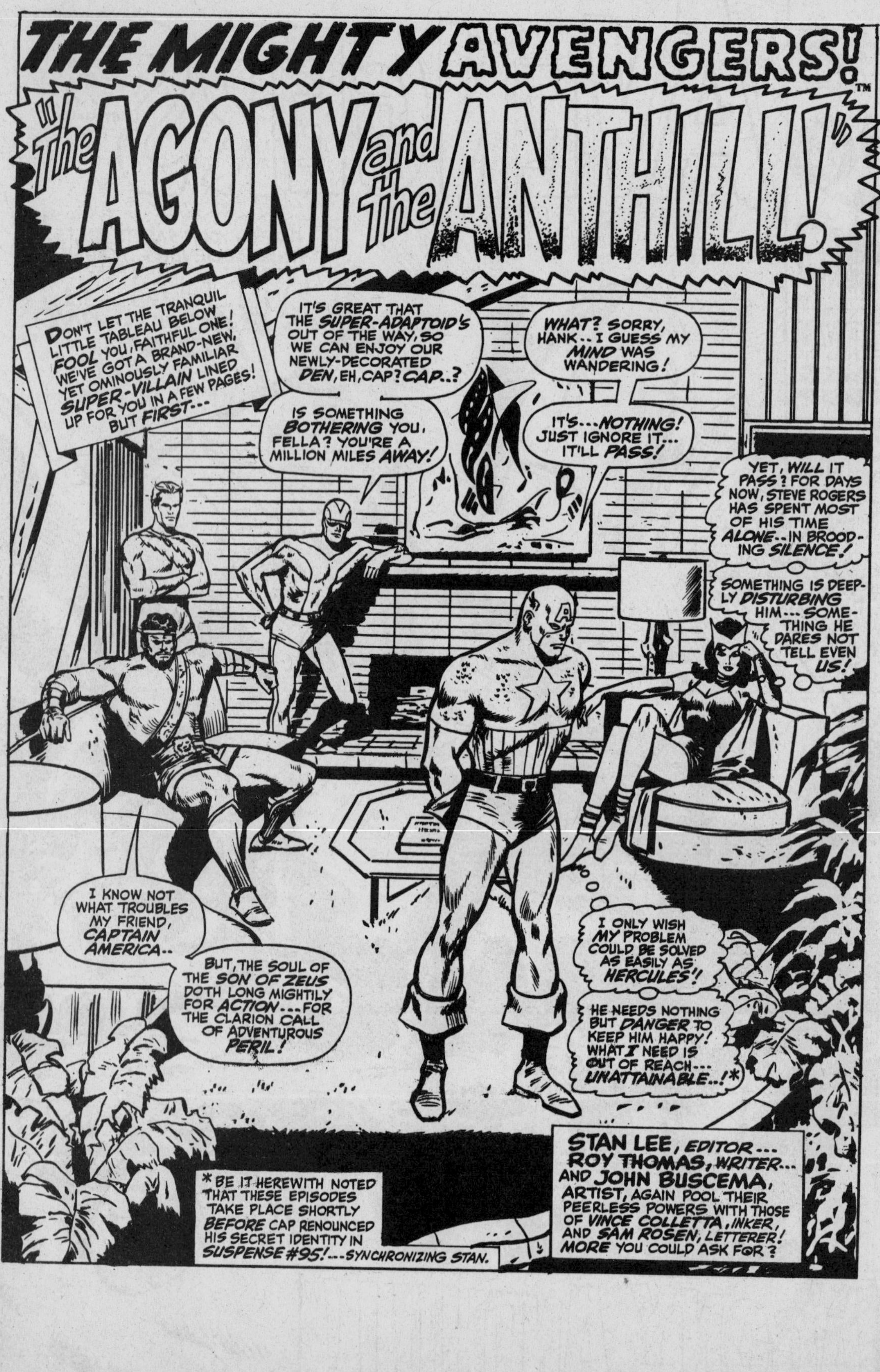

THE MIGHTY AVENGERS!
"The AGONY and the ANTHILL!"
DON'T LET THE TRANQUIL LITTLE TABLEAU BELOW FOOL YOU, FAITHFUL ONE! WE'VE GOT A BRAND-NEW, YET OMINOUSLY FAMILIAR SUPER-VILLAIN LINED UP FOR YOU IN A FEW PAGES! BUT FIRST--
IT'S GREAT THAT THE SUPER-ADAPTOID'S OUT OF THE WAY, SO WE CAN ENJOY OUR NEWLY-DECORATED DEN, EH, CAP? CAP..?
WHAT? SORRY, HANK.. I GUESS MY MIND WAS WANDERING!
IS SOMETHING BOTHERING YOU, FELLA? YOU'RE A MILLION MILES AWAY!
IT'S... NOTHING! JUST IGNORE IT... IT'LL PASS!
YET, WILL IT PASS? FOR DAYS NOW, STEVE ROGERS HAS SPENT MOST OF HIS TIME ALONE--IN BROODING SILENCE!
SOMETHING IS DEEPLY DISTURBING HIM--- SOMETHING HE DARES NOT TELL EVEN US!
I KNOW NOT WHAT TROUBLES MY FRIEND, CAPTAIN AMERICA..
BUT, THE SOUL OF THE SON OF ZEUS DOTH LONG MIGHTILY FOR ACTION... FOR THE CLARION CALL OF ADVENTUROUS PERIL!
I ONLY WISH MY PROBLEM COULD BE SOLVED AS EASILY AS HERCULES'!
HE NEEDS NOTHING BUT DANGER TO KEEP HIM HAPPY! WHAT I NEED IS OUT OF REACH--- UNATTAINABLE..!*
*BE IT HEREWITH NOTED THAT THESE EPISODES TAKE PLACE SHORTLY BEFORE CAP RENOUNCED HIS SECRET IDENTITY IN SUSPENSE #95! --- SYNCHRONIZING STAN.
STAN LEE, EDITOR... ROY THOMAS, WRITER... AND JOHN BUSCEMA, ARTIST, AGAIN POOL THEIR PEERLESS POWERS WITH THOSE OF VINCE COLLETTA, INKER, AND SAM ROSEN, LETTERER! MORE YOU COULD ASK FOR?

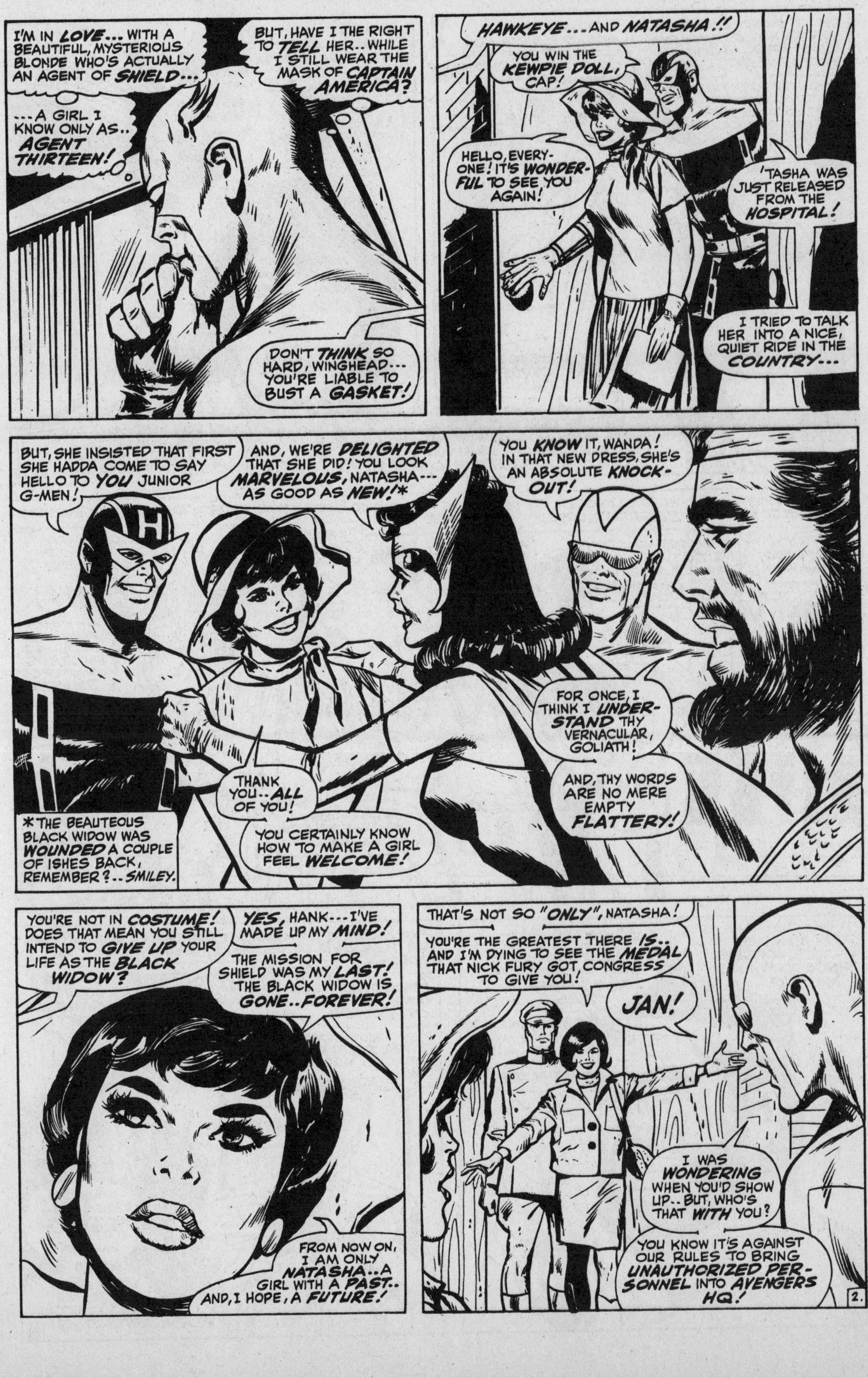

I'M IN LOVE... WITH A BEAUTIFUL, MYSTERIOUS BLONDE WHO'S ACTUALLY AN AGENT OF SHIELD...
BUT, HAVE I THE RIGHT TO TELL HER.. WHILE I STILL WEAR THE MASK OF CAPTAIN AMERICA?
...A GIRL I KNOW ONLY AS.. AGENT THIRTEEN!
DON'T THINK SO HARD, WINGHEAD--- YOU'RE LIABLE TO BUST A GASKET!
HAWKEYE... AND NATASHA!!
YOU WIN THE KEWPIE DOLL, CAP!
HELLO, EVERY-ONE! IT'S WONDER-FUL TO SEE YOU AGAIN!
'TASHA WAS JUST RELEASED FROM THE HOSPITAL!
I TRIED TO TALK HER INTO A NICE, QUIET RIDE IN THE COUNTRY---
BUT, SHE INSISTED THAT FIRST SHE HADDA COME TO SAY HELLO TO YOU JUNIOR G-MEN!
AND, WE'RE DELIGHTED THAT SHE DID! YOU LOOK MARVELOUS, NATASHA--- AS GOOD AS NEW!*
YOU KNOW IT, WANDA! IN THAT NEW DRESS, SHE'S AN ABSOLUTE KNOCK-OUT!
FOR ONCE, I THINK I UNDER-STAND THY VERNACULAR, GOLIATH!
AND, THY WORDS ARE NO MERE EMPTY FLATTERY!
THANK YOU.. ALL OF YOU!
YOU CERTAINLY KNOW HOW TO MAKE A GIRL FEEL WELCOME!
*THE BEAUTEOUS BLACK WIDOW WAS WOUNDED A COUPLE OF ISHES BACK, REMEMBER?.. SMILEY.
YOU'RE NOT IN COSTUME! DOES THAT MEAN YOU STILL INTEND TO GIVE UP YOUR LIFE AS THE BLACK WIDOW?
YES, HANK--- I'VE MADE UP MY MIND!
THE MISSION FOR SHIELD WAS MY LAST! THE BLACK WIDOW IS GONE.. FOREVER!
FROM NOW ON, I AM ONLY NATASHA.. A GIRL WITH A PAST.. AND, I HOPE, A FUTURE!
THAT'S NOT SO "ONLY", NATASHA!
YOU'RE THE GREATEST THERE IS.. AND I'M DYING TO SEE THE MEDAL THAT NICK FURY GOT CONGRESS TO GIVE YOU!
JAN!
I WAS WONDERING WHEN YOU'D SHOW UP.. BUT, WHO'S THAT WITH YOU?
YOU KNOW IT'S AGAINST OUR RULES TO BRING UNAUTHORIZED PER-SONNEL INTO AVENGERS HQ!
2.

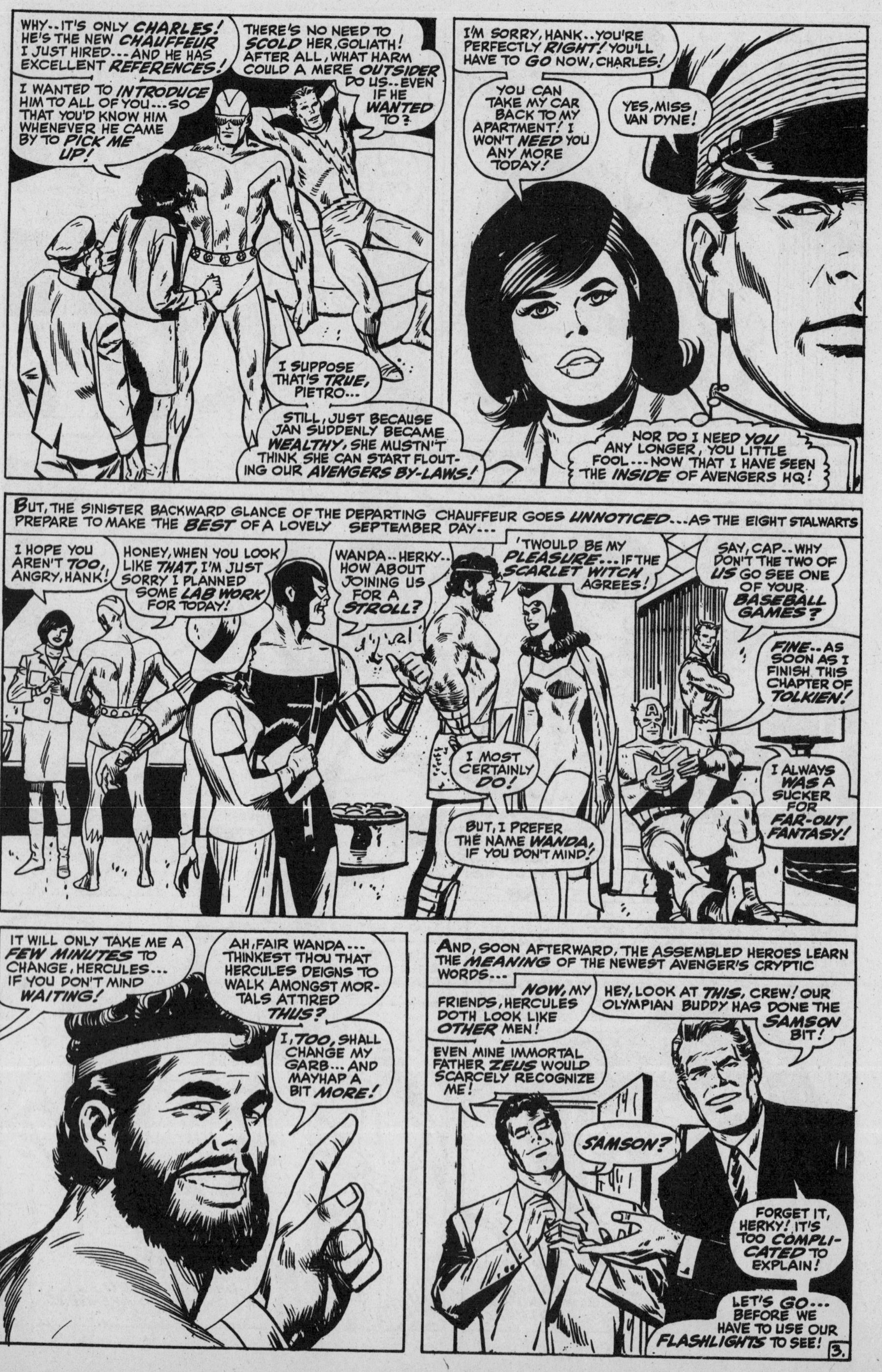

WHY..IT'S ONLY CHARLES! HE'S THE NEW CHAUFFEUR I JUST HIRED...AND HE HAS EXCELLENT REFERENCES!
I WANTED TO INTRODUCE HIM TO ALL OF YOU...SO THAT YOU'D KNOW HIM WHENEVER HE CAME BY TO PICK ME UP!
THERE'S NO NEED TO SCOLD HER, GOLIATH! AFTER ALL, WHAT HARM COULD A MERE OUTSIDER DO US...EVEN IF HE WANTED TO?
I SUPPOSE THAT'S TRUE, PIETRO...
STILL, JUST BECAUSE JAN SUDDENLY BECAME WEALTHY, SHE MUSTN'T THINK SHE CAN START FLOUTING OUR AVENGERS BY-LAWS!
I'M SORRY, HANK..YOU'RE PERFECTLY RIGHT! YOU'LL HAVE TO GO NOW, CHARLES!
YOU CAN TAKE MY CAR BACK TO MY APARTMENT! I WON'T NEED YOU ANY MORE TODAY!
YES, MISS VAN DYNE!
NOR DO I NEED YOU ANY LONGER, YOU LITTLE FOOL...NOW THAT I HAVE SEEN THE INSIDE OF AVENGERS HQ!
BUT, THE SINISTER BACKWARD GLANCE OF THE DEPARTING CHAUFFEUR GOES UNNOTICED...AS THE EIGHT STALWARTS PREPARE TO MAKE THE BEST OF A LOVELY SEPTEMBER DAY...
I HOPE YOU AREN'T TOO, ANGRY, HANK!
HONEY, WHEN YOU LOOK LIKE THAT, I'M JUST SORRY I PLANNED SOME LAB WORK FOR TODAY!
WANDA..HERKY..HOW ABOUT JOINING US FOR A STROLL?
'TWOULD BE MY PLEASURE...IF THE SCARLET WITCH AGREES!
I MOST CERTAINLY DO!
BUT, I PREFER THE NAME WANDA, IF YOU DON'T MIND!
SAY, CAP..WHY DON'T THE TWO OF US GO SEE ONE OF YOUR BASEBALL GAMES?
FINE..AS SOON AS I FINISH THIS CHAPTER OF TOLKIEN!
I ALWAYS WAS A SUCKER FOR FAR-OUT FANTASY!
IT WILL ONLY TAKE ME A FEW MINUTES TO CHANGE, HERCULES...IF YOU DON'T MIND WAITING!
AH, FAIR WANDA...THINKEST THOU THAT HERCULES DEIGNS TO WALK AMONGST MORTALS ATTIRED THUS?
I, TOO, SHALL CHANGE MY GARB...AND MAYHAP A BIT MORE!
AND, SOON AFTERWARD, THE ASSEMBLED HEROES LEARN THE MEANING OF THE NEWEST AVENGER'S CRYPTIC WORDS...
NOW, MY FRIENDS, HERCULES DOTH LOOK LIKE OTHER MEN!
EVEN MINE IMMORTAL FATHER ZEUS WOULD SCARCELY RECOGNIZE ME!
HEY, LOOK AT THIS, CREW! OUR OLYMPIAN BUDDY HAS DONE THE SAMSON BIT!
SAMSON?
FORGET IT, HERKY! IT'S TOO COMPLICATED TO EXPLAIN!
LET'S GO...BEFORE WE HAVE TO USE OUR FLASHLIGHTS TO SEE!
3.

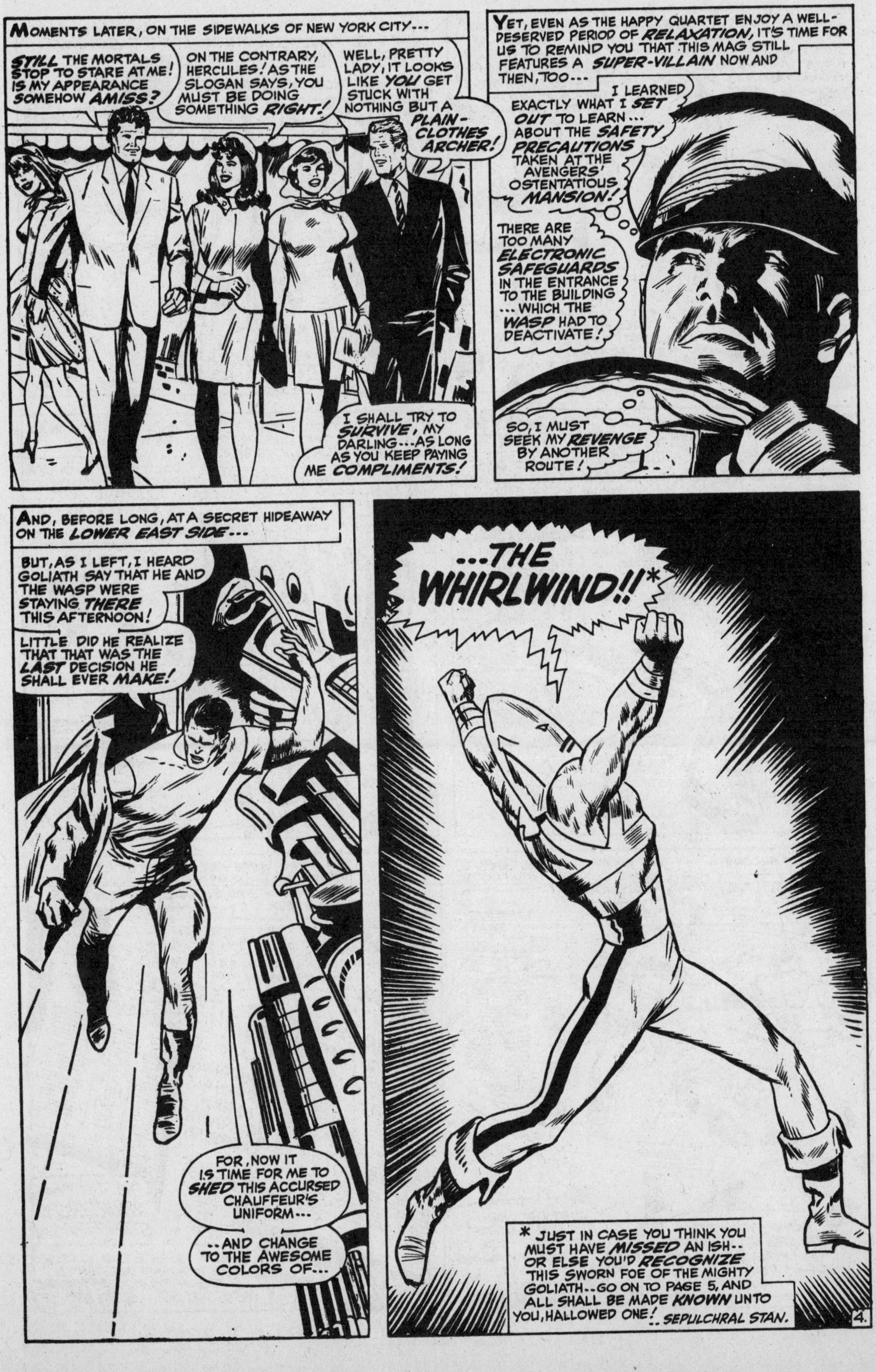

MOMENTS LATER, ON THE SIDEWALKS OF NEW YORK CITY...
STILL THE MORTALS STOP TO STARE AT ME! IS MY APPEARANCE SOMEHOW AMISS?
ON THE CONTRARY, HERCULES! AS THE SLOGAN SAYS, YOU MUST BE DOING SOMETHING RIGHT!
WELL, PRETTY LADY, IT LOOKS LIKE YOU GET STUCK WITH NOTHING BUT A PLAIN-CLOTHES ARCHER!
I SHALL TRY TO SURVIVE, MY DARLING...AS LONG AS YOU KEEP PAYING ME COMPLIMENTS!
YET, EVEN AS THE HAPPY QUARTET ENJOY A WELL-DESERVED PERIOD OF RELAXATION, IT'S TIME FOR US TO REMIND YOU THAT THIS MAG STILL FEATURES A SUPER-VILLAIN NOW AND THEN, TOO...
I LEARNED EXACTLY WHAT I SET OUT TO LEARN... ABOUT THE SAFETY PRECAUTIONS TAKEN AT THE AVENGERS' OSTENTATIOUS MANSION!
THERE ARE TOO MANY ELECTRONIC SAFEGUARDS IN THE ENTRANCE TO THE BUILDING ...WHICH THE WASP HAD TO DEACTIVATE!
SO, I MUST SEEK MY REVENGE BY ANOTHER ROUTE!
AND, BEFORE LONG, AT A SECRET HIDEAWAY ON THE LOWER EAST SIDE...
BUT, AS I LEFT, I HEARD GOLIATH SAY THAT HE AND THE WASP WERE STAYING THERE THIS AFTERNOON!
LITTLE DID HE REALIZE THAT THAT WAS THE LAST DECISION HE SHALL EVER MAKE!
FOR, NOW IT IS TIME FOR ME TO SHED THIS ACCURSED CHAUFFEUR'S UNIFORM...
..AND CHANGE TO THE AWESOME COLORS OF...
...THE WHIRLWIND!!*
* JUST IN CASE YOU THINK YOU MUST HAVE MISSED AN ISH--OR ELSE YOU'D RECOGNIZE THIS SWORN FOE OF THE MIGHTY GOLIATH..GO ON TO PAGE 5, AND ALL SHALL BE MADE KNOWN UNTO YOU, HALLOWED ONE! ..SEPULCHRAL STAN.
4.

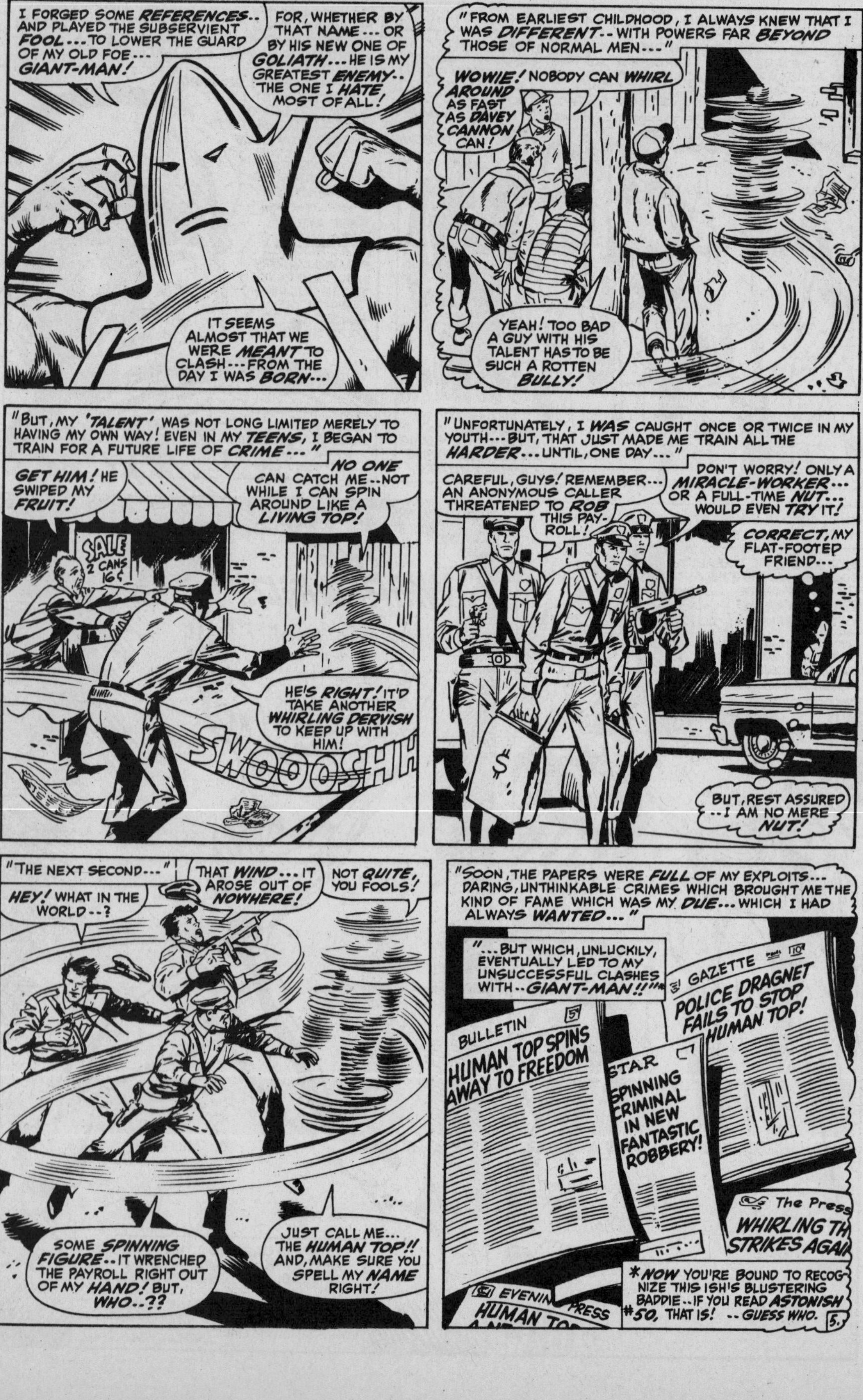

I FORGED SOME REFERENCES.. AND PLAYED THE SUBSERVIENT FOOL... TO LOWER THE GUARD OF MY OLD FOE--- GIANT-MAN!
FOR, WHETHER BY THAT NAME... OR BY HIS NEW ONE OF GOLIATH... HE IS MY GREATEST ENEMY.. THE ONE I HATE MOST OF ALL!
IT SEEMS ALMOST THAT WE WERE MEANT TO CLASH---FROM THE DAY I WAS BORN...
"FROM EARLIEST CHILDHOOD, I ALWAYS KNEW THAT I WAS DIFFERENT -- WITH POWERS FAR BEYOND THOSE OF NORMAL MEN---"
WOWIE! NOBODY CAN WHIRL AROUND AS FAST AS DAVEY CANNON CAN!
YEAH! TOO BAD A GUY WITH HIS TALENT HAS TO BE SUCH A ROTTEN BULLY!
"BUT, MY 'TALENT' WAS NOT LONG LIMITED MERELY TO HAVING MY OWN WAY! EVEN IN MY TEENS, I BEGAN TO TRAIN FOR A FUTURE LIFE OF CRIME---"
GET HIM! HE SWIPED MY FRUIT!
NO ONE CAN CATCH ME..NOT WHILE I CAN SPIN AROUND LIKE A LIVING TOP!
SALE 2 CANS 16¢
HE'S RIGHT! IT'D TAKE ANOTHER WHIRLING DERVISH TO KEEP UP WITH HIM!
SWOOOSHH
"UNFORTUNATELY, I WAS CAUGHT ONCE OR TWICE IN MY YOUTH---BUT, THAT JUST MADE ME TRAIN ALL THE HARDER... UNTIL, ONE DAY..."
CAREFUL, GUYS! REMEMBER... AN ANONYMOUS CALLER THREATENED TO ROB THIS PAYROLL!
DON'T WORRY! ONLY A MIRACLE-WORKER... OR A FULL-TIME NUT... WOULD EVEN TRY IT!
CORRECT, MY FLAT-FOOTED FRIEND...
BUT, REST ASSURED.. I AM NO MERE NUT!
"THE NEXT SECOND---"
HEY! WHAT IN THE WORLD--?
THAT WIND... IT AROSE OUT OF NOWHERE!
NOT QUITE, YOU FOOLS!
SOME SPINNING FIGURE.. IT WRENCHED THE PAYROLL RIGHT OUT OF MY HAND! BUT, WHO..??
JUST CALL ME... THE HUMAN TOP!! AND, MAKE SURE YOU SPELL MY NAME RIGHT!
"SOON, THE PAPERS WERE FULL OF MY EXPLOITS... DARING, UNTHINKABLE CRIMES WHICH BROUGHT ME THE KIND OF FAME WHICH WAS MY DUE... WHICH I HAD ALWAYS WANTED..."
"...BUT WHICH, UNLUCKILY, EVENTUALLY LED TO MY UNSUCCESSFUL CLASHES WITH..GIANT-MAN!!"*
GAZETTE
POLICE DRAGNET FAILS TO STOP HUMAN TOP!
BULLETIN
HUMAN TOP SPINS AWAY TO FREEDOM
STAR
SPINNING CRIMINAL IN NEW FANTASTIC ROBBERY!
The Press
WHIRLING TH STRIKES AGAI
EVENIN PRESS
HUMAN TO
*NOW YOU'RE BOUND TO RECOGNIZE THIS ISH'S BLUSTERING BADDIE..IF YOU READ ASTONISH #50, THAT IS! --GUESS WHO.
5.

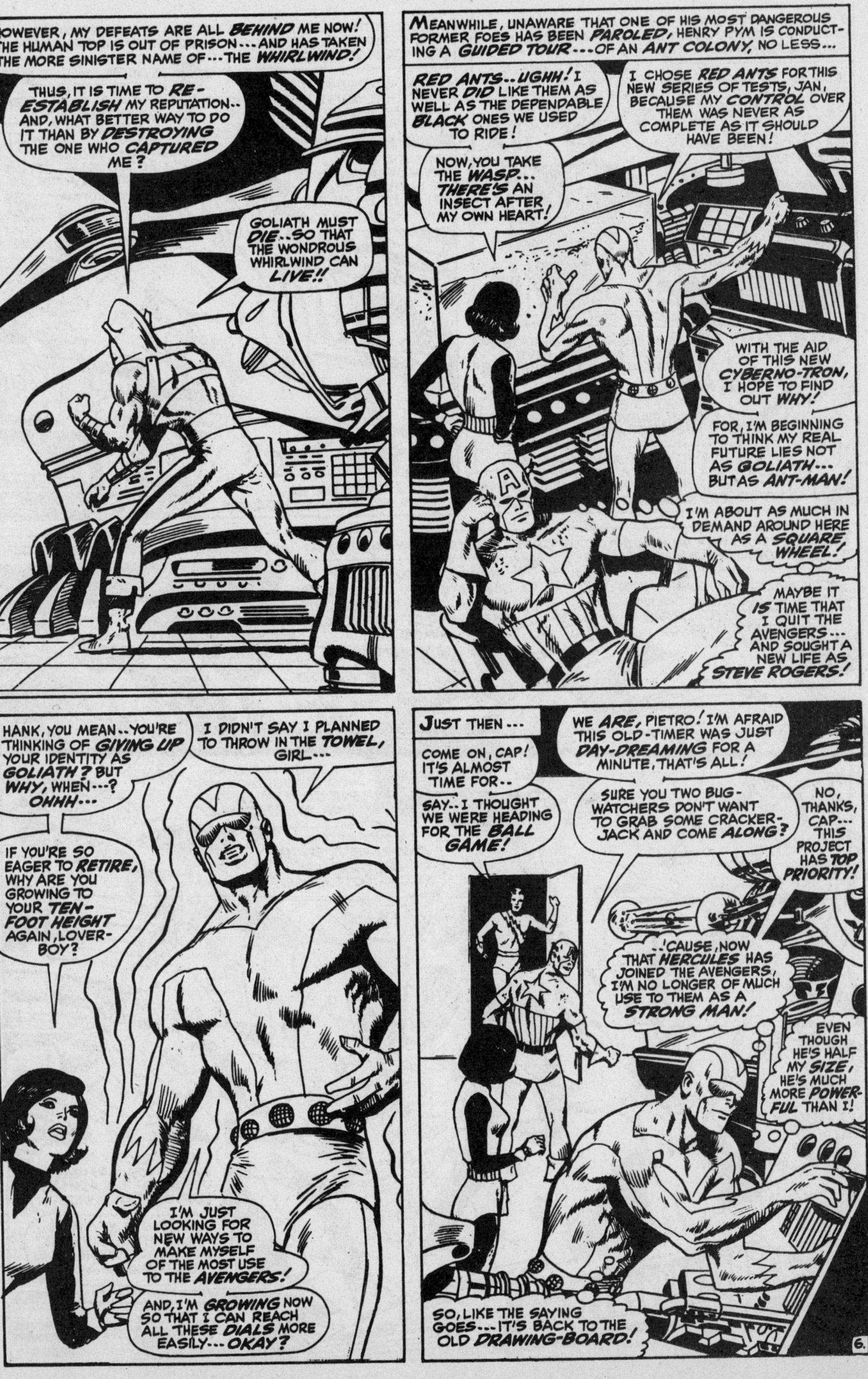
HOWEVER, MY DEFEATS ARE ALL BEHIND ME NOW! THE HUMAN TOP IS OUT OF PRISON... AND HAS TAKEN THE MORE SINISTER NAME OF... THE WHIRLWIND!
THUS, IT IS TIME TO RE-ESTABLISH MY REPUTATION.. AND, WHAT BETTER WAY TO DO IT THAN BY DESTROYING THE ONE WHO CAPTURED ME?
GOLIATH MUST DIE.. SO THAT THE WONDROUS WHIRLWIND CAN LIVE!!
MEANWHILE, UNAWARE THAT ONE OF HIS MOST DANGEROUS FORMER FOES HAS BEEN PAROLED, HENRY PYM IS CONDUCTING A GUIDED TOUR... OF AN ANT COLONY, NO LESS...
RED ANTS.. UGHH! I NEVER DID LIKE THEM AS WELL AS THE DEPENDABLE BLACK ONES WE USED TO RIDE!
I CHOSE RED ANTS FOR THIS NEW SERIES OF TESTS, JAN, BECAUSE MY CONTROL OVER THEM WAS NEVER AS COMPLETE AS IT SHOULD HAVE BEEN!
NOW, YOU TAKE THE WASP... THERE'S AN INSECT AFTER MY OWN HEART!
WITH THE AID OF THIS NEW CYBERNO-TRON, I HOPE TO FIND OUT WHY!
FOR, I'M BEGINNING TO THINK MY REAL FUTURE LIES NOT AS GOLIATH... BUT AS ANT-MAN!
I'M ABOUT AS MUCH IN DEMAND AROUND HERE AS A SQUARE WHEEL!
MAYBE IT IS TIME THAT I QUIT THE AVENGERS... AND SOUGHT A NEW LIFE AS STEVE ROGERS!
HANK, YOU MEAN.. YOU'RE THINKING OF GIVING UP YOUR IDENTITY AS GOLIATH? BUT WHY, WHEN...? OHHH...
I DIDN'T SAY I PLANNED TO THROW IN THE TOWEL, GIRL...
IF YOU'RE SO EAGER TO RETIRE, WHY ARE YOU GROWING TO YOUR TEN-FOOT HEIGHT AGAIN, LOVER-BOY?
I'M JUST LOOKING FOR NEW WAYS TO MAKE MYSELF OF THE MOST USE TO THE AVENGERS!
AND, I'M GROWING NOW SO THAT I CAN REACH ALL THESE DIALS MORE EASILY... OKAY?
JUST THEN...
COME ON, CAP! IT'S ALMOST TIME FOR..
SAY.. I THOUGHT WE WERE HEADING FOR THE BALL GAME!
WE ARE, PIETRO! I'M AFRAID THIS OLD-TIMER WAS JUST DAY-DREAMING FOR A MINUTE, THAT'S ALL!
SURE YOU TWO BUG-WATCHERS DON'T WANT TO GRAB SOME CRACKER-JACK AND COME ALONG?
NO, THANKS, CAP... THIS PROJECT HAS TOP PRIORITY!
..'CAUSE, NOW THAT HERCULES HAS JOINED THE AVENGERS, I'M NO LONGER OF MUCH USE TO THEM AS A STRONG MAN!
EVEN THOUGH HE'S HALF MY SIZE, HE'S MUCH MORE POWER-FUL THAN I!
SO, LIKE THE SAYING GOES... IT'S BACK TO THE OLD DRAWING-BOARD!
6.

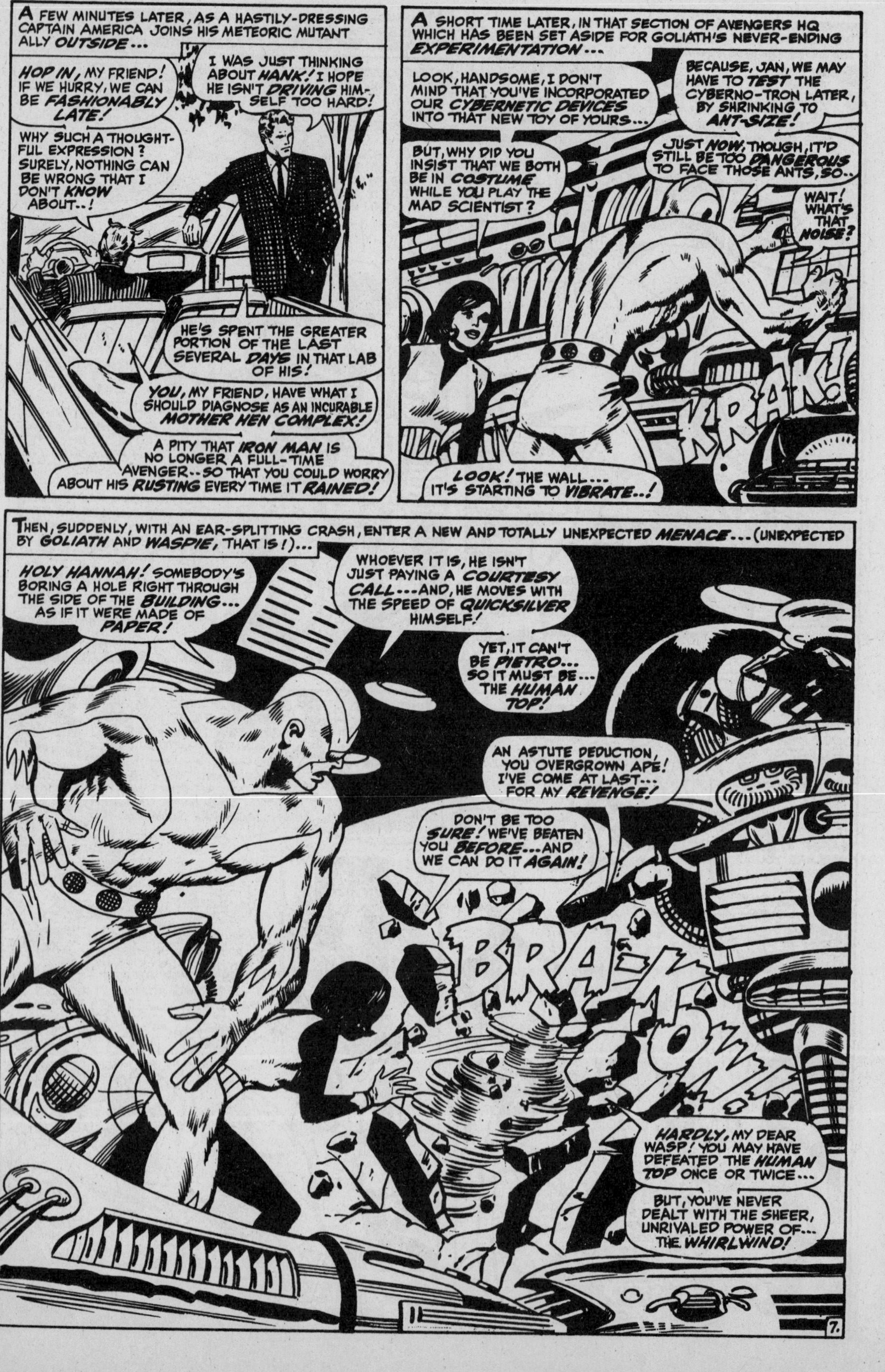

A FEW MINUTES LATER, AS A HASTILY-DRESSING CAPTAIN AMERICA JOINS HIS METEORIC MUTANT ALLY OUTSIDE...
HOP IN, MY FRIEND! IF WE HURRY, WE CAN BE FASHIONABLY LATE!
I WAS JUST THINKING ABOUT HANK! I HOPE HE ISN'T DRIVING HIMSELF TOO HARD!
WHY SUCH A THOUGHTFUL EXPRESSION? SURELY, NOTHING CAN BE WRONG THAT I DON'T KNOW ABOUT..!
HE'S SPENT THE GREATER PORTION OF THE LAST SEVERAL DAYS IN THAT LAB OF HIS!
YOU, MY FRIEND, HAVE WHAT I SHOULD DIAGNOSE AS AN INCURABLE MOTHER HEN COMPLEX!
A PITY THAT IRON MAN IS NO LONGER A FULL-TIME AVENGER.. SO THAT YOU COULD WORRY ABOUT HIS RUSTING EVERY TIME IT RAINED!
A SHORT TIME LATER, IN THAT SECTION OF AVENGERS HQ WHICH HAS BEEN SET ASIDE FOR GOLIATH'S NEVER-ENDING EXPERIMENTATION...
LOOK, HANDSOME, I DON'T MIND THAT YOU'VE INCORPORATED OUR CYBERNETIC DEVICES INTO THAT NEW TOY OF YOURS...
BUT, WHY DID YOU INSIST THAT WE BOTH BE IN COSTUME WHILE YOU PLAY THE MAD SCIENTIST?
BECAUSE, JAN, WE MAY HAVE TO TEST THE CYBERNO-TRON LATER, BY SHRINKING TO ANT-SIZE!
JUST NOW, THOUGH, IT'D STILL BE TOO DANGEROUS TO FACE THOSE ANTS, SO..
WAIT! WHAT'S THAT NOISE?
KRAK!
LOOK! THE WALL... IT'S STARTING TO VIBRATE..!
THEN, SUDDENLY, WITH AN EAR-SPLITTING CRASH, ENTER A NEW AND TOTALLY UNEXPECTED MENACE... (UNEXPECTED BY GOLIATH AND WASPIE, THAT IS!)...
HOLY HANNAH! SOMEBODY'S BORING A HOLE RIGHT THROUGH THE SIDE OF THE BUILDING... AS IF IT WERE MADE OF PAPER!
WHOEVER IT IS, HE ISN'T JUST PAYING A COURTESY CALL... AND, HE MOVES WITH THE SPEED OF QUICKSILVER HIMSELF!
YET, IT CAN'T BE PIETRO... SO IT MUST BE... THE HUMAN TOP!
AN ASTUTE DEDUCTION, YOU OVERGROWN APE! I'VE COME AT LAST... FOR MY REVENGE!
DON'T BE TOO SURE! WE'VE BEATEN YOU BEFORE... AND WE CAN DO IT AGAIN!
BRA-KOOM!
HARDLY, MY DEAR WASP! YOU MAY HAVE DEFEATED THE HUMAN TOP ONCE OR TWICE...
BUT, YOU'VE NEVER DEALT WITH THE SHEER, UNRIVALED POWER OF... THE WHIRLWIND!

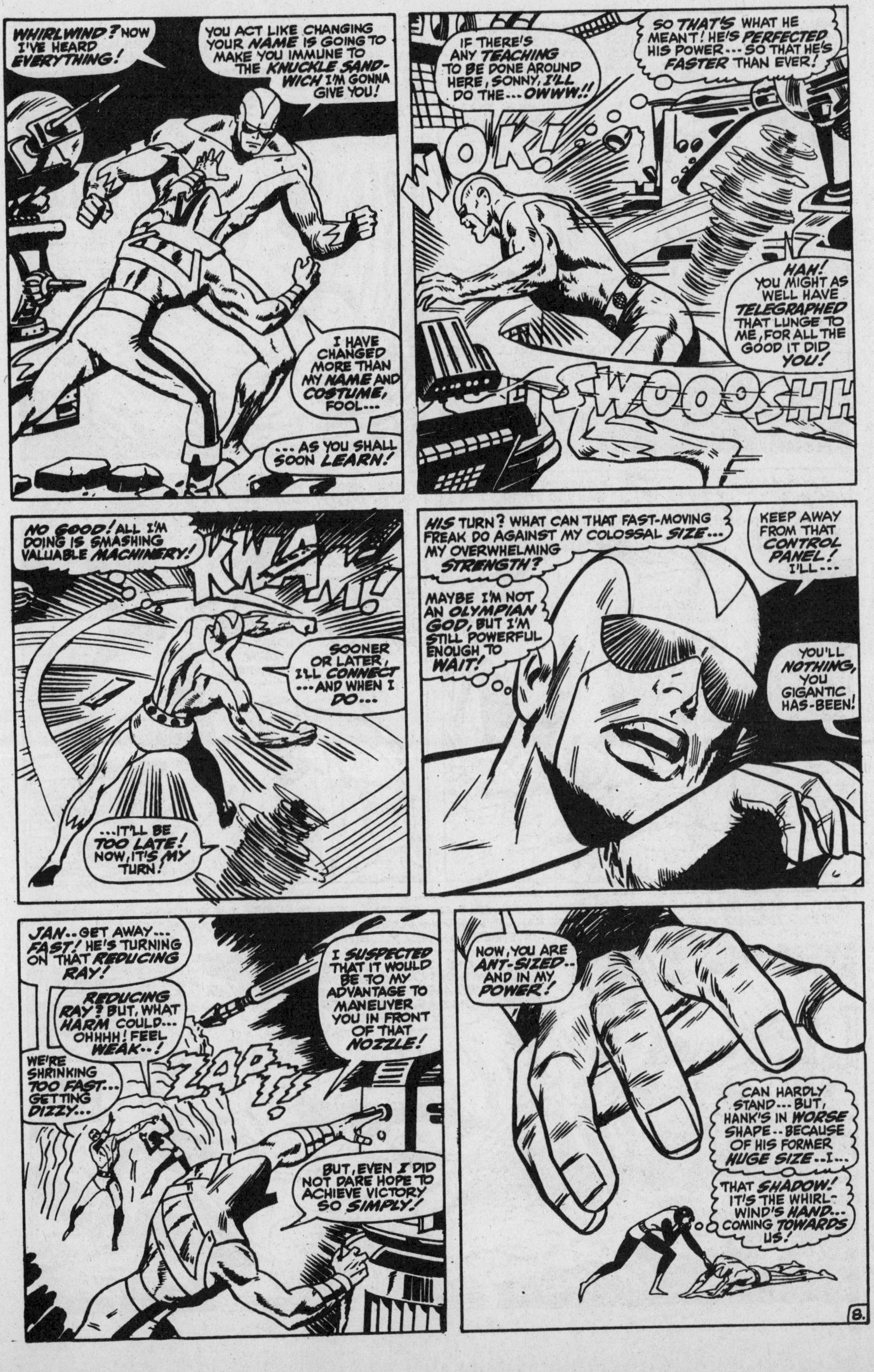
WHIRLWIND? NOW I'VE HEARD EVERYTHING!
YOU ACT LIKE CHANGING YOUR NAME IS GOING TO MAKE YOU IMMUNE TO THE KNUCKLE SANDWICH I'M GONNA GIVE YOU!
I HAVE CHANGED MORE THAN MY NAME AND COSTUME, FOOL...
...AS YOU SHALL SOON LEARN!
IF THERE'S ANY TEACHING TO BE DONE AROUND HERE, SONNY, I'LL DO THE... OWWW!!
SO THAT'S WHAT HE MEANT! HE'S PERFECTED HIS POWER... SO THAT HE'S FASTER THAN EVER!
WOK!
HAH! YOU MIGHT AS WELL HAVE TELEGRAPHED THAT LUNGE TO ME, FOR ALL THE GOOD IT DID YOU!
SWOOOSHH
NO GOOD! ALL I'M DOING IS SMASHING VALUABLE MACHINERY!
KWAM!
SOONER OR LATER, I'LL CONNECT ...AND WHEN I DO...
...IT'LL BE TOO LATE! NOW, IT'S MY TURN!
HIS TURN? WHAT CAN THAT FAST-MOVING FREAK DO AGAINST MY COLOSSAL SIZE... MY OVERWHELMING STRENGTH?
MAYBE I'M NOT AN OLYMPIAN GOD, BUT I'M STILL POWERFUL ENOUGH TO WAIT!
KEEP AWAY FROM THAT CONTROL PANEL! I'LL...
YOU'LL NOTHING, YOU GIGANTIC HAS-BEEN!
JAN.. GET AWAY... FAST! HE'S TURNING ON THAT REDUCING RAY!
REDUCING RAY? BUT, WHAT HARM COULD... OHHHH! FEEL WEAK..!
WE'RE SHRINKING TOO FAST... GETTING DIZZY...
I SUSPECTED THAT IT WOULD BE TO MY ADVANTAGE TO MANEUVER YOU IN FRONT OF THAT NOZZLE!
ZAPT!!
BUT, EVEN I DID NOT DARE HOPE TO ACHIEVE VICTORY SO SIMPLY!
NOW, YOU ARE ANT-SIZED.. AND IN MY POWER!
CAN HARDLY STAND... BUT, HANK'S IN WORSE SHAPE.. BECAUSE OF HIS FORMER HUGE SIZE..I...
THAT SHADOW! IT'S THE WHIRLWIND'S HAND... COMING TOWARDS US!
8.

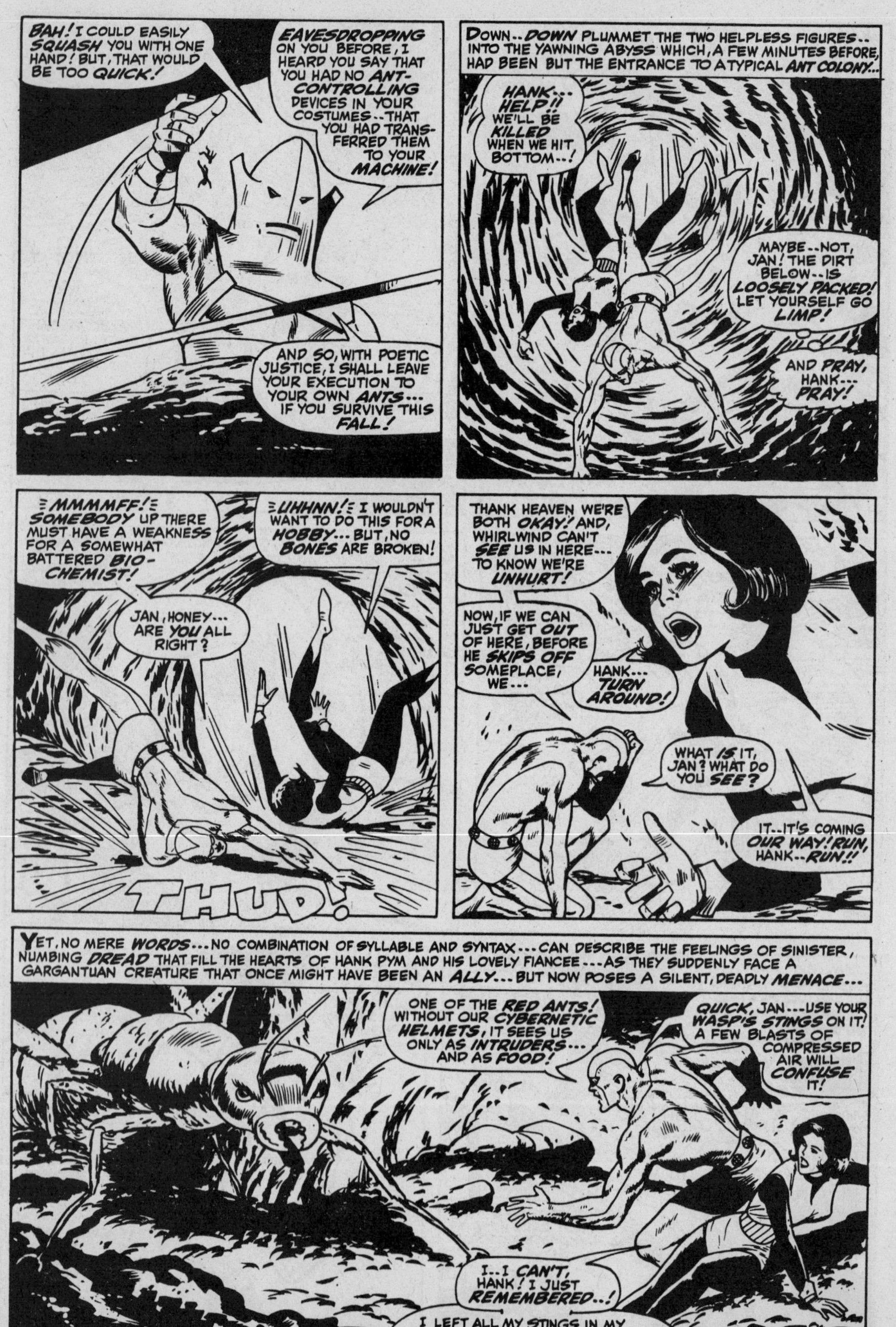

BAH! I COULD EASILY SQUASH YOU WITH ONE HAND! BUT, THAT WOULD BE TOO QUICK!
EAVESDROPPING ON YOU BEFORE, I HEARD YOU SAY THAT YOU HAD NO ANT-CONTROLLING DEVICES IN YOUR COSTUMES-- THAT YOU HAD TRANSFERRED THEM TO YOUR MACHINE!
AND SO, WITH POETIC JUSTICE, I SHALL LEAVE YOUR EXECUTION TO YOUR OWN ANTS... IF YOU SURVIVE THIS FALL!
DOWN.. DOWN PLUMMET THE TWO HELPLESS FIGURES.. INTO THE YAWNING ABYSS WHICH, A FEW MINUTES BEFORE, HAD BEEN BUT THE ENTRANCE TO A TYPICAL ANT COLONY...
HANK... HELP!! WE'LL BE KILLED WHEN WE HIT BOTTOM--!
MAYBE--NOT, JAN! THE DIRT BELOW--IS LOOSELY PACKED! LET YOURSELF GO LIMP!
AND PRAY, HANK--- PRAY!
MMMMFF! SOMEBODY UP THERE MUST HAVE A WEAKNESS FOR A SOMEWHAT BATTERED BIO-CHEMIST!
UHHNN! I WOULDN'T WANT TO DO THIS FOR A HOBBY... BUT, NO BONES ARE BROKEN!
JAN, HONEY... ARE YOU ALL RIGHT?
THUD!
THANK HEAVEN WE'RE BOTH OKAY! AND, WHIRLWIND CAN'T SEE US IN HERE... TO KNOW WE'RE UNHURT!
NOW, IF WE CAN JUST GET OUT OF HERE, BEFORE HE SKIPS OFF SOMEPLACE, WE...
HANK... TURN AROUND!
WHAT IS IT, JAN? WHAT DO YOU SEE?
IT--IT'S COMING OUR WAY! RUN, HANK--RUN!!
YET, NO MERE WORDS... NO COMBINATION OF SYLLABLE AND SYNTAX... CAN DESCRIBE THE FEELINGS OF SINISTER, NUMBING DREAD THAT FILL THE HEARTS OF HANK PYM AND HIS LOVELY FIANCEE... AS THEY SUDDENLY FACE A GARGANTUAN CREATURE THAT ONCE MIGHT HAVE BEEN AN ALLY... BUT NOW POSES A SILENT, DEADLY MENACE...
ONE OF THE RED ANTS! WITHOUT OUR CYBERNETIC HELMETS, IT SEES US ONLY AS INTRUDERS... AND AS FOOD!
QUICK, JAN... USE YOUR WASP'S STINGS ON IT! A FEW BLASTS OF COMPRESSED AIR WILL CONFUSE IT!
I--I CAN'T, HANK! I JUST REMEMBERED--!
I LEFT ALL MY STINGS IN MY OTHER COSTUME--THE NEW SEQUINED ONE! WE'RE DOOMED!!
9.

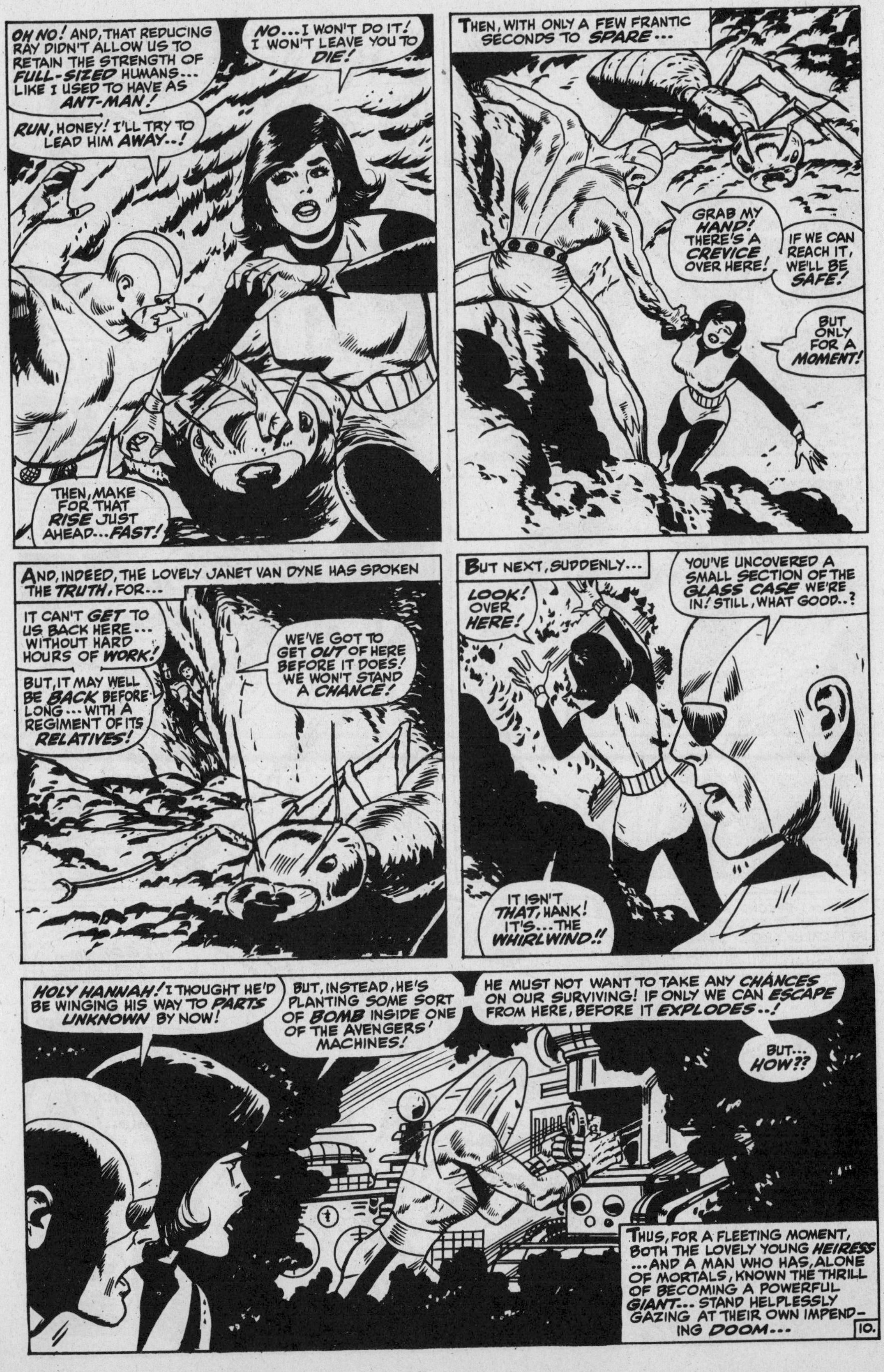

OH NO! AND, THAT REDUCING RAY DIDN'T ALLOW US TO RETAIN THE STRENGTH OF FULL-SIZED HUMANS... LIKE I USED TO HAVE AS ANT-MAN!
RUN, HONEY! I'LL TRY TO LEAD HIM AWAY..!
NO... I WON'T DO IT! I WON'T LEAVE YOU TO DIE!
THEN, MAKE FOR THAT RISE JUST AHEAD... FAST!
THEN, WITH ONLY A FEW FRANTIC SECONDS TO SPARE...
GRAB MY HAND! THERE'S A CREVICE OVER HERE!
IF WE CAN REACH IT, WE'LL BE SAFE!
BUT ONLY FOR A MOMENT!
AND, INDEED, THE LOVELY JANET VAN DYNE HAS SPOKEN THE TRUTH, FOR...
IT CAN'T GET TO US BACK HERE... WITHOUT HARD HOURS OF WORK!
BUT, IT MAY WELL BE BACK BEFORE LONG... WITH A REGIMENT OF ITS RELATIVES!
WE'VE GOT TO GET OUT OF HERE BEFORE IT DOES! WE WON'T STAND A CHANCE!
BUT NEXT, SUDDENLY...
LOOK! OVER HERE!
YOU'VE UNCOVERED A SMALL SECTION OF THE GLASS CASE WE'RE IN! STILL, WHAT GOOD..?
IT ISN'T THAT, HANK! IT'S... THE WHIRLWIND!!
HOLY HANNAH! I THOUGHT HE'D BE WINGING HIS WAY TO PARTS UNKNOWN BY NOW!
BUT, INSTEAD, HE'S PLANTING SOME SORT OF BOMB INSIDE ONE OF THE AVENGERS' MACHINES!
HE MUST NOT WANT TO TAKE ANY CHANCES ON OUR SURVIVING! IF ONLY WE CAN ESCAPE FROM HERE, BEFORE IT EXPLODES..!
BUT... HOW??
THUS, FOR A FLEETING MOMENT, BOTH THE LOVELY YOUNG HEIRESS ...AND A MAN WHO HAS, ALONE OF MORTALS, KNOWN THE THRILL OF BECOMING A POWERFUL GIANT... STAND HELPLESSLY GAZING AT THEIR OWN IMPENDING DOOM...
10.

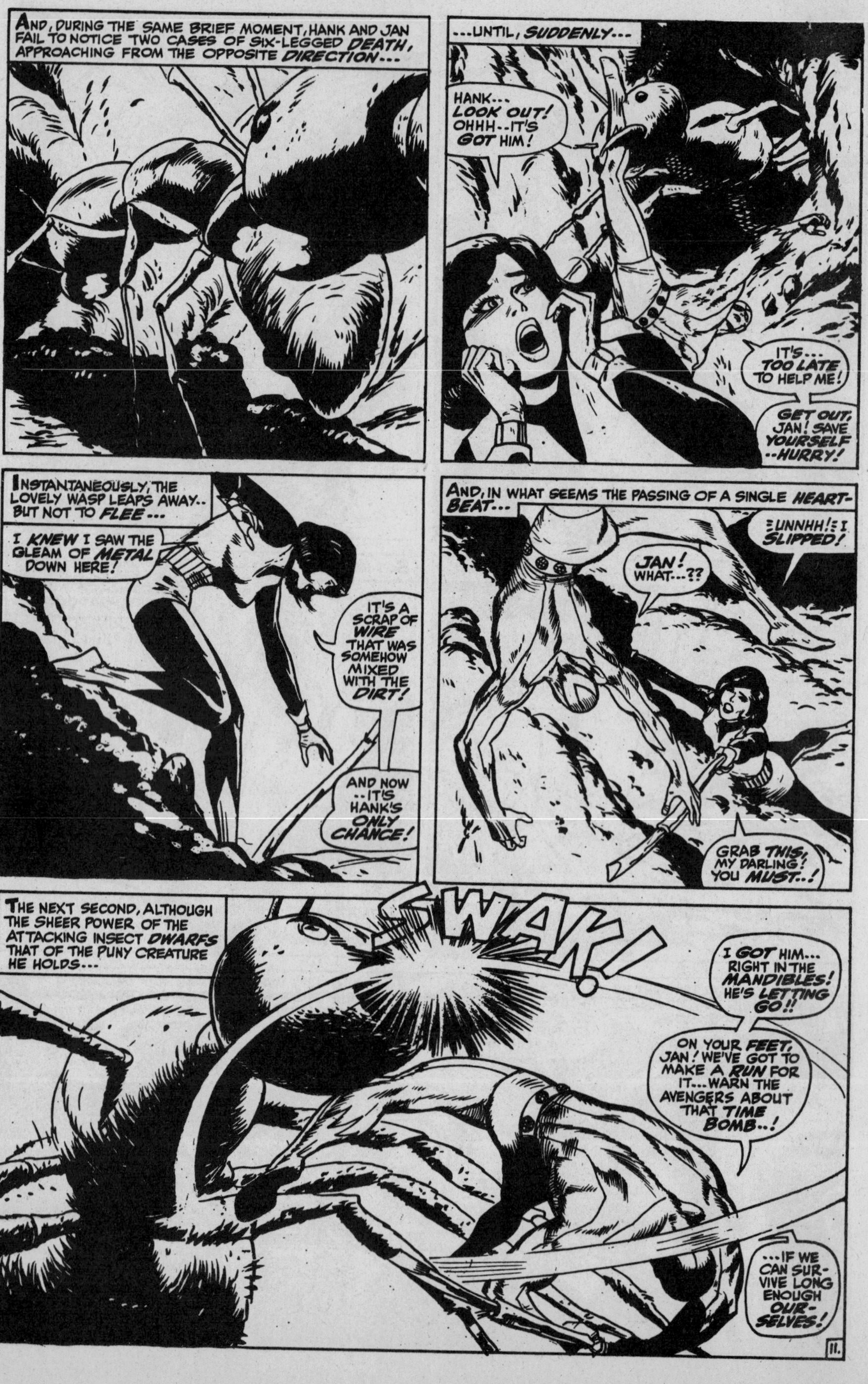
AND, DURING THE SAME BRIEF MOMENT, HANK AND JAN FAIL TO NOTICE TWO CASES OF SIX-LEGGED DEATH, APPROACHING FROM THE OPPOSITE DIRECTION...
...UNTIL, SUDDENLY...
HANK... LOOK OUT! OHHH--IT'S GOT HIM!
IT'S... TOO LATE TO HELP ME!
GET OUT, JAN! SAVE YOURSELF --HURRY!
INSTANTANEOUSLY, THE LOVELY WASP LEAPS AWAY.. BUT NOT TO FLEE...
I KNEW I SAW THE GLEAM OF METAL DOWN HERE!
IT'S A SCRAP OF WIRE THAT WAS SOMEHOW MIXED WITH THE DIRT!
AND NOW --IT'S HANK'S ONLY CHANCE!
AND, IN WHAT SEEMS THE PASSING OF A SINGLE HEART-BEAT...
UNNHH! I SLIPPED!
JAN! WHAT--??
GRAB THIS, MY DARLING! YOU MUST..!
THE NEXT SECOND, ALTHOUGH THE SHEER POWER OF THE ATTACKING INSECT DWARFS THAT OF THE PUNY CREATURE HE HOLDS...
SWAK!
I GOT HIM... RIGHT IN THE MANDIBLES! HE'S LETTING GO!!
ON YOUR FEET, JAN! WE'VE GOT TO MAKE A RUN FOR IT... WARN THE AVENGERS ABOUT THAT TIME BOMB..!
...IF WE CAN SUR-VIVE LONG ENOUGH OUR-SELVES!
11.

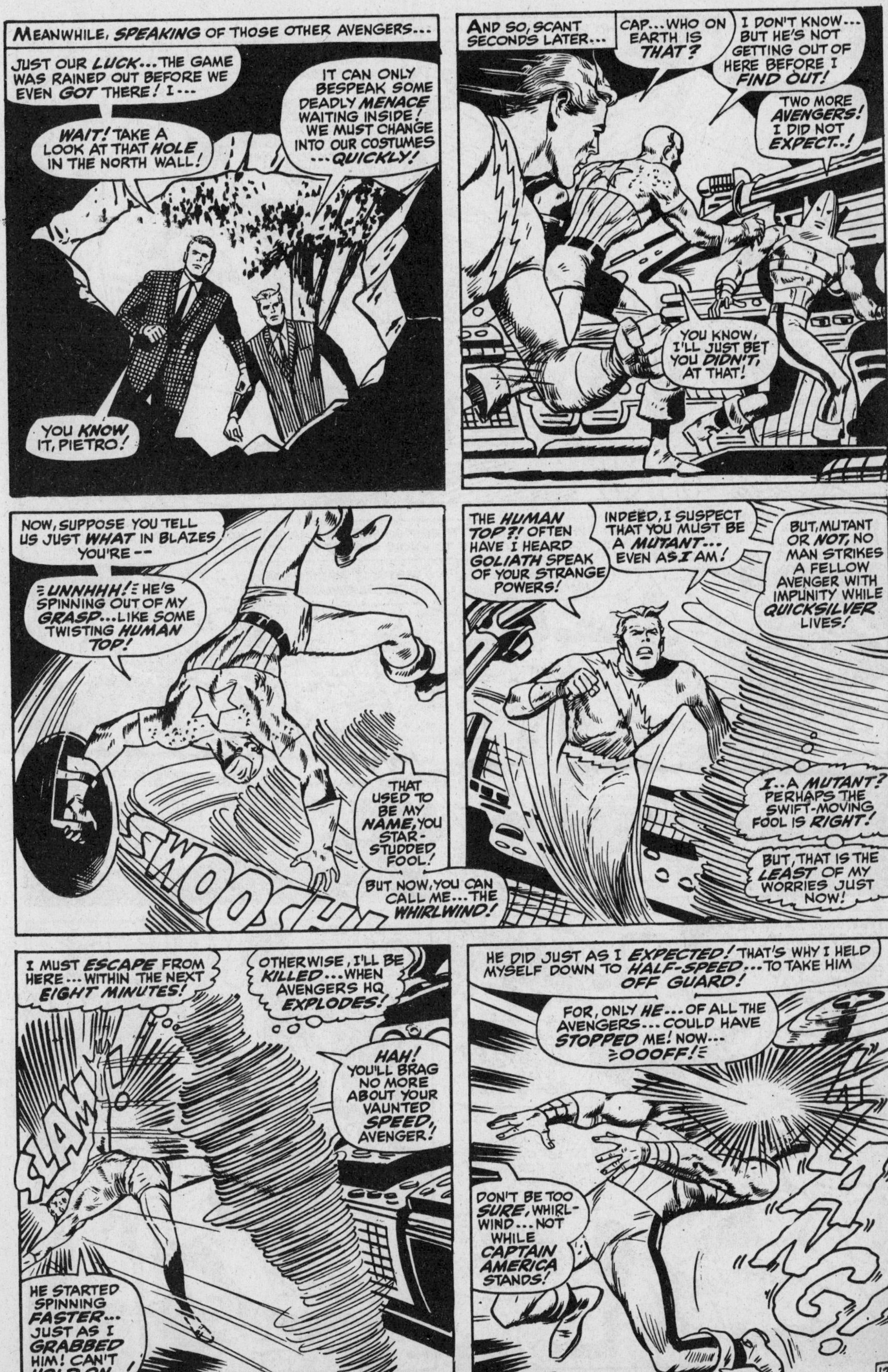
MEANWHILE, SPEAKING OF THOSE OTHER AVENGERS...
JUST OUR LUCK... THE GAME WAS RAINED OUT BEFORE WE EVEN GOT THERE! I ---
WAIT! TAKE A LOOK AT THAT HOLE IN THE NORTH WALL!
IT CAN ONLY BESPEAK SOME DEADLY MENACE WAITING INSIDE! WE MUST CHANGE INTO OUR COSTUMES ---QUICKLY!
YOU KNOW IT, PIETRO!
AND SO, SCANT SECONDS LATER...
CAP... WHO ON EARTH IS THAT?
I DON'T KNOW... BUT HE'S NOT GETTING OUT OF HERE BEFORE I FIND OUT!
TWO MORE AVENGERS! I DID NOT EXPECT..!
YOU KNOW, I'LL JUST BET YOU DIDN'T, AT THAT!
NOW, SUPPOSE YOU TELL US JUST WHAT IN BLAZES YOU'RE --
UNNHHH! HE'S SPINNING OUT OF MY GRASP... LIKE SOME TWISTING HUMAN TOP!
THAT USED TO BE MY NAME, YOU STAR-STUDDED FOOL!
BUT NOW, YOU CAN CALL ME... THE WHIRLWIND!
SWOOSH!
THE HUMAN TOP?! OFTEN HAVE I HEARD GOLIATH SPEAK OF YOUR STRANGE POWERS!
INDEED, I SUSPECT THAT YOU MUST BE A MUTANT... EVEN AS I AM!
BUT, MUTANT OR NOT, NO MAN STRIKES A FELLOW AVENGER WITH IMPUNITY WHILE QUICKSILVER LIVES!
I.. A MUTANT? PERHAPS THE SWIFT-MOVING FOOL IS RIGHT!
BUT, THAT IS THE LEAST OF MY WORRIES JUST NOW!
I MUST ESCAPE FROM HERE... WITHIN THE NEXT EIGHT MINUTES!
OTHERWISE, I'LL BE KILLED... WHEN AVENGERS HQ EXPLODES!
HAH! YOU'LL BRAG NO MORE ABOUT YOUR VAUNTED SPEED, AVENGER!
SLAM!
HE STARTED SPINNING FASTER... JUST AS I GRABBED HIM! CAN'T HOLD ON...!
HE DID JUST AS I EXPECTED! THAT'S WHY I HELD MYSELF DOWN TO HALF-SPEED... TO TAKE HIM OFF GUARD!
FOR, ONLY HE... OF ALL THE AVENGERS... COULD HAVE STOPPED ME! NOW... OOOFF!
DON'T BE TOO SURE, WHIRL-WIND... NOT WHILE CAPTAIN AMERICA STANDS!
12.

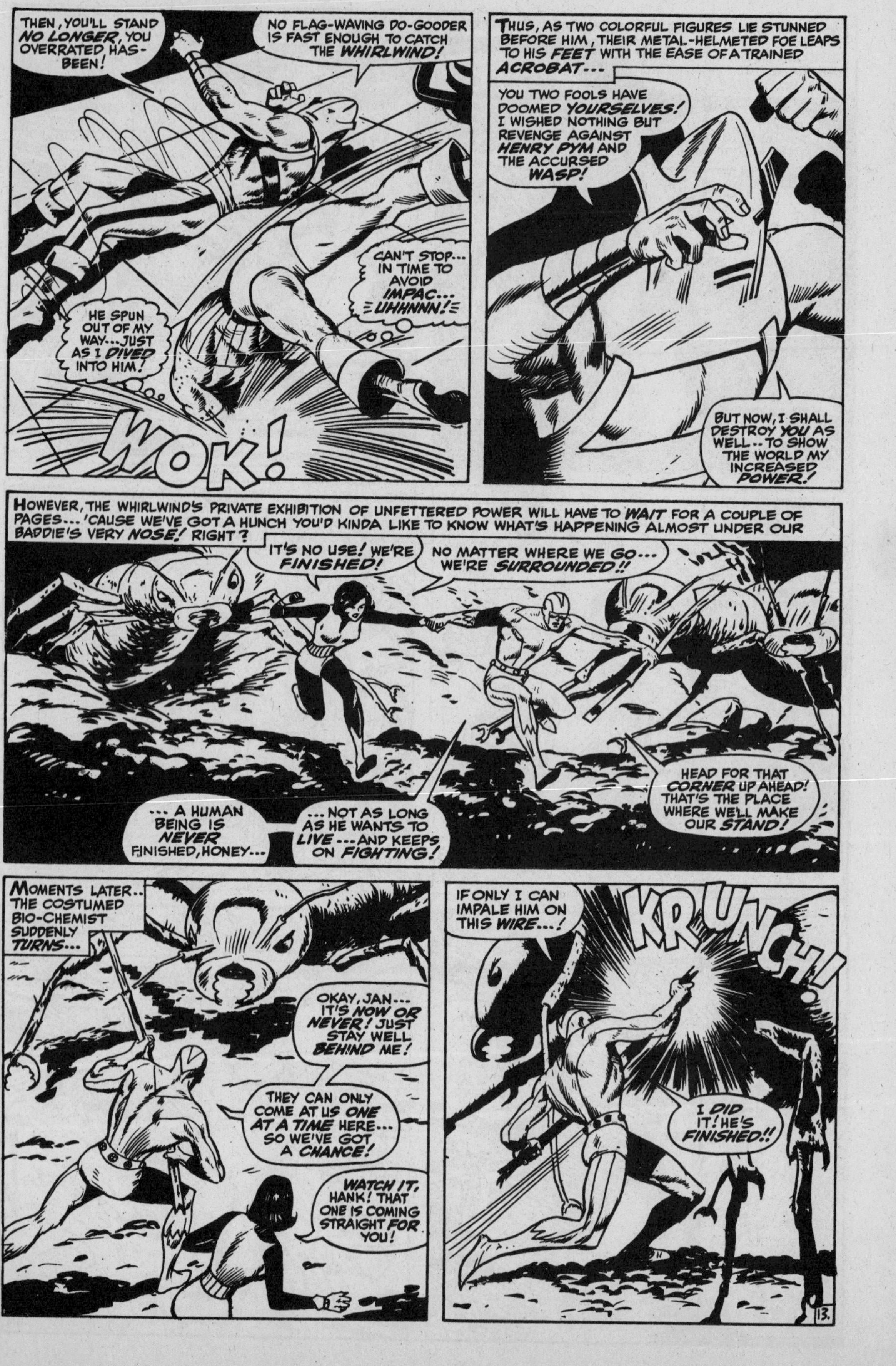
THEN, YOU'LL STAND NO LONGER, YOU OVERRATED HAS-BEEN!
NO FLAG-WAVING DO-GOODER IS FAST ENOUGH TO CATCH THE WHIRLWIND!
CAN'T STOP... IN TIME TO AVOID IMPAC... UHHNNN!
HE SPUN OUT OF MY WAY... JUST AS I DIVED INTO HIM!
WOK!
THUS, AS TWO COLORFUL FIGURES LIE STUNNED BEFORE HIM, THEIR METAL-HELMETED FOE LEAPS TO HIS FEET WITH THE EASE OF A TRAINED ACROBAT...
YOU TWO FOOLS HAVE DOOMED YOURSELVES! I WISHED NOTHING BUT REVENGE AGAINST HENRY PYM AND THE ACCURSED WASP!
BUT NOW, I SHALL DESTROY YOU AS WELL.. TO SHOW THE WORLD MY INCREASED POWER!
HOWEVER, THE WHIRLWIND'S PRIVATE EXHIBITION OF UNFETTERED POWER WILL HAVE TO WAIT FOR A COUPLE OF PAGES... 'CAUSE WE'VE GOT A HUNCH YOU'D KINDA LIKE TO KNOW WHAT'S HAPPENING ALMOST UNDER OUR BADDIE'S VERY NOSE! RIGHT?
IT'S NO USE! WE'RE FINISHED!
NO MATTER WHERE WE GO... WE'RE SURROUNDED!!
... A HUMAN BEING IS NEVER FINISHED, HONEY...
... NOT AS LONG AS HE WANTS TO LIVE --- AND KEEPS ON FIGHTING!
HEAD FOR THAT CORNER UP AHEAD! THAT'S THE PLACE WHERE WE'LL MAKE OUR STAND!
MOMENTS LATER.. THE COSTUMED BIO-CHEMIST SUDDENLY TURNS...
OKAY, JAN... IT'S NOW OR NEVER! JUST STAY WELL BEHIND ME!
THEY CAN ONLY COME AT US ONE AT A TIME HERE... SO WE'VE GOT A CHANCE!
WATCH IT, HANK! THAT ONE IS COMING STRAIGHT FOR YOU!
IF ONLY I CAN IMPALE HIM ON THIS WIRE...!
KRUNCH!
I DID IT! HE'S FINISHED!!
13.

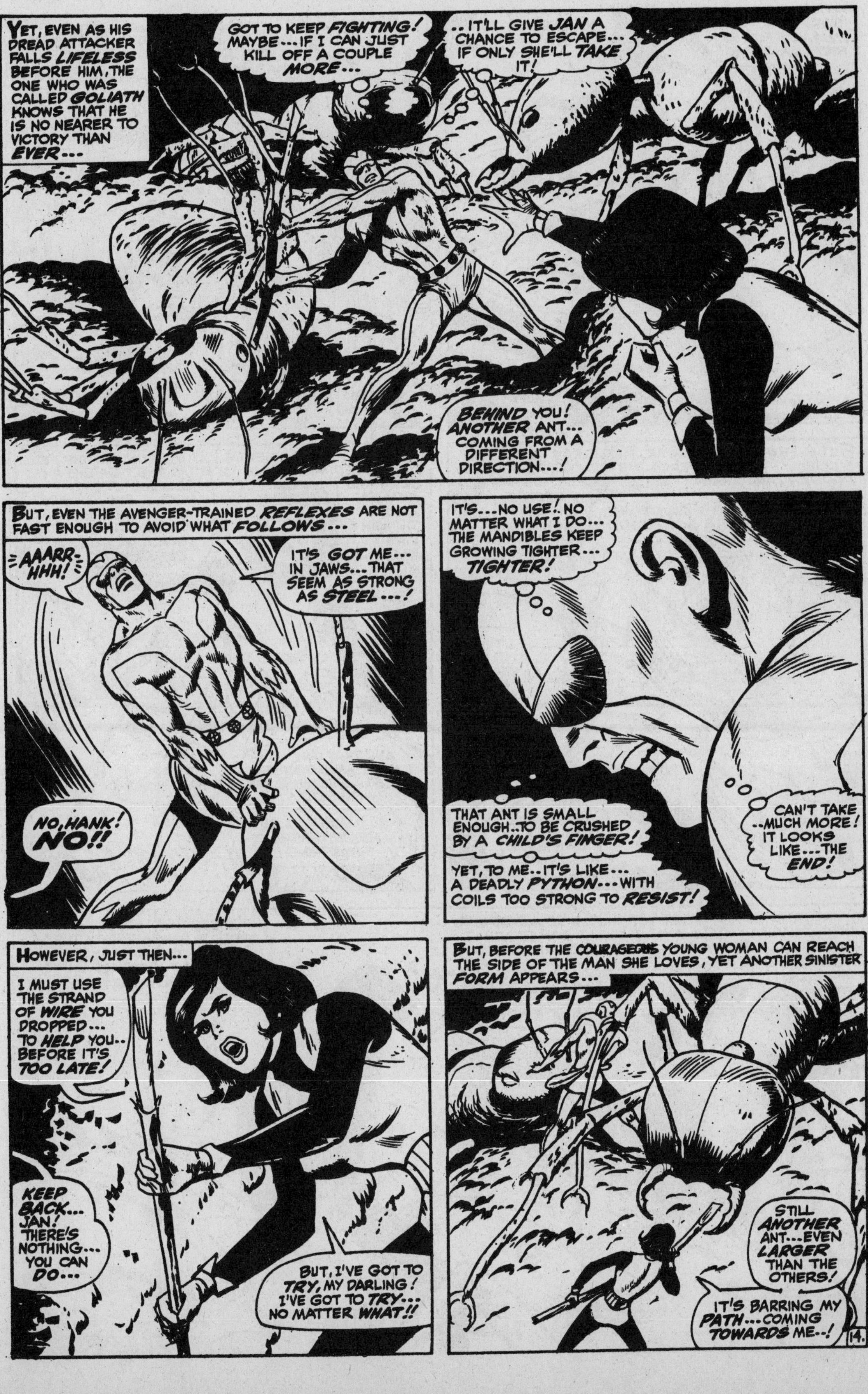
YET, EVEN AS HIS DREAD ATTACKER FALLS LIFELESS BEFORE HIM, THE ONE WHO WAS CALLED GOLIATH KNOWS THAT HE IS NO NEARER TO VICTORY THAN EVER...
GOT TO KEEP FIGHTING! MAYBE... IF I CAN JUST KILL OFF A COUPLE MORE...
..IT'LL GIVE JAN A CHANCE TO ESCAPE... IF ONLY SHE'LL TAKE IT!
BEHIND YOU! ANOTHER ANT... COMING FROM A DIFFERENT DIRECTION...!
BUT, EVEN THE AVENGER-TRAINED REFLEXES ARE NOT FAST ENOUGH TO AVOID WHAT FOLLOWS...
AAARR-HHH!
IT'S GOT ME... IN JAWS... THAT SEEM AS STRONG AS STEEL...!
NO, HANK! NO!!
IT'S... NO USE! NO MATTER WHAT I DO... THE MANDIBLES KEEP GROWING TIGHTER... TIGHTER!
THAT ANT IS SMALL ENOUGH..TO BE CRUSHED BY A CHILD'S FINGER!
YET, TO ME..IT'S LIKE... A DEADLY PYTHON... WITH COILS TOO STRONG TO RESIST!
CAN'T TAKE ..MUCH MORE! IT LOOKS LIKE... THE END!
HOWEVER, JUST THEN...
I MUST USE THE STRAND OF WIRE YOU DROPPED... TO HELP YOU.. BEFORE IT'S TOO LATE!
KEEP BACK... JAN! THERE'S NOTHING... YOU CAN DO...
BUT, I'VE GOT TO TRY, MY DARLING! I'VE GOT TO TRY... NO MATTER WHAT!!
BUT, BEFORE THE COURAGEOUS YOUNG WOMAN CAN REACH THE SIDE OF THE MAN SHE LOVES, YET ANOTHER SINISTER FORM APPEARS...
STILL ANOTHER ANT... EVEN LARGER THAN THE OTHERS!
IT'S BARRING MY PATH... COMING TOWARDS ME..!
14.

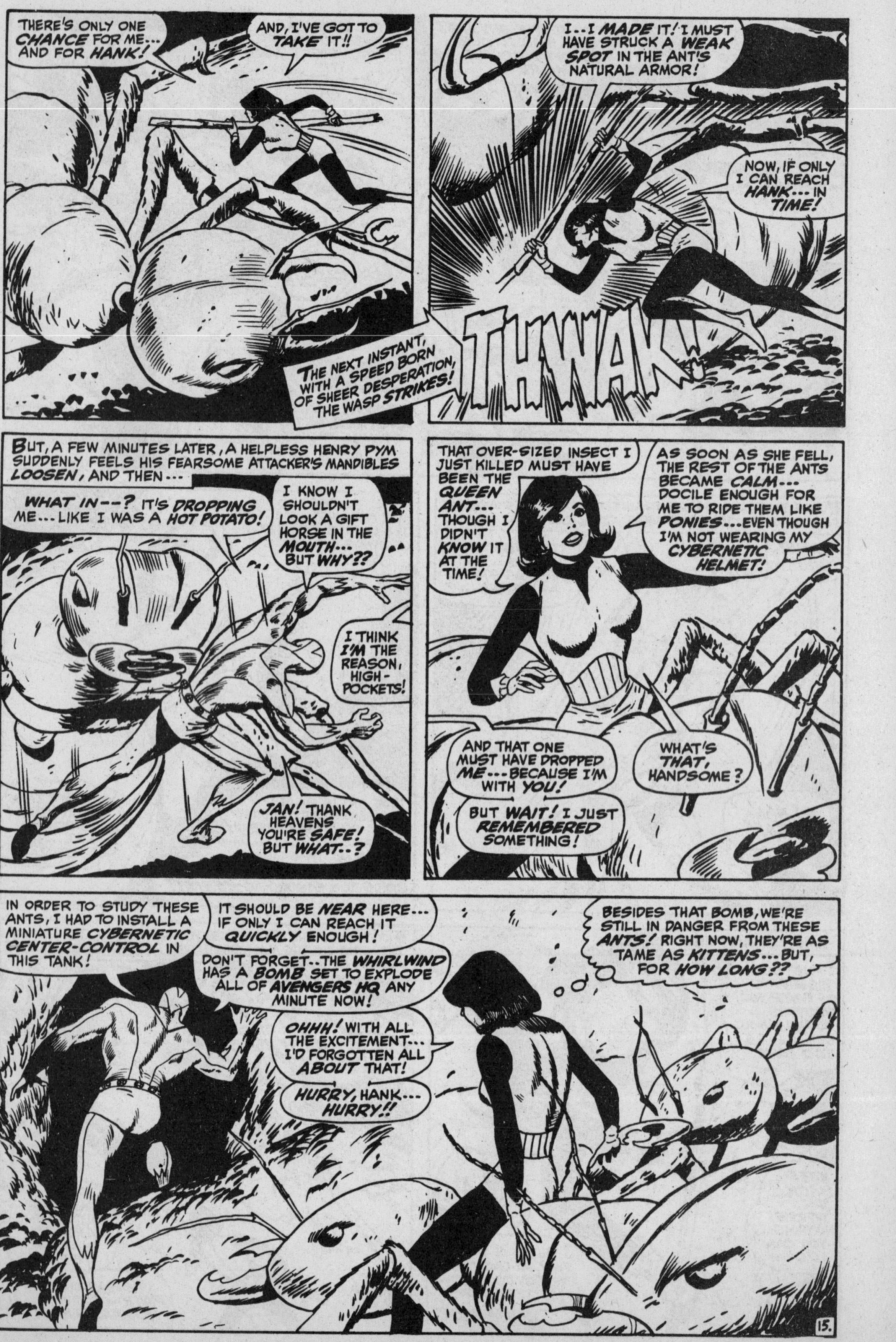
THERE'S ONLY ONE CHANCE FOR ME... AND FOR HANK!
AND, I'VE GOT TO TAKE IT!!
THE NEXT INSTANT, WITH A SPEED BORN OF SHEER DESPERATION, THE WASP STRIKES!
THWAK!
I..I MADE IT! I MUST HAVE STRUCK A WEAK SPOT IN THE ANT'S NATURAL ARMOR!
NOW, IF ONLY I CAN REACH HANK... IN TIME!
BUT, A FEW MINUTES LATER, A HELPLESS HENRY PYM SUDDENLY FEELS HIS FEARSOME ATTACKER'S MANDIBLES LOOSEN, AND THEN ---
WHAT IN--? IT'S DROPPING ME... LIKE I WAS A HOT POTATO!
I KNOW I SHOULDN'T LOOK A GIFT HORSE IN THE MOUTH... BUT WHY??
I THINK I'M THE REASON, HIGH-POCKETS!
JAN! THANK HEAVENS YOU'RE SAFE! BUT WHAT..?
THAT OVER-SIZED INSECT I JUST KILLED MUST HAVE BEEN THE QUEEN ANT... THOUGH I DIDN'T KNOW IT AT THE TIME!
AS SOON AS SHE FELL, THE REST OF THE ANTS BECAME CALM... DOCILE ENOUGH FOR ME TO RIDE THEM LIKE PONIES... EVEN THOUGH I'M NOT WEARING MY CYBERNETIC HELMET!
AND THAT ONE MUST HAVE DROPPED ME... BECAUSE I'M WITH YOU!
WHAT'S THAT, HANDSOME?
BUT WAIT! I JUST REMEMBERED SOMETHING!
IN ORDER TO STUDY THESE ANTS, I HAD TO INSTALL A MINIATURE CYBERNETIC CENTER-CONTROL IN THIS TANK!
IT SHOULD BE NEAR HERE... IF ONLY I CAN REACH IT QUICKLY ENOUGH!
DON'T FORGET.. THE WHIRLWIND HAS A BOMB SET TO EXPLODE ALL OF AVENGERS HQ ANY MINUTE NOW!
OHHH! WITH ALL THE EXCITEMENT... I'D FORGOTTEN ALL ABOUT THAT!
HURRY, HANK... HURRY!!
BESIDES THAT BOMB, WE'RE STILL IN DANGER FROM THESE ANTS! RIGHT NOW, THEY'RE AS TAME AS KITTENS... BUT, FOR HOW LONG??

BUT, EVEN AS SUCH SOMBRE THOUGHTS RUN THROUGH JANET VAN DYNE'S MIND... NOT FAR AHEAD, GOLIATH SEES...

THE CYBERNETIC CONTROL-CENTER!

IT'S OUR ONE HOPE OF GETTING OUT OF HERE... IN TIME!

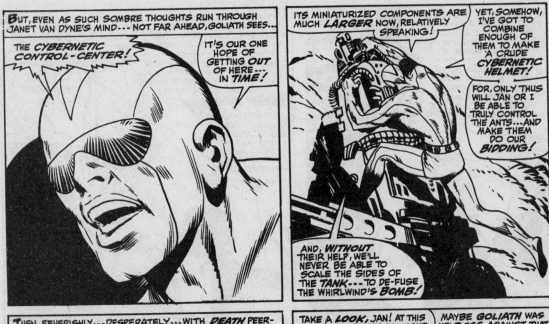

ITS MINIATURIZED COMPONENTS ARE MUCH LARGER NOW, RELATIVELY SPEAKING!

YET, SOMEHOW, I'VE GOT TO COMBINE ENOUGH OF THEM TO MAKE A CRUDE CYBERNETIC HELMET!

FOR, ONLY THUS WILL JAN OR I BE ABLE TO TRULY CONTROL THE ANTS...AND MAKE THEM DO OUR BIDDING!

AND, WITHOUT THEIR HELP, WE'LL NEVER BE ABLE TO SCALE THE SIDES OF THE TANK... TO DE-FUSE THE WHIRLWIND'S BOMB!

THEN, FEVERISHLY---DESPERATELY---WITH DEATH PEERING OVER HIS SHOULDER AND TIME HIS MOST DREAD ENEMY--- HE FASHIONS A STRANGE, GADGET-STUDDED HEADPIECE, AND---

IT WORKS! IT WORKS!!

I CAN HEAR THE ANTS' THOUGHTS... AND UNDERSTAND THEM... AS WELL AS EVER!

WONDERFUL! NOW, IF ONLY YOU CAN MAKE THEM OBEY YOU... LIKE THEY DO WHEN YOU WEAR YOUR REAL HELMET!

TAKE A LOOK, JAN! AT THIS CLOSE RANGE, MY COMMAND OVER THEM IS PERFECT!

MAYBE GOLIATH WAS HELPLESS AGAINST THAT WHIRLWIND CRUMB... BUT ANT-MAN IS ANOTHER STORY!

MOVE, MY SIX-LEGGED FRIENDS! WE'VE GOT A SUPER-VILLAIN TO TACKLE!

HOWEVER, ALTHOUGH OUR EMBATTLED BIO-CHEMIST HAS BEEN A BIT TOO BUSY TO NOTICE IT, OUR FLASHY FOE IS ALREADY BEING WELL TAKEN CARE OF, THANK YOU... BY THE STAR-SPANGLED AVENGER HIMSELF!

YOU MAY BE A REGULAR KANSAS TWISTER WHEN IT COMES TO SPINNING AROUND, WHIRLWIND...

BUT, WHEN IT COMES TO REFLEXES, YOU'RE NO FASTER THAN A HUNDRED OTHER NOGOODNIKS I'VE FLATTENED!

BOK!

≡UNNHHHH!

16.

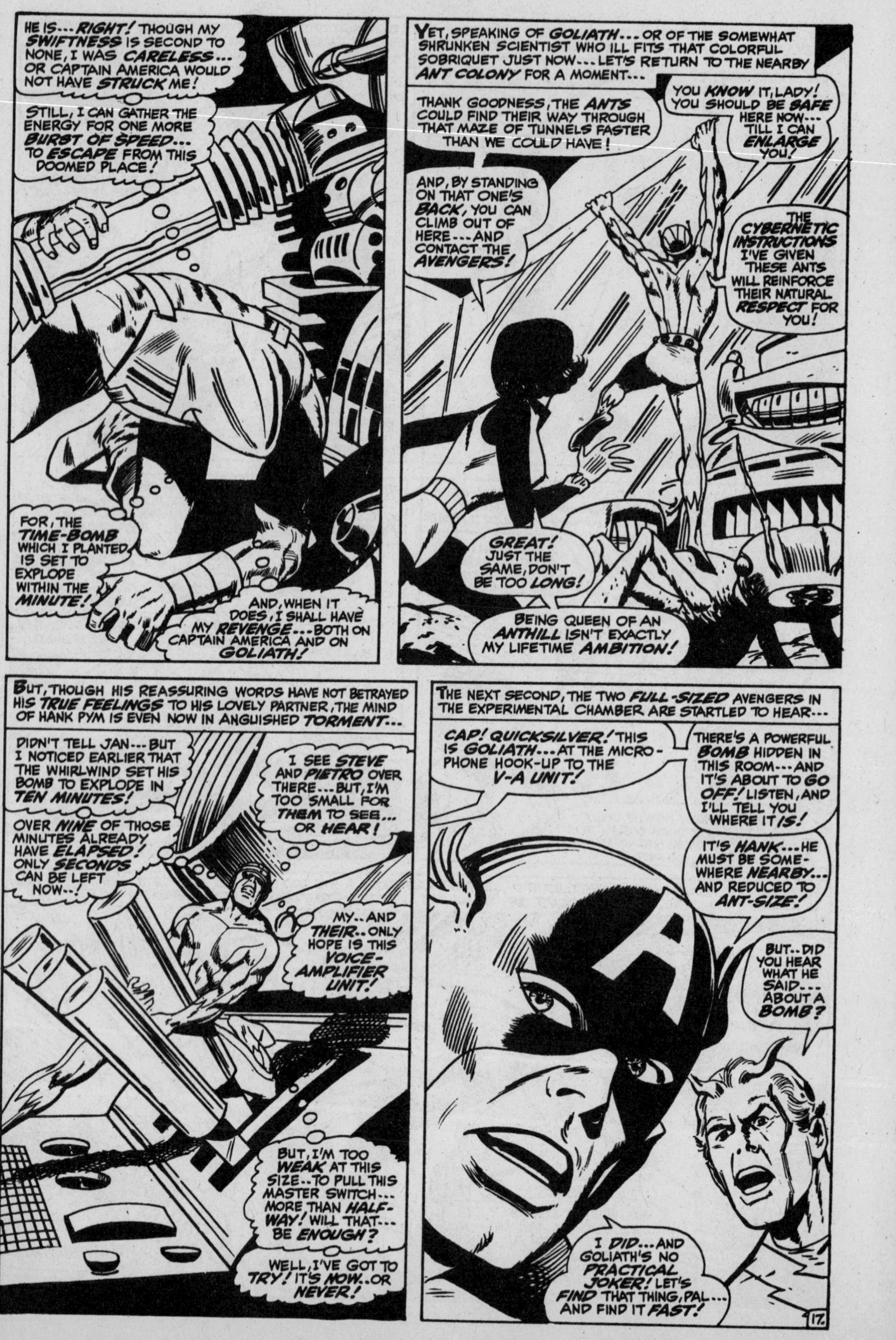

HE IS... RIGHT! THOUGH MY SWIFTNESS IS SECOND TO NONE, I WAS CARELESS... OR CAPTAIN AMERICA WOULD NOT HAVE STRUCK ME!
STILL, I CAN GATHER THE ENERGY FOR ONE MORE BURST OF SPEED... TO ESCAPE FROM THIS DOOMED PLACE!
FOR, THE TIME-BOMB WHICH I PLANTED IS SET TO EXPLODE WITHIN THE MINUTE!
AND, WHEN IT DOES, I SHALL HAVE MY REVENGE... BOTH ON CAPTAIN AMERICA AND ON GOLIATH!
YET, SPEAKING OF GOLIATH... OR OF THE SOMEWHAT SHRUNKEN SCIENTIST WHO ILL FITS THAT COLORFUL SOBRIQUET JUST NOW... LET'S RETURN TO THE NEARBY ANT COLONY FOR A MOMENT...
THANK GOODNESS, THE ANTS COULD FIND THEIR WAY THROUGH THAT MAZE OF TUNNELS FASTER THAN WE COULD HAVE!
YOU KNOW IT, LADY! YOU SHOULD BE SAFE HERE NOW... TILL I CAN ENLARGE YOU!
AND, BY STANDING ON THAT ONE'S BACK, YOU CAN CLIMB OUT OF HERE... AND CONTACT THE AVENGERS!
THE CYBERNETIC INSTRUCTIONS I'VE GIVEN THESE ANTS WILL REINFORCE THEIR NATURAL RESPECT FOR YOU!
GREAT! JUST THE SAME, DON'T BE TOO LONG!
BEING QUEEN OF AN ANTHILL ISN'T EXACTLY MY LIFETIME AMBITION!
BUT, THOUGH HIS REASSURING WORDS HAVE NOT BETRAYED HIS TRUE FEELINGS TO HIS LOVELY PARTNER, THE MIND OF HANK PYM IS EVEN NOW IN ANGUISHED TORMENT...
DIDN'T TELL JAN... BUT I NOTICED EARLIER THAT THE WHIRLWIND SET HIS BOMB TO EXPLODE IN TEN MINUTES!
OVER NINE OF THOSE MINUTES ALREADY HAVE ELAPSED! ONLY SECONDS CAN BE LEFT NOW..!
I SEE STEVE AND PIETRO OVER THERE... BUT, I'M TOO SMALL FOR THEM TO SEE... OR HEAR!
MY.. AND THEIR.. ONLY HOPE IS THIS VOICE-AMPLIFIER UNIT!
BUT, I'M TOO WEAK AT THIS SIZE.. TO PULL THIS MASTER SWITCH... MORE THAN HALF-WAY! WILL THAT... BE ENOUGH?
WELL, I'VE GOT TO TRY! IT'S NOW.. OR NEVER!
THE NEXT SECOND, THE TWO FULL-SIZED AVENGERS IN THE EXPERIMENTAL CHAMBER ARE STARTLED TO HEAR...
CAP! QUICKSILVER! THIS IS GOLIATH... AT THE MICRO-PHONE HOOK-UP TO THE V-A UNIT!
THERE'S A POWERFUL BOMB HIDDEN IN THIS ROOM... AND IT'S ABOUT TO GO OFF! LISTEN, AND I'LL TELL YOU WHERE IT IS!
IT'S HANK... HE MUST BE SOME-WHERE NEARBY... AND REDUCED TO ANT-SIZE!
BUT.. DID YOU HEAR WHAT HE SAID... ABOUT A BOMB?
I DID... AND GOLIATH'S NO PRACTICAL JOKER! LET'S FIND THAT THING, PAL... AND FIND IT FAST!
17.

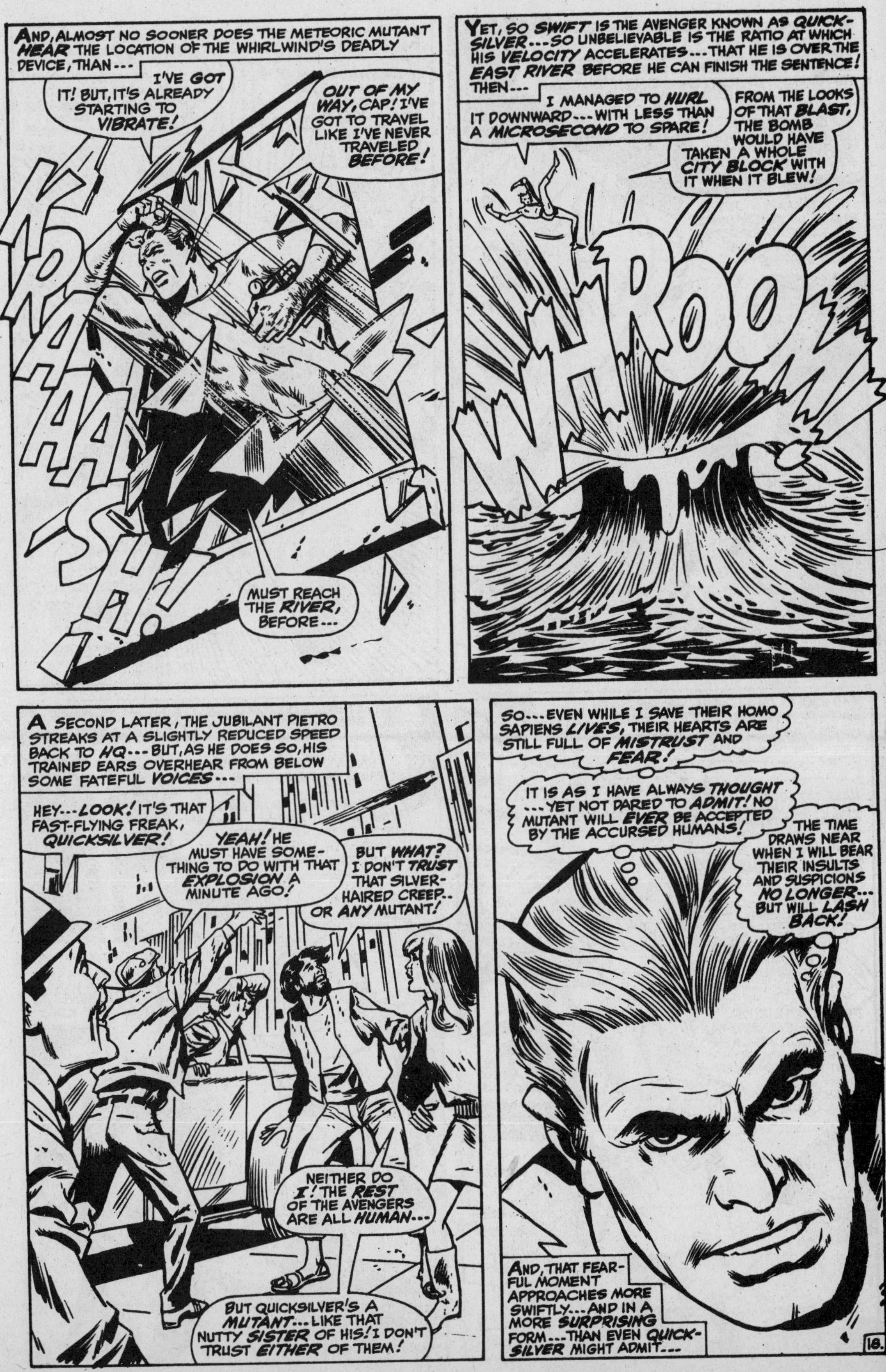

AND, ALMOST NO SOONER DOES THE METEORIC MUTANT HEAR THE LOCATION OF THE WHIRLWIND'S DEADLY DEVICE, THAN---
I'VE GOT IT! BUT, IT'S ALREADY STARTING TO VIBRATE!
OUT OF MY WAY, CAP! I'VE GOT TO TRAVEL LIKE I'VE NEVER TRAVELED BEFORE!
KRAAASH!
MUST REACH THE RIVER, BEFORE---
YET, SO SWIFT IS THE AVENGER KNOWN AS QUICK-SILVER---SO UNBELIEVABLE IS THE RATIO AT WHICH HIS VELOCITY ACCELERATES---THAT HE IS OVER THE EAST RIVER BEFORE HE CAN FINISH THE SENTENCE! THEN---
I MANAGED TO HURL IT DOWNWARD---WITH LESS THAN A MICROSECOND TO SPARE!
FROM THE LOOKS OF THAT BLAST, THE BOMB WOULD HAVE TAKEN A WHOLE CITY BLOCK WITH IT WHEN IT BLEW!
WHROOM
A SECOND LATER, THE JUBILANT PIETRO STREAKS AT A SLIGHTLY REDUCED SPEED BACK TO HQ---BUT, AS HE DOES SO, HIS TRAINED EARS OVERHEAR FROM BELOW SOME FATEFUL VOICES---
HEY---LOOK! IT'S THAT FAST-FLYING FREAK, QUICKSILVER!
YEAH! HE MUST HAVE SOME-THING TO DO WITH THAT EXPLOSION A MINUTE AGO!
BUT WHAT? I DON'T TRUST THAT SILVER-HAIRED CREEP.. OR ANY MUTANT!
NEITHER DO I! THE REST OF THE AVENGERS ARE ALL HUMAN---
BUT QUICKSILVER'S A MUTANT---LIKE THAT NUTTY SISTER OF HIS! I DON'T TRUST EITHER OF THEM!
SO---EVEN WHILE I SAVE THEIR HOMO SAPIENS LIVES, THEIR HEARTS ARE STILL FULL OF MISTRUST AND FEAR!
IT IS AS I HAVE ALWAYS THOUGHT ---YET NOT DARED TO ADMIT! NO MUTANT WILL EVER BE ACCEPTED BY THE ACCURSED HUMANS!
THE TIME DRAWS NEAR WHEN I WILL BEAR THEIR INSULTS AND SUSPICIONS NO LONGER--- BUT WILL LASH BACK!
AND, THAT FEAR-FUL MOMENT APPROACHES MORE SWIFTLY---AND IN A MORE SURPRISING FORM---THAN EVEN QUICK-SILVER MIGHT ADMIT---

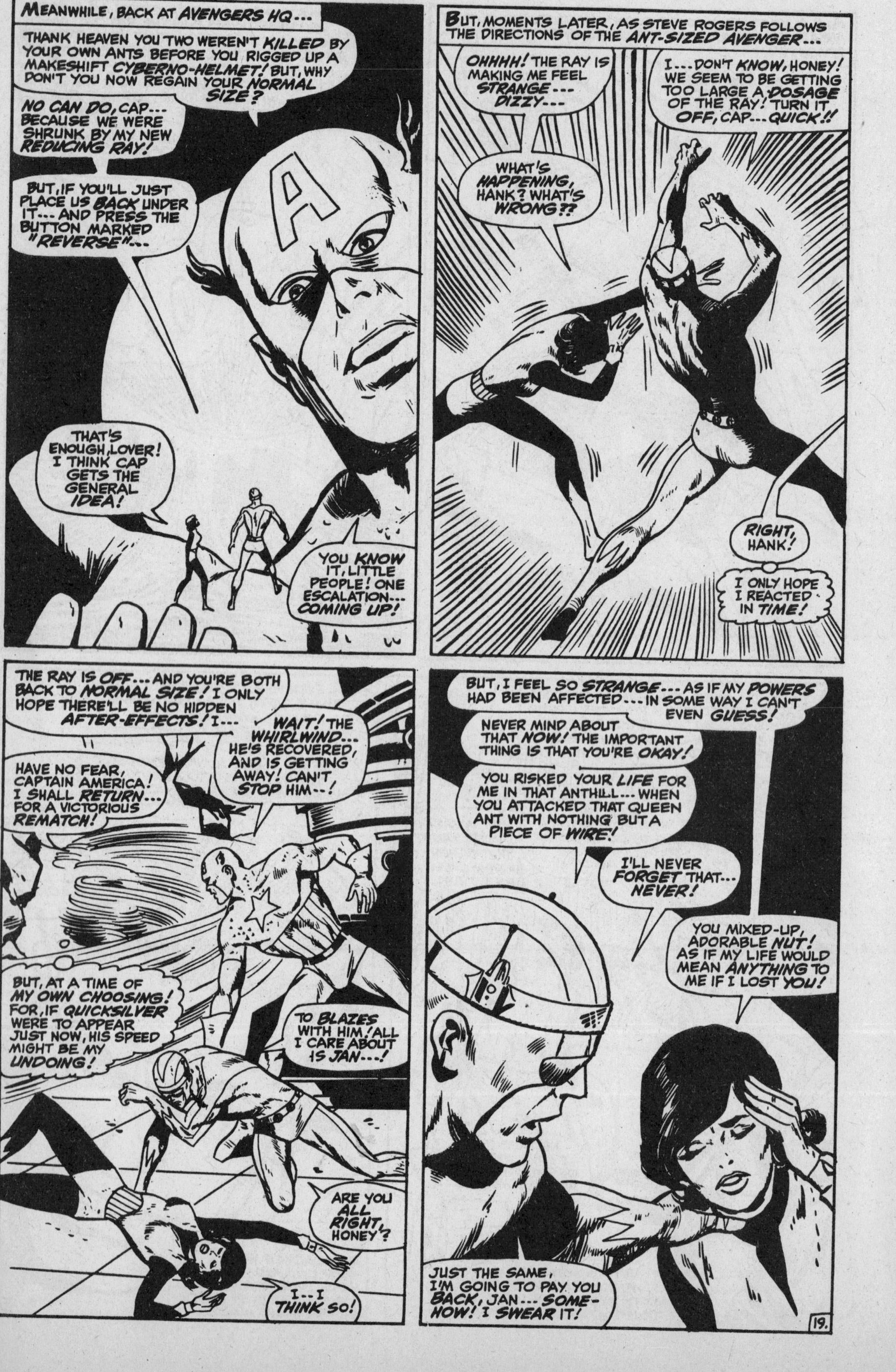
MEANWHILE, BACK AT AVENGERS HQ...
THANK HEAVEN YOU TWO WEREN'T KILLED BY YOUR OWN ANTS BEFORE YOU RIGGED UP A MAKESHIFT CYBERNO-HELMET! BUT, WHY DON'T YOU NOW REGAIN YOUR NORMAL SIZE?
NO CAN DO, CAP... BECAUSE WE WERE SHRUNK BY MY NEW REDUCING RAY!
BUT, IF YOU'LL JUST PLACE US BACK UNDER IT... AND PRESS THE BUTTON MARKED "REVERSE"...
THAT'S ENOUGH, LOVER! I THINK CAP GETS THE GENERAL IDEA!
YOU KNOW IT, LITTLE PEOPLE! ONE ESCALATION... COMING UP!
BUT, MOMENTS LATER, AS STEVE ROGERS FOLLOWS THE DIRECTIONS OF THE ANT-SIZED AVENGER...
OHHHH! THE RAY IS MAKING ME FEEL STRANGE--- DIZZY---
WHAT'S HAPPENING, HANK? WHAT'S WRONG??
I... DON'T KNOW, HONEY! WE SEEM TO BE GETTING TOO LARGE A DOSAGE OF THE RAY! TURN IT OFF, CAP... QUICK!!
RIGHT, HANK!
I ONLY HOPE I REACTED IN TIME!
THE RAY IS OFF... AND YOU'RE BOTH BACK TO NORMAL SIZE! I ONLY HOPE THERE'LL BE NO HIDDEN AFTER-EFFECTS! I...
WAIT! THE WHIRLWIND... HE'S RECOVERED, AND IS GETTING AWAY! CAN'T STOP HIM--!
HAVE NO FEAR, CAPTAIN AMERICA! I SHALL RETURN... FOR A VICTORIOUS REMATCH!
BUT, AT A TIME OF MY OWN CHOOSING! FOR, IF QUICKSILVER WERE TO APPEAR JUST NOW, HIS SPEED MIGHT BE MY UNDOING!
TO BLAZES WITH HIM! ALL I CARE ABOUT IS JAN...!
ARE YOU ALL RIGHT, HONEY?
I.. I THINK SO!
BUT, I FEEL SO STRANGE... AS IF MY POWERS HAD BEEN AFFECTED... IN SOME WAY I CAN'T EVEN GUESS!
NEVER MIND ABOUT THAT NOW! THE IMPORTANT THING IS THAT YOU'RE OKAY!
YOU RISKED YOUR LIFE FOR ME IN THAT ANTHILL... WHEN YOU ATTACKED THAT QUEEN ANT WITH NOTHING BUT A PIECE OF WIRE!
I'LL NEVER FORGET THAT... NEVER!
YOU MIXED-UP, ADORABLE NUT! AS IF MY LIFE WOULD MEAN ANYTHING TO ME IF I LOST YOU!
JUST THE SAME, I'M GOING TO PAY YOU BACK, JAN... SOME-HOW! I SWEAR IT!
19.

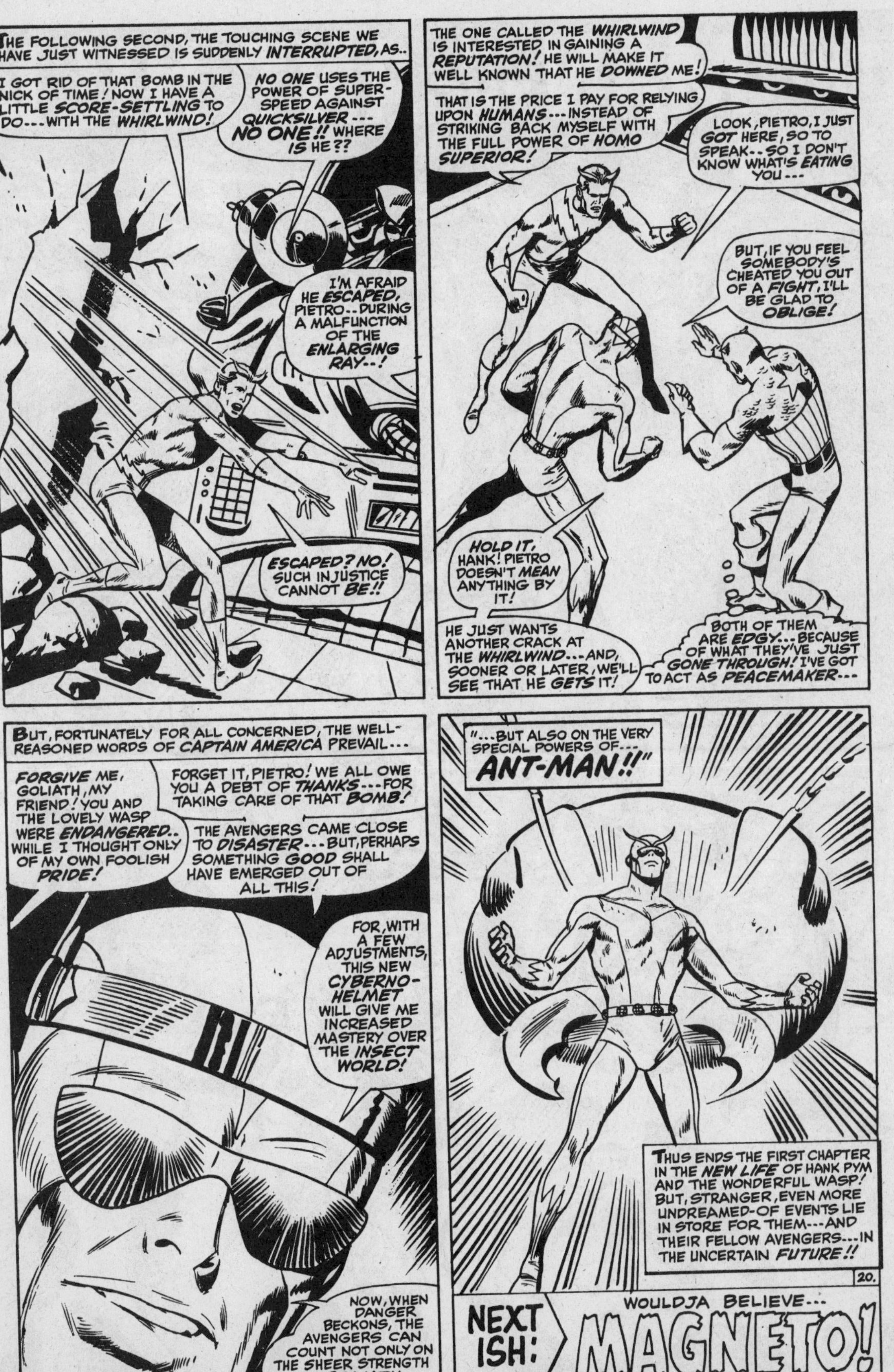

THE FOLLOWING SECOND, THE TOUCHING SCENE WE HAVE JUST WITNESSED IS SUDDENLY INTERRUPTED, AS..
I GOT RID OF THAT BOMB IN THE NICK OF TIME! NOW I HAVE A LITTLE SCORE-SETTLING TO DO--- WITH THE WHIRLWIND!
NO ONE USES THE POWER OF SUPER-SPEED AGAINST QUICKSILVER --- NO ONE!! WHERE IS HE??
I'M AFRAID HE ESCAPED, PIETRO-- DURING A MALFUNCTION OF THE ENLARGING RAY--!
ESCAPED? NO! SUCH INJUSTICE CANNOT BE!!
THE ONE CALLED THE WHIRLWIND IS INTERESTED IN GAINING A REPUTATION! HE WILL MAKE IT WELL KNOWN THAT HE DOWNED ME!
THAT IS THE PRICE I PAY FOR RELYING UPON HUMANS--- INSTEAD OF STRIKING BACK MYSELF WITH THE FULL POWER OF HOMO SUPERIOR!
LOOK, PIETRO, I JUST GOT HERE, SO TO SPEAK-- SO I DON'T KNOW WHAT'S EATING YOU ---
BUT, IF YOU FEEL SOMEBODY'S CHEATED YOU OUT OF A FIGHT, I'LL BE GLAD TO OBLIGE!
HOLD IT, HANK! PIETRO DOESN'T MEAN ANYTHING BY IT!
HE JUST WANTS ANOTHER CRACK AT THE WHIRLWIND---AND, SOONER OR LATER, WE'LL SEE THAT HE GETS IT!
BOTH OF THEM ARE EDGY... BECAUSE OF WHAT THEY'VE JUST GONE THROUGH! I'VE GOT TO ACT AS PEACEMAKER---
BUT, FORTUNATELY FOR ALL CONCERNED, THE WELL-REASONED WORDS OF CAPTAIN AMERICA PREVAIL---
FORGIVE ME, GOLIATH, MY FRIEND! YOU AND THE LOVELY WASP WERE ENDANGERED.. WHILE I THOUGHT ONLY OF MY OWN FOOLISH PRIDE!
FORGET IT, PIETRO! WE ALL OWE YOU A DEBT OF THANKS--- FOR TAKING CARE OF THAT BOMB!
THE AVENGERS CAME CLOSE TO DISASTER--- BUT, PERHAPS SOMETHING GOOD SHALL HAVE EMERGED OUT OF ALL THIS!
FOR, WITH A FEW ADJUSTMENTS, THIS NEW CYBERNO-HELMET WILL GIVE ME INCREASED MASTERY OVER THE INSECT WORLD!
NOW, WHEN DANGER BECKONS, THE AVENGERS CAN COUNT NOT ONLY ON THE SHEER STRENGTH OF GOLIATH---
"...BUT ALSO ON THE VERY SPECIAL POWERS OF--- ANT-MAN!!"
THUS ENDS THE FIRST CHAPTER IN THE NEW LIFE OF HANK PYM AND THE WONDERFUL WASP! BUT, STRANGER, EVEN MORE UNDREAMED-OF EVENTS LIE IN STORE FOR THEM---AND THEIR FELLOW AVENGERS...IN THE UNCERTAIN FUTURE!!
20.
NEXT ISH: WOULDJA BELIEVE--- MAGNETO!

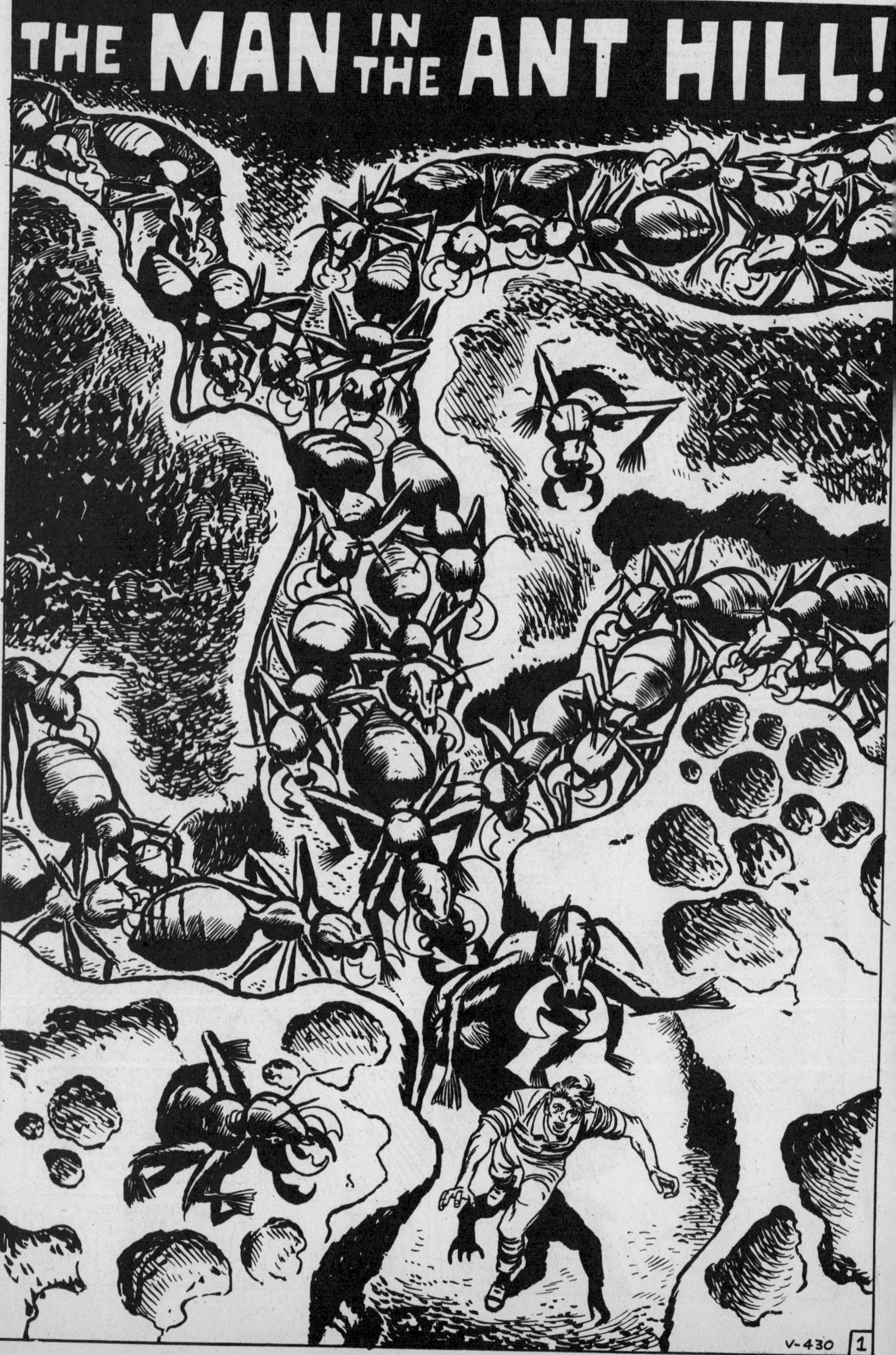
THE MAN IN THE ANT HILL!

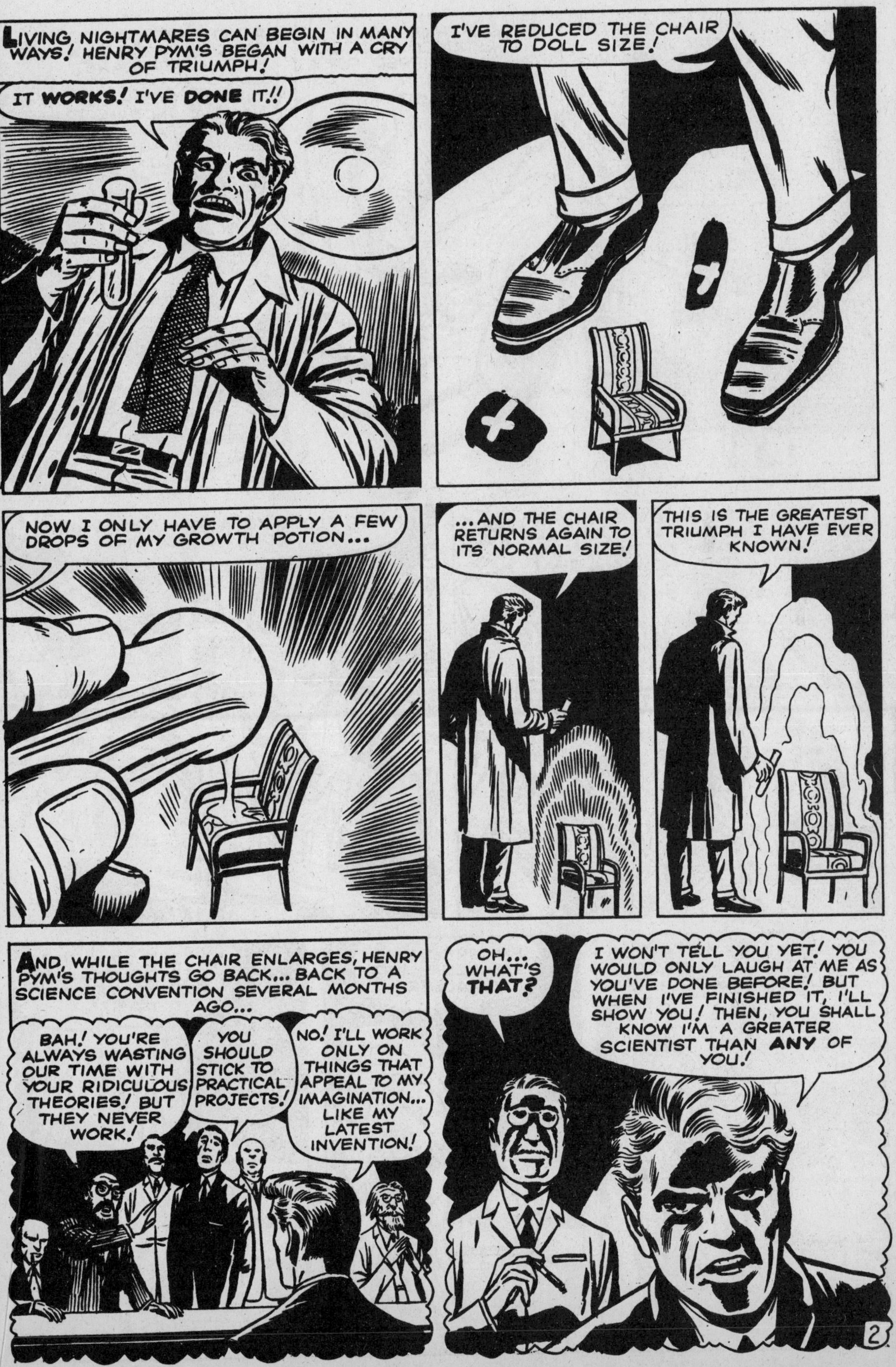
LIVING NIGHTMARES CAN BEGIN IN MANY WAYS! HENRY PYM'S BEGAN WITH A CRY OF TRIUMPH!
IT WORKS! I'VE DONE IT!!
I'VE REDUCED THE CHAIR TO DOLL SIZE!
NOW I ONLY HAVE TO APPLY A FEW DROPS OF MY GROWTH POTION...
...AND THE CHAIR RETURNS AGAIN TO ITS NORMAL SIZE!
THIS IS THE GREATEST TRIUMPH I HAVE EVER KNOWN!
AND, WHILE THE CHAIR ENLARGES, HENRY PYM'S THOUGHTS GO BACK... BACK TO A SCIENCE CONVENTION SEVERAL MONTHS AGO...
BAH! YOU'RE ALWAYS WASTING OUR TIME WITH YOUR RIDICULOUS THEORIES! BUT THEY NEVER WORK!
YOU SHOULD STICK TO PRACTICAL PROJECTS!
NO! I'LL WORK ONLY ON THINGS THAT APPEAL TO MY IMAGINATION... LIKE MY LATEST INVENTION!
OH... WHAT'S THAT?
I WON'T TELL YOU YET! YOU WOULD ONLY LAUGH AT ME AS YOU'VE DONE BEFORE! BUT WHEN I'VE FINISHED IT, I'LL SHOW YOU! THEN, YOU SHALL KNOW I'M A GREATER SCIENTIST THAN ANY OF YOU!

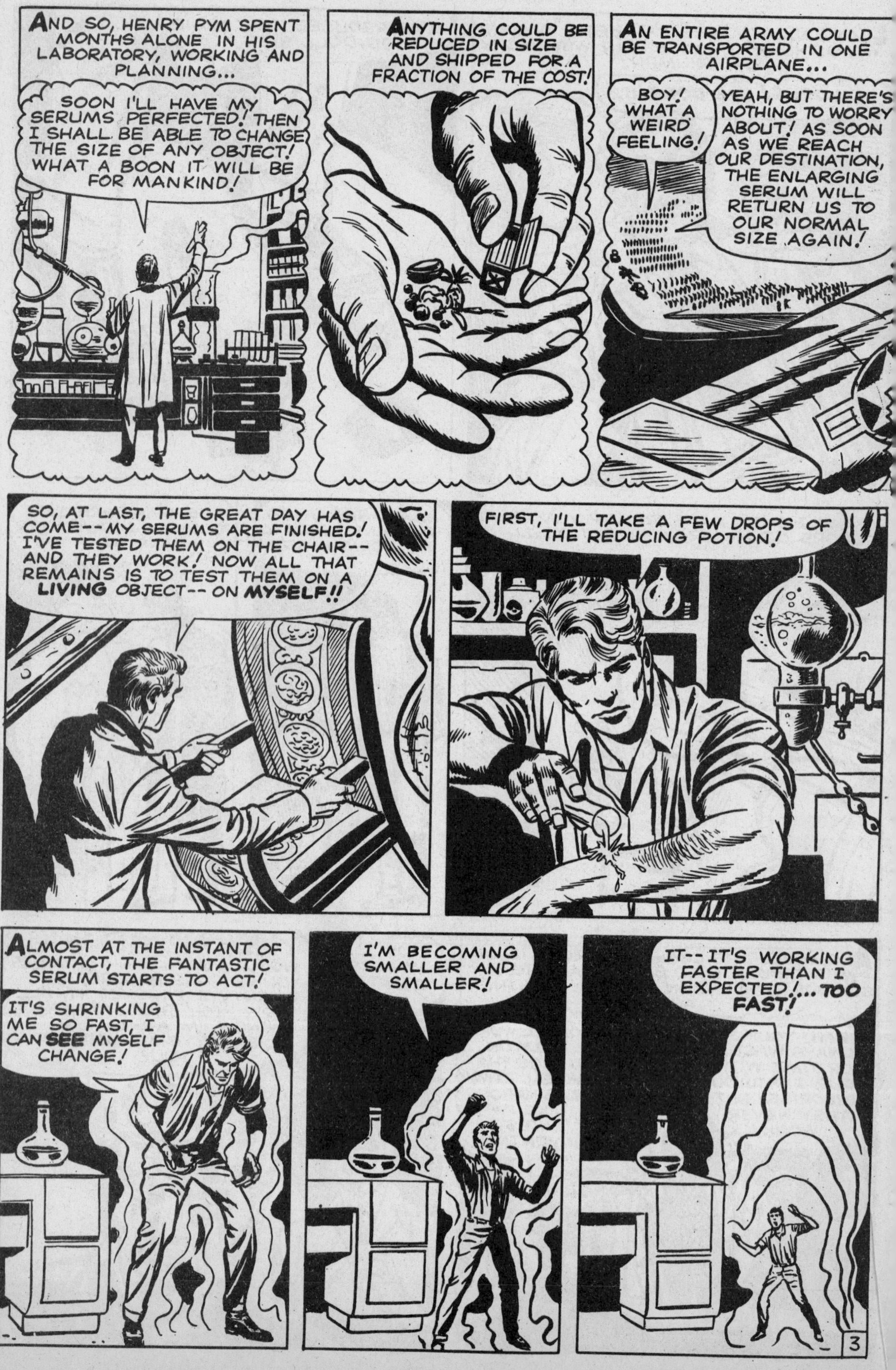
AND SO, HENRY PYM SPENT MONTHS ALONE IN HIS LABORATORY, WORKING AND PLANNING...
SOON I'LL HAVE MY SERUMS PERFECTED! THEN I SHALL BE ABLE TO CHANGE THE SIZE OF ANY OBJECT! WHAT A BOON IT WILL BE FOR MANKIND!
ANYTHING COULD BE REDUCED IN SIZE AND SHIPPED FOR A FRACTION OF THE COST!
AN ENTIRE ARMY COULD BE TRANSPORTED IN ONE AIRPLANE...
BOY! WHAT A WEIRD FEELING!
YEAH, BUT THERE'S NOTHING TO WORRY ABOUT! AS SOON AS WE REACH OUR DESTINATION, THE ENLARGING SERUM WILL RETURN US TO OUR NORMAL SIZE AGAIN!
SO, AT LAST, THE GREAT DAY HAS COME--MY SERUMS ARE FINISHED! I'VE TESTED THEM ON THE CHAIR--AND THEY WORK! NOW ALL THAT REMAINS IS TO TEST THEM ON A LIVING OBJECT--ON MYSELF!!
FIRST, I'LL TAKE A FEW DROPS OF THE REDUCING POTION!
ALMOST AT THE INSTANT OF CONTACT, THE FANTASTIC SERUM STARTS TO ACT!
IT'S SHRINKING ME SO FAST, I CAN SEE MYSELF CHANGE!
I'M BECOMING SMALLER AND SMALLER!
IT--IT'S WORKING FASTER THAN I EXPECTED!...TOO FAST!
3

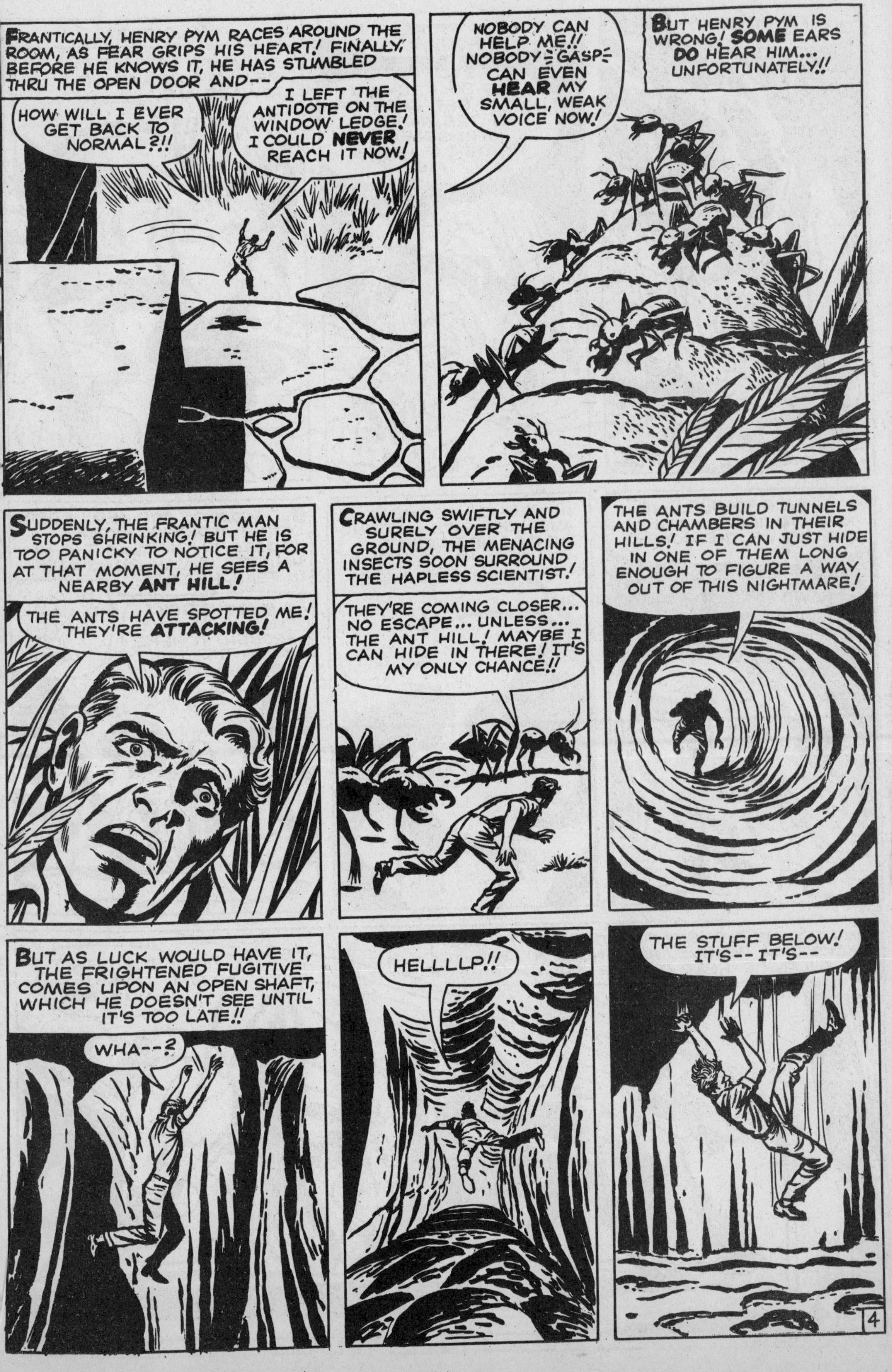

FRANTICALLY, HENRY PYM RACES AROUND THE ROOM, AS FEAR GRIPS HIS HEART! FINALLY, BEFORE HE KNOWS IT, HE HAS STUMBLED THRU THE OPEN DOOR AND--
HOW WILL I EVER GET BACK TO NORMAL?!!
I LEFT THE ANTIDOTE ON THE WINDOW LEDGE! I COULD NEVER REACH IT NOW!
NOBODY CAN HELP ME!! NOBODY -GASP- CAN EVEN HEAR MY SMALL, WEAK VOICE NOW!
BUT HENRY PYM IS WRONG! SOME EARS DO HEAR HIM... UNFORTUNATELY!!
SUDDENLY, THE FRANTIC MAN STOPS SHRINKING! BUT HE IS TOO PANICKY TO NOTICE IT, FOR AT THAT MOMENT, HE SEES A NEARBY ANT HILL!
THE ANTS HAVE SPOTTED ME! THEY'RE ATTACKING!
CRAWLING SWIFTLY AND SURELY OVER THE GROUND, THE MENACING INSECTS SOON SURROUND THE HAPLESS SCIENTIST!
THEY'RE COMING CLOSER... NO ESCAPE... UNLESS... THE ANT HILL! MAYBE I CAN HIDE IN THERE! IT'S MY ONLY CHANCE!!
THE ANTS BUILD TUNNELS AND CHAMBERS IN THEIR HILLS! IF I CAN JUST HIDE IN ONE OF THEM LONG ENOUGH TO FIGURE A WAY OUT OF THIS NIGHTMARE!
BUT AS LUCK WOULD HAVE IT, THE FRIGHTENED FUGITIVE COMES UPON AN OPEN SHAFT, WHICH HE DOESN'T SEE UNTIL IT'S TOO LATE!!
WHA--?
HELLLLP!!
THE STUFF BELOW! IT'S--IT'S--
4

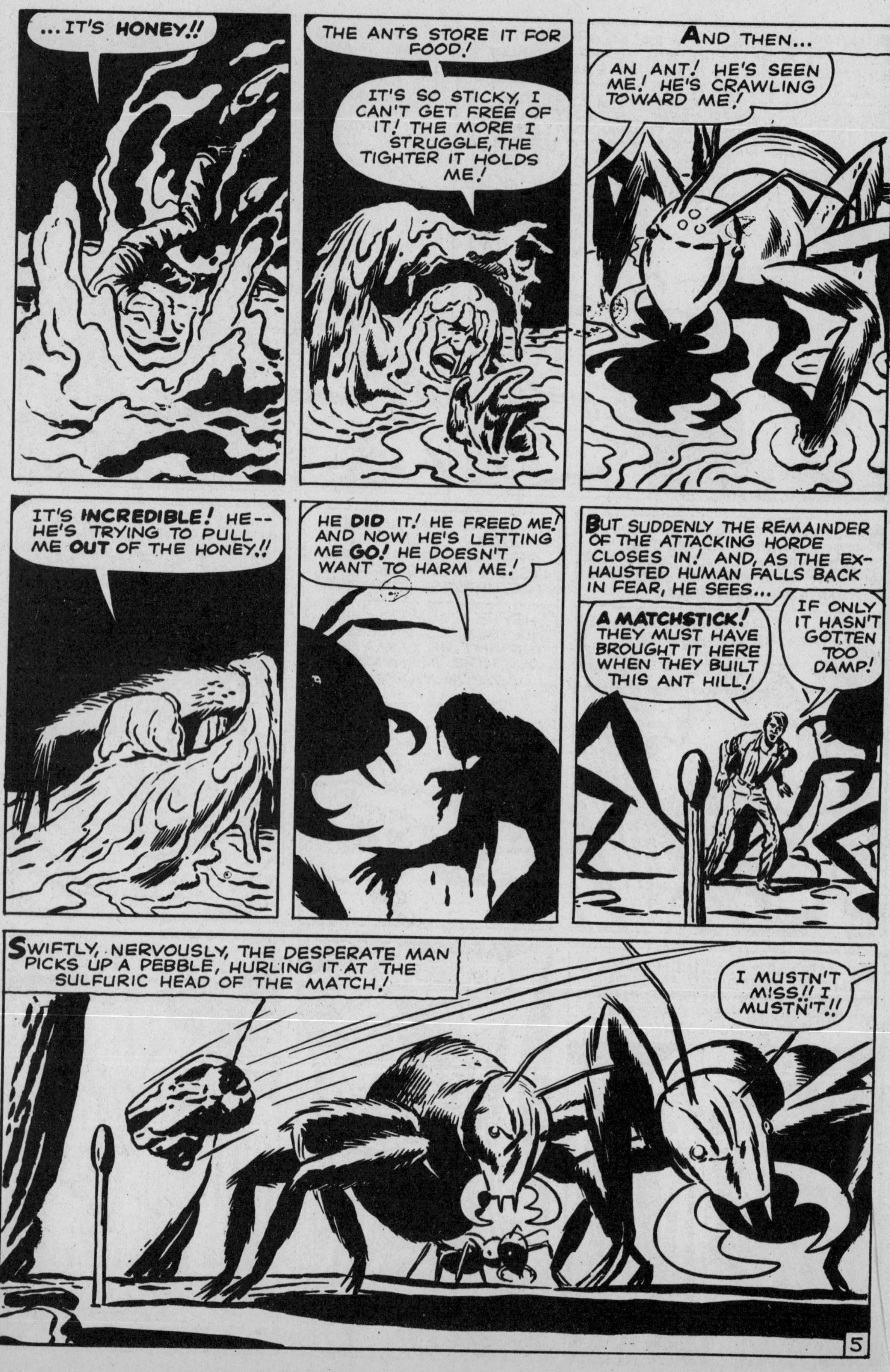
...IT'S HONEY!!
THE ANTS STORE IT FOR FOOD!
IT'S SO STICKY, I CAN'T GET FREE OF IT! THE MORE I STRUGGLE, THE TIGHTER IT HOLDS ME!
AND THEN...
AN ANT! HE'S SEEN ME! HE'S CRAWLING TOWARD ME!
IT'S INCREDIBLE! HE-- HE'S TRYING TO PULL ME OUT OF THE HONEY!!
HE DID IT! HE FREED ME! AND NOW HE'S LETTING ME GO! HE DOESN'T WANT TO HARM ME!
BUT SUDDENLY THE REMAINDER OF THE ATTACKING HORDE CLOSES IN! AND, AS THE EXHAUSTED HUMAN FALLS BACK IN FEAR, HE SEES...
A MATCHSTICK! THEY MUST HAVE BROUGHT IT HERE WHEN THEY BUILT THIS ANT HILL!
IF ONLY IT HASN'T GOTTEN TOO DAMP!
SWIFTLY, NERVOUSLY, THE DESPERATE MAN PICKS UP A PEBBLE, HURLING IT AT THE SULFURIC HEAD OF THE MATCH!
I MUSTN'T MISS!! I MUSTN'T!!
5

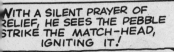

WITH A SILENT PRAYER OF RELIEF, HE SEES THE PEBBLE STRIKE THE MATCH-HEAD, IGNITING IT!

THE FIRE WILL KEEP THE ANTS AT BAY--LONG ENOUGH FOR ME TO USE THIS MAKE-SHIFT LASSO!

SO FAR, SO GOOD! B-BUT WHAT'S THAT ABOVE ME?

OH NO!!

ANOTHER ANT--WAITING FOR ME!

WITH ALL ITS FURY, THE PREDATORY INSECT ATTACKS THE TINY HUMAN!

UHHH-- STRONG-- TOO STRONG FOR ME!

BUT I HAVE ONE ADVANTAGE! A HUMAN BRAIN...

...WHICH HAS LEARNED THE ART OF JUDO!

UP AHEAD... A PATH OUT OF THIS ACCURSED ANT HILL!! IF I CAN ONLY MANAGE TO REACH SAFETY!

LONG, FRENZIED, FEAR-FILLED MINUTES LATER...

MADE IT!! AND NOW... THERE, UP ON THE WINDOW LEDGE IS MY ENLARGING SERUM! THE ONLY THING THAT CAN RETURN ME TO NORMAL SIZE! BUT HOW AM I GOING TO GET TO IT?? I CAN'T CLIMB UP THE WALL!!

IT'S HOPELESS! THEY'RE ALMOST UPON ME!

I--I JUST CAN'T RUN ANY MORE!

6

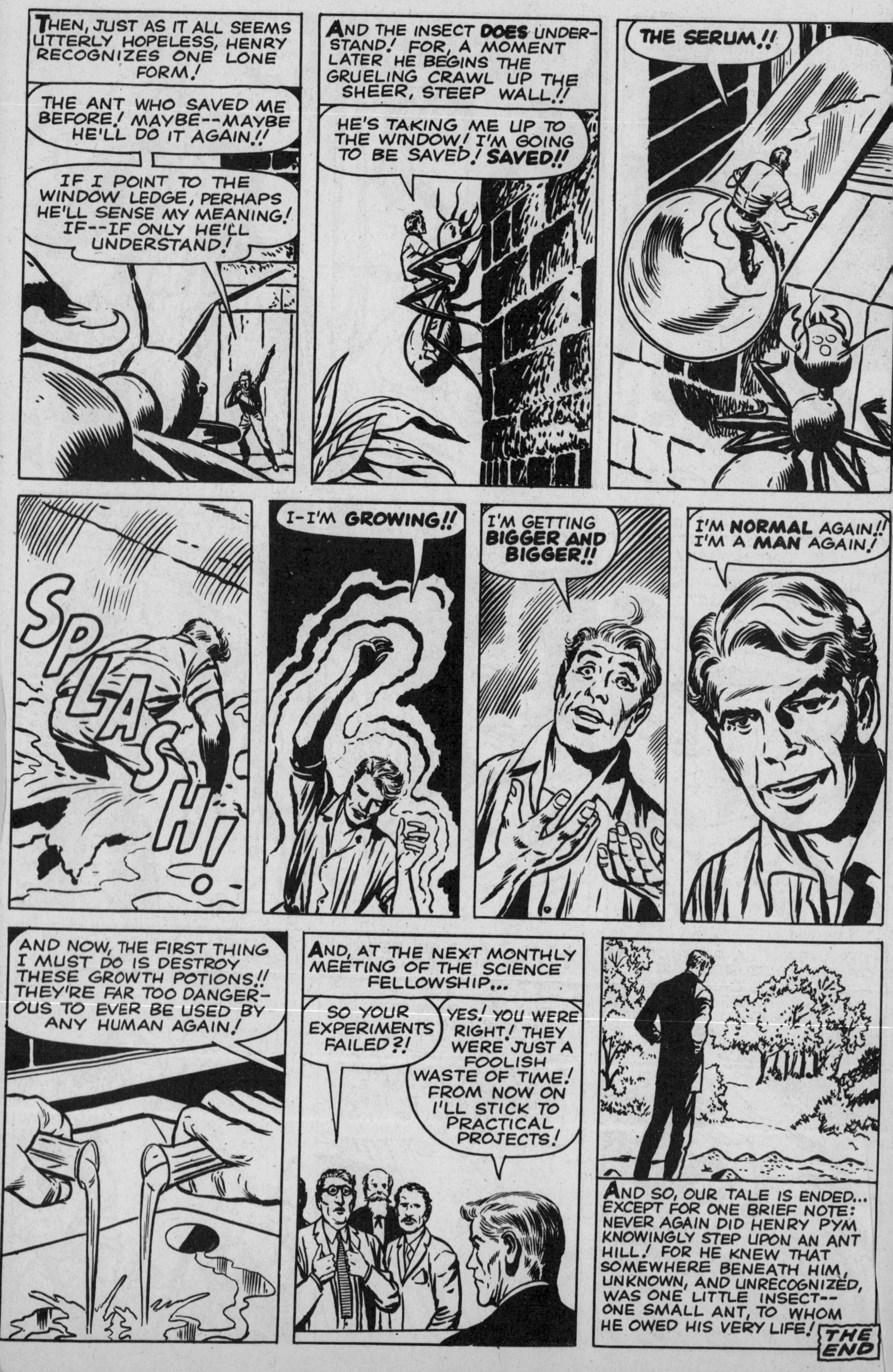
THEN, JUST AS IT ALL SEEMS UTTERLY HOPELESS, HENRY RECOGNIZES ONE LONE FORM!
THE ANT WHO SAVED ME BEFORE! MAYBE--MAYBE HE'LL DO IT AGAIN!!
IF I POINT TO THE WINDOW LEDGE, PERHAPS HE'LL SENSE MY MEANING! IF--IF ONLY HE'LL UNDERSTAND!
AND THE INSECT DOES UNDERSTAND! FOR, A MOMENT LATER HE BEGINS THE GRUELING CRAWL UP THE SHEER, STEEP WALL!!
HE'S TAKING ME UP TO THE WINDOW! I'M GOING TO BE SAVED! SAVED!!
THE SERUM!!
SPLASH!
I-I'M GROWING!!
I'M GETTING BIGGER AND BIGGER!!
I'M NORMAL AGAIN!! I'M A MAN AGAIN!
AND NOW, THE FIRST THING I MUST DO IS DESTROY THESE GROWTH POTIONS!! THEY'RE FAR TOO DANGEROUS TO EVER BE USED BY ANY HUMAN AGAIN!
AND, AT THE NEXT MONTHLY MEETING OF THE SCIENCE FELLOWSHIP...
SO YOUR EXPERIMENTS FAILED?!
YES! YOU WERE RIGHT! THEY WERE JUST A FOOLISH WASTE OF TIME! FROM NOW ON I'LL STICK TO PRACTICAL PROJECTS!
AND SO, OUR TALE IS ENDED... EXCEPT FOR ONE BRIEF NOTE: NEVER AGAIN DID HENRY PYM KNOWINGLY STEP UPON AN ANT HILL! FOR HE KNEW THAT SOMEWHERE BENEATH HIM, UNKNOWN, AND UNRECOGNIZED, WAS ONE LITTLE INSECT-- ONE SMALL ANT, TO WHOM HE OWED HIS VERY LIFE!
THE END